International Marketing Data and Statistics

International Marketing Data and Statistics

2004

28th edition

Euromonitor International Plc, 60-61 Britton Street, London EC1M 5UX

International Marketing Data and Statistics 2004

First published 1975

Twenty-eighth edition, 2004

Researched and published by:

EUROMONITOR INTERNATIONAL plc

60-61 Britton Street

London EC1M 5UX

United Kingdom

Telephone: +44 207-251-8024

Fax: +44 207-608-3149

EUROMONITOR INTERNATIONAL INC

122 South Michigan Avenue

Suite 810

Chicago

Illinois 60603, USA

Tel: + 1 312 922 1115

Fax: +1 312 922 1157

EUROMONITOR INTERNATIONAL (Asia) Pte Ltd

3 Lim Teck Kim Road

#08-02 Singapore Technologies Building

Singapore 088934

Tel: + 65 6429 0590

Fax: + 65 6324 1855

E-mail: info@euromonitor.com

http://www.euromonitor.com

International Marketing Data and Statistics 2004

A CIP catalogue record for this book is available from the British Library

ISBN 184 264 2901

Printed in Great Britain by Antony Rowe Ltd, Chippenham Wiltshire

Table of Contents

Section One
■ **Marketing Geography** **49**

List of Tables

Section Eleven
Energy Resources & Output 349

Section Twelve
Environmental Data 373

Section Thirteen
Foreign Trade 387

Section Fourteen
Health 431

Section Fifteen
Household Profiles 447

Section Sixteen
Income and Deductions 465

Section Twenty-four
▪ Travel and Tourism 619

Section Twenty-five
▪ Index 655

Foreword and Guide

Foreword

International Marketing Data and Statistics is a compendium of statistical information on the countries of the Americas, Asia, Africa and Oceania. Published annually, it provides a wealth of detailed and up-to-date statistical information relevant to international market planning. The information is regularly updated and held on an international database of market information comprising 24 subject areas.

Published annually since the mid-1970s, **International Marketing Data and Statistics** or IMDAS is now in its 28th edition. The data coverage includes a considerable number of 26-year time-series, which permit the analysis of socio-economic trends over a longer time span as a basis for forecasting. The book is published at the end of each year so that figures for the most recent complete year (in this edition 2002) can be included for key parameters.

In addition to major countries, the country coverage includes smaller international countries and states. Although the availability of statistical information on these countries is limited and they are minor markets, it assists in building up a more comprehensive picture of the total international market and will be of interest to academic users.

The data are presented in tabular form and in several sections a number of extrapolated tables have been included.

The handbook contains a full alphabetical index, and we have included a list of major sources of information on international markets. Readers requiring detailed guidance on sources of information are referred to the World Directory of Business Information Web Sites (Euromonitor, 2003), World Directory of Marketing Information Sources (Euromonitor, 2003), World Directory of Trade and Business Associations (Euromonitor, 2002) and the World Directory of Non-Official Statistical Sources (Euromonitor, 2002) for more comprehensive listings.

A companion volume of marketing data, European Marketing Data and Statistics (EMDAS) is also available in the same format. The data included in both volumes are also accessible as part of the Global Marketing Information Database (GMID) on the web.

As multinational companies extend their activities and developing countries and regions play an increasingly important role in international trade, statistical information on the countries of the world will become an essential pre-requisite for forward planning. **International Marketing Data and Statistics** aims to provide such a compilation in a handy format which allows easy access to key data drawn from hundreds of market sources and Euromonitor's own extensive information resources. Euromonitor has an important ongoing research programme in the world's emerging markets (concentrating primarily on Eastern Europe, Latin America and South-East Asia), and has published several new reports and directories concentrating on these areas.

All of the databases in this 28th edition of **International Marketing Data and Statistics** are still in a formative stage and will be expanded and developed over subsequent editions. User comments are welcomed. Also, whilst the editors have made every effort to ensure accuracy, Euromonitor cannot accept responsibility for any errors which may have occurred.

Guide to Using This Handbook

1 - Scope of the Handbook

International Marketing Data and Statistics (IMDAS) is a statistical yearbook of business and marketing information. This edition features a compilation of up-to-date and detailed marketing statistics on 24 principal subject areas. These sectors are stored on a database of international marketing information and are regularly updated by Euromonitor's research team.

The sections of IMDAS cover a wide variety of marketing topics, ranging from socio-economic trends and background information through to key consumer marketing parameters. There are also sections covering consumer expenditure, retailing, advertising, consumer market sizes and household composition. Key agro-industrial trends covering energy, automotives, industrial output and agricultural resources are included.

In IMDAS 2004, each statistical tabulation presents comparative information, either in the form of long-term time-series (dating back to 1977 as available), or single-year data for the latest year available. All the countries are listed down the left-hand column, grouped into regional entities. Where appropriate and available, regional subtotals and averages are included.

The country listing is either the full matrix or a "key countries" listing. This is dependent on data availability or relevance.

Where data is in values, units have been generally been left in national currencies unless initially compiled in US dollars. However, selected tables include calculations in US dollars. These are calculated only for the latest year available (usually 2002) as fluctuations in exchange rates and contrasts in rates of inflation render year-on-year conversions meaningless.

In addition, calculations have been made where deemed appropriate to show growth rates over a defined period, and per capita data. These permit rapid cross-comparisons between countries, regions and markets.

Using IMDAS 2004 is easy. Whatever topic is of interest, you simply look up the relevant tables (using the list of contents or index) and the table will show the relevant data for all countries. The heading shows the relevant section, title summary and title of the table, and unit. A guide to the sources used in the compilation of the data appears at the foot of the table, while any relevant notes are collected together at the end of each section.

The aim of IMDAS is to locate in one handbook the essential statistical information relevant to international market planning. The handbook will save the busy marketeer or researcher hours of time trawling through statistics from many sources and provides a wealth of hard-to-get information drawn from many sources. Business users and librarians will find the handbook especially useful.

2 - Subject Coverage

IMDAS 2004 is presented in 24 separate sections or "databases" which have all been specially updated by Euromonitor for this new edition. The subjects have been selected as those most appropriate for strategic planning and international market analysis, covering both background marketing parameters and detailed consumer market information. The 24 product databases are discussed below.

1 Marketing Geography

This database features a summary of basic data (population, area, main cities, currency, language(s), religion(s), economic and political structure, heads of state and government and last election results) for each country covered.

2 Advertising

This database features 7 tables covering advertising expenditure data.

3 Agricultural Resources

This section presents key data on land use and the output of various agricultural and forestry products. There are nine tables on the database, mostly including figures for 2002.

4 Automotives and Transport

This database covers the circulation, manufacture and sales of cars, commercial vehicles and two-wheelers; also major movements in the road, rail, air and shipping transport sectors.

5 Banking and Finance

This section features tabulations showing data from 1980-2002 and covering bank assets, liabilities, claims and interest rates.

6 Consumer Expenditure

The presentation of this section comprises total consumer spending, a consolidated breakdown by product sector, and a series of tables analysing each major consumer sector. New 2002 data have been included and all the data are presented in 13-year trends with growth rates and 2002 dollar comparisons.

7 Consumer Market Sizes

This section gives per capita consumption and retail market sizes in 17 tables for 2002. The information for the main countries is drawn from Euromonitor's market information database, which was published in 2003 in the companion volume Consumer International, which featured greater detail on a much wider range of product markets along with extensive calculated tables.

8 Consumer Prices and Costs

Trends in consumer prices and selected international living costs are portrayed in four tables of data.

9 Cultural Indicators

This section includes tables covering available data on libraries, museums, book publishing and cinema.

10 Economic Indicators

This database features tables of key economic data, again with several long-term time-series tables. The main economic indicators are all covered, including GDP, GNP, inflation, money supply, public and private consumption, government finance and exchange rates.

11 Energy Resources and Output

This section consists of tables on energy supply and demand. Coverage extends to household energy consumption and includes a number of tables trended over 20 or more years.

12 Environmental Data

This section includes tables covering various environmental factors. Data range from forest resources and protected areas to emissions of carbon dioxide and availability of fresh water.

13 Foreign Trade

This section features tables giving a cohesive and structured trade overview covering total imports and exports and external trade breakdowns by origin/destination and commodity.

14 Health

This database comprises seven tables covering major health indicators (including a table on the number of reported AIDS cases).

15 Household Profiles

This section comprises tables of comparative statistics on households. Data on housing stock and household composition are included.

16 Income and Deductions

This section includes five tables covering gross and disposable income parameters.

17 Industrial Markets

This section provides key industrial indices for a 26-year period and includes output tables covering major industrial materials.

18 IT and Telecommunications

This section features information on telecommunications and information technology including data concerning the number of Internet users.

19 Labour

This database covers the key employment indicators including numbers employed, unemployed and hours of work. The structure of the labour force by industry sector, age group and status is included for latest years available.

20 Literacy and Education

A range of literacy and educational statistics are included in this five-table section.

21 Population

This database features statistical compilations covering population trends, vital statistics, urbanisation, demographic analysis by age and sex, and population forecasts. Much of the data is in long-term trends, forming a basis for forecasting and projections.

22 Possession of Household Durables

In this section we give latest-year figures for household ownership of a range of consumer durable items.

23 Retailing

This section includes tables covering retail sales and channels and breakdowns for different retail sectors.

24 Travel and Tourism

This database consists of tabulations covering tourism values and movements, tourist accommodation and its usage.

3 - Data Coverage

Each of the statistical compilations is presented in one of four data periods:

(1) A 26-year trend table from 1977-2002, with data for each country drawn from the same consistent source. In most cases, some intermediary years have been excluded for reasons of space.

(2) A different period trend, eg 1980-2002 (23-year trend) or a recent period.

(3) Latest year available, with the years differing between countries. These are used where the information is drawn from occasional studies, eg a census, or where statistical offices vary in the speed of publishing statistics.

(4) A single year, eg 2002, where space does not permit trends or where an interactive range of information is provided (eg imports by origin, GDP by origin etc).

The statistics in this volume are as available during the compilation period (June-October 2003). Data for 2002 (in some cases provisional or estimated) have been included where possible. Various one-off surveys cover earlier years only.

4 - Country Coverage

The country coverage of IMDAS extends over 160 countries.

The countries appearing in the main matrix are grouped in 5 regional entities as follows:

North America

Canada	USA

Latin America and Caribbean

Anguilla	Antigua
Argentina	Aruba
Bahamas	Barbados
Belize	Bermuda
Bolivia	Brazil
British Virgin Islands	Cayman Islands
Chile	Colombia
Costa Rica	Cuba
Dominica	Dominican Republic
Ecuador	El Salvador
French Guiana	Grenada
Guadeloupe	Guatemala
Guyana	Haiti
Honduras	Jamaica
Martinique	Mexico
Netherlands Antilles	Nicaragua
Panama	Paraguay
Peru	Puerto Rico
St Kitts	St Lucia
St Vincent & Grenadines	Suriname
Trinidad and Tobago	Uruguay
Venezuela	

Asia-Pacific

Afghanistan	American Samoa
Armenia	Azerbaijan
Bangladesh	Bhutan
Brunei	Cambodia
China	Fiji
French Polynesia	Guam
Hong Kong, China	India
Indonesia	Japan
Kazakhstan	Kiribati
Kyrgyzstan	Laos
Macau	Malaysia
Maldives	Mongolia
Myanmar	Nauru
Nepal	New Caledonia
North Korea	Pakistan
Papua New Guinea	Philippines
Singapore	Soloman Islands
South Korea	Sri Lanka
Taiwan	Tajikistan
Thailand	Tonga
Turkmenistan	Tuvalu
Uzbekistan	Vanuatu
Vietnam	Western Samoa

Australasia

Australia	New Zealand

Middle East and Africa

Algeria	Angola
Bahrain	Benin
Botswana	Burkina Faso
Burundi	Cameroon
Cape Verde	Central African Republic
Chad	Comoros
Congo, Dem. Rep	Congo-Brazzaville
Côte d'Ivoire	Djibouti
Egypt	Equatorial Guinea
Eritrea	Ethiopia
Gabon	Gambia
Ghana	Guinea
Guinea-Bissau	Iran
Iraq	Israel
Jordan	Kenya
Kuwait	Lebanon
Lesotho	Liberia
Libya	Madagascar
Malawi	Mali
Mauritania	Mauritius
Morocco	Mozambique
Namibia	Niger
Nigeria	Oman
Qatar	Réunion
Rwanda	Sao Tomé e Principe
Saudi Arabia	Senegal
Seychelles	Sierra Leone
Somalia	South Africa
Sudan	Swaziland
Syria	Tanzania
Togo	Tunisia
Uganda	United Arab Emirates
Yemen	Zambia
Zimbabwe	

For some sections, only major markets are featured. These are drawn from the following list of 40 key countries:

Algeria	Argentina
Australia	Azerbaijan
Bolivia	Brazil
Canada	Chile
China	Colombia
Ecuador	Egypt
Hong Kong, China	India
Indonesia	Israel
Japan	Jordan
Kazakhstan	Kuwait
Malaysia	Mexico
Morocco	New Zealand
Nigeria	Pakistan
Peru	Philippines
Saudi Arabia	Singapore
South Africa	South Korea
Taiwan	Thailand
Tunisia	Turkmenistan
United Arab Emirates	USA
Venezuela	Vietnam

5 - Sources

International Marketing Data and Statistics is based on an extensive and ongoing programme of research into international markets and industries. A network of market analysts and researchers work to pull together available data on socio-economic patterns, market conditions and trends, living standards and background information relevant to business, export and market planning.

The principal sources used in the compilation of IMDAS are as follows:

- International organisations, such as the United Nations, OECD, and the International Monetary Fund.

- National statistical offices and central banks in each country.

- International and national trade and industry associations.

- Industry study groups and unofficial research publishers.

- Euromonitor's own research publications, including one-off reports and statistical compilations.

- Original research specially commissioned for the handbook, including consumer research, trade interviews and retail surveys.

A guide to the main sources used in the compilation of each table is included at the foot of each table. For reasons of space the main sources are only briefly cited; in some cases, many different publications are used in the preparation of just one table. In other cases, statistical compilations are from secondary sources which have in turn used a number of sources.

A brief guide to the main sources used in each of the 24 product databases follows.

1 Marketing Geography

Information mainly drawn from the business press, data from the yearbooks of the national statistical offices and various informal studies on the countries covered.

2 Advertising

Drawn from advertising associations and agents in various countries.

3 Agricultural Resources

Mainly based on the publications and databases of the Food and Agricultural Organisation of the United Nations (FAO).

4 Automotives and Transport

Automotives data are drawn from national statistics, and the publications of various motor trades organisations. Transport statistics are based on national statistics and on various UN publications; the International Civil Aviation Organisation; the International Road Federation and Lloyd's Register of Shipping.

5 Banking and Finance

The major source of comparative financial data is the IMF's International Financial Statistics.

6 Consumer Expenditure

Drawn from the OECD and the national accounts of each country (generally published by the national statistical offices). Euromonitor estimates have been used to reach levels of consolidation.

7 Consumer Market Sizes

Drawn from Euromonitor's consumer market database; primary sources include trade associations and industry leaders in all countries.

8 Consumer Prices and Costs

Mainly from national statistics, the International Monetary Fund and the OECD; living costs from the International Labour Organisation.

9 Cultural Indicators

Mainly drawn from the UN, UNESCO and national statistical offices.

10 Economic Indicators

The principal international sources are the OECD and the International Monetary Fund (IMF). National statistical offices (yearbooks, national accounts) and economic bulletins by leading banks are also used.

11 Energy Resources and Output

This compilation draws mainly on data from BP, the UN and the OECD/IEA, national statistics and various industry publications.

12 Environmental Data

Drawn largely from the OECD, United Nations, and the World Resources Institute, as well as national statistics.

13 Foreign Trade

The IMF, UN and OECD track external trade flows in some detail. National statistical yearbooks are also utilised.

14 Health

Compiled from various publications from national statistical offices, OECD and UN publications and incorporating Euromonitor estimates and calculations.

15 Household Profiles

Compiled from various publications from national statistical offices, UN publications and incorporating Euromonitor estimates and calculations.

16 Income and Deductions

Data from national statistical offices of each country. Specific sources include Household Budget Surveys and National Accounts. Euromonitor estimates have been used.

17 Industrial Markets

Mainly drawn from UN and OECD publications, and from national statistics. Various industry sectors are covered by associations as stated.

18 IT and Telecommunications

Mainly based on national statistics and UN data, particularly the publications of the International Telecommunication Union (ITU), and incorporating some data from the World Bank.

19 Labour

In addition to national statistics, the primary international source is the International Labour Organisation, which publishes both a statistical yearbook and quarterly bulletins.

20 Literacy and Education

The main source is UNESCO with data from national statistical offices incorporated as available.

21 Population

Drawn mainly from the statistical yearbooks of the national statistical offices supplemented with UN data and population forecasts.

22 Possession of Household Durables

National statistical office data has been drawn together and standardised.

23 Retailing

Reference was made to Retail Trade International (Euromonitor 2002), also original new research. Primary sources include retail trade censuses (various countries) by national statistical offices, retail trade associations, major retailers etc.

24 Travel and Tourism

A compilation sourced from the World Tourism Organisation and Euromonitor's own research.

6 - List of Abbreviations

ADB	Asian Development Bank
ASEAN	Association of South-East Asian Nations
EFTA	European Free Trade Association
EU	European Union
FAO	Food and Agriculture Organisation of the United Nations
FT	Financial Times
IAA	International Advertising Association
IATA	International Air Transport Association
IBRD	International Bank for Reconstruction and Development (World Bank)
ICAO	International Civil Aviation Organisation
IEA	International Energy Authority
IISS	International Institute for Strategic Studies
ILO	International Labour Organisation
IMF	International Monetary Fund
IMMA	International Motorcycle Manufacturers' Association
IRF	International Road Federation
ITU	International Telecommunication Union (a UN agency)
OECD	Organisation for Economic Co-operation and Development
SMMT	Society of Motor Manufacturers and Traders
UN	United Nations
UNESCO	United Nations Educational, Scientific and Cultural Organisation
WHO	World Health Organisation
WTO	World Tourism Organisation
EAP	Economically active population
GDP	Gross domestic product
GNP	Gross national product
LPG	Liquefied petroleum gases
NGL	Natural gas liquids
NIC	Newly Industrialised Country
PDR	People's Democratic Republic
SITC	Standard International Trade Classification
'000	thousand
gWh	gigawatt-hours
ha	Hectare
hl	Hectolitre
kg	kilogramme
km	kilometre
km2	square kilometre
kWh	kilowatt-hours
m2	square metre
m3	cubic metre
mn	million
MTOE	million tonnes of oil equivalent
MW	megawatts
R/P	reserves/production
TJ	terajoules
0	denotes less than 0.5 where no fraction given

Key International Marketing Information Sources

Introduction

This section identifies the major information sources for researching the international market. The listings are not intended as exhaustive; rather we aim to list some of the main international and national organisations publishing statistics, to locate some of the principal non-European libraries and to identify the main general business contacts.

Readers are referred to several other Euromonitor publications for further information on international sources:

- **Asian Marketing Information Sourcebook/Latin American Marketing Information Sourcebook**
  (1st edition, Euromonitor 2003)

  These brand new sourcebooks are the ideal resource to consult when researching Asian and Latin American markets. They provide full contact details for a wide variety of business information providers in each region, including trade associations, national statistical offices, government departments, business information libraries, trade and business journals and business websites.

- **World Directory of Business Information Web Sites**
  (6th edtion, Euromonitor 2003)

  Comprehensive coverage of over 2,000 web sites from 120 countries around the world. Web sites included offer access to the following types of information: socio-economic statistics; consumer market statistics; industrial market statistics; market research surveys and reports; company information; and business news sources.

- **World Directory of Marketing Information Sources**
  (4th edition, Euromonitor 2003)

  The directory has full contact details for more than 6,000 market information providers, together with details of their activities and publications. These include: official organisations; trade development bodies; business information libraries; leading market research companies; private research publishers; trade associations; major trade and business journals; and on-line database sources.

- **World Directory of Trade and Business Associations**
  (4th edition, Euromonitor 2002)

  This directory lists some 5,000 trade associations throughout the world from a broad range of sectors, with details of membership, key personnel, structure, aims and objectives, activities and publications.

- **World Directory of Business Information Libraries**
  (5th edition, Euromonitor, 2002)

  This directory details around 1,500 of the world's major libraries that provide public access to business information, including libraries belonging to national statistical offices, chambers of commerce, academic bodies, private companies, etc.

- **World Directory of Non-Official Statistical Sources**
  (4th edition, Euromonitor, 2002)

  This directory provides details of over 2,800 regularly produced statistical information publications from official and non-official organisations throughout the world, with special emphasis on the major industrialised nations including the USA, Canada, and Japan.

Official Organisations

International Official Organisations

Agence Internationale de l'Energie (AIE)

(International Energy Agency (IEA))

Address:	9, rue de la Fédération, 75739 Paris Cédex 15, France
Telephone:	+33 1 4057 6551
Fax:	+33 1 4057 6559
E-mail:	info@iea.org
Website:	www.iea.org

Website notes: compilation of news and articles on the latest developments and issues affecting the world's energy resources sector. Access to Oil Market Reports, and samples of Country Studies; environmental briefings and essays; and various statistics on world energy resources

Statistical Coverage: by entering the "Statistics Section", online access is provided to a series of annually and monthly updated publications: Key World Statistics 2000; Monthly Electricity Survey; Monthly Price Statistics; Monthly Natural Gas Survey; and Monthly Oil Survey. Access is also provided to IEA Energy Technology R&D Statistics database, 1974-1998, and to Energy Indicators per Country

Year Established: 1974

Obtaining Publications: same as above

Publications:
- ↳ **International Energy Agency** *(Website)*
- ↳ **Oil Market Report** — statistical data on current world oil market trends including: total stocks, crude stocks and product stocks in both barrels and days of forward demand; industry and government-controlled stocks in each region for crude oil and other main products; total stocks in each country in both barrels and days of forward consumption; a summary overview of stock levels and regional stock developments in North America, Europe and the Pacific. Covers crude oil, gasoline, middle distillates and fuel oil — *monthly*
- ↳ **World Energy Outlook 2002**

Food and Agricultural Organisation of the United Nations (FAO)

Address:	Viale delle Terme di Caracalla, 00100 Rome, Italy
Telephone:	+39 06 5705 4243
Fax:	+39 06 5705 6167
E-mail:	publications-sales@FAO.org
Website:	www.fao.org

Website notes: general information on the Food and Agricultural Organisation of the UN (FAO), plus news, articles and reports on latest developments and trends affecting the world's agricultural sector and food industry ("News Highlights", "Press Releases", "Global Watch", and "The State of..." sections)

Statistical Coverage: access to world-wide databases on food related sectors: agriculture; nutrition; fisheries; forestry; food quality control. International statistics covers: production; trade; fertiliser and pesticides; land use and irrigation; forest products; fishery products; population; agricultural machinery; and food aid shipments

Obtaining Publications: FAO Distribution and Sales Section, Viale delle Terme di Caracalla, 00100 Rome, Italy

Guides to Publications: FAO Books in print (annual catalogue of FAO publications in English on CD-Rom, free of charge); List of Documents (listing of publications in all languages); on-line database FAOSTAT (http://apps.fao.org)

Publications:
- ↳ **FAO** *(Website)*
- ↳ **Yearbook of Fisheries Statistics (Aquaculture/Commodities/Capture Production)** — three different volumes providing statistical data for the world aquaculture industry, world fish captures, and production and foreign trade of fishery commodities — *annual*
- ↳ **Yearbook of Forest Products** — statistical information on volume production and trade of forestry products in the world — *annual*

International Fund for Agricultural Development (IFAD)

Address:	Via de Serafico 107, 00142 Rome, Italy
Telephone:	+39 06 545 91
Fax:	+39 06 504 3463
E-mail:	ifad@ifad.org
Website:	www.ifad.org

Year Established: 1977

Guides to Publications: online catalogue of annual publications, books, booklets, brochures, manuals and periodicals published by the organisation

Publications:
- ↳ **Annual Report** — *annual*
- ↳ **International Fund for Agricultural Development**

International Labour Organisation (ILO)

Address:	4, route des Morillons, 1211 Geneva 22, Switzerland
Telephone:	+41 227 996 111
Fax:	+41 227 998 685
E-mail:	ilo@ilo.org or pubvente@ilo.org
Website:	www.ilo.org

Website notes: contains basic data on stocks and flows of migrant labour. Statistics are available for 1996 onward and tables are searchable by country and by type of information. Up to five countries can be compared for a specific year

Statistical Coverage: different databases covering a wide variety of topics and areas within the labour market sector: CISDOC; ILOLEX; LABORDOC; LABORSTA; NATLEX; etc. For details on contents and access requirements, enter "Library and Information Services" section

Obtaining Publications: Library and Information Services: tel: +41.22.799.8675; fax: +41.22.799.6516; e-mail: bibl@ilo.org

Guides to Publications: online catalogue

Publications:
- ↳ **International Labour Migration Database (ILM)** *(Website)*
- ↳ **International Labour Organisation (ILO)** *(Website)*
- ↳ **International Labour Review** — global view with the results of analysis by economists, lawyers, sociologists, policy-makers and other experts on the many factors determining the level, quality and distribution of employment — *quarterly*
- ↳ **LABORSTA** *(Website)*
- ↳ **World Labour Report** — analyses the global labour market — *irregular*
- ↳ **Yearbook of Labour Statistics** — evolution of labour and of living and working conditions throughout the world. The series presented in the Yearbook provide statistical information for more than 190 countries, areas and territories, usually covering the last ten years. Includes information on total and economically active population, employment, unemployment, hours of work, wages, labour costs, consumer prices, occupational injuries, and strikes and lockouts — *annual*

International Monetary Fund (IMF)

Address:	700 19th Street, Washington, DC 20431, USA
Telephone:	+1 202 623 7300
Fax:	+1 202 623 6278
E-mail:	publicaffairs@imf.org
Website:	www.imf.org

Website notes: global view of international monetary and economic affairs. Access to a series of news, fact sheets, briefings and databases on world economic growth, international capital markets and various online publications, including IMF's Annual Report

Statistical Coverage: statistics on different economic, financial and monetary issues can be found in various online publications and fact sheets. The Country Reports section includes individual country statistical appendixes for most IMF member nations

Obtaining Publications: International Monetary Fund, Publication Services, Catalog Orders, 700 19th Street, N.W., Washington, DC 20431, USA, Tel: +1 202 623 7430, Fax: +1 202 623 7201, E-mail: publications@imf.org

Guides to Publications: Publications Catalogue available online (under Publications section)

Publications:
- ↳ **Balance of Payments Statistics Yearbook** – balance of payments statistics covering most countries in the world – *annual*
- ↳ **Debt Relief for Low Income Countries**
- ↳ **Direction of Trade Statistics** – *quarterly*
- ↳ **Direction of Trade Statistics Yearbook** – *annual*
- ↳ **IMF Economic Reviews**
- ↳ **IMF Survey** – macroeconomic research and policy analyses, country analyses, issues in international finance, as well as the latest development in the IMF policies and activities – *fortnightly*
- ↳ **International Financial Statistics** – statistics covering international reserves, interest rates, exchange rates, prices, unit values and commodity prices, trade, national accounts – *monthly*
- ↳ **International Financial Statistics Yearbook** – contains some additional series to the monthly edition – *annual*
- ↳ **International Monetary Fund** *(Website)*
- ↳ **World Economic Outlook** – global outlook on the world's economy, analysing latest economic and financial developments in developed and developing countries, as well as emerging markets – *every two years*

International Telecommunication Union (ITU)

Address:	Place des Nations, 1211 Geneva 20, Switzerland
Telephone:	+41 22 730 5111
Fax:	+41 22 733 7256/730 6500
E-mail:	itumail@itu.int
Website:	www.itu.int

Website notes: highlights of the telecommunications' industry world-wide; access to several industry related databases and to online publications and online statistical documents (subscription required)

Year Established: 1865

Publications:
- ↳ **African Telecommunication Indicators** – overview of the telecommunications industry in the African continent, supported by various facts and figures for the region, covering a total of 55 different countries
- ↳ **Americas Telecommunication indicators** – analysis of the telecommunications industry in Central and South America and the Caribbean. Covers latest trends in mobile communications, internet and e-commerce, and regulatory and policy issues. Supported by key indicators on the regional telecommunications industry
- ↳ **Asia-Pacific Telecommunication Indicators** – overview of the telecommunications's industry in Asia and major players in the market. Provides statistical data for some 38 different countries, and includes a directory of leading companies and telecommunication related bodies and organisations
- ↳ **International Telecommunications Union (ITU)** *(Website)*
- ↳ **ITU Yearbook of Statistics** – compilation of annual statistical data relating to the development of the telecommunications industry worldwide – *annual*

International Trade Centre UNCTAD/WTO (ITC)

Address:	Palais des Nations, 1211 Geneva 10, Switzerland
Telephone:	+41 227 300 111
Fax:	+41 227 334 439
E-mail:	itcreg@intracen.org
Website:	www.intracen.org

Website notes: development and promotion of trade activities between developed and developing countries, as well as emerging economies. Information provided on: product-specific trade, from handicraft products to coffee, leather products, textiles, etc; trade in services; and access to ITC databases on Trade Information Index and Periodicals

Statistical Coverage: country-specific business information, including trade statistics for UN individual member nations: trade performance index; national export performance; national import profile; trade & employment; etc. Years covered vary from country to country, as well as amount of detail and sector coverage

Year Established: 1964

Obtaining Publications: It is possible to order online

Guides to Publications: online catalogue

Publications:
- ↳ **International Trade Centre (UNCTAD/WTO)** *(Website)*
- ↳ **International Trade Forum** – covers trade promotion and development of exporting and importing activities in developing countries and economies in transition
- ↳ **World Directory of Trade Promotion Organizations and Other Foreign Trade Bodies** – *annual*

Joint United Nations Programme on HIV/AIDS (UNAIDS)

Address:	20, avenue Appia, 1211 Geneva 27, Switzerland
Telephone:	+41 22 791 3666
Fax:	+41 22 791 4187
E-mail:	unaids@unaids.org
Website:	www.unaids.org

Website notes: online information, provided in most UN official languages, on the work and services of the Joint United Nations Programme on HIV/AIDS. Provides access to a wide range of publications and databases, including the online annually updated "Aids Epidemic Update", and the HIV/AIDS info database searchable by country and/or subject

Publications:
- ↳ **UNAIDS** *(Website)*

Organisation for Economic Co-operation and Development (OECD)

Address:	2, rue André Pascal, 75775 Paris Cédex 16, France
Telephone:	+33 1 4524 8200/8167
Fax:	+33 1 4524 1391/1950
E-mail:	sales@oecd.org
Website:	www.oecd.org

Website notes: online service which enables downloading of various OECD publications and periodicals. Sectors covered include: agriculture; food; biotechnology; education; energy; health; industry; telecommunications; transport; tourism; emerging markets; etc. Includes free access to annual Economic Surveys for most member countries

Statistical Coverage: statistical section includes a wide range of data on different socio-economic indicators for OECD member countries. Statistics are sold as hard-copy publications, on CD-ROM format, or online. Some of the data available online (subject to charge) covers: general OECD statistics (from demographic trends to environment and health); economic statistics; agricultural and food statistics (agricultural databases); energy statistics; development co-operation and public management; education, labour and social affairs; science, technology and industry statistics; health statistics; and transport statistics

Obtaining Publications: OECD Publications Services at above address and via National Sales Agents (HMSO in UK)

Guides to Publications: OECD Publications (annual catalogue) and quarterly supplement. News from OECD: monthly bulletin also lists publications appearing during the current month and is available on request

Publications:
- ↳ **Indicators of Industrial Activity** – overall view of short-term economic developments in different industries for all member countries: indices of output, new orders, unfilled orders, prices and employment – *quarterly*
- ↳ **International Trade by Commodities Statistics** – *annual*
- ↳ **Main Economic Indicators** – *monthly*
- ↳ **Monthly Statistics of International Trade** – statistics on trade of individual OECD member countries and main country groupings with most of their partner countries – *monthly*
- ↳ **OECD Economic Outlook** – surveys latest economic developments in the OECD area and assesses future prospects, including data on actual and forecast demand, costs and prices, employment and unemployment, foreign trade, etc. – *2 p.a.*
- ↳ **OECD Economic Surveys** – national economic survey and prospects for each OECD member country – *17 p.a.*
- ↳ **OECD Online** *(Website)*
- ↳ **Oil, Gas, Coal and Electricity** – detailed data on production of crude oil, natural gas, liquids and refinery feedstocks, crude oil and product trades, refinery intake and output, final consumption, stock levels and changes – *quarterly*
- ↳ **Quarterly Labour Force Statistics** – *quarterly*
- ↳ **Trends in International Migration** – international migration statistics and legislation – *annual*

United Nations (UN)

Address:	**United Nations Publications, Room DC2-853, 2 UN Plaza, New York, NY 10017, USA**
Telephone:	**+1 212 963 8302**
Fax:	**+1 212 963 3489**
E-mail:	**publications@un.org**
Website:	**www.un.org**

Website notes: official site of the United Nations. Access to information in the form of online publications, reports and briefings, news, surveys and press releases, covering a wide range of issues in the areas of human rights, socio-economic and human development, environment and poverty reduction. Provides links to UN official bodies and institutions and is available in all UN official languages: English, French, Spanish, Russian, Arabic and Chinese. (For more information on UN Statistics see UN Statistical Division site)

Obtaining Publications: at the above address for all orders from North America, Latin America and the Caribbean and Asia and the Pacific. Customers in Europe, Africa and the Middle East should send their orders to: United Nations Publications, Sales Office and Bookshop, CH-1211, Geneva 10, Switzerland, tel: +41 22 917 2614; fax: +41 22 917 0027; e-mail: unpubli@unog.ch.

Guides to Publications: Catalogue of United Nations Publications (annual, free) lists all publications currently in print from UN bodies and affiliated agencies whose publications are sold by UN Sales Sections; UNDOC Current Index (United Nations Document Index) is issued 10 times a year, on a subscription basis, and gives a comprehensive coverage of UN documentation

Publications:

↳ **Demographic Yearbook** – demographic statistics provided for some 200 countries, covering size, distribution and trends in population, fertility, mortality, marriage and divorce, international migration and population census data

↳ **Economic and Social Survey of Asia and the Pacific** – analyses recent economic and social developments in the region with particular emphasis on economic and social policy issues and broad development strategies – *annual*

↳ **Economic and Social Survey of Latin America and the Caribbean** – analyses the economic situation in the region – *irregular*

↳ **Economic Survey of Europe** – update on the current economic situation in Europe, North America and the Commonwealth of Independent States (CIS), focusing on regional disparities and economic convergence – *irregular*

↳ **Industrial Commodity Statistics Yearbook** – Yearbook consists of two parts. Part one contains annual quantity data on production of industrial commodities by country, geographical region, economic grouping and for the world. For some 200 countries, information has been presented for about 230 commodities over a ten-year period . Part two presents data by country on apparent consumption of about 530 industrial commodities over the same period – *annual*

↳ **International Trade Statistics Yearbook** – presents the basic information for individual countries' external trade performance in terms of the overall trends in current value, as well as in volume and price; the importance of trading partners and the significance of individual commodities imported and exported – *annual*

↳ **Monthly Bulletin of Statistics** – economic and social statistics from more that 200 countries and territories, as well as quarterly statistics on industrial production – *monthly*

↳ **Population and Vital Statistics Report** – estimates of world and regional populations as well as estimates for 218 countries. Data is compiled and collected by national statistical offices and related official organisations, based on latest national population census – *quarterly*

↳ **Statistical Yearbook for Asia and the Pacific** – statistics covering a total of 56 countries, covering a wide range of topics including: population, manpower, national accounts, agriculture, forestry and fishing, industry, energy production and consumption, transportation and communication, internal and external trade, wages, banking, finance and social statistics – *annual*

↳ **Statistical Yearbook for Latin America and the Caribbean** – annual compilation of a wide range of socio-economic statistics for a total of 33 Latin American countries. Data covers topics including: population, national accounts, employment, social conditions, agriculture, industry, import-export goods and services, balance of payments and infrastructure services – *annual*

↳ **UN Statistical Yearbook** – presents an overall comprehensive description of the world economy, its structure, major trends and recent performance – *annual*

↳ **United Nations** *(Website)*

↳ **United Nations Statistics Division** *(Website)*

↳ **World Economic and Social Survey** – assesses the current global economic situation, including a forecast of output, international trade and other key economic variables – *annual*

↳ **World Population Prospects** – presents population estimates and projections for the world, the more developed and less developed regions, the least developed countries, 5 major areas, 21 regions and 184 countries or areas – *irregular*

↳ **World Statistics Pocketbook** – international compilation of basic economic, social and environmental indicators for 208 countries and areas worldwide. It covers 57 key indicators in the areas of population, economic activity, agriculture, industry, energy, international trade, transport, communications, gender, education and environment – *annual*

United Nations Educational, Scientific and Cultural Organization (UNESCO)

Address:	**7, place de Fontenoy, 75352 Paris Cédex 07, France**
Telephone:	**+33 1 4568 1000**
Fax:	**+33 1 4567 1690**
Website:	**www.unesco.org**

Website notes: official web site of UNESCO - information on the Organisation and its mission; press releases; UNESCO legal instruments; publications and audiovisual materials; and link to related statistical web sites

Publications:

↳ **UNESCO** *(Website)*

↳ **Unesco Institute for Statistics** *(Website)*

United Nations Industrial Development Organisation (UNIDO)

Address:	**PO Box 300, Vienna International Centre, 1400 Vienna, Austria**
Telephone:	**+43 126 026**
Fax:	**+43 1269 2669**
E-mail:	**grobyn@unido.org**
Website:	**www.unido.org**

Website notes: offers information on UNIDO and its products and services: catalogue of publications and research documents; weekly news; business contacts; and access to different databases and statistical data (IDA - Industrial Development Abstracts Database; Industrial Statistics Database)

Statistical Coverage: "Reference Information" section includes country information data for most UN member nations: general annual macro-economic indicators (population; GDP; consumer price index; manufacturing value added; constant MVA; manufactured exports and imports; etc) plus industry related statistics on international comparison of manufacturing value added at 1990 constant prices in US$; labour productivity and wages; and selected real growth rates by manufacturing branch

Obtaining Publications: UNIDO Publications Sales Office, PO Box 300, A-1400 Vienna, Austria; tel: (+43) 1 26026 5031; fax: (+43) 1 21346 5031/26026 6843; E-mail: publications@unido.org

Publications:

↳ **Annual Report of UNIDO** – *annual*

↳ **Industrial Development Global Report** – focuses on the long-term dynamics of investment and economic growth in developing countries – *annual*

↳ **International Yearbook of Industrial Statistics** – worldwide statistics on current performance and trends in the manufacturing sector. Analyses patterns of growth, structural change and industrial performance in individual industries in over 120 countries – *annual*

↳ **United Nations Industrial Development Organisation (UNIDO)** *(Website)*

United Nations Statistics Division

Address:	**Statistics Division, United Nations, New York, NY 10017, USA**
Fax:	**+1 212 963 4116**
E-mail:	**statistics@un.org**
Website:	**www.un.org/Depts/unsd**

Website notes: wide range of world statistics, including: world economic statistics; environment statistics; demographic and social data

Statistical Coverage: UNSD statistical databases on-line provide different world socio-economic data, some of these subject to charge: e.g. Monthly Bulletin of Statistics; Population and Vital Statistics Report (Latest population census by sex and latest mid-year estimate; birth, deaths and infant deaths, numbers, rates and estimated rates); population of capital cities and cities of 100,000 and more inhabitants; social indicators; and World's Women 2000

Obtaining Publications: United Nations, Sales Section,

DC2-0853, New York 10017, USA e-mail: publications@un.org

Sales Section, Palais des Nations,

1211 Geneva 10, Switzerland e-mail: unpubli@unog.ch

Guides to Publications: a list of publications is available online. Alternatively a Catalogue and References for United Nations Statistical Publications and Documents is available on request to either of the Sales Offices, or to:

Director, United Nations Statistics Division, New York, e-mail: statistics@un.org.

Publications:
↳ **Population and Vital Statistics Report** – *Quarterly*
↳ **UN Statistical Division** *(Website)*

World Bank

Address:	1818 H Street NW, Washington, DC 20433, USA
Telephone:	+1 202 477 1234
Fax:	+1 202 477 6349
E-mail:	info@worldbank.org
Website:	www.worldbank.org

Website notes: official site of the World Bank, offering information on the organisation's main objectives; main products and services provided; poverty-reduction activities; data and statistics on most of the world's countries; information on research projects; and catalogue of publications published

Statistical Coverage: social, economic and financial statistics are provided online under different sections and/or databases. By entering the Data and Statistics section, one has direct access to different data grouped by country, by topic and by query. All data is extracted from the World Development Indicators Database. More than 200 countries are covered and figures are provided for various topics/areas, including: agriculture; domestic finance; early childhood development; education; environment; gender; governance; health and population; HIV/AIDS; informatics; infrastructures; industry; international economics; labour and employment; macro-economics and growth; poverty; private sector development; public sector management; rural, urban and social development; and transition to democratic systems

Year Established: 1944

Obtaining Publications: World Bank Publications: tel: +1 800 645 7247/+1 703 661 1580; fax:+1 703 661 1501; E-mail: books@worldbank.org

Guides to Publications: available online under: http://publications.worldbank.org/ecommerce/

Publications:
↳ **World Bank** *(Website)*
↳ **World Bank Annual Report** – *annual*
↳ **World Bank Atlas** – main social, economic and environmental indicators for 206 countries – *annual*
↳ **World Development Indicators** – overview of the world's economy, including some 600 indicators for 148 countries, with basic indicators for a further 59 countries – *annual*
↳ **World Development Report** – analysis of world development policies, world disparities and inequalities, poverty and sustainable growth, and policies for future global progress – *annual*

World Health Organisation (WHO)/Organisation Mondiale de la Santé

Address:	20 Avenue Appia, 1211 Geneva 27, Switzerland
Telephone:	+41 22 791 2111
Fax:	+41 22 791 3111
E-mail:	info@who.int
Website:	www.who.ch

Website notes: information on WHO and the present state of health services world wide. Provides online access to different publications, including the Bulletin of the World Health Organization, and the annual World Health Report. This last report includes basic macro-economic statistics for all WHO member countries, together with data more specific to health including: child immunization; health expenditures; infant mortality; maternal mortality; deaths by type of condition; etc.

Obtaining Publications: at the above address, or through e-mail: publications@who.ch.

Guides to Publications: the online catalogue covers over 900 formal WHO publications organized by subject category. In addition WHO issues around 300 informal technical documents each year (identified by WHO/ prefix). These can be located by searching the online library catalogue. www.who.int/dsa/cat98/zcon.htm

Publications:
↳ **Bulletin of the World Health Organization** – *monthly*
↳ **WHO Statistical Information System (WHOSIS)** *(Website)*
↳ **World Health Organisation (WHO)** *(Website)*
↳ **World Health Report** – in-depth statistical analysis of world health – *annual*

World Tourism Organisation (WTO)
(Organización Mundial del Turismo)

Address:	Capitán Haya 42, 28020 Madrid, Spain
Telephone:	+34 91 567 8100
Fax:	+34 91 571 3733
E-mail:	omt@world-tourism.org
Website:	www.world-tourism.org

Website notes: official site of the World Tourism Organisation. Global overview of latest trends affecting the travel and tourism industry; news and articles on developments within specific market sectors; trade in tourism services; quality of tourism development; sustainable development of tourism; etc. Information on WTO's main products and services and compilation of online statistics

Statistical Coverage: data on world tourism activities can be found under "Statistics" section and "Facts & Figures" section. The first one allows access to a Tourism Statistical Database (subject to charge), covering international outbound tourism, international inbound tourism, and a wide variety of indicators for the industry, searchable by country and/or year, e.g.: tourist arrivals; arrivals by air, car, road and sea; rooms in hotels; international tourism receipts; international tourism expenditure; etc. Facts & Figures section provides general figures on international, national and regional tourism, covering: global industry size; tourist arrivals by region and by country; international tourism by means of transportation; international tourism receipts by region and by country; and international tourism by purpose of visit

Obtaining Publications: it is possible to order online

Guides to Publications: online catalogue

Publications:
↳ **Compendium of Tourism Statistics** – tables on tourism in specific countries over a five year period with summary data over a 30 year period. Covers visitors, arrivals, nights stayed, mode of transport, purpose of visit, expenditure etc. – *annual*
↳ **Global Tourism Forecasts** – series of seven volumes covering different world regions as well as the whole world. Compiles information from different forecast studies for the industry, as well as WTO's own forecasts for the 21st century (regions covered include: Africa; Americas; East Asia and the Pacific; Europe; Middle East; and South Asia)
↳ **Tourism Economic Report** – analysis the importance and impact of tourism activities on global and regional economies. Statistics are provided for international tourism receipts and expenditure, tourism transactions, etc – *irregular*
↳ **Tourism Market Trends** – analysis of latest trends in the global tourism industry, with specific sections on selected regions and markets. Covers tourism results and economic impacts on national and regional markets; world hotel capacity; top destinations; origin of tourist flows; etc – *annual*
↳ **World Directory of Tourism Education and Training Institutions** – *annual*
↳ **World Tourism Organisation** *(Website)*
↳ **Yearbook of Tourism Statistics** – two-volume publication containing final data on tourism trends from over 190 countries and territories. Volume I covers countries from A-L. Volume II covers countries from M-Z – *annual*

World Trade Organisation (WTO)

Address:	Centre William Rappard, Rue de Lausanne 154, 1211 Geneva, Switzerland
Telephone:	+41 22 739 5111
Fax:	+41 22 731 4206
E-mail:	enquiries@wto.org or publications@wto.org
Website:	www.wto.org

Website notes: offers information on global trade, and rules defining international commercial activities around the world. Compilation of news on WTO and international trade; articles and briefings on different trade topics (e.g. General Agreement on Trade and Tariffs, textiles, agriculture, etc); access to free online publications on trade policies reviews, agreements, trade statistics, etc

Statistical Coverage: statistics compiled by WTO are provided online, by downloading some of its major statistical titles, including: International Trade Statistics (annual); Annual Report; and Historical Series. Data covers main features of trade activities around the world: global trade figures; merchandise trade by product; commercial services trade; trade by world region; trade by economic sector. The world is for this purpose divided into 7 different areas: 1) North America; 2) Latin America; 3) Western Europe; 4) Central and Eastern Europe; 5) Africa; 6) Middle East; and 7) Asia

Obtaining Publications: As above

Guides to Publications: on-line document database, 'Documents online', (opens in a new window) where it is possible to find and download the official documents of all the WTO bodies. http://docsonline.wto.org/gen_home

Publications:

↪ **Annual Report** — analysis of latest developments in World trade activities, trade policies and regulations, and trade statistics for the last two years — *annual*

↪ **International Trade Statistics** — compilation of annual statistics on world trade activities: data provided by country, region, and economic sector — *annual*

↪ **Special Study - Trade, Income Disparity and Poverty** — analysis of links between international trade, global income disparities, and poverty

↪ **World Trade Organisation (WTO)** *(Website)*

Pan-regional Official Organisations

□ ASIA

Asian Development Bank

Address:	PO Box 789, 0980 Manila, Philippines
Telephone:	+63 2 632 4444
Fax:	+63 2 636 2444
E-mail:	business@adb.org or adbpub@adb.org
Website:	www.adb.org

Website notes: covers ADB's products and services: catalogue of publications, news and major events releases, information on projects, online access to selected publications and statistical series

Year Established: 1966

Obtaining Publications: to order directly from the ADB headquarters, e-mail adbpub@adb.org using orderform.xls, which is provided on the website, as an attachment, or mail a completed PDF order form to Publications Unit, ADB, PO Box 789, 0980, Manila, Philippines, or fax it to +632 636-2648

Guides to Publications: publications catalogue for download; various on-line editions available free of charge

Publications:
  ↳ **Asian Development Bank** – data on all Asian countries including national accounts, external trade and direction of trade, price indices, population, labour force, balance of payments, government finance, money and banking, production and energy *(Website)*
  ↳ **Asian Development Bank Research Bulletin** – the findings of economic research and policy analysis undertaken by the Bank – *annual*
  ↳ **Asian Development Outlook** – survey of economic progress in developing member countries, examining growth, investment and employment, fiscal and monetary policies, external trade and balance of payments, and policy and development issues. Also devotes a special chapter to regional integration including intra-regional trade, foreign direct investment and portfolio investment, labour migration, environmental issues and policy developments – *annual*
  ↳ **Asian Development Review** – major development issues (results of research carried out by the bank and contributions from specialists in Asian and Pacific affairs) – *2 p.a.*

Association of South East Asian Nations (ASEAN)

Address:	PO Box 2072, 70a Jalan Sisingamangaraja, Jakarta 12110, Indonesia
Telephone:	+62 21 726 2991/724 3372
Fax:	+62 21 739 8234/724 3504
E-mail:	termsak@aseansec.org
Website:	www.aseansec.org

Website notes: general information on ASEAN main activities. Overview of political and security cooperation in South East Asia; economic cooperation; and external relations. Online access to Annual Report and other ASEAN titles

Statistical Coverage: data on trade and major socio-economic indicators provided under ASEAN Statistics section, for the period of 1993 up to 1999. Includes: overall ASEAN trade (exports and imports); intra-ASEAN trade; extra-ASEAN trade; transport and communication; and selected macro-economic indicators

Publications:
  ↳ **ASEAN Annual Report** – socio-economic overview of South East Asia: regional peace and stability; economic integration and cooperation; human and social development; ASEAN external relations and promotion campaigns – *annual*
  ↳ **ASEAN Statistical Indicators** – *annual*
  ↳ **Association of South East Asian Nations** *(Website)*

UN Economic and Social Commission for Asia and the Pacific (ESCAP)

Address:	UN Building, Rajadamnern Nok Avenue, Bangkok 10200, Thailand
Telephone:	+66 2 288 1234
Fax:	+66 2 288 1000
Website:	www.unescap.org

Website notes: information on socio-economic development issues in Asia and the Pacific. In-depth analysis and data on regional and country economic and financial structure; population trends; urban

vs rural development; environment and natural resources; tourism; and transports and infrastructures

Statistical Coverage: "Asia and the Pacific in Figures" section provides socio-economic data from 1980 to 1997 for a total of 56 countries. Includes population statistics; social indicators; employment; energy consumption; national accounts; external trade; central government expenditure by function; price index; tourism arrivals and receipts; etc

Obtaining Publications: from United Nations Sales Section, as described in main United Nations entry

Guides to Publications: details included in general Catalogue of United Nations Publications

Publications:
  ↳ **Asia-Pacific in Figures** – *annual*
  ↳ **Economic and Social Survey of Asia and the Pacific** – *annual*
  ↳ **Statistical Indicators for Asia and the Pacific** – *quarterly*
  ↳ **Statistical Yearbook for Asia and the Pacific** – *annual*
  ↳ **UN Economic and Social Commission for Asia and the Pacific** *(Website)*

□ CENTRAL & SOUTH AMERICA

Asociacin Latinamericana de Integracin/Associaāo Americana de Intergraāo (ALADI)

(Latin American Integration Association)

Address:	PO Box 577, Cebollati 1461, 11200 Montevideo, Uruguay
Telephone:	+598 2400 1121
Fax:	+598 2409 0649
E-mail:	sgaladi@aladi.org
Website:	www.aladi.org

Website notes: news, articles and statistics on the economic and financial climate in Central and South America, promoting trade and business activities between ALADI member countries (12 nations) and other world economic regions

Statistical Coverage: "Estadsticas" section provides socio-economic data for each member country and the ALADI region as a whole. Countries covered include: Argentina; Bolivia; Brazil; Chile; Colombia; Cuba; Ecuador; Mexico; Paraguay; Peru; Uruguay; and Venezuela. Data is provided for the period of 1990-2000, covering various socio-economic indicators e.g.: total population and general demographic trends; education, unemployment, and labour force structure; GDP; industrial & agricultural production; energy production and consumption rates; foreign investment; price indices; external trade indicators; and external debt

Year Established: 1980

Obtaining Publications: As above

Publications:
  ↳ **Asociacin Latinoamericana de Integracin/Associaāo Americana de Intergraāo (ALADI)** *(Latin American Integration Association) (Website)*

UN Economic Commission for Latin America and the Caribbean (ECLAC)

Address:	Edificio Naciones Unidas, Avenida Dag Hammarskjld s/n, Vitacura, Santiago, Chile
Telephone:	+56 2 210 2000/208 5051
Fax:	+56 2 208 0252
E-mail:	grosenthal@eclac.cl
Website:	www.eclac.cl

Website notes: information on major socio-economic projects developed by the UN in Latin America and the Caribbean. Access to various online publications covering a wide range of topics, from economic and social development to industrial resources, demographic studies, environmental issues, etc

Statistical Coverage: most statistics provided are included on selected on-line publications, covering different socio-economic topics. Access to the Annual Statistical Yearbook provides a wide range of country statistics on demographic trends and regional macro-economic indicators, production and trade, employment and labour force structure, etc. Other publications provide data on population dynamics and migrations, transports and economic forecasts for the region

Obtaining Publications: Unidad de Servicios de Informacin, add: Avenida Dag Hammarskjld s/n, Vitacura, Santiago de Chile; tel: (56-2) 210 2380/210 2149; fax: (56-2) 228 1947/210 2238; e-mail: dpisantiago@eclac.cl

Guides to Publications: online catalogue

Publications:

⮡ **Economic Survey of Latin America** – review of the latest most relevant economic and financial trends in Latin America – *annual*

⮡ **Social Panorama of Latin America** – assessment of social development in Latin America and the social agenda of the region's Governments – *annual*

⮡ **Statistical Yearbook for Latin America and the Caribbean** – economic and social trends in 25 to 30 countries of the Latin American and Caribbean region – *annual*

⮡ **UN Economic Commission for Latin America and the Caribbean** *(Comisin Econmica para Amrica Latina y el Caribe) (Website)*

◘ EASTERN EUROPE

Interstate Statistical Committee of the Commonwealth of Independent States

Address:	39, Myasnitskaya Str, 107450 Moscow, Russia
Telephone:	+7 952 074 237/4802
Fax:	+7 952 074 592
E-mail:	cisstat@online.ru or info@cisstat.com
Website:	www.cisstat.com

Website notes: official web site for the CIS: main macro-economic indicators (annual summary or current data) of Armenia, Azerbaijan, Belarus, Georgia, Kazakhstan, Kyrgyzstan, Moldova, Russia, Tajikistan, Turkmenistan, Ukraine and Uzbekistan

Statistical Coverage: statistical information section provides both monthly and annual data for all member countries. Covers general geographic statistics (country size, major cities, rivers, etc), population and unemployment and different economic data: GDP, industrial and agricultural production, capital investments, freight carried, retail trade turnover, industrial producers price index, consumer price index, exports and imports to CIS and other countries

Year Established: 1991

Obtaining Publications: as above

Guides to Publications: website provides online order form; online publications catalogue on new releases and publications already issued but still valid

Publications:

⮡ **CIS Statistical Yearbook** – detailed data on each state of the CIS by major industries; statistics on demographics and labour market, macro-economic and financial indicators, data on consumer market, prices, incomes and expenditures of population, standard of living – *annual*

⮡ **External Trade of the CIS & EU Countries** – information on foreign trade activities between CIS member countries and other world economic unions – *irregular*

⮡ **Industry of the CIS Countries** – provides main indicators on the development of the industrial sector in CIS countries: volume indices, output of industrial products, branch structure of industrial output, industrial producer's price indices, number of employees, average monthly wages, capital investments in industry through all sources of finance, financial performance of industrial enterprises and organisations, privatisation of industrial enterprises and units, use of enterprises production capacities – *irregular*

⮡ **Interstate Statistical Committee of the Commonwealth of Independent States** *(Website)*

⮡ **Labour Market in the CIS Countries in Figures and Diagrams** – overview of the labour market in the CIS countries. It contains information on labour supply and demand, employment and unemployment, labour migration, wages and salaries. Employment data is broken down by demographic criteria, sectors of activity (agriculture, industry, etc.) and occupational status – *irregular*

⮡ **National Accounts of the CIS Countries** – main tables and aggregates of the System of National Accounts (SNA) by CIS member states. Includes data on core accounts which show production, distribution, redistribution and final use of income as well as capital formation for the total economy, sectors and industries – *annual*

⮡ **Statistical Bulletin** – information on latest economic situation and progress of reforms in CIS member countries. It contains short-term data on different fields of economic and social activity as well as monthly report "Economy of the Commonwealth of Independent States" – *6 p.a.*

⮡ **Statistical Portrait** – brief statistics covering the economy, population, education, employment, consumption, etc. – *annual*

◘ MIDDLE EAST & AFRICA

African Development Bank

Address:	01 BP 1387, Rue Joseph Anoma, Abidjan 01, Cte d'Ivoire
Telephone:	+225 2020 4444
Fax:	+225 2020 4006
E-mail:	afdb@afdb.org
Website:	www.afdb.org

Website notes: information on all ADB member countries, including physical and social geographical data and basic economic indicators. Access to major publications and analysis of the bank's main activities and projects across the continent

Statistical Coverage: more detailed statistical information is provided by accessing the ADB Statistics Publications section. Besides a compendium of statistics on bank group operations, this same section includes selected statistics on African countries (human development indicators; macro-economic indicators; and external sector economic indicators); gender, poverty and environmental indicators; and comparative socio-economic indicators

Year Established: 1963

Obtaining Publications: publications and general information obtained at the Communication Unit, at the address above

Guides to Publications: a general guide to ADB's major publications is available in both English and French under the name ADB Brief/La BAD en Bref

Publications:

⮡ **ADB Statistics Pocket Book · 2002**

⮡ **AFB Statistics Publication** – compilation of different socio-economic statistics for each ADB member country, all of these available on-line – *annual*

⮡ **African Development Bank** *(Website)*

Afristat - Observatoire Economique et Statistique d'Afrique Subsaharienne

(Afristat - Subsaharan Africa's Institute of Economy and Statistics)

Address:	Bamako, Mali
Telephone:	+223 221 5500/221 6073
Fax:	+223 221 1140
E-mail:	afristat@afristat.org
Website:	www.afristat.org

Website notes: Afristat's official web site provides a series of economic, social, and environmental statistics for 17 sub-Saharan nations (Afristat works closely with national statistical offices of each country). Data is provided on: geography and climate; demographics; health and education; economic indicators and national accounts; transports and telecommunications; tourism; and the environment. It provides direct links to each national statistical organisation

Year Established: 1993

Publications:

⮡ **Afristat · Observatoire Economique et Statistique d'Afrique Subsaharienne** *(Afristat · Subsaharan Africa's Institute of Economy and Statistics) (Website)*

UN Economic and Social Commission for Western Asia (ESCWA)

Address:	PO Box 11-8575, Riad el-Solh Square, Beirut, Lebanon
Telephone:	+961 198 1301 ext 1845
Fax:	+961 1 981 510/511/512
E-mail:	unescwa@escwa.org.lb or gemayel.escwa@un.org
Website:	www.escwa.org.lb

Website notes: key research reports including statistical data on Western Asia and the Middle East region, with information on a wide range of major economic and social development issues for a total of 13 countries

Statistical Coverage: regional and country statistics provided focusing on major socio-economic indicators; data is provided on regional demographic trends; energy resources; trade; labour force and unemployment; literacy and education, etc

Obtaining Publications: as above

Guides to Publications: free and sales publications can be ordered on-line

Publications:
↳ **Demographic and Related Socio-Economic Data Sheets** — *annual*
↳ **Industry Review in ESCWA Countries**
↳ **Survey of Economic and Social Developments in the ESCWA Region**
↳ **UN Economic and Social Commission for Western Asia** *(Website)*

UN Economic Commission for Africa

Address:	**PO Box 3001, Africa Hall, Addis Ababa, Ethiopia**
Telephone:	**+251 1 515 826/517 200**
Fax:	**+251 1 510 365/514 416**
E-mail:	**ecainfo@uneca.org**
Website:	**www.uneca.org**

Website notes: wide range of key research reports on the economic and social development of 53 African countries, promoting international co-operation for Africa's development

Year Established: 1958

Obtaining Publications: same as above

Guides to Publications: details included in general Catalogue of United Nations Publications

Publications:
↳ **Africa in Figures** — *annual*
↳ **African Statistical Yearbook** — presents data arranged on a country basis for 53 ECA members states. Statistics cover: population, national accounts, agriculture, industry, transport and communications, foreign trade, prices, social statistics — *annual*
↳ **Compendium of Intra-African & Related Foreign Trade Statistics** — *irregular*
↳ **UN Economic Commission for Africa** *(Website)*

National Official Organisations

◻ AFGHANISTAN

Central Statistics Office

Address:	PO Box 2002, Ansari Watt, Kabul
Telephone:	+93 22 448/21 866 (through local operator)

◻ ALGERIA

Office National de la Statistique (ONS)
(National Statistical Office)

Address:	BP 2025, 8/10, rue des Mousebilinne, Algiers
Telephone:	+213 274 4141/100
Fax:	+213 274 3839
E-mail:	ons@onssiege.ons.dz
Website:	www.ons.dz

Website notes: provides information in Arabic, French, and English of most updated statistical titles and publications; includes general online statistics on: population; consumer price index; agricultural and industrial production price index; economic accounts; housing; education; motor vehicle park; etc

Year Established: 1964

Guides to Publications: online catalogue includes all publications. The establishment is in charge of collecting, processing and diffusing socio-economic statistical information such as population census, labour surveys, industrial enterprise surveys, etc

Publications:
↳ **Bulletin des Statistiques** *(Statistical Bulletin)* — quarterly updated socio-economic statistics — *quarterly*
↳ **Indice des prix à la consommation** *(Consumer Price Index)* — consumer price index by food and non-food products — *monthly*
↳ **L'Annuaire Statistique de l'Algérie** *(Statistical Yearbook of Algeria)* — annual compilation of national socioeconomic statistics covering a wide variety of topics, including: geography and climate; employment; health and education; agricultural and industrial resources; energy resources; external trade; transports and communications; tourism; price index; etc — *annual*
↳ **Office National des Statistiques** *(National Statistical Office) (Website)*

◻ ANGOLA

Instituto Nacional de Estatística
(National Institute of Statistics)

Address:	CP 1215, Luanda
Telephone:	+244 232 0430
Fax:	+244 232 0430
E-mail:	ine@angonet.gn.apc.org

Publications:
↳ **Anuario Estatistico** *(Statistical Yearbook)* — *annual*
↳ **Boletim Demografico** *(Demographic Bulletin)* — *annual*
↳ **Boletim Mensal** *(Monthly Bulletin)* — *monthly*
↳ **Estatisticas do Comercio Externo** *(Foreign Trade Statistics)* — foreign trade statistics — *irregular*
↳ **Inquerito sobre o Emprego e Desemprego** — employment and unemployment statistics — *annual*
↳ **Perfil Estatístico Económico e Social** *(Socio-economic Statistical Profile)* — socio-economic statistical profile — *annual*

◻ ANGUILLA

Statistics Unit Anguilla

Address:	PO Box 60, Old Court House, The Valley
Telephone:	+1264 497 3986
Fax:	+1264 497 3986
E-mail:	stats@gov.ai

Obtaining Publications: same as above
Guides to Publications: online catalogue

Publications:
↳ **Anguilla Statistics Unit** *(Website)*
↳ **Consumer Price Index** — *annual*

◻ ANTIGUA

Ministry of Finance Statistics Division

Address:	Redcliffe Street, St John's
Telephone:	+1268 462 4775/3233
Fax:	+1268 462 1622
E-mail:	anustats@candw.ag

◻ ARGENTINA

Instituto Nacional de Estadística y Censos (INDEC)
(National Institute of Statistics and Census)

Address:	Julio A. Roca 615 - PB, 1067 Buenos Aires
Telephone:	+54 114 349 9652/4
Fax:	+54 114 349 9621/52
E-mail:	ces@indec.mecon.gov.ar
Website:	www.indec.mecon.ar

Website notes: official web site of INDEC. Offers a wide variety of national statistical data covering socio-economic and financial indicators. Access to different online publications and list of statistical publications for sale produced by the Institute. Available both in English and Spanish

Statistical Coverage: statistics provided cover a wide range of indicators. A compilation of most relevant socio-economic data can be found by downloading the "Anuario Estadístico". Data coverage period varies from table to table, though most offer figures for the last 5 years. Statistics are provided on: general geographic country data; population (latest census, 1991); social indicators (household consumption; education; health services; labour force); economic sectors (agriculture; manufacturing industry; commerce; communications; etc); financial activities; public and external sectors; price index; and national accounts

Guides to Publications: online catalogue and publications plan

Publications:
↳ **Anuario Estadístico de la República Argentina** *(Annual Statistical Yearbook)* — annual socio-demographic and economic statistics — *annual*
↳ **Argentine Foreign Trade Statistics** — export and import statistics by destination and by country of origin — *quarterly*
↳ **Encuesta Industrial Annual** *(Annual Industrial Survey)* — information covering the industrial sector, including: production value; income levels; employment; hours worked; consumption of energy — *quarterly*
↳ **Instituto Nacional de Estadística y Censos (INDEC)** *(National Institute of Statistics and Census) (Website)*
↳ **Situación y Evolución Social** *(Social Development Statistics)* — series of socio-economic indicators covering: demographic trends; family and households; education and health services; labour force and unemployment; etc — *annual*

◻ ARMENIA

Ministry of Statistics State Register and Analysis of the Republic of Armenia

Address:	3 Government House, Republic Square, 375010 Yerevan
Telephone:	+374 524 213
Fax:	+374 521 921
E-mail:	armstat@sci.am
Website:	www.armstat.am

Year Established: 1921
Obtaining Publications: same as above
Guides to Publications: online catalogue

Publications:

↳ **Foreign Trade of the Republic of Armenia**

▫ ARUBA

Centraal Bureau voor de Statistiek

(Central Bureau of Statistics)

Address:	Sun Plaza Mall, L G Smith Boulevard 116, Oranjestad
Telephone:	+297 837 433
Fax:	+297 838 057
E-mail:	cbs@toaruba.com
Website:	www.arubastatistics.com

Website notes: socio-economic information and statistics on Aruba covering: labour force statistics, business structure and foreign trade statistics

Publications:

↳ **Centraal Bureau voor de Statistiek** *(Website)*
↳ **Economic Profile** — contains short-term economic indicators of Aruba — *quarterly*
↳ **Social Profile** — general statistical coverage of Aruba, including information on geography and climate, demography and population, social affairs, etc — *quarterly*
↳ **Statistical Yearbook** — contains statistics on the social and economic situation of Aruba — *annual*
↳ **Statistics of Foreign Trade** — contains global information on trade for Aruba by commodity codes and country of destination — *quarterly*

▫ AUSTRALIA

Australian Bureau of Statistics (ABS)

Address:	5th Floor QBE Building, 33-35 Ainslie Avenue, Canberra ACT 2616
Telephone:	+61 2 6207 0326
Fax:	+61 2 6207 0282
E-mail:	client.services@abs.gov.au
Website:	www.abs.gov.au

Website notes: general information on ABS and its products and services. Offers a wide range of online services, including: statistical profile of Australia; guide to publications and products/main publication features; and economic and social data. It also includes media releases (access to archives back to 1997) and weekly statistical releases on specific socio-economic and financial topics

Statistical Coverage: statistical section provides a wide range of online social, economic and financial data. Among others, the Key National Indicators sub-section includes latest national socio-economic statistics covering different topics such as: consumer price index; GDP; unemployment rate; retail trade; average weekly earnings; estimated resident population; building approvals; new motor vehicle registrations; and company profits. Other annual statistical databases, online publications and special articles are available, some of these are subject to charge

Guides to Publications: online catalogue

Publications:

↳ **Agriculture, Australia** — structure of Australian farming sector, details of land use, crop and horticultural activity, livestock numbers and financial results — *annual*
↳ **Australian Bureau of Statistics (ABS)** *(Website)*
↳ **Australian Demographic Statistics** — estimates of total population for States, Territories and the whole of Australia — *quarterly*
↳ **Consumer Price Index** — movements in retail prices of services and goods in urban Australia. Goods and services are divided into the following groups: food; clothing; housing; household equipment and operation; transportation; tobacco and alcohol; health and personal care; recreation and education — *quarterly*
↳ **International Merchandise Trade, Australia** — statistics on trade activities (exports and imports) between Australia and its main trade partners. Data provided by commodity, state, major economic category and industry of origin, with some tables covering a period of 12 years — *annual*
↳ **Labour Statistics, Australia** — statistical overview of the labour force in Australia: socio-demographic characteristics; employment, unemployment and underemployment; earnings, labour costs and employment benefits; working hours, industrial relations, training and international comparisons — *annual*
↳ **Manufacturing Industry, Australia** — compilation of final results from the Manufacturing Survey for establishments across Australia. Data on employment and wages; turnover; and industry value-added (IVA) classified by industry class — *annual*
↳ **Manufacturing Production, Australia** — estimates of production quantities for 28 major indicators, including food, wood products, fuels, building materials and metals. Contains original, seasonally adjusted and trend data for quarterly items — *quarterly*

↳ **Manufacturing Production, Australia: Food, Drink, Tobacco, Stock and Poultry Food** — annual production statistics for a wide range of food and drink products, as well as tobacco and cigarettes — *annual*
↳ **Motor Vehicles in Australia** — overview of the Australian Automotive market: statistics including Motor Vehicle Census counts; annual new motor vehicle registration data, information; vehicle ownership; and vehicle manufacturing, retailing and trade data. Most tables and graphs are complemented by an analytical commentary on the statistics — *annual*
↳ **Retail Trade Australia** — statistics covering the Australian retail industry: estimates turnover for retail and selected service establishments for all States and Australia in current prices — *monthly*
↳ **Sales of Australian Wine and Brandy by Winemakers** — quantity of wine sales classified by type (fortified, table, sparkling, etc.) and brandy. Sales of table wine further classified by container type. Wine and brandy exports and imports cleared for home consumption. Includes seasonally adjusted and trend estimates — *annual*
↳ **Tourism Indicators, Australia** — overview of the tourism industry in Australia, combining data from the Survey of Tourist Accommodation (STA) and Overseas Arrivals and Departures (OAD) collections — *annual*
↳ **Yearbook Australia** — compilation of annual statistics, combining data from various publications and surveys.Covers Australia's geography and climate, government, international relations and defence and a wide range of socio-economic indicators — *annual*

▫ AZERBAIJAN

State Statistical Committee of Azerbaijan Republic

Address:	Inshatchilar Str., 370136 Baku
Telephone:	+994 1238 6498/9376
Fax:	+994 1238 2442
E-mail:	ssc@azstat.org
Website:	www.azstat.org

Obtaining Publications: same as above
Guides to Publications: online catalogue

Publications:

↳ **State Statistical Committee of Azerbaijan Republic** *(Website)*
↳ **Statistical Yearbook of Azerbaijan** — *Annual (Website)*

▫ BAHAMAS

Department of Statistics

Address:	PO Box 3904, Nassau
Telephone:	+1242 325 6520
Fax:	+1242 325 5149

Obtaining Publications: same as above
Guides to Publications: online catalogue

Publications:

↳ **Annual Review of Prices** — *annual*
↳ **Bahamas in Figures** — *annual*
↳ **External Trade** — *annual*
↳ **Hotels, Motels and Guesthouses and Restaurants: New Providence, Paradise Island and Grand Bahama** — *annual*
↳ **Household Income Report** — includes Labour Force Report — *annual*
↳ **Statistical Abstract** — *annual*
↳ **Statistical Summary** — *quarterly*
↳ **Summary of External Trade Statistics** — *quarterly*

▫ BAHRAIN

Central Statistics Organisation

Address:	PO Box 5835, Manama
Telephone:	+973 725 725
Fax:	+973 728 169
Website:	www.bahrain.gov.bh/English/stats/index.asp

Obtaining Publications: same as above
Guides to Publications: online catalogue

Publications:

↳ **Bahrain in Figures** — *yearly (Website)*

◻ BANGLADESH

Bangladesh Bureau of Statistics

Address:	E-27/A, Agargaon, Sher-e-Bangla Nagar, Dhaka 1207
Telephone:	+880 2911 8045/811 5942
Fax:	+880 2911 1064
E-mail:	ndbp@bangla.net
Website:	www.bbsgov.org

Obtaining Publications: same as above

Guides to Publications: online catalogue

Publications:
- ↳ **Agricultural Production Levels in Bangladesh** — *annual*
- ↳ **Bangladesh Bureau of Statistics** *(Website)*
- ↳ **Monthly Indicators of Current Economic Situation of Bangladesh** — money and banking, foreign aid and trade, agriculture, food production and consumption — *monthly*
- ↳ **Statistical Yearbook of Bangladesh** — *annual*
- ↳ **Yearbook of Agricultural Statistics of Bangladesh** — *annual*

◻ BARBADOS

Barbados Statistical Service

Address:	3rd Floor, National Insurance Building, Fairchild Street, Bridgetown
Telephone:	+1246 427 7841
Fax:	+1246 435 2198
E-mail:	barstats@caribsurf.com
Website:	www.bgis.gov.bb/stats

Website notes: general socio-economic statistical information on Barbados, focusing on the travel and tourism industries

Obtaining Publications: same as above

Guides to Publications: online catalogue

Publications:
- ↳ **Barbados Statistical Service** *(Website)*
- ↳ **Digest of Tourism Statistics** — *annual*
- ↳ **Monthly Digest of Statistics** — *monthly*

◻ BELIZE

Central Statistical Office, Ministry of Finance

Address:	New Administration Building, Cayo District, Belmopan
Telephone:	+501 822 207/352
Fax:	+501 823 206
E-mail:	csogob@blt.net
Website:	www.belize.gov.bz/cabinet/s_musa/welcome.shtml

Obtaining Publications: same as above

Guides to Publications: online catalogue

Publications:
- ↳ **Abstract of Statistics** — *annual*
- ↳ **Central Statistical Office, Ministry of Finance**
- ↳ **Consumer Price Index of Belize** — *quarterly*
- ↳ **Labour Force Indicators** — *annual*
- ↳ **National Census Report** — *irregular*
- ↳ **Social Indicators Report** — *annual*

◻ BENIN

Institut National de la Statistique et de l'Analyse Economique (INSAE)
(Institute of National Statistics and Economic Analysis)

Address:	BP 323, Cotonou
Telephone:	+229 308 243/4
Fax:	+229 308 246
E-mail:	insae@planben.intnet.bj
Website:	www.demographie.refer.org/benin.htm

Year Established: 1994

Obtaining Publications: same as above

Guides to Publications: online catalogue

Publications:
- ↳ **Annuaire Statistique de Benin** *(Statistical Yearbook of Benin)* — *annual*
- ↳ **Institut National de la Statistique et de l'Analyse Economique**

◻ BERMUDA

Ministry of Finance Statistical Department

Address:	PO Box HM 3015, 30 Parliament Street, Hamilton, HM 12
Telephone:	+1441 295 5151
Fax:	+1441 295 5727
E-mail:	gvstats@ibl.bm

Obtaining Publications: same as above

Publications:
- ↳ **Retail Sales Index** — *monthly*

◻ BHUTAN

Ministry of Communications, Department of Information-Bhutan

Address:	PO Box 204, Motithang, Thimphu
Telephone:	+975 22 483/925
Fax:	+975 22 975

◻ BOLIVIA

Instituto Nacional de Estadística (INE)
(National Institute of Statistics)

Address:	PO Box 6129, Calle José Carrasco Nº 1391, La Paz
Telephone:	+591 222 333
Fax:	+591 222 2693
E-mail:	ceninf@ine.gov.bo
Website:	www.ine.gov.bo

Website notes: key figures of Bolivia: geography and population; social statistics; macroeconomic statistics; environment and development

Guides to Publications: online catalogue

Publications:
- ↳ **Anuario de Comercio Exterior** *(Foreign Trade Yearbook)* — *annual*
- ↳ **Anuario de Estadísticas Industriales** *(Industrial Statistics Yearbook)* — *annual*
- ↳ **Anuario Estadístico** *(Statistical Yearbook)* — contains information on: social and economic statistics, production, prices, exchange rates, banking and finance, stock market, municipal infrastructure, foreign investment — *annual*
- ↳ **Bolivia en Cifras** *(Bolivia in Figures)* — *annual*
- ↳ **Censo de Población y Vivienda 2001** *(Population and Home Census 2001)* — *annual*
- ↳ **Comercio Exterior** *(External Trade)* — import/export information — *annual*
- ↳ **Encuesta Nacional Agropecuaria. Campana** *(Agroindustry Survey)* — results from the national farming survey
- ↳ **Indice de Precios al Consumidor** *(Consumer Price Index)* — consumer price index — *annual*
- ↳ **Instituto Nacional de Estadística** *(National Institute of Statistics)* *(Website)*

↳ **Resultados de la Produccion Agricola** *(Agricultural Production - Results)* — annual

↳ **Turismo en Cifras Flujo de Viajeros via Aerea** *(Tourism in Figures)* — tourism figures — *annual*

▫ BOTSWANA

Central Statistics Office

Address:	**Private Bag 0024, Gaborone**
Telephone:	**+267 352 200**
Fax:	**+267 352 201**
E-mail:	**csobots@gov.bw**
Website:	**www.cso.gov.bw**

Obtaining Publications: same as above

Guides to Publications: online catalogue

Publications:
↳ **Central Statistics Office** *(Website)*
↳ **Consumer Price Statistics** — *monthly*
↳ **Demographic Statistics** — contains demographic data — *annual*
↳ **Household Surveys** — statistical indicators covering seven topics including household income and consumption, household resources for production and income earning, health, and education
↳ **Industrial Statistics** — basic indicators on the economic performance of the industrial sectors in the economy and information pertaining to their contribution to the Gross Domestic Product
↳ **Labour Force Survey** — data on economic activity, unemployment, income, etc. — *annual*
↳ **National Accounts of Botswana** — provide objective measures of the country's level of economic activity and performance. They measure production, consumption, accumulation and external trade of the economy. — *annual*
↳ **Statistical Bulletin** — summary of major demographic, social and economic indicators — *monthly*
↳ **Trade Statistics** — compiled as a by-product from customs documents. Goods declared at ports of entry/exit are classified according to the Harmonised Commodity and Coding System (HS) of Botswana, which is an adapted version of the internationally recognised Harmonised Commodity and Coding System
↳ **Transport and Communications Statistics** — *annual*

▫ BRAZIL

Instituto Brasileiro de Geografia e Estatística (IBGE)

(Brazilian Agency for Statistical and Geographic Information)

Address:	**Biblioteca, Rua General Canabarro, 706, térreo - Bairro Maracanã, 20271-201 Rio de Janeiro RJ**
Telephone:	**+55 212 514 4715/0123**
Fax:	**+55 212 514 0123**
E-mail:	**bibliotecacddi@ibge.gov.br**
Website:	**www.ibge.gov.br**

Website notes: compilation of different socio-economic statistics on Brazil, covering: demography and population; industry and commerce; national accounts and finances; etc

Obtaining Publications: same as above

Publications:
↳ **Anuário Estatístico do Brasil** *(Statistical Yearbook of Brazil)* — statistical yearbook covering all sectors of the Brazilian economy — *annual*
↳ **Instituto Brasileiro de Geografia e Estatística** *(Brazilian Institute for Statistical and Geographic Information)* (Website)

▫ BRITISH VIRGIN ISLANDS

The Development Planning Unit

Address:	**Road Town, Tortola**
Telephone:	**494 3701**
Fax:	**494 3947**
E-mail:	**dpu@dpu.org**
Website:	**dpu.org**

Guides to Publications: online guide to publications

Publications:
↳ **Development Planning Unit**

↳ **Main Economic Indicators. Quarterly Bulletin** — *Quarterly*

▫ BURKINA FASO

Institut National de la Statistique et de la Demographie

(National Institute of Statistics and Demography)

Address:	**BP 374, 555 Boulevard de la Révolution, Ouagadougou 01**
Telephone:	**+226 324 801/803/976**
Fax:	**+226 310 760**

Publications:
↳ **Bulletin Annuaire d'Information Statistique et Economique** *(Annual Statistical Yearbook of Economy and Finance)* — annual

---

▫ BURUNDI

Institut de Statistiques et d'Etudes Economiques du Burundi (ISTEEBU))

(Institute of Statistics and Economic Studies of Burundi)

Address:	**BP 1156, Bujumbura**
Telephone:	**+257 226 729**

Publications:
↳ **Annuaire Statistique** *(Statistical Yearbook)* — annual
↳ **Annuaire Statistique des Prix** *(Annual Price Statistics)* — annual
↳ **Bulletin Mensuel des Prix** *(Monthly Price Bulletin)* — monthly
↳ **Bulletin Statistique Trimestriel** *(quarterly Statistical Bulletin)* — quarterly
↳ **Comptes Economiques** *(Economic Accounts)* — national accounts — annual

---

▫ CAMBODIA

National Institute of Statistics of Cambodia, Ministry of Planning

Address:	**Sankat Boeung Keng Kong 2, 386 Monivong Boulevard, Phnom Penh**
Telephone:	**+855 23 216 538**
Fax:	**+855 23 213 650**
E-mail:	**census@camnet.com.kh**
Website:	**www.nis.gov.kh**

Website notes: statistics mainly on demographic and development issues

Statistical Coverage: population figures; population density; age distribution; gender ratios; marital status; adult literacy; educational attainment; migration; labour force participation rates; main source of drinking water; main source of electricity; main source of cooking fuel; population projections; province profiles

Obtaining Publications: same as above

Guides to Publications: online catalogue

Publications:
↳ **Cambodia Demographic and Health Survey 2000**
↳ **General Population Census of Cambodia - Final Census Results**
↳ **National Institute of Statistics** *(Website)*

▫ CAMEROON

Direction de la Statistique et de la Comptabilité Nationale

(Directorate of Statistics and National Accounts)

Address:	**PO Box 660, Yaoundé**
Telephone:	**+237 220 912/221 441**
Fax:	**+237 232 437**

Obtaining Publications: same as above

Publications:
↳ **Bulletin Mensuel de Statistique** *(Monthly Statistical Bulletin)* — monthly
↳ **Bulletin Trimestriel de Conjoncture** *(quarterly Conjunctural Bulletin)* — quarterly
↳ **Comptes Nationaux du Cameroun** *(Cameroun Economic Accounts)* — annual

↳ **Note Annuelle de Statistique** – *annual*

▣ CANADA

Statistique Canada
(Statistics Canada)

Address:	**Statistical Reference Centre, Holland Avenue, Ottawa, ON K1A 0T6**
Telephone:	**+1 613 951 8116**
Fax:	**+1 613 951 0581**
E-mail:	**infostats@statcan.ca**
Website:	**www.statcan.ca**

Website notes: available in French and English, provides general information on new products and services of the national statistical institute of Canada: daily news; selected articles; conferences and seminars; online publications; and access to statistical databases

Statistical Coverage: "Canadian Statistics" section provides latest data on land and population, economy and government and politics: 1) Land and population statistics cover: geography and environment; population; education and health; labour force and unemployment; travel and leisure; etc. 2) Economic section includes data on: daily updated indicators on national accounts, trade and labour; general economic conditions; primary industries; communications, transport, and national and international trade; manufacturing and construction; etc; 3) State statistics provide data on governmental issues; justice; and crime

Obtaining Publications: same as above

Guides to Publications: Statistics Canada Publications List (annual, free of charge)

Publications:
- ↳ **Agriculture Economic Statistics** – *2 p.a.*
- ↳ **Beverage and Tobacco Products Industries** – analyses recent development and market trends. Information is based on the results of the Annual Survey of Manufactures – *annual*
- ↳ **Canada Year Book** – overview of Canada's socio-economic structure, government policies and general living conditions – *every two years*
- ↳ **Canada's Food Processing Industry** – provides an overview of the performance and trends of Canada's food processing industry – *irregular*
- ↳ **Canadian Social Trends** – discusses the social, economic and demographic changes affecting the lives of Canadians. Contains the latest figures for major social indicators – *quarterly*
- ↳ **Consumer Price Index** – national coverage plus detail on 15 regional cities – *monthly*
- ↳ **Dairy Review** – a statistical summary of the dairy situation in Canada, including farm sales of milk for fluid and manufacturing purposes; cash receipts from farm sales; and production and stocks of creamery butter, cheddar cheese and other dairy products – *quarterly*
- ↳ **Food Consumption in Canada** – contains supply, disposition and per capita data for the following food groups: cereals, sugars and syrups, pulses and nuts, beverages, dairy products and by-products, poultry, eggs and meats – *annual*
- ↳ **Food Expenditure Survey** – provides estimates of food expenditures and quantities purchased by households – *irregular*
- ↳ **Retail Chain and Department Stores** – retail sales of such stores by kind of business, province, selected localities, number of stores operated annually, sales volume, stocks, cost of goods sold, etc. – *annual*
- ↳ **Retail Trade** – total retail sales by province and kind of business, for chain and independent stores – *monthly*
- ↳ **Statistics Canada** *(Website)*
- ↳ **Tourism Statistical Digest** – incorporates data on travel and tourism in the form of analytical texts, charts and tables on demand and supply of tourism products and services. Data is presented at the national, provincial and regional/municipal levels – *every two years*
- ↳ **Wholesaling and Retailing in Canada** – contains statistical information on 16 retail trade groups and 11 wholesale trade groups – *annual*

▣ CAPE VERDE

Instituto Nacional de Estatística (INE)
(National Institute of Statistics)

Address:	**Avenida Amílcar Cabral, CP 116, Praia**
Telephone:	**+238 613 960/827**
Website:	**www.ine.cv**

Website notes: information on INE services and products available in Portuguese only; catalogue of publications; news

Statistical Coverage: statistics provided focusing on major demographic and socio-economic indicators, health and education, transport and tourism, geography and climate

Guides to Publications: on-line catalogue of publications

Publications:
- ↳ **Boletim Trimestral de Estatística** *(Statistical Bulletin)* – covers demographics, production, external trade, public finances and prices – *4 p.a.*
- ↳ **Instituto Nacional de Estatística** *(National Institute of Statistics)* – *annual* *(Website)*

▣ CAYMAN ISLANDS

Finance and Economic Development. Statistics Office

Address:	**4th Floor, Elizabethan Square, George Town, Grand Cayman**
Telephone:	**+1345 949 0940**
Fax:	**+1345 949 8782**

▣ CENTRAL AFRICAN REPUBLIC

Division des Statistiques et des Etudes Economiques (DSEE)
(Statistics and Economic Studies Division)

Address:	**Boite Postal 696, Bangui**
Telephone:	**614 574/612 554**
Fax:	**614 711/617 387**

Obtaining Publications: same as above

Publications:
- ↳ **Bulletin Trimestriel de Statistique** *(quarterly Statistical Bulletin)* – *quarterly*

▣ CHILE

Instituto Nacional de Estadísticas (INE)
(National Institute of Statistics)

Address:	**Casilla 498-3, Avenida Presidente Bulnes 418, Santiago**
Telephone:	**+56 2 366 7777/7504**
Fax:	**+56 2 671 2169/4349**
E-mail:	**cedoc@ine.cl**
Website:	**www.ine.cl**

Website notes: official site of the National Institute of Statistics of Chile, including information on products and services; latest news, press releases and statistical documents

Statistical Coverage: a wide range of both annual and monthly statistics is provided online, covering different topics within Chile's social and economic structure. "Estadísticas Territoriales" provides a general overview of Chile's main socio-economic regions between 1997-2001; "Indicadores Mensuales" includes monthly updated statistics for different indicators covering: price indices; industrial production by industry/sector; and labour force, unemployment and wages. "Chile en Cifras" (Chile in Numbers) provides 2001 statistics on population, industry, society, economy, services and agriculture

Guides to Publications: publications catalogue

Publications:
- ↳ **Instituto Nacional de Estadísticas** *(National Institute of Statistics)* *(Website)*

▣ CHINA

National Bureau of Statistics

Address:	
Telephone:	**+86 106 857 3311/86328/86327**
Fax:	**+86 106 852 5899**
E-mail:	**info@stats.gov.cn**
Website:	**www.stats.gov.cn**

Website notes: access to the latest online editions of the publication "China Statistical Yearbook", including various statistics on: national accounts; population; employment and wages; investment; production and consumption of energy; agriculture; industry; construction; education and health; and general economic indicators

Publications:

↳ **National Bureau of Statistics** *(Website)*

▫ COLOMBIA

Departamento Administrativo Nacional de Estadística (DANE)
(National Department of Statistics)

Address:	Apartado Aéreo 80043, Zona Postal 611, Transversal 45 No. 26-70 Interior 1 - CAN, Bogotá DC
Telephone:	+57 1 597 8300
Fax:	+57 1597 8399
E-mail:	dane@dane.gov.co
Website:	www.dane.gov.co

Website notes: general information on the Institute, its products and services provided. Includes press releases, links to other national and international statistical institutes and a wide range of national socio-economic statistics

Statistical Coverage: "Información Estadística" section provides annual and monthly figures for a wide range of socio-economic areas: demography and population; labour force; standard of living; education; consumer prices; services; building and construction; finances; and national and external trade

Guides to Publications: online catalogue

Publications:
↳ **Anuario de Comercio** *(Trade Yearbook) – annual*
↳ **Boletín de Estadística** *(Statistical Bulletin) – quarterly*
↳ **Departamento Administrativo Nacional de Estadística** *(National Department of Statistics) (Website)*
↳ **Encuesta Annual Manufacturera** *(Manufacturing Industry Survey) – annual*
↳ **Indicadores de Coyuntura** *(Economic Indicators) – monthly*

▫ COMOROS

Direction Centrale de la Statistique
(Central Directorate of Statistics)

Address:	BP 131, Moroni
Fax:	732 629

▫ CONGO, DEMOCRATIC REPUBLIC

Institut National de la Statistique
(National Institute of Statistics)

Address:	BP 20, Kinshasa
Telephone:	123 1401

Obtaining Publications: same as above

▫ CONGO-BRAZZAVILLE

Centre National de la Statistique et des Etudes Economiques, Direction des Statistiques Démocratiques et Sociales
(Centre for National Statistics and Economic Studies)

Address:	BP 2031, Ministère du Plan, Brazzaville
Telephone:	+242 834 324/815 909
Fax:	+242 815 909
E-mail:	cnsee@hotmail.com

Obtaining Publications: same as above

Guides to Publications: online catalogue

Publications:
↳ **Annuaire Statistique** *(Statistical Yearbook)* – statistical coverage includes subjects such as demography, prices and household expenditure; labour, social welfare; public health; environment; education; rural industry; forestry and fisheries; mining; manufacturing; energy; housing and building; transport and communication; recreation and travel – *annual*
↳ **Bulletin de Statistique** *(Statistical Bulletin)* – key socio-economic statistics – *quarterly*
↳ **Cadre Comptable National** – national account statistics – *annual*

↳ **Compte de la Nation** *(National Accounts)* – national accounts data – *annual*
↳ **Indice des prix à la consommation** *(Consumer Price Index)* – *monthly*
↳ **Rapport d'Activités des Entreprises du Secteur Moderne** – information on companies operating in Congo-Brazzaville – *annual*

▫ COSTA RICA

Instituto Nacional de Estadística y Censos
(National Statistical Office)

Address:	Apartado 10163, Ministerio de Economia Industria y Comercio, Avenida 4, Calle Central, Edificio Rex, 1000 San José
Telephone:	+506 221 9656
Fax:	+506 223 0813
E-mail:	inecinfo@racsa.co.cr
Website:	www.meic.go.cr/inec

Website notes: provides access to various publications, including the Anuario Estadístico, including annual data on: demographic trends; education and health; agricultural and industrial resources; labour force; public finances; tourism; etc

Guides to Publications: online publications

Publications:
↳ **Anuario Estadístico de Costa Rica** *(Statistical Yearbook of Costa Rica)* – compilation of annual main socio-economic indicators – *annual*
↳ **Instituto Nacional de Estadística y Censos** *(National Institute of Statistics and Census) (Website)*

▫ CÔTE D'IVOIRE

Direction de la Statistique, Ministère du Plan
(Directorate of Statistics, Ministry of Planning)

Address:	01 BP V55, Abidjan 01
Telephone:	+225 210 566/538
Fax:	+225 214 401
E-mail:	statistique@aviso.ci or edsci2@netafric.ci

Obtaining Publications: same as above

Publications:
↳ **Bulletin Mensuel de Statistiques** *(Monthly Statistical Bulletin)* – *monthly*

▫ CUBA

Comité Estatal de Estadísticas
(State Commitee of Statistics)

Address:	PO Box 6016, Paseo 60 y 5a Vedado, Havana 12300
Telephone:	+53 731 5171
Fax:	+53 733 3083

Obtaining Publications: same as above

Publications:
↳ **Anuario Estadístico de Cuba** *(Statistical Yearbook of Cuba)* – annual data covering the main social and economic indicators – *annual*
↳ **Censo de Población y Viviendas** *(Demographic Census)* – population and housing statistics – *annual*
↳ **Revista Estadística** *(Statistical Journal)* – statistical journal covering social and economic statistics

---

▫ DJIBOUTI

Direction Nationale de la Statistique
(National Directorate of Statistics)

Address:	BP 1846 and 67, Djibouti
Telephone:	+253 351 682
Fax:	+253 350 949

Obtaining Publications: same as above

□ DOMINICAN REPUBLIC

Oficina Nacional de Estadísticas y Censos
(National Institute of Statistics and Census)

Address:	Apartado de Correos 1342, Edificio de Oficinas Gubernamentales "Juan Pablo Duarte" 8 y 9 piso, Avenida México, Santo Domingo
Telephone:	+1809 682 7777
Fax:	+1809 685 4424
E-mail:	ofic.estadis@codetel.net.do
Website:	www.estadistica.gov.do

Website notes: key socio-economic indicators: demography; population; education; labour market. Includes national and regional data

Obtaining Publications: same as above

Publications:
- ↳ **Anuario estadistico de la Republica Dominicana** *(Dominican Republic Statistical Yearbook)* – annual
- ↳ **Oficina Nacional de Estadísticas y Censos** *(National Office of Statistics and Census) (Website)*

□ ECUADOR

Instituto Nacional de Estadística y Censos (INEC)
(Institute of National Statistics and Census)

Address:	Juan Larrea N° 534, Riofrío, Quito
Telephone:	+593 2 529 858/544 326
Fax:	+593 2 509 836
E-mail:	inec1@ecnet.ec or inec2@ecua.net.ec
Website:	www.inec.gov.ec

Website notes: key socio-economic indicators: manufacturing and mining industries; commerce; services; demography; housing; national accounts; prices

Guides to Publications: List of Publications

Publications:
- ↳ **Actividad Industrial** *(Industrial Activity)* – annual
- ↳ **Encuesta Anual de Comercio Interno** *(Internal Trade Survey)* – internal trade survey – annual
- ↳ **Encuesta de Condiciones de Vida** *(Living Standards Survey)* – annual
- ↳ **Encuesta de Restaurantes, Hoteles y Servicios** *(Hotels and Catering Survey)* – hotel, restaurant and catering survey – annual
- ↳ **Instituto Nacional de Estadística y Censos** *(Institute of National Statistics and Census) (Website)*
- ↳ **Sistema Estadistico Agropecuario** *(Agricultural Statistics)* – agricultural statistics – annual

□ EGYPT

Central Agency for Public Mobilisation and Statistics

Address:	PO Box 2086, Salah Salem St., Cairo
Telephone:	+20 2 402 3031/402 4229
Fax:	+20 2 402 4099
E-mail:	capmas@capmas.gov.eg
Website:	www.capmas.gov.eg

Year Established: 1964

Obtaining Publications: same as above

Guides to Publications: online catalogue available

Publications:
- ↳ **Central Agency for Public Mobilisation and Statistics**
- ↳ **Statistical Yearbook** – annual

□ EL SALVADOR

Dirección General de Estadísticas y Censos (DIGESTYC)
(Office of Statistics and the Census)

Address:	Apartado Postal 2670, Avenida Juan Bertis #79, Delgado, San Salvador
Telephone:	+503 276 5900 (ext. 127)
Fax:	+503 276 5900 (ext. 128)
E-mail:	dmc_ernesto@yahoo.com

Obtaining Publications: same as above

Publications:
- ↳ **Anuario Estadistico** *(Statistical Yearbook)* – social and economic statistical data – annual
- ↳ **Boletin Estadistico** *(Statistical Bulletin)* – monthly socio-economic statistics – monthly
- ↳ **Indice de Precios al Consumidor** *(Consumer Price Index)* – consumer price index – monthly

□ EQUATORIAL GUINEA

Dirección General de Estadistica

Address:	Calle Mongomo 163, Malabo

Obtaining Publications: same as above

□ ETHIOPIA

Central Statistical Authority

Address:	PO Box 1143, Addis Ababa
Telephone:	+251 1 553 011/115 131/550 450
Fax:	+251 1 550 334
E-mail:	csa@telecom.net.et

Obtaining Publications: same as above

Publications:
- ↳ **Average Retail Prices of Goods and Services by Rural Areas** – quarterly
- ↳ **Consumer Price Indices of Ethiopia at Country, Rural and Urban Levels** – monthly
- ↳ **Statistical Abstract of Ethiopia** – annual
- ↳ **Statistical Pocket Book of Ethiopia**

□ FIJI

Bureau of Statistics

Address:	PO Box 2221, Government Buildings, Suva
Telephone:	+679 315 144
Fax:	+679 303 656
Website:	www.statsfiji.gov.fj

Obtaining Publications: same as above

Publications:
- ↳ **Census of Distribution and Services** – irregular
- ↳ **Current Economic Statistics** – quarterly
- ↳ **Fiji Bureau of Statistics** *(Website)*
- ↳ **Fiji Facts & Figures** – annual
- ↳ **Fiji Household Income and Expenditure Survey** – irregular
- ↳ **Survey of Employment** – irregular

■ FRENCH POLYNESIA

Institut statistique de la Polynésie française
(French Polynesia Statistics Institute)

Address:	BP 395, Papeete, 98713 Tahiti
Telephone:	+689 473 434
Fax:	+689 473 474
E-mail:	bertrando@ispf.pf
Website:	www.ispf.pf

Obtaining Publications: same as above

Publications:
- ↳ **Institute Statistique de la Polynésie Française** *(French Polynesia Statistics Institute) (Website)*
- ↳ **Spécial Indice des prix de détail à la consommation** *(Special Consumer Price Index) — monthly*

■ GABON

Direction Générale de la Statistique et des Etudes Economiques, Ministère de la Planification et de l'Economie
(Directorate of Statistics and Economic Studies, Ministry of Planning and the Economy)

Address:	BP 2119, Libreville
Telephone:	+241 760 671/763 511
Fax:	+241 720 457/773 499
E-mail:	plandgsee@internetgabon.com

Obtaining Publications: same as above

Publications:
- ↳ **Bulletin Mensuel de Statistique** *(Monthly Statistical Bulletin)* — monthly statistical bulletin — *monthly*
- ↳ **Projet du Budget General**

■ GAMBIA

Central Statistics Department

Address:	Ministry of Economic Planning and Industrial development (MEPID), Central Bank Building, 32 Buckle Street, Banjul
Telephone:	+220 272 30/228 364/229 655
E-mail:	gamcens@qanet.gm

Obtaining Publications: same as above

Publications:
- ↳ **Consumer Price Index** — *monthly*
- ↳ **External Trade Statistics of Gambia** — *annual*
- ↳ **Monthly Bulletin of Prices** — *monthly*
- ↳ **Statistical Abstract of the Gambia** — *annual*

■ GHANA

Ghana Statistical Service (GSS)

Address:	PO Box 1098, Accra
Telephone:	+233 21 682 692/663 578
Fax:	+233 21 671 731/667 069

Obtaining Publications: same as above

Publications:
- ↳ **Consumer Price Index Numbers** — *monthly*
- ↳ **External Trade Statistics of Ghana** — *annual*
- ↳ **Motor Vehicle Registration** — *quarterly*

■ GRENADA

Central Statistical Office

Address:	Ministry of Finance, Lagoon Road, St Georges
Telephone:	+1473 440 2731/1369
Fax:	+1473 440 4115
E-mail:	tdh33@hotmail.com

Obtaining Publications: same as above

■ GUADELOUPE

Institut National des Statistiques et des Etudes Economiques. INSEE
(National Institute of Statistics and Economic Studies)

Address:	BP 96, Avenue Paul Lacavé, 97102 Basse-Terre
Telephone:	+590 811 786
Fax:	+590 810 715

■ GUATEMALA

Instituto Nacional de Estadística
(National Institute of Statistics)

Address:	8a calle 9-55, Zona 1, 01001 Guatemala City
Telephone:	+502 232 6136/238 2587
Fax:	+502 232 4790
E-mail:	info-ine@ine.gob.gt
Website:	www.ine.gob.gt

Website notes: provides a wide range of socio-economic statistics on Guatemala including: demographic trends; gross domestic product; inflation and price index; external trade; transport; education; water and energy supply; health services; and environment. Access to INE's monthly bulletin

Obtaining Publications: same as above

Guides to Publications: online catalogue

Publications:
- ↳ **Compendio Estadistico sobre Variables Economico-sociales** *(Socio-Economic Statistics)* — compendium of key socio-economic statistics — *annual*
- ↳ **Directorio Nacional de Establecimientos Industriales** *(Industrial National Directory)* — directory of industrial companies — *annual*
- ↳ **Instituto Nacional de Estadística** *(National Institute of Statistics) (Website)*

■ GUINEA

Direction Générale de la Statistique, Ministère du Plan et Coopération Internationale
(Directorate General of Statistics, Ministry of Planning and International Cooperation)

Address:	Boite Postale 373, Conakry
Telephone:	+224 413 127/442 148
Fax:	+224 414 356

Obtaining Publications: same as above

■ GUINEA-BISSAU

Instituto Nacional de Estatistica e Censos (INEC)
(National Institute of Statistics and Census (INEC))

Address:	CP 6, Bissau, Bissau
Telephone:	+245 222 054/53
Fax:	+245 222 122

Obtaining Publications: same as above

Publications:
- ↳ **Anuario estatistico** *(Statistical Annual)* — *annual*

□ GUYANA

Statistical Bureau, Ministry of Economic Planning and Finance

Address:	PO Box 542, Home Stretch Avenue, Georgetown
Telephone:	+592 2 561 50/711 55
Fax:	+592 2 589 95

Obtaining Publications: same as above

Publications:
↳ **Annual Account Relating to External Trade** — *annual*

□ HAITI

Institut Haitien de Statistique et d'Informatique
(Haitian Institute of Statistics and Information Technology)

Address:	BP 1796, Cité de l'Exposition, Boulevard Harry Truman, Port-au-Prince
Telephone:	+509 231 011/22 2 669
Fax:	+509 222 669

Obtaining Publications: same as above

Publications:
↳ **Bulletin Trimestriel de Statistique** *(quarterly Statistical Bulletin)* — economic, social and demographic statistical data — *quarterly*

□ HONDURAS

Dirección General de Estadística y Censos
(General Directorate of Statistics and Census)

Address:	Avenida Centenario 6 y 8 Calles, Comayaguela DC
Telephone:	+504 228 450
Fax:	+504 227 880

Year Established: 1950

Obtaining Publications: same as above

Publications:
↳ **Anuario Estadistico** *(Statistical Annual)* — *annual*

□ HONG KONG, CHINA

Census and Statistics Department

Address:	16/F - 22/F & 25/F, Wanchai Tower, 12 Harbour Road, Wanchai
Telephone:	+852 2582 3025
Fax:	+852 2827 1708
E-mail:	publications@censtatd.gov.hk
Website:	www.info.gov.hk/censtatd

Website notes: official site of Hong Kong's Census and Statistics Department: information on products and services; latest press releases; catalogue of publications; web links to other national and international statistical offices; educational materials; and online statistical data on Hong Kong

Statistical Coverage: annual socio-economic statistics on Hong Kong can be found in the "Hong Kong in Figures" section. Online data provided both in Chinese and English covers: geography and climate; population and labour structure; national and public accounts and balance of payments; prices; money and finance; foreign trade; production and commerce; health and education; social welfare; information technology; transports, communication and tourism; land, housing, building and construction; and law and order

Obtaining Publications: Government Publications Centre; G/F, Low Block, Queensway Government Offices; 66 Queensway, Hong Kong; (Tel.: (852) 2537 1910; Fax.: (852) 2523 7195)

Guides to Publications: statistical products of the C&SD are available online (some of them are for free distribution) in separate Chinese and English versions. Both online and hardcopy publications can be purchased in the section Statistical Bookstore (www.statisticalbookstore.gov.hk/desc_eng.htm).

Publications:
↳ **Annual Review of Hong Kong External Trade** — statistical compilation on Hong Kong's foreign trade activities — *annual*
↳ **Consumer Price Index Report** — statistics and analysis of price movements of consumer goods and services — *annual*
↳ **Hong Kong Annual Digest of Statistics** — socio-economic portrait of Hong Kong, covering the last seven years — *annual*
↳ **Hong Kong Energy Statistics Annual Report** — statistics on the supply and consumption of oil products, coal products, electricity and gas in terms of volume, prices, suppliers and storage capacity — *annual*
↳ **Hong Kong In Figures** — booklet of annual socio-economic statistics on Hong Kong — *annual*
↳ **Hong Kong in Figures** *(Website)*
↳ **Hong Kong Social and Economic Trends** — statistical overview of Hong Kong's social and economic trends in the last ten years — *every two years*
↳ **Hong Kong Trade Statistics** — series of publications providing two different types of statistics, one on imports and another on domestic exports and re-exports. For each type of statistic, there are monthly publications and an annual supplement — *annual*
↳ **Monthly Report on the Consumer Price Index** — *monthly*
↳ **Quarterly Report of Wage and Payroll Statistics** — summary statistics extracted from the Labour Earnings Survey, providing a breakdown of wage and payroll data by major industrial sector — *quarterly*
↳ **Quarterly Textile Production Statistics** — statistics on the textile industry covering production, employment and imports of raw materials — *quarterly*
↳ **Report on Annual Survey of Industrial Production** — general overview and analysis of Hong Kong's industrial sector — *annual*
↳ **Report on Annual Survey of Wholesale, Retail and Import and Export Trades, Restaurants and Hotels** — statistical analysis of wholesaling and retailing activities in Hong Kong, as well as foreign trade matters and travel and tourism sectors — *annual*
↳ **Report on Monthly Survey of Retail Sales** — monthly data on retail volume and value sales by type of outlet — *monthly*

□ INDIA

Central Statistical Organisation

Address:	Sardar Patel Bhavan, Parliament Street, New Delhi 110 001
Telephone:	+91 11 374 2026
Website:	ospi.nic.in

Obtaining Publications: available from statistical information and publications division at the address above or from agents authorised for sale of Government of India Publications

Publications:
↳ **Ministry of Statistics and Programme Implementation**

Directorate General of Commercial Intelligence and Statistics

Address:	1 Council House Street, Calcutta 700 001
Telephone:	+91 33 248 3111/4
Fax:	+91 33 248 6528

□ INDONESIA

Badan Pusat Statistik
(Central Bureau of Statistics)

Address:	Jalan Dr Sutomo 6-8, Jakarta 10710
Telephone:	+62 21 350 7057
Fax:	+62 21 385 7046
E-mail:	bpshq@bps.go.id
Website:	www.bps.go.id

Website notes: general information on the Bureau's main products and services: catalogue of publications; abstracts and papers; official releases; links to other national and international statistical organisations; and compilation of both national and regional statistics

Statistical Coverage: statistics, covering mainly social, economic and financial indicators, are provided in three major sections: 1) Statistics by Subject: annual statistics for the last three years, covering topics such as population, employment, agriculture, manufacturing, tourism, foreign trade, social welfare, etc; 2) Statistics by Region: data on Indonesia's main regions, including data on population structure (2000), labour force (1996-2000), GDP (1995-2000) and inflation rates by product and service (2001); and 3) Macro-economic Statistics: monthly analysis of latest economic and financial trends

Guides to Publications: List of Publications sold by BPS Bookstore, queries to be forwarded to Sri Hartani (koperasi@mailhost.bps.go.id)

Publications:
- ↳ **Biro Pusat Statistik** *(Central Bureau of Statistics) (Website)*
- ↳ **Consumer Price of Selected Goods and Services in all Provincial Capital Cities in Indonesia** — *annual*
- ↳ **Economic Indicators** — *monthly*
- ↳ **Export Statistics** — *annual*
- ↳ **Statistik Hotel dan Akomodasi Lainnya di Indonesia** *(Hotel and Other Accommodation Statistics in Indonesia)* — *annual*
- ↳ **Statistik Tahunan Indonesia** *(Indonesian Statistical Yearbook)* — annual socio-economic indicators on Indonesia — *annual*
- ↳ **Statistik Wisatawan Internasional di Indonesia** *(International Tourism Statistics in Indonesia)* — *annual*
- ↳ **Wholesale Price Indices of Indonesia** — *annual*

▫ IRAN

Statistical Centre of Iran

Address:	PO Box 14155-6133, Dr Fatemi Avenue, 14144 Tehran
Telephone:	+98 21 655 061-9
Fax:	+98 21 656 082/653 451
Website:	www.sci.or.ir

Year Established: 1918

Obtaining Publications: publications available from address above

Publications:
- ↳ **Iran Statistical Yearbook** — contains 518 tables and 22 chapters according to international classifications about, land and climate, population, manpower, agriculture, mining and quarrying, manufacturing, water and electricity, financial markets, housing, trade, transport and communication, judicial affairs, welfare, education, health and treatment, culture and tourism, price indices, government budget, household expenditure and income, national accounts and international statistics — *annual*
- ↳ **Statistical Centre of Iran** — national and international affairs, culture and tourism, trade, finance, agriculture, etc *(Website)*

▫ IRAQ

Central Statistical Organisation, Ministry of Planning

Address:	PO Box 8001, No. 8 February Post Office, Baghdad
Telephone:	+964 1 719 60 37

Publications:
- ↳ **Annual Abstract of Statistics**

▫ ISRAEL

Central Bureau of Statistics

Address:	PO Box 34525, 66 Kanfei Nesharim St, Jerusalem
Telephone:	+972 2 659 2222
Fax:	+972 2 652 1340
E-mail:	cbs@cbs.gov.il
Website:	www.cbs.gov.il

Website notes: information on the CBS main products and services; online access to various regularly updated publications, including the "Annual Statistical Abstract" and the "Monthly Bulletin of Statistics" covering a wide range of socio-economic statistics, such as demographics, health, foreign trade and financial markets

Obtaining Publications: publications can be purchases from the address above

Publications:
- ↳ **Central Bureau of Statistics** *(Website)*
- ↳ **Monthly Bulletin of Statistics** — wide range of monthly updated statistics covering: climate; population and demographics; health; migration and tourism; national accounts; balance of payments; foreign trade; financial and capital markets; prices; labour and wages; agriculture; industry; energy; construction; commerce; transports; etc — *quarterly*
- ↳ **Price Statistics Monthly** — monthly summary of price indices; consumer prices; wholesale prices of manufacturing output; input prices in residential building and road construction; etc — *monthly*

↳ **Statistical Abstract of Israel** — annual statistics on Israel covering latest demographic trends and household data — *annual*

Palestinian Central Bureau of Statistics

Address:	PO Box 1647, Ramallah, Palestine
Telephone:	+972 2 240 6340
Fax:	+972 2 240 6340
E-mail:	diwan@pcbs.pna.org
Website:	www.pcbs.org

Website notes: main socio-economic indicators of the Palestinian economy: population; labour and wages; education; living conditions; health; housing; crime; national accounts. Also statistics on: trade; services; industry; construction; prices; agriculture; tourism; environment. Latest labour force survey results can also be found online for July-September 2002. Consumer price indices can be accessed online. Publications are available under the titles of Economic Publications, Population and Social Publications, Area Publications and Special Publications

Statistical Coverage: statistics are available on demographic, social, economic and environmental states and trend to serve the Palestinian citizenry, and to serve the instrumental needs of businesses and their organisations for statistical information on states and trends.

Obtaining Publications: contact the address above

Guides to Publications: some publications can be purchased by filling out the on-line order form

Publications:
- ↳ **Bulletin of Consumer Prices**
- ↳ **Palestinian Central Bureau of Statistics** *(Website)*
- ↳ **Population in the Palestinian Territory**
- ↳ **Population, Housing, and Establishments Census**

▫ JAMAICA

Statistical Institute of Jamaica

Address:	Information Centre, 9 Swallowfield Road, Kingston 5
Telephone:	+1876 926 2175/2199
Fax:	+1876 926 4859
E-mail:	library.sales@statinja.com
Website:	www.statinja.com

Website notes: information on the Institute's products and services, publications, and selected tables from the Statistical Yearbook of Jamaica: general statistical data covering demographic trends; major economic indicators; labour force indicators; and trade figures

Statistical Coverage: statistics covering commercial, industrial, social, economic and general activities and condition of the people,

Year Established: 1984

Obtaining Publications: as above or fill out the online publication order form

Guides to Publications: Catalogue of Publications and Services

Publications:
- ↳ **Consumer Price Indices Annual Review** — statistics on rate of inflation recorded — *annual*
- ↳ **External Trade** — *quarterly*
- ↳ **Statistical Institute of Jamaica** *(Website)*
- ↳ **Statistical Yearbook of Jamaica** — on the country's physical and natural resources, social and economic conditions, resources, government organisations, industry and judicial system — *annual*

▫ JAPAN

Statistics Bureau, Management and Co-ordination Agency

Address:	19-1 Wakamatsu-cho, Shinjuku-ku, Tokyo 162-8668
Telephone:	+81 3 3202 1111
Fax:	+81 3 5273 1180
Website:	www.stat.go.jp

Website notes: official site of the Japanese Statistics Bureau, providing information on its products and services and the overall national statistical system; catalogue of publications; links to other official statistical organisations; and online data on Japan

Statistical Coverage: online statistics are provided in both English and Japanese, under three different sections: 1) Summary of Survey Results: summaries of major surveys conducted by the Bureau covering population; labour force; service industries; household income and expenditure; consumer and retail price indices; etc; 2) Statistical Compendia: online access to two online publications covering major socio-economic and financial indicators - "Japan in Figures" and "Japan Statistical Yearbook", both annual publications; and 3) Economic and Financial Data on Japan: data collected by the International Monetary Fund on the real sector; fiscal and financial sector; external sector; and population

Obtaining Publications: Japan Statistical Association, Tel. +813 5332 3151; Fax +8 353 890 691; E-Mail jsa@jstat.or.jp

Guides to Publications: List of Recent Publications prepared by the Statistics Bureau, Management and Coordination Agency (free); A Guide to Statistics Bureau and Statistics Center is a guide to the organisation and functions including details of topics covered by the various census and surveys

Publications:
- ↳ **Annual Report on Family Income and Expenditure** – *annual*
- ↳ **Annual Report on Population Estimates** – population statistics by age and sex
- ↳ **Annual Report on the Labour Force Survey** – employment status of the population and changes in employment and unemployment, nationally and regionally – *annual*
- ↳ **Annual Report on the Retail Price Survey** – annual statistics derived from the monthly Retail Price Survey – *annual*
- ↳ **Consumer Price Index Japan** – *monthly*
- ↳ **Japan Statistical Yearbook** – detailed socio-economic statistics on Japan – *annual*
- ↳ **Japan Statistics Bureau, Management and Co-ordination Agency** *(Website)*
- ↳ **Monthly Statistics of Japan** – *monthly*

◘ JORDAN

Department of Statistics (DOS)

Address:	PO Box 2015, Amman
Telephone:	+962 6 530 0700
Fax:	+962 6 530 0710
Telex:	24117 STATIS JO
E-mail:	stat@dos.gov.jo
Website:	www.dos.gov.jo

Website notes: compilation of statistical information on Jordan, including data on: geography and climate; population and general demographic trends; agricultural resources; labour force; major economic indicators; and external trade

Statistical Coverage: socio-economic and democratic data

Year Established: 1949

Obtaining Publications: The Hashemite Kingdom Of Jordan, Department Of Statistics, Public Relations, PO Box 2015, Amman; publications available in printed form or on floppy disk

Guides to Publications: List of Recent Publications prepared by DOS

Publications:
- ↳ **Department of Statistics (DOS)** *(Website)*
- ↳ **Jordan in Figures** – *annual*
- ↳ **Statistical Yearbook** – *annual*

◘ KAZAKHSTAN

Committee on Statistics and Analysis of the Republic of Kazakhstan

Address:	125, Abay Avenue, 480008 Almaty
Telephone:	+732 72 626 645/420 505
Fax:	+732 72 420 824/424 338
E-mail:	kazstat@mail.banknet.kz
Website:	www.kazstat.asdc.kz

Website notes: general information on the Agency's main products and services; free online statistics on socio-economic and financial topics from 1913 up to 1999. Data available in Russian and English

Statistical Coverage: statistics on banking and finance, agriculture, industrial production, construction, investment, trade, economics, demographics, population and households

Obtaining Publications: special order form can be printed out from the internet and is to send back to the above address

Guides to Publications: access to all electronical statistical publications of the Agency on Statistics Analysis of the Republic of Kazakhstan for constant subscribers (monthly license fee US$ 50 (excl VAT))

Publications:
- ↳ **Economics and Statistics** – *quarterly*
- ↳ **National Statistical Agency of Kazakhstan** *(Website)*
- ↳ **Socioeconomic Development of the Republic of Kazakhstan** – *monthly*
- ↳ **Statistical Yearbook of Kazakhstan** – *annual*

◘ KENYA

Central Bureau of Statistics, Ministry of Economic Planning and National Development

Address:	PO Box 30007, Harambee Avenue, Nairobi
Telephone:	+254 2 338 111
Fax:	+254 2 214 511
E-mail:	info@treasury.go.ke
Website:	www.cbs.go.ke

Publications:
- ↳ **Central Bureau of Statistics, Ministry of Economic Planning and National Development** *(Website)*
- ↳ **Economic Survey** – *annual*
- ↳ **Kenya Statistical Digest** – *quarterly*
- ↳ **Statistical Abstract** – includes coverage of retail trade – *annual*

◘ KIRIBATI

Statistics Office, Ministry of Finance

Address:	PO Box 67, Bairiki, Tarawa
Telephone:	+686 210 82
Fax:	+686 213 07
E-mail:	statistics@tskl.net.ki

◘ KUWAIT

Statistical & Information Sector, Ministry of Planning

Address:	PO Box 26188, Safat
Telephone:	+965 242 8200
Website:	www.mop.gov.kw

Website notes: statistics section on Kuwait includes data on demographics, labour force indicators, macro-economic indicators, agriculture and fisheries, petroleum and other industries, tourism, education and health services. Data available up to 1995 only

Guides to Publications: List of publications available online (all of these irregularly updated)

Publications:
- ↳ **Central Statistical Office** *(Website)*

◘ KYRGYZSTAN

National Statistical Committee of the Kyrgyz Republic (NSC)

Address:	374 Frunze street, Bishkek 720033
Telephone:	+733 312 226 363
Fax:	+733 312 220 759/660 138
E-mail:	zkudabaev@nsc.bishkek.su or 311@nsc.bishkek.su
Website:	nsc.bishkek.su

Website notes: general statistics on major national economic indicators, industrial resources, and agricultural resources

Statistical Coverage: population censuses, household surveys, demographic statistics and a wide range of economic statistics involving establishment and enterprise surveys, as well as prices, international trade (in collaboration with the customs department), the national accounts, government finance, agricultural, labour and social statistics

Obtaining Publications: as above

Guides to Publications: on-line statistics on real, fiscal, financial, external and social sectors (free); publication list including details of topics covered by the various census and surveys

Publications:
↳ **Demographic Yearbook of the Kyrgyz Republic** — contains administrative data on: territorial division, population, ethnicity, gender, age groups, birthrates, mortality, marriage, divorce, migration and other data — *annually*
↳ **National Statistical Committee of the Kyrgyz Republic (NSC)** *(Website)*
↳ **The Program of Statistics Development of the Kyrgyz Republic 2001-2005** — statistics and committee activities and plans

---

▫ LEBANON

Central Administration for Statistics

Address:	5th Floor, Commerce and Finance Building., Kantari St., Beirut
Website:	www.cas.gov.lb

Website notes: free access to monthly bulletin providing statistical data on different areas such as: geography and climate; economy and finance; agricultural and industrial production; retail prices; foreign trade; energy production and consumption; etc

Year Established: 1959

Publications:
↳ **Central Administration for Statistics** *(Website)*

▫ LESOTHO

Lesotho Bureau of Statistics

Address:	Box 455, Maseru 100
Telephone:	+266 22323852
Fax:	+266 22310177
E-mail:	library@bos.gov.ls

Year Established: 1964

▫ LIBERIA

Bureau of Statistics, Ministry of Planning and Economic Affairs

Address:	PO Box 10-9016, 1000 Monrovia 10
Telephone:	+231 226 962/227 987/222 121

Publications:
↳ **Annual Report to the People's Redemption Council** — *annual*
↳ **Survey of Liberia** — *annual*

▫ LIBYA

Census and Statistical Department, Secretariat of Planning

Address:	PO Box 600, 2nd Floor, 40 Sharia Damascus, Tripoli
Telephone:	+218 317 31

Publications:
↳ **External Trade Statistics** — *annual*
↳ **Report of the Annual Survey of Large Manufacturing Establishments** — *annual*
↳ **Statistical Handbook of the Libyan Arab Jamahariya** — *annual*
↳ **Trends of External Trade** — *monthly*
↳ **Vital Statistics of the Socialist People's Libyan Arab Jamahariya** — *annual*
↳ **Wholesale Prices in Tripoli Town** — *quarterly*

▫ MACAU

Direcção dos Serviços de Estatística e Censos (DSEC)
(Census and Statistics Department of Macau)

Address:	Edifício "Dynasty Plaza", 17 andar, Alameda Dr. Carlos de Assumpção, nos. 411-417, Macau
Telephone:	+853 399 5311
Fax:	+853 307 825
E-mail:	info@dsec.gov.mo
Website:	www.dsec.gov.mo

Website notes: general information on DSEC main products and services, including details on major publications; press releases; data base of external trade statistics; and wide range of online figures on the ex-Portuguese colony

Statistical Coverage: detailed socio-economic data on Macau available at "Statistical Indicators" section covering: demography, education, health, labour force, travel and tourism, construction, external trade, communication and transport, banking and finance, prices, energy, industry, GDP

Obtaining Publications: as above

Guides to Publications: Guide for Statistical Publications; some data can be downloaded directly from the homepage of Statistics and Census Service, under the title "Statistical publications in homepage"

Publications:
↳ **Demographic Statistics** — *annual*
↳ **Direcção dos Serviços de Estatística e Censos (DSEC)** *(Census and Statistics Department of Macau) (Website)*
↳ **External Trade Statistics** — *annual*
↳ **Industrial Survey** — *annual*
↳ **Macau in Figures** — *annual*
↳ **Monthly Bulletin of Statistics** — *monthly*
↳ **Statistical Yearbook** — key social and economic statistics — *annual*
↳ **Wholesale and Retail Survey** — *annual*

▫ MADAGASCAR

Institut National de la Statistique
(National Institute of Statistics)

Address:	Boite Postal 485, Anosy, 101 Antananarivo
Telephone:	+261 2 216 52
Fax:	+261 2 332 50

Publications:
↳ **Analyse des Donnees** *(Data Analysis)* — socio-economic statistics and analyses — *annual*
↳ **Bulletin Mensuel de Statistique** *(Monthly Statistical Bulletin)* — monthly statistical bulletin — *monthly*

▫ MALAWI

National Statistical Office

Address:	PO Box 333, Zomba
Telephone:	+265 152 4377
Fax:	+265 152 5130
E-mail:	enquiries@statistics.gov.mw
Website:	www.nso.malawi.net

Statistical Coverage: provides access to statistical information on Malawi. Includes national accounts, census data, poverty trends, demographic trends, health figures, etc.

Obtaining Publications: as above

Guides to Publications: list of recent publications on the website

Publications:
↳ **Annual Statement of External Trade** — detailed statements on commodity exports and imports — *annual*
↳ **Annual Survey of Economic Activities** — covers large scale profit making industry, and forms the main source of information for compiling the national accounts — *annual*
↳ **Monthly Statistical Bulletin** — *monthly*
↳ **National Statistical Office** *(Website)*
↳ **Urban Household Expenditure Survey**

◘ MALAYSIA

Jabatan Perangkaan Malaysia
(Department of Statistics Malaysia)

Address:	Blok C6, Pusat Pentadbiran Kerajaan Persekutuan, 62514 Putrajaya
Telephone:	+60 3 8885 7000/7710
Fax:	+60 3 8888 9248
E-mail:	jpbpo@stats.gov.my
Website:	www.statistics.gov.my

Website notes: up-to-date information on the overall services and products provided by the Malaysian Department of Statistics, including: list of major statistical titles; latest releases; special data dissemination standard, and links to national and international statistical organisations

Statistical Coverage: "Key Statistics Section" provides data on different social, economic and financial topics, for the last three years. Indicators covered include: total population and demographic dynamics; GDP and Gross National Income; balance of payments; external trade; major exports; production; index of industrial production; consumer and producer price index; and employment. Available in Malay and English

Year Established: 1949

Obtaining Publications: as above

Guides to Publications: website contains complete list of all statistical publications

Publications:
- ↳ **Consumer Price Index for Malaysia (CPI)** – *monthly*
- ↳ **Jabatan Perangkaan Malaysia** *(Department of Statistics Malaysia) (Website)*
- ↳ **Labour Force Survey Report** – analysis of labour force structure and unemployment rates in Malaysia – *annual*
- ↳ **Monthly External Trade Statistics** – *monthly*
- ↳ **Monthly Statistical Bulletin** – contains basic socio-economic indicators – *monthly*
- ↳ **Report on Household Expenditure Survey** – information on the levels and patterns of consumption expenditure by private households on a comprehensive range of goods and services – *annual*
- ↳ **Yearbook of Statistics** – *annual*

◘ MALDIVES

Ministry of Planning and National Development. Statistics Section

Address:	Ghaazee Building, 4th floor, Ammer Ahned Magu, Malé 20-25
Telephone:	+960 315 347
Fax:	+960 327 351
E-mail:	stats@planning.gov.mv
Website:	www.planning.gov.mv

Guides to Publications: online guide to publications and services available

Publications:
- ↳ **Ministry of Planning and National Development** – Statistical reports on living standards, demographic indicators, economic indicators and annual statistical yearbooks, all available to download from the website *(Website)*
- ↳ **Statistical Yearbook** – *Annual*

◘ MALI

Direction Nationale de la Statistique et de l'Informatique, Ministère du Plan
(National Statistical and Information Office, Ministry of Planning)

Address:	BP 12, Bamako
Telephone:	+223 225 780/204
Fax:	+223 228 853

Publications:
- ↳ **Annuaire Statistique** *(Statistical Yearbook)* – annual compendium of social and economic indicators – *annual*
- ↳ **Statistiques Douanières du Commerce Exterieur** *(Foreign Trade Statistics)* – foreign trade statistics – *irregular*

◘ MAURITANIA

Office National de la Statistique
(National Statistical Office)

Address:	BP 240, Nouakchott
Telephone:	+222 525 2880
Fax:	+222 525 5170
E-mail:	sidna@ons.mr or dg-ons@iiardd.mr
Website:	www.ons.mr

Website notes: online statistics provided in French

Statistical Coverage: regional and country statistics provided focusing on major socio-economic and demographic indicators, as well as on institutional development, agriculture, fisheries

Obtaining Publications: all publications can be subscribed at the above address

Guides to Publications: The National Statistical Offices provides a PDF document for download containing a list off all statistical publications.

Publications:
- ↳ **Annuaire statistique de la Mauritanie** *(Statistical Yearbook of Mauritania)* – *annually*
- ↳ **Office National de la Statistique** *(National Statistical Office) (Website)*

◘ MAURITIUS

Central Statistical Office

Address:	LIC Center, President John Kennedy Street, Port-Louis
Telephone:	+230 208 0859/212 2316
Fax:	+230 211 4150
E-mail:	cso@intnet.mu
Website:	ncb.intnet.mu/cso.htm

Website notes: general information on CSO's main products and services, including catalogue of publications, data collection and data dissemination. Compilation of socio-economic statistics.

Statistical Coverage: statistical data on Mauritius is found under "Economic Indicators" and "Mauritius in Figures". The first section includes series of quarterly updated macroeconomic statistics, including: consumer & producer price index, external trade activities, industrial and agricultural production figures, etc. "Mauritius in Figures" covers different social, economic, and financial data for the last five to ten years, depending on the indicator/area in question: climate, population & vital statistics, health & education, labour force, price indexes, household income and expenditure, agricultural and industrial production, national accounts and general finance, etc

Year Established: 1945

Obtaining Publications: as above

Guides to Publications: digital list of all regular publications provided by the CSO website

Publications:
- ↳ **Annual Digest of Statistics** – *annual*
- ↳ **Central Statistical Office** *(Website)*
- ↳ **Digest of Industrial Statistics**
- ↳ **External Trade Statistics** – *quarterly*

◘ MEXICO

Instituto Nacional de Estadística, Geografía e Informática (INEGI)
(National Institute of Statistics, Geography and Informatics)

Address:	Avenida Héroe de Nacozari Sur, Número 2301, Fracc. Jardines del Parque, 20270 Aguascalientes
Telephone:	+52 44 918 1948
Fax:	+52 44 918 0739
E-mail:	ventas@cis.inegi.gob.mx
Website:	www.inegi.gob.mx

Website notes: details on INEGI's main products and services: catalogue of publications; structure, programmes and latest statistical projects; electronic library and national information centres. Includes various free online statistics

Statistical Coverage: wide range of different economic, financial and social statistics is provided on a free basis, under different sections: 1) "Acerca del Territorio" section provides latest data on Mexico's natural and environmental resources; 2) "Estadísticas Sociodemográficas" section offers access (registration required) to a database covering major social and demographic indicators by Federal State and municipality; 3) "Estadísticas Económicas" covers main economic indicators, including results of major national annual economic surveys; and 4) "Información por Entidad Federativa" provides a general socio-economic and industrial portrait of each of Mexico's Federal states. Data is available in Spanish and English

Obtaining Publications: online order service

Guides to Publications: online catalogue of all publications

Publications:
- ↳ **Anuario Estadístico de los Estados Unidos Mexicanos** *(Statistical Yearbook of Mexico)* — statistical overview of socio-economic conditions in Mexico and its federal states. Covers wide range of subjects, from population and demography to labour force; education and health services; agriculture; tourism; etc — *annual*
- ↳ **Boletín de Información Oportuna del Sector Alimentario** *(Food Sector Bulletin)* — covers the Mexican food and drinks industries, providing latest data on production, consumption, retail distribution and external trade
- ↳ **El Sector Alimentario en México** *(Food Industry in Mexico)* — overview of the food industries in Mexico and related sectors: agriculture and fisheries; wholesaling, retail distribution and trade; consumption trends; etc
- ↳ **Encuesta Industrial** *(Industrial Survey)* — statistics cover 205 classes of economic activity in the manufacturing sector, according to subsector, branch and class of activity — *annual*
- ↳ **Encuesta Nacional de la Dinamica Demográfica** *(Demographic Trends Survey)* — statistical analysis of latest demographic trends in Mexico · population growth rate; birth and mortality rates; marriages; population structure by age and gender; etc — *irregular*
- ↳ **Estadísticas del Comercio Exterior de México** *(Mexican Foreign Trade Statistics)* — import and exports statistics by commodity and by country of origin/destination
- ↳ **Estadísticas Demograficas y Socioeconómicas de México** *(Mexican Demographic and Socio-economic Statistics)* — annual socio-economic and financial portrait of Mexico, including data on general population structure and demographic dynamics; health and social security services; infrastructures; national accounts and public finance; etc — *annual*
- ↳ **Indicadores de Empleo y Desempleo** *(Employment and Unemployment Statistics)* — employment and unemployment statistics — *quarterly*
- ↳ **Instituto Nacional de Estadística, Geografía e Informática (INEGI)** *(National Institute of Statistics, Geography and Informatics) (Website)*
- ↳ **Mexican Bulletin of Statistical Information** — provides updated statistics on various socio-economic indicators on a quarterly basis — *quarterly*

▫ MONGOLIA

National Statistical Office of Mongolia

Address:	Government Building 3, Ulaanbaatar-20A, Ulan Bator
Telephone:	+976 11 322 424/328 414
Fax:	+976 11 324 518
E-mail:	info@nso.mn
Website:	www.nso.mn

Website notes: key socio-economic statistics covering; population; labour force; GDP; industry; agriculture; trade; transport and communications; education; health. Also includes full online access to the Mongolian Statistical Yearbook and Mongolia in Figures

Obtaining Publications: online order service

Guides to Publications: on-line catalogue contains information on both publications planned to arrive and publications already issued but still valid

Publications:
- ↳ **Mongolian Statistical Yearbook** — contains major indicators of the socio-economic situation of the country with respect to labour market and earnings, households and social benefits, population, prices, money and finance, agriculture, industry and construction, transport and trade — *annual*
- ↳ **Monthly Bulletin of Statistics** — key socio-economic statistics — *monthly*
- ↳ **National Statistical Office of Mongolia** *(Website)*
- ↳ **Statistical Profile on Agriculture**

▫ MOROCCO

Direction de la Statistique
(Directorate of Statistics)

Address:	BP 178, Rue Bel Hassan El Ouazzani Haut-Agdal, 1001 Rabat
Telephone:	+212 37 773 606
Fax:	+212 37 773 217
E-mail:	statguichet@statistic.gov.ma
Website:	www.statistic.gov.ma

Website notes: general information on products and services provided; catalogue of publications; databases; online access to latest annual statistical publications

Statistical Coverage: available only in French, "Chiffres Clés" section provides key annual statistics on socio-economic and financial indicators for Morocco, including: geography and population, health and education, labour force and wages, agriculture, mines and energy, industry, transports and communications, external trade, tourism, stock market and public finances, etc

Year Established: 1942

Guides to Publications: online catalogue

Publications:
- ↳ **Annuaire Statistique du Maroc** *(Statistical Yearbook of Morocco)* — detailed socio-economic statistics including population and cultur, climate, fishery, mining, energy, industry, construction, transport and tourism, education, prices, finance, etc — *annual*
- ↳ **Bulletin of Statistics** — statistical data covering different economic sectors, including manufacturing industry, mining and construction, transports and tourism, external trade, public finances, etc — *quarterly*
- ↳ **Direction de la Statistique** *(Directorate of Statistics) (Website)*

▫ MOZAMBIQUE

Instituto Nacional de Estatística
(National Institute of Statistics)

Address:	CP 493, Av Ahmed Sekou Touré 21, Maputo
Telephone:	+258 1 491 054/5/490 930
Fax:	+258 1 493 547
E-mail:	info@ine.gov.mz or joao.loureiro@ine.gov.mz
Website:	www.ine.gov.mz

Website notes: offers information on the Instituto's main products and services in Portuguese only, including catalogue of publications and different online socio-economic statistics

Statistical Coverage: compilation of statistics on Mozambique's climate, geography and natural resources, population and general demographic trends, economy, agricultural and industrial output, building and construction, education and health systems

Guides to Publications: on-line catalogue of publications

Publications:
- ↳ **Estatísticas de Comercio Externo** *(External Trade Statistics)* — *irregular*
- ↳ **Estatísticas Industriais** *(Industrial Statistics)* — *irregular*
- ↳ **Instituto Nacional de Estatística** *(National Institute of Statistics) (Website)*
- ↳ **Statistical Yearbook** — annual review of major socio-economic indicators, covering: population; labour force; agricultural and industrial resources; national accounts and finances; etc — *annual*

▫ MYANMAR

Central Statistical Organisation, Ministry of National Planning and Economic Development

Address:	Six Storey Building, Strand Road, PBDN Tsp, Yangon
Telephone:	+95 128 3535/286 933/277 274
Fax:	+95 250 351

Publications:
- ↳ **Myanmar Data** — *annual*

□ NAMIBIA

Central Statistics Office

Address:	Private Bag 13356, 14-16 Krupp Street, Windhoek 9000
Telephone:	+264 61 239 360
Fax:	+264 61 239 376

Publications:
↳ Statistical Abstract

□ NAURU

Nauru Bureau of Statistics

Address:	Ministry of Finance, Government Buildings, Yaren District, Nauru
Telephone:	+674 444 3125
Fax:	+674 444 3217

Obtaining Publications: same as above

□ NEPAL

National Planning Commission Central Bureau of Statistics

Address:	Ramshah path, Thapathali, Kathmandu
Telephone:	+977 1 213 422/212 606/748
Fax:	+977 1 227 720
E-mail:	cbscls@wlink.com.np
Website:	www.census.gov.np

Website notes: socio-economic statistics

Publications:
↳ **National Planning Commission Central Bureau of Statistics** – statistics provided focusing on major socio-economic indicators such as household, population, agriculture, national accounts, prices, industry, health and education *(Website)*
↳ **Statistical Pocket Book** – *every two years*
↳ **Statistical Year Book of Nepal** – *every two years*

□ NETHERLANDS ANTILLES

Central Bureau of Statistics

Address:	Fort Amsterdam, Curaçao
Telephone:	+599 9 461 1031/461 1549
Fax:	+599 9 461 1696/5004

Obtaining Publications: same as above

Publications:
↳ **Statistical Quarterly Bulletin** – statistics on: area and climate, population, manufacturing industry, traffic transport and communication, money and banking, public finance, prices, justice and security, internal trade, comparative international data on wholesale prices and stock market prices – *quarterly*
↳ **Statistical Yearbook** – statistics on: area and climate, population, public health, housing, religion and politics, education, labour, manufacturing industry, foreign trade, traffic transport and communication, money and banking, national accounts, balance of payments, public finance, prices, social affairs, justice and security, and internal trade – *annual*

□ NEW CALEDONIA

Institut Territorial de la Statistique et des Etudes Economiques (ITSEE)

(Institute of Statistics and Economic Studies)

Address:	BP 823, 98845 Nouméa
Telephone:	+687 275 481
Fax:	+687 288 148

Year Established: 1974

Publications:

↳ **Comptes Economiques** *(Economic Accounts)* – annual
↳ **Tableaux de l'Economie Caledonienne** *(Caledonian Economic Tables)* – quarterly

□ NEW ZEALAND

Te Tari Tatau

(Statistics New Zealand)

Address:	PO Box 2922, Aorangi House, 85 Molesworth Street, Wellington 1
Telephone:	+64 4 931 4731
Fax:	+64 4 473 2626
E-mail:	info@stats.govt.nz or publications@stats.govt.nz
Website:	www.stats.govt.nz

Website notes: presentation of Statistics New Zealand and products and resources provided to the general public and researchers: listing of major statistical titles, latest press releases and online access to various statistical publications, articles and databases

Statistical Coverage: social, economic and financial data on New Zealand is available free of charge by downloading a range of different articles and publications covering a wide variety of topics and indicators. Depending on the topic covered, data may be updated on an annual, quarterly or monthly basis. Areas covered include population and demographic trends, labour market, environment, economy, agricultural resources, industry and manufacturing activities, price indexes, etc

Obtaining Publications: Dissemination Unit, Statistics New Zealand, Freepost 10 007, PO Box 2922, Wellington

Guides to Publications: annual catalogue (free, available online)

Publications:
↳ **Agricultural Production Statistics** – *irregular*
↳ **Business Activity Statistics** – statistical analysis of a wide range of business activities in New Zealand, covering the agricultural, industrial, manufacturing and services sectors – *annual*
↳ **Business and Trade** – information and statistics on New Zealand external trade activities, as well as consumer and producer price indices; overseas debt; GDP; retail sales figures and general business activities – *annual*
↳ **Consumer Expenditure Statistics** – analysis of latest trends in household expenditure and national consumption patterns – *annual*
↳ **Demographic Trends** – statistical overview of the overall structure of New Zealand's population and present demographic trends: includes data on population change; migrations; fertility rates; births and deaths; marriages and divorces; etc – *annual*
↳ **Information Network for Official Statistics Database (INFOS Database)** *(Website)*
↳ **Labour Market Statistics** – analysis of the national labour market structure, providing statistics on employment and unemployment, labour costs and hours of work – *annual*
↳ **New Zealand in Profile** – statistics on population, production and trade – *annual*
↳ **New Zealand Official Yearbook** – *annual*
↳ **Te Tari Tatau** *(Statistics New Zealand) (Website)*

□ NICARAGUA

Instituto Nacional de Estadística y Censos

(National Institute of Statistics and Census)

Address:	Frente al Hospital Lenín Fonseca, Los Arcos, Managua
Telephone:	+505 266 6178/2825
Website:	www.inec.gob.ni

Website notes: available in Spanish only; provides information on products and services; access to online database providing statistical information

Statistical Coverage: censuses and surveys on socio-demographic and economic indicators related to Nicaragua

Publications:
↳ **Indicadores Sociales de la Niñez Nicaragüense** *(Social Indicators of Nicaraguan Children)* – information and analyses on the economic and social situation of children and youth in Nicaragua
↳ **Instituto Nacional de Estadística y Censos** *(National Institute of Statistics and Census) (Website)*
↳ **Un Paso Arriba y dos Abajo** *(One step up and two steps down)* – information on the poverty level in Nicaragua

▫ NIGER

Direction de la Statistique et de L'Informatique, Ministere des Finances et du Plan

(Central Statistical Office, Ministry of Finance and Planning)

Address:	Boite Postal 235, Niamey
Telephone:	+227 723 560/722 374
Fax:	+227 733 371

▫ NIGERIA

Federal Office of Statistics (FOS)

Address:	36 - 38 Broad Street, PMB 12528, Lagos
Telephone:	+234 1 260 1710-4
Fax:	+234 1 263 5077
E-mail:	fos@infoweb.abs.net
Website:	www.nigeriabusinessinfo.com/fos.htm

Website notes: information on the Institute's products and services, publications, and selected statistical tables

Year Established: 1947

Publications:
↳ **Federal Office of Statistics** – provides statistical information relating to social and economic activities as well as living conditions of the inhabitants of Nigeria *(Website)*

▫ OMAN

Ministry of National Economy, Department of Statistics

Address:	Oman
Telephone:	+968 699 483
E-mail:	mone@omantel.net.om

Obtaining Publications: same as above

Guides to Publications: online catalogue

Publications:
↳ **Statistical Yearbook** – *annual*

▫ PAKISTAN

Government of Pakistan, Statistics Division - Federal Bureau of Statistics

Address:	5-SLIC Building, F-6/4, Blue Area, Islamabad
Telephone:	+92 51 921 1406/1585
Fax:	+92 51 920 5287
E-mail:	secstats@isb.paknet.com.pk
Website:	www.statpak.gov.pk

Website notes: information on the Federal Bureau of Statistics and its products and services. Includes monthly and annually updated statistics covering different socio-economic indicators including monthly price indices, rate of inflation, external trade, statistics, etc

Statistical Coverage: Collection, compilation and analysis of statistical data relating to various sectors of economy

Year Established: 1950

Guides to Publications: Catalogue of Publications (annual, free)

Publications:
↳ **Foreign Trade Statistics of Pakistan** – *annual*
↳ **Government of Pakistan, Statistics Division** *(Website)*
↳ **Monthly Statistical Bulletin** – monthly socio-economic statistics – *monthly*
↳ **Pakistan Statistical Yearbook** – annual updated figures covering Pakistan major socio-economic indicators, including population, labour force, prices, national accounts, transport, external trade and tourism – *annual*
↳ **Statistical Pocket Book of Pakistan** – summary of statistics extracted from the Statistical Yearbook – *annual*

▫ PANAMA

Dirección de Estadística y Censos

(Directorate of Statistics and Census)

Address:	Apartado 5213, Panamá 5 RP
Telephone:	+507 264 3734
Fax:	+507 269 7294
E-mail:	cgrdec@contraloria.gob.pa

Guides to Publications: Catalogo de Estadística Panamena y de Publicaciones Censales (free)

Publications:
↳ **Fiscia de Situación Económica: Indice de la Producción · Industria Manufactura** – *annual*
↳ **Indicadores Económicos y Sociales** – social and economic indicators – *monthly*
↳ **Panama en Cifras** – key socio-economic statistics – *annual*
↳ **Situación Demográfica: Estadísticas Vitales** *(Demographic Statistics)* – demographic statistics – *annual*
↳ **Situación Económica: Anuario de Comercio Exterior** *(Foreign Trade Yearbook)* – in 4 parts: imports; exports; Canal Free Trade Zone; re-exports – *annual*
↳ **Situación Económica: Indice de Precios al por Mayor al Consumidor** *(Consumption Price Index)* – retail and wholesale price indices – *quarterly*
↳ **Situación Económica: Industria** *(Industry Report)* – industry economic overview – *2 p.a.*
↳ **Situación Económica: Producción Agropecuaria** *(Agricultural Production Report)* – agricultural production report – *annual*

▫ PAPUA NEW GUINEA

National Statistical Office

Address:	PO Box 337, Waigani, NCD
Telephone:	+675 301 1229/1283/1226
Fax:	+675 325 1869
E-mail:	nsuvulo@nso.gov.pg or nsopub@nso.gov.pg
Website:	www.nso.gov.pg

Website notes: details on the Institute's main products and services; catalogue of publications; selected online statistics

Statistical Coverage: statistics focusing on major socio-economic indicators such as business, household and international trade

Guides to Publications: on-line catalogue containing information on publications; on-line subscription order form

Publications:
↳ **Abstract of Statistics** – covers economic indicators including monthly or quarterly figures for current year and two proceeding years – *quarterly*
↳ **Consumer Price Index** – *annual*
↳ **Economic Indicators** – data on balance of payments, trade, export prices, consumer price indices, banking and finance, and international tourism – *monthly*
↳ **Export Price Indices** – *quarterly*
↳ **Gross Domestic Product and Expenditure** – data on all economic activity in Papua New Guinea – *annual*
↳ **Import Price Indexes** – *annual*
↳ **National Statistical Office** *(Website)*

▫ PARAGUAY

Dirección General de Estadística y Censos

(Directorate General of Statistics and Census)

Address:	PO Box 1118, Herrera 1010, Asunción
Telephone:	+595 21 205 424
Fax:	+595 21 205 442
E-mail:	info@dgeec.gov.py

Obtaining Publications: PO Box 1118, Asunción, Paraguay

Publications:
↳ **Anuario Estadistico del Paraguay** *(Statistical Yearbook of Paraguay)* – *annual*
↳ **Boletin Estadistico del Paraguay** *(Paraguay's Statistical Bulletin)* – *annual*
↳ **Dirección General de Estadística y Censos** *(Statistics and Census Office)* *(Website)*

□ PERU

Instituto Nacional de Estadística e Informática (INEI)
(National Institute of Statistics and Information)

Address:	Avenida Gral Garzón 654-658 Jesús María, Lima 11
Telephone:	+51 1 433 6565
Fax:	+51 1 431 1340
E-mail:	infoinei@inei.gob.pe
Website:	www.inei.gob.pe

Website notes: information on INE's main products and services: catalogue of publications, news and press releases, list of major events, online library and access to publications and statistical series

Statistical Coverage: statistics provided online cover different social, economic and financial areas. "Peru en Cifras" section is subdivided into three categories of data: 1) Demographic indicators - data on population structure from the 1940s up to 2001, and latest demographic trends; 2) Social indicators - statistics on education & health services, households, poverty, employment: gender and youth issues, crime, human development, and 3) Economic Indicators - data covering annual inflation for the last ten years, investment and finances, money and tourism, production and external trade. Data available in Spanish only

Obtaining Publications: as above

Guides to Publications: access to online databases and online catalogue

Publications:
↳ **Estado de la Población Peruana** *(Demographic Statistics of Peru)*
↳ **Evolución de la Actividad Productiva** *(Development of Production)* — monthly statistics on production results for different industries and markets, including: agriculture; fishing; mining ; manufacturing; electricity and water; construction; and commerce — *monthly*
↳ **Instituto Nacional de Estadística e Informática (INEI)** *(National Institute of Statistics) (Website)*
↳ **Perú: Compendio Estadístico Económico Financiero** *(Peru: Economic and Financial Statistics)* — statistical coverage of main economic and financial areas in Peru, including data on: agricultural resources and fisheries; manufacturing industries; mining and petroleum; commerce; prices; transports and communications; tourism; public finances and national accounts; external trade; and international panorama — *annual*
↳ **Perú: Compendio Estadístico Socio-Demográfico** *(Peru: Socio-demographic Statistics)* — statistical analysis of different socio-economic indicators in Peru covering: population; education & health services; gender and youth issues; environment; violence; poverty; and general social and human development
↳ **Perú: Mercado Laboral Urbano y Género** *(Peru: Urban Labour Market)* — statistical overview of the labour market in Peru, focusing on the urban labour force sector — *annual*
↳ **Sistema de Precios** *(Price Index)* — *monthly*

□ PHILIPPINES

National Statistics Office (NSO)

Address:	PO Box 779, Solicarel Building 1, R Magsaysay Boulevard, Sta Mesa, Manila 1008
Telephone:	+63 2 716 0807/713 7074/715 6502
Fax:	+63 2 713 7073/715 6503
E-mail:	info@mail.census.gov.ph or v.abuan@mail.census.gov.ph
Website:	www.census.gov.ph

Website notes: offers information on NSO's main products and services, including catalogue of publications, latest press releases and free online statistics

Statistical Coverage: socio-economic data can be found on the NSO main page, under "Site Map". Monthly, quarterly and annual statistics are provided for a series of different social and economic sectors, including: population, labour force and child labour, agriculture and fisheries, inflation rates, wholesale price index, foreign trade, manufacturing, income and expenditure, housing, energy consumption and poverty indicators

Year Established: 1941

Obtaining Publications: Information Dissemination Section, address as above

Guides to Publications: online catalogue providing detailed informations on various publications and compilations

Publications:
↳ **Annual Poverty Indicators Survey (APIS)** — data and analysis of social, economic and demographic situation on Filipino families living in poverty — *annual*

↳ **Annual Survey of Establishments - Wholesale and Retail Trade - Small** — statistical tables on national and regional levels that include data on number of establishments, employment, compensation, revenue, costs, fixed assets, capital expenditures — *annual*
↳ **Census of Agriculture and Fisheries** — data on the overall structure and resources of the national agricultural and fishing sectors — *irregular*
↳ **Census of Establishments - Wholesale and Retail Sales - Large** — compilation of statistical information pertaining to business operations of establishments — *every five years*
↳ **Consumer Price Index** — *annual*
↳ **Family Income and Expenditures Survey** — data on household incomes and consumption patterns in the Philippines — *every two years*
↳ **Foreign Trade Statistics of the Philippines** — *annual*
↳ **Integrated Survey of Households** — *quarterly*
↳ **Monthly Bulletin of Statistics** — monthly updated data on social, demographic, and economic variables — *monthly*
↳ **Monthly Integrated Survey of Selected Industries (MISSI)** — *monthly*
↳ **National Demographic and Health Survey** — demographic data on fertility, family planning, and maternal and child health — *every five years*
↳ **National Statistics Office (NSO)** *(Website)*
↳ **Philippine Yearbook** — annual statistical compilation of main geographic, demographic, social, and economic indicators for the Philippines — *annual*
↳ **Philippines in Figures** — annual compilation of statistics produced by the NSO and other government agencies, focusing on macro-economic indicators and financial statistics — *annual*

□ PUERTO RICO

Puerto Rico Agricultural Statistics Service

Address:	
Telephone:	+1787 723 1190
Fax:	+1787 787 721 8355
E-mail:	ewaldhaus@nass.usda.gov
Website:	www.nass.usda.gov/pr

Guides to Publications: online guides to publications and services

Publications:
↳ **Puerto Rico Agricultural Statistics Service**

□ QATAR

Central Statistical Organisation (CSO)

Address:	PO Box 7283, Doha
Telephone:	+974 491 497
Fax:	+974 445 573

Obtaining Publications: same as above

□ RWANDA

Direction Générale des Statistiques, Ministère du Plan
(Directorate General of Statistics, Ministry of Planning)

Address:	BP 46, Kigali
Telephone:	+250 754 02

Publications:
↳ **Bulletin de Statistique** *(Statistical Bulletin)* — statistical bulletin containing social and economic statistics — *quarterly*
↳ **Comptes Economiques Nationaux du Rwanda** *(Rwanda Economic Accounts)* — national accounts — *annual*
↳ **Rapport Annuel** *(Annual Report)* — detailed financial, economic and social statistics — *annual*

□ SAO TOMÉ E PRÍNCIPE

Direccao de Estatistica
(Statistics Centre)

Address:	CP 256, Sao Tome
Telephone:	21 982

◘ SAUDI ARABIA

Central Department of Statistics, Ministry of Finance and National Economy

Address:	PO Box 3735, Off Airport Road, behind the Ministry of Finance Building, Riyadh 11187
Telephone:	+966 1 405 9638/401 4528
Fax:	+966 1 405 9493
Website:	www.saudinf.com

Publications:
- ↳ **Central Department of Statistics, Ministry of Finance and National Economy** *(Website)*

◘ SENEGAL

Direction de la Prévision et de la Statistique
(Directorate of Forecasting and Statistics)

Address:	BP 116, Corner Rue 1 and Boulevard l'Est Pt E, Dakar
Telephone:	+221 825 0743
Fax:	+221 824 9001
E-mail:	sdiarisso@finances.gouv.sn or dps@telecomplus.sn

Publications:
- ↳ **Analyse du commerce exterieur** *(Foreign Trade Analysis)* – foreign trade – *annual*
- ↳ **Banque de Données économiques et financières** *(Database of Financial and Economic Information)* – 3 volumes covering company activities and performance, sector by sector – *annual*
- ↳ **Indice de la Production Industrielle** *(Industrial Production Index)* – indices of industrial production – *quarterly*
- ↳ **Rapport sur les Perspectives Economiques** *(Economic Outlook Report)* – economic trend data – *2 p.a.*
- ↳ **Situation Economique du Sénégal** *(Senegal Economic Situation)* – economic review of Senegal. – *annual*
- ↳ **Tableau de Bord de l'Economie Sénégalaise** – recent data on Senegal economy – *monthly*

◘ SEYCHELLES

Ministry of Administration and Manpower, Management and Information Systems Division

Address:	PO Box 206, Independence House, Victoria, Mahé
Telephone:	+248 224 041
Fax:	+248 225 339
E-mail:	hris@seychelles.net

Obtaining Publications: same as above

Publications:
- ↳ **Migration and Tourism Statistics** – *annual*
- ↳ **Statistical Abstract** – *annual*
- ↳ **Statistical Bulletin** – *quarterly*

◘ SIERRA LEONE

Central Statistics Office, Ministry of Development and Economic Planning

Address:	P.M.B. 595, A. J. Momoh Street, Tower Hill, Freetown
Telephone:	+232 22 223 287
Fax:	+232 22 223 897
E-mail:	cso@sierratel.sl
Website:	www.statistics-sierra-leone.org

Publications:
- ↳ **Central Statistics Office** *(Website)*

◘ SINGAPORE

Department of Statistics

Address:	#05-01 Treasury Building, 100 High Street, Singapore 179434
Telephone:	+65 6323 7686
Fax:	+65 6332 7689
E-mail:	info@singstat.gov.sg
Website:	www.singstat.gov.sg

Website notes: offers information on Singapore Statistics main products and services, including: catalogue of most recent publications; press releases; analytical papers; links to other national and international statistical organisations; and various online statistics

Statistical Coverage: "Key Facts & Figures" section includes monthly, quarterly and annual data covering different social, economic and financial indicators for Singapore. Latest monthly and quarterly indicators cover: real sector; fiscal and financial sector; external sector; and population. Other monthly statistics provided include: Singapore population structure by age, sex and ethnic group; labour force productivity; industrial GDP; and consumer and wholesale price indices. Annual statistics online include highlights and tables from some of the Institute's main socio-economic statistical titles such as the "Yearbook of Statistics" and "Singapore in Figures"

Year Established: 1871

Obtaining Publications: selected publications are available at Shop@AsiaOne and AsianConnect

Guides to Publications: website

Publications:
- ↳ **Economic Surveys Series · Hotels & Catering** – *irregular*
- ↳ **Economic Surveys Series · Wholesale & Retail** – *irregular*
- ↳ **Monthly Consumer Price Index** – *monthly*
- ↳ **Monthly Digest of Statistics** – monthly and/or quarterly updated statistics covering main physical, socio-economic and demographic indicators – *monthly*
- ↳ **Monthly Retail Sales and Catering Trade Indices** – *monthly*
- ↳ **Singapore Census of Population**
- ↳ **Singapore in Figures** – annual compilation of social and economic statistics covering: population; labour force; national income; balance of payments; foreign investment; manufacturing industries; foreign trade; tourism; education and health; etc – *annual*
- ↳ **Singapore Statistics** *(Website)*
- ↳ **Statistics Singapore Newsletter** – information and highlights of most recent surveys – *quarterly*
- ↳ **Yearbook of Statistics** – annual socio-economic statistical data on Singapore, covering a wide range of topics, from population and demographics to employment; health and education; transport and communications; etc – *annual*

◘ SOLOMON ISLANDS

Statistics Office

Address:	PO Box G6, Honiara
Telephone:	+677 237 00
Fax:	+677 231 10
Website:	www.commerce.gov.sb/Ministries/statistics_office.htm

Publications:
- ↳ **reports of varying lengths** – *irregular*
- ↳ **Solomon Islands Statistics Office** *(Website)*
- ↳ **Statistical Yearbook** – *yearly*
- ↳ **Trade Report** – *irregular*

□ SOUTH AFRICA

Statistieke Suid-Afrika
(Statistics South Africa)

Address:	Private Bag X44, 274 Schoeman Street, Pretoria 0001
Telephone:	+27 12 310 8911
Fax:	+27 12 310 8500-3
E-mail:	info@statssa.pwv.gov.za
Website:	www.statssa.gov.za

Website notes: general presentation of main products and services of the Central Statistical Service, including: list of statistical releases; statistical reports; discussion and technical papers; links to other statistical organisations; and online data on South Africa

Statistical Coverage: "Economic Indicators" section provides data on consumer and producer price indexes from 1975 to 2000. The "Bulletin of Statistics" (under Statistical Reports section) includes quarterly updated figures on different social and economic topics: population and demography; labour market; agriculture and manufacturing industries; internal trade; national accounts; etc

Obtaining Publications: Can be ordered online

Guides to Publications: online catalogue of publications

Publications:
- ↳ **Agricultural Census** – *annual*
- ↳ **Bulletin of Statistics** – quarterly updated statistics providing a general socio-economic portrait of South Africa. Areas covered include: population and demography; labour market; agriculture, manufacturing and construction; public and private finance; internal trade; and national accounts – *quarterly*
- ↳ **Demographic Statistics - Mid-Year Estimates** – *annual*
- ↳ **Household Survey** – statistical analysis of household sizes, poverty and general standards of living of the South African population – *annual*
- ↳ **Labour statistics: Survey of Total Employment and Earnings** – employment statistics by industry sector – *annual*
- ↳ **Products Manufactured: Food, Beverages and Tobacco** – statistics covering the volume of goods manufactured in the food, drinks and tobacco industries – *annual*
- ↳ **Retail Prices** – retail prices of selected goods and services – *monthly*
- ↳ **Retail Trade Sales** – retailing data by kind of business and type of merchandise – *monthly*
- ↳ **Statistics South Africa** *(Website)*
- ↳ **Tourism and Migration** – *annual*

□ SOUTH KOREA

National Statistical Office (NSO)

Address:	71 Nonhyon-dong, Kangnam-gu, Seoul-teukbyeolsi, 135-010
Telephone:	+82 2 3443 5382
Fax:	+82 2 3443 5384
Website:	www.nso.go.kr

Website notes: information on the National Statistical Office main products and services: catalogue of publications; KOSIS (Korean Statistical Information System); NSO surveys; and online statistics

Statistical Coverage: "Korea in Graph" section provides data in both English and Korean for a series of different socio-economic areas: land and population; agriculture; mining and manufacturing; energy; construction; wholesale, retail trade and services; transports and communications; labour and wages; prices and household economy; money and banking; public finance; national accounts; balance of payments and economic co-operation; education, science and health; society, tourism and environment; and international statistics

Year Established: 1948

Obtaining Publications: Dong-Sook Kim (kosa@nso.go.kr), Korea Statistical Association

Guides to Publications: online catalogue with summary of contents for publications

Publications:
- ↳ **Annual Report of the Wholesale and Retail Trade Survey** – national and regional statistics focusing on outlet/company number and size (number of outlets and workers); floor space; annual sales; etc – *annual*
- ↳ **Annual Report on Monthly Industrial Production Statistics** – provides information on the output and structure of national production industries – *annual*
- ↳ **Consumer Price Survey** – consumer price data – *monthly*
- ↳ **Family Income and Expenditure Survey** – *annual*
- ↳ **Korea Statistical Yearbook** – compilation of annual statistics on Korea covering a wide range of areas, from population to general macro-economic indicators, agricultural and industrial resources, etc – *annual*

- ↳ **Major Statistics of Korean Economy** – *2 p.a.*
- ↳ **National Statistical Office** *(Website)*
- ↳ **Service Industry Survey** – statistical information covering: number of workers by status, sex and group of industry; amount of annual receipts and expenses by group of industry; amount of receipts by size of floor space – *annual*
- ↳ **Social Indicators in Korea** – contains statistics covering: population; family; income and consumption; labour; education; health; housing and transportation; telecommunications; environment; welfare; culture and leisure – *annual*

□ SRI LANKA

Department of Census and Statistics

Address:	PO Box 563, Information Unit, Colombo
Telephone:	+94 1 675 297
E-mail:	dcensus@lanka.ccom.lk
Website:	www.statistics.gov.lk

Website notes: list of main products and services provided by the Department, including publications catalogue; press releases; and online statistics

Statistical Coverage: basic socio-economic statistics on Sri Lanka are provided by sector, with period coverage depending on area/topic in question: population; labour market; agricultural and industrial resources; education and social conditions; prices and wages; national accounts; and trade

Obtaining Publications: Publications Division (Mr. R.Balakrishnan, Deputy Director), Tel: +94 1 508 818

Guides to Publications: online catalogues

Publications:
- ↳ **Bulletin of Selected Retail Prices** – *irregular*
- ↳ **Demographic Survey** – *irregular*
- ↳ **Department of Census and Statistics** *(Website)*
- ↳ **Sri Lanka Labour Force Survey** – *irregular*
- ↳ **Statistical Abstract** – *irregular*
- ↳ **Statistical Pocketbook** – *irregular*

□ ST LUCIA

St Lucia Statistical Department

Address:	Chreiki Building, Micoud Street, Castries
Telephone:	+1758 452 3716
Fax:	+1758 451 8254
E-mail:	statsdept@candw.lc
Website:	www.stats.gov.lc

Statistical Coverage: main socio-economic indicators and statistical data on national accounts; labour force; agriculture; tourism; foreign trade; population; health; industrial production; construction; prices; banking and finance; education; public finance

Guides to Publications: online catalogue and summary of publications by sectors

Publications:
- ↳ **Annual Overseas Trade** – external trade by sectors and years – *yearly*
- ↳ **Labour Force Report** – economic and social conditions of the employed, the unemployed and persons not in the labour force – *irregular*
- ↳ **St Lucia Statistical Department** *(Website)*
- ↳ **Tourism By Numbers** – *erratic*

□ ST VINCENT AND THE GRENADINES

Statistical Office

Address:	Central Planning Division, Ministry of Finance and Planning, Administrative Building, Kingstown
Telephone:	457 2921
Fax:	456 2430
E-mail:	statssvg@vincysurf.com

Publications:
- ↳ **Digest of Statistics** – *annually*

■ SUDAN

Department of Statistics, Ministry of Finance and Economic Planning

Address:	PO Box 700, Khartoum
Telephone:	+249 1177 7131
Fax:	+249 1177 1860

Publications:
- ↳ Foreign Trade Statistics
- ↳ Internal Trade and Other Statistics

■ SURINAME

Algemeen Bureau voor de Statistiek

(National Statistical Office)

Address:	PO Box 244, Kromme Elleboogstraat 10, Paramaribo
Telephone:	+597 473 927/474 861
Fax:	+597 421 056
E-mail:	statistics@cq-link.sr

Publications:
- ↳ Statistical Yearbook — *annual*

■ SWAZILAND

Central Statistical Office

Address:	PO Box 456, Mbabane
Telephone:	+268 268 421 51/459 82
Fax:	+268 268 433 00
E-mail:	cso@realnet.co.sz

Publications:
- ↳ Annual Statistical Bulletin — *annual*
- ↳ Annual Survey of Swazi Nation Land — *annual*
- ↳ Census of Industries — *annual*
- ↳ Employment and Wages — *annual*
- ↳ National Accounts — *annual*

■ SYRIA

Central Bureau of Statistics

Address:	Abou Rumaneh, Abdel Malek Ben Marwan Street, Damascus
Telephone:	+963 11 335 830/31/32
Fax:	+963 11 332 2292
E-mail:	cbs@mail.sy

Publications:
- ↳ Statistical Abstract — comprehensive socio-economic indicators — *annual*
- ↳ Summary of Foreign Trade — *quarterly*

■ TAIWAN

Directorate General of Budget Accounting and Statistics - National Statistics

Address:	
Telephone:	+886 233 566 500
E-mail:	edp@dgbas.gov.tw
Website:	www.dgbasey.gov.tw

Website notes: information on the National Institute's main products and services and online statistics covering: key economic and social indicators; national economic statistics; price indices; labour force data; earnings and productivity statistics; and online monthly bulletin of statistics

Obtaining Publications: It is possible to order online.

Guides to Publications: online catalogue

Publications:
- ↳ Monthly Bulletin of Statistics of the Republic of China — present social and economic conditions in Taiwan area, and the latest figures which incorporate all the important statistical series published in the country — *Monthly*
- ↳ National Statistics of Taiwan, the Republic of China *(Website)*
- ↳ Social Indicators of the Republic of China
- ↳ Statistical Abstract of National Income in Taiwan Area — *annual*
- ↳ Statistical Yearbook of the Republic of China — *annual*

■ TANZANIA

Bureau of Statistics

Address:	PO Box 796, Dar es Salaam
Telephone:	+255 22 212 2722/213 7834
Fax:	+255 211 2352
Telex:	41576 TANSTAT
E-mail:	nbs.dg@raha.com
Website:	www.tanzania.go.tz/statisticsf.html

Statistical Coverage: It covers national demographic and economic statistics

Guides to Publications: online catalogue

Publications:
- ↳ Quarterly Statistical Bulletin — *quarterly*
- ↳ Survey of Employment
- ↳ The United Republic of Tanzania

■ THAILAND

National Statistical Office

Address:	Larn Luang Road, Bangkok 10100
Telephone:	+66 2 281 0333
Fax:	+66 2 281 3814
E-mail:	onsoadm@nso.go.th or binfopub@nso.go.th
Website:	www.nso.go.th

Website notes: overview of the NSO's main products and services, including list of publications; links to other national statistical offices; and free access to Thai socio-economic statistics

Statistical Coverage: by entering the "Statistics" section, one has free access to a wide range of online publications and surveys, covering several social, economic and financial sectors. The section is divided into three main types of statistics: 1) Summary statistics from major census and surveys - covering mainly population and demographics; household income and expenditure; agricultural and industrial resources; and general socio-economic living conditions; 2) Statistics by Subject: including annually compiled data on population and labour market; agriculture, forestry, fisheries and industry; wholesale and retail trade; foreign trade and balance of payments; money and finance; etc; and 3) Subject and Analytical Reports: covering specific topics within broader socio-economic areas such as gender and youth issues

Obtaining Publications: As above. It is also possible to order online

Guides to Publications: online catalogue

Publications:
- ↳ Monthly Statistical Newsletter — *monthly*
- ↳ National Statistical Office *(Website)*
- ↳ Statistical Yearbook Thailand — detailed social and economic statistics — *annual*

□ TOGO

Direction de la Statistique
(Statistical Office)

Address:	BP 118, Lomé
Telephone:	+228 212 287/216 224
Fax:	+228 213 753
E-mail:	togostat@ecowasmail.net

Publications:
- ↳ **Annuaire Statistique du Togo** *(Statistical Yearbook of Togo)* – socio-economic statistics – *annual*
- ↳ **Bulletin Mensuel de Statistique** *(Monthly Statistical Bulletin)* – monthly statistical bulletin – *monthly*
- ↳ **Enquete sur les Entreprises Industrielles et Commerciales du Togo** *(Industrial and Commerical Survey)* – industrial and commercial survey – *annual*

□ TONGA

Statistics Department, Ministry of Finance

Address:	PO Box 149, Treasury Building, Vuna Road, Nuku'alofa
Telephone:	+676 233 00/239 13
Fax:	+676 243 03
Telex:	66244 MINFIN TS
E-mail:	minfin@kalianet.to or statdept@tongatapu.net.to

Tonga Statistics Department

Address:	PO Box 149, Vuna Road, Nuku'alofa
Telephone:	+676 24 303/21 010
Fax:	+676 23 300
E-mail:	statdept@tongatapu.net.to

Year Established: 1971

Obtaining Publications: same as above

□ TRINIDAD AND TOBAGO

Central Statistical Office

Address:	PO Box 98, 35/41 Queen Street, Port of Spain
Telephone:	624 2436
Fax:	625 3802

Guides to Publications: List of Publications (free)

Publications:
- ↳ **Annual Statistical Digest** – *annual*
- ↳ **International Travel Report** – *annual*
- ↳ **Labour Force** – *quarterly*
- ↳ **Overseas Trade Report** – *annual*
- ↳ **Population and Vital Statistics** – *annual*

□ TUNISIA

Institut National de la Statistique
(National Institute of Statistics)

Address:	BP 265, 70 rue Ech Cham, Tunis
Telephone:	+216 71 891 002
Fax:	+216 71 792 559
E-mail:	INS@Email.ati.tn
Website:	www.ins.nat.tn

Website notes: online information on the Institute's main products and services: contacts, list of publications, and selected online statistical data

Statistical Coverage: statistical data is provided under two main sections: 1) Social and Demographic data and 2) Economic and Financial data. The first section covers: population and demographic indicators (e.g. total population, 1990-2000; age segmentation, 1990-2000, and projections up to 2029; infant mortality, fertility rates, and life expectancy); labour force indicators (employment and unemployment rates, 1994-2001); consumption and expenditure data (e.g. household expenditure by consumer good, %, 1995-1995); health and education indicators (e.g. literacy rates, 1966-2000; health infrastructures; medical staff; etc); and household structure and habits indicators. The second section provides statistics on: national accounts; public finances and the monetary system; external trade; industrial production and output; and prices. Data is available in French only

Year Established: 1969

Obtaining Publications: As above

Guides to Publications: online catalogue

Publications:
- ↳ **Comptes de la nation** *(Statistical Yearbook)* – *annual*
- ↳ **Institut National de la Statistique** *(National Institute of Statistics) (Website)*
- ↳ **Rapport annuel sur les indicateurs d'infrastructure** *(Infrastructure Indicators Annual Report)* – *annual*
- ↳ **Statistique du commerce extérieur** *(External Trade Statistics)* – annually updated statistics covering: lexternal trade – *annual*

□ TURKMENISTAN

National Institute of Statistics and Forecasting of Turkmenistan

Address:	72 Makhtumkuli Avenue, Ashkhabad 744000
Telephone:	+993 12 394 265/353 596
Fax:	+993 12 354 379
E-mail:	office@natstat.gov.tm

□ TUVALU

Tuvalu Central Statistics Division

Address:	PO Box 33, Ministry of Finance and Economic, Vaiaku, Funafuti Island
Telephone:	+688 20 107
Fax:	+688 20 107
E-mail:	csd_stats@yahoo.com or mchris@tuvalu.tv

Obtaining Publications: same as above

Publications:
- ↳ **Population and Housing Census 2002**

□ UGANDA

Uganda Bureau of Statistics

Address:	PO Box 13, Plot 10/11 Airport Road, Entebbe
Telephone:	+256 4132 0741
Fax:	+256 4132 0147
E-mail:	ubos@infocom.co.ug or unhs@infocom.co.ug
Website:	www.ubos.org/

Year Established: 1998

Obtaining Publications: As above

Guides to Publications: online catalogue including prices

Publications:
- ↳ **Consumer Price Index** – *monthly*
- ↳ **Consumer Price Indexes** – *monthly*
- ↳ **Migration and Tourism Statistics** – *annual*
- ↳ **Statistical Abstract** – *Annual*
- ↳ **Uganda Bureau of Statistics** – Covers all aspects of a national statistic centre, with data from housing and demographic indicators to statistics referring to industrial resources and revenues.

▪ UNITED ARAB EMIRATES

Ministry of Information and Culture, Department of External Information

Address:	PO Box 17, Abu Dhabi
E-mail:	admin@uaeinteract.com
Website:	www.uaeinteract.com

Website notes: presentation of the United Arab Emirates, providing a wide variety of information and data on: government and politics, travel and tourism, culture, and education

Publications:
↳ **UAE Interact** *(Website)*

▪ URUGUAY

Instituto Nacional de Estadística

(National Institute of Statistics of Uruguay)

Address:	Rio Negro 1520, 11100 Montevideo
Telephone:	+598 2 902 7303/1007/1014
Fax:	+598 2 903 2780
E-mail:	difusion@ine.gub.uy
Website:	www.ine.gub.uy

Website notes: information on the institute's main products and services, including free access to online publications and statistical data

Statistical Coverage: data and figures are available under different sections, covering several social, economic, and financial topics. Online publications include the "Anuario Estadístico", as well as surveys on population structure and demographic trends, and household income and expenditure patterns. The Statistical Yearbook covers: population; health and education; social security and general living conditions; agriculture and fisheries; industry and commerce; transports; tourism; external trade; prices and salaries; energy resources; and banking and financial matters

Year Established: 1852

Obtaining Publications: same as above

Guides to Publications: online catalogue

Publications:
↳ **Anuario Estadístico** *(Statistical Yearbook)* – annual overview of main social, economic and financial indicators, providing a general portrait of Uruguay and its human and economic resources – *annual*
↳ **Encuesta Industrial Annual** *(Annual Industrial Survey)* – *annual*
↳ **Estadísticas Vitales** *(Vital Statistics)* – socio-economic indicators – *annual*
↳ **Indice Medio de Salarios** *(Average Wage Index)* – average wage index – *quarterly*
↳ **Instituto Nacional de Estadística** *(National Institute of Statistics of Uruguay)* *(Website)*

▪ USA

Banco Interamericano de Desarollo

(Inter-American Development Bank)

Address:	1300 New York Avenue, NW, Washington, DC 20577
Telephone:	+1 202 623 1000
Fax:	+1 202 623 3096
E-mail:	pic@iadb.org
Website:	www.iadb.org

Website notes: news and articles on the Latin American pan-regional business environment, financial structure, and general economic situation. online access to IDB America Magazine, press releases, and a series of statistics on member countries

Statistical Coverage: "Statistics and Quantitative Analysis Unit": A wide range of statistics on Latin America as a whole and specific countries are provided, covering various different socio-economic sectors: agricultural statistics (FAO data); general economic and social data (IDB); education statistics (UNESCO); external trade (IDB); and labour statistics (ILO)

Year Established: 1959

Obtaining Publications: Online ordering facilities. Alternatively IDB Bookstore, 1300 New York Ave., NW, Washington, D.C. 20577

USA.

Guides to Publications: online catalogue

Publications:
↳ **Annual Report** – comprehensive review of the Bank's operations during the year and a summary of the economic situation of Latin America and the Caribbean. Presents descriptions by country of Bank loans and technical cooperation operations. Includes regional statistical information and financial statements of the Bank – *annual*
↳ **Development Beyond Economics · Economic and Social Progress in Latin America** – *annual*
↳ **Inter-American Development Bank** *(Website)*

Bureau of Economic Analysis, US Department of Commerce

Address:	US Department of Commerce, Washington, DC 20230
Telephone:	+1 202 606 9900/9666
Website:	www.bea.doc.gov

Website notes: provides key national, international and regional statistics on the US economy including: GDP and related data; industry accounts statistics; regional and international accounts data; and statistical releases. Information on BEA's main products and services, including catalogue of publications and online products

Obtaining Publications: Superintendent of Documents, PO Box 371954, Pittsburgh, PA 15250-7954 or US Government Printing Office, Washington DC. (Tel: +1 202 512 1800; Fax: +1 202 512 2250). It also offers the possibility of online ordering through http://bookstore.gpo.gov

Guides to Publications: online catalogue with year by year sections

Publications:
↳ **Bureau of Economic Analysis (BEA)** *(Website)*
↳ **Foreign Direct Investment in the United States**
↳ **National Income and Product Accounts of the United States**
↳ **Survey of Current Business** – general analysis of the US and international economic scene and business activities. Includes monthly estimates of national income and product accounts – *monthly*
↳ **US Direct Investment Abroad**

Bureau of Labor Statistics, US Department of Labor

Address:	Division of Information Services, 2 Massachusetts Avenue, NE, Room 2860, Washington, DC 20212
Telephone:	+1 202 691 5200
Fax:	+1 202 691 7890
E-mail:	blsdata_staff@bls.gov or labstat.helpdesk@bls.gov
Website:	www.bls.gov

Website notes: information on the Bureau's main products and services and access to various online publications, including BLS News; Occupational Outlook Handbook; and most recent press releases

Statistical Coverage: site contains different socio-economic statistics directly related to the national labour market. Data covered includes: inflation and spending - consumer and producer prices; inflation rates; employment costs; consumer spending; employment and unemployment rates, employment projections; productivity; and international comparisons. "Economy at a Glance" section provides monthly updated figures on macro-economic indicators; employment data for 9 major national industrial sectors; and combined economic and industrial employment statistics at regional, state and metropolitan area levels

Obtaining Publications: Bureau of Labor Statistics, Publications Sales Center PO Box 2145, Chicago, IL 60690, Tel: +1 312 353 1880. To order subscriptions: GPO Superintendent of Documents:P.O. Box 371954; Pittsburgh, PA 15250-7954; (202) 512-1800

Guides to Publications: US Government Publications Catalogue (monthly and annual, priced, from US Government Printing Office)

Publications:
↳ **Bureau of Labor Statistics** *(Website)*
↳ **Compensation and Working Conditions** – information and results of the national compensation survey and detailed analysis of working conditions in the US – *monthly*
↳ **Monthly Labor Review** – monthly updated news on the US labour market, covering employment structure and unemployment rates; wages; productivity and costs; etc – *monthly*
↳ **Occupational Outlook Handbook** – *annual*

↳ **Report on the American Workforce** – *annual*

Bureau of Transportation Statistics, US Department of Transportation

Address:	400 Seventh Street, SW, Room 3103, Washington, DC 20590
Telephone:	+1 202 366 1270
Fax:	+1 202 366 3640
E-mail:	answers@bts.gov
Website:	www.bts.gov

Website notes: offers information on the Bureau's main products and services including: access to different online publications including the "Journal of Transports and Statistics" and the "National Household Travel Survey"; information on transport industry related databases, such as - Commodity Flow Survey; Highway Statistics; National Transportation Atlas; National Transportation Statistics; etc

Obtaining Publications: it offeres the possibility to order online

Guides to Publications: online search engine for publications

Publications:
↳ **Airport Activity Statistics**
↳ **Bureau of Transportation Statistics** *(Website)*
↳ **FAA Aviation Forecasts** – forecasts for the coming 12 years of activity at FAA facilities – *annual*
↳ **FAA Statistical Handbook of Aviation** – historical statistics on airports, airport activity, US civil airline fleet, US airline operating data, production of aircraft and related products, imports and exports – *annual*
↳ **National Household Travel Survey** – survey on internal traveling in the USA, covering inter-state and inter-metropolitan passenger travel by trip and traveler characteristics – *every five years*
↳ **North American Transportation In Figures** – statistical data on the transport industries in USA, Canada and Mexico
↳ **Transportation Statistics Annual Report** – overview of the national transports system and analysis of latest trends and developments affecting the sector – *annual*
↳ **US International Air Travel Statistics** – *annual*

International Trade Administration (ITA), US Department of Commerce

Address:	Public Affairs Office, Room 3414, Washington, DC 20230
Telephone:	+1 202 482 3809
Fax:	+1 202 482 5819
E-mail:	tic@ita.doc.gov
Website:	www.ita.doc.gov

Website notes: offers information on US external trade activities and foreign commercial services. Includes statistics on exports and imports at both national and international levels, collected by other sections of the US Department of Commerce and other official organisations, such as the US Bureau of Census

Guides to Publications: online information about services provided and guide to some of the publications and statistical reports they publish

Publications:
↳ **Big Emerging Markets** *(Website)*
↳ **International Trade Administration, US Department of Commerce** *(Website)*
↳ **Showcase Europe** *(Website)*

National Agricultural Statistics Service (NASS), US Department of Agriculture (USDA)

Address:	14th & Independence Avenue SW, Washington, DC 20250-1000
Telephone:	+1 202 720 3878
E-mail:	nass@nass.usda.gov
Website:	www.usda.gov/nass

Website notes: statistical information and analysis of latest trends and developments affecting the national agricultural market. Access to wide range of reports, surveys and databases, covering different sectors within the market, at both national and state levels. Includes catalogue of products; latest news and information on coming events; and links to related official bodies and organisations

Statistical Coverage: data on the US agricultural resources and general market structure can be found by downloading several of

NASS's online reports and surveys. A wide range of market sectors are covered, with figures being collected on either an annual, quarterly, or monthly basis. For some sectors, data is provided at both national and state level. Areas covered include: agricultural prices and land value; livestock; fresh produce production (statistics for a wide range of fruit and vegetables); crop production; dairy products; structure of the agricultural labour market; and chemical usage

Obtaining Publications: it offers the possiblity to order online

Guides to Publications: online catalogue and shop

Publications:
↳ **Agricultural Prices** – listing of prices paid to US farmers for main agricultural commodities (crops, livestock and livestock products) – *annual*
↳ **Crop Production** – statistical data on crop production by state (planted area, harvested area, yield and production) – *monthly*
↳ **Dairy Products** – monthly updated information on the production of dairy products, covering milk (evaporated, condensed and dry), butter, cheese and frozen dairy goods – *monthly*
↳ **Farm Labor** – analysis of the labour market' structure in the US agricultural sector – *quarterly*
↳ **Milk Production** – monthly updated statistics on liquid milk production and livestock (milk cows) by major producing state – *monthly*
↳ **National Agricultural Statistics Service (NASS), US Department of Agriculture** *(Website)*

National Center for Health Statistics

Address:	6525 Belcrest Road, Hyattsville, MD 20782-2003.
Telephone:	+1 301 458 4636
Website:	www.cdc.gov/nchswww/

Website notes: this governmental site covers all issues about health in the US providing information on subjects such as diseases, vaccinations and disabilities. It also has sections on news, press releases and up-coming events

Statistical Coverage: offers surveys and data that include: national health interview survey; national health and nutrition examination survey; national health care survey; national vital statistics system; national immunisation survey; state and local area integrated telephone survey. The site also offers a detailed range of statistics searchable in alphabetical order

Publications:
↳ **National Center for Health Statistics** *(Website)*

US Census Bureau

Address:	4700 Silver Hill Road, Suitland, MD 20746
Telephone:	+1 301 457 4608
E-mail:	pop@census.gov
Website:	www.census.gov

Website notes: offers information on the Census Bureau and the collection of social and economic data in the USA. Listing of main products and services, including catalogue of major statistical titles and online products; free access to different databases and online reports; and links to major national and international statistical agencies

Statistical Coverage: access to a series of different databases and publications, including a wide range of social, economic, financial and demographic statistics on the US. Databases include "American Factfinder"; "Foreign Trade Statistics"; and "State and Country Quick Facts". Data is provided at both national and state levels, covering topics such as: population structure and demographic trends; household income, expenditure and general living conditions; macro-economic indicators; geographic maps; census of governments; etc

Obtaining Publications: It is possble to order online

Guides to Publications: detailed online catalogue

Publications:
↳ **Annual Survey of Manufacturers** – *annual*
↳ **Census of Agriculture - Geographic Area Series** – general statistical overview of the US agricultural sector, with data provided at a national, state, and county levels. It covers land use and farm sizes; cereals production; livestock; market value of agricultural products; machinery and equipment; etc – *every five years*
↳ **Census of Manufacturing: Geographic Area Series** – *every five years*
↳ **Census of Manufacturing: Industry Series** – *every five years*
↳ **Census of Population and Housing**
↳ **Census of Retail Trade - Area Series** – *every five years*
↳ **Census of Service Industries - Geographic Area Series** – statistical data at a national, state and county level for a wide range of service industries and sectors. It covers: the hotels and catering industry; personal and business services;

automotives repairs; leisure centres; health and educational services; etc — *every five years*

↳ **Census of Wholesale Trade · Area series** — *every five years*

↳ **Economic census · Accommodation and Foodservices (Geographic Area Series)** — hotel, catering and restaurant statistics covering: number of establishments; industry turnover; number of employees. Statistics are broken down by state and county — *every five years*

↳ **Monthly Wholesale Trade Report: Sales and Inventories** — *monthly*

↳ **Population · Household Economic Studies**

↳ **Population Characteristics**

↳ **Statistical Abstract of the United States** — statistical publication providing a wide range of social, economic & financial, and demographic data on the USA, collected and produced by several government agencies and private organisations. Includes both historic data and selected projections (issued since 1878) — *annual*

↳ **US Census Bureau** *(Website)*

↳ **US Census Bureau · Foreign Trade Statistics** *(Website)*

↳ **US Merchandise Trade: U.S. Exports and Imports by Harmonized Commodity** — *annual*

↳ **USA Statistics in Brief** — summary of the Annual Statistical Abstract, it includes selected socio-economic statistics at a national, state, and metropolitan areas level — *annual*

▫ UZBEKISTAN

Ministry of Macroeconomy and Statistics

Address:	Bujuk Ipak Yuli 63, Tashkent 700077
Telephone:	+7 87 1267 0494/97
Fax:	+7 87 1267 7816/2509
E-mail:	Gds@uzstat.org.uz
Website:	www.gov.uz

Website notes: socio-economic data and analysis covering: geography; population; labour force; industry; agriculture; construction; transport and communications; economy

Publications:
↳ **Ministry of Macroeconomy and Statistics** *(Website)*

▫ VANUATU

Statistics Office (NPSO)

Address:	Private Mail Bag 019, Port Vila
Telephone:	+678 21 10/21 11
Fax:	+678 24 583
Website:	www.spc.int/stats/vanuatu/indexold.htm

Publications:
↳ **Vanuatu National Statistics Office** *(Website)*

▫ VENEZUELA

Instituto Nacional de Estadistica

(National Institute of Statistics)

Address:	
E-mail:	ocei@platino.gov.ve
Website:	www.ine.gov.ve

Statistical Coverage: covers national economic and demographic indicators, lifestyles, and internal and external trade. Provides annual reports and decennial population reports

Year Established: 1871

Publications:
↳ **Instituto Nacional de Estadística** *(Website)*

Oficina Central de Estadística e Informática

(Central Office of Statistics)

Address:	Apartado 4593, Edificio Fundación La Salle, Avenida Boyaca, 1010 Caracas
Telephone:	+58 212 782 1133/1212
Fax:	+58 212 782 1156/781 5412
E-mail:	ocei@platino.gov.ve
Website:	www.ocei.gov.ve

Website notes: overview of the office's main products and services and access to series of online statistics covering: main socio-economic indicators; socio-demographic statistics; and selected data from the last and previous population census

Statistical Coverage: online data is grouped under different sections, according to each indicator in question: 1) Economic data, covering: external trade; main economic indicators (e.g. GDP; wages; industry statistics; etc); 2) Socio-demographic data, covering: social indicators (e.g. education; health; culture; etc); national and regional population projections; labour force data; and environmental data; and 3) Population census data: census 1873-1990; indigenous populations census

Year Established: 1978

Publications:
↳ **Anuario Estadístico de Venezuela** *(Statistical Yearbook of Venezuela)* — includes statistics on demography, economic and social situation, culture, science and technology — *annual*

↳ **Boletín** *(Bulletin)* — *quarterly*

↳ **Comercio Exterior de Venezuela** *(Venezuelan External Trade)* — foreign trade statistics by region and commodity — *annual*

↳ **Oficina Central de Estadística e Informática** *(Central Office of Statistics)* *(Website)*

▫ VIETNAM

Vietnamese General Statistical Office

Address:	2 Hoang Van Thu Street, Ba Dinh District, Hanoi
Telephone:	+84 4 823 4072/834 8027/826 3522
Fax:	+84 4 846 4345

▫ WESTERN SAMOA

Department of Statistics

Address:	PO Box 1151, Apia
Telephone:	+685 21 371
Fax:	+685 21 716/24 675
Telex:	221 Malo SX

Year Established: 1963

▫ YEMEN

Central Statistical Organisation, Ministry of Planning and Development

Address:	PO Box 13434, Sana'a
Telephone:	+967 1 250 108/618-9
Fax:	+967 1 250 664

▫ ZAMBIA

Central Statistical Office

Address:	PO Box 31908, Lusaka
Telephone:	+260 1 211 231/212 121
Fax:	+260 1 253 609
Telex:	ZA40242
E-mail:	censtat@zamnet.zm

Publications:
↳ **Consumer Price Statistics** — *quarterly*

↳ **Financial Statistics of Public Corporations** — *annual*
↳ **Manpower Survey** — *annual*

◻ ZIMBABWE

Central Statistical Office

Address:	**PO Box CY 342, Kaguvi Building, 4th Street Central Avenue Causeway, Harare**
Telephone:	**+263 4 706 681**
Fax:	**+263 4 728 529**

Publications:
↳ **Annual Statistical Digest** — *annual*
↳ **Census of Production** — *annual*
↳ **Monthly Bulletin** — *monthly*
↳ **Monthly Migration and Tourist Statistics** — *quarterly*
↳ **Quarterly Digest of Statistics** — *quarterly*

Marketing Geography

□ Afghanistan

Capital City	Kabul	*Capital population: 2,034,000 (1995)*
Population ('000)	23,337 *(2002)*	
Urban population (%)	22.68 *(2002)*	
Land area (km²)	65209	
Languages	Dari (Persian dialect); Pushtu. Also a number of minority languages.	
Religion	Mainly Islam	
Currency	Afghani (AFA)	
Head of State	Hamid Karzai (2002)	
Head of Government	Hamid Karzai (2002)	
Ruling Party	The government is led by a loose coalition of Pushtuns, Tajiks and other ethnic groups with strong support from the international community.	

Main Urban Areas	Population
Kabul (capital)	2,034,000 (1995)

Afghanistan divides the Middle East from the Indian subcontinent. It borders on China in the northeast, Pakistan in the east and south, Iran in the west and the former Soviet Union republics of Turkmenistan, Uzbekistan and Tajikistan in the north. It is this central location that has largely accounted for the successive invasions of the country over the centuries. The capital is Kabul.

Afghanistan remains a divided country. Various faction leaders, in particular the mainly-Tajik Northern Alliance, have immense power behind the scenes. According to the Bonn Agreement, negotiated in 2002, the country's loya jirga has the power to approve key personnel in the government as well as its structure.

The loya jirga, a group of 1,500 delegates from across the country, met in June 2002 and chose Karzai as president for the next 18 months. Karzai then selected his cabinet, which was eventually approved by the loya jirga with a few changes.

Any assessment of recent economic performance is necessarily tentative since the underlying information base is extremely weak. Estimates made in 2001 placed Afghanistan's per capita income at about US$300, for a population of 23 million, giving an aggregate GDP of about US$6.9 billion. However, this is likely to have declined substantially during the past year. Current assessments of assistance start from the assumption of a per capita GDP of only US$200 in 2001. According to the latest available estimates, the bulk of national production consists of agriculture and forestry products (53%), followed by mining and light industry (28%), trade (8%) and construction (6%). Transport, communications and services account for the remaining 5%. There is no effective banking system and the central government raises almost no revenues. Warlords siphon off customs revenue at source, sending only a fraction of the receipts to Kabul. The government hopes to rebuild 6,000 kilometres of roads by 2006, employing thousands of workers at $2 per day.

Agriculture is the mainstay of the economy. Most Afghans used to be settled farmers, herders, or both. In addition to the war, farmers have suffered from a three-year drought which has devastated much of the country, particularly in the south. A survey completed in 2002 indicates that the total livestock population in Afghanistan has declined by about 60% from 1998 levels. Opium has once again become more important than traditional crops. Over 2,000 tonnes (an amount roughly double annual output in the Taliban years) were harvested in 2002 with a value of $1.2 billion. At the end of 2002, farmers could get $540 a kilo, a price which no other crop can match. Increasingly, the opium is being processed into heroin, which has a higher value and is easier to conceal, before it is exported. The production of traditional products such as meat, fruits, wheat and livestock will not increase substantially while high-yield poppies hold sway. Farming is also limited by the seven million landmines that have been planted in the country. Mining and light industry constitute the second major sector of the economy after agriculture. Among manufactured products, carpets, leather goods, and gold and silver jewellery are the main items. With the restoration of political and economic stability, production of these goods should recover fairly quickly. Afghanistan is believed to have substantial hydrocarbon reserves, both oil and gas, in the north. Exploration started in 1967 with collaboration from the former Soviet Union, but ended with the Soviet withdrawal in 1989. With the restoration of peace, prospects for the resumption of hydrocarbon exploration are good, as well as for the transit flow of oil and gas from the Central Asian republics to India and Pakistan, on the basis of foreign capital. The mining sector is also underdeveloped but has the most potential for growth. Afghanistan has silver, copper, iron, gold, chrome, lapis lazuli and talc.

Afghanistan's proven and probable natural gas reserves are estimated to be up to five trillion cubic feet. Production, however, has been declining since the mid-1970s. At its peak, Afghanistan supplied 70-90% of its natural gas output to the Soviet Union's gas grid. Pakistan has signed a deal with Turkmenistan and Afghanistan to build a $3.2 billion gas pipeline through Afghanistan but for the moment there are no investors.

□ Algeria

Capital City	Algiers	*Capital population: 2,423,694 (1998)*
Population ('000)	30,623 *(2002)*	
Urban population (%)	60.73 *(2002)*	
Land area (km²)	238174	
Languages	Arabic (official), French	
Religion	Islam	
Currency	Algerian dinar (DZD)	
Head of State	Abdelaziz Bouteflika (1999)	
Head of Government	Ali Benflis (2000) National Liberation Front (FLN)	
Ruling Party	The government is formed by a coalition of six parties.	

Main Urban Areas	Population	
Algiers (capital)	2,423,694	(1998)
Setif	1,299,116	(1998)
Oran	1,208,171	(1998)
Tizi-Ouzoa	1,100,297	(1998)
Batna	987,475	(1998)
Chlef	874,917	(1998)
Tlemcen	873,039	(1998)
Medea	859,273	(1998)
Bejaia	836,301	(1998)
M'sila	835,701	(1998)

Algeria, one of the largest countries in Africa, occupies most of the western Mediterranean coast of North Africa, and faces Spain and Italy across the Mediterranean at a distance of no more than 150km. It is bordered to the west by Morocco and Mauritania, to the south by Mali and Niger, and to the east by Tunisia and Libya. The climate is warm and has a dry desert character. The capital is Algiers.

The president is elected for a five-year term by the people. Parliament has two chambers. The National People's Assembly has 380 members, elected for a five-year term in multi-seat constituencies by proportional representation. Eight seats in the national assembly are reserved for Algerians abroad. The National Council has 144 members, 96 members elected by communal councils and 48 members appointed by the president.

Presidential elections were held in April 1999 but six of the seven candidates withdrew, citing massive fraud. In that election, Bouteflika of the RND took 74% of the vote. Elections to the National Assembly were held in May 2002. The FLN won 199 seats while the RND took 47 seats. The Movement of the Society for Peace, an Islamic party, captured 39 seats with the remainder being scattered among several minor parties. All recent elections have been boycotted by the two Berber parties, the Front of Socialist Forces and Rally for Culture and Democracy.

GDP grew by 4.1% in 2002 while prices rose by 1.4%. Growth in 2003 is expected to be 5.9% with growth of 3.8% in 2004. Inflation should be about 2.3% in 2002 and 3.5% in 2004. Faced with mounting social demands, the government decided to ease fiscal policy starting in 2001 until private activity generates sufficient employment opportunities. It adopted a fiscal stimulus plan covering the period 2001-2004. As a result, the overall budget balance weakened in 2002. This deterioration mainly reflected higher spending and a decline in hydrocarbon revenues due to a reduction in volumes and prices. The fiscal stimulus will boost growth only temporarily, and cannot substitute for the more fundamental reforms that are needed to achieve a lasting improvement in growth and employment creation. The most prominent of these structural reforms is a comprehensive tariff reform that was implemented in 2002 as part of Algeria's Association Agreement with the EU. Continued economic, social and political problems for Algeria include: high unemployment (around 30% and reportedly still rising), labour unrest and a large black market (possibly 20% of the country's GDP). Efforts to address these problems are hampered by state inefficiencies and corruption.

Agriculture accounts for just over 10% of GDP with most farming being limited to the coastal regions where wheat, maize and sugar beet are grown. Agricultural output declined in 2002 due to adverse weather conditions but there was a pickup in construction and service activities as a result of the government's fiscal stimulus. Algeria remains highly dependent on oil and natural gas exports, which account for more than 90% of all export earnings, and about 30% of GDP. The country also has a substantial petrochemical and fertiliser industry. There are a number of other downstream, oil-using industries, as well as plants producing steel, paper products, metal manufactures and even motor vehicles. Together, oil and gas revenues make up 60% of the state budget. Lower hydrocarbon output in 2002 was partly offset by a better performance in non-hydrocarbon sectors. In 2003, legislation intended to reform the energy sector was scrapped, constituting a major blow to the overall economic reform bill and underlining the power of the conservative military elite. Most non-oil industries are located in the northern part of the country. Few of these industries are profitable and a majority operate with considerable excess capacity.

Algeria is considered to be under-explored although significant oil and gas discoveries have been made over the last few years. The government hopes to increase crude oil production capacity significantly but that will require large amounts of foreign capital and expertise. The goal is to double the number of companies operating in Algeria by 2005. Official estimates of Algeria's proven oil reserves remain at 9.2 billion barrels. But with recent oil discoveries, plans for more exploration drilling, improved data on existing fields, and use of enhanced oil recovery systems, proven oil reserve estimates are expected to be revised upward in coming years. Algeria expects a sharp increase in crude oil exports due to a rapid shift towards domestic natural gas consumption and planned increases in oil production.

◦ American Samoa

Capital City	Pago Pago	*Capital population: 3,200 (1992)*
Population ('000)	76 *(2002)*	
Urban population (%)	53.58 *(2002)*	
Land area (km²)	20	
Languages	English, Samoan	
Religion	Mainly Christian	
Currency	US dollar (US$)	
Head of State	President George W. Bush (2000)	
Head of Government	Governor: Tauese P. Sunia (1996)	
Ruling Party	None.	

Main Urban Areas	Population
Pago Pago (capital)	3,200 (1992)

American Samoa is a cluster of islands within the Samoan group, to the east of the state of Western Samoa. Apart from Tutuila, Tau, Aunu'u, Ofu, Olosega and Rose, American Samoa includes the more northerly Swain's Island, which is closer to Tokelau, a dependent territory of New Zealand. The climate is warm, with limited rainfall but occasional danger of cyclones. The capital is Pago Pago.

American Samoa is an unincorporated territory of the US, whose executive authority rests in the Governor, appointed for a four-year term. The Legislature has two chambers. The House of Representatives has 21 members, elected for a two-year term, 20 in single-seat constituencies and one by a public meeting on Swain's Island. The Senate has 18 members, elected for a four-year term by and from the chiefs of the islands. One observer is sent to the US Congress in Washington.

Elections to the legislature were last held in November 2000 when only non-partisans were elected. In gubernatorial elections held at the same time, Tauese Sunia was re-elected with 51% of the vote.

The islands are highly dependent on the US, which provides about a third of the government's budget. Attempts by the government to develop a larger and more broadly-based economy are held back by the country's remote location, its limited transportation and devastating hurricanes. Growth was no more than 1.5% in 2002. Unemployment is high - typically 15-16% and over half the population live below the poverty line. American Samoa receives certain tax advantages and some immunity from US import restrictions. Average per capita income is about US$3,200 per year.

Fishing - primarily tuna fishing and tuna canning - is the most important economic activity in American Samoa and the main source of income. Fishing operations employ a third of the workforce and account for more than 90% of exports, which are valued at US$250-300 million per annum. There are two large American-owned canneries that comprise the greater part of the country's industrial base. More than 90% of the land is communally owned. The main agricultural products are bananas, coconuts, vegetables, taro, breadfruit, yams, copra, pineapples and papayas; dairy farming is also important. With no natural mineral resources and limited scope for manufacturing exports, the country depends heavily on fishing and agriculture. The tourist sector has also added a number of new hotels and hopes to attract more Japanese visitors but development has been held back by the Asian financial crisis in the late 1990s and the anti-terrorism focus of the US government.

American Samoa has at least twice as much generating capacity it actually needs at present. Apart from geothermal sources and natural resources such as timber, the country has ready access to oil supplies from the US.

◦ Angola

Capital City	Luanda	*Capital population: 2,207,000 (1995)*
Population ('000)	14,184 *(2002)*	
Urban population (%)	35.22 *(2002)*	
Land area (km²)	124670	
Languages	Portuguese (official); Ovimbundu, Kimbundu, Bakongo, Chokwe spoken	
Religion	Roman Catholic (majority)	
Currency	New kwanza (AON)	
Head of State	President José Eduardo dos Santos	
Head of Government	Fernando da Piedade Dias dos Santos (2002)	
Ruling Party	The People's Movement for the Liberation of Angola - Worker's Party (MPLA-PA) leads a coalition.	

Main Urban Areas	Population
Luanda (capital)	2,207,000 (1995)

Angola lies on the western (Atlantic) coast of southern Africa. It is bounded in the south by Namibia, in the east and north by the Democratic Republic of the Congo (formerly Zaire), and in the east by Zambia. The capital is Luanda.

After more than 21 years of armed conflict, virtually all national institutions have been destroyed. In 1998, dos Santos temporarily suspended the post of Prime Minister, creating a parallel ministry of defence within the office of the presidency and sacked a number of political figures who might have threatened his monopoly on power. He appointed Dias dos Santos as prime minister in 2002. In theory, the president is elected for a five-year term by the people but the elections due in 1997 have been put off indefinitely.

Elections were last held in October 1992, when the government of the ruling MPLA-PA faced competition for the first time from opposition parties. The MPLA-PA received more than 60% of the national vote - though much less in many rural areas. The UNITA rebels, who won the remaining 40%, denounced the result as a sham and reopened the war.

GDP grew at the astounding pace of 15.3% in 2002 but that figure is somewhat misleading. Most of the country's capacity had been idle during the civil war, and the sudden growth spurt mainly represents the resumption of economic activity as peace returned. Growth of 4.4% is forecast in 2003 and 11.4% in 2004. Meanwhile, Angola is experiencing one of the highest rates of inflation in the world - 109% in 2002, an expected 95.2% in 2003 and a forecast rate of inflation of 30.1% in 2004. Even though the war is over, rebuilding Angola will be arduous. Despite a massive increase in oil and diamond-related income, the country continues to face pressing economic and social problems. Its fiscal deficits amount to more than 7% of GDP and insufficient controls on public spending prevent the authorities from assembling a credible anti-inflationary policy. The budgetary situation appears to have deteriorated further during 2002, when the government used almost all of its deposits at the central bank, and the bank itself lost about half of its foreign exchange reserves. Meanwhile, the humanitarian situation has reached dire proportions; there is an urgent need to reallocate expenditures in favour of the social sectors, including humanitarian assistance. Angola is potentially one of the richest countries in southern Africa but more than three-quarters of the population now live below the poverty line. The situation is worst in Luanda, which is home to over 40% of Angolans as a result of wartime displacement.

Angola is the second largest oil producer in sub-Saharan Africa after Nigeria. Most of this oil comes from offshore fields. A number of oil analysts believe that new discoveries could soon make the country Africa's leading producer. The economy is highly dependent on oil, which accounts for about half of the country's GDP and over 90% of export revenues. However, the sector has very few linkages to other parts of the economy. Over the past year, allegations have arisen that suggest large portions of Angola's oil revenue has been embezzled or channelled to military purposes. According to the IMF, about $1.2 billion of Angola's oil revenue for the year 2001 is "unaccounted for". Though the government strongly denies these allegations, aid agencies accuse the Angolan government of using the missing money to support its efforts to fight UNITA. In times past, agriculture accounted for 12-15% of GDP and employed almost 60% of the workforce. However, during the civil war the government has followed a policy of systematically emptying the countryside of people in order to starve UNITA into submission. In mid-2002, farming was carried out on no more than 2% of the country's land. Sporadic water supplies, yearly outbreaks of cholera and the abysmal condition of the roadways are other complications that have contributed to the sharp fall in agricultural output. In peacetime, bananas, coffee, palm products and timber are the sector's main exports while maize, cassava and potatoes are grown for domestic consumption.

Angola is sub-Saharan Africa's second largest oil producer behind Nigeria. The province of Cabinda produces about 70% of Angola's oil and accounts for nearly all of its foreign exchange earnings. Political tensions are high in some areas of Cabinda as separatist groups demand a greater share of oil revenue. Crude oil production averaged 897,000 barrels per day (bbl/d) in 2002, and production is expected to exceed one million bbl/d in 2003. Several additional deepwater discoveries were announced in 2002. Angola is developing plans for a new 200,000-bbl/d refinery, to be located in the central coastal city of Lobito. The majority of products refined at the new facility (80%) would be exported regionally.

◦ Anguilla

Capital City	The Valley	*Capital population: 500 (1992)*
Population ('000)	8 *(2002)*	
Urban population (%)	12.54 *(2002)*	
Languages	English	
Religion	Mainly Christian	
Currency	East Caribbean dollar (EC$)	
Head of State	HM Queen Elizabeth II	
Head of Government	Osbourne Fleming (2000)	
Ruling Party	Anguilla National Alliance (ANA) and Anguilla Democratic Party (ADP) form a coalition.	

Main Urban Areas	Population
The Valley (capital)	500 (1992)

Anguilla is located at the northern limit of the Leeward Islands group, north of St Kitts and to the east of the British Virgin Islands and Puerto Rico. The island is built on coral and is entirely low-lying. The climate is equable, with occasional threat from hurricanes. The capital is The Valley.

As a Dependent Territory of the UK, ultimate sovereignty rests with the British monarch, although in practice the Chief Minister governs. Until 1980, Anguilla was technically a part of St Christopher (St Kitts)/Nevis/Anguilla, but this proved to be an unhappy union and the Anguillans repudiated the St Kitts administration. The 1982 Constitution came into operation in May 1990. The House of Assembly has 11 members, seven members elected for a five-year term in single-seat constituencies, two ex officio members and two nominated members.

General elections were held in March 2000. The Anguilla National Alliance won three seats, the ADP won two seats and the AUP took the remaining two seats.

The level of economic activity contracted in 2002 by 1-2%. The main reason for this decline was the poor performance of the tourist sector and the weakness in construction activity on the island. The consumer price index also fell by 0.5% in 2002. The fall was mainly the result of lower prices for housing, food and clothing and footwear. The country's trade deficit was reduced by more than 10%, owing mainly to a correspondingly large fall in the value of imports. Unemployment remains high and each year more inhabitants leave the island in search of better jobs elsewhere. Anguilla has few natural resources, and the economy depends heavily on high-class tourism, remittances from Anguillans employed in other countries and grants from the British Government.

Anguilla's burgeoning tourist industry dominates the economy, eclipsing all traditional activities such as farming and fishing. Tourism performed poorly in 2002, however, with the number of visitors falling by 4.7%. Gross visitor expenditures in 2002 were estimated to be $118 million, representing a 12.8% decline over the previous year. Construction activity, which is also driven by the tourist industry, suffered a similar contraction. Farming is for subsistence purpose and consists mainly of small holdings. Productivity in this sector is very low. The agricultural products include peas, corn, sweet potatoes; sheep, goats, pigs, cattle and poultry. Major export crops are lobster, fish, livestock and salt. Agricultural output fell by 0.6% in 2002. The island aspires to be a domicile for offshore banks, trusts and international business companies. Although problems of inadequate regulation and charges of money laundering have slowed development of the financial sector, net foreign assets of the banking system rose by more than 20% during the year, amounting to $204 million by the end of 2002.

The bulk of Anguilla's energy derives from oil, most of it imported from Venezuela. Firewood and geothermal resources are other sources of fuel.

▫ Antigua

Capital City	St John's	Capital population: 38,000 (1992)
Population ('000)	70 (2002)	
Urban population (%)	37.34 (2002)	
Land area (km²)	44	
Languages	English	
Religion	Mainly Christian	
Currency	East Caribbean dollar (EC$)	
Head of State	HM Queen Elizabeth II	
Head of Government	Lester Bird	
Ruling Party	The Antigua Labour Party (ALP) leads the government.	

Main Urban Areas	Population
St John's (capital)	38,000 (1992)

Antigua, along with Barbuda (25 miles to Antigua's north) forms part of the Leeward Islands in the Eastern Caribbean. Also included in the Leeward Islands is the uninhabited islet of Redonda (25 miles southwest of Antigua). The capital is St John's.

Antigua is a member of the British Commonwealth and the British monarch is the titular head of state. In practice, the Prime Minister appoints the British Governor. Parliament has two chambers. The House of Representatives has 19 members, 17 members elected for a five-year term in single-seat constituencies, one ex-officio member and a Speaker. The Senate has 17 appointed members.

In March 1999, elections to the 17-member House of Representatives resulted in another win for the ALP, which has held power since 1976. The ALP claimed 12 seats (up from 11 in the previous administration) while the opposition United National Democratic Party took four seats. The remaining seat went to the Barbuda People's Movement. Lester Bird was again named Prime Minister.

Antigua's economy grew by 2.2% in 2002 while inflation also measured 2.2%. Growth in 2003 will be an estimated 2.5%, slowing to 1% in 2004. Meanwhile, prices are expected to rise by 2.5% in both 2003 and 2004. The fall in economic activity in 2002 is attributed mainly to the weak performance of the tourist industry owing to a drop in the number of overnight visitors and cruise-ship arrivals, particularly in the first half of 2002. The number of tourists is expected to recover in 2003 with an increase in air services and an expansion of hotel capacity. The government's capital expenditures are estimated to have risen by more than 23% in 2002. The surge was mainly due to spending for several infrastructure projects including roads. The government is actively promoting policies to alleviate poverty. Critics argue that these programmes are really intended to enrich supporters of the ALP and the Bird family. Investment in public projects is increasing rapidly, however.

Tourism accounts for almost three quarters of GDP and is the driving economic force. The number of tourists fell more than 18% in 2002, with the biggest decline coming in the number of cruise-ship passengers. The sector has ample capacity, but existing facilities require refurbishment and other improvements in quality. Activity in the construction sector rose in 2002, partly attributable to an expansion in private sector real estate development. Farming suffers from recurrent droughts

and soil erosion. The agriculture sector accounts for only about 5% of GDP and its share is falling. Sugar, maize, fruit and vegetables are grown for domestic consumption, and bananas and coconuts for export. The country also has considerable mineral resources, including limestone and clay, but these have never been developed, partly for environmental reasons. The financial services sector is small but growing.

Nearly all of Antigua's energy needs are met through imports. Oil from Venezuela is refined in Trinidad and Tobago and then supplied to Antigua. There are opportunities to develop geothermal energy but little capital is available for development.

▫ Argentina

Capital City	Buenos Aires	Capital population: 2,877,630 (2002)
Population ('000)	37,715 (2002)	
Urban population (%)	89.91 (2002)	
Land area (km²)	273669	
Languages	Spanish	
Religion	Roman Catholic (90%)	
Currency	Peso argentino (Pesos)	
Head of State	Nestor Kirchner (2003)	
Head of Government	Nestor Kirchner (2003)	
Ruling Party	The government is led by the Justicialist Party (JP).	

Main Urban Areas	Population	
Buenos Aires (capital)	2,877,630	(2002)
Cordoba	1,311,339	(2002)
San Justo	1,284,304	(2002)
Rosario	961,952	(2002)
Lomas de Zamora	619,290	(2002)
Mar de Plata	610,589	(2002)
Almirante Brown	589,811	(2002)
La Plata	566,425	(2002)
Quilmes	562,796	(2002)
San Miguel de Tacuman	537,190	(2002)

Argentina is the second largest state in South America and occupies most of the continent south of the Tropic of Capricorn and east of the Andes. With its only coastline facing the Atlantic, Argentina's terrain varies from the vast prairies of the north to the mountains of the east and the sub-Antarctic south. The capital is Buenos Aires.

A new constitution was introduced in August 1994 which effectively cemented the country's departure from the military system that ran the country in the 1960s and 1970s. Argentina comprises a Federal District, 23 provinces and the National Territory of Tierra del Fuego, all of which enjoy varying degrees of autonomy. The executive president is elected every six years, answering to a 257-seat Chamber of Deputies and a 72-seat Senate.

In presidential elections held in April 2003 Kirchner and former president Carlos Menem emerged as the front-runners. They were to face a run-off in May 2003 but Menem withdrew before the vote. Parliamentary elections were held in October 2001. In the Chamber of Deputies the JP won 116 seats, the Alliance took 88 seats and the Alternative for a Republic of Equals received 17 seats. The remainder were spread among smaller parties. In the Senate, the JP won 40 seats and the Alliance won 21 seats. Other seats were dispersed among several parties.

Real GDP fell by 11% in 2002 and is expected to rise by 5.5% in 2003. In 2004, growth of 4% is predicted. Prices rose by 25.9% in 2002 and are expected to rise by 14.3% in 2003. Inflation is forecast to be 7.7% in 2004. In 2002, the government threatened to default on its debts to the IMF (and did default on loans from the World Bank). However, under pressure from the US, the IMF eventually granted another $6.6 billion loan in 2003. Prospects for recovery remain fragile. The exchange rate was stable during the second half of 2002 and actually strengthened in the early part of 2003. Unemployment has fallen (albeit from 22% at the beginning of 2002 to 18% in early 2003). Consumer confidence has also risen but fears of a return to hyperinflation are widespread. In nominal terms, public spending has remained constant, which means that it has fallen sharply in real terms. A danger is that the 2003 budget has weakened the government's grip on spending, and there has been growing pressure to spend in the run-up to the election. The government must still renegotiate its debt to private creditors, which amounted to $100 billion in January 2003. Hopefully, Argentineans will gradually begin to repatriate some of the US$100 billion or more they moved abroad when the exchange rate plummeted. Restoring public trust in government will take much longer, however.

In comparison with other parts of the economy, agricultural output has remained buoyant with good harvests for both wheat and maize. The country's favourable climate and fertile soils have traditionally made Argentina a leading agricultural power. However, the sector has been squeezed by lower international prices, higher domestic costs and the collapse of the banking system at home. Up to a third of all farmers have been bankrupted, while the rest have accumulated huge amounts of debt. Private consumption accounts for a very high share of GDP (close to 70%) and that share has increased since the economy plunged into recession. The services sector accounts for around 60% of GDP, and privatisation has helped to raise efficiency in communications, electricity distribution, finance and transport. However, in many of these markets competition is still limited. Tourism is traditionally a big earner of foreign exchange but the number of visitors has fallen sharply over the past year. In manufacturing, the Argentinean automotive sector is a key player but is heavily dependent on the Brazilian market for exports.

Argentina has around 2.9 billion barrels of proven oil reserves and is the region's fourth largest oil producer, behind Venezuela, Mexico and Brazil. The country is also the region's third largest oil consumer, after Mexico and Brazil. Argentina's production increased rapidly throughout the 1990s, allowing exports to grow from negligible levels in the 1980s to exceed 400,000 barrels per day in the late 1990s. The oil sector is completely privatised. Although the country is widely considered to be too mature to offer significant exploration potential, there are opportunities for further development of existing reserves. Most of Argentina's oil is produced in two onshore basins, Neuquén in western Argentina, and Golfo San Jorge in the southeast. In August 2002, a new hydrocarbon discovery was announced in the Rio Negro province. Exploratory drilling continues in order to determine the size of the discovery and the characteristics of the oil. Among the consequences of the 2002 financial crisis was a fuel oil shortage as the currency devaluation encouraged exports and severely restricted the importation of petroleum products.

◻ Armenia

Capital City	Yerevan	*Capital population: 1,305,000 (1995)*
Population ('000)	3,815 *(2002)*	
Urban population (%)	70.51 *(2002)*	
Land area (km²)	2820	
Languages	Armenian	
Religion	Mainly Christian	
Currency	Dram (AMD)	
Head of State	President Robert Kocharian (1998)	
Head of Government	Andranik Markaryan (2000)	
Ruling Party	The government is formed by a coalition of minority parties and non-partisans.	

Main Urban Areas	Population
Yerevan (capital)	1,305,000 (1995)

Geographically, the Republic of Armenia occupies the south-western sector of the land mass known as Transcaucasia, and borders Turkey and Iran in the south; politically, it spans the gulf between the former Soviet Union and the Islamic states of the Middle East. Armenia was formed as a protective haven for members of the Armenian Church from all parts of the region. The capital is Yerevan.

Armenia declared its unilateral independence from the Soviet Union in 1990, a decision confirmed by a national referendum later that year when 94% voted in favour. Armenia's executive President is elected by popular vote and serves a four-year term. The National Assembly has 131 members, elected for a four-year term, with 56 members in single-seat constituencies and 75 chosen by proportional representation. The seats determined by proportional representation are distributed among those party lists which have received at least 5 % of the total of the number of votes.

In presidential elections held in March 2003, Kocharian was returned to office with 68% of the vote. Elections to the National Assembly were held in May 2003. The Republican Party of Armenia took 23 seats, the Justice party received 14 seats and the centrist Rule of Law Party won 12 seats. The Armenian Revolutionary Federation won 11 seats, the National Unity Party won nine seats and the United Labour Party took six seats.

GDP grew by 12.9% in 2002 and a gain of 7% is expected in 2003. The forecast rate of growth for 2004 is 6%. Inflation was 1.1% in 2002 and should be about 2.2% in 2003. Prices are forecast to rise by 3% in 2004. Continued gains in labour productivity have been instrumental in containing the rate of inflation. Unemployment has fallen slightly but is still high (9.2% in 2002) despite rapid economic growth in the preceding few years. The government's 2003 budget calls for a fiscal deficit of 2.5% of GDP with tax revenues forecast to rise to 15% of GDP thanks to improvements in administration. The deficit in 2002 was well above 3% (one of the highest in Central Europe). If the target for 2003 is met, it will represent a important step in stabilising the economy. The government is also committed to clear remaining arrears by mid-2003 and to reduce expenditures below budgeted amounts by up to 0.7% of GDP in the event of a shortfall in external financing. Armenia became a member of the WTO in February 2003 and is committed to maintain a liberal trade regime with no restrictions on payments and transfers. Armenia's small- and medium-sized enterprises, most of which have already been privatised, are the main sources of much of the country's economic growth. At its current growth rate, by 2005, Armenia's absolute GDP will reach the same level as in 1991, the year that the Soviet Union and its central economic planning system collapsed.

Agriculture accounts for about a third of GDP and is the backbone of the Armenian economy. Farmers produce grain, sugar beet, potatoes and other vegetables, as well as grapes and other fruit. Cattle, sheep and pigs are the main forms of livestock. Industry accounts for another third of GDP. Traditionally, most operations in this sector have been under the control of the state but the number of privately-owned farms now exceeds state-run farms. In industry, over 70% of large enterprises and 80% of small enterprises have been privatised. The government has also imposed a system to monitor the financial operation of state-owned firms on a regular basis. Industrial activity is limited to basic manufactures and suffers from power shortages. Industrial output increased by 16% in 2002 but this rate is misleading as much of the increase was due to the resumption of production in previously idle plants. Meanwhile, retail trade rose by 15% as consumers returned to markets. The government plans to take several

steps to strengthen its financial system in 2003. At least five banks are scheduled for liquidation and the system of banking supervision will be strengthened. In January 2003, the value of imported goods exempted from VAT at the border was reduced from 25% to 20% of total imports. There is a four-year economic programme aimed at modernising decaying infrastructure and generally reforming the economy in a market-oriented direction. The performance of the energy sector improved in 2002, reflecting increased use of hydropower, measures undertaken to enhance efficiency, and the privatisation of the electricity distribution company. Such developments follow years of mismanagement that have raised the indebtedness of the sector to unsustainable levels and crippled its ability to deliver reliable and cost-effective power. At end-2002, domestic and foreign banks had claims of nearly $31 million on state-owned energy sector companies.

Armenia has no oil production and is completely dependent on imports of refined products. Since there are no petroleum product pipelines into the country, all imports must be transported either by railcars or trucks. Most of Armenia's estimated 13,000 barrels per day in petroleum product imports comes from Georgia. The country's hopes of becoming an important part of an energy trans-shipment system are opposed by Azerbaijan and Turkey. Because Armenia does not expect to benefit substantially from the east-west pipelines that are in development, it is cultivating closer ties with Iran in order to diversify its energy sources. In addition, Armenia and Iran are developing a natural gas pipeline to connect the two countries, with the pipeline possibly continuing further northwards to connect to Georgia and then to the Russian pipeline system.

◻ Aruba

Capital City	Oranjestad	*Capital population: 23,000 (2001)*
Population ('000)	117 *(2002)*	
Land area (km²)	19	
Languages	Dutch, Papiamento, Spanish, English	
Religion	Mainly Roman Catholic	
Currency	Aruban florin (AGL)	
Head of State	HM Queen Beatrix (Netherlands)	
Head of Government	Nelson Oduber (2001)	
Ruling Party	The government is formed by People's Electoral Movement (MEP).	

Main Urban Areas	Population
Oranjestad (capital)	23,000 (2001)

Aruba is located in the Leeward Islands chain within the Caribbean Sea, about 70km west of Curacao, the capital island of the Netherlands Antilles and no more than 30km north of the Venezuelan coast. The country enjoys a warm tropical climate, with relatively little susceptibility to hurricanes. The capital is Oranjestad.

Aruba is an overseas territory of the Netherlands. It was formerly part of the Netherlands Antilles but became a separate political entity in January 1986. In 1990, Aruba requested and received from the Netherlands cancellation of the agreement that would have automatically given independence to the island in 1996. The Parliament has 21 members, elected for four-year terms by proportional representation. The prime minister and deputy prime minister are elected by parliament for four-year terms.

Parliamentary elections were held in September 2001. The MEP took 12 seats while the Aruban People's Party won six seats. Smaller parties won the remainder.

After growing at over 4% per year in 1996-2000, the Aruban economy experienced two years of retrenchment, with GDP growing by 1.5% in 2001 and falling 3.8% in 2002. This downturn reflected a lull in investment activity, but especially weak tourism following the US recession and the terrorist attacks of September 11, 2001. In 2003, sharply higher private and public investment and a modest revival in tourism should boost economic growth to over 4%. With higher tourism capacity and continued sustained investment, economic growth should remain around 3% in the medium term. The exchange rate is pegged to the US dollar and inflation has been low, averaging 2.7% in the 1990s. Higher energy prices, indirect taxes and faster credit growth, as a result of controls being suspended, caused inflation to accelerate in the second half of 2002, reaching 4.5% in December 2002. Weak growth and the introduction of universal health care exacerbated existing fiscal imbalances, resulting in a marked worsening of the government deficit, from 0.2% of GDP in 2000 to an estimated 4.9% in 2002. To stem this deterioration, the government froze public sector wage indexation for three years and raised excise rates in the second half of 2002.

Aruba's small agricultural sector produces aloes and raises livestock. Fishing also generates some income but the land is poorly adapted to farming. Tourism is a major earner of income and provides most employment opportunities. The island hosts large numbers of visitors from the Netherlands, the US, Venezuela, Canada and other Caribbean countries but the number has fallen sharply in 2002. Offshore banking and oil refining and storage are the other mainstays of the economy. The banking sector is highly liquid and well capitalised despite the downturn, but interest rates remain high because of a lack of competition. A new indirect tax on imports and services is planned for 2003. A New Fiscal Regime for corporate income was also introduced, which will result in more uniform taxation of corporate profits and dividends. Although the previous offshore and tax holiday regime will be phased out, incentives for export-oriented activities will remain through an imputation system. The island has no fresh water supplies and every litre has to be imported.

Aruba has no oil deposits but does have some of the largest oil refining capacity in the Caribbean as well as substantial storage capacity. The bulk of the country's oil supplies come from other islands in the Netherlands Antilles group.

▫ Australia

Capital City	Canberra	Capital population: 312,400 (2002)
Population ('000)	19,442 (2002)	
Urban population (%)	84.73 (2002)	
Land area (km²)	768230	
Languages	English	
Religion	Mainly Christian	
Currency	Australian dollar (A$)	
Head of State	HM Queen Elizabeth II	
Head of Government	John Howard (1996)	
Ruling Party	The Liberal Party (LP) leads a coalition with the National Party (NP).	

Main Urban Areas	Population
Sydney	4,204,000 (2002)
Melbourne	3,541,600 (2002)
Brisbane	1,677,200 (2002)
Perth	1,424,400 (2002)
Adelaide	1,105,400 (2002)
Newcastle	506,600 (2002)
Canberra-Queanbeyan	375,600 (2002)
Canberra (capital)	312,400 (2002)
Hobart	192,600 (2002)
Darwin	94,200 (2002)

Some 3,680km from its eastern tip to its western extreme, Australia is the world's second largest island. The country lies about 1,000km from New Zealand, and about 500km south of Indonesia. Thus its climate ranges from the subtropical in the north to the significantly colder regions of the south. The capital is Canberra.

Australia is a federation of six states and two territories (Northern Territory and Capital Territory of Canberra), each of which exercises considerable autonomy over its own affairs. The country's central affairs are run by a Cabinet which answers to a 150-member House of Representatives, elected for a term of three years. The Senate has 76 members, elected through a preferential system in 12-seat state constituencies and two-seat territorial constituencies. The territorial senators are elected for a three-year term. The state senators are elected for a six-year term, with half of the seats renewed every three years. The question of Australia's status in the Commonwealth emerged as a key issue during the previous administration but in November 1999, Australians voted to retain its membership, with Queen Elizabeth as their head of state.

Elections to the House of Representatives took place in November 2001. The LP won 68 seats, the Australian Labour Party (ALP) took 65 seats and the NP won 13 seats. The remainder were spread among smaller parties. Elections to the Senate occurred at the same time and the ALP claimed 28 seats while the ruling coalition took 34 seats. Smaller parties won the remainder. Howard, the leader of the coalition, was re-appointed as prime minister.

Real GDP grew by 3.6% in 2002. Growth of 3% is expected in 2003 and 3.5% in 2004. Meanwhile, inflation was 3% in 2002 and is expected to fall to 2.9% in 2003. Prices are forecast to increase by 2.3% in 2004. At present, Australia has one of the fastest growing industrialised economies in the world. Income growth is brisk, employment is expanding and public finances are healthy. Rapidly rising house prices and strong consumer spending have been other key economic drivers. All indications are that the continuing effects of previous reforms will help the economy to combat any shocks in the immediate future. Nevertheless, the delayed global recovery has led to a slowdown in exports, compounded by the increasing strength of the Australian dollar, which rose 8% against the US dollar in the first quarter of 2003. Australia's current account deficit has also risen and in early 2003 stood at 6.3% of GDP. The government is under pressure to simplify its tax system and make it more equitable. In particular, the large gap between the top personal income tax rate and the company tax rate must be addressed. Currently, the top personal tax rate is 48.5%, compared with just 30% for companies.

The structure of the Australian economy has been dramatically transformed over the past ten years. As growth has continued, the share of the manufacturing sector in GDP has fallen. Finance, business services and communications are believed to account for up to a third of total economic growth experienced over the ten years to 2001. Meanwhile, the manufacturing sector continues to move from the processing of agricultural and mineral raw materials into more sophisticated types of products and markets. Despite this economic transformation, Australia is still one of the world's major producers of commodities. A large agricultural sector specialises in wheat and sheep rearing, and together, these two activities account for more than half of the sector's export revenues. Farming suffered in 2002, however, as a result of a severe drought. Australia also has vast amounts of natural resources. It has approximately 30% of the world's recoverable uranium and is a major producer of copper, iron ore, manganese, nickel, lead, limestone and gemstones. In addition, Australia is a major player in world energy markets.

Australia is a significant energy producer, and one of the few OECD countries that is a net energy exporter. It is the world's fourth largest producer of coal. The commodity is one of Australia's most important exports and supplies 44% of total domestic energy needs. Australia is a major producer of liquid natural gas and the

third-largest exporter of this commodity in the Asia-Pacific region, behind Indonesia and Malaysia. Despite these increases in energy production, the country is becoming increasingly dependent upon foreign oil. A rapidly expanding economy and declining domestic oil production have led some observers to forecast an energy supply crisis in the decade from 2002-2011. Most of the country's 1.8 billion barrels of oil reserves are located offshore. It also has approximately 30% of the world's recoverable uranium.

▫ Azerbaijan

Capital City	Baku	Capital population: 1,731,520 (2002)
Population ('000)	8,150 (2002)	
Urban population (%)	57.81 (2002)	
Land area (km²)	8660	
Languages	Azerbaijani (Azeri)	
Religion	Mainly Islam	
Currency	Azerbaijani Manats (AZM)	
Head of State	President Heidar Aliev (June 1993)	
Head of Government	Ilham Aliev (2003)	
Ruling Party	Yeni Azerbaycan Partiyasi (YAP)	

Main Urban Areas	Population
Baku (capital)	1,731,520 (2002)
Gandja	304,140 (2002)
Sumgayit	273,620 (2002)
Mingachevir	98,060 (2002)
Ali Bayramli	70,700 (2002)

The Republic of Azerbaijan lies in the eastern Transcaucasian region, bordering the Caspian Sea from Grozny to Baku. It includes the autonomous provinces of Nagorny-Karabakh (mainly Armenian in character) and Nakhichevan, which was obtained from Iran recently. The capital is Baku.

Azerbaijan was one of the last states to declare its independence from the Soviet Union. The move came in August 1991 and was later confirmed by a 99.6% vote in a referendum. The president is elected by the people for a five-year term. The National Assembly has 125 members, 100 members elected for a five-year term in single-seat constituencies and 25 members elected by proportional representation. In practice, Azerbaijan aligns itself more closely with Russia than do other countries in this volatile region.

Elections to the National Assembly took place in January 2001 and were dominated by members of the Yeni Azerbaycan Partiyasi (YAP), which took 75 seats. All the remaining seats were widely scattered among several parties. In October 1998, Aliev was re-elected as president after first taking office in 1993 following a military-backed coup. In August 2003, parliament elected the president's son, Ilham Aliev, prime minister. He replaces Artur Rasi-Zade.

Azerbaijan's economy has performed impressively in the past two years with GDP growing by 10.6% in 2002. Growth of 9.2% is expected in 2003 and growth of 9.1% is forecast in 2004. Prices rose by 2.8% in 2002 and should increase by another 2.7% in 2003. Inflation is forecast to be 2.5% in 2004. The country's external position improved during 2002. Oil sector exports grew 11% (largely due to higher oil prices) and non-oil exports grew by about 25%, led by agricultural and chemical products exports. The country's critical financial policies remain on track, with money and credit both growing somewhat faster than programmed and net international reserves well in excess of targets. Net direct investment has steadily increased and the rise is expected to continue over the medium term, as major energy sector projects are being developed. Foreign capital continues to be the major source of deficit financing. There have been some modest tax reforms, consisting of small reductions in the payroll and profit tax rates, as well as several measures aimed at broadening the tax base. Government officials concede that in the future they will need to accentuate efforts at economic diversification in order to combat instability and poverty in the country. Despite the strong economic growth, unemployment remains high because much of this growth has been in capital-intensive areas that create few jobs. In addition, nearly half of all Azerbaijani earn less than $25 per month.

Both the oil and the non-oil sector, including agriculture, have experienced strong growth in recent years. The country is still a relatively insignificant producer of oil and gas in the global network but production is expected to rise dramatically after 2005. Even today, crude oil and oil product exports make up over 70% of Azerbaijan's exports, and oil-related revenue accounts for nearly 50% of budget revenues. Since 1994, foreign investment in the energy sector has totalled roughly $3.5 billion. To promote non-oil trade activities, the government has allowed a gradual depreciation of the manat. The backbone of the manufacturing sector is a number of heavy industries that were established more than 20 years ago. The more important of these are steel, aluminium and cement. Revenue from many of these state-owned enterprises has declined due to the switch from pre-negotiated tax targets to payments according to the tax code. Baku, Azerbaijan's largest city and port, has the potential to become a major regional transportation and communications hub for the Trans-Caucasus and Central Asian republics.

Following Azerbaijan's independence in 1991, the country's oil production began to decline. Yet, with 1.2 billion barrels of proven oil reserves, as well as enormous possible reserves in undeveloped offshore Caspian fields, international investors and multinational energy companies have been returning to the country. The government expects investment in the country's oil sector to surpass US$60 billion in the next few years. In 2002, Azerbaijan posted its fifth consecutive annual increase in its average oil production, as output rose to 318,000 barrels per day. Over 80% of Azerbaijan's oil production currently comes from offshore, with a significant percentage coming from a shallow-water section, located 60 miles off the Azeri coast. Development of new fields in the Caspian Sea is likely to boost Azerbaijan's oil production well beyond its previous best, with predictions that Azerbaijani oil exports could exceed one million barrels per day by 2010 and two million within 20 years. Despite boasting one of the world's largest natural gas field discoveries of the last 20 years, Azerbaijan is currently a net natural gas importer. The country produced 200 billion cubic feet (Bcf) of natural gas in 2001, while consuming roughly 240 Bcf. In 2003, a new consortium agreed to invest $3.2 billion to develop the Caspian's largest gas field, which will eventually send gas to Turkey.

□ Bahamas

Capital City	Nassau	Capital population: 190,000 (1992)
Population ('000)	325 *(2002)*	
Urban population (%)	89.01 *(2002)*	
Land area (km²)	1001	
Languages	English	
Religion	Mainly Christian	
Currency	Bahamian dollar (BS$)	
Head of State	HM Queen Elizabeth II	
Head of Government	Perry Christie (2002)	
Ruling Party	The government is formed by the Progressive Liberal Party (PLP).	

Main Urban Areas	Population
Nassau (capital)	190,000 (1992)

The Bahamas are made up of some 700 islands in the Atlantic Ocean, of which 30 are inhabited. They extend from just off the coast of Florida (US) to within a short distance of Cuba and Haiti. The capital is Nassau.

The Bahamas are an independent member of the British Commonwealth with a British-appointed governor-general who exercises only nominal powers. The Prime Minister and his Cabinet are answerable to a 40-member House of Assembly (Lower House of Parliament) and to a 16-member Senate. Elections to the House of Assembly are normally held every five years while members of the Senate are appointed.

Elections to the House of Assembly were held in May 2002. The PLP, led by Perry Christie, took 29 seats, the Free National Movement won seven and the remainder went to non-partisans.

Growth was 0.7% in 2002 but in 2003 GDP should increase by 0.9%. In 2004, growth of 2.5% is forecast. Inflation was running at about 2.2% in 2002. In 2003, prices should increase by 1.7% and are forecast to rise by another 2.5% in 2004. The Bahamas enjoys a per capita income that is among the world's top 30, but there are serious imbalances in the distribution of wealth, most of which is concentrated in the country's main commercial and tourist centres. The administration's policy of gradual fiscal consolidation has been a key factor in turning the economy around. The government has increased tourism taxes, eliminated some import duty exemptions and reduced both current and capital outlays. The main challenge for the future will be to build on current accomplishments by maintaining a prudent fiscal stance, enhancing competitiveness and pressing ahead with pending structural reforms. Additional efforts will be needed to ensure an adequate level of public investment to sustain growth. Overall growth prospects will depend heavily on the fortunes of the tourism sector and an economic recovery in the US, which accounts for the majority of tourist visitors.

The tourist sector is the heart of the economy but suffered severely in the fourth quarter of 2001 and the first half of 2002. Occupancy levels dropped to as low as 30% and important investments have been postponed. Tourist numbers have now recovered, although many hotel workers are still on a part-time basis. Driven by tourism, the service sector has seen tremendous growth over the past decade, leading to a migration of people from fishing and farming villages to commercial centres in New Providence Island, Grand Bahama and Great Abaco. The financial sector, which is the other cornerstone of the economy, continues to flourish, although parliament has introduced a number of new measures to curb money laundering and tax evasion. The Bahamas has the world's largest fleet of cruise ships and the fifth largest fleet of tankers. Manufacturing and agriculture together contribute less than 10% of GDP and show little growth, despite government incentives aimed at those sectors.

Most of the country's energy needs are met by imports of oil and gas, or by natural materials such as firewood. All electricity generation is derived from thermal plants.

□ Bahrain

Capital City	Manama	Capital population: 142,500 (1992)
Population ('000)	641 *(2002)*	
Urban population (%)	92.64 *(2002)*	
Land area (km²)	71	
Languages	Arabic	
Religion	Islam	
Currency	Bahraini dinar (BHD)	
Head of State	Sheikh Hamad ibn 'Isa Al Khalifah (1999)	
Head of Government	Sheikh Khalifa bin Al Khalifa	
Ruling Party	There are no political parties in Bahrain.	

Main Urban Areas	Population
Manama (capital)	142,500 (1992)

Bahrain is made up of a group of islands located in the midst of the Gulf, about 24km off the eastern coast of Saudi Arabia. The main urban centre is on Bahrain Island, but the country's airport is located on the island of Muharraq. The capital is Manama.

Bahrain is an absolute monarchy in which traditional consultative procedures, involving senior figures in the tribal hierarchy, are preferred to a formal parliamentary system. In addition, a 40-member Parliament has been established with limited powers In March 1999, Sheikh Khalifa bin Sulman Al Khalifa died suddenly and was replaced by his eldest son, Sheikh Hamad ibn 'Isa Al Khalifah. The previous ruler's brother is Prime Minister.

Parliamentary elections were held in October 2002. According to the government, secular representatives or independents secured a total of 21 seats. Islamists, including moderate Sunni Islamists, took the remainder. The Khalifa family holds half the cabinet posts and its members chair most public sector organisations. In 2001 Bahrainis gave overwhelming support to proposals put by the Emir - now the King - to turn the country into a constitutional monarchy with an elected parliament and an independent judiciary by 2004.

Bahrain's economy grew by 4.1% in 2002 and the same rate is forecast for 2003. In 2004, growth of 4.3% is expected. Prices increased just 1.2% in 2002 but are expected to grow by 3.3% in 2003. Inflation is forecast to be 5% in 2004. Over the longer term however, growth has not kept pace with the annual 3% rise in population, most of which consists of expatriates. In the ten years to 2001, the country's population rose by 31%. The government claims that unemployment is under 3% but the actual figure is much higher. Unofficial estimates put the figure at 15-30%. Most Bahrainis work in the public sector, but it is clear that many cannot find work. In addition, the expatriates send much of their earnings abroad. In a typical year, remittances are about US$1 billion. The capital drain is compounded by the practice of wealthy Bahrainis, who prefer to keep the bulk of their money abroad. In mid-2002, between US$15 and US$20 billion was invested overseas. Not surprisingly, the country is short of cash. Total government domestic and foreign debt stands at 30% of GDP. This is not high by the region's standards but it has almost doubled since 1996. The island also receives revenues in the form of gifts of Saudi crude oil and cash and handouts from Kuwait and Abu Dhabi. However, it has done nothing to curb the rising cost of expatriate remittances or the share of recurrent expenditures in the budget.

The country's economy depends heavily on the oil industry, but it also is an important centre for financial services and banking. Oil prices affect Bahrain's economy both directly, as revenues, and indirectly, due to banking and export links to neighbouring Persian Gulf countries which depend on oil revenues. The island's principal activity is the extraction of oil from its own fields, along with the processing of other countries' oil at its Sipra refinery. All the island's main industries are still firmly in the hands of the state. Hidden subsidies distort the viability of local industries, creating uncertainties that discourage many investors. The government has partially privatised just 14 companies and only one, Bahrain Aluminium, is a large one. Agriculture is of marginal importance, although there are fishing industries and pearl culture. Bahrain has had more success in attracting international banks with tax-haven facilities. The offshore banking sector presently has assets in excess of US$90 billion.

Bahrain has proven oil reserves of only 125 million barrels, all in the Awali field. The field was discovered in 1932 and was the first oilfield developed in the Persian Gulf. Production peaked at more than 75,000 barrels per day (bbl/d) in the early 1970s, but the field is now nearing depletion. Current production is around 35,000 bbl/d of crude oil. Bahrain also has untapped potential oil reserves offshore in the Gulf of Bahrain. In 2001, the International Court of Justice resolved a territorial dispute between Bahrain and Qatar over islands located between the two countries. Sovereignty over the Hawar Islands was awarded to Bahrain, while Qatar retained the neighbouring islands of Zubarah and Janan. More important than crude oil production, however, is Bahrain's refining industry. The country has a refinery south of Manama with a capacity of 248,900 bbl/d. The national petroleum company has recently has announced a $900 million modernisation programme that entails the addition of supplemental hydro-cracking facilities, which will allow the refinery to produce a wider range of petroleum products including low sulphur diesel and gasoline.

▫ Bangladesh

Capital City	Dhaka	*Capital population: 7,832,000 (1995)*
Population ('000)	131,587 *(2002)*	
Urban population (%)	25.49 *(2002)*	
Land area (km²)	13017	
Languages	Bengali	
Religion	Islam	
Currency	Taka (Taka)	
Head of State	President Lajuddin Ahmed (2002)	
Head of Government	Khaleda Zia (2001)	
Ruling Party	The government is formed by a coalition led by the Bangladesh Nationalist Party (BJD).	

Main Urban Areas	Population
Dhaka (capital)	7,832,000 (1995)
Chittagong	2,410,000 (1995)
Khulna	998,000 (1995)

Bangladesh is a low-lying and densely populated territory lying in the Bay of Bengal between India and Myanmar. The country occupies most of the delta of the river Ganges, and has a tropical and humid climate. The capital is Dhaka.

Bangladesh is an independent member of the Commonwealth, with an executive President elected by parliament. National Parliament has 330 members, 300 members elected for a five-year term in single-seat constituencies and 30 women elected by the parliamentarians.

Parliamentary elections were held in October 2001. The BJD won 191 seats and the Awami League won 62 seats. The remainder were spread among several smaller parties. Zia was then appointed as the new Prime Minister. In September 2002, parliament endorsed the nomination of Lajuddin Ahmed as president of the country.

GDP rose by 4.9% in 2002 and an increase of 5.4% is expected in 2003. In 2004, growth of 5.8% is forecast. Meanwhile, inflation was 6.8% in 2002 and should be around 4.5% in 2003. Prices are forecast to rise by 4.1% in 2004. The unemployment rate is thought to be as high as 11%, while underemployment stands at around 35%. Higher unemployment will also make it harder for the government to achieve its goal of reducing income poverty by 25% by 2005, from the levels that prevailed in 2000. Revenue collection is up in 2003 and the fiscal deficit is expected to fall to 4.7% of GDP as the effects of revenue measures and greater fiscal discipline take hold. Exports are also on the rise in 2003, due mainly to large increases in exports for jute and jute goods, frozen foods, and knitwear and hosiery products. Exchange restrictions have recently been eased, and exchange rate management has been more flexible, helping to strengthen the external position. The current account balance is expected to again revert to a deficit of about 1.3% of GDP, as import growth recovers and growth in remittances remains stable. Foreign exchange reserves could come under some pressure with the worsening current account balance. In 2004, the current account deficit is likely to widen to 2.5% of GDP as import growth picks up. Such a deficit would be historically high for Bangladesh, but should be manageable, given the increased availability of concessional aid. Progress nevertheless remains elusive because of political conflicts, the slow pace of reforms and the government's extensive involvement in most industries.

Overall, foreign aid provides Bangladesh with around 40% of government revenues and 50% of foreign exchange. The economy's recent improvements have been led by the agricultural and industrial sectors, aided by the strength of domestic and external demand. Following a fall in exports in 2002, due to a sharp decline in the prices of ready-made garments, exports have recovered, rising by 6% in the ten months to April 2003. During the same period, remittances continue to be strong, growing at an annual rate of 24%, reflecting in part a further shift in such flows to official channels. Industrial activities that are less dependent on global demand - such as small-scale industry, electricity generation, and gas production - have also experienced relatively robust growth. Currently, cotton textiles and garments account for around 80% of Bangladeshi exports. Growth in construction activity, however, slowed due to an oversupply of commercial buildings and apartments. Wholesale and retail trade was weaker owing to the fall in manufacturing exports and the service sector as a whole grew by 5.2% (down from 5.5% the previous year). In manufacturing, the government has initiated a four-year programme to phase out state-owned enterprises, starting with the closure or privatisation of key loss-making units. Most investment is going into natural gas, electricity and physical infrastructure. Exports of natural gas could provide a major additional revenue source for Bangladesh, but the issue remains controversial, and no final decision has been made on whether to allow exports.

Bangladesh possesses small proven oil reserves of 56.9 million barrels and produces around 6,200 bbl/d. Over the past few years, the government has encouraged foreign oil companies to enter the industry. To date, oil exploration has proven largely unsuccessful, although hopes continue, especially onshore. Bangladesh does possibly have very large natural gas resources but there is much uncertainty about the amount. Both major political parties are officially committed to considering natural gas exports only if Bangladesh has proven reserves sufficient to cover 50 years of domestic demand. Only around 18% of the population (25% in urban areas and 10% in rural areas) has access to electricity, and per capita commercial energy consumption is among the lowest in the world. Non-commercial energy sources, such as wood, animal wastes and crop residues, are estimated to account for over half of the country's energy consumption. Consumption of wood for fuel has contributed to deforestation and other environmental problems. The World Bank has estimated that Bangladesh loses around US$1 billion per year due to power outages and unreliable energy supplies.

▫ Barbados

Capital City	Bridgetown	*Capital population: 7,670 (1992)*
Population ('000)	274 *(2002)*	
Urban population (%)	50.95 *(2002)*	
Land area (km²)	43	
Languages	English	
Religion	Mainly Christian	
Currency	Barbados dollar (BB$)	
Head of State	HM Queen Elizabeth II	
Head of Government	Hon. Owen Arthur (September 1994)	
Ruling Party	Barbados Labour Party	

Main Urban Areas	Population
Bridgetown (capital)	7,670 (1992)

Barbados, the most easterly of the Caribbean islands, is some 30km long and 20km wide. With its pleasant climate (subject to occasional storms in the autumn months), it has proved popular as a tourist venue. The capital is Bridgetown.

Barbados, an independent member of the Commonwealth, has a 28-seat House of Assembly whose members are elected by universal suffrage for a term of five years, and a 21-member Senate whose members are appointed for five-year terms. Queen Elizabeth II is represented by a governor-general who appoints the Prime Minister on the advice of Parliament. Barbados is likely to change its political status in the next few years, removing the Queen of England as head of state and converting itself to a republic with an elected president.

General elections to the House of Assembly were held in May 2003 when the Barbados Labour Party (BLP) of Owen Arthur took 23 seats in the 28-seat Assembly. The Democratic Labour Party (DLP) won five seats.

GDP contracted by 1.8% in 2002 but growth of 1.6% is expected in 2003. In 2004, GDP is forecast to increase by 2.3%. Prices rose by 0.15% in 2002 and are expected to increase by 1.5% in 2003 and 2.4% in 2004. To address the recent recession, the government has employed fiscal policies. Increased capital spending, as well as public wage increases and a reduction in the finances of public enterprises are being used to spur growth but have also widened the fiscal deficit. In late 2002, authorities turned to a programme of fiscal tightening and structural reforms. These policies include: reforms of the tax and social security system, financial sector liberalisation and other steps to encourage private investment. Increases in public sector wages will also be limited. Liberalisation of the capital market is also expected in order to bolster capital inflows and as part of the Caribbean effort to create a single market. Unemployment continues to rise, reaching 10.3% in mid-2002, up from 8.5% in 2001. Over the medium term, authorities intend to reverse recent tariff increases which have penalised several import-dependent industries.

During the 1990s, economic activity in Barbados shifted towards services, notably tourism and offshore financial services. However, the country suffered a recession in 2002 owing mainly to a sharp drop in tourism revenues and continuing declines in agricultural and manufacturing output. The recession also reflected a deterioration in competitiveness as wage increases in Barbados exceeded productivity gains and inflation. To offset the economic decline, authorities boasted spending to promote tourism, reintroduced import licences for selected agricultural products to protect domestic production and accelerated implementation of public investment projects. Public sector wages rose by nearly 3% in 2002 despite the recession. The country's offshore banking sector contracted in 2002 due to the inclusion of Barbados in the OECD's list of non-cooperative tax havens. To strengthen the finances of the public sector, authorities intend to close additional operations in the sugar industry, to curtail subsidies to other publicly-owned firms, to privatise some tourist projects and to deregulate the telecommunications industry.

Barbados has about 2.5 million barrels of proven reserves and produces small amounts of natural gas. The country plans to expand production to 3,000 barrels per day in the next few years and has begun to employ horizontal-drilling techniques. The island, along with the Dominican Republic, Haiti and Jamaica, is party to the San Jose pact under which Mexico and Venezuela supply crude oil and refined products on favourable terms.

□ Belize

Capital City	Belmopan *Capital population: 3,927 (1994)*
Population ('000)	256 *(2002)*
Urban population (%)	55.35 *(2002)*
Land area (km²)	2280
Languages	English (official); Spanish is the mother tongue of 15% of the population.
Religion	Mainly Christian (Roman Catholic 60%)
Currency	Belize dollar (BZ$)
Head of State	HM Queen Elizabeth II
Head of Government	Said Musa (1998)
Ruling Party	People's United Party (PUP)

Main Urban Areas	Population
Belmopan (capital)	3,927 (1994)

Belize lies on the Caribbean coast of Central America, bounded in the north by Mexico and in the south and west by Guatemala. The coastal areas are mainly swamp, although inland they rise to meet the Maya mountain range. The country has a subtropical climate and is subject to hurricanes in the autumn months. The capital is Belmopan.

Belize, an independent member of the Commonwealth since 1981, has a bicameral National Assembly. The country's 29-member House of Representatives is elected by popular vote for a five-year term, while its nine-member Senate is appointed by the governor-general. The possibility of political union with Dominica, St Lucia and St Vincent and the Grenadines has been discussed.

Elections to the House of Representatives were held in March 2003. The PUP took 53% of the vote and won 22 of the 29 seats. The remaining seats are held by members of the United Democratic Party.

Growth was 3.5% in 2002 and is expected to be 4.5% in 2003. Growth of 4.4% is forecast in 2004. Inflation was 2.2% in 2002 and is expected to slow to 1.5% in 2003 and 2004. Belize's small economy is based on agriculture, agro-based industry and merchandising, with tourism and construction assuming increasing importance. Growth has been sluggish for more than a decade. The present government is attempting to accelerate economic growth through tax cuts, government investment, expansionary monetary policy, and the provision of subsidised credit to the private sector. These expansionary policies have contributed to a growing government deficit which reached 12% of GDP in 2002. The deficit is being financed mainly through privatisation receipts and external borrowing, mostly on commercial terms. The increase in public investment has also led to a rapid rise in imports and the current account deficit has increased to 20% of GDP. Mounting concern about the sustainability of these policies has led officials to announce some changes in macroeconomic policy. In 2003, the government intends to reduce the budget deficit and tighten monetary policy. They also intend to bolster government revenues by taking further steps to boost tax collection and reduce exemptions.

Agriculture is the dominant sector in Belize, accounting for 18% of GDP and employing more than 40% of the workforce. Bananas, coca, citrus, sugarcane, fish, cultured shrimp and fruit are the major products, while bananas, citrus fruits and sugar cane are grown for export. Sugar, the chief crop, accounts for more than one third of exports, but tourism is the major foreign-exchange earner. However, returns from tourism declined in 2002 for the second consecutive year owing to adverse weather conditions and the drop in travel because of terrorism. Citrus production is rising sharply and officials hope this will be a major foreign-exchange earner in the future. Fishery products, especially lobsters and conches, are exported to the US. The manufacturing sector is small with most almost all firms geared solely to the domestic market. The main manufacturing activities consist of garment production, food processing and construction Altogether, industry makes up about 28% of GDP but output fell in 2002. The country has no railway system and this factor hinders the development of exports and economic progress in general. Belize has good prospects for the development of a thriving tourist industry but needs investment in this field and better planning.

Belize is highly dependent on electricity imported from Mexico to meet domestic demand. Besides the approximately 50% of electric power that is purchased from Mexico, another 30% comes from Belize's Mollejon dam, and the remainder from the country's thermal plants. A project is underway to build a new dam upstream from the Mollejon dam with a capacity of 7 megawatts. The project has attracted much opposition from environmental groups.

□ Benin

Capital City	Porto Novo *Capital population: 177,600 (1992)*
Population ('000)	6,656 *(2002)*
Urban population (%)	43.59 *(2002)*
Land area (km²)	11062
Languages	French
Religion	Mainly traditional; some Christian (15%) and Muslim (13%)
Currency	CFA franc (CFAF)
Head of State	President Mathieu Kerekou (1996)
Head of Government	Mathieu Kerekou (1996)
Ruling Party	A multiparty coalition leads the government.

Main Urban Areas	Population
Porto Novo (capital)	177,600 (1992)

Benin, one of the poorest countries in Africa, is located on the West African coastline with the Gulf of Guinea to the south. The country is bounded by Togo in the west, Burkina Faso and Niger in the north and Nigeria in the east. The capital is Porto Novo.

Benin's transition to multiparty democracy began in 1991 when the first elections were held under the terms of the 1990 Constitution. In practice, all power rests with the president who is elected by universal suffrage for a five-year term, and answers to the 83-seat National Assembly (itself elected for a four-year term). The president has organised a multiparty coalition, although splits and defections are commonplace in Benin politics.

Parliamentary elections were held in March 2003. A coalition of eight parties known as the Presidential Movement received 56% of the vote and took 52 seats. A group of opposition parties received 44% of the vote and 31 seats. Presidential elections were held in March 2001 when Mathieu Kerekou was re-elected with 84% of the vote. Opposition candidates, including ex-president Nicéphore Soglo, boycotted the final round of the elections.

Benin's economy grew by 6% in 2002 and prices increased by 2.5%. GDP is expected to grow by about 5.6% in 2003 while prices rise by 2.5%. In 2004, growth of 6.5% is forecast with inflation of 2.4%. Although growth remains strong, the current account deficit widened, as a result of a sharp drop in the world cotton price. The government continues to implement its agenda of structural reform. The primary fiscal objective for 2003 is to broaden the tax base and limit non-priority outlays. Authorities are also working to encourage development of the private sector and to broaden the country's production base in order to reduce the economy's vulnerability. Reforms focus on divesting public utilities and enhancing the cotton sector reform through the privatisation. Meanwhile, reform of the civil service has stalled and more efforts to garner public support for this programme are needed.

Benin's economy is primarily agricultural. The most important crop is cotton but production slumped for several years before recovering in 2001. Authorities have launched a major reorganisation of the cotton sector to bolster its long-term competitiveness. Other agricultural products include corn, sorghum, cassava (tapioca), yams, beans, rice, palm oil, peanuts; and poultry and livestock. Aside from cotton, the country's only other export of significance is palm oil. Benin's parched soil will not normally support conventional fruit or vegetable crops. The manufacturing sector consists mainly of textiles, cigarettes, beverages, food, construction materials and petroleum and is geared almost exclusively to serving the domestic market. By 2003, the country had made sufficient progress in structural reforms to qualify for $460 million in debt relief. Additional reforms are planned, including the privatisation of the state-owned ginning company. Commercial and transport activities make up nearly 40% of GDP, but are extremely vulnerable to market conditions in Nigeria. There are deposits of gold, chrome and iron, although these are of only limited size. Oil has been extracted since the early 1980s, but again the scale of the deposits is not large.

Benin derives virtually all of its almost negligible energy requirements from imported oil and gas resources.

□ Bermuda

Capital City	Hamilton *Capital population: 6,000 (1992)*
Population ('000)	67 *(2002)*
Urban population (%)	100. *(2002)*
Land area (km²)	5
Languages	English
Religion	Mainly Anglican/Episcopal
Currency	Bermudian dollar (BM$)
Head of State	HM Queen Elizabeth II
Head of Government	Jennifer Smith (1998)
Ruling Party	Progressive Labour Party (PLP)

Main Urban Areas	Population
Hamilton (capital)	6,000 (1992)

Bermuda comprises a group of some 150 small islands, of which 20 are inhabited. The group lies in the Western Atlantic, over 900km off the coast of South Carolina. The climate is variable, with a susceptibility to hurricanes during the autumn. The capital is Hamilton.

Bermuda, a British Dependent Territory, has a 36-member House of Assembly which exercises legislative authority and is elected by universal suffrage for a term of five years. There is also an 11-member Senate whose members are nominated by the Governor. The Governor also appoints the Prime Minister, on the basis of advice from the House of Assembly, and the Premier then appoints his own Cabinet. There has been intense discussion about the possibility of declaring independence from the UK, but in August 1995 the government lost a referendum on the subject.

General elections were held in July 2003. The PLP received 52% of the vote and 22 of the 36 seats in the Assembly. The United Bermuda Party won 48% of the vote and the remaining 14 seats. The PLP supports total independence from the UK.

Bermuda's economy is among the most affluent in the Atlantic/Caribbean nexus with per capita income exceeding $34,000. Nevertheless, the island remains vulnerable to any recession in North America. At present, GDP is estimated to be growing at about 2-2.5% per year while inflation is around 3%. Unemployment is low, though the number of jobs being created is rising very slowly. The significance of tourism is crucial, since no other activity has the same employment potential. Competition is fierce, but the island's planners are placing more emphasis on the need to match the quality of its tourism product to the premium it charges. The island's tax and regulatory system has made it an attractive base for insurers since the 1950s. Companies pay no tax on their profits or their investment income, allowing them to build up reserves for future losses more quickly. There are presently more than 10,000 international businesses on the islands making use of various corporate forms, and they generate over 60% of Bermuda's economic output. However, figures released in October 2002 revealed that the number of exempted companies formed in the second quarter of 2002 was down to 223 - 30% lower than in the previous year, and 55% lower than the number recorded during the second quarter of 2000. Some observers drew a link between falling applications for exempted company status and the ongoing "corporate inversion" debate in the US, which concerns the relocation of companies to avoid American taxes. Sophisticated telecommunications, the island's proximity (900km) to the US and new laws designed to strengthen confidence in the financial sector are some of the reasons for Bermuda's success.

Bermuda enjoys one of the highest per capita incomes in the world, having successfully exploited its location by providing financial services for international firms and luxury tourist facilities for 400,000 visitors annually. The tourist industry draws more than 80% of its business from North America. Agriculture is severely limited by a lack of suitable land. Consequently, more than 80% of the country's food needs are imported. The industrial sector is small, although over 60% of all non-tourist activity is the result of international business. Manufacturing tends to centre on perfumes, flowers and pharmaceuticals. About 80% of food needs are imported. International business contributes over 60% of Bermuda's economic output and the failed independence vote in late 1995 can be partially attributed to Bermudian fears of scaring away foreign firms. Government economic priorities are the further strengthening of the tourist and international financial sectors. Bermuda's economy is a high-cost one, a characteristic due in part to the need to import everything from fuel to food.

Like most of its counterparts in the Atlantic, Bermuda is entirely dependent on imports to meet its energy needs.

▫ Bhutan

Capital City	Thimphu	*Capital population: 29,000 (1992)*
Population ('000)	2,198 *(2002)*	
Urban population (%)	7.54 *(2002)*	
Land area (km²)	4700	
Languages	Dzongkha (Tibetian dialect). English is also widely used and there are a number of local dialects.	
Religion	Mahayana Buddhist	
Currency	Ngultrum (BTN)	
Head of State	HM King Jigme Singye Wangchuk	
Head of Government	Lyonpo Kinzang Dorji (2002)	
Ruling Party	There are no legal political parties in Bhutan.	

Main Urban Areas	Population
Thimphu (capital)	29,000 (1992)

Bhutan is a small and sparsely populated state located in the Himalayan mountain range, between India and Tibet, which is part of China. The mountainous character of the landscape precludes all possibility of intensive agriculture, forcing much of the workforce to seek employment abroad. The capital is Thimphu.

The Kingdom of Bhutan is a hereditary limited monarchy in which the King shares power with the Council of Ministers, the National Assembly and the chief priest of the Buddhist religion in Bhutan. The 150-member National Assembly includes 105 elected representatives and 45 appointed members. After nearly a century of absolute rule by a monarchy, King Jigme Singye Wangchuk took a step towards increased political participation by recently giving the legislature the right to remove him from leadership and to appoint his cabinet. An income tax also was introduced for the first time.

There are no general elections in Bhutan. The 105 elective delegates to the National Assembly are elected in their various constituencies when the need arises and are not allowed to represent political groups.

Growth has been strong in recent years and this trend is expected to continue over the short term. GDP grew by 7.7% in 2002 and should increase by another 7.3% in 2003. In 2004, growth of 7.6% is forecast. Inflation was 2.5% in 2002 and should be 5% in 2003. Prices are forecast to rise by 5% once again in 2004. The trade deficit has narrowed, reflecting an increase in energy exports to India as several major hydro-power projects near completion, and a decline in imports from that country. There has also been a rationalisation of import tariffs and export duties. A key objective of the Ninth Five-Year Plan is the decentralisation of economic power to local governments so as to facilitate implementation of reforms and improve the effectiveness of public spending. Fiscal policy is very prudent, while the exchange rate peg to the Indian Rupee allows Bhutan to share in the stable monetary conditions that prevail in India. Authorities continue to maintain a surplus on the fiscal current account. To improve the buoyancy of the tax system and to promote social equity, personal income taxation was introduced in 2002. The 2003 budget targets a deficit of 4.8% of GDP, with higher tax receipts and lower current expenditure expected to more than offset a drop in non-tax revenues. Aside from the tourist sector, the economy is relatively well insulated from the direct effects of global economic volatility, although it is vulnerable to the effects of major developments in India. The key medium-term challenges are to diversify the economy in order to increase employment opportunities, and to expand the private sector.

Agriculture accounts for 45% of GDP, industry makes up another 20% and services contribute the remainder. The economy is based on agriculture and forestry, which provide the main livelihood for more than 90% of the population. Agriculture consists largely of subsistence farming and animal husbandry. Rugged mountains dominate the terrain and make the building of roads and other infrastructure difficult and expensive. Tourism, which registered double-digit growth in the 1990s, has performed especially poorly as a result of slower tourist arrivals following the events of 11 September 2001 and other terrorist threats in Asia. The industrial sector is technologically backward, with most production of the cottage industry type. Most development projects, such as road construction, rely on Indian migrant labour. Bhutan's hydropower potential and its attraction for tourists are key resources. Detailed controls and uncertain policies in areas like industrial licensing, trade, labour, and finance continue to hamper foreign investment. Electricity and related construction will continue to boost the industry sector, while private sector development will determine the prospects for mining and manufacturing. The services sector will also benefit from an expected recovery in tourism.

Bhutan does not produce or consume much energy, but it has hydroelectric power potential and is a hydropower exporter (to India). Several new power generation projects are nearing completion and should be operational by 2005. These investments should not only boost revenues and exports, but also create new business opportunities in the country, and benefit rural communities through expansion of rural electrification. Bhutan's coal industries provide the greater part of the Kingdom's modest energy needs.

▫ Bolivia

Capital City	Sucre	*Capital population: 205,396 (2002)*
Population ('000)	8,610 *(2002)*	
Urban population (%)	62.95 *(2002)*	
Land area (km²)	108438	
Languages	Spanish (official) although a majority speak Indian languages: Quechua or Aymara	
Religion	Roman Catholic (65%)	
Currency	Boliviano (Bvs)	
Head of State	Gonzalo Sanchez de Lozada (2002)	
Head of Government	Gonzalo Sanchez de Lozada (2002)	
Ruling Party	The centre-right Nationalist Revolutionary Movement (MNR) leads a coalition with the Movimiento Izquierda Revolucionaria (MIR).	

Main Urban Areas	Population
Santa Cruz	1,092,975 (2002)
La Paz	1,059,799 (2002)
Cochabamba	647,223 (2002)
El Alto	602,398 (2002)
Oruro	241,018 (2002)
Sucre (capital)	205,396 (2002)
Potosi	153,896 (2002)
Tarija	145,561 (2002)
Quillacollo	111,808 (2002)
Trinidad	82,518 (2002)

Bolivia, a landlocked republic located in central South America, is bordered by Brazil in the north and east, by Argentina and Paraguay in the south, and by Chile and Peru in the west. Its mountainous terrain, though well stocked with minerals, makes for poor farming. There are, however, some 20,000km of navigable rivers. La Paz is the seat of government while Sucre is the legal capital and seat of judiciary.

The president and the vice president are elected for a five-year term by the people (1st round) or parliament (2nd round). The National Congress has two chambers. The Chamber of Deputies has 130 members, elected for a five-year term by proportional representation. The Chamber of Senators has 27 members, elected for a five-year term by proportional representation.

After elections in July 2002, Gonzalo Sanchez de Lozada was confirmed as president by the parliament. He defeated Evo Morales, the leader of a long-running campaign to thwart US-led efforts to wipe out coca leaf production. In elections to the National Congress held at the same time, the MNR and the MIR, together took two thirds of the seats while Morales' Party, the Socialist Movement, won the remaining third.

Bolivia's GDP rose by 2.8% in 2002 and growth of 2.9% is expected in 2003. In 2004, GDP is forecast to rise by about 4.3%. Inflation was 0.9% in 2002 and should be around 2.6% in 2003. Inflation is forecast to be 3.1% in 2004. Problems in neighbouring countries, along with the American-backed drive to reduce coca production, have slowed the pace of growth. The government was slow to recognise that two of its major policies - coca eradication and a reform of customs procedures - removed several hundred million dollars from the informal economy, in which many unskilled workers make their living. The latest round of violence was triggered by the government's decision (under pressure from the IMF) to cut its deficit from 8.6% of GDP in 2002 to 5.5% in 2003. The move entailed a freeze on public-sector pay and an unpopular income tax. A large majority of Bolivians are bitterly opposed to foreign investment in the country's natural resources. This leaves Bolivia dependent on foreign aid, while it sits on an abundance of undeveloped wealth. Foreign direct investment in Bolivia peaked in 1999, as privatisation brought in record revenues of about US$1 billion. Investment is estimated to be about half that amount for 2001 and 2002, with increased activity in the oil and gas sectors as the driving force. An ambitious natural gas project could almost double the country's legal exports if it receives more support. Meanwhile, unemployment remains high and the real value of wages is falling. Prospects for some parts of the economy are good but the problem is that that these areas of growth are capital-intensive and generate very few jobs.

Bolivia's agricultural sector accounts for 14% of GDP. Programmes to boost productivity and encourage exports have had some positive effects, but productivity is low. Exports of non-traditional products, such as soya, have increased. Subsistence farmers produce rice, barley, oats, wheat and sugar cane, but coca and cocaine are the dominant crops. The major export crops (aside from coca) are soybeans, natural gas, zinc, gold, silver, lead, tin, antimony, wood and sugar. Industry contributes 31% to GDP and depends mainly on mining activities. In the industrial sector, the government has pushed through an aggressive programme of privatisation involving the sale of the state airline, a telephone company, railroad, electric power company, and oil company. Rather than pay the government for their stakes, the buyers are required to make investment pledges in the businesses they purchase. Bolivia is considering expanding its natural gas exports to include liquefied natural gas, which could be shipped worldwide from a port in Chile. Mining is the single largest sector in the country and accounts for more than half of all exports. Bolivia is the world's largest producer of tin and has deposits of copper, lead, silver, zinc, antimony, wolfram and gold in considerable quantity.

In 2002, Bolivia's total proven oil reserves amounted to 440.5 million barrels. Bolivia is relatively self sufficient in oil, consuming an estimated 43,000 barrels per day, about the same amount that it produces. Almost all crude oil produced in Bolivia is for domestic consumption, except for a small amount that is exported to Chile through the Sica-Arica pipeline. Bolivia's main hope for future economic growth hinges on increasing natural gas exports and becoming a major energy hub for South America's Southern Cone in coming years. Possible markets for Bolivian natural gas include Brazil, Mexico, Argentina, and the United States. Progress has been slow to date, however.

Legislative elections were held in October 1999, when the ruling BDP was returned to power with 54% of the vote and 33 seats in the National Assembly. Most of the remaining seats went to the Botswana National Front (BNF). The BDP has held power without a break since independence but is losing its influence in urban areas to the BNF. Although the government spends freely in the towns, its supporters are mostly rural Batswana - a group of eight ethnic clans defined by the constitution as the "majority tribe". Unlike other ethnic groups, this majority tribe is officially represented in a special chamber and their presence helps to preserve the government's core support.

GDP grew by 2.6% in 2002 and prices increased by 8.1%. Growth of 3.7% is forecast in 2003 while prices rise by 4.7%. In 2004, growth of 3.6% is forecast and inflation is expected to be 4.5%. Over the past 30 years, real per capita GDP growth averaged more than 7% a year, so that Botswana, once one of the poorest countries in the world, ranks as a middle-income country today. Botswana remains heavily dependent on its diamond sector. The economy faltered somewhat in 2002 owing to a downturn in the global diamond market and a drop in Botswana's diamond production. Unemployment remains a problem, running at more than 20% of the labour force. Inflation has been kept under control because of a tight monetary policy and a modest appreciation of the pula. The overall fiscal balance moved into deficit 2002 as a result of a decline in mineral revenue and a 16% rise in government spending. Foreign exchange reserves at the end of 2002 were $5.9 billion (equivalent to 32 months of imports). The country's development plan places a great emphasis on diversification, which is considered critical for generating employment, alleviating poverty and reducing income inequality. Botswana's medium-term growth prospects will depend on the continued sustained development of the non-mining economy, as diamond production and revenue reach a plateau, and on decisive action to contain the enormous social and economic costs of the HIV/AIDS pandemic.

Abundant diamond resources, coupled with sound macroeconomic policies, have enabled Botswana to achieve one of the highest growth rates in the world. Diamonds account for more than one third of GDP, 70% of export earnings and about two thirds of the central government's revenue. Mining and government services are the other foundations and together account for 52% of the country's GDP. The economic health of the non-mining sectors has improved in recent years, especially the service industries. Their success is in part a product of Botswana's market-friendly environment, sound macroeconomic policies, and investments in education and physical infrastructure. Agricultural is the main employer with cattle herding contributing over 85% of total farming production. This activity has suffered in recent years as a result of recurrent disease in cattle herds. Aside from cattle farming, the land is generally too dry to permit much arable crop production. In 2002, Botswana's economy was hit by several negative shocks, including a temporary decline in global diamond demand, the near 40% depreciation in the South African rand in 2001, and the regional food crisis. Many analysts want to see an easing of monetary policy in order to promote business investment and support the medium-term diversification objective.

Botswana's coal resources, together with natural fuels such as brushwood, account for most of its needs. A sizeable proportion of its electricity is of hydroelectric origin, although some of this is imported.

Botswana

Capital City	Gaborone	Capital population: 137,522 (1992)
Population ('000)	1,713 (2002)	
Urban population (%)	51.12 (2002)	
Land area (km²)	56673	
Languages	English (official), Setswana (national)	
Religion	Mainly traditional	
Currency	Pula (Pula)	
Head of State	President Festus Mogae (1998)	
Head of Government	Ian Khama (1998)	
Ruling Party	Botswana Democratic Party (BDP)	

Main Urban Areas	Population
Gaborone (capital)	137,522 (1992)

Botswana is a landlocked territory in central southern Africa. It is bounded by South Africa in the south and east, by Zimbabwe in the northeast, and by Namibia in the west and north. There is also a short northern border with Zambia. The country has a varied climate, ranging from the swamplands of the Okavango and Limpopo to the deserts of the Kalagadi. The capital is Gaborone.

Botswana is an independent member of the Commonwealth with an executive president who is elected by universal suffrage for a term of five years. Legislative power is vested in the National Assembly, which has 47 members. Of these, 40 members are elected for a five-year term in single-seat constituencies, four members co-opted by the elected members and two members ex officio and the Speaker (if elected from outside Parliament).

Brazil

Capital City	Brasilia	Capital population: 2,189,243 (2002)
Population ('000)	172,782 (2002)	
Urban population (%)	81.78 (2002)	
Land area (km²)	845651	
Languages	Portuguese	
Religion	Mainly Roman Catholic (90%)	
Currency	Real (R$)	
Head of State	President Luiz Inácio Lula da Silva (2003)	
Head of Government	Luiz Inácio Lula da Silva (2003)	
Ruling Party	The government is formed by the Workers Party (PT) and its allies.	

Main Urban Areas	Population	
Sao Paulo	9,919,598	(2002)
Rio de Janeiro	5,969,170	(2002)
Salvador	2,549,868	(2002)
Belo Horizonte	2,293,779	(2002)
Fortaleza	2,215,051	(2002)
Brasilia (capital)	2,189,243	(2002)
Curitiba	1,639,555	(2002)
Manaus	1,509,533	(2002)
Recife	1,455,494	(2002)
Porto Alegre	1,348,930	(2002)

Brazil, the largest country in South America, occupies some two thirds of the continent's entire Atlantic coast and has a wide range of climatic conditions, from the humid equatorial states of the north to the cooler and drier south. Much of the country is made up of dense tropical forest and jungle, and apart from the capital, Brasilia, there are no settlements of any size in the interior of the country.

Brazil has an executive president who is elected by popular mandate for a term of four years and is answerable to a bicameral National Congress which has two chambers. The Chamber of Deputies is composed of 513 members, elected for a four-year term by proportional representation. The Federal Senate has 81 members, elected for eight-year terms, with elections every four years for alternately one-third and two-thirds of the seats.

In October 2002, Lula was elected with 61% of the vote. He defeated José Serra of the Social Democratic Party (PSDB). In Congressional elections held at the same time, the PT took 91 seats in the Chamber of Deputies and 14 in the Senate. The PSDB won 71 seats in the Chamber and 11 in the Senate. The Brazilian Democratic Movement (PMDB) won 74 votes in the Chamber and 19 in the Senate. The remaining seats were scattered among a number of parties. The seats awarded to major parties mean little, since no fewer than 18 different political parties are represented in Congress and they operate without any real form of party discipline.

Brazil's GDP rose by a meagre 1.5% in 2002 and is expected to repeat this performance in 2003. Growth of 3% is forecast for 2004. Inflation was 8.4% in 2002 but is expected to rise to 15% in 2003. In 2004, prices are forecast to increase by 6.2%. At present, the government is under considerable pressure from two very different sources. Radicals within the ruling Workers' Party want to see increased spending but investors and financial markets are growing more fearful of risk. The government has announced that it intends to raise its fiscal surplus (before interest payments) to 4.25% of GDP. The aim is to show that Brazil means to cur its public debt, which stands at 56% of GDP. Higher domestic energy prices will help to generate more public funds and civil servants will see very small increases in their wages. Social spending will also fall. To appease the radicals, the government will redistribute over 200,000 hectares of land to farmers. The financial plan could go off the rails if there is a sharp devaluation of the real. In 2002, Brazil's currency lost about a quarter of its value. The current account deficit has been steadily rising and now exceeds $252 billion, almost entirely financed by net inflows of FDI. The government has made some progress on its agenda of structural reform, including the privatisation of federalised state banks. The government is attempting to address its energy problems by attracting more foreign investment to the energy sector and by promoting increased supply in the medium and long term.

Brazil has a vibrant agricultural sector. The sector's stellar performance has helped to keep inflation under control. Brazil is the world's top producer of orange juice, sugar cane and coffee. It ranks second in world production of soya and meat (beef and poultry) and third for fruits and corn. Coffee, one of the main cash crops, has been hurt by low world prices, but growers are diversifying, especially into fruits. Altogether, agro-business accounts for over a quarter of total GDP. The country also has an abundance of mineral deposits (for example, bauxite, iron ore, manganese, chrome, lead, zinc, tungsten and nickel). Brazil's industrial base is one of the largest and most diversified of any emerging economy. The country's big manufacturers include producers of automobiles, consumer electronics, computers and software, and heavy industries making everything from steel to planes. With the stagnation of government activities as a result of the steps taken to curtail expenditure, services expanded only moderately. The country's stunning natural beauty - from rainforests to beaches - offers opportunities to expand tourism. So far, however, the sector has not lived up to its potential, relying too heavily on local visitors rather than international tourists. The country has built up a streamlined and competitive private sector but growth will only be strong if policy makers manage to further reduce the underlying economic imbalances.

Brazil contains the second largest oil reserves in South America (after Venezuela), at 8.4 billion barrels. Although Brazil continues to strive for self-sufficiency in oil production, it is unlikely that the country will reach this goal within the next few years. Production has been rising steadily since the early 1990s, reaching 1.6 million barrels per day in 2002. The offshore Campos Basin, north of Rio de Janeiro, is the country's most prolific production area. Brazil's oil consumption is estimated at 2.2 million barrels per day. A combination of factors contributed to the problem including a failure to expand grid limits, partial privatisation and Californian-style bungling of tariffs. To modernise, Brazil will need an estimated US$38 billion worth of investment in its energy sector. The country's state-owned oil company has announced plans to invest $5 billion by 2010 to upgrade its refineries and increase capacity.

▫ British Virgin Islands

Capital City	Road Town	*Capital population: 2,510 (1992)*
Population ('000)	22 *(2002)*	
Urban population (%)	62.53 *(2002)*	
Land area (km²)	34	
Languages	English	
Religion	Mainly Christian	
Currency	US dollar (US$)	
Head of State	HM Queen Elizabeth II	
Head of Government	Ralph T. O'Neal (1995)	
Ruling Party	Virgin Islands Party	

Main Urban Areas	Population
Road Town (capital)	2,510 (1992)

The British Virgin Islands lie in the Eastern Caribbean, to the east of Puerto Rico and northeast of St Kitts and Nevis. Only about 16 of the 60-plus islands administered by Britain (as distinct from those run by the US) are inhabited. All except the coral island of Anegada are hilly or mountainous. The capital is Road Town.

The British Virgin Islands, a UK Crown Colony, are governed to a large extent by the local assembly (Legislative Council), despite the presence of a Governor appointed by the Crown who formally presides over an Executive Council. The Legislative Council has 15 members, 13 members elected for a four-year term in single-seat constituencies, one ex officio member and one speaker chosen from outside the council.

General elections were held in May 1999. The ruling Virgin Islands Party took 38% of the vote and seven seats in the Legislative Council. The National Democratic Party received 37% of the vote and five council seats. Ralph O'Neal was returned as head of the government.

GDP is growing by less than 3% per year while prices are rising by around 5% per annum. The economy, one of the most prosperous in the Caribbean, is highly dependent on tourism but the sector performed poorly in 2001. The government's efforts to diversify the financial sector beyond its traditional base of focusing on international business companies has yielded encouraging, but far from spectacular results. However, more than 90% of government revenues are still derived from international business companies. There is some discussion of changing the laws governing these entities but officials insist that the proposals are not in response to international action on tax havens. The only significant tax in the country is income tax, which applies to the relatively few local companies and to individuals. The government is planning to abolish the income tax in 2004.

Agriculture accounts for only 2% of GDP and industry contributes just 6%. Agriculture is a minor activity consisting mainly of livestock. Poor soils limit the islands' ability to meet domestic food requirements but there is some cultivation of fruit and vegetables and fish are exported. Industry centres on the processing of agricultural products, especially rum manufacturing, although there is a stone quarry and a paint factory. The economy is nevertheless one of the most stable and prosperous in the Caribbean. Income and wealth depend on tourism, which generates an estimated 45% of the national income. Unlike most other tourist destinations, the country did not suffer significantly from the effects of 11 September 2001. The British Virgin Islands are also home to over 140,000 international business companies and the number is growing steadily. The islands are regarded as the world capital for setting up international business companies. However, these opaque identities have raised the concerns of regulators in Western nations. The government is actively trying to broaden the financial sector to include new areas such as insurance and mutual funds. The islands' small number of expensive resorts is complemented by a growing number of others aimed at the mass market.

The islands have no domestic sources of energy and rely entirely on imports.

▫ Brunei

Capital City	Bandar Seri Begawan	*Capital population: 55,000 (1992)*
Population ('000)	337 *(2002)*	
Urban population (%)	73.08 *(2002)*	
Land area (km²)	527	
Languages	Malay, Chinese, English	
Religion	Muslim (64%), Buddhist (14%), Christian (10%)	
Currency	Brunei dollar (BN$)	
Head of State	HM Sultan Sir Muda Hassanal Bolkiah Mu'izzadin Waddaulah	
Head of Government	HM Sultan Sir Muda Hassanal Bolkiah Mu'izzadin Waddaulah	
Ruling Party	There are no legal political parties.	

Main Urban Areas	Population
Bandar Seri Begawan (capital)	55,000 (1992)

The Sultanate of Brunei lies on the northwestern coast of the island of Borneo and is surrounded on all sides by Malaysian territory. The country has a humid and tropical climate. The capital is Bandar Seri Begawan.

Brunei achieved full independence from the UK in 1984 and is ruled by an executive monarch, the Sultan, in whose hands all legal powers are vested. The Sultan is assisted by a Council of Ministers, a Religious Council and a Privy Council. However, part of the Constitution has been revoked since 1962, when massive protests developed, and a state of emergency was declared which has yet to be revoked. The Sultan disbanded the Legislative Council in 1984 and now rules by decree.

There are no elections in Brunei.

Brunei's small, wealthy economy is a mixture of foreign and domestic entrepreneurship, government regulation and welfare measures, and village tradition. It is almost totally supported by exports of crude oil and natural gas, with revenues from the hydrocarbons sector accounting for over 50% of GDP, around 80-90% of exports, and 75-90% of government revenues. Substantial income from overseas investment supplements income from domestic sources. GDP grew by about 2.3% in 2001 while prices rose by around 1.8%. The government provides for all medical services and subsidises food and housing. Expatriates - mainly engaged in the oil and gas industries - account for over 40% of the workforce. The Brunei Investment Agency, which at one point was worth around US$110 billion, has now fallen in value to an estimated US$30-40 billion. Brunei's main economic problems include rising unemployment (especially among recent college graduates), huge state subsidies, a civil service which employs around 75% of Brunei's workforce, extensive state economic controls, a chronic budget deficit, a small tax base and a heavy reliance on the hydrocarbons sector.

Brunei's income is almost entirely derived from its oil and gas resources, which account for around 70% of annual revenues in a typical year and employs two-fifths of the workforce. Farming is largely limited to yams, bananas and cassava, mainly for the domestic market, but there are also considerable stocks of hardwoods, which are exported. Agriculture accounts for only 5% of GDP. There are very few industries other than those related to oil and gas. The government had hoped to develop a financial centre, based on the country's policy of low taxation and banking secrecy. This ambition, however, is likely to be strongly opposed by Western countries. Brunei would like to diversify away from hydrocarbons into areas like tourism (the country boasts unspoiled tropical forests, beaches, shipwrecks, the world's largest palace and gilded mosques, among other things) and energy-intensive industries like petrochemicals, oil refining and aluminium smelting.

Brunei contains proven crude oil reserves of 1.35 billion barrels and produces 173,000 barrels per day, plus around 22,000 barrels per day of natural gas liquids. This is down from production of around 270,000 barrels per day in 1980. Crude oil production peaked in 1979 at about 240,000 barrels per day, but was cut back deliberately to extend life of the fields and to improve recovery rates. Brunei has seven offshore oil fields. Major customers for Brunei's oil include Japan, South Korea, Singapore, Taiwan and Thailand. In November 2000, Brunei signed an agreement with China to export 10,000 barrels per day, the first time Brunei has exported to mainland China. In 2001, Brunei launched its first deepwater petroleum exploration areas. Long-term prospects for the development of natural gas are excellent. The government has a master plan to expand its capacity with an additional four million metric tons per year by 2008.

□ Burkina Faso

Capital City	Ouagadougou	*Capital population: 634,479 (1994)*
Population ('000)	13,156 *(2002)*	
Urban population (%)	19.45 *(2002)*	
Land area (km²)	27360	
Languages	French, Mossi	
Religion	traditional (more than 50%)	
Currency	CFA franc (CFAF)	
Head of State	President Blaise Compaoré (1991)	
Head of Government	Paramanga Ernest Yonli (2000)	
Ruling Party	Congress for Democracy and Progress (CDP) leads a coalition.	

Main Urban Areas	Population
Ouagadougou (capital)	634,479 (1994)

Burkina Faso, the former Upper Volta, is a landlocked state in northwest Africa, which is bounded in the north and west by Mali, in the east by Niger, and in the south by Côte d'Ivoire, Ghana, Benin and Togo. The country's especially arid climate and hard soil makes farming difficult. The capital is Ouagadougou.

Burkina Faso, which was known until 1984 as Upper Volta, has an executive president who is elected by universal suffrage for a seven-year term. The National Assembly consists of 111 members and is also elected by universal suffrage. Members serve five-year terms. There is also a House of Representatives made up of 178 members appointed for three-year terms.

Presidential elections were last held in November 1998 when Blaise Compaoré won with more than 87% of the vote. Elections to the National Assembly were held in May 2002. The CDP won 57 seats in the National Assembly. The main other parties are the centrist Alliance for Democracy and Federation-African Democratic Rally which won 17 seats and the Social Democratic Party for Democracy and Progress/Socialist Party which took ten seats.

Burkina Faso saw growth of 4.6% in 2002 with inflation of 2.2%. In 2003, growth of 3.2% is expected while prices again rise by 3%. In 2004, GDP is forecast to increase by 4% while prices rise by 2.8%. An increase in tax revenue, and in particular import duties, has served to reduce the financial pressure on the government. The government had previously agreed to abolish tariffs on about 60 items in 2002 but this was not done. The country's main challenge is to move ahead with its reform programme, so as to create the conditions for sustainable and equitable growth. Structural reforms focus on the adoption of an automatic pricing policy for petroleum products in line with international prices, pursuit of the reform of the cotton sector and completion of the privatisation programme. Modest efforts have been made to strengthen the country's public finances and widen its revenue base, but there has been little progress in attempts to scale back public spending or alter its composition.

One of the poorest countries in the world, landlocked Burkina Faso has a high population density, few natural resources and a fragile soil. About 90% of the population is engaged in (mainly subsistence) agriculture which is highly vulnerable to variations in rainfall. Farming accounts for about a third of GDP with animal husbandry being the main source of farm income. The government's attempts to spur agricultural progress have been only half-heartedly implemented. Industry accounts for 28% of GDP and is dominated by unprofitable government-controlled corporations. The main manufactured products are cotton lint, beverages, agricultural processing, soap, cigarettes and textiles. Burkina Faso has some mineral deposits that are being actively mined. These include gold, copper, bauxite, manganese and graphite. However, the country's gold mining operations have been hit by falling prices, forcing it to close down its biggest gold mine.

The bulk of Burkina Faso's very modest fuel requirements are met by natural resources such as brushwood. In the absence of coal deposits, oil remains the main source of thermally generated energy.

□ Burundi

Capital City	Bujumbura	*Capital population: 220,100 (1992)*
Population ('000)	7,097 *(2002)*	
Urban population (%)	9.54 *(2002)*	
Land area (km²)	2568	
Languages	Kirundi, French, Kiswahili	
Religion	Mainly Christian (60%)	
Currency	Burundi franc (BIF)	
Head of State	Domitien Ndayizeye (April 2003)	
Head of Government	vacant	
Ruling Party	Burundi has a power-sharing government that includes the Uprona and Frodebu Parties.	

Main Urban Areas	Population
Bujumbura (capital)	220,100 (1992)

The tiny landlocked republic of Burundi is located to the northeast of Tanzania, with Rwanda to the north and the Democratic Republic of the Congo (formerly Zaire) to the west. It lies along the rivers that feed into Lake Tanganyika further south. The climate is tropical, although there is an ample supply of water available from the rivers. The capital is Bujumbura.

Officially, the National Assembly has 81 members, elected for a five-year term by proportional representation with a 5% barrier. In July 1998, the Assembly was reformed into the National Transition Assembly, whereby 40 additional members were appointed, belonging to political parties and civil society.

In April 2003, Pierre Buyoya handed over power to Ndayizeye in accordance with the 2002 peace agreement. The country's last elections were held in 1993. In that poll, Sylvestre Ntibantunganya was confirmed as head of state. He led an uneasy coalition between the Tutsi-dominated Uprona Party and the mainly Hutu Frodebu Party. The break-up of the coalition contributed to a coup d'état and the assassination of Ntibantunganya. Buyoya's representatives subsequently held 65 seats in the National Transition Assembly.

Burundi's GDP increased by 4.5% in 2002 while prices fell by 1.4%. In 2003, negative growth of -0.5% is expected and prices could rise by 11%. Growth of 5.4% is forecast for 2004 with prices increasing by 7.2%. The programme to stabilise the economy has been hampered by continued instability and a consequent hesitance on the part of donors. The fiscal situation has deteriorated owing to expenditure overruns and a rise in the overall budget deficit increased to 5.2% of GDP. Confronted with lower-than-expected donor support, the government resorted to domestic bank financing and arrears in external debt service mounted, reaching $116 million at the end of 2001. The external current account deficit also worsened (rising to 16.2% of GDP). In the near term, the government's priority is to restore a measure of fiscal discipline through stricter budget implementation, tighter monetary conditions, and more flexible exchange rate management. The authorities hope that progress in the implementation of their economic and financial programme will help them mobilise external assistance, including budgetary support.

Burundi is a landlocked, resource-poor country with an underdeveloped manufacturing sector. The economy is predominantly agricultural with roughly 90% of the population dependent on subsistence agriculture. Its economic health depends on the coffee crop, which accounts for 80% of foreign exchange earnings, but cotton and tea were sold on the international markets until the civil war disrupted production. The ability to pay for imports rests largely on the vagaries of the climate and the international coffee market. Agricultural output rebounded in 2001 and 2002 but this positive development was offset by a sharp drop in world coffee prices. Large losses in 2002 by the country's coffee parastatal, equivalent to about 1% of GDP, have been covered by budget subsidies Only one in four children go to school, and one in nine adults has HIV/AIDS. Foods, medicines and electricity remain in short supply. There has been some prospecting for minerals, and major deposits of zinc have been located. However, their difficult location would make them uneconomic to extract.

The greater part of Burundi's very modest energy needs is met by solid fuels such as coal, or by natural fuels such as brushwood. Hydroelectric power accounts for virtually all of its limited electricity consumption.

◻ Cambodia

Capital City	Phnom-Penh	*Capital population: 900,000 (1992)*
Population ('000)	11,487 *(2002)*	
Urban population (%)	16.51 *(2002)*	
Land area (km²)	17652	
Languages	Khmer	
Religion	Theravada Buddhist	
Currency	Riel (KHR)	
Head of State	King Norodom Sihanouk	
Head of Government	Hun Sen	
Ruling Party	The Cambodian People's Party (CPP) leads a coalition with its main rival, the royalist United National Front party, known as Funcinpec.	

Main Urban Areas	**Population**
Phnom-Penh (capital)	900,000 (1992)

◻ Cameroon

Capital City	Yaoundé	*Capital population: 1,121,000 (1995)*
Population ('000)	16,583 *(2002)*	
Urban population (%)	50.19 *(2002)*	
Land area (km²)	46540	
Languages	French, English	
Religion	Christian (53%), traditional (23%), Muslim (22%)	
Currency	CFA franc (CFAF)	
Head of State	President Paul Biya (1982)	
Head of Government	Peter Mafany Musonge Mafani (1996)	
Ruling Party	The Rassemblement Démocratique du Peuple Camerounais (RDPC) leads a coalition.	

Main Urban Areas	**Population**
Douala	1,322,000 (1995)
Yaoundé (capital)	1,121,000 (1995)

Cambodia, the former Kampuchea, is located at the centre of the Indochinese peninsula with Vietnam to the south and east, Laos to the north and Thailand to the northwest. Its access to the sea is through a 300-kilometre stretch of land adjoining the Gulf of Thailand. Most of the country is near-impenetrable jungle. The climate is tropical and extremely humid. The capital is Phnom-Penh.

The State of Cambodia resumed its traditional title in 1990, having been known since the late 1970s as Kampuchea or Democratic Kampuchea. Prince Ranariddh, the leader of Funcinpe, was ousted in a coup in 1997. The National Assembly has 122 members, elected for a five-year term by proportional representation. The Senate has 61 members, appointed by the king on recommendation of the parties in the National Assembly.

Hun Sen claimed victory in the July 2003 elections, defeating the royalist Funcinpe Party and its leader Prince Norodom Ranariddh. The CPP won 69 of the 122 seats in the National Assembly. The liberal Sam Rainsy Party took 28 seats and Funcinpec secured 26 seats. The Senate was last appointed in March 1999.

GDP increased by 5.5% in 2002 and should rise by another 4.7% in 2003. In 2004, growth of 5.8% is forecast. Prices rose by 3.2% in 2002 and are expected to rise by 2.6% in 2003. Inflation is forecast to be 3.5% in 2004. The government is maintaining a tight fiscal policy, underpinned by steady increases in fiscal revenues and reductions in spending on defence and security. However, revenue performance suffered in 2002 owing to a drop in trade taxes, an erosion of the tax base after a backlog of applications for tax exemptions were cleared and recently signed public contracts that have reduced transfers to the Treasury. The 2002 revenue shortfall was met through a reduction in non-wage expenditures and larger-than-expected foreign financing. International reserves have risen steadily from US$390 million at end-1998 to about US$665 million at end-2002 (equivalent to 3.5 months of imports). Cambodia has also made progress in implementing key structural reforms, although slippages have occurred in several areas. Trade liberalisation has proceeded smoothly in the context of the ASEAN Free Trade Area and in preparation for World Trade Organisation membership. However, further implementation of civil service reform has been delayed. The government is committed to maintain fiscal stability in the coming years, with an overall fiscal deficit of around 6% of GDP. The incidence of poverty remains high. The number of people below the poverty line is in the range of 35-39%.

Cambodia's growth is very narrowly based on the performance of the agricultural sector (which accounts for a third of all economic activity) and production of garments. Farm output has grown very slowly because the country's irrigation system is underdeveloped. This limitation is of particular concern, given that over 80% of the population live in rural areas and depend largely on agriculture for their livelihoods. Wages of skilled workers, who are in comparatively short supply, are improving while those of unskilled workers decline due to the difficulty of the labour market in absorbing new entrants. Many of the country's highways and rural roads are in poor condition. Current and proposed infrastructure projects could substantially improve the situation by helping to improve access to market for many rural households and increasing the country's attractiveness as a tourist destination. The financial sector is weak and is not effectively serving as an intermediary between savers and potential lenders. The lack of access to credit is a commonly cited limitation to growth for the private sector. The country's important logging industry is the centre of a controversy with international donors. In 2003, the World Bank suspended a $15 million loan until charges of corruption and graft in the industry are resolved.

Cambodia's best chance to achieve some measurable improvement in living standards is that one of the energy consortiums exploring off its coast will find oil and/or gas. Preliminary wells proved the existence of hydrocarbons but it is still uncertain that these are available in commercial quantities. Most of the country's energy needs are met either from coal or natural fuels such as firewood. Its electricity production, however, is almost 40% derived from hydroelectric power plants.

Cameroon lies on the West African Atlantic coast facing south-westwards into the Gulf of Guinea. With Nigeria to the west, Gabon, Equatorial Guinea and Congo to the south, and the Central African Republic and Chad to the east and northeast, it has a tropical but dry climate. The capital is Yaoundé.

Cameroon was a one-party socialist state from 1964 (when all but the ruling party were banned) until 1992. Under the 1990 Constitution, an executive president is elected by popular mandate. Members of the 180-member National Assembly are elected for a five-year term by popular mandate. In December 1995 a new constitution was approved, with provisions included to increase the president's term from five to seven years with a maximum presidential tenure of two terms.

Elections to the national assembly were held in June 2002 and the RDPC won 149 seats. The Social-Democratic Front took 21 seats with the remainder spread among several small parties. Presidential elections last held in October 1997 returned Biya to power. He claimed to have won over 90% of the vote but international observers put the turnout at 30%. Biya stood without opposition, leaving foreigners with little basis to criticise the results. In practice, the president continues to rule by decree.

Cameroon's GDP increased by 6.5% in 2002. In 2003, growth of 4% is expected and an increase of another 4.4% is forecast for 2004. Prices rose by 2.8% in 2002 and are expected to increase by 2.5% in 2003. Inflation is forecast to be 2.1% in 2004. The government's fiscal surplus rose to about 5.6% of GDP in 2002, thanks to higher oil prices and a strong performance in the non-oil sector. In an effort to attract more investment, Cameroon has adopted a national investment charter, which is consistent with the Central African Economic and Monetary Community's common investment charter. Cameroon's external position has strengthened considerably in more recent years. In the budget area, progress has been made in realising fiscal sustainability through the strengthening of the collection of both oil and non-oil revenues. A weak expenditure management system has also been strengthened. The country's growth prospects depend on its success in increasing investment (both domestic and foreign), raising the domestic tax revenue base, rebuilding infrastructure and implementing structural reforms that will bolster its external competitiveness.

Cameroon is richly endowed with natural resources and has a diversified, commodity-based economy. In recent years the services sector has grown and now accounts for just over 40% of GDP. Industry accounts for 31% of GDP while agriculture makes up the remainder. Many farms are extremely small but the government hopes to develop larger-scale agro-industrial complexes that will boost productivity. Petroleum products contribute about 60% of export receipts. Timber, coffee, and cocoa are the country's principal non-oil exports. The economy benefited in 2002 from the spillover effects of the construction of the Chad-Cameroon pipeline, a strong expansion in the textile and other light manufacturing industries and in construction, and increased private sector income. Industrial development centres on bauxite, with a large aluminium smelter at Edéa. There is also an oil refinery which processes part of Cameroon's crude oil production. Delays persist in the privatisation of major public companies, including the state-owned fixed telecommunications company and the water company. The implementation of most of the structural reforms, notably in the transport and forestry sectors, has also encountered further delays

Cameroon is sub-Saharan Africa's fifth largest oil producer with crude oil production of almost 71,200 barrels per day (bbl/d) in 2002. Oil output is expected to fall to between 50,000 bbl/d and 60,000 bbl/d by 2005. However, the government is confident in the development potential of two basins that remain largely unexplored. In 2000, construction of the Chad-Cameroon pipeline began. A related component of this project is the development of several oil fields and export facilities. The consortium in charge of the project plans to drill 300 wells. Production is forecast to continue for 25 to 30 years, with peak production projected at 225,000 bbl/d to 250,000 bbl/d. Crude oil from the fields will be gathered, treated and blended at the new facility. Production is set to begin in early 2004, with the cost of the field development estimated to be $1.5 billion.

□ Canada

Capital City	Ottawal *Capital population: 1,096,976 (2002)*
Population ('000)	31,027 *(2002)*
Urban population (%)	77.34 *(2002)*
Land area (km²)	922097
Languages	English (60.6%), French (24.3%), American Indian (0.4%), other European (14.7%)
Religion	Mainly Christian
Currency	Canadian dollar (C$)
Head of State	HM Queen Elizabeth II
Head of Government	Jean Chrétien (1993)
Ruling Party	The Liberal Party leads the government.

Main Urban Areas	Population
Toronto	4,780,555 (2002)
Montréal	3,494,706 (2002)
Vancouver	2,170,625 (2002)
Ottawa (capital)	1,096,976 (2002)
Calgary	939,114 (2002)
Edmonton	900,772 (2002)
Québec	705,988 (2002)
Winnipeg	672,893 (2002)
Hamilton	660,418 (2002)
London	420,647 (2002)

Extending some 3,000 miles from the Pacific Ocean in the west to the Arctic Atlantic in the east, Canada occupies virtually the entire northern half of the North American continent. The capital is Ottawa.

Canada comprises a federation of 12 provinces and territories, each of which exercises considerable political autonomy over its own affairs. The Northwest Territories are to be divided so as to create an Indian territory, to be known as Nunavut. The province of Québec, which is French-speaking, narrowly rejected a referendum on secession from the Federation in 1995. Parliament consists of the House of Commons in Ottawa with 301 elected members from individual constituencies and the Senate which has 104 members appointed by the Prime Minister. A governor- general represents the monarch.

Elections to the House of Commons were held in November 2000. The Liberal Party took 172 seats while the Reform Conservative Alliance won 66 seats. The remaining seats were scattered among numerous parties.

The Canadian economy grew by 3.3% in 2002. In 2003, growth should be about 1.9% while in 2004 GDP should rise by around 3%. Inflation was 2.2% in 2002 and will rise to 2.8% in 2003. In 2004, inflation is forecast to be 1.7%. The Canadian economy has outperformed that of most other large industrialised countries in the past two years. Despite weak demand abroad, Canada's external current account has remained in significant surplus and net foreign liabilities have continued to fall. Modest gains in world commodity prices and gradual recoveries abroad would leave the current account surplus in the range of 2-3% of GDP, a level consistent with Canada becoming a net foreign creditor for the first time in its history by the end of the decade. Recent tax measures have lowered the tax burden and improved the incentives to work, save, and invest. Other reforms have put the Canadian Pension Plan on a sound footing and improved labour market flexibility. Nonetheless, given its proximity and close integration with the US, the Canadian economy has been negatively affected by the new security measures related to the war on terrorism. The impact on the Canadian economy has included a significant disruption of commercial traffic in the Canada-US border area, a decline in business confidence and interruptions in activities such as air travel and tourism.

Canada's economy has been shifting away from being primarily resource-based, and now boasts a larger portion of manufacturing and high-technology industries. Meanwhile, the country's dependence on the US has grown. America's share of Canada's exports has climbed from 73% to 85% since the two countries signed a free-trade agreement in 1988, reinforced six years later by NAFTA, which also includes Mexico. In 2002, the car industry, based mostly in Ontario, has seen record sales on both sides of the border. Western Canada's oil and gas producers have also flourished as energy prices have risen. Finally, low interest rates have kept the housing market strong. However, in the early part of 2003 these engines of growth began to show weakness. Demand for cars slumped and housing starts fell. Agriculture accounts for less than 5% of GDP but the sector's exports provide an important boost to the economy. In the mineral sector, Canada is the world's largest producer of zinc and uranium and has substantial reserves of nickel, potash, cobalt, silver and gold.

Canada has proven conventional oil reserves of 4.9 billion barrels. Oil production averaged 2.9 million barrels per day (bbl/d) during 2002, with estimated consumption of two million bbl/d. The province of Alberta, located in western Canada, is by far the country's leading oil producer. While Alberta's light oil reserves are declining (the province now contains an estimated 45% of the country's light oil reserves), there are huge oil sands deposits. Meanwhile, projects and potential projects in other provinces are shifting the oil industry focus to include the eastern and northern parts of the country. Some analysts estimate that the region off Canada's east coast could hold upwards to 20 trillion cubic feet of gas. Canada's oil sector has seen significant mergers and acquisitions in recent years, with US firms purchasing over $35 billion in Canadian oil and gas assets during 2001. Although most Canadian oil is produced in western Canada (mainly Alberta), oil is consumed primarily in central and eastern Canada. As a result, Canada exports mostly crude oil from Alberta and imports crude oil and petroleum products on the east coast.

□ Cape Verde

Capital City	Praia *Capital population: 69,000 (1992)*
Population ('000)	460 *(2002)*
Urban population (%)	64.14 *(2002)*
Land area (km²)	403
Languages	Portuguese, Crioulo
Religion	Roman Catholic (97%)
Currency	Escudo (CVE)
Head of State	Pedro Verona Rodrigues Pires (2001)
Head of Government	José Maria Neves (2001)
Ruling Party	The government is formed by the African Party of Independence of Cape Verde (PAICV).

Main Urban Areas	Population
Praia (capital)	69,000 (1992)

Cape Verde, one of the smallest African states, consists of two groups of islands (known as the Windward and Leeward Islands) off the Atlantic coast of West Africa, some 500km west of Senegal. The capital is Praia.

The Republic of Cape Verde became independent from Portugal in 1985 and quickly established itself as a one-party state with a socialist orientation. Under the 1990 Constitution the country has an executive president, elected by popular mandate for a five-year term. He answers to a 72-member National Assembly, also elected for five years.

Elections to he National Assembly were held in January 2001 when the PAICV received 47% of the votes and 40 seats. The Movement for the Democracy won 40% of the votes and 30 seats. Presidential elections occurred in February 2001. Pires received just over 50% of the vote, narrowly defeating Carlos Alberto Wahnon de Carvalho Veiga.

Growth of GDP was 4.6% in 2002 while inflation was 1.9%. In 2003, GDP should increase by around 5% and prices will rise by 2.8%. In 2004, growth of 5.1% is forecast while inflation should be 2%. Economic performance has been better than anticipated, thanks to a rise in exports, tourism receipts and private transfers. The fiscal outcome has also been better than expected, reflecting stronger revenue performance across all categories and the restraint of recurrent expenditures. The rescheduling of external payment arrears has helped to re-establish foreign credit lines and increase the pace of implementing the public investment programme. Monetary policy continues to be guided by the need to sustain the exchange rate peg, which has been the key to the country's price stability. A new value-added tax and a revised customs tariff schedule was approved in 2002 and implemented in 2003. The government is also proposing to reduce the corporate income tax rate from 35% to 30%.

Although nearly 70% of the population lives in rural areas, the share of agriculture in GDP is only 11%. Only the farms in the country's irrigated valleys are reliable producers of basic foodstuffs. The main agricultural products are bananas, corn, beans, sweet potatoes, sugarcane, coffee and peanuts. About 82% of food must be imported. The fishing potential, mostly lobster and tuna, is not fully exploited. Since the mid-1990s, droughts have cut the islands' grain crop by 80%, and in 1998 an outbreak of African swine fever threatened to wipe out the country's pig population, an important element in the diet of poorer islanders. Cape Verde has very little domestic industry of any importance, the main activities revolving around the processing of agricultural raw materials (flour milling, rum manufacture, garment production, fish processing) and ship repair. Industry accounts for 17% of GDP but the sector's only exports are garments, hides and shoes. The government is liquidating two large loss-making public enterprises engaged in food import and distribution and municipal transport. The mining industry centres on the extraction of pozzuolana, a volcanic rock, and the production of sea salt, which is obtained by an evaporation process.

Cape Verde is entirely dependent on imported energy supplies, mainly in the form of oil and natural gas. All electricity is produced by thermal power stations.

□ Cayman Islands

Capital City	George Town *Capital population: 13,150 (1992)*
Population ('000)	41 *(2002)*
Urban population (%)	100. *(2002)*
Land area (km²)	26
Languages	English
Religion	Mainly Christian
Currency	Cayman Islands dollar (CI$)
Head of State	HM Queen Elizabeth II
Head of Government	McKeeva Bush (2001)
Ruling Party	The government is formed by the United Democratic Party.

Main Urban Areas	Population
George Town (capital)	13,150 (1992)

The Cayman Islands lie in the Caribbean, about 230km south of Cuba and 300km northwest of Jamaica. The climate is consistently warm, with only light rainfall. The capital is George Town.

The Cayman Islands were a dependency of Jamaica until 1962 and have been a UK Dependent Territory ever since. There has been no serious move to replace the system created by the 1972 Constitution, which awards all executive power to the Governor and the eight-member Executive Council (of which four members are elected by the Legislative Assembly, with the Governor and the other three ex officio members). The Legislative Assembly has 18 members, of whom three are officials and the other 15 are elected by universal suffrage for a term of five years. A move introduced in 1987 granted resident Cayman Islanders certain electoral privileges over immigrants.

Elections to the Legislative Assembly were last held in November 2000, when all the candidates presented themselves as independents. After the election members of parliament formed the United Democratic Party.

Affluence is high, thanks to the considerable revenues derived from tourism, import duties and other fee incomes and the operations of the financial sector. Growth, however, has slowed in recent years while inflation has been rising and exceeds 3% per year. There are no taxes in the Cayman Islands: Government revenue comes from customs duties, stamp duty and annual fees levied on corporations. More than 75% of the economy is service-based, principally financial services and tourism. The number of registered companies is approaching 60,000. The figure represents one-and-a-half companies per person. The currency is often stronger than the US dollar, a factor which periodically impacts on the tourism sector.

Tourism is the main source of income in the Caymans, with a wide range of facilities on offer. Tourist revenues are also the primary source of funding for the country's development. The sector accounts for about three quarters of all economic activity and employs a third of the workforce. There were more than 100,000 visitors in a typical year but the number plummeted in 2001 and 2002. A majority of tourist arrivals (close to 70%) are passenger visits from cruise ships. Tourism, however, has reached its saturation point. The islands' financial services industry has been under constant pressure to stop money laundering and has imposed stringent new regulations. International offshore funds, attracted by a complete absence of income tax or other corporate taxes, are the driving force for growth in this sector. The Cayman Islands are the largest offshore banking centre in the world with 600 banks and deposits worth US$500 billion. It is the second largest captive insurance base after Bermuda, with assets worth $R 25511 billion. Mutual funds are a growing sector, especially since the opening of the Cayman Islands Stock Exchange in 1997.

All of the country's energy requirements are imported, with oil predominating. All electricity generation is derived from thermal stations.

Central African Republic

Capital City	Bangui	Capital population: 600,000 (1992)
Population ('000)	3,814 *(2002)*	
Urban population (%)	42.05 *(2002)*	
Land area (km²)	62298	
Languages	Sangho, French	
Religion	Traditional (60%), Christian (35%), Muslim (5%)	
Currency	CFA franc (CFAF)	
Head of State	President Francois Bozize (2003)	
Head of Government	Abel Boumba (2003)	
Ruling Party	Central African People's Liberation Party leads a four-party coalition.	

Main Urban Areas	Population
Bangui (capital)	600,000 (1992)

The Central African Republic is located in the geographic centre of the continent. It borders on Congo and the Democratic Republic of the Congo (formerly Zaire) in the south, Chad in the north, Sudan in the east and Cameroon in the west. Although there are important watercourses in the east of the country, much of the rest is semi-desert, and climatic conditions are dry tropical. The capital is Bangui.

Talks to restore multiparty democracy were held in 1993 and 1994 following the collapse of the "Grand National Debate" during 1992. Under the present version of the constitution the people elect the president for a six-year term. The National Assembly consists of 109 members, elected for a five-year term in three- and four-seat constituencies.

In presidential elections held in September 1999, Ange-Felix Patasse received 52% of the vote and was returned to office. The latest elections to the National Assembly took place in December 1998. The Central African People's Liberation Party took 47 seats with the remainder spread among several minor parties. After the coup in March 2003, Goumba was appointed prime minister.

Growth of GDP was 0.8% in 2002 and prices rose by 3.4%. In 2003, negative growth of -0.7% is expected while prices should rise by 3.2%. GDP is forecast to rise by another 5.8% in 2004 while prices are expected to increase by 1.7%. The authorities have managed to regain a measure of control over public finances. A key challenge facing the authorities is to raise revenue collection. The revenue ratio in the Central African Republic remains one of the lowest in sub-Saharan Africa and constrains the functioning of the central administration. The government has responded by implementing measures to strengthen tax and customs administrations and streamlining the tax system. The agenda for structural reform is focused on measures designed to improve economic efficiency and increase growth potential. A tiny domestic market prevents the development of many manufacturing operations and related activities. Other barriers to

development include the country's landlocked position, a poor transportation system, a largely unskilled workforce and a legacy of misdirected macroeconomic policies.

Subsistence agriculture, together with forestry, remains the backbone of the economy of the Central African Republic, with more than 70% of the population living in outlying areas. The agricultural sector generates about 55% of GDP. Cattle herding is the major activity, although cotton and coffee are other important commodities. The small industrial sector accounts for 20% of GDP. The main activities are sawmilling, breweries, textiles, footwear, and the assembly of bicycles and motorcycles. The privatisation of petroleum distribution has been completed and the national oil company was sold in 2001. Authorities hope to place the large public companies in the electricity and telecommunications sectors under private management and to divest or liquidate the remaining public enterprises. However, there has been little progress in the past year. Mining provides much of the impetus for the economy, with diamonds, gold, uranium, copper and manganese being extracted in the west of the country. In the late 1980s, the mineral sector provided half of GDP but its share has declined over the past 15 years.

The country has no domestic sources of energy, relying entirely on imports.

Chad

Capital City	N'Djaména	Capital population: 615,000 (1992)
Population ('000)	8,234 *(2002)*	
Urban population (%)	24.45 *(2002)*	
Land area (km²)	125920	
Languages	French and Arabic (official), some 25 others	
Religion	Muslim (50%), Christian (7%), traditional	
Currency	CFA franc (CFAF)	
Head of State	President Idriss Déby (2001)	
Head of Government	Haroun Kabadi (2002)	
Ruling Party	The Patriotic Salvation Movement (MPS) leads a three-party coalition.	

Main Urban Areas	Population
N'Djaména (capital)	615,000 (1992)

Chad, one of the largest and most sparsely populated countries in Africa, is located in central North Africa. Libya is to the north, Sudan to the east, and Niger and Cameroon to the west. The Central African Republic borders on the country's more fertile southern regions. The climate is dry tropical, with little rainfall. The capital is N'Djaména.

The president is elected for a five-year term by the people. The National Assembly has 155 members, elected for a four-year term in 25 single-member constituencies and 34 multi-member constituencies. The president can serve a maximum of two five-year terms in office.

Elections to the National Assembly took place in April 2002. The MPS won 102 seats, the Rally for Democracy and Progress took 12 seats and the remainder were scattered among several smaller parties. Elections for president occurred in May 2001 when Déby was easily re-elected with 63% of the vote.

Chad's economy grew impressively in 2002, with GDP increasing by 9.7%. Inflation was 5.2% in that year. In 2003, growth of 10.9% is expected with inflation of 4.3%. GDP is forecast to rise by an impressive 42.7% in 2004 while prices increase by 4%. The strong rate of growth was mainly because of the acceleration of the construction of the Chad-Cameroon pipeline. The overall fiscal deficit reached 16.2% of GDP in 2002, mainly due to the postponement of some foreign-financed investment and an increase in domestically financed investment expenditures. In 2003, the government has adopted a more restrictive fiscal stance as external budgetary support diminishes. The external current account deficit is projected to widen from 39% of GDP in 2001 to 46% of GDP in 2003. The upward trend is due to rising imports relating to the acceleration of investment related to various oil projects and a general increase in public investment. A large part of this deficit is financed by foreign direct investment. Various bodies to oversee oil revenues (which will begin in 2004) were also created in 2003. The purpose is to ensure that the use of these revenues will be transparent to all.

Chad's economy is dominated by the agricultural sector, which accounts for over 38% of GDP and employs roughly 80% of the population. Cotton, the major cash crop, accounts for 60% of Chad's exports. Cotton is grown in the south of the country, while cattle herding, the other main source of foreign revenues, is conducted in the central regions. Reform of the cotton industry is underway, despite the difficult financial situation of the state cotton company. The industrial sector accounts for only 13% of GDP. The major industries are simple ones such as textiles, meatpacking, beer brewing, soap, cigarettes and construction materials. Chad is rich in natural and mineral resources. Currently, only deposits of sodium carbonate and kaolin are utilised commercially. Deposits of other minerals have been discovered in Chad, including gold, bauxite, tin, tungsten, titanium, iron ore and petroleum. A consortium led by two US companies is investing $3.7 billion to develop oil reserves estimated at a billion barrels in southern Chad. The country has received financing from the World Bank for the project, plus a pipeline to transport the oil to the Cameroon coast. Oil exports are expected to begin in 2004.

With its large undeveloped oil reserves, Chad has the potential to become a significant energy producer. Development includes plans to drill up to 300 wells. Production is forecast to continue for 25-30 years, with peak production projected at 225,000 to 250,000 barrels per day. Construction is also underway on a 650-mile pipeline which will allow Chad to export 225,000 barrels per day of crude by the middle of the decade. The total cost of field development and construction of the pipeline and export facilities is estimated to be US$3.5 billion. Chad's downstream oil sector is currently totally dependent on petroleum product imports from neighbouring Nigeria and Cameroon.

Chile

Capital City	Santiago	Capital population: 4,931,600 (2002)
Population ('000)	15,496 (2002)	
Urban population (%)	85.35 (2002)	
Land area (km²)	74880	
Languages	Spanish	
Religion	Mainly Roman Catholic (85%)	
Currency	Chilean peso (CH$)	
Head of State	President Ricardo Lagos Escobar (2000)	
Head of Government	President Ricardo Lagos Escobar (2000)	
Ruling Party	The Christian Democratic Party leads a broad-based coalition of Parties for Democracy.	

Main Urban Areas	Population	
Santiago (capital)	4,931,600	(2002)
Puente Alto	473,200	(2002)
Concepcion	396,000	(2002)
Vina del Mar	355,200	(2002)
Talcahuano	295,200	(2002)
Valparaiso	288,800	(2002)
Temuco	286,000	(2002)
San Bernardo	265,000	(2002)
Antofagasta	264,400	(2002)
Rancagua	222,400	(2002)

Although never more than about 200km wide, Chile occupies the greater part of South America's Pacific coastline, with Argentina to its east over the Andes mountains and Peru and Bolivia to the north. In the south its Tierra del Fuego regions are sub-Antarctic in character. The extraordinary range of climatic conditions that result is one of the most striking features of the country. The capital is Santiago.

An executive president serves a six-year term. The National Congress has two chambers - a 48-member Senate and a 117-member Chamber of Deputies, elected for four years.

In presidential elections held in January 2000, Lagos took 51% of the vote. He defeated Joaquín Lavín Infante, who received 49%. Congressional elections were held in December 2001. The coalition led by Lagos took 51 seats while the Independent Democratic Union gained 35 seats. The remainder of the seats were dispersed among various other parties.

GDP grew by 2.1% in 2002 and growth of 3.3% is expected in 2003. In 2004, growth of 4.5% is forecast. Inflation was 2.5% in 2002. In 2003, prices are expected to rise by 3.4% and are forecast to rise by 3% in 2004. Chile has maintained a very open trade regime and has continued to reduce its external tariff rate, which is now down to 8%. Authorities recently intensified trade agreement negotiations with the US and have concluded an agreement with the EU. Despite progress in diversifying exports, copper still represents 47% of exports by value and will continue for some time yet to play a major role in generating export earnings. Although the share of non-traditional products in total exports has risen over time, there remain doubts about the ability of the current export structure (highly concentrated in natural resource-based products) to sustain high rates of growth over the medium and long term. With tighter fiscal controls, the combined public sector deficit narrowed moderately to less than 2% of GDP by the end of 2002. Despite general success, the country's level of unemployment remains high. Many analysts believe that it is important that the government do more in this area. Authorities are under pressure to ensure that any new labour market reform measures do not introduce rigidities that would limit the economy's ability to generate employment. There is much support for a policy of granting adjustments to the minimum wage where this will help to boost employment.

Despite frequent efforts to diversify, the mining sector remains the backbone of Chile's economy. Codelco, the giant state-owned copper firm, is the dominant firm but there are other large mining operations. The government is trying to redress Chile's dependence on copper and mining in general by channelling more capital into non-traditional areas such as seafood and wine. Manufacturing has faired well in recent years as the private sector took hold. Most firms are either small or of medium size but nevertheless have rapidly won new foreign markets, with processed fruits and vegetables and fine wines becoming important foreign-exchange earners. Chile's agricultural sector depends on livestock rearing in the plateau and extensive crop farming in the central region. Products such as tomato paste, wine, shoes and textiles are expected to benefit as the pattern of trade changes to reflect Chile's new associate membership in Mercosur. Chile has been privatising major government holdings since the 1970s. The last two major companies to remain under state control are the oil company, Empresa Nacional de Petróleo, and the copper company, Codelco, Chile's largest company. The degree of inequality in income distribution remains among the highest in Latin America. This attribute further restricts the size of the domestic market.

Chile is a small oil producer, with an output of only 14,000 barrels per day, and proven reserves of 150 million barrels. Domestic production is only 6% of total consumption. The country also has natural gas reserves of 3.5 trillion cubic feet. The energy sector is largely in private hands. Chile's electricity sector has served as a model for subsequent privatisations throughout the world and is improving its efficiency and reliability. The country has three refineries, the largest of which is undergoing a significant expansion, with numerous new facilities under construction.

China

Capital City	Beijing	Capital population: 12,606,000 (2002)
Population ('000)	1,293,934 (2002)	
Urban population (%)	32.98 (2002)	
Land area (km²)	932742	
Languages	Putonghua (Mandarin), Cantonese, Hakka, Amoy, Foochow and numerous other dialects	
Religion	Mainly Buddhism	
Currency	Renminbi (RMB)	
Head of State	President Hu Jintao (2003)	
Head of Government	Wen Jiabao (2003)	
Ruling Party	Chinese Communist Party.	

Main Urban Areas*	Population	
Chongqing	31,074,960	(2002)
Shanghai	13,203,660	(2002)
Beijing (capital)	12,606,000	(2002)
Chengdu	10,378,380	(2002)
Harbin	9,889,460	(2002)
Tianjin	9,233,360	(2002)
Wuhai	7,635,000	(2002)
Guangzhou	7,144,280	(2002)
Shenyang	6,902,300	(2002)
Nanjing	5,478,280	(2002)

*Counties under the jurisdiction of city governments are included

Occupying the entire 5,000-km spread from the Sea of Japan and the East China Sea in the east to the Afghan border in the west, China has one of the longest international boundaries in the world. In the north and northwest, its border is shared with Mongolia, Russia, Tajikistan, Kyrgyzstan and Kazakhstan. In the west, it meets Afghanistan and Pakistan, while India, Nepal, Bhutan, Myanmar, Laos and Vietnam lie to the south. The capital is Beijing.

China's 1992 constitution vests all legislative authority in the 3,000-member National People's Congress, which is elected every five years. The Congress, however, meets only once a year, and the Communist Party undertakes most political decisions.

In March 2003, Hu Jiontao was elected Premier, replacing Jiang Zemin. At the same time, Wen Jiabao, who was previously a vice-premier, was elevated to head of government, replacing Zhu Rongji.

China's rate of growth has been exceptionally high during the past decade but is now gradually falling. Real GDP rose by 8% in 2002 and was expected to increase by 7.5% in both 2003 and 2004. Prices fell by 0.8% in 2002 and are expected to recover by 0.8% in 2003. Inflation in 2004 is forecast to be 1.5%. Beginning in 2003, consumer spending has assumed a larger role in driving Chinese growth. In the past, spending by the central government has played that role. This shift is essential if Beijing is to realise its overriding goal to quadruple GDP to more than $4,000 billion by 2020. Growth slowed sharply in the second quarter of 2003 (falling to 6.7%), owing mostly to the effects of SARS. WTO accession has propelled foreign direct investment, which rose to a record $52.7 billion in 2002 and climbed by 57% to $13.1 billion in the first quarter of 2003 compared with the same period in 2002. China is coming under increasing pressure (especially from the US) to adjust its currency which is estimated to be more than 20% undervalued against the dollar. Analysts expect the government to eventually expand the trading range with the dollar, allowing it to vary within about 3.5 percentage points on either side of the current peg. The country's current-account surplus rose by 2.2% of GDP in 2002. Meanwhile, China's trade surplus soared to $50 billion, up from $30.3 billion in 2001. Exports rose by 19.6%, thanks in part to the country's undervalued currency. Based on official statistics, the urban registered unemployment rate rose from 3.6% in 2001 to 4.0% in 2002. If workers at state-owned enter-prises who had not been re-employed were included, the adjusted unemployment rate would have been more than 7%.

Despite a spring drought, agricultural performance improved slightly compared with the previous two years. Grain output, which dropped by 2.1% in 2001, rose by 1%. Although agriculture is no longer the dominant sector, the government gives farming a high priority. Over 900 million people live in rural China and their contentment is essential to national stability. Rice is the main food crop, but tea, sugar, cotton and fibre crops are all important cash earners. Industry (including construction) was the key engine of economic growth, with value added accelerating to 9.9% in 2002 from 8.7% in 2001. Electronic equipment, transportation equipment and chemical products all did well. A surge in FDI and export growth resulted in the value added of foreign-funded enterprises increasing by 13.3%. The service sector grew by 7.3% in 2002, thanks to a strong performance in transportation, telecommunications and real estate. The profitability of both private and state-owned enterprises has improved as a result of increased demand and reform measures such as debt-equity swaps. Selected parts of the manufacturing sector are performing particularly well. The frenetic desire to buy cars is a major reason for the brisk retail sales. Nearly, 440,000 cars were produced in China in the first quarter of 2003 as manufacturers raced to keep pace with sales that grew by 56% in 2002 to 1.13 million units. Steel sales have also risen sharply, in part to supply the car sector. Much of the boom in foreign investment that is flowing into the country is being lured by the partial liberalisation of investment regulations in various industries since Beijing joined the WTO. Retail sales rose by 8.8% in 2002 and the pace accelerated in the first quarter of 2003. Tourism, transport and catering have suffered during 2003 as a result of the outbreak of severe acute respiratory syndrome (SARS) in the early part of the year.

China is expected to surpass Japan as the second largest world oil consumer within the next decade and reach a consumption level of 10.9 million barrels per day by 2025, making it a major factor in the world oil market. Experts estimate that Beijing will have to import 40% of its oil by the 2010 - up from less than 20% today. China's petroleum industry has undergone major changes in recent years. In 1998, the Chinese government reorganised most state-owned oil and gas assets into two vertically integrated firms - the China National Petroleum Corporation (CNPC) and the China Petrochemical Corporation (Sinopec). This created two regionally focused firms, CNPC in the north and west, and Sinopec in the south, though CNPC is still tilted toward crude oil production and Sinopec toward refining. The intention of the restructuring was to make these state firms more like similar vertically integrated corporate entities elsewhere. Recent offshore oil exploration has identified fields believed to hold more than 1.5 billion barrels in reserves. With China's expectation of growing future dependence on oil imports, the country has been acquiring interests in exploration and production abroad. This includes oil concessions in Kazakhstan, Venezuela, Sudan, Iraq, Iran, and Peru, and Azerbaijan. Russia's Far East is seen as another potential source of Chinese crude oil imports.

◻ Colombia

Capital City	Bogotá	Capital population: 7,059,871 (2002)
Population ('000)	40,104 (2002)	
Urban population (%)	75.01 (2002)	
Land area (km²)	103870	
Languages	Spanish	
Religion	Roman Catholic (95%)	
Currency	Colombian peso (Col$)	
Head of State	President Alvaro Uribe Velez (2002)	
Head of Government	President Alvaro Uribe Velez (2002)	
Ruling Party	The government is formed by the Colombian Conservative Party (PCC), the Liberal Party of Colombia (PLC) and non-partisans.	

Main Urban Areas	Population	
Bogotá (capital)	7,059,871	(2002)
Cali	2,256,558	(2002)
Medellin	1,993,768	(2002)
Barranquilla	1,299,625	(2002)
Cartagena	883,876	(2002)
Cucuta	671,272	(2002)
Bucaramanga	568,205	(2002)
Ibaque'	408,909	(2002)
Santa Marta	401,318	(2002)
Pereira	396,275	(2002)

Colombia forms the geographical link between Central and South America. Meeting the Isthmus of Panama in the west, it is bordered on the south and east by Ecuador, Peru, Venezuela and Brazil, and has coastlines on both the Caribbean and the Pacific. Its climate is warm and temperate in the coastal strip, but arid in the inland plateau. The capital is Bogotá.

Colombia has an executive president who answers to a 102-member Senate and a House of Representatives with 161 elected members. Constitutional reform has been under way for many years, but in practice the issue has been repeatedly overshadowed by concerns about the eradication of the gangs who operate the drug trade.

In presidential elections held in May 2002, the independent candidate Alvaro Uribe Velez won in the first round 53% of the vote. The main other contender was Horacio Serpa of the Liberal Party who took 32% of the vote. Elections to the House were held in March 2002. The PLC won 54 seats followed by the PCC which took 21 seats. The remainder of the seats went to numerous smaller parties.

GDP grew by just 1.5% in 2002 and an increase of only 2% is forecast for 2003. In 2004, growth of 3.3% is forecast. Inflation was 6.3% in 2002 and an increase of 6.9% is expected in 2003. Inflation in 2004 is forecast to be 5.3%. In 2002, the economy suffered as a result of problems being experienced by other countries (mainly Argentina but also Brazil) in the region. To rein in fiscal imbalances, the government imposed an austere budget for 2003. In addition, it levied a one-off tax on net wealth, as well as introducing a package of other tax measures and structural reforms. The wealth tax, which will yield about 1% of GDP, will be used to help finance additional security needs. Net debt of the non-financial public sector increased from the equivalent of 38.8% of GDP in 1999 to 50.7% in 2002, partly because of the recent and especially sharp depreciation of the peso. The current account deficit was unchanged at about 1.8% of GDP in 2002. However, conditions in international capital markets have deteriorated sharply, leading to a fall in public and private capital inflows. In 2003, the government intends to

pursue additional reforms in the pension system including an increase in contribution rates and retirement ages. Exemptions to the income tax are expected to be phased out and an increase in the VAT will be proposed. In order to boost employment, the government intends to reduce overtime charges and severance payments. There are also plans to encourage the diversification of Colombia's exports, especially in view of the weak coffee prices and the continuing decline in oil production. Non-traditional exports have increased in importance in recent years to over 50 percent of total exports. They are expected to receive a further boost following the renewal and expansion of the Andean Trade Preferences Act, which widens significantly the duty free access of Colombian exports to the United States

Farming is the mainstay of the Colombian economy with production of coffee, sugar, bananas, cotton and meat. Coffee is grown by 400,000 farmers, mainly smallholders who employ a similar number of labourers. Agriculture accounts for about 20% of GDP, as does manufacturing. Manufacturing is concentrated around the cities of Medellin, Bogota, Cali and Barranquilla, and is dominated by large private conglomerates. These firms produce everything from soft drinks to glass, televisions and textiles. The manufacturing sector has been hit hard in recent years by high interest rates, a strong peso and moves towards trade liberalisation. Manufacturing's annual share of GDP has been falling for several years and this decline is expected to continue. Although mining-mainly coal and oil-accounts for just 5% of GDP, it is one of the country's most important export industries. Oil is Colombia's top export product (followed by coal and coffee), accounting for about 25% of government revenues. Coffee prices fell, however, with the advent of new, low-cost producers (for example, Vietnam and Brazil) and many Colombian farmers are losing money. The banking system has continued its recovery since the crisis of 1999, but weaknesses remain. The banks' operating environment has been strengthened significantly with the adoption of tighter regulations for loan-loss provisions, loan classification and capital adequacy, consistent with international best practices. Colombia has vast and still under-exploited reserves of minerals including coal and oil and deposits of gold, silver, copper, nickel, iron ore, platinum, bauxite, gypsum, limestone, phosphates, sulphur and uranium.

Colombia has about 1.75 billion barrels of proven oil reserves, down from 2001 estimates of 1.97 billion barrels. Potential oil reserves are much larger but estimates indicate that, without new discoveries, Colombia could become a net oil importer in the medium term. Oil and natural gas development is regulated by the state oil company (Ecopetrol) and the Energy and Mines Ministry. Private companies may operate in joint ventures with the state but Ecopetrol must have an interest of at least 30% in any project. Security problems continue to plague the Colombian oil industry. Oil production has failed to meet annual targets in recent years. In part, this is due to the mature nature of the largest producing fields. However, repeated industry infrastructure attacks have further reduced production.

◻ Comoros

Capital City	Moroni	Capital population: 22,000 (1992)
Population ('000)	765 (2002)	
Urban population (%)	34.22 (2002)	
Land area (km²)	223	
Languages	Arabic and French (official), Comoran	
Religion	Islam	
Currency	Comoros franc (KMF)	
Head of State	Azali Assoumani (2002)	
Head of Government	Azali Assoumani (2002)	
Ruling Party	Rassemblement National pour la Développement (RND).	

Main Urban Areas	Population
Moroni (capital)	22,000 (1992)

The Comoros are an archipelago of islands in the Indian Ocean, situated between Mozambique and the island of Madagascar. They retain both French and Islamic cultural traditions - with the latter becoming more important in recent years. The climate is tropical and many islands are heavily forested. The capital is Moroni.

The president is elected for a four-year term by the people. The Union of the Comoros has no federal parliament.

The presidential elections held in April 2002 were marred by violence and a boycott by two of the three candidates and one of the archipelago's three main islands. Assoumani polled more than 80% in the second round and was then declared elected. Parliament has been dissolved.

GDP grew by 2.5% in 2002, while inflation was 3.3%. In 2003, growth of 2.5% is again expected while prices also rise by 2.5%. Growth of 3% is forecast for 2004 while inflation is expected to be 2%. One of the world's poorest countries, the Comoros' three islands have inadequate transportation links, a young and rapidly increasing population, and few natural resources. The low educational level of the labour force contributes to a subsistence level of economic activity, high unemployment, and a heavy dependence on foreign grants and technical assistance. Per capita income in some parts of the county is only US$30 and unemployment is near 90%. The deficit in the balance of payments has been erased as a result of a large increase in private transfers from the Comorian community living abroad. Some progress had been made in strengthening tax administration but further efforts in this regard are essential. International donors have pledged money to help reduce the Comoros' high population growth rate but very little to improve the standard of living. The country remains highly dependent on its trade relationship with France, and its lack of self-sufficiency in food products is another source of concern. In years when the economy performs poorly, French aid accounts for around 35% of GDP.

Agriculture accounts for 40% of GDP, industry contributes 14% and services make up the remainder. Agriculture employs over 80% of the workforce, with most people engaged in subsistence farming. Farm production consists mainly of vanilla, cloves, perfume essences, copra, coconuts, bananas and cassava (tapioca). The sector's exports are primarily vanilla, cloves, perfume oil and copra. The country is not self- sufficient in food production; rice, the main staple, accounts for the bulk of imports. The Comoros has a large natural forest that offers substantial scope for timber exporting but is not developed. The industrial sector is largely limited to the processing of essential oils, but there are also a few factories making soft drinks, plastics and timber products.

All of the country's fuel requirements, apart from brushwood and similar fuels, are imported. A hydroelectric dam is under construction, and this should provide some degree of self-sufficiency in electricity.

◻ Congo, Democratic Republic

Capital City	Kinshasa	*Capital population: 4,214,000 (1995)*
Population ('000)	56,123 *(2002)*	
Urban population (%)	31.12 *(2002)*	
Land area (km²)	226705	
Languages	Bantu, Lingala, Kikongo, French	
Religion	Mainly Roman Catholic (55%); also traditional	
Currency	Congolese franc (CDF)	
Head of State	Joseph Kabila (2000)	
Head of Government	Joseph Kabila (2000)	
Ruling Party	All political parties have been dissolved.	

Main Urban Areas	**Population**
Kinshasa (capital)	4,214,000 (1995)

The Democratic Republic of the Congo, formerly known as Zaire, is the largest country in Central Africa. Its boundaries extend from the Central African Republic and Sudan in the north to Zambia and Angola in the south, with Tanzania, Uganda and the tiny states of Rwanda and Burundi to the east and Congo to the west. Despite its size, it has only one coastal access, a channel running to the Atlantic between Congo and Angola. The terrain ranges from the vast plains of the north and far south to the dry Zaire River valley in the west. The capital is Kinshasa.

Until the AFDL's takeover in 1997, the then Zaire had a nominally executive president who was elected for a seven-year term by universal vote along with a 310-member Legislative Council (Parliament). The president was the de facto head of the ruling party. This system was scrapped when Mobutu Sese Seko seized power in 1972. When Mobutu's health failed, he lost influence and was replaced by Laurent Kabila, who was assassinated in 2000 and replaced by his son, Joseph. Kabila Sr. appointed a 300 member Assembly in 2000.

Legislative elections have not been held since September 1987. Upon gaining power, Kabila committed himself to new elections but there now appears to be little chance that the regime will allow a vote.

The Congo experienced a recovery in 2002 with growth of 3%. In 2003, growth of 5% is expected. GDP is forecast to rise by 6% in 2004. Prices rose by 31.5% in 2002 and are expected to rise by another 9.1% in 2003. Inflation in 2004 is forecast to be 6%. With much international help, the government has succeeded in stabilising the macroeconomic situation but the country's encouraging growth prospects will still depend heavily on maintaining the uneasy peace. A number of structural policies have been put in place including the unification of multiple exchange rates and the liberalisation of prices. There has also been a profound change in the judicial and regulatory environment so as to create an institutional framework propitious for private sector-led growth. The external current account balance, including grants and after debt relief, went from a deficit in 2001 into a small surplus in 2002, mainly as a result of an upturn in diamond exports. The central bank's dubious practice of lending to the government has been discontinued but the bank continues to finance government expenditure that has not been authorised by the Ministry of Finance, in violation of a presidential decree in 2002.

Farming, which is carried out mainly on a subsistence basis, continues to be the dominant sector. The sector accounts for about 55% of GDP. Oil palms, coffee, rubber, cocoa and timber are grown for export, while cassava, cereals, fruit and tobacco are grown for the domestic market. However, present levels of production remain below the pre-war levels. Industry makes up only 9% of GDP. The country's key industries - copper and cobalt mining and diamond extraction - were nearly destroyed during the war. Copper prices remain depressed but there is considerable optimism about a turnaround. Foreign businesses have curtailed operations due to uncertainty about the possible resumption of the conflict, lack of infrastructure, and the difficult operating environment. The war has intensified the impact of such basic problems as an uncertain legal framework, corruption, and lack of openness in government economic policy and financial operations. The government has made some progress in implementing reforms, however. The country's diamond export monopoly was abolished in 2001 and the industry's export earnings have risen sharply in the past two years. A new, investor-friendly mining law has also been drafted. A number of small and medium-sized companies have reopened since the end of the war. The country's large informal economy is already thriving.

The Democratic Congo has a limited amount of proven oil reserves located offshore, and some gas. There are expectations that more reserves could be located but the country's problems and its desperate economic situation deters investors.

◻ Congo-Brazzaville

Capital City	Brazzaville	*Capital population: 1,009,000 (1995)*
Population ('000)	3,029 *(2002)*	
Urban population (%)	63.59 *(2002)*	
Land area (km²)	34150	
Languages	French	
Religion	traditional (50%), Roman Catholic (40%)	
Currency	CFA franc (CFAF)	
Head of State	Denis Sassou-Nguesso (1997)	
Head of Government	Denis Sassou-Nguesso (1997)	
Ruling Party	Congolese Labour Party (PCT)	

Main Urban Areas	**Population**
Brazzaville (capital)	1,009,000 (1995)

Congo is a long triangle of land, dominated by tropical forest, which follows the Congo River south from Cameroon and the Central African Republic, between Gabon and the Democratic Republic of the Congo (formerly Zaire), to meet the sea just north of Angola. The climate is hot and humid. The capital is Brazzaville.

The constitution calls for the president to be elected for a five-year term by the people. The National Assembly consists of 153 members, elected for a five-year term in single-seat constituencies. The Senate had 66 members, elected partially every two years for a six-year term by district, local and regional councils.

In presidential elections held in March 2002, Denis Sassou-Nguesso was re-elected with 89% of the vote. Elections to the National Assembly were held in June 2002. The PCT 53 seats, the United Democratic Forces won 30 seats and the remainder were divided among more than 30 other parties.

GDP rose by 3.5% in 2002 and prices rose by 4.6%. In 2003, GDP is expected to increase by around 2% while prices also increase by about 2%. Growth of 7% is forecast for 2004 along with further inflation of 2%. Congo's business and administrative infrastructure was badly damaged during the country's two recent civil wars, increasing the petroleum sector's dominance of the economy (since oil production was not directly harmed by the fighting). Economic activity was further hampered by the fact that nearly 30% of the population fled their homes during the 1998-1999 conflict. In return for international loans, the government has committed itself to improve the management of its fiscal balance and external arrears (ie by reducing fraud in the customs area), and to reduce cost overruns for civil service salaries. In general, priorities for Congo in the next few years include structural reform (in the banking sector, for instance) and macroeconomic stabilisation. The country still operates under a heavy debt burden, amounting to more than 150% of GDP.

Congo's economy consists mainly of village agriculture, an urban informal sector (unregulated business, commerce and service activities), and an industrial sector dominated by oil and oil-related services. Since the 1980s, the oil industry has provided the major share of government revenues and exports, replacing timber production and exports as the main source of growth. Oil accounts for over 50% of Congo's real GDP, 60-80% of the government budget and about 90% of Congo's export earnings. Oil exports grew sharply, from approximately US$820 million in 1994 to around US$2.5 billion in 2001. Agriculture accounts for only about 10% of GDP and is poorly developed with less than 1% of the land area under cultivation. Most farming involves the cultivation of subsistence crops such as cassava, yams, groundnuts and manioc. Coffee, cocoa, sugar and tobacco are grown for export. The industrial sector makes up another 48% of GDP. There is considerable scope for further development of mineral extraction operations but investors are hesitant.

Congo is sub-Saharan Africa's fourth largest oil producer (after Nigeria, Angola and Gabon), with estimated proven reserves of 1.5 billion barrels. The majority of Congo's crude production is located offshore and is heavily reliant on foreign personnel and technology. Congo's crude production has nearly doubled since 1988 and annual output now is about 265,000 barrels per day. Roughly one-third of this oil goes directly to the government and is sold on the state's behalf. New offshore oil fields are being developed at a cost of US$135 million. The new fields have reserves of 180 million barrels and are expected to be in production by 2004. The Congo also has at least 3.2 trillion cubic feet of natural gas reserves, making it the third largest oil and second largest natural gas source in sub-Saharan Africa. At present, however, all of this natural gas output is vented or flared because of a lack of infrastructure. The government plans to reduce this by utilising the natural gas for electric power production over the next several years.

▫ Costa Rica

Capital City	San José	Capital population: 1,220,412 (1996)
Population ('000)	3,908 (2002)	
Urban population (%)	48.32 (2002)	
Land area (km²)	5106	
Languages	Spanish	
Religion	Roman Catholic	
Currency	Colón (CRC)	
Head of State	Abel Pacheco de la Espriella (2002)	
Head of Government	Abel Pacheco de la Espriella (2002)	
Ruling Party	Christian Social Unity Party (PUSC)	

Main Urban Areas	Population
San José (capital)	1,220,412 (1996)

Costa Rica meets the Isthmus of Panama at its northern extreme. Nicaragua lies to the north. The country has coasts facing both the Caribbean and the Pacific. However, its coastal lowlands are too humid for intensive development while its upland plains have a pleasant climate. The capital is San José.

Costa Rica has an executive president elected by universal suffrage for a term of four years. He is answerable to the 57-member Legislative Assembly, also elected for four years. The president is assisted by two vice presidents and appoints the Cabinet personally.

In parliamentary elections held in February 2002, the conservative PUSC became the largest party winning 19 seats. The social/democratic National Liberation Party received 17 seats and the Citizens' Action Party claimed 14 seats. Presidential elections held in February and April 2002 led to a victory for the conservative candidate Abel Pacheco de la Espriella.

GDP grew by 2.8% in 2002, while prices rose by 9.2%. In 2003, GDP should increase by 3% while inflation is 10.5%. Growth of 2.5% is forecast for 2004 and inflation should be 10%. Since 2000, economic growth has slowed, inflation has remained high, and unemployment has not fallen below 6%. The external current account deficit has increased to about 5.5% of GDP, reflecting a sharp increase in imports of capital goods by public enterprises, and a loss of dynamism of exports. Behind this deterioration is a loss of competitive strength. Net official international reserves are no more than 2.5 months of imports Tax revenues total just 12% of GDP and the public debt is on the rise. To correct the situation, the government proposes to tax income earned abroad, levy the sales tax on services as well as goods, and introduce a single form for income tax. The goal is to raise tax revenue by 1% per year. Progress in other areas of structural reform has also slowed in recent years. In particular, the privatisation process lost dynamism following the failure in 2000 of efforts to several key industries. A ceiling has been placed on nominal growth in discretionary government expenditures for 2003, and limits placed on public enterprise wage and investment spending. The authorities are facing strong resistance in implementing some of these measures, but they still hope to achieve an important reduction of the fiscal deficit in 2003. The benefits of growth are spread very unevenly across the economy. One result is that the number of families in extreme poverty continues to rise.

Costa Rica's economy relies largely on its agricultural sector, with coffee, bananas, sugar, cut flowers and cattle being exported. The country is the world's second largest exporter of bananas. Agriculture accounts for 11% of GDP and employs nearly half the work force. Cocoa, rice, maize, cassava, ginger, melons, pineapples and flowers are produced for domestic consumption. There has been some progress in agricultural diversification and farm exports have been increasing rapidly. Industry accounts for 37% of GDP but many of the country's traditional industries are still publicly owned. Efforts to develop private sector initiatives in the telecommunications sector and other key fields dominated by large public enterprises have been stymied. There is also a need to strengthen the health of the financial sector. There are weaknesses in prudential regulations as well as risk and liquidity management, while bank supervision, especially of the large offshore banking system, must be strengthened further. Returns on FDI, which had been significant in the past, are lower owing to the drop in the profits of high-technology industries.

Costa Rica needs an estimated US$3 billion of investment in its power sector by 2011, and demand is forecast to grow by 10% annually. Approximately 80% of the population has access to electricity. Nearly 90% of Costa Rica's electricity is generated by hydroelectric plants. The country's electricity sector is dominated by the state-owned electricity monopoly. Numerous new hydropower plants are being developed

▫ Côte d'Ivoire

Capital City	Yamoussoukro	Capital population: 2,797,000 (1995)
Population ('000)	15,767 (2002)	
Urban population (%)	47.39 (2002)	
Land area (km²)	31800	
Languages	French	
Religion	Muslim (23%), Christian (12%), traditional	
Currency	CFA franc (CFAF)	
Head of State	Laurent Gbagbo (2000)	
Head of Government	Seydou Diarra (2003)	
Ruling Party	The government is formed by a three-party coalition led by the Ivorian People's Front (FPI).	

Main Urban Areas	Population
Yamoussoukro (capital)	2,797,000 (1995)

Côte d'Ivoire is located on the Atlantic coast of West Africa, with a short coastal stretch facing southward into the Gulf of Guinea. Inland, the country broadens out considerably to meet Guinea, Burkina Faso and Mali in the north, Ghana in the east and Liberia in the west. The climate is tropical and humid, but a rich soil means that agriculture is strong. The capital isernment is Yamoussoukro.

Côte d'Ivoire, the former Ivory Coast, became fully independent from France in 1960. The executive president exercises a large degree of power and is elected for five years by universal suffrage. Legislative authority is vested in the 225-member National Assembly, which is also elected for five years.

In February 2003, Diarra was sworn in as Prime Minister at the Paris Peace Conference and will form a new government. Presidential elections were held in October 2000 when Gbagbo defeated General Robert Gueri with 59% of the vote. Gueri had, in 1999, seized power from Felix Houphouet-Boigny, who had led the country for three decades. Elections to the National Assembly were held in January 2001. The FPI took 96 seats, the Democratic Party of Ivory Coast won 94 seats and the remainder were divided among several parties.

GDP declined by 1.8% in 2002 and a contraction of 3% is expected in 2003. In 2004, GDP is forecast to grow by 3%. Such a high rate now seems highly unlikely, however, in view of the recent civil war. Inflation was 3.1% in 2002 and will be about 3.5% in 2003. Prices are forecast to rise by 2.9% in 2004. The government recently came close to defaulting on its external debt just before the civil war broke out. As the situation gradually improves, officials hope to stabilise the current account deficit (including official transfers) at about 1% of GDP by 2004. Steps are also planned to boost domestic saving and to increase domestic investment, which had fallen to less than 10% of GDP. These moves are all part of an internationally-led initiative to create a business environment in which private enterprise can flourish. With the help of international aid, an increase in public investment is anticipated to rehabilitate the country's infrastructure and to launch new projects in the social sector. The country's programme of privatisation has faltered owing to mismanagement and a lack of investor interest.

Côte d'Ivoire's economy is heavily reliant on agriculture Together, agriculture, forestry and fisheries account for over one third of GDP and two thirds of exports. Côte d'Ivoire produces 35-40% of the world's cocoa crop every year, and is a major exporter of bananas, coffee, cotton, palm oil, pineapples, rubber, tropical wood products and tuna. However, a fall in cocoa prices and the growing pressure of more people on the land have caused serious problems in agriculture. Measures to diversify the economy, including the introduction of non-traditional cash crops and expansion of the industrial sector, have not met with much success. Manufacturing consists mainly of the processing of agricultural raw materials, with textiles, matting, carpets, footwear and leather goods being major activities. Private sector development continues to fall short of expectations and further liberalisation of the coffee sector is badly needed.

Côte d'Ivoire contains an estimated 100 million barrels of recoverable oil reserves, with offshore reserves first discovered in the 1970s. Offshore oil discoveries in Ghanaian waters in the past two years have raised hopes that the oil-bearing structures continue into Ivorian waters Natural gas reserves in Cote d'Ivoire have recently have begun to be developed. Current estimates of Cote d'Ivoire's recoverable natural gas reserves stand at 1.1 trillion cubic feet. Over the next four years, the government estimates that natural gas consumption will grow by 50%. Natural gas production is expected to average 35 million cubic feet per day over 20 years. Côte d'Ivoire is self-sufficient in producing refined petroleum products and is a major supplier to the West African region.

◻ Cuba

Capital City	Havana	Capital population: 2,241,000 (1995)
Population ('000)	11,257 (2002)	
Urban population (%)	75.6 (2002)	
Land area (km²)	10982	
Languages	Spanish	
Religion	Mainly Roman Catholic	
Currency	Cuban peso (Cu$)	
Head of State	President Fidel Castro Ruz (1976)	
Head of Government	President Fidel Castro Ruz	
Ruling Party	Communist Party of Cuba	

Main Urban Areas	Population
Havana (capital)	2,241,000 (1995)

◻ Djibouti

Capital City	Djibouti	Capital population: 310,000 (1992)
Population ('000)	669 (2002)	
Urban population (%)	83.67 (2002)	
Land area (km²)	2318	
Languages	Arabi,C French	
Religion	Islam	
Currency	Djibouti franc (DJF)	
Head of State	President Ismail Omasr Guelleh (1999)	
Head of Government	Dileita Mohamed Dileita (2001)	
Ruling Party	Rassemblement Populaire pour le Progress (RPP)	

Main Urban Areas	Population
Djibouti (capital)	310,000 (1992)

The Republic of Cuba is an archipelago that includes Cuba, the largest island in the Caribbean. Extending more than 800km from east to west, the country lies just 145km south of the Florida coast. Its proximity has drawn the ire of successive US administrations - on account of both its communist ideology and the thousands of refugees who seek sanctuary in the US. The capital is Havana.

The National Assembly of People's Power has 601 members, elected for a five-year term out of the list of the Communist Party of Cuba (PCC). However, most of the power is vested in the Council of Ministers, which is the highest executive body in the country. The Executive Committee of the Council makes most of the decisions and the president of the country is the chairman of the Executive Committee.

In January 2003, Castro was re-elected by the National Assembly of Popular Power (Parliament) for another five years as president. In accordance with tradition, delegates to the National Assembly itself were appointed by the country's 14 provincial assemblies.

After a brief spurt of growth in the late 1990s, Cuba's economy is once again in trouble. The government forecasts growth of just 1.5% in 2003 after growth of 1.1% in 2002. The economy has undergone a substantial restructuring in the past decade. In 1990, more than 90% of Cuba's foreign exchange came from sugar sales to the Soviet Union, which provided the island with generously priced oil supplies in return. Today, tourism accounts for around 50% of Cuba's foreign exchange earnings and the country produces 50%of the oil it consumes. Nickel is the island's main export. Tourism is improving and nickel prices are strong but a serious shortage of foreign exchange persists. Public transportation has noticeably declined and power outages increased, while many Cubans remain hard pressed to meet their basic food, clothing and other needs. Dollarisation has created a massive gulf in Cuban society. Approximately 50% of the population have access to foreign currency - mainly through remittances or self-employment but also through tourism and hard currency incentive schemes for workers. The result is a growing inequality which undermines the country's social cohesion. Havana continues to maintain its spending on health and education and the country retains its position as a leader in social fields with one of the lowest rates of poverty and illiteracy on the continent.

Tourism, the country's main foreign currency earner and the hope of so many government officials, was down by around 25% in 2002 but is making a strong recovery in 2003. Through April of 2003, the number of visitors is up by 19% over 2002 and 2% over the number in the same period in 2001, which was a record year. Most visitors come from the EU and Canada. Cuba's biggest employer, the sugar industry, is suffering as world prices stay low. Sugar production is 2003 is expected to be down by 40% over the level in 2002. Castro agreed to close half the country's inefficient sugar mills in 2002 but the country is still the world's fourth largest sugar producer. The government is desperately seeking foreign investment but the inflows have failed to make up for the steady deterioration of Cuba's infrastructure that followed the Soviet collapse. The informal economy (which is made up of small-time private entrepreneurs, both legal and clandestine) is now so extensive that it threatens to undermine efforts to bolster efficiency in the formal state sector. The manufacturing sector is starved of cash with many state-owned firms operating at far less than full capacity (but fully staffed). Havana claims that the percentage of state companies that are not profitable fell sharply over the past several years but foreign analysts dismiss these claims.

Cuba has about 750 million barrels of crude oil reserves and produces about 42,000 barrels per day. Reserves of natural gas are estimated to be around 2,500 billion cubic feet. The country also generates significant amounts of power from renewable sources (geothermal, solar, wind, wood and waste). There are four refineries in the country with a combined capacity of just over 300,000 barrels per day. Most domestic production consists of heavy oil whose sulphur content is so high that it can only be used for converted power and cement plants. Refineries process imported crude oil, mainly from Venezuela and Mexico. The US maintains an economic embargo against Cuba, and oil companies from other countries may be subject to US sanctions.

The Republic of Djibouti is a tiny country on the northeast African approach from the Indian Ocean to the Red Sea (the so-called Horn of Africa). It is bounded in the north, west and southwest by Eritrea and Ethiopia, and in the southeast by Somalia. Across the Gulf of Aden it faces the Republic of Yemen. The capital is Djibouti.

Djibouti became independent from France in 1977. The president is elected by popular vote for a six-year term. There is a National Assembly of 65 members, elected for five-year terms in multi-seat constituencies.

Elections to the National Assembly took place in January 2003. The RPP and the Front pour la Restauration de l'Unité et de la Démocratie (FRUD) won 63% of the vote and claimed all the seats in the Assembly. Presidential elections took place in April 1999 when Guelleh received 74% of the vote, defeating Moussa Ahmed Iddris.

GDP grew by 2.6% in 2002 while inflation was 0.6%. In 2003, growth of 3% is expected while inflation should be 2%. Growth of 3.1% is forecast for 2004 with prices rising by 2%. Per capita incomes have been falling in recent years because of recession, civil war and a high population growth rate (including immigrants and refugees). Unemployment is a very serious problem - as much as 40-50% of the workforce is without a job. The government deficit continues to grow, owing mainly to a shortfall in revenues. In 2002, authorities undertook a comprehensive programme of budgetary reforms. The income tax was unified and simplified, and new legal instruments for collecting taxes were established. The government has also settled all arrears on its external debt to both multilateral and bilateral creditors. A privatisation programme is underway but progress has been slow. Foreign assistance is a major source of income and an important supplement to GDP. These funds help Djibouti support its balance of payments and to finance development projects.

The economic recovery in Djibouti is being driven by the service sector, which benefited from the sizeable foreign military contingents stationed in Djibouti as part of the fight against international terrorism and by a rebound in the construction sector. The competitive advantage of the service sector is the country's strategic location and status as a free trade zone in northeast Africa. Much of Djibouti's income derives from its port facilities and its strategic position in the approaches to the Red Sea. The country provides services as both a transit port for the region and an international transhipment and refuelling centre. The management of the Djibouti international airport was privatised in 2002 and is now being operated by the same group that manages the Djibouti port. Agriculture accounts for a meagre 2% of GDP. Two thirds of the inhabitants live in the capital city, the remainder being mostly herders. Scanty rainfall limits crop production to fruits and vegetables. Owing mainly to the poor climate and the nomadic lifestyle of rural inhabitants, 95% of all food requirements are imported. Djibouti has few natural resources and industry represents no more than 20% of GDP. Djibouti has a substantial construction sector that feeds a large cement industry. Smaller industries that are being encouraged include water bottling, tanning, paint processing and meat processing. There are some mineral deposits, mainly copper, gypsum and sulphur, but these are not mined commercially. More important has been the discovery of an offshore gas field.

There is currently no upstream (exploration or production) oil activity in Djibouti. However, the downstream oil sector is an important aspect of Djibouti's economy, given the role the capital city plays as a significant regional bunkering and refuelling facility. Total storage capacity at the port facility is 1.26 million barrels (200,000 cubic metres). There are plans to increase Djibouti's handling capacity from 125,000 metric tonnes to 300,000 metric tonnes per year, and to make it the leading transhipment point on the African continent. Planned port expansion and modernisation will also entail an upgrade to the petroleum receiving and storage facilities. Djibouti currently has installed electricity generating capacity of 85 megawatts (MW), all of which is oil-fired. There are plans to boost capacity to 100 MW by 2015.

□ Dominica

Capital City	Roseau	*Capital population: 16,535 (1991)*
Population ('000)	71 *(2002)*	
Urban population (%)	71.58 *(2002)*	
Land area (km²)	75	
Languages	English	
Religion	Mainly Roman Catholic	
Currency	East Caribbean dollar (EC$)	
Head of State	President Vernon Shaw (1998)	
Head of Government	Rosie Douglas (2000)	
Ruling Party	The government is formed by the Dominica Labour Party (DLP) and the Dominica Freedom Party (DFP).	

Main Urban Areas	**Population**
Roseau (capital)	16,535 (1991)

□ Dominican Republic

Capital City	Santo Domingo	*Capital population: 2,580,000 (1995)*
Population ('000)	8,688 *(2002)*	
Urban population (%)	65.98 *(2002)*	
Land area (km²)	4838	
Languages	Spanish	
Religion	Roman Catholic (80%)	
Currency	Dominican Republic peso (Do$)	
Head of State	President Hipolito Mejia (2000)	
Head of Government	President Hipolito Mejia (2000)	
Ruling Party	Dominican Revolutionary Party (PRD)	

Main Urban Areas	**Population**
Santo Domingo (capital)	2,580,000 (1995)
Santiago	1,007,000 (1995)

Dominica forms part of the Lesser Antilles, in the Windward Islands group, lying between Guadeloupe and Martinique. Its volcanic soil is very fertile and its climate is generally equable, although subject to hurricanes. The capital is Roseau.

Dominica, an independent republic within the Commonwealth, is formally ruled by an executive president, who in practice hands most of his legislative authority to the prime minister and her cabinet. There is a unicameral House of Assembly with 32 members. They include 21 members elected for a five-year term in single-seat constituencies, nine appointed senators, the Speaker and one ex-officio member. The House then elects the president, for a maximum of two five-year terms.

Elections were held in January 2000 to the House of Assembly. The United Workers' Party (UWP) took 43% of the vote and nine seats in the Assembly. The DLP won 43% of the vote and ten seats while the DFP received 14% of the vote and two seats. The parliament elected Vernon Shaw as president in 1998.

The Dominican economy contracted by 3.6% in 2002 and is expected to decline by another 1% in 2003. Growth of just 0.5% is forecast for 2004. Prices rose by just 0.2% in 2002 and are expected to rise by 0.5% in 2003. Inflation is forecast to be 1.5% in 2004. The sluggish economic performance is attributed to retrenchment of the banana industry and a slowdown in tourism receipts. As the economy has worsened, the island's public finances have deteriorated. Capital expenditures have increased sharply, while saving has been declining. The deficit of the public sector almost quadrupled since 1999, reaching 12.5% of GDP in 2002. The public sector's serious cash shortage is the main impediment to output and employment growth, and poses a threat to economic stability. Unemployment has risen in recent years and is estimated to exceed 25%. A tight public expenditure policy is crucial to support fiscal consolidation. Officials have acknowledged the need to implement a prudent government wage policy and, in the medium term, to put in place a wage policy based on performance and productivity gains. Many of the economy's problems stem from low levels of public investment in infrastructure, structural impediments which prevent economic diversification and the adverse effects of a series of natural calamities such as hurricanes, droughts and windstorms.

Dominica's fertile volcanic soil provides ample opportunity for the development of an excellent agricultural industry. Agriculture accounts for almost 30% of GDP and employs 40% of the labour force. The main agricultural product is bananas although limes, oranges, grapefruit, copra and bay oil are also produced for export. Dominica exports 25-35 tonnes of bananas in a year and this is the main earner of foreign exchange. Banana production began to recover in the latter half of 2002 following a drought. Output for the year, however, was below the level in 2001. Dominica relies on the EU to pay grants equal to almost 2% of GDP a year until 2004 to help its banana farmers switch to other crops. Construction activity declined in 2002, due mainly to the completion of several public sector projects. Tourism, although growing fast, is less developed than in other Caribbean states. The problem is due partly to the poor provision of roads, airports and other infrastructure facilities, and partly to the fact that nearly all beaches comprise black volcanic sand. The number of tourists fell by nearly 30% in 2002. Most industrial enterprises are geared to the processing of agricultural raw materials: rum manufacture is a major activity. There are also fruit canning plants, tobacco processing sheds and plants making soap and other light products. The financial sector remains under pressure from OECD and other international sources. The authorities have taken steps to prevent money laundering, but more initiatives are demanded on outstanding issues.

Dominica imports all of its fuel requirements, with oil and gas predominating. Just over half of its electricity derives from hydroelectric schemes, with thermal stations providing the rest.

The Dominican Republic lies in the Greater Antilles, north of Venezuela. It occupies the eastern half of the island of Hispaniola, with the state of Haiti in the west. The climate is equable, although often humid at sea level, and the soil is adequate for agriculture. The capital is Santo Domingo.

The Dominican Republic has an executive president who is elected for a four-year term by parliament. Parliament has two chambers. The Chamber of Deputies has 150 members, elected for four-year terms by proportional representation in each of the provinces. The Senate has 32 members, elected for a four-year term in single-seat constituencies. The country consists of 26 provinces, each of which is run by an appointed governor, and the National District around the capital Santo Domingo.

Presidential elections were held in May 2000 when Hipolito Mejia defeated two other candidates with 50% of the vote. Parliamentary elections were last held in May 2002. The PRD won 73 seats in the Chamber of Deputies and 29 in the Senate. The other parliamentary parties are the centrist Dominican Liberation Party (41 seats in the Chamber and two in the Senate) and the conservative Social Christian Reformist Party (36 seats in the Chamber and one in the Senate).

GDP increased by 4.1% in 2002, but negative growth of up to -3% is expected to be registered in 2003. In 2004, growth of 0.5% is forecast. Inflation was 5.2% in 2002 and is expected to rise to around 26.1% in 2003. Prices are forecast to rise by 20.1% in 2004. In recent years, the economy has suffered severely from the slowdown in the US and Europe and the consequences of the terrorist attacks. These shocks broadly coincided with the introduction of a package of fiscal measures, which had been designed in response to an overheating of the economy. The net effect of the fiscal reform was minimal as spending on social services had to be increased. Falling oil prices led to some narrowing of the current account deficit but this was partly offset by a fall in export and tourism receipts (as a result of the external shocks). Rural and urban poverty remains widespread and the benefits of economic growth are not enjoyed by many. The Dominican Republic's economy is closely tied with that of the US. The island is the US's seventh largest export market in the Western Hemisphere and a major destination for US foreign direct investments.

Agriculture accounts for 11% of GDP, industry contributes 34% and services make up the remainder. Although the country has long been viewed primarily as an exporter of sugar, coffee and tobacco, in recent years the services sector overtook agriculture as the economy's largest employer, due to growth in tourism and free-trade zones. In 2002, growth was supported by rising investment, including substantial foreign direct investment in the electricity, telecommunications, free-trade-zone, and tourism sectors The Dominican Republic suffers from marked income inequality; the poorest half of the population receives less than 20% of GNP, while the richest 10% enjoys 40% of national income. The country receives more tourists each year than any other Caribbean holiday destination, but like other destinations, it suffered a sharp drop in arrivals after 11 September 2001. The island has made a determined start in its privatisation programme. A top reform priority is now the electricity sector, where high costs and complex financial arrangements are having negative effects on the rest of the economy.

The Dominican Republic has sought to alleviate chronic electricity shortages by buying power from private producers and also by privatising selected power plants. Still power cuts remain a problem for businesses and the general population. Power demand is growing at about 7% per year and already outstrips supply. One reason is that droughts have periodically reduced hydroelectric power available from dams. Another is that private generators have taken about 300 MW out of production because of non-payment by the government - the current debt owed to them is about $100 million. The Dominican Republic, along with Barbados, Haiti and Jamaica is party to the San Jose pact, under which Mexico and Venezuela supply crude oil and refined products on favourable terms. Small deposits of crude oil have been located at Chaco Largo, but the country remains dependent on oil imports for most of its energy needs and all of its electricity generating requirements.

◘ Ecuador

Capital City	Quito	Capital population: 1,738,064 (2002)
Population ('000)	13,112 (2002)	
Urban population (%)	66.76 (2002)	
Land area (km²)	27684	
Languages	Spanish (also Quechua Indian)	
Religion	Roman Catholic (80%)	
Currency	Sucre (S)	
Head of State	Lucio Edwin Gutierrez Borbua (2003)	
Head of Government	Lucio Edwin Gutierrez Borbua (2003)	
Ruling Party	The National Pachakutik United Movement - New Country (MUPP-NP) leads a coalition.	

Main Urban Areas	Population
Guayaquil	2,340,863 (2002)
Quito (capital)	1,738,064 (2002)
Cuenca	298,637 (2002)
Machala	233,952 (2002)
Santo Domingo de los Colorados	222,656 (2002)
Portoviejo	204,790 (2002)
Ambato	177,636 (2002)
Manta	175,249 (2002)
Quevedo	143,678 (2002)
Milagro	132,622 (2002)

Ecuador lies on the western (Pacific) coast of South America, where it is bordered in the north and east by Colombia and in the south and east by Peru. The republic also includes the territory covered by the Galapagos Islands, about 1,000km off the coast. The country has some of the highest mountains in South America, peaking at over 6,000 metres, and is extensively forested - although the coastal regions are often damp and humid. The capital is Quito.

Ecuador has an executive president who is chosen by universal suffrage for a single, non-renewable four-year term and appoints his own cabinet. The president is answerable to the National Congress which has 100 members elected for a five-year term.

In elections held in October 2002, Gutierrez won 58.7% of the vote for president, defeating Alvaro Noboa who took 41.3% of the vote. Noboa had previously held the office after a coup. Parliamentary elections were also held in October 2002 when the Social-Christian Party won 24 seats in Congress, the Ecuadorian Populist Party took 15, the Party of the Democratic Left won 13, the Institutional Renewal Party of National Action received 10, the MUPP-NP captured five and the remainder were spread among other small parties.

Ecuador's GDP increased by 3.4% in 2002 and growth of 3.1% is anticipated in 2003. A growth rate of 5% is forecast for 2004. Inflation was 12.5% in 2002 but will fall to around 8.2% in 2003. Prices are forecast to rise by 4.4% in 2004. Unemployment remains relatively high, however, at around 15%, and around 70% of the country's population is considered poor. In addition, the country has a very high debt-to-GDP ratio of around 78%. In December 2001, the IMF disbursed the final $95 million of a $304 million loan package. The IMF deal with Ecuador had been conditioned on Ecuador's pursuit of structural reforms (i.e. reduction of domestic fuel subsidies, loosened restrictions on foreign investment). In line with IMF lending guidelines, Ecuador continues to stress structural reform, increased foreign investment, privatization, and fiscal stabilisation. Progress in these areas has been slowed by political opposition from unions, indigenous groups, nationalists, and others. Over 90% of foreign investment goes to the oil sector. In 2002, the government experienced a shortfall in its funds for debt repayments of US$500 million on top of a budget deficit of US$500 million - in all an obligation equivalent to 6% of GDP. Since the government adopted the US dollar in 2000, it can no longer print money to pay these debts. Seeking to make the labour market more flexible, the government introduced contracts based on the number of hours worked and began a process of wage consolidation. In 2003, the new government raised fuel prices, cut public sector wages and imposed a value added tax on medicines and electricity.

Agriculture employs almost half the workforce but farm productivity is low. Despite the favourable climate and good soil quality, farms are small, vulnerable to hurricanes and flooding and rather inefficient. Fishing is an important foreign exchange earner with tuna, sardines and shrimps dominating. Ecuador's oil sector accounts for around one-fifth of the country's economy, and is the country's most important source of foreign exchange, ahead of coffee, fish, and bananas. This reliance on oil exports makes Ecuador's economy vulnerable to sharp fluctuations in oil prices. Ecuador also is vulnerable to any economic downturn in the United States, since remittances from Ecuadorian workers living in the United States are Ecuador's second largest source of foreign exchange earnings (around $1.4 billion in 2001). Meanwhile, revenues from construction of a $1.1 billion heavy oil pipeline (see Energy section) are helping to fund the country's fiscal stabilisation fund and to help pay off the country's huge debt. Industry depends mainly on agro-processing activities such as fish canning, rum manufacture and palm oil milling. The financial system remains fragile with a high percentage of the portfolio in arrears. Around 95% of banking credit is extended to just 5% of depositors, many of them linked to political contacts.

Since oil was discovered in Ecuador in the 1970s, it has become an increasingly important part of the Ecuadorian economy. The country has 4.6 billion barrels of proven oil reserves, with crude production of around 390,000 barrels per day (bbl/d) during the first 10 months of 2002, down from 422,000 bbl/d in 2001. Of this production, the state-owned oil company (Petroecuador) accounts for about

55% of Ecuador's total output, with private companies contributing the remainder. In 2002, Petroecuador reported that its oil output was at a 10-year low point, due mainly to underinvestment and ageing fields. The company hopes to increase production in 2003, but its exploration and production investment budget is expected to be cut by more than 40%. Recurring problems between oil producers and the government on one side, and indigenous peoples on the other, continue to plague the development of oil supplies. Native tribes inhabit most of the highly productive south-eastern area of Ecuador, and get no monetary compensation for the drilling that occurs in the territory.

◘ Egypt

Capital City	Cairo	Capital population: 14,872,204 (1996)
Population ('000)	64,392 (2002)	
Urban population (%)	46.14 (2002)	
Land area (km²)	99545	
Languages	Arabic	
Religion	Mainly Islam (80%)	
Currency	Egyptian pound (E£)	
Head of State	President Muhammad Hosni Mubarak (1981)	
Head of Government	Atif Muhammad Ubaid (1999)	
Ruling Party	The government is led by the National Democratic Party (HDW).	

Main Urban Areas	Population
Cairo (capital)	14,872,204 (1996)
Giza	4,779,865 (1996)
Alexandria	3,800,000 (1996)
Assuan	973,671 (1996)
Damietta	914,614 (1996)
Ismailia	715,009 (1996)

The Arab Republic of Egypt is situated at the extreme eastern end of North Africa's Mediterranean coast. Bordering on Israel to the north and east, with Sudan to the south and Libya to the west, it is in fact more closely linked with Saudi Arabia, with which it shares the strategically important Red Sea. Egypt is the keeper of the Suez Canal, one of its main sources of income. There is agriculture around the Nile delta, elsewhere the terrain is mostly desert. The capital is Cairo.

Egypt's 1972 Constitution provides for an executive president who answers to a unicameral People's Assembly with 454 members, ten of whom he appoints personally. The People's Assembly is elected by universal suffrage for a term of five years and then elects the president for a six-year term. There is also a 210-member Consultative Council which consists of 140 elected members with 70 appointed by the president.

Elections to the People's Assembly took place in November 2000. The HDW won 353 seats while independents aligned with the HDW took another 35 seats. Other seats were scattered among several parties and independents.

Egypt's GDP grew by 2% in 2002 and in 2003 growth of 2.8% is expected. In 2004, GDP is forecast to rise by 3%. Prices rose by 2.7% in 2002. In 2003, inflation is expected to be 3.2% and is forecast at 4.2% in 2004. After several years of strong growth in the late 1990s, Egypt's economic growth has slowed markedly. The country's private sector remains weak owing to a recent tightening of credit conditions and a cautious monetary policy. Falling bank earnings in 2002 suggest that private sector investment is likely to remain sluggish in the near term. Some of Egypt's key sources of hard currency revenue have been negatively impacted as a result of regional tensions and fears of war and terrorism. The tourism sector has been hit hardest, and revenues from the Suez Canal also have declined. Egyptian officials have taken several significant steps to reform specific aspects of the economy during the past 18 months. These include the extension of the general sales tax to the retail and wholesale levels and the conclusion of an association agreement with the EU which provides for multi-year reductions in EU imports. In the financial sector, a law to promote the development of a mortgage market has been implemented and regulations to criminalise money laundering have been approved. Moreover, a small number of companies have been privatised, although few are of any great economic significance. Over the longer term, Egypt's macroeconomic prospects may be more favourable, provided progress is made on such structural issues as privatisation, trade liberalisation, and deregulation. Egypt's main challenge is matching employment growth to the nearly 800,000 new job seekers coming into the labour market each year. Unofficial estimates put Egypt's unemployment rate in the 15%-25% range, roughly twice the official figure. To lower unemployment, Egypt needs to maintain a high rate of GDP growth and to bring in more foreign investment.

Egypt's economy is well diversified and it has a large, consumer-oriented domestic market. It also has several important sources of foreign exchange, each bringing in US$2-3 billion per year. These include remittances from expatriate Egyptians, dues from ships passing through the Suez Canal and oil exports. Tourism revenues account for about 5% of Egypt's GDP, and are among the country's five main sources of hard currency inflows. Tourism is critical since one in seven Egyptians depend on the industry for their livelihood. The average growth rate for tourism between 1993 and 2000 was 12.5%. The number of tourists fell 41% (calculated at an annual rate) during the fourth quarter of 2001 and receipts are still far below the level attain prior to September 11th 2001. Agriculture is the mainstay of the economy. Farming is still concentrated in the fertile Nile delta where cotton is the major cash crop and a big earner of foreign exchange. The government plans to accelerate its programme for the privatisation of state-owned enterprises, though to date the privatisation programme has moved slowly due to the large debts of these firms and severe overstaffing (layoffs are still difficult due to labour regulations). In recent years, the private sector percentage of overall Egyptian GDP has been growing by around 1.5% per year, with 110 state-owned enterprises having been privatised since 1994. In the future, the government plans to target "strategic" areas for privatisation, including telecommunications and other utilities such as the Egyptian Electricity Authority

Egypt produced an average of about 632,000 barrels per day (bbl/d) of crude oil in 2002, down sharply from 748,000 bbl/d in 2000, but only slightly below the 639,260 bbl/d produced in 2001. Domestic demand for petroleum products has declined slightly since 1998, after rapid growth during the previous five-year period. This is due in part to the weakness of the economy, but also to reductions in subsidies for petroleum products consumption and the increased use of compressed natural gas as a fuel for motor vehicles. Egypt is hoping that exploration activity, particularly in new areas, will discover sufficient oil in coming years to slow the decline in output.

▫ El Salvador

Capital City	San Salvador	*Capital population: 422,570 (1992)*
Population ('000)	6,513 *(2002)*	
Urban population (%)	47.28 *(2002)*	
Land area (km²)	2072	
Languages	Spanish	
Religion	Roman Catholic (87%)	
Currency	Salvadorean colón (SVC)	
Head of State	Francisco Flores (March 1999)	
Head of Government	Francisco Flores (March 1999)	
Ruling Party	Alianza Republicana Nacionalista (ARENA)	

Main Urban Areas	Population
San Salvador (capital)	422,570 (1992)

El Salvador is a long coastal strip, never more than 80km in width, which extends for some 250km along the Pacific coast of Central America, with Guatemala to the north and west and Honduras to the east and northeast. Its favourable climate and important position have helped to make it one of the most densely populated areas of the developing world. The terrain is mainly mountainous, with several extinct volcanoes. The capital is San Salvador.

The executive president is elected by universal suffrage for a term of five years, and answers to a unicameral Legislative Assembly whose membership was expanded from 60 to 84 seats in March 1991.

The second presidential elections since the end of the civil war were held in March 1999, when Francisco Flores defeated six other candidates with 52% of the votes cast. Elections to the 84-seat Legislative Assembly were held in March 2003, when ARENA won 27 seats with 32% of the vote. The Marti National Liberation Front (a former guerrilla movement) won 31 seats with 34% of the vote.

GDP increased by 2.3% in 2002 and is expected to grow by 2.5% in 2003. Growth of 3% is forecast for 2004. Inflation was 1.9% in 2002 and is expected to be about 2.9% in 2003. Prices are forecast to rise by 2.7% in 2004. After a promising spurt in the mid-1990s, El Salvador's economy has slumped owing to the adoption of more restrictive monetary policies, a rise in fuel prices and a slowdown in key economic sectors. Remittances from overseas workers (mainly in the US) have been a crucial factor contributing to the stability of the economy. In foreign trade, the government focuses on trade negotiations, while maintaining the tariff reduction programme. El Salvador is part of the new negotiations involving a Central American Free-Trade Agreement with the US. The aim is to conclude these discussions before the end of 2003. In addition, negotiations are continuing with the Andean Community and with Canada. The government has made considerable progress in restructuring the economy, although the country must boost its growth rate in order to reduce its widespread poverty. The fiscal deficit is high and remains a concern to policy makers.

Agriculture accounts for almost 11% of GDP. Farming dominates the economy but plots are small, farms are relatively inefficient and productivity is low. Most farming is for subsistence but cash crops include sugar, cotton and especially coffee. Farmers have suffered in recent years owing to the fall in world coffee prices. Products grown for the domestic market include maize, rice, sesame and fruit. Industry makes up about 30% of GDP and has expanded in the past few years. An exception is the many clothing factories set up in the country over the past decade. They now face stiff competition from factories in Mexico and elsewhere in Central America. Leading industries include textiles, food processing, beverages, petroleum, chemicals, fertiliser and furniture manufacture. The country has made significant progress in its programme of privatisation.

El Salvador is Central America's largest consumer of geothermal energy. The country has two main geothermal facilities. Power generated in El Salvador can be exported to Guatemala via an existing interconnection, and a connection to Honduras is planned. El Salvador relies on imports for its entire supply of petroleum and petroleum products and has little refining capacity.

▫ Equatorial Guinea

Capital City	Malabo	*Capital population: 34,890 (1992)*
Population ('000)	490 *(2002)*	
Urban population (%)	50. *(2002)*	
Land area (km²)	2805	
Languages	Spanish	
Religion	Roman Catholic (94%)	
Currency	CFA franc (CFAF)	
Head of State	President Teodoro Obiang Nguema Mbasogo	
Head of Government	Cándido Muatetema Rivas (2001)	
Ruling Party	Partido Democràtico de Guinea Ecuatorial (PDGE)	

Main Urban Areas	Population
Malabo (capital)	34,890 (1992)

Equatorial Guinea comprises the mainland territory of Rio Muni, located on the West African Atlantic coast between Cameroon and Gabon, and also the islands of Bioko, Pagalu and the Corisco group. The region has a warm, dry climate and has suffered from drought and environmental mismanagement in recent years. The capital is Malabo.

The president is elected for a seven-year term by the people. The Chamber of People's Representatives has 80 members, elected for a five-year term by proportional representation in multi-member constituencies. Although officially a multiparty state, Equatorial Guinea's politics is completely dominated by the PDGE. Four other political parties exist, but no serious opposition to the president is tolerated.

Teodoro Obiang Nguema Mbasogo was elected unopposed in December 2002. Elections to the Chamber of People's Representatives took place in March 1999 when the PDGE took 75 of the 80 seats. Each recent poll has been criticised as unrepresentative by both domestic and foreign observers, and the percentage of those voting is very low.

The country's GDP increased by an impressive 13.3% in 2002 while prices rose by 12%. In 2003, growth of 15.6% is expected and inflation should be 10%. In 2004, growth of 10.2% is forecast along with inflation of 8%. The tremendous surge in growth was due predominately to the development of new oil fields. The external current account deficit (including official transfers) narrowed from more than 80% of GDP in 1998 to less than 20% of GDP in 2002. The abrupt turnaround was due to a rapid increase in oil output. The government's cash flow situation improved considerably, reflecting growing oil revenue, but fiscal policy performance continued to weaken, as evidenced by the lack of control over government financial operations. The management of oil contracts lacks transparency, and there is no fiscal control over the payments due from, and paid by the oil companies. Government oil revenue is paid into treasury accounts held abroad. Moreover, large extra-budgetary expenditures have been financed since 1996 through advances on oil revenue, and the oil companies have been withholding government oil revenue at source to repay these advances. Opposition groups complain of escalating corruption and say the diversion of oil money will help perpetuate clan dictatorship and the abuse of human rights. Standards of living certainly remain low, even in urban areas. Malaria and a host of other diseases are some of the reasons why life expectancy is 48 years.

Recent economic developments in Equatorial Guinea have been dominated by rapid growth in the country's oil sector and subsequent sharp increases in government expenditure. Over 60% of GDP and over 90% of total exports originate in the oil sector. Expansion of the petroleum sector, mainly the result of exploration and foreign investment, has been the main impetus behind the country's high rates of growth in recent years. Annual oil investment now tops US$2 billion. While oil sector expansion has spurred new construction in the capital, Malabo, other sectors of the economy have stagnated, with the exception of the growing timber export industry. The government has largely liberalised the economy, with the exception of major agricultural exports. The country's sparse landscape offers little scope for intensive farming. Cocoa and coffee are the major exports but can be grown in only a small area of the country. Elsewhere, cassava, sweet potatoes, palm oil and bananas are produced as subsistence crops. Gradually, the country has become a large importer of food.

Oil production in Equatorial Guinea is up to about 190,000 barrels per day (bbl/d) and is expected to rise further in the next few years. The present level of output represents an increase of more than tenfold since 1996, when production averaged just 17,000 bbl/d. The government estimates that US$3.4 billion will be invested in offshore field development projects in Equatorial Guinea during 2000-2004. Production currently comes from three offshore fields. Equatorial Guinea should soon replace Gabon as sub-Saharan Africa's third largest producer of crude oil. Plans are also being made to expand the utilisation of natural gas from offshore fields.

□ Eritrea

Capital City	Asmara	*Capital population: 1,000,000 (1992)*
Population ('000)	4,301 *(2002)*	
Urban population (%)	19.41 *(2002)*	
Land area (km²)	10100	
Languages	Amharic (official); also English, Tigrigna, Arabic	
Religion	Islam (50%), Coptic (50%)	
Currency	Nafka (ERN)	
Head of State	President Issaias Afewerki (May 1993)	
Head of Government	President Issaias Afewerki	
Ruling Party	People's Front for Democracy and Justice (PFDJ) is the only legal political party.	

Main Urban Areas	Population
Asmara (capital)	1,000,000 (1992)

□ Ethiopia

Capital City	Addis Ababa	*Capital population: 2,209,000 (1995)*
Population ('000)	67,147 *(2002)*	
Urban population (%)	18.45 *(2002)*	
Land area (km²)	100000	
Languages	Amharic (official); also English, Tigrigna, Arabic	
Religion	Islam (45%), Ethiopian Orthodox (40%)	
Currency	Birr (Birr)	
Head of State	Girma Wolde-Giyorgis (2001)	
Head of Government	Meles Zenawi (1995)	
Ruling Party	Ethiopian People's Revolutionary Democratic Front (EPRF) leads a broad-based coalition.	

Main Urban Areas	Population
Addis Ababa (capital)	2,209,000 (1995)

Eritrea, a large and predominantly mountainous area of the old Ethiopian republic, became independent in May 1993. The state lies in northeast Africa along the Red Sea coast, facing Saudi Arabia and the Republic of Yemen across the water. In the west it borders on Djibouti, in the south on Kenya, in the east on Sudan and in the southwest on Somalia. The country has a warm and desert climate and is prone to periodic drought. The capital is Asmara.

Eritrea has an executive president. The National Assembly has 104 members, 60 members appointed and 44 members representing the members of the Central Committee of the People's Front for Democracy and Justice. There is also a parliament which has 150 indirectly elected members.

In January-March 1997, voters elected 399 representatives in a lengthy process that led to the formation of a constituent assembly. Only representatives of the PFDJ were permitted to stand.

Eritrea's GDP increased 1.6% in 2002 and prices rose by 18.8%. In 2003, growth of 8.6% is expected while inflation is put at 23.9%. Growth of 7.8% is forecast for 2004 along with inflation of 9%. The country's debt has soared during its war with Ethiopia. Government revenues come from custom duties and income and sales taxes. Eritrea has inherited the entire coastline of Ethiopia and has long-term prospects for revenues from the development of offshore oil, offshore fishing and tourism. The country's territory also contains much of the good arable land in the former Ethiopia, though like Ethiopia, it has faced recurrent droughts in recent years. Foreign investment remains very limited.

Eritrea is facing a critical food situation that is expected to worsen appreciably during 2003. Agricultural production could fall by as much as 70% below the level in 2001. The cereal deficit in 2003 is estimated at 400,000 tons. Some experts believe that Eritrea could quickly attain food self-sufficiency if the government would focus on the economy and not its disputes with Ethiopia. However, such a turnaround would require major improvements in irrigation systems to compensate for the lack of regular rainfall. Revival and expansion of traditional agricultural products such as beef, mutton, leather, citrus fruits and cotton are critical to a prosperous economy. Aside from agriculture, construction, communications and energy are other key sectors that require immediate investment. Rehabilitation of the country's two major ports in the Red Sea, Massawa and Assab, is underway. Eritrea's coastline, stretching over 1,200km, is rich with commercially important marine life and the government hopes to revitalise the fishing industry, though efforts continue to be hampered by the limited number of storage and processing facilities. Tourism is another sector with great potential. Eritrea's close proximity to both Europe and the Middle East, the abundance of historical and archaeological sites, and rich supply of natural resources that can be enjoyed by all visitors are distinct advantages. Given the country's low labour costs and domestic availability of raw materials, light manufacturing of finished leather goods and cotton clothing has the potential to become a significant export earner. Eritrea also has some mineral reserves, mainly copper, potash, gold and platinum, but these have not yet been exploited seriously.

Hydrocarbon exploration, primarily offshore in the Red Sea, began in the 1960s when Eritrea was still federated with Ethiopia. Several companies have been granted offshore exploratory rights but little oil of commercial volumes has been discovered. Eritrea has crude refining capacity of 18,000 barrels per day, but the refinery located in the Red Sea port of Assab has been shutdown since 1997 due to the high operating and maintenance costs. Geothermal energy is a potential source of development in the eastern escarpment area of Eritrea and is being actively investigated by foreign investors. Eritrea also has substantial hydroelectric power generating capacity but electricity is only available in Eritrea's larger cities and towns. This leaves about 80% of the Eritrean population without access to electricity. Some smaller villages have community diesel generators which can provide small amounts of electricity to households.

Ethiopia is a large, landlocked country with much mountainous terrain. It lies in northeast Africa and is bordered in the north by Eritrea. In the west it borders on Djibouti, in the south on Kenya, in the east on Sudan and in the southwest on Somalia. The country has a warm and desert climate and is prone to periodic drought. The capital is Addis Ababa.

Ethiopia has an executive president who serves a four-year term and is elected by parliament. The Federal Parliamentary Assembly has two chambers. The Council of People's Representatives has a maximum of 550 members, elected for five-year terms, and one from each professional sector. Members are designated by the regional councils, which may elect them directly or provide their direct elections.

Elections to the Council of People's Representatives were held in May and August 2000. The Oromo People's Democratic Organisation won 178 seats, the Amhara National Democratic Movement took 134 seats, the Tigray Peoples Liberation Front claimed 38 seats and the remainder were scattered among a number of parties. Wolde-Giyorgis was subsequently selected as president by parliament.

Ethiopia's GDP grew by 1.2% in 2002 and prices rose by 1.6%. In 2003, the economy is expected to contract by 3.8% but growth of 6.7% is forecast in 2004. Prices are forecast to rise by as much as 14.6% in 2003 and a further increase of 5.5% is forecast for 2004. Since it took power, the government has focused much of its attention on farming through what it calls "agricultural development through industrialisation". Although Ethiopia posted bumper crops in 2000 and 2001, food prices fell massively, leading to deflation. Signs of growth have begun to re-emerge but much of this reflects pent-up demand and investment which has now plateaued. Moreover, the drop in interest among foreign investors during the war has not resumed. Structural reforms include a reduction in the average import tariff and modifications to the investment code allowing foreign participation in the telecommunications and power sectors. The government's agenda also extends to reform of the financial sector, trade liberalisation and improvements in health and education standards. In the financial sector, the immediate focus is on building up the supervisory capacity of the central bank.

Ethiopia's agricultural sector employs some 85% of the workforce, produces about half of the country's GDP and generates most of its export earnings. The sector has suffered dearly through war and drought. In 2002, almost half the livestock in drought-affected areas died. Land is still owned by the government, and taxation on it remains a problem for many farmers. Moreover, taxes must be paid in cash, shortly after harvest time. The government argues that privatisation of land would lead to a social crisis, with farmers selling their last assets and migrating to over-populated urban areas. Ethiopia is Africa's leading producer of arabica coffee, which accounts for about 60% of export earnings. The country has 1.2 million coffee farmers, and the government estimates that about 15 million households are either directly or indirectly dependent on coffee for their livelihoods. A steep decline in the world price for coffee - down by 70% since 1998 - has left farmers, exporters and their financial backers in deep trouble. Most manufacturing is carried out only on a local scale and caters to the domestic market. There are mineral reserves, mainly copper, potash, gold and platinum, but these have not yet been exploited seriously.

Ethiopia's current proven hydrocarbon reserves are minimal, but the potential to increase reserves to commercial viability is seen as promising. The country's geology is similar to that of its oil-producing neighbours to the east (on the Arabian Peninsula) and the west (Sudan). The government plans to conduct feasibility studies to establish the extent and viability of the deposits have yet to be implemented. Ethiopia's petroleum consumption was estimated to be 22,000 barrels per day in 2000. Since the closure of the Assab refinery in 1997, Ethiopia is totally reliant on imports to meet its petroleum requirements. Petroleum imports are received at the port of Djibouti, and shipped via rail and tanker truck to Ethiopia.

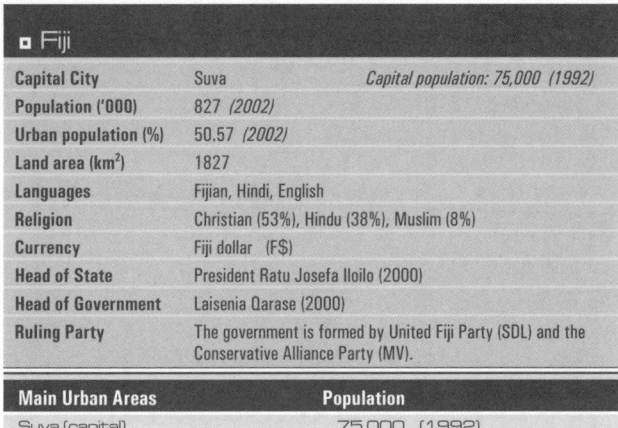

□ Fiji	
Capital City	Suva *Capital population: 75,000 (1992)*
Population ('000)	827 *(2002)*
Urban population (%)	50.57 *(2002)*
Land area (km²)	1827
Languages	Fijian, Hindi, English
Religion	Christian (53%), Hindu (38%), Muslim (8%)
Currency	Fiji dollar (F$)
Head of State	President Ratu Josefa Iloilo (2000)
Head of Government	Laisenia Qarase (2000)
Ruling Party	The government is formed by United Fiji Party (SDL) and the Conservative Alliance Party (MV).

Main Urban Areas	Population
Suva (capital)	75,000 (1992)

Fiji lies in the South Pacific, about 1,600km north of New Zealand and northeast of Tonga. The country comprises 332 islands and some 500 atolls and reefs, of which about 100 are inhabited. The terrain is mainly low-lying, although there are large volcanic ranges on most of the larger islands. The climate is warm and tropical, with some risk of cyclones. The capital is Suva.

Fiji left the Commonwealth in 1987 after two successive coups in which ethnic Fijians asserted their precedence over the ethnic Chinese and Indians who were effectively running the country at the time. Eventually, international pressure led to changes in the constitution which ensure that all Fijians (including Indians) have equal rights of representation. That constitution was again scrapped in 2000, following a coup led by indigenous Fijians. The House of Representatives is now made up of 71 members elected for a five-year term in single-seat constituencies, divided in 23 Fijian communal, 19 Indian communal, three general communal, one Rotuman and 25 open seats. The Senate has 32 members, elected for a five-year term: 14 members elected by the Council of Chiefs, nine members appointed by the prime minister, eight nominated by the leader of the opposition and one Rotuma representative.

Elections to the House of Representatives occurred in September 2001. The SDL received 32 seats, the Fiji Labour Party won 27 seats and the remaining seats were divided among several parties. Iloilo was subsequently appointed president.

Fiji's economy slumped badly in the past two years but a modest recovery is expected as the resumption of development assistance projects begins to take effect. GDP grew by around 4.4% in 2002 and is expected to increase by another 5.2% in 2003. In 2004, growth of 3.2% is forecast. Inflation was 0.8% in 2002 and is expected to rise to 2% in 2003. Prices are forecast to rise by 2.5% in 2004. Authorities maintained a highly expansionary fiscal stance in 2002, which led to a net budget deficit (including asset sales) of 7.0% of GDP. Growth has recovered and most macroeconomic parameters have improved following the political instability and civil disorder of 2000. However, the strengthened performance partly reflects the strong fiscal stimulus and accommodative monetary policy of the past two years. This raises the issue of growth sustainability. Private investment - including foreign direct investment - also remains very weak, reflecting the uncertainties of borrowers and lenders regarding the longer-term political and economic outlook. In an attempt to secure greater macroeconomic stability, the government is targeting a net deficit of 4.0% of GDP for 2003. The medium-term target for the debt-to-GDP ratio is 40.0% by the end of 2005. The 2003 budget contains measures to both strengthen revenues and restrain expenditures. The major revenue-raising measure announced was an increase in VAT from 10% to 12.5%. Together with some excise tax and tariff increases, this will mean an increase in indirect tax revenues of 30%.

The agricultural sector (including forestry and fisheries) recorded modest growth of 1.1% in 2002. The fisheries subsector grew by 8.0% following a 25.0% surge in 2001, supported by new export markets in Asia. However, the sugar industry continued to be beset by land lease, quality and transportation problems and mill inefficiencies. Manufacturing grew by 3.9%, while construction activity expanded by 8.0%, mainly as a result of public investment projects. The trade, restaurant and hotel subsector expanded by 8.6% supported by both tourism and resilient local demand. Despite this expansion, private investment continued to be weak, prolonging the trend of the last decade. However, there were signs that investor confidence was improving in 2002. Many private sector projects remained in the pipeline. Infrastructure constraints and uncertainty related to important constitutional issues seem to be holding back these projects. For 2002 as a whole, exports increased by 3.6%, reflecting a rise in gold exports. This is a continuation of a recovery that started in the previous year. Total merchandise imports increased by about 9.8%, due largely to increased imports of minerals and fuels, and machinery and transport equipment. Skills shortages became more apparent in both the public and private sectors, as qualified and skilled citizens emigrated. Mining is expected to continue to expand very strongly over the next couple of years, while the fisheries and construction subsectors are also projected to register strong improvements.

Fiji relies on imported oil and gas for most of its energy needs which it cannot cover with indigenous resources such as brushwood or timber. There may be scope for geothermal power in the future. Meanwhile, three-quarters of the country's electricity is produced by hydroelectric plants.

□ French Guiana	
Capital City	Cayenne *Capital population: 41,067 (1990)*
Population ('000)	205 *(2002)*
Urban population (%)	78.64 *(2002)*
Land area (km²)	8815
Languages	French
Religion	Mainly Roman Catholic (75%)
Currency	Euro (€)
Head of State	President Jacques Chirac (France)
Head of Government	Stephan Phinera-Horth (1994)
Ruling Party	Parti Socialiste Guyanais (PSG)

Main Urban Areas	Population
Cayenne (capital)	41,067 (1990)

Located on the northeastern Atlantic coast of South America, between Suriname in the west and Brazil in the east and south, French Guiana is a predominantly forested region with a number of large rivers flowing down from a high sierra in the south. The climate is humid and tropical. The capital is Cayenne.

French Guiana is an external department of France and is therefore governed to a considerable degree from Paris. The country sends deputies to the French Assemblée Nationale, and is represented at the EU. Since being accorded regional status in 1974, however, it elects its own 31-member Regional Council for a term of six years, with responsibility for economic and social planning. Other executive power rests in a 19-member General Council.

Elections to the Regional Council were held in March 1998 and the PSG took 11 seats. Elections to the General Council took place in 1994 with the PSG taking eight seats. The last full elections to the French Assemblée Nationale were in 1998, when the Rassemblement pour la République returned one delegate and the left wing returned one "dissident" member.

The rate of growth has been less than 2% in recent years while inflation probably exceeds 5%. Unemployment is well over 20% and much higher among younger workers. The economy is closely tied to that of France through subsidies and imports. The European Space Agency's launch site at Kourou is the single most important contributor to GDP. Dependence on Paris has not always proved to the country's advantage and it has been difficult to attract foreign investors.

French Guiana relies almost exclusively on its agricultural sector to employ and feed the population, and yet only 0.1% of the land surface is actually cultivated - most of the remainder being jungle. Export crops are limited to sugar and fish products. Most of the population is engaged in subsistence farming of rice, maize and bananas. There are also, a small number of cattle farms. Timber, the most obvious natural asset, is only marginally exploited because of a lack of infrastructure facilities. The hardwoods that are harvested support an expanding sawmill industry that provides sawn logs for export. There is also a growing fishing fleet and shrimp processing is an important industry. Industry tends to be restricted to the small area around the European Space Agency's launch site at Kourou - which alone generates a fifth of GDP. The mining sector produces a modest quantity of gold.

Much of the French Guiana's energy is hydroelectric. Otherwise, the country relies almost entirely on imports for all fuel supplies except natural resources such as brushwood and timber.

□ French Polynesia	
Capital City	Papeete *Capital population: 26,000 (1992)*
Population ('000)	240 *(2002)*
Urban population (%)	52.84 *(2002)*
Land area (km²)	366
Languages	French
Religion	Mainly Christian (55%)
Currency	Franc CFP (CFPF)
Head of State	President Jacques Chirac (France)
Head of Government	Gaston Flosse (1991)
Ruling Party	People's Rally for the Republic

Main Urban Areas	Population
Papeete (capital)	26,000 (1992)

French Polynesia consists of five separate groups of islands in the South Pacific. Included are Tahiti and Moorea, the remaining Society Islands, the Leeward Islands, the Tuamotu Islands, the Gambier Islands and the Marquesa Islands. With most of the territory composed of coral reefs, the land seldom rises far above sea level. The capital is Papeete.

French Polynesia is one of the four French Overseas Territories, which does not enjoy full department status but are regarded as an integral part of France. As such, most important decisions are taken in France rather than locally. The 49-member Territorial Assembly is elected by universal suffrage and elects its own representatives to the National Assembly in Paris. Executive power is wielded locally by the President of the Territorial Government, who approximates to a Prime Minister.

The most recent election was held in May 2001 when the People's Rally for the Republic (Gaullist) captured 28 seats in the Territorial Assembly. The People's Servant Party won 13 seats with the remainder spread among several parties.

GDP has been growing by 5-6% in recent years but growth fell sharply as a result of the worldwide slump in tourism. Since 1962, when France stationed military personnel in the region, French Polynesia has changed from a subsistence economy to one in which a high proportion of the workforce is either employed by the military or supports the tourist industry. It is possible that the French military presence will be reduced over the course of this decade and, if so, the islands' economy will suffer greatly. The tourist sector accounts for a fifth of GDP and is the primary source of foreign exchange, although it employs only a small proportion of the population. The territory substantially benefits from development agreements with France aimed principally at creating new businesses and strengthening social services.

Farm land is of poor quality and agriculture remains underdeveloped, accounting for no more than 6% of GDP but the government is seeking to expand the sector. Copra, vanilla and fruit are grown for the export market, and pineapples, bananas, mangoes, paw paws and cereals for the home market. Timber is grown for export. Industry contributes 18% of GDP and services make up the remainder. The country's industries consist mainly of pearls, handicrafts, fruit canning, soap-making with coconut oil, and brewing. Tourism, alone, contributes about 20% to GDP and is a primary source of hard currency earnings, although it employs only a small proportion of the population. The country is particularly popular with French, German and American visitors but a sharp decline in the number of visitors occurred in the latter part of 2001 and 2002. The islands have cobalt and phosphate reserves, although there has been little mining since the 1930s.

The country relies on imports for the greater part of its energy needs, except for timber and fuel wood.

Gabon

Gabon		
Capital City	Libreville	Capital population: 395,000 (1992)
Population ('000)	1,325 (2002)	
Urban population (%)	82.37 (2002)	
Land area (km²)	25767	
Languages	French	
Religion	Mainly Christian (60%), traditional	
Currency	CFA franc (CFAF)	
Head of State	President El Hadj Omar Bongo (1967)	
Head of Government	Jean-François Ntoutoume (1999)	
Ruling Party	Parti Democratique Gabonais (PDG)	

Main Urban Areas	Population
Libreville (capital)	395,000 (1992)

The Gabonese Republic straddles the equator on the Atlantic coast of Africa between Equatorial Guinea and Cameroon in the north and Congo in the south and southeast. It has a warm and occasionally humid equatorial climate. The capital is Libreville.

Gabon, which achieved independence from France in 1960, was run as a single-party socialist system from 1968 until March 1991, when a new multiparty Constitution came into force. The country has an executive president who is elected by universal suffrage for a seven-year term. Parliament has two chambers. The National Assembly has 120 members, 111 members elected for a five-year term in single-seat constituencies and nine members appointed by the president. The Senate has 91 members, elected for a six-year term in single-seat constituencies.

Omar Bongo was re-elected as president in December 1998 with 67% of the vote. Bongo has been in power since 1967. Elections to the National Assembly were held in December 2001. The PDG took 85 seats with the remainder scattered among several parties and non-partisans. Elections to the Senate were last held in February 1997 when the PDG took 54 seats and the National Woodcutters Rally won 20 seats. The remainder were divided among several parties.

GDP registered no growth in 2002 and inflation was 0.2%. Growth of 1% is expected in 2003 while prices should rise by 2%. In 2004, GDP is forecast to rise by 1.7% with inflation of 2%. Gabon continues to have one of the highest per capita incomes (around $3,700) in sub-Saharan Africa, but its income distribution is extremely uneven and almost half of the population lives below the poverty line. The informal sector has grown dramatically due to higher domestic prices, relatively lower salaries, and a scarcity of official or formal employment opportunities. The economy suffers from erratic public expenditure, dependence on diminishing oil output and negligible diversification. In the medium term, the biggest problem is declining oil revenue which threatens government resources, the country's investment capacity and the stability of the banking sector. In 2002, the government has been forced to continue subsidising loss-making public firms because of a delay in privatisation. As a result, the country's deficit now exceeds 14% of GDP. Oil and tax revenues were less than expected due to lower world oil prices and poor customs receipts. Foreign exchange reserves have fallen sharply because of lower export revenue and especially high debt repayments. The value of exports has declined by 15% due to the smaller amount of oil and timber sold, and lower world prices for both commodities. Meanwhile, imports have risen by 11% owing to the strength of the non-oil sector and additional investment aimed at slowing the decline in oil production. Because only 3% of the population have a bank account, a significant portion of savings is not being channelled into the financial system. Prospects for sustained growth and poverty reduction depend on

the development of the non-oil sector. This objective will require significant efforts to mobilise domestic savings, enhanced access to foreign financing and further improvements in the environment for private sector activity.

Gabon's economy continues to rely heavily on exports of crude oil, which account for nearly 65% of the government's budget, 80% of total export revenues, and 43% of GDP. Timber products typically have been Gabon's second largest export, comprising around 12% of total exports and about 5% of GDP. Exports of manganese also contribute significantly to Gabon's GDP, and are expected to grow by 600,000 metric tonnes per year now that the new Industrial Complex of Moanda has been built. Agriculture accounts for no more than 5% of GDP and less than 1% of the total land area is under cultivation. Cocoa, coffee, rubber, sugar cane and coffee are the major exports while cassava, maize, groundnuts and vegetables are produced for the domestic market. Industrial development is very limited, consisting mainly of food and beverages, textiles, lumbering and plywood, cement, petroleum extraction and refining, chemicals and ship repairs. Gabon contains substantial natural resources and is currently the eighth largest supplier of uranium ore in the world, producing an average of 500-600 tonnes of uranium dioxide yearly. In 2001, following a ten-year debate, legislation was enacted to create a duty free zone in a 5.8 square mile area surrounding Port-Gentil. Companies operating within the zone will be exempt from minimum investments, customs duties on imports and exports, price controls, import/export quotas, and licences.

Gabon is sub-Saharan Africa's third largest oil producer. The country's oil production was 302,000 barrels per day in 2002 and has been declining in recent years. However, Gabon's proven oil reserves increased to 2.5 billion barrels in 2002 from 1.3 billion barrels in 1996. The Gabonese government is promoting increased petroleum exploration and investment in the oil and non-oil sectors. To help boost reserves and production, Gabon's oil ministry has revised its production-sharing contracts to attract new investors and has increased the number of exploration permits issued. Several foreign oil companies have invested in Gabon's oil sector in recent years. Gabon's natural gas reserves total 1.2 trillion cubic feet. The majority of the natural gas produced in Gabon is used in the generation of electricity or as a refinery fuel.

Gambia

Gambia		
Capital City	Banjul	Capital population: 1,371 (2002)
Population ('000)	1,429 (2002)	
Urban population (%)	33.66 (2002)	
Land area (km²)	1000	
Languages	English (official); Mandinka, Fula, Wolof	
Religion	Islam (85%)	
Currency	Dalasi (GMD)	
Head of State	Captain Yahya Jameh (July 1994)	
Head of Government	Captain Yahya Jameh (July 1994)	
Ruling Party	The Provisional Revolutionary Council (PRC) is the dominant party.	

Main Urban Areas	Population
Banjul (capital)	1,371 (2002)

The state of The Gambia takes the form of a narrow strip bordering the banks of the River Gambia on the Atlantic coast of West Africa. It has a short coastline but is otherwise surrounded by the republic of Senegal. The climate is generally hot and extremely dry, although there is rain in the spring. The capital is Banjul.

The Gambia has been independent since 1965 and became a republic in 1970. The constitution provides for an executive president who is elected for a five-year term by universal suffrage, along with a 53-member unicameral legislative assembly, the House of Representatives. Among the representatives, 48 are elected for five-year terms and five are appointed. In 1994, the constitution was suspended when President Alhaji Sir Dawda Kairaba Jawara was deposed in a bloodless coup led by Captain Yahya Jameh who continues to rule with an iron hand.

In presidential elections held in October 2001, President Jameh received 53% of the vote, defeating Ousinou Darboe who received 33%. Elections to the House of Representatives were held in January 2002. The PRC secured 45 seats and the Peoples' Democratic Organisation won 3. The remainder were appointed. The centrist United Democratic Party boycotted the elections.

GDP contracted by 3.1% in Gambia in 2002 and inflation was 8.6%. In 2003, growth of 7.4% is expected while inflation will rise to 13%. Growth of 5.5% is forecast for 2004 with prices rising by 8%. Although its economic prospects are reasonably bright, Gambia remains one of the poorest countries in the world with a very high (but undetermined) rate of unemployment. Important strides were made in implementing economic and structural reforms during 2002. However, there were budgetary slippages leading to a sizeable increase in the overall budget deficit which now stands at more than 8% compared with a target of just 3%. Monetary policy is lax, with domestic credit expansion, both for the government and the private sector, exceeding targets. There has been significant progress in implementing structural reforms including tighter control over expenditures and closer links between sectoral priorities and spending. The government has also approved a fast-track privatisation programme for a number of public enterprises that do not require regulation. A comprehensive reform programme that targets judicial reforms, government decentralisation and civic education is underway.

Agriculture accounts for 21% of GDP and three-quarters of employment. Industry makes up 12% of GDP and services account for the remainder. The main agricultural products include peanuts, millet, sorghum, rice, corn, cassava (tapioca) and palm kernels. Cattle, sheep and goats are also raised. Farm productivity is low and suffers from climatic problems. Thanks to favourable climatic conditions, farm output has been on the rise over the past two years. Peanuts and peanut products are the dominate crops and account for more than 70% of the country's exports. The government has also placed a renewed emphasis on implementing agricultural marketing reforms and providing extension services, improved inputs, and access to credit for farmers with support from donors. Gambia's forestry and fishing resources are modest but are not fully exploited. There are no important mineral or other natural resources and the country's agricultural sector suffers from deforestation and desertification. Small-scale manufacturing activity is limited to the processing of agricultural products, tanning and related activities dependent on agricultural inputs. There are known deposits of kaolin, but little extraction at present.

All energy requirements except for fuel wood are imported. The country's electricity is generated by thermal power stations, although hydroelectric resources are to be developed if investment funds or international aid can be obtained.

▫ Ghana

Capital City	Accra	Capital population: 1,687,000 (1995)
Population ('000)	21,898 *(2002)*	
Urban population (%)	39.25 *(2002)*	
Land area (km²)	22754	
Languages	English, Akan, several other dialects	
Religion	Christian (43%), traditional (38%), Muslim (12%)	
Currency	Cedi (Cedis)	
Head of State	John Agyekum Kufuor (2000)	
Head of Government	Alhaji Aliu Mahama (2000)	
Ruling Party	New Patriotic Party (NPP)	

Main Urban Areas	Population
Accra (capital)	1,687,000 (1995)

Ghana, the former Gold Coast, lies on the Atlantic coast of West Africa, facing southward in the Gulf of Guinea. Côte d'Ivoire lies to the east, Burkina Faso to the north and Togo to the east. The climate is warm and tropical and occasionally humid. The capital is Accra.

Ghana has an executive president who governs through an essentially benevolent military administration. The current administration seized power in a military coup in 1981. However, political dissent has been allowed for some time under the freedom of association laws. The Fourth Republic was pronounced in January 1993, following the 1992 elections. The president is elected for a four-year term by the people. Parliament has 200 members, elected for four-year terms in single-seat constituencies.

Presidential elections took place in January 2001, when Kufuor took 57% of the vote, defeating John Mills who garnered 43%. Parliamentary elections were also held In January 2001. The NPP won 45% of the vote and 100 seats while the National Democratic Congress received 41% of the vote and 92 seats.

Real GDP grew by 4.5% in 2002 and growth will be about 4.7% in 2003. Growth of 5% is forecast in 2004. Inflation was 14.8% in 2002. Prices should rise by 26.4% in 2003 and are forecast to increase by another 8.6% in 2004. The economic recovery that began in 2001 owes much to the substantial improvements in economic management. Improvements in the system of taxation and collection have been another key component in the country's success. Government revenues nevertheless depend very heavily on a small number of large taxpayers, a group which accounts for about 60% of all income tax and over 90% of VAT taxes. Thus the tax base is very narrow and revenues can be uncertain in turbulent times. The country's privatisation programme dates back to 1988, when 300 companies were slated for sale. By mid-2002, some 212 of these had been divested. Discouragingly, however, the pace of sales has slowed significantly in recent years. An improvement in the balance of payments in 2001 and 2002 has enabled Ghana to increase its limited foreign exchange reserves to cover at least 1.5 months of imports. The performance of the external sector also improved in 2002 despite unfavourable market conditions for some of the country's major exports. The country's trade deficit has narrowed accordingly.

Ghana's economy is heavily reliant on agriculture and mining. Agriculture accounts for 35% of the country's GDP and has recorded steady gains in recent years thanks to higher output of good crops, livestock and fisheries. The industrial sector contributes 25% of GDP but has underperformed since 2001. Manufacturers are hampered by the high cost of credit, depressed local demand and what many firms see as unfair competition from abroad due to distortions in the tariff and tax systems. The mining industry (especially gold) is contracting and several mines have been closed. The service sector accounts for about 40% of GDP and has performed well in the past two years. The wholesale and retail trade, as well as restaurants and hotels, have all recorded strong rates of growth. Tourism, too, has experienced an upswing. Ghana, which is a relatively new destination, has apparently benefited from the decline in visits to established tourist destinations following the events of September 11th 2001 and the terrorist attacks in East Africa.

Ghana's estimated 16.5 million barrels of recoverable oil reserves are located in five sedimentary basins. Exploration offshore began in the 1970s but the results have not been promising and potential levels of commercial production are very low. The government has reorganised the Ghana National Petroleum Company, the parastatal primarily responsible for the importation of crude and petroleum products, and intends for its activities to focus solely on the exploration of Ghana's hydrocarbon resources in the future. Domestic prices for electricity and petrol have also been hiked as subsidies are withdrawn.

▫ Grenada

Capital City	St George's	Capital population: 7,000 (1992)
Population ('000)	95 *(2002)*	
Urban population (%)	38.82 *(2002)*	
Land area (km²)	34	
Languages	English	
Religion	Roman Catholic (60%), Anglican (20%)	
Currency	East Caribbean dollar (EC$)	
Head of State	HM Queen Elizabeth II	
Head of Government	Keith Mitchell (May 1995)	
Ruling Party	The New National Party (NNP) leads the government.	

Main Urban Areas	Population
St George's (capital)	7,000 (1992)

The island of Grenada lies at the southernmost tip of the archipelago known as the Windward Islands, in the Eastern Caribbean, about 140km north of Trinidad and Tobago and 170km northwest of Barbados. The territory includes some of the Grenadines islets. The climate is equable, although increasingly subject to hurricanes. The capital is St George's.

As an independent member of the Commonwealth, Grenada is essentially self-governing, with the British Crown being represented by a governor-general. The prime minister is answerable to a 15-member Parliament elected by popular mandate for a term of five years. There is also a 13-member Senate, appointed by the governor-general.

New elections were required in January 1999 following the defection of several key members of the NNP. Despite charges of corruption, Mitchell easily won re-election and the NNP took all 15 seats in the Assembly. This is the first time any party has held all seats in the Assembly since the restoration of parliamentary government in 1984.

GDP fell by 0.5% in 2002 but a recovery is expected in 2003 with growth of 2.5%. GDP is forecast to rise by another 4.5% in 2004. Inflation was 3% in 2002 and is forecast to be 2.5% in both 2003 and 2004. The recession in 2002 was the result of a combination of factors including the global slowdown, the completion of a number of large infrastructure and tourist projects and the effects on tourism of the terrorist attacks on September 11th. The fiscal situation deteriorated markedly in 2001 and 2002 with the central government deficit rising to 8.5% of GDP, reflecting a sharp increase in spending (about 6% of GDP) on social programmes. Authorities have responded with plans to curtail public spending over the next two years. Structural reforms are focused on efforts to improve the efficiency of the public sector through increasing the commercialisation of public services; outsourcing the work of more public agencies; and reducing the number of workers. The unemployment rate remains high at around 12%, reflecting structural rigidities in the labour market. To enhance the flexibility of the labour market, the government plans to amend the dispute resolution law to prevent solidarity strikes by workers in essential services. The tourist industry faces stiff competition over the next few years and foreign investment is needed if the sector is to thrive.

Agriculture and tourism are the dominant sectors of the economy. Farming accounts for over half of all merchandise exports, and a large portion of the population is employed, either directly or indirectly, in that sector. In 2002, tropical storm Lili inflicted considerable damage on crops and infrastructure. The total cost was estimated to be €21 million, equivalent to nearly 2% of GDP, in addition to a potential loss of €15 million of export earnings. Bananas is one of the main exports but suffers due to falling prices, low production and poor quality. Tourism, the leading foreign exchange earner, has done well in most years. Revenues contracted after 11 September 2001 but began to recover by the fourth quarter of 2002. Officials are trying to develop the island's financial sector. In 2001, the government shut down eight banks as part of its effort to eliminate institutions that could be conduits for laundered money.

Grenada has no domestic energy sources, importing most its supplies from other Caribbean countries. Reluctantly, the government agreed to ratify a privatisation agreement initiated by the previous administration after international arbitration ruled against it.

▫ Guadeloupe

Capital City	Basse Terre	Capital population: 12,410 (1999)
Population ('000)	485 *(2002)*	
Urban population (%)	99.73 *(2002)*	
Land area (km²)	169	
Languages	French	
Religion	Mainly Roman Catholic	
Currency	Euro (€)	
Head of State	Jacques Chirac (France)	
Head of Government	Marcellin Lubeth (President of the General Council, 1998)	
Ruling Party	Federation Guadeloupéenne du Rassemblement pour la République (RPG)	

Main Urban Areas	Population
Basse Terre (capital)	12,410 (1999)

The French overseas department of Guadeloupe is the northernmost territory of the Windward Islands group of the Caribbean. It comprises the two islands of Grande-Terre and Basse-Terre, together with Marie-Galante, La Dísirade and Iles des Saintes, and the St Martin and St Barthélemy group, which lie within the Leeward group. The climate is tropical/Caribbean, with some tendency toward hurricanes in the autumn months. The capital is Basse-Terre.

As a part of the French Antilles, Guadeloupe is an external department of France and is governed to a considerable degree from Paris. The country sends deputies to the French Assemblée Nationale, and is represented at the EU. Since being accorded regional status in 1974, however, Guadeloupe elects its own 41-member Regional Council for a term of six years, with responsibility for economic and social planning. Other executive power rests in a 42-member General Council.

The last full elections were to the French Assemblée Nationale in 2002, when the Rassemblement pour la République returned one delegate, dissents gained two seats and the Progressive Democratic Party received one. Elections to the General and Regional Council were held in March 1998. The RPG and the Progressive Democratic Party both won eight seats in the General Council. The RPG won control of the Regional Council with 49% of the vote.

Guadeloupe's agricultural sector, although the largest part of the economy, is far from self-sufficient. A large proportion of the country's food is imported from France. The island's perennial trade deficit is only partially covered by its tourism revenues and these fell sharply in 2002. For the most part, the country is forced to rely on remittances from France. Unemployment exceeds 30% and is especially high among the young.

The economy consists mainly of agriculture, tourism, light industry, and services. It is heavily dependent on France for large subsidies and imports. Tourism is the most important activity, with most visitors coming from the US. In addition, an increasingly large number of cruise ships visit the islands. Agriculture contributes 6% of GDP and employs 15% of the work force. The industrial sector employs 22% of the workforce and contributes 9% of GDP. Services, which is dominated by the tourist sector, accounts for 85% of GDP. The traditionally important sugarcane crop is slowly being replaced by other crops, such as bananas (which now account for more than half of all export earnings), eggplant and flowers. Other vegetables and root crops are cultivated for local consumption, although Guadeloupe is still dependent on imported food, which comes mainly from France. The most important industries are sugar processing and rum production. Some processing of food and timber production is also carried out. There is an industrial free port at Jarry, and a fair-sized ship repair business. Most manufactured goods and fuel are imported.

The country's fuel needs are met exclusively with imports, the only viable local resource being fuel wood and brushwood. Thermal stations generate all electricity.

▫ Guam

Capital City	Agaña	Capital population: 4,000 (1992)
Population ('000)	172 *(2002)*	
Urban population (%)	39.78 *(2002)*	
Land area (km²)	55	
Languages	Chamorro, English	
Religion	Mainly Roman Catholic	
Currency	US dollar (US$)	
Head of State	President George W. Bush (US)	
Head of Government	Felix Camacho (2003) (Governor)	
Ruling Party	Republican Party.	

Main Urban Areas	Population
Agaña (capital)	4,000 (1992)

Guam is the largest island in the Mariana group, lying 5,300km west of Honolulu and 2,170km south of Japan. The climate is characterised by hot wet weather from June to November, but is cooler and drier in the winter months. The capital is Agaña.

Guam's status as a US unincorporated territory is currently under review in the light of the general US withdrawal from the Pacific region. A referendum in 1982 produced a majority in favour of commonwealth status, but since then opinion has shifted back toward the status quo. The Guam authorities are particularly anxious to acquire a right of veto over the extraterritorial application of US law. The Governor is elected every four years and the 21-member Legislature for two years. Guam also elects one non-voting delegate to the US Congress in Washington.

Elections to the Guam Legislature took place in October 2001. The Republicans won eight seats and the Democrats won seven. In 2002, Camacho was elected governor, defeating his democratic opponent, Robert Underwood.

Guam's economy grew by less than 2% in 2002. The tiny economy was hit by two major typhoons during the year, Chatahan in July and Pongsona in December. The tourist industry suffered once again, after seeing the number of visitors drop sharply after September 11th 2001. The local economy is heavily dependent on the US military presence, which provides a big boost to the island's income and once provided most of the employment. However, this source of growth is declining. Tourism is Guam's best hope for the future and already accounts for a substantial portion of GDP. In a normal year, the industry would welcome more than 1.5 million visitors. However, several hotels were substantially damaged during 2002 and additional investment is needed. The government hopes to encourage foreign investment with a range of incentives aimed at widening the economic base. More than 300 US foreign sales corporations have established offices in Guam and the interest of foreign and domestic companies continues to grow. Although Guam receives no foreign aid, it does receive large transfer payments from the general revenues of the US Federal Treasury into which Guamanians pay no income or excise taxes. Under the provisions of a special law of Congress, the Guamanian Treasury, rather than the US Treasury, receives federal income taxes paid by military and civilian Federal employees stationed in Guam.

Agriculture is only of modest significance, with most farms being run on a part-time basis. The country is a producer of cassava, bananas, coconuts, sugar cane, fruit, vegetables, sweet potatoes and breadfruit. Fishing is important, and animals are grown for local consumption. Guam's most prominent and profitable activities have traditionally centred on servicing the US troop presence, which once provided most of the employment on the island. These activities are gradually declining in importance as the number of troops is scaled back. Otherwise, tourism is the main activity, with substantial revenues especially from the Japanese who comprise 70% of all visitors. More than one million tourists visit Guam in a typical year but the number dropped sharply in 2002. Japanese visitors normally make up over 90% of all visitors but with the recession in that country, the number of tourists began to fall in early 2002. The island has over 8,000 hotel rooms, and the number is expected to reach 12,000 by 2005. Industry is modest in scope, employing less than 4% of the workforce although it offers a wide range of activities: cement production, food processing, textiles and clothing, oil processing and even watch manufacture.

Guam imports all of its fuel needs, although it has an ample supply of petroleum products on tap as a result of its own oil processing activities.

▫ Guatemala

Capital City	Guatemala City	Capital population: 946,000 (1995)
Population ('000)	11,841 *(2002)*	
Urban population (%)	40.22 *(2002)*	
Land area (km²)	10843	
Languages	Spanish, Indian dialects	
Religion	Mainly Christian (Roman Catholic 75%, Protestant 25%)	
Currency	Quetzal (GTQ)	
Head of State	President Alfonso Antonio Portillo Cabrera (2000)	
Head of Government	Alfonso Antonio Portillo Cabrera	
Ruling Party	Republic Guatemalan Front (FRG)	

Main Urban Areas	Population
Guatemala City (capital)	946,000 (1995)

Guatemala lies directly across the Central American isthmus to the south of Mexico. It has a short coastline on the Caribbean Sea and a much longer one on the Pacific Ocean. The southern part of the country is mountainous, while the northern areas, bounded by Mexico and Belize, are relatively flat. The climate is generally humid and much of the country is forested. Earthquakes are frequent, as a result of the volcanic activity in the country. The capital is Guatemala City.

Guatemala is a republic with an executive president who is elected by popular mandate for a four-year term. The congress has 80 members elected for four-year terms; 64 members represent departmental constituencies and 16 are determined by proportional representation.

In general elections held in December 1999, Cabrera defeated Óscar Berger Perdomo, receiving 68% of the vote. Elections to Congress were last held in November 1999. The FRG captured 63 seats while the National Progress Party received 37. In May 1999, voters rejected amendments to the constitution that would recognise Guatemala's multi-ethnic society. The amendments had the support of all the main political parties in Congress.

GDP rose by 2.2% in 2002 and should increase by 2.4% in 2003. Growth of 3.5% is forecast for 2004. Prices rose by 8% in 2002 and the rate of price increase in 2003 will be 5%. Inflation is forecast to be 4% in 2004. The government has taken several steps to strengthen its financial base. These include a reduction in the public sector deficit, a cut in the income tax rate from 31% to 25% and policy changes to widen the tax base. Monetary policy remains tight in order to control inflation. Persistent problems of non-performing loans continue to restrict credit to the private sector. Guatemala is part of the new negotiations involving a Central American Free-Trade Agreement with the US and hopes to bolster the performance of its exporters. The aim is to conclude these discussions before the end of 2003. Guatemala is also reportedly negotiating a trade agreement with the Andean Community.

Agriculture accounts for 23% of GDP and provides jobs for almost 60% of all workers. Industry makes up another 20% of GDP and services account for the remainder. Coffee, sugar cane, bananas and cotton are the main cash crops. The country's main exports are coffee, sugar, bananas, cardamom and beef, but coffee is by far the most important. However, coffee prices on world markets have fallen significantly and Guatemala's coffee production is expected to be halved, leaving only the high-quality coffee that can fetch a premium on the international market. Sugar exports also fell in both value and volume. On the other hand, non-traditional exports have grown briskly. The industrial sector is dominated by small-scale manufacturing geared mainly to serve the domestic economy.

Guatemala, Central America's largest oil producer, produces approximately 19,000 barrels per day and has 526 million barrels of proven oil reserves located primarily in the country's northern jungles. Since the cessation of violence in 1996, the government has been opening areas for bidding and granting concessions for oil exploration. Oil production has subsequently increased dramatically. Efforts are also underway to explore and exploit potential reserves near Lake Izabal, Guatemala's largest lake. Just over half of all households have access to electricity and demand is growing rapidly. The availability of electricity is virtually non-existent in many rural areas. Even those who do have electricity experience inadequate supplies and brownouts.

▫ Guinea		
Capital City	Conakry	*Capital population: 1,508,000 (1995)*
Population ('000)	7,662 *(2002)*	
Urban population (%)	33.99 *(2002)*	
Land area (km²)	24572	
Languages	French	
Religion	Muslim (95%), Christian	
Currency	Franc guinéen (GNS)	
Head of State	President Maj.-Gen. Lansana Conté (1984)	
Head of Government	Laimine Sidime (1999)	
Ruling Party	Party for Unity and Progress (PUP)	

Main Urban Areas	**Population**
Conakry (capital)	1,508,000 (1995)

Guinea lies on the Atlantic coast of West Africa with Senegal and Guinea-Bissau to the north, Mali and Côte d'Ivoire to the east, and Liberia and Sierra Leone to the south. The climate is dry, despite the presence of the sources of major African rivers such as the Senegal, the Niger and the Gambia. The capital is Conakry.

Guinea's 1982 Constitution was suspended after the military takeover of 1984 that brought the present administration to power. A new draft was approved by a national referendum in December 1990. The current version of the constitution provides for the president to be elected for a five-year term by the people. The National Assembly has 114 members, elected for four-year terms, 38 members in single-seat constituencies and 76 members by proportional representation.

Presidential elections were last held in December 1998 when Conté retained his office with 54% of the vote. In 2001, a referendum was held which abolished presidential term limits. Elections to the National Assembly took place in June 2002, with the PUP gaining 85 seats. The Union for Progress and Renewal took 20 seats and the remainder were divided among several parties. Most opposition parties boycotted the election.

One of the poorest countries in the world, Guinea has struggled to implement a reform programme. GDP grew by 4.2% in 2002 and inflation was 3%. Growth of 3.6% is expected in 2003 and prices should rise by 6.2%. In 2004, GDP is forecast to increase by 5% while inflation should be 3%. The economy has been adversely affected by conflicts in neighbouring countries that have imposed severe humanitarian costs. Corruption is rampant with as much as one-fifth of all government revenues being pilfered and much of the rest being misspent. The country's modest programme of privatisation has attracted some foreign investment (mainly in the mining sector) but this has just nourished corruption. The dangerous security situation in neighbouring countries has required increasing financial commitments to peacekeeping forces and continued expenditure to defend the country's borders and host a refugee community between 5-10% of its population.

Over 80% of Guinea's population depend on subsistence farming for their livelihood. Nevertheless, agriculture accounts for less than a quarter of GDP. Only 3% of the land is cultivated with the main products being bananas, groundnuts, oil palm, cotton and pineapples. Coffee is grown for export. Cassava, rice and maize are the staples for the domestic market. Industry accounts for almost a third of GDP but production is geared to serve the domestic market. The only large-scale manufacturing installation is a bauxite smelting plant though many small-scale plants are engaged in light manufacturing and food processing. Mining generates a quarter of GDP and accounts for practically all the country's export revenues. Guinea has a third of the world's bauxite reserves and is the world's second largest bauxite producer. It also has significant diamond stocks, iron ore, vast hydroelectric potential and some gold. Foreign investment is minimal, however, except in the bauxite industry.

Although the country is actively searching for offshore petroleum resources, its only indigenous energy source is its considerable hydroelectric potential.

▫ Guinea-Bissau		
Capital City	Bissau	*Capital population: 145,000 (1992)*
Population ('000)	1,303 *(2002)*	
Urban population (%)	24.52 *(2002)*	
Land area (km²)	2812	
Languages	Portuguese	
Religion	Traditional (54%), Muslim (38%), Christian (8%)	
Currency	Guinea peso (XOF)	
Head of State	General Verissimo Correia Seabre (2003)	
Head of Government	Mario Pires (2002)	
Ruling Party	The government is formed by the Party for Social Renewal (PRS), the Resistance of Guinea-Bissau-Bafatá Movement (RGB) and several smaller parties.	

Main Urban Areas	**Population**
Bissau (capital)	145,000 (1992)

Guinea-Bissau, the former Portuguese Guinea, is a small triangle of land lying on the Atlantic coast of West Africa, between Senegal to the north and Guinea to the south and east. Until the 19th century, it shared a political union with Cape Verde. Attempts to revive that union were hurriedly dropped in the mid-1980s after a coup attempt. The country is low-lying, yet suffers from recurrent drought. The capital is Bissau.

The democratic system was restored in 1994. The president is elected for a five-year term by the people. The People's National Assembly has 102 members, elected for four-year terms in multi-member constituencies.

General Seabre seized power in a bloodless coup in September 2003. He took over from Kumba Ialá, who had been elected president with a large majority in 2000. Ialá has frequently been accused of erratic and authoritarian behaviour. Seabre has come under international pressure to return power to Ialá but insists he will remain in office until free elections are held. Elections to the National Assembly were held in November 1999. The PRS won 38 seats while the RGB took 28 seats. The African Independence Party of Guinea and Cape Verde (PAIGC) took 24 seats.

Guinea-Bissau is one of the poorest countries in the world. Its situation was only worsened by the military conflict that took place in Guinea-Bissau in 1998-2000. The conflict caused severe damage to the infrastructure and disrupted economic activity, in addition to bringing intense hardship and suffering to the civilian population. Today, the country's fortunes fluctuate mainly with the price of groundnuts. The economy contracted by 7.2% in 2002 and prices rose by 0.9%. In 2003, growth should be 2.4% and prices are expected to rise by another 3%. Growth of 2.9% is forecast for 2004 with inflation of 3%. After several false starts, the government and the IMF managed to piece together a recovery programme that is now being implemented. The country's large amounts of domestic arrears are gradually being eliminated and budgetary controls are in place. However, delays in implementing the agreed structural reforms continue to create problems for the economy. Programmes for military demobilisation and civil service reform are key features of the fiscal policy framework.

Agriculture and fishing employ over 80% of the population and account for around 55% of the country's GDP. Only about 8% of the land area is under cultivation, and subsistence farming predominates — with intermittent and frequent serious droughts. Cashews and groundnuts are grown for export, together with tobacco, sugar and palm kernels. Agricultural production has been significantly reduced as a result of the war. The domestic population relies on cassava, millet, sorghum and maize. The industrial sector contributes only about 15% of GDP. The inequality of income distribution is one of the most extreme in the world. The country's main industrial belt is a wasteland of derelict factories and broken machinery. Because of high costs, the development of petroleum, phosphate, and other mineral resources is not a near-term prospect. However, unexploited offshore oil reserves could provide much-needed revenue in the long run. Guinea-Bissau has bauxite resources, but it is uneconomic at present to exploit them.

Guinea-Bissau depends entirely on imported oil at present, but there are moves to develop the country's hydroelectric potential.

□ Guyana

Capital City	Georgetown	*Capital population: 200,000 (1992)*
Population ('000)	881 *(2002)*	
Urban population (%)	38.27 *(2002)*	
Land area (km²)	19685	
Languages	English	
Religion	Christian (50%), Hindu (33%), Muslim (10%)	
Currency	Guyana dollar (G$)	
Head of State	Bharrat Jagdeo (1999)	
Head of Government	Sam Hinds (December 1997)	
Ruling Party	The People's Progressive Party-Civic (PPP)	

Main Urban Areas	Population
Georgetown (capital)	200,000 (1992)

Guyana, the former British Guiana, lies on the north-eastern coast of South America, its coast facing north-east into the Atlantic. It is bordered in the west by Venezuela, in the east by Suriname (the former Dutch Guiana), and in the far south by Brazil. The terrain is heavily forested, and the climate is humid and sub-tropical. The capital is Georgetown.

Guyana, an independent member of the Commonwealth, has a semi-executive president who exercises considerable powers. The president also leads a 65-member National Assembly, which includes 53 members elected for a five-year term and 12 regional deputies. The country was for many years so firmly identified with the policies of the former ruling People's National Congress (PNC) that it amounted to a single- party state.

Elections to the National Assembly were held in March 2001. The PPP-Civic 35 seats, the Peoples' National Congress took 27 seats with the other seats divided among several parties.

GDP rose by 1.1% in 2002 and a contraction of 0.2% is forecast for 2003. In 2004, GDP is forecast to grow by 2%. Inflation was 5.3% in 2002 and is expected to be about 5.8% in 2003. Prices are forecast to rise by 4.6% in 2004. Guyana's per capita output has been falling over the past five years as a result of adverse movements in the terms of trade, a real appreciation of the currency, and a slowdown in the implementation of critical structural reforms. Exports have declined, mainly reflecting lower bauxite exports, and this has led to a larger current account deficit. Net capital inflows have also fallen, primarily as a result of lower private sector inflows. However, over the past two years the government has begun to take corrective actions to contain the fiscal deficit and tighten monetary policy. Most analysts now expect stronger rates of growth over the medium term as the implementation of structural reforms begins to impact positively on productivity and competitiveness. The prime sectors of growth are expected to be agriculture, mining and construction, and related services

Guyana's economy depends heavily on sugar and rice production, gold and bauxite mining, and logging. Agriculture accounts for 36% of GDP while industry contributes 32% and services make up the remainder. Farming is mainly for subsistence purposes. Most cash crops are grown near the coast since the inland terrain is too elevated and hostile. Domestic markets consume mainly cereals, fruit and vegetables. In the past, reduced output of sugar and rice, caused by lower acreage, mismanagement and adverse weather, has restricted growth and worsened the country's fiscal situation. However, in 2002 the government agreed on a comprehensive plan to modernise the sugar industry. The Guyana National Cooperative Bank has also been put up for sale and procedures put in place to strengthen government procurement operations. Officials are anxious to diversify the economy, but foreign investors remain aloof. Export performance reflects a decade of terms of trade deterioration, for which adjustment was made more difficult by the sustained appreciation of the exchange rate.

Efforts to exploit offshore oil fields were derailed in 2000 when the navy from Suriname chased a Canadian rig from a concession granted by Guyana, but which Suriname claims. Guyana had hoped to bolster its domestic production of energy with a massive hydro-electricity project but investors remain wary. Meanwhile, Guyana remains heavily dependent on imported oil supplies, despite some promising oil finds on its own territory.

□ Haiti

Capital City	Port-au-Prince	*Capital population: 1,266,000 (1995)*
Population ('000)	8,209 *(2002)*	
Urban population (%)	36.77 *(2002)*	
Land area (km²)	2756	
Languages	French, Creole	
Religion	Roman Catholic (75%)	
Currency	Gourde (HTG)	
Head of State	Jean Bertrand Aristide (2001)	
Head of Government	Yvon Neptune (2002)	
Ruling Party	The Lavalas Party (FL)	

Main Urban Areas	Population
Port-au-Prince (capital)	1,266,000 (1995)

Haiti shares the large Caribbean island of Hispaniola with the Dominican Republic, occupying the western half. At its western extreme the country is no more than 80km from Cuba and 160km from Jamaica. The terrain is largely mountainous with fertile valleys. The climate is tropical and generally constant in character. The capital is Port-au-Prince.

The constitution calls for the president to be elected by popular vote for a five-year term. The National Assembly has two chambers. The Chamber of Deputies has 82 members, elected for four years in single-seat constituencies. The Senate has 27 members, elected for six years, one third renewed every two years, in single-seat constituencies.

Presidential elections were held in November 2000 when Aristide received 92% of the vote. Elections to the Chamber of Deputies took place at the same time. The Lavalas Party received 73 out of 82 seats with the remainder dispersed among several parties. In elections to the Senate (also in November 2000), the Lavalas Party won 26 of the 27 seats.

GDP contracted by 0.9% in real terms in 2002 and is expected to register no real growth in 2003. Growth in 2004 should be about 1%. Prices rose by 9.9% in 2002 and are expected to increase by a huge 32.3% in 2003. The forecast for 2004 is for inflation of 20%. Fiscal performance worsened markedly during the last two years, with rising deficits financed mainly by the central bank and through an accumulation of external arrears. The overall central government deficit rose to 3% of GDP in 2002. Central government revenue declined to a historically low level (7.3 %of GDP) in 2001, but increased to 8% of GDP in 2002, owing in part to enhanced collection efforts. With monetary policy accommodating the increased fiscal deficit through a substantial increase in central bank financing, net international reserves declined in 2002 and the exchange rate depreciated. By mid-2002, international reserves covered only about two weeks of imports. Two-thirds of Haiti's inhabitants live in poverty, half of all adults are illiterate, and less than a quarter of rural children attend primary school. Haiti also produces more cases of HIV-AIDS each year than the entire US. International economists estimate that as much as 70% of the workforce is unemployed or working only part -time.

Drug-running continues to be the main money-earner in Haiti. Legally, the economy relies overwhelmingly on the agricultural sector, which employs 70% of the workforce. Farm productivity, however, is very low. Drought and erosion have destroyed much of the arable land. Today, agriculture accounts for only about 30% of GDP. Coffee is grown for export, but foreign exchange earnings have shrunk as world prices fell. Other exports include sugar and mangoes; yet most people rely on the subsistence farming of maize, sorghum, rice, beans and fruit. The most dynamic sectors are construction and manufacturing, but growth in these fields is not strong enough to offset the contraction in agriculture and other parts of the economy. International lenders are pressing the government to move ahead with its programme of privatisation in the energy, telecommunications, and transportation sectors, and to improve public infrastructure. Little, however, has been done. Efforts to expand Haiti's tourism sector are impeded by poor infrastructure and inadequate capacity. The only significant investment is a US$40 million Hilton hotel being built near the airport. Industry contributes about 15% of GDP in a typical year but its share, too, is declining. Food processing and related activities involving raw materials dominate, and there is some manufacturing of other low-cost goods. Haiti has deposits of copper, silver, bauxite, gold, marble, lignite and asphalt, but only bauxite has ever been mined, and there is virtually no foreign investment in the country at present.

With no natural fuels except for lignite, Haiti must rely almost completely on imports to meet its energy needs. The country, along with Barbados, the Dominican Republic and Jamaica, is party to the San Jose pact, under which Mexico and Venezuela supply crude oil and refined products on favourable terms.

□ Honduras

Capital City	Tegucigalpa	*Capital population: 775,300 (1994)*
Population ('000)	6,742 *(2002)*	
Urban population (%)	54.18 *(2002)*	
Land area (km²)	11189	
Languages	Spanish (English is first language in certain areas)	
Religion	Mainly Roman Catholic	
Currency	Lempira (HNL)	
Head of State	Ricardo Maduro (2002)	
Head of Government	Ricardo Maduro	
Ruling Party	National Party of Honduras (PNH)	

Main Urban Areas	Population
Tegucigalpa (capital)	775,300 (1994)

Honduras occupies a central position in the Central American isthmus, located between Guatemala in the west and Nicaragua in the east, with El Salvador on its southern border. Consequently, its Caribbean coastline is significantly longer than its Pacific frontage, which is less than 80km in total. The country has a largely mountainous character, and three- quarters of the land is covered by forest. The climate is tropical and generally humid. The capital is Tegucigalpa.

Honduras has an executive president who is directly elected by popular mandate for a four-year term. He and his cabinet are answerable to a 128-member National Assembly.

Presidential elections were held in November 2001. Ricardo Maduro received 52% of the vote, defeating Pineda Ponce of the Liberal Party. Elections to the National Congress were held at the same time. The PNH gained 61 seats, followed by the Liberal party which won 55 seats. The remainder were spread among several smaller parties.

GDP grew by 2% in 2002 and is expected to increase by the same rate in 2003. Growth of 2.5% is forecast for 2004. Prices rose by 7.7% in 2002 and should increase by another 8.4% in 2003. The forecast is for inflation of 7.9% in 2004. Macroeconomic policies have remained sound in the period since presidential elections in November 2001. The central government recorded a deficit of 1.2% of GDP and monetary policy has been tight. However, fiscal consolidation will require the maintenance of a cautious wage policy and the pressure to raise wages is mounting. An adjustment in exchange rate policy is designed to prevent any further real appreciation of the currency. Tax revenues are growing at a slightly slower rate than inflation and this puts pressure on government spending. Honduras is part of the new negotiations involving a Central American Free-Trade Agreement with the US. The aim is to conclude these discussions before the end of 2003. The government has also adopted a strategy to reduce the overall rate of poverty from 66% of the population to 42% by 2015.

Agriculture is the largest sector of the economy. In a typical year, farming accounts for about a quarter of GDP and up to 60-70% of export revenues. Agriculture is also the fastest- growing sector, a fact which is largely attributable to an upturn in export crops (bananas, coffee and African palm). Authorities have faced a number of difficult economic conditions associated with the economic slowdown in the US, the collapse in world coffee prices and the drought affecting most of Central America. Aside from farming, Honduras has a relative abundance of natural resources. These include timber, gold, silver, copper, lead, zinc, iron ore, antimony and coal. There are no funds to develop these industries, however, and for the present the country must concentrate on feeding itself. The country's tiny tourism sector has potential but is underdeveloped. Industry consists mainly of small-scale establishments that process agricultural products including sugar, coffee, textiles, timber and food.

In addition to the extensive damage sustained from hurricanes, a fire at a large dam knocked out 60% of the country's electrical supply. Electricity is frequently rationed, highlighting Honduras' over-dependence on hydro power.

▫ Hong Kong, China

Capital City	Hong Kong	Capital population: 7,217,885 (2002)
Population ('000)	7,218 (2002)	
Urban population (%)	100. (2002)	
Land area (km²)	99	
Languages	English, Putonghua (Mandarin), Cantonese	
Religion	Mainly Buddhist	
Currency	Hong Kong dollar (HK$)	
Head of State	Jiang Zemin	
Head of Government	Tung-Chee-hwa (1997)	
Ruling Party	Chinese Communist Party	

Main Urban Areas	Population
Hong Kong (capital)	7,217,885 (2002)
Kowloon	2,259,283 (2002)
Victoria	1,223,261 (2002)
Tuen Mun	555,062 (2002)
Sha Tin	441,220 (2002)
Tai Po	351,806 (2002)
Tseun Wan	300,560 (2002)
Kwai Chung	285,010 (2002)

Hong Kong occupies an important strategic position at the mouth of the Pearl River where it conducts an active trading business on behalf of the People's Republic of China. Hong Kong, which is now part of China, includes the Kowloon island area and the so-called New Territories. It has a mild climate, but summers and early autumns are very wet.

Hong Kong was a Crown Colony until it was returned to China in July 1997. At that time, Hong Kong's democratically elected Legislative Council (Legco) was replaced with a curious "provisional" legislature of 60 seats. Half the legislators are chosen by "functional" constituencies made up of narrowly defined professional groups including even corporations. Another ten are selected by a pro-China group of supporters. The remaining 20 seats are filled by universal franchise.

Tung won re-election in February 2002 when no rival candidates were nominated to challenge him.

Real GDP rose by 2.3% in 2002 and growth of 1.5% is anticipated in 2003. In 2004, growth of 2.8% is forecast. Prices declined by 3% in 2002 and are expected to fall 2.6% in 2003. The forecast for 2004 calls for another fall in prices of 1.9%. Deflation continues with prices falling by 2.5% in the year to May 2003. The main reason for the continuing decline is a drop in property prices and rentals. The budget for 2003 indicates that the prime objective for authorities is to contain the budget deficit. The government is committed to bring the budget into balance by 2006. They intend to do this by boosting economic growth, cutting public expenditures, and raising revenues. A series of revenue-generating measures has been proposed, including selling public assets; increasing payroll, profit, and property taxes; and boosting fees and charges for public services. Over the longer term, the economy will continue to suffer the restructuring pains of intensifying integration with lower-cost production centres in mainland China. Structural

unemployment will likely remain high as displacement of employees in traditional manufacturing and low-end services continues. Unemployment reached a record-high level of 8.7% in the three months to July 2003 and will continue to exert a downward pressure on prices. The unemployment rate should begin to fall in 2004 as stronger exports and strengthening domestic demand gradually lift labour market performance.

Hong Kong's growth was underpinned by strong export performance. After a sluggish start to the year, merchandise and services exports registered double-digit growth rates in the second half of 2002. Exports benefited from strong demand in mainland China and other Asian economies, and growth in offshore trade and transportation services. The recent weakening of the Hong Kong dollar, along with the US dollar to which it is pegged, also assisted export growth. Output growth in services was strong while manufacturing output fell due to the relocation of labour-intensive production to the mainland. Hong Kong's industrial sector covers a range of activities from heavy chemicals and steel manufacturing to electronic goods, textile and clothing/apparel, and industrial machinery. Industrial output slumped by 8.8% in the year to April 2003 owing largely to the impact of SARS. Services dominate Hong Kong's economy, accounting for 85% of GDP and employing more than 80% of the workforce. Major sectors include the trade and travel related sector (wholesale trade, retail trade, import-export operations, restaurants and hotels), which, together, account for a quarter of GDP. The bursting of the property bubble has caused a significant decline in the real estate sector. In mid-2003, analysts estimated that 25-30% of residential mortgage loans were in negative equity. The fact that properties in neighbouring Shenzhen are only one-third to one-fifth the price of their Hong Kong equivalents means that the property market is likely to fall further, especially as border restrictions are lowered in coming years. Tourism is typically Hong Kong's largest earner of foreign exchange after the textile and apparel industries. However, tourist revenues fell in 2002 as a result of SARS and the terrorist attacks in the US and Asia.

Hong Kong is entirely dependent on imports for all its fuel needs. Electricity and coal are imported from China, and oil from Southeast Asia. Hong Kong has benefited from the opening of a Chinese nuclear power station in Shenzhen, but the development has aroused environmental fears in the ex-colony.

▫ India

Capital City	New Delhi	Capital population: 7,626,133 (1993)
Population ('000)	1,036,389 (2002)	
Urban population (%)	29.11 (2002)	
Land area (km²)	297319	
Languages	Hindi, English, 14 recognised regional languages	
Religion	Mainly Hindu	
Currency	Indian rupee (Rs)	
Head of State	President A. P. J. Abdul Kalam (July 2002)	
Head of Government	Atal Behari Vajpayee (1999)	
Ruling Party	The Hindu-nationalist Bharatiya Janata (BJP) leads a coalition.	

Main Urban Areas	Population
Mumbai	10,503,576 (1993)
New Delhi (capital)	7,626,133 (1993)
Calcutta	4,655,888 (1993)
Chennai	4,064,965 (1993)
Hyderabad	3,137,179 (1993)
Ahmedaba	3,044,134 (1993)
Bangalore	2,814,905 (1993)
Kanpur	1,983,499 (1993)
Nagpur	1,719,312 (1993)
Lucknow	1,713,347 (1993)

India occupies the central northern coast of the Indian Ocean, where it is bounded in the west by Pakistan, in the north by Tibet (a region of China), Bhutan and Nepal, and in the east by Myanmar and Bangladesh. Spanning the equator, its climate is tropical and occasionally prone to violent storms. The capital is New Delhi.

India is essentially a federation of 25 states and seven union territories, encompassing a large number of ethnic groups. The President holds all executive power, and appoints the Prime Minister and his cabinet on the basis of election results to the Lok Sabha (Parliament). The Parliament has 545 seats while the Council of States has 245 members.

In parliamentary elections in October 1999, the BJP won only 182 seats in the Lok Sabha and 41 in the Council of States. The Indian National Congress took 112 seats in the Lok Sabha and 81 in the Council. Kalam was elected president by parliament in 2002.

GDP grew by 4.7% in 2002 and should accelerate to 5.6% in 2003. In 2004, GDP is forecast to rise by 5.9%. The annual inflation rate in 2002 was 4.4% and in 2003 prices are expected to rise by about 4%. Inflation is forecast to be 4.8% in 2004. The country faces a large and growing budget deficit. At almost 11% of GDP, India's fiscal deficit is one of the highest in the world. Although a quarter of the country's billion people live below the poverty line, interest payments are still the biggest single expense, account for 60% of recurrent expenditures (including defence spending and subsidies). New Delhi has begun to restructure its international debt (valued at $54 billion). It paid off $3 billion in 2002 and plans to double that reduction in 2003. Behind these moves is a huge rise in foreign exchange reserves, which reached $84 billion in mid-2003. The increase is attributed to a strong inflow in foreign capital. Meanwhile, there is pressure on officials to improve India's paltry level of tax collection, which remains below 10% of GDP. The government has deferred the long hope-for overhaul of the tax system, although it has made some minor changes which will help the middle class. The target for India's current five-year plan is for average annual growth of 8%, the minimum needed to create enough jobs for the country's young. That goal is unlikely to be met any time soon.

India's rural sector accounts for 25% of GDP but provides a living to almost 70% of the country's population. The countryside suffered one of the worst droughts in decades in the first quarter of 2003 but a good monsoon promises to boost agricultural output. The economy has received a boost from the industrial sector where housing and some manufacturing industries are showing signs of strong growth. The country's information technology and business process outsourcing industries also expect to record another year of double digit export growth. Meanwhile, the government has introduced a number of reforms. These include a new law to make it easier for banks to recover assets from defaulters, deregulation of petrol prices and the continued attrition of the bloated public sector payroll. The government has also revived its privatisation programme, selling off 13 state-owned companies between 2000 and 2003. The state's residual stakes in telecoms and internet companies and in petrochemicals are also to be sold or floated on the stock market. In June 2003, the government significantly reduced its stake in Maruti, India's largest car maker. Despite these efforts, analysts estimate that as much as 83% of the economy remains untouched by the liberalisation process. In 2003 India announced its intention to refuse foreign aid from 22 donor countries. Multilateral sources and diplomatically influential countries like Russia and the US are excluded. The big losers will be state governments and services like the railways, which have been receiving much of the money from the 22 countries.

India is the world's sixth largest energy consumer and plans major energy infrastructure investments to keep up with increasing demand. Reform of the energy sector has been slow, however. Electricity consumption is supported by heavy subsidies, and the formal end of the Administered Pricing Mechanism for petroleum products in 2002 did not completely end government controls on petroleum product prices. Oil accounts for about 30% of India's total energy consumption with the majority of domestic production being offshore. Future oil consumption in India is expected to reach 3.2 million barrels per day (bbl/d) by 2010, up from 2 million bbl/d in 2002. India is attempting to limit its dependence on oil imports somewhat by expanding domestic exploration and production. To this end, the government is pursuing a new licensing policy which permits foreign involvement in exploration, an activity long restricted to Indian state-owned firms. The country's consumption of natural gas is also expected to increase sharply. From only 0.6 trillion cubic feet (Tcf) per year in 1995, natural gas use rose to nearly 0.8 Tcf in 2000 and is projected to reach 1.6 Tcf in 2010.

□ Indonesia

Capital City	Jakarta	*Capital population: 10,245,837 (2002)*
Population ('000)	216,136 *(2002)*	
Urban population (%)	42.17 *(2002)*	
Land area (km²)	181157	
Languages	English, 27 local languages	
Religion	Mainly Islam (87%)	
Currency	Rupiah (Rp)	
Head of State	Megawati Sukarno-putri (2001)	
Head of Government	Megawati Sukarno-putri (2001)	
Ruling Party	The government is formed by the Indonesian Democratic Party (PDIP), the Sekretariat Bersana Golongan (Golkar) and others.	

Main Urban Areas	Population	
Jakarta (capital)	10,245,837	(2002)
Surabaya	2,941,578	(2002)
Bandung	2,788,032	(2002)
Medan	2,135,458	(2002)
Tangerang	1,795,026	(2002)
Palembang	1,441,016	(2002)
Ujungpandang	1,250,574	(2002)
Semarang	1,221,561	(2002)
Malang	824,880	(2002)
Depok	781,945	(2002)

Indonesia, the largest Muslim state in the world, is also one of the most geographically dispersed nations. It consists of a group of archipelagos which range from the large islands of Sumatra and Java (in the west), through Sulawesi (in the centre) to the territory of Irian Jaya (Western New Guinea). To this is added the territory of Kalimtan and the Molucca Islands. The capital is Jakarta.

The 1,000-member People's Consultative Assembly elects the president for a five-year term. Half the assembly is elected by universal franchise with the remainder appointed by the president, often from the armed forces.

The first elections in the post-Suharto era were held in June 1999. The PDIP received 37% of the vote and 154 seats in the Assembly. Golkar got 21% of the vote and 120 seats. Abdurrahman Wahid then became president. In July 2001, Wahid was impeached and Sukarno-putri, the vice president and daughter of Indonesia' first president, assumed office.

GDP grew by 3.7% in 2002 and growth of 3.5% is expected in 2003. GDP is forecast to rise by 4% in 2004. Inflation was 11.5% in 2002 and should be 6.6% in 2003. Prices are forecast to rise by 5.4% in 2004. The government's top priority is to bring badly needed capital back to south-east Asia's largest market. Indonesia was the country hardest hit by the Asian financial crisis in the late 1990s and must absorb two million new workers who enter the labour force each year. So far, these efforts have not been rewarded. The government estimates that only 10-20% of the $9.7 billion in foreign investments approved in 2002 will be realised. Foreign investment in the first half of 2003 was $4.4 billion but has slowed following the terrorist attack in Jakarta. Critics argue that the economy's real problem is the endemic corruption and bureaucratic chaos which is slowing economic reform. In response, the government is emphasising structural reforms in areas that impact on macroeconomic stability, such as financial sector reforms, privatisation and asset recovery, and legal and governance issues. Fiscal policy is on track to achieve the 2003 deficit target of 1.8% of GDP. In the first quarter of the year, the budget unexpectedly recorded a surplus. Bilateral creditors have agreed to reschedule $5.4 billion of interest and principal due between April 2002 and December 2003. This achievement has significantly reduced the impact of external debt servicing. However, the government continues to face large external repayment obligations in 2004-2005. The outlook for the Indonesian economy is highly promising but subject to considerable risks.

Manufacturing recorded growth of 3.7% in 2002. However, a slowdown was already evident by the end of the third quarter, reflecting the impact of floods early in the year and continuing softness in investment spending. Utilities and some services subsectors showed strong growth, albeit slowing during the year. Agriculture grew by 2.3%, substantially up from the recent 0.7% annual growth trend. The growth was remarkable given the flooding in the early part of the year and the dislocation to markets, including those for agricultural inputs, due to heavy rainfall. The total production of paddy (wetland and dry land) for 2002 was up by 1.8% from the 2001 level with a 0.3% increase in the harvested area and a 1.6% increase in productivity. Non-food production benefited from increases in the prices of palm oil, rubber, and Robusta coffee. Private spending, equivalent to more than 70% of GDP, grew by 4.7%, a slightly slower pace than in 2001. A poor investment climate is harming the economy. The level of government approvals for foreign and domestic investment in the first 8 months of 2002 were more than 60% lower than in the equivalent period in 2001-a clear negative indicator of business and investment sentiment. The level of open unemployment rose from 8.1% in 2001 to 9.1% in 2002 while the number of unemployed increased to 9.1 million. Despite the generally rising level of unemployment and underemployment, formal sector wages have risen rapidly owing to a succession of steep rises in minimum wages, including a 30% increase in 2002. Higher wages are having a negative impact on the competitiveness of labour-intensive industries, such as textiles and electronics.

Indonesia currently holds proven oil reserves of five billion barrels. This represents a 14% decline since 1994. During 2002, crude oil production averaged 1.1 million bbl/d, having decreased from just over 1.2 million bbl/d in 2001. Sizeable, but as yet unproven, reserves may lie in the numerous basins located in eastern Indonesia. Companies producing from existing fields are also investing in programmes to increase recovery rates and to prolong the life of the fields. Despite these efforts, Indonesia's oil production is not likely to rise markedly due to the continuing decline of mature fields. The country could possibly become a net oil importer by the end of the current decade. Indonesia also has eight refineries, with a combined capacity of 992,745 barrels per day (bbl/d). One new project currently under consideration is a 300,000-bbl/d joint venture refinery planned for Pare-Pare in South Sulawesi.

□ Iran

Capital City	Tehran	*Capital population: 6,830,000 (1995)*
Population ('000)	69,236 *(2002)*	
Urban population (%)	62.45 *(2002)*	
Land area (km²)	163620	
Languages	Farsi	
Religion	Islam	
Currency	Iranian rial (IRR)	
Head of State	President Mohammad Khatami (1997)	
Head of Government	President Mohammad Khatami (1997)	
Ruling Party	The Islamic Iran Participation Front leads a coalition of reformers.	

Main Urban Areas	Population	
Tehran (capital)	6,830,000	(1995)
Mashhad	2,011,000	(1995)
Esfahan	1,915,000	(1995)
Tabriz	1,450,000	(1995)
Shiraz	1,022,000	(1995)

Iran, the largest non-Arab country in the Middle East, occupies the land mass between the Caucasus in the north (Turkey, Azerbaijan and Turkmenistan), the Afghan and Pakistani borders to the east and southeast, and Iraq to the west. It lies on the coast of the Persian (Arabian) Gulf, facing Saudi Arabia, Bahrain and the United Arab Emirates. The capital is Tehran.

Modern Iran has its foundations in the Islamic revolution supporters of Ayatollah Ruhollah Khomeini. Political power rests loosely in the clerical and religious hierarchy, which exercises authority through the 76-member Assembly of Experts. The country's Majlis consists of 290 members which are popularly elected. There is also a 12-member Council of Guardians, which includes six clerical members appointed by Ayatollah Sayed Ali Khamenei. The council has to pass all legislation coming from parliament and vets all would-be candidates.

In presidential elections in June 2001, Khatami was re-elected with 77% of the vote. In parliamentary elections held in May 2000, the Reformist Party won 189 seats, the Radical Islamists won 54 seats and independents took 42 seats. The remainder went to religious minorities.

Iran's economy, which relies heavily on oil export revenues, was hit hard by record-low oil prices during 1998 and early 1999, but improved once oil prices strengthened. GDP rose by 6.7% in 2002. Growth of 6.1% is expected in 2003 while the forecast for 2004 is for growth of 5.7%. Inflation was 14.3% in 2002. In 2003, prices are expected to rise by another 18%. Inflation in 2004 is forecast to be 17%. The current account should remain in surplus in 2003, but is expected to fall sharply into deficit in 2004 as oil prices decline. Iran's programme of economic reform will move forward over the next couple of years, but the pace of change will be slow and uneven in many crucial areas. About one million Iranians enter the labour market each year, but there are jobs for less than half of them. Unemployment is unofficially estimated to be 18% and rising. Since 2000, about 285,000 qualified Iranians have emigrated. The present administration is sympathetic to economic reform but is not powerful enough to dismantle the socialist-style economy. It continues to dole out more than US$1 billion each year in the form of soft loans to employers who hire extra workers. The government has managed to cut corporate tax and income tax for the poor, and has removed many import barriers. In 2002, however, spending has gone up by 54%.

Agriculture generates 20% of GDP and employs about 22% of the work force. Farming is concentrated in the fertile valleys of the north and west. Iran's budget shortfall, which is a chronic problem, is due in part to large-scale state subsidies - totalling some US$11 billion per year - which are mainly for foodstuffs. Wheat, barley, rice, cotton and sugar beet are grown for domestic consumption; there are also timber resources in the north and west. The oil sector's share of GDP has declined from 30-40% in the 1970s to 10-20%, mainly as a result of war damage to production facilities (Iranian output still stands below its pre-war highs) and OPEC output ceilings, but oil revenue still provides some 80% of export earnings and around 40-50% of the government budget. The non-oil industrial sector has been undermined by the uncertain implementation of the privatisation process, together with import suppression imposed in the mid-1990s as Iran sought to conserve foreign exchange to meet its high external debt-repayment obligations. The services sector has seen the greatest long-term growth in terms of its share of GDP, but currency-exchange restrictions, excessive bureaucracy and the uncertainty of long-term planning have made this a volatile sector. Despite the high returns on oil, Iran continues to face budgetary pressures due to expensive state subsidies (billions of dollars per year) on many basic goods; a large, inefficient public sector and state monopolies which control at least a quarter of the economy and constitutionally are answerable only to supreme leader Ayatollah Ali Khamenei. The present five-year plan (which began in 2000) calls for the creation of 750,000 new jobs per year and a reduction in subsidies for basic commodities (bread, rice, sugar, vegetable oil, wheat, fuels), plus a wide range of fiscal and structural reforms. Implementation of these plans, however, has been delayed by lack of domestic political consensus (as well as the Iranian constitution).

Iran holds 90 billion barrels of proven oil reserves, or roughly 9% of the world's total. The vast majority of crude oil reserves are located in giant onshore fields in south-western Khuzestan near the Iraqi border and the Persian Gulf. Domestic oil consumption is increasing rapidly (about 7% per year) as the economy and population grow. In addition, Iran subsidises the price of oil products, resulting in a large amount of waste and inefficiency in oil consumption. Currently, Iran is forced to spend around US$1 billion per year to import oil products (mainly gasoline) which it cannot produce locally. Over the next few years, Iran is aiming to double foreign investment in the hydrocarbons sector to $24 billion. The country reportedly also hopes to increase its oil production capacity to 4.5 million barrels per day by 2004.

▢ Iraq

Capital City	Baghdad	Capital population: 4,478,000 (1995)
Population ('000)	25,358 *(2002)*	
Urban population (%)	77.45 *(2002)*	
Land area (km²)	43737	
Languages	Arabi,C English	
Religion	Mainly Islam (95%)	
Currency	Iraqi dinar (IQD)	
Head of State	President Saddam Hussein (1979)	
Head of Government	vacant	
Ruling Party	There is no government at present.	

Main Urban Areas	Population	
Baghdad (capital)	4,478,000 (1995)	

Iraq, situated across the Persian (Arabian) Gulf from Iran, is much less of a desert state, being watered by the Tigris and Euphrates rivers. The country borders on Saudi Arabia and Kuwait in the south, on Syria and Jordan in the west, and on Turkey in the north. It has substantial oil resources. The capital is Baghdad.

The form of the new government is under negotiation. In the previous administration of Saddam Hussein the president was elected by the Revolutionary Command Council (RCC) from among its members, and appoints the cabinet. The RCC shared legislative powers with the 250-member National Assembly,

which was elected by universal suffrage for a term of four years. The Kurdish parliament has 115 members, elected by proportional representation, 100 seats reserved for Kurds, five for Assyrians and ten for Turkmens.

A national referendum to affirm Hussein as president for seven more years took place in October 2002. The Kurdish minority held their own (officially unrecognised) elections to the (equally unrecognised) Iraqi Kurdistan parliament in May 1992, when the Kurdistan Democratic Party and the Patriotic Union of Kurdistan each obtained 50 seats.

With the resumption of oil production and exports, and the inflow of aid and reconstruction money, the economy will strengthen. By 2004, significant increases in oil production and export volumes, and ongoing reconstruction assistance, could yield growth of 20-25%. This will be reflected in an improvement in the current-account surplus, which is forecast to rise from $2.1 billion in 2003 to more than $4 billion in 2004.

Before the war and the previous embargo, the oil industry contributed 98% of all export revenues in a typical year. At that time, agriculture in Iraq was diversified and well developed. However, limited rainfall meant that there were only two harvests a year. Farming is on the decline now, owing to a lack of investment, access to the necessary inputs and the deterioration in the quality of the soil. Industry was once moderately well developed but with the embargo Iraqi's industrial capability has declined markedly.

Iraq contains 112 billion barrels of proven oil reserves, the second largest in the world (behind Saudi Arabia) along with roughly 220 billion barrels of probable and possible resources. Iraq's true resource potential may be far greater than this, however, as the country is relatively unexplored due to years of war and sanctions. Deep oil-bearing formations located mainly in the vast Western Desert region, for instance, could yield large additional oil resources, but have not been explored. Industry experts generally assess Iraq's sustainable production capacity at no higher than 280,000 barrels per day. The long squeeze on investment in Iraqi oil fields keeps its production capacity far below the potential of a country with the world's second largest oil reserves.

▢ Israel

Capital City	Jerusalem	Capital population: 679,800 (2002)
Population ('000)	6,422 *(2002)*	
Urban population (%)	91.34 *(2002)*	
Land area (km²)	2062	
Languages	Hebrew, Arabic	
Religion	Jewish (82%)	
Currency	New shekel (NIS)	
Head of State	President Moshe Katzav (2000)	
Head of Government	Ariel Sharon (2001)	
Ruling Party	The Likud Party leads a multi-party coalition.	

Main Urban Areas	Population	
Jerusalem (capital)	679,800	(2002)
Tel Aviv-Yafo	346,400	(2002)
Haifa	270,600	(2002)
Rishon LeZiyyon	227,860	(2002)
Ashdod	192,640	(2002)
Be'er Sheva	176,460	(2002)
Petah Tiqwa	176,300	(2002)
Netanya	165,140	(2002)
Holon	163,820	(2002)
Bat Yam	136,580	(2002)

Israel, which occupies the lower third of the eastern Mediterranean coastline, was formed in 1948 as a thin strip of mainly Jordanian and Palestinian-owned land. But its territory was extended in the Six-Day War of 1967 to include territories seized from Jordan on the West Bank of the Jordan River, as well as some Syrian and Egyptian land. The country has a typically Middle Eastern climate, with warm summers. The capital is Jerusalem.

The territory of Israel was created in 1948 to provide a homeland for displaced Jews. Carved out of mainly Palestinian-owned land, it was effectively extended after the 1967 war to the West Bank territory, including East Jerusalem (formerly in Jordan). A seven-year campaign of Palestinian disruption and non-co-operation was partially resolved in 1994 with Israeli recognition of Palestinian autonomy in the West Bank and the creation of a Palestinian parliament. Israel also withdrew from the Gaza Strip in 1994, after occupying it since 1967. Israel has a non-executive president and a parliament (Knesset) of 120 members. In 1996, a change was introduced which allows voters to cast two ballots, one for the prime minister and the other for a party. Until now, people only voted for one of 30-odd parties which then haggled over the prime minister. The change is meant to reduce the negotiating power of the small parties.

Elections to the 120-member parliament took place in January 2003. Sharon's Likud Party took 37 seats, nearly double the number in the previous parliament. The Labour Party won 19 seats and the anti-clericalist Shinui took 15 seats. The remainder were widely distributed among several parties. Presidential elections took place in February 2001 when Sharon defeated Ehud Barak with 62% of the vote. In July 2000, parliament elected Moshe Katzav as president following the resignation of Ezer Weizmann, who had been involved in a political scandal.

GDP contracted by 1% in 2002. In 2003, growth of just 0.7% is expected while the forecast for 2004 calls for growth of 2.1%. Prices rose by 5.6% in 2002. In 2003, inflation should be 1.1%. Prices are forecast to rise by just 0.2% in 2004. The Israeli economy continues to stagnate as a result of the global slowdown, especially the high-tech slump, and the increasingly worsening security situation. Macroeconomic policies cannot fully offset these negative shocks. In fact, too vigorous policy reactions to these shocks could cause adverse consequences elsewhere, such as high inflation, a loss of fiscal discipline and financial market instability. Rather, their main task is to attenuate the impact of these shocks by providing a stable, transparent and supportive environment to economic activity, until the economy begins a solid recovery. The country's deficit is soaring and now seems to be out of control. In the first two months of 2003, it reached $1.1 billion, a third of the total budgeted for the entire year of 2003. The sum is equivalent to 6% of GDP - double the budget target. In March 2003, the government unveiled an economic austerity plan that included proposals to cut the budget deficit by $2.3 billion and reduce wages in the public sector. Opponents immediately attacked the plan as evidence of further erosion in support for the poor. Israel is seeking $8 billion in loan guarantees and up to $4 billion in defence aid from Washington, which has made help conditional on Israel acting to boost the private sector.

The country's agricultural sector accounts for just 2% of GDP but is highly productive due to the mild climate and fertile soil. Wheat, avocados, millet, sorghum and a wide variety of fruits are produced. The area under cultivation includes a substantial part of the occupied West Bank. Industry makes up 26% of GDP and includes an impressive array of high-technology manufacturers. Exports include machinery and mechanical equipment, cut diamonds, chemicals, textiles and apparel, and processed agricultural products. Some traditional industries, especially the larger textile firms, have gone through a structural change and have been outsourcing labour-intensive activities to neighbouring countries such as Jordan and Egypt, where wages are substantially lower than in Israel. This has enabled Israeli manufacturers to focus on their relative advantage in product design and make the most use of their country's trade agreements with the US and the EU as part of a free-trade zone. Other industries that have been unable to make a similar transition are slowly being phased out. Infrastructure investments are likely to remain high in the near term, in response to annual population growth of 2.5%.

Until recently, with a significant offshore natural gas discovery, Israel had no commercial fossil fuel resources and has been forced to depend on energy imports. Israel has attempted to diversify its supply sources and to utilise alternatives like solar and wind energy. Traditionally, Israel has relied on expensive, long-term contracts with nations like Mexico (oil), Norway (oil), the UK (oil), Australia (coal), South Africa (coal) and Colombia (coal) for its energy supplies. The government has estimated that the country could contain five billion barrels of oil reserves, most likely located underneath gas reserves, and that offshore gas potentially could supply Israel's short-term energy needs. Geologically, Israel appears to be connected to the oil-rich petroleum system stretching from Saudi Arabia through Iraq to Syria.

worsened significantly. In 2003, the debt amounts to 152% of GDP and foreign analysts fear that the country risks default. At present, the country is spending 65% of its budget on debt service. The government aims to reduce the deficit to 4% of GDP by 2005 and zero by 2006 but few outside the government take these goals seriously. Jamaica has ample international reserves totalling $1.4 billion, which is high for a small economy. However, reserves have been steadily falling and were about $2 billion as recently as 2002. The rate of unemployment has hovered at about 16% for the past several years. In 2003, authorities managed to stabilise the economy and were successful in borrowing on the international bond market. Analysts see this result as an encouraging sign of the credibility of the authorities' economic policies. Despite progress, the structure of the island's economy is still a barrier to development. It also suffers from an excess of crime and violence which has been a problem for the island's tourist industry. Jamaica's medium-term prospects will depend upon encouraging investment, maintaining a competitive exchange rate, selling off reacquired firms.

Agriculture contributes only 7% of GDP, though it employs a quarter of the workforce. Sugar cane, coffee, pineapples and bananas are grown for export, while rice, maize and vegetables are produced for domestic consumption. The tropical climate makes for rapid growth, but vulnerability to hurricanes is a problem. Manufacturing makes up 28% of GDP and is growing slowly. The industrial base is fairly well diversified with food processing, textiles, clothing and timber and wood products being especially important. Jamaica also has a major petrochemicals plant, and export-free zones have been established to encourage further diversification. The service sector, which contributes 65% of GDP and about 60% of employment, is dominated by Jamaica's most important industry, tourism. In the fallout after September 11th 2001, there are fears that some parts of this sector are growing too quickly. Initial plans to add 2,650 rooms to the island's complement of 15,500 have now been scaled back somewhat. Jamaica also faces increasing competition from other Caribbean destinations. A sizeable portion of the tourist sector is state-owned. Mining and quarrying output has been subject to much volatility since 1999 when most of the country's bauxite processing facilities sustained damage. These facilities have now resumed operation and bauxite production and exports have rebounded.

Imports provide for almost all of Jamaica's energy needs. In 2001, a US-based utility completed an 80% acquisition of the island nation's main power provider. The new investor promised that it will eliminate capacity bottlenecks that have led to blackouts around the country. The island, along with Barbados, the Dominican Republic and Haiti, is party to the San Jose pact, under which Mexico and Venezuela supply crude oil and refined products on favourable terms.

□ Jamaica

Capital City	Kingston	Capital population: 643,801 (1991)
Population ('000)	2,675 *(2002)*	
Urban population (%)	56.92 *(2002)*	
Land area (km²)	1083	
Languages	English	
Religion	Mainly Christian	
Currency	Jamaican dollar (J$)	
Head of State	HM Queen Elizabeth II	
Head of Government	Percival Patterson (March 1989)	
Ruling Party	People's National Party (PNP)	

Main Urban Areas	Population
Kingston (capital)	643,801 (1991)

Jamaica is centrally located in the western Caribbean, lying some 145km south of Cuba and 160km south-west of Haiti. The country has a pleasant climate, although subject to hurricanes and heavy rains in the October-November period. The capital is Kingston.

Jamaica, an independent member of the Commonwealth, is ruled by a prime minister and cabinet who are drawn from a 60-member House of Representatives (Lower House), elected by universal suffrage for a five-year term. The governor-general, who represents the Crown, has only formal functions. There is a 21-member Senate (Upper House), whose functions are mainly advisory. The constituency character of the electoral system means that parliamentary representation is often out of proportion to the levels of actual electoral support.

General elections were held in October 2002, when Patterson and his People's National Party were returned to power with a majority of 34 parliamentary seats. The opposition Labour Party took the remaining seats.

Jamaica's GDP rose by 1.5% in 2002 and should increase by another 2.2% in 2003. Growth of 1.6% is also forecast for 2004. Inflation was 7.1% in 2002 and should be 7% in both 2003 and 2004. For years Jamaica has struggled with sluggish growth while the government's debt has snowballed. Jamaica's economy was hit by a series of shocks including the impact of the terrorist attacks on September 11th 2001 on tourism, the outbreak of violence in 2002 and heavy floods in late November of that year. The government responded to these shocks through steps to cushion the impact on the economy. However, partly as a result, public finances

□ Japan

Capital City	Tokyo	Capital population: 11,898,400 (2002)
Population ('000)	127,044 *(2002)*	
Urban population (%)	79.21 *(2002)*	
Land area (km²)	36450	
Languages	Japanese	
Religion	Shinto (70%), Buddhist	
Currency	Yen (¥)	
Head of State	HM Emperor Akihito (1989)	
Head of Government	Junichiro Koizumi (2001)	
Ruling Party	The Liberal Democratic Party (LDP) leads a coalition.	

Main Urban Areas	Population	
Tokyo (capital)	11,898,400	(2002)
Osaka	8,802,600	(2002)
Kanagawa	8,583,000	(2002)
Saitamaok	7,060,400	(2002)
Chiba	6,014,600	(2002)
Hokkaido	5,691,200	(2002)
Fukuoka	5,043,400	(2002)
Hiroshima	2,885,800	(2002)
Kyoto	2,640,800	(2002)
Nagano	2,239,600	(2002)

Located (at its nearest point) 150km east of the Korean peninsula and about 1,500 km northeast of the Chinese mainland, Japan is situated in the northern Pacific Ocean with the Sea of Japan to its east. The country mainly comprises four volcanic islands - Hokkaido, Honshu, Shikoku and Kyushu, of which Honshu is the largest. There are also a considerable number of smaller islands. The climate is temperate, with mild winters. The capital is Tokyo.

Japan is a constitutional monarchy in which the Emperor Akihito plays only a ceremonial role. All political power is vested in a Diet (Parliament). Parliament includes a 480-member House of Representatives elected by universal suffrage for a term of four years, and a 247-member House of Councillors that serves a six-year term of office with half of its members coming up for election every three years.

In elections to the House of Representatives held in June 2000, the LDP lost support, winning 233 seats (down from 271 in the previous parliament). Elections to the House of Councillors were held in July 2001. The LDP won 110 seats, the Social-Democratic Party won 59 seats, the Communist Party of Japan won 20 seats and the remainder were scattered among various other parties.

GDP rose by only 0.2% in 2002 and growth of 2% is expected in 2003. In 2004, growth of 1.4% is forecast. Meanwhile, prices fell by 0.9% in 2002 and will decline by 0.3% in 2003. Prices are forecast to fall by another 0.6% in 2004. A slowdown in export growth brought Japan's modest economic expansion to a halt in 2002. Since

2000, consumer spending has been rising even as incomes have shrunk. As a result, the country's persistently high savings rate has plummeted. Although the outlook for domestic demand remains weak, the economy experienced a mild rebound in 2003. Profits are up, wages are rising and business investment is improving. However, these signs are by no means sufficient to pull the economy out of its rut. The slight upturn is partly due to a surge in exports to China, at a time when exports to Japan's largest market, the US, have declined. Unemployment has still risen to 5.5%, which is historically a very high level for Japan. Strong deflationary pressures continue to pose a downside risk for the economy, as does continued financial sector fragility and the strains associated with a further rise in public debt. The government has reversed the previous policy of increasing government spending to stimulate the country's economy, and has set a deficit ceiling of 30 trillion yen. Spending on public works projects, which had been funded as part of previous stimulus packages, has been scaled back significantly. The Bank of Japan, however, has adopted a more expansionary monetary policy, which has provided some stimulus to the economy.

Japanese agriculture is small and steadily contracting. Efficiency is hampered by the small and scattered nature of farmlands and by inordinately high input costs. Manufacturing is the mainstay of Japan's economy, accounting for just over 20% of GDP. The electronics and car industries dominate the manufacturing sector and have had huge success in penetrating international markets. Both, however, have suffered in recent years from the strength of the yen. This has led many firms to relocate their factories in lower-cost countries, mainly in Asia. Japan is also the world's largest maker of machine tools. Japan also exhibits a low degree of openness to foreign trade, mainly due to official and unofficial restrictions on merchandise imports. This lack of openness to foreign trade has often been cited as one of the reasons for the persistence of the structural problems in the country's economy in general and the poor productivity of companies in the non-tradable sectors in particular. By the year 2025, more than one of every four Japanese will be 65 or older (up from about one in every six in 2002). As a result, manufacturers are designing production to minimise labour inputs and ensure increased demand for capital-intensive, high value-added manufacturing.

Japan contains almost no oil reserves of its own but is the world's second largest oil consumer. Oil provides Japan with around 52% of its total energy needs. About half of all energy is used by industry and about one-fourth by transportation, with nearly all the rest used by the residential, agricultural, and service sectors. Japan's energy intensity (energy use per unit of GDP) is among the lowest in the developed world. The government is trying to develop more activities in the Caspian Sea region in order to offset its dependence on oil supplies from the Middle East. Since 1997, the country's oil consumption has declined as its economic slump caused demand by industrial and other users to fall. In 2002, Japan had 4.8 million barrels per day (bbl/d) of oil refining capacity at 33 refineries, down from five million bbl/d in 2001. Japan's economic stagnation has led to a period of consolidation in the energy sector. Energy demand has been stable, and Japan's energy industries, particularly the downstream oil sector, have undergone a period of downsizing and consolidation.

▫ Jordan

Capital City	Amman	*Capital population: 1,134,235 (1994)*
Population ('000)	5,355 *(2002)*	
Urban population (%)	74.72 *(2002)*	
Land area (km²)	8893	
Languages	Arabic	
Religion	Mainly Islam (90%)	
Currency	Jordanian dinar (JOD)	
Head of State	King Abdullah ibn Hussein as-Hashemi (1999)	
Head of Government	Ali Abu Rageb (1999)	
Ruling Party	The government is formed by non-partisans and Islamists.	

Main Urban Areas	**Population**	
Amman (capital)	1,134,235	(1994)
Zarqa	422,628	(1994)
Irbid	243,816	(1994)
Aqaba	77,409	(1994)
Madaba	67,484	(1994)
Salt	64,758	(1994)
Mafraq	48,474	(1994)
Maan	27,613	(1994)
Jerash	24,880	(1994)
Tafileh	24,790	(1994)

The Hashemite Kingdom of Jordan lies just to the east of Israel, at the eastern end of the Mediterranean, and would have been landlocked by the creation of Israel in 1948 if it did not have access to a narrow channel running into the Red Sea. Jordan is bounded in the north by Syria, in the south by Saudi Arabia and in the east by Iraq. It lost much of its West Bank territory to Israel after the 1967 war. The capital is Amman.

Jordan is a constitutional monarchy in which the King plays an especially active role. In February 1999, King Hussein ibn Talal died after ruling the country for more than 40 years. Just before his death, he appointed his son, Abdullah, to succeed him. Jordan has a bicameral national Assembly. The Chamber of Deputies is made up of 110 members who are directly elected, while the king appoints a Senate of 40 members.

The elections held in June 2003 resulted in the restoration of a parliament that King Abdullah had dissolved in June 2001 and ended two years of rule by decree. Tribal independents and pro-government candidates took a majority of 62 seats in the Chamber of Deputies. The Islamic Action Front (IAF) received 22% of the popular vote and won 21 seats. The IAF will also have the support of two Islamic Palestinians who won office. The remaining seats are scattered among non-partisans and minor parties.

GDP increased by 4.9% in 2002. Growth in 2003 is expected to be 3% and growth of 5.5% is forecast for 2004. Prices increased by 1.8% in 2002. Inflation in 2003 will be 2.5% and prices are forecast to increase by 1.8% in 2004. Exports of goods to neighbours Iraq and Saudi Arabia have made a significant contribution to Jordan's economy, and growth in regional exports is also helping to further Jordan's economic recovery. Both these growth sources are in jeopardy, however, as tensions between the US and Iraq mount. Remittances from Jordanian workers in the Persian Gulf countries are another important contributor to Jordan's balance of payments. At home, the government faces a stifling bureaucracy and a web of vested interests and other obstacles to liberalisation. It is important that these barriers be quickly overcome because Jordan needs even faster growth to absorb the unemployed, which are estimated to exceed 20%. The country's budget deficit is another serious concern. Excluding grants, in mid-2002 it stood at a high 7.5% of GDP. The government hopes to bring the budget deficit under control by 2005 but policymakers have limited room for manoeuvre. About 70% of the budget is tied up in military spending, interest payments on Jordan's US$7.2 billion of foreign debt, wages and pensions. Revenues, meanwhile, will come under increased pressure as Jordan brings down trade barriers and implements free-trade accords, including one signed with the EU to create a Mediterranean free-trade zone by 2010. To compensate, a value-added tax has been introduced, following on the reform of the general sales tax. Ultimately, Jordan's economy remains a hostage to wider developments in the Middle East. Events in Iraq, Israel and Palestinian territories have significant effects on the country.

Jordan's economy relies mainly on farming, with smallholders producing wheat, barley, olives, lentils, tobacco, fruit and vegetables. A persistent shortage of water and a lack of irrigation facilities keep farm productivity low and prevent any large-scale operations. The country is seeking to increase its fresh water supplies, as its underground aquifers are being depleted as the country's water consumption rises along with the rapidly growing population. One proposal is for a US$5 billion canal linking the Red Sea with the Dead Sea, where desalination plants would produce water. Typically, the country is able to meet only a quarter of its food needs. A privatisation programme has been undertaken to reduce the government's stake in sectors of the economy previously dominated by state-controlled firms. The government sold a 40% stake in the Jordan Telecommunications Company in 2000, in the most significant privatisation to date. Oil and electric power generation, as well as the country's large phosphate and potash industries, also are targeted for privatisation. As part of its preparations for admission to the WTO, Jordan has lifted most limits on foreign ownership of formerly state-owned companies. The country's large phosphate and potash industries are also slated for privatisation. The manufacturing sector is well diversified with production of cement, steel, glass, paints, plastics, fertilisers, food products and pharmaceuticals being prominent. Almost all manufacturing firms are small and few are capable of exporting. Amman is also working hard to develop its tourism sector but the number of visitors fell sharply in 2002.

Jordan has no significant oil resources of its own. In the past, it relied on Iraqi oil for nearly all of its needs (currently around 100,000 barrels per day - bbl/d). Jordan expects that these supplies will be quickly resumed once an interim government is in place in Iraq. The country has one refinery, at Zarqa, with a capacity of 90,400 bbl/d. An expansion of the facility to a capacity of 150,000 bbl/d is under consideration, but has not yet been implemented. Jordan does possess a significant quantity of oil shale resources, possibly as much as 40 billion tonnes. Foreign investors have conducted limited exploration digging in the Lajjun area, southwest of Amman. If the project is implemented, it could be in production by 2006 at a rate of 17,000 bbl/d.

□ Kazakhstan

Capital City	Astana	Capital population: 342,040 (2002)
Population ('000)	16,094 (2002)	
Urban population (%)	56.8 (2002)	
Land area (km²)	269970	
Languages	Kazakh	
Religion	Islam	
Currency	Tenge (KZT)	
Head of State	President Nursultan Nazarbayev (1991)	
Head of Government	Daniyal Akmetov (2003)	
Ruling Party	Republican Party Otan (OTAN)	

Main Urban Areas	Population	
Almaty	1,146,900	(2002)
Karaganda	402,840	(2002)
Shymkent	353,580	(2002)
Taraz	342,520	(2002)
Astana (capital)	342,040	(2002)
Ust-Kamenogorsk	306,940	(2002)
Pavlodar	290,040	(2002)
Semipalatinsk	260,420	(2002)
Aktobe	251,160	(2002)
Kostanai	220,380	(2002)

Until it achieved independence in 1991, Kazakhstan was one of the largest states in the old USSR. Lying directly to the south of Russia, it extends some 2,500km from the Caspian Sea in the west to the Chinese/Mongolian border in the east, and borders on the almost dried out Aral Sea and Lake Balkash. The land is mainly of steppe type, or of desert, and is richly endowed with minerals. The capital is Astana.

Kazakhstan declared its independence only in October 1990, having tried in vain to campaign for the vanishing Soviet Union. The president is elected for a five-year term by the people. Parliament has two chambers. The Assembly has seven seats, elected for a four-year term in single-seat constituencies. The Senate has 47 members, 40 members elected for a four-year term in double-seat constituencies by the local assemblies, half renewed every two years, and seven presidential appointees.

Presidential elections took place in January 1999 when Nazarbayev received 80% of the vote. In October 1999, elections to the Assembly gave 24 seats to the OTAN, 13 seats to the Civil Party of Kazakhstan, with the remainder distributed among small parties and non-aligned candidates. Elections to the Senate have been postponed with the last voting held in January 1996. The Peoples' Party of Kazakhstan took six seats, the Democratic Party gained five seats and the remainder went to non-aligned candidates. In June 2003, Imangali Tasmagambetov resigned his post as prime minister and was replaced by Akmetov.

Kazakhstan's recovery continued with growth of 9.5% in 2002 and expected growth of 9% in 2003. GDP is forecast to rise by another 8% in 2004. Inflation was 5.8% in 2002 and should be about 6.4% in 2003. Prices are forecast to rise by 5.9% in 2004. Living standards improved as continuing economic growth helped raise real incomes. In 2002, average monthly wages reached T 20,305 (equivalent to $131), a 16.6% increase over the 2001 figure in nominal terms and 10.0% in real terms. Today, Kazakhstan is the richest country in the region but nearly one person in four still lives below the poverty line. There are also severe regional disparities with 95% of the rural population in Mangystau province (which borders the Caspian Sea) living in poverty while in Astana, the capital, only 2% lack basic necessities. The unemployment rate declined from 10.4% to 9.4% in 2002, mainly due to greater employment in construction and services. However, unemployment is still a major problem, especially in rural areas and among women. Analysts have recently highlighted the growing danger of possible over-reliance on the oil sector, predicting that without more investment in the country's non-oil sectors, Kazakhstan's economic capacity will be strained by 2007 and growth will suffer. The fiscal position is expected to continue to be strong. General government revenues are projected at 20.9% of GDP in 2003 and 20.5% in 2004. Continued economic growth is expected to improve living standards as the average real wage is projected to rise by 8-9% annually over the 2002 level. The government recently approved a state programme on poverty reduction for 2003-2005, which aims to bring down the number of people living below the subsistence minimum to 25.0% in 2005 from 27.5% in 2002. Government plans to diversify agriculture and help depressed areas mean that it can no longer put off land reform. However, it is thought that the newly-approved law, which would affect 44% of the population, would benefit only the rich and ruin many farmers. Despite rapid growth in recent years, progress is hampered by a weak judicial system and a poor investment climate outside the oil and financial sectors, particularly for small and medium-size domestic and foreign investors

The oil sector, which is still in a phase of investment-led expansion, is the main engine of economic growth in Kazakhstan. Oil and gas account for more than a quarter of GDP and government revenues. Production will keep on rising as new fields come on stream. The country's imports have increased significantly as oil sector developments push up import volumes (primarily capital technology and services imports). The non-oil economy has also grown strongly, by an annual 8% on average in 2000-2002. Agricultural output grew by 2.7%; growth in the livestock subsector was strong, but the grain subsector recorded only a modest rise due to a decline in crop productivity. Construction output rose sharply by 19.3%, largely as a result of rapid infrastructure development for the new capital, Astana, and rapid

continued growth (at over 9%) in the services sector, mainly due to large rises in transport and telecommunications. Fixed capital investment at 19% of GDP remained high, though somewhat below the 21.0% of GDP peak recorded in 2001.

Kazakhstan's combined onshore and offshore proven hydrocarbon reserves have been estimated to be between 9 and 17.6 billion barrels. Between 1999 and 2002, annual oil production grew by approximately 16% per year. Although only a minor world oil exporter in 2002, Kazakhstan is poised to become a more significant supplier in the future. Massive increases in foreign investment have helped to boost oil production The government expects that the country will produce 2.4 million bbl/d (120 million tons per year) by 2010, and 3.6 million bbl/d (180 million tons per year) by 2015. Most of this growth will come from just three enormous fields. The country also has proven reserves of 65 trillion cubic feet of natural gas, ranking it in the top 20 countries in the world in terms of this energy resource. However, the natural gas industry is significantly underdeveloped and hampered by a lack of infrastructure.

□ Kenya

Capital City	Nairobi	Capital population: 2,079,000 (1995)
Population ('000)	32,768 (2002)	
Urban population (%)	34.56 (2002)	
Land area (km²)	56914	
Languages	Swahili, English	
Religion	Mainly traditional	
Currency	Kenya shilling (KES)	
Head of State	President Emilio Mwai Kibaki (2002)	
Head of Government	President Emilio Mwai Kibaki (2002)	
Ruling Party	The government is formed by the National Rainbow Coalition (NARC).	

Main Urban Areas	Population	
Nairobi (capital)	2,079,000	(1995)

Kenya lies on the Indian Ocean coast of central East Africa, where it is bounded in the north by Eritrea, Ethiopia, Sudan and Somalia, in the west by Uganda and in the south by Tanzania. Although subject to occasional drought, the country has an equable climate and numerous major watercourses. The capital is Nairobi.

Kenya has an executive president who is elected for a five-year term by the people. The National Assembly has 224 members, 210 members elected for five-year terms in single-seat constituencies, 12 members appointed and two ex officio members.

Presidential elections took place in December 2002 when Kibaki of the NARC took 62% of the vote, defeating Uhuru Kenyatta of the Kenya African National Union Party (KANU). Legislative elections at the same time gave the NARC 132 seats to 68 for the KANU. The remaining seats were divided among several smaller parties.

GDP grew by 1% in 2002. Growth in 2003 is expected to be 1.3% and GDP is forecast to grow by 2.6% in 2004. Inflation was 2% in 2002. Prices are expected to rise by 12.4% in 2003 and are forecast to increase by another 3.9% in 2004. Kenya's poor economic performance is aggravating unemployment and increasing poverty. The growth in wage employment has decelerated since 2001 for the first time since independence. Meanwhile, the percentage of those living in poverty rose to 56% in 2002, up from 52% in 1997. These developments have been accompanied by a sharp deterioration in the country's budgetary position. The downward trend is expected to continue at least during 2003. Total public expenditures declined to 21.9% of GDP in 2002 but public revenues fell even faster. The weak economy, the government's failure to complete several large privatisation deals and the suspension of international assistance are the main reasons for the drop in public revenues. Kenya has had better results in liberalising its trade regime. After reducing the most important tariffs, the trade deficit narrowed in 2002. Imports fell slightly while total export receipts rose by 9.7%. Non-traditional exports were the main source of growth, while exports of major commodities such as coffee and tea performed poorly. Nonetheless, analysts expect the trade deficit to rise to 13.1% of GDP in 2003. Kenya's record with restructuring and privatisation of public enterprises has remained an issue of contention between the government and its major development partners. Several large public firms are to be put up for sale in 2003 and the government has announced its intention to concentrate on attracting private sector participation in the provision of infrastructure services.

The agricultural sector remains the cornerstone of the economy, accounting for 19% of GDP and employs abut three-quarters of the workforce. Coffee, tea, cotton, sugar, tobacco and pyrethrum are produced for export. Domestic crops include maize, sorghum, cassava and beans, and there are substantial livestock herds. Improved weather conditions have led to a rise in production after several years of drought. However, coffee producers are suffering owing to a drop in world prices while exports of tea have fallen. The manufacturing sector accounts for 13% of GDP and is growing slowly thanks to a cessation of power rationing and the gains in agricultural output. Agro-based industries are performing best, along with producers of wood, cork and basic chemical products. Kenya also has a significant engineering industry along with producers of textiles, glass and construction materials. In the service sector, the transport and communications subsectors all reported strong growth. The tourist industry faces a very uncertain future following the terrorist attacks in November 2002. The attacks could not have happened at a worse time as the number of visitors was just beginning to rise again after earlier terrorist attacks around the world. Poor management of the country's game reserves and the growth of crime are other problems that handicap the tourist sector.

Kenya has no oil of its own, and must import all of its daily consumption of 50,000 barrels. The government has sought to bring in partners to assist with oil exploration in the country. Recent oil surveys have indicated that more than half of the country has oil potential. Limited oil exploration has been going on for the last 40 years, but only 30 wells have been drilled so far with little success.

□ Kiribati

Capital City	Bairiki	Capital population: 25,300 (1992)
Population ('000)	86 (2002)	
Urban population (%)	39.99 (2002)	
Land area (km²)	73	
Languages	I-Kiribati, English	
Religion	Mainly Christian	
Currency	Australian dollar (A$)	
Head of State	Anote Tong (2003)	
Head of Government	Anote Tong (2003)	
Ruling Party	Boutokaan Te Koaua (BTK) Party	

Main Urban Areas	Population
Bairiki (capital)	25,300 (1992)

Kiribati (pronounced Kiribass), the former Gilbert Islands, is a group of 33 islands and atolls in the southwest central Pacific, of which the largest is Banaban, the former Ocean Island. The climate is warm and equable, but the terrain is extremely flat, seldom rising more than 4m above sea level. The capital is Bairiki.

Kiribati is an independent republic within the Commonwealth. The people elect the executive president for a four-year term. The House of Assembly has 42 members, 40 elected for four-year terms in single-seat and multi-seat constituencies, one delegate from Banaba Island and one ex-officio member.

Presidential elections were held in July 2003 when Anote Tong won 47.4% of the vote, defeating two other candidates. Elections to the House of Assembly were held in May 2003. The Protect the Maneaba Party took 24 seats in the Assembly and the BTK won 16 seats.

Kiribati's economy grew by 1% in 2002 and growth of 2.5% is expected in 2003. The forecast for 2004 is for growth of 1.8%. Inflation was 3.2% in 2002 and will be about 1.4% in 2003. Prices are forecast to rise by 2.3% in 2004. Economic growth in recent years has generally been less than population increases, leading to a gradual decline in per capita incomes. Central government revenues amounted to 119.1% of GDP during 2002, lower than the previous year's 148.2%. Fishing revenues typically account for half of internal revenues. Income from the overseas investments of the government's Revenue Equalization Reserve Fund, valued at $325 million, and local taxes and duties (mainly on wages and salary income, company profits, and imports) provides the remainder. Public expenditures have also risen in the past two years, due mainly to an increase in public sector wages and the larger subsidies being paid to public enterprises. The economy is dominated by the public sector and future growth will depend heavily on developments in this field. The outlook for foreign trade is somewhat brighter than it has been. Exports are expected increase to $5.1 million in 2003, though achieving this forecast rests heavily on developments in the copra industry. The recent improvement in world copra prices and the scheduled completion of the new copra mill in mid-2003 should help provide a somewhat improved outlook for copra in the medium term.

Kiribati's small-scale economy relies heavily on its agricultural sector, which produces copra - dried coconut albumen, the raw material used in the manufacture of coconut oil - and fish for world markets. Export products consisted of copra, live fish for aquariums, and seaweed. Economic growth has been held back in part by a poor agricultural performance, with a decline in copra production. Growth was also slowed by continued infrastructure problems and lack of progress in creating an enabling environment for private sector investment. There has been almost no foreign direct investment since 2000. Tourism continues to thrive in the outer islands, consisting mainly of cruise ship vacationers visiting Fanning Island and sports-fishermen. Nearly 20% of the formally employed labour force work on foreign merchant or fishing vessels and generate a substantial amount of factor income. This is an important source of income, particularly for people from the outer islands where poverty levels are higher and opportunities for formal employment are very limited. The government provides a subsidy to the copra industry of about $2 million per year. In addition, it has committed US$2 million to build a copra mill. The mill, to be operated by a private firm, is intended to increase value added from Kiribati's copra and reduce the subsidy required.

Kiribati's limited energy needs are met in part by domestic resources such as fuel wood and brushwood. Otherwise, all requirements have to be imported.

□ Kuwait

Capital City	Kuwait City	Capital population: 28,747 (1995)
Population ('000)	2,343 (2002)	
Urban population (%)	97.7 (2002)	
Land area (km²)	1782	
Languages	Arabi,C English	
Religion	Mainly Islam	
Currency	Kuwaiti dinar (KWD)	
Head of State	HH Shaikh Jaber al-Ahmed al-Sabah	
Head of Government	HH Sheikh Saad Abdullah al-Salem al-Sabah	
Ruling Party	There are no political parties in Kuwait. The government is formed by royalists.	

Main Urban Areas	Population
Kuwait City (capital)	28,747 (1995)
Ahmadi City	21,587 (1995)

The tiny state of Kuwait includes a mainland area and several small islands. It lies at a strategically important point on the northern extreme of the Persian (Arabian) Gulf, which allows it to serve as a transhipment point for oil supplies from Saudi Arabia (and formerly Iraq). Lacking any fresh river water or other natural water supplies, it is obliged to manufacture its own through massive desalination plants. The greater part of the population lives in the capital, Kuwait City.

Kuwait became an independent state in 1961, having been a British protectorate since 1899. The Emir exercises almost complete political control. In 1986, he dissolved the National Assembly (Parliament), and ruled by decree for some years thereafter. In April 1991, following the Gulf War, the Emir appointed an interim government and the democratic process was later resumed. The National Assembly has 50 members elected for four-year terms in double-seat constituencies and the ministers who sit as ex-officio members. The Emir again dissolved the National Assembly in 1999 in an effort to end a long paralysis between parliament and government. In May 1999, he decreed that women could vote and stand in elections, with the same rights as men.

Elections to the National Assembly took place in July 2003. Islamists won 21 of 50 seats, government supporters 14, liberals 3, and non-partisans 12. The country is the only one in the Gulf to have an elected legislature — a source of great pride for Kuwaitis.

GDP contracted by 0.9% in 2002. In 2003, growth of 4.7% is expected while the forecast for 2004 is for an increase of 2.2%. Inflation was 1.4% in 2002 and should be 2% in both 2003 and 2004. The country's external position remains solid. Although the surplus of the external current account has declined, a substantial surplus remains (equivalent to about 26% of GDP in 2002). Every year, the government siphons off 10% of its revenues to the Fund for Future Generations. The country's savings abroad amounts to US$200,000 for every citizen. But with population growing by 3.5% a year, the state is always hard pressed to keep its people in the style they expect. This includes free health and education, generous housing, cheap petrol, power and water, subsidised food and a job for the asking. Kuwait's other investments abroad - which contribute substantial income to the government - have been falling sharply as world markets slide. An estimated 93% of all Kuwaitis work in the public sector. Their incomes are unlikely to change in the medium term, whatever the level of international oil prices or returns on foreign investments. The government has made some progress in creating the necessary institutional framework for the implementation of structural reforms. The reform package includes measures to increase private sector investment, privatise state enterprises and utilities, allow foreigners to own 100% equity, open up the upstream oil sector to foreign investment under operating service agreements, reduce implicit subsidies by increasing fees and charges on government-provided services, and reform the labour market.

Kuwait hopes to attract additional foreign investment, and as part of this effort is considering a reduction in the income tax cap on non-Kuwaiti companies. Kuwait has started a programme to privatise state-owned businesses (outside the oil sector) as a way of reducing subsidies. As part of this programme, the Kuwaiti government has begun privatising healthcare, electricity and telecommunications assets. Privatisation is complicated by the need to protect the jobs of Kuwaiti citizens, who are employed in state-owned enterprises and the government. The government hopes to address emerging unemployment pressures through the development of skills that will be needed by the private sector in the years ahead. Eventually, the government will also have to take steps to better integrate the labour markets in the public and private sector, possible by reducing public-sector wages and introducing civil service reforms. In the oil sector, the constitution forbids foreign ownership of mineral resources, but the government may allow foreign investment in upstream oil development under terms which provide for per-barrel fees rather than traditional production sharing agreements.

Kuwait contains 96.5 billion barrels of proven oil reserves (including its share of the Neutral Zone), or roughly 9% of the world's total oil reserves. Along with Saudi Arabia and the United Arab Emirates, Kuwait remains one of the few oil-producing countries with significant excess oil production capacity. Most of Kuwait's oil reserves are located in the 70-billion barrel Greater Burgan area, which comprises the Burgan, Magwa and Ahmadi structures. Greater Burgan is widely considered the world's second largest oil field, surpassed only by Saudi Arabia's Ghawar field, and has been producing oil since 1938. Kuwait's Raudhatain, Sabriya and Minagish fields have large proven reserves as well, with 6 billion, 3.8 billion, and 2 billion barrels of oil, respectively. Kuwait has completed major renovations of its main port for the export of crude oil, which was virtually destroyed during the Gulf War.

The country also is planning a $900 million expansion at the port in order to add storage capacity and increase export capacity in conjunction with plans for expanded oil production.

◻ Kyrgyzstan		
Capital City	Bishkek	*Capital population: 589,400 (1997)*
Population ('000)	4,714 *(2002)*	
Urban population (%)	33.29 *(2002)*	
Land area (km²)	19180	
Languages	Kyrgyz	
Religion	Islam	
Currency	Kyrgyzstani Som (KGS)	
Head of State	President Askar Akayev (1990)	
Head of Government	Nikolay Tanayev (2002)	
Ruling Party	The government is formed by non-partisans, loyal to the president.	

Main Urban Areas	**Population**
Bishkek (capital)	589,400 (1997)

Kyrgyzstan is a mountainous region lying in the northern part of Soviet Central Asia, and borders on China, from which it is separated by the Pamir-Altai mountain range. The capital is Bishkek.

Kyrgyzstan declared independence in December 1990. The country has an executive president who is elected by universal suffrage for a maximum of two five-year terms, and who leads a Cabinet of Ministers. The Supreme Council has two chambers. The Legislative Assembly has 60 members, elected for five-year terms in single-seat constituencies. The Assembly of People's Representatives has 45 members, elected for five-year terms in single-seat constituencies.

In presidential elections held in October 2000, Askar Akayev was returned to power with 74% of the vote. Elections to the Assembly of People's Representatives were held in February 2000. The Communist Party received 28% of the vote and 15 seats, the Union of Democratic Forces received 19% of the vote and four seats and the Women's' Democratic Party of Kyrgyzstan took 13% and two seats. The remaining votes were distributed among several parties. Voting for the Legislative Assembly took place at the same time, when all 45 elected officials were non-partisan.

GDP fell by 0.5% in 2002 and is expected to increase by 5.6% in 2003. In 2004, growth of 4% is forecast. Meanwhile, inflation was 2.1% in 2002 and will be about 3.3% in 2003. Prices are forecast to rise by 3.8% in 2004. Kyrgyzstan is one of the poorest countries in the region. After independence, the proportion of those living in poverty jumped from a third to over 55% in 1999 before dropping to around 50% in 2001. Excessive deficits threaten to trigger macroeconomic imbalances by rekindling inflation, and increasing debt. It is essential that higher rates of growth be realised to avoid unsustainable external debt. The high dependency on a few export commodities calls for diversification of the economy, and policies to achieve this aim must be put in place urgently. Exports to neighbouring Uzbekistan have also been cut by half when the latter recently introduced harsh trade restrictions. Kyrgyzstan became a member of WTO in 1998 but this has brought few trade benefits since most of its neighbours remain outside that organisation. The government intends to focus on strengthening structural policies, especially in governance and banking, to increase economic efficiency. Containing the growth of unit labour costs relative to trade partners will be critical for maintaining the competitive edge of Kyrgyz exports. At the same time, financial policies will need to contain consumer price inflation. In 2003-2006, an increase in national savings by three percentage points of GDP is anticipated. This goal is to be achieved through additional fiscal adjustments and improvements in enterprise profitability through productivity gains. The use of foreign savings to finance investment should increase by 1.3 percentage points in the same period. In 2002, the fiscal deficit rose to 5.6% of GDP, up from 5% in 2001. This weakening of the fiscal balance reflects the lower-than-expected growth in that year. However, in 2003, the deficit should be reduced to 4.7% of GDP. This goal is to be achieved mainly through an increase in state budget revenue from the projected 13.4% of GDP in 2002 to 14.6% in 2003. The level of unemployment is not officially available, but on the basis of estimates of the registered unemployed, it appears that there has been very little reduction in unemployment. However, the incidence of poverty has declined as a result of stronger export prices and stable food prices in the domestic market.

The agricultural sector performed satisfactorily in 2002, although the harvest was delayed. In the industrial sector, growth was again uneven, masking a decline in the output of several subsectors. The mining sector is an important source of foreign exchange but total earnings fell in 2002 owing to a landslide at the country's Kumtor gold mine. However, the reduction in gold exports was partially offset by higher gold prices. The Kumtor mine, alone, accounts for 40% of Kyrgyzstan's industrial production. The country is one of the largest producers of mercury and antimony, for which there is high demand in world markets. Energy exports also declined in 2002. Within the manufacturing sector, a few industries - notably, textiles, glass, leather and food processing - reported a strong turnaround in 2002. Meanwhile, government officials are focused on reforms of the banking sector. These reforms are mainly designed to reduce the vulnerability of commercial banks. They are expected to improve the business and investment climate and facilitate access to credit. A commercial dispute has delayed the privatisation of the country's state-owned telecommunications firm, but the sale is expected to proceed in 2003. Efforts to broaden the tax base continue with the

addition of a new tax on property. Agriculture accounts for 40% of GDP but only 5% of tax revenue and in the future it is expected that the VAT will be extended to cover large producers' direct sales to the domestic market.

With estimated petroleum reserves of only 40 million barrels, Kyrgyzstan is reliant on imports to meet its domestic supply needs. The country has seven developed oil fields and two oil/gas fields but the mountainous topography makes extraction difficult. Water encroachment means that recovery rates are low. Although oil consumption has declined steadily for the past ten years, Kyrgyzstan still needs to import supplies to meet domestic demand. Kyrgyzstan is looking to increase its oil production, and the government is undertaking a programme of intensive oil extraction in order to meet the country's domestic petroleum needs. Drilling of exploration wells began in 2002 with an initial investment of $30 million. As part of the programme, Kyrgyzstan is planning to produce 3,000 barrels per day by 2005.

◻ Laos		
Capital City	Vientiane	*Capital population: 449,000 (1992)*
Population ('000)	5,606 *(2002)*	
Urban population (%)	24.55 *(2002)*	
Land area (km²)	23080	
Languages	Laotian, French, tribal languages including Meo	
Religion	Mainly Buddhist	
Currency	Kip (Kip)	
Head of State	President Khamtai Siphandone (1998)	
Head of Government	Boungnang Vorachith (2001)	
Ruling Party	Revolutionary People's Party of Laos (dictatorial communist)	

Main Urban Areas	**Population**
Vientiane (capital)	449,000 (1992)

Laos runs from northeast to southwest through the northernmost part of the central Indochina peninsula. The country borders on China and Myanmar in the north, on Thailand in the west and on Cambodia in the south. In the east, Vietnam follows its entire length in such a way as to shut it off from the South China Sea. The country has a tropical and generally humid climate. The capital is Vientiane.

The Lao Constitution, approved in August 1991, provides in principle for the creation of a National Assembly to be elected by universal suffrage and to serve for five years. The Assembly consists of 109 members and elects the executive President, who also serves for five years.

In parliamentary elections held in February 2002, the Revolutionary People's Party of Laos (PPPL) won 108 seats. Only one (approved) non-partisan candidate won a seat.

GDP grew by 5.9% in 2002 and growth of 5.5% is expected in 2003. In 2004, growth of 6% is forecast. Inflation, which peaked at 134% in 1999, dropped to 10.6% in 2002 and should be around 11.3% in 2003. Prices are forecast to rise by 7% in 2004. In recent years, the government has made concerted efforts to reduce its fiscal deficit. It has had some success and inflation rates have fallen as a consequence. However, the fiscal deficit remains substantial, but is now almost entirely financed through grants and external borrowings, rather than through credit creation. In the area of private sector development, reforms to the foreign investment framework were carried out in 2002, including streamlining approval procedures for the establishment and operation of foreign investment and simplifying the regulations and procedures for establishing businesses. Reforms are also under way among state-owned enterprises, including restructuring as well as tariff hikes for electricity and water. In the medium term, government revenues are expected to rise modestly, provided that reforms in tax collection continue and coordination with provincial tax authorities improves. Imports are forecast to rise due to higher capital goods requirements. With higher imports, it is expected that the trade and current account balances in 2003-2004 will deteriorate.

Agriculture employs an estimated 80% of the workforce and accounts for about half of GDP. The sector expanded by 4.0% in 2002. Industry remained the fastest growing sector - with construction and garments playing a key role - expanding by 9.8%. The services sector, which accounts for a quarter of the economy, grew by 5.8%. Tourism continued to play a major role, contributing both to GDP growth and the balance of payments. Income from tourism has increased steadily since the mid-1990s. The value of new foreign investment projects approved in 2002 rose due to a gradual recovery in developing Asia and improved investment conditions domestically. More public sector resources were allocated to the social sector, with the share of expenditures for education and health increasing to 19.1% in 2002. Banking reform has been initiated with measures to stop the deterioration in performance and reduce the level of new non-performing loans. The country's leading exports in 2002 included hydroelectric power, garments and wool products. Both the trade deficit and the current account deficit decreased in 2002 while foreign exchange reserves rose and were now sufficient to cover 3.5 months of imports of goods and services by mid-2003.

Laos manages to meet only a small proportion of its own oil needs, relying mainly on domestically mined coal. The country has a number of agreements to develop hydroelectric plants but work has been halted and the interest of foreign investors has diminished.

▪ Lebanon

Capital City	Beirut	Capital population: 702,000 (1983)
Population ('000)	3,464 (2002)	
Urban population (%)	90.21 (2002)	
Land area (km²)	1023	
Languages	Arabi,C French, English	
Religion	Muslim, Christian, Jewish	
Currency	Lebanese pound (L£)	
Head of State	President Émile Lahoud (1998)	
Head of Government	Rafiq al-Hariri (2000)	
Ruling Party	Parti Socialiste Progressiste leads a coalition.	

Main Urban Areas	Population
Beirut (capital)	702,000 (1983)

Lebanon is a narrow (100km wide) strip of land running from north to south for about 220km along the eastern coastline of the Mediterranean. In the south it is bordered by Israel and in the north and east by Syria. The country has a temperate Mediterranean climate with warm summers but occasionally cool winters, especially in the hills. The capital is Beirut.

The electoral system has been only recently restored, having been effectively shelved since 1979. In May 2000, the government announced its plans for a complicated new electoral system. Each sectarian group will receive a fixed number of the 128 seats in parliament. Voters must cast ballots not only for candidates from their own sect, but also vote for candidates from other sects. The president is elected for a six-year term. The prime minister is chosen by the president after consultation with parliamentary deputies. The Assembly of Representatives has 128 members, elected for a term of four years by the religious communities.

In August-September 2000, elections to the Assembly of Representatives were held. The Resistance and Development Party won 23 seats, the Dignity Party took 18 seats and the Baalbeck-Hermel Coalition captured nine seats. Other seats were distributed among a number of parties.

GDP rose by 2% in 2002 and a further increase of 2% is anticipated in 2003. In 2004, growth of 3% is forecast. Inflation was 1.8% in 2002 and should be 2% in 2003. In 2004, inflation is forecast to be 2.5%. Macroeconomic conditions became particularly difficult in the spring of 2002, when the country's international reserves reached their lowest level, but have since improved considerably. Market confidence was bolstered after industrialised countries agreed in November 2002 to mobilise international financial assistance. The authorities' economic strategy for the medium term aims at reducing the government debt (as well as service costs) and restoring growth. The strategy includes further fiscal adjustment, large-scale privatisation and external financial assistance on concessional terms. The authorities expect proceeds from privatisation and securitisation in 2003-2007 to total US$8.9 billion, and have made extensive preparations in the telecommunications, power, and water sectors. To restore competitiveness and spur economic growth, the authorities rely on structural reforms and improvements in the business environment. Ending patronage is proving very difficult for a government whose members are appointed on political lines. Meanwhile, the reconstruction programme to rebuild Lebanon after the civil war is far behind schedule. The costs were to be paid off by 1999, but it now appears that this will not be done before the year 2005.

Lebanon has much fertile farmland, producing wheat, barley, maize, fruit, potatoes, tobacco and olives. Farms are small but relatively efficient and there is little need to import foodstuffs. Manufacturing is concentrated around the coastal urban areas. The more important industries include textiles, cement, chemicals, refining and light industries making goods for the domestic consumer market. All these types of industries have flourished since 2000, but reconstruction has proven to be a much bigger problem for the more capital-intensive industries and country's infrastructure. Many of the country's manufacturers are also expected to suffer following the war in Iraq. Prior to the war, Lebanon had a free-trade agreement with Iraq and in 2002 7% of total exports went to that country. Since 1997 firms received $1.3 billion in contracts under the UN oil-for-food programme. Such sums were substantial for high-cost Lebanese manufacturers who find it difficult to compete in other foreign markets. Most analysts expect the Iraqi market will be lost when a new government assumes power there. Lebanon's banking sector contributes 8% to GDP and most of the sector is profitable despite considerable fragmentation. Petroleum refining and financial services were two of the mainstays of the Lebanese economy prior to the war but the country will probably never regain its position in these two industries.

Lebanon is self-sufficient in hydrocarbons and has a number of electricity generating stations, 90% of which are thermal with the remainder hydroelectric. The country's energy companies are very inefficient, however. Several oil refineries have been out of operation since the early 1990s.

▪ Lesotho

Capital City	Maseru	Capital population: 130,000 (1992)
Population ('000)	2,314 (2002)	
Urban population (%)	29.33 (2002)	
Land area (km²)	3035	
Languages	English, Sesotho	
Religion	Roman Catholi,C Lesotho Evangelical and Anglican	
Currency	Loti (LSL)	
Head of State	HM King Letsie III (1996)	
Head of Government	Pakalitha Mosisili (1998)	
Ruling Party	Lesotho Congress for Democracy (LCD)	

Main Urban Areas	Population
Maseru (capital)	130,000 (1992)

Lesotho is a small mountainous territory situated in southern Africa. It is surrounded on all sides by the Republic of South Africa. Although a third of its land is classified as lowland, the remainder is all above 2,000 metres and rises to more than 3,500 metres. The capital is Maseru.

The country's parliament has two chambers. The National Assembly has 120 members, elected for a five-year term, 80 in single-seat constituencies and 40 by proportional representation. The Senate has 33 nominated members.

In parliamentary elections held in May 2002, the ruling LCD won 77 seats. The conservative Basotho National Party took 21 seats and the remainder were spread among several parties.

GDP increased by 4.2% in 2002 and the same rate of growth is expected in 2003. The forecast for 2004 is for growth of 4.4%. Prices rose by 33.8% in 2002 and are expected to increase by another 9.3% in 2003. Inflation is forecast to be 10.1% in 2004. Lesotho has struggled to rebuild its economy ever since a period of political instability in 1998. Like many of its neighbours, Lesotho has been in the grip of food shortages in recent years. The government's efforts to develop the economy and reduce poverty have met with varying degrees of success. The medium-term strategy is to concentrate on increasing export-led growth, with prudent fiscal management and a cautious monetary policy. Lesotho would also benefit from a stronger economy in South Africa, one of Lesotho's major export markets. Unemployment is estimated at over 40%, and poverty is widespread. The fiscal and balance of payments situations have also deteriorated. Declining public revenue and one-off expenditures associated with the restructuring of a public enterprise and state banks have caused the budget deficit to rise to 16% of GDP. Additional investment in the manufacturing sector is desperately needed to reduce the country's high rate of unemployment and to provide employment for miners released from jobs in South Africa.

Agriculture accounts for most of the employment in Lesotho but productivity is low and the sector contributes no more than 12% to GDP. A combination of bad weather and late deliveries of seeds and fertiliser could condemn Lesotho to another disastrous harvest in 2003. Some 445,000 people are estimated to be in need of food aid in Lesotho. Most farming is for subsistence purposes. Maize, sorghum and beans dominate, though livestock herding is also important. Droughts and persistent mismanagement have reduced yields in recent years. The industrial sector makes up 44% of GDP and produces textiles, clothing, food products and pharmaceuticals. Many of these manufactured items are exported. Lesotho's diamond mining activities have been closed down after many years of decline, although there is still some freelancing. The country has deposits of peat, iron ore, uranium and lead.

Apart from firewood, Lesotho depends on imports for all its fuel resources. Completion of the US$4 billion Highlands Water Scheme should provide enough hydroelectricity for the whole country and allow it to become a substantial exporter of electricity. The construction phase of this project accounts for as much as 15% of Lesotho's GDP.

▪ Liberia

Capital City	Monrovia	Capital population: 490,000 (1992)
Population ('000)	4,021 (2002)	
Urban population (%)	45.97 (2002)	
Land area (km²)	9632	
Languages	English	
Religion	Christian, Muslim	
Currency	Liberian dollar (L$)	
Head of State	Charles Taylor (1997)	
Head of Government	Gyude Bryant (2003)	
Ruling Party	A broad-based coalition leads the interim government.	

Main Urban Areas	Population
Monrovia (capital)	490,000 (1992)

Located on the Atlantic coast of West Africa, Liberia lies between Sierra Leone in the north-west, Guinea in the north-east, and Côte d'Ivoire in the south-east. The country has a mixed landscape, rising from the coastal plains to the upper plateau further inland. The climate is tropical, and is often humid. The capital is Monrovia.

Liberia's political system disappeared during the first half of the 1990s. Two peace treaties signed in 1993 and 1995 respectively failed to hold. West African (mainly Nigerian) peacekeepers eventually managed to restore order. The constitution calls for the president to be elected for a six-year term by the people. Parliament has two chambers. The House of Representatives has 64 members, elected for a six-year term in single-seat constituencies. The Senate has 26 members, elected for a nine-year term in two-seat constituencies. The recent compromise which created the new interim government has dispensed with these two chambers in favour of a single 76-member parliament. The nature of the future political system remains uncertain.

In August 2003, the warlord and president, Charles Taylor, bowed to international pressure and left the country. Government officials and rebel groups then agreed on a transitional government led by Bryant, leader of the Liberia Action Party. He was selected over Ellen Johnson-Sirleaf, the runner-up in the 1997 election. The transitional government will remain in power until elections in 2005. Under the agreement, two rebel groups will each have 12 members in the new parliament. The remaining seats will be filled by civil groups, members of unarmed political parties and other interest groups.

Liberia's previous government did little to improve the economy. The war took a heavy toll on the population and the country's infrastructure was largely destroyed. Outside the urban areas only 13% of people are estimated to have access to clean water and 4% to sanitation. Domestic production has rebounded strongly, although it still remains far below the pre-war level. The country's economic policy objectives are to achieve economic growth of some 15-20%, largely reflecting continued recovery in the forestry and agriculture sectors, with inflation in the range of 5% and the exchange rate stable, despite the recent decline in donor financing. Achievement of these ambitious goals is highly unlikely in view of the muddled macroeconomic policies currently in place.

Richly endowed with water, mineral resources, forests, and a climate favourable for agriculture, Liberia had been a producer and exporter of basic products before the civil war. For most people, farming is still the most important activity. Employing nearly 80% of the workforce, the sector produces rubber, coffee, cocoa and timber for export. A combination of the war and reckless farming has brought deforestation to the country's tropical rain forest, while soil erosion is an increasing problem for farmers. Liberia's main industrial activity is the mining of iron ore, and to a lesser extent, diamonds and gold. These three minerals contribute two-thirds of export revenues although they account for only 5% of all employment. There has been an environmental cost with these activities, however. Pollution of rivers from the dumping of iron ore tailings and of coastal waters from oil residue is a growing problem. A majority of the population lives on a subsistence basis, growing cassava, rice and various root vegetables. Manufacturing is at a very rudimentary stage, with mainly small companies producing textiles, food products, timber goods, chemicals and cement.

Liberia relies on imports for all its petroleum needs, although exploration is under way for domestic resources. The general lack of hydroelectric capacity means that oil is still the most popular means of generating electricity.

▫ Libya

Capital City	Tripoli	*Capital population: 3,272,000 (1995)*
Population ('000)	5,871 *(2002)*	
Urban population (%)	88.08 *(2002)*	
Land area (km²)	175954	
Languages	Arabic	
Religion	Islam	
Currency	Libyan dinar (LYD)	
Head of State	President Col Muammar al-Qaddafi	
Head of Government	Muhammad Ahmad al-Mangoush (Secretary of the General People's Congress)	
Ruling Party	There are no parties, with the Arab Socialist Union the sole authorised political group.	

Main Urban Areas	Population
Tripoli (capital)	3,272,000 (1995)
Benghazi	1,059,000 (1995)

The Arab Jamahiriya of Libya occupies the centre of the North African Mediterranean coast, lying between Algeria and Tunisia in the west, Egypt and Sudan in the east and Niger and Chad in the south. The interior of the country consists almost entirely of rocky and sandy deserts. The south forms part of the Sahara desert, peopled mainly by nomads. On the coast, however, the terrain becomes much milder and greener. Temperatures are generally Saharan. The capital is Tripoli.

Strictly speaking, Qaddafi has no formal post and no title except "Leader of the Revolution and Supreme Commander of the Armed Forcesø0. In practice, he is effectively the country's president. Power is nominally vested in the Libyan people, acting through some 1,500 "basic people's congresses" at local level, and influencing the activities of the national General People's Congress (GPC) and its Secretariat. The GPC meets for about one week every year. In 1994, the country took a step toward Islamic rule, when Sharia law was introduced throughout the country and the clergy were empowered to issue decrees for the first time.

There have been no multi-party elections in recent years.

GDP declined by 0.2% in 2002 while prices rose by 2.8%. Growth of 5.6% is forecast in 2003 with prices increasing by 2.8%. In 2004, growth of 2.8% is anticipated with inflation of 2.9%. Per capita levels of income are high but little of this wealth (which is generated almost entirely from oil revenues) reaches the lower income classes. Import restrictions and inefficient resource allocations have led to periodic shortages of basic goods and foodstuffs. The non-oil manufacturing and construction sectors, which account for about 20% of GDP, have expanded from processing mostly agricultural products to include the production of petrochemicals, iron, steel, and aluminium. Stronger economic growth is badly needed to help reduce Libya's 30% unemployment rate and make it easier for the country to maintain a budget surplus. Libya's relatively poor infrastructure, unclear legal structure, often-arbitrary government decision-making process, bloated public sector (as much as 60% of government spending goes towards paying public sector employees' salaries) and various structural rigidities all have been impediments to foreign investment and economic growth. The suspension of UN sanctions in 1999 and a 51% devaluation of the dinar in 2002 will provide an economic boost, though it could also bring higher inflation. The government has eased foreign exchange controls and has established a free-trade zone. The country's development plan calls for US$35 billion in investments in 2000-2005, 30-40% of which would come from private investors, mainly foreigners. With the country's youthful population set to double by 2025, job-creation has much to do with the new plan. Life is not as easy as might be expected in an oil-rich state that subsidises food, health and education. The state undertakes to find jobs for 30,000 new workers each year.

Oil export revenues account for about 95% of Libya's hard currency earnings and 75% of government receipts. Libya is hoping to reduce its dependency on oil as the country's sole source of income, and to increase investment in agriculture, tourism, fisheries, mining and natural gas. The country has invested much of its oil profits in the development of other parts of its economy, including agriculture, industry and mining. Agriculture is expanding south from the coast to newly irrigated areas of desert. At present, agriculture accounts for a meagre 2% of GDP, though it employs 15-20% of the workforce. Most of the large farms are government-owned and have begun to produce foods that were formerly imported, including corn, wheat and citrus fruits as well as cattle, sheep and poultry. Local forms of industry include traditional handicrafts, food processing and construction. The government is also looking for foreign investment for vast projects in transport, power generation and telecommunications and is welcoming businessmen who offer capital or want to start up their own ventures. The tourist sector is another target for development. With its long Mediterranean coast and Roman antiquities, Libya has much to attract tourists.

Libya's oil industry is run by the state-owned National Oil Corporation (NOC), along with smaller subsidiary companies. Libya has 12 oil fields, each with reserves of one billion barrels or more. There are two others with reserves of 500 million-1 billion barrels. In order to achieve its oil sector goals, Libya will require as much as $10 billion in foreign investment by 2010. Around $6 billion of this is to go towards exploration and production, with the rest going towards refining and petrochemicals. In addition, NOC has earmarked $1.5 billion for oil infrastructure investment. During 2002, Libyan oil production was estimated at just over 1.3 million barrels per day (bbl/d), only about two-fifths of the 3.3 million bbl/d produced in 1970. With reserve replacement slipping since the 1970s, Libya's challenge is maintaining production at mature fields while at the same time bringing new fields online.

▫ Macau

Capital City	Macau	*Capital population: 356,000 (1992)*
Population ('000)	486 *(2002)*	
Urban population (%)	98.83 *(2002)*	
Land area (km²)	2	
Languages	Portuguese (official), Cantonese, English	
Religion	Buddhist, Roman Catholic	
Currency	Pataca (MOP)	
Head of State	President Jiang Zemin	
Head of Government	Edmund Ho (1999)	
Ruling Party	Chinese Communist Party	

Main Urban Areas	Population
Macau (capital)	356,000 (1992)

Macau (Macao) is a tiny territory at the mouth of the Pearl River in southern China. It is adjacent to Hong Kong, with which it has a ferry link. Consisting almost entirely of a port and two small islands, Taipa and Coloane, the entire country is only 16 sq km in size. Like Hong Kong, it was built to service Portugal's trade with China in the 19th century. The capital is Macau.

Macau was a Special Territory of Portugal but returned to Chinese rule on 19 December 1999 when it became the Chinese Special Administrative Region (SAR) of Macau.

In May 1999, elections were held to determine Macau's leader once it returned to Chinese rule. Edmund Ho, a local banker, easily won the contest, which was dominated by Beijing-appointed voters.

GDP grew by less than 2% in 2002 and the outlook is not for any substantial improvement in the short term. Macau's economy is becoming extensively dominated by Beijing. Mainland interests have a half ownership in the new airport while the state-owned Bank of China and its affiliates account for over 40% of Macau's banking deposits. Easy money policies in China during the early 1990s led to a wave of real estate investments in Macau. By 1996 there were some 30%

more homes than there were households in the city and roughly half of all households were owned by mainland Chinese. Competition for jobs is intense. The neighbouring economic zone of Zhuhai has a workforce six times that of Macau's and the average pay is only a sixth of the rate in the city-state. Chinese officials hope to turn Macau into a service hub for the southern part of the Pearl River Delta.

Agriculture accounts for just 1% of GDP, industry contributes 40% and services make up the remainder. Macau's principal industry is tourism, which attracts visitors from all over the world to its gambling centres. Officials expect tourism to suffer significantly from the threat of SARS. Gambling taxes account for almost two thirds of all government revenues. There are a number of manufacturing companies making textiles and high-technology goods. Efforts to diversify have spawned other small industries such as toys and artificial flowers. The city earns considerable revenues from foreign trade, especially with Hong Kong and China. A huge land reclamation project, funded with mainland money, will double the amount of acreage available to Macau.

Macau depends entirely on imports for all forms of energy.

□ Madagascar

Capital City	Antananarivo	*Capital population: 805,450 (1992)*
Population ('000)	17,507 *(2002)*	
Urban population (%)	30.72 *(2002)*	
Land area (km²)	58154	
Languages	Malagasy, French	
Religion	Traditional (50%); Christian (43%); Muslim	
Currency	Franc malgache (MGF)	
Head of State	President Marc Ravalomanana (2002)	
Head of Government	Jean-Jacques Rasolondraibe (2002)	
Ruling Party	Government is formed by followers of the president.	

Main Urban Areas	Population
Antananarivo (capital)	805,450 (1992)

The island of Madagascar lies in the Indian Ocean, about 500km off the coast of Mozambique. It is the fourth largest island in the world, measuring some 2,000km from north to south. The country has a mountainous elevation, with substantial lowland areas, and enjoys a warm and moderate climate. The capital is Antananarivo.

Madagascar, which was known until 1975 as the Malagasy Republic, became independent from France in 1960. The president is elected by universal suffrage for a five-year term. The National Assembly has 160 members, elected for a four-year term in single-member and two-member constituencies. The Senate has 90 members, 60 members elected for a six-year term, ten for each province by provincial electors, and 30 members appointed In 1995, a referendum was approved which gives the president - and not parliament - the right to appoint the prime minister. A new constitution was approved in 1998.

Presidential elections held in December 2001 produced much confusion. Marc Ravalomanana competed in the election against the standing president, Didier Ratsiraka. Ravalomanana claimed to have won the election outright though official results gave him only a plurality. Ratsiraka and Ravalomanana later agreed to a recount. The result confirmed the absolute majority of Ravalomanana. Ratsiraka continued to fight on until July 2002 when he fled the country. In the final vote count, Ravalomanana apparently received 67% of the vote and has assumed office as president. Elections to the National People's Assembly were last held in December 2002. The Love Madagascar Party took 103 seats while the National Union won 22 seats. The remainder of seats was widely dispersed among several parties.

Real GDP contracted by 12.7% in 2002, while prices rose by 15.9%. In 2003 and 2004, the economy should recover with annual growth of 6% and inflation of 3.5% each year. Madagascar's economy was severely hurt by the political crisis in the first half of 2002. Beginning in July 2002, the new Malagasy authorities moved to ameliorate the situation with the introduction of various temporary tax measures to promote economic recovery and financial support measures designed to alleviate the impact of the crisis on the most vulnerable social groups. Since then, the country has made significant progress in terms of macroeconomic stabilisation and structural reform. Spurred by foreign direct investment in the export processing zone and growth in non-traditional exports, Madagascar's balance of payments position strengthened. Public finances have also improved and there has been significant progress in an ambitious public enterprise and regulatory reform agenda. Growth prospects are constrained by structural impediments and governance-related problems. Weaknesses in tax administration limit the government's ability to mobilise revenue, leaving Madagascar with limited resources for crucial projects and dependent on foreign assistance. The government's efforts to attract private savings and investment, both domestic and foreign, also met with some success but this support disappeared following the post-election dispute.

Agriculture, including fishing and forestry, is the mainstay of the economy, accounting for almost a third of GDP and contributing more than 70% to export earnings. Farming is mainly in a subsistence capacity and most is in the drier, western half of the island where rice, maize, bananas and sweet potatoes are grown for the domestic market. Forestry is important, though conservationists are pressing for restraint. Industry is limited and dominated by small-scale activities such as food processing, soap making, textile manufacture and brewing. The sector's share of GDP has declined in recent years to around 13%. The largest manufacturing operations are plants making cement and fertilisers. The mounting

losses of several inefficient state enterprises, in particular the cotton and sugar companies, are placing an increasingly heavy burden on the state budget. Despite the good economic performance since mid-2002, poverty remains pervasive. The government needs to improve productivity in agriculture, diversify the production base, and build rural infrastructure, including roads, schools, and clinics.

Madagascar has offshore oil deposits of up to 200 million barrels, but these are not adequate for self-sufficiency. All supplies are imported. There are hydroelectric resources, which generate some 60% of the country's electricity requirements.

□ Malawi

Capital City	Lilongwe	*Capital population: 395,500 (1994)*
Population ('000)	12,045 *(2002)*	
Urban population (%)	26.85 *(2002)*	
Land area (km²)	9408	
Languages	Chichewa, English	
Religion	Christian (50%); Muslim; Hindu	
Currency	Kwacha (MWK)	
Head of State	President Baktili Muluzu (May 1994)	
Head of Government	Baktili Muluzu	
Ruling Party	The United Democratic Party (UDP) dominates a coalition.	

Main Urban Areas	Population
Lilongwe (capital)	395,500 (1994)

Malawi is a long, landlocked triangular strip of country in central southeast Africa. It is bounded in the south by Mozambique, in the north by Tanzania and in the west by Zambia. The territory is fertile and permeated with large rivers, and has a pleasant subtropical climate. The capital is Lilongwe.

Malawi has an executive president who is elected for a five-year term and appoints his own cabinet. Theoretically, all legislative power is vested in the National Assembly with 192 officials elected for five-year terms. The constitution of 1995 also provides for a Senate of 80 seats to be installed in the near future.

Presidential elections were held in June 1999 when Muluzu retained his position with 52% of the vote. Elections to the National Assembly were held at the same time. The UDP received 47% of the vote and gained 93 seats. The Malawi Congress Party took 34% of the vote and 66 seats. Other parties received smaller proportions.

Malawi is one of the world's poorest countries, income is unequally distributed and about half of the population lives below the poverty line. One-third of the population (about 3.2 million people) required humanitarian aid in 2002 (including about 200,000 metric tons of food). GDP rose by 1.8% in 2002, while prices increased by 14.7%. In 2003, growth of 6.5% is expected while inflation is 5%. Forecasts for 2004 put growth at 5.2% and inflation of 4.3%. The country's problems have been compounded by occasional inconsistencies in the application of its macroeconomic policies. Slippages involving excess public spending, the accumulation of domestic spending arrears and an increase in the fiscal deficit have all complicated the economic environment. The country's privatisation programme has also faltered, despite assistance from the IMF and other international institutions. Malawi is a member of the Southern African Development Community and the Common Market for Eastern and Southern Africa, both of which launched free-trade agreements in 2000.

Agriculture contributes around 45% of GDP and employs almost 90% of the country's workforce. Most of the country's population is engaged in subsistence farming. Export crops such as tobacco, tea or sugar account for over 75% of export revenues and have traditionally been produced by the larger farms. The harvest in 2001 left a shortfall of at least 800,000 tonnes of maize, the main stable, out of a total requirement of about two million tonnes. The harvest in 2002 would have been better, except for the fact that many starving people ate the maize before it was fully grown. A large part of the population was unable to afford maize at import prices, so the government distributed it a subsidised price. The cost in 2002 was about 1.5% of GDP. Industry accounts for up 30% of GDP and consists mainly of sugar processing, sawmill products, cement and the production of consumer goods (for example, processed foods, pharmaceuticals, cement and tobacco products). Tourism has considerable potential but facilities remain rudimentary. Malawi has an abundance of natural resources with large reserves of coal, some of which is extracted. There are also known deposits of uranium, phosphates, bauxite, graphite and asbestos.

Half of the country's fuel requirements are met with domestic coal mining. Otherwise, the country depends on imports of oil. Most of Malawi's electricity is supplied by hydroelectric power stations.

□ Malaysia

Capital City	Kuala Lumpur	*Capital population: 1,361,807 (2002)*
Population ('000)	23,168 *(2002)*	
Urban population (%)	58.16 *(2002)*	
Land area (km²)	32855	
Languages	Bahasa Malaysia (Malay); also English, dialects of Chinese, Tamil and native languages	
Religion	Muslim (53%), Buddhist (19%), Christian	
Currency	Malaysian dollar (RM)	
Head of State	Syed Sirajuddin ibni al-Marhum Syed Putra Jamalullail (2001)	
Head of Government	Datuk Seri Dr Mahathir Mohamed	
Ruling Party	The government is formed by the member-parties of the Barisan Nasional.	

Main Urban Areas	Population	
Kuala Lumpur (capital)	1,361,807	(2002)
Klang	668,031	(2002)
Johor Bahru	661,409	(2002)
Ipoh	606,054	(2002)
Ampang Jaya	503,455	(2002)
Petaling Jaya	458,343	(2002)
Kuching	450,196	(2002)
Subang Jaya	443,555	(2002)
Shah Alam	334,776	(2002)
Kota Kinabalu	319,102	(2002)

Malaysia, one of the largest countries in the Asia-Pacific group, comprises the 11 states of Peninsular Malaysia, where the bulk of the population live, as well as the predominantly forested areas of Sabah and Sarawak, across the South China Sea on the northern coast of Borneo. Its climate is tropical and often humid. The capital is Kuala Lumpur.

Malaysia is a constitutional monarchy in which the monarch is elected every five years from among the tribal elders of peninsular Malaysia. The influence of the monarchy is limited, however. All effective power is actually exercised by the Prime Minister, who reports to a bicameral legislature. The House of Representatives (or Lower House) is composed of 193 members elected for five years, while the 69-member Senate consists of 26 representatives of the States, elected for a six-year term, and 43 appointed members. Constitutional amendments in 1993 reduced the legal immunity of the nine Malay rulers. A new federal capital, to be called Putrajaya, is now being built near Kuala Lumpur, and is due for completion in 2008.

The sultans elected Putra as king in 2001. In November 1999, elections to the House of Representatives were held. UMNO, the leading party of the Barisan Nasional, won 71 seats, the Malaysian/Chinese Front took 29 seats and the United Traditional Bumiputera Party won ten seats.

Malaysia's GDP rose by 4.1% in 2002 and should increase by 4.2% in 2003. In 2004, growth of 5.3% is forecast. Inflation was 1.8% in 2002, and prices should rise by 1.7% in 2003 and by 2.2% in 2004. During the 1980s and 1990s, at least $80 billion in foreign investment poured into Malaysia, turning it into an export-dependent economy. Only Singapore and Hong Kong sell more abroad as a proportion of GDP. More recently, foreign investment has been diverted to China and the amounts going to Malaysia have fallen below $1 billion per year. The slowdown in the US market (particularly in the electronics sector) has hit Malaysia hard. The problem could also worsen. Between 2005 and 2007, Malaysia will have to start complying with new regional and WTO trading rules that will throw its markets open to competition. For the time being, increases in consumption and public investment have kept the economy growing. Public spending on infrastructure has been an especially important economic driver in the past two years. With a high savings ratio and reserves of more than $33 billion (and growing), Malaysia has been able to finance the building of dams, airports and much else. Public investment, which accounted for 58.0% of gross fixed capital formation in 2001, continued to provide the major impetus for growth, increasing by 5.0% in 2002. This strategy has led to a government deficit in each of the last six years, but government debt still amounts to only 45% of GDP. The government still needs to find ways to boost the investment ratio, but Malaysian banks (still wary after the 1998 crash) are reluctant to lend. Private consumption is projected to expand by more than 6% in 2004, boosted by rising disposable incomes, continued accommodative monetary and fiscal policies and improving consumer confidence. The growth rate of public consumption may fall to about 6%, reflecting the government policy stance to focus expenditures on physical investment and construction activities, rather than on direct government consumption.

Manufacturing still accounts for more than 30% of GDP but has suffered during the present slowdown. Malaysia's economy depends on exports and is overwhelmingly based on foreign direct investment, much of it in the electronics sector. Overseas sales of these producers have fallen sharply in the past two years. Automobile manufacture is another key industry, but the country's domestic carmaker, Proton, depends on the huge import taxes payable on foreign cars. These will disappear in the next 3-5 years as Malaysia complies with WTO trading rules. In response, the government is encouraging more development of services. Tourism is an important part of this plan and already accounts for more than 5% of GDP. International terrorist attacks have certainly hurt the sector, but Malaysians are now targeting Chinese and Middle East tourists rather than Americans and Europeans. Tourist revenues were up slightly in 2002 and faster growth is expected in the future. Malaysia is also returning to the commodities that originally made it rich. Demand for palm oil is strong and the industry is

profitable, thanks in part to the increasing affluence in India and China. Malaysians are also boosting the profitability of their rubber trees by growing more cost-effective varieties. However, the agricultural sector as a whole continued to grow very slowly (only 0.3% in 2002) and accounts for just 8% of GDP. Banking and corporate sector reforms have been given a renewed impetus and the percentage of non-performing loans had fallen to about 10.6% of the total by the end of 2002.

Malaysia contains proven oil reserves of three billion barrels, down from 4.3 billion barrels in 1996. Despite this downward trend (due to a lack of major new discoveries in recent years), Malaysia's crude oil production has been stable, with monthly production numbers fluctuating between 650,000 barrels per day (bbl/d) and 730,000 bbl/d between 1996 and 2002. As a result of declining oil reserves, the state oil and gas company has embarked on an international exploration and production strategy. Currently, it has invested in oil exploration and production projects in Syria, Turkmenistan, Iran, Pakistan, China, Vietnam, Burma, Algeria, Libya, Tunisia, Sudan, and Angola. Malaysia also has six refineries, with a total processing capacity of 514,500 bbl/d. In addition, the country contains 75 trillion cubic feet of proven natural gas reserves. Domestic consumption of gas has been steadily rising in recent years.

□ Maldives

Capital City	Malé	*Capital population: 60,105 (1992)*
Population ('000)	296 *(2002)*	
Urban population (%)	27.07 *(2002)*	
Land area (km²)	30	
Languages	Maldivian (Dhivehi)	
Religion	Islam	
Currency	Rufiyaa (MVR)	
Head of State	President Maumoon Abdul Gayoom (1978)	
Head of Government	President Maumoon Abdul Gayoom	
Ruling Party	There are no political parties in the Maldives.	

Main Urban Areas	Population	
Malé (capital)	60,105	(1992)

The Maldives are a group of 1,190 coral islands lying in the central Indian Ocean, some 675km southwest of Sri Lanka and extending for almost 1,000km from one extreme to the other. Only about 200 of the islands are inhabited and none extends more than 2.5 metres above sea level. The capital is Malé.

The Republic of Maldives is an independent member of the Commonwealth in which all executive functions are vested in the president and his cabinet. The president is elected for a five-year term by parliament and confirmed in a referendum by the people. He reports to a 48-member Citizens' Assembly (Majlis) and appoints eight members of that group. The remainder are elected by universal adult suffrage for a term of five years.

The latest referendum on the presidency took place in October 1998 when 91% voted in favour of Gayoom. Elections to the Citizens' Assembly were held in November 1999, when all candidates were obliged to campaign on independent tickets in the absence of political parties.

GDP grew by 6% in 2002 and gains of about 6.2% are forecast in 2003. In 2004, growth of 4% is forecast. Inflation was just 0.9% in 2002 and a price contraction of 1.5% is expected in 2003. Prices are forecast to rise by 2% in 2004. The Maldivian economy has prospered over the past decade with the rapid expansion of tourism and the modernisation of the fisheries sector. During the 1990s, annual GDP growth averaged around 8%, raising per capita income to about US$2,200 in 2002. Economic growth slowed, however, in recent years, and continues to be dampened by the tourism slowdown that began in mid-2001. After a loss of international reserves in 2001, the balance of payments has improved. Reserves recovered to about 3.5 months of imports by November 2002. The external current account deficit is expected to remain large, but capital inflows, both public and private, have provided the necessary financing. External debt had risen to around 42% of GDP in 2002. Meanwhile, debt service amounts to only about 5.5% of exports. After several years of improving fiscal performance, the budget deficit has widened, reaching 7% of GDP in 2002. The larger deficit reflects strong capital expenditures, increasingly financed externally on commercial terms. The growing fiscal deficits financed by central bank resources pose a threat to the fixed exchange rate regime, and a risk to the Maldives' ability to compete in external markets. Economic performance remains reliant on tourism. A gradual recovery in tourist arrivals is expected to continue in 2004 due to a better outlook for the EU, the main market for tourism.

The economy is being driven by a gradual recovery in tourism and an improving fish catch, as well as government spending. The devaluation of the rufiyaa in 2001 does not appear to have affected the competitiveness of these key industries. However, the banking system is being challenged by slower rates of growth, the removal of credit ceilings, and stronger competition. Tourism accounts for more than one third of GDP and is the largest source of foreign exchange earnings. The tourism sector, which had shown annual growth of about 6% in recent years, contracted slightly in 2001 but began to recover in 2002. Fisheries expanded by 13.7% in 2002, based on a recovery in international tuna prices that led to greater fishing and a strong export performance. Construction activity increased substantially owing to the jump in public expenditures for the Hulhumalé project, a large-scale infrastructure development initiative to create a land mass and develop a new town on an island near to the capital city of Malé. The Maldives' financial market is still underdeveloped and major industries, particularly tourism, must depend heavily on foreign financing. Total exports in 2002 surged by 18.1%

over the 2001 level, mainly reflecting the recovery of international fish prices and stimulus provided by the lagged effects of the currency devaluation in 2001. In contrast, total imports decreased by 2.4%, despite the modest pickup in the economy, and the trade deficit decreased to $R 55208 million.

The Maldives produces no oil, although the government has searched without success. The country consumes only about 2,000 barrels per day, all of which is imported.

□ Mali

Capital City	Bamako	Capital population: 440,000 (1992)
Population ('000)	12,098 (2002)	
Urban population (%)	31.16 (2002)	
Land area (km²)	122019	
Languages	French	
Religion	Islam (80%); traditional	
Currency	CFA franc (CFAF)	
Head of State	President Amadou Toumani Touré (2002)	
Head of Government	Ahmed Mohamed Ag Hamani (2002)	
Ruling Party	The government is formed by followers of the president.	

Main Urban Areas	Population
Bamako (capital)	440,000 (1992)

Mali, the former French colony of Soudan, lies in the geographic centre of northwest Africa, an area of almost unbroken desert except for the marshlands of the upper Niger and the slightly more hospitable Niger valley further down towards the capital Bamako. With Algeria to the north, Mauritania and Senegal to the west, Burkina Faso and Niger to the east and Côte d'Ivoire and Guinea to the south, its only access to the sea is through Senegal, Guinea or The Gambia. The capital is Bamako.

Mali was ruled by military-backed autocrats from 1968 until 1991 when the regime was overthrown by Alpha Oumar Konaré. The people elect the president for a five-year term. The National Assembly has 160 members, elected for five-year terms, with 147 members elected in single-seat constituencies and 13 members elected by the Malinese abroad.

Touré was elected president in May 2002 with 64% of the vote. He defeated Soumaïla Cissé of the Alliance for Democracy in Mali and Ibrahim Boubacar Keita of the Rally for Mali. In parliamentary elections in July 2002, Spirit 2002 took 66 seats. The Alliance for Democracy won 51 seats. Minor parties claimed the remainder.

GDP grew by 9.7% in 2002, while prices rose by 5%. In 2003, a contraction of 1.1% is expected while prices rise by 3.8%. The forecast for 2004 calls for growth of 5.7% and inflation of 2.5%. The external current account deficit declined from 14.2% of GDP in 2001 to 10.7% in 2002. Thanks to increased gold exports, the volume of exports rose by 24.5% in 2002. The growth in the volume of imports is estimated to have been somewhat less than real GDP growth. The deterioration in the terms of trade was less severe than expected because the price of cotton rose slightly and the price of gold held steady on international markets. The fiscal deficit was financed without recourse to the banking system, since the government received the proceeds from the sale of a licence for operating a telephone network. The volume of exports is expected to fall by 5.8% in 2003, owing to lower cotton and gold production (despite the shipment of the large stock of cotton that remained at end-2002). Given the importance of regional integration for a landlocked country, the government will take all steps needed to ensure strict compliance with the West African Economic and Monetary Union convergence criteria.

About 10% of the population are nomadic and some 80% of the labour force is employed in agriculture and fishing. Most farmers are engaged in a subsistence capacity. Altogether, agriculture accounts for 47% of GDP. Cotton, groundnuts, wheat, sorghum and fruit and vegetables are grown for export, while rice, millet, sorghum, maize and groundnuts are the staples for the domestic population. There is a substantial amount of cattle herding in the dry zones. Mali's economy greatly depends on rainfall conditions and access to the ports of neighbouring countries for its foreign trade. This largely explains the significant swings in the level of activities during 2002 and those expected during 2003. The government is particularly concerned by the crisis in Côte d'Ivoire and the effects on Mali's economy of the closing of the Bamako-Abidjan road, which carried about 70% of the country's foreign trade. Strong growth during 2002 came mainly from three sectors. First, cotton production more than doubled after the producer price was raised and sector reforms took effect. Second, production of cereals increased by 10% in 2002. Finally, gold production increased by 17% following the discovery of new deposits in one of the mines. However, the closing of the Bamako-Abidjan road since September and the need to redirect foreign trade to other more distant and more expensive ports have led to a slowdown of activity in some sectors, increased costs, and supply shortages. The mining sector is an important source of foreign currency, with uranium, salt, gold and phosphates being mined. There are known deposits of bauxite, iron, manganese and tin, but these are only marginally exploited. Industry remains limited to the fulfilment of local needs, and centres on the processing of agricultural raw materials.

Mali relies on imports for the greater part of its modest energy requirements. It does, however, have enough electricity to meet its own needs. The electricity sector, however, has encountered serious problems in recent years. Officials have also raised the retail price of petroleum in order to reduce losses.

□ Martinique

Capital City	Fort de France	Capital population: 101,540 (1990)
Population ('000)	407 (2002)	
Urban population (%)	95.21 (2002)	
Land area (km²)	106	
Languages	French	
Religion	Mainly Roman Catholic	
Currency	Euro (€)	
Head of State	President Jacques Chirac (France)	
Head of Government	Claude Lise (President of General Council, 1992)	
Ruling Party	Union pour la Démocratie Francaise (RPR-UDF)	

Main Urban Areas	Population
Fort de France (capital)	101,540 (1990)

The French overseas department of Martinique is a single island in the Windward Islands group, situated between Dominica in the north and St Lucia in the south. With a benign climate and relatively little hurricane risk, it is a popular tourist resort. The capital is Fort de France.

As an external department of France, Martinique is governed to a considerable degree from Paris. The country sends four deputies to the French National Assembly and is represented at the EU. Since being accorded regional status in 1974, Martinique elects its own 41-member Regional Council for a term of six years, with responsibility for economic and social planning. Other executive power rests in a 42-member General Council.

The Regional Council elections of 1998 produced a victory for the RPR-UDF, which won 14 of the 41 seats. The Martinique Independence Movement captured 13 seats and the Martinique Progressive Party took seven seats. Other seats were divided among various parties. In elections to the General Council, the Martinique Progressive Party won a plurality. The last full elections to the French Assemblée Nationale returned two delegates for the RPR, one for the Socialists and one for other left-wing groupings.

Martinique, like many other French overseas territories, has occasionally felt left out of the mainstream of the decision-making process with regard to its own economy, although it has achieved a better development than most. Unemployment remains very high (well over 30%) and is the major cause of concern among public officials. The bulk of the island's exports consist of refined petroleum products, bananas, rum and pineapples. The tourism sector is the fastest growing area of the economy, with French tourists providing the great majority of the country's annual total of 500,000 visitors.

The economy is based on sugar cane, bananas, tourism and light industry. Agriculture accounts for about 6% of GDP, the industrial sector contributes another 11% and services make up the remainder. The majority of the workforce is employed in the services sector and in administration. Sugar production has experienced a secular decline, with most of the sugar cane now being used for the production of rum. Just over a quarter of the total land area is cultivated. Banana exports are increasing, going mostly to France. The bulk of meat, vegetable and grain requirements must be imported - contributing to a chronic trade deficit that requires large annual transfers of aid from France. Fishing is important, with lobsters, crabs and octopus among the major export activities. Tourism has great potential and has become more important than agricultural exports as a source of foreign exchange. Major industries consist of construction, rum, cement, oil refining and sugar. Industry is only moderately developed, although it employs 15% of the workforce. There is also a major ship repair yard and an industrial free port at Jarry.

Martinique relies on imports for all its energy requirements. There is no hydroelectric capacity, with all electricity being supplied by oil-fired generators.

□ Mauritania

Capital City	Nouakchott	Capital population: 600,000 (1992)
Population ('000)	2,916 (2002)	
Urban population (%)	59.43 (2002)	
Land area (km²)	102522	
Languages	Arabi,C French	
Religion	Islam	
Currency	Ouguiya (MRO)	
Head of State	President Maaouiya Ould Sidi Mohamed Taya (1984)	
Head of Government	Sghair Ould M'Bareck (2003)	
Ruling Party	Democratic and Social Republican Party (PRDS)	

Main Urban Areas	Population
Nouakchott (capital)	600,000 (1992)

Mauritania occupies a substantial part of central West Africa, meeting the Atlantic Ocean between Senegal and the disputed territory known as Western Sahara, but extending eastward as far as Mali. It shares a border with Algeria in the northeast. The country is mainly of Saharan type with most of its major settlements located on or near the coast. The capital is Nouakchott.

Faced with growing pressure from abroad, Mauritania has been gradually liberalising its political institutions. Political parties were legalised for the first time in July 1991 and the first free elections were held the following spring. The president is elected for a six-year term by the people. Parliament has two chambers. The National Assembly has 81 members, elected for five-year terms in single-seat constituencies. The Senate has 56 members, 53 members elected for six-year terms by municipal councillors with one third renewed every two years and three members elected by Mauritanians abroad.

In presidential elections held in December 1997, Taya was returned to office with 90% of the vote. Parliamentary elections were held in October 2001. The ruling PRDS won 64 seats in the National Assembly. The remainder were scattered among six parties. Elections to the Senate took place in April 2000 and the PRDS won 52 seats. In July 2003, the president appointed M'Bareck as prime minister. He replaced Cheikh El Afia Ould Mohamed Khouna who was suspected of participating in an attempted coup in June 2003.

Mauritania's GDP increased by 3.3% in 2002, while inflation was 3.8%. In 2003, growth of 5.4% is expected with inflation of 6.4%. Forecasts for 2004 call for growth of 6.1% and inflation of 3.7%. The government continues to push ahead with economic reforms efforts, including the planned privatisation of the state power company. International lenders recently eased Mauritania's debt service burden as a reward for the country's moves towards economic reform. Despite this positive sign, Mauritania is a very country with more than half the population living on less than $1 per day, a rapidly growing population and many social and economic problems. Mauritania also remains heavily reliant on foreign aid. Fiscal policy is being eased in order for the government to address the needs of the poorest segment of the population. The economy's narrow export base leaves it vulnerable to external shocks. In the future, policy makers hope to introduce policies to foster private sector development, liberalise markets and promote competition, all with the goal of stimulating employment and promoting growth.

Mauritania's agricultural sector employs well over 80% of the workforce. Farm productivity, however, is very low and the sector accounts for just a fifth of GDP. Arable or fruit crops are grown only around the Senegal River. Cattle are raised in some parts of the country. Fishing is particularly important, with a large fleet producing a substantial proportion of foreign exchange revenues but over-exploitation by foreigners threatens this source of revenue. In 2002, Mauritania was hit by torrential rains which caused significant damage to crops, livestock, and grazing land in southern regions of the country Mining offers great potential, with extensive deposits of iron ore accounting for almost 50% of the country's total exports. There is also some copper mining, as well as gold and uranium. Industry (including mining) accounts for 30% of GDP. Most manufacturers are geared mainly to serve the local market and are engaged in the processing of agricultural products, raw fish processing, iron smelting, the production of footwear and sugar. Both the manufacturing and tourism sectors are regarded as underdeveloped.

Mauritania has not traditionally been regarded as a promising hydrocarbons area, but this may now be changing as exploration has yielded some positive signs. In 2001, a consortium of energy companies made a significant oil discovery in deep waters off the country's southwest coast, and in October 2002, the presence of oil-bearing geological structures was confirmed. In addition, there is a second find that is believed to contain as much as 100 million barrels of oil plus several trillion cubic feet of natural gas. In general, it is now expected that Mauritania may contain significant oil deposits off its coast. For the present, the overwhelming majority (99%) of Mauritania's commercial energy consumption consists of imported oil.

Elections to the Assembly took place in September 2000, when the MSM and the MMM together received 52% of the vote and 55 seats. Karl Auguste Offmann was appointed prime minister. Following the election, party leaders struck a power-sharing deal which left Jugnauth as prime minister until September 2003. AT that time, he would assume the largely ceremonial post of president while his deputy, Bérenger, would become prime minister.

One of the richest countries in Africa, Mauritius largely avoided the disastrous problems existing in other parts of the continent. GDP grew by 4% in 2002 and prices rose by 6.7%. Growth of 3.3% is forecast for 2003 with prices rising by 6.4%. In 2004, growth of 6.1% is forecast with inflation of 3.7%. The long-term rise in unemployment continues with the number of jobless approaching 9% in 2002. The upward trends suggests a mismatch between the requirements of the workplace and either the job aspirations or skills of the unemployed workforce, as well as rigidities in the labour market and more general problems in education and training. Government finances continued to deteriorate further in 2002, following a sharp deterioration in 2001. The main cause is higher capital expenditure on education and environmental projects and an increase in net lending. Significant reductions in external tariffs have been put into effect, mainly on raw materials and intermediates, along with certain income tax and indirect tax reductions. The economy's main weakness is that a sizeable proportion of the population is excluded from the island's increasing wealth.

The farming sector is enjoying its second consecutive year of strong growth. Sugar product in 2002 reached its highest level since 1987. Agriculture accounts for 6% of GDP and is the country's main employer, with sugar cane, tea and tobacco grown for export. Staples produced for the indigenous population include cereals, fruit and coconut products. Growth is broad based, with significant contributions recorded in manufacturing (especially in the export processing zone), financial and business services (including offshore activities), and other services (particularly transport and communications). Industry contributes a third of GDP and is primarily export oriented. Mauritius has a strong textiles sector but other manufacturing activities are generally small scale. Recent political upheavals in neighbouring Madagascar, and the resulting disruption in production and trade, have hurt the profitability of Mauritius's export processing zones because of their sizeable investments and integration with Madagascar's export processing zones. The tourist industry is very important and was performing well until the terrorist attacks in the US and around Asia led to a fall in the number of visitors. However, the industry began to recover in 2003 thanks to Mauritius' reputation as a safe destination. Tourism is already approaching a saturation point in any case, with local operators admitting the islands may not be able to handle more than 500,000 visitors without suffering serious environmental damage. The island's tax treaty with India has spurred the development of a thriving financial services sector with more than 9,000 offshore entities.

Mauritius relies on imports for all its energy needs, except for a small amount of fuel wood. All but one sixth of its electricity derives from thermal power stations.

◘ Mexico

Capital City	Mexico City	Capital population: 18,199,543 (2002)
Population ('000)	101,847 (2002)	
Urban population (%)	74.77 (2002)	
Land area (km²)	190869	
Languages	Spanish (95%), Indian languages (Náhuati, Maya, Zapote,C Otomí, Mixtec)	
Religion	Mainly Roman Catholic	
Currency	Mexican new peso (Mx$)	
Head of State	President Vicente Fox (December 2000)	
Head of Government	Vicente Fox (December 2000))	
Ruling Party	National Action Party (PAN)	

Main Urban Areas	Population
Mexico City (capital)	18,199,543 (2002)
Guadalajara	3,737,732 (2002)
Monterrey	3,375,865 (2002)
Ciudad de Puebla	2,661,662 (2002)
Toluca, Mex.	1,323,974 (2002)
Leon, Gto.	1,317,321 (2002)
Ciudad Juarez, Chih.	1,297,965 (2002)
Tijuana, B.C.	1,297,369 (2002)
Torreon-Gomez Palacio, Coah., Dgo.	932,382 (2002)
San Luis Potosi, S.L.P.	874,863 (2002)

◘ Mauritius

Capital City	Port Louis	Capital population: 143,509 (1993)
Population ('000)	1,185 (2002)	
Urban population (%)	41.84 (2002)	
Land area (km²)	203	
Languages	English, French, Creole	
Religion	Hindu; Christian; Muslim	
Currency	Mauritian rupee (MUR)	
Head of State	Anerood Jugnauth (2003)	
Head of Government	Paul Bérenger (2003)	
Ruling Party	The government is formed by the Militant Socialist Movement (MSM) and the Mauritian Militant Movement (MMM).	

Main Urban Areas	Population
Port Louis (capital)	143,509 (1993)

Mauritius comprises a group of islands lying in the Indian Ocean, some 800km off the eastern coast of Madagascar. It has a mixed population of Asian, European and some African origin. The country has a subtropical climate with high humidity throughout the year. The capital is Port Louis.

Mauritius became an independent republic in March 1992. Shortly thereafter, it left the Commonwealth. The president is elected for a five-year term by the parliament. The National Assembly has 66 members, 62 elected for a four-year term in single-seat constituencies and four additional members appointed by the Supreme Court. Operation of the political system is sometimes hampered by serious differences between the minority Creoles and the dominant Hindus.

Mexico, perhaps the most affluent state in Latin America, extends for well over 2,000km from its northern border with the US down to the boundaries with Guatemala and Belize in the south. It has coastlines on both the Atlantic and the Pacific and embraces a wide range of territorial types. The landscape is partly volcanic and is subject to earthquakes, although in the south it becomes jungle. The capital is Mexico City.

Mexico, a parliamentary democracy with an executive president, has one of the longest democratic traditions in Latin America. Yet its politics - until the latest elections - have been dominated completely by the Partido Revolucionario Institucional (PRI) since 1917. The president is elected for a six-year term by universal suffrage. Parliament has two chambers. The Chamber of Deputies has 500 members, elected for three-year terms, 300 members elected in single-seat constituencies and 200 members elected by proportional representation, 300 members in single-seat constituencies and 200 members by proportional representation. The Chamber of Senators has 128 members, elected for three-year terms in four-seat constituencies, three seats going to the plurality winner and one to the first runner-up.

Parliamentary elections were held in July 2003. The PRI won 223 seats while Fox's PAN took only 155 seats. The Revolutionary Democratic Party (PRD) garnered 96 seats and the remainder were scattered among several other parties. Presidential elections were held in July 2000. For the first time in many decades, the candidate of PAN, Vicente Fox, defeated the PRI candidate, Francisco Labastida. Fox received 43% of the vote. Labastida got 36% and Cardenas, representing the PRD, won 16%.

GDP increased 0.7% in 2002 and will grow by 1.5% in 2003. Inflation was 5% in 2002 and prices are expected to rise by 4.6% in 2003. In 2004, growth of 3.5% is forecast with inflation of 3.4%. Fellow NAFTA member the United States consumes over 80% of Mexico's exports. The latest downturn, unlike previous ones, has not been associated with macroeconomic instability or a crisis of confidence, but rather reflects the increasing integration of Mexico into NAFTA and the resulting synchronisation between Mexico and the US economic cycles. Mexico's exports to the US include significant quantities of crude oil, as well as manufactured goods and machinery. Mexico's merchandise exports increased modestly in 2002 over the previous year, but were still below the level attained in the year 2000. In addition, Mexico's maquiladora sector, which comprises Mexican corporations that work in government sanctioned partnerships with foreign investors to export goods, mainly to the US, suffered declining production in 2002 after being a major contributor to economic growth for a number of years. A number of structural weaknesses persist. A large informal sector co-exists with formal employment. Poverty is widespread and acute poverty remains significant. The productive sector continues to be characterised by a dual structure, with a dynamic export sector made of large firms with easy access to financing including from abroad, and a less efficient domestic market-oriented sector.

The share of agriculture has declined owing to the rapid growth of other sectors. Farm production is stagnating but around a fifth of the nation's workforce is employed in this sector. Major exports are citrus crops, tomatoes, peppers, cotton, coffee and sugar cane. In 2001, agricultural output shrank slightly and a drought in large parts of the country in 2002 may lead to another decline. Pemex, the state oil company, is the world's fifth largest oil company, the single most important entity in the Mexican economy. The government relies on Pemex for approximately one-third of its fiscal revenues, as an estimated 60% of the company's revenues are turned over to federal authorities. This financial responsibility has left the company with little ability to invest in exploration and development. Congress allocated $23.9 billion to the Pemex budget in 2002, providing $14.7 billion for new investment. The 2002 budget represented Pemex's largest annual investment increase in twenty years. Manufacturing has replaced oil as the country biggest exporter, accounting for around 90% of all export earnings. Mexico has a sophisticated industrial base, but output has stagnated in recent years. There are a large number of companies making consumer durables for both the home and export markets. Industries producing clothing and household goods have benefited greatly from Mexico's membership in NAFTA and have gained market share in the US at the expense of their Caribbean competitors. Altogether, industry contributes 25% to GDP while services accounts for 70%. The legislative session in 2003 will have to deal with several crucial reform packages proposed by the current administration. The most important of these deal with the electricity market and reform of the labour market.

In 2002, Pemex revised its crude oil reserve estimate downwards by 26% to 12.6 billion barrels. Mexico still has the second largest proven crude oil reserves in the Western Hemisphere after Venezuela. Petroleum production is expected to increase to 3.8 million barrels per day in 2003, slightly exceeding 2002 levels. The government aims to increase Mexican crude oil output by 34% between 2001 and 2006. With the Mexican economy predicted to grow at an average rate of just over 5% per year for the next two decades, energy demand is expected to rise significantly. Oil and natural gas will likely remain the dominant energy sources through 2020, accounting for well over 80% of total energy consumed.

◘ Mongolia

Capital City	Ulan Bator	Capital population: 680,000 (1994)
Population ('000)	2,705 (2002)	
Urban population (%)	64.35 (2002)	
Land area (km²)	156650	
Languages	Khalkha Mongolian, Kazakh	
Religion	Buddhist	
Currency	Tugruk (MNT)	
Head of State	President N. Bagabandi (1997)	
Head of Government	Nambarlin Enkhbayar (2000)	
Ruling Party	The government is formed by the Revolutionary People's Party of Mongolia, (MAKN)	

Main Urban Areas	Population
Ulan Bator (capital)	680,000 (1994)

The Mongolian Republic extends some 1,800km across the eastern centre of the Asian landmass, running from the Kazakh/Russian border in the west to the start of the Yablonovy mountain range in the east, with Russia always to the north and with China always to the south. The terrain is mountainous, with the south giving way to the Gobi desert. The capital is Ulan Bator.

Mongolia's semi-executive President is elected for a four-year term by the people. The State Assembly has 76 members, elected for four-year terms in single-seat constituencies.

Elections to the State Assembly in June 2000 returned the former communist party, the MPRP, to power. The Party won 72 of the 76 seats in the Assembly. Presidential elections in May 2001 produced another victory for the former communists led by Bagabandi. He received 58% of the vote compared to 37% for Radnaasumbereliyn Gonchigdorj.

Mongolia's economy began a recovery with GDP rising by 3.9% in 2002 and growth of 5% in 2003. Inflation was 0.9% in 2002 and is expected to be 5% in 2003. In 2004, growth of 5.3% is forecast with prices rising by 5%. The improved economic performance had a favourable impact on the labour market. Actual unemployment is much higher than suggested by the official estimate of 3.6%, with high job losses in rural Mongolia driving migration to Ulaanbaatar. Moreover, employment estimates are also distorted by the size of the informal sector (around 35% of GDP). To promote export-led growth and investment, the authorities need to streamline Mongolia's trade and investment regime and simplify methods of customs administration and licensing. Exports declined by 3.9% in 2002 while imports grew by 3.3%, widening the trade deficit to about 14% of GDP. Cumulatively, FDI inflows have amounted to $734 million since 1991, with inflows from China accounting for 90% of the country's FDI stock. External debt stood at 88.3% of GDP in 2002, and debt service remains low at 4.9% of exports, partly due to the fact that most debt is concessional. However, concerns are growing over debt sustainability in the short to medium term. Despite the concessional nature and long-term structure of the debt, the debt service burden is increasing. This is particularly worrisome given Mongolia's vulnerability to external price shocks. Growing demand for capital goods to fuel expansion of manufacturing, mining, and construction in the private sector will mean that the current account experiences rather large deficits over the next several years. Rising unemployment, with only a poor social safety net, is another concern and a primary cause of poverty.

Agricultural output, which still accounts for about 30% of GDP, posted another poor year. A milder than expected winter helped cushion losses in the livestock subsector, and agricultural output declined by a less steep 10.5%, after an 18.5% contraction in 2001. Despite strong manufacturing activity, principally in textiles and meat processing, industrial output grew moderately in 2002 by 4.7%, down from 11.9% growth in 2001, reflecting the impact of the poor performance of the mining sector. Lower copper production, triggered by falling prices in international markets, depressed both industrial output and exports receipts. Informal gold mining has become a popular activity for farmers who have lost their herds and for those who have failed to find employment in urban areas. Between 50,000 and 100,000 make their living from this occupation. Construction expanded by 11% as a result of the ongoing real estate boom in Ulaanbaatar. Services accounts for about half of GDP and grew by 12% in 2002, propelled by the solid outcome in financial services, transport and communications, and wholesale and retail trade. The banking system is now subject to more stringent methods of supervision and a few of the country's loss-making banks have been restructured. However, the privatisation of other large enterprises which are still carrying out loss-making activities has been delayed, while the energy sector's persistent financial imbalances continue to pose a fiscal threat in the medium-term.

Mongolia has substantial coal resources, which are being developed to encourage industrial expansion; otherwise the country depends on imports for its energy needs. Exploration continues for indigenous hydrocarbon resources.

◘ Morocco

Capital City	Rabat	Capital population: 1,606,540 (2002)
Population ('000)	29,208 (2002)	
Urban population (%)	56.66 (2002)	
Land area (km²)	44630	
Languages	Arabi,C Berber, French, Spanish	
Religion	Islam	
Currency	Moroccan dirham (Dh)	
Head of State	HM King Mohammed (1999)	
Head of Government	Driss Jettou (2002)	
Ruling Party	The government is formed by a multiparty coalition.	

Main Urban Areas	Population
Casablanca	3,351,360 (2002)
Rabat (capital)	1,606,540 (2002)
Fez	924,520 (2002)
Marrakech	746,930 (2002)
Agadir	612,350 (2002)
Tangier	593,370 (2002)
Meknes	565,150 (2002)
Oujda	342,630 (2002)
Knitra	336,520 (2002)
Tetuan	331,140 (2002)

Although one of the smaller countries in northwest Africa, Morocco is probably the most affluent. Its rocky terrain almost meets with Europe across the Strait of Gibraltar, and most of the settlements of any size are located along the Atlantic coast just southwest of Gibraltar. The capital is Rabat.

Morocco is a constitutional monarchy with a parliament of two chambers. The Assembly of Representatives has 325 members elected for a five-year term, comprising 295 members elected in multi-seat constituencies and 30 in national lists consisting only of women. The Assembly of Councillors has 270 members, elected for a nine-year term, elected by local councils (162 seats), professional chambers (91 seats) and wage-earners (27 seats). The prime minister is appointed by the monarch. King Hassan died in 1999 and was replaced by his son, Mohammed.

Elections to the Assembly of Representatives were held in September 2002. The Socialist Union of Popular Forces took 50 seats, the Independence Party won 48 seats and the Islamist Justice and Development Party received 42 seats. The remainder was divided among more than ten parties.

Morocco's GDP grew by 3.2% in 2002 and growth of 5.5% is expected in 2003. In 2004, growth of 3.4% is forecast. Inflation was 2.8% in 2002 and should be 2% in 2003 and 2004. The current five-year economic plan, which runs from 1999 through 2004, calls for promoting job creation (unemployment is a serious problem in Morocco, at 13% or higher), exports and tourism, upgrading infrastructure, and reducing social inequalities (especially between urban rich and rural poor). The government also has considered imposing a value-added tax (VAT), as well as direct taxes on business and individual income. In some areas, economic reforms have made significant progress. For example, the government has liberalised the foreign exchange regime, lowered tariffs and other trade barriers, reformed the banking system, and encouraged foreign investment (now permitted in most sectors of the economy). Morocco also has signed several agreements with the European Union on economic co-operation, including one establishing a free trade zone for industrial goods over a 12-year transition period. There has been much less progress in the field of privatisation. For example, privatisation of the domestic oil market was promised in 1997 but not yet carried out. State-owned sugar and tobacco companies are reported to be scheduled for sale in 2003. Morocco maintains relatively tight fiscal and monetary policies, with the 2003 budget calling for only a small increase in spending, and this has helped sharply reduce the country's fiscal deficit.

Agriculture makes up a large share (around 17-20%) of Morocco's economy and accounts for a substantial portion of the country's workforce (around 40-50%). Farming, however, is heavily dependent on rainfall patterns. In November 2002, Morocco was afflicted by heavy rains and severe flooding which caused major infrastructure damage near Casablanca. This flooding has now occurred two years in a row, following three years of drought. Farmers have suffered significantly during this period. Morocco's vulnerability to erratic rainfall patterns, and therefore agricultural output, has encouraged the government in its attempts at economic diversification, particularly towards manufacturing and services (including tourism). In the meantime, the government has initiated a $100 million emergency programme to repair damaged infrastructure and protect vulnerable areas from future floods. Tourism is the country's second largest earner of foreign exchange (after mining), employing one out of every ten workers. The opportunities for tourism are substantial although the sector is underdeveloped and has suffered after the terrorist attacks in September 2001. For example, the country has 3,800km of coastline but not one seaside resort. Tourism has also been hurt by the general perception of Middle East political instability. Morocco also has a strong manufacturing base which accounts for around 17% of GDP. The mineral sector is the mainstay of the economy, producing phosphates, fluorite, manganese, cobalt, lead, zinc, copper and antimony. The country is estimated to hold three quarters of the world's phosphate reserves.

Morocco contains insignificant proven oil reserves of 1.6 million barrels, although most sedimentary basins (especially offshore on the Atlantic continental shelf or in deep waters off the shelf) in the country have not been explored, and Morocco is actively pursuing expansion of its upstream oil and natural gas sector. At present, the country relies on imports for nearly all of its oil consumption needs (around 150,000 barrels per day). This could change in coming years with a possibly significant discovery of oil near the border with Algeria. So far, however, estimates suggest that the filed has proven reserves of ten million barrels or less of total hydrocarbons (the exact mix of oil and natural gas is unknown). Meanwhile, exploration in other parts of Morocco continues.

□ Mozambique

Capital City	Maputo	Capital population: 2,227,000 (1995)
Population ('000)	21,338 *(2002)*	
Urban population (%)	41.9 *(2002)*	
Land area (km²)	78409	
Languages	Portuguese (official), Ronga, Shangaan, Muchope spoken	
Religion	Traditional; Christian; Muslim	
Currency	Metical (MZM)	
Head of State	President Joaquim Alberto Chissano (1986)	
Head of Government	Pascoal Mocumbi (December 1994)	
Ruling Party	Frelimo (Mozambique Liberation Front)	

Main Urban Areas	Population
Maputo (capital)	2,227,000 (1995)

Mozambique extends for as much as 2,500km along the Indian Ocean coast of East Africa, running from the borders with South Africa and Swaziland in the south to Tanzania in the north. Inland, it borders on Malawi, Zimbabwe and Zambia. Less elevated than other countries in the region, the most fertile areas are in the west, where the Zambezi River is dammed at Cabora Bassa, and on the coast. The climate is tropical but prone to devastating drought. The capital is Maputo.

Mozambique's 1990 constitution marked a significant departure from the single-party collectivist state, which had dominated the country since 1975. The executive president is elected by universal suffrage for a maximum of two five-year terms. The Assembly of the Republic has 250 members, elected for five-year terms by proportional representation.

Presidential elections were held in December 1999. Chissano was re-elected president with 52% of the vote. He defeated Afonso Marceta Macacho Dhlakama. In parliamentary elections occurring at the same time, Frelimo took 49% of the vote and 133 seats. Renamo (National Resistance of Mozambique) received 39% of the vote and won 117 seats.

GDP rose by 8.3% in 2002, while inflation was 16.8%. In 2003, the rate of growth is expected to be about 7% with prices rising by 12.9%. Forecasts for 2004 call for growth of 8% and inflation of 9.7%. Macroeconomic stability is still highly dependent on aid inflows. In 2001, foreign aid represented 46% of total public expenditure and, in particular, two thirds of public capital expenditure. In 2002, the government attempted to achieve a substantial reduction of total expenditures, below 30% of GDP, aided by the end of the emergency and reconstruction costs relating to recent floods and the bail out of several banks. A new fiscal incentive code was introduced in 2002 in order to limit the type and scale of tax exemptions granted to investors thereby allowing for effective control and tracking. A new income tax law was submitted to parliament and its full application is expected in 2003. Mozambique is also one of the most open trade policy regimes in Southern Africa. Import licensing was abolished in the early 1990s, and administrative requirements in 1998. The tariff structure has been simplified and ad valorem tariffs have been re-grouped for different kinds of goods. In 2003, the government reduced the top tariff rate from 30% to 25%.

Agriculture represents the bulk of the economy involving some 80% of the work force and 22% of GDP. The sector comprises a large smallholder sector that produces around 95% of value-added in agriculture, mainly as food crops, such as maize and cassava and some cash crops such as cotton, cashews and, more recently, sugar. Far from reaching their full potential, sugar and cotton have done reasonably well in recent years, although cotton production is highly dependent on world market prices. The sugar industry is currently protected and is being rehabilitated with major foreign investment. Mega-projects and development corridors appear to be the principal means by which the authorities seek to promote the structural changes in the economy. Major examples include an $840 million expansion of an existing aluminium facility, the $1 billion construction of a gas pipeline to supply South Africa, and several large mineral developments. The government has also undertaken programmes aimed at modernising transport infrastructure (port, rail network, road network) of the Maputo, Nacala, and Beira corridors, connecting with South Africa, Malawi and Zimbabwe. The authorities have faced difficult challenges in the banking system. The government is committed to recovering non-performing loans and improving accountability. There are also plans to tighten banking regulations and strengthen banking supervision.

Mozambique has coal deposits but no oil has been discovered. It does have vast and still only partially developed hydroelectric potential.

□ Myanmar

Capital City	Yangon	Capital population: 3,851,000 (1995)
Population ('000)	46,260 *(2002)*	
Urban population (%)	28.55 *(2002)*	
Land area (km²)	65755	
Languages	Burmese; also Shan, Karen, Chin, Kayeh, Kachin, English	
Religion	Mainly Buddhist (87%)	
Currency	Kyat (Kyats)	
Head of State	Gen. Than Shwe	
Head of Government	Gen. Khin Nyunt (2003)	
Ruling Party	The National Unity Party is in power. No other parties are allowed.	

Main Urban Areas	Population
Yangon (capital)	3,851,000 (1995)

Myanmar (Burma) occupies most of the westward-facing coastline of the Indochinese peninsula, extending from the northern Chinese/Laotian border, with Assam (India) and Bangladesh to the west, down to the 600-km-long finger of coastal territory which effectively seals off most of Thailand from the Indian Ocean. The climate is tropical and mainly humid. The capital is Yangon.

Myanmar, or Burma as it was known until 1988, was run as a one-party socialist state until September 1988, when a military coup overthrew the administration and declared martial law. A 485-member Constituent Assembly was formed in May 1990, but never met. In 1996, a military-run constitutional convention decreed that a newly elected assembly would choose its president from among three vice-presidents that it elects. All three are to serve five-year terms.

Multi-party elections to the newly created Constituent Assembly were held in 1990 and contested by some 93 different parties, as well as 87 independents. The election produced a crushing defeat for the ruling junta, the State Law and Order Restoration Council, whose own favoured party, the National Unity Party, collected less than 20% of the vote. Meanwhile, the opposition National League for Democracy (NLD) led by Aung San Suu Kyi received more than 50% of the ballots. Shortly afterwards, the junta banned the new Assembly and refused to allow Aung San to assume office. In 2003, General Shwe, who is widely thought to resist "reconciliation" talks with Aung San Suu Kyi, relinquished his position as prime minister to Nyunt.

GDP grew by 5.5% in 2002 and growth of 5.1% is expected in 2003. In 2004, growth of 4.3% is forecast. Meanwhile, inflation remains high, running at 57.1% in 2002 and an expected rate of 40% in 2003. Prices are forecast to rise by 43% in 2004. Prospects for sustained reductions in poverty and broad-based improvements in the quality of life for the people of Myanmar are impaired by macroeconomic imbalances and impediments to structural adjustment. Despite recorded growth, there has been little change in the structure of the economy for more than a decade. Large fiscal deficits have underpinned perennially high inflation in Myanmar. The deficits are fuelled by large military expenditures and inefficient state enterprises that receive direct budgetary support and a poor track record in mobilising public sector revenues. A pervasive system of implicit subsidies and taxes, as well as the dual exchange rate system, also contribute to fiscal stress. The government has targeted 6% GDP growth over the latest five-year planning period. However, the immediate prospects for fast economic expansion are uncertain. Over the long term, prospects for growth and for lasting poverty reduction remain uncertain in a context where macroeconomic and structural distortions are acute.

Widespread flooding in 2002 probably had an adverse impact on agricultural activity, which still accounts for over 40% of GDP. Also, yields of important agricultural crops (including rice) have fallen recently against a backdrop of shortages of imported fertilisers and other inputs. On the demand side, royalties from gas production supported increased capital expenditures by state enterprises. Continuing power shortages are another constraint on growth. Private capital inflows to Myanmar have all but evaporated in the face of international sanctions and domestic economic uncertainties. It is estimated that gross international reserves at the end of 2001 were sufficient to cover about 2.3 months of imports. In sectors where state enterprises benefit from large exchange rate subsidies, it is impossible for the private sector to compete. Political and economic sanctions limit prospects for exports and FDI, and any significant easing of foreign exchange constraints is unlikely in the near future. The removal of administrative and other impediments to private sector activity and enterprise could generate large supply-side gains.

Much of the foreign investment going to Myanmar is associated with the oil and gas sector. Gas exports have risen with the completion of several major projects in 2000 and 2001. The country's reserves are dwindling, however, and there have been no promising new finds in recent years. Half of all electricity is generated by hydroelectric systems.

▫ Namibia

Capital City	Windhoek	*Capital population: 126,000 (1992)*
Population ('000)	1,831 *(2002)*	
Urban population (%)	31.72 *(2002)*	
Land area (km²)	82329	
Languages	English (official, but most African ethnic groups have their own language), Afrikaans, German	
Religion	Mainly Christian (90%)	
Currency	Namibian dollar (N$)	
Head of State	President Sam Nujoma (1990)	
Head of Government	Theo-Ben Gurirab (2002)	
Ruling Party	South West Africa People's Organisation (SWAPO)	

Main Urban Areas	**Population**
Windhoek (capital)	126,000 (1992)

Namibia, the former South West Africa, lies on the southern Atlantic coast of the continent, where it is bounded in the south by its former occupying power, South Africa, in the north by Angola and in the east by Botswana. The country's climate is generally dry, although drought is rare. The capital is Windhoek.

The Republic of Namibia became fully independent in March 1990, having been effectively annexed by South Africa in 1966 after the UN ended that country's right to act as administrator to the territory. Namibia has an executive president who is elected by the people for a maximum of two five-year terms. Parliament has two chambers. The National Assembly has 78 members, elected for five-year terms, 72 members elected by proportional representation and 68 members appointed by the president. The National Council has 26 members, elected for six-year terms in double-seat constituencies (regions).

Sam Nujoma was re-elected as president in December 1999 with 77% of the vote. Elections to the National Assembly were held at the same time. SWAPO delegates won 76% of the vote and 55 seats. The Congress of Democrats received 10% of the vote and seven seats, while the right-wing Democratic Turnhalle Alliance also obtained 10% of the vote and seven seats.

Growth in Namibia's economy has slowed as a result of the slump in neighbouring South Africa. Namibia's economic ties with its larger neighbour have been very close since South Africa granted Namibia independence in 1990. GDP grew by 2.7% in 2002 and prices rose by 11.3%. In 2003, growth of 3.7% is anticipated while prices are expected to increase by 9.5%. Forecasts for 2004 call for growth of 4.7% with prices rising by 8.5%. A major problem is unemployment which has remained high, at about 35% of the labour force. Nor has economic growth in recent years been sufficient to achieve gains in per capita income or a reduction in poverty. In 2002, the budget deficit rose to 5.4% of GDP. The budgets for 2003 and 2004 (expressed in constant prices for 2001) targeted deficits of 3% of GDP. The government's main goals are to strengthen the agricultural and industrial sectors, upgrade education and improve the rural infrastructure. Although per capita GDP is three to six times the level in Africa's poorest countries, the

majority of Namibia's people live in pronounced poverty because of the great inequality of income distribution and the large amounts of income controlled by foreigners.

Agriculture accounts for 11% of GDP, industry (including mining) contributes 28% and services make up the remainder. Half of the population depends on agriculture (largely subsistence agriculture) for its livelihood. Namibia must import some of its food. The main agricultural crops are millet, sorghum and peanuts. The economy's performance has been hurt by slower agricultural growth and a fall in fishing output, despite buoyant diamond receipts. The major source of income and foreign exchange is the extraction of its vast wealth in minerals, particularly diamonds, uranium and tin and lithium. Other natural resources are copper, gold, lead, cadmium, zinc, salt, vanadium, natural gas and fish. Deposits of oil, natural gas, coal and iron ore are also thought to exist, while the country has the world's largest open cast uranium mine at Rossing. The extraction and processing of minerals for export is a significant activity. Industry is still on a small scale but is growing fast. The main industries include meatpacking, fish processing and dairy products. The prospects for stronger growth beyond 2003 depend on the expansion of offshore mining activity, the operation of a new zinc mine expected and foreign direct investment inflows. Namibia also has strong tourism potential, but this has yet to be fully developed.

Namibia is entirely dependent on imports of energy supplies, although prospecting is under way for petroleum. In 2000, Namibia renewed a stalled agreement with Russia granting Moscow the right to explore for oil and natural gas along Namibia's northern coastline. Namibia's government also awarded oil and gas exploration licences in 2000 to a consortium led by US companies. The country has natural gas reserves of 3,000 billion cu ft. Although natural gas is still in early stages of use in the region, some projects have been identified. Namibia is also developing a programme to utilise solar energy.

▫ Nauru

Capital City	Yaren	*Capital population: 700 (1996)*
Population ('000)	14 *(2002)*	
Urban population (%)	100. *(2002)*	
Land area (km²)	2	
Languages	Nauruan, English	
Religion	Nauruan Protestant Church	
Currency	Australian dollar (A$)	
Head of State	President Derog Gioura (2003)	
Head of Government	Derog Gioura (2003)	
Ruling Party	The Democratic Party of Nauru is the only legal political party.	

Main Urban Areas	**Population**
Yaren (capital)	700 (1996)

Nauru is a single island, located between Kiribati, the Marshall Islands and the Solomon Islands. Almost circular in shape, it is remarkable for its low-lying terrain and for the virtual exhaustion of viable agricultural land. The climate is warm and dry. The capital is Yaren District.

The Republic of Nauru is an associate member of the Commonwealth, in which the executive president governs with the aid of a cabinet whose number may not exceed six people. The president is elected for a period of three years from the 18-member unicameral parliament, which is also elected, by universal suffrage, for a period of three years. Voting is compulsory in all elections.

Parliamentary elections were held in May 2003. Non-partisans won 15 seats. The remaining three seats were taken by members of the Nauru First Party. The elections were held following the death of President Bernard Dowiyogo in March 2003.

GDP grew very little in 2002 and will probably fall in 2003. The medium-term outlook is bleak, given the adverse effect of declining phosphate reserves and many years of poor fiscal management. The provision of basic public services is regularly disrupted and is at serious risk over the medium term. In 2003, the government was not always able to pay its employees and can not afford the fuel to run the island's power plant. The government is behind payments for Air Nauru's one aircraft and can not maintain its telephone system. Another pressing problem is the frequent disruptions of supplies of food, fuel, equipment and materials. Public services, notably power, water and healthcare also face growing problems.

Power, water, telephone, post, banking and air transport services are all provided by state-owned enterprises. The government also owns the country's phosphate mining operation. This was the main income-earner for years, but almost all of the phosphate is now gone. The loss of phosphate has left the island increasingly dependent on the government wages, compensation and royalty payments to landowners and other initiatives as the main stimulus to demand. The financial sector is essentially non-operational. The country's main bank has operated for a number of years on a limited basis even though it is insolvent by international standards. Needless to say, weak fiscal management is constraining the country's ability to obtain external assistance.

All energy requirements are imported at present. There is no scope for hydroelectric development.

□ Nepal

Capital City	Kathmandu	*Capital population: 255,000 (1992)*
Population ('000)	24,616 *(2002)*	
Urban population (%)	12.51 *(2002)*	
Land area (km²)	14300	
Languages	Nepali, Maithir, Bhojpuri	
Religion	Hindu (90%)	
Currency	Nepalese rupee (NPR)	
Head of State	HM King Gyanendra (2001)	
Head of Government	Surya Bahadur Thapa (2003)	
Ruling Party	The National Congress Party of Nepal leads the government.	

Main Urban Areas	**Population**
Kathmandu (capital)	255,000 (1992)

Nepal is a 700-km strip of land lying along the summit of the Himalayan mountain range between India and the Tibet Autonomous Region of China. Only a small proportion of the country is less than 2,000 metres above sea level, and the highest peaks approach 9,000 metres. Half the population lives in the lowlands, however, with three major rivers feeding into the Ganges river basin. The capital is Kathmandu.

The Kingdom of Nepal is a constitutional monarchy in which the King, as the "symbol of Nepalese nationality and the unity of the people of Nepal", has extensive powers. Parliament has two chambers. The House of Representatives has 205 members elected for five year term in single-seat constituencies. The House of the States has 60 members, 35 members elected by the House of Representatives, 15 representatives of Regional Development Areas and 10 appointed members. In 2002 King Gyanendra sacked Prime Minister Sher Bahadur Deuba of the NCP, abolished the Council of Ministers, and assumed executive powers himself. He appointed Lokendra Chand as prime minister in 2002 but replaced him with Thapa in June 2003.

Parliamentary elections were held in May 1999. The Congress Party secured a comfortable majority, winning 110 seats. The Communist Party took 67 seats and the right-wing National Party captured 11. Deuba was appointed as Prime Minister in July 2001 following the assassination of the king.

The economy contracted by 0.5% in 2002 but the pace should rise to 2.3% in 2003. In 2004, growth of 4% is anticipated. Inflation was 2.8% in 2002 and should be 4.7% in 2003. The forecast for 2004 is for prices to rise by 5.4%. Labour market conditions, characterised in 2000 by a 47% underemployment rate and a 7% urban unemployment rate, likely deteriorated somewhat in 2002, given the high annual rate of population growth (2.3%) and the weakness of the economy. The current account deficit widened significantly to 7% of GDP in 2002 (from 5.4% in 2001). However, the value of officially recorded remittances from abroad is known to be a significant understatement. Analysts estimate that the current account would be surplus at 2.5% of GDP in 2002 if informal remittances were taken into account. The increase in the deficit was due to a drop in net services receipts, stemming from the plunge in tourism receipts, as recorded net transfers and remittances from workers abroad rose. Economic performance over the medium term will depend heavily on the domestic security and political scenario, the vagaries of the weather, and developments in the global economy and, especially, in the Indian economy. While the announcement of a ceasefire in January 2003 is clearly a welcome breakthrough, any positive impact on the economy will likely take some time before it becomes evident. Historically, high population growth rates and low economic growth rates have limited progress in poverty reduction. To achieve the level of growth necessary to reduce poverty in the country, Nepal must accelerate the process of economic reforms. The extent of the recovery will be largely determined by export growth and domestic political stability. A major upturn in the services sector is unlikely unless the ceasefire leads to a significant improvement in the security situation.

Agricultural growth slipped to 2.2% in 2002 owing to an irregular monsoon season and the effects of the insurgency. Agricultural growth is expected to slow further to about 2% in 2003, but should recover in 2004. The irregular monsoon in July-August 2002 will adversely affect summer crop production in 2003. Tourist arrivals fell by 40% in 2002, resulting in an estimated 34% fall in tourism receipts and a 1.8% decline in services sector output. The external trade sector also suffered as both exports and imports sharply declined. Exports fell by 18.0% with most of the decline due to the sharp drop in exports of readymade garments, woollen carpets, and shawls. Production disruptions, weak external demand, and intensified competition were factors behind the weak performance. Imports fell by 11.4% during the year, reflecting a decline in manufacturing activity, sluggish development activities, and lower aid inflows. In the financial sector, after considerable delays, external contracts to manage and develop restructuring plans for the two largest commercial banks in the country have been completed. These state-owned banks account for about 52% of banking system assets and because of a very large amount of non-performing loans are technically insolvent, with a combined estimated negative net worth of 7-9% of GDP. External audit and operational review of the Agricultural Development Bank and Nepal Industrial Development Bank are under way to address similar issues. Although SOE finances have continued worsening in recent years, little progress in reforming their operations is evident.

Nepal relies almost exclusively on hydroelectricity for its power needs. Nepal also has large untapped hydroelectric potential, which could be developed both for domestic consumption (only about 15% of Nepal's population currently has access to electricity) as well as for export. Non-commercial energy sources, such as wood,

animal wastes and crop residues, account for a significant share of the country's total energy consumption. Nepal produces a small amount of coal and also imports coal, mainly from China, Bhutan and India.

□ Netherlands Antilles

Capital City	Willenstad	*Capital population: 2,345 (1992)*
Population ('000)	225 *(2002)*	
Urban population (%)	70.94 *(2002)*	
Land area (km²)	80	
Languages	Dutch, Papiamento, English, Spanish	
Religion	Mainly Christian	
Currency	Netherlands Antilles guilder (ANG)	
Head of State	HM Queen Beatrix (Netherlands)	
Head of Government	Etienne Ys (2002)	
Ruling Party	The Party for the Restructured Antilles (PAR) leads a six-party coalition.	

Main Urban Areas	**Population**
Willemstad (capital)	2,345 (1992)

The Netherlands Antilles consists of two groups of islands lying in the Caribbean Sea about 800km apart. The principal group, which includes the capital Curacao, lies just 150km off the coast of Venezuela. Being some 600km from the nearest other island states (Grenada, to the west), the group has acquired its own character under Dutch domination. Aruba, which once belonged to the group under Dutch sovereignty, negotiated its independence in 1986. The capital is Willemstad.

The Netherlands Antilles is a Dutch overseas dependency ruled by the Dutch monarch through an appointed governor. In practice, the country enjoys a high degree of political autonomy and is edging toward independence. The country has a unicameral Parliament (Staten) of 22 members elected by universal suffrage for a four-year term. Aruba, which was part of the group until 1986, became fully independent in 1996. In June 2000, the island of St Maarten voted to become independent. This move would eventually give it the same status as Aruba. Much attention now focuses on the question of secession by Curacao, the most affluent island. But like, St Eustatius and Saba, Curacao has voted to remain within the Netherlands Antilles in previous ballots.

General elections were held in January 2002. The Party Workers' Liberation Front 30th of May won five seats, the PAR claimed four seats, the National People's Party took three seats with the remaining seats divided among five minor parties.

Growth was 0.2% in 2002 and GDP is expected to increase by 0.5% in 2003. The forecast for 2004 is for growth of 1%. Prices rose by 0.4% in 2002 and are expected to increase by 2% in 2003. In 2004, the forecast is for prices to rise by 2.5%. The Antillean economy is relatively undiversified and has suffered from the global recession. Adjustment to these shocks has been hampered by labour and product market rigidities, high administrative and tax burdens, and inefficiencies in public enterprises. Unemployment has risen sharply, and many people have emigrated Tourism and oil refining are the country's two most important sectors. Tourism is the most dynamic sector but has experienced a fall in visitors after 11 September 2001. Nevertheless, the sector probably holds the most potential for the future, with most facilities being located on Curacao and St. Maarten. Visitors from the Netherlands, the US and other parts of the Caribbean make up the bulk of visitors. The Netherlands Antilles' offshore financial sector currently handles over US$65 billion of assets and a significant portion of total income is derived from these activities. Economic conditions are volatile, being influenced by erratic movements in world commodity prices (especially oil) and conditions in international financial markets.

The agricultural sector is tiny, accounting for only 1-2% of GDP. Poor soil and inadequate water supplies hamper the development of farming. Industry accounts for 15% and services contribute the remainder. Tourism, petroleum transhipment and offshore finance are the mainstays of the economy, which is closely tied to the outside world. The islands enjoy a high per capita income and a well-developed infrastructure as compared with other countries in the region. The main industries are petroleum refining (Curacao), petroleum, transhipment facilities (Curacao and Bonaire) and light manufacturing (Curacao). Almost all consumer and capital goods are imported.

The country has no indigenous energy resources and depends on imports for all its fuel needs.

▫ New Caledonia

Capital City	Nouméa	Capital population: 65,110 (1989)
Population ('000)	220 (2002)	
Urban population (%)	78.56 (2002)	
Land area (km²)	1828	
Languages	French	
Religion	Mainly Roman Catholic (60%)	
Currency	Franc CFP (CFPF)	
Head of State	President Jacques Chirac (France)	
Head of Government	Pierre Frogier (2001)	
Ruling Party	The government is led by the Rassemblement pour la Caledonie dans la Republique (RPCR) in coalition with two smaller parties.	

Main Urban Areas	Population
Nouméa (capital)	65,110 (1989)

New Caledonia, situated in the Western Pacific about 1,500km east of Australia, is basically a single large island which controls numerous smaller coral reefs and islets. Vanuatu lies directly to the northeast. The capital is Noumea.

New Caledonia is an external department of France and is governed, in part, from Paris. The country sends deputies to the French national Assembly and is represented at the EU. Since being accorded regional status in 1974, the country elects its own regional council. There are 56 members who serve for a term of six years. A referendum on independence from France was held in 1987, but the vote was boycotted by the Kanak majority, which opposed the move. Another referendum was scheduled for 1998 but a last-minute compromise by Paris postponed the vote for at least 15 years. Under the new agreement, New Caledonia will have control over employment rights, trade, natural resources and primary education while Paris retains responsibility for foreign policy, justice, public order and defence.

Elections to the regional council were held in May 1999. The RPCR won 24 seats and the Front de Liberation Nationale Kanake Socialiste captured 18 seats. The remaining seats were divided among anti-independence and pro-independence parties.

The economy continues to struggle with growth of around 1% in 2003. Inflation has begun to rise and is expected to be 3-4% in 2003. Many decisions regarding New Caledonia's economy are made in Paris rather than Noumea. Export earnings rose in recent years as world prices strengthened. The local government, however, remains terribly short of cash and demands more aid from France. The island's mining operations represent the most important sector of the economy, with nickel and chrome extraction accounting for the bulk of national income. New Caledonia's reserves of nickel account for over 40% of known world deposits.

New Caledonia's mining operations represent the most important sector of the economy, with nickel and chrome extraction earning well over US$8 million a year. The country is the world's third largest nickel producer, with over 40% of known world deposits. There are also reserves of iron ore, manganese, cobalt, zinc and lead. Agriculture performs poorly and productivity in the sector is low owing to a lack of investment which is related to the continuing political uncertainty in the country. Only a negligible amount of the land is suitable for cultivation, and food accounts for more than a quarter of all imports. Farmers nevertheless have some export crops including copra and coffee, while sweet potatoes, bananas, papaws and vegetables are grown for the domestic market. Cattle are raised in various parts of the country and there are extensive timber removal programmes under way. Industry is varied, ranging from heavy activities like nickel smelting to light industries, textiles and electronics. The tourist industry is also extremely important, but is performing poorly. Travel fears following the events of 11 September 2001 and the terrorist attacks in Bali, coupled with more competition from other destinations in the region, has led to a slump in the number of arrivals.

The country relies on imports for all its basic requirements. Demand for electricity has been generally falling since the mid-1980s.

▫ New Zealand

Capital City	Wellington	Capital population: 170,040 (2002)
Population ('000)	3,902 (2002)	
Urban population (%)	86.73 (2002)	
Land area (km²)	26799	
Languages	English	
Religion	Mainly Christian (75%)	
Currency	New Zealand dollar (NZ$)	
Head of State	HM Queen Elizabeth II	
Head of Government	Helen Clark (1999)	
Ruling Party	The Labour Party leads a coalition.	

Main Urban Areas	Population
Auckland	399,100 (2002)
Christchurch	329,820 (2002)
Manukau	298,520 (2002)
North Shore	195,960 (2002)
Waitakere	181,000 (2002)
Wellington (capital)	170,040 (2002)
Hamilton	122,200 (2002)
Dunedin	118,740 (2002)
Lower Hutt	97,680 (2002)
Palmerston North	75,260 (2002)

The two large islands which make up the greater part of New Zealand are located between the southern Tasmanian Sea and the South Pacific. They have a total length of almost 1,500km and extend to a maximum altitude of just over 4,000 metres along the volcanic ridges. The climate is pleasant, though cool in winter. The capital is Wellington.

New Zealand, an independent member of the Commonwealth, is ruled by the Crown acting through a Governor-General. Executive power is exercised by the prime minister, who is appointed by the unicameral House of Representatives (Parliament). The 120 members of the House are elected by universal suffrage for a term of three years. A proportional representation system was introduced in 1995. The present government has raised the possibility of abolishing its link to the Queen.

Elections to the House of Representatives were held in July 2002. The Labour Party won 52 seats while its coalition partner, the Alliance Party, took only two seats. The National Party took 27 seats, the anti-immigration New Zealand First Party received 13 seats and the remainder were divided among several smaller parties. Helen Clark retained her position as prime minister.

New Zealand's GDP grew by 4.4% in 2002. In 2003, growth is expected to be 2.6% while in 2004 the forecast is for a gain of 2.9%. Inflation was 2.7% in 2002 and should fall to about 2% in 2003. Prices are forecast to rise by 2% in 2004. Although the economy has performed well in recent years, the pace of economic growth is expected to ease, given the weak external environment, the fall in commodity prices, and the sizeable currency appreciation in 2001 and 2002. Private consumption will account for most of the slowdown in growth, reflecting weaker disposable income growth and slower population growth. Uncertainty about the strength of external demand and recent dry weather conditions in some parts of the country are some of the downside risks. By 2004, the current account deficit is projected to return to its average level of the 1990s of around 4-4.5% of GDP. Over the longer term, the country's finances are likely to come under pressure owing to the ageing of the population. Measures to deal with these costs must be adopted soon in order to spread the fiscal burden over time and to enable households to adapt their savings behaviour appropriately.

Agriculture accounts for 11% of GDP but is an especially important contributor to the country's exports. Half the country's land area consists of pasture land for sheep and cattle, with much of the remainder being woodlands and forests which are used for the extraction of hardwoods. There are nearly 70 million sheep in the country. The country continues to be heavily reliant on commodity production in agriculture, fishing and forestry. Although these sectors account directly for only around 8% of GDP, they provide a far greater share of export earnings and also supply inputs for processing industries. There has been a shift in recent years towards further processing of primary commodities, to add value and to counter fluctuating world commodity prices. The industrial sector contributes a third of GDP. Until the mid-1980s, manufacturing was focused on production for the small domestic market and was aided by import protection. More recently, it has been geared towards export markets. Activities range from heavy smelting to light industry, with the production of light engineering and consumer goods being the most prominent. New Zealand is reasonably well endowed with mineral resources, which include sulphur, iron ore and iron sand, titanium, gold, silver, limestone and dolomite. It also has ample energy reserves which mainly consist of coal and lignite along with a massive offshore gas field. As this field is developed, New Zealand should have an exportable surplus of energy supplies.

With ample reserves of coal and lignite and a massive offshore gas field, New Zealand should have an exportable surplus of energy supplies. However, it relies on imports for its oil supplies while exporting both gas and coal. At least 80% of all electricity comes from hydroelectric installations.

□ Nicaragua

Capital City	Managua	*Capital population: 1,195,000 (1995)*
Population ('000)	4,872 *(2002)*	
Urban population (%)	56.7 *(2002)*	
Land area (km²)	12140	
Languages	Spanish (English in certain coastal areas)	
Religion	Mainly Roman Catholic (90%)	
Currency	Cordoba oro (NIC)	
Head of State	Enrique Bolaños Geyer (2001)	
Head of Government	Enrique Bolaños Geyer (2001)	
Ruling Party	The government is supported by the Constitutional Liberal Party (PLC).	

Main Urban Areas	**Population**
Managua (capital)	1,195,000 (1995)

Nicaragua is the second largest state in Central America, after Mexico. It bridges the section of the Panamanian isthmus that lies between Costa Rica and Honduras and has coastlines on both the Pacific and the Caribbean. The terrain is mountainous to the west, but descends to lowlands in the coastal east. There are two huge inland lakes situated to the northwest and southeast of the capital Managua. The capital is Managua.

The 1987 Constitution provides for an executive president, directly elected for a five-year term and a unicameral National Assembly (Parliament) of 93 members, elected by universal suffrage every six years.

Presidential elections in November 2001 produced a victory for Geyer, leader of the PLC. He received 56% of the vote. José Daniel Ortega, leader of the Sandinista Front, was second with 42% of the vote. In parliamentary elections held at the same time, the PLC won 47 seats while the Sandinistas took 43. The remainder went to the Conservative Party.

In 2002, GDP grew by 1% and growth of 2.3% is expected in 2003. The forecast for 2004 is for growth of 3.7%. Inflation was 4% in 2002 and should be about 5.2% in 2003. In 2004, prices are forecast to rise by 5.2%. The government is aggressively fighting corruption and tax evasion. In 2002, tax revenues rose by 9% even though the economy grew by just 1.5%. However, the financial position of the central bank deteriorated sharply in 2001. In addition to a large loss of reserves, the central bank's dollar-indexed domestic debt jumped by US$520 million (21% of GDP) as it absorbed the cost of resolving four banks that failed in 2000 and 2001. Gross official reserves at the end of 2002 stood at just US$362 million (equivalent to 2.7 months of imports of goods and services). Fortunately, the government has moved quickly to address these imbalances. Government spending has been reined in and the public sector deficit was reduced to 9.2% of GDP in 2002. At the urging of international analysts, further trade liberalisation and renewed efforts to strengthen regional integration are expected. Meanwhile, there has been some progress in structural reform. The national assembly approved legislation to reform the social security system and improve the process of government procurement. Nicaragua joined with El Salvador and Guatemala in signing a tri-national declaration calling for the establishment of a regional system for ensuring economic and social justice, the formation of a customs union and the consolidation of the financial system.

Nicaragua's agricultural sector accounts for 33% of GDP and employs 42% of the workforce. Food processing, coffee roasting, textiles, timber and handicrafts are all important. The long-term decline in coffee prices is a trend that greatly concerns both farmers and public officials. The manufacturing sector contributes 23% of GDP and produces chemicals, metal products, textiles, clothing, refined petroleum, beverages, footwear and wood products. On the demand side, the main contributors to growth are public expenditures (on consumption and, to a lesser degree, investment) and a recovery of exports. Although the construction industry has remained buoyant, its pace of activity has gradually been declining because government allocations for the special reconstruction programme launched in the wake of Hurricane Mitch in 1998 are being scaled back and because private investment in non-residential construction is decreasing as a number of major hotel projects have reached their final stages. Distribution of income is extremely unequal. The country has only limited mineral resources, notably salt, gold, silver, tungsten and lead and zinc.

In 2002, the government announced legislation opening the country to foreign oil exploration. Included are onshore concessions, as well as offshore blocks in the Atlantic and Pacific Oceans. With electricity demand expected to continue growing rapidly (a projected 6.1% annually over the next 20 years), Nicaragua will require large amounts of investment in new power plants. This growth is from a very low level, however, and a significant portion of the population still does not have electricity. For the present, Nicaragua's main domestic source of energy is geothermal. The country hopes to boost generation capacity by 1,200 megawatts over the next 20 years.

□ Niger

Capital City	Niamey	*Capital population: 450,000 (1992)*
Population ('000)	11,805 *(2002)*	
Urban population (%)	21.48 *(2002)*	
Land area (km²)	126670	
Languages	French, Hausa, Tuareg, Djerma, Fulani	
Religion	Muslim (85%)	
Currency	CFA franc (CFAF)	
Head of State	President Mamadou Tandja (1999)	
Head of Government	Hama Amadou (2000)	
Ruling Party	The government is formed by the National Movement for the Development Society (MNSD) and the Democratic and Social Convention (CDS).	

Main Urban Areas	**Population**
Niamey (capital)	450,000 (1992)

Niger, occupying much of the centre of northwest Africa, is a large and landlocked state which borders on Algeria in the northwest, Libya in the far north, Chad in the east, Nigeria in the south and Benin, Burkina Faso and Mali in the west and southwest. The only cultivable soil in the country lies along the Niger River; elsewhere it is mainly desert or savanna. The capital is Niamey.

From 1974 until the return of parliamentary democracy in 1993, Niger was run by a military administration. Ibrahim Bare Mainassara assumed the presidency in 1996 and was assassinated in 1999. Under the present constitution, the people elect the president for a five-year term. The National Assembly has 83 members, elected for five-year terms, 75 members elected in multi-seat constituencies and eight members elected in single-seat national minority constituencies.

Presidential elections were held in November 1999 Mamadou Tandja received 60% of the vote, defeating Mahamane Ousmane. In parliamentary elections occurring in November 1999, the MNSD took 38 seats while the CDS won 17 seats. The remainder were scattered among several parties.

GDP rose by 3% in 2002 and prices increased by 2.6%. In 2003, the rate of growth is expected to be 4% and prices are expected to rise by just 0.5%. Forecasts for 2004 call for growth of 4.1% and inflation of 1.7%. The government's programme of economic reforms is being implemented against in a relatively hostile environment. Business leaders frequently protested against the new tax legislation imposed in 2002, there were frequent strikes by labour unions and a mutiny by army officers. In response, the government initiated a process of dialogue and negotiation with economic agents and labour unions which led to a reduction in direct taxes on business profits and the income tax on wages and salaries. In 2003, the government hopes to encourage growth through increased public investment and further reductions in its domestic payments arrears. The tax will be broadened and the scope of exemptions reduced during 2003. Most of the major enterprises in Niger are presently eligible for one or more special tax exemptions and this situation will be rectified. No upward adjustments in public-sector wages are anticipated during 2003 and the annual wage bill is projected to amount to 3.5% of GDP, or 35% of tax receipts. This benchmark compares favourably to a level of over 50% of tax receipts in 2000. During 2002, the government signed debt-relief agreements totalling $45 million and expects to conclude additional agreements in 2003.

With a per capita income of about US$200, Niger is one of the poorest countries in Africa and is ranked very low on all social indicators. The country is highly vulnerable to external and weather-related shocks. Its main economic activities are agriculture and livestock. The recent improvement in economic performance is partly due to a good harvest after two years of adequate rainfall. Agriculture accounts approximately for 40% of output, while the export base is largely limited to a few minerals. Niger has coal, iron ore, gold, molybdenum, tin and phosphates but produces very little of these minerals. Minerals account for no more than 8% of GDP. Uranium revenues have dropped sharply since the mid-1980s with the end of the uranium boom. The main exports are uranium ore (67%), livestock products (20%) and a few agricultural products. Employing over 90% of the workforce, the agricultural sector produces cotton, hides, leather goods, sorghum, millet, rice and vegetables. Industry generates about 2% of GDP, mainly producing goods for the domestic market. These operations include processed foods, plastics and construction materials and chemicals. The privatisation programme has met with repeated delays and none of the larger public enterprises have yet been sold.

Despite recent oil finds, Niger relies on imports for nearly all its petroleum needs. The only alternatives, apart from coal, are the country's considerable timber resources for fuel wood.

◻ Nigeria

Capital City	Abuja	Capital population: 5,840,180 (1993)
Population ('000)	124,501 (2002)	
Urban population (%)	45.03 (2002)	
Land area (km²)	91077	
Languages	English, Igbo, Yoruba, Hausa	
Religion	Muslim (47%); Christian; traditional	
Currency	Naira (NGN)	
Head of State	Olusegun Obasanjo (1999)	
Head of Government	Olusegun Obasanjo (1999)	
Ruling Party	People's Democratic Party (PDP)	

Main Urban Areas	Population
Abuja (capital)	5,840,180 (1993)
Kano	2,435,508 (1993)
Ibadan	2,063,132 (1993)
Kaduna	1,116,992 (1993)
Benin City	857,402 (1993)
Port Harcourt	790,743 (1993)
Maiduguri	695,030 (1993)
Zaira	688,262 (1993)
Ilorin	598,142 (1993)
Jos	573,648 (1993)

Nigeria is located on the Atlantic coast of West Africa, where it is bounded in the north by Niger, in the west by Benin, in the east by Chad and on the southeast by Cameroon. It has a generally warm and pleasant tropical climate, although conditions along the 100-km-wide mangrove swamps of the coast are less favourable. The capital is Abuja.

Nigeria, an independent member of the Commonwealth, has been ruled by civilian administrations for only nine of its 36 years of independence. General Abacha, who seized power in 1993, jailed most leading politicians including Obasanjo. In June 1998, Abacha died in office and was replaced by Gen. Abbdulsalami Abubakaar, who oversaw the return to civilian rule that brought Obasanjo to office.

Presidential elections were held in April 2003. Obasanjo was re-elected with 62% of the vote, defeating the former military dictator, Muhammadu Buhari. Numerous outside observers conceded that the vote was seriously flawed. In parliamentary elections held in 1999, Obasanjo's party, the PDP, won 208 of the 360 seats in the House of Representatives and 59 out of 109 in the Senate. The two main opposition parties, the All People's Party (APP) and the Alliance for Democracy (AD), together won 145 seats in the House and 44 in the Senate.

GDP rose by just 0.5% in 2002 but growth is expected to be 5.2% in 2003. In 2004, growth of 2.8% is forecast. Inflation was 12.9% in 2002 and is expected to be 12.3% in 2003. Prices are forecast to rise by 10.6% in 2004. Fiscal policy was highly expansionary in 2002, despite efforts by the executive to contain capital spending. The fiscal deficit is to be financed by a drawdown in government deposits in the banking system and the issuance of short-term debt. Monetary policy has been equally accommodating, thus risking even higher rates of inflation. Aggregate bank credit to the federal government increased tenfold during 2002. These lax policies led to a steep loss of international reserves, forcing the government to undertake a series of small devaluations during 2002. Meanwhile, progress on structural reforms has been mixed. The trade and tariff policies adopted in 2002 suggest an increase in overall tariff and non-tariff protection of domestic producers of finished goods, thus representing a setback to the government's goal of liberalisation. The results as regards public enterprise reform have also been mixed. While the privatisation of enterprises in the early phases of the programme is all but complete, there have been setbacks in recent privatisation efforts, especially with regard to privatising public utilities. There are also serious concerns about the soundness and stability of the banking system. The structure of investment is equally disconcerting. Since 1995, when investment averaged 21% of GDP, the private sector share has been less than 8%. In turn, such low levels of private sector investment help to explain why productivity has been so low.

Nominally the wealthiest state in sub-Saharan Africa, Nigeria owes most of its riches to its oil deposits. Over two million barrels are produced each day, accounting for a fifth of GDP and the great majority of all export revenues. Oil contributes nearly 80% of government revenues, 90-95% of export revenues and over 90% of foreign exchange earnings. At one time, 50% of all oil revenues were retained locally but the official figure has fallen to less than 5%. The agricultural sector depends on exports of cocoa, coffee, cotton, palm oil and rubber. Farming has stagnated in recent years but recovered in 2002 because of good rains. Nigeria also has four refineries with a combined capacity one third greater than domestic requirements. Yet these refineries still produce at only about a third of capacity. Recurrent shortages of power in all the country's larger cities have hurt business and increased tensions. Medium-sized enterprises are thought to spend up to 30% of their operating costs on private power-generation. The Nigerian financial system is vulnerable to a number of risks, such as fiscal indiscipline, the economy's high dependence on volatile oil prices, and financial abuse. The country has deposits of coal, tin, iron ore, uranium, lead, zinc and gold, not all of which are being exploited.

Nigeria contains estimated proven oil reserves of 22.5 billion barrels and production is currently 2.3 million barrels per day. Almost all reserves are found in relatively simple geological structures along the country's coastal Niger River Delta. The majority of this oil lies in about 250 small fields, most of which hold

reserves of less than 50 million barrels each. Nigerian crude oil production typically exceeds two million barrels per day but sabotage and ethnic disputes forced cutbacks in 2002 and 2003. Domestic shortages of oil are also due in part to the current system of price controls, which make it more attractive to sell oil outside the country. Other problems facing Nigeria's oil sector are insufficient government funding of its joint venture commitments and corruption.

◻ North Korea

Capital City	Pyongyang	Capital population: 2,470,000 (1995)
Population ('000)	24,548 (2002)	
Urban population (%)	60.64 (2002)	
Land area (km²)	12041	
Languages	Korean	
Religion	Buddhist; Christian; Chundo Kyo	
Currency	North Korean Won (KPW)	
Head of State	President Kim Jong II	
Head of Government	Pak Pong-ju (2003)	
Ruling Party	The Korean Workers' Party is the only legal political party.	

Main Urban Areas	Population
Pyongyang (capital)	2,470,000 (1995)

North Korea occupies slightly more than half of the Korean peninsula, which lies to the south of the Chinese city of Shenyang. Like South Korea, it has a mixed and often mountainous landscape with extensive tree cover. The climate is temperate and often wet. The capital is Pyongyang.

The Democratic People's Republic of Korea has been a communist one-party state since 1948. The 1972 Constitution provides for an executive president who is elected by the Supreme People's Assembly, or Parliament, composed of 687 members. The Assembly's members are elected every four years by universal suffrage, from a single list, but they meet only occasionally. In effect, power is exercised by the Central People's Committee, in which the Korean Workers' Party dominates.

Parliamentary elections were held in August 2003 when over 600 deputies were selected. Among them was Kim Jong II. Kim was elected general secretary of the ruling Workers' Party in October 1997. Only members of the Democratic Front for the Reunification of the Fatherland, which consists of the Workers' Party and its satellites, are permitted to stand for elections. In September 2003, Kim changed the prime minister, appointing Pak.

North Korea's economy remains under tight state control. The country's communist ideology is based on the concept of "juche", or self-reliance. Severe economic problems have, however, forced the country to accept international food aid and embark on a series of limited market reforms. In the current increasingly tense atmosphere, these reforms have largely been forgotten. In 2002, the government increased wages by as much as 20-30 fold. With far too many North Korean won chasing far too few goods, the country's currency was trading privately in 2003 at around 700 won to the US dollar. In 2002, in an effort to close the gap with the black market rate, the government devalued the won to a rate of 151 to the dollar from 2.16 to the dollar. As the won become increasingly worthless, the government ordered that all dollars be swapped for euros, a curious decree that was ignored. Despite incentives by the Seoul government for companies to invest in and trade with North Korea, interest has trailed off. The number of new projects approved by the South Korean government fell to just three in 2002, down from 13 in 1998. of 52 Southern companies allowed to invest in the North, half have dropped out of the programme.

North Korea's economy remains under tight state control. State-owned companies in agriculture and industry account for about 90% of all economic activity in the country. The economy relies heavily on agriculture, which employs 45% of the workforce although its contribution to GDP is somewhat smaller. Rice, maize, potatoes, millet, sorghum, vegetables, fruit and tobacco are grown for the domestic market. Silk is the only export. In 2002, food rationing was partially abandoned and prices were raised by 20-40 fold for staples like rice, corn and pork. The result has been hyperinflation - at least in the small part of the economy that runs on money. North Korea's heavy industry has been affected by a severe energy shortage, which has forced production cutbacks at some plants. Few consumer durables are manufactured in North Korea. The country's mineral resources include coal, lignite, clays, phosphates, iron ore, magnesium and tungsten but extraction techniques are very rudimentary.

North Korea relies on two domestic sources of commercial energy - coal and hydropower - for most of its energy needs. In 2000, coal accounted for 86% of primary energy consumption. The country's total electricity consumption in 2000 was only 65% of what it had been in 1991. As a result of the electricity shortage, North Korea has resorted to a rationing system. The country often experiences blackouts for extended periods of time, and power losses due to an antiquated transmission grid are high. Rainfall improved in 2001, but some hydroelectric facilities are believed to be out of operation due to flood damage.

Oman

Capital City	Muscat	*Capital population: 622,506 (1993)*
Population ('000)	2,813 *(2002)*	
Urban population (%)	85.63 *(2002)*	
Land area (km²)	30950	
Languages	Arabi,C English	
Religion	Islam	
Currency	Omani rial (OR)	
Head of State	Sultan Qaboos Bin-Said (1970)	
Head of Government	Sultan Qaboos Bin-Said	
Ruling Party	There are no legal political parties in Oman.	

Main Urban Areas	**Population**
Muscat (capital)	622,506 (1993)

Oman, which lies in the southeastern extremity of the Arabian peninsula, actually consists of two separate pieces of land. The larger lies on the Arabian Sea, controlling the southern access to the Gulf through the Gulf of Oman; the smaller, but more significant territory, is on the headland which demarcates the boundary between the two related waterways on the tip of the United Arab Emirates territory in the Gulf. The capital is Muscat.

The Sultanate of Oman is ruled by decree by the Sultan who deposed his father in the coup of 1970. The Sultan is also prime minister and is advised by a cabinet that he appoints. Oman has a bicameral parliament. The Consultative Assembly has 82 elected members with only consultative tasks. The Council of State has 40 appointed members. Although the Council has no powers whatever, its introduction was seen as a move toward greater democratisation. Oman favours closer co-operation within the Gulf region.

The last elections were 14 September 2000.

GDP increased by 2.3% in 2002 and prices fell by 0.7%. In 2003, growth is expected to be about 2.2% while prices rise by 1%. Forecasts for 2004 call for growth of 4.8% while inflation is 1.1%. Oman remains heavily dependent on oil revenues, which account for nearly 80% of the country's export earnings and 40% of GDP. The government has made privatisation and diversification of its economy top policy priorities. Expanded utilisation of natural gas is central to Omani diversification plans, for export as well as for domestic use. In recent years, Oman also has put forth great efforts to attract foreign investments, particularly in light industry, tourism, and electric power generation. Foreign investment incentives include a five-year tax holiday for companies in certain industries, an income tax reduction for publicly held companies with at least 51% Omani ownership, and soft loans to finance new and existing projects. The country's total external debt remains manageable at less than 45% of GDP. Oman became a member of the World Trade Organisation in 2000.

Agriculture accounts for a mere 3% of GDP while industry (including oil) makes up 69%. The country's non-oil exports, including many agricultural products and textiles, have increased sharply, although they still account for less than 10% of total exports. The main products are alfalfa, dates, bananas, wheat, mangoes and limes together with tomatoes and other water-dependent crops. Fishing is a traditional activity with a long history in Oman. Manufacturing is limited, accounting for just 1% of GDP. There are factories producing cement, steel sections, cattle feed plants and a variety of consumer goods. Among the new projects being implemented are several natural gas investments, an aluminium smelter and petrochemicals plant, and a urea fertiliser plant. These projects are intended not only to help alleviate Oman's dependence on oil, but also reduce dependence on governmental spending and employment. There is also an important mining industry, producing chromate, copper and manganese, and deposits of many more metals have been located. Expanded utilisation of natural gas is central to Omani diversification plans, both for export as well as for domestic use.

In many ways, Oman is atypical of Persian Gulf oil producers. Oil was not discovered in commercial quantities until 1962 - decades after most of Oman's neighbours. Most of Oman's 5.5 billion barrels in proven oil reserves are located in the northern and central regions The country's oil fields are also generally smaller, more widely scattered, less productive and more costly per barrel than in other countries. This means that the average well in Oman produces about one tenth the volume per well compared to neighbouring countries. Oman continues to use a variety of enhanced oil recovery techniques in order to minimise the costs of exploration and further development at new and existing oil fields. Using these technologies, Oman has succeeded in bringing down the cost of oil production to US$3 per barrel in some fields and US$4 per barrel in others - but these figures, while still low by world standards, are substantially above most other Persian Gulf oil fields. At current production rates, Oman is projected to exhaust its oil reserves by around 2020. It is for this reason that government officials put together a plan to spend US$4 billion in oil exploration and development. Roughly 18% of this amount has been targeted for exploration, 44% for the development and installation of production facilities and the remaining 38% for operating expenses. Oman is not a member of OPEC but has agreed in recent years to cooperate with OPEC countries by reducing its oil production in an effort to restore stability to world oil prices. The government has made natural gas - both for export as well as for domestic gas-intensive industries - the cornerstone of its diversification and economic growth strategy. Through an extensive exploration programme, Oman has consistently increased its natural gas reserves in recent years. In 2002, estimated proven natural gas reserves were approximately 29.3 trillion cubic feet, up from only 12.3 trillion cu ft in 1992.

Pakistan

Capital City	Islamabad	*Capital population: 574,424 (1993)*
Population ('000)	162,784 *(2002)*	
Urban population (%)	38.05 *(2002)*	
Land area (km²)	77088	
Languages	Urdu is the official language, but is only in everyday use among about 8% of the population. Other languages in more general use include Punjabi (48%), Pushto (13%), Sindhi (12%), Saraiki (10%); English is also widely spoken.	
Religion	Islam (97%)	
Currency	Pakistani rupee (PKR)	
Head of State	General Pervez Musharraf (1999)	
Head of Government	Mir Zafarullah Khan Jamali (2002)	
Ruling Party	The government is formed by supporters of the president.	

Main Urban Areas	**Population**
Karachi	10,137,499 (1993)
Lahore	5,583,258 (1993)
Faisalabad	2,180,616 (1993)
Rawalpindi	1,530,302 (1993)
Multan	1,299,759 (1993)
Huderabad	1,266,662 (1993)
Gujranwala	1,229,337 (1993)
Peshawar	1,066,846 (1993)
Quetta	613,456 (1993)
Islamabad (capital)	574,424 (1993)

Pakistan lies in the northwest corner of the Indian Ocean, where it is bounded in the south and east by India and in the north and west by Afghanistan and Iran. The country is partially low-lying, although its northwestern border with Afghanistan is extremely mountainous. The climate is subtropical, with heavy rains. The capital is Islamabad.

Pakistan, an independent member of the Commonwealth, has an executive president who is elected by universal suffrage and reports to an elected parliament. The constitution also allows the president to dismiss any prime minister without notice. Musharraf restored a number of presidential powers after taking office and appointing Aziz as prime minister in 2001. The National Assembly has 342 members, elected for a five-year term, 272 members elected in single-seat constituencies, ten members elected by non-Muslim minorities and 60 seats or women nominated by political parties in accordance to their share of National Assembly seats per province. The Senate had 87 members, elected for a six-year term.

Musharraf was confirmed as president in a referendum in 2002. Elections to the National Assembly were held in October 20002. The Pakistan People's Party Parliamentarians won 71 seats, the Pakistan Muslim League took 69 seats, the Islamist Muttahhida Hajlis-e-Amal Pakistan received 53 seats and several smaller parties took the remainder.

GDP rose by 4.4% in 2002 and should increase by 5.4% in 2003. In 2004, growth of 5.1% is forecast. Inflation was 3.3% in 2002 and is expected to rise to 3.6% in 2003. Prices are forecast to increase by 4% in 2004. Remittances from Pakistanis working abroad (many of them in the Middle East) were strong in 2002. These inflows, combined with large bilateral and multilateral support, have allowed authorities to build official reserves to R 2$7.6 billion by end-December 2002, equivalent to about 6.5 months of projected imports in 2003. The persistence of unexpectedly high private capital/remittances inflows is putting upward pressure on the exchange rate, posing a dilemma for monetary and exchange rate policy. Pakistan's external debt is equal to around 60% of GDP and its debt payments due each year exceed its receipts from exports. The government also suffers from a relatively ineffective system for tax collection, with only 1% of the population paying income taxes. The government has begun a programme to increase tax collection rates, and the effort is showing some signs of success. With regard to fiscal issues, non-tax revenue exceeded the target for 2002, owing to larger payments by the coalition against terrorism. However, net lending was much higher than programmed on account of non-payment by public sector enterprises. In general, macroeconomic policy aims at continued budget deficit reduction to enhance public debt sustainability, reduce vulnerability to shocks, and create room over the medium term for the needed increase in human development and infrastructure expenditure. The unemployment rate stands at about 8% but the number of unemployed is very large.

Agriculture has begun to recover from the severe drought in 2001 which is estimated to have caused a loss of about 2% in national income. The drought also had adverse impacts on hydropower generation. The country's textile industry has been adversely affected since September 2001, but an inflow of aid has improved the short-term financial situation. The US has also agreed to reduce or suspend some tariffs on imports of Pakistani textile products. New rules and procedures on General Sales Tax and customs duties refunds were implemented in September 2002, with a view to closing loopholes and reducing scope for abuse. The tax reforms being implemented in 2003 include the abolition of a sizeable number of income tax exemptions, as well as all remaining withholding tax exemptions for income. The country's privatisation programme has produced mixed results with several smaller enterprises being sold to private investors while the sale of a few larger firms has been delayed or postponed. A plan to revamp the railways through corporatisation, downsizing, and partial privatisation is being prepared. The country's national airline is scheduled for privatisation by 2004. A decision on the restructuring of the National Bank and further reform of the financial sector should be made during 2003.

Pakistan produced 53,000 bbl/d of oil in 2002 and consumed 365,000 bbl/d of petroleum products. While there is no prospect for Pakistan to reach self sufficiency in oil, the government has encouraged private (including foreign) firms to develop domestic production capacity. Pakistan's net oil imports are projected to rise substantially as demand growth outpaces increases in production. Demand for refined petroleum products also greatly exceeds domestic oil refining capacity, so nearly half of Pakistani imports are refined products. The Pakistani government had planned to move forward with the sale of a significant number of the production assets, but has postponed the sales due to investor concerns about the country's stability.

□ Panama

Capital City	Panama City	*Capital population: 948,000 (1995)*
Population ('000)	2,921 *(2002)*	
Urban population (%)	56.79 *(2002)*	
Land area (km²)	7443	
Languages	Spanish (English is widespread)	
Religion	Mainly Roman Catholic	
Currency	Balboa (PAB)	
Head of State	President Mireya Moscoso (1999)	
Head of Government	President Mireya Moscoso (1999)	
Ruling Party	The government is formed by a multiparty coalition.	

Main Urban Areas	Population
Panama City (capital)	948,000 (1995)

Panama forms the longest and most slender section of the isthmus which divides Central America from South America, and extends in an S-shape, some 700km from east to west, between Costa Rica and Colombia. The land is traversed by the Panama Canal, the all-important marine link that connects the Caribbean Sea (and thus the Atlantic Ocean) with the Pacific Ocean. The capital is Panama City.

The 1983 Constitution provides for an executive president who is elected by universal suffrage for a term of five years and a unicameral National Assembly with 71 members who are also elected for five years. Panamanian politics have changed considerably since the US invasion in 1989 and the removal of Gen. Manuel Noriega as president. In December 1991 the Assembly approved a constitutional amendment which abolished the national army.

Presidential elections were held in May 1999 and were won by Mireya Moscoso, the widow of a former president. She took 45% of the vote, easily defeating other candidates. Voting for the National Assembly was held at the same time with the ruling coalition receiving 57% of the vote and 42 seats.

GDP grew by 0.8% in 2002 and growth of 1.5% is forecast for 2003. Forecasts for 2004 call for growth of 3%. Prices rose by 1% in 2002 and should rise by another 1.7% in 2003. Inflation is forecast to be 1.4% in 2004. The economic slowdown has sent Panama's unemployment rate soaring to more than 14%. By independent estimates, the government's deficit presently stands at 3-4% of GDP, about double what is permitted. The new accounting methods, which incorporate some $90 million in revenues from the Panama Canal, would reduce the deficit to the 2% which is allowed by the constitution. Critics argue that the government's accounting methods seriously underestimate the deficit. Cutbacks in public investment expenditure have reduced the fiscal deficit, and measures were taken to curb the country's large deficit on the balance-of-payments current account. Panamanians have the eighth highest average income in the continent but the wealth distribution is one of the most unequal. Two fifths of the population live in poverty.

Agriculture accounts for about 10% of GDP and employs a quarter of the workforce. However, the country's exports of farm products are of critical importance, generating a substantial amount of foreign exchange. Panama's banana exports have been one of the country's major exports but have declined sharply. Exports of domestically-produced goods have increased, thanks to higher sales of products such as flour and fish oil, shrimp larvae, coffee and sugar. Domestic crops include rice, maize, potatoes, beans and beef. The fishing industry is another major source of foreign exchange revenues as Panama is the world's third biggest shrimp exporter. Panama stands apart from the rest of Central America by virtue of its services-based economy and its control over the Panama Canal. In 1996, the government began expansion and modernisation of the ports at each end of the canal. More than US$120 million has been spent so far with another US$200 million on related projects. Ambitious new plans to modernise and expand the canal are now being considered by the Panama Canal Authority. The new plans involve a $5-8 billion expansion, including the dredging of a new lake and a third set of locks. This would be the largest upgrade since the opening of the canal in 1914. With the completion of these modernisation programmes in 2005, canal transit capacity would increase by approximately 20%. Manufacturing establishments are mostly small-scale and consist mainly of producers of clothing, footwear, textiles, paper, plastics and electronics products. Mineral deposits are also arousing interest from international investors. The country has copper reserves of some six million tonnes, which rank it ninth in the world in this category. Optimists predict that mining could account for 15% of GDP within the next 10-15 years.

Panama and Guatemala are the only oil producers in Central America. Panama is the smaller of the two suppliers, producing only 1,000 barrels per day. The country imports over 70% of its energy. Electricity generation accounts for most of Panama's domestic energy production, with hydroelectric generation alone accounting for 75% of the country's total energy production In 2000, neighbouring

Colombia approved a bill allowing natural gas exports, which previously had been banned. This paves the way for the possible construction of a gas pipeline leading from offshore Colombian gas sources directly to Panama.

□ Papua New Guinea

Capital City	Port Moresby	*Capital population: 147,000 (1992)*
Population ('000)	4,940 *(2002)*	
Urban population (%)	17.98 *(2002)*	
Land area (km²)	45286	
Languages	Pidgin, English, Motu; more than 700 native languages	
Religion	Mainly Christian (93%)	
Currency	Kina (Kina)	
Head of State	HM Queen Elizabeth II	
Head of Government	Sir Michael Somare (2002)	
Ruling Party	The government is formed by the People's Democratic Movement (PDM) and allies.	

Main Urban Areas	Population
Port Moresby (capital)	147,000 (1992)

Papua New Guinea, one of the more important island states in the Asia-Pacific region, occupies the eastern half of the old island of New Guinea. It also includes territories in the Solomon Islands group, in the Trobriands and in the Louisiade Archipelago. The capital is Port Moresby.

Papua New Guinea, a member of the British Commonwealth, has a Governor-General who represents the Queen. However, executive power is exercised by a prime minister and a national executive council. The council is appointed by the Governor on the advice of the unicameral national parliament. The 109 members of parliament are elected by universal suffrage for a period of not more than five years.

Parliamentary elections occurred in June 2002 when the National Alliance Party took 19 seats and the PMD won 13 seats. The People's Progress Party received eight seats with the remainder divided among many minor parties. Somare subsequently became prime minister.

The economy suffered a strong contraction in 2002, with real GDP falling by 3.3%. However, growth of 2.5% is anticipated in 2003. In 2004, the rate of growth is forecast to be 2.3%. Inflation was 11.8% in 2002 and is likely to be even higher, at 17.2%, in 2003. Prices are forecast to rise by 8% in 2004. The rise in inflation in 2002 was partly due to the depreciation of the kina, the country's currency. A sharp deterioration in fiscal conditions also contributed to the rise in prices. The decline forced the government to adopt a supplementary budget in 2002 to accommodate the shortfall. Papua New Guinea recorded a current account deficit in 2002 after more than two years of surpluses. The new government formed in 2002 subsequently announced its intention to strengthen fiscal responsibility and remove barriers to investment and growth. At the same time, however, the government initiated a review of the privatisation process, which it subsequently suspended temporarily. Periods of weak fiscal management that trigger macroeconomic instability have been a feature of the economy since the 1990s. Fiscal and monetary policies were tightened in 2003, primarily through sizeable cuts in goods and services expenditure. The fiscal deficit for the year is expected to be around 2% of GDP. Much more needs to be done in this field, however. The country's medium-term prospects remain highly dependent on the fiscal stance. The most likely source of a favourable economic outcome over the medium term is continued higher prices for gold and oil. This development can provide a boost to government revenues and lessen macroeconomic pressures. Privatisation is expected to provide an important source of financing in the future. However, the government's domestic debt will have to rise thereafter, as increased domestic financing is required to offset rising external obligations.

The agriculture sector remained subdued in 2002 because of delay in harvesting some major crops (mainly coffee) while the declining trend in minerals continued. However, the non-mining sector grew by 2.4%, after contracting the two previous years. The improvement in the non-mining sector is in part a result of a turnaround in the prices of key commodities, notably palm oil, cocoa, and, to a lesser extent, coffee. Construction shrank by 2.1% in 2002. Stronger domestic expenditures lifted manufacturing output by an estimated 7.5% over the year, as it did the transport and services sectors to a degree. This surge in activity was largely met with existing capacity. Consequently, business investment outside the mining and oil sector remained subdued. The commercial banks faced weak private demand for lending in 2002, with private sector credit at year-end 2002 approximately 4.6% below the level at the start of the year. Exports fell by 14.7% in 2002. The decline was caused mainly by a 24.3% fall in oil exports, reflecting the natural decline in output of the major field of Kutubu. Agricultural exports rose by 35.5% from the 2001 level, helped by higher world prices for major agricultural commodities. Log exports increased by 16.5%, largely as a consequence of a delayed wet season that improved access to logging areas. Total merchandise imports fell by 12.8% in 2002, reflecting the depreciation of the kina and continued weakness in the economy. However, the increased competitiveness provided by the steady depreciation of the kina is bringing some changes. There are some signs of local products displacing imports, particularly in fresh and processed foods, but also in new areas of economic activity - for example, oil refining, where the country's first oil refinery is now being constructed.

The country has four huge and potentially oil-filled basins offshore, although their exact content remains uncertain. Meanwhile, it is dependent on thermal energy for three-quarters of its electricity.

▫ Paraguay

Capital City	Asunción	*Capital population: 825,000 (1992)*
Population ('000)	5,707 *(2002)*	
Urban population (%)	57.12 *(2002)*	
Land area (km²)	39730	
Languages	Spanish, Guarani	
Religion	Mainly Roman Catholic (90%)	
Currency	Guaraní (PYG)	
Head of State	Nicanor Duarte Frutos (2003)	
Head of Government	Luis González Macchi (1999)	
Ruling Party	The government is formed by the Republican National Alliance (ANR) and the Colorado Party.	

Main Urban Areas	Population
Asunción (capital)	825,000 (1992)

Paraguay, the geographic centre of South America, is a landlocked state bordered in the north by Bolivia, in the east by Brazil, and in the south and southwest by Argentina. Its terrain is, however, less mountainous than any of these countries. Most of it consists of a marshy plain through which the Paraguay and Pilcomayo rivers flow, interspersed with vast tracts of forest and jungle. The capital is Asunción.

The Republic of Paraguay has an executive president who is directly elected by universal suffrage for a five-year term of office. The president answers to a bicameral national Congress comprising a 45-member Senate and an 80-member Chamber of Deputies - both similarly elected for five years. In elections to the Chamber of Deputies, the party receiving the most votes is automatically granted two thirds of the seats in both Houses.

Frutos defeated Pedro Niella in presidential elections held in April 2003. In the congressional elections held at the same time, the ANR/Colorado Party won 34 seats in the Chamber of Deputies and 16 seats in the Senate. The Radical Liberal Party took 20 seats in the Chamber and 12 in the Senate. The remaining seats were scattered among several parties.

GDP fell by 3.9% in 2002 and should grow by just 0.6% in 2003. In 2004, growth of 1% is forecast. Prices increased by 10.5% in 2002 and are expected to rise by 17.4% in 2003. The forecast is for prices to increase by another 12.1% in 2004. These figures are evidence of an increasingly serious situation. Successive governments have blocked repeated attempts to reform a state which employs more than 200,000 people. Now, the government is also running out of cash. Tax revenues in 2002 were 20% below budgeted levels. The government is struggling to pay salaries and has unpaid bills of at least $120 million. Both the finance minister and the central bank governor resigned in November 2002, after failing to persuade Congress to approve fiscal reforms. Urban unemployment remains high - more than 10%. Monetary policy continues to be expansionary, with interest rates falling. The value of total exports has fallen in response to lower demand for exports linked to the informal border trade with Brazil and Argentina. In most years, these transactions (referred to as "unregistered and re-export trade") represent around three quarters of total exports and are facing increasingly stringent customs restrictions in Paraguay's neighbouring countries. The country's best hope may be its membership in Mercosur. Paraguay's taxes, as well as its labour and energy costs, are the lowest in the organisation. These advantages should attract investment in labour-intensive industries such as shoes, textiles and food processing if the country can ever bring its rampant corruption under control.

Paraguay's economy is dominated by the agricultural sector, which accounts for 29% of GDP and 90% of exports. These consist mainly of soya, cotton, vegetable oils and increasingly timber. Farming is subject to recurrent drought and only 5% of the land area is under cultivation. Industry contributes 26% to GDP and depends mainly on the processing of raw materials, including textiles and timber products. Cement, steel and oil refining are other prominent industries. The government's plans for privatisation had to be scrapped in 2002 following violent protests. The sale of the country's telecommunications monopoly was stopped, and the new law for privatisation was repealed. The case for privatisation has been undermined by allegations of corruption. Paraguay has a market economy marked by a large informal sector. The informal sector features both re-export of imported consumer goods to neighbouring countries as well as the activities of thousands of micro-enterprises and urban street vendors. The country's varied and often-inaccessible landscape discourages large-scale exploitation of the mineral sector, which is currently limited to limestone and salt - although ample deposits of copper, iron ore and manganese are known to exist.

Paraguay has no oil of its own. The country relies entirely on imports to meet its crude oil demand, which totalled 29,000 barrels per day in 2001, a 48% increase since 1991. Exploration by both local and North American companies continues, encouraged by the discovery in 1984 of substantial deposits in the Argentine province of Formosa. Paraguay is a co-owner (with Brazil) of two of the world's largest hydroelectric dams. Paraguay and Argentina are planning to build another hydroelectric dam on the Paraná River. There has been considerable opposition to the project among the local community and among environmentalists.

▫ Peru

Capital City	Lima	*Capital population: 7,803,735 (2002)*
Population ('000)	26,521 *(2002)*	
Urban population (%)	73.28 *(2002)*	
Land area (km²)	128000	
Languages	Spanish, Quechua, Aymara	
Religion	Mainly Roman Catholic	
Currency	New sol (n/s)	
Head of State	President Alejandro Toledo (2001)	
Head of Government	Beatriz Merino (2003)	
Ruling Party	The Peru Posible Party leads a diverse coalition.	

Main Urban Areas	Population	
Lima (capital)	7,803,735	(2002)
Arequipa	802,351	(2002)
Trujillo	697,521	(2002)
Chiclayo	546,987	(2002)
Iquitos	393,751	(2002)
Chimbote	356,383	(2002)
Huancayo	346,767	(2002)
Piura	338,694	(2002)
Cusco	299,365	(2002)
Tacna	234,477	(2002)

Peru's 2,000-km Pacific coastline extends from the Ecuadorian border in the north to Chile in the south. Its northeastern border abuts with Colombia and its eastern frontiers with Brazil and Bolivia. The country includes the northern part of the Andes, although there are also deep jungles in the northwest. The capital is Lima.

Under the 1993 Constitution, the president is elected by universal suffrage for a term of five years and reports to the 240-member Congress (120 in the Lower House and 120 in the Upper House) - also elected by universal suffrage for a five-year term.

Alejandro Toledo of the Peru Posible Party won a narrow victory in a run-off ballot for the presidency in June 2001, defeating Alan Garcia, a former president. Toledo received 45.7% of the vote to Garcia's 40.6%. The vote was said by observers to be possibly the cleanest in Peru's history. In the congressional elections in April 2000, the Nuevo Majoridad-Cambio 90 party received 42% of the vote and 52 seats, the Peru Posible Party got 23% of the vote and 26 seats, the Independent Front took 7% of the vote and eight seats. Minor parties accounted for the remainder. In June 2003, Toledo appointed Merino as the country's first woman premier, replacing Luis Solari. The move was part of a broader effort by Toledo to revive his sagging popularity following the resignation of the entire cabinet.

GDP increased by 5.3% in 2002, with growth of 4% expected in 2003. In 2004, growth of 4% is forecast. Inflation was 0.2% in 2002. In 2003, prices are expected to rise by 2.5% and to increase by another 2.5% in 2004. The Peruvian economy was recovering in 2002 after several years of slow growth. Employment rose 2.3% over the level in 2001. After a sizeable fiscal stimulus in the second half of 2001, fiscal policy was tightened, and the combined public sector deficit is projected at 2.3% of GDP for the year. The external position is robust, with an expected accumulation of official international reserves of over US$1 billion. During 2002, progress was made in introducing structural reforms in the fiscal area, including on tax and pension system reform, fiscal transparency, and fiscal rules. The authorities also introduced an inflation targeting framework for monetary policy. Further tax reform measures are planned in 2003, as are continued efforts to fortify the financial position of the pension system, improve debt management, and strengthen bank supervision. The number of jobless continues to be a serious problem. Only around 40% of the workforce has a proper job and 54% of Peruvians are classified as poor. In 1997, Peru joined the Asia Pacific Economic Co-operation (APEC) forum. Peru also hopes to join Mercosur, the South American common market group now consisting of Brazil, Argentina, Uruguay and Paraguay. Being a member of both APEC and Mercosur could encourage Peru's hope of becoming an economic link between Asia and Latin America.

Peru's agricultural sector accounts for 9% of GDP. The sector employs 40% of the workforce who survive on subsistence farming but farming is also an important earner of foreign exchange. Fishmeal and fish oil exports are also significant. Coca farming, once endemic throughout the region, has been reduced but even now is thought to account for 30% of total exports. Cotton, sugar cane, coffee and soya are grown for export while rice, maize, sorghum, potatoes and vegetables are produced for the domestic market. Industry accounts for about 26% of GDP. The sector is widely diversified, including rubber, vehicle assembly, engineering, food processing and chemicals. Peru's privatisation earnings have been disappointing but revenues could increase through the sale of some large state assets, including the Talara oil refinery and the Mantaro hydroelectric complex, possibly in 2003. Mining is important for the balance of payments, providing 46% of Peru's export earnings. The proportion is expected to rise as new investments-particularly the huge Antamina copper and zinc mine-come on stream. The country has vast mineral potential, including copper, silver, zinc, gold, iron ore, phosphorus and manganese.

Oil production has been gradually falling and was about 95,000 barrels per day (bbl/d) in 2002. With oil consumption at 180,000 bbl/d, the country has become a significant net oil importer. The main areas of current and potential oil activity are in the northern jungle as well as some offshore areas located from the northern city of Tumbes to Pisco, south of Lima. Peru's 37 million acres of offshore basins are largely unexplored. Peru has proven natural gas reserves of about 8.7 trillion cu ft, and production of around 14.8 billion cu ft per year. This production is likely to increase sharply in coming years with development of the giant Camisea natural gas field, the largest in South America, which contains an estimated 9-13 trillion cu ft of gas.

▫ Philippines

Capital City	Manila	*Capital population: 1,547,833 (2002)*
Population ('000)	79,335 *(2002)*	
Urban population (%)	59.63 *(2002)*	
Land area (km²)	29817	
Languages	Filipino, English, also Spanish, Cebuano and other local dialects	
Religion	Mainly Roman Catholic (84%); Muslim	
Currency	Philippine peso (Ps)	
Head of State	President Gloria Macapagal-Arroyo (2001)	
Head of Government	Gloria Macapagal-Arroyo (2001)	
Ruling Party	The government is formed by the Struggle of the Philippine Masses (LMP).	

Main Urban Areas	Population
Quezon City	2,249,747 (2002)
Manila (capital)	1,547,833 (2002)
Caloocan City	1,233,938 (2002)
Cebu	742,479 (2002)
Pasig City	517,199 (2002)
Valenzuela	505,292 (2002)
Taguig	503,828 (2002)
Las Pinas	495,493 (2002)
Paranaque	471,524 (2002)

Composed of 11 large islands and some 7,000 smaller islands and atolls, the Philippines lies some 800km off the coast of Indo-China, north-east of Papua New Guinea and north of Indonesia. The group of islands is some 900km in length from north to south. The capital is Manila.

The Republic of the Philippines has an executive president who is elected for a six-year term by universal mandate and then appoints a cabinet. The Congress has two chambers. The House of Representatives has at most 260 seats elected for a three-year term, 208 seats in single-seat constituencies and at most 52 seats allotted to party-lists according to proportional representation. The Senate has 24 members, elected for a six-year term by proportional representation, half of them renewed every three years.

Joseph Estrada easily won the presidential elections held in 1998. In Senatorial elections held at the same time, the LMP took ten seats while the alliance of the National Union of Christian Democrats and the United Muslim Democratic Party each won five seats. In 2001, Estrada was convicted of embezzlement and replaced by the vice president, Macapagal-Arroyo. Elections to the House of Representatives were also held in 2001 when the National Union of Christian Democrats won 86 seats, the Nationalist People's Coalition received 54 seats and the LMP took 21 seats. The remainder was dispersed among several parties.

GDP rose by 4.4% in 2002 and should increase by a further 4% in 2003. In 2004, growth of 4% is again forecast. Inflation was 3.1% in 2002 and is expected to rise to 3% in 2003 and 3.4% in 2004. The fiscal deficit rose in 2002, reaching 5.3% of GDP. The increase was mainly due to a shortfall in revenues. The government's ability to use fiscal expansion to spur additional growth is now limited because of this rise in the deficit and the negative market sentiment it has evoked. The contribution of domestic demand to growth continues to be relatively important. With employment growing slowly, unemployment remained high at 11.4% in 2002, edging up from 9.8% in the previous year. The unemployment rate remains one of the highest among ASEAN members, and has been exacerbated by rapid growth in the labour force and by relatively slow economic growth in recent years. This has led to fewer job opportunities in urban areas, despite additional jobs created by the services sector. Since 1998, the fiscal deficit has been large and increasing. The main problem lies with the shortfalls in tax revenues, and indeed the government has focused on reforms directed at improving the revenue base and tax effort. The overall balance of payments is forecast to be in surplus in 2003. Increases in the current account surplus will more than offset capital outflows. In 2004, the current account surplus is expected to rise to 2.5% of GNP. Capital outflows are likely to reverse direction as the effect of higher investment incentives and financial reforms starts to be felt. Peace and order are among the primary prerequisites for sustaining economic growth and development, as they remain a major concern for investors in the country. Conflicts in Mindanao, the second-largest island in the south of the country, have contributed to a loss of business confidence.

Industrial growth strengthened to 4.1% in 2002, largely as a result of a recovery in manufacturing. The improved performance was due to stronger external demand for electronics and garments. The services sector, which grew strongly by 5.4%, remained the main pillar of economic growth, driven by the transport and communications subsectors. The sector's rapid rate of growth is expected to continue for several more years as the economy moves toward high-technology services including computer software. Although agricultural growth decelerated in 2002 to 3.5%, it picked up strongly toward the end of the year. On the demand side, personal consumption expenditure continued to be the main driver of rising GDP. Propelled by strong demand for household furnishing, transport, and communications, personal consumption expenditure rose by 3.9%. Investment grew by 2.1%, after a 2.2% decline in 2001. After a contraction of 16.2% in 2001, merchandise exports rose by 12.2% in 2002, boosted by some recovery in global

demand for electronics, which account for half total exports. Exports were also helped by improved markets for garments and agricultural products. The trade and current account balances should improve further in the future as export growth continues to outpace import growth. Workers' remittances amount to $7-8 billion per year and are another major reason for the anticipated surpluses.

The Philippines' energy sector is relatively dynamic. Major reforms include projects to electrify isolated villages and to reduce the Philippines' dependence on imported oil. The country was producing only 1,000 barrels per day (bbl/d) of oil in 2001 but in 2002 production was nearing 25,000 bbl/d. This increase was due primarily to the discovery of new deep-sea oil deposits beneath the natural gas-bearing structures. But while new hydrocarbon discoveries will significantly reduce the Philippines' oil import bill, the country is still a highly dependent net oil importer. This dependence on imported oil makes the Philippine economy vulnerable to sudden spikes in world oil prices. The Philippines also has 3.693 trillion cubic feet of proven natural gas reserves, but no significant production at the present. While in the past the gas sector has not been developed extensively, the government has made expanding gas use a priority, particularly for electric power generation, in an effort to cut oil import expenses.

▫ Puerto Rico

Capital City	San Juan	*Capital population: 1,101,000 (1995)*
Population ('000)	3,996 *(2002)*	
Urban population (%)	75.81 *(2002)*	
Land area (km²)	887	
Languages	Spanish, English	
Religion	Mainly Roman Catholic (81%)	
Currency	US dollar (US$)	
Head of State	Governor Sila Maria Calderon (2001)	
Head of Government	Governor Sila Maria Calderon (2001)	
Ruling Party	Popular Democratic Party (PDP)	

Main Urban Areas	Population
San Juan (capital)	1,101,000 (1995)

Puerto Rico is one of the larger islands in the Antilles group, located about 80km east of Haiti and about 800km off the coast of Venezuela. With a pleasant Caribbean climate, but with some vulnerability to hurricanes, it has a large population for its size. The capital is San Juan.

The Commonwealth of Puerto Rico, an external territory of the US, has a Resident Commissioner who is elected by universal suffrage for a four-year term, and who has a non-voting seat in the US House of Representatives. Executive authority is vested in an elected Governor and his cabinet, while legislative power rests with the bicameral Legislative Assembly - which consists of a 28-member Senate and a 54-member House of Representatives, both popularly elected for a four-year term. In December 1998, voters rejected plans for full US statehood for the third time in the last decade. Thus Puerto Rico's "commonwealth" status, which provides people with US citizenship but limited control over the island's affairs, remains intact.

Elections to the office of governor took place in November 2000. Calderon narrowly defeated Carlos Pesquera. Elections to the House and Senate took place at the same time. In the House, the PDP received 49% of the vote and garnered 27 seats. The New Progressive Party won 46% of the vote and 23 seats. In the Senate, the PDP got 49% of the vote and 19 seats while the New Progressive Party won 46% of the vote and seven seats. The Puertorican Independentists Party holds one seat in each chamber.

Puerto Rico's economy grew by 2% in 2002 and the pace is expected to fall in 2003. The US government has phased out a programme of tax and wage credits which had attracted American companies to Puerto Rico and stimulated rapid expansion of its manufacturing sector. With this phase-out, local officials want to broaden the economy and reduce its dependence on manufacturing and tourism. The Free Trade Area of the Americas, proposed for creation in 2005, is regarded by Puerto Rico as both a challenge and an opportunity. The island would face competition for markets in the mainland US from other nations in the free-trade area, many of which could be more competitive because of lower production costs. Officials hope to expand the amount of high technology manufacturing on the island. The unemployment rate was 10% in 2002.

Manufacturing makes up 40% of GDP and is dominated by industries such as pharmaceuticals, electronics, textiles, petrochemicals, metal products and machinery, motor vehicles, glass, cement and processed foods. There are also many assembly operations that are allowed to import components and materials from the US and, after assembly, can re-export to the mainland duty-free. Much of the manufacturing investment in Puerto Rico was stimulated by tax breaks provided by the US which were discontinued in 1996. Most industries are geared to the export market. The country is a major exporter of pharmaceuticals Farming is a major source of employment although it accounts for only 1% of GDP. The government plans to develop a huge new port on the western side of the island and has begun to restore the colonial district in the capital city. Puerto Rico already has a good basis for shipping as it handles 1.8 million containers a year. The new mega-port will include a transhipment facility which is a free-trade zone for manufacturing and distributive services. Experts forecast that within ten years between 21 and 26 million containers will pass close to Puerto Rico and the new facility should capture most of this traffic.

Puerto Rico consumes about 170,000 barrels per day (bbl/d) of petroleum, all of which was imported. In 2002, the island's refining capacity was 93,000 bbl/d. Power consumption is increasing by about 3% per year, and authorities are investing $2 billion in new capacity to meet growing demand. Another effort at fuel diversification is a $815-million, 454-MW coal-fired plant, presently under construction. Two more projects are planned, one to re-power ageing power stations in San Juan and another for a new power station, built by American firms.

▫ Qatar

Capital City	Doha	Capital population: 243,000 (1992)
Population ('000)	635 (2002)	
Urban population (%)	92.77 (2002)	
Land area (km²)	1100	
Languages	Arabi,C English	
Religion	Islam	
Currency	Qatar riyal (QR)	
Head of State	HH Shaikh Hamad bin Khalifa al Thani (June 1995)	
Head of Government	Sheikh Abdullah ibn Khalifah ath-Thani (1996)	
Ruling Party	There are no political parties in Qatar.	

Main Urban Areas	Population
Doha (capital)	243,000 (1992)

Qatar is a small peninsula protruding northward into the Persian (Arabian) Gulf from the northwestern extreme of the United Arab Emirates. It also has a very short border with Saudi Arabia. Most of the terrain is sandy and inhospitable and, except for a dwindling number of nomadic tribesmen, virtually all of the population now lives in the capital, Doha.

HH Shaikh Hamad Khalifa al Thani assumed power in June 1995, following a palace coup against his father, HH Shaikh Khalifa bin Hamad al Thani, who had ruled since 1972. The coup was prompted by a prolonged period of disagreement between the two men, although it was not clear whether it also related to the growing calls for a democratisation of the country. As before, Qatar is ruled exclusively by the Emir and his immediate family. There is a Consultative Assembly of 35 appointed members.

There are no elections in Qatar, although the Emir has promised municipal elections and is considering a direct poll to determine the membership of his consultative council.

GDP grew by 3% in 2001, while prices rose by 1.7%. In 2003, growth of 4% is expected with inflation of 2.9%. The forecasts for 2004 call for growth of 8.2% and inflation of 1.2%. Qatar suffers from many of the same problems as other oil-dependent Persian Gulf states, especially the need to diversify economic development beyond crude oil exports and scale back the generous state subsidies for consumers, which date from the oil boom of the 1970s and early 1980s. Qatar has begun to pay off its large external debt, which peaked at nearly $12 billion in 1999. The country accumulated this debt largely for infrastructure investment in oil and gas projects, which sharply increased Qatar's oil production capacity, construction of facilities for the export of LNG, and petrochemical plants. Qatar's external debt is currently around $7 billion, still equal to more than half of the country's GDP. Qatar recorded a large budget surplus for the 2001/2002 fiscal year, which ended in March 2002. The Qatari government for the short term has concentrated on reducing its international debts, rather than increasing public expenditures, and has based its budgets on very conservative projections of oil and gas export revenues. Lenders remain confident of the country's ability to make good on these debts and claims. Much will depend on future trends in the price of oil since the price of Qatar's natural gas is tied to oil prices. Despite these difficulties, the income of the average Qatari (excluding expatriates) is more than US$60,000. This level is twice as high as that for any other country in the Middle East apart from Kuwait and the UAE.

Qatar's policy of economic diversification has led to a surge in investment in projects for the export of liquefied natural gas and petrochemicals. The government expects that it will be able to earn more per barrel of crude oil produced if it can export refined products and petrochemicals, as well as create private sector jobs - in a country which has been overly dependent on government ministries to provide employment for the population. Qatar has twice the natural gas reserves of either Saudi Arabia or Abu Dhabi and, unlike these countries, all its gas is clean and easy to exploit. Altogether, the country's oil and gas industries employ the greater part of the active workforce and provide well over 90% of export revenues. Qatar also has a limited industrial sector, concentrating on basic materials such as cement, steel, ammonia, fertiliser and petrochemicals. Farming is generally restricted by a shortage of suitable land, but the government has ploughed vast resources into irrigation projects aimed at expanding the scope for vegetable cultivation. Fishing is a major industry.

Qatar contains the third largest natural gas reserves and the largest non-associated gas field in the world. Qatar is also emerging as a major exporter of liquefied natural gas. An OPEC member, Qatar exports over 800,000 barrels of oil per day. Qatar has proven, recoverable oil reserves of 15.2 billion barrels. In 2002, Qatar produced 807,777 barrels per day (bbl/d) of liquids (including crude oil, natural gas liquids, and condensate), down from 863,918 bbl/d in 2001. The reversal of the previous upward trend was the result of production cuts undertaken in coordination with OPEC. Qatar exports almost all of its oil production to Asia, with Japan by far its largest customer. With proven reserves of 394 trillion cu ft, Qatar's natural gas resources are just behind those of Russia and Iran. Most this gas is located in the North Field, which contains 380 trillion cu ft of gas in-place and 239 trillion cu ft of recoverable reserves, making it the largest known non-associated gas field in the world.

▫ Réunion

Capital City	St Denis	Capital population: 121,922 (1990)
Population ('000)	727 (2002)	
Urban population (%)	71.78 (2002)	
Land area (km²)	250	
Languages	French	
Religion	Mainly Roman Catholic (87%0	
Currency	Euro (€)	
Head of State	President Jacques Chirac (France)	
Head of Government	Christophe Payet (President of General Council, 1994)	
Ruling Party	At the national level, the Gaullist Rassemblement pour la République leads a coalition with the Union pour la Démocratie Francaise. At the regional level, the Parti Socialiste dominates.	

Main Urban Areas	Population
St Denis (capital)	121,922 (1990)

Réunion, an overseas department of France, is located in the Indian Ocean about 800km east of the island of Madagascar. The local government also administers a number of other, largely uninhabited islands on behalf of the French authorities. With a warm and pleasant climate, Réunion has a thriving tourist industry. The capital is St Denis.

Réunion is an external department of France and is governed to a considerable degree from Paris. The country sends deputies to the French Assemblée Nationale and is represented at the EU. Since being accorded regional status in 1974, Réunion elects its own 45-member Regional Council for a term of six years, with responsibility for economic and social planning. Other executive powers rest in a 47-member General Council.

Elections to the Regional Council were held in March 1998. The Communist Party of Reunion captured seven seats, the Union for French Democracy won eight and the Socialist Party took 6. The remaining seats were dispersed among several parties. General Council elections were held in March 1994, when the Socialist Party won control and Christophe Payet became president of the General Council.

Réunion's economy is heavily dependent on aid from France, which accounts for as much as half of the country's GDP. Government officials have long tried to develop a tourist industry in order to relieve the high rate of unemployment which exceeds 40%. The gap in Réunion between the well-off and the poor is extraordinary and accounts for the persistent social tensions.

Réunion's economy has traditionally been based on agriculture. Sugarcane has been the primary crop for more than a century, and in some years it accounts for 85% of exports. This is the only significant crop apart from vegetables grown for domestic consumption. There is also an important fishing industry. The government has been pushing the development of a tourist industry to relieve high unemployment, which amounts to more than 40% of the labour force. Industry is limited to the processing of agricultural raw materials. The major manufacturing activities include production of rum, cigarettes, handicraft items and flower oil. Over 70% of the workforce is employed in the services sector, another 8% in agriculture and the remainder in industry.

Réunion has only a limited amount of domestic energy resources, although there are some natural gas deposits. It produces more than two thirds of its electricity from hydroelectric sources.

▫ Rwanda

Capital City	Kigali	Capital population: 170,000 (1992)
Population ('000)	9,634 (2002)	
Urban population (%)	4.09 (2002)	
Land area (km²)	2467	
Languages	Kinyarwanda, French, Kiswahili	
Religion	Traditional (50%); Roman Catholic (40%)	
Currency	Rwanda franc (RWF)	
Head of State	Paul Kagame (April 2000)	
Head of Government	Bernard Makuza (2000)	
Ruling Party	The government is formed by a coalition of five parties.	

Main Urban Areas	Population
Kigali (capital)	170,000 (1992)

Rwanda, a small state to the west of Tanzania, lies just north of Burundi and is bounded in the west by the Democratic Republic of the Congo (formerly Zaire) and in the north by Uganda. Its position on Lake Kivu has helped to ensure an adequate water supply for irrigation. The capital is Kigali.

Under the agreement set up during the Arusha peace negotiations, the government will have a 70-member parliament and a president who is elected for seven years. The new parliament will have two chambers. One, the Chamber of Deputies, will have 80 members, 53 of them elected for a five year term by proportional representation. There will also be 24 female members elected by provincial councils, two by the National Youth Council and one by the Federation of the Associations of the Disabled. The Senate will have 26 members elected or appointed for eight-year terms.

Kagame was elected president in August 2003, receiving more than 95% of all votes. This was the first time that the country's voters had a chance to back opposition candidates since independence from Belgium in 1962. The poll was marred by allegations of voter intimidation. No parliamentary elections have yet been held but a National Transitory Assembly exists.

GDP grew 9.4% in 2002 and inflation was 2.5%. Growth of 3.2% is expected in 2003 with inflation of 4.7%. Forecasts for 2004 call for growth of 6% and inflation of 3%. While Rwanda's present and expected rates of growth are encouraging, the turnaround is mainly due to the fact that much idle capacity is simply being brought back into operation. An even larger amount of the country's capital was destroyed or has become too dilapidated to use. Rwanda badly need investment or more aid but the prospects of additional capital inflows are not good. The government is still trying to eliminate debts incurred before or during the 1994 war. Some of Rwanda's massive foreign debt has been written off by donors but it remains a problem. External security remains a serious problem and foreign donors still have serious concerns about defence spending when debt services are so high.

The agricultural sector dominates the economy, accounting for half of GDP. Coffee and tea are the most important farm products but coffee prices have fallen in recent years. Food production is still depressed in what would otherwise be a highly fertile country and a breadbasket for East Africa. In normal times, other cash crops were sugar cane, vegetables and fruit. Industry makes up 21% of GDP and was traditionally specialised in the processing of agricultural raw materials, such as timber, textiles, beverages and soap. The economy continues to suffer massively from the failure to maintain the infrastructure and the lack of healthcare facilities. Government spending is under control, and revenue collection is improving. Food, however, is in short supply and few industries operate at anything near full capacity.

The country has limited indigenous fuel resources and relies heavily on imports. It derives the greater part of its electricity needs from the hydroelectric sector.

□ Sao Tomé e Príncipe

Capital City	Sao Tomé	Capital population: 36,000 (1992)
Population ('000)	156 *(2002)*	
Urban population (%)	47.46 *(2002)*	
Land area (km²)	96	
Languages	Portuguese	
Religion	Mainly Roman Catholic	
Currency	Dobra (STD)	
Head of State	President Fradique de Menzes (2001)	
Head of Government	Manuel Pinto da Costa (2002)	
Ruling Party	The government is formed by the Movimento de Libertaçao de Sao Tomé e Príncipe (MLSTP) and the Democratic Convergence Party-Reflection Group (PCD).	

Main Urban Areas	Population
Sao Tomé (capital)	36,000 (1992)

Sao Tomé e Príncipe is a federation of two eponymous islands and several islets in the Gulf of Guinea, some 300km off the Atlantic coast of West Africa. The nearest land point is Libreville in Gabon. The capital is Sao Tomé.

The Democratic Republic of Sao Tomé e Príncipe was an overseas territory of Portugal until 1975, and quickly became a single-party state run by the socialist Movimento de Libertaçao de Sao Tomé e Príncipe. In 1990, a new Constitution was introduced which provided for a semi-executive president who is elected for a five-year term by the people. The National People's Assembly has 55 members, elected for a four-year term in twelve multi-member constituencies by proportional representation. There are plans to award Príncipe a substantial degree of regional autonomy, including the creation of a regional assembly.

Elections to the 55-member National People's Assembly were held in March 2002, when the MLSTP won 24 of the 55 seats. The Force for Change Democratic Movement gained 23 seats with the remainder scattered among smaller parties. In January 2003, the president dissolved the parliament, promising elections in April. Presidential elections were held in July 2001 when de Menzes received 56% of the vote, defeating Manuel Pinto da Costa of the Movimiento de Libertaçao de São Tomé e Príncipe who received 34% of the vote.

GDP increased by 4.1% in 2002 and prices rose by 9.2%. In 2003, GDP should grow by around 5% once again while prices are forecast to rise by 9%. Forecasts for 2004 also call for growth of 5% and inflation of 8%. The country's current account deficit reached 16% of GDP in 2001 but the government hopes to reduce this to 10% in 2003. Authorities also want to reduce the budget deficit to 8% of GDP in 2003. To bolster government revenues, the country's sales tax will be modified and extended to include more domestic goods and services (notably in the tourist industry). Petrol prices will be freed to bring them in line with the price of imports and new incentives will be offered for investors in the private sector. At

the moment, Sao Tomé is one of the most heavily indebted of the world's poorer countries, but will receive about US$200 million in debt relief over the next few years.

Agriculture is the mainstay of the economy, with cocoa providing 75% of GDP. However, production has been gradually declining as a result of drought and mismanagement. Output of minor crops such as coffee, copra and palm kernels has also been falling. There are some moves toward encouraging alternative crops but these have made little headway. Industry is limited in scale and is restricted to the coverage of domestic needs: soap, beverages and timber products. Most other products have to be imported. Considerable potential exists for the development of a tourist industry, and the government took a few steps to expand facilities in recent years.

At present, the country has little domestic energy resources, but oil firms think billions of barrels may lie beneath the island's territorial waters.

□ Saudi Arabia

Capital City	Riyadh	Capital population: 2,915,000 (1993)
Population ('000)	22,840 *(2002)*	
Urban population (%)	86.12 *(2002)*	
Land area (km²)	214969	
Languages	Arabic	
Religion	Islam	
Currency	Saudi riyal (SR)	
Head of State	HM King Fahd ibn Abdul Aziz (1982)	
Head of Government	HM King Fahd ibn Abdul Aziz	
Ruling Party	There are no political parties in Saudi Arabia.	

Main Urban Areas	Population
Riyadh (capital)	2,915,000 (1993)
Jiddah	2,148,000 (1993)
Makkah	1,014,000 (1993)
Al-Madinah	638,000 (1993)
Ad-Dammam	506,000 (1993)
At-Ta'if	436,000 (1993)
Tabuk	307,000 (1993)
Buraydah	261,000 (1993)
Al-Hufuf	237,000 (1993)
Al-Mubarraz	229,000 (1993)

Saudi Arabia, the largest country in the Middle East, occupies the greater part of the Arabian peninsula and borders on both the Persian (Arabian) Gulf and the Red Sea. It faces Iran across the Gulf to the east, and Egypt, Sudan and Ethiopia across the Red Sea to the west. In the south, it borders on Yemen and Oman. Its most crucial borders are in the north, where it meets Iraq, Jordan and Kuwait. The capital is Riyadh.

Saudi Arabia is an absolute monarchy with most senior government posts filled by members of the royal family. Technically, there is no constitution except for the Koran, reflecting the country's role as keeper of the shrines of Mecca and Medina. Saudi Arabia is a Sunni state. Representation takes place through personal petitions to royal figures, but royal audiences are common. A new constitution with a 60-member Consultative Council is contemplated.

There are no general elections in Saudi Arabia.

GDP grew by 1% in 2002. In 2003, growth is expected to be 4.7% while the forecast for 2004 is for growth of 2.1%. Prices fell by 0.5% in 2002 and are expected to rise by 1.1% in 2003. Inflation is forecast to be 1% in 2004. The recovery of oil prices resulted in a much smaller than expected budget deficit in 2002 and increased liquidity throughout the economy. In the non-oil private sector, growth in 2002 is estimated to have been much higher (about 3.5%) than in any recent year. However, with a continued reliance on oil and a population growing at more than 3% a year, the future is troubling. Roughly 71% of the population is under the age of 29 and the country needs much higher growth than the 1-2% recorded in recent years. Unemployment is estimated by the government to be 10% and by private economists to be about 15%.for males. Nearly half the Saudi workforce is made up of expatriates who could gradually be replaced by locals. Meanwhile, the country intends to move towards a policy of "Saudiisation", which is intended to increase employment of its own citizens by replacing 60% of the estimated 5-6 million foreign workers that presently work in Saudi Arabia. The government finds it much easier to respond to economic issues than political or social ones. It has begun to court foreign investment, passing favourable legislation, launching a wide-ranging privatisation drive, and opening new fields to foreign participation.

The government is searching for ways to enhance the role of the private sector. Laws to streamline regulation of capital labour markets have been tabled, as well as others covering insurance, commerce, taxation and monopolies. There has also been progress in modernising the country's peculiar legal system. In the labour market, most sectors now operate under rules to raise quotas of Saudi employees every year. This can be difficult since expatriate labour costs, on average, a third of what it costs to hire Saudi nationals. State subsidies and losses by unprofitable state-owned enterprises are large contributors to Saudi Arabia's budget deficit. Prior to the sharp downturn in oil prices and the resulting financial pressures on the Saudi budget during 1998 and early 1999, Saudi Arabia had been investing in refinery upgrades and expansions. The projects have now resumed but are far behind schedule. Diversification into oil-related industries such as bulk and fine chemicals, plastics and other heavy industries is being encouraged. Saudi Arabia has one of the world's harshest climates, but maintains a large and heavily subsidised agricultural sector.

Saudi Arabia contains 264 billion barrels of proven oil reserves (more than 25% of the world total) and up to one trillion barrels of ultimately recoverable oil. Saudi Arabia is the world's leading oil producer and exporter, and its location in the politically volatile Gulf region adds an element of concern for its major customers. During 2002, Saudi Arabia produced around 8.1 million barrels per day (bbl/d) of oil, compared to production capacity of around 10.0-10.5 million bbl/d. Although Saudi Arabia has around 80 oil and gas fields (and over 1,000 wells), more than half of its oil reserves are contained in only eight fields, including Ghawar (the world's largest onshore oil field, with estimated remaining reserves of 70 billion barrels) and Safaniya (the world's largest offshore oilfield, with estimated reserves of 19 billion barrels). The government has approved spending of $15 billion per year between 2000 and 2004, in order to boost Saudi oil production capacity as well as to increase gas output. Saudi Arabia also has ambitious plans for expanding petrochemical production using natural gas as a feedstock. The country's state-owned company is the Middle East's largest non-oil industrial company and is expected to become one of the world's top five ethylene producers by 2005. The company, known as SABIC, accounts for around 10% of the world's total petrochemical production.

◻ Senegal

Capital City	Dakar	Capital population: 1,986,000 (1995)
Population ('000)	10,291 (2002)	
Urban population (%)	48.5 (2002)	
Land area (km²)	19253	
Languages	French	
Religion	Mainly Muslim (90%)	
Currency	CFA franc (CFAF)	
Head of State	President Abdoulaye Wade (2000)	
Head of Government	Idrissa Seck (2002)	
Ruling Party	The Senegalese Democratic Party (PDS) leads a multiparty coalition.	

Main Urban Areas	Population
Dakar (capital)	1,986,000 (1995)

Located on the Atlantic coast of West Africa, Senegal is the continent's westernmost point. With Mauritania to the north, Mali to the southeast, and Guinea and Guinea-Bissau to the south, it lies in a deeply depressed and drought-ridden belt with poor soil. Indeed, virtually all the cultivable ground lies along the banks of the River Gambia, which is enclosed for most of its useful length by the political enclave of The Gambia. The capital is Dakar.

The Republic of Senegal was proclaimed in September 1960, having seceded from the Federation of Mali, which in turn had left French domination in June 1960. The executive president is elected by direct popular vote for a seven-year term. There is a 120-member National Assembly, which is elected by universal suffrage for a term of five years. The Senate has 60 members, 45 elected by legislators and local, municipal and regional councillors, 12 appointed by the president and three members elected by Senegalese living abroad.

Abdoulaye Wade won the presidency in March 2000, defeating Abdou Diouf. Wade received 60% of the popular vote. Elections to the National Assembly were held in April 2001. The coalition led by the PDS won 89 seats, the Alliance of Progress Forces took 11 seats and Socialist Party of Senegal (PSS) won ten seats. The few remaining seats are divided among several parties. The Senate was elected in January 1999. The 45 elected members are all member of the PSS.

GDP rose by 2.4% in 2002, while prices increased by 2.2%. In 2003, growth of 6.6% is expected with prices rising by 2%. The forecast for 2004 is for growth of 5.6% and inflation of 1.8%. The economy slowed in 2002 after several years of strong growth. However, Senegal should benefit from investment and trade redirected from Côte d'Ivoire because of the fighting there. The tax system has been streamlined through the introduction of a uniform sales tax (VAT) and other improvements which have raised tax revenues to 17% of GDP. The government began its privatisation programme more than a decade ago but its holdings still include several problem firms. The government, which is very much in favour of a free market, has two overriding objectives. One is to transform Senegal's essentially peasant economy into a private sector-driven centre of agro-industry and services. The other is to capitalise on the country's relative proximity to Europe and the US to build a regional trading crossroads. A longer-term challenge is to build on the country's macroeconomic performance by boosting productivity and diversifying an economy which still relies on a limited number of commodities. Unemployment, even among well-qualified school-leavers, remains high. The country is vulnerable to external shocks and poverty is still widespread.

Senegal's agricultural sector accounts for only 11% of GDP and even less in years when rainfall is below average. Yet the sector provides employment for three-quarters of the work force. The country's savannah grasslands make it most suitable for cattle herding, mainly by nomadic farmers. Groundnuts are the major crop but problems with the operation of the marketing board have held back profits. Agricultural exports include fish, ground nuts (peanuts), petroleum products, phosphates and cotton. Senegal's industrial base is more diverse than its neighbours and accounts for 21% of GDP. However, the sector is still mainly processing food crops and minerals, such as chemical phosphate plants. The government's aim is to reduce raw phosphate exports and step up processing them into acid and fertiliser for export. Production of phosphoric acid is expected to

double by 2004. A new mine at Tobène started up in 2002, triggering an 11% growth in extractive industries. The service sector, which accounts for the bulk of GDP, is fuelled by steady migration from the countryside and the development of small businesses arising from urbanisation. The government has been obliged to help two large state-owned operations in the groundnut and electricity industries. The cost of bailing these two firms out in 2002 totalled more than $R 55135 million.

Senegal is a net energy importer. By itself, and in conjunction with neighbouring countries, Senegal is promoting increased offshore petroleum exploration. The country depends heavily on imports for all requirements that brushwood cannot fulfil. Senegal's natural gas reserves, which are primarily located onshore, are estimated at 106 billion cubic feet. The country has no hydroelectric capacity.

◻ Seychelles

Capital City	Victoria	Capital population: 30,000 (1992)
Population ('000)	78 (2002)	
Urban population (%)	65.04 (2002)	
Land area (km²)	45	
Languages	Creole (official), English, French	
Religion	Roman Catholic (90%)	
Currency	Seychelles rupee (SCR)	
Head of State	President France Albert Ren (1977)	
Head of Government	President France Albert Ren	
Ruling Party	Seychelles People's Progressive Front (FPPS)	

Main Urban Areas	Population
Victoria (capital)	30,000 (1992)

The Seychelles are a group of 115 islands located in the Indian Ocean, to the east of Tanzania and Kenya. Most of the population inhabit the Mah group of islands, which are of granite and contrast with the low-lying terrain of the other, mainly coral islands. The climate is tropical with the cooler season occurring during the southeast monsoons (late May to September). The capital is Victoria.

The rule of Sir James Mancham was overthrown in 1977 by a coup led by France Albert Ren, who thereupon suspended all political parties except for his own Seychelles People's Progressive Front and declared himself president. After fighting off a coup attempt by South African-backed mercenaries in 1981, Ren went on to institute an executive presidency in which the president, like all but 11 of the 34-member unicameral National Assembly, is elected for a five-year term, renewable three times. Multiparty politics were readmitted in 1992 and a new constitution was approved by referendum in 1993.

Ren and his Seychelles People's Progressive Front have dominated local politics since the coup in 1977. He easily won another election in September 2001 with 54% of the vote. Elections to the National Assembly were last held in December 2002 when the FPPS won 23 seats in the National Assembly. The Seychelles National Party took the remaining 11 seats.

Seychelles has achieved one of the highest standards of living in Africa. In recent years, however, the sustainability of these achievements has been threatened by growing macroeconomic imbalances and structural problems that have made the economy less efficient and competitive. The economy grew by just 0.3% in 2002 while inflation was 0.2%. In 2003, the economy is expected to contract by as much as 5.1%, while prices rise by 7%. The forecast for 2004 is for a further contraction of 2% coupled with price rises of 5%. A major problem is the large fiscal deficit incurred in recent years which has led to a huge increase in government debt. Steps have been taken to correct the problem but they have been offset by growth in capital spending. The government encourages private investment to upgrade its tourist industry and make it more competitive in international markets. However, public officials also want to reduce the country's dependence on this sector. Tax breaks and other benefits have been used to induce some 4,000 companies to register in the islands. The state continues to dominate the economy, with nearly 70% of all economic activity found in government-run businesses. This lack of competition is hurting efficiency and making the islands far too expensive.

The economy rests on tourism and fishing. Presently, tourism accounts for about 12.7% of the GDP and the manufacturing and construction sectors (including industrial fishing) account for about 28.8%. Industrial fishing has surpassed tourism as the most important foreign exchange earner in recent years. Employment, foreign earnings, construction, banking, and commerce are all dominated by tourism-related industries. Despite attempts to improve its agricultural base and emphasise locally manufactured products and indigenous materials, Seychelles continues to import 90% of what it consumes. The exceptions are some fruits and vegetables, fish, poultry, pork, beer, cigarettes, paint, and a few locally made plastic items. Imports of all kind are controlled by the Seychelles Marketing Board, a government parastatal which operates all the major supermarkets and is the distributor and licensor of most other imports. Most industrial establishments are geared to meeting domestic needs for basic products such as timber, cement, tobacco and food processing. Seychelles faces serious structural impediments to economic growth, many of which arise from the extensive intervention of the government. These include controlled prices, a cumbersome system of foreign exchange allocation, a restrictive import licensing system and a practice of frequently intervening in manufacturing activities.

The country has only limited fuel resources, apart from brushwood, and relies on imports to meet its energy needs. There is no hydroelectric capacity.

◘ Sierra Leone

Capital City	Freetown	*Capital population: 505,000 (1992)*
Population ('000)	5,322 *(2002)*	
Urban population (%)	37.79 *(2002)*	
Land area (km²)	7162	
Languages	English, Mende and Temba dialects	
Religion	Mainly traditional	
Currency	Leone (SLL)	
Head of State	Ahmad Tejan Kabbah (1997)	
Head of Government	Solomon Berewa (2002)	
Ruling Party	The government is formed by Sierra Leone Peoples' Party (SLPP).	

Main Urban Areas	Population
Freetown (capital)	505,000 (1992)

Sierra Leone is located on the Atlantic coast of West Africa, where it is bounded in the north and east by Guinea and in the south by Liberia. The climate is tropical and humid, but affords significant agricultural possibilities. The capital is Freetown.

The president is elected for a five-year term by the people. The House of Representatives has 124 members, 112 members elected for a four-year term and 12 Paramount chiefs.

Both presidential and parliamentary elections were held in May 2002. Ahmad Tejan Kabbah was re-elected president with 70% of the vote. His party, the SLPP, took 83 seats in the House. The socialist All Peoples Party gained 22 seats and the remainder went to a minor party.

GDP grew by 6.3% in 2002 and prices fell by 3.3%. In 2003, growth of 6.5% is expected with prices rising by 7.4%. Forecasts for 2004 call for growth of 6.8% and inflation of 3.5%. Although the economy is rebounding, the situation is still tense. The government is engaged in the resettlement of the internally displaced population and refugees. At the same time, the reintegration of ex-combatants continues. These efforts, together with the restoration of government services and authority in the rural areas, have strained the government's limited capacity and resources. The country's overall deficit (excluding grants) in 2002 was 20% of GDP. Although this is high, it was substantially lower than programmed. The implementation of structural reforms in 2002 accelerated, beginning with the establishment of a national tax authority and a commission to organise the programme of privatisation. Government domestic revenue in 2003 is projected at 14.6% of GDP, while total expenditure is budgeted to rise to about 40% of GDP. The overall budget deficit (excluding grants), is programmed to widen to about 26% of GDP. Sierra Leone will continue to require substantial amounts of foreign aid for several more years.

In peaceful times the farming sector produces cocoa, coffee, ginger and palm kernels. Agriculture is still the biggest contributors to exports but production fell to less than a quarter of its pre-war levels. Rice, cassava, maize and vegetables are grown for domestic consumption. At present, much farming is for subsistence but agricultural exports picked up significantly, albeit from a very low level. There was once a sizeable fishing industry and in 2003 the government announced a new plan intended to develop marine resources and boost fish exports. Aid agencies are providing funding for training of the thousands of ex-soldiers and rebels but it will be some time before these people become workers again. Manufacturing activities in Sierra Leone are primarily concerned with the processing of raw materials. The country's mining sector suffered during the war but still manages to produce various minerals such as gold, bauxite and diamonds. The export sector continues to be depressed, apart from the substantial increase in diamonds exported through official channels. The rehabilitation of the country's largest mine has been delayed, pending the finalisation of financing arrangements.

The country is entirely dependent on imports for most of its requirements, although there is some coal. There are no hydroelectric facilities.

◘ Singapore

Capital City	Singapore City	*Capital population: 3,737,000 (1997)*
Population ('000)	3,341 *(2002)*	
Urban population (%)	100. *(2002)*	
Land area (km²)	61	
Languages	Malay, Mandarin, Tamil, English	
Religion	Buddhist/Daoist (53%); Muslim (16%); Christian (12%)	
Currency	Singapore dollar (S$)	
Head of State	President S. R. Nathan (1999)	
Head of Government	Goh Chok Tong (1991)	
Ruling Party	People's Action Party (PAP)	

Main Urban Areas	Population
Singapore City (capital)	3,737,000 (1997)

Singapore, although only a tiny and highly urbanised city state on the south-eastern corner of Peninsular Malaysia, owes its extraordinary wealth entirely to its position. Its harbour facilities, oil processing and - most recently - its highly developed telecommunications systems gave it a central role in the development of the region.

The Republic of Singapore, an independent member of the Commonwealth, achieved independence in 1965. The president is elected for a six-year term by the people. The prime minister and the cabinet are appointed by the president and are responsible to parliament. Parliament has 93 members, 84 members elected for a five-year term in single-seat and multi-seat constituencies and nine members appointed by the president.

Parliamentary elections were held in November 2001. The PAP won 82 seats, the Workers' Party of Singapore gained one seat and the National Solidarity Party took the other with the remainder being appointed. Chok Tong has said that he will step down before the end of his present term in 2007 and that his successor would be Lee Hsien Loong, deputy prime minister and son of the city-state's foundering father, Lee Kuan Yew. However, the prime minster is critical of Yew and will not leave office until the economy recovers.

GDP rose by 2.2% in 2002 and should increase by just 0.5% in 2003. In 2004, growth of 4.2% is anticipated. Prices fell by 0.4% in 2002 and should increase by no more than 0.6% in 2003, rising to 1.2% in 2004. A downside risk in these forecasts is the impact of Severe Acute Respiratory Syndrome (SARS) on consumer and business confidence, with the disease undermining commercial activity in the country. This has been exacerbated by a fall in tourism activity. Gross fixed investment is projected to grow by 3.5% in 2003 and by 5.7% in 2004. This reflects the recent increase in new FDI commitments in manufacturing and services. Noteworthy is the sharp increase in FDI commitments from the EU for petrochemical products and chip design services in the second half of 2002. Fiscal policy will remain broadly expansionary, with the budget remaining in deficit until 2004. Unemployment is expected to reach 4.5% in 2003 before falling back to around 4.1% in 2004. Merchandise exports are forecast to pick up by 7.5% in 2003 and by 10.2% in 2004, with growth led by strong demand for chemicals, instrumentation equipment, and pharmaceuticals. The trade and current account balances are forecast to deteriorate slightly as import growth exceeds export growth. Important changes in both the tax and expenditure sides are planned. Tax measures include the reduction of the corporate income tax rate to 22% in 2003 from 24.5% in 2002, with further reductions to 20% by 2004; tax deductions for approved R&D expenses of all services companies and cuts in the top marginal personal income tax rate from 26% in 2002 to 20% by 2004. These moves should help boost domestic demand but falling residential property prices will also have a negative effect on consumption.

Weak domestic demand meant that growth was generally slower in Singapore than in most other Asian economies in 2002. Manufacturing experienced high growth across a broad spectrum of industries, due to improved external demand. The subsector grew by 8.3% in 2002, with recoveries in electronics, rubber and plastic products, and instrumentation equipment. Electronics grew by 4.1%, after a decline of 21.3% in 2001, due to increased production of semiconductors and of data storage and office automation equipment. The growth was boosted by a modest recovery in the global electronics market. The construction subsector, which declined by 3.2% in 2001, fell by a further 10.8% in 2002. Industrial performance has suffered in recent months, however, mainly as a result of SARS. Industrial output fell by 9.5% in the 12 months to May 2003. A recovery is forecast for 2004 with industrial output expanding by around 5.6%. Both public and private construction activities remain weak. Nearly all segments in public investment declined, but the shrinkage in private construction was largely attributed to weak levels of commercial, industrial, and civil engineering works. Finance, one of the economy's key industries, fell by 4.8% in 2002, compared with modest growth of 3.7% in 2001. The wholesale and retail trade sector grew by 2.7%, a significant improvement from a decline of 3.3% in 2001. The rebound was aided by better performance in entrepot trade, with a substantial increase in non-oil re-exports. Private consumption has remained weak throughout 2002 and the first half of 2003. This measure is forecast to grow by 3.8% in 2003 and 4.7% in 2004.

Singapore is one of the major petroleum refining centres of Asia, with total crude oil refining capacity of 1.3 million barrels per day. Recent refinery expansions in several of its traditional markets also are hurting Singapore's exports. The overall outlook for Singapore's refiners is still uncertain, with so much capacity being built elsewhere in Asia. In response to these pressures, individual refinery operators in Singapore have been exploring different restructuring measures.

◘ Solomon Islands

Capital City	Honiara	*Capital population: 37,000 (1992)*
Population ('000)	461 *(2002)*	
Urban population (%)	20.65 *(2002)*	
Land area (km²)	2799	
Languages	English, Pidgin	
Religion	Mainly Christian (95%)	
Currency	Solomon Island dollar (SI$)	
Head of State	HM Queen Elizabeth II	
Head of Government	Allan Kemakeza (2001)	
Ruling Party	The government is formed by the People's Action Party (PAP).	

Main Urban Areas	Population
Honiara (capital)	37,000 (1992)

The Solomon Islands extend some 1,400km from Bougainville (part of Papua New Guinea) in the north-west to the Santa Cruz islands in the south-east. Although the terrain varies significantly, typical landscapes are mountainous with dense tree cover. The capital is Honiara.

The Solomon Islands are an independent member of the Commonwealth, in which the Crown is represented by a Governor-General. Legislative authority is vested in the 50-member unicameral Parliament, which is elected by universal adult suffrage for a term of up to four years. The prime minister is elected from among the parliament's members, by secret ballot.

Parliamentary elections were last held in December 2001. The PAP won 20 seats, the Association of Independent Members took 13 seats and the Solomon Island Alliance for Change claimed 12 seats. Minor parties took the few remaining seats. Kemakeza was then elected prime minister by parliament.

The economy shrank by 2% in 2002, the fourth consecutive year in which there has been a contraction. GDP is expected to rise by 1.9% in 2003 and growth of 3.1% is forecast for 2004 but these figures seem optimistic in view of the country's plight. Inflation was 9.8% in 2002. The forecast is for prices to rise by 12.1% in 2003 and 11% in 2004. The mainly subsistence economy has collapsed. Export earnings fell by 80% between 1997 and 2002. Australian aid, which has increased threefold over the past four years to $23 million a year, has reached barely any of the local population. Nor has income from timber, one of the Solomons' main resources. After four years of civil war, the country's meagre infrastructure has been destroyed. No employee contributions to the national pensions fund have been made in some years. In addition, the government has defaulted on international debts and domestic debts held by local commercial banks and the pension fund.

Major export-oriented business related to fisheries, copra, cocoa, palm oil and gold have been closed in recent years. The Japanese owner pulled out of the large fish cannery at Noro, timber exports were hit by the Asian slump, the large mining conglomerate closed it Gold Ridge Mine and Guadalcanal's palm-oil plantations have been abandoned. These supply disruptions, together with generally weaker world prices, have significantly depressed exports and, along with the internal strife, are major reasons for the decline in GDP. The finance sector is under great strain due to increased non-performing assets. Maintenance of stable and efficient financial intermediation will remain crucial during the reconstruction period for sustainable economic development. Insurance will be very difficult to obtain for any future venture, particularly in mining, and this will create an added hurdle to investors seeking to restart closed operations.

Most of the country's fuel needs are met from firewood or similar sources. All oil has to be imported.

Somalia

Capital City	Mogadishu	Capital population: 982,000 (1995)
Population ('000)	11,561 (2002)	
Urban population (%)	28.28 (2002)	
Land area (km²)	62734	
Languages	Arabic	
Religion	Muslim	
Currency	Somali shilling (SOS)	
Head of State	Abdiqasim Salad Hassan (2000)	
Head of Government	Hassan Abshir Farah (2001)	
Ruling Party	Main parties are the two factions of the United Somali Congress, the Somali National Movement, the Somali Democratic Movement and the Somali Patriotic Movement.	

Main Urban Areas	Population
Mogadishu (capital)	982,000 (1995)

Somalia occupies the entire eastern tip of the Horn of Africa, with Kenya to its west, Ethiopia to the northwest and Djibouti to the north. Its northern coastline follows the Gulf of Aden, while its eastern coast lies on the Indian Ocean. Somalia's terrain is mixed, with plains toward the Indian Ocean coast but with hills and mountains in the north. Soil quality is poor and a large proportion of the population is nomadic. The capital is Mogadishu.

The Republic of Somalia was ruled from 1969 until January 1991 by Maj.-Gen. Siyad Barre, who seized power in a coup and created a socialist state. The constitution was suspended from 1969 until 1991, when it was reintroduced in its unaltered form. A ruinous inter-ethnic feuding followed Barre's removal in 1991, and the situation eventually deteriorated into full-scale guerrilla war. Hassan has been appointed by an interim-parliament formed in 2000 as a result of the peace conference in Djibouti. This National Assembly has 245 members appointed by clan chiefs. Hasan is recognised by most factions, but is not supported by Somaliland and the region of Puntland. De facto, the state is in anarchy without any governmental structures.

The elections held in April 1996 were of no real significance since the results were immediately disputed and fighting resumed with even greater intensity. By 1999, Somalia appeared to be breaking apart into two countries. One is southern Somalia with its capital in Mogadishu. The other is Somaliland in the north with its capital in Hargeisa. In June 2001, a huge majority of this breakaway state voted in favour of independence from the rest of Somalia.

Somalia's traders have been doing remarkably well and their economic success threatens the power of some of the small fiefs created by the war. Malnutrition is widespread and water supplies in much of the country do not operate. Growth in the war-devastated south is nil but in the north (in Somaliland) there is more progress with trading, small-scale manufacturing and farming all recovering.

Agriculture is the most important sector, with livestock accounting for about 40% of GDP and about 65% of export earnings. Nomads and semi-nomads, who are dependent upon livestock for their livelihood, make up a large portion of the population. After livestock, bananas are the principal export; sugar, sorghum, corn and fish are products for the domestic market. The small industrial sector is based on the processing of agricultural products (including hides, wool and leather products) and accounts for 10% of GDP. In the north, in Somaliland, farmers produce frankincense (an aromatic oil), mangoes, henna and other exotic products. The country may have deposits of precious stones. The recent discovery of high-quality emerald deposits bears this optimism out.

Somalia has no proven oil reserves, and only 200 billion cu ft of proven natural gas reserves. At present, there is no hydrocarbon production in the country. Exploration activity remains hindered by the internal security situation, and the multiple sovereignty issues.

South Africa

Capital City	Pretoria	Capital population: 692,348 (1996)
Population ('000)	44,396 (2002)	
Urban population (%)	50.91 (2002)	
Land area (km²)	122104	
Languages	Afrikaans, English (official languages); principal African languages are Xhosa, Zulu and Sesotho	
Religion	Mainly Christian	
Currency	Rand (R)	
Head of State	President Thabo Mbeki (1999)	
Head of Government	Thabo Mbeki (1999)	
Ruling Party	The African National Congress (ANC) leads a coalition with the Inkatha Freedom Party (IFP).	

Main Urban Areas	Population
Soweto	904,165 (1996)
Johannesburg	760,791 (1996)
Port Elizabeth	753,156 (1996)
Mitchells Plain	728,914 (1996)
Pretoria (capital)	692,348 (1996)
Inanda	642,945 (1996)
Durban	566,120 (1996)
Wynberg	538,561 (1996)
Vanderbijl	483,360 (1996)
Kempton Park	446,106 (1996)

South Africa shares borders with Namibia in the northwest, Botswana and Zimbabwe in the north, Mozambique in the northeast and Swaziland in the east. Apart from the sovereign enclaves of Lesotho and Swaziland, it includes various "independent republics" which have no international recognition. The climate is warm and generally dry, but is well suited to agriculture; there are also vast areas of bush and scrub. The capital is Pretoria.

A full system of universal suffrage was introduced for the first time in 1994, thus ending the apartheid system under which only white electors had the vote. The "homelands" where black citizens were officially confined under apartheid were effectively disbanded. The executive president is elected by universal suffrage for a five-year term of office. A new constitution was agreed in May 1996. Parliament has two chambers. The National Assembly has 400 members, elected for a five-year term by the proportional representation. The National Council has 90 members, elected for a five-year term by the provincial parliaments.

The country's second non-racial parliamentary election took place in June 1999. The ANC won 66% of the vote and 266 seats. The Democrat Party garnered 10% of the vote and 38 seats, while the IFP won 9% of the vote and 34 seats.

GDP grew by 3% in 2002 and growth of 2.2% is anticipated in 2003. In 2004, growth of 3% is forecast. Inflation was 9.2% in 2002 and prices are expected to rise by 7.7% in 2003. In 2004, prices are forecast to increase by 4.9%. Ten years after apartheid ended, South Africa still faces the challenges of reducing inequality and enhancing growth performance. The policies implemented so far have had somewhat limited results. The sharp depreciation of the exchange rate at the end of 2001 mitigated the slowdown and boosted exports but it also resulted in a rise in inflation. The government has worked to contain the deficit, which was just 1.4% of GDP (well below the target of 2.5%) at the end of 2002. With some improvement n the financial situation, government spending is expected to rise in 2003 and a more generous tax regime for small businesses will be implemented. Tax cuts of $1.73 billion are also scheduled through a restructuring of personal income taxes affecting particularly the middle-income class. Unemployment is very high and continues to rise. Over the past decade the economy has lost more than one million jobs. One concern has been the steady increase in labour costs owing to increasing wages, without corresponding increases in productivity. However, the major reasons behind the unemployment problem are skills constraints and low demand in the economy. More reforms are necessary to make the labour market more competitive, to ensure that investment increases employment and that privatisation and continued trade liberalisation raise productivity growth and labour demand over time.

Agriculture contributes just 3% to GDP but accounts for more than 11% of total employment. Farm output rose in 2002 after a sharp drop in the previous year. Manufacturing accounts for 18% of GDP and benefited greatly from the devaluation of the rand in late 2001. Following the depreciation, some sub-sectors, such as chemicals, basic metals and motor vehicles manufacturing, and the related leather and rubber products, have raised output substantially. The mining sector, which makes up 8% of GDP, is in turmoil following passage of the Minerals and Petroleum Development Act in 2002. This law is significant because it is the first time in the country's history that mineral rights have been vested with the state. The law has been opposed by mining conglomerates which believe it offers insufficient protection for the billions of dollars in investments which the mining industry requires. South Africa's large mining sector offers diamonds, iron ore, copper, manganese, limestone and chrome but it is gold that dominates. The country is also the third leading coal exporter in the world, and coal is the country's second largest foreign exchange earner after gold. South Africa also has a highly developed synthetic fuels industry, which takes advantage of the country's abundant coal resources and offshore natural gas and condensate production. Tourism increased substantially in 2002 (the number of non-residents visiting South Africa rose from 4.8 million in the first ten months of 2001 to 5.3 million in the same period of 2002), boosted by the rand depreciation. A number of initiatives in environmental and tourism policy are expected to boost tourism even further in the future.

South Africa has recently begun to develop and exploit its reserves of conventional oil. Several discoveries have been made offshore, within the Bredasdorp Basin. An offshore natural gas discovery has also been made near the coast of Namibia. However, the importance of oil and natural gas are dwarfed by coal, which is the country's primary energy source. South Africa's recoverable coal reserves are presently estimated at 61 billion short tons (6% of the world reserves). The country is also is the world's second largest net exporter of coal. Finally, the country has a highly developed synthetic fuels industry, which takes advantage of its abundant coal resources.

▫ South Korea	
Capital City	Seoul — *Capital population: 10,395,200 (2002)*
Population ('000)	48,165 *(2002)*
Urban population (%)	82.82 *(2002)*
Land area (km²)	9873
Languages	Hangul (Korean)
Religion	Mahayana Buddhist; Christian
Currency	South Korean Won (Won)
Head of State	Roh Moo-hyun (December 2002)
Head of Government	Kim Suk-soo (2002)
Ruling Party	The government is formed by the Democratic Party (MD), the United Liberal Democrats (JMY) and non-partisans.

Main Urban Areas	**Population**
Seoul (capital)	10,395,200 (2002)
Pusan	3,967,800 (2002)
Inchon	2,629,600 (2002)
Taegu	2,532,000 (2002)
Kwangju	1,437,800 (2002)
Taejon	1,396,600 (2002)

The Republic of Korea (South Korea) is located about 500km off the coast of mainland China, and forms the entire southern half of the Korean peninsula. There are many hundreds of small islands to the south, most of them uninhabited. The territory is mixed in character, with considerable mountainous areas. Consequently, most of the largest settlements are on the southern and eastern coasts, the capital city of Seoul being the notable exception. The capital is Seoul.

South Korea has a prime minister but real power lies with the executive president. The National Assembly has 273 members, elected for a four-year term, 227 members in two-seat constituencies and 46 members by proportional representation.

Elections to the National Assembly were held in April 2000. The Grand National Party received 39% of the vote and 133 seats. The MD received 36% of the vote and gained 115 seats. The JMY captured 10% of the vote and 17 seats. In December 2002, Roh Moo-hyun won the presidency defeating Lee Hoi Chang.

GDP grew by around 6.3% in 2002 and growth of 2.5% is expected in 2003. In 2004, growth of 4.7% is forecast. Inflation was 2.8% in 2002 and should be about 3.3% in 2003. In 2004, prices are forecast to rise by 3%. South Korea's recovery in 2002, which occurred despite a sluggish world economy, reflects the success of its economic restructuring programme and the underlying dynamism of the economy. The slowdown in consumer spending growth arising from tighter consumer credit and mortgage terms will be largely offset by rising exports and a moderate revival of savings and business investment. There is, however, a downside risk stemming from rising uncertainty over developments in North Korea. While monetary policy is focused on inflation, fiscal policy aims at a balanced budget. The budget had a surplus in 2002 of 0.2% of GDP. A slight fiscal tightening is planned for 2003. Weaknesses in the pension system make it essential to enact fundamental reforms, particularly given the rapid pace of population ageing. Outlays on public pensions and healthcare are likely to rise with an ageing population, thus necessitating increased revenues for the public sector. At present, the generous allowances and tax credits that are offered mean that half of all individual income earners do not pay income tax. The tax bases of the corporate and value-added taxes must be broadened by reducing preferences and exemptions and capital

income will have to be taxed more evenly across sources to enhance equity. The system of public expenditures must also more efficient and effective. At 22.5% of GDP, South Korea has one of the lowest levels of public spending among all industrialised countries. Unemployment had risen to 3.2% in May 2003 but averaged 7.1% for those aged 20-29. Many of the larger companies plan to slash hiring by up to 30% in 2003 compared with the previous year. The government has belatedly decided to double its supplementary budget for creating jobs.

A moderation in growth of exports and domestic demand is expected in 2003. Consumer spending is expected to recede to a more sustainable pace, after booming through most of 2002 with the help of aggressive bank lending to households that has since been tempered. There has been significant progress in strengthening financial supervision and regulation in Korea since the 1997 financial crisis. The government is gradually forcing many smaller banks to consolidate and is slowly reducing its ownership in the banking sector. The present administration has also promised more extensive reform of the Korean conglomerates known as chaebols. Manufacturing is now highly export oriented as well as cyclical in nature, and most investment is concentrated in this subsector. In response, the government has begun to utilise tax policy to stabilise consumption. Less dependence on export industries and on investment in plant and equipment will have an impact not only on the composition of GDP but also on the volatility of the equity market. Further reduction of trade barriers, particularly in the service sector, is expected to enhance competition and promote South Korea's ambition of becoming a regional hub. The agricultural sector, which receives large-scale assistance equivalent to 5% of GDP, is another priority for trade liberalisation. Exports are expected to rise by 8.0% and imports by 9.0% in 2004. Nevertheless, the current account is expected to slip back into the red as the services account deficit and recovery-driven imports increase.

With no domestic reserves, South Korea must import all of its crude oil. Oil makes up the largest share of South Korea's total energy consumption, though its share has been declining in recent years. South Korea is the sixth largest oil consumer and fourth largest crude oil importer in the world. South Korea's total reliance on oil imports has led to a policy of securing and diversifying the country's oil supply. South Korea has both a short-term and a long-term approach to fulfilling its oil needs. In the short term, it has developed a strategic petroleum reserve. Strategic stocks are roughly equivalent to a 90-day supply, and are expanded in proportion to consumption levels. In the long term, the country is pursuing equity stakes in oil and gas exploration around the world. South Korea has 19 overseas exploration and production projects in 12 countries. The country relies on imported liquefied natural gas (LNG) to meet its entire demand for natural gas, though a project currently under development will make the country a minor natural gas producer in 2003.

▫ Sri Lanka	
Capital City	Colombo — *Capital population: 2,007,000 (1994)*
Population ('000)	19,022 *(2002)*
Urban population (%)	24.35 *(2002)*
Land area (km²)	6463
Languages	Sinhala, Tamil, English
Religion	Mainly Buddhist (70%)
Currency	Rupee (LKR)
Head of State	Chandrika Bandaranaika Kumaratunga (1994)
Head of Government	Ratnasiri Wickremanayake (2000)
Ruling Party	The government is formed by the United National Party (EJP).

Main Urban Areas	**Population**
Colombo (capital)	2,007,000 (1994)
Gampaha	1,696,000 (1994)
Kurunegala	1,376,000 (1994)
Kandy	1,219,000 (1994)
Galle	954,000 (1994)
Ratnapura	918,000 (1994)
Kegalle	756,000 (1994)
Matara	754,000 (1994)

Sri Lanka lies in the Indian Ocean, some 80km off the southern coast of India. Most of the island is forested, although the soil is ideally suited to agriculture. The climate is humid and tropical. The capital is Colombo.

The Democratic Socialist Republic of Sri Lanka, which has been independent in its present form since 1978, is a member of the Commonwealth. The country elects an executive president who serves a six-year term. The president appoints a cabinet in accordance with the parliament. The parliament has 225 members, elected for a six-year term, 196 members elected in multi-seat constituencies and 29 by proportional representation. The country's politics are dominated by ethnic differences; Tamils in the north and east want their own independent republic.

Elections to parliament were held in December 2001. The EJP won 109 seats while the Bahejana Nidasa Party (BNP) 77 seats. The remaining seats were dispersed among five parties. Presidential elections held in December 1999 gave Kumaratunga the presidency with 51% of the vote. She defeated Ranil Wickremesinghe, who received 43% of the ballots.

Sri Lanka's economy grew by 4% in 2002 and growth of 5.5% is expected in 2003. Growth of 6.5% is forecast for 2004. Inflation was 9.6% in 2002 and prices are expected to rise by another 7.5% in 2003. In 2004, prices are forecast to increase by 7%. The economy recovered in 2002 after a sharp contraction the previous year. Growth was modest, but the government's progress in stabilising the economy provides a firm foundation for a better performance in the medium term. Savings and investment rates recovered somewhat in 2002, but significantly higher savings rates will only materialise as fiscal consolidation progresses. The private sector did not generate many new investments, owing mainly to the existence of excess capacity following the 2001 recession. The current account deficit is expected to widen over the medium term, a reflection of the rising investment needs which outstrip saving in the public and private sector. The demand for labour has been weak despite the recovery in production. The unemployment rate rose by a percentage point to 9.0% for the year. More than 60% of the unemployed have at least a middle school education and nearly 32% have at least a high school education. While conscious of the need to create jobs, the government is reluctant to turn to the short-term solution of expanding public sector employment, which already accounts for nearly one fifth of the total. The stability arising from the ongoing peace process is a key element for sustaining development. While a breakthrough is unlikely in the near term, steady progress needs to be made in the peace talks to target the needs of the poor in the north and east and to foster investor confidence in the country generally.

The end of the drought brought relief to the agricultural sector, which grew by 2.4% during 2002, compared with a decline of 3.0% in the previous year. As long as a ceasefire is in place, tourism and shipping flourish. In 2002, services were the leading growth sector, expanding by 4.6%. The one area of continued weakness was the industry sector, where the level of output remained largely unchanged from the previous year, growing by only 0.5%. Power cuts, of up to four hours a day, due to system failures and low water levels in the reservoirs, led to an almost 10% reduction in output from utilities in the first half of 2002. Even once this power crisis had subsided, the sector had still not fully recovered lost ground by year-end. The power cuts, combined with weaker than expected global recovery, led to lacklustre performance in manufacturing, with this subsector contracting over the first 6 months of 2002 and growing by a mere 1.5% for the whole year. Although an improvement from the 4% contraction in 2001, there is still excess capacity in the manufacturing sector. Exports slumped badly in 2002 and the early part of 2003. Textiles and apparel, which are heavily dependent on demand in the US and EU, have been particularly hard hit.

Sri Lanka is overwhelmingly dependent on petroleum to meet its energy needs. The country imports all of its crude oil, which is used largely for electricity generation and transportation, and has refining capacity of 50,000 barrels per day. In recent years, Sri Lanka has increased its oil imports in an effort to diversify away from over reliance on hydroelectricity, which varies depending upon rainfall amounts. Between 1991 and 2000, Sri Lankan oil consumption roughly doubled. In addition, Sri Lanka consumes large amounts of non-commercial fuel, specifically biomass, nearly all of which is wood. Biomass consumption is increasing by about 3% annually. Overall, biomass accounts for about 55% of Sri Lanka's total energy consumption. Biomass is consumed mainly by households, and Sri Lanka has, in the past, run successful wood stove programmes. The petroleum sector has been liberalised, and competitors to the state-owned petroleum company began operations in 2003.

St Kitts

Capital City	Basseterre	Capital population: 14,900 (1992)
Population ('000)	38 (2002)	
Urban population (%)	34.41 (2002)	
Land area (km²)	36	
Languages	English	
Religion	Mainly Anglican	
Currency	East Caribbean dollar (EC$)	
Head of State	HM Queen Elizabeth II	
Head of Government	Dr. Denzil Douglas (1995)	
Ruling Party	St. Kitts-Nevis Labour Party (SKNLP)	

Main Urban Areas	Population
Basseterre (capital)	14,900 (1992)

St Kitts and Nevis comprises the islands of St Christopher and Nevis, situated in the northern Leeward Islands, in the Eastern Caribbean. The two are separated by a three-km maritime strait, and are mountainous and densely forested. The climate is equable, although subject to storms in the autumn months. The capital is Basseterre.

St Kitts (St Christopher and Nevis) has been a fully independent member of the Commonwealth since 1983. The Crown is represented by a Governor-General who appoints the prime minister and cabinet in accordance with the wishes of parliament. The unicameral National Assembly consists of a speaker, three senators appointed by the Governor-General, and 11 members who are elected by universal suffrage for a term of five years. The island of Nevis has a separate eight-member legislature and a cabinet with certain internal powers.

Elections to the National Assembly were held in March 2000 when the SKNLP won eight seats in the Assembly. The Concerned Citizens' Movement took two seats and the Peoples Action Movement received the remaining seat. In August 1998, Nevis held a referendum on secession from the federation. Although 62% backed secession, a two thirds majority was needed and the referendum failed.

GDP contracted by 0.8% in 2002 but growth of 1.2% is expected in 2003. In 2004, a rate of 1.4% is forecast. Prices rose by 2.1% in 2002 and are expected to rise by another 1.4% in 2003. In 2004, inflation is forecast to be 1.5%. A combination of hurricanes and terrorist-induced cuts in tourism led to the contraction in 2002. The deficit widened to 33% of GDP in 2002, reflecting the weakening markets for tourism demand and exports. There has also been a sharp increase in public debt,

reaching 122% of GDP in 2002. This is one of the highest debt levels in the Caribbean. In the field of structural reform, priority in 2002 was given to the liberalisation of the telecommunications sector and the break-up of the monopoly on domestic cellular services. The government is also working to improve revenue collection in order to provide more funding for social programmes. Living standards, however, are still low in comparison with those in neighbouring countries. St. Kitts depends on the UK for almost all its exports and foreign exchange earnings and its economic prospects are therefore extremely vulnerable to conditions in the latter country.

Nevis's economy is based on tourism and offshore financial services, while St. Kitts's economy is larger and more diversified. Agriculture contributes just 4% of GDP, and is spread around the coastal areas. Bananas, copra and cotton are the main export products but sugar cane is the dominant product. Manufacturing accounts for 26% of GDP and consists of light industries (mainly textiles) and the processing of agricultural commodities. Services account for 70% of GDP and depend mainly on tourism. Tourism is not fully developed but has considerable potential. It is typically one of the fastest growing sectors of the economy but suffered significantly after two hurricanes and the terrorist attacks on September 11th 2001. In addition, exports to the US were virtually halted in the twelve months after the attacks. Neither St. Kitts nor Nevis has any significant indigenous resources.

The islands have no fuel except timber. They rely on imports from Venezuela and Mexico for most of their energy needs.

St Lucia

Capital City	Castries	Capital population: 53,883 (1992)
Population ('000)	160 (2002)	
Urban population (%)	38.24 (2002)	
Land area (km²)	61	
Languages	English	
Religion	Mainly Roman Catholic	
Currency	East Caribbean dollar (EC$)	
Head of State	HM Queen Elizabeth II	
Head of Government	Kenny Anthony (1997)	
Ruling Party	St. Lucia Labour Party (SLP)	

Main Urban Areas	Population
Castries (capital)	53,883 (1992)

St Lucia, situated in the Windward Islands of the Eastern Caribbean some 32km north of St Vincent and 40km south of Martinique, is no more than 40km long at its greatest extent, yet its important strategic role has made it much sought after over the years. This is due partly to its record as a safe harbour during the annual hurricane season which afflicts other parts of the region. The capital is Castries.

St Lucia, a member of the Commonwealth, is one of the Windward Islands group which favours political integration with Dominica, Grenada and St Vincent and the Grenadines. Parliament consists of two chambers. The House of Assembly has 17 members, elected for a five-year term in single-seat constituencies. The Senate has 11 appointed members.

In elections held in December 2001, the SLP won 14 of the 17 seats in the island's legislature. The United Workers Party took three seats.

GDP fell by 0.5% in 2002 but growth of 1.5% is expected in 2003. In 2004, growth of 2% is forecast. Inflation was 1.6% in 2002 and is expected to be 2% in 2003. The forecast calls for the same rate in 2004. The island's National Development Corporation is working hard to develop tourism and promote St. Lucia as an investment location. It has plans for development of 600 acres of government land, formerly used as a US military base. The site is to be converted into golf courses and several major resorts. Despite these efforts, earnings from bananas are the only source of income for entire communities in some parts of the country. St Lucia is trying to diversify production, and has begun to promote the growth of tree crops such as mangoes and avocados. The island presently has more than 10,000 small farms that depend almost entirely on bananas, with annual exports exceeding 70,000 tonnes. Though foreign investment in manufacturing and information processing is rising, the pace of diversification is too slow. St Lucia has recently opened a dedicated container terminal at Vieux Fort and has established a free-trade zone there. The intention is to offer transhipment connections for Central and South America, Europe and West Africa.

Agriculture accounts for 12% of the GDP but over 40% of all employment. Industry makes up a third of GDP and services contribute the remainder. Tourism attracts about 200,000 visitors in most years but the numbers have fallen since September 11th 2001. Tourism is restricted only to the larger resorts and its benefits are spread unevenly. However, the sector has much potential with forests, sandy beaches, minerals (pumice), mineral springs and geothermal sources. Though foreign investment in manufacturing and information processing is rising, the island's industrial base depends heavily on the production of bananas. St Lucia continues to be the largest supplier of bananas in the Windward Islands. Nevertheless, production costs are about three times higher than in Central and South America.

St Lucia has no indigenous energy resources and relies on imports for all fuel requirements.

▫ St Vincent and the Grenadines

Capital City	Kingstown	*Capital population: 15,670 (1991)*
Population ('000)	118 *(2002)*	
Urban population (%)	56.7 *(2002)*	
Land area (km²)	39	
Languages	English	
Religion	Mainly Christian	
Currency	East Caribbean dollar (EC$)	
Head of State	HM Queen Elizabeth II	
Head of Government	Ralph Gonsalves (2001)	
Ruling Party	Unity Labour Party (ULP)	

Main Urban Areas	Population
Kingstown (capital)	15,670 (1991)

▫ Sudan

Capital City	Khartoum	*Capital population: 2,429,000 (1995)*
Population ('000)	32,018 *(2002)*	
Urban population (%)	37.66 *(2002)*	
Land area (km²)	237600	
Languages	Arabi,C English	
Religion	Muslim; Traditional; Christian	
Currency	Sudanese pound (SD£)	
Head of State	President Omar Hassan Ahmad Al-Bashir	
Head of Government	President Omar Hassan Ahmad Al-Bashir	
Ruling Party	The government is dominated by the National Congress Party.	

Main Urban Areas	Population
Khartoum (capital)	2,429,000 (1995)

St Vincent, a 30-km island, is the main island in a group of some 100 islets which extend for more than 60km through the Grenadines group in the Windward Islands. Other islands in the Grenadines are part of the state of Grenada. St Vincent itself is about 160km west of Barbados and 34km southwest of St Lucia. The capital is Kingstown.

St Vincent and the Grenadines has been a Commonwealth member since gaining independence from the UK in 1979. The Crown is represented by a Governor-General who appoints the prime minister in accordance with the wishes of parliament. The unicameral National Assembly consists of six appointed senators and 15 members who are elected by universal suffrage for a term of five years.

Elections to the National Assembly were held in March 2001 when the ULP took 12 seats with 58% of the vote. The New Democratic Party won three seats. Ralph Gonsalves of the ULP became prime minister.

GDP rose by just 1.1% in 2002 and growth of 2.2% is expected in 2003. In 2004, growth of 2.8% is forecast. Prices increased by 0.8% in 2002 and should rise by 0.3% in 2003. In 2004, inflation is forecast to be 2%. The government's counter-cyclical policy has helped to avoid recession and mitigate employment losses. This result, while positive, has led to degeneration in the overall fiscal position. The deficit of the public sector reached 6% of GDP in 2002. Meanwhile, public investment rose from 7% in 2000 to around 12% of GDP in 2002. The central government's overall balance recorded a deficit of 3.5% in 2002, as the wage bill and capital increased significantly. The external current account deficit remains broadly unchanged at 11.8% of GDP in 2002, largely financed by official capital inflows and foreign direct investment. With the deadlines imposed by the Caribbean Community and the Free Trade Area of the Americas, the authorities will come under pressure to broaden the tax base and reduce reliance on trade tariffs. In this connection, a VAT-type tax is likely to be introduced in advance of the trade liberalisation. Unemployment is thought to be around 20% or higher.

Farming accounts for just over 10% of GDP but productivity is low. Approximately a quarter of all workers are employed in the agricultural sector. Bananas are the most important export, though farmers also export arrowroot, coconuts, cocoa and spices, while cassava and vegetables are grown for the domestic market. Preliminary estimates for 2002 indicate a strong rebound in agriculture prior to tropical storm Lili, which occurred in September 2002. Industry makes up 19% of GDP. Growth in this sector has been driven by construction activity as public sector projects were implemented. Manufacturing centres on the processing of raw materials for domestic use, but a range of light activities including woodworking and furniture and clothing are also prominent. There is also a growing services sector including tourism, telemarketing, and a small offshore financial centre. The authorities are strengthening the regulatory and supervisory framework of the offshore banking sector in order to bring it in line with international best practices. The number of offshore banks fell from 38 in 2001 to around 20 at end-2002. Export receipts from bananas, despite an increase in volume, will remain flat because of lower international prices. Tourist receipts are expected to drop reflecting significant declines in excursionists, yacht, and cruise passenger arrivals.

St Vincent and the Grenadines have no indigenous fuels except for firewood, and the country imports nearly all its requirements. However, hydroelectric power accounts for three quarters of all electricity generation.

Sudan, the largest country in Africa, lies in central northeast Africa where it shares borders to the north with Egypt, to the east with Eritrea and Ethiopia, to the south with Kenya, Uganda and the Democratic Republic of the Congo (formerly Zaire), and to the west with the Central African Republic, Chad, and to a small extent Libya. Very little of its terrain is suitable for cultivation, except for a limited area around the River Nile and its tributaries, the Atbara, the Blue Nile and the White Nile. The capital is Khartoum.

The elected regime was overthrown in 1989 and the leaders of the coup have dominated Sudanese politics since then. The president is elected for a five-year term by the people. The National Assembly has 360 members, 270 directly elected for a four-year term in single-seat constituencies, 35 members representing women, 26 members representing university graduates and 29 representatives of trade unions.

Presidential elections took place in December 2000 when Al-Bashir was returned to office with 87% of the vote. Elections to the National Assembly were held at the same time and the National Congress Party captured 355 seats.

Despite considerable natural resources, Sudan is one of the world's poorest countries. GDP grew by 5% in 2002 and prices increased by 8.3%. In 2003, GDP should increase by another 5.8% with prices rising by 7%. Forecasts for 2004 call for growth of 6.5% and inflation of 5%. Exports have grown sharply since 1999, when the oil export pipeline was completed, turning the country's trade balance from negative to positive. Sudan's government has been negotiating the payment of its substantial debts to the IMF so that the nation can improve its relations with the institution. Sudan's debt to the IMF was rescheduled in 2002, and arrears payments were deferred. Despite its economic progress, Sudan still faces developmental obstacles, including a limited infrastructure and an external debt estimated to be around $15 billion in 2001, representing a debt-to-GDP ratio of just over 122%. The government has announced that it intends to accelerate and broaden the country's privatisation programme. Khartoum also is moving to cut costs, reduce subsidies on gasoline and benzene and scale back support to state-owned enterprises. These moves should help to bring the budget closer into balance.

Traditionally, Sudan's economy has been mainly agricultural - a mix of subsistence farming and production of cash crops such as cotton and gum arabic. Farming is the main source of income for the great majority of the population but has been severely disrupted by the war. Sugar, wheat, millet and sorghum are grown for domestic consumption, while groundnuts and oilseeds are some of the main export crops. Cattle are herded, mainly by nomads, in the desert. With the start of significant oil production (and exports) beginning in late 1999, however, Sudan's economy is changing dramatically, with oil export revenues now accounting for around 70% of Sudan's total export earnings. Sudan no longer relies on expensive imported oil products, which has helped the country's trade balance, while foreign investment has started to flow into the country (US$7 billion in 2001). Manufacturing accounts for only about 5% of GDP. Cement, timber processing, textiles and leather goods being the main products. Development of Sudan's oil resources remains controversial and problematic. Numerous international human rights organisations have accused the Sudanese government of financing wide-scale human rights abuses with oil revenues, including the mass displacement of civilians living near the oil fields. The SPLA has declared that it considers oil installations a "legitimate military target", as oil development has provided the Sudanese government the financial resources to expand its war effort. The SPLA says it destroyed the main oil well at one field in September 2002.

In 2003, Sudan's estimated proven reserves of crude oil stood at 563 million barrels, more than twice the 262.1 million barrels estimated in 2001. Crude oil production averaged 227,500 barrels per day (bbl/d) during 2002, a figure that has been rising steadily since the completion of the export pipeline in 1999. By 2003, oil output could surpass 300,000 bbl/d, with plans to reach 450,000 bbl/d by 2005. Sudan has been self-sufficient in producing petroleum products (except jet fuel) since 2000.

Suriname

Suriname	
Capital City	Paramaribo *Capital population: 240,000 (1992)*
Population ('000)	424 *(2002)*
Urban population (%)	75.25 *(2002)*
Land area (km²)	15600
Languages	Dutch
Religion	Christian; Hindu; Muslim
Currency	Suriname guilder (SRG)
Head of State	Runaldo Ronald Venetiaan (2000)
Head of Government	Runaldo Ronald Venetiaan (2000)
Ruling Party	The government is formed by New Front for Democracy.

Main Urban Areas	Population
Paramaribo (capital)	240,000 (1992)

Suriname is located on the north-eastern Atlantic coast of South America, where it is flanked in the west by Guyana, in the east by French Guiana and in the south by Brazil. The major settlements are on the coast. Further inland, the dense jungle gives way to a high sierra where the only cultivable crop is balata, a rubbery sap obtained from certain trees. The capital is Paramaribo.

The Republic of Suriname gained its independence from the Netherlands in 1975 and has close ties to that country today. A protracted civil war led to a succession of coups and counter-coups but the situation had eased by the mid-1990s, following another military coup. The executive president is chosen by an electoral college based on the parliament which, in turn, is elected by popular vote for a five-year term. The National Assembly has 51 members, elected every five years by proportional representation per district.

In general elections held in May 2000, Ronald Venetiaan, and his New Front coalition received 47% of the vote and 25 seats. The Millennium Combination won 15% of the votes and ten seats. The remainder of the seats were scattered among several parties.

GDP rose by 2.7% in 2002 and growth of 3.8% is expected in 2003. In 2004, an increase of 4.3% is forecast. Inflation was 28.3% in 2002 and is expected to be 20% in 2003. Prices are forecast to rise by 18% in 2004. With an IMF programme for macroeconomic stabilisation in place, Suriname's economy is improving though inflation is expected to remain high. A breakdown in the fiscal plan occurred in 2002 when the government implemented an agreement with the civil service unions for an average increase of 60% in civil service salaries. This increase, together with the 30% wage increase granted in 2001, will result in an increase in the wage bill in 2002 of 80%, or 6.5% of GDP. Central government revenue has also been adversely affected by a go-slow in the tax administration department. As a result of these factors, the fiscal deficit for the first half of 2002 was 1.4% of GDP, compared with a surplus of 3.4% for the corresponding period in 2001. Investors' concerns about the direction of macroeconomic policy have resulted in pressures on the guilder. The currency depreciated by more than 35% during the period of January to August 2002. In 2002, a new law was passed placing a 60% ceiling on the ratio of total government debt to GDP.

Agriculture makes up 13% of GDP, industry accounts for 22% and services contribute the remainder. Agriculture is viable only along the coastal regions where the terrain is more accessible. Products range from sugar and banana plantations to rice (the staple crop) and vegetables. Further inland, timber and forestry are found. In the high sierras, balata (a form of ersatz rubber) is extracted from trees. The country's main industries include lumbering, food processing and commercial fishing. Suriname has an abundance of natural resources including: timber, hydropower potential, fish, shrimp, bauxite, iron ore, and small amounts of nickel, copper, platinum and gold. However, the economy is dominated by the bauxite industry, which accounts for around 15% of GDP and more than 65% of export earnings in recent years. After reaching over US$400 per tonne in early 2000, the international price of alumina slumped to around US$150 per tonne in late 2001. The country's gold fields support many freelance miners but most these are Brazilians, many of them heavily armed.

Suriname has immense and largely unrealised hydroelectric potential in its upland jungle areas, as well as some oil resources offshore.

Swaziland

Swaziland	
Capital City	Mbabane *Capital population: 42,400 (1992)*
Population ('000)	1,102 *(2002)*
Urban population (%)	26.95 *(2002)*
Land area (km²)	1720
Languages	English, Siswati
Religion	Christian (60%), remainder Mainly traditional beliefs
Currency	Lilangeni (SZL)
Head of State	HM King Mswati III (1986)
Head of Government	Barnabas Sibusiso Dlamini (1996)
Ruling Party	All political parties are banned under the 1978 constitutional amendments.

Main Urban Areas	Population
Mbabane (capital)	42,400 (1992)

Swaziland is a landlocked state in southern Africa, bordered in the east by Mozambique and on all other sides by South Africa. Four rivers ensure a satisfactory flow of irrigation to the lowlands; higher up the land turns to mountain ranges. The climate is tropical but pleasant. The capital is Mbabane.

The Kingdom of Swaziland, an independent member of the Commonwealth, is the only absolute monarchy in sub-Saharan Africa. All political activity has been banned since 1973, when King Sobhuza II took "supreme power". His successor, the current king, has relaxed the rules a bit. He appoints the prime minister and cabinet directly and they answer to him rather than to the 65-member House of Assembly or the 30-member Senate. Current practice is for 55 members of the House of Assembly and ten Senators to be elected by the 40 traditional tribal communities, with the King appointing all the others.

Non-party elections took place in September and October 1998. As a result of those elections, Barnabas Dlamini was reinstated as prime minister after a one-year absence.

GDP grew by 1.6% in 2002 and prices rose by 12%. In 2003, growth is expected to be around 1.5% and prices are forecast to rise by 9.5%. Forecasts for 2004 call for growth of 1.6% and inflation of 6.7%. Swaziland's growth performance has weakened since the early 1990s as the emergence of South Africa from economic isolation has eroded some of the country's advantage as a location for investment. The poor economic performance in 2002 also reflected a fall in export demand associated with the economic slowdown in South Africa, foreign disinvestment in some industries, and poor weather. Unemployment rose in 2002 to about 33%. A deterioration in public finances is attributed to a decline in Southern African Customs Union receipts. In 2003, the authorities expect that the deficit could widen to 4-4.5% of GDP, largely due to an increase in the civil service wage bill and supplementary expenditures equivalent to around 2% of GDP. Gross international reserves also declined slightly to 3 months of imports. In 2002, the government took some steps to broaden the tax base, which would help compensate for an envisaged decline in Southern African Customs Union receipts Although Swaziland is regarded as a middle-income country with a per capita GDP of US$1,340, adult per capita consumption for the poorest 40% of its population is equivalent to US$230 or less. Moreover, Swaziland's HIV prevalence is estimated at 22.5% of the population aged 15-49.

The agricultural sector is the most important area of the economy for most of the population, supporting subsistence crops such as sugar cane, cereals and fruit, as well as cash crops such as pineapples and cotton. Other farm products include maize, tobacco, rice, citrus, pineapples, corn, sorghum, peanuts, cattle, goats and sheep. Exports of sugar and forestry products are the main earners of hard currency. Roughly 60% of the workforce is employed in agriculture. Productivity is very low, however, and farming makes up only 16% of GDP. Farmers suffer from overgrazing, soil depletion and drought. Farm expansion is hobbled by the fact that the king owns most land "in trust" for the nation, and can evict tillers on a whim. Swaziland faces a food shortage with over a quarter of the population in need of emergency food assistance. Manufacturing makes up 40% of GDP. Exports of manufactures are few with most of the production being destined for domestic consumption. Major activities include brewing, timber products, textiles and various crafts. The manufacturing sector weakened in 2002 as a result of additional closures by foreign firms and agricultural output being affected by the drought in the region. Swaziland has a well-developed banking system. Banks' capitalisation and risk management are sound and the share of nonperforming loans is relatively low. Mining has declined in importance in recent years as high-grade iron ore deposits were depleted and health concerns cut world demand for asbestos. The country earns much of its foreign exchange from the weekend visits of South Africans who come for gambling and the wildlife, and from remittances by Swazis working in South Africa's mines and factories.

Swaziland depends almost entirely on South Africa to meet its energy needs. However, it has an ample supply of hydroelectric power, but otherwise few natural energy resources, all of which have to be imported.

Syria

Syria	
Capital City	Damascus *Capital population: 2,052,000 (1995)*
Population ('000)	17,453 *(2002)*
Urban population (%)	55.32 *(2002)*
Land area (km²)	18378
Languages	Arabic; also Kurdish, Turkish, Aramaic
Religion	Mainly Muslim
Currency	Syrian pound (SYP)
Head of State	President Bashar al Assad (2000)
Head of Government	Naji al-Otari (2003)
Ruling Party	Ba'ath Party leads the National Progressive Front coalition.

Main Urban Areas	Population
Damascus (capital)	2,052,000 (1995)
Aleppo	1,855,000 (1995)

Syria owes its unusual political influence to its position in the extreme northeast of the Mediterranean, where the Islamic Middle East meets with Israel on the one hand and secular Turkey on the other. Its Mediterranean coastline, in fact, is no more than 150km. More important is the country's long eastern and south-eastern border with Iraq and Jordan, and that with Lebanon and Israel in the southwest. The climate is cool Middle Eastern, with occasional cold winters. The capital is Damascus.

The country's 1973 Constitution calls for an executive president who is formally elected by universal suffrage every seven years. In principle, the president answers to a People's Assembly of 250 members who are elected for four years. However, the Alawite group has dominated Syrian politics since Hafez al Assad seized power in 1970. Most decisions are taken by the ruling Ba'ath Arab Socialist Renaissance party.

Elections to the People's Assembly were held in March 2003 when the Ba'ath Party and its allies won 167 seats - the same number it has held in the seven previous elections. The remaining 85 seats went to independents. Opponents boycotted the election, arguing that the process was not democratic. Hafez al Assad was reconfirmed as president after being approved in an uncontested national referendum in February 1999. He died in June 2000 and was replaced by his son, Bashar al Assad. In September 2003, Bashar appointed Mohammed Naji al-Otari as prime minister.

GDP increased by 2.7% in 2002 and inflation was 1.5%. In 2003, growth is expected to be 1% and inflation should be 2.5%. Forecasts for 2004 call for growth of 2.9% and inflation of 3%. With its rapidly rising population (around 2.5% per year), Syria's current growth rate is far below the estimated 5% rate the country is estimated to need in order to make significant economic progress. Unemployment is also high. According to the Syrian government, the country's jobless rate is under 10%, although private analysts put the figure at more than 20%. Syria's trade with Iraq (mostly illegal) prior to the war amounted to more than $2 billion. All of that is now lost to the economy. The ultimate goals of economic reform in Syria are to move the country away from a state-run economy and towards a more market-based, modernised one, to reduce the rate of unemployment and to diversify the country's economic base for the day when oil reserves run out. In recent years, Syria has moved extremely slowly and cautiously in this direction. For the most part, large state corporations continue to control all strategic sectors, including oil, electricity, banking, and chemicals. The Syrian government announced in 2002 that it had put on hold any immediate moves to privatise large state-owned enterprises, concentrating instead on increasing state revenue. The main economic reform of the past year was the decision in October 2002 to allow banks to trade foreign currencies at rates closer to the "market-based" rates against the Syrian pound prevailing in neighbouring Lebanon. Economists estimate that more than US$50 billion has been sent abroad by Syrians, rendering the country short of capital. Foreign debt is another problem, although perhaps US$10 billion of the country's approximately US$1.2 billion debt is owed to the former Soviet Union and is considered unlikely to be repaid.

Farming, which is the main activity, is concentrated mainly on the Mediterranean coastline. In recent years, the agriculture sector has recovered from years of government inattentiveness and drought. Most farms are privately owned, but important elements of marketing and transportation are controlled by the government. The government has redirected its economic development priorities from industrial expansion into the agricultural sectors in order to achieve food self-sufficiency, enhance export earnings, and stem rural migration. Thanks to sustained capital investment, infrastructure development, subsidies of inputs, and price supports, Syria has gone from a net importer of many agricultural products to an exporter of cotton, fruits, vegetables, and other foodstuffs. One of the prime reasons for this turnaround has been the government's investment in huge irrigation systems in northern and north-eastern Syria, part of a plan to increase irrigated farmland by 38% over the next decade. Cotton and tobacco are cash crops, while wheat, barley and fruit are grown for the domestic market. Development of the manufacturing sector is constrained by a host of obstacles including export taxes, a shortage of credit and a corrupt and sluggish bureaucracy. Private investors, with financial backing from the Gulf States, have been expanding into various sectors (textiles, pharmaceuticals, food-processing and other light industries), many built by wealthy Syrians from abroad. Tourism was growing prior to the terrorist attacks on the US and the war in Iraq, but collapsed in 2003. Along with agriculture, foreign aid and remittances from Syrian workers abroad, Syria relies heavily on the oil sector - for around 55-60% of total export revenues. Foreign banks are being allowed to set up, but the state institutions that have monopolised banking since 1963 remain so inept that it can take weeks to transfer money between branches. Phosphates and asphalt are mined but the country has ample deposits of other natural resources that have yet to be developed.

Syria's oil industry faces many challenges in the years to come. Oil output and production continues to decline due to technological problems and depletion of oil reserves. Since peaking at 590,000 barrels per day (bbl/d) in 1996, Syria's oil output has fallen steadily, to an estimated 525,682 bbl/d in 2002, as older fields have reached maturity. Syrian oil production is expected to continue its decline over the next several years, while consumption rises, leading to a reduction in Syrian net oil exports. If this trend continues, it is feared Syria could become a net oil importer within a decade. Syria hopes to reverse this trend through intensified oil and natural gas exploration and production efforts, plus a switch from oil-fired to natural-gas fired electric power plants. Syria also has opened up new blocks for oil and natural gas exploration. However, oil exploration activity has been slow in recent years due to unattractive contract terms by the government and poor exploration results. Only a few companies out of more than a dozen operating in the country in 1991 remain.

□ Taiwan		
Capital City	Taipei	*Capital population: 2,580,075 (2002)*
Population ('000)	22,569 *(2002)*	
Urban population (%)	77.89 *(2002)*	
Languages	Mandarin	
Religion	Mainly Buddhist	
Currency	New Taiwan dollar (NT$)	
Head of State	President Chen Shui-bian (2000)	
Head of Government	Yu Shyi-kun (2002)	
Ruling Party	The government is formed by the Democratic Progressive Party (MCT) and non-partisans.	

Main Urban Areas	Population	
Taipei (capital)	2,580,075	(2002)
Kaohsiung Municipality	1,446,194	(2002)
Taichung City	1,047,017	(2002)
Tainan City	749,851	(2002)
Panchiao Shih	505,711	(2002)
Keelung City	402,357	(2002)
Chungho Shih	391,444	(2002)
Hsinchuang Shih	391,244	(2002)
Sanchung Shih	381,013	(2002)
Hsinchu City	378,447	(2002)

Taiwan is principally located on what was formerly known as the island of Formosa. This is a territory no more than 400km from north to south which lies between the South China Sea and the East China Sea about 200km off the coast of mainland China and about 700km north-east of Hong Kong. The capital is Taipei.

The president is elected for a four-year term by the people. Parliament has two chambers. The Legislative Yuan has 225 members, 168 members elected for three-year terms in multi-seat constituencies, eight members representing the aboriginals, 41 members elected by proportional representation and eight members representing the overseas Chinese elected by proportional representation. When necessary, a National Assembly with some constitutional tasks has to be elected by proportional representation on an ad hoc basis.

The presidential election was held in March 2000. Chen Shui-bian received 39% of the ballots, James Soong got 38% and Lien Chan received 23%. Elections to parliament took place in December 2001. The MCT took 87 seats in the Yuan, the Nationalist Party won 68 seats and the People First Party claimed 13 seats. The remainder was divided among three smaller parties.

GDP increased by 3.5% in 2002 and growth of 2.7% is anticipated in 2003. In 2004, an increase of 3.8% is forecast. Prices contracted by 0.2% in 2002 and should increase by just 0.1% in 2003 and 0.8% in 2004. The employed labour force rose by 0.8% in 2002, but the unemployed labour force increased by 14.5%, resulting in an unemployment rate of 5.2%, the highest in the past three decades. The major factor was the closure or downsizing of enterprises in response to sluggish economic performance and ongoing structural transition. Accordingly, average monthly earnings for manufacturing workers fell by 1.2% in 2002. In 2002, the relatively high levels of non-performing loans and of public debt remained the two pressing issues for the authorities. On the first point, a new law was passed in 2001 to allow financial institutions to have greater flexibility to merge and to provide a wider range of financial services. On the second point, the public debt-to-GDP ratio has worsened as a result of the continued large central government budget deficit in 2002. Taiwan was admitted to membership in the World Trade Organisation in November 2001, concurrently with China's admission. Unlike China, Taiwan has been admitted as a "developed country," which imposes more stringent requirements for reducing barriers to foreign competition. Taiwan recently has lifted some restrictions on direct trade with and investment in mainland China. The weak economy, combined with accumulated tax incentives offered by the authorities, caused tax revenues to decline by 2.6% in 2002. The government's commitment not to raise taxes through 2004 has made it difficult to widen the tax base. In the future, the process of restructuring will require Taiwan to become a provider of high value-added services to the region, rather than a manufacturing hub.

Agriculture accounts for just 2% of GDP and 8% of employment. Farmers are producing sugar, yams, rice, tea and bananas, as well as vegetables and fruit. The industrial sector strengthened in 2002 due to increased exports. Growth was 5.4%, driven largely by a 6.6% broad-based expansion in manufacturing: production in electronics (11.4%), basic metals (10.3%), machinery (5.8%), and chemicals (4.4%). Production related to the food industry contracted by 4.5% and construction declined by 2.9%. Growth of services was a modest 2.7% in 2002. Exports grew by 6.4% in 2002 and the pace is expected to accelerate further in 2003 and 2004. The economy's information technology exports account for more than 50% of exports of goods and services. Strong demand from China, particularly for information technology-related goods, provided support for exports, offsetting soft demand from the US and Japan. Imports rose by 3.2% compared with 2001, due largely to higher levels of imported intermediate goods and higher oil prices; this was despite the fact that household spending remained weak. Further stimulus through additional public spending has been hindered by the sluggish economy, while the president's promise not to raise taxes in the next two years has made the widening of the tax base difficult. Instead of tax cuts, reform of the tax system has been directed to rationalising the tax system, such as reducing some of the tax breaks that used to be enjoyed by high-tech companies, and improving the overall efficiency of the tax.

Taiwan's current crude oil production is less than 1,000 barrels per day. Most oil imports come from the Persian Gulf, though West African countries also are important suppliers for Taiwan. To ensure against a supply disruption, Taiwan's refiners are under a regulatory requirement to maintain stocks of no less than 60 days of consumption. Refiner-held strategic petroleum stocks are the norm in Asia, and Taiwan's policy is similar to those of Japan and South Korea. Taiwan's legislature passed the Petroleum Administration Act in 2001, which will permit the eventual sale of a majority stake in the Chinese Petroleum Corporation (CPC), a government-operated firm, to take place by mid-2004. Foreign firms will be allowed to acquire stakes in CPC on an equal basis with domestic investors. Despite the lack of formal ties between Taipei and Beijing, the two countries have developed a co-operative relationship in the field of energy. CPC and Beijing's state-owned China National Offshore Oil Corporation signed a deal to explore a 5,939-sq mile area in the Tainan Basin of the Taiwan Strait. Geologists have reportedly identified several structures considered worthy of exploration, and the two firms have expressed interest in forming a joint venture company to carry out exploratory drilling in the area.

◻ Tajikistan

Capital City	Dushanbe	*Capital population: 605,000 (1992)*
Population ('000)	6,298 *(2002)*	
Urban population (%)	27.64 *(2002)*	
Land area (km²)	14060	
Languages	Tajik	
Religion	Mainly Islam	
Currency	Tajik rouble (TJRb)	
Head of State	Imamali Sharipovich Rakhmonov	
Head of Government	Akil Akilov (1999)	
Ruling Party	The government is formed by the People's Democratic Party of Tajikistan (HDKT).	

Main Urban Areas	**Population**
Dushanbe (capital)	605,000 (1992)

Tajikistan, almost the southernmost point of the former Soviet Union, is a predominantly Muslim state which borders on Afghanistan and China in the south. But for the Hindu Kush, a narrow tongue of Afghan territory, it would also meet Pakistan. In the west it borders on Uzbekistan and in the north-east on Kyrgyzstan. With a mainly dry climate but with well-irrigated soil, it produces cotton and similar crops. The capital is Dushanbe.

Tajikistan declared its independence from the Soviet Union in August 1991. A civil war followed when ex-communists from the west of the country deposed an alliance of Islamists and secular democrats from the east. Parliament has two chambers. The Assembly of Representatives has 63 members, elected for a five-year term - 22 by proportional representation and 41 in single-seat constituencies. The National Assembly will have 33 members, 25 elected for a five-year term by local deputies and eight appointed by the president. The president is elected for a five-year term by the people.

The country held its first parliamentary election in March 2000. The HDKT won 30 seats while the communists took 13 seats. Non-partisans claimed another 15 with the remainder being divided among smaller parties. Presidential elections were held in November 1999, when Rakhmonov, a former chairman of the Supreme Soviet, was re-elected as head of state with 97% of the vote. In June 2003, voters approved a new constitution which would allow the president up to 14 more years in power.

Tajikistan has the lowest per capita GDP in the former Soviet Union. However, its economy has performed reasonably well. GDP rose by 9.1% in 2002 and should increase by another 6% in 2003. The forecast for 2004 is for growth of 4%. The pace of inflation has slowed with prices rising by around 12.2% in 2002 and 14.5% in 2003. In 2004, inflation is forecast to be 5%. Public external debt is very high at over 87% of GDP (a total of $R 255962 million, with about one third owed to the Russian Federation). The debt is a major obstacle in fiscal management: in 2002, total scheduled debt service amounted to 5.3% of GDP. In early 2002, the government renegotiated concessional terms on debts with Kazakhstan and Uzbekistan, and a major breakthrough was achieved by the restructuring of debt to the Russian Federation on concessional terms in December (this lowered debt service due in 2002 from 41% to 18% of fiscal revenues). Regional surveys suggest that non-cash, cash and non-cash incomes have increased substantially since the finalisation of the peace agreement in 2000. However, people's wages are extremely low. More than 80% of the population fall below the poverty line, and 17% live on less than $1 a day. Only a small share of the labour force is engaged in formal sector employment-an area that has shown little growth. While the official unemployment rate rose only slightly from 2.3% to 2.7% in 2002, unofficial estimates place unemployment or underemployment much higher, at over 30% of the labour force. For many Tajiks, informal activity, agricultural labour, and jobs abroad are the most likely sources of employment. The country's exports must travel through Uzbekistan and Kazakhstan to reach Russia and Europe and the neighbours' harsh new trading restrictions have sharply reduced this flow. Corruption and extortion at border posts and along roads add to the problem. Tajikistan has managed to improve revenue collection rates steadily from 12% of GDP in 1998 to over 15% in 2001. In 2002, fiscal performance was better than anticipated: faster than expected economic growth, an increase in cotton exports (leading to an increase of cotton sales tax collection), and a more systematic implementation of the new VAT regime. Assuming that the goodwill of the international community persists, the inflow of additional funds and grants may well continue, significantly relieving pressure on the budget and current account.

Growth of the agricultural sector was 15% in 2002. Cotton production rose by 13.9% in 2002 while the end of a drought pushed up production of wheat, which is rain fed and not irrigated. For the first time in many years, the country produced enough wheat to avoid dependence on foreign aid to supplement domestic production. The economy depends heavily on the enormous Tadaz aluminium smelter which contributes around 70% of export revenues. Light industry, mostly textiles, and cotton processing grew markedly by about 27%. Construction was another major growth area, up 30%, but its 4% share of GDP somewhat limited its impact on overall growth. Domestic demand and economic growth were boosted by worker remittances, estimated at $R 55120 million or about 10% of GDP. It is estimated that up to a million Tajiks, almost 17% of the population, live abroad either permanently or temporarily, and mainly in the Russian Federation. After a trough in 2001, when the signing of several FDI contracts was delayed because of the crisis in Afghanistan, FDI inflows in 2002 picked up, doubling to $21 million. FDI continues to be concentrated in textiles and mining. The health of the banking sector has not improved significantly. Two of the four major banks have effective negative net capital, and two are severely under-provisioned. Only five (out of 14) banks meet the minimum capital requirements. The external sector performed significantly better in 2002 than a year earlier. Exports grew by 11.0% (to $723 million) while imports rose by only 6.0% (to $819 million). Stagnant or even slightly decreasing prices of the major exports (due to slower global demand for aluminium and large global stocks of cotton) are expected to lead to reduce export growth over the next two years. Two opposite pressures will influence import growth. The demand for imported consumer goods will increase, financed in part by remittances, but import growth will be constrained by a slowdown in capital goods imports.

Tajikistan has proven oil reserves of only 12 million barrels. Tajikistan's civil war, coupled with economic contraction and a lack of investment to maintain the oil sector's infrastructure, has resulted in a 73% decline in national oil production. Almost all the country's consumption of petroleum products is imported. In 2001, Tajikistan opened its first refinery which produces gasoline, diesel, kerosene and fuel oil. Uzbekistan supplies more than 70% of Tajikistan's oil demand.

◻ Tanzania

Capital City	Dodoma	*Capital population: 1,734,000 (1995)*
Population ('000)	35,792 *(2002)*	
Urban population (%)	34.14 *(2002)*	
Land area (km²)	88359	
Languages	Kiswahili, English	
Religion	Muslim (35%); Christian (32%); Roman Catholic (22%)	
Currency	Tanzanian shilling (TZS)	
Head of State	President Benjamin Mkapa (1996)	
Head of Government	Frederick Sumaye (1996)	
Ruling Party	The government is formed by the Revolutionary Party of Tanzania (CCM).	

Main Urban Areas	**Population**
Dodoma (capital)	1,734,000 (1995)

Tanzania is located on the central east African coast bordering the Indian Ocean, and comprises the mainland territory of Tanganyika and the islands of Zanzibar and Pemba. Tanganyika is bounded in the north by Uganda and Kenya, in the west by Rwanda, Burundi and the Democratic Republic of the Congo (formerly Zaire), and in the south by Zambia, Malawi and Mozambique. The capital is Dodoma.

The Republic of Tanzania is an independent member of the Commonwealth, whose executive president is elected for a maximum of two five-year terms by popular vote. Legislative authority is vested in a unicameral National Assembly, which serves for a five-year term. The 274-member Assembly includes 232 directly elected with 37 seats allocated to women nominated by the president and five seats are allocated to members of the Zanzibar House of Representatives. Zanzibar has its own House of Representatives of 59 members, which legislates on internal matters. Until 1992 the CCM was the only legal political party.

Elections to the National Assembly were held in October 2000. The Revolutionary Party of Tanzania (CCM) won 244 seats. The remaining seats are scattered among several parties. Presidential elections were held in October 2000. Benjamin Mkapa was declared the winner with 71% of the vote.

Tanzania's GDP rose by 6.3% in 2002 and should increase by another 5.5% in 2003. In 2004, growth of 6.3% is forecast. Inflation was 4.6% in 2002 and should be 5.3% in 2003. The forecast for 2004 calls for inflation of 5%. Tanzania's fiscal policy is intended to control the growth of the budget deficit and reduce the incidence of waste and abuse in the public sector. These goals have been achieved by strict adherence to a cash budgeting system and large inflows of external assistance, without which Tanzania would have suffered large budget deficits. At the same time, several laws were enacted in 2002 to improve supervision, control, and auditing of public funds and the acquisition of goods and services by the government. The revenue measures put in place so far yielded some dividend as the tax/GDP ratio rose to an estimated 11.1% in 2002 from 10.7% the previous year. The government also made headway in its policy of directing expenditure towards priority social services for poverty alleviation. This was achieved at the expense of capital spending, which fell to 3.2% of GDP in 2002 from 3.5% the year earlier. The recent downward trend of inflation has been helped by a tight monetary policy, improvements in domestic food production and the large food imports that relieved the food situation. The country's present phase of privatisation is focused on relatively big enterprises in the telecommunication, transport, energy and mineral, water and finance sectors. By the end of 2002, the government had divested itself of 260 out of the total 395 enterprises that formed the core of the programme. The country's low levels of saving are the main drag on growth but dilapidated infrastructure (poor roads, costly electricity and inadequate water) also push up the costs of doing business. Other problems include a bloated bureaucracy and a culture that thrives on petty corruption. Tanzania remains one of the world's poorest countries.

Agriculture is the backbone of the economy, accounting for 45% of GDP and providing a livelihood for 85% of the population. Farming is subject to frequent droughts and flooding but the country has huge fertile zones which are still untouched and could be a major food producer if its farming system can be better organised. The mainland's leading exports include: coconuts, coffee, tea, cotton and groundnuts, while Zanzibar is a worldwide supplier of spices. Among the cash crops, the output of coffee, tea, lint cotton and cashew increased in 2002 while tobacco output decreased on account of declining tobacco prices and poor crop husbandry. Most food crops recorded significant increases on the 2001 levels. Nonetheless, Tanzania faced a difficult food situation. The Food and Agricultural Organisation reported that in the latest marketing season the country ran a cereal deficit of around 840,000 tonnes, necessitating the import of about 600,000 tonnes of cereal and about 150,000 tonnes of food aid. The industrial sector accounts for about 11% of GDP and has been growing thanks to higher electricity generation as a result of good rains experienced in areas where hydroelectricity is generated. Production increases were reported in industries such as sheet iron, paint and cement. Total consumption is on the rise, with increases in both private and public consumption. The resurgence of total consumption in GDP emphasises Tanzania's dependence on foreign savings for investment. The outlook for the composition of demand is further increases in consumption (public and private) that will lead to decline in gross investment. Tanzania is rich in mineral deposits, including gold and diamonds. Investors from Australia, Canada and South Africa are all putting money into the mining sector. Spending on exploration is beginning to fall but investment in mining has risen substantially since 1998. The country has huge potential for tourism, with bigger herds of wildlife in better game parks than its neighbour, Kenya. The government aims to increase the total number of visitors to more than half a million in the next few years.

Tanzania relies exclusively on imports for its oil needs. Although foreign oil prospectors have spent millions in search of oil in Tanzania without success since 1981, the government continues to encourage oil exploration. Experts have long suspected that there are considerable hydrocarbon reserves off Tanzania's coast. Tanzania plans to develop two offshore gas fields to provide fuel for power generation. Gas from these fields will be transported to Dar es Salaam by a 160-mile (250-km) pipeline, where it will be used to generate electricity. The pipeline could be extended to the Kenyan port city of Mombasa to supply gas for industrial usage and power generation.

Thailand

Capital City	Bangkok	Capital population: 6,617,137 (2002)
Population ('000)	62,253 (2002)	
Urban population (%)	22.31 (2002)	
Land area (km²)	51089	
Languages	Thai	
Religion	Buddhism (95%); Muslim (4%)	
Currency	Baht (Bt)	
Head of State	HM King Bhumibol Adulyadej (1946)	
Head of Government	Thaksin Shinawatra (2001)	
Ruling Party	The government is formed by a three-party coalition led by the Thai Love Thai Party (TRT).	

Main Urban Areas	Population	
Bangkok (capital)	6,617,137	(2002)
Samut Prakan	390,521	(2002)
Nonthaburi	300,046	(2002)
Udon Thani	244,459	(2002)
Nakhon Ratchasima	204,418	(2002)
Hat Yai	201,648	(2002)
Chon Buri	184,947	(2002)
Phra Pradaeng	169,463	(2002)
Chiag Mai	166,821	(2002)
Lampang	150,970	(2002)

Thailand, although the largest state in the Indo-Chinese peninsula, has access to the sea only in the far south. With Myanmar accounting for almost all of its shoreline with the Bay of Bengal, its access to that sea is limited to a long but narrow (150-km wide) isthmus to the south which eventually links up with Malaysia. Its more extensive coastline is on the Gulf of Thailand, where it borders Cambodia in the east. In the north-east it shares a border with Laos. The capital is Bangkok.

The National Assembly has two chambers. The House of Representatives has 438 members, elected for a four-year term, 100 members by proportional representation and 338 members in multi-seat constituencies. The Senate has 200 members elected in single-seat constituencies. Only non-partisans are allowed to run for office.

General elections to the House of Representatives were held in January 2001. The TRT won 248 seats and the Democratic Party took 128 seats. The remainder were scattered among several minor parties. The TLT appointed Thaksin Shinawatra as prime minister. The Election Commission disqualified some victors on grounds of vote fraud. Elections to the Senate were last held in July 2000. The Election Commission disqualified a number of victors on grounds of vote fraud.

Real GDP rose by 5.3% in 2002 and an increase of 5% is expected in 2003. Growth in 2004 is forecast to be 5.1%. Prices rose by only 0.6% in 2002 and are expected to increase by 1.4% in 2003. Inflation is forecast to be 0.1% in 2004. Unemployment continued to trend downward, falling to a five-year low of 1.4% in December 2002. At these levels, unemployment is no longer a major policy issue for the government, though poverty is. Based on consumption of $2 per day, the World Bank estimates that poverty rose significantly from 28.2% in 1996 to 35.6% in 2000, but that its incidence declined slightly to 32.5% in 2002. A substantial package of farm, village, and small enterprise-oriented programmes designed to expand productive opportunities for low-income groups has been introduced. In addition, a low-cost universal health scheme has been brought in to cover the uninsured. External debt totalled $59.3 billion at end-2002, down from $67.5 billion at end-2001. Investment spending is expected to slow down a little but remain strong in the future, having shot up in 2002 from a relatively low base. The budget deficit is forecast to continue narrowing, especially in 2004, in line with buoyant tax collections driven by strong growth and a possible increase in VAT. Government spending is expected to remain relatively stable over the next two years. With private consumption spending remaining healthy, the need for fiscal pump priming will abate. The main risk for Thailand's economic prospects is the possibility of a rise in oil prices. As a major net importer, the country would be one of the hardest hit in Asia.

The main contributor to growth in 2002 was the manufacturing sector, which expanded by 7.7% in 2002. While output of iron and steel products and cement was boosted by greater domestic construction activity, production of electronic goods and electrical appliances rose in line with the measured upturn in the global electronics cycle. The agriculture sector did not contribute to overall economic expansion, with zero growth in 2002 compared with 3.3% in 2001. A major underlying factor was a 4.8% drop in fisheries output. Major crops continued to perform well, however, despite somewhat erratic weather conditions - droughts in the first half of the year and floods in the second. The services sector grew by 4.1% in 2002. This sector is dominated by tourism, which accounts for almost 5% of GDP. The tourism industry has recovered from the sharp drop-off due to terrorist attacks in Bali and Jakarta and fears of SARS. Tourist arrivals improved by 7.3% in 2002, with a significant rise in the number of tourists from nearby countries, such as Korea and Malaysia. Private consumption spending is expected to remain strong in 2004. The sharp pickup in consumer spending has been a major factor underlying the return to growth and this is likely to continue. The low interest rate environment will probably continue to stimulate private consumption spending. Higher consumer confidence, resulting from falling unemployment and rising farm and non-farm incomes, is also likely to boost consumption expenditures.

Thailand has just over 500 million barrels of proven oil reserves. The country produces about 175,000 barrels per day (bbl/d) of oil. Consumption has fallen slightly because the government has been raising taxes on petroleum products to promote conservation and reduce oil imports. There have been a number of significant recent oil discoveries, most notably offshore in the Gulf of Thailand. Thailand also has four oil refineries, with a combined capacity of more than 681,000 bbl/d. In response to low refining margins, Thai refiners have been trying to reduce operating costs. Thailand contains about 12.7 trillion cubic feet of proven natural gas reserves. Much of the country's natural gas is used for generating electricity, and Thailand completed its programme for the conversion of almost all oil-fired electric power plants to natural gas in 2001.

Togo

Capital City	Lomé	Capital population: 590,000 (1992)
Population ('000)	5,017 (2002)	
Urban population (%)	34.25 (2002)	
Land area (km²)	5439	
Languages	French	
Religion	Traditional (50%); Christian (35%); Muslim (15%)	
Currency	CFA franc (CFAF)	
Head of State	President Gnassingbe Eyadema (1967)	
Head of Government	Koffi Sama (2002)	
Ruling Party	The Rally of the Togolese People (RPT)	

Main Urban Areas	Population	
Lomé (capital)	590,000	(1992)

Togo is a narrow strip of land stretching north from the Atlantic coast of West Africa. It meets the Gulf of Guinea between Ghana in the west and Benin in the east. With a tropical climate, but with lower elevation than either Benin or Burkina Faso, the country has substantial agricultural capabilities. The capital is Lomé.

Although Togo has a non-executive president, he has retained significant power during periods of unrest. The president is elected by popular vote and serves a five-year term. The National Assembly has 81 members, elected for five-year terms in single-seat constituencies.

Parliamentary elections were held in October 2002, when the RPT gained 72 of the 81 seats. The main opposition parties boycotted the elections. Presidential elections took place in June 2003. Eyadema, Africa's longest-serving ruler, was once again returned to office in a poll that was deemed fraudulent by opponents and foreign observers alike.

Growth was 2.9% in 2002, while inflation was 3.1%. In 2003, growth of 3.5% is anticipated with inflation of 4.3%. Forecasts for 2004 call for growth of 4.4% and inflation of 3.1%. The Togolese economy has suffered from various economic and political shocks in recent years, exacerbated by the suspension of external assistance. In addition, the relaxation of fiscal discipline resulted in an accumulation of domestic and external arrears. Delays in implementing structural reforms further weakened the financial situation of the public enterprises and the banking sector. The overall deficit has continued to increase and reached the equivalent of 5.8% of GDP in 2001.

Agriculture is the dominant sector in Togo, accounting for more than 40% of GDP and employing 60% of the workforce. The majority of the population depend on the cultivation of subsistence crops such as cassava, manioc and vegetables. Palm kernels, cocoa and copra are the main exports. A decline in the prices paid to cotton farmers and delays in payments by the state-run marketing monopoly for cotton has seriously hampered production in recent years. Moreover, the continued deterioration of the Togolese phosphate company's financial situation has also resulted in a sharp decline in phosphate production. Manufacturing activity is constrained by weak domestic demand and low levels of capacity utilisation, while growth in the services sector is modest. Progress in the implementation of the privatisation programme has been mixed. The authorities recently took steps to accelerate the privatisation of the banking sector, and progress has been made in the reform of the telecommunications and postal services. However, the reform of the remaining key public enterprises has been slow.

Togo has limited domestic fuel resources, apart from firewood, and is forced to import nearly all of its requirements from abroad. Electricity generation is of a low order and there is little exploitation of the country's hydroelectric potential.

Tonga

Capital City	Nuku'alofa	Capital population: 28,500 (1992)
Population ('000)	99 *(2002)*	
Urban population (%)	39.14 *(2002)*	
Land area (km²)	72	
Languages	Tongan, English	
Currency	Pa'anga (TOP)	
Head of State	HM King Taufa'ahau Tupou IV (1961)	
Head of Government	Prince Lavaka Ata Ulukalala (2000)	
Ruling Party	There are no official political parties in Tonga at present, although unofficial groupings exist.	

Main Urban Areas	Population
Nuku'alofa (capital)	28,500 (1992)

Tonga lies in the south-east of the important South Pacific Group which also includes Vanuatu, Fiji and the Solomon Islands. Its nearest major neighbour is New Zealand, more than 1,500km to the south. The capital is Nuku'alofa.

The Kingdom of Tonga is a constitutional monarchy and an independent member of the Commonwealth. The King, who exercises full executive powers, is assisted by a 10-member Privy Council, or cabinet. Legislative powers are held by a 30-member unicameral Legislative Assembly. Apart from the King, the Privy Council and nine hereditary nobles, the Assembly includes nine members elected by universal adult suffrage. The issue of constitutional reform sharply divides members of the Assembly.

Elections to the nine available seats in the National Assembly were held in March 2002. The nine successful candidates belong to the democratic Human Rights and Democracy Movement.

GDP rose by 1.6% in 2002 and should increase by another 2.5% in 2003. In 2004, a contraction of 0.5% is forecast. Meanwhile, prices rose by 10.4% in 2002 and should increase by 20% in 2003 and 2004. External shocks and competing demands on the budget have exerted extensive pressure on fiscal policy. Over the past two fiscal years, annual budget deficits - estimated at around 1.5% of GDP - reflected primarily increased support to public enterprises and rapid growth in current expenditures, as public wages were adjusted by 20% for cost of living in 2001. The government expects a deficit equivalent to 2.9% of GDP in 2003, which is to be financed entirely with external concessional funds. Expansionary macroeconomic policies have resulted in a marked decline in net foreign assets and a weaker pa'anga. Officials are under pressure from international agencies to restore macroeconomic stability. Analysts want the government to eliminate some exemptions on import duties for personal and household goods and petroleum products, broaden the sales tax base and increase the rate of the tax, and reduce current expenditures, particularly the public wage bill. Net private transfers from Tongans living abroad continue to be the major source of foreign exchange, at about four times the value of exports. If the high level of remittances recorded in 2002 does not continue, the economy could easily slump, jeopardising efforts to improve the fiscal and external positions and placing further pressure on the currency.

Conditions in agriculture improved owing to record-high prices for squash and vanilla. Construction rebounded sharply with the assistance provided by the international community to rebuild structures destroyed by Cyclone Waka. Tourism and the service sector have been sluggish during most of the past two years, partly owing to the unwinding of the stimulus from the new millennium celebrations and the impact of September 11 events, but tourism has been recovering markedly in recent months. The most promising industry in the country is tuna fishing, primarily for export. Tourism could also perform well in the next few years as Tonga has the potential to benefit from the diversion of tourists from other locations in the Asia-Pacific region perceived to suffer from greater public security risks.

All of Tonga's fuel requirements, except for fuel wood, have to be imported at present.

Trinidad and Tobago

Capital City	Port-of-Spain	Capital population: 60,450 (1992)
Population ('000)	1,319 *(2002)*	
Urban population (%)	74.61 *(2002)*	
Land area (km²)	513	
Languages	English (official); French, Spanish, Hindi and Chinese are also spoken	
Religion	Roman Catholic (34%); Hindu (25%); Anglican (15%); Islam (6%)	
Currency	Trinidad and Tobago dollar (TT$)	
Head of State	Linda Baboolal (2002, acting president)	
Head of Government	Patrick Manning (2002)	
Ruling Party	The People's National Movement (PNM) leads the government.	

Main Urban Areas	Population
Port-of-Spain (capital)	60,450 (1992)

Trinidad is the most southerly island in the West Indies group, and lies just off the northern coast of Venezuela. Tobago, 32km northeast of Trinidad, is the more popular area for tourism, but there are also numerous small islands. The climate is warm, with a dry spring and a wet and often stormy autumn. The capital is Port-of-Spain.

The Republic of Trinidad and Tobago is an independent member of the Commonwealth. The executive president is elected by parliament for a term of five years. Legislative power rests with the bicameral parliament, which consists of a 31-member Senate and a 36-member House of Representatives. The House is elected by universal suffrage for five years while the Senate is appointed - 16 members by the prime minister, six by the leader of the opposition and nine by the president. Tobago, the smaller of the two islands, has been independent from the UK since 1987 and has its own 12-member House of Assembly with some autonomous powers. In Tobago, politics run to quite a different agenda from those of Trinidad and the political complexion is very different.

Elections to the House of Representatives were held in October 2002. The PNM, which is mainly black and has nearly always ruled, took 20 of the 36 seats. The Indian-based United National Congress won the remaining seats.

The economy grew by 2.7% in 2002 and growth of 3.8% is anticipated in 2003. In 2004, growth of 4% is forecast. Prices rose by 4.2% in 2002 and are expected to increase by 3.5% in 2003. Prices are forecast to rise by 2.8% in 2004. Once an economy of "boom and bust" depending on the fortunes of oil, Trinidad and Tobago has entered a period of more stable growth as it shifts towards the utilisation of its expanding gas reserves. The country's per capita income is one of the highest in the Caribbean. Unemployment remains high, running at about 13%. In 2002, the government implemented a series of measures to make the tax system more efficient and increased the number of tax exemptions. As a result, the fiscal surplus in 2001 became deficit, estimated at 1% of GDP. Since 1995, Trinidad and Tobago has received foreign direct investment of more than US$5.6 billion and these inflows are expected to accelerate over the next few years. A series of steps to promote exports including the liberalisation of the trade and the foreign exchange market have been introduced with modest success.

Agriculture accounts for just 2% of GDP and 10% of the work force. Farming is important, however, with sugar, citrus fruits and copra being grown for export, while rice, coconuts, yams and bananas are produced for the domestic market. The non-oil sector now contributes 75% of GDP. Output of the petroleum sector (which consists of exploration and extraction of gas and oil, refining, petrochemical production and asphalt production) is slowly rising although oil production, itself, is falling. Oil revenues alone account for over a quarter of GDP and 77% of foreign exchange. The country's move from oil to liquid natural gas has spawned a growing petrochemical industry to make use of this resource. Most manufacturers cater for local consumer needs, including textiles, food products, textiles and clothing. Tourism is a growing sector, although not proportionately as important as in many other Caribbean islands.

Trinidad and Tobago is the largest producer of oil and gas in the Caribbean, with oil production averaging about 140,000 barrels per day. Oil production, however, is slowly declining. Crude oil reserves, at an estimated 716 million barrels, are expected to last only another decade. Natural gas reserves are estimated to be 23.5 trillion cubic feet and are expected to last for about 60 years. Both natural gas and oil exploration activities in Trinidad and Tobago have continued at a fast pace and several small new discoveries were announced in 2002. New discoveries of natural gas are eventually expected to push reserves up by another 100 trillion cu ft. Already, Trinidad and Tobago has become one of the major natural gas development centres in the world. Gas is expected to surpass oil as the main revenue earner for the country in the near future.

▫ Tunisia

Capital City	Tunis	*Capital population: 698,800 (2002)*
Population ('000)	9,689 *(2002)*	
Urban population (%)	66.55 *(2002)*	
Land area (km²)	15536	
Languages	Arabi,C French	
Religion	Muslim	
Currency	Tunisian dinar (TND)	
Head of State	President Gen. Zine el-Abidine Ben-Ali (1987)	
Head of Government	Mohamed Ghannouchi (1999)	
Ruling Party	Rassemblement Constitutionnel Democratique (RCD)	

Main Urban Areas	Population	
Tunis (capital)	698,800	(2002)
Safaqis	268,478	(2002)
Ariana	208,755	(2002)
At-Tadaman Dawwar Hisar	184,833	(2002)
Susah	152,368	(2002)
Kairouan	117,084	(2002)
Binzart	112,504	(2002)
Gabes	109,065	(2002)
Gafsa	80,077	(2002)
Halq el Oued	78,398	(2002)

Tunisia, one of the smaller but more influential states in North Africa, lies on the Mediterranean coast with Algeria to its west and Libya to the east. Equally important, however, is its proximity to Italy (a sea voyage of only 200km from Tunis to Sicily) or to France, the governing power until 1956. The country's fertile northern soil enjoys adequate irrigation from numerous rivers; in the south, however, it gives way to desert terrain. The capital is Tunis.

The Republic of Tunisia became independent from France in 1957 and was ruled until 1981 as a one-party state by the Parti Socialiste Destour. Now known as the Rassemblement Constitutionnel Democratique, the party still rules the country with little opposition. The executive president is elected for a maximum of three five-year terms by universal suffrage, although in practice he has always stood unopposed. The Chamber of Deputies has 182 members, elected for a five-year term in single-seat constituencies. 34 seats are guaranteed to the opposition. In April 2002, Tunisia's parliament passed a new constitution that will allow Ben Ali to stand for a fourth five-year term in 2004.

Presidential elections were held in 1999, when Gen. Ben-Ali was re-elected with 99% of the vote. Elections to the National Assembly took place at the same time. The RCD received 92% of the votes and controls parliament as well as municipalities. The six legal opposition parties are virtually weightless compared with Ben Ali's RCD.

Tunisia's economy grew by 1.7% in 2002 and is expected to grow by 5.5% in 2003. The forecast for 2004 is for growth of 5.8%. Prices rose by 2.7% in 2002 and rises of 2.5% is expected in 2003 and 2004. The improved economic outlook for 2003 and 2004 can be attributed to economic reforms implemented over the last ten years. The external current account deficit was reduced to around 3.8% of GDP in 2002, down from 4.3% in the previous year. Despite a decline in revenues due to the economic slowdown and a decrease in imports, significant expenditure cuts, particularly in capital expenditures, and higher non-tax revenues have limited the budget deficit. The draft budget for 2003 provides for a further reduction in the deficit (excluding privatisation revenues and grants) and goes further in the direction of fiscal consolidation. Structural reforms have been proceeding at a cautious but steady pace. Though per capita income is only US$2,000, Tunisia does not face the serious income inequalities that exist in other North African countries. The country's unemployment rate remains at high levels (officially 15%, but unofficially much higher).

Agriculture accounts for around 13% of GDP. The bulk of the country's population depends on farming, which takes place mainly along the northern coasts and valleys. Cereals such as wheat and barley, and olives, vines and citrus fruits produce heavy exportable crops. Further inland, farming is limited to cattle herding. Agricultural activity fell significantly in 2002 as a result of a drought but this was offset by higher levels of economic activity in other parts of the economy. Industry contributes almost a third of GDP. The IMF is pushing Tunisia to accelerate programmes of economic reform in the industrial sector. Emphasis is given to privatisation, liberalisation of trade and diversification. Privatisation is moving ahead slowly, despite both international pressure and the president's call for an acceleration of the process. The country's tourism sector has suffered since the September 2001 terrorist attacks in the United States, as well as the April 2002 bombing of an ancient synagogue on the island of Djerba. Tunisia began reducing tariffs against EU manufactured goods in 1996, but overall trade protection remains high and significant restructuring is still needed to meet the challenges of free trade with the EU.

During 2002, Tunisia produced around 78,000 barrels per day (bbl/d) of oil. This represents a 32% decline from the country's peak oil output, of 114,000 bbl/d, in 1992. Meanwhile, domestic petroleum demand is increasing rapidly, and Tunisia became a net oil importer in 2000 for the first time in over 20 years. Because Tunisia's refining capacity is low, the country exports crude oil and imports refined products. Currently, Tunisia has over 300 million barrels in proven oil reserves, and few new discoveries have been made in recent years. The government is seeking to encourage exploration, especially in the northern part of the country, the northern coast, and the Gulf of Hammamet. Tunisia also has 2.8 trillion cubic feet of proven natural gas reserves, with around two-thirds located offshore.

▫ Turkmenistan

Capital City	Ashgabad	*Capital population: 646,400 (2002)*
Population ('000)	4,610 *(2002)*	
Urban population (%)	45.14 *(2002)*	
Land area (km²)	46993	
Languages	Turkmen	
Religion	Mainly Islam	
Currency	Turkmenistani Manats (TMM)	
Head of State	President Saparmurat Niyazov (October 1990)	
Head of Government	Saparmurat Niyazov	
Ruling Party	Democratic Party of Turkmenistan (DPT)	

Main Urban Areas	Population	
Ashgabad (capital)	646,400	(2002)
Chärjew	211,000	(2002)
Dashhowuz	178,800	(2002)
Nebidag	145,200	(2002)
Mary	143,000	(2002)
Turkenbashi	77,000	(2002)
Bayramaly	63,000	(2002)
Tedjen	57,000	(2002)
Gyzylarbat	54,600	(2002)
Buzmeyin	38,200	(2002)

Turkmenistan is located in the far south of the former Soviet empire, bordering Iran and Afghanistan in the south and the Caspian Sea in the west, with Uzbekistan and Kazakhstan to the north. The terrain is dominated by the Kara-Kum desert, and the climate is accordingly arid for most of the year. The capital is Ashgabad.

Turkmenistan declared its independence from the Soviet Union in October 1991. Despite the country's strong economic performance in recent years (due mainly to greater exports of oil and natural gas), it is still ruled by the Communist Party, albeit under the new name of the Democratic Party of Turkmenistan. The 1991 Constitution allows for an executive president, who is the Chairman of the Supreme Soviet, and who was first elected by that body, although he was subsequently confirmed by popular vote. In a subsequent referendum, he was named president for life. In practice, the country is a one-party state. Turkmenistan has two parliamentary chambers. The Majlis (Assembly) has 50 members, elected for a five-year term in single-seat constituencies. The People's Council has as members the 50 members of the Majlis, 50 directly elected members and additional executive and judicial officials.

In accordance with the wishes of President Niyazov, a referendum held in 1994 approved the decision to abolish the 1997 elections. Ominously, the official reports of the poll declared that 99% of the electorate voted in favour. The last elections to the Majlis were held in December 1999. The DPT was the only allowed party and won all seats.

Turkmenistan is believed to be one of the poorest countries in all of central and east Europe. GDP grew by 6% in 2002, with a forecast of 4.8% for 2003. Inflation continues to be a problem with prices rising by 15% in 2002. The 2002 state budget was essentially balanced. However, this is difficult to assess because of large off-budget accounts including the foreign exchange reserve fund that is managed by the President's Office. Non-budget funds managed by various ministries and government agencies received about TMM40.5 trillion, or more than three times the budget revenues. The trade surplus almost doubled to $1 billion from $535 million in 2001 with the $465 million improvement about equally due to the export gain and the import decline. The decline in imports is worrisome as it reflects, perhaps, Turkmenistan's growing disengagement from global trade and investment flows and a slowdown in industrial expansion and diversification. The most deleterious aspect of macroeconomic policy regime is the more than 300% spread between official and market exchange rates, which effectively translates into a regime of arbitrarily determined multiple exchange rates. This is a severe impediment for private sector growth and inhibits FDI. Unemployment and social stress may well increase in the next few years unless a more active policy is pursued both to stimulate private sector-led growth and to diversify exports. Reconstruction of Afghanistan and trade expansion with neighbouring Iran could provide new sources of external demand for Turkmenistan's hydrocarbon, energy, textiles, and light industry exports. There are reports also of new, larger contracts under negotiation for natural gas exports with Russia and Iran that will help improve utilisation of existing production capacities. Domestic demand is unlikely to show significant improvement in a policy regime characterised by strict price controls, a pervasive industrial licensing system, and tight control of banking and foreign transactions. As part of the diversification strategy, some public sector investment and foreign exchange earnings have been used for establishing textile and garment manufacturing plants, often in collaboration with Turkish partners. These joint ventures are now exporting to the US and Europe.

Performance in the agriculture sector, which provides a livelihood for over half of the population, was boosted by expansion of wheat and rice output bringing grain production up by 15% for the year to meet its official target. However, there was an extremely poor cotton harvest which declined to a mere 0.5 tons from 1.1

million tons in 2001, and against an official target of 2.0 million tons for the year. There was a further increase in the export and oil products and an increase in the output of food processing and light industry. Despite these reported gains, there are hardly any signs of greater private sector activity, except for the continuing boom in construction of luxury housing in Ashgabat. The officially estimated shares in GDP for 2001 are about 35% for industry, 25% for agriculture, 32% for services, and 6% for construction. The natural gas subsector is estimated to account for nearly three quarters of the industry sector value added. The services sector has lagged behind industry and agriculture, as a result of weak development in private financial and retail trade activities. The government's policy of heavily subsidising consumption of basic necessities, combined with an increase in average nominal wages by about 20% during 2002, has ensured maintenance of welfare levels. However, this masks the increasing gap in living standards in urban centres like Ashgabat. The worsening state of education and health facilities in rural areas, which is a result of a decline in their share of budgeted expenditures, is another area of concern reflecting growing welfare disparities. Growth and income prospects in the longer term are being undermined by education policies that have cut the number of years of education to nine and generally caused deterioration in educational facilities and standards. This issue is emerging as a source of discontent.

Turkmenistan has 546 million barrels in proven oil reserves, with possible reserves (mainly in the western part of the country and in undeveloped offshore areas in the Caspian Sea of up to 1.7 billion barrels. The country's oil production, which steadily declined after independence, from 110,000 barrels per day (bbl/d) in 1992 to 81,000 bbl/d in 1995, has increased dramatically in the past six years. Under a 10-year programme, Turkmenistan aims to raise its oil production to nearly one million bbl/d by 2010. Although the country has attempted to ease restrictions on foreign investment, many layers of regulation remain in place. Turkmenistan maintains prohibitive rules that prevent companies using subsurface resources to export hydrocarbons. Since foreign investors do not have access to export pipelines, they are forced to sell the oil and natural gas they produce in Turkmenistan through the state commodities exchange or send it to refineries. Oil and natural gas are sold in Turkmenistan at fixed prices that are well below world market levels. As a result, several projects that could substantially increase Turkmenistan's oil production have stalled.

Tuvalu

Capital City	Funafuti	Capital population: 2,860 (1992)
Population ('000)	13 (2002)	
Urban population (%)	53.83 (2002)	
Land area (km²)	3	
Languages	Tuvaluan, English	
Religion	Protestant (98%)	
Currency	Australian dollar (A$)	
Head of State	HM Queen Elizabeth II	
Head of Government	Saufatu Sopoanga (2002)	
Ruling Party	The government is formed by the non-partisans.	

Main Urban Areas	Population
Funafuti (capital)	2,860 (1992)

Tuvalu is a group of nine coral islands and atolls formerly known as the Ellice Islands and located in the South Pacific to the north of Fiji, south of Kiribati and east of the Solomon Islands. With a total land area of just 25 sq km, and with hardly any of its land reaching more than four metres above sea level, the islands are mainly suitable only for coconut growing. The capital is Funafuti.

Tuvalu, an independent special member of the Commonwealth since 1978, is formally ruled by the British monarch acting through a Governor-General. In practice, all executive power is exercised by a prime minister and cabinet which are elected from the parliament. The parliament of Tuvalu has 13 members, 12 members elected for a four-year term in four double- and four single-seat constituencies and one ex-officio member.

At the last elections in July 2002, only non-partisans were elected.

GDP grew by 3% in 2002 and the same rate is forecast for 2003. Inflation was 1.5% in 2002. Prices are forecast to rise by 2.1% in 2003. The budget for 2003 assumes a significant increase in grants and fishing licence fees, along with a budget deficit of 6.5% of GDP. All tariffs are to be gradually removed by 2016. Import duties are currently around 14% of total non-grant revenues, so that the eventual removal of tariffs will create a need for new revenue sources. Public enterprise reform has been under way since the mid-1990s but there is still a need to develop an effective governance framework to help improve the financial situation. No more operating subsidies will be paid to state-owned enterprises until they have signed operating agreements with the government. In an effort to reduce the disparity between household income in Funafuti and the outer islands, the government is implementing an Island Development Programme. This aims to decentralise administration, improve public service delivery, promote small business development and encourage the sustainable augmentation of financial resources for outer island development.

A sharp cutback in public spending in 2002 led to a slowdown in construction and retailing while agriculture grew only marginally. Special development spending was only A$3.8 million, against an original estimate of about A$11 million. In 2002, a substantial one-off boost to revenues came as a result of the sale of DotTV Corporation for A$20 million, but spending was curtailed in an effort to prevent a replication of the deficit of the preceding year. The combination of expanded revenues and a significant reduction in overall government expenditures led to a

very large budget surplus of around 85% of GDP. Unfortunately, it also slowed economic growth. Foreign trade statistics for Tuvalu are unavailable. However, that the country's non-merchandise account is dominated by seafarers' remittances, estimated at about 20% of GDP a year. Another source income is the Tuvalu Trust Fund (TTF). With recent weakness in world equity markets, the market value of the TTF in 2002 was 10% less than the maintained value. Consequently, there was no distribution of earnings in 2002 and none is expected in 2003. The financial sector is dominated by the government-owned National Bank of Tuvalu, which continued to be highly profitable, reflecting its monopoly position.

Tuvalu has no oil or gas, and apart from firewood all energy requirements are imported.

Uganda

Capital City	Kampala	Capital population: 954,000 (1995)
Population ('000)	24,064 (2002)	
Urban population (%)	14.81 (2002)	
Land area (km²)	19710	
Languages	English, Bantu, Kiswahili	
Religion	Christian (60%); Muslim (5%)	
Currency	New Uganda shilling (UGS)	
Head of State	President Yoweri Museveni (1986)	
Head of Government	Apolo Nsibambi (1999)	
Ruling Party	The government is formed by the National Resistance Movement (NRM), the Democratic Party (DP), Uganda National Rescue Front and Uganda People's Congress (UPC).	

Main Urban Areas	Population
Kampala (capital)	954,000 (1995)

Uganda is a landlocked country in central east Africa, bordered in the east by Kenya, in the south by Rwanda, Tanzania and the shore of Lake Victoria, in the north by Sudan and in the west by the Democratic Republic of the Congo (formerly Zaire). The country has a mountainous terrain with ample rainfall, and has numerous large rivers that converge in the Lake Victoria complex to the south. The capital is Kampala.

Uganda is an independent member of the Commonwealth ruled by an executive president who is assisted by a cabinet. The National Parliament has 292 members, 214 are elected without party-label in single-seat constituencies, while 78 members are elected from special interest groups.

Presidential elections were held in March 2001. Museveni received 69% of the vote and was re-elected. Parliamentary elections were held in June 2001, though only non-partisan candidates were allowed to participate.

Uganda's GDP increased by 6.6% in 2002 with growth of 5.4% expected in 2003. In 2004, growth of 6% is forecast. Prices fell by 0.3% in 2002 and are expected to rise by 5.9% in 2003 and 2004. In comparison with its neighbours, Uganda is an open, deregulated economy, with investor-friendly conditions and a record of fiscal discipline. Inflows of aid and private capital have so far offset a widening gap in the balance of payments current account. However, a large part of its growth is needed just to keep up with a population increase of more than 3% a year. Uganda needs growth of at least 7% a year if it is to reduce the number living in poverty. So far, the country can point to real progress. The proportion of the population living on less than $1 a day has fallen to 35% in 2003 from 56% a decade ago. But to stay on course, more private investment and better use of aid funds will be essential. The government's own revenue collection programme has fallen below expectations, partly because of corruption and fuel smuggling from Kenya to avoid higher Ugandan taxes. The economy depends to a substantial degree on coffee, tea and cotton, the three main export crops and diversification will be necessary.

Agriculture accounts for 42% of GDP and employs as much as 80% of the work force. However, the sector's share in GDP is falling. Farm output is a major earner of foreign exchange, with coffee, tea and cotton being especially important. The main products for the domestic market are plantains, bananas, cassava, sweet potatoes, potatoes, sorghum and maize. Rising coffee production in Vietnam and the impact on world prices of EU and US cotton subsidies have combined to place traditional cash crops at their lowest price levels in years. Manufacturing accounts for just 10% of GDP. Uganda has attracted the bulk of foreign investment in East Africa in recent years and much of this has benefited manufacturers. Capital inflows, however, are concentrated around the country's capital. Tourism and tea production are the only industries located in the countryside that have received significant amounts of foreign investment. To support new industry, the government is finalising plans for an export-processing zone while supporting initiatives aimed at exploiting openings in the US textile market. Tourism has much to offer, though hotels and marketing are primitive. Uganda has numerous mineral deposits. The country's largest single foreign investment is in the development of its cobalt reserves in the Rwenzori foothills. Rehabilitation of copper mines closed in the 1970s is also underway. To further this effort, a new mining code has been put in place. The planned privatisation of electricity distribution and the railways could help ease some of the infrastructure weaknesses that presently constrain expansion.

Although Uganda has no proven oil or gas resources, some exploration is taking place, and there are signs that the western Rift Valley may contain hydrocarbon deposits. The landlocked country is dependent on the importation of all oil products in their refined form. Oil accounts for more than 80% of Uganda's commercial energy needs.

□ United Arab Emirates

Capital City	Abu Dhabi	Capital population: 398,695 (1995)
Population ('000)	3,268 (2002)	
Urban population (%)	86.18 (2002)	
Land area (km²)	8360	
Languages	Arabi,C English	
Religion	Muslim	
Currency	UAE dirham (AED)	
Head of State	Zayd ibn Sultan al Nahayan of Abu Dhabi	
Head of Government	Maktum bin Rachid al Maktum of Dubai	
Ruling Party	There are no legal political parties in the United Arab Emirates.	

Main Urban Areas	Population
Dubai	669,181 (1995)
Abu Dhabi (capital)	398,695 (1995)
Sharjah	320,095 (1995)
Al-Ain	225,970 (1995)
Ajman	114,395 (1995)
Ras-Al-Khaimah	77,550 (1995)
Al-Fujeirah	33,176 (1995)
Umm-Al-Quwain	25,052 (1995)
Khor-Fakkan	22,594 (1995)

The United Arab Emirates (UAE) is a confederation of nominally independent states which form a crescent running along the southern Persian (Arabian) Gulf coast of Saudi Arabia - although its eastern edge also incorporates an access to the Gulf of Oman. With the main land area of Oman to the east, and with the enclave which is the urban capital of Oman lying at its extreme eastern tip (in the Straits of Hormuz), the UAE occupies a position of immense strategic importance. The capital is Abu Dhabi.

The UAE is a federation of seven emirates - Abu Dhabi, Dubai, Sharjah, Ajman, Fujairah, Ras al-Khaimah and Umm al-Qaiwain. Political power is concentrated in Abu Dhabi, which controls the vast majority of the UAE's economic and resource wealth. The two largest emirates - Abu Dhabi and Dubai - provide over 80% of the UAE's income. In 1996, the UAE's Federal National Council approved a permanent constitution. The establishment of Abu Dhabi as the UAE's permanent capital was one of the new framework's main provisions.

There have been no elections to any of the UAE's bodies in recent decades.

With per capita incomes exceeding US$20,000, the standard of living in the United Arab Emirates is one of the highest in the world. GDP grew by just 1.5% in 2002 but growth of 6.3% is expected in 2003. An increase of 3.9% is forecast in 2004. Prices rose by 1.4% in 2002 and are expected to increase by another 2.4% in 2003. The inflation forecast for 2004 is for prices to rise by 1.9%. The anti-terrorist campaign has raised the heat on smuggling and money laundering, lucrative staples of the UAE's free-wheeling economy. Growth in the non-oil sectors of the economy is expected to outpace growth in the oil sector over the next several years, as a result of increasing capital investment and the government's expansionary monetary policy. The UAE also has one of the more diversified economies among the major oil-producing Persian Gulf states. This diversity has helped to cushion the economic impact of the collapse of crude oil prices. Nevertheless, oil and derivative products account for about 75% of the UAE's total exports. Like other Gulf States, the UAE is trying to restrict the employment of foreign workers. As the number of foreigners grows, fears that they may demand more rights increases proportionally.

In recent years, the UAE undertook several projects to diversify its economy and to reduce its dependence on oil and gas revenues. The non-oil sectors of the UAE's economy presently contribute more than two thirds of the UAE's total GDP, and about 30% of its total exports. The federal government has invested heavily in sectors such as aluminium production, tourism, aviation, re-export commerce and telecommunications. As part of its strategy to further expand its tourism industry, the UAE is building new hotels, restaurants and shopping centres, and expanding airports and duty-free zones. In 2002, Dubai announced the construction of the world's largest luxury housing estate to cost over US$3 billion. Dubai has become a central Middle East hub for trade and finance, accounting for about 70% of the Emirates's non-oil trade. However, its flourishing transit trade through its ports has suffered from the general spending caution in the region, plus the steep rises in insurance rates. For its part, Abu Dhabi plans to develop an offshore financial and commodity trade centre on Saadiyat Island, which will include storage facilities, a port, a freight centre and a financial and insurance centre to facilitate trading. Agriculture also makes up only a small portion of the UAE's economy.

The UAE contains proven crude oil reserves of 97.8 billion barrels, or slightly less than 10% of the world total. Abu Dhabi holds 94% of this amount, or about 92.2 billion barrels. Dubai contains an estimated 4 billion barrels, followed by Sharjah and Ras al-Khaimah, with 1.5 billion and 100 million barrels of oil, respectively. Proven oil reserves in Abu Dhabi have doubled in the ten years to 2001, mainly due to significant increases in rates of recovery. Abu Dhabi has continued to identify new finds, especially offshore, and to discover new oil-rich structures in existing fields. Under the UAE's constitution, each emirate controls its own oil production and resource development. The UAE's total production capacity is 2.60 million barrels per day, making it second only to Saudi Arabia in excess production capacity among OPEC member states. Several projects to upgrade infrastructure at existing oilfields are planned or underway. These projects are part of an overall goal of raising the UAE's production capacity to three million barrels per day within the next four years. The UAE's natural gas reserves of 212 trillion cu ft are the world's fifth largest after Russia, Iran, Qatar and Saudi Arabia.

Over the last decade, natural gas consumption in Abu Dhabi has doubled, and is projected to reach four billion cu ft per day by 2005. The development of natural gas fields also results in increased production and exports of condensates, which are not subject to OPEC quotas.

□ Uruguay

Capital City	Montevideo	Capital population: 1,303,182 (1996)
Population ('000)	3,302 (2002)	
Urban population (%)	91.64 (2002)	
Land area (km²)	17502	
Languages	Spanish	
Religion	Mainly Roman Catholic (77%)	
Currency	New Uruguayan peso (Uy$)	
Head of State	President Jorge Luis Batlle Ibáñez (2000)	
Head of Government	President Jorge Luis Batlle Ibáñez (2000)	
Ruling Party	Colorado Party leads a coalition with the National (Blanco) Party.	

Main Urban Areas	Population
Montevideo (capital)	1,303,182 (1996)

Uruguay, the smallest republic in South America, lies on the central Atlantic coast between Argentina in the south and west, and Brazil in the north. With an equable climate and with generally adequate rainfall despite occasional droughts, the area consists largely of grassy plains with lush forests in some parts. The capital is Montevideo.

Uruguay has an executive president who is elected every five years, together with a 99-member House of Deputies and a 31-member Senate. The political system was effectively suspended from 1973, when a military dictatorship took over the country, until 1985, when civilian rule was restored.

Presidential elections took place in November 1999 when Ibáñez won office with 54% of the vote. Elections to the House and Senate occurred in October 1999. The Christian-Democratic Party received 39% of the vote earning them 40 seats in the House and 12 in the Senate. The Colorado Party got 31% of the vote giving them 31 seats in the House and ten in the Senate. The National Party received 21% of the vote which accorded them 22 seats in the House and seven in the Senate.

Uruguay's economy contracted by a huge 10.8% in 2002 and a further contraction of 1% is expected in 2003. In 2004, growth of 4.5% is forecast. Prices rose by 14% in 2002 and are expected to increase by more than 21.6% in 2003. The forecast for 2004 is for inflation of 18.9%. Many analysts thought that a default was inevitable in 2002 and the IMF did not provide a loan until August of that year. The peso, having lost half its value in the first half of 2002, then stabilised but the damage had been done. Unemployment climbed to 20% and the burden of public debt (all of which is in dollars) has doubled. To avoid default, the government had to impose harsh fiscal restraints. The state pays the wages or pensions of a million people, accounting for 62% of government spending. By law, civil servants can not be sacked, so the eventual adjustment had to come through higher inflation. In real terms, average wages fell by 11% in 2002. In 2003, the government will aim for a fiscal surplus (before interest payments) of around 3.3% of GDP. Eventually, it may be forced to seek a "voluntary" restructuring of some of its debt. Technically, that would amount to a default but there is a chance the financial community may not regard it as such and Uruguay would not be unduly penalised.

Agriculture's share in GDP amounts to just 8% and has been falling in recent years. Farms, however, are very productive. The sector's main products include wheat, rice, corn, sorghum; and livestock. Cattle herding is the main farming activity and the biggest single source of foreign exchange. Uruguay's merchandise exports have fallen sharply, due mainly to the economic problems of its important neighbours. The public sector in Uruguay is unusually large, having avoided the wave of privatisation that swept its neighbours in the 1990s, but the country has begun some reforms. Privatisation activities in recent years have included concessions for cellular telephone networks, a container terminal at the Port of Montevideo, a major private toll road between Montevideo and the resort town of Punta del Este, and a new US$40-million airport for Punta del Este. Many industries face serious problems relating to a continued fall in the peso, a decline in tourism, and an exodus of Argentine funds from Uruguayan banks. Manufacturing, which accounts for almost a fifth of GDP, includes various agro-processing industries such as meat processing, wool and hides, sugar, textiles, wine, footwear and leather apparel. Other industries manufacture industrial components and industrial intermediates such as vehicle tyres, cement, plywood and petroleum products and a range of more sophisticated consumer goods. A $1-billion, 22-mile bridge - the longest of its kind in the world - between Buenos Aires, Argentina, and Colonia, Uruguay, is planned. This would further open up Uruguay as a major trade and transit centre between Argentina and Brazil. Mineral extraction is of little significance in comparison with most other South American economies. Uruguay has iron ore, dolomite, marble and granite.

Uruguay has no fossil fuel resources and only a small amount of hydroelectric power (compared to its neighbours), and thus relies heavily on imports to meet its energy needs. About 57% of total energy consumption comes from imported sources. Uruguay imports 43,000 barrels of oil per day. Seismic studies of Uruguayan waters near the border with Brazil began in 2002 in order to determine hydrocarbon potential in the area. The role of natural gas in Uruguay's energy sector is expected to grow over the next few years. Approximately 850 megawatts (MW) of new gas-fired generating capacity is expected to be installed in Uruguay over the next ten years. Present plants using oil are to be converted to dual use (oil and gas). Natural gas is to come from new pipelines linking gas-rich Argentina to Uruguay, including the $170 million Cruz del Sur ("Southern Cross") line being built to enhance natural gas trade between Argentina, Brazil and Uruguay.

USA

Capital City	Washington, DC	*Capital population: 570,898 (2002)*
Population ('000)	279,054 *(2002)*	
Urban population (%)	77.54 *(2002)*	
Land area (km²)	915896	
Languages	English	
Religion	Mainly Christian	
Currency	US dollar (US$)	
Head of State	President George Bush (2001)	
Head of Government	George Bush (2001)	
Ruling Party	The Republican Party controls the government.	

Main Urban Areas	Population	
New York	7,557,400	(2002)
Los Angeles	4,003,200	(2002)
Chicago	2,658,200	(2002)
Houston	1,865,200	(2002)
Philadelphia	1,471,400	(2002)
Phoenix	1,337,600	(2002)
San Diego	1,317,600	(2002)
San Antonio	1,202,000	(2002)
Dallas	1,157,400	(2002)
Detroit	891,200	(2002)
Washington, DC (capital)	570,898	(2002)

The US is a federation of 50 states which spans the land mass between the Pacific Ocean and the northern Atlantic. As such, it occupies most of the North American continent, extending from the Alaskan enclave in the west to Maine in the extreme northeast. In the north it borders on Canada, and in the south with Mexico. The west and southwest consist mainly of mountain ranges. The capital is Washington, DC.

The US has an executive president, elected for a four-year term of office by universal suffrage, who then selects and directs his own cabinet ("Administration"). The US Congress comprises a 435-member House of Representatives, half of whom are elected every two years, and a 100-member Senate, which serves for six years but a third of which is re-elected every two years. The country has a strong federal structure, and devolves its legal and fiscal system to a considerable extent.

Elections to the House and Senate were held in November 2002. In the House, the Republican Party received 49% of the vote and won 221 seats while the Democrats took 47% of the vote and 212 seats. Two seats went to non-partisans. In the Senate, the Republicans hold 51 seats. In presidential elections held in November 2000, the Republican, George Bush, defeated Al Gore despite the fact that Gore won the popular vote. One Republican later became an independent, giving the Democrats control of the Senate.

GDP grew by just 2.4% in 2002. In 2003, growth of 2.6% is expected while the forecast for 2004 is for growth of 3.9%. Inflation was 1.6% in 2002 and should be 2.1% in 2003 and 1.3% in 2004. Monetary policy is very supportive of the weak economy. Interest rates may fall even further during 2003 as the authorities scramble to avoid deflation. The proposed tax cuts and further increases in expenditure, not least the jump in defence purchases, will widen the federal government deficit sharply. This will have to be reversed in coming years. Unemployment continues to rise and exceeded 6% in mid-2003. Household spending stagnated when energy prices were rising in the run-up to the war in Iraq. Spending should begin to rise once again now that energy prices are falling. Business investment has stabilised following the end of the war in Iraq, while rising military expenditures are providing a boost to demand. Household, business and foreign demand - the latter buoyed by the drop in the dollar - are all expected to strengthen in 2004.

Agriculture accounts for 2% of GDP and is predominately large scale and generally efficient. The US is a major exporter of foodstuffs and processed foods. Nevertheless, the government programme has substantially increased subsidies to the farmers. The move means the US programme of agricultural support is almost as protectionist as the much-criticised Common Agricultural Policy of the EU. The country's manufacturing sector contributes 17% of GDP and leads the way in the information technology revolution. Leading industries include motor vehicles, aerospace, telecommunications, chemicals, electronics and computers. Some traditional manufacturing sectors have showed adaptability and grown strongly by embracing new technology and increasing labour productivity. But others have struggled, relying increasingly on imported components and even finished products. Among the latter are older industries such as steel, textiles, clothing and assembly-based operations. The most important activities in the service sector include real estate, transport, finance, healthcare and business services. In the so-called new economy, which is driven by information and communications technology, it is becoming increasingly difficult to distinguish between services and manufacturing in the traditional sense. The US faces several wide-ranging disputes with the EU. In 2003, the WTO ruled against the US regarding its practice of subsidising exporters. Unless a compromise can be reached, this will allow the EU to impose billions of dollars in penalties.

The US has 22.4 billion barrels of proved oil reserves, the twelfth highest total in the world. Proven oil reserves have declined by around 20% since 1990. During 2002, the US produced around 8.2 million barrels of oil per day (MMBD), of which 5.9 MMBD was crude oil, and the rest natural gas liquids and other liquids. Total oil production in 2002 was down sharply (around 2.4 MMBD, or 23%) from the 10.6 MMBD averaged in 1985. The US is estimated to have consumed an average of about 19.7 MMBD of oil in 2002. Of this, 8.9 MMBD (or 45% of the total) is motor gasoline. Since the mid-1990s, US refinery capacity has increased, from 15.0 MMBD in 1994 to 16.8 MMBD in 2002. As of November 2002, utilisation of operating capacity at refineries reportedly was averaging around 88%-92%. Although financial, environmental, and legal considerations make it unlikely that new refineries will be built, expansion at existing refineries likely will increase total US refining capacity in the long-run.

Uzbekistan

Capital City	Tashkent	*Capital population: 2,288,000 (1995)*
Population ('000)	24,736 *(2002)*	
Urban population (%)	36.97 *(2002)*	
Land area (km²)	41424	
Languages	Uzbek	
Religion	Mainly Islam	
Currency	Uzbekistani Som (UZS)	
Head of State	President Islam Karimov (1990)	
Head of Government	Utkur Sultonov (December 1995)	
Ruling Party	The government is formed by the People's Democratic Party (CDP).	

Main Urban Areas	Population	
Tashkent (capital)	2,288,000	(1995)

Uzbekistan, one of the southernmost of the former Soviet republics, runs southeast in a broad sweep, from the dried-out Aral Sea to the Afghan border in the south and the Tajikistan border in the east. Kazakhstan remains to the north; a further finger of land extends eastward to meet Kyrgyzstan. The land is mostly desert or at best plain, and the climate is warm and mainly dry. The capital is Tashkent.

Uzbekistan, a predominantly Sunni Muslim state, has an executive president who is directly elected by universal suffrage for a term of eight years (recently extended from five years). He answers to a National Assembly with 250 members, elected for a five-year term, 83 members directly and 167 members by the local councils. Most parties are excluded.

Presidential elections took place in January 2000, when Karimov was returned to office with 92% of the vote. Elections to the Supreme Soviet were held in December 1999. The CDP took 48 seats, the Fatherland Progress Party won 20, the Self Sacrifice Party received 34 and the remainder was divided among minor parties.

Uzbekistan is one of the poorest areas of the former Soviet Union with more than 60% of its population living in poverty-ridden rural communities. GDP has been growing in recent years but the pace is slowing. Growth was 3.2% in 2002 and an increase of about 0.3% is expected in 2003. In 2004, growth of 2.5% is forecast. Inflation continues to be high with prices rising by 38.7% in 2002 and an expected 21.9% in 2003. The forecast is for inflation of 20.7% in 2004. A brief flurry of economic reforms in the early 1990s has been followed by a tightening of controls, including the introduction of a multiple exchange rate system. In 2002, the government decided to re-nationalise several companies it had previously sold off but in 2003 it announced it was ready to sell its remaining 25% holding in most privatised companies that were not "strategic". Such stop-and-go measures create serious problems for the business community. FDI fell to $65 million in 2002 - one of the lowest levels of all former communist economies. In 2002, officials also imposed high tariffs on imports, temporarily closed markets and prevented traders from crossing into neighbouring countries. Unemployment is not reported but is thought to be very high and rising. The country's economic prospects have grown consistently dimmer as the government turns away from economic reforms.

Agriculture and industry recorded moderately improved performances in 2002, though expansion in other sectors, mainly services (accounting for about 50% of GDP), slowed markedly to about 1.5% from 14.2% in 2001. Agriculture, which is the largest employer and exporter, saw output rise by 6.1% 2001. Productivity and area increases raised grain production by 38% to 5.3 million tons, exceeding domestic consumption needs. Adverse weather lowered the cotton harvest by 80,000 metric tons to 3.2 million tons, but most of it was of premium quality. Cotton makes up 27% of the country's exports. The country is the world's largest exporter of cotton after the US. In 2003, the government introduced a new system allowing cotton farmers to sell half their production without going through the cumbersome official system for distribution. The industry sector reportedly grew by 8.5%, up from 8.1% growth in 2001, though the data are unclear on what drove it. The transport and communications subsector posted stronger performance, of 6.8% compared with 3.3% in 2001, driven mainly by the operations of Uzbekistan Airways. Retail trade output contracted by 0.5%, against 8.6% growth in 2001, as the impact of intensified trade restrictions on imports disrupted trade. The number of private small and medium scale enterprises continued to rise during the year with most new entrants in the agriculture sector. However, small businesses are reported to pay up to 23% of their gross revenues in taxes. Not surprisingly, many admit to cheating. Regional disparities in incomes are another problem. Per capita incomes in Tashkent were the highest at R 2$40 per month (at the official exchange rate) and the lowest were in Samarkand at just $10 per month. Most government expenditures, 38% of the total, were on welfare and social programmes, while subsidies and investment take up 7% and 20%, respectively, of the total, with most of this going to state-owned industry.

Uzbekistan is estimated to contain 594 million barrels of proven oil reserves, with 171 discovered oil and natural gas fields in the country. The Bukhara-Khiva region contains over 60% of Uzbekistan's known oil fields, including the Kokdumalak field, which accounts for about 70% of the country's oil production. In addition, the Fergana region contains another 20% of the country's oilfields. Oil deposits in other parts of the country are being developed rapidly. In an effort to stem the decline in Uzbekistan's oil production, the Uzbek government is seeking foreign investment in the country's oil sector. Since independence, the Uzbek government has invested over $1.2 billion in modernising the energy sector, but the flow of money has been far slower than in other Central Asian nations due to Uzbekistan's strict currency controls. The government is eager to attract $400 million through production-sharing agreements as well, with over 80 fields on offer. In addition, Uzbekistan is seeking investment to boost production at existing fields. The country also has three refineries, with a total refining capacity of 222,000 barrels per day. Finally, Uzbekistan is the second largest natural gas producer in the Commonwealth of Independent States (after Russia) and one of the top ten natural gas-producing countries in the world. Uzbekistan produces natural gas from 52 fields in the country.

□ Vanuatu

Capital City	Port Vila	Capital population: 20,000 (1992)
Population ('000)	196 (2002)	
Urban population (%)	20.58 (2002)	
Land area (km²)	1219	
Languages	Bislama (pidgin), English, French	
Religion	Mainly Christian	
Currency	Vatu (VUV)	
Head of State	President John Bani (1999)	
Head of Government	Edward Natapei (2001)	
Ruling Party	A coalition led by the Union of Moderate Parties (UMP) leads the government.	

Main Urban Areas	Population
Port Vila (capital)	20,000 (1992)

Vanuatu, which was formerly run as an Anglo-French condominium under the name New Hebrides, consists of about 80 islands in the south-west Pacific located about 1,000km west of Fiji. Most of the islands are uninhabited and many are active volcanoes. The country has a moderate tropical climate, and is occasionally susceptible to cyclones. The capital is Port Vila.

The Republic of Vanuatu is an independent member of the Commonwealth. The executive president is elected for a five-year term by an electoral college, which includes not only the Parliament but also the presidents of the numerous regional councils. These councils enjoy a considerable degree of regional autonomy. The 52 members of the unicameral national Parliament are elected by universal adult suffrage.

Parliamentary elections were held in April 2002. The UMP won 15 seats while the Party of Our Land (socialist) took 14 seats. Other representatives in the Parliament include the Vanuatu National United Party (8 seats), non-partisans and several smaller parties.

GDP declined by 2.8% in 2002 and growth of 1% is anticipated in 2003. In 2004, growth of 2.2% is forecast. Inflation was 2.2% in 2002 and is expected to be 4% in 2003. Prices are forecast to rise by 3.2% in 2004. Vanuatu is characterised by numerous long-standing structural weaknesses that raise costs relative to those of competitors, by fiscal limitations, and by vulnerability to external shocks and political developments. A tight cash situation persisted in 2002 with the government still using a system of monthly warrants to control spending. Revenues were also lower than originally estimated, reflecting the impact of weaker than expected economic growth. However, the impact of improvements in VAT and customs administration was also evident in 2002. Exports grew by 7% in 2002, following a steep fall in 2001; imports rose by 2.9%, following weak growth in 2001. The current account deficit narrowed slightly to 2% of GDP. Tariff revenues constituted 35% of total revenues (including grants) in 2002 and are projected still to be 33% of total revenues in 2005. In 2002, the average implicit tariff was 24%. However, the government has agreed that all tariffs would be gradually removed by 2016. Tourism is expected to pick up over the medium term with the recent completion of two new hotels and ongoing advertising campaigns. A switch in the focus of the tourism market from certain other Asian locations as a result of security concerns, to the South Pacific and the flow-on effects of sporting events in this part of the world, will help support tourism in Vanuatu, but the cost aspect remains a consideration. The government sector is projected to decline in real terms by 5-5.7% in the medium term, contributing to relatively weak overall economic growth but helping secure a more sustainable fiscal position and facilitating longer-term private sector development. The government is aiming to achieve GDP growth of 4.5% over the medium term by encouraging private, including foreign, investment. Accordingly, the Foreign Investment Act was amended to promote investment from overseas. The high level of international reserves and prospects of a rebuilding of export revenues during 2002 mean that a stable exchange rate and a sustainable balance-of-payments position should be achievable over the medium term.

The contraction in 2002 reflected the effects on agriculture and tourism of several major cyclones. The forestry subsector contracted by 34% in 2002. The cocoa subsector was also depressed, though copra production grew by 7.1%, boosted by subsidised prices and, despite the cyclones, generally favourable weather. The construction sector expanded by 5%, stimulated by government expenditures on upgrading the airports on Efate and Santo, while the services sector as a whole contracted by 0.9%, with the hotels and restaurants subsector and government services leading the decline. Total visitors in 2002 were 7.4% lower than a year earlier, attributable to a decline in tourist arrivals due to a combination of greater competition from other destinations in the Pacific and, to a lesser extent, a relatively high real exchange rate. Output of the industrial and service sectors has stagnated, largely because of reduced wholesale and retail trade. Industry accounts for around 13% of GDP and tends to centre on the processing of food products, notably canned or frozen meat, or timber products. All other manufactures are imported. Several privatisations that had been planned for 2002 (including the national airline, the national bank and the country's telecoms facilities) were delayed.

Vanuatu has no indigenous oil, gas or coal resources and will remain dependent for the foreseeable future on imports for its energy requirements.

□ Venezuela

Capital City	Caracas	Capital population: 1,738,026 (2002)
Population ('000)	25,093 (2002)	
Urban population (%)	87.57 (2002)	
Land area (km²)	88205	
Languages	Spanish	
Religion	Mainly Roman Catholic	
Currency	Bolivar (Bs)	
Head of State	President Hugo Chavez (1999)	
Head of Government	Hugo Chavez (1999)	
Ruling Party	The Movimiento Quinta República (MVR) leads a coalition.	

Main Urban Areas	Population
Maracaibo	1,791,522 (2002)
Caracas (capital)	1,738,026 (2002)
Valencia	1,476,414 (2002)
Barquisimeto	929,105 (2002)
Ciudad Guayana	792,532 (2002)
Petare	508,357 (2002)
Maracay	484,651 (2002)
Ciudad Bolivar	361,771 (2002)
Barcelona	350,153 (2002)
Turmero	304,758 (2002)

Venezuela, perhaps the most oil-rich state in South America, lies on the northeast Atlantic and Caribbean coast of the continent, with Brazil to the south, Colombia to the west and Guyana to the east. Much of the south and west of the country comprises the high sierras of the Guiana highlands, and in the northwest the land rises again to the Sierra Nevada. Elsewhere, there are low forested areas, especially along the Orinoco River which winds slowly northeast through the country. The capital is Caracas.

President Chávez has made important changes in the political structure. A 131-member Constituent Assembly rewrote the 1961 constitution, and the new constitution passed overwhelmingly in a December 1999 public referendum. The new constitution increases the presidential term from five years to six and allows the president to run for re-election. National Assembly has 165 members, elected for a five-year term. The country has an extensively devolved political structure, with 20 autonomous states and 72 dependencies.

Hugo Chavez of the MVR was re-elected as president in July 2000, winning a landslide victory and another six years in office. The former coup leader took 59% of the vote, compared to 37% for his main rival. Elections to the National Assembly took place in July 2000. The MVR received 76 seats, the Democratic Action Party won 29, the Movement towards Socialism won 21 seats and the remainder were dispersed among several factions.

Venezuela's troubled economy contracted by 8.9% in 2002 and the IMF predicts another contraction of 16.7% in 2003. The forecast for 2004 is for growth of 7.7%. Prices rose by 22.4% in 2002 and should increase by another 34% in 2003. In 2004, inflation of 40.8% is forecast. The forecasts of private economists are even gloomier. They predict that the economy will shrink by more than 40% in the first quarter of 2003 because of the unprecedented collapse in oil production and the resultant dearth of foreign currency. Private analysts also expect unemployment rate to rise to 25%, up from 18% in 2002. Chávez's policies have prompted massive movements of capital out of the country. In February 2002, the Venezuelan currency band was abandoned. The bolivar was floated, and by mid-year the currency was worth about 20% less than it was before the float. In January 2003, the government - faced with a steep drop in the value of the Bolivar and a sharp fall in international reserves - introduced exchange controls. These are expected to result in a big increase in retail prices. Royalty rates on oil production have been increased from 16.6% to 30% (the global average is a reported 7.1%). FDI flows had been relatively large, but are now dwindling and are not sufficient to compensate for the capital flight that Chávez's policies have produced. Attempts to diversify the economy and reduce its dependence on oil have not been successful.

Agriculture is fragmented and lacking in investment. Half the country's 500,000 farms occupy just 1.6% of the arable land. At the other end of the scale, just 1% of the farms account for over 46% of the land. When elected, Chávez promised a radical land reform. Now, both the landowners and the landless have turned to violence. The resultant disruptions have stopped investment in agriculture and reduced production. The sector produces cotton, coffee, cocoa, rice, sugar, tobacco and bananas both for domestic consumption and for export. Meat production is of an unusually high order. Oil dominates the economy, accounting for more than three quarters of total Venezuelan export revenues, about half of total government revenues and about one third of gross domestic product. Oil sector activity, however, is expected to decline by 69% in the first quarter of 2003. Meanwhile, the non-oil sector is forecast to decline by 33%. Manufacturing includes several heavy, energy-intensive industries such as steel and aluminium. The government has banned privatisation of social security, healthcare and the state oil company, and previously-planned privatisations, for instance, in the electricity sector, have stalled.

Venezuela controls the Western Hemisphere's largest proven oil reserves, 77.7 billion barrels. The general strike, which began in December 2002, reduced average production from 2.9 million barrels per day (bbl/d) to just over 600,000 per day in the first two months of 2003. The strike has been ended but Venezuelan supplies may not approach pre-crisis levels for a number of months, and it is possible that several hundred thousand barrels per day of production capacity will be permanently lost because of the shut-down. Venezuela operates one of the Western Hemisphere's largest refining systems and is one of the world's largest oil refiners. Domestic refinery capacity is about 1.3 million bbl/d, with significant additional holdings in Curaçao, the US and Europe.

◻ Vietnam

Capital City	Hanoi	Capital population: 1,035,288 (2002)
Population ('000)	82,446 (2002)	
Urban population (%)	20.01 (2002)	
Land area (km²)	32549	
Languages	Vietnamese	
Religion	Buddhist	
Currency	New dông (VND)	
Head of State	President Tran Duc Luong (1997)	
Head of Government	Phan Van Khai (1997)	
Ruling Party	Communist Party of Vietnam (CPV)	

Main Urban Areas	Population	
Ho Chi Minh	3,771,693	(2002)
Hai Phong	1,585,063	(2002)
Hanoi (capital)	1,035,288	(2002)
Da Nang	437,752	(2002)
Biên Hoa	335,514	(2002)
Nha Trang	254,420	(2002)
Can Tho	250,895	(2002)
Nam Dinh	249,349	(2002)
Hue	246,725	(2002)
Buon Ma	114,847	(2002)

Vietnam is located on the South China Sea coast of the Indo-Chinese peninsula. The country follows the coast for more than 2,000km from the Chinese border in the north to the far south where it joins Cambodia on the Gulf of Thailand. There is also a western border with Laos. The climate is tropical and extremely humid. The capital is Hanoi.

The influence of the communist party remains dominant despite attempts at economic and political reform. The country has a semi-executive president who has until recently been elected from single-candidate lists, and a 498-member National Assembly which is formally vested with all legislative power. In practice, the CPV controls the armed forces and the judiciary.

At the last elections in May 2002, only a few groups dominated by the Vietnamese Fatherland Front (VFF), a front of the Communist Party of Vietnam, were allowed to participate. Others participants included selected organisations and affiliates, and some non-partisans. In all, 51 seats were won by non-party candidates with the remainder of more than 400 seats going to the VFF. The National Assembly choose Phan Van Khai and Tran Duc Luong to be the country's Prime Minister and President.

GDP grew by 5.8% in 2002 and growth of 6% is anticipated in 2003. In 2004, growth of 7% is forecast. Inflation was 4% in 2002 and prices are expected to rise by 4% again in 2003. In 2004, inflation of 3.5% is forecast. The economy has maintained its relatively high levels of growth despite the global economic slowdown, largely due to the fact that it is less integrated into the world economy and less vulnerable to declines in demand for its exports. Domestic consumption and investment have been the main reasons for the steady growth in aggregate demand. The government is making efforts to further diversify the tax base and improve collections. These efforts include strengthening the nascent VAT system and generating more revenues from income taxes. VAT, which has replaced turnover tax and is levied on imports, rose as a proportion of revenues to 21.9% in 2002 from 18.6% in 2001. Currently, the revenue base for income tax is narrow and tax collections are low. Inflows of foreign direct investment were down by 41% in 2002 over the previous year, to $1.3 billion, but the number of projects approved was higher. Most income tax is produced by a profit tax on firms in the state sector. Vietnam's youthful population distribution continues to add 1.4 million

people to the workforce annually. Thus the workforce is rising by 3.0% a year, despite a population growth rate of about 1.4%. Official unemployment figures show little change year on year, but have limited meaning for a poor, developing, and still largely agricultural country. The high costs of doing business in Vietnam imply the need to introduce greater competition into certain sectors such as telecommunications, power, and shipping (to help reduce costs); ease restrictions on the transfer of technology and accelerate deregulation. It is likely that the trade deficit will widen, to over 3% of GDP in 2003 and to over 5% in 2004. This is grounded in the fact that imports are projected to continue growing more rapidly than exports because of a positive response to further reductions in import tariffs. The fiscal deficit is also expected to be substantially higher at around 5.3% of GDP in 2003.

Higher rice prices coupled with increased output helped the agriculture sector post 3.0% growth for 2002. Strong expansion in the output of high-value seafood products drove up fisheries by 6.0%, but as a result of deforestation and bush fires, the forestry sector remained virtually unchanged. Food prices are expected to continue their recent rise in 2004. Cash crop prices are also likely to increase, except coffee and sugar where world stocks are high. Services sector growth of 6.0% in 2002 was driven by financial services, which gained 7.6%; by wholesale and retail trade; and by real estate, both of which grew by 6.5%. Tourism was another buoyant area, with more than two million tourists visiting Vietnam in 2002 and representing an important source of foreign exchange. There was increased confidence in the business sector, resulting in a surge in registrations of new private businesses. Much new investment is going into manufacturing, notably the labour-intensive textile and garment sector Exports contracted during the first eight months of 2002 but have recorded a brisk recovery since then. Strong increases in exports of garments, footwear, and seafood led the recovery, although the value of agricultural exports also rose, thanks mainly to higher prices for rice. The outstanding debt of the country's state-owned enterprises now totals about $6 billion. It amounts to 40% of total domestic credit, although the share of new loans to this group of companies is down to 25%. Private remittances from Vietnamese overseas amounted to about $2 billion in 2002, and these inflows are emerging as an important source of foreign exchange earnings.

Vietnam has 600 million barrels of proven oil reserves, and further discoveries are likely. Crude oil production averaged 339,000 barrels per day (bbl/d) in 2002, a 5% decline from 357,000 bbl/d in 2001. The country has six operating oil fields. Production grew rapidly in recent years, from only 175,000 bbl/d as recently as 1996. The government has issued around 44 investment licences for oil and gas exploration since the industry was opened to foreign partners in 1998. About 30 companies, including American, European, Korean, and Japanese firms, now operate in offshore Vietnam. However, several foreign companies have withdrawn from their contracts. Reasons include problems with the Vietnamese regulatory framework and disappointment at recovering smaller quantities of oil and gas than anticipated. During 2002, large oil and gas deposits were discovered in two fields. Currently, Vietnam does not have a major refinery, but it is in the process of building its first. The $1.3 refinery, which is located in Quang Ngai province, will have a capacity of about 140,000 bbl/d.

◻ Western Samoa

Capital City	Apia	Capital population: 37,000 (1992)
Population ('000)	183 (2002)	
Urban population (%)	21.7 (2002)	
Land area (km²)	283	
Languages	Samoan, English	
Religion	Mainly Christian	
Currency	Tala (WST)	
Head of State	HH King Susuga Malietoa Tanumafili II (1962)	
Head of Government	Tuilaepa Sailele Malielegaoi (1998)	
Ruling Party	Human Rights Protection Party (HRPP)	

Main Urban Areas	Population	
Apia (capital)	37,000	(1992)

Western Samoa consists of nine islands, of which the two largest are Savai'i and Upolu, lying in the South Pacific north of Tonga and some 2,400km north of New Zealand. The country has a pleasant climate, although it is susceptible to cyclones. The capital is Apia.

Western Samoa, an independent member of the Commonwealth, has a constitutional monarch who may dissolve the 49-member Fono (Parliament) at any time and who appoints the prime minister on the recommendation of the Fono. A system of full universal voting was introduced in December 1990, prior to the country's first fully franchised elections. However, the voting mechanism was changed in 1993 to extend the life of the parliament from three years to five. The head of state is presently appointed for a life term but in the future the occupant will be elected for a five-year term by the parliament.

Legislative elections were last held in March 2001. The HRPP won 23 seats, the Samoan National Development Party won 13 seats and independents captured the remainder.

GDP increased by 1.8% in 2002 and is expected to rise by 3.1% in 2003. In 2004, growth of 3.2% is forecast. Inflation was 8.1% in 2002 and should be 4.2% in 2003. The forecast for 2004 is for inflation of 2.4%. Concerned about overheating in the economy, the government has deferred the implementation of some of its public investments. A small current account deficit of 1.4% of GDP is expected in 2003, with the growth in imports outstripping the continued growth in commodity exports, tourism revenues, and remittances. The overall balance is expected to weaken slightly in 2003, reflecting lower private capital flows with foreign reserves declining slightly to less than 4.5 months cover for import. A number of changes in tariff and tax policy are underway in Western Samoa. They include an increase in the VAT from 10.0% to 12.5%, a reduction in import tariffs on goods from 10.0% to 8.0%, higher excise rates and motor vehicle registration and license fees, and application of the corporate income tax to the commercial fishing sector.

Economic activity picked up in the second half of 2002, when fresh fish exports recovered, remittances strengthened, tourism expanded, and construction activity turned up, assisted by an increase in credit to the private sector. Tourism also expanded with the participation of visitors in various sporting competitions and the 40th anniversary of Samoa's independence. Agricultural production is improving in 2003 and the fishing sector should continue to expand as capacity increases. Further growth in construction activity will likely be seen, reflecting public infrastructure investment activity and private housing and other construction activities. The central bank expects that bank credit to the private sector will grow less quickly than in recent years. Manufacturing will continue to register strong growth as garment production strengthens and copra-processing activity recovers somewhat. Total exports declined by 9.4% in 2002, mainly due to a fall of about 17% in the export value of the two main export commodities, fresh fish and garments. The fish harvest was lower than normal early in the year, and export values were also lower because of weaker prices. The decline in garment exports reflected weaker demand in international markets. Imports were 4.3% higher than in 2001, causing the merchandise trade deficit to widen by 6.1%.

Apart from firewood, the country is entirely dependent on imports for its fuel requirements.

□ Yemen

Capital City	Sana'a	Capital population: 500,000 (1992)
Population ('000)	20,344 (2002)	
Urban population (%)	34.02 (2002)	
Land area (km²)	52797	
Languages	Arabic	
Religion	Islam	
Currency	Yemeni riyal (YR)	
Head of State	President Ali Abdullah Saleh	
Head of Government	Abdul-Qader Bagammal (2001)	
Ruling Party	The government is formed by the General People's Congress (MSA).	

Main Urban Areas	Population
Sana'a (capital)	500,000 (1992)

The Republic of Yemen, which took its present form in 1990, occupies the entire southern tip of the Arabian Peninsula, controlling the strategically important access from the Arabian sea through the Gulf of Aden, to the Red Sea. With Saudi Arabia to its north and Oman to the northeast, it faces Djibouti, Ethiopia and Somalia across the Gulf of Aden. The capital is Sana'a.

The current state of Yemen was the result of a federation in May 1990, when the Republic of Yemen was formed by the union of the Yemen Arab Republic (North Yemen) with the People's Democratic Republic of Yemen (South Yemen). In 1994, the southern states declared their own secession from the federation. However, the rebellion was crushed and by mid-1995 the country appeared to be stabilising. The president is elected for a seven-year term by the people. The parliament (or Assembly of Representatives) has 301 members, elected for a six-year term in single-seat constituencies. In February 2001, a national referendum was held in which voters agreed to the postponement of parliamentary elections. The referendum also extended Saleh's possible time in office until 2013. This voting, like previous ones, was accompanied by violence.

Parliamentary elections took place in April 2003. The MSA won 238 of the 301 seats in the House of Representatives while the Islah Party won 46 seats. The Yemen Socialists Party gained eight seats, with the remainder being scattered among several small parties and non-partisans. Presidential elections occurred in September 1999 when Saleh received 96% of the ballots. The election was boycotted by the main opposition Yemen Socialist party, some of whose leaders launched the bid that triggered the civil war, and three other parties.

Yemen's economy grew by 3.9% in 2002 while inflation was 12.2%. In 2003, growth of 3.8% is anticipated with prices rising by 9.1%. The forecasts for 2004 are for growth of 3.3% and inflation of 6.6%. Widespread poverty (42% of population in 1998), inadequate per capita growth and a projected steady decline of oil revenues represent serious challenges for the government over the medium term. Concerns about security and project risk have heightened a result of terrorist attacks in Yemen and elsewhere. As a result, the government intends to increase its spending for defence, and border demarcation. Over the longer term, the primary objective is to diversify the economy away from oil. Yemen remains one of the poorest countries in the world, with a per capita income of only $500. Structural reforms that are currently underway focus on further tax reform, including the introduction of a value-added tax, civil service reform and the restructuring of public financial institutions.

Agriculture accounts for 17% of GDP and employs a majority of the work force. The main agricultural products are fruits, vegetables, pulses, qat (a mildly narcotic shrub), coffee, cotton and livestock. Industry accounts for 40% of GDP and consists primarily of petroleum refining, small-scale production of cotton textiles and leather goods, food processing, handicrafts and small aluminium products. Income from oil accounts for approximately 40% of Yemen's total government revenues and is the country's main source of foreign currency. Growth of non-oil

GDP (equivalent to about 60% of GDP) has been weak. Large increases in the prices of diesel and electricity and inadequate rainfall are the main reasons Yemen's government continues to implement an economic reform programme which includes banking reform, privatisation of state-run industries, major infrastructure investment and reduction or elimination of government subsidies, including wheat, flour, gasoline and electricity. Privatisation has resumed, notably for small- and medium-sized enterprises, for which tenders are under way. However, the privatisation of larger public enterprises, such as the National Bank of Yemen, the Aden refinery, and cement factories is still under discussion.

Yemen's oil output is about 450,000 barrels per day (bbl/d) and provides the country's main source of hard currency revenue. Proven oil reserves, which are concentrated in the north, are four billion barrels. Yemen currently has a crude refining capacity of 130,000 bbl/d from two ageing refineries. Yemen's border demarcation treaty with Saudi Arabia has opened up new areas to exploration. With natural gas reserves of 16.9 trillion cu ft, Yemen has considerable potential as a producer and exporter. However, there is currently no production of natural gas in the country, and the gas which is extracted as a by-product of oil production is reinjected.

□ Zambia

Capital City	Lusaka	Capital population: 1,327,000 (1995)
Population ('000)	10,052 (2002)	
Urban population (%)	43.24 (2002)	
Land area (km²)	74339	
Languages	English (official); Nyanja, Bemba, Tonga, Lozi, Lunda and Luvale	
Religion	Mainly traditional (70%); Christian (20%)	
Currency	Zambian kwacha (ZMK)	
Head of State	Levy Patrick Mwanawasa (2002)	
Head of Government	Levy Patrick Mwanawasa (2002)	
Ruling Party	Movement for Multiparty Democracy (MMD)	

Main Urban Areas	Population
Lusaka (capital)	1,327,000 (1995)

Zambia is a landlocked country lying in the centre of Central Southern Africa. It borders in the south on Zimbabwe, Botswana and Namibia. In the north are the Democratic Republic of the Congo (formerly Zaire) and Tanzania, in the west is Angola and in the east is Malawi. The country has a varied terrain, ranging from mountain ranges to the lowlands of the Zambezi, Luapula, Kafue and Luangwa rivers. The climate is subtropical, but humidity is not excessive. The capital is Lusaka.

The executive president is elected by universal suffrage for a five-year term, and answers to a National Assembly. The National Assembly has 159 members, 150 members elected for a five-year term in single seat-constituencies, eight appointed members and the Speaker.

Presidential and parliamentary elections both took place in December 2001. Mwanawasa, leader of the MMD, defeated Anderson Mazoka of the United Party for National Development. In the parliamentary elections, the MMD won 69 seats, the United Party for National Development won 49 seats and the United National Independence Party claimed 13 seats. The remainder were distributed among several parties.

GDP increased by 3% in 2002 and inflation was 22.2%. In 2003, growth of 4.5% is expected and inflation should be 18.4%. Forecasts for 2004 call for growth of 4.5% and inflation of 5.2%. During the 1990s, Zambia suffered from large deficits in the budget and current account and significant exchange rate volatility. Accordingly the government's current strategy is to reduce the fiscal deficit to 6.4% of GDP by 2004. However, massive maize purchases - necessary to avoid famine - have put pressure on government finances. The government's wage bill also rose in 2002 following a pay hike for public servants in 2001. The central bank is tightening the money supply to bring down inflation but its efforts are hindered by its need to accommodate the government's borrowing requirements. The latter are driven by debt servicing obligations and the losses being piled up by public enterprises. The privatisation programme, which is strongly supported by donors, has led to the sale of 257 enterprises by the end of 2002. Most these firms, however, are small and have been purchased by Zambians. A long-term objective for the government is to diversify the country's export base away from copper. So far, these efforts have not met with much success.

Zambia's agricultural sector contributes 20% to GDP. The country has much agricultural potential and a good rainfall pattern, other than in the southern part of the country, which is prone to drought. Farming centres on maize, vegetables and livestock, mainly for domestic consumption. Sugar, tobacco and cotton are produced for export. The rural population is scattered over a large area and farms tend to be comparatively large. The government that took over in 2002 made agriculture the priority sector to promote growth and announced radical moves to tackle shortages, including contracting with large-scale farmers to produce maize under irrigation, constructing dams, and providing fertilisers and pesticides to smallholders. Another objective is to encourage private sector investment in agriculture, light manufacturing, small-scale mining and tourism. The manufacturing sector accounts for 11% of GDP and has been growing slowly. Food, beverages and tobacco are the largest sub-sectors. Increased mining activity also led to additional demand for the manufacture of basic metals. The sector's development is constrained by a series of bottlenecks. These include a narrow export base, unfair competition from smuggling and export subsidies in some neighbouring countries. Other constraints are the lack of long-term capital, the high cost of energy and inadequate infrastructure. Mineral extraction involves mainly copper, the single most abundant deposit in Africa, which generally accounts for around 75% of Zambia's foreign exchange earnings. The mines, however, are in poor condition. The country's copper mines were privatised in 2000 but the energy, telecommunications and financial sectors have yet to be privatised.

Zambia has no indigenous oil or gas reserves, though it has some coal. The country is obliged to depend on imports for most of its fuel needs. The vast bulk of its electricity derives from hydroelectric sources.

◻ Zimbabwe

Capital City	Harare	*Capital population: 1,044,000 (1995)*
Population ('000)	12,307 *(2002)*	
Urban population (%)	36.52 *(2002)*	
Land area (km²)	38685	
Languages	English (official); Chishona, Sindebele	
Religion	Christian (55%); traditional	
Currency	Zimbabwe dollar (ZW$)	
Head of State	President Robert G. Mugabe (1987)	
Head of Government	President Robert G. Mugabe	
Ruling Party	Zimbabwe African National Union-Patriotic Front (ZANU-PF)	

Main Urban Areas	Population
Harare (capital)	1,044,000 (1995)

Zimbabwe is a landlocked country lying in east-central southern Africa. It is separated from the Indian Ocean by Mozambique - a factor which proved crucially awkward during the decades of civil war in that country. In the north it borders on Zambia, in the southwest on Botswana and in the south on South Africa. The climate is dry and tropical, yet there is usually enough water thanks to the numerous large rivers which flow through the country. The capital is Harare.

Zimbabwe, an independent member of the Commonwealth, has an executive president who is elected by universal suffrage for a six-year term and presides over a single-chamber House of Assembly. The Assembly's 150 members, who also serve for six years, include 120 elected members, ten tribal chiefs, eight provincial governors appointed by the president, and 12 other presidential appointees. In 1999, the president announced his intention to form a commission to draw up a new constitution.

In parliamentary elections held in June 2000, Mugabe's ZANU-PF coalition was returned to power but with only a slim majority. The opposition Movement for Democratic Change swept most urban areas, winning 57 of the country's 120 constituencies. The ZANU-PF coalition received just over 50% of the vote and 62 seats. A total of 37 court challenges to the results in various constituencies were subsequently made, most to no avail. In March 2002, presidential elections were held. The violence-marred poll returned Mugabe to power with 56% of the vote. He defeated Morgan Tsvangirai, leader of the Movement for Democratic Change.

Zimbabwe's economy contracted by 12.8% in 2002 while inflation was 140.1%. In 2003, GDP is expected to contract further by 11% while prices will soar by 420%. In 2004, growth is forecast to be 5.1% with inflation of 380%. Zimbabwe faces a severe shortage of foreign currency, affecting almost every sector and impeding the country's ability to import items necessary for the agriculture and manufacturing industries. The National Oil Company must raise $185 million to import the fuel needed in 2003. Energy imports from Mozambique were cut off in April 2003 because of Zimbabwe's failure to pay for previous supplies. A number of small companies have closed as a result. By the middle of 2003, almost five million people in the south of the country were in need of food aid and the country's per capita GDP was estimated to have fallen by 28% since 1997. Zimbabwe's economic and social problems are spilling over to other countries in the region in the form of increased illegal immigration, weakened investor confidence and financial market turmoil.

With its fertile lands, Zimbabwe was traditionally regarded as the breadbasket of southern Africa. In normal times, the sector accounts for 20% of GDP with production being equally divided between black- and white-owned farms. However, Mugabe's policy of land confiscation, coupled with his erratic macroeconomic policies, has devastated the farm sector. Many farmers now face destitution. The country's crucial tobacco farmers had another poor harvest in 2002 owing to a shortage of fuel. They are demanding assurances that fuel and input shortages will be remedied before the next harvest. The manufacturing sector is small but was growing rapidly until credit dried up and the Zimbabwean dollar plummeted. Most firms still cater mainly to the domestic market and exports are modest. Tourism has great potential but the number of visitors has dropped off sharply as a consequence of the present unrest. The mining sector is especially important to the economy, producing gold, silver, asbestos and copper but exports of these minerals have also suffered from the government's erratic policies on exchange rates. Many banks are very weak and have almost stopped lending.

The bulk of Zimbabwe's energy needs are met by importing petroleum from South Africa, although the country does have some coal and uses this for electricity generation. About a third of Zimbabwe's electricity comes from hydroelectric resources.

Advertising

◘ Advertising

Table 2.1

Advertising Expenditure by Medium 2002

● Million units of national currency

	Television	Radio	Print	Cinema	Outdoor	Online
Algeria						
Argentina	752	164	626	45	189	
Australia	2,527	702	3,943	64	274	63
Azerbaijan						
Bolivia						
Brazil	7,989	730	4,637		400	577
Canada	2,770	1,168	3,921	14	349	
Chile	162,699	37,756	128,932	1,111	23,712	
China	53,533	5,380	20,369			
Colombia	634	178	338			
Ecuador						
Egypt						
Hong Kong, China	13,531	749	14,913	64	1,242	111
India	37,785	2,267	43,484	348	6,557	443
Indonesia	8,415,804	447,109	4,202,000	12,100	103,786	2,037
Israel	888	448	2,637		277	41
Japan	1,960,201	178,951	1,476,000		493,464	94,385
Jordan						
Kazakhstan						
Kuwait						
Malaysia	930	136	2,292	13	83	
Mexico	19,793	4,010	8,119			
Morocco						
New Zealand	516	203	801	8	37	
Nigeria						
Pakistan	3,624	204	3,224	36	543	
Peru	2,670	140	490		116	
Philippines	15,168	4,412	3,670			
Saudi Arabia						
Singapore	548	164	753	25	105	
South Africa	4,354	1,368	3,894	52	431	
South Korea	3,240,424	313,031	3,445,600		46,146	
Taiwan	32,207	2,561	19,671			
Thailand	35,040	5,543	20,100	417	2,570	291
Tunisia						
Turkmenistan						
United Arab Emirates						
USA	110,672	42,180	60,294		10,661	18,655
Venezuela						
Vietnam						

Source: *Euromonitor from World Association of Newspapers*

TV Adspend 1985-2002

- Million units of national currency

	1985	1990	1995	1996	1997	1998	1999	2000	2001	2002	2002 (US$ million)
Algeria											
Argentina		300	1,140	1,148	1,290	1,259	1,370	1,181	1,051	752	245.4
Australia	1,096	1,475	2,022	2,084	2,248	2,400	2,454	2,746	2,490	2,527	1,373.0
Azerbaijan											
Bolivia											
Brazil			3,273	4,582	5,643	5,741	5,874	5,704	6,797	7,989	2,735.1
Canada	1,716	1,726	1,850	1,982	2,103	2,312	2,387	2,456	2,560	2,770	1,765.1
Chile	16,386	41,212	118,816	128,628	140,405	131,609	129,081	141,472	152,475	162,699	236.2
China	144	960	6,498	9,079	11,441	13,564	15,615	16,891	17,937	53,533	6,467.7
Colombia	3,172	75,469	365	472	512	636	592	598	593	634	0.3
Ecuador											
Egypt											
Hong Kong, China	1,341	3,086	7,433	8,437	9,563	10,515	11,101	11,608	13,291	13,531	1,734.9
India	364	1,925	11,200	15,520	19,724	21,358	23,765	28,098	33,400	37,785	777.3
Indonesia	13,077	147,231	1,638,000	2,203,000	2,678,000	2,213,000	3,445,000	4,933,000	6,057,000	8,415,804	903.8
Israel			791	950	1,018	997	1,077	1,098	1,018	888	187.5
Japan	1,528,743	1,696,460	1,755,000	1,916,000	2,008,000	1,951,000	1,912,000	2,079,000	2,068,000	1,960,201	15,633.1
Jordan											
Kazakhstan											
Kuwait											
Malaysia	254	380	654	774	780	698	823	936	878	930	244.8
Mexico			5,358	7,936	13,425	9,983	13,135	18,779	19,634	19,793	2,049.8
Morocco											
New Zealand	242	343	476	478	465	473	487	501	479	516	238.6
Nigeria											
Pakistan	130	507	2,021	2,420	2,958	3,401	3,738	2,875	3,264	3,624	60.7
Peru			3,094	3,133	3,165	2,861	2,535	2,293	2,481	2,670	759.3
Philippines	2,048	3,444	7,428	9,320	9,872	10,100	11,648	13,437	14,346	15,168	293.9
Saudi Arabia											
Singapore	93	183	355	379	440	434	410	504	557	548	306.2
South Africa	265	697	1,808	1,938	2,398	2,936	3,311	3,567	4,146	4,354	413.1
South Korea	399,498	673,518	1,281,725	1,591,476	1,555,005	1,049,898	1,532,773	2,242,200	2,229,364	3,240,424	2,590.1
Taiwan	12,038	18,919	28,948	24,306	25,685	34,832	32,234	30,670	27,682	32,207	931.7
Thailand	1,753	6,141	18,633	22,962	24,603	21,150	26,042	30,472	32,879	35,040	815.6
Tunisia											
Turkmenistan											
United Arab Emirates											
USA	21,842	29,303	35,680	38,472	40,709	43,471	47,299	52,258	49,714	110,672	110,671.7
Venezuela											
Vietnam											

Source: Euromonitor from World Association of Newspapers

Radio Adspend 1985-2002

- Million units of national currency

	1985	1990	1995	1996	1997	1998	1999	2000	2001	2002	2002 (US$ million)
Algeria											
Argentina		92	205	227	220	215	204	231	226	164	53.6
Australia	291	384	510	525	540	557	644	684	695	702	381.4
Azerbaijan											
Bolivia											
Brazil			269	257	373	389	514	481	564	730	249.9
Canada	810	761	748	792	856	930	964	1,014	1,062	1,168	744.2
Chile	12,558	13,794	20,284	33,889	36,907	33,867	28,782	34,012	34,408	37,756	54.8
China	7	77	738	873	1,058	1,330	1,252	1,574	1,828	5,380	650.0
Colombia	1,353	27,730	97	126	155	177	166	167	166	178	0.1
Ecuador											
Egypt											
Hong Kong, China	113	345	978	917	1,089	1,024	915	1,010	821	749	96.0
India	181	415	1,000	1,100	1,119	998	1,470	1,800	2,250	2,267	46.6
Indonesia	34,735	73,606	170,000	189,000	206,000	136,000	187,000	257,000	341,000	447,109	48.0
Israel			193	219	278	286	324	412	429	448	94.5
Japan	424,035	277,462	208,000	218,000	225,000	215,000	204,000	207,000	200,000	178,951	1,427.2
Jordan											
Kazakhstan											
Kuwait											
Malaysia	6	18	59	71	67	56	85	102	120	136	35.7
Mexico			334	726	3,271	3,511	4,452	5,011	4,611	4,010	415.3
Morocco											
New Zealand	144	142	158	165	172	170	178	190	196	203	93.9
Nigeria											
Pakistan	5	24	129	151	169	119	123	173	190	204	3.4
Peru			157	141	155	121	141	111	125	140	39.7
Philippines	569	854	2,409	2,736	2,640	2,700	3,113	3,607	4,022	4,412	85.5
Saudi Arabia											
Singapore	4	16	55	65	63	54	62	77	115	164	91.6
South Africa	88	236	574	658	726	794	926	1,223	1,206	1,368	129.8
South Korea	69,180	107,771	187,225	216,619	189,031	110,297	145,895	250,400	222,283	313,031	250.2
Taiwan	1,148	2,133	3,969	2,200	2,500	2,750	2,146	2,310	2,231	2,561	74.1
Thailand	462	1,514	4,690	5,400	4,076	3,799	4,112	5,059	5,136	5,543	129.0
Tunisia											
Turkmenistan											
United Arab Emirates											
USA	5,602	8,833	11,470	12,412	13,794	15,411	18,581	20,819	18,800	42,180	42,179.8
Venezuela											
Vietnam											

Source: *Euromonitor from World Association of Newspapers*

Print Adspend 1985-2002

- Million units of national currency

	1985	1990	1995	1996	1997	1998	1999	2000	2001	2002	2002 (US$ million)
Algeria											
Argentina		348	1,362	1,480	1,722	1,871	1,396	985	1,079	626	204.4
Australia	1,691	2,166	3,092	3,055	3,479	3,777	3,870	4,196	3,904	3,943	2,142.3
Azerbaijan											
Bolivia											
Brazil			2,234	2,869	3,023	3,103	3,392	3,157	3,764	4,637	1,587.6
Canada	3,662	3,201	2,795	2,875	3,285	3,524	3,604	3,835	3,837	3,921	2,498.5
Chile	15,884	39,077	99,522	116,260	130,443	120,998	116,799	127,882	127,512	128,932	187.1
China	27	550	6,850	8,330	10,210	11,148	12,125	15,781	16,956	20,369	2,460.9
Colombia	465	19,272	251	293	305	298	266	266	316	338	0.1
Ecuador											
Egypt											
Hong Kong, China	620	2,356	6,172	7,070	9,137	8,977	11,362	13,856	14,300	14,913	1,912.2
India	2,737	8,055	24,500	27,950	32,396	26,360	29,796	35,064	39,857	43,484	894.5
Indonesia	62,484	262,368	1,286,000	1,472,000	1,851,000	1,147,000	1,707,000	2,430,000	3,048,000	4,202,000	451.3
Israel			2,182	2,279	2,482	2,410	2,667	3,150	2,918	2,637	556.6
Japan	1,931,424	1,763,557	1,540,000	1,645,000	1,704,000	1,605,000	1,572,000	1,684,000	1,621,000	1,476,000	11,771.5
Jordan											
Kazakhstan											
Kuwait											
Malaysia	75	332	1,247	1,528	1,722	1,371	1,575	1,997	2,119	2,292	603.2
Mexico			2,760	3,875	6,241	7,475	8,553	8,822	9,022	8,119	840.8
Morocco											
New Zealand	330	460	665	692	715	693	725	753	772	801	370.5
Nigeria											
Pakistan	95	409	1,892	2,242	2,538	1,743	1,820	3,000	3,140	3,224	54.0
Peru			251	455	472	481	548	413	451	490	139.3
Philippines	59	516	3,411	4,822	2,688	2,500	2,812	3,182	3,495	3,670	71.1
Saudi Arabia											
Singapore	198	350	604	646	711	633	672	819	752	753	420.5
South Africa	774	1,185	1,998	2,338	2,760	3,162	3,417	3,693	3,799	3,894	369.4
South Korea	441,398	934,117	2,007,739	2,268,301	3,113,566	2,465,514	3,126,591	3,867,500	3,043,300	3,445,600	2,754.1
Taiwan	24,007	29,433	43,239	16,786	22,900	27,043	24,957	25,946	22,916	19,671	569.0
Thailand	789	3,871	15,337	15,309	12,388	8,267	16,176	21,609	19,230	20,100	467.9
Tunisia											
Turkmenistan											
United Arab Emirates											
USA	32,770	41,513	47,427	50,071	52,827	55,914	59,290	66,400	61,708	60,294	60,294.0
Venezuela											
Vietnam											

Source: Euromonitor from World Association of Newspapers

▣ Cinema Adspend

Table 2.5

Cinema Adspend 1985-2002

- Million units of national currency

	1985	1990	1995	1996	1997	1998	1999	2000	2001	2002	2002 (US$ million)
Algeria											
Argentina		1	41	52	50	49	54	48	44	45	14.8
Australia	15	21	37	41	47	53	58	69	64	64	34.8
Azerbaijan											
Bolivia											
Brazil											
Canada	6	7	8	8	8	8	9	11	12	14	8.6
Chile	62	193	495	783	850	900	1,300	945	1,012	1,111	1.6
China											
Colombia											
Ecuador											
Egypt											
Hong Kong, China	227	107	47	44	85	77	23	12	56	64	8.2
India	94	106	90	100	104	217	245	350	310	348	7.2
Indonesia	7,977	9,341	11,000	10,000	9,000	4,000	6,000	8,000	9,000	12,100	1.3
Israel											
Japan											
Jordan											
Kazakhstan											
Kuwait											
Malaysia	2	3	7	7	9	11	10	10	11	13	3.4
Mexico											
Morocco											
New Zealand	0	1	8	7	8	10	12	13	9	8	3.7
Nigeria											
Pakistan	1	4	11	13	18	28	28	30	33	36	0.6
Peru											
Philippines											
Saudi Arabia											
Singapore	2	4	8	10	15	15	18	22	22	25	13.9
South Africa	27	30	34	47	70	77	66	69	62	52	4.9
South Korea											
Taiwan											
Thailand	300	53	23	24	176	223	261	325	370	417	9.7
Tunisia											
Turkmenistan											
United Arab Emirates											
USA											
Venezuela											
Vietnam											

Source: Euromonitor from World Association of Newspapers

Outdoor Adspend 1985-2002

- Million units of national currency

	1985	1990	1995	1996	1997	1998	1999	2000	2001	2002	2002 (US$ million)
Algeria											
Argentina		7	150	178	193	207	204	228	168	189	61.7
Australia	321	279	150	178	193	207	204	228	271	274	148.9
Azerbaijan											
Bolivia											
Brazil			197	257	301	428	514	511	260	400	136.9
Canada	75	102	167	200	220	250	269	293	310	349	222.7
Chile	1,088	3,220	17,233	19,005	20,971	19,294	19,192	22,570	21,935	23,712	34.4
China											
Colombia											
Ecuador											
Egypt											
Hong Kong, China	59	185	484	516	525	514	659	1,019	1,135	1,242	159.3
India	469	1,110	2,300	2,600	2,908	4,732	4,900	6,000	6,200	6,557	134.9
Indonesia	9,544	31,450	230,000	266,000	350,000	261,000	269,000	269,000	188,000	103,786	11.1
Israel			261	248	265	273	294	328	303	277	58.4
Japan			571,000	585,000	581,000	563,000	547,000	556,000	547,000	493,464	3,935.5
Jordan											
Kazakhstan											
Kuwait											
Malaysia	13	27	57	65	68	54	59	62	70	83	21.9
Mexico											
Morocco											
New Zealand			9	12	9	14	18	28	32	37	17.1
Nigeria											
Pakistan	5	30	247	299	331	431	531	400	470	543	9.1
Peru						119	127	123	114	116	32.9
Philippines											
Saudi Arabia											
Singapore	22	25	30	35	44	49	54	78	96	105	58.6
South Africa	18	55	145	149	195	211	251	326	382	431	40.9
South Korea							24,319	27,193	35,991	46,146	36.9
Taiwan			4,820								
Thailand	39	333	3,540	3,689	4,418	2,042	1,043	1,610	1,999	2,570	59.8
Tunisia											
Turkmenistan											
United Arab Emirates											
USA	1,201	1,525	3,369	3,597	3,802	4,027	4,565	4,912	4,814	10,661	10,660.5
Venezuela											
Vietnam											

Source: Euromonitor from World Association of Newspapers

☒ Online Adspend

Table 2.7

Online Adspend 1995-2002

● Million units of national currency

	1995	1996	1997	1998	1999	2000	2001	2002	US$ million 2002
Algeria									
Argentina									
Australia					35	83	61	63	63
Azerbaijan									
Bolivia									
Brazil					81	192	290	577	577
Canada									
Chile									
China									
Colombia									
Ecuador									
Egypt									
Hong Kong, China						111	111	111	111
India					50	250	350	443	443
Indonesia				500	500	835	1,280	2,037	2,037
Israel						13	29	41	41
Japan		2,000	6,000	11,000	24,000	59,000	74,000	94,385	94,385
Jordan									
Kazakhstan									
Kuwait									
Malaysia									
Mexico									
Morocco									
New Zealand									
Nigeria									
Pakistan									
Peru									
Philippines									
Saudi Arabia									
Singapore									
South Africa							53		
South Korea									
Taiwan						870	850		
Thailand					90	225	150	291	291
Tunisia									
Turkmenistan									
United Arab Emirates									
USA	100	300	906	1,920	4,600	6,000	6,600	18,655	18,655
Venezuela									
Vietnam									

Source: Euromonitor from World Association of Newspapers / Jupiter research

Agricultural Resources

▣ Indices of Agricultural Output								Table 3.1	

Indices of Agricultural Output 1985-2002

● 1989-1991 = 100

	1985	1990	1995	1996	1997	1998	1999	2000	2001	2002
North America										
Canada	91.9	103.5	111.8	118.0	117.7	125.7	131.4	132.8	120.4	115.5
USA	101.8	102.5	109.2	114.5	118.6	119.1	120.6	123.4	121.6	120.9
Latin America										
Anguilla										
Antigua		100.7	101.7	99.6	98.8	97.9	97.1	98.3	101.4	103.2
Argentina	101.0	101.8	117.0	121.1	123.1	131.5	138.1	136.4	136.9	138.5
Aruba										
Bahamas		100.3	123.6	142.4	133.3	167.0	174.9	127.1	133.9	159.5
Barbados	91.5	102.7	90.3	105.4	96.6	97.2	100.0	107.0	103.2	98.3
Belize		108.4	140.2	151.8	166.0	157.3	170.2	186.5	195.4	178.5
Bermuda		100.7	84.7	78.1	78.4	78.4	78.4	78.4	78.4	78.4
Bolivia	79.5	100.4	123.8	128.4	134.1	136.4	137.2	150.3	148.1	156.6
Brazil	89.8	97.3	121.6	122.0	126.8	129.0	139.6	143.8	149.4	160.3
British Virgin Islands		94.9	104.0	104.0	104.0	104.0	104.0	104.0	104.0	104.0
Cayman Islands		84.8	84.9	84.9	84.9	84.9	84.9	84.9	84.9	84.9
Chile	75.7	101.1	126.1	128.2	129.8	132.8	129.7	132.9	142.0	141.9
Colombia	79.1	101.4	110.2	108.7	110.0	110.2	109.6	111.3	112.5	115.6
Costa Rica	80.8	100.1	120.6	125.0	125.2	133.3	139.4	141.7	141.8	142.7
Cuba	98.0	102.8	55.0	64.8	63.4	59.5	67.0	72.5	70.6	70.6
Dominica		99.8	78.0	92.5	91.5	83.2	83.1	83.0	79.3	79.6
Dominican Republic	93.7	97.8	97.0	102.4	103.0	104.3	96.3	99.6	105.5	109.1
Ecuador	81.4	100.3	130.0	141.5	147.4	125.4	144.1	146.9	151.9	151.5
El Salvador	100.0	102.4	100.9	103.1	106.3	102.8	113.5	105.0	104.2	99.1
French Guiana		98.8	126.5	141.2	135.0	135.6	127.2	127.4	117.0	117.0
Grenada		102.5	94.6	92.6	97.9	90.4	101.8	98.4	87.3	94.2
Guadeloupe	113.7	87.7	83.1	89.8	111.3	95.8	114.3	114.3	114.3	114.3
Guatemala	85.3	101.7	113.1	116.9	122.9	125.6	127.3	131.2	132.2	128.4
Guyana	120.0	86.4	179.9	192.1	196.8	172.3	186.2	194.6	187.0	180.1
Haiti	110.3	98.2	88.0	91.2	94.1	93.4	95.9	101.9	98.2	100.0
Honduras	83.3	101.9	115.2	127.5	125.3	125.9	114.1	125.1	126.6	133.9
Jamaica	87.4	104.0	124.1	131.5	122.1	119.3	127.3	120.2	128.2	127.8
Martinique	100.4	96.3	91.4	116.3	122.8	114.2	122.2	123.4	123.4	123.0
Mexico	96.7	101.2	120.1	118.1	122.3	122.7	128.6	129.1	135.6	133.5
Netherlands Antilles		101.4	188.1	145.0	158.6	167.0	153.3	166.1	170.6	162.7
Nicaragua	108.9	96.0	111.3	114.2	118.5	124.2	127.8	143.7	143.6	145.8
Panama	96.0	99.7	102.8	104.0	102.6	102.4	104.0	103.3	105.6	108.5
Paraguay			109.6	106.5	109.3	113.7	117.3	116.6	130.6	123.8
Peru	90.5	99.8	124.2	133.3	140.8	142.1	161.2	166.0	168.5	176.7
Puerto Rico		102.4	87.1	83.3	81.7	83.2	83.9	84.4	84.4	84.4
St Kitts		100.9	94.3	102.4	134.5	113.9	98.0	97.2	97.3	97.3
St Lucia		99.1	97.2	91.6	81.1	67.4	76.8	69.4	55.3	55.6
St Vincent and the Grenadines		108.6	88.5	82.7	73.2	77.4	76.1	78.1	78.6	78.6
Suriname	115.2	104.1	101.0	89.2	90.3	77.5	77.9	75.4	80.5	83.3
Trinidad and Tobago	94.2	100.2	110.7	110.6	106.2	91.9	106.8	126.6	123.0	129.0
Uruguay	88.6	100.1	111.7	121.7	130.0	129.8	129.9	121.9	105.8	117.5
Venezuela	87.8		105.3	110.7	117.8	116.7	119.2	128.4	133.8	135.0

Source: UN Food and Agriculture Organisation, FAOSTAT

■ Indices of Agricultural Output

Indices of Agricultural Output 1985-2002

- 1989-1991 = 100

	1985	1990	1995	1996	1997	1998	1999	2000	2001	2002
Asia Pacific										
Afghanistan		99.8	122.6	136.2	148.6	160.5	142.6	132.2	132.0	
American Samoa		103.6	96.2	96.2	96.2	96.2	96.2	96.2	96.2	96.2
Armenia			79.5	82.8	73.5	80.5	79.6	75.6	80.0	82.8
Azerbaijan			52.5	57.1	53.5	57.4	61.2	68.4	72.7	77.4
Bangladesh	89.9	99.5	103.2	109.4	111.5	114.4	129.2	136.9	134.2	138.2
Bhutan	98.8	101.2	115.2	118.7	120.9	120.0	117.0	116.2	116.1	96.1
Brunei		100.4	144.1	125.1	156.0	183.5	229.0	256.0	295.0	346.2
Cambodia	76.0	99.1	125.6	127.4	130.9	133.0	148.2	151.6	157.1	142.4
China	80.5	101.1	136.5	144.4	154.1	160.2	167.2	173.5	179.4	184.6
Fiji	85.1	104.7	102.8	108.9	97.6	84.7	98.4	99.3	94.0	96.8
French Polynesia		103.0	101.8	97.9	95.7	79.5	87.8	97.0	94.6	101.2
Guam		96.9	110.8	129.0	129.0	129.0	129.0	129.0	129.1	129.1
Hong Kong, China		98.1	55.9	25.9	20.3	41.0	58.0	63.0	65.0	67.0
India	84.1	99.5	115.2	119.7	121.7	124.9	130.2	130.6	132.6	128.9
Indonesia	82.8	101.1	124.6	124.2	118.6	117.9	120.0	123.8	122.6	123.1
Japan	103.0	100.8	96.9	95.0	95.3	91.1	92.4	92.0	90.0	91.0
Kazakhstan			63.6	61.3	60.8	49.8	67.5	63.9	74.0	77.2
Kiribati		85.0	109.0	127.2	127.2	133.1	134.6	126.5	128.4	130.5
Kyrgyzstan		119.5	80.0	89.2	96.9	102.1	108.2	114.5	120.1	121.0
Laos	92.0		109.4	111.3	124.5	128.6	149.7	174.0	181.2	184.2
Macau		104.8	106.2	105.9	115.8	158.9	160.3	161.5	162.0	
Malaysia	77.7	97.7	117.2	120.6	120.9	118.0	120.1	120.6	125.5	129.8
Maldives		99.6	115.2	117.4	124.7	127.0	131.5	147.3	148.8	148.8
Mongolia	92.8	96.2	83.5	91.2	88.2	91.0	105.8	103.2	81.6	92.6
Myanmar	112.2	105.5	131.2	136.1	136.6	138.9	154.4	166.6	180.2	180.6
Nauru		97.0	105.5	105.4	105.6	105.6	105.6	105.6	105.6	105.6
Nepal	82.5	99.9	112.8	115.5	118.4	120.8	127.3	132.0	136.1	138.2
New Caledonia		98.7	116.6	121.7	125.9	129.4	129.7	128.4	130.7	130.6
North Korea		99.7	77.2	69.6	69.8	83.2	83.7	82.3	90.1	90.4
Pakistan	77.8	103.8	123.2	130.2	132.6	136.5	142.7	145.6	142.8	143.6
Papua New Guinea	99.7	98.5	107.2	115.2	114.6	117.7	124.8	129.0	122.6	120.3
Philippines	87.3	102.8	111.0	120.3	123.0	114.0	124.0	128.8	133.9	141.4
Singapore		97.0	43.3	42.3	37.5	41.4	27.7	33.4	34.9	27.4
Solomon Islands	123.8		122.3	125.5	131.1	134.6	138.2	148.3	151.3	152.1
South Korea		95.0	113.0	120.0	125.3	124.3	131.1	131.2	131.5	130.2
Sri Lanka	107.2	98.0	115.0	105.7	109.3	113.3	117.2	120.8	117.0	118.1
Taiwan										
Tajikistan		100.2	59.8	51.7	49.9	47.3	46.6	52.0	57.2	56.5
Thailand	95.0		112.4	115.0	117.6	114.4	117.2	123.4	127.7	125.8
Tonga	98.7	100.5	91.6	89.3	96.0	91.5	98.3	97.5	97.5	97.5
Turkmenistan		96.8	103.5	66.3	76.9	84.8	98.3	96.5	91.4	87.4
Tuvalu		101.9	95.9	99.6	105.5	107.0	110.3	110.6	100.4	100.4
Uzbekistan		101.2	102.0	93.2	94.4	98.7	95.1	98.4	100.1	102.8
Vanuatu	99.8	98.4	103.1	104.0	121.6	126.0	106.2	100.7	83.7	87.6
Vietnam	82.1	113.9	130.0	137.2	146.2	152.3	164.7	175.0	178.4	189.0
Western Samoa		105.4	88.3	90.6	93.1	97.4	96.6	101.5	102.9	104.4
Australasia										
Australia	94.1	102.6	108.1	118.0	119.4	125.5	133.5	128.8	132.6	110.9
New Zealand	107.9	100.4	112.6	114.0	120.2	120.7	114.2	121.8	125.6	127.8

Source: UN Food and Agriculture Organisation, FAOSTAT

◻ Indices of Agricultural Output

Indices of Agricultural Output 1985-2002

● 1989-1991 = 100

	1985	1990	1995	1996	1997	1998	1999	2000	2001	2002
Africa and Middle East										
Algeria	90.0	93.3	120.3	141.9	113.5	129.9	132.4	126.3	139.4	136.8
Angola	97.2	97.9	122.0	126.9	127.5	147.3	140.7	158.5	175.1	173.6
Bahrain		96.9	111.5	109.4	115.2	104.6	131.9	121.8	73.9	73.9
Benin	77.0	99.0	141.0	156.6	163.8	166.2	168.2	182.5	179.7	189.8
Botswana	96.6	99.7	111.5	106.4	94.6	90.4	79.1	84.0	92.8	92.6
Burkina Faso	82.9	94.6	122.7	137.8	135.7	154.7	156.3	134.4	171.1	176.8
Burundi	90.5	102.2	95.3	95.0	94.0	89.2	91.7	85.8	94.0	93.6
Cameroon	92.4	99.2	118.0	124.9	118.8	126.4	135.9	138.5	137.4	134.9
Cape Verde		102.6	124.0	110.3	113.4	128.4	162.2	143.8	142.3	144.6
Central African Republic	83.0	99.8	112.6	129.6	124.7	128.0	130.4	141.8	138.3	143.1
Chad	81.8	92.0	115.7	123.2	139.4	151.8	140.5	131.7	154.9	148.4
Comoros		99.3	113.4	118.4	117.2	123.2	126.4	129.6	132.2	132.5
Congo Dem Rep	85.6	100.8	92.5	91.7	89.6	90.6	88.2	86.4	84.8	82.9
Congo-Brazzaville	94.5	101.0	113.6	117.8	118.3	116.2	125.1	127.3	128.8	132.2
Côte d'Ivoire	86.0	102.2	114.8	121.4	127.9	134.2	140.6	146.0	132.5	124.5
Djibouti		107.6	85.4	87.0	87.7	88.4	89.7	89.1	89.2	89.2
Egypt	84.1	101.5	123.2	135.7	140.3	139.0	147.5	154.5	154.0	155.2
Equatorial Guinea		100.6	98.5	98.2	96.3	93.6	101.1	100.0	98.0	98.0
Eritrea		107.3	104.0	103.4	148.5	133.8	116.6	124.0	107.4
Ethiopia		100.0	117.9	136.9	137.5	126.3	134.1	142.1	155.3	148.8
Gabon	86.8	97.7	105.5	109.1	112.7	116.1	117.1	119.6	119.8	119.8
Gambia	88.3	84.4	87.8	69.8	89.7	85.0	123.8	137.2	149.5	89.7
Ghana	83.6	88.1	138.3	149.4	145.2	158.8	167.3	171.8	175.9	198.3
Guinea	91.5	99.6	128.3	131.7	138.4	145.8	152.9	155.0	163.3	170.5
Guinea-Bissau	87.7	103.1	112.1	116.1	125.1	128.2	135.9	141.3	143.6	141.0
Iran	83.6	104.2	132.4	139.5	137.7	157.5	153.2	153.0	151.1	159.8
Iraq	111.7	118.2	100.2	101.6	94.1	97.7	83.6	73.6	78.0	79.3
Israel	104.6	108.0	107.7	112.4	111.5	115.2	110.4	112.6	112.6	112.2
Jordan	94.7	106.7	150.8	116.4	134.6	137.0	106.3	142.0	127.6	163.2
Kenya	80.7	100.0	106.0	107.2	107.2	113.6	117.3	116.6	121.0	123.8
Kuwait	147.1		123.0	144.4	153.6	178.5	196.0	194.8	243.8	242.3
Lebanon	68.4		125.5	130.0	118.9	113.4	111.8	117.7	110.7	107.9
Lesotho	92.2	99.4	96.2	110.7	109.2	94.4	96.2	107.5	95.4	126.0
Liberia		111.2	66.4	76.5	100.4	108.9	117.9	125.5	125.2	130.4
Libya	90.5	92.1	119.2	125.5	130.8	136.5	136.3	133.3	132.1	133.8
Madagascar	92.9		106.0	107.8	109.3	109.1	111.6	110.4	114.7	114.5
Malawi	90.7	100.0	109.6	125.2	121.5	134.1	142.3	161.6	162.4	128.1
Mali	73.0	104.4	115.9	120.8	122.6	130.8	134.9	119.4	137.3	147.6
Mauritania	86.3	105.9	101.5	107.7	105.8	107.1	106.7	110.2	108.0	106.9
Mauritius	98.7	100.2	103.3	103.7	110.6	105.8	82.6	101.0	111.8	98.1
Morocco	66.7	99.8	74.0	113.4	96.6	112.3	104.8	96.9	103.6	110.3
Mozambique	91.8	93.6	108.5	122.3	131.0	140.9	142.5	126.6	132.4	132.7
Namibia	83.7	101.0	105.3	115.7	83.5	95.5	101.0	105.9	93.1	93.2
Niger	78.3	100.6	110.2	123.6	102.2	153.1	140.5	129.7	151.1	141.5
Nigeria	71.0	97.7	131.7	138.6	142.2	148.4	153.8	155.0	152.8	158.3
Oman		77.9	111.7	128.4	137.9	151.4	164.6	159.0	162.6	163.8
Qatar		99.7	154.9	166.3	185.6	147.5	161.0	173.0	127.3	160.5
Réunion	77.6	104.5	112.9	114.8	123.6	118.2	124.9	125.1	127.4	131.0
Rwanda	109.7	94.7	65.9	74.8	77.7	84.1	89.4	108.3	109.5	127.4
Sao Tomé e Príncipe		106.1	124.1	142.9	160.0	179.5	187.1	191.0	198.1	198.0
Saudi Arabia	64.2	100.0	81.6	76.1	89.1	108.3	85.0	84.2	106.6	106.9
Senegal	85.9	96.6	114.7	107.1	101.1	98.8	135.1	133.7	129.4	101.2
Seychelles		104.4	141.0	137.2	142.1	128.0	133.8	133.8	130.2	132.9
Sierra Leone	89.2	101.7	92.0	97.1	103.0	95.0	82.8	76.9	84.0	85.3
Somalia		97.9	101.4	111.9	105.5	106.4	108.9	107.6	110.4
South Africa	90.2	97.0	86.8	102.0	103.2	98.0	104.4	109.8	105.3	109.1
Sudan	109.9	102.6	138.3	151.7	152.6	157.8	154.8	157.3	169.7	160.8
Swaziland	91.4	91.4	82.1	94.2	84.6	84.9	90.2	97.1	97.4	94.5
Syria	101.6	106.7	131.7	146.5	136.4	164.0	135.4	154.3	162.0	170.0
Tanzania	90.4	105.0	106.5	107.6	95.0	107.2	107.9	112.1	114.0	113.5
Togo	80.3	99.1	110.9	134.3	139.0	137.7	137.6	129.4	134.7	139.7
Tunisia	87.5	95.8	81.6	141.3	97.4	123.1	134.3	131.0	114.0	96.6
Uganda	82.9	83.1	112.0	108.9	108.9	120.7	132.6	132.9	141.3	141.6
United Arab Emirates		100.0	173.2	195.4	240.4	236.9	392.1	597.4	515.8	525.4
Yemen	79.3	132.3	113.8	114.5	121.9	133.2	132.0	139.0	148.3	147.8
Zambia	82.2	101.1	90.9	112.8	105.6	100.1	121.4	110.7	104.5	110.9
Zimbabwe	101.1	93.7	82.8	110.4	114.8	110.4	110.8	127.9	119.8	98.8

Source: *UN Food and Agriculture Organisation, FAOSTAT*

□ Indices of Agricultural Output								Table 3.2	

Indices of Food Output 1985-2002

● 1989-1991 = 100

	1985	1990	1995	1996	1997	1998	1999	2000	2001	2002
North America										
Canada	91.0	103.2	111.2	118.1	117.6	125.4	131.6	133.7	120.9	115.9
USA	102.3	101.1	109.1	114.3	118.5	120.3	121.3	124.3	121.6	121.7
Latin America										
Anguilla										
Antigua		100.6	102.0	99.9	99.1	98.2	97.4	98.6	101.7	103.4
Argentina	102.0	101.5	118.9	122.9	125.8	134.7	142.6	141.4	141.8	144.1
Aruba										
Bahamas		100.3	123.6	142.4	133.3	167.0	174.9	127.1	133.9	159.5
Barbados	91.5	102.7	90.3	105.4	96.6	97.2	100.0	107.0	103.2	98.3
Belize		108.4	140.2	151.8	166.0	157.2	170.1	186.4	195.0	178.1
Bermuda		100.7	84.7	78.1	78.4	78.4	78.4	78.4	78.4	78.4
Bolivia	78.6	100.6	123.7	127.3	133.5	136.1	137.3	151.1	147.4	156.3
Brazil	87.1	97.2	125.2	125.2	130.4	131.6	142.6	146.0	151.5	162.2
British Virgin Islands		94.9	104.0	104.0	104.0	104.0	104.0	104.0	104.0	104.0
Cayman Islands		84.8	84.9	84.9	84.9	84.9	84.9	84.9	84.9	84.9
Chile	74.9	101.0	126.6	128.9	130.9	133.9	130.6	133.9	143.4	143.4
Colombia	78.9	101.6	113.9	114.0	116.9	115.0	117.8	118.4	119.4	123.2
Costa Rica	80.7	100.5	124.7	129.4	132.0	139.5	147.4	148.6	149.8	151.6
Cuba	97.8	102.9	54.4	64.2	62.6	58.5	66.4	72.2	70.2	70.3
Dominica		99.9	77.2	91.8	90.7	82.4	82.3	82.2	78.5	78.7
Dominican Republic	91.1	98.4	99.0	103.8	103.4	102.5	99.6	102.1	109.3	112.0
Ecuador	81.0	100.1	132.3	142.2	154.0	132.2	148.2	151.1	155.1	155.2
El Salvador	91.6	101.8	102.5	103.6	112.5	109.1	115.0	112.9	112.5	109.8
French Guiana		98.8	126.5	141.2	135.0	135.6	127.2	127.4	117.0	117.0
Grenada		102.5	94.6	92.6	97.8	90.4	101.8	98.4	87.2	94.1
Guadeloupe	113.7	87.7	83.1	89.8	111.3	95.8	114.3	114.3	114.3	114.3
Guatemala	80.2	101.6	119.6	123.1	127.9	131.8	129.7	132.6	136.5	139.6
Guyana	119.8	86.4	180.4	192.6	197.4	172.9	186.9	195.4	187.6	180.7
Haiti	110.7	98.2	88.8	92.7	95.8	94.9	97.5	103.6	100.0	101.6
Honduras	84.4	100.5	113.9	126.6	122.0	121.3	109.8	117.5	117.5	128.2
Jamaica	87.7	104.1	124.5	132.1	122.4	120.0	128.0	120.6	128.8	128.3
Martinique	100.5	105.9	91.4	116.3	122.8	114.2	122.2	123.4	123.4	123.0
Mexico	96.8	101.2	121.3	118.3	123.3	123.8	130.7	131.5	138.6	136.9
Netherlands Antilles		98.7	188.1	145.0	158.6	167.0	153.3	166.1	170.6	162.7
Nicaragua	97.1	104.5	116.2	121.4	122.7	130.2	128.8	149.7	153.3	159.8
Panama	96.5	102.5	103.2	104.3	102.8	102.4	104.0	103.7	105.6	108.2
Paraguay	78.4	102.8	117.9	117.4	125.4	128.7	133.9	132.5	147.3	143.3
Peru	88.3	96.4	126.8	134.7	144.8	146.6	165.7	170.1	172.7	182.1
Puerto Rico		97.9	86.8	83.0	81.5	82.6	83.5	84.0	84.0	84.0
St Kitts		87.9	94.5	102.6	134.8	114.2	98.2	97.5	97.6	97.6
St Lucia		108.6	97.2	91.6	81.1	67.4	76.8	69.4	55.3	55.6
St Vincent and the Grenadines		106.2	88.2	82.2	72.6	76.9	75.5	77.6	78.0	78.0
Suriname	115.2	93.5	101.0	89.2	90.3	77.5	77.9	75.3	80.5	83.4
Trinidad and Tobago	93.2	102.7	111.6	112.2	106.7	93.1	108.3	128.1	124.6	130.8
Uruguay	90.2		115.5	128.3	137.0	138.0	141.0	132.3	113.3	128.7
Venezuela	87.6	100.1	106.6	111.9	119.5	118.6	121.2	131.1	136.4	137.6

Source: UN Food and Agriculture Organisation, FAOSTAT

■ Indices of Agricultural Output

Indices of Food Output 1985-2002

● 1989-1991 = 100

	1985	1990	1995	1996	1997	1998	1999	2000	2001	2002
Asia Pacific										
Afghanistan		100.3	122.9	136.5	149.2	161.3	143.3	132.4	130.5	
American Samoa		103.5	96.2	96.2	96.2	96.2	96.2	96.2	96.2	96.2
Armenia			80.1	83.6	74.2	81.3	79.9	74.9	80.0	83.0
Azerbaijan			53.7	60.2	59.0	63.7	69.3	77.1	83.7	90.3
Bangladesh	87.6	99.6	103.7	109.7	111.2	115.2	131.2	139.0	135.8	140.1
Bhutan	99.0	101.2	115.2	118.7	120.9	120.0	117.0	116.2	116.1	96.0
Brunei		100.4	144.8	125.6	156.7	184.4	230.4	257.6	297.1	348.8
Cambodia	76.0	99.0	125.6	127.5	131.0	133.0	149.2	152.6	159.1	144.2
China	80.0	101.6	139.7	148.1	157.4	165.9	174.0	180.1	185.8	191.8
Fiji	85.1	104.5	103.1	109.1	97.8	84.9	98.6	99.4	94.0	96.9
French Polynesia		103.1	101.8	97.9	95.7	79.5	87.8	96.9	94.6	101.2
Guam		96.9	110.8	129.0	129.0	129.0	129.0	129.0	129.1	129.1
Hong Kong, China		98.1	55.9	25.9	20.3	41.0	58.0	63.0	65.0	67.0
India	83.6	99.7	115.3	119.6	122.4	125.3	130.8	132.0	133.6	129.8
Indonesia	82.1	100.9	125.5	124.6	119.0	117.8	119.8	124.0	122.8	123.9
Japan	102.0	100.8	97.4	95.5	95.8	91.6	92.9	92.6	90.6	91.6
Kazakhstan			64.0	62.1	62.2	50.8	70.0	65.2	75.7	79.6
Kiribati		85.0	109.0	127.2	127.2	133.1	134.6	126.5	128.4	130.5
Kyrgyzstan			87.4	99.2	107.0	113.3	120.2	126.6	134.4	136.5
Laos	93.1	106.1	113.2	112.3	126.2	130.4	156.2	178.9	188.2	192.2
Macau		99.7	104.8	106.2	105.9	115.8	158.9	160.3	162.4	162.3
Malaysia	70.6	100.0	124.6	128.6	130.8	128.7	133.0	136.0	142.9	147.3
Maldives		104.4	115.2	117.4	124.7	127.0	131.5	147.3	148.8	148.8
Mongolia	93.0	99.8	79.1	90.9	88.2	90.8	106.3	103.0	80.2	92.6
Myanmar	110.9	101.2	132.0	135.9	136.2	138.2	154.8	167.0	181.1	181.5
Nauru		99.9	105.5	105.4	105.6	105.6	105.6	105.6	105.6	105.6
Nepal	82.2	101.9	113.0	115.7	118.7	121.2	127.7	132.4	136.4	138.5
New Caledonia		100.0	118.1	123.4	127.6	131.1	131.4	130.2	132.0	132.3
North Korea		99.7	76.9	69.1	69.4	83.5	83.9	82.4	90.5	90.9
Pakistan	78.7	99.5	127.2	138.0	141.2	146.5	149.6	154.0	151.0	153.2
Papua New Guinea	100.1	99.5	108.3	116.3	115.8	115.8	122.9	127.6	124.0	121.4
Philippines	87.3	103.9	112.1	121.9	124.6	115.4	126.1	131.0	136.3	144.1
Singapore		104.9	43.3	42.3	37.5	41.4	27.7	33.4	34.9	27.4
Solomon Islands	123.9	97.0	122.4	125.6	131.2	134.8	138.3	148.4	151.4	152.3
South Korea		101.8	113.2	121.1	126.6	125.6	132.2	132.3	132.9	131.6
Sri Lanka	109.1	104.6	117.4	103.3	106.4	111.9	117.0	119.7	116.1	115.7
Taiwan										
Tajikistan			64.1	55.0	53.5	47.9	50.5	59.5	58.6	63.3
Thailand	95.9	94.4	110.7	113.2	115.8	112.5	115.5	121.3	125.7	123.6
Tonga	98.7	95.8	91.6	89.4	96.0	91.6	98.4	97.6	97.5	97.5
Turkmenistan			114.3	94.0	102.9	125.2	133.9	131.8	131.1	131.9
Tuvalu		83.1	95.9	99.6	105.5	107.0	110.3	110.6	100.4	100.4
Uzbekistan			114.4	107.2	108.9	113.2	112.8	119.3	121.4	126.3
Vanuatu	99.7	113.9	103.1	104.0	121.6	126.0	106.1	100.6	83.6	87.6
Vietnam	82.2	99.8	128.1	134.4	141.8	148.0	158.2	165.5	168.1	180.5
Western Samoa		100.2	87.6	90.1	92.6	97.0	96.2	101.2	102.6	104.2
Australasia										
Australia	93.5	102.4	118.6	131.6	129.8	138.2	148.4	141.6	148.8	126.1
New Zealand	106.0	95.8	117.1	120.1	127.2	128.4	121.4	130.3	136.2	139.1

Source: *UN Food and Agriculture Organisation, FAOSTAT*

▣ Indices of Agricultural Output

Indices of Food Output 1985-2002

● 1989-1991 = 100

	1985	1990	1995	1996	1997	1998	1999	2000	2001	2002
Africa and Middle East										
Algeria	89.9	92.9	121.3	143.9	114.5	131.4	134.7	128.2	141.7	138.7
Angola	96.5	98.1	123.5	128.6	129.0	149.6	143.0	161.3	178.8	177.4
Bahrain		96.9	111.5	109.4	115.2	104.6	131.9	121.8	73.9	73.9
Benin	79.9	98.8	128.0	136.0	147.6	151.6	161.7	170.1	170.0	181.6
Botswana	96.6	99.7	111.6	106.4	94.6	90.5	79.2	83.9	92.8	92.7
Burkina Faso	85.2	92.3	127.0	139.6	126.3	149.4	154.4	131.5	172.4	169.9
Burundi	90.0	102.5	96.4	96.3	96.5	91.3	91.9	87.3	96.1	96.1
Cameroon	92.8	99.8	119.0	124.7	121.7	126.3	137.2	139.7	137.8	137.4
Cape Verde		102.6	124.4	110.6	113.7	128.8	162.7	144.2	142.8	145.0
Central African Republic	81.6	99.6	115.0	129.3	124.6	130.4	132.8	147.8	143.9	147.8
Chad	84.6	91.1	118.1	121.1	135.6	158.8	143.5	137.0	160.9	155.8
Comoros		98.8	114.5	120.1	118.9	125.3	128.8	132.3	135.2	135.5
Congo Dem Rep	84.6	100.8	92.8	92.2	90.2	91.8	89.6	87.9	86.4	84.6
Congo-Brazzaville	92.9	101.2	114.0	118.4	119.1	117.3	126.0	128.2	129.6	133.1
Côte d'Ivoire	83.9	100.9	122.6	131.4	131.4	133.2	140.4	145.9	137.0	126.7
Djibouti		107.6	85.4	87.0	87.7	88.4	89.7	89.1	89.2	89.2
Egypt	80.4	101.6	125.6	137.0	141.9	142.7	151.6	159.1	157.2	158.4
Equatorial Guinea		100.9	108.3	110.5	111.1	107.9	117.0	115.5	112.8	112.8
Eritrea		107.5	104.1	103.5	149.5	134.5	117.0	124.4	107.5	
Ethiopia	85.1	99.9	118.7	139.0	140.2	128.1	137.1	145.5	159.8	152.4
Gabon	86.4	98.2	105.0	107.5	109.9	113.0	114.0	116.6	116.8	116.7
Gambia	88.6	84.5	87.8	69.6	90.3	86.1	125.6	139.2	151.7	90.8
Ghana	83.9	88.1	137.9	148.5	144.3	157.4	166.5	171.0	175.0	197.6
Guinea	94.7	99.6	129.6	134.4	141.0	147.2	153.4	153.3	162.2	169.9
Guinea-Bissau	86.8	103.0	112.1	116.2	125.4	128.6	136.1	141.5	143.9	141.2
Iran	83.1	104.3	132.5	139.6	137.8	158.3	153.4	152.7	150.7	161.0
Iraq	112.2	118.4	101.5	103.4	95.3	99.0	84.2	74.0	78.6	79.9
Israel	98.1	107.1	107.7	111.7	110.5	114.8	112.5	115.8	115.0	115.2
Jordan	95.4	107.0	150.8	115.6	136.4	139.6	108.1	144.9	130.9	166.5
Kenya	80.4	99.8	104.4	105.0	108.0	112.6	118.4	117.2	125.2	124.2
Kuwait	144.2	120.0	124.5	146.1	155.2	180.7	198.2	196.4	246.3	244.4
Lebanon	67.8	99.4	123.9	127.7	116.3	111.4	109.6	115.1	107.3	104.4
Lesotho	90.4	111.3	87.2	110.1	107.7	95.5	97.4	109.2	95.9	129.7
Liberia		96.5	74.2	80.2	95.6	103.2	104.9	112.2	110.3	116.7
Libya	89.7	100.4	120.2	126.5	131.9	138.5	137.5	134.3	133.0	134.8
Madagascar	92.5	100.0	107.7	109.5	111.7	111.3	113.7	113.1	117.3	117.0
Malawi	93.6	97.1	105.7	122.5	114.1	141.2	160.2	184.1	190.9	146.8
Mali	75.8	97.8	110.1	113.0	111.2	120.5	128.1	123.6	126.3	136.0
Mauritania	86.3	100.2	101.5	107.7	105.8	107.1	106.7	110.2	108.0	106.9
Mauritius	96.2	101.4	105.6	107.6	116.0	111.2	86.2	106.4	117.7	103.0
Morocco	66.1	93.3	73.5	114.1	96.5	112.6	105.2	96.7	103.6	110.6
Mozambique	92.6	106.0	108.1	122.3	130.0	139.2	140.9	124.9	128.7	128.9
Namibia	83.1	96.8	105.2	115.8	82.8	95.2	100.4	105.4	92.4	92.5
Niger	78.2	89.3	109.5	123.3	101.7	153.0	138.7	128.1	150.4	141.9
Nigeria	71.7	97.5	132.3	139.1	142.7	148.9	154.3	155.5	153.2	158.8
Oman		99.1	112.1	129.0	138.8	152.4	165.9	160.2	163.9	165.1
Qatar		95.4	154.9	166.3	185.6	147.5	161.0	173.0	127.3	160.5
Réunion	77.0	99.1	113.5	115.4	124.4	118.9	125.6	125.8	128.1	131.8
Rwanda	109.8	100.4	66.0	75.8	78.1	84.7	90.2	110.6	110.8	130.6
Sao Tomé e Príncipe		96.5	124.2	143.0	159.8	179.5	186.8	191.2	198.3	198.2
Saudi Arabia	63.6	104.5	80.8	75.1	88.3	107.8	84.1	83.4	105.9	106.2
Senegal	86.3	95.2	115.5	107.2	101.0	100.6	137.8	135.7	130.2	101.4
Seychelles		96.3	142.8	138.9	142.7	128.2	134.9	134.5	131.2	134.0
Sierra Leone	88.2	99.6	91.5	97.2	101.9	94.7	85.4	78.7	86.0	87.4
Somalia		103.7	97.8	101.4	111.8	105.4	106.4	108.8	107.5	110.3
South Africa	89.5	98.1	88.3	104.5	106.1	100.3	106.8	113.2	107.9	112.1
Sudan	107.2	91.8	140.9	154.6	156.7	162.8	159.7	162.3	174.7	165.6
Swaziland	93.7	96.8	88.5	99.5	86.4	88.5	93.1	100.7	101.1	97.9
Syria	103.0	106.8	134.4	149.0	130.9	164.7	133.1	151.6	162.2	177.0
Tanzania	91.8	99.6	105.4	106.0	93.0	107.3	108.4	113.0	113.0	112.4
Togo	83.9	103.1	112.2	132.8	136.4	129.4	139.6	130.6	131.2	132.4
Tunisia	87.5	96.6	81.8	143.4	98.1	124.6	136.3	132.8	115.2	97.2
Uganda	81.3	101.0	110.5	101.8	104.8	117.4	127.6	132.0	139.0	139.2
United Arab Emirates		102.4	173.9	196.3	241.7	238.2	394.5	601.5	519.2	528.9
Yemen	78.9	100.8	113.2	113.2	120.3	131.3	130.1	137.0	145.7	145.2
Zambia	83.2	93.6	93.2	114.3	104.5	98.9	112.3	109.5	102.7	109.4
Zimbabwe	104.3	103.8	74.5	103.2	106.5	94.0	103.7	118.0	111.9	95.8

Source: UN Food and Agriculture Organisation, FAOSTAT

| ▣ Total Surface Area (Land and Water) | | | | | | Table 3.3 |

Land Use and Irrigation 2002

● '000 hectares

	Total Area	Land Area	Arable Land	Permanent Crops	Permanent Pasture	Irrigated Land	Irrigated as % of Land Area
North America							
Canada	997,061	922,097	45,560	140	29,000	720	0.1
USA	962,909	915,896	176,950	2,050	239,250	22,400	2.4
Latin America							
Anguilla	9						
Antigua	44	44	8		4		
Argentina	278,040	273,669	25,000	2,200	142,000	1,561	0.6
Aruba	19	19	2				
Bahamas	1,388	1,001	6	4	2		
Barbados	43	43	16	1	2	1	2.3
Belize	2,296	2,280	64	25	50	3	0.1
Bermuda	5	5					
Bolivia	109,858	108,438	1,935	275	33,831	132	0.1
Brazil	854,740	845,651	53,200	12,000	185,000	2,910	0.3
British Virgin Islands	34	34	3	1	5		
Cayman Islands	26	26			2		
Chile	75,663	74,880	1,979	321	12,935	1,800	2.4
Colombia	113,891	103,870	2,965	1,710	40,520	850	0.8
Costa Rica	5,110	5,106	225	280	2,340	108	2.1
Cuba	11,086	10,982	3,630	835	2,200	870	7.9
Dominica	75	75	3	12	2		
Dominican Republic	4,873	4,838	1,100	500	2,100	275	5.7
Ecuador	28,356	27,684	1,574	1,427	5,107	865	3.1
El Salvador	2,104	2,072	560	250	794	40	1.9
French Guiana	9,000	8,815	9	4	10	2	0.0
Grenada	34	34	1	10	1		
Guadeloupe	171	169	19	6	24	6	3.6
Guatemala	10,889	10,843	1,360	545	2,602	130	1.2
Guyana	21,497	19,685	480	16	1,230	150	0.8
Haiti	2,775	2,756	560	350	490	75	2.7
Honduras	11,209	11,189	1,068	359	1,506	80	0.7
Jamaica	1,099	1,083	174	100	229	25	2.3
Martinique	110	106	12	8	12	3	2.8
Mexico	195,820	190,869	24,800	2,500	81,000	6,500	3.4
Netherlands Antilles	80	80	8				
Nicaragua	13,000	12,140	2,457	289	4,815	88	0.7
Panama	7,552	7,443	500	155	1,477	35	0.5
Paraguay	40,675	39,730	2,290	88	21,700	67	0.2
Peru	128,522	128,000	3,700	510	27,100	1,195	0.9
Puerto Rico	895	887	35	46	210	40	4.5
St Kitts	36	36	7	1	2		
St Lucia	62	61	3	14	2	3	4.9
St Vincent and the Grenadines	39	39	4	7	2	1	2.6
Suriname	16,327	15,600	57	10	21	51	0.3
Trinidad and Tobago	513	513	75	47	11	3	0.6
Uruguay	17,622	17,502	1,310	39	13,520	180	1.0
Venezuela	91,205	88,205	2,440	960	18,240	575	0.7

Source: *UN Food and Agriculture Organisation, FAOSTAT*

Land Use and Irrigation 2002

● '000 hectares

	Total Area	Land Area	Arable Land	Permanent Crops	Permanent Pasture	Irrigated Land	Irrigated as % of Land Area
Asia Pacific							
Afghanistan	65,209	65,209	7,910	144	30,000	2,386	3.7
American Samoa	20	20	2	3			
Armenia	2,980	2,820	495	65	834	287	10.2
Azerbaijan	8,660	8,660	1,655	263	2,640	1,455	16.8
Bangladesh	14,400	13,017	8,050	345	600	4,220	32.4
Bhutan	4,700	4,700	140	20	300	40	0.9
Brunei	577	527	3	4	6	1	0.2
Cambodia	18,104	17,652	3,700	107	1,500	270	1.5
China	959,805	932,742	124,135	11,478	400,001	54,402	5.8
Fiji	1,827	1,827	200	85	175	3	0.2
French Polynesia	400	366	3	20	20	1	0.3
Guam	55	55	6	6	8		
Hong Kong, China	107	99	5	1	1	2	2.0
India	328,726	297,319	161,800	7,950	10,910	54,800	18.4
Indonesia	190,457	181,157	20,500	13,046	11,177	4,815	2.7
Japan	37,780	36,450	4,470	360	405	2,640	7.2
Kazakhstan	272,490	269,970	21,180	132	185,098	2,350	0.9
Kiribati	73	73		37			
Kyrgyzstan	19,990	19,180	1,368	67	9,291	1,072	5.6
Laos	23,680	23,080	877	83	890	175	0.8
Macau	2	2					
Malaysia	32,975	32,855	1,820	5,785	285	365	1.1
Maldives	30	30	1	2	1		
Mongolia	156,650	156,650	1,170	1	129,294	84	0.1
Myanmar	67,658	65,755	9,800	595	316	1,990	3.0
Nauru	2	2					
Nepal	14,718	14,300	2,898	70	1,757	1,135	7.9
New Caledonia	1,858	1,828	7	6	216		
North Korea	12,054	12,041	1,700	300	50	1,460	12.1
Pakistan	79,610	77,088	10	652	4	18,300	23.7
Papua New Guinea	46,284	45,286	205	670	90		
Philippines	30,000	29,817	5,550	4,500	1,280	1,550	5.2
Singapore	62	61	1				
Solomon Islands	2,890	2,799	42	18	40		
South Korea	9,926	9,873	1,725	200	54	1,159	11.7
Sri Lanka	6,561	6,463	895	1,020	440	667	10.3
Taiwan	3,599						
Tajikistan	14,310	14,060	730	130	3,500	719	5.1
Thailand	51,312	51,089	14,700	3,300	800	5,020	9.8
Tonga	75	72	17	31	4		
Turkmenistan	48,810	46,993	1,630	65	30,700	1,800	3.8
Tuvalu	3	3					
Uzbekistan	44,740	41,424	4,475	375	22,800	4,281	10.3
Vanuatu	1,219	1,219	30	90	42		
Vietnam	33,169	32,549	5,750	1,600	642	3,000	9.2
Western Samoa	284	283	55	67	1		
Australasia							
Australia	774,122	768,230	51,000	310	404,500	2,370	0.3
New Zealand	27,053	26,799	1,555	1,725	13,300	282	1.1

Source: *UN Food and Agriculture Organisation, FAOSTAT*

Total Surface Area (Land and Water)
Land Use and Irrigation 2002

● '000 hectares

	Total Area	Land Area	Arable Land	Permanent Crops	Permanent Pasture	Irrigated Land	Irrigated as % of Land Area
Africa and Middle East							
Algeria	238,174	238,174	7,675	521	31,200	560	0.2
Angola	124,670	124,670	3,000	300	54,000	75	0.1
Bahrain	71	71	3	3	4	4	5.6
Benin	11,262	11,062	1,950	260	550	12	0.1
Botswana	58,173	56,673	382	3	25,600	1	0.0
Burkina Faso	27,400	27,360	3,900	50	6,000	25	0.1
Burundi	2,783	2,568	900	375	935	74	2.9
Cameroon	47,544	46,540	5,960	1,200	2,000	33	0.1
Cape Verde	403	403	39	2	25	3	0.7
Central African Republic	62,298	62,298	1,930	90	3,125		
Chad	128,400	125,920	3,520	30	45,000	20	0.0
Comoros	223	223	78	50	15		
Congo Dem Rep	234,486	226,705	6,700	1,180	15,000	11	0.0
Congo-Brazzaville	34,200	34,150	175	45	10,000	1	0.0
Côte d'Ivoire	32,246	31,800	2,950	4,400	13,000	73	0.2
Djibouti	2,320	2,318			1,300	1	0.0
Egypt	100,145	99,545	2,821	466		3,280	3.3
Equatorial Guinea	2,805	2,805	130	100			
Eritrea	11,760	10,100	498	3	6,967	21	0.2
Ethiopia	110,430	100,000	10,000	721	20,000	190	0.2
Gabon	26,767	25,767	325	170	4,665	15	0.1
Gambia	1,130	1,000	230	5	459	2	0.2
Ghana	23,854	22,754	3,609	2,250	8,350	11	0.0
Guinea	24,586	24,572	885	600	10,700	95	0.4
Guinea-Bissau	3,612	2,812	300	50	1,080	17	0.6
Iran	164,820	163,620	14,324	2,005	44,000	7,500	4.6
Iraq	43,832	43,737	5,200	340	4,000	3,525	8.1
Israel	2,106	2,062	333	85	140	194	9.4
Jordan	8,921	8,893	244	145	791	75	0.8
Kenya	58,037	56,914	4,000	520	21,300	67	0.1
Kuwait	1,782	1,782	8	1	136	7	0.4
Lebanon	1,040	1,023	190	143	16	104	10.2
Lesotho	3,035	3,035	325		2,000	1	0.0
Liberia	11,137	9,632	380	215	2,000	3	0.0
Libya	175,954	175,954	1,815	335	13,300	470	0.3
Madagascar	58,704	58,154	2,900	600	24,000	1,090	1.9
Malawi	11,848	9,408	2,150	142	1,850	28	0.3
Mali	124,019	122,019	4,640	44	30,000	138	0.1
Mauritania	102,552	102,522	488	12	39,250	49	0.0
Mauritius	204	203	100	6	7	20	9.9
Morocco	44,655	44,630	8,623	970	21,000	1,305	2.9
Mozambique	80,159	78,409	3,900	235	44,000	107	0.1
Namibia	82,429	82,329	816	4	38,000	7	0.0
Niger	126,700	126,670	4,490	10	12,000	66	0.1
Nigeria	92,377	91,077	28,200	2,580	39,200	233	0.3
Oman	30,950	30,950	19	61	1,000	62	0.2
Qatar	1,100	1,100	18	3	50	12	1.1
Réunion	251	250	34	4	12	12	4.8
Rwanda	2,634	2,467	940	250	541	5	0.2
Sao Tomé e Príncipe	96	96	4	45	1	10	10.4
Saudi Arabia	214,969	214,969	3,594	195	170,000	1,620	0.8
Senegal	19,672	19,253	2,362	39	5,650	71	0.4
Seychelles	45	45	1	6			
Sierra Leone	7,174	7,162	490	60	2,200	30	0.4
Somalia	63,766	62,734	1,043	24	43,000	200	0.3
South Africa	122,104	122,104	14,753	959	83,928	1,500	1.2
Sudan	250,581	237,600	16,200	200	117,180	1,950	0.8
Swaziland	1,736	1,720	178	12	1,200	70	4.1
Syria	18,518	18,378	4,600	820	8,400	1,270	6.9
Tanzania	94,509	88,359	4,000	950	35,000	168	0.2
Togo	5,679	5,439	2,510	120	1,000	7	0.1
Tunisia	16,361	15,536	2,909	2,105	4,062	380	2.4
Uganda	24,104	19,710	5,060	1,920	1,800	9	0.0
United Arab Emirates	8,360	8,360	55	192	305	76	0.9
Yemen	52,797	52,797	1,545	125	16,065	500	0.9
Zambia	75,261	74,339	5,260	19	30,000	46	0.1
Zimbabwe	39,076	38,685	3,220	130	17,200	117	0.3

Source: UN Food and Agriculture Organisation, FAOSTAT

Number of Livestock 2002

● '000 head

	Asses	Cattle	Goats	Horses	Pigs	Sheep
North America						
Canada		13,699.5	30.0	385.0	14,367.1	993.6
USA	52.0	96,700.0	1,250.0	5,300.0	59,074.0	6,685.0
Latin America						
Anguilla						
Antigua	1.5	13.8	35.0	0.5	5.3	18.5
Argentina	95.0	50,669.0	3,550.0	3,650.0	4,250.0	14,000.0
Aruba						
Bahamas		0.7	13.9		4.9	6.4
Barbados	2.0	21.0	5.0	1.0	35.0	41.3
Belize		56.9	1.6	5.1	22.9	6.4
Bermuda	0.0	0.6	0.3	0.9	0.6	
Bolivia	632.0	6,576.3	1,500.5	323.0	2,850.5	8,901.6
Brazil	1,250.0	176,000.0	9,800.0	5,900.0	30,000.0	15,000.0
British Virgin Islands	0.3	2.4	10.0	0.1	1.5	6.1
Cayman Islands		1.3	0.3		0.4	
Chile	28.5	3,566.0	900.0	660.0	2,750.0	4,100.0
Colombia	723.0	27,000.0	1,120.0	2,650.0	2,150.0	2,260.0
Costa Rica	7.6	1,219.0	1.7	114.5	475.0	2.5
Cuba	7.0	4,038.4	291.4	400.0	1,307.3	970.0
Dominica		13.4	9.7		5.0	7.6
Dominican Republic	150.0	2,159.6	188.0	342.0	577.0	121.3
Ecuador	275.0	5,578.4	278.3	528.0	2,805.6	2,380.7
El Salvador	3.2	1,392.1	10.7	96.0	153.5	5.1
French Guiana		9.2	0.8	0.3	10.5	2.6
Grenada	0.7	4.4	7.1	0.0	5.9	13.1
Guadeloupe	0.1	85.0	28.0	1.0	19.0	3.1
Guatemala	9.9	2,540.0	111.6	122.0	778.0	250.0
Guyana	1.0	100.0	79.0	2.4	20.0	130.0
Haiti	215.0	1,450.0	1,943.0	500.5	1,001.1	153.0
Honduras	23.0	1,859.7	32.0	180.0	538.0	13.7
Jamaica	23.0	400.0	440.0	4.0	180.0	1.4
Martinique		25.0	17.0	2.0	35.0	34.0
Mexico	3,260.0	30,600.0	9,400.0	6,255.0	17,000.0	6,700.0
Netherlands Antilles	2.6	0.6	13.0		2.4	7.5
Nicaragua	8.8	3,350.0	6.7	250.0	420.0	4.3
Panama		1,533.5	6.2	170.0	280.0	
Paraguay	33.0	9,900.0	125.0	358.0	2,750.0	406.5
Peru	580.0	4,950.0	2,010.0	710.0	2,800.0	14,300.0
Puerto Rico	2.0	390.0	9.0	26.0	118.0	16.0
St Kitts		4.3	14.4		4.0	14.0
St Lucia	0.5	12.4	9.8	1.0	15.0	12.5
St Vincent and the Grenadines	1.3	6.2	6.0		9.5	13.0
Suriname	0.0	136.0	7.0	0.4	24.0	7.6
Trinidad and Tobago	2.1	31.6	60.5	1.1	64.0	12.8
Uruguay	1.4	11,667.0	15.0	390.0	344.0	11,250.0
Venezuela	440.0	14,500.0	4,000.0	500.0	5,655.0	820.0

Source: UN Food and Agriculture Organisation, FAOSTAT

▫ Livestock

Number of Livestock 2002

● '000 head

	Asses	Cattle	Goats	Horses	Pigs	Sheep
Asia Pacific						
Afghanistan	920.0	2,000.0	5,000.0	104.0		11,000.0
American Samoa		0.1			10.7	
Armenia	2.6	520.0	10.5	12.1	105.0	555.0
Azerbaijan	38.0	2,097.9	556.0	63.0	16.9	6,002.9
Bangladesh		24,000.0	34,400.0			1,143.0
Bhutan	18.2	355.4	31.3	29.9	41.4	22.8
Brunei		2.0	2.5		6.5	4.0
Cambodia		2,924.5		27.0	2,105.4	
China	8,815.0	106,175.0	161,492.2	8,262.3	464,695.0	136,972.4
Fiji		340.0	247.0	44.0	138.0	7.0
French Polynesia		10.8	16.5	2.2	34.0	0.4
Guam		0.1	0.7	0.0	5.0	
Hong Kong, China		31.0	0.2	1.5	110.0	0.0
India	750.0	221,900.0	124,000.0	800.0	18,000.0	58,800.0
Indonesia		11,200.0	12,400.0	450.0	6,000.0	7,350.0
Japan		4,564.0	35.0	20.0	9,612.0	11.0
Kazakhstan	30.0	4,281.7	1,271.1	985.5	1,123.8	9,207.5
Kiribati					12.0	
Kyrgyzstan	7.4	988.0	661.3	350.0	87.2	3,104.1
Laos		1,150.0	260.0	30.0	1,425.9	
Macau						
Malaysia		747.6	247.6	4.5	1,824.2	118.1
Maldives						
Mongolia		2,053.7	8,858.0	3,100.0	15.0	11,937.3
Myanmar		11,551.0	1,541.7	120.0	4,498.7	431.5
Nauru					2.8	
Nepal		6,978.7	6,606.9		934.5	840.1
New Caledonia		123.0	1.5	11.5	40.0	0.5
North Korea		575.0	2,693.0	48.0	3,152.0	170.0
Pakistan	3,900.0	22,857.0	50,900.0	300.0		24,398.0
Papua New Guinea		89.0	2.4	2.0	1,650.0	6.5
Philippines		2,547.8	6,250.0	230.0	11,652.7	30.0
Singapore		0.2	0.3		190.0	
Solomon Islands		13.0		0.1	68.0	
South Korea	0.0	1,951.0	435.0	11.0	8,811.0	0.6
Sri Lanka		1,565.0	490.0	1.5	67.0	11.7
Taiwan						
Tajikistan	123.0	1,090.7	779.4	71.2	0.7	1,489.9
Thailand	0.0	4,640.4	150.0	8.0	6,688.9	42.7
Tonga		11.3	12.5	11.4	80.9	
Turkmenistan	25.0	860.0	375.0	17.0	45.0	6,000.0
Tuvalu					13.2	
Uzbekistan	160.0	5,400.0	830.0	145.0	90.0	8,220.0
Vanuatu		151.0	12.0	3.1	62.0	
Vietnam		4,063.0	621.9	124.0	23,169.5	
Western Samoa	7.0	28.0		1.8	201.0	
Australasia						
Australia	2.0	30,500.0	310.0	220.0	2,912.0	113,000.0
New Zealand		9,632.5	182.8	78.0	358.1	43,141.9

Source: *UN Food and Agriculture Organisation, FAOSTAT*

■ Livestock

Number of Livestock 2002

• '000 head

Africa and Middle East	Asses	Cattle	Goats	Horses	Pigs	Sheep
Algeria	170.0	1,600.0	3,200.0	44.0	5.7	17,300.0
Angola	4.5	4,150.0	2,050.0	1.0	780.0	340.0
Bahrain		11.0	16.3			17.5
Benin	0.6	1,550.0	1,270.0	1.0	550.0	670.0
Botswana	330.0	1,700.0	2,250.0	33.0	8.0	370.0
Burkina Faso	502.0	4,800.0	8,700.0	26.5	630.0	6,800.0
Burundi		315.0	750.0		70.0	230.0
Cameroon	38.0	5,900.0	4,400.0	16.5	1,350.0	3,800.0
Cape Verde	14.0	22.0	112.0	0.5	200.0	8.5
Central African Republic		3,273.0	2,921.0		738.0	246.0
Chad	370.0	5,900.0	5,500.0	205.0	24.0	2,450.0
Comoros	5.0	52.0	115.0			21.0
Congo Dem Rep		761.3	4,003.9		953.1	896.9
Congo-Brazzaville		93.0	294.2	0.1	46.2	96.0
Côte d'Ivoire		1,476.0	1,191.0		356.0	1,522.0
Djibouti	8.7	270.0	512.0			475.0
Egypt	3,050.0	3,810.0	3,470.0	45.7	30.0	4,671.5
Equatorial Guinea		5.0	9.0		6.1	37.6
Eritrea		2,200.0	1,700.0			1,575.0
Ethiopia	3,414.0	35,500.0	9,622.1	1,254.0	26.0	11,438.2
Gabon		35.0	90.0		212.0	195.0
Gambia	35.0	326.6	262.0	17.0	17.2	145.6
Ghana	13.1	1,430.0	3,410.0	2.7	350.0	2,970.0
Guinea	2.0	3,128.0	1,119.0	2.7	60.0	948.5
Guinea-Bissau	4.9	515.0	325.0	1.9	350.0	285.0
Iran	1,600.0	8,738.0	25,757.0	150.0		53,900.0
Iraq	380.0	1,400.0	1,650.0	47.0		6,200.0
Israel	5.0	390.0	65.0	4.0	155.0	392.0
Jordan	18.0	68.1	557.3	4.0		1,457.9
Kenya		13,500.0	9,000.0	1.8	380.0	8,000.0
Kuwait		18.0	130.0	1.2		800.0
Lebanon	25.0	79.0	385.0	6.0	20.0	350.0
Lesotho	154.0	540.0	650.0	100.0	65.0	850.0
Liberia		36.0	220.0		130.0	210.0
Libya	30.0	220.0	1,265.0	46.0		4,130.0
Madagascar	0.1	11,000.0	1,350.0	0.5	1,600.0	790.0
Malawi	2.2	750.0	1,700.0	0.0	456.3	115.0
Mali	700.0	6,818.9	8,850.0	170.0	85.0	6,150.0
Mauritania	157.5	1,500.0	5,100.0	19.5		7,600.0
Mauritius	0.1	28.0	93.0	0.1	13.5	11.5
Morocco	1,000.0	2,669.6	5,090.4	155.0	8.0	16,335.5
Mozambique	23.0	1,320.0	392.0		180.0	125.0
Namibia	169.3	2,508.6	1,769.1	52.5	21.9	2,370.0
Niger	580.0	2,260.0	6,900.0	105.0	39.0	4,500.0
Nigeria	1,000.0	20,000.0	27,000.0	205.0	5,500.0	22,000.0
Oman	28.5	314.0	998.0			354.0
Qatar		15.0	179.0	3.8		200.0
Réunion	0.0	30.0	37.0	0.5	78.0	1.7
Rwanda		815.0	760.0	0.0	180.0	260.0
Sao Tomé e Príncipe	0.0	4.1	4.8	0.2	2.1	2.6
Saudi Arabia	100.0	330.0	4,650.0	3.0		8,000.0
Senegal	420.0	3,230.0	4,000.0	492.0	300.0	4,900.0
Seychelles		1.4	5.2		18.5	
Sierra Leone		400.0	220.0		55.0	370.0
Somalia	21.0	5,300.0	12,700.0	0.8	4.2	13,100.0
South Africa	150.0	13,722.0	6,849.0	270.0	1,600.0	29,090.0
Sudan	750.0	38,325.0	40,000.0	26.0		47,043.0
Swaziland	14.8	615.0	422.0	1.4	30.0	27.0
Syria	217.0	866.7	931.9	27.0	0.8	13,497.5
Tanzania	182.0	17,700.0	11,650.0		455.0	3,550.0
Togo	3.3	278.5	1,460.0	1.6	300.0	1,700.0
Tunisia	230.0	760.0	1,450.0	56.2	6.0	6,850.0
Uganda	17.9	5,900.0	6,600.0		1,550.0	1,200.0
United Arab Emirates		100.0	1,300.0	0.4		510.0
Yemen	500.0	1,400.6	4,452.5	3.0		5,029.0
Zambia	1.8	2,600.0	1,270.0		340.0	150.0
Zimbabwe	108.0	5,753.0	2,970.0	27.0	605.0	600.0

Source: UN Food and Agriculture Organisation, FAOSTAT

■ Food Production

Table 3.5

Production of Selected Crops 2002

● '000 tonnes

	Apples	Bananas	Grapes	Hops	Potatoes	Rapeseed	Sugar Beet	Tomatoes
North America								
Canada	460.0		70.0		4,645.6	3,577.1	540.0	690.0
USA	3,857.0	8.6	6,479.0	26.5	21,011.0	706.3	24,992.9	12,266.8
Latin America								
Anguilla								
Antigua		0.1						0.2
Argentina	1,000.0	180.0	2,460.0	0.3	2,132.5	9.4		667.8
Aruba								
Bahamas		3.3						3.4
Barbados		0.6						0.7
Belize		43.0						
Bermuda					0.6			0.1
Bolivia	9.8	714.2	36.4		944.2			153.4
Brazil	857.8	6,369.5	1,099.5		2,865.1	41.0		3,518.2
British Virgin Islands		0.3						
Cayman Islands		0.2						0.0
Chile	1,050.0		1,720.0		1,303.3	3.5	3,540.0	1,287.0
Colombia		1,650.0	19.2		2,698.0			394.1
Costa Rica		2,140.0			82.2			49.8
Cuba		678.7			345.4			258.6
Dominica		29.0			0.1			0.2
Dominican Republic		502.9			48.6			154.9
Ecuador	12.9	6,500.0	0.6		349.4		2.6	48.6
El Salvador		65.0			17.0			21.5
French Guiana		4.5						3.8
Grenada	0.5	4.1						0.1
Guadeloupe		115.5						3.1
Guatemala	28.9	940.4	14.3		248.0			187.2
Guyana		17.0						2.7
Haiti		295.0			11.5			2.5
Honduras	0.1	965.1	0.2		19.1			53.0
Jamaica		130.0			6.7			24.1
Martinique		310.0						6.1
Mexico	428.2	2,076.7	354.7		1,536.4	14.0		2,083.6
Netherlands Antilles								
Nicaragua		53.5			28.5			6.6
Panama		600.0			25.7			17.5
Paraguay	0.6	65.0	8.5		1.1			55.5
Peru	123.6		136.1		3,299.2			129.8
Puerto Rico		50.0						5.0
St Kitts					0.2			0.1
St Lucia		92.0						
St Vincent and the Grenadines	0.6	46.0						
Suriname		43.0						1.1
Trinidad and Tobago		6.5						1.2
Uruguay	45.8		120.0		122.0			37.5
Venezuela		750.0	11.5		330.0		16.8	182.0

Source: *UN Food and Agriculture Organisation, FAOSTAT*

◻ Food Production

Production of Selected Crops 2002

● '000 tonnes

	Apples	Bananas	Grapes	Hops	Potatoes	Rapeseed	Sugar Beet	Tomatoes
Asia Pacific								
Afghanistan	17.5		365.0		240.0		1.0	
American Samoa		0.8						
Armenia	35.2		104.0		374.3			171.0
Azerbaijan	313.0		62.0		694.9		115.8	403.9
Bangladesh		606.0			3,216.0	233.0		103.0
Bhutan	5.1				22.0			
Brunei		0.6						
Cambodia		146.0						
China	20,434.8	5,651.7	3,830.0	16.0	65,052.1	10,530.0	11,562.0	25,466.2
Fiji		6.5			0.1			2.8
French Polynesia		0.5			0.9			1.1
Guam		0.2						0.1
Hong Kong, China								0.0
India	1,420.0	16,450.0	1,200.0		24,000.0	5,040.4		7,420.0
Indonesia		3,696.0			850.0			600.0
Japan	911.9	0.5	231.7	0.7	2,980.0	0.2	4,098.0	800.0
Kazakhstan	110.5		26.3		2,257.0	2.1	372.2	448.9
Kiribati		4.6						
Kyrgyzstan	97.2		17.7		1,244.0		524.5	183.5
Laos		23.5			35.0			
Macau								
Malaysia		500.0						10.0
Maldives		2.6						
Mongolia					65.6			
Myanmar					318.6			
Nauru								
Nepal					1,472.8			
New Caledonia		1.2			1.6			
North Korea	660.0			1.8	1,884.0			70.0
Pakistan	367.1	149.7	52.6		1,721.6	230.0	316.5	294.1
Papua New Guinea		725.0			0.5			0.4
Philippines		5,264.5	0.2		68.0			146.0
Singapore								
Solomon Islands		0.3						
South Korea	403.6		454.0	1.8	750.0	4.5		200.0
Sri Lanka					57.7			40.4
Taiwan								
Tajikistan	75.0		100.0		400.0			170.4
Thailand		1,750.0	40.0		84.1			246.0
Tonga		0.7						0.5
Turkmenistan	20.0		130.0		28.0			150.0
Tuvalu		0.3						
Uzbekistan	500.0		570.0		730.0	1.5		1,000.0
Vanuatu		13.0						
Vietnam		1,044.4			377.5			
Western Samoa		21.5						
Australasia								
Australia	295.0	250.0	1,753.9	2.0	1,260.0	621.0		400.0
New Zealand	537.0		118.7	0.7	500.0	4.0		87.0

Source: *UN Food and Agriculture Organisation, FAOSTAT*

▢ Food Production

Production of Selected Crops 2002

● '000 tonnes

	Apples	Bananas	Grapes	Hops	Potatoes	Rapeseed	Sugar Beet	Tomatoes
Africa and Middle East								
Algeria	100.0		196.0		1,000.0	100.0		830.0
Angola		300.0			27.0			13.0
Bahrain		0.7	0.1		0.0			3.4
Benin		13.0			0.1			141.3
Botswana								
Burkina Faso					1.5			10.0
Burundi		1,548.9			27.3			
Cameroon		630.0			130.0			370.0
Cape Verde		6.0			3.4			4.5
Central African Republic		118.0			1.0			
Chad					33.0			
Comoros		60.0			1.0			0.6
Congo Dem Rep		313.4			91.4			40.0
Congo-Brazzaville		84.4			4.6			3.2
Côte d'Ivoire		270.0						170.0
Djibouti								1.1
Egypt	484.1	849.3	1,103.8		1,903.1		3,168.3	6,328.7
Equatorial Guinea		20.0						
Eritrea					40.0			
Ethiopia		82.0	4.0		415.0	14.7		55.0
Gabon		12.0						0.3
Gambia								
Ghana		10.0						200.0
Guinea		150.0						
Guinea-Bissau		4.0						
Iran	2,353.4	40.6	2,516.7		3,500.0		5,250.0	3,000.0
Iraq	75.0		265.0		625.0		7.5	500.0
Israel	95.0	106.0	114.0		375.0			352.0
Jordan	39.2	47.4	34.8		105.3			359.8
Kenya		210.0			1,000.0			270.0
Kuwait			0.0		32.6			35.1
Lebanon	112.0	66.7	116.2		257.0		15.2	247.0
Lesotho					90.0			
Liberia		110.0						1.0
Libya	47.0		39.5		195.0			160.0
Madagascar	6.9	290.0	10.4		296.0			22.0
Malawi		93.0			1,082.3			35.0
Mali								49.7
Mauritania					2.0			
Mauritius		6.7			14.2			11.7
Morocco	372.5	162.3	275.0		1,334.4	0.3	2,985.9	991.0
Mozambique		90.0			80.0			8.5
Namibia			5.5					
Niger					4.2			99.2
Nigeria					629.0			879.0
Oman		33.7			12.7			46.5
Qatar			0.1		0.1			11.0
Réunion	0.1	10.2	0.2		4.0			5.4
Rwanda					1,038.9			
Sao Tomé e Príncipe		35.0						
Saudi Arabia			117.0		400.0			310.0
Senegal		6.0			7.5			13.2
Seychelles		2.0						0.2
Sierra Leone								13.5
Somalia		60.0						
South Africa	579.3	280.0	1,350.0	0.3	1,606.0			446.1
Sudan		73.0			15.5			245.0
Swaziland		0.5			6.0			3.4
Syria	215.8	0.7	368.9		515.2		1,480.5	546.0
Tanzania		150.4	14.0		596.0			140.0
Togo		16.1						5.5
Tunisia	100.0		113.0		310.0	2.5		810.0
Uganda		988.8			510.0			14.0
United Arab Emirates		0.1	0.1		12.0			400.0
Yemen	2.7	95.9	162.7		208.6			261.7
Zambia		0.7			11.0			25.0
Zimbabwe	6.2	85.0	2.5		33.0			12.0

Source: UN Food and Agriculture Organisation, FAOSTAT

     Table 3.6

Production of Dairy Products and Eggs 2002

- '000 tonnes

	Butter and Ghee	Cheese	Fresh Cows' Milk	Hens' Eggs
North America				
Canada	93.0	337.7	8,130.0	390.0
USA	614.2	4,239.4	77,021.3	5,128.0
Latin America				
Anguilla				
Antigua			5.1	0.2
Argentina	65.0	444.0	8,200.0	330.0
Aruba				
Bahamas			0.6	0.9
Barbados			9.0	1.0
Belize			1.9	1.8
Bermuda			1.4	0.3
Bolivia	0.6	6.8	190.0	38.7
Brazil	70.0	39.0	22,635.0	1,550.0
British Virgin Islands				
Cayman Islands				0.0
Chile	11.6	59.7	2,170.0	112.0
Colombia	19.2	54.0	5,750.0	355.0
Costa Rica	5.5	8.8	790.5	47.8
Cuba	7.2	14.5	620.7	67.5
Dominica			6.1	0.2
Dominican Republic	1.8	3.7	517.7	82.4
Ecuador	4.9	7.3	2,433.2	73.5
El Salvador	0.2	2.4	408.0	53.0
French Guiana			0.3	0.5
Grenada			0.5	0.9
Guadeloupe			0.1	1.7
Guatemala	0.6	11.3	270.0	85.0
Guyana			30.0	1.5
Haiti			42.5	4.3
Honduras	4.4	9.0	595.5	43.4
Jamaica			28.5	5.8
Martinique			2.2	1.5
Mexico	18.0	158.9	9,597.6	1,896.0
Netherlands Antilles			0.4	0.5
Nicaragua	0.5	16.1	263.5	25.0
Panama	0.1	10.0	146.8	12.7
Paraguay			332.0	72.0
Peru	0.8	8.7	1,194.3	181.6
Puerto Rico			377.0	15.2
St Kitts				0.2
St Lucia			1.0	0.5
St Vincent and the Grenadines			1.4	0.6
Suriname	0.0		13.5	2.6
Trinidad and Tobago			10.0	3.7
Uruguay	16.0	28.6	1,490.0	39.0
Venezuela	1.5	97.2	1,450.0	181.5

Source: UN Food and Agriculture Organisation, FAOSTAT

Production of Dairy Products and Eggs 2002

- '000 tonnes

	Butter and Ghee	Cheese	Fresh Cows' Milk	Hens' Eggs
Asia Pacific				
Afghanistan	27.7	18.1	1,200.0	18.3
American Samoa			0.0	0.0
Armenia	0.1	3.0	477.5	19.1
Azerbaijan	5.2	11.2	1,119.8	31.4
Bangladesh	17.8	1.0	782.0	133.5
Bhutan		0.1	41.1	0.2
Brunei				5.5
Cambodia			20.4	12.8
China	88.0	217.6	10,843.3	20,616.4
Fiji	1.8		57.5	2.7
French Polynesia			1.2	1.6
Guam				0.7
Hong Kong, China			0.2	0.0
India	2,400.0		35,700.0	2,000.0
Indonesia			550.0	655.0
Japan	86.3	122.8	8,380.0	2,512.2
Kazakhstan	3.9	11.2	4,068.2	116.6
Kiribati				0.2
Kyrgyzstan	1.4	4.7	1,140.3	13.4
Laos			6.0	11.0
Macau				0.7
Malaysia			37.0	432.0
Maldives				
Mongolia	0.5	1.8	175.5	0.4
Myanmar	11.6	33.0	525.1	101.7
Nauru				0.0
Nepal	20.3		352.1	25.0
New Caledonia			3.6	1.6
North Korea			92.0	130.0
Pakistan	599.6		6,840.0	345.6
Papua New Guinea			0.2	4.8
Philippines			11.0	495.0
Singapore				16.0
Solomon Islands			1.4	0.5
South Korea	57.1		2,390.0	510.0
Sri Lanka	0.5		224.5	53.7
Taiwan				
Tajikistan	0.0	6.7	412.0	2.6
Thailand			580.0	504.2
Tonga			0.4	0.0
Turkmenistan	0.8	1.6	830.0	15.0
Tuvalu				0.0
Uzbekistan	3.1	17.3	3,549.0	73.9
Vanuatu			3.1	0.3
Vietnam			78.5	200.5
Western Samoa			1.5	0.3
Australasia				
Australia	164.0	431.0	11,610.0	171.0
New Zealand	395.0	311.0	14,078.5	44.3

Source: *UN Food and Agriculture Organisation, FAOSTAT*

◻ Food Production

Production of Dairy Products and Eggs 2002

• '000 tonnes

	Butter and Ghee	Cheese	Fresh Cows' Milk	Hens' Eggs
Africa and Middle East				
Algeria	1.6	1.5	1,150.0	114.0
Angola	0.5	1.2	195.0	4.3
Bahrain			14.0	3.0
Benin			24.2	7.2
Botswana	1.0	4.5	101.5	3.2
Burkina Faso	1.3		170.0	17.5
Burundi	0.1		19.3	3.0
Cameroon			125.0	13.8
Cape Verde			5.3	1.9
Central African Republic			65.0	1.4
Chad	0.4		159.3	4.5
Comoros			4.5	0.8
Congo Dem Rep			5.0	7.0
Congo-Brazzaville			1.1	1.2
Côte d'Ivoire			25.9	31.2
Djibouti			8.1	
Egypt	96.7	489.5	1,900.0	199.6
Equatorial Guinea				0.2
Eritrea	0.7	0.3	52.0	2.0
Ethiopia	17.6	5.9	1,450.0	37.8
Gabon			1.6	2.0
Gambia			7.6	0.7
Ghana			37.2	23.3
Guinea	0.2		77.0	16.7
Guinea-Bissau			13.3	1.0
Iran	146.4	228.3	4,975.1	580.0
Iraq	7.8	30.1	300.0	14.0
Israel	7.5	104.3	1,250.5	86.0
Jordan	2.1	2.6	176.9	58.9
Kenya	2.3	0.3	2,650.0	60.7
Kuwait			36.0	23.5
Lebanon		16.7	167.2	37.5
Lesotho			23.8	1.5
Liberia			0.7	4.3
Libya			138.0	59.0
Madagascar			535.0	14.9
Malawi			35.0	19.5
Mali			166.6	9.6
Mauritania	0.8	2.2	115.5	4.9
Mauritius			4.7	5.2
Morocco	20.5	7.9	1,331.0	235.0
Mozambique			60.4	14.0
Namibia	0.3	0.1	88.5	1.7
Niger	5.1	14.7	184.0	10.4
Nigeria	9.7	7.8	432.0	450.0
Oman	0.2	0.5	17.6	10.0
Qatar			11.2	3.6
Réunion			22.5	5.8
Rwanda	0.3		85.0	2.3
Sao Tomé e Príncipe			0.1	0.4
Saudi Arabia	2.6		740.0	140.0
Senegal	0.5		116.3	33.0
Seychelles			0.3	2.2
Sierra Leone			21.3	8.3
Somalia	11.1		557.0	2.5
South Africa	11.5	36.0	2,646.0	366.3
Sudan	16.2	152.2	3,216.0	46.0
Swaziland	0.2		37.5	1.1
Syria	15.3	91.2	1,173.5	166.0
Tanzania	5.1	2.0	724.0	65.0
Togo			9.0	6.3
Tunisia	2.8	14.4	960.0	78.0
Uganda	0.0		511.0	20.0
United Arab Emirates	0.4		10.0	14.8
Yemen	4.8	11.8	189.5	31.8
Zambia	0.2	0.8	64.2	46.4
Zimbabwe	1.8	2.1	310.0	22.0

Source: UN Food and Agriculture Organisation, FAOSTAT

■ Food Production

Production of Meat 2002

Table 3.7

● '000 tonnes

	Beef and Veal	Goat Meat	Horse Meat	Mutton and Lamb	Pig Meat	Poultry	Total (including others)
North America							
Canada	1,290.0		18.0	13.0	1,835.0	1,133.3	4,290.0
USA	12,438.0		20.5	100.2	8,937.0	17,331.0	39,026.7
Latin America							
Anguilla							
Antigua	0.5	0.1		0.0	0.2	0.2	1.0
Argentina	2,700.0		55.5	50.3	215.0	972.9	4,058.1
Aruba							
Bahamas	0.0	0.1		0.0	0.2	10.0	10.3
Barbados	0.6	0.0		0.1	4.6	11.7	17.0
Belize	1.8	0.0		0.0	1.0	13.1	16.0
Bermuda		0.0			0.1	0.1	0.2
Bolivia	164.6	5.8		16.0	76.5	143.1	413.9
Brazil	7,136.0	39.8	21.0	77.0	2,100.0	7,229.2	16,605.2
British Virgin Islands	0.1	0.0		0.1	0.0		0.3
Cayman Islands							
Chile	200.0	6.5	11.7	9.9	350.7	370.6	949.3
Colombia	775.0	6.4	5.6	7.0	75.0	524.0	1,396.2
Costa Rica	68.8	0.0		0.0	36.3	78.8	183.9
Cuba	77.0	0.7	1.1	1.0	116.0	60.0	255.8
Dominica	0.5	0.0		0.0	0.4	0.3	1.4
Dominican Republic	71.7	0.7		0.4	64.0	185.3	322.2
Ecuador	190.0	1.4		6.5	115.0	209.5	531.0
El Salvador	38.0	0.1		0.0	8.7	50.0	96.8
French Guiana	0.5	0.0		0.0	1.2	0.6	2.3
Grenada	0.1	0.0		0.1	0.2	0.6	1.1
Guadeloupe	3.3	0.2	0.0	0.0	1.1	0.9	5.5
Guatemala	63.0	0.5	2.3	1.2	25.5	155.0	247.4
Guyana	1.0	0.3		0.5	0.5	14.0	16.3
Haiti	42.0	6.5	5.6	0.8	29.1	8.5	96.0
Honduras	62.0	0.2	0.6	0.1	8.0	80.0	150.9
Jamaica	13.0	1.7	0.0	0.0	6.4	83.0	104.2
Martinique	2.3	0.1		0.3	1.7	1.1	5.4
Mexico	1,450.9	42.3	78.9	37.4	1,085.9	2,059.0	4,758.5
Netherlands Antilles	0.0	0.0		0.0	0.2	0.3	0.6
Nicaragua	60.1	0.0	1.9	0.0	6.3	56.1	124.5
Panama	57.9				21.0	83.0	161.9
Paraguay	250.0	0.7	0.6	2.6	153.0	58.8	465.7
Peru	141.5	6.2		31.8	84.9	609.4	906.2
Puerto Rico	15.0	0.1		0.1	14.5	60.0	89.7
St Kitts	0.1	0.1		0.1	0.3	0.1	0.7
St Lucia	0.5	0.1		0.1	0.7	0.7	2.1
St Vincent and the Grenadines	0.2	0.0		0.1	0.6	0.4	1.3
Suriname	2.5	0.0		0.0	1.3	5.4	9.3
Trinidad and Tobago	0.9	0.4		0.1	3.0	47.8	52.1
Uruguay	421.0		7.5	48.0	26.6	53.7	557.6
Venezuela	450.0	7.8		2.6	114.0	730.0	1,304.3

Source: UN Food and Agriculture Organisation, FAOSTAT

◘ Food Production

Production of Meat 2002

• '000 tonnes

	Beef and Veal	Goat Meat	Horse Meat	Mutton and Lamb	Pig Meat	Poultry	Total (including others)
Asia Pacific							
Afghanistan	108.0			88.0		12.2	250.1
American Samoa	0.0				0.3	0.0	0.3
Armenia	32.1			6.7	9.4	3.3	53.2
Azerbaijan	63.0			40.6	1.1	19.9	124.6
Bangladesh	173.0	130.0		2.7		115.0	433.2
Bhutan	4.7	0.1		0.1	1.2	0.3	6.5
Brunei	3.9	0.0			0.2	15.4	19.8
Cambodia	53.4				87.5	26.5	180.8
China	5,320.0	1,444.1	156.0	1,600.0	44,599.0	13,523.5	67,849.4
Fiji	9.1	1.0		0.0	3.9	8.4	22.4
French Polynesia	0.2	0.1		0.0	1.2	0.7	2.2
Guam	0.0	0.0			0.1	0.0	0.2
Hong Kong, China	16.0	0.1			154.0	74.0	255.1
India	1,462.6	470.0		230.4	612.5	1,401.1	5,743.5
Indonesia	339.0	44.3	1.5	33.4	471.4	871.0	1,802.6
Japan	535.1	0.2	6.0	0.1	1,235.9	1,221.2	3,001.5
Kazakhstan	297.1	7.2	65.0	93.9	186.9	36.1	687.1
Kiribati					0.9	0.5	1.3
Kyrgyzstan	98.1	3.8	24.6	41.5	25.7	4.5	198.5
Laos	25.0	0.6			32.0	14.4	89.0
Macau	1.5	0.0			7.8	5.0	
Malaysia	21.1	0.4	0.1	0.2	107.0	835.6	1,068.0
Maldives							1.1
Mongolia	83.8	30.1	33.0	129.5	0.6	0.0	286.4
Myanmar	108.0	7.8		2.2	122.7	256.6	518.6
Nauru					0.1	0.0	0.1
Nepal	46.8	38.6		2.8	15.6	14.4	246.1
New Caledonia	4.0	0.0		0.0	1.4	0.8	6.2
North Korea	21.8	11.0		1.0	145.7	33.7	214.0
Pakistan	437.0	360.0		172.0		359.7	1,838.6
Papua New Guinea	3.2	0.0	0.1	0.0	46.5	5.5	74.3
Philippines	182.8	33.6	0.7	0.1	1,332.3	650.9	2,289.7
Singapore	0.0	0.0		0.2	50.0	69.6	119.8
Solomon Islands	0.6				2.2	0.3	3.2
South Korea	180.0	2.7		0.0	1,030.0	451.0	1,671.1
Sri Lanka	27.5	1.6		0.2	1.7	82.2	119.3
Taiwan							
Tajikistan	15.0			13.2	0.2	1.7	30.1
Thailand	172.3	0.6		0.2	485.8	1,449.8	2,161.3
Tonga	0.3	0.0			1.5	0.3	2.2
Turkmenistan	67.0	3.0		57.0	0.6	5.0	134.6
Tuvalu					0.1	0.0	0.1
Uzbekistan	404.0			82.0	15.0	16.4	519.4
Vanuatu	3.0	0.0	0.0		2.8	0.5	6.4
Vietnam	102.5	5.4	2.4		1,653.6	383.8	2,262.1
Western Samoa	1.0				3.8	0.3	5.1
Australasia							
Australia	2,034.0	10.6	21.3	631.0	395.0	702.1	3,794.0
New Zealand	576.3	1.6	1.4	520.9	46.7	129.3	1,307.7

Source: *UN Food and Agriculture Organisation, FAOSTAT*

◻ Food Production

Production of Meat 2002

● '000 tonnes

	Beef and Veal	Goat Meat	Horse Meat	Mutton and Lamb	Pig Meat	Poultry	Total (including others)
Africa and Middle East							
Algeria	133.0	12.4	0.4	165.0	0.1	531.3	551.5
Angola	85.0	9.2		1.3	27.9	7.7	138.6
Bahrain	0.8	1.8		5.5		5.7	13.8
Benin	18.8	4.3		2.5	6.9	11.6	50.1
Botswana	32.0	6.1		1.7	0.4	9.4	61.7
Burkina Faso	55.0	23.5	0.4	13.6	8.9	27.0	136.2
Burundi	9.1	2.9		1.1	4.2	6.1	23.4
Cameroon	94.8	15.4	0.3	16.4	16.2	28.0	217.2
Cape Verde	0.5	0.5		0.0	7.0	0.4	8.4
Central African Republic	58.3	11.0		1.4	13.3	4.1	96.9
Chad	73.2	21.9	0.1	12.5	0.5	4.7	117.4
Comoros	1.0	0.4		0.1		0.5	1.9
Congo Dem Rep	12.5	18.4		2.8	23.7	10.5	211.9
Congo-Brazzaville	3.0	0.8		0.3	2.1	5.8	28.0
Côte d'Ivoire	45.0	4.3		5.1	11.1	68.2	161.8
Djibouti	5.6	2.4		2.2			10.8
Egypt	247.0	32.7		75.0	3.1	643.1	1,435.5
Equatorial Guinea	0.0	0.0		0.1	0.1	0.2	0.6
Eritrea	16.7	5.8		5.7		2.1	31.0
Ethiopia	304.0	28.6		37.8	1.5	49.8	548.8
Gabon	1.1	0.3		0.7	3.1	3.7	31.6
Gambia	3.1	0.7		0.4	0.4	0.9	6.6
Ghana	26.8	11.3		10.2	11.8	21.2	171.2
Guinea	33.8	4.9		3.8	1.8	4.4	52.6
Guinea-Bissau	4.5	0.9		0.7	10.8	1.4	18.3
Iran	284.3	104.7		345.0		812.1	1,571.5
Iraq	46.6	8.3		20.0		41.0	118.3
Israel	53.0	0.8		5.4	12.0	306.5	377.7
Jordan	2.8	1.4		3.9		110.1	118.7
Kenya	295.0	27.5		25.8	13.0	54.0	450.6
Kuwait	1.6	0.5		34.0		42.8	79.3
Lebanon	36.7	2.7		8.8	2.2	112.0	162.4
Lesotho	8.7	1.9		3.1	2.8	1.8	22.2
Liberia	1.0	0.7		0.7	4.4	8.2	21.4
Libya	6.5	6.0		27.4		98.8	142.5
Madagascar	153.0	7.0	0.0	2.9	70.0	61.6	299.1
Malawi	16.0	6.0		0.4	20.0	15.3	57.7
Mali	97.5	34.3	0.5	26.3	2.7	29.6	218.5
Mauritania	10.5	12.0	0.2	18.0		4.6	65.5
Mauritius	2.7	0.2		0.0	1.1	22.1	26.7
Morocco	150.0	21.0	2.0	120.0	0.6	280.0	608.6
Mozambique	38.1	1.9		0.8	12.8	36.8	90.5
Namibia	57.8	4.2		7.1	0.6	3.4	77.2
Niger	42.0	25.2	0.7	14.9	1.4	26.9	135.2
Nigeria	376.0	142.2		96.8	173.3	190.0	1,078.3
Oman	5.1	6.5		13.1		4.4	35.5
Qatar	0.5	0.7		8.2		4.2	14.7
Réunion	1.8	0.1	0.0	0.0	12.0	19.0	37.2
Rwanda	19.4	2.7		0.8	3.3	1.4	36.0
Sao Tomé e Príncipe	0.1	0.0		0.0	0.1	0.6	0.8
Saudi Arabia	23.3	23.1		70.0		445.7	615.1
Senegal	52.5	16.8	6.8	16.4	7.7	64.1	170.8
Seychelles	0.0	0.0			1.1	0.9	2.1
Sierra Leone	5.0	0.5		1.2	2.4	10.6	22.0
Somalia	61.6	37.7		45.5	0.1	3.5	185.8
South Africa	579.0	36.0	1.5	104.0	118.0	722.1	1,576.6
Sudan	325.0	118.3		144.0		30.5	697.5
Swaziland	14.0	2.9		0.4	1.1	1.2	19.6
Syria	47.0	5.0		183.6		130.4	367.4
Tanzania	230.3	29.4		10.3	13.2	44.9	342.1
Togo	5.7	3.7		3.7	4.6	10.4	32.6
Tunisia	55.0	8.2	0.5	50.0	0.2	110.5	232.6
Uganda	96.8	25.3		5.9	80.9	41.7	268.6
United Arab Emirates	7.8	8.5		14.4		37.2	81.0
Yemen	56.2	23.6		25.4		78.3	186.4
Zambia	40.8	4.7		0.5	11.0	36.5	127.1
Zimbabwe	101.3	12.8		0.6	25.9	41.5	209.1

Source: *UN Food and Agriculture Organisation, FAOSTAT*

Production of Cereals 2002

- '000 tonnes

	Barley	Maize	Millet	Oats	Rice	Rye	Sorghum	Wheat	Total (including others)
North America									
Canada	7,282.6	9,065.3		2,748.8		132.8		15,689.9	35,439.9
USA	4,940.0	228,805.1	75.0	1,729.2	9,569.0	177.4	9,392.0	43,992.3	298,744.6
Latin America									
Anguilla									
Antigua		0.0							0.0
Argentina	570.0	14,710.4	25.3	560.0	713.4	65.0	2,847.4	12,500.0	32,023.1
Aruba									
Bahamas		0.4							0.4
Barbados		2.1							2.1
Belize		33.5			11.0		12.1		56.5
Bermuda									
Bolivia	62.1	724.6		4.7	248.2	0.2	165.6	143.5	1,373.1
Brazil	300.3	35,478.7		372.1	10,489.4	7.3	814.7	2,925.9	50,436.4
British Virgin Islands									
Cayman Islands									
Chile	77.2	923.7		416.3	141.9	0.2		1,818.7	3,378.0
Colombia	6.3	1,331.2			2,353.4		233.4	29.4	3,953.6
Costa Rica		11.6			250.0				261.6
Cuba		233.3			325.5		1.0		559.8
Dominica		0.2							0.2
Dominican Republic		30.3			730.7		5.2		766.1
Ecuador	26.4	386.3		1.2	1,283.4	0.1	10.0	13.6	1,721.3
El Salvador		637.0			28.8		139.2		805.0
French Guiana		0.0			19.9				19.9
Grenada		0.3							0.3
Guadeloupe									
Guatemala	1.5	1,050.1			39.9		54.2	9.1	1,154.9
Guyana		2.0			450.0				452.0
Haiti		185.0			104.0		85.0		374.0
Honduras		392.2			7.5		42.6	1.0	443.3
Jamaica		1.7			0.0				1.7
Martinique									
Mexico	838.6	17,500.0	0.0	94.0	225.9		5,800.0	3,272.7	27,733.8
Netherlands Antilles									
Nicaragua		483.3			263.7		89.9		836.9
Panama		95.5			320.2		2.8		418.5
Paraguay		783.5			100.7		45.0	355.0	1,284.2
Peru	200.0	2,099.5		12.9	2,124.1	0.1	0.0	186.3	4,659.7
Puerto Rico		1.0							1.0
St Kitts									
St Lucia									
St Vincent and the Grenadines		2.0							2.0
Suriname		0.1			192.0				192.1
Trinidad and Tobago		5.0			3.9				8.9
Uruguay	217.4	163.4		45.0	939.5		62.0	270.0	1,699.7
Venezuela		1,805.0			790.0		552.8	0.6	3,148.3

Source: UN Food and Agriculture Organisation, FAOSTAT

◻ Food Production

Production of Cereals 2002

● '000 tonnes

	Barley	Maize	Millet	Oats	Rice	Rye	Sorghum	Wheat	Total (including others)
Asia Pacific									
Afghanistan	345.0	298.0	22.0		388.0			2,686.0	3,739.0
American Samoa									
Armenia	113.3	13.1		1.1		0.6		280.5	412.7
Azerbaijan	295.2	128.0		0.5	16.6	0.0		1,692.8	2,133.2
Bangladesh	3.0	10.0	57.0		38,134.0		1.0	1,606.0	39,811.0
Bhutan	1.7	48.5	3.8		44.3			4.4	106.9
Brunei					0.4				0.4
Cambodia		168.1			3,740.0				3,908.1
China	2,470.0	123,175.0	2,070.8	600.0	176,553.0	650.0	2,731.0	91,290.2	402,000.6
Fiji		1.3			14.7		0.0		16.0
French Polynesia									
Guam		0.0							0.0
Hong Kong, China									
India	1,415.8	10,570.0	6,150.0		116,582.0		7,060.0	71,814.3	213,590.1
Indonesia		9,277.3			51,603.7				60,881.0
Japan	217.2	0.2	0.3	2.0	11,111.0			827.8	12,184.5
Kazakhstan	2,208.9	435.2	39.2	183.2	199.1	106.5	0.3	12,700.0	15,952.1
Kiribati									
Kyrgyzstan	165.9	428.2		4.7	19.0	0.0	0.0	1,305.5	1,923.3
Laos		113.0			2,410.0				2,523.0
Macau									
Malaysia		70.0			2,091.0				2,161.0
Maldives			0.0						0.0
Mongolia	2.0							149.3	151.3
Myanmar		660.0	170.0		21,900.0			103.0	22,849.0
Nauru									
Nepal	30.8	1,510.8	282.6		4,130.0			1,258.0	7,212.2
New Caledonia		2.5					0.1	0.0	2.6
North Korea	69.0	1,651.0	45.0	11.0	2,190.0	75.0	10.0	130.0	4,181.0
Pakistan	99.8	1,689.0	180.0		6,343.0		230.0	18,226.1	26,767.9
Papua New Guinea		8.5			0.8		3.5		12.8
Philippines		4,319.3			13,270.7				17,589.9
Singapore									
Solomon Islands					5.2				5.2
South Korea	382.8	60.0	1.5		6,650.0	0.0	1.4	2.8	7,105.5
Sri Lanka		28.8	4.3		2,794.0		0.1		2,827.1
Taiwan									
Tajikistan	15.0	35.0		0.0	29.0	0.1		361.0	440.3
Thailand	5.0	4,170.0			25,945.0		300.0	0.8	30,484.4
Tonga									
Turkmenistan	26.6	11.0			45.0			2,023.0	2,105.6
Tuvalu									
Uzbekistan	129.0	232.0	3.6		143.1	10.2	34.2	4,956.0	5,510.4
Vanuatu		0.7							0.7
Vietnam		2,314.7			34,063.5		2.7		36,378.2
Western Samoa									
Australasia									
Australia	3,268.0	521.0	63.0	725.0	1,275.0	21.0	2,123.0	9,385.0	17,655.5
New Zealand	406.0	156.5		27.2				355.0	954.7

Source: UN Food and Agriculture Organisation, FAOSTAT

◻ Food Production

Production of Cereals 2002

● '000 tonnes

	Barley	Maize	Millet	Oats	Rice	Rye	Sorghum	Wheat	Total (including others)
Africa and Middle East									
Algeria	550.0	1.1		45.0	0.3		0.6	1,502.0	2,099.0
Angola		430.0	100.0		16.0			4.0	550.0
Bahrain									
Benin		622.1	40.6		66.2		195.5		926.5
Botswana		10.0	1.1				15.0	0.6	26.7
Burkina Faso		653.1	994.7		89.1		1,373.3		3,119.1
Burundi		124.4	10.0		60.9		70.0	8.7	274.0
Cameroon		750.0	71.0		62.0		450.0	0.4	1,333.4
Cape Verde		20.0							20.0
Central African Republic		113.0	12.0		27.4		52.9		205.3
Chad		115.0	369.0		115.0		428.0	4.0	1,166.0
Comoros		4.0			17.0				21.0
Congo Dem Rep	0.5	1,154.0	36.1		314.6		60.0	8.4	1,573.6
Congo-Brazzaville		6.7			1.4				8.1
Côte d'Ivoire		625.0	70.0		818.0		30.0		1,558.0
Djibouti		0.0							0.0
Egypt	100.8	6,800.0			5,600.0	30.0	750.0	6,183.2	19,464.0
Equatorial Guinea									
Eritrea	7.5	0.1	3.6				33.6	2.2	57.1
Ethiopia	830.0	2,600.0	378.0	36.0			1,820.0	1,250.0	8,699.0
Gabon		26.0			1.0				27.0
Gambia		18.6	84.6		20.5		15.2		138.9
Ghana		1,407.0	159.1	0.0	280.0		316.1		2,162.2
Guinea		103.0	9.5		842.5		5.2		1,088.2
Guinea-Bissau		22.8	26.1		79.9		14.3		144.9
Iran	2,000.0	1,200.0	8.0		2,115.0			12,000.0	17,232.0
Iraq	500.0	60.0	4.0	0.5	90.0		0.7	800.0	1,455.2
Israel	5.0	58.0		0.4			16.2	175.0	254.6
Jordan	56.8	10.0					0.4	6.5	73.6
Kenya	47.0	2,800.0	45.0	3.5	45.0		130.0	280.0	3,350.5
Kuwait	3.1	0.8						0.5	4.4
Lebanon	8.1	3.8		0.6			1.8	139.5	153.8
Lesotho	0.2	300.0		0.4			46.0	51.0	397.6
Liberia					190.0				190.0
Libya	80.0	0.5	7.5					130.0	218.0
Madagascar		180.6			2,670.6		1.0	10.0	2,862.2
Malawi		1,603.3	20.9		94.2		39.2	1.5	1,759.1
Mali		320.5	1,034.2		926.5		951.4	10.1	3,256.5
Mauritania	0.3	6.0	0.4		67.9		25.4	0.4	100.4
Mauritius		0.3							0.3
Morocco	1,669.0	198.9	8.0	14.7	16.8	2.4	9.8	3,356.7	5,283.2
Mozambique		1,150.0	49.0		166.9		313.8	1.0	1,680.7
Namibia		27.7	65.0				8.1	6.1	106.9
Niger		6.4	2,000.0		76.4		655.7	6.3	2,746.8
Nigeria		4,934.0	6,100.0		3,192.0		7,704.0	77.0	22,089.0
Oman							3.0	1.4	5.8
Qatar	4.7	1.0						0.2	5.8
Réunion		17.0			0.1				17.1
Rwanda		91.7	4.0		21.0		194.4	7.4	318.4
Sao Tomé e Príncipe		2.5							2.5
Saudi Arabia	100.0	4.0	7.0				200.0	1,800.0	2,111.0
Senegal		97.9	414.7		177.8		143.9		835.0
Seychelles									
Sierra Leone		10.0	4.5		250.0		9.0		275.7
Somalia		210.0			4.0		90.0	0.9	304.9
South Africa	142.4	9,123.0	12.0	35.0	3.3	1.6	237.5	2,400.0	11,955.1
Sudan		53.0	618.0		15.7		2,800.0	247.0	3,733.7
Swaziland		85.0			0.2		0.6	0.3	86.1
Syria	919.5	231.9	2.5	0.0			2.8	4,775.4	5,929.6
Tanzania	5.5	2,700.5	200.0		514.0		650.0	77.0	4,147.0
Togo		463.9	41.2		63.7		141.7		714.9
Tunisia	90.2			1.0			1.0	422.2	533.4
Uganda		1,174.0	590.0		114.0		430.0	14.0	2,322.0
United Arab Emirates								0.2	0.2
Yemen	46.0	50.0	68.6				360.0	150.0	675.0
Zambia	2.2	900.0	38.0		12.0		17.0	75.0	1,044.2
Zimbabwe	16.5	498.5	14.6	0.4	0.6		80.0	150.0	760.7

Source: *UN Food and Agriculture Organisation, FAOSTAT*

■ Forestry Production

Production of Forestry and Paper Products 2002

Table 3.9

- Units as stated

	Fuelwood and Charcoal ('000 cu m)	Household and Sanitary Paper ('000 tonnes)	Paper and Paperboard ('000 tonnes)	Printing and Writing Paper ('000 tonnes)	Roundwood ('000 cu m)	Sawnwood and Sleepers ('000 cu m)	Wood Pulp ('000 tonnes)
North America							
Canada	2,953	692	20,226	6,345	200,326	52,896	25,744
USA	73,086	6,447	81,792	20,964	477,821	89,151	53,569
Latin America							
Anguilla							
Antigua							
Argentina	3,965	177	1,374	344	9,970	821	1,363
Aruba							
Bahamas					17	1	
Barbados					5		
Belize	126				188	35	
Bermuda							
Bolivia	2,184		2		2,743	308	
Brazil	134,473	619	7,354	2,150	237,467	23,100	7,436
British Virgin Islands							
Cayman Islands							
Chile	12,326	116	879	111	38,008	5,872	2,668
Colombia	7,827	129	771	252	9,568	539	197
Costa Rica	3,463	20	20		5,150	812	3
Cuba	2,810	5	57	14	3,618	190	
Dominica							
Dominican Republic	556	62	130	10	562		
Ecuador	5,274	14	91		10,993	1,455	2
El Salvador	4,122	3	56	3	4,804	58	
French Guiana	84				144	15	
Grenada							
Guadeloupe	15				15	1	
Guatemala	15,207	21	31	2	15,674	220	
Guyana	873				1,185	30	
Haiti	1,978				2,217	14	
Honduras	8,710	6	95	13	9,542	417	7
Jamaica	584				867	66	
Martinique	10				12	1	
Mexico	37,913	689	4,056	670	45,333	3,387	334
Netherlands Antilles							
Nicaragua	5,827				5,920	65	
Panama	1,248	18			1,321	42	
Paraguay	5,743		13		9,787	550	
Peru	8,857		63	11	9,928	494	
Puerto Rico							
St Kitts							
St Lucia							
St Vincent and the Grenadines							
Suriname	44				200	57	
Trinidad and Tobago	36				92	41	
Uruguay	4,076	11	88	49	5,675	203	35
Venezuela	3,697	165	589	275	4,667	211	348

Source: UN Food and Agriculture Organisation, FAOSTAT

Production of Forestry and Paper Products 2002

● Units as stated

	Fuelwood and Charcoal ('000 cu m)	Household and Sanitary Paper ('000 tonnes)	Paper and Paperboard ('000 tonnes)	Printing and Writing Paper ('000 tonnes)	Roundwood ('000 cu m)	Sawnwood and Sleepers ('000 cu m)	Wood Pulp ('000 tonnes)
Asia Pacific							
Afghanistan	1,351				3,111	400	
American Samoa							
Armenia	46		2		54	4	
Azerbaijan	6	140	143		14	0	
Bangladesh	27,763		46	30	28,386	70	19
Bhutan	4,348				4,482	31	
Brunei	12				229	90	
Cambodia	9,737				9,858	5	
China	191,047	2,521	37,929	8,310	284,908	8,549	4,075
Fiji	37				510	79	
French Polynesia							
Guam							
Hong Kong, China					21	441	15
India	300,564	40	3,973	1,530	319,418	7,900	1,590
Indonesia	82,556	175	6,995	2,697	116,052	6,400	5,482
Japan	124	1,711	30,717	11,163	16,232	15,485	10,792
Kazakhstan	315	0	23	0		224	
Kiribati							
Kyrgyzstan	16	2	16		26	6	
Laos	5,899				6,469	227	
Macau							
Malaysia	3,228	115	851	123	16,289	4,700	123
Maldives							
Mongolia	186				631	300	
Myanmar	35,403	1	42	15	39,365	671	
Nauru							
Nepal	12,728		13		13,988	630	
New Caledonia					5	3	
North Korea	5,620		80		7,120	280	56
Pakistan	25,013	21	1,165	731	27,692	1,180	25
Papua New Guinea	5,533				8,597	218	
Philippines	13,328	27	1,056	296	16,013	199	175
Singapore			87			25	
Solomon Islands	138				692	12	
South Korea	2,458	347	9,332	2,134	3,991	4,420	554
Sri Lanka	5,774		25	11	6,468	61	3
Taiwan							
Tajikistan							
Thailand	20,250	92	2,445	638	27,351	233	919
Tonga					2	2	
Turkmenistan							
Tuvalu							
Uzbekistan	19						
Vanuatu	91				119	28	
Vietnam	26,547	60	384	70	30,730	2,950	240
Western Samoa	70				131	21	
Australasia							
Australia	7,104	204	2,652	554	31,312	3,525	1,074
New Zealand	50	59	839	4	20,523	3,807	1,501

Source: UN Food and Agriculture Organisation, FAOSTAT

◻ Forestry Production

Production of Forestry and Paper Products 2002

● Units as stated

	Fuelwood and Charcoal ('000 cu m)	Household and Sanitary Paper ('000 tonnes)	Paper and Paperboard ('000 tonnes)	Printing and Writing Paper ('000 tonnes)	Roundwood ('000 cu m)	Sawnwood and Sleepers ('000 cu m)	Wood Pulp ('000 tonnes)
Africa and Middle East							
Algeria	7,305		41	14	7,513	13	
Angola	3,320				4,436	5	15
Bahrain							
Benin	5,966				6,298	13	
Botswana	645				750		
Burkina Faso	11,400				11,994	1	
Burundi	8,095				8,428	83	
Cameroon	9,256				11,065	1,150	
Cape Verde							
Central African Republic	2,000				3,058	150	
Chad	6,119				6,880	2	
Comoros					9		
Congo Dem Rep	67,285		3		67,455	70	
Congo-Brazzaville	1,186				2,437	95	
Côte d'Ivoire	8,581				12,112	630	
Djibouti							
Egypt	16,484	90	460	100	16,752	4	
Equatorial Guinea	447				811	4	
Eritrea	2,323				2,325		
Ethiopia	90,202		12	3	92,660	60	
Gabon	520				3,104	142	
Gambia	620				733	1	
Ghana	20,678				21,979	480	
Guinea	11,537				12,188	26	
Guinea-Bissau	422				592	16	
Iran	257		46		1,317	106	
Iraq	53		20	8	112	12	
Israel	2	50	275	95	27		
Jordan	237	22	27	2	241		
Kenya	20,002	6	129	18	21,979	185	66
Kuwait							
Lebanon	82	6	42		89	9	
Lesotho	2,034				2,034		
Liberia	5,133				5,470	20	
Libya	536		6		652	31	
Madagascar	10,202	0	4	2	10,295	400	1
Malawi	5,029				5,549	45	
Mali	4,846				5,258	13	
Mauritania	1,502				1,508		
Mauritius	9				17	3	
Morocco	6,932	1	129	34	7,507	83	177
Mozambique	16,724				18,043	28	
Namibia							
Niger	8,190				8,601	4	
Nigeria	60,064		19	1	69,482	2,000	23
Oman							
Qatar							
Réunion	31				36	2	
Rwanda	7,500				7,836	79	
Sao Tomé e Príncipe					9	5	
Saudi Arabia							
Senegal	5,178				5,972	23	
Seychelles							
Sierra Leone	5,374				5,497	5	
Somalia	9,827				9,937	14	
South Africa	12,000	150	2,267	533	30,616	1,498	2,276
Sudan	17,068		3		19,241	51	
Swaziland	560				890	102	191
Syria	16		1		50	9	
Tanzania	21,125		25	6	23,439	24	54
Togo	5,600				5,835	15	
Tunisia	2,116	4	94	38	2,329	20	
Uganda	35,142		3		38,317	264	
United Arab Emirates							
Yemen	326				326		
Zambia	7,219		4	2	8,053	157	
Zimbabwe	8,115		80	7	9,108	397	42

Source: *UN Food and Agriculture Organisation, FAOSTAT*

Automotives and Transport

◘ Automotives

Commercial Vehicles in Use 1977-2002

Table 4.1

● '000

	1977	1980	1985	1990	1996	1997	1998	1999	2000	2001	2002	per '000 persons 2002
North America												
Canada	2,494.3	2,955.3	3,148.5	3,931.0	3,540.7	3,591.2	3,694.1	748.7	739.0	742.1	746.0	24.0
USA	29,805.0	34,165.4	39,582.6	55,097.4	76,636.8	78,005.0	79,778.0	83,876.6	87,853.8	91,038.3	94,408.1	338.3
Latin America												
Anguilla												
Antigua	1.9	1.5	2.5	2.8	4.9	4.9	5.0	5.0	5.0	5.1	5.2	74.2
Argentina	1,138.7	1,187.2	1,350.0	1,484.8	1,238.1	1,379.0	1,496.6	1,535.0	1,550.8	1,578.5	1,597.4	42.4
Aruba						10.0	10.0	10.5	11.0	11.5	11.5	98.4
Bahamas	5.7	7.0	12.0	15.0	14.0	17.9	17.9	18.3	18.6	18.8	19.2	59.0
Barbados	4.3	5.1	7.5	8.0	7.2	7.3	7.4	7.4	7.4	7.4	7.4	27.0
Belize	3.4	3.8	5.4	3.5	9.3	12.2	12.3	12.2	12.3	12.7	12.8	49.9
Bermuda	2.6	2.8	3.5	3.3	4.0	4.5	4.5	4.5	4.5	4.5	4.5	67.2
Bolivia	42.9	47.6	90.0	177.2	221.5	234.4	220.6	220.6	220.6	220.4	217.0	25.2
Brazil	1,875.0	1,987.9	2,100.0	2,400.0	2,520.0	2,540.0	2,561.5	2,578.0	2,561.5	2,572.0	2,580.0	14.9
British Virgin Islands												
Cayman Islands												
Chile				178.2	229.0	234.0	362.0	534.5	785.5	946.2	1,087.5	70.2
Colombia	106.7	270.7	280.0	665.0	805.0	810.0	812.0	815.0	812.0	813.8	814.7	20.3
Costa Rica	57.1	64.1	65.0	95.1	140.0	141.4	143.5	148.3	151.1	152.6	154.1	39.4
Cuba	40.0	40.0	37.0	33.0	30.0	30.0	30.0	30.0	30.0	30.0	30.0	2.7
Dominica	1.2	1.3				3.3	3.3	3.4	3.4	3.5	3.5	49.3
Dominican Republic	45.8	63.1	65.0	75.0	170.0	171.0	171.5	172.9	174.9	175.4	178.6	20.6
Ecuador	123.2	160.7	175.6	168.0	245.0	245.0	246.0	278.0	312.2	335.4	364.5	27.8
El Salvador	31.9	69.0	70.0	65.0	135.8	135.8	135.8	182.0	209.8	224.5	234.5	36.0
French Guiana	3.9	4.8	6.0	7.0	10.7	11.2	11.2	11.2	11.2	11.2	11.2	54.8
Grenada												
Guadeloupe	20.6	22.9										
Guatemala	71.0	93.0	100.0	135.0	97.8	98.0	98.0	98.0	98.0	98.0	98.0	8.3
Guyana	12.6	12.9	12.5	9.0	9.0	10.6	10.6	10.6	10.6	10.6	10.6	12.0
Haiti	5.8	9.5	15.0	20.0	21.0	21.0	21.0	29.4	35.0	37.4	39.1	4.8
Honduras	38.1	49.3	50.0	18.0	102.0	103.0	103.6	103.6	103.6	103.8	104.2	15.5
Jamaica	27.3	27.2	30.0	17.5	51.0	52.1	52.3	55.2	56.1	56.7	56.9	21.3
Martinique	20.0	21.6										
Mexico	1,118.8	1,622.6	2,100.0	2,982.0	4,110.7	4,298.6	4,453.0	4,640.2	4,568.6	4,690.8	4,794.3	47.1
Netherlands Antilles	8.1	8.8	14.0	15.0	15.0	15.0	15.0	15.0	15.0	15.0	15.0	66.7
Nicaragua	30.0	30.7	35.0	33.9	66.0	66.0	66.2	69.1	72.2	73.5	74.8	15.4
Panama	29.2	37.5	50.0	72.7	60.0	60.4	60.6	63.1	64.2	65.3	67.2	23.0
Paraguay		81.9	83.6	74.6	79.7	77.6	76.2	92.1	112.9	134.5	148.8	26.1
Peru	164.7	176.6	220.3	237.4	379.5	389.3	390.6	402.1	390.6	393.4	394.5	14.9
Puerto Rico	147.5	192.4	200.0	230.0	240.0	242.0	243.4	273.5	298.8	305.6	308.2	77.1
St Kitts	0.5	0.7	1.0	1.0	2.2	2.3	2.3	2.4	2.4	2.5	2.5	66.4
St Lucia	2.1	2.0	3.0	4.5	9.1	9.1	9.2	10.3	11.0	11.5	11.9	74.2
St Vincent and the Grenadines	0.8	1.0	2.0	1.3	3.2	3.7	3.8	4.0	4.1	4.3	4.4	37.3
Suriname	7.3	9.8	12.6	14.2	18.0	20.5	20.8	20.8	20.8	20.8	20.8	49.0
Trinidad and Tobago	29.7	39.4	60.0	80.0	35.0	38.0	38.4	38.4	38.4	38.5	38.7	29.3
Uruguay	91.2	91.2	125.0	146.4	45.0	45.8	46.8	49.5	53.9	57.2	59.1	17.9
Venezuela	488.0	659.3	900.0	464.0	480.0	581.0	594.0	601.2	594.0	602.5	603.6	24.1

Source: *Euromonitor from SMMT/national statistics*
Notes: *There may be wide variations from year to year in SMMT estimates and in other figures due to interpretation of definitions*

Automotives

Commercial Vehicles in Use 1977-2002

- '000

	1977	1980	1985	1990	1996	1997	1998	1999	2000	2001	2002	per '000 persons 2002
Asia Pacific												
Afghanistan	24.6	28.7	30.0	27.5	26.0	26.2	26.5	26.5	26.5	26.5	26.5	1.1
American Samoa	0.6	1.0										
Armenia				13.6								
Azerbaijan				113.6	90.8	89.6	87.0	85.9	84.8	83.4	81.9	10.0
Bangladesh		50.0							126.8			
Bhutan												
Brunei	5.2	7.4	12.0	12.5	15.0	17.6	17.7	18.1	18.3	18.5	18.8	55.8
Cambodia	10.0	15.0	15.0	15.0	15.0	15.0	15.0	19.0	22.4	24.9	26.1	2.3
China	700.0	870.0	1,700.0	3,539.7	4,721.0	4,720.0	4,718.6	5,017.7	6,012.3	6,959.4	7,865.3	6.1
Fiji	12.6	16.7	25.0	25.0	37.0	37.0	39.6	40.8	42.4	43.7	44.5	53.8
French Polynesia	7.0	9.2	14.0	15.0	15.0	16.0	16.2	16.5	16.8	17.4	18.1	75.4
Guam	11.0	15.1	25.0	30.0	31.0	34.7	35.1	31.5	26.8	22.4	20.1	116.7
Hong Kong, China	53.7	69.0	90.0	136.9	171.6	136.3	139.9	158.0	139.7	140.5	141.6	19.6
India	834.0	700.0	980.0	1,608.0	2,488.0	2,567.0	2,610.0	2,650.7	2,610.0	2,741.9	2,787.5	2.7
Indonesia	339.5	564.2	1,040.3	1,492.8	2,030.2	2,159.8	2,220.5	2,296.1	2,305.0	2,379.3	2,437.6	11.3
Japan	12,182.2	14,196.7	18,312.7	22,773.5	21,933.0	21,392.5	20,918.8	20,558.6	20,211.7	20,783.5	20,634.0	162.4
Kazakhstan				112.0	48.5	42.3	32.7	34.5	35.3	32.6	30.6	1.9
Kiribati												
Kyrgyzstan				616.0								
Laos	3.0	3.0	8.0	10.7	9.0	9.0	9.0	9.0	9.0	9.0	9.0	1.6
Macau									7.1			
Malaysia	122.6	167.6	250.0	407.1	788.8	888.0	931.7	994.8	1,029.6	1,084.5	1,135.5	49.0
Maldives									2.5			
Mongolia					27.0	27.0	27.0	30.2	33.2	34.5	35.8	13.2
Myanmar	41.0	43.2	45.0	40.0	42.0							
Nauru												
Nepal												
New Caledonia	12.9	14.7	15.0	17.5	18.5	17.0	32.6	34.6	36.5	37.2	39.5	179.5
North Korea												
Pakistan	97.0	106.0	250.0	126.0	360.0	363.0	366.0	378.4	378.0	382.6	387.7	2.4
Papua New Guinea	23.8	36.2	50.0	65.0	60.0	60.0	60.0	60.0	60.0	60.0	60.0	12.1
Philippines			108.7	149.3	207.0	235.3	252.1	267.2	273.5	289.5	304.9	3.8
Singapore	54.6	83.8	140.0	123.6	168.4	171.1	170.4	169.3	168.3	168.9	168.3	50.4
Solomon Islands												
South Korea	149.7	269.4	556.8	1,319.9	2,659.5	2,804.3	2,888.7	2,955.1	3,327.1	3,518.7	3,724.0	77.3
Sri Lanka	54.4	81.3	120.0	163.7	175.0	198.0	198.9	198.9	198.9	201.5	202.6	10.7
Taiwan					843.0	882.0	885.0	850.0	883.3	866.8	863.1	38.2
Tajikistan				16.1								
Thailand					2,256.1	2,587.3	2,779.3	2,897.5	4,075.5	3,301.8	3,418.7	54.9
Tonga	0.7	0.9			3.8	5.9	6.1	7.3	8.7	9.2	9.7	98.0
Turkmenistan				8.1	10.4	10.0	10.2	10.6	11.2	11.4	11.8	2.6
Tuvalu												
Uzbekistan												
Vanuatu				2.0	2.5	2.5	2.5	2.0	1.8	1.9	2.1	10.7
Vietnam					68.0	69.0	83.6	83.6	83.6	84.2	83.7	1.0
Western Samoa						3.3	3.2					
Australasia												
Australia	1,317.7	1,462.5	1,886.5	1,953.9	2,075.8	2,111.7	2,177.3	2,382.0	2,528.0	2,655.7	2,812.3	144.6
New Zealand	234.1	259.3	302.4	317.5	363.6	370.8	378.7	386.1	440.7	469.5	506.6	129.8

Source: Euromonitor from SMMT/national statistics
Notes: There may be wide variations from year to year in SMMT estimates and in other figures due to interpretation of definitions

◻ Automotives

Commercial Vehicles in Use 1977-2002

● '000

	1977	1980	1985	1990	1996	1997	1998	1999	2000	2001	2002	per '000 persons 2002
Africa and Middle East												
Algeria	134.0	231.0	325.0	535.0	810.0	875.0	936.2	942.9	950.0	961.6	984.7	32.2
Angola	42.0	43.5	50.0	42.0	43.0	43.5	42.0	42.0	43.5	44.1	44.6	3.1
Bahrain	10.2	19.0	20.0	24.7	31.0	32.6	32.8	35.8	39.7	43.5	47.9	74.8
Benin	5.0	10.5	12.0	12.0	25.0	28.5	25.0	25.0	25.0	25.0	25.0	3.8
Botswana	13.4	17.3	25.0	23.0					73.2			
Burkina Faso	11.8	13.0	15.0	13.0	24.0	24.0	24.0	24.0	24.0	24.0	24.0	1.8
Burundi	2.6	4.0	7.5	9.2	12.3	13.6	14.4	14.4	14.4	14.4	14.4	2.0
Cameroon	30.8	47.1	50.0	80.0	79.0	81.0	82.2	82.2	82.2	82.2	82.2	5.0
Cape Verde												
Central African Republic	3.5	4.8	6.0	5.7	4.1	3.5	3.7	3.7	3.7	3.8	3.8	1.0
Chad	7.5	4.0	7.0	8.4					12.4			
Comoros												
Congo Dem Rep	87.1	84.9	70.0						20.4			
Congo-Brazzaville							20.4					
Côte d'Ivoire	65.5	77.8	80.0	90.0		93.6	93.6	93.6	93.6	93.6	93.6	5.9
Djibouti	2.3	2.5	5.0	5.0	3.0	3.0	3.1	3.1	3.1	3.2	3.2	4.8
Egypt	67.0	128.0	200.0	430.8	470.0	476.0	478.1	480.2	508.0	518.1	529.2	8.2
Equatorial Guinea	3.0	3.0	3.0	4.0	3.6	3.6	3.6	3.6	3.6	3.6	3.6	7.3
Eritrea												
Ethiopia	8.3	14.2	20.0	25.2	23.0	30.4	30.4	30.4	30.4	30.4	30.4	0.5
Gabon	10.0	14.6	25.0	15.9	17.0	17.0	17.0	17.0	17.0	17.0	17.0	12.8
Gambia				2.5	3.0	3.5	3.6	3.6	3.6	3.6	3.6	2.5
Ghana	47.9	47.6	40.0	42.1	47.0	47.4	47.6	47.6	47.6	47.6	47.8	2.2
Guinea	11.0	8.0	12.0	12.5	13.0	13.3	13.3	13.3	13.3	13.3	13.3	1.7
Guinea-Bissau	1.0	2.1	2.0	2.0	2.5	2.5	2.5	2.5	2.5	2.5	2.5	1.9
Iran	528.2	406.0	515.0	550.0	1,558.0	589.5	590.4	590.4	590.4	590.4	590.4	8.5
Iraq	83.0	192.7	189.0	320.0	673.0	371.0	375.0	375.0	375.0	375.0	375.0	14.8
Israel	108.0	97.0	130.0	165.6	220.0	276.0	279.5	337.3	298.0	374.3	354.7	55.2
Jordan	19.0	29.0	60.0	86.4	87.0	89.7	89.8	90.3	106.9	112.5	119.1	22.2
Kenya	77.7	110.5	125.0	50.8	150.0	163.0	165.0	182.2	204.3	216.4	234.6	7.2
Kuwait	100.0	144.0	200.0	200.0	149.0	153.0	153.0	154.0	167.2	172.1	177.2	75.6
Lebanon	27.1	40.7	55.0	50.0	83.0	84.7	96.0	96.0	96.0	96.3	97.2	28.1
Lesotho					13.0	13.0	13.0	13.0	13.0	13.0	13.0	5.6
Liberia					15.0	11.5	12.5	12.5	12.5	12.5	12.5	3.1
Libya	181.6	278.9	275.0	325.0	452.0	334.0	350.0	350.0	350.0	350.0	350.0	59.6
Madagascar	48.0	49.2	45.0	29.1	37.0	38.4	38.5	38.5	38.5	39.1	39.4	2.3
Malawi	13.4	15.4	17.5	10.3	18.0	18.2	19.2	19.2	19.2	19.2	19.1	1.6
Mali	5.2	6.4	7.5	8.0	8.6	8.6	8.6	8.6	8.6	8.6	8.6	0.7
Mauritania	5.5	3.4	5.0	5.0	5.7	5.7	5.7	5.7	5.7	5.7	5.7	2.0
Mauritius									66.6			
Morocco	140.0	180.0	200.0	227.9	319.0	343.0	348.0	350.0	382.0	399.6	415.2	14.2
Mozambique	24.7	24.7	20.0	24.0	26.8	26.8	28.5	28.5	28.5	29.1	30.5	1.4
Namibia				51.9	60.0	60.0	62.0	62.0	62.0	62.5	63.1	34.5
Niger	13.4	17.3	15.0	18.0	18.0	18.0	18.1	18.1	18.1	18.2	18.2	1.5
Nigeria	282.0	459.0	600.0	625.0	640.0	645.0	656.0	658.0	661.1	663.8	668.6	5.4
Oman	21.0	45.0	100.0	110.0	90.0	101.2	101.8	107.2	110.7	112.6	114.2	40.6
Qatar	16.1	30.5	33.4	47.2	63.5	67.0	67.2	67.2	67.2	67.7	68.3	107.6
Réunion	25.1	31.2	30.0	50.0		62.7	62.9	62.9	62.9	63.2	63.7	87.6
Rwanda			8.0	15.0	5.6	5.8	6.1	6.1	6.1	6.2	6.3	0.7
Sao Tomé e Príncipe												
Saudi Arabia	500.0	947.0	1,450.0	2,272.8	3,198.4	3,467.5	3,768.3	4,056.4	4,375.0	4,545.5	4,865.5	213.0
Senegal	32.0	34.2	17.5	25.0	35.1	38.9	40.7	45.2	48.0	53.5	57.1	5.5
Seychelles	1.2	1.3	1.3	1.5	2.7	2.3	2.4	2.4	2.4	2.6	2.6	33.3
Sierra Leone	5.8	10.8	11.0	11.3	12.0	12.0	12.3	12.3	12.3	12.4	12.6	2.4
Somalia	5.5	6.0	20.0	9.0	11.5	11.5	10.8	10.8	10.8	10.5	10.4	0.9
South Africa	900.6	966.3	1,228.7	1,497.6	1,790.0	1,853.0	1,883.0	1,915.0	1,946.0	1,665.9	1,710.5	38.5
Sudan	30.0	71.0	40.0	56.9	57.0	57.8	58.2	58.2	58.2	58.1	57.4	1.8
Swaziland	4.5	8.0	15.0	24.3	20.0	36.2	36.3	36.3	36.3	36.4	36.7	33.3
Syria	55.7	69.1	200.0	130.5	202.5	224.0	226.5	243.5	269.1	281.3	294.2	16.9
Tanzania	47.2	52.1	45.0	88.8	60.0	60.0	63.0	63.0	63.0	63.0	63.0	1.8
Togo	4.4	10.4	12.0	12.3	16.1	16.1	16.1	16.1	16.1	16.1	16.1	3.2
Tunisia	79.0	103.0	150.0	175.0	220.0	245.7	249.0	256.0	255.0	264.6	269.5	27.8
Uganda	12.4	12.9	15.0	14.9	35.0	42.3	44.0	44.0	44.0	44.0	44.0	1.8
United Arab Emirates	55.0	40.0	75.0	155.0	180.0	193.0	194.2	193.9	194.2	197.9	199.2	60.9
Yemen		50.3	78.0	237.0	300.0	304.0	306.7	363.5	422.1	456.2	487.5	24.0
Zambia	62.5	66.3	50.0	65.0	68.0	68.0	68.0	68.0	68.0	68.0	68.0	6.8
Zimbabwe	70.0	70.6	80.0	75.0	88.0	88.0	89.0	89.0	89.0	89.0	89.0	7.2

Source: *Euromonitor from SMMT/national statistics*
Notes: *There may be wide variations from year to year in SMMT estimates and in other figures due to interpretation of definitions*

Table 4.2

Automotives

Passenger Cars in Use 1977-2002

- '000

	1977	1980	1985	1990	1996	1997	1998	1999	2000	2001	2002	per '000 persons 2002
North America												
Canada	9,554.3	10,255.5	11,118.1	12,622.0	13,251.1	13,487.0	13,887.3	16,732.2	16,832.2	16,953.1	17,125.1	551.9
USA	112,287.5	121,630.8	131,864.0	133,700.5	129,728.4	129,748.7	131,838.5	132,432.0	133,621.4	134,612.8	135,724.0	486.4
Latin America												
Anguilla												
Antigua	5.8	7.0	7.5	12.0	15.5	16.0	15.6	17.5	20.0	21.5	23.7	338.0
Argentina	2,649.2	3,005.0	3,700.0	4,352.1	4,783.9	4,904.2	5,047.7	5,051.0	5,056.1	5,067.0	5,081.9	134.7
Aruba						40.5	40.6	40.6	40.6	40.6	40.6	347.4
Bahamas					46.0	58.5	69.5	82.6	97.6	105.1	112.9	347.0
Barbados	23.8	24.6	30.0	35.0	35.0	42.5	56.9	60.8	44.1	32.6	29.4	107.2
Belize				6.8	9.3	10.0	9.9	11.5	13.0	14.1	15.5	60.7
Bermuda	13.2	14.2	17.5	20.0	21.4	22.3	22.5	22.5	22.5	22.5	22.5	336.1
Bolivia	32.2	32.1	50.0	165.2	223.8	198.4	156.5	193.0	235.7	238.8	239.7	27.8
Brazil	6,926.9	8,302.9	9,500.0	10,250.0	12,500.0	12,800.0	12,906.0	13,010.0	12,906.0	13,243.0	13,308.0	77.0
British Virgin Islands												
Cayman Islands			8.0	8.8	12.3	13.5	13.4	14.7	16.0	17.4	17.9	434.5
Chile	288.8	405.0	550.0	676.0	1,121.2	1,175.8	1,236.9	1,326.8	1,250.0	1,197.5	1,176.5	75.9
Colombia					818.9	884.3	964.1	988.2	969.5	953.4	904.7	22.6
Costa Rica				168.8	277.9	294.1	316.8	326.5	272.8	301.5	318.7	81.5
Cuba	80.0	80.0	160.0		216.6	172.6			16.8			
Dominica	2.4	2.5	2.5	2.7	2.8	3.8	5.7	7.2	8.7	9.4	10.3	145.1
Dominican Republic				148.0	224.0	250.5	274.6	291.4	330.9	365.5	378.5	43.6
Ecuador				313.5	464.9	483.9	495.1		268.2			
El Salvador				88.2	168.2	177.5	152.6	143.2	121.0	115.4	112.7	17.3
French Guiana	15.1	18.3	21.0	24.0	29.5	29.8	29.9	29.9	29.9	29.9	30.0	146.7
Grenada												
Guadeloupe	45.7	53.2										
Guatemala					429.6	470.0	508.9	578.7	104.5	669.5	713.9	60.3
Guyana	31.3	32.5	33.0	22.0	24.0	25.1	25.3	25.3	25.3	25.3	25.3	28.7
Haiti	21.0	25.5	30.0	32.0	32.0	32.0	32.0	41.5	59.0	55.6	58.1	7.1
Honduras						26.8	30.6	32.7	40.5	42.4	45.3	6.7
Jamaica	107.3	103.6	110.0	95.0	104.0	109.3	109.5	126.5	156.8	186.5	197.5	73.8
Martinique	55.0	62.7										
Mexico	2,829.1	4,032.0	5,000.0	6,839.3	8,706.8	8,997.5	9,378.6	9,842.0	10,281.1	10,717.2	11,196.3	109.9
Netherlands Antilles	49.7	51.1	65.0	68.5	70.0	70.0	70.0	70.0	70.0	70.0	70.0	311.5
Nicaragua	38.0	36.6	40.0	39.8	72.4	48.0	52.2	62.7	72.4	73.4	75.1	15.4
Panama				143.1	203.8	214.9	228.7	208.4	198.7	193.4	189.7	65.0
Paraguay		110.8	169.2	149.1	145.1	163.5	194.8	221.5	250.2	268.4	294.7	51.6
Peru					557.0	595.8	645.9	684.5	602.5	619.9	632.3	23.8
Puerto Rico	698.6	931.5	1,150.0	1,300.0	878.0	1,156.4	1,467.5	1,756.9	2,048.4	2,356.4	2,687.2	672.5
St Kitts	2.7	2.5	2.5	2.5	3.7	5.2	5.3	5.9	6.3	6.5	6.9	183.3
St Lucia	4.4	5.0	4.5	7.5	14.6	15.1	14.8	14.2	13.5	13.3	13.1	81.7
St Vincent and the Grenadines	3.9	4.0	4.0	4.4	5.5	6.0	6.2	7.5	8.0	8.2	8.5	72.1
Suriname	21.6	23.5	31.2	36.2	50.2	50.2	55.4	55.4	55.4	55.8	55.9	131.7
Trinidad and Tobago					122.0	132.1	149.5	153.9	168.7	172.4	177.9	134.9
Uruguay				379.6	485.1	516.9	541.5	463.8	571.6	583.7	595.5	180.4
Venezuela	1,172.4	1,463.8	1,750.0	1,550.0	1,520.0	1,625.0	1,845.0	1,853.1	1,845.0	1,863.6	1,875.5	74.7

Source: Euromonitor from SMMT/national statistics
Notes: There may be wide variations from year to year in SMMT estimates and in other figures due to interpretation of definitions

■ Automotives

Passenger Cars in Use 1977-2002

● '000

	1977	1980	1985	1990	1996	1997	1998	1999	2000	2001	2002	per '000 persons 2002
Asia Pacific												
Afghanistan	36.0	34.1	32.0	32.5	31.0	33.5	33.5	33.5	33.5	33.5	33.5	1.4
American Samoa	2.7	3.5										
Armenia				3.1	1.3							
Azerbaijan				260.2	273.7	271.3	281.3	307.0	335.2	369.2	402.0	49.3
Bangladesh				43.0	55.0	54.8	57.1	56.2	55.8	55.3	55.4	0.4
Bhutan												
Brunei	28.2	38.2	72.0	107.8	100.7	106.7	94.1	124.5	163.1	179.8	189.4	562.5
Cambodia					3.7	46.8	52.9	48.5	45.6	42.3	43.5	44.8	3.9
China			19.3	240.7	1,430.4	1,912.7	2,306.5	3,040.9	5,805.6	6,060.3	6,359.4	4.9
Fiji	24.6	26.7	32.0	33.0	30.0	37.4	42.1	49.8	58.0	63.4	72.1	87.2
French Polynesia	22.0	25.7	30.0	37.5	41.5							
Guam	51.0	57.4	90.0	130.0	84.0	86.0	86.2	74.5	66.4	61.4	59.7	346.7
Hong Kong, China	131.7	204.8	185.6	238.5	349.3	373.0	384.0	389.8	350.4	361.5	367.4	50.9
India				2,056.7	4,189.4	4,429.0	4,624.5	4,820.0	4,820.0	4,905.2	5,032.0	4.9
Indonesia	443.4	729.5	965.2	1,313.2	2,409.1	2,639.5	2,772.5	3,018.5	2,900.0	2,825.1	2,486.0	11.5
Japan	19,825.7	23,659.5	27,844.6	34,924.2	46,868.4	48,610.7	49,895.7	51,164.2	52,437.4	53,850.6	55,251.7	434.9
Kazakhstan				809.7	997.5	973.3	971.2	987.7	995.6	1,027.4	1,052.0	65.4
Kiribati												
Kyrgyzstan				194.6	172.4	176.1	187.7	187.3	190.4	198.7	212.0	45.0
Laos				25.3	16.3	14.7	13.9	11.5	9.0	8.7	8.5	1.5
Macau					38.9	42.9	46.3	47.8	48.9	50.3	52.7	108.4
Malaysia	503.2	729.1	1,000.0	1,845.6	2,946.0	3,333.4	3,517.5	3,852.7	4,212.6	4,606.9	4,995.1	215.6
Maldives				0.8	1.1	1.3	1.2	1.4	1.5	1.6	1.7	5.6
Mongolia				12.0	30.0	35.6	37.8	39.9	44.1	44.2	46.5	17.2
Myanmar	34.0	31.5	32.0	27.5	27.0	30.0						
Nauru												
Nepal												
New Caledonia	30.5	37.6	40.0	47.5	50.0	50.0	40.8	43.8	47.0	49.2	51.7	234.9
North Korea												
Pakistan	209.0	286.0	380.0	427.7	577.7	606.3	636.9	669.0	736.5	801.6	923.0	5.7
Papua New Guinea	19.0	24.6	27.0	30.0	31.0	35.0	36.0	36.0	36.0	36.0	36.0	7.3
Philippines	431.0	478.6	350.0	412.2	641.7	666.7	667.0	688.7	691.2	700.6	709.3	8.9
Singapore	135.8	164.5	240.0	272.5	362.1	373.3	370.8	378.0	413.5	398.8	405.4	121.4
Solomon Islands												
South Korea	125.6	249.1	556.7	2,074.9	6,893.6	7,586.5	7,580.9	7,598.1	7,837.3	8,092.7	8,224.4	170.8
Sri Lanka				105.9	246.5	261.6	284.3	274.5	268.5	264.5	262.8	13.8
Taiwan	209.9	425.4	915.6	2,263.4	4,147.0	4,412.0	4,545.0	4,509.0	4,716.2	4,702.4	4,777.9	211.7
Tajikistan				1.9	0.7							
Thailand	344.0	397.0	575.0	804.8	1,567.3	1,812.4	1,974.3	2,153.7	2,044.6	2,185.1	2,289.6	36.8
Tonga	0.6	0.6								8.4		
Turkmenistan				164.1	226.8	231.4	237.5	243.5	252.9	259.9	267.5	58.0
Tuvalu												
Uzbekistan												
Vanuatu				3.8	4.0	4.0	4.0	5.7	7.4	7.7	8.2	41.8
Vietnam					123.0	135.0	142.0	143.5	142.0	140.1	141.4	1.7
Western Samoa						3.5	3.4					
Australasia												
Australia	5,343.8	5,800.6	6,842.5	7,672.3	9,021.5	9,239.5	9,560.6	9,750.0	10,000.0	10,260.8	10,542.8	542.3
New Zealand	1,210.2	1,307.4	1,500.0	1,500.0	1,718.9	1,771.5	1,841.7	1,921.3	2,221.7	2,321.8	2,486.2	637.1

Source: *Euromonitor from SMMT/national statistics*
Notes: *There may be wide variations from year to year in SMMT estimates and in other figures due to interpretation of definitions*

□ Automotives

Passenger Cars in Use 1977-2002

- '000

	1977	1980	1985	1990	1996	1997	1998	1999	2000	2001	2002	per '000 persons 2002
Africa and Middle East												
Algeria	224.0	490.0	650.0	800.0	1,390.0	1,490.0	1,585.0	1,602.0	1,625.0	1,637.0	1,651.0	53.9
Angola	147.0	142.1	110.0	134.0	207.0	186.2	163.5	142.5	123.0	112.4	109.8	7.7
Bahrain				104.7	143.9	149.6	157.2	166.7	159.3	153.4	149.2	232.9
Benin				11.3	37.8	35.2	31.2	26.4	22.0	19.7	18.3	2.7
Botswana	4.6	7.9	13.5	12.6	26.7	28.2	37.0	47.9	44.5	42.1	39.4	23.0
Burkina Faso	10.9	12.5	15.0	15.5	38.2	37.3	36.2	34.1	32.0	30.7	29.4	2.2
Burundi	5.1	6.0	6.5	11.4	19.2	19.8	19.8	19.8	19.8	19.8	19.8	2.8
Cameroon				72.0	98.0	97.0	97.5	97.5	97.5	97.5	97.5	5.9
Cape Verde				2.0	3.3							
Central African Republic				1.5	1.0	1.0						
Chad				4.5	10.6	10.3	9.9	9.6	9.0	8.7	8.9	1.1
Comoros					9.1							
Congo Dem Rep									26.2			
Congo-Brazzaville				27.0	37.2							
Côte d'Ivoire	105.2	127.7	155.0	182.0	293.0							
Djibouti				5.8	9.2	10.4	11.3	12.6	13.4	14.2	15.7	23.5
Egypt				1,082.1	1,354.0	1,376.5	1,406.4	1,423.7	1,435.0	1,453.1	1,473.9	22.9
Equatorial Guinea				1.0	1.5	2.1	2.7	3.4	4.0	4.5	4.7	9.6
Eritrea				3.2	5.9							
Ethiopia	43.9	40.4	40.0	40.7	49.7	52.5	54.2	50.2	45.6	46.0	47.5	0.7
Gabon				17.8	24.7	25.6	25.6	25.6	25.6	25.6	25.6	19.3
Gambia				6.0	8.6	8.6	8.5	8.1	7.4	7.1	7.2	5.0
Ghana	66.7	65.9	60.0	82.2	90.0	91.2	93.2	93.2	93.2	93.3	93.7	4.3
Guinea				11.8	14.1	16.3	18.2	20.4	23.1	25.1	26.8	3.5
Guinea-Bissau	3.2	2.8	2.9	3.6	7.1	6.1	5.4	4.2	3.5	3.2	3.3	2.6
Iran				1,340.0	1,793.0	1,623.5	1,603.5	1,583.5	1,566.0	1,534.2	1,513.4	21.9
Iraq					773.0	754.3	723.5	707.5	685.0	664.5	637.5	25.1
Israel	313.0	402.0	610.0	811.7	1,184.8	1,240.4	1,298.0	1,341.3	1,298.0	1,460.9	1,482.8	230.9
Jordan				161.9	213.9	224.3	239.0	225.0	200.0	174.4	148.9	27.8
Kenya				239.9	278.0	264.5	251.4	246.8	236.1	227.6	222.7	6.8
Kuwait				500.0	696.6	742.3	768.6	794.8	787.0	811.4	829.6	354.1
Lebanon				1,090.0	1,217.0	1,299.4	1,273.0	1,263.2	1,256.0	1,249.4	1,253.7	361.9
Lesotho				5.3	12.6	10.5	9.8	7.2	5.0	4.9	4.8	2.1
Liberia				17.8	9.4	11.4	12.9	15.8	17.4	18.2	19.1	4.8
Libya	386.0	367.4	400.0	425.0	809.5	735.5	664.5	573.5	469.5	405.6	375.6	64.0
Madagascar	54.7	55.7	53.5	42.0	60.5	57.2	56.3	55.1	54.5	53.7	52.2	3.0
Malawi	15.0	16.2	25.0	17.3	27.0	25.4	22.1	19.5	17.9	17.1	16.3	1.4
Mali	21.0	21.9	12.5	18.8	26.2	24.3	22.1	21.7	21.0	20.4	19.8	1.6
Mauritania				13.0	18.8	17.3	14.5	11.1	8.9	7.6	7.1	2.4
Mauritius	24.5	32.0	34.0	46.8	69.9	75.4	80.6	85.2	54.9	43.2	39.8	33.6
Morocco	326.0	425.0	450.0	669.6	1,018.1	1,089.4	1,108.7	1,162.0	1,108.7	1,304.2	1,365.8	46.8
Mozambique	107.9			41.0	27.7				86.5			
Namibia				53.9	74.9	73.2	68.2	62.1	56.8	54.1	52.7	28.8
Niger	11.1	15.8	20.0	37.0	38.2	32.6	28.6	22.6	18.2	17.5	16.2	1.4
Nigeria					885.1	825.9	864.7	879.4	884.3	916.8	941.1	7.6
Oman	35.4	40.0	100.0	134.9	211.0	227.4	251.6	268.1	279.1	287.9	301.5	107.2
Qatar	26.9	43.9	80.0	115.1	126.0	138.5	138.9	138.9	138.9	139.2	140.6	221.4
Réunion	72.4	75.0	100.0	145.0	178.0	181.0	184.2	184.2	184.2	185.6	186.7	256.9
Rwanda				7.5	13.0	12.1	11.3	10.2	9.5	9.1	8.9	0.9
Sao Tomé e Príncipe	355.0				4.0							
Saudi Arabia	376.0	764.0	1,200.0	1,550.0	1,744.0	1,978.0	2,212.3	2,385.7	2,689.0	2,996.4	3,414.0	149.5
Senegal				57.1	85.5	91.0	93.4	97.5	106.0	109.5	112.7	11.0
Seychelles	4.8	4.0	3.5	5.8	7.1	7.0	6.9	6.9	6.8	6.7	6.7	85.8
Sierra Leone	12.8	23.2	20.0	29.8	20.7	23.5	27.2	31.5	36.2	38.2	41.5	7.8
Somalia	5.0	5.0	20.0	5.8	10.2	10.7	11.3	11.6	12.0	12.3	12.7	1.1
South Africa	2,163.5	2,333.2	2,936.1	3,403.6	3,750.0	3,850.0	3,900.0	3,950.0	4,100.0	4,170.2	4,254.3	95.8
Sudan	55.0	57.6		198.0	285.0	253.5	216.5	164.8	124.2	98.5	87.4	2.7
Swaziland	4.0	13.0	15.0	26.7	30.3	31.9	34.1	39.4	45.0	48.2	51.7	46.9
Syria	57.4	65.5	100.0	121.0	139.6	139.0	138.6	157.0	175.9	183.7	194.2	11.1
Tanzania	42.8	42.9	45.0	36.7	23.8	27.4	31.5	38.4	49.5	61.2	73.5	2.1
Togo				62.1	63.7	59.4	46.2	38.4	25.0	19.4	16.4	3.3
Tunisia	110.0	112.0	150.0	190.0	269.0	286.0	316.2	349.6	386.5	423.2	466.7	48.2
Uganda	32.7	33.0	31.0	12.3	35.4	42.0	46.9	48.4	48.5	51.6	53.8	2.2
United Arab Emirates				178.0	201.0	235.5	267.8	302.5	348.0	368.4	379.5	116.1
Yemen		47.2	92.0	163.0	240.6	258.0	283.1	326.0	380.6	397.5	435.2	21.4
Zambia				66.0	157.0	146.5	128.5	113.5	100.0	97.4	93.4	9.3
Zimbabwe	180.0	172.5	175.0	210.0	323.0	342.2	361.2	376.5	386.0	394.2	405.5	32.9

Source: Euromonitor from SMMT/national statistics
Notes: There may be wide variations from year to year in SMMT estimates and in other figures due to interpretation of definitions

Table 4.3

Two-Wheelers in Use 1985-2002

● '000

	1985	1990	1996	1997	1998	1999	2000	2001	2002	per '000 persons 2002
North America										
Canada	487.9	335.0	310.8	319.2	333.5	327.7	329.7	334.6	338.6	10.9
USA	7,700.0	4,259.3	3,871.2	3,765.8	3,734.9	3,709.9	3,684.0	3,638.6	3,607.5	12.9
Latin America										
Anguilla										
Antigua										
Argentina	760.0	32.2	35.6							
Aruba										
Bahamas										
Barbados					1.4	1.4	1.5	1.5	1.6	5.9
Belize		0.6	0.6	0.7	0.7	0.7	0.7	0.7	0.7	2.6
Bermuda										
Bolivia		56.0	66.1	67.5	69.0	69.8	70.6	71.8	72.9	8.5
Brazil	1,088.9									
British Virgin Islands										
Cayman Islands										
Chile	31.0	30.0	32.2	34.1	30.9	31.4	32.2	34.0	37.0	2.4
Colombia	337.9	270.2	334.3	385.4	450.3	479.1	493.0	519.3	548.3	13.7
Costa Rica	35.0	41.6	51.4	58.6	60.5	81.6	93.4	107.2	125.3	32.1
Cuba			215.9	180.4						
Dominica										
Dominican Republic										
Ecuador	8.7		20.9	25.2	23.8	28.2	29.8	32.6	34.6	2.6
El Salvador	41.1	2.4	38.3	27.5						
French Guiana										
Grenada										
Guadeloupe										
Guatemala			105.3	111.4	117.5	129.7	142.5	153.8	167.9	14.2
Guyana										
Haiti										
Honduras		8.5		74.4	82.8	90.9	99.5	108.6	118.7	17.6
Jamaica										
Martinique										
Mexico		249.8	270.0	271.5	273.2	274.8	276.4	278.0	279.7	2.7
Netherlands Antilles										
Nicaragua	15.5	12.3	23.2	17.4	19.3	17.8	17.7	17.8	18.5	3.8
Panama		5.1	7.2	7.5						
Paraguay										
Peru										
Puerto Rico	11.3									
St Kitts										
St Lucia		0.2	0.6							
St Vincent and the Grenadines										
Suriname		27.2	30.0							
Trinidad and Tobago	11.0									
Uruguay		230.0	328.4	359.8						
Venezuela	473.0	301.0			310.9	312.7	314.5	317.5	316.7	12.6

Source: Euromonitor from SMMT/national statistics
Notes: Two-wheelers consist of motorcycles and mopeds

Automotives

Two-Wheelers in Use 1985-2002

• '000

	1985	1990	1996	1997	1998	1999	2000	2001	2002	per '000 persons 2002
Asia Pacific										
Afghanistan										
American Samoa										
Armenia										
Azerbaijan		45.2	9.6	3.2	9.3	9.3	10.5	13.1	15.2	1.9
Bangladesh		106.0	140.8	145.3	145.3	147.5	149.2	152.1	154.3	1.2
Bhutan										
Brunei		0.5	1.0	1.2	1.1	1.1	1.2	1.2	1.2	3.6
Cambodia		83.7	397.3	456.8						
China		564.4	3,585.2	4,871.8	5,952.3	8,436.0	8,280.8	10,208.5	12,282.3	9.5
Fiji										
French Polynesia										
Guam										
Hong Kong, China	19.3	20.7	30.2	31.2	32.0	33.1	34.8	36.1	38.4	5.3
India	3,512.0	13,000.1	23,111.0	25,692.6	26,906.6	29,382.0	31,757.4	34,383.6	37,259.5	36.0
Indonesia	4,765.1	6,083.0	10,090.8	11,735.7	12,651.8	13,077.3	13,502.8	14,522.7	15,317.3	70.9
Japan	18,180.4	17,771.8	15,262.0	14,882.5	14,525.1	14,324.0	14,372.9	14,158.8	14,348.7	112.9
Kazakhstan		650.9	301.6	271.3	247.1	246.3	243.0	230.2	221.0	13.7
Kiribati										
Kyrgyzstan										
Laos			231.0							
Macau			36.7	45.9	53.4	58.1	62.5	64.8	66.9	137.6
Malaysia	2,289.7	3,035.9	3,951.9	4,329.0	4,692.2	5,082.5	5,506.3	5,982.4	6,486.3	280.0
Maldives		3.2	5.6							
Mongolia		46.7	26.0	26.1	26.4	26.7	26.8	27.1	28.0	10.3
Myanmar										
Nauru										
Nepal										
New Caledonia										
North Korea										
Pakistan	456.0	896.2	1,593.2	1,710.8	1,843.7	1,987.1	2,053.2	2,146.3	2,257.3	13.9
Papua New Guinea										
Philippines			331.3	373.1	410.1	453.2	491.1	541.9	571.5	7.2
Singapore	127.6	121.3	131.3	131.6	132.3	133.4	131.9	131.9	131.7	39.4
Solomon Islands										
South Korea	711.4	1,327.5	2,437.8	2,552.7	2,729.7	2,933.4	3,137.1	3,341.2	3,573.8	74.2
Sri Lanka	161.4	391.7	673.1	709.8	751.9	762.5	763.5	764.5	768.5	40.4
Taiwan		8,460.1	9,284.0	10,052.0	10,529.0	10,958.0	11,419.0	12,025.4	12,576.6	557.3
Tajikistan										
Thailand	1,841.9	4,778.2	10,713.7	11,650.0	12,464.5	12,846.2	13,390.0	14,157.7	14,864.8	238.8
Tonga										
Turkmenistan										
Tuvalu										
Uzbekistan										
Vanuatu										
Vietnam		3,000.0	3,369.0	3,428.5	3,488.1	3,548.1	3,608.1	3,670.5	3,733.6	45.3
Western Samoa										
Australasia										
Australia	361.6	304.0	303.9	313.1	328.8	333.8	312.4	314.5	314.9	16.2
New Zealand	122.8	82.3	47.2	38.3	39.1	38.4	39.5	40.1	40.6	10.4

Source: Euromonitor from SMMT/national statistics
Notes: Two-wheelers consist of motorcycles and mopeds

□ Automotives

Two-Wheelers in Use 1985-2002

- '000

	1985	1990	1996	1997	1998	1999	2000	2001	2002	per '000 persons 2002
Africa and Middle East										
Algeria			9.5	9.3	9.0	9.0	9.0	8.9	8.8	0.3
Angola										
Bahrain		1.3	1.7	1.8	1.9	2.1	2.1	2.2	2.3	3.6
Benin		162.4	250.0							
Botswana	1.6		0.8	0.8	0.8	1.0	1.3	1.3	1.5	0.9
Burkina Faso			105.0							
Burundi										
Cameroon	57.4	20.8								
Cape Verde										
Central African Republic		1.3	1.1							
Chad		1.1	3.6							
Comoros										
Congo Dem Rep										
Congo-Brazzaville										
Côte d'Ivoire										
Djibouti										
Egypt	247.0	339.2	418.0	439.8	456.1	462.0	471.4	485.8	498.0	7.7
Equatorial Guinea										
Eritrea										
Ethiopia	1.4	2.0	1.7	1.1	1.2	1.2	1.2	1.2	1.3	0.0
Gabon										
Gambia	2.0									
Ghana										
Guinea										
Guinea-Bissau										
Iran			2,565.6							
Iraq										
Israel		38.1	69.0	72.4	75.0	75.6	76.3	78.3	79.1	12.3
Jordan		1.3								
Kenya		24.6	32.0							
Kuwait	4.0	4.7	6.4	6.4	6.7	7.1	7.2	7.4	7.7	3.3
Lebanon		48.5	54.4	61.5	63.4	66.1	67.8	68.2	70.8	20.4
Lesotho										
Liberia	0.2									
Libya			1.1							
Madagascar	2.4									
Malawi										
Mali										
Mauritania										
Mauritius	28.5	57.1	101.8	105.4	109.1	112.9	115.3	118.7	123.8	104.5
Morocco		19.4	19.9	20.0	20.1	20.2	20.5	20.7	20.8	0.7
Mozambique										
Namibia		1.3	1.5							
Niger	8.1	0.2								
Nigeria			441.6							
Oman		4.5	4.5							
Qatar										
Réunion										
Rwanda		8.1								
Sao Tomé e Príncipe										
Saudi Arabia		7.5	8.5	8.6	8.8	8.9	8.9	9.0	9.1	0.4
Senegal		1.8	4.1							
Seychelles										
Sierra Leone		9.9	10.1							
Somalia										
South Africa	335.9	298.9	262.0	254.5	247.2	246.2	245.2	241.2	237.9	5.4
Sudan	8.0									
Swaziland		2.5	2.7	2.6	2.6	2.5	2.5	2.5	2.5	2.2
Syria										
Tanzania										
Togo		27.4	59.0							
Tunisia	12.0	12.7	13.6	13.5	13.6	13.7	13.7	13.7	13.8	1.4
Uganda	4.8									
United Arab Emirates										
Yemen	20.9									
Zambia										
Zimbabwe	25.1		362.0							

Source: Euromonitor from SMMT/national statistics
Notes: Two-wheelers consist of motorcycles and mopeds

Table 4.4

□ Automotives

Production of Commercial Vehicles 1977-2002

● '000

	1977	1980	1985	1990	1996	1997	1998	1999	2000	2001	2002
Algeria					2.9	2.9	2.8	2.8	2.7	2.7	2.6
Argentina	67.2	54.3	21.2	18.5	43.7	79.8	104.9	80.1	100.7	103.9	108.9
Australia	73.3	47.2	27.6	23.2	27.3	30.3	33.9	37.5	41.1	45.5	50.4
Azerbaijan											
Bolivia											
Brazil	455.3	323.0	207.6	251.4	345.8	391.8	328.7	325.4	323.2	318.2	325.2
Canada	612.9	527.5	854.8	850.3	1,117.4	1,197.8	1,089.2	1,430.3	1,412.6	1,497.9	1,584.0
Chile				8.0	16.8	21.5	16.2	12.5	14.0	13.4	11.9
China				328.8	1,081.9	1,096.3	1,146.7	1,264.5	1,440.8	1,547.8	1,687.1
Colombia	8.9	10.5	10.3	12.7	12.4	13.2	14.2	6.8	3.3	2.4	1.5
Ecuador				15.1	11.1	11.4	10.2	9.8	9.4	9.0	8.5
Egypt											
Hong Kong, China											
India	42.0	68.0	101.0	145.6	289.6	186.4	129.3	168.4	154.6	160.5	164.2
Indonesia				151.7	290.2	378.1	323.5	294.3	265.1	259.2	235.8
Israel	2.0	2.0	1.0	1.1	1.1	1.1	1.2	1.2	1.3	1.4	1.4
Japan	3,083.5	4,004.8	4,624.3	3,538.8	2,482.0	2,483.6	1,994.0	1,795.3	1,781.4	1,660.0	1,613.0
Jordan											
Kazakhstan					0.0	0.1	0.1	0.1	0.1	0.1	0.2
Kuwait											
Malaysia	10.3	19.5	37.3	58.0	74.8	80.4	93.2	101.8	110.4	121.6	134.9
Mexico	93.2	187.0	161.6	203.7	398.3	474.8	457.2	462.0	548.4	526.9	540.8
Morocco					5.7	6.0	6.2	6.3	6.7	7.0	7.3
New Zealand			80.3								
Nigeria				1.9	2.2	2.2	2.2	2.3	2.4	2.5	2.5
Pakistan				13.8	52.5	53.6	54.6	57.9	56.7	57.8	58.9
Peru				3.0	0.6	0.6	0.5	0.5	0.4	0.4	0.3
Philippines											
Saudi Arabia											
Singapore											
South Africa			101.0	124.9	188.4	105.0	119.9	120.7	121.5	125.5	131.2
South Korea	40.7	65.9	113.7	334.9	573.2	509.8	329.4	481.4	513.0	475.0	436.0
Taiwan				74.2	100.3	95.9	85.1	78.4	80.5	76.2	81.2
Thailand	80.5	77.3	74.9	121.5	147.2	142.3	145.3	151.9	158.5	161.5	166.6
Tunisia				0.5	3.3	3.1	2.8	2.5	2.5	2.3	2.2
Turkmenistan											
United Arab Emirates											
USA	3,482.3	1,634.3	3,485.4	3,702.8	5,749.4	6,196.7	6,448.3	7,387.0	7,235.3	7,663.3	8,081.3
Venezuela	64.6	60.8	43.7	23.5	23.1	46.5	34.0	31.0	33.1	34.8	33.7
Vietnam											

Source: Euromonitor from SMMT/national statistics

■ Automotives   **Table 4.5**

Production of Passenger Cars 1977-2002

● '000

	1977	1980	1985	1990	1996	1997	1998	1999	2000	2001	2002
Algeria					0.5	0.4	0.4	0.4	0.3	0.3	0.2
Argentina	168.1	227.5	118.0	81.1	269.4	366.5	353.1	224.7	238.9	246.4	258.4
Australia	316.4	318.0	383.8	360.9	304.7	301.3	335.7	350.7	365.7	382.8	406.4
Azerbaijan											
Bolivia											
Brazil	463.9	600.7	759.1	663.5	1,458.6	1,677.9	1,244.5	1,103.5	1,347.9	1,393.2	1,442.0
Canada	1,162.5	846.8	1,077.9	1,076.1	1,279.8	1,372.6	1,481.1	1,626.3	1,551.2	1,627.6	1,698.4
Chile				3.0	5.0	4.9	5.1	5.1	5.2	5.3	5.4
China				42.4	382.9	486.0	507.1	571.3	607.0	681.1	741.1
Colombia	27.9	32.3	28.8	36.5	63.2	68.5	49.8	24.7	12.1	8.0	4.7
Ecuador				16.7	18.9	25.0	26.6	19.8	12.9	11.7	12.5
Egypt											
Hong Kong, China											
India	48.0	46.0	129.0	218.8	472.5	549.6	588.4	649.4	632.2	679.9	717.0
Indonesia				57.4	35.3	39.4	40.3	41.7	43.1	45.3	46.9
Israel	4.0	2.0		0.9	2.0	1.9	2.0	2.1	2.2	2.3	2.4
Japan	5,431.0	7,038.1	7,646.8	9,948.0	7,863.8	8,491.5	8,055.8	8,100.2	8,363.5	8,118.0	7,995.0
Jordan											
Kazakhstan											
Kuwait											
Malaysia	52.5	81.4	61.2	130.9	49.5	55.7	63.1	70.8	78.6	88.2	98.9
Mexico	7.0	303.1	297.1	611.1	802.1	857.8	947.4	987.8	1,294.8	1,278.4	1,258.5
Morocco					13.8	12.3	13.8	13.9	13.9	13.9	14.4
New Zealand			80.3								
Nigeria				10.2	2.4	2.4	2.5	2.6	2.6	2.7	2.7
Pakistan				25.7	22.5	21.0	19.5	17.9	18.2	17.3	18.0
Peru				0.7							
Philippines											
Saudi Arabia											
Singapore											
South Africa			204.3	241.6	293.0	239.8	248.4	252.6	256.8	248.5	250.7
South Korea	42.3	57.2	264.5	986.8	2,239.5	2,308.5	2,325.1	2,362.7	2,602.0	2,471.0	2,309.0
Taiwan				362.8	366.0	381.1	404.6	350.3	372.6	271.7	
Thailand	27.6	28.0	36.1	73.8	166.3	187.6	208.9	225.7	242.5	266.4	290.9
Tunisia				0.1	0.3	0.3	0.3	0.2	0.2	0.2	0.2
Turkmenistan											
United Arab Emirates											
USA	9,213.6	6,375.5	8,184.8	6,077.4	6,080.4	5,927.3	5,554.1	5,636.7	5,542.2	5,415.2	5,294.3
Venezuela	98.7	94.3	71.8		35.4	84.5	69.2	57.5	47.8	51.5	45.5
Vietnam											

Source: *Euromonitor from SMMT/national statistics*

Table 4.6

Production of Two-Wheelers 1985-2002

● '000

	1985	1990	1995	1996	1997	1998	1999	2000	2001	2002
Algeria										
Argentina			41.0	38.2	37.1	37.9	38.4	38.9	39.1	39.6
Australia										
Azerbaijan										
Bolivia										
Brazil										
Canada										
Chile										
China				4,277.9	4,032.7	6,902.9	9,782.0	9,601.9	11,752.7	14,141.5
Colombia										
Ecuador										
Egypt										
Hong Kong, China										
India			2,658.1	2,980.2	3,300.0	3,550.0	3,755.9	3,861.8	4,120.3	4,355.4
Indonesia										
Israel		38.1		69.0	72.4	75.0	77.6	76.6	78.6	80.3
Japan	4,536.0	2,807.0	2,753.0	2,584.0	2,546.3	2,475.8	2,403.7	2,331.6	2,272.5	2,315.5
Jordan										
Kazakhstan										
Kuwait										
Malaysia			328.6	329.9	339.4	348.9	358.1	367.3	377.2	387.3
Mexico										
Morocco										
New Zealand										
Nigeria										
Pakistan			96.0	94.6	117.5	134.3	148.6	185.7	219.8	257.0
Peru										
Philippines										
Saudi Arabia										
Singapore										
South Africa										
South Korea										
Taiwan										
Thailand										
Tunisia										
Turkmenistan										
United Arab Emirates										
USA									482.3	539.6
Venezuela										
Vietnam										

Source: Euromonitor from SMMT/national statistics

New Registrations of Commerical Vehicles 1977-2002

● '000

	1977	1980	1985	1990	1996	1997	1998	1999	2000	2001	2002
Algeria					2.6	1.1	0.8	0.7	0.7	0.6	0.6
Argentina			20.7	17.8	76.9	104.9	133.4	106.1	82.0	78.5	71.5
Australia	131.1	121.5	159.2	126.5	158.0	182.3	223.3	239.2	233.4	229.1	221.7
Azerbaijan											
Bolivia											
Brazil			161.1	179.9	260.8	279.1	220.0	176.5	233.2	282.9	333.3
Canada	333.6	335.8	393.4	416.0	541.6	662.8	694.7	739.6	748.0	810.9	852.8
Chile				24.0							
China				489.2	1,067.9	1,093.3	1,118.7	1,147.8	1,176.9	1,205.8	1,235.7
Colombia				18.4	25.0	26.4	27.7	29.4	30.4	31.9	33.5
Ecuador				0.2							
Egypt											
Hong Kong, China			20.0	15.9	12.1	14.7	9.7	7.6	9.8	9.5	9.4
India			99.0	201.8	282.1	183.8	133.6	167.1	155.8	161.5	156.3
Indonesia				218.5	293.5	319.0	154.8	103.4	112.0	124.4	129.5
Israel				14.4	40.0	39.8	39.6	39.8	39.8	39.8	39.7
Japan	1,694.2	2,161.3	2,452.7	2,674.8	2,409.0	2,233.0	1,786.3	1,707.1	1,703.2	1,613.0	1,642.0
Jordan					89.1						
Kazakhstan											
Kuwait					8.9	7.9	7.2	7.0	7.3	7.0	6.7
Malaysia			28.2	25.0	89.1	96.9	26.2	32.7	46.6	39.6	31.7
Mexico			149.5	366.8	133.8	185.0	215.8	218.8	268.3	335.6	389.4
Morocco					6.9	10.6	12.3	15.1	13.3	15.7	17.4
New Zealand				19.0	14.7	12.9	11.8	14.0	16.3	19.1	22.7
Nigeria			28.0	2.5	24.9	33.0	38.8	39.2	39.0	40.1	42.1
Pakistan				22.0	30.9	26.0	24.6	24.1	24.2	24.9	24.6
Peru				5.0	10.3	10.5	9.9	4.7	6.7	6.0	5.2
Philippines			3.5	15.5	73.1	68.8	48.9	18.0	19.7	18.8	19.5
Saudi Arabia											
Singapore			5.4	8.4	7.6	8.2	9.0	10.9	21.0	27.1	36.6
South Africa	90.0	127.7	101.0	125.2	143.1	127.1	110.6	106.4	117.0	111.2	115.5
South Korea	62.1	65.2	114.0	216.0	558.9	522.6	345.9	481.9	504.8	506.5	511.5
Taiwan				79.5	100.3	113.0	111.5	104.3	109.6	112.1	111.8
Thailand				293.4	416.4	231.1	107.9	84.3	60.7	62.2	67.6
Tunisia				8.9	12.7	13.9	15.0	16.3	16.1	17.1	18.0
Turkmenistan											
United Arab Emirates											
USA	3,509.3	2,476.8	4,681.7	4,798.5	6,938.0	7,196.4	7,731.5	8,529.6	9,172.5	9,835.5	10,634.6
Venezuela			46.2	20.2	33.0	43.4	40.9	18.8	23.6	24.9	21.6
Vietnam											

Source: Euromonitor from SMMT/national statistics

Table 4.8

New Registrations of Passenger Cars 1977-2002

• '000

	1977	1980	1985	1990	1996	1997	1998	1999	2000	2001	2002
Algeria					10.6	6.4	5.2	4.8	4.4	3.5	3.0
Argentina			125.6	83.3	299.2	321.4	322.0	274.0	225.0	331.5	334.1
Australia	430.4	453.4	530.2	487.7	492.1	540.4	584.4	547.6	553.7	684.6	691.5
Azerbaijan											
Bolivia											
Brazil			602.1	532.8	1,246.0	1,361.6	967.1	897.0	1,067.2	1,089.4	1,097.8
Canada	953.1	949.0	1,146.3	867.8	660.5	725.8	740.7	806.5	849.2	816.5	840.9
Chile				42.3	105.6	131.0	152.7	167.8	168.6	172.5	184.7
China				61.0	385.9	474.2	562.5	645.2	727.9	853.0	987.9
Colombia				32.7	63.2	72.9	77.5	83.0	88.0	95.6	102.3
Ecuador				13.3							
Egypt											
Hong Kong, China			16.3	28.9	22.2	38.9	31.4	35.4	33.1	34.5	33.5
India			124.0	176.2	479.8	568.4	517.9	689.9	730.5	811.5	887.1
Indonesia				55.7	43.9	73.2	72.4	75.6	75.3	75.2	74.7
Israel				61.0	86.8	88.7	89.6	93.0	96.6	99.2	102.0
Japan	2,500.1	2,854.2	3,104.1	5,102.7	4,668.7	4,492.0	4,093.1	4,154.1	4,259.9	4,290.0	4,315.0
Jordan					203.7						
Kazakhstan											
Kuwait					47.0	45.4	45.8	45.9	50.3	51.2	52.7
Malaysia			59.7	134.3	275.7	307.9	137.7	255.9	296.6	302.0	300.6
Mexico			242.2	352.6	200.1	303.4	430.2	465.1	603.0	781.8	990.5
Morocco					35.1	42.2	45.6	47.9	50.1	54.7	58.4
New Zealand				74.4	64.4	58.6	54.2	58.2	57.6	58.3	61.5
Nigeria			28.0	1.1	62.5	53.8	53.5	53.4	53.5	54.1	54.2
Pakistan				32.1	43.2	26.5	25.0	26.6	26.2	25.5	25.3
Peru				3.0	27.6	29.8	23.0	8.2	5.4	6.5	7.6
Philippines			8.6	42.4	89.0	75.7	37.9	30.5	31.2	32.5	33.5
Saudi Arabia											
Singapore			14.4	32.1	29.3	26.6	28.5	36.2	55.1	64.5	80.5
South Africa	166.8	277.1	204.3	209.6	275.7	239.8	203.8	189.4	224.1	218.1	220.6
South Korea	50.9	61.4	255.4	516.3	2,295.3	2,307.2	1,796.2	2,300.8	2,602.1	2,685.0	2,788.7
Taiwan				359.1	264.0	268.1	293.0	246.0	263.0	262.8	261.5
Thailand				169.2	172.7	132.1	57.8	65.3	72.8	75.0	77.5
Tunisia				9.6	30.7	30.8	30.9	31.1	31.0	31.1	31.1
Turkmenistan											
United Arab Emirates											
USA	10,826.2	8,760.9	10,888.6	9,103.2	8,526.8	8,220.3	8,042.7	8,472.1	8,847.0	8,913.1	9,095.2
Venezuela			77.3	21.1	48.8	134.5	134.8	85.6	121.7	131.5	130.7
Vietnam											

Source: Euromonitor from SMMT/national statistics

■ Automotives

Table 4.9

New Registrations of Two-Wheelers 1985-2002

- '000

	1985	1990	1995	1996	1997	1998	1999	2000	2001	2002
Algeria			49.0	25.0	24.0	23.5	17.9	14.7	12.9	11.0
Argentina		89.9								
Australia	45.9	20.5	20.5	22.3	22.8	26.8	30.1	32.6	35.1	39.0
Azerbaijan										
Bolivia										
Brazil	114.0									
Canada	722.0									
Chile										
China										
Colombia	23.8									
Ecuador			0.8	0.8	0.8	0.8	0.8	0.8	0.8	0.8
Egypt										
Hong Kong, China		3.3	3.7	3.8	3.9	3.1	3.5	3.9	3.9	4.0
India	1,103.0	1,607.4	1,150.0	1,072.9	1,098.5	1,124.0	1,144.3	1,182.3	1,211.4	1,241.4
Indonesia										
Israel		4.7	11.7	12.4	13.1	13.7	14.3	15.5	16.4	17.3
Japan	2,096.3	1,608.1	1,040.0	945.5	998.6	953.3	920.1	887.0	873.0	844.1
Jordan				0.4						
Kazakhstan										
Kuwait										
Malaysia		173.3	235.0	242.7	251.4	260.2	271.1	282.0	292.9	304.2
Mexico	159.4									
Morocco			106.0	68.0	89.0	129.0	128.0	171.0	215.3	268.6
New Zealand		4.9	3.5	3.8	4.1	4.1	4.8	5.0	5.3	5.7
Nigeria	17.0	4.9	5.8	6.1	6.4	6.8	6.3	6.7	6.9	7.0
Pakistan		77.8	75.5	87.8	72.6	61.8	51.5	56.8	57.9	60.7
Peru										
Philippines	17.0	70.0	145.4	180.2	229.3	202.3	190.3	214.8	224.4	223.2
Saudi Arabia										
Singapore		8.1	7.7	8.8	8.8	8.8	8.7	8.6	8.6	8.5
South Africa		5.3	6.2	6.3	6.4	6.6	6.8	7.0	7.1	7.3
South Korea		324.9	317.6	367.1	409.3	451.4	482.6	513.8	558.8	604.1
Taiwan	71.1	417.6	1,339.1	1,247.9	987.3	896.0	903.9	845.6	910.5	892.2
Thailand		645.8		1,247.9	1,187.9	1,134.6	1,099.3	1,064.0	1,022.4	984.8
Tunisia		0.1	0.2	0.3	0.3	0.3	0.4	0.4	0.4	0.5
Turkmenistan										
United Arab Emirates										
USA	718.3	269.5	230.0	238.9	241.9	245.0	233.0	221.0	216.7	210.9
Venezuela	414.1	269.5								
Vietnam	29.0									

Source: Euromonitor from SMMT/national statistics

Airline Freight Traffic 1980-2002

● Million tonne-kilometres

	1980	1985	1990	1995	1996	1997	1998	1999	2000	2001	2002
Algeria	7.3	8.8	13.7	14.3	16.0	16.8	18.8	15.4	11.7	10.4	8.6
Argentina	18.4	27.5	27.1	173.1	176.6	220.3	251.0	241.0	295.1	296.5	328.9
Australia	513.4	713.4	1,093.6	1,605.9	1,833.7	1,953.8	1,904.4	1,693.0	1,860.2	1,924.0	2,051.1
Azerbaijan				24.2	27.6	33.0	92.5	58.2	47.2	51.5	48.4
Bolivia	32.3	36.2	8.0	50.6	47.3	46.9	42.0	19.3	16.2	13.5	11.2
Brazil	594.9	867.3	1,197.0	1,531.3	1,644.8	1,789.9	1,642.8	1,462.9	1,523.3	1,624.6	1,712.0
Canada	750.9	1,083.4	1,907.6	1,722.7	1,781.0	1,956.5	1,805.7	1,881.6	1,806.3	1,802.5	1,764.2
Chile	88.4	109.6	342.6	778.7	806.2	1,071.2	1,246.2	1,139.4	1,312.0	1,278.5	1,354.4
China	93.1	228.7	517.3	1,568.9	1,688.6	2,083.6	2,474.2	3,295.4	3,900.1	3,512.0	3,625.6
Colombia	116.0	212.8	250.3	358.3	311.2	812.0	790.2	636.9	595.4	612.6	600.7
Ecuador	26.5	36.5	58.6	30.0	32.9	53.8	82.2	33.0	14.6	17.6	12.8
Egypt	22.5	71.0	111.2	149.1	198.0	208.6	255.1	269.5	278.1	240.4	227.1
Hong Kong, China						2,325.3	4,151.1	4,545.7	4,840.7	5,210.6	5,578.7
India	245.5	442.3	561.4	464.9	565.0	528.0	531.3	531.2	544.8	498.5	482.9
Indonesia	76.4	162.5	419.4	705.3	749.4	710.0	429.4	362.0	422.6	421.7	455.2
Israel	316.2	584.7	901.8	1,056.0	1,112.9	1,135.8	1,117.3	1,034.3	885.7	655.3	521.6
Japan	1,541.9	2,653.6	4,865.0	6,865.1	6,801.3	7,504.6	7,514.1	8,225.6	8,549.4	7,080.3	6,569.0
Jordan	83.1	173.6	255.6	272.5	296.6	271.0	219.2	193.6	204.0	199.8	201.5
Kazakhstan				4.5	16.7	16.7	24.0	9.8	11.8	15.6	19.5
Kuwait	61.2	174.0	237.5	335.6	333.8	364.6	364.6	267.7	243.2	226.3	208.1
Malaysia	105.5	295.8	620.1	1,202.0	1,414.6	1,425.7	1,375.6	1,424.6	1,863.8	1,535.4	1,594.0
Mexico	131.8	158.0	123.9	155.1	156.1	165.1	162.3	155.0	173.2	161.4	164.7
Morocco	36.1	45.2	40.4	58.5	57.0	53.9	58.0	57.8	62.5	60.6	62.0
New Zealand	205.9	336.8	370.6	648.8	745.0	928.4	826.2	855.6	817.1	825.1	810.2
Nigeria	1.7	15.7	6.7	4.3	4.7	5.0	27.0	9.7	9.5	9.8	9.9
Pakistan	171.1	215.7	333.7	453.8	427.2	422.7	402.4	331.8	339.4	377.7	403.0
Peru	18.9	33.6	15.9	11.8	14.1	9.5	8.7	6.0	3.5	4.5	3.8
Philippines	106.0	242.8	325.1	393.3	384.5	471.6	184.9	240.9	241.0	234.7	231.6
Saudi Arabia	148.9	439.8	579.7	776.0	862.8	926.4	934.0	1,000.0	999.6	1,005.5	1,008.3
Singapore	621.5	1,066.1	1,819.1	3,773.3	4,115.0	4,740.8	4,724.0	5,451.0	6,004.9	5,762.6	5,925.0
South Africa	337.0	629.8	292.4	393.2	328.5	420.4	535.6	688.4	687.5	693.6	696.1
South Korea	828.4	1,673.7	2,941.1	5,774.1	6,550.9	7,889.2	7,290.0	8,098.4	7,773.6	8,105.5	8,109.1
Taiwan											
Thailand	152.7	346.3	531.6	1,345.8	1,387.0	1,628.3	1,522.2	1,670.6	1,712.9	1,669.2	1,668.5
Tunisia	11.9	19.8	20.3	19.7	18.4	18.7	20.3	19.2	20.8	20.1	20.6
Turkmenistan				0.4	2.1	2.1	3.3	6.9	11.9	10.0	12.1
United Arab Emirates	15.4	33.8	129.6	570.9	651.3	809.4	902.0	1,129.7	1,427.5	1,493.8	1,717.8
USA	8,641.3	10,117.2	14,674.5	22,991.5	25,219.8	28,627.0	29,056.4	27,014.9	30,155.4	28,546.2	29,344.1
Venezuela		108.5	156.4	207.2	116.6	82.6	48.0	68.0	33.1	45.6	37.3
Vietnam		0.6	0.7	29.8	82.9	103.6	95.6	98.5	116.3	127.6	145.2

Source: Euromonitor from International Civil Aviation Authority/national statistics

◻ Civil Aviation   **Table 4.11**

Airline Passenger Traffic 1980-2002

● Million passenger-kilometres

	1980	1985	1990	1995	1996	1997	1998	1999	2000	2001	2002
Algeria	2,419.0	3,761.3	4,163.3	3,073.1	2,863.0	3,130.0	3,012.0	3,091.5	3,224.6	2,859.2	3,229.7
Argentina	7,587.8	8,089.2	10,107.9	12,494.8	13,360.0	14,338.0	14,376.0	15,188.4	17,580.6	18,008.1	19,532.5
Australia	27,531.8	29,071.9	41,200.9	68,016.1	72,594.0	75,873.0	73,647.0	78,520.4	77,568.3	78,419.3	76,794.8
Azerbaijan				2,037.7	1,743.0	1,283.0	843.0	1,448.0	1,506.2	1,518.6	1,588.4
Bolivia	1,138.8	1,161.3	1,366.5	1,508.2	1,634.0	2,143.0	2,179.0	2,311.5	2,296.3	2,213.1	2,255.2
Brazil	15,849.9	18,824.5	30,529.2	35,237.8	37,671.0	42,385.0	46,978.0	50,403.5	52,135.1	52,740.0	57,021.2
Canada	42,289.4	42,458.7	85,133.8	81,800.3	56,018.0	61,862.0	63,801.0	66,585.4	68,976.0	69,391.8	70,047.6
Chile	1,661.1	1,740.4	3,008.2	5,785.0	6,787.0	8,597.0	9,698.0	10,700.8	11,436.0	11,514.7	12,390.6
China	3,590.9	8,535.2	19,357.6	57,161.8	70,605.0	72,964.0	75,823.0	93,032.0	104,723.1	112,058.5	117,242.9
Colombia	5,162.9	5,527.1	5,582.5	6,982.7	5,991.0	7,219.0	7,350.0	7,587.6	7,798.6	7,897.6	7,646.8
Ecuador	947.4	1,009.6	1,366.8	1,594.0	1,663.0	2,035.0	2,282.0	2,459.1	2,601.1	2,619.8	3,032.3
Egypt	3,087.6	5,121.9	7,223.9	7,385.0	8,742.0	9,018.0	8,036.0	9,576.0	9,561.0	9,548.0	9,794.0
Hong Kong, China						20,283.0	42,964.0	53,094.6	59,766.9	65,150.1	71,998.2
India	11,904.3	17,287.4	21,848.2	21,353.8	22,317.0	24,069.0	24,646.0	25,842.3	25,908.0	25,052.4	24,755.5
Indonesia	5,166.7	9,359.6	15,583.6	23,279.4	25,081.0	23,517.0	15,974.0	17,232.1	17,002.0	16,982.6	18,209.8
Israel	6,609.2	7,326.0	9,013.6	11,466.6	11,793.0	11,776.0	12,418.0	12,946.7	12,268.0	11,692.0	12,065.5
Japan	53,486.4	64,868.9	98,543.1	128,110.8	141,812.0	151,048.0	154,402.0	165,170.2	185,926.8	198,793.9	215,520.3
Jordan	2,341.0	3,958.3	4,034.0	4,555.9	4,750.0	4,900.0	4,065.0	4,376.3	4,015.9	4,060.0	4,054.2
Kazakhstan				1,351.2	1,330.0	1,330.0	1,533.0	1,321.6	1,374.8	1,527.9	1,578.3
Kuwait	2,189.4	4,539.9	4,714.3	5,466.3	6,073.0	5,997.0	6,207.0	6,806.1	6,132.0	6,080.0	6,178.0
Malaysia	3,005.3	6,803.1	11,482.4	23,219.5	23,436.0	28,704.0	29,376.0	33,708.0	37,944.0	41,111.7	44,835.5
Mexico	12,185.6	17,591.7	16,251.8	23,803.5	19,636.0	23,668.0	25,976.0	27,586.5	27,168.0	26,987.0	28,066.2
Morocco	1,970.3	1,707.2	2,645.7	4,489.3	4,665.0	5,321.0	5,868.0	6,298.1	5,878.9	5,691.3	5,695.3
New Zealand	6,064.5	7,125.9	11,636.7	18,580.6	22,052.0	20,983.0	19,014.0	20,386.0	21,356.7	22,012.5	22,828.8
Nigeria	338.4	656.5	263.6	257.8	273.0	221.0	245.0	249.1	245.5	245.8	235.9
Pakistan	4,670.1	6,419.4	8,535.2	9,732.0	10,580.0	11,658.0	10,972.0	11,582.3	12,048.0	11,872.8	10,617.7
Peru	1,567.6	1,434.9	1,788.6	2,271.6	2,634.0	2,964.0	3,014.0	3,192.5	3,101.6	2,984.2	3,157.0
Philippines	4,931.1	8,830.2	11,177.0	14,752.1	15,132.0	16,392.0	7,503.0	7,890.3	8,881.9	9,331.9	9,813.2
Saudi Arabia	8,990.0	16,324.1	16,522.0	19,211.6	18,980.0	18,949.0	18,820.0	20,177.9	24,587.7	26,238.3	26,796.5
Singapore	13,723.5	23,149.7	34,700.1	51,193.6	53,640.0	55,452.0	58,176.0	64,416.0	71,784.0	70,232.0	71,224.4
South Africa	10,255.7	11,732.5	11,286.1	15,151.1	15,957.0	16,825.0	16,997.0	17,715.7	22,206.0	25,506.9	26,444.8
South Korea	11,320.4	13,949.9	22,570.1	49,182.4	55,751.0	59,372.0	47,711.0	52,955.8	59,610.6	63,858.6	66,305.9
Taiwan											
Thailand	4,768.2	9,684.9	19,151.1	25,668.4	29,801.0	30,827.0	34,340.0	38,623.6	42,240.0	40,582.0	39,629.8
Tunisia	1,372.6	1,618.0	1,599.7	1,956.0	2,118.0	2,484.0	2,683.0	2,760.0	2,688.0	2,695.0	2,785.6
Turkmenistan				1,088.1	1,093.0	1,093.0	832.0	767.0	797.9	813.7	832.7
United Arab Emirates	781.5	1,435.7	4,350.0	10,731.5	11,352.0	13,519.0	15,633.0	18,573.9	20,424.0	23,126.0	24,652.2
USA	452,376.1	515,069.8	745,496.6	858,624.0	919,752.0	964,536.0	946,968.0	1,039,296.0	1,110,060.0	1,106,347.4	1,132,265.5
Venezuela	2,931.9	2,309.4	4,570.5	4,556.3	5,800.0	4,444.0	3,133.0	3,178.0	3,258.5	3,226.1	3,194.9
Vietnam		48.3	62.0	1,710.3	2,954.0	3,785.0	3,644.0	7,073.5	7,962.4	8,079.3	9,138.1

Source: *Euromonitor from International Civil Aviation Authority/national statistics*

Distance Flown on Scheduled Flights 1980-2002

- Million kilometres

	1980	1985	1990	1995	1996	1997	1998	1999	2000	2001	2002
Algeria	22.6	30.4	31.8	30.4	30.5	33.6	30.9	31.8	32.6	28.7	32.2
Argentina	87.9	73.6	81.9	108.9	133.2	154.7	157.2	164.0	173.6	170.0	180.3
Australia	185.5	186.7	240.6	423.1	466.3	499.7	479.5	505.1	499.4	505.2	494.9
Azerbaijan				21.3	21.4	15.7	9.5	7.9	10.5	12.0	13.3
Bolivia	19.7	16.2	16.2	20.3	23.8	28.1	27.8	28.9	28.0	26.6	27.0
Brazil	209.1	251.4	325.5	386.5	427.8	471.0	534.7	563.7	619.5	645.9	709.0
Canada	426.8	444.3	596.9	543.1	497.0	519.3	547.3	558.2	562.0	557.4	558.7
Chile	22.0	23.4	45.2	83.5	96.8	108.9	139.3	153.5	178.7	187.8	206.5
China	68.5	107.9	204.6	531.2	589.7	639.5	729.9	867.9	981.2	1,052.3	1,102.1
Colombia	60.6	74.7	86.0	119.3	97.3	119.3	123.9	129.8	132.6	133.9	129.4
Ecuador	12.8	11.9	13.1	13.7	14.5	23.4	23.1	24.4	28.1	29.6	35.0
Egypt	29.0	37.1	44.3	56.4	62.2	64.5	63.4	66.8	66.1	69.2	72.7
Hong Kong, China						112.0	227.6	316.5	422.2	501.0	577.6
India	116.8	139.5	179.6	191.0	171.1	188.9	199.6	206.0	209.9	211.1	212.7
Indonesia	89.7	125.5	156.9	237.5	256.1	196.5	154.7	161.1	146.2	140.0	147.0
Israel	37.4	38.4	51.1	66.7	74.0	75.4	79.2	82.4	86.9	87.4	92.6
Japan	349.2	375.5	494.8	649.7	726.9	776.8	828.0	872.3	939.0	981.8	1,052.6
Jordan	21.1	28.6	36.3	41.2	42.1	40.3	34.8	36.5	35.5	36.9	37.3
Kazakhstan				20.2	20.2	20.2	35.3	48.5	60.4	73.4	79.3
Kuwait	21.3	30.4	32.5	40.6	42.8	42.7	45.5	48.7	51.0	50.4	51.1
Malaysia	41.1	55.3	88.7	157.7	172.9	183.4	188.8	205.2	219.2	231.3	249.0
Mexico	138.6	193.7	158.6	280.9	245.5	300.4	360.1	384.3	415.7	431.9	459.3
Morocco	23.1	20.1	28.3	46.3	45.2	48.9	55.6	58.3	61.7	63.7	65.8
New Zealand	51.1	50.3	83.6	136.3	155.6	172.8	174.0	186.2	201.3	210.8	220.4
Nigeria	7.7	9.4	5.1	4.2	4.3	4.7	5.3	5.4	5.5	5.6	5.4
Pakistan	46.9	45.1	58.2	67.9	73.8	78.3	74.8	77.6	80.2	81.3	73.7
Peru	22.1	22.5	20.6	24.1	32.9	39.5	40.8	42.4	48.8	51.1	56.4
Philippines	51.5	57.1	66.3	80.5	81.3	96.0	40.4	40.7	34.3	31.2	30.5
Saudi Arabia	76.6	109.5	98.5	113.9	117.6	117.1	120.3	125.6	128.7	125.9	123.2
Singapore	76.5	84.1	127.2	222.9	245.4	269.8	292.7	319.6	349.7	369.4	389.3
South Africa	74.1	82.4	81.5	112.0	121.1	131.0	128.4	133.2	139.0	145.8	144.4
South Korea	66.5	88.9	145.0	296.6	323.0	364.7	319.2	351.1	366.2	377.6	384.7
Taiwan											
Thailand	37.4	60.5	97.9	130.4	140.3	153.0	157.8	170.7	182.6	192.1	196.3
Tunisia	11.8	13.9	13.3	16.4	17.9	23.7	26.6	28.0	32.1	34.6	37.2
Turkmenistan				15.0	15.0	15.0	11.0	9.5	8.5	8.0	9.1
United Arab Emirates	7.2	10.5	29.4	77.7	81.7	84.7	94.0	108.7	118.3	117.5	121.4
USA	4,833.4	5,294.3	7,252.8	8,635.2	8,664.9	8,976.8	9,157.7	9,524.4	9,760.7	9,732.6	9,651.5
Venezuela	74.7	63.4	84.5	94.8	80.0	62.8	51.8	52.5	45.3	41.1	39.0
Vietnam				27.2	28.8	35.1	32.7	34.6	36.8	36.2	40.4

Source: *Euromonitor from International Civil Aviation Authority/national statistics*

◻ Civil Aviation

Table 4.13

Scheduled Airlines: Departures, Load Factor and Passengers Carried 2002

● As stated

	Aircraft Departures ('000)	Passengers Carried ('000)	Passenger Load Factor (%)
North America			
Canada	312	26,404	77
USA	8,938	673,517	72
Latin America			
Anguilla			
Antigua	66	1,510	67
Argentina	204	9,273	71
Aruba			
Bahamas	29	1,818	70
Barbados			
Belize			
Bermuda			
Bolivia	22	1,653	63
Brazil	827	37,195	77
British Virgin Islands			
Cayman Islands			
Chile	96	5,324	61
Colombia	182	8,142	68
Costa Rica	33	820	60
Cuba	13	1,009	79
Dominica			
Dominican Republic	1	14	89
Ecuador	21	1,170	55
El Salvador	40	2,345	78
French Guiana			
Grenada			
Guadeloupe			
Guatemala		521	61
Guyana	0	98	88
Haiti			
Honduras			
Jamaica	28	2,342	68
Martinique			
Mexico	316	22,231	78
Netherlands Antilles			
Nicaragua	1	73	61
Panama	24	1,248	72
Paraguay	7	266	39
Peru	51	2,404	84
Puerto Rico			
St Kitts			
St Lucia			
St Vincent and the Grenadines			
Suriname	3	216	70
Trinidad and Tobago	34	1,591	76
Uruguay	10	639	66
Venezuela	131	3,869	47

Source: Euromonitor from International Civil Aviation Authority/national statistics

Civil Aviation
Scheduled Airlines: Departures, Load Factor and Passengers Carried 2002

- As stated

	Aircraft Departures ('000)	Passengers Carried ('000)	Passenger Load Factor (%)
Asia Pacific			
Afghanistan	3	122	79
American Samoa			
Armenia	5	267	81
Azerbaijan	8	540	58
Bangladesh	6	1,398	74
Bhutan	1	38	56
Brunei	17	1,117	59
Cambodia			
China	596	68,480	65
Fiji	57	637	57
French Polynesia			
Guam			
Hong Kong, China	93	17,538	72
India	199	18,395	70
Indonesia	178	11,608	69
Japan	717	116,953	82
Kazakhstan	9	509	53
Kiribati	4	30	51
Kyrgyzstan	6	205	75
Laos	7	235	69
Macau			
Malaysia	194	19,301	81
Maldives	6	367	66
Mongolia	6	282	63
Myanmar	11	629	73
Nauru			
Nepal	12	670	70
New Caledonia			
North Korea	2	106	41
Pakistan	60	5,891	68
Papua New Guinea	28	1,186	44
Philippines	45	5,845	65
Singapore	76	18,576	70
Solomon Islands	15	72	67
South Korea	233	37,842	63
Sri Lanka	6	2,484	120
Taiwan			
Tajikistan	4	166	79
Thailand	104	18,972	57
Tonga	4	58	102
Turkmenistan	22	1,535	79
Tuvalu			
Uzbekistan	32	1,699	76
Vanuatu	1	106	70
Vietnam	32	3,267	81
Western Samoa			
Australasia			
Australia	344	32,685	73
New Zealand	228	10,464	70

Source: Euromonitor from International Civil Aviation Authority/national statistics

◻ Civil Aviation

Scheduled Airlines: Departures, Load Factor and Passengers Carried 2002

● As stated

	Aircraft Departures ('000)	Passengers Carried ('000)	Passenger Load Factor (%)
Africa and Middle East			
Algeria	36	2,949	79
Angola	5	205	63
Bahrain	24	1,536	79
Benin	2	73	64
Botswana	7	212	81
Burkina Faso	4	142	67
Burundi	1	12	
Cameroon	6	261	56
Cape Verde	16	304	44
Central African Republic	2	77	77
Chad	1	70	70
Comoros			
Congo Dem Rep			
Congo-Brazzaville	6	119	
Côte d'Ivoire	7	275	82
Djibouti			
Egypt	55	4,929	64
Equatorial Guinea		28	62
Eritrea			
Ethiopia	36	1,202	77
Gabon	7	414	57
Gambia			
Ghana	6	358	52
Guinea	1	77	63
Guinea-Bissau	1	21	72
Iran	75	8,575	79
Iraq			
Israel	49	4,202	75
Jordan	18	1,405	78
Kenya	35	1,890	49
Kuwait	17	2,051	68
Lebanon	11	887	68
Lesotho	0	2	28
Liberia			
Libya	6	587	67
Madagascar	26	749	93
Malawi	4	115	86
Mali	1	72	71
Mauritania	4	195	74
Mauritius	15	1,157	54
Morocco	46	3,974	74
Mozambique	7	295	80
Namibia	7	297	45
Niger	2	80	77
Nigeria	9	400	33
Oman	21	2,417	74
Qatar	25	2,864	79
Réunion			
Rwanda			
Sao Tomé e Príncipe	1	34	68
Saudi Arabia	100	11,979	63
Senegal	3	102	81
Seychelles	23	484	71
Sierra Leone	0		
Somalia			
South Africa	109	8,523	63
Sudan	7	411	32
Swaziland	0	70	40
Syria	11	725	49
Tanzania	6	174	
Togo	2	73	80
Tunisia	22	1,989	63
Uganda	4	224	60
United Arab Emirates	42	7,131	74
Yemen	13	1,025	63
Zambia	7	107	55
Zimbabwe	14	570	37

Source: *Euromonitor from International Civil Aviation Authority/national statistics*

⊡ Merchant Shipping   **Table 4.14**

Size of Merchant Shipping Fleet 1977-2002

● '000 gross tons

	1977	1980	1985	1990	1995	1996	1997	1998	1999	2000	2001	2002
North America												
Canada	2,822.9	3,180.1	3,343.8	2,744.2	2,401.0	2,406.2	2,526.6	2,501.3	2,495.9	2,490.5	2,727.0	2,779.5
USA		18,464.3	19,517.6	21,328.1	12,760.8	12,024.6	11,788.8	11,851.7	12,025.8	11,765.3	10,907.2	10,697.3
Latin America												
Anguilla		1.1	4.0	2.5	2.4	2.1	1.9	1.5	1.2	1.1	0.7	
Antigua		0.4		958.0	1,842.0	2,176.2	2,214.3	2,787.8	3,621.9	4,456.0	4,688.3	5,655.4
Argentina	1,677.2	2,546.3	2,457.0	1,890.0	594.9	586.3	579.4	498.8	477.3	455.7	421.6	389.4
Aruba												
Bahamas	106.3	87.3	3,907.3	13,626.3	23,602.8	24,408.8	25,523.2	27,515.8	29,482.5	31,449.2	33,385.7	35,704.0
Barbados		5.3	8.4	7.8	291.9	497.0	887.6	687.6	724.8	762.0	687.3	644.8
Belize						1,015.8	1,760.6	2,382.5	2,368.2	2,015.7	1,828.2	1,845.5
Bermuda	1,814.5	499.0	980.7	4,258.3	3,047.5	3,035.0	3,619.7	3,750.8	3,998.4	4,279.3	5,312.8	5,847.7
Bolivia									178.9	175.3	174.0	173.1
Brazil	3,330.0	4,533.7	6,057.4	6,015.7	5,076.7	4,530.0	4,372.4	4,170.6	3,933.3	3,696.1	3,687.1	3,533.2
British Virgin Islands											3.3	
Cayman Islands						690.0	1,011.7	1,333.5	1,655.2	1,977.0	2,053.9	2,451.7
Chile		614.4	413.8	616.3	761.0	690.9	721.9	753.4	820.0	886.6	880.3	925.0
Colombia		283.5	365.6	372.2	144.2	121.7	117.7	111.7	96.9	82.1	65.6	56.7
Costa Rica		20.3	19.9	13.9	6.5	5.9	5.9	5.6	5.7	5.8	3.0	2.5
Cuba		881.3	965.1	836.1	410.0	291.4	202.7	157.8	130.0	102.2	100.7	84.5
Dominica			1.4	2.4	1.6	1.6	2.5	2.5	2.2	2.2	2.2	2.3
Dominican Republic		37.7	46.7	35.8	12.0	12.0	11.3	9.0	10.1	11.2	9.4	9.0
Ecuador		275.1	443.9	384.9	347.8	368.4	378.2	345.1	309.2	307.7	305.9	301.6
El Salvador		0.5		1.5	1.5	1.5	1.5	1.5	1.6	1.7	1.5	1.5
French Guiana				0.7								
Grenada		0.2	0.4	0.6	5.0	0.9	0.9	0.9	1.0	1.1	1.0	1.0
Guadeloupe				4.1								
Guatemala		13.6	16.0	5.3	0.8	0.8	0.8	0.8	4.6	4.5	4.6	4.7
Guyana		18.3	23.4	15.0	15.2	16.2	17.1	16.3	14.0	14.8	15.2	14.7
Haiti		1.1	2.7	0.7	0.4	1.0	1.6	1.3	1.2	1.2	1.2	1.1
Honduras		213.4	356.6	711.9	1,206.0	1,197.8	1,053.0	1,083.2	1,219.6	1,126.5	966.5	946.0
Jamaica											23.1	
Martinique				8.1								
Mexico		1,006.4	1,467.2	1,319.6	1,129.2	1,128.3	1,144.6	1,085.2	918.0	912.5	908.1	879.7
Netherlands Antilles					1,196.8	1,168.0	1,067.4	970.6	965.9	980.1	1,249.8	1,300.0
Nicaragua		15.7	18.0	5.1	3.9	4.2	4.2	4.3	4.3	3.9	3.6	3.5
Panama	19,458.4	24,190.7	40,674.2	39,298.1	71,921.7	82,130.7	91,127.9	98,222.4	105,248.1	112,273.8	122,352.1	131,704.7
Paraguay		23.0	42.9	37.2	39.1	43.6	43.8	44.9	43.4	41.9	47.1	47.9
Peru		740.5	818.1	616.7	340.6	345.6	336.8	269.7	284.9	264.9	239.6	220.1
Puerto Rico												
St Kitts		0.3	0.6	0.3	0.3	0.3	0.3	0.3	0.3	0.3	0.3	0.3
St Lucia		2.4	1.8	1.9	1.4	0.9	0.4	0.4	0.4	0.4	0.4	0.4
St Vincent and the Grenadines		19.7	235.2	1,936.8	6,164.9	7,134.2	8,374.5	7,875.5	7,105.5	7,100.5	7,072.9	6,780.4
Suriname		14.9	15.2	12.6	7.6	7.8	7.8	6.2	6.5	6.2	5.2	4.7
Trinidad and Tobago		17.5	19.0	22.3	28.2	18.5	18.7	18.6	21.6	24.6	26.6	29.0
Uruguay		198.5	173.4	103.8	124.4	100.1	121.3	106.9	61.8	71.6	72.8	64.1
Venezuela		848.5	984.9	934.9	787.1	697.2	704.9	665.3	657.4	649.5	872.2	919.9

Source: *Euromonitor from Lloyd's Register/national statistics*
Notes: *Ships of 100 gross tons or more. Gross tonnage (gt) is a measure of the total volume within the hull, and above deck, available for cargo, passengers, crew, fuel, stores etc. 1gt = 100 cu ft*

▫ Merchant Shipping

Size of Merchant Shipping Fleet 1977-2002

● '000 gross tons

	1977	1980	1985	1990	1995	1996	1997	1998	1999	2000	2001	2002
Asia Pacific												
Afghanistan												
American Samoa				0.3								
Armenia												
Azerbaijan					654.9	636.1	632.7	651.0	654.2	657.4	641.2	643.3
Bangladesh		353.6	358.1	464.4	379.1	435.7	419.2	413.8	377.7	341.6	387.6	380.0
Bhutan												
Brunei		0.9	1.2	3.6	366.3	368.0	368.6	361.9	362.0	362.1	362.7	361.2
Cambodia					60.0	206.2	438.7	616.4	998.7	1,381.0	1,996.7	2,305.2
China	4,245.4	6,837.6	10,568.2	13,899.5	16,943.2	16,992.9	16,338.6	16,503.3	16,314.5	16,125.7	16,646.1	16,723.9
Fiji		14.8	30.6	55.5	31.9	36.3	36.1	29.3	28.7	28.1	28.7	27.1
French Polynesia				20.1								
Guam				4.3								
Hong Kong, China	609.7	1,717.2	6,858.1	6,564.9	8,794.8	8,832.0	5,770.6	6,170.8	7,972.6	10,656.1	13,709.7	15,846.3
India	5,482.2	5,911.4	6,604.5	6,475.6	7,126.9	7,127.3	6,934.3	6,777.1	6,914.8	6,846.5	6,688.2	6,628.0
Indonesia	1,214.5	1,411.7	1,936.4	2,178.6	2,770.5	2,972.6	3,195.0	3,252.1	3,241.5	3,230.8	3,613.1	3,726.0
Japan	40,035.9	39,015.0	38,141.0	25,186.0	19,030.0	19,200.9	18,516.4	17,780.4	17,062.6	16,344.7	14,564.8	13,716.5
Kazakhstan					11.7	9.2	9.5	9.3	9.3	11.5	13.1	14.2
Kiribati		1.0	2.1	3.5	6.4	6.4	6.2	6.3	4.2	4.2	4.2	3.8
Kyrgyzstan												
Laos				0.5	2.9	2.9	2.9	2.4	2.4	2.4	2.4	2.3
Macau											3.7	
Malaysia		702.1	1,773.1	1,717.5	3,282.9	4,175.3	4,842.1	5,209.0	5,244.7	5,280.3	5,207.1	5,302.6
Maldives		136.0	138.3	77.9	84.5	96.0	97.5	101.1	89.9	78.7	66.6	60.6
Mongolia												
Myanmar	87.5	87.5	116.6	827.4	522.7	687.2	568.3	492.3	540.2	462.5	379.8	343.4
Nauru		54.0	66.7	32.2								
Nepal												
New Caledonia				14.3								
North Korea		230.7	512.6	442.3	715.3	692.9	667.0	631.0	657.8	684.6	697.8	705.7
Pakistan		478.0	451.0	354.1	397.9	444.1	434.7	401.2	307.9	294.4	247.4	214.9
Papua New Guinea		24.9	28.5	37.2	48.7	56.8	60.4	61.0	64.8	68.6	77.0	81.9
Philippines	1,146.5	1,927.9	4,594.0	8,514.9	8,743.8	9,033.8	8,849.2	8,508.3	7,650.1	6,791.8	6,029.9	5,478.5
Singapore	6,791.4	7,664.2	6,504.6	7,927.9	13,610.8	16,448.5	18,874.8	20,370.4	21,780.1	23,189.8	21,022.6	21,596.7
Solomon Islands		2.7	5.8	8.2	8.0	9.9	9.9	10.4	10.4	10.4	8.4	8.1
South Korea	2,494.7	4,334.1	7,168.9	7,783.1	6,972.1	7,557.9	7,429.5	5,694.2	5,734.8	5,775.4	6,395.0	6,159.7
Sri Lanka		93.5	634.7	350.0	226.9	241.6	216.9	189.2	194.6	200.0	153.7	141.0
Taiwan	1,415.0	1,806.0	4,267.0	5,923.0	5,992.0	6,174.5	5,931.3	5,941.7	5,371.4	4,801.1	4,617.9	4,337.8
Tajikistan					11.0	11.0	11.0	11.0	11.0	11.0	11.0	11.0
Thailand	320.4	391.5	586.3	614.8	1,743.4	2,042.2	2,157.8	1,998.8	1,956.1	1,913.3	1,771.4	1,686.1
Tonga											337.6	
Turkmenistan					32.1	40.2	38.8	38.4	43.6	48.9	45.7	47.6
Tuvalu		0.4	0.5	1.2	64.3	57.0	54.6	48.7	43.1	37.5	35.5	31.9
Uzbekistan												
Vanuatu			138.0	2,163.6	1,874.2	1,711.3	1,577.5	1,602.2	1,444.2	1,286.2	1,496.4	1,476.8
Vietnam		240.9	298.6	470.3	700.1	808.3	765.5	784.0	864.7	945.4	1,073.6	1,168.3
Western Samoa		4.8	26.1	27.3	6.2	6.2	5.5	6.9	7.5	8.4	9.7	11.1
Australasia												
Australia	1,374.2	1,642.6	2,088.3	2,511.8	2,853.1	2,717.9	2,606.6	2,188.1	2,084.2	1,980.3	1,887.8	1,741.5
New Zealand		263.5	295.9	260.2	307.3	385.7	366.6	336.3	265.0	193.7	174.9	145.4

Source: Euromonitor from Lloyd's Register/national statistics
Notes: Ships of 100 gross tons or more. Gross tonnage (gt) is a measure of the total volume within the hull, and above deck, available for cargo, passengers, crew, fuel, stores etc. 1gt = 100 cu ft

◻ Merchant Shipping

Size of Merchant Shipping Fleet 1977-2002

● '000 gross tons

	1977	1980	1985	1990	1995	1996	1997	1998	1999	2000	2001	2002
Africa and Middle East												
Algeria											963.9	
Angola		65.7	91.0	93.1	89.6	81.9	68.0	73.9	65.7	64.1	63.1	62.0
Bahrain		10.2	47.6	46.6	165.8	164.3	193.6	233.7	291.7	312.2	338.1	351.6
Benin		4.6	4.9	4.7	1.0	1.0	1.2	0.9	1.1	1.3	1.0	1.0
Botswana												
Burkina Faso												
Burundi												
Cameroon		62.1	76.4	33.1	37.1	36.7	11.4	12.9	13.6	14.3	13.6	14.2
Cape Verde		11.4	14.1	20.7	16.5	14.9	20.6	19.9	20.5	18.6	16.5	15.6
Central African Republic												
Chad												
Comoros		1.1	1.3	2.3	8.3	15.9	25.6	32.3	38.2	45.1	53.8	
Congo Dem Rep		91.9	84.7	56.4	14.9	14.9	14.9	12.9	12.9	12.9	12.9	12.5
Congo-Brazzaville				8.6							3.4	
Côte d'Ivoire		186.1	141.7	82.5	40.1	12.7	11.4	9.5	9.5	9.5	8.6	8.1
Djibouti		3.1	2.8	3.1	3.5	3.8	4.0	4.0	4.4	3.7	2.5	2.2
Egypt		555.8	952.6	1,257.1	1,268.8	1,230.2	1,287.7	1,367.8	1,368.0	1,368.3	1,350.4	1,366.6
Equatorial Guinea		6.4	6.4	6.4	3.5	20.6	35.0	58.5	43.9	42.2	37.2	37.8
Eritrea					12.4	0.8	6.8	7.3	15.9	19.5	20.7	21.3
Ethiopia		23.8	56.7	74.9	79.5	86.0	86.0	82.5	96.2	109.9	89.3	90.1
Gabon		77.1	97.5	24.1	32.2	33.2	35.0	26.5	15.7	14.7	12.5	9.7
Gambia		3.9	2.6	1.9	1.5	1.5	1.6	1.9	1.9	1.9	1.9	2.0
Ghana		250.4	162.6	125.5	113.5	134.7	129.7	115.5	117.5	119.5	123.1	121.5
Guinea		5.6	7.2	9.1	6.9	6.7	9.0	11.2	10.7	11.0	11.4	12.1
Guinea-Bissau		0.8	3.7	4.3	4.9	5.9	5.6	6.1	6.4	6.7	6.5	6.7
Iran		1,283.7	2,380.0	4,738.2	2,902.4	3,566.8	3,553.0	3,347.4	3,546.2	3,745.0	3,943.5	4,047.6
Iraq		1,465.9	1,011.9	1,044.4	857.8	856.9	572.0	511.1	510.6	510.1	240.6	193.7
Israel		450.2	549.7	529.5	598.7	678.9	793.9	751.6	728.4	705.3	611.4	572.7
Jordan	3.2	0.5	48.3	42.2	21.3	40.9	42.8	42.1	42.1	42.1	42.1	41.9
Kenya		17.4	8.1	7.1	18.0	19.8	20.6	20.9	20.6	20.3	19.1	18.8
Kuwait		2,529.5	2,349.9	1,854.6	2,057.0	2,027.9	1,984.0	2,459.0	2,456.5	2,453.9	2,291.7	2,375.8
Lebanon		267.8	505.0	307.1	285.0	275.2	297.4	263.5	322.2	380.9	301.7	302.7
Lesotho												
Liberia	79,983.0	80,285.2	58,179.7	54,699.6	59,800.7	59,988.9	60,058.4	60,492.1	54,107.2	52,068.5	51,784.0	49,900.1
Libya		890.0	853.9	834.7	732.8	680.5	686.2	567.0	438.9	310.8	250.8	195.0
Madagascar		91.2	74.2	73.6	38.1	39.3	40.1	41.7	42.6	43.5	43.4	44.3
Malawi												
Mali		0.2										
Mauritania		0.9	17.1	40.9	39.4	42.7	43.0	48.0	48.6	49.2	47.4	48.6
Mauritius		37.7	37.7	99.2	238.3	243.6	274.5	206.0	149.9	93.8	96.9	74.7
Morocco		359.6	460.9	488.1	382.6	403.4	416.7	444.0	448.5	452.9	461.5	473.4
Mozambique		37.9	40.9	39.6	38.3	44.8	38.7	35.3	36.3	37.3	38.0	37.9
Namibia					51.8	58.6	55.3	54.8	55.3	60.1	65.8	68.8
Niger												
Nigeria		498.2	443.4	495.9	478.7	447.2	452.3	451.9	432.4	413.0	404.2	393.0
Oman		6.9	17.5	22.6	16.3	16.3	15.2	15.2	16.7	18.2	19.7	21.1
Qatar		91.9	353.2	359.5	482.5	561.7	647.7	744.1	748.9	732.0	690.8	702.0
Réunion				21.3								
Rwanda												
Sao Tomé e Príncipe											190.4	
Saudi Arabia	1,018.7	1,589.7	3,137.2	1,682.8	1,186.8	1,208.3	1,163.7	1,277.6	1,207.5	1,137.4	1,132.5	1,124.9
Senegal		34.5	51.0	52.3	48.0	49.6	50.7	50.6	47.6	44.6	48.0	47.4
Seychelles		4.6	1.7	3.2	5.0	3.7	4.7	17.7	24.0	30.3	34.0	35.5
Sierra Leone		3.7	5.9	21.3	23.2	19.4	19.2	18.8	17.4	16.0	13.1	12.0
Somalia		45.6			16.4	13.9	11.4	11.4	6.3	6.3	6.3	6.4
South Africa		728.9	632.5	352.3	340.3	213.0	382.6	383.7	379.3	374.9	381.9	381.7
Sudan		104.8	95.7	57.9	47.8	42.1	42.1	43.1	43.1	43.1	43.0	43.2
Swaziland												
Syria		39.3	58.0	79.8	351.7	420.2	414.9	427.5	440.1	452.7	498.2	521.5
Tanzania		55.9	50.6	31.7	46.1	45.2	46.3	35.5	36.2	36.9	37.6	38.5
Togo		25.4	54.0	52.3	1.1	1.1	1.8	1.6	4.3	8.4	8.1	8.2
Tunisia	105.7	131.1	284.3	277.6	159.7	157.9	180.4	193.5	199.5	200.6	202.8	208.8
Uganda		5.5	3.4	5.1		2.0	2.0	2.0	2.0	2.0	2.0	2.0
United Arab Emirates	154.6	158.2	868.6	749.6	960.7	890.4	923.5	932.8	786.5	640.1	746.4	707.7
Yemen		15.2	15.1		26.6	25.1	26.2	25.3	25.6	50.8	73.8	95.5
Zambia												
Zimbabwe												

Source: *Euromonitor from Lloyd's Register/national statistics*
Notes: *Ships of 100 gross tons or more. Gross tonnage (gt) is a measure of the total volume within the hull, and above deck, available for cargo, passengers, crew, fuel, stores etc. 1gt = 100 cu ft*

Length of Public Railway Network 1977-2002

- Kilometres at end-year

	1977	1980	1985	1990	1995	1996	1997	1998	1999	2000	2001	2002
Algeria	3,891	3,890	4,000	4,300	4,290	4,290	4,290	4,290	4,291	4,293	4,293	4,297
Argentina	36,996	34,077	34,500	35,750	35,750	35,750	35,750	37,910	37,900	37,893	37,888	37,856
Australia	40,133	39,463	39,000	33,600	33,700	33,400	36,100	37,902	39,930	39,844	39,844	39,857
Azerbaijan				2,080	2,120	2,120	2,120	2,120	2,120	2,120	2,120	2,120
Bolivia	3,633	3,330	3,600	3,900	3,691	3,700	3,700	3,723	3,731	3,781	3,810	3,815
Brazil	28,756	28,671	28,680	30,320	30,400	30,400	30,410	30,400	30,400	30,403	30,383	30,382
Canada	69,967	67,076	22,400	21,800	32,421	33,891	35,015	36,114	36,890	37,359	38,935	39,104
Chile	6,372	6,302	6,700	6,850	6,450	6,000	6,000	6,000	6,000	6,000	6,220	6,220
China		49,900	52,119	53,400	54,600	56,700	57,600	57,600	57,922	58,700	59,174	59,724
Colombia	3,403	3,403	3,260	2,110	2,110	2,110	2,100	2,100	2,110	2,110	2,110	2,110
Ecuador	1,200	965	1,000	970	960	960	960	1,000	1,000	1,000	1,050	1,050
Egypt		4,446		4,200	4,000	4,000	4,000	4,000	4,000	4,000	4,000	4,105
Hong Kong, China		92	100	600	1,800	2,000	2,200	2,400	2,600	2,790	2,987	3,182
India	60,874	60,933	61,850	62,200	65,000	66,500	67,890	68,202	69,362	70,654	71,858	73,084
Indonesia	6,637	6,637										
Israel					609	628	640	652	663	670	684	693
Japan	22,215	22,235	20,789	20,300	20,000	20,000	20,000	20,000	20,000	20,000	20,000	20,000
Jordan											677	677
Kazakhstan				14,400	14,400	14,400	13,700	13,600	13,500	13,399	13,299	13,198
Kuwait												
Malaysia	2,223	2,215	2,200	1,700	1,791	1,791	1,791	1,791	1,949	1,949	2,054	2,133
Mexico	19,996	20,058	20,000	26,360	26,610	26,780	26,780	26,900	27,000	27,100	27,255	27,351
Morocco	1,756	1,756	1,779	1,900	1,900	1,900	1,900	1,900	1,900	1,900	1,907	1,917
New Zealand	4,668	4,449	4,273									
Nigeria					3,957	3,825	3,693	3,610	3,574	3,561	3,557	3,578
Pakistan	8,815	8,823	8,775		12,625	12,625	12,900	13,000	13,066	13,155	13,228	13,306
Peru	2,510	2,099	2,200	2,200	2,120	2,120	1,980	2,000	2,000	2,000	2,020	2,020
Philippines			9,000									
Saudi Arabia			1,392	1,400	1,400	1,400	1,400	1,400	1,400	1,400	1,390	1,405
Singapore												
South Africa											20,384	20,391
South Korea	3,142	3,135	3,100	3,081	3,101	3,120	3,118	3,125	3,119	3,123	3,120	3,119
Taiwan			1,100	1,100	1,100	1,100	1,100	1,100	1,100	1,100	1,100	1,100
Thailand	3,765	3,735	3,735	3,700	3,600	3,600	3,500	3,500	3,500	3,500	3,500	3,500
Tunisia	1,688	2,013	1,402	2,162	2,162	2,162	2,162	2,162	2,100	2,100	2,168	2,197
Turkmenistan				2,150	2,150	2,310	2,310	2,310	2,310	2,310	2,310	2,310
United Arab Emirates												
USA	311,000	292,000	269,000	244,000	228,000	228,000	225,000	224,000	225,750	207,000	209,100	210,105
Venezuela	202	202	300	540	630	630	630	630	630	630	630	630
Vietnam		·					2,414	2,400	2,400	2,400	2,400	2,400

Source: *Euromonitor from national statistics*

Table 4.16

Rail Transport

Railway Statistics of Major National Carriers 2002

● As Stated

	Locomotives (number)	Rail motor vehicles (number)	Passengers carried (million)	Average journey length (km)	Total goods carried (million tonnes)
Algeria			29.4	36.7	
Argentina	706		404.8	24.4	17.4
Australia	2,381		631.1	0.8	519.0
Azerbaijan			4.3	159.0	14.8
Bolivia					
Brazil	1,691	46,212.0	1,275.6	13.7	270.7
Canada					
Chile	183		8.2	105.1	21.5
China	13,054	484,130.7	1,150.9	459.3	1,683.9
Colombia					
Ecuador					
Egypt	947	757.0			
Hong Kong, China			485.8	10.2	0.5
India					
Indonesia			2,066.0	10.3	30.6
Israel		10,709.0	14.2	85.6	11.0
Japan			506,195.7	0.4	
Jordan					
Kazakhstan			19.3	448.2	203.5
Kuwait					
Malaysia			4.0	266.0	7.0
Mexico	1,318		4.7	17.0	44.5
Morocco	204				29.0
New Zealand	210	7,026.4	12.0		13.0
Nigeria					
Pakistan			76.5	11.8	7.0
Peru	73	3,247.7	0.9	189.5	2.4
Philippines					
Saudi Arabia					
Singapore					
South Africa					
South Korea	542	2,288.2	800.5	35.6	48.5
Taiwan			183.7	56.7	27.0
Thailand			51.7	171.4	7.8
Tunisia	155	27.0	17.1	74.5	13.8
Turkmenistan			7.5	138.3	10.9
United Arab Emirates					
USA	16,602		3,510.0	2.4	1,910.0
Venezuela	18	274.0	0.2		0.4
Vietnam			9.8	339.7	7,833.3

Source: *Euromonitor from International Road Federation/national statistics*

■ Rail Transport

Table 4.17

Railway Freight Traffic 1977-2002

- Million net tonne-kilometres

	1977	1980	1985	1990	1995	1996	1997	1998	1999	2000	2001	2002
Algeria	1,940	2,461	3,048	2,674	1,946	1,801	1,757	1,747	1,752	1,757	1,767	1,774
Argentina	11,567	9,492	9,530	7,578	7,613	8,506	9,835	9,824	9,623	9,120	8,295	8,381
Australia	31,955	36,366	52,914	63,488								
Azerbaijan				37,288	2,765	2,777	3,515	3,813	3,844	4,032	4,287	4,526
Bolivia	583	658	494	541	758	780	839	998	1,079	1,090	1,050	1,044
Brazil	60,721	40,603	99,881	120,432	136,437	139,240	142,703	147,879	153,794	161,631	170,598	180,394
Canada	212,416	234,972	245,284	250,117	309,475	324,384	333,187	338,187	351,484	365,886	371,381	383,251
Chile	2,508	1,445	2,580	2,787	2,262	2,366	2,330	2,650	2,896	3,141	3,318	3,277
China	455,733	570,732	812,566	1,062,238	1,287,025	1,309,300	1,325,330	1,251,707	1,283,840	1,390,200	1,447,075	1,516,322
Colombia	1,215	862	777	396	356	858	732	648	473	403	381	374
Ecuador					3	3	3	3	3	3	3	3
Egypt	2,415	2,174	2,594	2,828	3,934	4,127	4,302	4,506	4,603	4,705	4,816	4,916
Hong Kong, China	49	67	72	72	41	39	37	35	33	31	29	27
India	150,250	147,652	196,488	233,292	238,446	270,000	277,567	287,285	297,627	308,638	319,204	329,881
Indonesia	853	961	1,332	3,192	4,172	4,700	5,030	4,963	5,035	4,997	5,032	5,049
Israel					1,222	1,354	1,497	1,619	1,702	1,771	1,821	1,907
Japan	41,317	37,428	21,920	27,196	25,101	25,702	26,113	26,677	27,477	28,639	29,560	30,542
Jordan	310	376	692	711	698	713	723	733	741	749	748	751
Kazakhstan				407,000	124,500	112,700	106,425	103,045	102,300	102,643	102,261	102,060
Kuwait												
Malaysia	1,209	1,195	1,020	1,404	1,421	1,398	1,338	993	909	918	865	828
Mexico	36,232	41,323	45,444	34,408	37,242	41,723	42,442	46,873	49,955	48,333	49,790	51,495
Morocco	3,474	3,834	4,560	5,112	4,621	4,757	4,835	4,827	4,795	4,650	4,732	4,805
New Zealand	3,723	3,226	3,192	2,744	2,963	3,207	3,505	3,777	3,985	4,131	4,232	4,319
Nigeria				221	68	61	60	48	47	47	47	48
Pakistan	7,857	8,598	7,200	7,193	5,078	4,538	4,300	4,162	4,098	4,067	4,107	4,137
Peru		742	1,049	848	864	856	1,034	1,068	1,124	1,232	1,186	1,179
Philippines	49	37	12	16	15	17	19	21	23	25	27	29
Saudi Arabia	125	261	415	645	728	691	675	609	610	617	617	620
Singapore												
South Africa	69,331	96,523	92,616	90,845	99,338	99,806	110,174	111,481	113,562	115,889	117,989	119,432
South Korea	10,294	10,798	12,084	13,663	13,838	12,947	12,564	11,989	11,349	10,694	10,049	9,402
Taiwan	2,658	2,716	2,300	1,877	1,900	1,585	1,514	1,404	1,395	1,421	1,463	1,442
Thailand	2,912	2,805	2,712	3,120	3,242	3,326	3,397	2,874	2,643	2,470	2,382	2,360
Tunisia	1,339	1,698	1,704	1,834	2,317	2,329	2,338	2,351	2,365	2,380	2,327	2,341
Turkmenistan					8,568	7,004	7,649	8,245	9,005	10,002	10,840	11,719
United Arab Emirates												
USA	1,206,366	1,341,717	1,310,388	1,513,776	1,930,796	1,945,345	1,969,394	1,988,987	2,111,708	2,249,961	2,321,564	2,416,487
Venezuela	20	21	14	36	53	46	55	80	88	90	92	93
Vietnam	980			847	1,751	1,684	1,758	1,795	1,840	1,884	1,929	1,973

Source: *Euromonitor from national statistics*

Table 4.18

Railway Passenger Traffic 1977-2002

- Million passenger-kilometres

	1977	1980	1985	1990	1995	1996	1997	1998	1999	2000	2001	2002
Algeria	1,506	2,070	1,938	2,991	1,574	1,220	1,054	1,021	1,047	1,079	1,081	1,079
Argentina	12,011	13,510	11,510	10,638	7,017	8,524	9,324	9,652	9,102	9,332	9,624	9,888
Australia					436	444	450	453	458	462	473	476
Azerbaijan				1,827	791	558	489	533	572	608	646	684
Bolivia	397		748	388	240	195	225	267	319	390	377	356
Brazil	11,699	13,390	16,362	18,209	14,498	14,971	15,434	15,878	16,307	16,730	17,124	17,476
Canada	2,966	3,280	3,040	2,004	1,307	1,287	1,414	1,486	1,441	1,396	1,300	1,343
Chile	2,382	1,421	1,522	1,077	691	644	552	519	637	736	814	863
China	102,015	138,037	241,614	261,263	354,570	334,760	358,486	377,342	413,593	453,260	490,650	528,609
Colombia	391	315	229	141	4	3	2	2	2	2	2	2
Ecuador	72	65	40	82	20	18	16	16	16	15	15	15
Egypt	9,300	10,995	16,854	34,876	48,243	50,665	52,928	54,859	56,774	58,666	60,124	60,349
Hong Kong, China	279	434	1,776	2,532	3,803	3,755	4,216	4,752	4,812	4,863	4,920	4,976
India	176,635	208,558	240,000	277,272	272,491	300,000	357,013	375,935	406,009	434,456	463,988	493,249
Indonesia	3,809	6,088	6,768	9,288	15,500	15,223	15,518	16,196	17,829	19,228	20,783	21,299
Israel					269	294	346	382	529	781	1,016	1,211
Japan	311,859	313,340	332,772	383,700	230,552	227,537	224,106	217,777	211,434	205,194	198,885	192,594
Jordan	5	5	1	2	3	3	3	3	3	3	3	3
Kazakhstan				19,700	13,200	14,200	12,802	10,669	9,987	9,692	9,139	8,651
Kuwait												
Malaysia	1,273	1,587	1,404	1,840	1,279	1,385	1,508	1,411	1,333	1,241	1,158	1,073
Mexico	5,040	5,296	4,014	5,336	1,899	1,799	1,508	460	254	82	84	80
Morocco	835	936	1,932	2,237	1,564	1,776	1,836	1,895	1,902	1,901	1,903	2,003
New Zealand	497	437										
Nigeria					340							
Pakistan	13,199	17,315	17,808		18,905	19,114	18,774	18,980	19,360	19,105	18,937	906
Peru				469	231	222	206	180	161	165	171	179
Philippines	692	416	144	264	55	52	51	50	49	47	46	44
Saudi Arabia	94	82	72	159	159	170	176	184	187	189	190	201
Singapore												
South Africa					7,844	9,310	10,776	11,242	11,758	12,334	13,156	13,842
South Korea	17,099	21,640	22,596	29,864	29,292	29,580	30,073	32,976	28,606	27,787	28,028	28,461
Taiwan	8,122	7,971	8,309	8,323	9,499	8,975	9,263	9,793	10,353	10,459	10,434	10,424
Thailand	5,649	8,861	9,144	11,832	12,975	12,205	11,804	10,947	10,021	9,794	9,160	8,858
Tunisia	713	862	744	1,019	996	1,023	1,032	1,158	1,223	1,268	1,284	1,274
Turkmenistan					1,876	2,104	970	910	940	974	1,005	1,037
United Arab Emirates												
USA				9,864	9,215	9,089	8,916	8,747	8,574	8,402	8,350	8,412
Venezuela	39	28	8	64	13	0						
Vietnam	4,043			1,913	2,133	2,261	2,476	2,685	2,873	2,999	3,166	3,323

Source: Euromonitor from national statistics

◻ Road Transport   **Table 4.19**
Car Traffic Volume 1978-2002

● Million car-kilometres

	1978	1980	1985	1990	1995	1996	1997	1998	1999	2000	2001	2002
Algeria												
Argentina			31,160	14,881	19,234	16,877	17,573	17,940	18,571	19,138	19,479	19,216
Australia												
Azerbaijan												
Bolivia		219		523	697	770	815	869	912	936	955	971
Brazil												
Canada	194,277	205,515	135,657			79,200	73,500	71,074	72,926	73,681	74,298	75,188
Chile	2,518	3,170	7,040						23,829			
China						214,730	267,060	307,770	362,710	418,330	485,925	564,478
Colombia	3,363	9,408	13,115			21,991	24,628	29,198	29,886	32,684	33,913	35,743
Ecuador			308	6,949	9,935	10,352	10,774	11,023	11,849	12,465	12,595	13,036
Egypt					6,120	6,570	6,982	7,440	7,990	8,342	8,823	9,315
Hong Kong, China	2,406	3,001	3,497	4,781	6,324	6,324	6,686	6,473	6,506	6,516	6,497	6,496
India												
Indonesia						2,115,093	2,368,466	2,543,157	2,758,463	2,942,312	3,159,565	3,390,989
Israel	6,238	6,895	13,574	20,391	21,532	20,391	21,317	23,011	23,275	24,361	25,345	26,300
Japan	220,363	241,459	300,606	387,015	464,123	464,123	475,599	482,551	501,532	515,906	519,322	529,408
Jordan				1,523	1,303	1,572	1,684	1,855	1,976	2,183	2,382	2,599
Kazakhstan				1,361	1,268	1,337	1,081	1,293	1,064	1,230	1,294	1,356
Kuwait		7,978	8,413									
Malaysia												
Mexico				38,229								
Morocco					12,374	12,932	13,279	14,242	15,177	15,896	16,813	17,747
New Zealand	17,378	16,545				28,000						
Nigeria					820,069	885,080	935,080	985,170	998,730	1,010,450	1,030,036	1,046,411
Pakistan				10,712	11,624	12,132	12,731	13,367	14,040	14,743	14,935	15,407
Peru												
Philippines					2,883	3,126	3,859	3,536	3,548	3,656	3,665	3,708
Saudi Arabia												
Singapore												
South Africa	29,872	34,752	40,364									
South Korea	2,535	2,861	6,272	11,756	26,665	29,676	29,601	31,583	33,526	36,754	39,687	42,952
Taiwan	7,654											
Thailand	4,168	5,076	8,012	15,438	34,100	39,200	44,430	49,148	53,429	57,432	62,267	67,348
Tunisia	1,137	2,531	3,533	5,340	6,384	7,272	7,777	8,347	9,046	9,685	10,416	11,199
Turkmenistan												
United Arab Emirates												
USA	1,884,287	1,789,412	2,028,249	2,434,713	2,315,653	2,366,465	2,418,133	2,487,763	2,529,267	2,531,796	2,559,292	2,581,158
Venezuela			98	100		98	99					
Vietnam												

Source: *Euromonitor from International Road Federation/national statistics*

Goods Transported by Road 1980-2002

- Million tonne-kilometres

	1980	1985	1990	1995	1996	1997	1998	1999	2000	2001	2002
Algeria											
Argentina											
Australia											
Azerbaijan				404	480	902	1,392	2,968	3,513	3,721	3,824
Bolivia											
Brazil											
Canada				65,767	71,473	72,240	76,694	79,056	82,500	84,973	87,133
Chile											
China					501,120	527,150	548,340	582,430	612,940	645,803	681,083
Colombia								31			
Ecuador				3,390	3,558	3,753	3,959	4,176	4,405	4,426	4,558
Egypt				31,400	31,500	31,600	31,680	31,750	31,820	31,935	32,085
Hong Kong, China				14	15	18	18	18	18	19	19
India					720	792	871	958	1,054	1,131	1,228
Indonesia											
Israel											
Japan	179,000	206,000	274,000	294,648	305,510	306,263	300,670	307,149	308,715	310,779	313,463
Jordan											
Kazakhstan			44,800	10,800	9,594	6,481	4,637	4,506	4,603	4,391	4,301
Kuwait											
Malaysia											
Mexico				162,827	170,838	154,083	179,085	197,958	198,879	203,576	209,871
Morocco				2,136	2,086	2,262	2,557	3,035	3,085	3,161	3,315
New Zealand											
Nigeria											
Pakistan				73,195	78,493	84,174	90,268	96,802	103,809	106,525	111,775
Peru											
Philippines											
Saudi Arabia											
Singapore											
South Africa											
South Korea				52,825	54,834	74,504	82,340	86,942	89,457	93,986	98,146
Taiwan	7,690	9,223	11,543	12,500	11,991	12,165	17,426	18,470	18,131	19,634	20,523
Thailand											
Tunisia											
Turkmenistan											
United Arab Emirates											
USA				1,344,634	1,419,093	1,534,430	1,581,236	1,654,673	1,745,476	1,829,265	1,920,791
Venezuela											
Vietnam			1,631	2,968	3,498	4,005	4,512	4,876	5,101	5,464	5,815

Source: *Euromonitor from International Road Federation/national statistics*

▢ Road Transport   **Table 4.21**

Average Annual Distance Travelled by Car 1990-2002

● Kilometres

	1990	1992	1993	1994	1995	1996	1997	1998	1999	2000	2001	2002
Algeria												
Argentina												
Australia												
Azerbaijan						231	151	240	182	185	190	186
Bolivia												
Brazil												
Canada												
Chile									18,000	18,000	18,000	18,000
China						44,000	46,000	47,000	49,000	49,000	49,873	50,670
Colombia									14,370	14,370	14,370	14,370
Ecuador		45,090	44,229	39,929	32,280	32,323	32,675	31,531	26,826	25,856	25,241	24,008
Egypt												
Hong Kong, China		18,268	17,977	17,658	18,232	18,196	18,488	16,943	16,795	16,299	15,783	15,356
India												
Indonesia												
Israel		17,100	17,100	17,800	17,900	17,700	17,600	17,700	17,600	17,100	16,841	16,538
Japan		10,413	10,300	9,971	9,991	9,903	9,784	9,671	9,802	9,811	9,841	9,881
Jordan	15,000	15,000	15,000	15,000	15,000	15,000	15,000	15,000	15,000	15,000	15,000	15,000
Kazakhstan						65,886	54,443	57,542	48,167	48,192	46,044	43,776
Kuwait												
Malaysia												
Mexico												
Morocco		14,235	13,870	13,505	11,680	9,198	8,460	6,804	6,403	6,302	5,923	5,655
New Zealand												
Nigeria												
Pakistan					14,000	14,000	14,000	14,000	14,000	14,000	14,000	14,000
Peru												
Philippines				5,191	4,601	4,449	5,192	4,720	4,495	4,350	4,145	3,969
Saudi Arabia				30,794								
Singapore												
South Africa												
South Korea	27,304	25,971	25,696	25,264	24,863	24,309	23,433	23,101	22,953	22,310	21,897	21,467
Taiwan												
Thailand							7,520	7,520	7,520	7,520	7,520	7,520
Tunisia						25,000	25,000	25,000	25,000	25,000	25,000	25,000
Turkmenistan												
United Arab Emirates												
USA		17,800	18,925	17,199	18,037	18,242	18,637	18,870	19,099	19,118	19,245	19,354
Venezuela												
Vietnam												

Source: *Euromonitor from International Road Federation/national statistics*

Road Network 2002

● Kilometres

	Total	Motorway	National Highway	Secondary Regional	Other Local	% Paved	Density (km per sq km of land)
North America							
Canada	901,903						
USA	6,392,820	89,645	1,886,312	4,416,863		58.8	0.65
Latin America							
Anguilla							
Antigua	250						0.60
Argentina	216,558	875	39,056	176,627		29.4	0.08
Aruba							
Bahamas	2,717					57.4	0.18
Barbados	2,028		336	195	1,497	96.8	
Belize	3,029		545		2,484	17.0	
Bermuda							
Bolivia	54,366	13	10,397	4,213	39,743	7.0	0.06
Brazil	1,738,431		88,593	1,649,838		5.3	0.20
British Virgin Islands							
Cayman Islands							
Chile	80,659		16,048	34,258	30,353	20.7	0.10
Colombia	114,271		17,819	72,015	24,437	15.1	0.10
Costa Rica	36,026		7,698	28,328		23.0	0.70
Cuba	60,856	638	4,353	7,272	48,593	49.0	0.55
Dominica	788					50.4	1.03
Dominican Republic	19,705					51.2	
Ecuador	43,183		5,684	37,499		18.9	0.17
El Salvador	10,029	327	553	1,109	8,040	19.8	0.48
French Guiana							
Grenada	1,059					61.3	3.01
Guadeloupe							
Guatemala	14,891	74		5,433	9,384	37.6	0.13
Guyana	7,970					7.4	0.05
Haiti	4,160					24.3	0.16
Honduras	13,603		3,199	2,565	7,839	20.4	0.12
Jamaica	18,746					70.1	
Martinique							
Mexico	347,677	6,796	44,587	66,116	230,178	34.8	0.18
Netherlands Antilles							
Nicaragua	19,488		2,033	9,067	8,388	12.2	0.16
Panama	11,575	30				39.5	0.22
Paraguay	29,500					53.9	
Peru	75,456		16,478	14,066	44,912	13.0	0.06
Puerto Rico	14,400					100.0	1.55
St Kitts	383					42.5	1.18
St Lucia	1,210		150	150	910	5.2	1.93
St Vincent and the Grenadines	1,164					31.8	3.01
Suriname	4,667		1,243	1,192	2,232	26.0	0.03
Trinidad and Tobago	8,320					51.1	1.60
Uruguay	8,984		2,612	5,246	1,126	90.0	4.90
Venezuela	96,155		34,301	27,336	34,518	33.6	

Source: *Euromonitor from International Road Federation/national statistics*

■ Road Network
Road Network 2002
● Kilometres

	Total	Motorway	National Highway	Secondary Regional	Other Local	% Paved	Density (km per sq km of land)
Asia Pacific							
Afghanistan	21,000					13.3	0.03
American Samoa							
Armenia	16,215	7,726	3,360	4,261	868	96.5	0.29
Azerbaijan	24,981		6,897	18,084		92.3	0.29
Bangladesh	216,614		20,585	17,986	178,043	9.5	1.45
Bhutan	4,415		1,599		2,816	60.7	0.05
Brunei	3,218	37	2,597	378	206	100.0	
Cambodia	12,323		4,180	3,615	4,528	16.2	
China	1,501,937	18,643	24,520	171,065	1,287,709	19.6	0.17
Fiji	3,440					49.2	0.19
French Polynesia							
Guam							
Hong Kong, China	1,857					100.0	
India	3,905,442		54,289	1,813,036	2,038,117	40.1	
Indonesia	343,697		26,990	39,911	276,796	46.3	
Japan	1,181,059	6,527	54,639	130,278	989,615	42.0	3.10
Kazakhstan	107,859		20,134	59,225	28,500	96.8	0.04
Kiribati	670						
Kyrgyzstan	18,470	140	3,174	6,375	8,781	91.1	0.10
Laos	21,716		4,459	7,650	9,607		
Macau	330					100.0	14.79
Malaysia	70,834		17,383	34,200	19,251	76.8	0.20
Maldives							
Mongolia	49,250		11,063	38,187		3.5	0.04
Myanmar	35,892					12.9	
Nauru	30					80.6	
Nepal							
New Caledonia							
North Korea	31,200					6.4	
Pakistan	281,393	381	7,396	234,216	39,400	43.0	0.38
Papua New Guinea	19,600					3.5	0.05
Philippines	224,569		33,149	55,373	136,047	23.0	0.57
Singapore	3,152	155	583	379	2,035	100.0	
Solomon Islands	1,360					2.5	0.06
South Korea	88,643	2,028	12,714	17,515	56,386	74.5	0.90
Sri Lanka	112,724		14,061	13,709	84,954	95.0	1.46
Taiwan	37,038	618	4,588	2,537	29,295	88.5	0.58
Tajikistan	27,158		9,243	11,510	6,405		
Thailand	64,600		64,600			97.5	0.13
Tonga	680					27.0	0.98
Turkmenistan	58,592		27,850	30,742		81.2	
Tuvalu	8						0.04
Uzbekistan	86,496					87.3	0.19
Vanuatu	1,070					23.9	0.08
Vietnam	93,430		11,600	73,000	8,830	25.1	0.33
Western Samoa	790		235	103	452	42.0	0.26
Australasia							
Australia	812,456	19,842	110,674	681,940		38.8	0.13
New Zealand	92,121	190	10,582	15,986	65,363	64.7	0.50

Source: *Euromonitor from International Road Federation/national statistics*

■ Road Network
Road Network 2002
● Kilometres

Africa and Middle East

	Total	Motorway	National Highway	Secondary Regional	Other Local	% Paved	Density (km per sq km of land)
Algeria	104,000	640	25,760	23,900	53,700	68.9	0.04
Angola	51,454		7,944	13,278	30,232	5.9	0.06
Bahrain	2,560		429	383	1,748	78.3	5.15
Benin	6,787	10	3,425	3,352		20.0	0.06
Botswana	10,964		3,121	2,633	5,210	58.0	0.20
Burkina Faso	12,264				5,408	16.0	0.05
Burundi	14,480		1,950	2,530	10,000	7.1	
Cameroon	34,300				4,313	12.5	0.07
Cape Verde	1,110		450	240	420	78.0	0.27
Central African Republic	23,417		5,200	3,766	14,451	3.6	0.04
Chad	33,360		7,880	5,380	20,100	0.8	0.03
Comoros	880		430	227	223	76.5	0.41
Congo Dem Rep	157,030	30	33,100	40,500	83,400		0.07
Congo-Brazzaville	12,800					9.7	0.04
Côte d'Ivoire	50,481		7,375	7,927	35,179	9.7	0.17
Djibouti	2,890		1,090	1,800		12.6	0.12
Egypt	64,000		26,000	25,000	13,000	78.1	0.07
Equatorial Guinea	2,880						0.10
Eritrea	4,010					21.8	0.03
Ethiopia	33,670		16,418		17,252	10.7	0.03
Gabon	8,639		2,200	6,439		9.9	0.03
Gambia	2,700		850	520	1,330	35.4	0.25
Ghana	42,138	30	5,732	10,761	25,615	32.6	0.16
Guinea	30,500		4,368	7,979	18,153	16.5	0.13
Guinea-Bissau	4,400		2,400	2,000		10.3	0.13
Iran	167,394	811	24,875	68,062	73,646	55.7	0.11
Iraq	44,888		10,607		29,199	84.3	
Israel	16,584	56	5,410		11,118	100.0	0.80
Jordan	7,381		2,975	2,089	2,317	100.0	0.08
Kenya	63,942		6,251	11,339	35,311	12.1	0.11
Kuwait	4,450					80.6	0.25
Lebanon	8,529		2,915	1,842	3,772	84.9	0.61
Lesotho	7,091		1,275	2,288	3,528	19.8	0.16
Liberia	10,600					6.2	0.10
Libya	100,024					57.2	
Madagascar	65,663		16,003	22,807	26,853	11.6	0.09
Malawi	40,195		11,605	7,107	21,483	18.5	21.30
Mali	15,100		5,825	5,714	3,561	12.1	0.02
Mauritania	7,660		2,800	4,000	860	11.3	0.01
Mauritius	1,945	41	919	590	395	98.0	1.03
Morocco	57,643	449	11,224	10,191	35,779		0.08
Mozambique	30,370		4,570	8,500	17,300	18.7	0.04
Namibia	69,322		4,564	9,868	54,890	14.1	0.08
Niger	10,090		3,620	3,320	3,150	7.9	0.01
Nigeria	194,394	1,194	26,500	32,300	134,400	30.9	0.21
Oman	32,830	550	2,160	3,720	26,400	30.0	0.10
Qatar	1,230					90.0	0.11
Réunion							
Rwanda	9,497		3,750	365	5,382	8.1	
Sao Tomé e Príncipe	384					71.2	
Saudi Arabia	162,135		15,959	146,176		31.4	0.07
Senegal	14,583	7	3,361	1,194	10,021	29.3	0.07
Seychelles	463					87.9	
Sierra Leone	11,458		3,342	3,348	4,768	7.9	0.16
Somalia	22,100					11.8	0.03
South Africa	367,459	2,055				20.3	0.30
Sudan	11,900		3,280	2,020	6,600	36.3	0.01
Swaziland	5,256		2,034	2,077	1,145		
Syria	45,161	992	30,879	10,175	3,115	23.8	0.23
Tanzania	88,200		10,355	17,851	59,994	4.2	0.09
Togo	7,520		1,687	689	5,144	31.6	0.13
Tunisia	18,168	142	3,900	6,235	7,891	65.1	0.11
Uganda							
United Arab Emirates	1,145		285	338	522	100.0	0.06
Yemen	67,735		6,135	5,946	55,654	10.3	0.12
Zambia	66,781		7,081	13,700	46,000	19.4	
Zimbabwe	18,338		6,781	1,668	9,889	47.4	0.05

Source: Euromonitor from International Road Federation/national statistics

Banking and Finance

◘ Bank Claims on the Private Sector

Table 5.1

Bank Claims on the Private Sector 1980-2002

- Million units of national currency

	1980	1985	1990	1995	1997	1998	1999	2000	2001	2002
North America										
Canada	136,543.0	216,847.0	334,547.0	474,889.0	607,315.0	617,217.0	643,277.0	714,836.0	757,170.0	799,476.0
USA	989,410.0	1,563,950.0	2,494,290.0	3,223,070.0	3,750,340.0	4,125,600.0	4,403,890.0	4,849,230.0	5,075,120.0	5,424,720.0
Latin America										
Anguilla										
Antigua	102.7	258.3	503.1	706.9	1,027.0	1,103.3	1,196.0	1,308.6	1,348.7	1,413.7
Argentina	0.0	0.9	10,702.0	50,779.7	63,131.4	70,524.9	68,431.4	65,842.7	54,158.6	47,227.3
Aruba			609.1	1,018.0	1,185.5	1,248.2	1,376.1	1,502.4	1,581.7	1,783.6
Bahamas	402.8	592.3	1,122.4	1,777.3	2,488.2	2,767.4	3,071.5	3,511.2	3,781.9	3,925.6
Barbados	521.5	769.4	1,104.3	1,470.6	1,839.1	2,138.1	2,445.4	2,508.2	2,504.3	2,583.9
Belize	77.3	120.5	268.4	436.4	540.0	610.7	641.1	679.7	771.0	884.1
Bermuda										
Bolivia	0.0	290.5	3,320.4	15,151.9	21,016.8	26,103.0	27,330.8	26,402.7	24,152.2	23,753.3
Brazil	0.0	0.0	3.6	210,488.0	254,585.0	296,921.0	301,955.0	315,948.0	345,315.0	386,930.0
British Virgin Islands										
Cayman Islands										
Chile	412,061.0	1,448,420.0	4,152,080.0	13,429,800.0	18,837,300.0	20,577,100.0	22,483,000.0	25,060,600.0	27,263,100.0	28,819,000.0
Colombia (a)	220,699.0	747,830.0	3,142,100.0	15,162,000.0	26,167,900.0	33,048,800.0	31,334,500.0	32,452,500.0	36,215,600.0	40,461,100.0
Costa Rica	10,205.4	34,144.0	78,944.0	222,996.0	434,257.0	670,628.0	914,333.0	1,180,050.0	1,493,280.0	1,824,370.0
Cuba										
Dominica	49.8	89.0	211.1	344.6	386.3	410.0	419.8	454.1	439.6	433.2
Dominican Republic	1,165.8	1,851.6	8,923.8	27,688.4	44,404.1	52,743.9	66,876.5	82,119.7	101,941.0	123,242.0
Ecuador	42,372.0	159,452.7	831,650.9	11,058,875.9	22,153,694.4	30,846,594.7	48,688,442.0	111,105,173.3	137,459,500.0	
El Salvador	849.8	1,590.9	914.7	3,378.7	4,520.6	5,039.4	5,475.9	5,857.3	5,456.4	5,639.4
French Guiana										
Grenada	72.3	109.7	270.7	437.3	588.0	684.7	767.9	878.4	886.4	896.2
Guadeloupe										
Guatemala	1,222.2	2,037.1	4,299.9	13,898.6	16,603.7	21,142.4	24,115.9	26,416.0	30,155.3	32,502.5
Guyana	196.3	520.4	4,159.6	21,107.1	44,863.3	51,838.3	55,823.3	58,341.0	58,943.0	59,199.7
Haiti	726.0	885.4	1,800.6	5,072.4	8,511.2	9,156.2	10,128.9	12,074.3	12,914.0	16,785.7
Honduras	945.3	1,617.2	3,026.0	7,711.4	16,744.2	23,247.0	28,014.0	32,020.5	35,524.5	38,000.9
Jamaica	904.0	2,601.7	8,582.6	44,407.6	57,482.1	74,777.3	84,592.8	102,602.0	42,311.5	56,046.9
Martinique										
Mexico	695.6	4,591.0	113,321.0	464,075.0	560,405.0	670,501.0	665,989.0	625,007.0	561,969.0	637,514.0
Netherlands Antilles	746.8	1,041.1	1,549.5	2,130.2	2,262.8	2,299.8	2,529.3	2,677.4	2,686.9	2,782.5
Nicaragua	0.0	0.0	57.1	5,159.0	6,707.4	9,715.5	13,270.5	15,240.8	9,783.2	11,228.2
Panama	1,803.2	2,277.1	2,233.5	5,852.4	7,294.0	9,010.2	10,507.1	11,092.3	11,842.8	10,881.9
Paraguay	77,341.5	128,664.0	768,442.0	3,795,040.0	5,217,410.0	5,093,490.0	5,654,330.0	5,937,320.0	6,757,090.0	6,777,930.0
Peru	0.0	0.0	436.6	19,090.4	37,812.0	45,834.7	49,220.6	47,568.9	45,463.5	45,229.1
Puerto Rico										
St Kitts	52.8	104.8	231.9	440.9	521.1	563.7	610.2	680.5	675.3	658.9
St Lucia	163.5	251.6	578.5	946.4	1,171.8	1,258.2	1,394.2	1,481.7	1,541.8	1,553.5
St Vincent and the Grenadines	68.0	107.4	204.3	347.0	447.2	486.4	545.6	592.1	605.5	633.4
Suriname	460.5	689.8	1,453.8	20,120.4	63,382.5	79,103.2	106,702.0	93,295.9	147,134.0	401,942.0
Trinidad and Tobago	3,310.3	5,843.6	6,428.3	8,739.4	11,835.3	13,433.3	14,498.6	16,353.1	16,922.7	17,645.6
Uruguay	34.3	216.7	3,382.3	32,241.8	58,466.5	107,288.0	118,105.0	124,044.0	133,636.0	171,869.0
Venezuela	69,328.0	115,386.0	376,465.0	1,184,610.0	5,287,720.0	6,021,810.0	6,655,060.0	8,350,970.0	10,310,000.0	10,406,600.0

Source: *International Monetary Fund (IMF), International Financial Statistics*
Notes: *(a) New series starting 1990, (b) New series starting 1992, (c) New series starting 1996, (d) New series starting 1988*

□ Bank Claims on the Private Sector

Bank Claims on the Private Sector 1980-2002

- Million units of national currency

	1980	1985	1990	1995	1997	1998	1999	2000	2001	2002
Asia Pacific										
Afghanistan										
American Samoa										
Armenia				37,946.4	48,486.2	70,790.6	86,188.5	102,406.0	91,826.4	93,477.7
Azerbaijan				126,518.0	386,809.0	530,059.0	559,688.0	1,391,760.0	1,327,530.0	1,662,150.0
Bangladesh	16,204.6	75,530.0	167,104.0	318,484.0	411,731.0	465,130.0	509,760.0	577,077.0	667,883.0	779,577.0
Bhutan		55.4	215.9	750.7	1,472.4	1,472.3	1,490.1	1,747.5	2,424.3	3,147.3
Brunei										
Cambodia				293,403.0	636,785.0	654,601.0	763,230.0	898,457.0	936,107.0	1,058,910.0
China		594,440.0	1,586,180.0	5,097,180.0	7,693,400.0	8,951,610.0	9,986,660.0	11,132,400.0	12,180,300.0	14,281,000.0
Fiji	188.7	350.4	676.4	1,112.2	1,013.9	963.8	997.0	1,145.9	1,081.8	1,136.1
French Polynesia										
Guam										
Hong Kong, China			962,035.0	1,671,930.0	2,324,350.0	2,181,930.0	1,964,830.0	2,010,950.0	1,968,190.0	1,890,330.0
India	302,118.0	698,920.0	1,435,460.0	2,713,860.0	3,639,990.0	4,196,400.0	5,054,730.0	6,064,340.0	6,626,090.0	8,052,760.0
Indonesia	4,253,650.0	17,280,500.0	97,145,200.0	243,067,000.0	381,741,000.0	508,558,000.0	225,236,000.0	270,301,000.0	298,901,000.0	352,378,000.0
Japan	203,016,000.0	318,501,000.0	524,378,000.0	569,199,000.0	578,790,000.0	583,345,000.0	570,911,000.0	559,373,000.0	538,909,000.0	510,316,000.0
Kazakhstan				71,988.0	85,866.2	102,887.0	153,534.0	288,856.0	515,735.0	699,029.0
Kiribati										
Kyrgyzstan				2,024.5	1,047.3	1,803.8	2,448.0	2,678.8	2,780.0	3,098.2
Laos			4,175.0	118,456.0	247,352.0	460,770.0	728,691.0	1,074,910.0	1,354,490.0	1,329,220.0
Macau										
Malaysia (b, c)	20,352.8	47,849.0	82,657.3	185,472.0	289,853.0	298,162.0	303,657.0	322,206.0	336,825.0	359,802.0
Maldives	16.5	184.0	255.3	655.1	996.8	1,253.2	1,302.8	1,407.1	1,827.2	2,100.8
Mongolia				51,837.6	44,255.6	77,292.5	75,820.9	83,959.1	139,989.0	232,768.0
Myanmar	2,131.0	2,762.0	7,208.0	45,956.0	115,505.0	155,760.0	188,649.0	266,966.0	416,676.0	609,101.0
Nauru										
Nepal	1,960.7	4,335.7	12,897.0	49,493.9	65,540.5	84,875.3	97,305.9	114,913.0	128,410.0	
New Caledonia										
North Korea										
Pakistan	51,903.4	132,590.0	210,491.0	464,913.0	613,944.0	686,932.0	761,793.0	868,069.0	929,064.0	978,492.0
Papua New Guinea	277.6	563.8	878.4	900.8	1,223.1	1,578.0	1,554.9	1,668.2	1,601.5	1,503.6
Philippines	76,637.5	115,033.0	206,558.0	715,322.0	1,370,070.0	1,279,190.0	1,249,580.0	1,316,590.0	1,293,290.0	1,303,350.0
Singapore	17,823.0	35,790.0	55,798.0	109,885.0	143,409.0	154,844.0	150,199.0	159,083.0	185,048.0	169,048.0
Solomon Islands	17.3	47.1	82.3	122.0	141.3	177.0	191.7	195.2	152.7	171.3
South Korea	15,787,500.0	39,990,800.0	94,331,800.0	200,769,000.0	293,812,000.0	318,667,000.0	383,884,000.0	457,258,000.0	520,733,000.0	628,230,000.0
Sri Lanka	11,343.5	32,792.5	63,051.6	206,783.0	261,359.0	291,969.0	323,374.0	362,435.0	395,216.0	452,054.0
Taiwan			4,324,500.0							
Tajikistan										
Thailand	195,323.0	481,234.0	1,408,840.0	4,089,200.0	5,729,590.0	5,299,620.0	5,014,490.0	4,211,560.0	3,774,670.0	4,404,670.0
Tonga	5.2	15.3	33.3	57.2	68.1	79.7	87.4	102.8	112.8	134.1
Turkmenistan										
Tuvalu										
Uzbekistan										
Vanuatu	2,646.0	3,286.9	5,966.3	9,074.6	9,579.8	10,605.0	12,157.9	11,556.3	12,295.2	13,264.9
Vietnam				18,198,500.0	31,220,200.0	34,888,900.0	112,730,000.0	155,720,000.0	189,103,000.0	231,078,000.0
Western Samoa	11.3	22.4	58.8	97.4	137.7	163.8	192.9	231.2	264.4	292.4
Australasia										
Australia	38,015.3	86,990.6	255,618.0	355,318.0	427,280.0	477,178.0	532,435.0	591,739.0	639,941.0	
New Zealand (d)	4,229.6	10,019.8	55,582.9	85,149.5	105,189.0	112,124.0	121,884.0	129,301.0	138,805.0	149,070.0

Source: International Monetary Fund (IMF), International Financial Statistics
Notes: (a) New series starting 1990, (b) New series starting 1992, (c) New series starting 1996, (d) New series starting 1988

◘ Bank Claims on the Private Sector

Bank Claims on the Private Sector 1980-2002

- Million units of national currency

	1980	1985	1990	1995	1997	1998	1999	2000	2001	2002
Africa and Middle East										
Algeria	68,195.0	174,530.0	246,979.0	103,471.0	108,556.0	128,856.0	173,886.0	245,310.0	289,053.0	
Angola				0.7	90.6	90.0	432.9	1,802.7	7,106.2	22,849.1
Bahrain	434.9	598.4	474.6	947.8	1,074.3	1,164.2	1,302.5	1,380.5	1,411.3	1,606.6
Benin	85,000.0	145,429.0	102,071.0	80,447.1	71,695.0	100,130.0	161,655.0	194,030.0	192,837.0	222,228.0
Botswana	93.1	181.5	661.8	1,559.7	1,775.1	2,460.8	3,518.4	4,344.3	4,914.6	6,155.4
Burkina Faso	58,653.0	91,147.0	141,431.0	78,975.0	163,212.0	180,921.0	186,533.0	217,588.0	247,910.0	293,629.0
Burundi	5,592.1	4,811.6	16,437.1	29,161.5	39,515.6	52,948.4	69,384.5	101,356.0	110,418.0	142,849.0
Cameroon	416,613.0	878,287.0	894,448.0	371,390.0	348,135.0	428,815.0	481,464.0	543,950.0	605,776.0	676,259.0
Cape Verde	506.3	2,110.2	3,444.5	9,292.1	13,540.5	15,308.7	17,289.2	18,252.2	21,099.2	23,778.0
Central African Republic	23,468.0	35,032.0	29,150.0	23,159.0	24,174.0	27,952.0	27,770.0	30,903.0	34,519.0	41,320.0
Chad	37,479.0	64,950.0	34,439.0	27,790.0	29,160.0	34,033.0	33,885.0	34,311.0	43,287.0	56,483.0
Comoros		3,428.0	9,023.0	9,452.0	8,458.0	6,948.0	8,600.0	9,480.0	9,223.4	10,277.9
Congo Dem Rep	0.0	0.0	0.0	3.5		9,643.8			9,643.8	11,842.1
Congo-Brazzaville	55,996.0	201,244.0	119,575.0	85,683.0	106,527.0	112,010.0	157,999.0	109,594.0	101,025.0	60,624.0
Côte d'Ivoire	861,240.0	1,053,780.0	1,062,730.0	997,071.0	1,147,400.0	1,186,670.0	1,084,520.0	1,136,170.0	1,192,250.0	1,192,340.0
Djibouti		32,965.0	36,165.0	37,783.0	38,469.0	42,098.0	27,491.0	31,413.0	26,898.0	25,629.0
Egypt	2,174.4	10,145.1	24,453.6	66,777.0	105,545.0	133,799.0	159,958.0	176,693.0	197,038.0	207,089.0
Equatorial Guinea		6,528.0	7,867.0	3,397.0	12,017.0	14,131.0	21,287.0	27,059.0	36,486.0	52,768.0
Eritrea										
Ethiopia	288.8	373.6	408.7	3,706.0	8,007.1	8,693.6	11,216.2	11,836.2	12,187.0	12,057.4
Gabon	142,586.0	303,196.0	210,542.0	196,080.0	269,888.0	285,118.0	286,057.0	313,789.0	375,038.0	415,735.0
Gambia	98.5	212.4	265.4	342.4	425.3	489.8	591.4	652.2	873.2	1,203.1
Ghana	939.6	10,663.3	94,670.0	393,287.0	1,156,610.0	1,591,870.0	2,553,010.0	3,751,120.0	4,460,500.0	5,813,200.0
Guinea		71,648.0	181,410.0	184,070.0	156,383.0	178,654.0	203,379.0	210,107.0	215,213.0
Guinea-Bissau		1,517.5	4,612.3	7,651.1	9,859.2	9,858.9	12,121.4	4,435.9	4,210.7
Iran	2,005,600.0	3,044,500.0	8,728,800.0	32,937,600.0	52,579,100.0	63,716,100.0	85,701,200.0	112,986,000.0	155,268,000.0	206,970,000.0
Iraq										
Israel	79.0	17,051.5	60,956.7	185,123.0	254,886.0	303,434.0	347,382.0	390,938.0	439,228.0	480,699.0
Jordan	541.6	1,193.4	1,716.1	3,192.5	3,526.5	3,803.2	4,050.2	4,230.7	4,709.9	4,833.4
Kenya	11,758.7	19,491.0	36,647.7	117,350.0	182,253.0	182,976.0	202,657.0	210,268.0	201,934.0	207,549.0
Kuwait	2,629.1	4,736.0		2,436.3	4,324.2	4,801.6	5,015.1	5,251.7	6,125.3	6,953.4
Lebanon	16,165.9	57,707.0	1,548,260.0	10,320,000.0	15,451,300.0	18,681,500.0	20,994,300.0	22,243,200.0	22,192,000.0	22,757,700.0
Lesotho	21.4	89.2	208.8	665.5	979.3	829.7	845.3	869.1	927.4	1,062.8
Liberia	88.7	77.5		176.0	82.7	1,148.1	900.9	663.2	877.0	1,064.4
Libya	1,087.1	1,942.7	2,484.8	3,468.1	3,109.1	3,123.4	3,989.1	4,004.0	4,039.0	4,004.9
Madagascar	155,098.0	362,679.0	757,243.0	1,550,400.0	1,797,640.0	1,811,770.0	1,937,490.0	2,303,270.0	2,500,770.0	2,434,510.0
Malawi	184.0	212.6	517.0	1,252.7	1,603.3	3,186.2	3,365.3	5,043.7	5,289.1	6,009.8
Mali	81,991.5	83,203.0	84,115.0	130,270.0	195,893.0	250,964.0	286,522.0	283,626.0	342,180.0	412,191.0
Mauritania	8,868.9	15,518.7	35,411.0	30,722.0	37,279.0	39,835.0	46,942.0	58,486.0	68,939.0	82,534.0
Mauritius	1,881.1	4,615.5	13,043.4	32,878.6	43,360.3	56,653.0	62,520.7	70,569.6	77,891.5	83,976.7
Morocco	11,038.0	22,920.0	34,095.0	81,777.0	151,203.0	167,602.0	183,531.0	199,576.0	208,026.0	214,949.0
Mozambique		7,077.0	95,303.0	2,373,300.0	5,114,800.0	6,466,960.0	8,552,660.0	10,987,700.0	1,893,090.0	1,768,910.0
Namibia			1,372.6	4,742.8	6,553.5	7,129.3	7,434.2	8,699.8	10,115.5	12,161.2
Niger	89,107.0	101,182.0	83,040.0	41,980.1	35,547.0	49,369.0	47,718.0	61,446.0	66,011.0	75,803.0
Nigeria	6,046.3	11,253.1	24,475.1	201,181.0	309,883.0	365,609.0	446,959.0	580,442.0	817,690.0	931,137.0
Oman	283.2	675.2	926.1	1,357.5	2,170.9	2,563.1	2,783.9	2,809.7	3,001.5	3,012.7
Qatar	3,693.2	6,445.0	9,905.5	10,266.6	12,548.2	14,451.3	15,663.5	17,337.5	17,614.3	19,373.8
Réunion										
Rwanda	5,689.4	13,140.3	14,629.2	28,381.3	44,948.0	54,079.0	59,686.4	69,289.0	75,307.0	
Sao Tomé e Príncipe				6,614.3	11,896.9	22,429.1	24,968.8	26,568.8	29,346.1	45,154.9
Saudi Arabia	37,248.7	63,493.2	70,985.7	121,153.0	133,684.0	160,655.0	162,190.0	172,238.0	187,064.0	205,829.0
Senegal	268,250.0	394,545.0	410,268.0	355,639.0	428,299.0	437,078.0	483,012.0	619,549.0	651,783.0	682,004.0
Seychelles	160.1	104.6	137.2	245.1	387.6	460.0	503.5	565.6	643.5	753.5
Sierra Leone	82.6	133.1	3,092.0	17,276.1	24,505.6	26,894.5	24,233.9	27,035.3	32,973.7	50,558.7
Somalia										
South Africa [b]	26,849.0	69,118.5	151,879.0	324,111.0	434,884.0	506,140.0	553,159.0	637,212.0	779,804.0	818,889.0
Sudan	59.3	188.2	766.7	13,068.1	39,351.3	44,336.2	43,583.0	71,483.4	101,136.0	178,425.0
Swaziland	97.1	151.9	466.0	915.6	1,095.0	1,159.4	1,223.4	1,308.2	1,383.6	1,770.1
Syria	2,943.5	6,824.5	20,009.4	63,667.0	73,351.2	72,616.9	75,345.0	76,611.0	78,737.0	83,676.0
Tanzania	1,136.7	2,404.0	115,483.0	201,015.0	166,754.0	239,861.0	302,165.0	333,264.0	403,494.0	570,668.0
Togo	64,130.0	69,715.0	99,091.0	130,390.0	154,762.0	161,876.0	146,551.0	147,593.0	137,348.0	127,657.0
Tunisia	1,334.4	3,480.7	5,956.9	9,273.8	10,539.8	11,542.3	12,652.1	15,716.8	17,423.2	18,306.5
Uganda	49.0	608.4	49,363.8	245,818.0	319,964.0	424,824.0	491,896.0	531,353.0	503,512.0	596,502.0
United Arab Emirates	25,173.0	33,627.6	46,897.0	71,759.0	89,925.0	102,416.0	110,276.0	119,828.0	130,549.0	145,592.0
Yemen			7,723.1	23,864.5	34,379.7	45,956.7	62,426.0	75,746.6	95,317.6	108,949.0
Zambia	433.4	612.9	9,117.9	240,010.0	386,060.0	392,748.0	522,048.0	825,538.0	902,792.0	958,347.0
Zimbabwe	561.1	672.2	2,502.6	15,059.9	27,097.9	36,810.5	41,357.1	62,036.8	101,184.0	293,379.0

Source: International Monetary Fund (IMF), International Financial Statistics
Notes: (a) New series starting 1990, (b) New series starting 1992, (c) New series starting 1996, (d) New series starting 1988

Mastercard Statistics 2002

- '000/as stated

	Mastercard accepting ATMs	Mastercard accepting outlets	Expenditure by mastercard cardholders (US$ million)	Mastercard cards	Mastercard Transactions
Algeria					
Argentina	6.0	272	980	9,080	43,150
Australia	12.5	499	13,630	18,630	202,650
Azerbaijan					
Bolivia	0.3	4	20	110	380
Brazil	7.4	589	8,100	26,900	354,560
Canada	35.3	619	32,270	31,670	492,220
Chile	2.5	61	840	2,920	18,080
China					
Colombia	4.1	107	1,580	6,960	32,820
Ecuador	0.5	31	250	460	4,730
Egypt	0.3	16	440	200	2,650
Hong Kong, China	2.2	88	5,700	5,300	56,910
India	3.7	105	790	7,430	24,080
Indonesia	6.1	52	860	11,210	18,410
Israel					
Japan	24.7	2,987	36,600	84,000	300,670
Jordan					
Kazakhstan					
Kuwait	0.1	5	270	80	1,500
Malaysia	3.8	50	3,260	5,990	67,810
Mexico	20.7	112	16,020	13,370	179,680
Morocco	0.2	16	110	40	1,270
New Zealand	1.9	85	3,090	2,450	59,470
Nigeria					
Pakistan	0.2			320	
Peru	0.3	12	60	480	1,680
Philippines	2.2	52	820	4,020	25,360
Saudi Arabia	1.7	20	420	2,660	1,860
Singapore	1.5	25	1,360	1,440	17,710
South Africa	6.4	105	4,450	9,830	120,060
South Korea					
Taiwan	9.6	122	10,010	37,590	140,060
Thailand	6.8	119	2,020	2,930	24,790
Tunisia	0.4	10	30	40	560
Turkmenistan					
United Arab Emirates	0.4	18	550	540	4,840
USA	352.0	4,293	602,220	351,980	6,884,200
Venezuela	2.9	65	900	7,610	13,680
Vietnam		8	10	10	100

Source: *Mastercard*
Notes: *Expenditure and transaction data refer only to credit cards*

Assets of Deposit Money Banks 1980-2002

● US$ million

	1980	1985	1990	1995	1997	1998	1999	2000	2001	2002
North America										
Canada	35,194.0	44,169.4	52,070.2	64,061.1	84,432.0	86,453.1	79,191.0	91,440.7	102,502.0	106,690.0
USA	176,908.0	417,315.0	578,439.0	606,460.0	791,263.0	813,157.0	860,504.0	961,554.0	1,126,710.0	1,159,890.0
Latin America										
Anguilla										
Antigua	4.5	27.6	30.3	77.5	58.8	71.3	160.1	172.2	187.3	256.6
Argentina	2,155.0	1,067.5	2,234.3	6,301.7	17,732.5	16,895.2	15,007.4	17,910.7	7,179.2	3,628.7
Aruba			160.7	208.0	257.4	269.6	280.5	299.2	297.2	303.2
Bahamas	33,447.5	29,384.6	33,938.1	35,144.4	41,309.8	46,328.8	58,681.7	77,649.0	103,669.0	136,339.0
Barbados	26.2	50.1	77.4	204.0	309.5	277.7	338.8	263.1	335.7	599.7
Belize	13.5	10.2	19.4	26.2	35.8	37.9	45.6	71.6	69.2	58.9
Bermuda										
Bolivia	43.2	15.0	61.3	103.6	137.9	409.8	471.8	552.8	693.9	604.1
Brazil	1,489.0	1,983.0	8,627.7	18,682.1	19,550.0	17,620.7	16,754.3	15,877.9	16,524.8	12,696.7
British Virgin Islands										
Cayman Islands										
Chile	548.2	413.0	507.0	490.0	1,257.2	2,111.6	4,961.5	4,544.0	3,282.6	2,146.7
Colombia	169.6	272.2	268.6	442.9	1,030.9	944.4	552.3	458.1	356.6	336.1
Costa Rica	30.0	48.5	96.5	203.9	251.6	324.6	284.4	330.7	362.8	335.2
Cuba										
Dominica	4.4	6.9	23.2	28.1	43.1	51.8	60.3	44.7	51.2	77.0
Dominican Republic	127.4	41.9	219.6	183.8	236.7	307.0	322.5	416.4	527.0	515.5
Ecuador	115.4	63.6	91.0	373.6	866.7	901.4	740.8	813.1	1,007.1	
El Salvador	43.0	148.4	86.9	69.9	113.4	121.3	125.3	280.0	793.8	867.0
French Guiana										
Grenada	10.9	7.6	18.5	59.1	57.1	55.0	72.7	69.8	113.2	137.9
Guadeloupe										
Guatemala	20.1	76.7	4.3	66.3	72.6	65.6	84.1	123.6	203.4	245.2
Guyana	23.1	8.2	53.4	27.0	24.3	23.9	40.1	38.8	46.4	63.1
Haiti	20.7	30.0	42.4	98.1	133.1	124.4	150.7	199.1	177.0	137.8
Honduras	9.2	3.3	24.6	123.5	228.0	275.7	379.8	451.9	487.8	565.5
Jamaica	37.8	59.9	113.0	489.0	542.0	457.9	571.8	593.8	811.8	898.8
Martinique										
Mexico	1,319.6	939.7	1,412.7	953.5	2,629.6	4,686.8	5,734.6	6,408.2	12,626.6	8,476.0
Netherlands Antilles	2,634.1	1,197.2	554.7	442.3	396.5	471.3	472.6	551.7	861.5	652.7
Nicaragua	23.8	11.6	5.5	45.0	211.3	162.2	144.0	65.7	88.4	92.5
Panama	18,970.3	22,555.2	6,857.4	15,663.9	16,595.2	13,208.7	12,362.1	12,620.5	12,521.1	10,061.4
Paraguay	53.7	43.1	158.2	503.0	378.5	416.2	402.4	498.8	447.9	288.3
Peru	387.3	241.1	527.9	1,544.9	1,215.7	1,245.8	1,388.6	1,298.7	1,365.7	1,218.1
Puerto Rico										
St Kitts	33.1	27.9	32.6	76.7	121.9	123.3	112.6	148.5	165.6	222.1
St Lucia	10.1	19.5	43.7	30.0	32.6	53.1	54.3	50.4	65.2	84.5
St Vincent and the Grenadines	8.8	12.7	48.6	45.8	47.8	53.5	89.9	106.0	105.2	116.1
Suriname	51.9	11.5	22.0	68.8	128.9	122.4	180.6	131.0	188.3	142.1
Trinidad and Tobago	48.0	56.3	114.8	216.4	265.2	298.4	381.7	456.2	538.3	602.5
Uruguay	376.2	667.2	2,469.9	3,479.4	4,758.4	5,015.1	5,803.1	6,252.0	7,271.1	4,137.6
Venezuela	769.6	927.2	1,268.1	646.6	767.0	859.2	1,192.4	1,159.2	976.0	1,096.1

Source: *International Monetary Fund (IMF), International Financial Statistics*
Notes: *(a) Monetary authorities' other assets*

Assets of Deposit Money Banks 1980-2002

● US$ million

	1980	1985	1990	1995	1997	1998	1999	2000	2001	2002
Asia Pacific										
Afghanistan										
American Samoa										
Armenia				24.3	33.3	33.1	70.3	96.1	101.0	126.0
Azerbaijan				167.7	154.5	97.3	152.1	379.5	193.1	211.8
Bangladesh	272.2	289.0	431.7	730.6	827.9	794.9	917.0	1,203.4	1,081.0	916.2
Bhutan		34.6	25.5	7.2	38.9	72.2	93.2	100.9	105.4	110.5
Brunei										
Cambodia				161.6	162.1	139.6	154.4	167.3	216.7	173.3
China (a)			2,006.0							
Fiji	8.4	44.4	77.9	50.1	89.3	136.3	200.1	81.1	84.2	93.3
French Polynesia										
Guam										
Hong Kong, China	34,518.0	101,171.0	464,087.0	655,578.0	600,631.0	501,171.0	475,783.0	450,481.0	405,221.0	394,415.0
India										
Indonesia	4,364.3	5,546.0	6,223.0	7,407.3	10,066.7	14,412.1	16,966.7	10,649.2	10,555.2	10,083.6
Japan	65,666.0	194,620.0	950,578.0	1,217,870.0						
Kazakhstan				440.9	273.8	344.6	570.6	383.5	556.0	1,331.9
Kiribati										
Kyrgyzstan				1.8	2.0	0.8	0.4	0.4	0.7	1.5
Laos			0.1	0.1	0.1	0.0	0.0	0.0	0.0	0.0
Macau										
Malaysia	872.8	1,247.0	2,804.0	4,178.0	6,003.2	5,517.3	6,519.0	7,470.4	7,161.4	7,460.5
Maldives	2.4	2.2	10.7	14.0	11.5	23.7	19.1	21.9	24.9	32.1
Mongolia				53.7	81.7	29.0	38.9	48.9	47.5	62.9
Myanmar	0.7	1.5	26.0	195.4	144.6	232.3	223.5	184.8	173.3	236.0
Nauru										
Nepal	59.3	83.5	128.9	208.9	246.1	299.0	345.3	459.9	335.8	339.4
New Caledonia										
North Korea										
Pakistan	309.9	563.8	1,459.0	1,608.6	1,409.6	1,281.5	1,364.9	1,439.5	1,771.0	1,574.4
Papua New Guinea	16.0	16.2	20.6	100.1	117.4	136.3	103.2	95.8	112.2	153.1
Philippines	2,170.3	2,158.5	3,910.3	6,402.4	8,878.0	9,153.2	10,114.1	8,181.0	7,468.3	8,074.5
Singapore	3,705.8	9,594.8	25,141.9	39,115.5	46,963.3	45,152.7	55,854.1	52,296.9	58,855.2	62,319.0
Solomon Islands	1.0	2.5	1.2	1.3	3.9	1.3	6.1	2.4	5.5	5.4
South Korea	3,615.8	4,848.0	9,532.0	27,806.0	32,749.0	34,310.0	34,748.0	34,562.0	28,086.0	25,851.0
Sri Lanka	130.4	209.0	421.6	838.8	1,103.0	916.0	941.5	1,049.7	899.7	795.3
Taiwan			13,080.0							
Tajikistan										
Thailand	757.2	1,262.9	2,228.8	9,364.8	8,665.3	12,605.2	15,158.3	16,642.0	16,922.9	14,683.4
Tonga	0.1	0.3	1.7	2.0	1.6	4.3	2.9	11.5	10.3	5.1
Turkmenistan										
Tuvalu										
Uzbekistan										
Vanuatu	35.0	288.4	235.1	183.9	204.8	190.0	164.3	160.6	192.6	215.7
Vietnam				869.2	999.2	1,347.0	2,119.0	4,221.9	5,261.4	4,589.2
Western Samoa	2.3	2.0	5.5	4.7	7.0	8.0	11.4	14.6	12.3	7.4
Australasia										
Australia	367.2	1,483.0	10,601.9	12,049.2	15,734.7	13,064.5	18,751.6	18,559.7	21,330.4	
New Zealand	434.7	473.7	1,821.4	1,955.3	1,914.8	2,828.7	4,786.2	6,952.7	8,963.1	11,786.0

Source: International Monetary Fund (IMF), International Financial Statistics
Notes: (a) Monetary authorities' other assets

◻ International Liquidity

Assets of Deposit Money Banks 1980-2002

• US$ million

	1980	1985	1990	1995	1997	1998	1999	2000	2001	2002
Africa and Middle East										
Algeria	682.1	382.4	741.0	638.2	395.6	455.7	402.4	375.8	415.7	
Angola				264.6	833.3	682.2	747.4	878.1	1,168.8	1,453.8
Bahrain	851.0	1,560.6	2,505.1	2,592.0	2,863.0	3,164.1	3,410.6	3,419.9	3,327.9	3,387.9
Benin	0.0	0.0	0.1	0.5	0.5	0.5	0.4	0.3	0.3	0.4
Botswana	3.3	17.5	80.4	69.6	211.3	317.7	290.5	267.6	319.5	284.4
Burkina Faso	0.0	0.0	0.2	0.5	0.3	0.3	0.4	0.3	0.3	0.3
Burundi	3.5	5.2	5.3	17.1	12.0	5.2	13.4	18.4	14.3	18.2
Cameroon	34.3	431.1	142.8	131.1	105.2	122.8	163.3	163.1	153.2	248.7
Cape Verde				10.6	23.9	33.4	30.7	42.4	43.0	43.3
Central African Republic	14.6	21.9	12.6	6.4	5.0	5.9	10.5	8.0	4.5	5.8
Chad	14.3	27.0	57.2	9.9	32.4	24.2	39.7	27.7	42.5	41.2
Comoros		3.8	3.9	2.4	4.3	2.0	8.1	5.7	8.7	6.8
Congo Dem Rep	171.6	77.5	131.6	69.2		93.4			93.4	95.6
Congo-Brazzaville	13.9	32.2	48.9	33.2	27.8	29.0	34.1	140.7	21.8	130.8
Côte d'Ivoire	0.4	0.4	0.7	0.7	0.5	0.5	0.6	0.4	0.3	0.5
Djibouti		195.9	209.4	210.0	167.2	170.0	178.3	166.0	201.8	251.4
Egypt	4,633.7	8,774.9	10,365.5	11,070.3	9,153.2	7,815.1	7,441.2	7,297.1	5,915.0	6,279.5
Equatorial Guinea										
Eritrea										
Ethiopia	50.8	57.4	43.6	454.2	672.1	647.8	536.1	592.9	619.1	693.6
Gabon	17.7	26.5	89.4	75.7	64.5	71.6	74.9	239.7	132.3	115.9
Gambia	10.0	5.4	4.5	5.6	10.7	6.5	10.9	9.2	0.9	24.3
Ghana	0.8	7.5	289.9	327.9	392.3	242.9	194.4	168.6	181.4	207.5
Guinea			70.4	90.9	73.1	85.3	77.5	80.3	68.5	73.9
Guinea-Bissau			0.1	0.1	0.0	0.0	0.0	0.0	0.0	0.0
Iran	2,218.0	2,004.1	3,109.9	3,353.7	4,402.9	4,647.9	2,258.2	3,112.3	6,298.0	7,244.2
Iraq										
Israel	5,522.5	6,256.3	8,316.7	12,055.9	10,823.5	12,746.6	14,146.6	16,095.4	15,644.9	16,194.8
Jordan	665.2	1,046.6	986.9	2,655.3	3,077.5	3,607.1	4,101.5	5,235.2	6,104.3	6,336.7
Kenya	70.4	39.3	68.7	439.6	594.2	501.6	313.6	500.7	395.0	546.6
Kuwait	6,930.1	9,537.1		7,127.8	6,945.2	5,928.5	5,873.8	6,444.9	6,582.7	8,148.5
Lebanon	3,673.9	2,559.0	2,820.1	3,970.7	6,014.4	6,620.8	5,910.8	8,159.3	8,615.7	9,503.2
Lesotho	45.2	43.9	79.9	65.0	41.8	73.0	80.4	80.5	65.1	76.3
Liberia	24.3	14.7		12.0	15.6	10.4	16.7	12.4	11.0	10.3
Libya	1,052.0	521.6	272.7	380.2	979.4	618.6	735.3	937.2	927.7	636.6
Madagascar	75.3	46.9	93.0	176.6	151.7	142.0	140.5	180.4	158.4	188.5
Malawi	6.8	7.8	11.3	29.4	41.6	60.0	47.3	53.9	59.8	43.0
Mali	0.0	0.0	0.3	0.3	0.2	0.2	0.2	0.2	0.3	0.3
Mauritania	9.2	3.3	28.7	25.9	24.7	24.1	22.1	21.6	19.0	19.4
Mauritius	13.3	41.1	121.9	264.2	327.4	361.0	383.8	400.2	427.0	465.5
Morocco	246.0	322.2	780.9	653.3	381.2	496.2	477.1	598.6	568.0	888.2
Mozambique		1.4	5.9	275.4	243.0	205.4	192.8	315.9	341.1	383.0
Namibia			146.0	38.6	110.3	93.6	142.6	231.7	121.4	130.6
Niger	0.1	0.0	0.1	0.1	0.1	0.1	0.1	0.1	0.1	0.1
Nigeria	458.1	414.7	737.1	3,490.3	3,179.6	4,394.8	1,651.4	2,035.5	2,700.6	3,150.4
Oman	402.6	680.9	758.7	999.1	1,776.8	1,222.7	992.3	1,215.5	997.9	1,241.9
Qatar	732.7	1,918.7	2,273.6	3,093.7	2,643.4	2,324.3	2,455.5	3,193.1	3,163.5	4,102.9
Réunion										
Rwanda	21.3	28.9	32.4	51.9	73.2	75.2	56.2	76.5	73.7	
Sao Tomé e Príncipe				7.1	8.0	6.8	6.1	5.4	6.1	8.0
Saudi Arabia	9,691.9	19,384.0	32,967.4	26,160.5	26,572.8	22,948.9	24,429.2	27,023.8	26,525.9	25,497.7
Senegal	0.3	0.1	0.2	0.3	0.3	0.4	0.4	0.3	0.3	0.5
Seychelles	7.5	4.8	11.2	9.9	31.0	29.4	43.7	51.4	51.1	59.2
Sierra Leone	14.0	10.0	8.7	22.5	15.6	19.2	17.9	24.4	21.9	26.6
Somalia										
South Africa	541.6	733.5	465.1	798.6	1,603.5	2,874.4	5,121.8	5,432.4	7,338.2	10,267.2
Sudan	435.0	618.1	616.9	32.1	25.8	26.9	266.1	286.2	343.2	488.8
Swaziland	4.2	7.3	58.2	47.5	91.8	99.2	135.5	84.1	71.9	89.3
Syria	108.5	152.2	991.7	13,364.8	19,818.7	22,775.5	25,457.6	35,517.2	44,742.0	51,819.3
Tanzania	172.1	52.5	61.0	309.2	373.9	392.4	377.6	511.7	588.3	585.4
Togo	0.2	0.1	0.3	0.2	0.1	0.1	0.1	0.1	0.1	0.1
Tunisia	125.4	223.7	610.0	451.6	607.8	643.6	621.1	669.9	550.0	641.0
Uganda	18.5	11.5	27.3	132.5	160.8	190.2	199.8	265.6	248.6	240.1
United Arab Emirates	5,286.4	12,070.1	17,134.0	17,377.8	20,735.7	22,108.9	22,010.3	24,454.7	26,822.6	30,595.0
Yemen			520.2	861.1	455.9	457.9	446.2	624.1	695.5	849.0
Zambia	56.1	48.2	165.7	116.5	155.0	198.9	201.4	239.5	233.3	293.5
Zimbabwe	94.5	8.3	16.4	31.7	26.0	7.6	4.1	3.7	2.7	4.2

Source: International Monetary Fund (IMF), International Financial Statistics
Notes: (a) Monetary authorities' other assets

Liabilities of Deposit Money Banks 1980-2002

- US$ million

	1980	1985	1990	1995	1997	1998	1999	2000	2001	2002
North America										
Canada	42,959.0	64,636.6	77,946.5	77,142.9	108,978.0	111,723.0	92,324.9	94,728.4	109,353.0	116,856.0
USA	151,448.0	381,255.0	733,396.0	1,011,910.0	1,207,310.0	1,265,470.0	1,311,600.0	1,411,340.0	1,523,660.0	1,683,460.0
Latin America										
Anguilla										
Antigua	14.8	49.2	55.8	46.6	101.7	112.6	209.5	262.9	231.7	208.9
Argentina		6,732.2	7,010.7	13,649.2	21,047.7	21,440.4	22,830.8	24,170.3	16,296.9	12,825.9
Aruba			132.8	161.1	217.1	190.8	191.9	221.4	228.8	259.1
Bahamas	33,246.2	29,647.2	35,819.5	35,542.3	41,661.8	47,052.8	59,126.5	78,346.2	104,135.0	136,804.0
Barbados	48.4	88.3	126.2	274.9	382.4	401.0	450.0	373.0	440.9	607.9
Belize	17.3	21.7	4.6	39.6	43.7	50.7	43.1	59.8	71.6	71.3
Bermuda										
Bolivia	161.0	156.6	60.0	544.0	721.4	879.7	744.6	461.3	214.7	181.1
Brazil	11,291.9	14,053.0	15,695.9	42,493.8	54,756.2	50,580.3	41,889.6	40,646.2	39,837.0	31,651.2
British Virgin Islands										
Cayman Islands										
Chile	3,535.3	6,572.0	2,972.0	3,962.0	2,116.7	2,203.7	1,419.0	1,166.4	1,926.7	3,212.1
Colombia	1,093.4	1,096.0	984.4	2,135.9	3,315.7	2,867.9	1,712.0	1,365.1	1,120.0	1,104.2
Costa Rica	126.7	79.4	58.6	167.0	293.5	333.7	388.0	529.3	651.7	727.4
Cuba										
Dominica	7.6	8.8	20.4	34.5	43.0	45.7	45.4	49.5	46.0	47.8
Dominican Republic	154.8	13.3	220.5	55.0	188.6	401.4	458.9	739.3	684.5	924.5
Ecuador	40.3	51.6	262.9	792.7	1,316.2	1,484.4	853.8	588.9	506.4	
El Salvador	9.1	42.2	17.1	361.7	534.9	514.4	549.7	671.2	949.9	1,085.1
French Guiana										
Grenada	11.0	10.3	20.6	39.0	68.3	69.1	74.0	76.9	99.9	104.4
Guadeloupe										
Guatemala	53.6	78.7	26.6	266.2	413.4	500.9	452.5	613.8	656.6	689.2
Guyana	27.6	15.2	19.8	20.5	34.5	31.9	22.2	20.7	17.5	25.9
Haiti	13.3		20.3	4.9	17.9	8.3	16.7	21.8	18.7	20.8
Honduras	47.0	31.2	16.3	103.2	271.4	345.0	297.6	272.0	228.0	230.6
Jamaica	65.1	71.1	138.4	336.2	371.6	328.0	267.2	219.7	368.7	360.2
Martinique										
Mexico	7,173.9	2,202.6	1,339.7	7,947.7	6,909.1	5,461.7	4,141.3	4,422.2	3,064.2	2,181.8
Netherlands Antilles	2,631.0	1,155.3	548.5	390.5	391.9	420.6	454.5	568.4	664.1	496.2
Nicaragua	270.5	98.4	2.2	31.3	54.7	55.1	109.9	90.4	102.6	107.0
Panama	19,508.4	22,385.2	6,533.1	13,929.8	14,825.0	11,744.7	11,844.5	11,775.8	12,081.2	9,568.0
Paraguay	34.1	44.2	23.3	453.0	304.7	232.0	119.9	105.3	96.6	69.1
Peru	624.2	298.2	250.2	1,566.1	3,473.6	3,291.0	2,286.3	2,029.9	1,562.9	1,002.1
Puerto Rico										
St Kitts	13.7	24.2	22.5	77.5	106.1	105.1	125.2	137.1	133.7	171.1
St Lucia	18.6	15.8	30.1	56.3	94.2	87.3	96.6	84.1	108.8	137.4
St Vincent and the Grenadines	12.2	14.2	20.0	32.1	29.7	25.0	51.9	56.7	71.9	67.6
Suriname	19.0	27.8	78.3	45.7	86.0	96.3	160.5	128.1	181.1	5.3
Trinidad and Tobago	76.1	85.7	49.7	98.7	154.1	182.2	239.8	256.0	549.9	596.3
Uruguay	244.5	1,066.1	2,601.0	3,363.6	4,696.9	5,314.7	6,076.4	6,815.3	7,969.4	3,586.3
Venezuela	837.1	1,956.4	838.9	181.4	208.7	169.7	130.7	315.6	432.8	227.8

Source: *International Monetary Fund (IMF), International Financial Statistics*
Notes: *(a) New series starting 1984*

◘ International Liquidity

Liabilities of Deposit Money Banks 1980-2002

● US$ million

	1980	1985	1990	1995	1997	1998	1999	2000	2001	2002
Asia Pacific										
Afghanistan										
American Samoa										
Armenia				24.6	73.4	96.1	111.5	119.9	105.3	93.1
Azerbaijan				34.0	53.2	56.1	69.3	96.5	92.6	110.6
Bangladesh	171.0	127.0	237.6	327.0	510.7	437.3	463.7	571.4	673.5	633.6
Bhutan		4.4	6.5						20.2	
Brunei										
Cambodia				65.8	58.0	59.5	56.9	44.2	50.3	41.6
China	5,667.0	6,634.0	12,868.0	50,370.0	59,034.9	54,685.3	47,057.1	49,536.0	37,476.9	47,317.1
Fiji	16.3	55.6	83.0	73.9	123.5	108.0	159.5	114.1	120.6	148.1
French Polynesia										
Guam										
Hong Kong, China	32,594.0	83,325.0	402,694.0	620,403.0	597,324.0	447,348.0	371,867.0	319,154.0	264,386.0	244,739.0
India	290.0	620.0	1,930.0							
Indonesia	617.6	523.0	6,737.0	11,677.6	15,147.1	12,192.1	14,167.3	9,658.6	6,577.5	5,804.8
Japan	80,209.0	179,306.0	958,478.0	738,324.0						
Kazakhstan				414.2	207.5	390.5	232.2	379.6	982.2	1,802.5
Kiribati										
Kyrgyzstan				2.8	13.1	8.3	1.8	3.0	3.4	36.4
Laos			0.0	0.1	0.0	0.0	0.0	0.0	0.0	0.0
Macau										
Malaysia	1,302.9	2,633.0	3,500.0	8,242.0	12,339.4	9,160.5	7,296.3	6,772.2	6,079.7	8,343.4
Maldives	1.6	30.7	27.9	19.0	12.2	15.1	26.9	32.4	27.6	35.0
Mongolia				14.1	15.1	22.1	9.1	10.2	11.6	14.6
Myanmar	407.0	744.5	441.9	2,119.7	1,706.0	1,640.0	1,705.2	1,698.9	1,645.1	1,606.6
Nauru										
Nepal	6.3	24.4	32.8	67.4	111.3	149.8	174.9	206.8	224.9	237.0
New Caledonia										
North Korea										
Pakistan	124.4	936.7	2,328.8	3,014.7	2,335.4	2,090.8	1,614.0	1,331.2	898.1	584.8
Papua New Guinea	9.9	56.2	113.2	41.4	8.0	54.5	37.4	18.1	24.2	26.0
Philippines	4,846.4	2,500.2	2,378.4	6,419.8	15,406.0	12,751.3	11,977.6	10,302.4	8,729.9	8,254.8
Singapore	4,513.0	12,829.5	24,936.7	46,753.2	62,783.6	50,466.1	53,565.4	58,923.5	61,941.7	67,103.9
Solomon Islands	2.1	2.1	3.8	1.8	2.6	2.6	5.6	3.1	4.4	4.0
South Korea	7,145.9	15,867.0	10,181.0	31,446.0	27,975.0	29,455.0	27,547.0	24,805.0	21,290.0	36,681.0
Sri Lanka	26.2	149.0	303.0	1,003.9	1,093.7	858.8	764.0	909.4	1,009.4	864.9
Taiwan			11,120.0							
Tajikistan										
Thailand	1,378.6	1,722.0	4,340.0	46,214.1	40,307.3	29,057.9	19,164.7	13,070.1	10,439.2	9,575.2
Tonga	0.3	0.6	0.5	1.2	4.3	4.9	4.4	6.9	5.1	5.8
Turkmenistan										
Tuvalu										
Uzbekistan										
Vanuatu	5.8	190.5	64.1	32.0	48.0	25.0	33.9	26.2	28.5	65.2
Vietnam				865.0	868.7	679.0	664.7	682.6	679.6	640.1
Western Samoa	3.1	0.3	0.6	0.3	2.4	1.4	6.8	6.6	6.8	5.0
Australasia										
Australia (a)	655.3	2,921.7	33,997.4	49,238.1	64,258.4	73,409.4	88,291.1	90,027.5	98,049.4	
New Zealand	182.0	446.9	7,563.5	14,438.7	17,024.3	20,030.7	25,260.9	25,553.9	27,632.3	33,990.3

Source: *International Monetary Fund (IMF), International Financial Statistics*
Notes: *(a) New series starting 1984*

International Liquidity
Liabilities of Deposit Money Banks 1980-2002

- US$ million

	1980	1985	1990	1995	1997	1998	1999	2000	2001	2002
Africa and Middle East										
Algeria	2,953.0	5,091.8	7,940.9	2,749.5	1,215.5	1,068.3	1,014.6	720.4	766.9	
Angola				69.7	137.3	199.5	119.1	49.1	157.4	126.9
Bahrain	627.7	339.5	762.8	1,136.4	1,583.2	1,522.1	2,305.3	1,672.9	1,480.6	1,536.0
Benin	0.4	0.1	0.3	0.1	0.1	0.2	0.2	0.1	0.1	0.1
Botswana	4.0	10.3	34.1	35.1	31.6	38.5	34.8	41.9	52.6	53.3
Burkina Faso	0.3	0.1	0.3	0.1	0.1	0.1	0.2	0.1	0.2	0.2
Burundi	6.2	6.7	5.5	11.0	7.5	7.5	7.7	14.3	19.2	21.3
Cameroon	326.0	268.4	338.3	82.0	62.5	85.9	84.5	70.8	67.4	96.1
Cape Verde				6.3	9.9	11.2	15.5	16.4	14.1	18.5
Central African Republic	23.8	3.3	16.2	7.9	6.4	7.4	8.8	9.4	8.1	9.6
Chad	6.8	3.2	23.0	17.4	14.8	8.6	14.6	13.0	15.5	29.5
Comoros		1.2	6.3	0.3		2.0	2.5	4.3	4.2	4.8
Congo Dem Rep	44.0	18.0	53.1	16.8		48.8			48.8	42.0
Congo-Brazzaville	56.8	138.9	59.3	28.9	14.1	41.8	39.2	18.0	17.8	68.7
Côte d'Ivoire	2.9	0.9	2.3	0.8	0.5	0.6	0.6	0.4	0.5	0.4
Djibouti		102.7	68.9	91.1	83.3	88.5	45.3	50.1	38.7	43.0
Egypt	2,598.9	6,239.3	3,714.3	1,500.2	3,555.7	4,995.3	4,318.3	4,232.6	4,268.9	4,264.0
Equatorial Guinea										
Eritrea										
Ethiopia	40.7	59.2	67.9	216.0	249.6	252.6	282.3	257.1	206.1	215.0
Gabon	80.9	94.5	143.7	79.9	50.6	56.7	77.8	91.6	81.4	131.8
Gambia	20.9	3.6	0.4	2.5	14.5	12.9	17.0	8.9	10.4	18.2
Ghana	21.3	38.3	110.1	45.8	75.7	26.1	140.4	116.3	51.7	66.3
Guinea			48.8	79.9	53.9	58.7	62.7	40.9	27.3	38.7
Guinea-Bissau			0.0	0.0	0.0	0.0	0.0	0.0	0.0	0.0
Iran	692.8		1,860.4	4,014.9	2,128.2	2,770.5	3,409.8	3,486.4	6,695.1	8,656.6
Iraq										
Israel	7,593.4	10,038.0	11,024.5	14,514.4	16,738.3	18,334.0	20,452.0	21,872.6	22,106.4	22,305.0
Jordan	480.5	917.9	691.5	2,926.5	3,084.7	3,079.7	3,285.2	3,819.1	4,213.6	4,718.1
Kenya	68.7	50.0	70.5	103.8	165.2	195.8	218.2	173.0	162.3	142.1
Kuwait	4,181.0	5,258.3		2,239.0	4,009.2	3,595.3	3,971.0	3,913.3	5,101.3	6,782.3
Lebanon	1,577.1	1,019.0	901.3	2,063.4	4,189.3	5,908.2	6,392.5	7,190.2	7,347.2	7,339.9
Lesotho	8.3	3.1	9.6	16.5	11.7	8.1	6.5	18.5	8.5	11.5
Liberia	49.4	46.2		15.3	8.4	2.5	3.0	10.0	11.9	9.6
Libya	112.7	1.0	1,017.0	109.0	2,964.6	2,164.9	1,834.2	1,461.1	2,483.9	1,475.6
Madagascar	111.5	27.8	48.3	33.5	32.0	40.0	50.9	62.2	57.7	50.8
Malawi	56.4	40.8	21.6	9.8	10.7	13.8	16.0	16.9	15.1	12.8
Mali	0.2	0.1	0.4	0.2	0.0	0.1	0.1	0.1	0.1	0.2
Mauritania	81.3	56.8	120.6	67.4	26.4	15.0	13.6	12.5	12.1	12.1
Mauritius	19.7	6.0	12.8	67.5	38.4	127.9	104.3	106.6	98.3	196.7
Morocco	69.3	49.1	226.2	442.2	350.9	462.0	456.5	407.0	335.7	269.5
Mozambique		0.0	5.3	69.3	87.9	65.7	33.6	56.3	81.9	38.6
Namibia			107.5	137.3	172.3	116.2	68.0	129.6	129.1	255.3
Niger	0.6	0.3	0.4	0.1	0.1	0.1	0.1	0.1	0.0	0.0
Nigeria	162.2	259.8	27.6	136.5	137.5	298.8	55.9	137.8	152.2	149.9
Oman	320.1	249.2	203.0	441.4	1,326.5	1,522.2	1,662.4	1,641.8	1,532.5	1,401.8
Qatar	174.4	246.6	578.7	1,768.2	1,274.4	1,497.6	1,605.5	611.3	586.9	655.0
Réunion										
Rwanda	8.4	24.8	7.5	4.1	12.6	11.9	5.3	8.2	10.1	
Sao Tomé e Príncipe				1.5	0.4	1.3	0.3	0.4	0.3	0.3
Saudi Arabia	2,752.2	2,848.4	8,056.7	10,594.9	12,294.8	11,510.1	13,659.0	17,207.9	15,918.4	11,481.7
Senegal	1.0	0.4	0.7	0.3	0.2	0.2	0.2	0.1	0.1	0.2
Seychelles	1.2	3.6	11.5	10.4	33.4	34.7	47.1	61.4	55.9	48.1
Sierra Leone		2.1	0.0	3.1						
Somalia										
South Africa	804.3	1,750.0	2,612.6	9,183.6	9,675.8	10,483.1	8,878.4	8,884.6	8,147.9	6,568.6
Sudan	144.1	215.5	154.6	5.3	2.6	2.0	13.4	14.8	34.8	52.4
Swaziland	4.7	3.3	12.3	17.6	20.9	6.1	9.4	13.8	1.9	8.4
Syria	376.7	1,165.5	919.0	496.6	247.9	325.4	437.8	408.3	346.6	990.3
Tanzania	23.0	511.3	21.0	51.4	7.8	3.6	2.2	5.2	17.6	36.0
Togo	0.4	0.2	0.3	0.2	0.1	0.1	0.1	0.1	0.1	0.1
Tunisia	410.1	471.6	753.9	1,740.8	1,845.2	1,979.9	2,091.3	2,618.5	2,608.8	3,198.6
Uganda	4.2	3.4	14.5	0.1	2.0	2.1	25.5	41.7	32.1	38.7
United Arab Emirates	4,571.2	5,422.6	6,779.1	7,653.5	12,351.5	14,446.6	14,577.8	14,133.4	8,137.0	8,136.7
Yemen			404.9	479.1	60.8	50.2	45.6	56.5	26.9	18.7
Zambia	77.7	90.5	49.3	9.3	13.2	29.2	34.9	25.9	24.5	26.0
Zimbabwe	88.1	27.2	39.5	94.0	51.5	19.4	6.4	3.8	2.3	3.4

Source: International Monetary Fund (IMF), International Financial Statistics
Notes: (a) New series starting 1984

□ Lending Rates

Table 5.5

Lending Rates 1980-2002

● % per annum

	1980	1985	1990	1995	1997	1998	1999	2000	2001	2002
North America										
Canada [a]	14.25	10.58	14.06	8.65	4.96	6.60	6.44	7.27	5.81	4.21
USA [b]	15.27	9.93	10.01	8.83	8.44	8.35	7.99	9.23	6.92	4.67
Latin America										
Anguilla										
Antigua	10.00	13.17	12.67	12.70	11.98	12.20	12.07	12.17	11.62	11.39
Argentina				17.85	9.24	10.64	11.04	11.09	27.71	51.68
Aruba [c]			10.60	10.60	10.00		13.14	12.07	12.10	13.08
Bahamas [b]	10.83	10.33	9.00	6.75	6.75	6.75	6.38	6.00	6.00	6.00
Barbados [b]		10.56	11.42	10.00	9.83	9.75	9.40	10.19	9.58	8.50
Belize	16.50		14.04	15.69	16.29	16.50	16.27	16.00	15.45	14.83
Bermuda										
Bolivia	28.00	172.15	41.81	51.02	50.05	39.41	35.37	34.60	20.06	20.63
Brazil				53.37	78.19	86.36	80.44	56.83	57.62	62.88
British Virgin Islands										
Cayman Islands										
Chile	47.14	39.97	48.87	18.16	15.67	20.17	12.62	14.84	11.89	7.76
Colombia			45.25	42.72	34.22	42.24	25.77	18.79	20.72	16.33
Costa Rica [d]		20.92	32.56	36.70	22.48	22.47	25.74	24.89	23.83	26.42
Cuba										
Dominica	8.50	10.04	10.50	11.50	11.17	11.27	11.40	11.68	11.14	10.96
Dominican Republic				30.68	21.01	25.64	25.05	26.80	24.26	26.06
Ecuador	9.00	18.00	37.50	55.67	43.02	49.55	16.53	16.26	15.46	15.08
El Salvador		14.00	21.17	19.08	16.05	14.98	15.46	13.96		
French Guiana										
Grenada	9.50	11.42	10.50	11.08	11.24	11.73	11.62	11.60	10.19	11.13
Guadeloupe										
Guatemala [e]	11.00	12.00	23.27	21.16	18.64	16.56	19.51	20.88	18.96	16.86
Guyana	13.50	15.00	32.75	19.22	17.04	16.77	17.11	17.30	17.01	16.32
Haiti					21.00	23.62	22.88	25.09	28.63	25.67
Honduras		16.30	17.05	26.95	32.07	30.69	30.15	26.82	23.76	22.69
Jamaica	15.63	24.92	30.50	43.58	32.86	31.59	27.00	23.35	20.61	18.50
Martinique										
Mexico				58.59	24.55	28.70	25.87	18.23	13.87	9.38
Netherlands Antilles [b]	11.88	11.46	9.25	12.93	13.29	13.58	13.60	9.98	10.44	10.14
Nicaragua			22.00	19.89	21.02	21.63	22.15	21.35	22.81	23.16
Panama [f]			11.98	11.10	10.63	10.82	10.05	10.48	10.97	10.58
Paraguay			31.00	33.94	27.79	30.49	30.21	26.78	28.25	38.66
Peru			4,774.53	27.16	29.96	30.80	30.79	27.91	20.43	14.73
Puerto Rico										
St Kitts		11.58	12.00	10.89	11.16	11.42	11.21	11.10	11.08	10.89
St Lucia	11.00	14.00	10.71	12.68	12.68	11.40	12.79	13.06	12.97	12.59
St Vincent and the Grenadines [b]	10.00	12.08	12.88	11.07	11.29	11.31	11.55	11.46	11.63	11.56
Suriname				40.18	33.13	27.50	27.32	28.95	25.76	22.18
Trinidad and Tobago	10.00	12.69	12.87	15.17	15.33	17.33	17.04	16.50	15.67	12.48
Uruguay [g]	66.62	94.58	174.45	99.10	71.55	57.93	53.28	49.05	51.71	126.07
Venezuela		9.33	35.53	39.74	23.68	46.35	32.13	25.20	22.45	36.58

Source: International Monetary Fund (IMF), International Financial Statistics
Notes: *(a) Prime commercial lending rate, (b) Prime rate, (c) Current account lending rate, (d) Commercial lending rate, agricultural, (e) Maximum commercial bank lending rate, (f) 1-5 year lending rate, (g) Ordinary*

Lending Rates 1980-2002 (continued)

● % per annum

	1980	1985	1990	1995	1997	1998	1999	2000	2001	2002
Asia Pacific										
Afghanistan										
American Samoa										
Armenia				111.86	54.23	48.48	38.85	31.57	26.69	21.14
Azerbaijan				162.50			19.48	19.66	19.71	17.37
Bangladesh [a]	11.33	12.00	16.00	14.00	14.00	14.00	14.13	15.50	15.83	16.00
Bhutan		15.00	15.00	16.00						
Brunei										
Cambodia				18.70	18.40	18.33	17.56	17.34	16.50	16.23
China	5.04	7.92	9.36	12.06	8.64	6.39	5.85	5.85	5.85	5.31
Fiji [b]	12.00	13.50	11.86	11.06	11.03	9.66	8.77	8.40	8.34	8.05
French Polynesia										
Guam										
Hong Kong, China			10.00	8.75	9.50	9.00	8.50	9.50	5.13	5.00
India [c]	16.50	16.50	16.50	15.46	13.83	13.54	12.54	12.29	12.08	11.92
Indonesia [d]			20.82	18.85	21.82	32.15	27.66	18.46	18.55	18.95
Japan	8.35	6.60	6.95	3.51	2.45	2.32	2.16	2.07	1.97	1.86
Kazakhstan				52.50	19.50	21.40	23.70	19.40		
Kiribati										
Kyrgyzstan					49.38	73.44	60.86	51.90	37.33	24.81
Laos				25.67		29.28	32.00	32.00	26.17	29.33
Macau										
Malaysia [e]	7.75	11.54	7.17	7.63	9.53	10.61	7.29	6.77	6.66	6.39
Maldives										
Mongolia [f]				134.37	82.05	46.77	39.29	32.75	30.24	28.38
Myanmar	8.00	8.00	8.00	16.50	16.50	16.50	16.13	15.25	15.00	15.00
Nauru										
Nepal [g]	14.00	17.00	14.42		14.54	14.00	11.33	9.46	7.67	
New Caledonia										
North Korea										
Pakistan	10.00	10.00	10.00	13.00	13.00					
Papua New Guinea [g]	11.15	11.54	15.52	13.14	10.45	17.70	18.90	17.54	16.21	13.89
Philippines [h]	14.00	28.61	24.12	14.68	16.28	16.78	11.78	10.91	12.40	9.14
Singapore [i]	11.72	7.93	7.36	6.37	6.32	7.44	5.80	5.83	5.66	5.37
Solomon Islands [i]		12.83	18.00	16.59	15.71	14.84	14.50	15.49	15.72	16.42
South Korea [k]	18.00	10.00	10.00	9.00	11.88	15.28	9.40	8.54	7.71	6.77
Sri Lanka [l]	19.00	13.40	13.00	18.04	14.69	15.03	14.72	16.16	19.39	
Taiwan	14.58	5.09	9.60	7.40	6.30	7.20				
Tajikistan										
Thailand	16.15	16.08	14.42	13.25	13.65	14.42	8.98	7.83	7.25	6.88
Tonga [i]	10.00	10.00	13.50	9.82	10.02	10.40	10.32	10.35	11.43	11.43
Turkmenistan										
Tuvalu										
Uzbekistan										
Vanuatu [g]		15.75	17.33	10.50	10.50	10.96	10.29	9.85	8.81	7.41
Vietnam					14.42	14.40	12.70	10.55	9.42	9.06
Western Samoa [g]		19.00	13.25	12.00	12.00	11.50	11.50	11.00	9.93	9.75
Australasia										
Australia [m]	10.50	15.24	18.17	11.12	9.31	8.04	7.51	8.78	8.13	7.96
New Zealand [e]	12.63		16.01	12.09	11.35	11.22	8.49	10.22	9.88	9.81

Source: *International Monetary Fund (IMF), International Financial Statistics*
Notes: *(a) Short-term agricultural rate, scheduled banks, (b) Maximum commercial bank lending rate, (c) Prime commercial lending rate, (d) Working capital lending rate, (e) Base lending rate, (f) End of period, (g) Commercial lending rate, (h) Average commercial lending rate, (i) Minimum rate, (j) Overdraft rate, (k) Minimum lending rate on Deposit Money Banks, (l) Minimum unsecured rate, (m) Maximum overdraft rate less $100,000*

▣ Lending Rates
Lending Rates 1980-2002 (continued)

● % per annum

	1980	1985	1990	1995	1997	1998	1999	2000	2001	2002
Africa and Middle East										
Algeria				19.00	12.50	11.00	10.00	10.00	9.50	8.50
Angola				206.25	37.75	45.00	80.30	103.16	95.97	97.34
Bahrain (a)			8.50	11.83	12.33	11.92	11.86	11.73	10.81	8.50
Benin	14.50	14.50	16.00							
Botswana	8.47	11.50	7.88	14.29	14.08	13.53	14.63	15.31	15.75	15.96
Burkina Faso	14.50	14.50	16.00							
Burundi (b)	12.00	12.00	12.34	15.26	9.30	9.60	15.24	15.77	16.82	19.47
Cameroon	13.00	14.50	18.50	16.00	22.00	22.00	22.00	22.00	20.67	18.00
Cape Verde	6.50	10.00	10.00	12.00	12.06	12.51	12.03	11.94	12.85	13.17
Central African Republic	10.50	12.50	18.50	16.00	22.00	22.00	22.00	22.00	20.67	18.00
Chad	11.00	11.50	18.50	16.00	22.00	22.00	22.00	22.00	20.67	18.00
Comoros										
Congo Dem Rep				293.88	134.58	29.00	124.58	165.00	167.92	66.79
Congo-Brazzaville	11.00	12.00	18.50	16.00	22.00	22.00	22.00	22.00	20.67	18.00
Côte d'Ivoire	14.50	14.50	16.00							
Djibouti										
Egypt	13.33	15.00	19.00	16.47	13.79	13.02	12.97	13.22	13.29	13.79
Equatorial Guinea		15.00	18.50	16.00	22.00	22.00	22.00	22.00	20.67	18.00
Eritrea										
Ethiopia		8.50	6.00	15.08	10.50	10.50	10.58	10.89	10.87	8.66
Gabon	12.50	12.67	18.50	16.00	22.00	22.00	22.00	22.00	20.67	18.00
Gambia (c)	15.00	14.48	26.50	25.04	25.50	25.38	24.00	24.00	24.00	24.00
Ghana										
Guinea (d)			21.17	21.50		19.56	19.88	19.38		
Guinea-Bissau			45.75	32.92						
Iran										
Iraq										
Israel (e)	176.93	503.42	26.45	20.22	18.71	16.18	16.36	12.87	10.03	9.89
Jordan (f)			10.31	10.66	12.25	12.61	12.33	11.80	10.92	10.18
Kenya (g)	10.58	14.00	18.75	28.80	30.25	29.49	22.38	22.34	19.67	18.45
Kuwait (h)	6.80	8.75		8.37	8.80	8.93	8.56	8.87	7.88	6.48
Lebanon		17.29	39.94	24.69	20.29		19.48	18.15	17.19	16.58
Lesotho	11.00	19.67	20.42	16.38	18.03	20.06	19.06	17.11	16.55	17.11
Liberia (i)	18.40	19.34		15.57	16.82	21.74	16.72	20.53	22.14	20.21
Libya (i)	7.00	7.00	7.00				7.00	7.00	7.00	7.00
Madagascar			25.80	37.50	30.00	27.00	28.00	26.50	25.25	25.25
Malawi (g)	16.67	18.38	21.00	47.33	28.25	37.67	53.58	53.13	56.17	50.54
Mali	14.50	14.50	16.00							
Mauritania	12.00	12.00	10.00							
Mauritius (k)		13.83	18.00	20.81	18.92	19.92	21.63	20.77	21.10	21.00
Morocco (l)	7.00	7.75	9.00			13.50	13.50	13.31	13.25	13.13
Mozambique						24.35	19.63	19.04	22.73	26.71
Namibia				18.51	20.18	20.72	18.48	15.28	14.53	13.84
Niger	14.50	14.50	16.00		5.00	5.00	5.00	5.00		
Nigeria (m)	8.43	9.43	25.30	20.23	17.80	18.18	20.29	21.27	23.44	24.77
Oman		10.24	9.68	9.38	9.30	10.09	10.32	10.06	9.23	8.55
Qatar	9.50	9.50	9.50							
Réunion										
Rwanda (n)	13.50	13.88	13.17							
Sao Tomé e Príncipe (o)			20.00	52.00	51.50	55.58	40.33	39.67	37.00	37.08
Saudi Arabia										
Senegal	14.50	14.50	16.00							
Seychelles			15.65	15.76	14.88	14.39	12.01	11.45	11.14	11.09
Sierra Leone (p)	11.00	17.00	52.50	28.83	23.87	23.83	26.83	26.25	24.27	22.17
Somalia										
South Africa (q)	9.50	21.50	21.00	17.90	20.00	21.79	18.00	14.50	13.77	15.75
Sudan										
Swaziland	9.50	20.63	14.50	17.05	19.50	19.50	17.42	14.00	13.25	15.25
Syria										
Tanzania (g)	11.50	12.29		42.83	26.27	22.89	21.89	21.58	20.26	16.43
Togo	14.50	14.50	16.00							
Tunisia	7.25	9.63		8.80	6.90	6.90	5.90	5.90		
Uganda (r)	10.80	24.00	38.67	20.16	21.37	20.86	21.55	22.92	22.66	19.10
United Arab Emirates										
Yemen					22.52	14.71	24.08	19.54	17.50	17.71
Zambia (s)	9.50	18.60	35.10	45.53	46.69	31.80	40.52	38.80	46.23	45.20
Zimbabwe (t)	17.54	17.17	11.71	34.73	32.55	42.06	55.39	68.21	38.02	36.48

Source: International Monetary Fund (IMF), International Financial Statistics
Notes: (a) Prime commercial lending rate, (b) Short-term commercial lending rate, (c) Maximum rate for industrial credit, (d) Deposit rate, (e) Overall cost of unindexed credit, (f) End of period, (g) Maximum commercial bank lending rate, (h) Loans against commercial bank bills, (i) Average overdraft rate, (j) Secured loan and advances, (k) Upper margin prime rate, (l) Maximum export credit, (m) First class advances, (n) Overdraft rate, (o) Period average, (p) Minimum commercial bank lending rate, (q) Prime rate, (r) Lending rate for exports and manufacturing, (s) Commercial overdraft rate, (t) Commercial lending rate

| ▣ Reserves of Deposit Money Banks | | | | | | | | | **Table 5.6** | |

Reserves of Deposit Money Banks 1980-2002

● Million units of national currency

	1980	1985	1990	1995	1997	1998	1999	2000	2001	2002
North America										
Canada	7,281	5,676	6,581	4,669	4,792	4,892	8,556	6,870	6,070	5,956
USA	47,243	50,255	67,861	67,463	74,060	66,486	86,102	61,776	62,538	67,366
Latin America										
Anguilla										
Antigua	15	61	63	117	99	116	131	117	191	173
Argentina (a, b)	0	0	1,342	2,637	2,673	2,905	3,101	2,826	8,429	13,968
Aruba			83	181	119	210	224	181	246	314
Bahamas	36	54	86	128	146	183	226	208	250	292
Barbados	58	83	181	145	166	217	196	256	328	533
Belize	8	21	38	54	59	65	59	101	103	84
Bermuda										
Bolivia	0	111	664	1,450	3,588	1,426	1,459	1,797	1,827	1,753
Brazil	0	0	0	22,126	42,494	32,716	38,029	38,342	46,389	153,456
British Virgin Islands										
Cayman Islands										
Chile	55,540	96,040	178,119	721,655	564,103	897,920	896,659	864,429	930,236	911,641
Colombia (a)	106,008	268,840	1,000,600	2,736,300	3,544,700	2,157,100	3,242,870	3,008,240	3,201,230	4,112,940
Costa Rica	3,305	23,685	78,950	232,321	248,784	282,462	294,010	282,132	275,244	288,494
Cuba										
Dominica	12	25	38	46	45	56	69	57	58	98
Dominican Republic	346	770	4,268	10,654	12,964	16,947	17,331	26,692	30,405	28,653
Ecuador	12,679	25,937	216,947	1,039,662	2,145,716	3,439,585	1,954,959	5,608,396	5,895,750	
El Salvador	203	361	292	967	1,222	1,338	1,465	782	712	660
French Guiana										
Grenada	10	45	46	57	73	76	92	98	108	138
Guadeloupe										
Guatemala	246	583	1,450	4,019	5,731	4,823	3,122	5,132	6,120	9,052
Guyana	126	628	1,802	10,326	13,316	16,070	12,419	15,510	18,340	21,031
Haiti	326	611	1,517	3,608	3,324	3,411	4,394	6,297	7,714	8,805
Honduras	104	129	274	1,118	5,021	6,018	6,374	7,134	8,091	11,269
Jamaica	392	1,304	4,273	25,624	29,167	30,812	26,972	32,236	40,378	44,099
Martinique										
Mexico	515	3,927	6,637	114,111	54,841	71,425	114,882	72,160	105,728	156,789
Netherlands Antilles	85	156	138	210	232	263	251	305	432	596
Nicaragua	0	0	33	1,112	2,324	2,753	2,627	2,729	4,114	4,644
Panama										
Paraguay	38,661	84,280	301,071	1,032,560	1,189,090	1,421,920	1,636,090	1,740,620	2,106,190	2,250,360
Peru	0	0	267	6,846	12,135	11,126	11,897	12,382	13,252	14,353
Puerto Rico										
St Kitts	4	27	35	65	66	79	90	99	113	140
St Lucia	9	36	85	97	105	109	129	121	152	174
St Vincent and the Grenadines	11	27	61	54	61	87	73	111	140	108
Suriname	53	544	1,339	29,584	18,531	31,462	32,392	122,759	124,630	220,338
Trinidad and Tobago	869	1,673	1,196	2,245	2,773	3,059	3,022	3,214	3,936	3,535
Uruguay	2	76	2,534	9,420	15,781	17,772	21,390	23,777	37,790	39,549
Venezuela	11,608	22,043	108,248	483,542	1,874,690	2,392,370	2,921,310	3,566,150	4,031,120	3,827,130

Source: *International Monetary Fund (IMF), International Financial Statistics*
Notes: *(a) New series starting 1990, (b) New series starting 1994, (c) New series starting 1988*

◻ Reserves of Deposit Money Banks

Reserves of Deposit Money Banks 1980-2002

● Million units of national currency

	1980	1985	1990	1995	1997	1998	1999	2000	2001	2002
Asia Pacific										
Afghanistan										
American Samoa										
Armenia				3,987	13,681	12,033	11,082	12,593	14,717	22,092
Azerbaijan				303,170	301,943	204,066	177,853	391,513	318,494	361,198
Bangladesh	3,378	9,312	31,368	43,333	48,678	64,661	63,584	65,494	96,995	94,687
Bhutan		119	1,009	2,382	3,009	2,901	3,675	4,669	4,924	6,473
Brunei										
Cambodia				88,152	199,150	346,001	503,743	737,125	866,848	1,270,840
China		96,070	263,810	1,006,410	1,645,680	1,511,150	1,610,780	1,619,320	1,817,140	2,041,320
Fiji	22	41	83	126	126	112	237	174	233	244
French Polynesia										
Guam										
Hong Kong, China			6,050	12,094	12,373	13,848	32,665	14,343	12,532	11,909
India	47,718	130,692	287,420	646,910	604,300	783,690	661,670	747,420	769,810	733,560
Indonesia	1,262,450	2,039,800	4,892,800	7,371,000	24,172,000	50,229,000	68,479,000	66,536,800	93,356,500	94,632,700
Japan	5,484,000	6,298,000	10,610,000	7,085,000	9,355,000	10,026,000	30,217,000	11,325,500	19,281,000	26,586,700
Kazakhstan				14,771	22,361	12,144	21,794	24,359	42,344	45,362
Kiribati										
Kyrgyzstan				113	381	449	739	700	343	792
Laos			2,815	44,161	77,702	212,415	402,962	688,771	714,460	939,280
Macau										
Malaysia	1,587	2,552	6,205	32,421	45,197	30,814	58,149	53,269	43,114	53,759
Maldives	10	72	199	613	1,174	1,347	1,553	1,695	1,563	2,094
Mongolia				12,531	13,457	17,921	24,171	33,858	34,637	54,531
Myanmar	2,419	879	22,962	-17,511	14,570	44,356	57,339	70,591	99,973	113,696
Nauru										
Nepal	369	914	2,943	8,488	9,972	15,673	14,096	18,376	18,742	16,257
New Caledonia										
North Korea										
Pakistan	6,167	13,871	28,931	109,689	100,518	119,696	145,480	81,205	169,195	150,861
Papua New Guinea	26	23	35	56	67	106	310	251	279	310
Philippines	12,188	45,138	83,747	123,927	161,055	168,168	190,987	178,088	181,182	216,574
Singapore	1,192	2,219	3,951	7,152	8,498	6,423	10,076	7,174	8,199	7,633
Solomon Islands	12	8	6	22	22	52	52	61	65	81
South Korea	1,323,910	1,016,290	6,716,900	14,091,600	6,797,600	6,610,000	8,957,600	10,433,800	14,063,100	17,903,800
Sri Lanka	2,049	8,228	9,406	35,449	36,500	39,667	40,110	39,542	49,760	53,234
Taiwan		177,132	930,500							
Tajikistan										
Thailand	10,431	21,172	51,563	117,827	203,595	145,737	142,993	112,829	185,971	201,571
Tonga	12	25	40	35	38	34	34	22	30	38
Turkmenistan										
Tuvalu										
Uzbekistan										
Vanuatu	105	236	546	2,033	1,742	1,238	2,215	2,547	2,496	2,563
Vietnam				7,409,260	9,451,430	9,920,040	16,881,100	20,390,500	18,426,200	20,165,700
Western Samoa	2	17	75	41	60	24	30	36	31	41
Australasia										
Australia	2,619	4,280	4,281	5,830	8,789	9,052	5,052	4,228	8,532	8,205
New Zealand (c)	93	182	558	606	409	448	1,592	818	908	944

Source: *International Monetary Fund (IMF), International Financial Statistics*
Notes: *(a) New series starting 1990, (b) New series starting 1994, (c) New series starting 1988*

Reserves of Deposit Money Banks

Reserves of Deposit Money Banks 1980-2002

- Million units of national currency

	1980	1985	1990	1995	1997	1998	1999	2000	2001	2002
Africa and Middle East										
Algeria	701	2,315	4,035	5,576	18,774	15,851	13,374	42,737	182,935	
Angola				1	82	92	1,045	2,964	7,509	16,100
Bahrain	38	56	197	125	127	89	154	139	178	204
Benin	1,442	3,384	36,142	32,355	31,926	31,493	16,517	37,110	77,028	86,329
Botswana	36	16	99	166	271	331	353	229	263	311
Burkina Faso	1,616	20,191	22,322	17,651	15,701	14,358	19,847	18,057	35,415	30,081
Burundi	79	2,075	737	1,290	2,852	2,839	4,754	3,625	6,289	6,453
Cameroon	8,941	27,503	41,245	37,490	70,566	68,599	62,663	141,594	201,244	301,040
Cape Verde				5,987	5,701	5,820	5,648	7,111	7,869	9,760
Central African Republic	428	235	1,285	2,068	2,381	860	844	963	1,439	1,529
Chad	3,420	439	2,175	10,076	12,765	10,127	10,352	9,887	12,889	28,586
Comoros		66	1,637	1,631	4,024	5,195	3,796	5,257	8,806	12,547
Congo Dem Rep	0	0	0	1		4,359			4,359	3,072
Congo-Brazzaville	4,666	2,749	4,089	7,409	15,081	13,851	12,716	105,987	30,070	29,340
Côte d'Ivoire	31,510	78,090	24,830	58,052	45,440	67,233	60,701	64,693	96,135	106,408
Djibouti		551	894	1,065	778	575	743	718	1,056	1,221
Egypt	1,325	7,164	14,726	28,094	30,241	33,262	34,636	46,432	61,180	62,156
Equatorial Guinea		439	843	1,946	4,380	2,996	5,107	10,370	29,015	22,856
Eritrea										
Ethiopia	325	703	941	2,197	2,173	2,312	1,315	3,197	2,213	3,833
Gabon	9,206	5,293	7,070	27,056	44,098	27,471	34,754	75,731	56,103	54,185
Gambia	21	15	38	118	130	178	222	162	250	368
Ghana	1,854	10,848	44,710	106,784	219,250	365,315	559,044	779,055	1,398,040	1,576,190
Guinea			7,407	28,310	46,130	50,064	59,859	66,492	101,186	138,767
Guinea-Bissau			230	3,362	4,392	2,728	2,728	6,256	2,397	1,667
Iran	556,300	2,909,400	6,779,500	22,519,400	36,562,700	40,385,100	47,189,600	51,535,700	58,558,600	72,743,000
Iraq										
Israel	45	11,107	15,911	12,425	48,103	54,578	68,029	67,882	65,788	52,630
Jordan	117	162	567	1,800	2,164	2,016	2,389	2,518	2,383	2,827
Kenya	1,204	2,272	5,353	35,316	39,736	34,970	36,081	31,763	37,062	34,165
Kuwait	222	376		158	79	98	141	119	120	144
Lebanon	2,168	8,848	178,002	3,541,480	6,224,600	6,513,380	6,826,700	7,330,800	10,655,900	11,959,800
Lesotho	33	78	136	166	245	491	574	507	127	159
Liberia	30	71		202	240	769	815	1,175	1,403	1,532
Libya	876	852	1,073	2,337	2,706	2,776	2,428	2,357	2,346	2,459
Madagascar	7,270	12,284	80,906	400,234	721,529	678,721	887,120	823,385	1,225,250	1,204,930
Malawi	18	96	222	1,312	1,804	2,176	2,762	1,985	3,483	3,545
Mali	516	12,780	54,032	17,146	32,108	16,531	47,652	70,738	59,189	99,747
Mauritania	719	1,226	2,291	12,486	3,083	2,390	2,984	2,887	3,105	3,884
Mauritius	388	649	1,955	5,232	3,697	3,900	4,365	5,030	5,513	6,523
Morocco	389	695	8,086	9,018	11,936	13,380	17,100	18,980	27,466	27,535
Mozambique		13,621	102,532	838,600	1,389,880	1,309,960	1,013,080	1,545,230	3,306,840	3,773,600
Namibia			81	175	276	266	510	369	412	426
Niger	3,827	24,909	44,819	8,311	8,126	7,665	8,804	10,529	15,238	22,072
Nigeria	1,552	824	4,777	60,281	64,903	65,895	120,585	170,099	318,986	321,495
Oman	50	86	88	68	116	132	99	130	136	164
Qatar	335	192	581	739	919	1,064	1,169	1,368	1,678	2,068
Réunion										
Rwanda	999	1,391	1,040	8,590	16,035	11,835	15,845	10,823	2,872	
Sao Tomé e Príncipe				5,488	30,646	30,486	26,620	35,474	62,633	75,299
Saudi Arabia	8,190	12,560	11,636	11,178	12,555	12,573	16,545	18,883	19,147	43,863
Senegal	10,143	22,364	62,336	31,059	32,380	27,148	35,743	55,870	93,425	153,792
Seychelles	27	31	59	536	731	262	264	264	286	416
Sierra Leone	121	418	3,963	4,701	26,240	8,088	23,229	20,543	17,047	21,696
Somalia										
South Africa	2,582	3,171	5,407	10,356	13,514	14,726	17,969	19,761	23,757	26,304
Sudan	20	201	832	8,014	28,072	30,624	37,909	57,149	57,411	67,682
Swaziland	45	93	133	232	194	151	177	145	131	196
Syria	1,622	25,334	17,503	29,366	25,946	21,403	23,716	31,419	42,242	71,788
Tanzania	321	1,618	6,890	66,032	59,710	113,202	123,199	172,096	177,329	195,153
Togo	4,373	77,589	72,629	12,530	17,741	7,886	8,960	13,419	12,803	33,713
Tunisia	40	67	118	275	816	356	853	468	749	700
Uganda	46	715	11,989	79,600	104,216	129,412	121,020	188,933	233,787	205,795
United Arab Emirates	2,295	4,394	5,247	12,258	12,923	12,127	16,256	25,893	27,849	25,711
Yemen			20,533	44,055	28,052	35,714	43,631	45,545	50,647	55,710
Zambia	567	1,096	8,323	34,631	87,841	134,732	175,586	322,673	475,500	731,302
Zimbabwe	82	208	472	1,819	4,279	6,045	10,109	9,720	30,625	88,691

Source: International Monetary Fund (IMF), International Financial Statistics
Notes: (a) New series starting 1990, (b) New series starting 1994, (c) New series starting 1988

Consumer Expenditure

| ▫ Consumer Expenditure | | | | | | Table 6.1 |

Consumer Expenditure 1977-2002

● Million units of national currency/as stated

	1977	1980	1985	1990	1995	1996	1997
North America							
Canada				363,980	438,992	457,713	486,746
USA				3,831,501	4,968,988	5,237,499	5,529,283
Latin America							
Anguilla			21	45	107	111	118
Antigua	116	194	390	504	672	784	774
Argentina				57,402	179,131	188,471	205,161
Aruba					842	892	955
Bahamas	521	578	898	2,027	2,077	2,220	2,330
Barbados	742	1,081	1,392	2,189	2,302	2,355	2,760
Belize	154	280	293	490	766	765	822
Bermuda			781	1,140	1,407	1,538	1,620
Bolivia				11,901	24,504	28,280	31,240
Brazil				7	385,703	483,440	542,040
British Virgin Islands						326	357
Cayman Islands			166	369	413	439	465
Chile				5,719,556	16,187,130	18,411,100	20,514,772
Colombia				14,880,448	55,150,267	65,838,528	78,847,940
Costa Rica	17,171	27,140	118,974	321,143	8,411,060	8,616,860	9,060,530
Cuba		6,692	9,683			284,119	328,418
Dominica	77	148	193	291	377	389	364
Dominican Republic	3,589	5,109	12,562	47,290	127,819	147,252	166,323
Ecuador				5,621,876	31,133,554	38,790,849	53,152,490
El Salvador	4,634	6,405	11,640	32,435	72,683	79,719	85,218
French Guiana					354	382	399
Grenada	97	161	264	371	503	551	591
Guadeloupe	598	866					3,123
Guatemala	4,127	6,217	9,296	28,692	72,899	83,072	93,804
Guyana	707	1,010	1,071	9,537	40,897	44,224	47,147
Haiti	4,592	6,835	9,471	11,661	38,167	41,719	49,393
Honduras	2,314	3,612	5,412	8,379	23,819	30,782	39,732
Jamaica	2,030	3,147	8,247	21,408	139,785	162,340	174,685
Martinique	828	933			1,399	1,700	1,776
Mexico				515,605	1,256,545	1,677,399	2,075,459
Netherlands Antilles			1,376		2,801	2,956	3,032
Nicaragua	0	0	0	1,005	12,118	14,984	17,782
Panama	1,243	2,039	3,033	3,029	4,090	4,297	4,699
Paraguay	190,060	399,400	1,056,120	4,996,500	15,089,200	16,853,300	17,704,300
Peru				3,997	86,229	99,290	111,780
Puerto Rico	11,600	19,000	29,900			20,427	21,289
St Kitts	47	92	147	255	355	408	404
St Lucia			83,000		860	921	928
St Vincent and the Grenadines	84	141	176	341	456	488	632
Suriname	609	916	961	1,707	36,578	162,281	212,741
Trinidad and Tobago	3,605	6,865	9,824	11,576	17,020	19,536	22,302
Uruguay	15	70	328	7,607	89,265	117,977	148,387
Venezuela				1,351,453	9,150,162	17,637,115	27,143,682

Source: Euromonitor from national statistics

Consumer Expenditure 1977-2002 (continued)

- Million units of national currency/as stated

	1998	1999	2000	2001	2002	Total US$ million 2002	US$ per capita 2002
North America							
Canada	508,629	537,728	569,798	594,635	623,627	397,386.8	12,807.9
USA	5,856,036	6,246,513	6,683,745	6,987,044	7,314,966	7,314,966.0	26,213.4
Latin America							
Anguilla	120	121	123	130	133	49.7	6,213.6
Antigua	751	711	780	785	801	296.7	4,231.5
Argentina	209,372	203,290	201,006	188,381	196,696	64,211.3	1,702.5
Aruba	995	1,074	1,113	1,155	1,218	680.4	5,821.4
Bahamas	2,099	2,180	2,270	2,304	2,381	2,381.0	7,318.7
Barbados	2,963	3,206	3,545	3,458	3,655	1,827.4	6,660.8
Belize	850	884	1,110	1,156	1,291	645.3	2,519.2
Bermuda	1,722	1,832	1,844	1,924	2,002	2,003.1	29,923.4
Bolivia	35,442	37,197	39,018	40,505	42,150	5,878.6	682.7
Brazil	570,008	640,056	735,681	804,151	881,569	301,821.5	1,746.8
British Virgin Islands	382	423	438	480	520	520.1	23,694.2
Cayman Islands	495	524	536	574	603	740.2	17,966.6
Chile	22,032,081	22,067,452	23,917,162	25,208,758	26,466,835	38,417.0	2,479.2
Colombia	92,092,644	97,291,150	111,922,823	123,102,839	132,848,955	53,049.6	1,322.8
Costa Rica	9,549,710	9,757,120	1,000,800	1,015,490	4,145,570	11,521.3	2,948.0
Cuba	341,333	375,429	381,619	393,730	413,264	38,294.7	3,401.8
Dominica	383	448	447	455	485	179.5	2,528.2
Dominican Republic	187,557	209,068	250,209	277,448	300,799	16,163.5	1,860.4
Ecuador	75,610,129	105,659,158	217,564,040	291,097,544	321,916,198	12,876.6	982.1
El Salvador	89,305	93,686	101,547	105,702	110,857	12,669.4	1,945.2
French Guiana	427	459	511	534	578	543.9	2,659.2
Grenada	697	544	759	780	835	309.3	3,262.7
Guadeloupe	3,240	3,197	3,370	3,667	3,838	3,612.2	7,452.7
Guatemala	105,429	114,554	124,568	136,867	156,809	20,048.1	1,693.1
Guyana	48,571	52,936	57,396	56,216	59,307	311.1	352.9
Haiti	57,148	62,157	72,446	82,353	90,433	3,091.7	376.6
Honduras	46,930	53,240	62,909	71,684	79,837	4,858.2	720.6
Jamaica	181,900	196,641	223,341	245,990	272,163	5,621.4	2,101.4
Martinique	1,918	2,102	2,210	2,331	2,489	2,342.7	5,758.3
Mexico	2,629,332	3,116,390	3,728,916	4,087,115	4,330,901	448,521.0	4,403.9
Netherlands Antilles	2,368	2,309	2,455	2,509	2,561	1,430.7	6,366.1
Nicaragua	20,395	24,878	27,711	30,144	33,378	2,342.1	480.7
Panama	5,283	5,332	5,673	5,968	6,217	6,217.4	2,128.9
Paraguay	20,101,400	19,762,500	22,406,800	25,912,000	27,527,000	4,815.6	843.7
Peru	119,659	123,214	132,817	137,839	144,147	40,991.6	1,545.6
Puerto Rico	22,616	24,178	25,482	27,320	29,210	29,209.9	7,309.9
St Kitts	413	519	671	691	828	306.5	8,140.4
St Lucia	955	985	1,007	1,044	1,079	399.5	2,490.4
St Vincent and the Grenadines	676	593	569	571	542	200.8	1,703.1
Suriname	286,820	507,790	767,482	1,163,188	1,860,372	792.7	1,868.2
Trinidad and Tobago	23,862	25,407	29,283	32,796	36,622	5,860.7	4,443.5
Uruguay	169,442	173,360	179,327	184,905	190,853	8,978.4	2,719.3
Venezuela	35,978,351	41,579,635	50,289,544	58,749,426	69,295,999	59,689.0	2,378.7

Source: *Euromonitor from national statistics*

■ Consumer Expenditure

Consumer Expenditure 1977-2002 (continued)

- Million units of national currency/as stated

	1977	1980	1985	1990	1995	1996	1997
Asia Pacific							
Afghanistan							
American Samoa	145,729	222,690	597,581		208	214	225
Armenia					555,056	664,002	832,638
Azerbaijan					9,080,979	12,067,057	12,377,834
Bangladesh	94,600	180,690	366,340	832,090	1,254,360	1,342,160	1,440,770
Bhutan		749	1,507	2,806	3,428	5,171	7,138
Brunei						11,979	12,808
Cambodia					3,366,531	4,010,145	4,544,910
China				919,786	2,735,368	3,262,070	3,516,921
Fiji	415	575	838	1,443	1,777	1,855	1,910
French Polynesia		59,491	119,842	178,697	46,544	59,357	63,781
Guam	426,802	767,742	1,261,580		681	709	753
Hong Kong, China				343,583	676,768	747,457	807,225
India				3,493,580	6,871,560	7,901,280	9,273,660
Indonesia				117,119,967	286,747,752	341,250,050	395,574,063
Japan				228,294,800	269,271,300	275,240,500	280,621,200
Kazakhstan					769,236	1,018,028	1,241,004
Kiribati		161	249		41	42	43
Kyrgyzstan					12,111	19,212	21,151
Laos	54,610	114,910	158,590		12,111	20,009	21,150
Macau	4,590	6,840	9,471	10,190		20,592	21,291
Malaysia				62,262	109,834	120,595	127,799
Maldives	199	416	701	518	1,457	1,913	2,213
Mongolia	631	1,048	3,616	5,746	364,720	412,897	518,851
Myanmar	26,132	31,774	49,532	134,188	523,876	701,220	987,513
Nauru	9,269	12,911	17,553		167	168	171
Nepal	13,689	19,195	35,977	86,314	166,443	191,469	216,364
New Caledonia		49,575	76,497	143,470			172,743
North Korea		118	152				
Pakistan				621,343	1,452,780	1,666,431	1,932,428
Papua New Guinea	770	1,168	1,469	1,816	2,454	3,375	4,119
Philippines				767,061	1,411,904	1,595,346	1,762,008
Singapore				41,026	53,925	56,668	59,515
Solomon Islands		118	152		795	793	871
South Korea				91,954,075	201,629,715	227,294,917	248,623,225
Sri Lanka	26,698	53,399	126,503	244,288	489,057	569,416	643,839
Taiwan				2,358,684	4,124,738	4,539,920	4,936,084
Tajikistan					52	246	522
Thailand				1,301,608	2,331,001	2,634,326	2,753,444
Tonga		381,700	510,200		101	113	113
Turkmenistan					215,532	2,206,671	3,544,516
Tuvalu	26,700	53,400	126,500		5	5	5
Uzbekistan					254,146	455,158	734,063
Vanuatu			6,079	11,267	12,777	14,299	16,872
Vietnam				73,685,715	168,492,000	202,509,000	225,084,000
Western Samoa		177			242	265	285
Australasia							
Australia				227,797	292,477	307,632	324,792
New Zealand				42,122	51,421	55,431	58,278

Source: *Euromonitor from national statistics*

◻ Consumer Expenditure

Consumer Expenditure 1977-2002 (continued)

- Million units of national currency/as stated

	1998	1999	2000	2001	2002	Total US$ million 2002	US$ per capita 2002
Asia Pacific							
Afghanistan							
American Samoa	236	248	250	263	273	273.3	3,615.1
Armenia	956,322	951,565	985,821	1,107,600	1,215,830	2,120.6	555.9
Azerbaijan	13,386,376	13,497,829	14,201,045	14,921,421	15,814,049	3,253.4	399.2
Bangladesh	1,558,560	1,707,130	1,838,530	1,979,930	2,105,130	36,365.6	276.4
Bhutan	9,322	10,067	11,329	12,695	14,104	290.1	132.0
Brunei	13,561	13,560	13,543	14,099	14,327	8,001.3	23,762.6
Cambodia	5,274,256	5,487,777	6,083,375	6,810,881	7,429,728	1,899.2	165.3
China	3,720,500	3,956,836	4,316,584	4,619,745	4,829,873	583,532.3	451.0
Fiji	2,123	2,105	2,181	2,321	2,399	1,097.1	1,326.2
French Polynesia	68,836	72,957	77,470	84,387	90,561	680.1	2,833.6
Guam	794	838	915	931	985	985.1	5,721.4
Hong Kong, China	748,299	715,458	726,279	730,512	709,159	90,930.4	12,597.9
India	10,223,470	11,726,560	13,171,580	13,858,070	15,347,206	315,719.2	304.6
Indonesia	667,331,065	826,828,342	882,473,533	1,015,630,051	1,170,828,543	125,744.2	581.8
Japan	279,340,700	277,343,100	277,217,600	277,744,600	281,017,500	2,241,183.4	17,641.0
Kazakhstan	1,319,145	1,505,248	1,678,402	1,992,772	2,214,523	14,447.7	897.7
Kiribati	40	42	47	51	56	30.2	350.7
Kyrgyzstan	30,163	37,848	49,952	55,766	50,838	1,083.1	229.8
Laos	30,164	37,848	49,952	55,766	68,692	6.8	1.2
Macau	20,630	21,751	23,855	24,855	26,525	3,177.0	6,534.4
Malaysia	116,736	127,091	147,095	152,902	160,454	42,224.7	1,822.6
Maldives	2,636	2,681	3,097				
Mongolia	598,793	701,284	757,677	839,518	942,704	849.0	313.9
Myanmar	1,419,710	1,906,140	39,245	40,750	32,657	4,968.0	107.4
Nauru	172	189	213	236	263	142.5	10,276.7
Nepal	231,392	264,944	287,947	309,107	326,108	4,187.5	170.1
New Caledonia	173,715	188,754	195,731	212,079	226,917	1,704.1	7,741.8
North Korea							
Pakistan	2,025,309	2,329,813	2,454,383	2,689,234	2,926,721	49,004.3	301.0
Papua New Guinea	4,620	6,123	5,431	5,791	6,331	1,625.3	329.0
Philippines	1,980,088	2,161,645	2,335,535	2,575,150	2,838,416	55,004.2	693.3
Singapore	56,363	60,065	67,627	66,749	67,407	37,645.0	11,268.2
Solomon Islands	477	508	883	933	1,204	178.5	387.2
South Korea	241,858,261	268,229,646	293,678,318	319,224,520	348,455,122	278,521.2	5,782.7
Sri Lanka	723,506	790,379	906,186	1,023,990	1,175,240	12,285.3	645.9
Taiwan	5,334,143	5,641,313	5,981,274	6,042,628	6,199,029	179,319.9	7,945.4
Tajikistan	807	1,035	1,373	1,933	2,590	937.0	148.8
Thailand	2,699,679	2,803,121	2,971,311	3,144,704	3,304,401	76,917.9	1,235.6
Tonga	116	121	189	195	237	107.9	1,089.9
Turkmenistan	4,326,900	6,095,134	7,800,125	10,667,385	12,818,629	2,054.3	445.7
Tuvalu	6	6	7	7	7	3.9	307.6
Uzbekistan	1,189,792	1,747,465	2,608,315	3,666,021	5,352,699		
Vanuatu	17,821	18,961	19,790	21,417	22,797	163.8	835.8
Vietnam	255,409,159	274,553,000	289,207,496	310,280,908	341,915,549	22,377.4	271.4
Western Samoa	296	316	454	497	597	176.8	967.7
Australasia							
Australia	344,726	364,470	388,929	414,966	441,055	239,630.9	12,325.4
New Zealand	59,946	62,207	65,410	68,411	71,920	33,262.6	8,524.0

Source: *Euromonitor from national statistics*

▣ Consumer Expenditure

Consumer Expenditure 1977-2002 (continued)

• Million units of national currency/as stated

	1977	1980	1985	1990	1995	1996	1997
Africa and Middle East							
Algeria				344,313	1,154,150	1,387,301	1,497,866
Angola			0	0			
Bahrain	337	370	407	611	1,165	1,229	1,277
Benin	139,127	220,024	374,128	404,106	791,158	913,892	1,017,200
Botswana	223	409	785	2,063	4,259	4,715	5,315
Burkina Faso	161,900	231,300	563,900	617,800	891,100	988,600	1,041,200
Burundi	38,227	70,133	109,478	163,216	228,920	215,243	283,030
Cameroon	545,300	985,300	2,466,300	2,298,200	3,018,900	3,354,800	3,537,200
Cape Verde	2,955	5,386	11,471		21,330	23,074	25,008
Central African Republic	162,000	231,300	411,900	317,000	292,608	298,367	332,311
Chad	38,227	70,133	109,478		273,839	308,038	369,164
Comoros					75,902	78,104	80,499
Congo Dem Rep	0	0		0	324		
Congo-Brazzaville	123,200	147,900	403,583	403,200	510,500	524,100	611,100
Côte d'Ivoire	811,900	1,349,800	1,836,400	1,761,800	3,367,000	3,592,600	3,898,800
Djibouti		38,600			58,665	65,372	66,519
Egypt				71,661	157,800	184,774	208,043
Equatorial Guinea			30,566	23,593	52,433	78,305	168,117
Eritrea							
Ethiopia	5,461	6,881	10,661	12,258	27,942	31,291	32,831
Gabon	162,100	236,600	501,200	617,000	1,119,300	1,169,100	1,348,200
Gambia					2,023	2,297	2,694
Ghana	8,638	35,953	284,621	1,736,080	5,909,900	8,629,000	11,267,000
Guinea		1,296			2,689,397	3,322,136	3,647,251
Guinea-Bissau				64,190	117,485	132,206	141,323
Iran	2,146,200	3,488,100	9,509,000	21,478,000	95,702,000	117,271,000	148,833,000
Iraq	3,670	3,602	8,099	11,761			
Israel				64,077	159,818	183,231	202,739
Jordan				2,092	3,168	3,663	3,876
Kenya	20,680	32,178	58,435	121,655	322,622	360,177	450,664
Kuwait				2,631	2,611	3,382	3,412
Lebanon	363,600	504,100	925,500		15,222,895	16,686,498	17,660,181
Lesotho	264	387	838	2,211	4,075	4,835	5,359
Liberia	363	430	707		1,390	1,432	1,653
Libya	1,482	2,795	3,224	3,964	6,276	6,809	8,368
Madagascar	343,100	526,100	1,703,100	3,965,100	12,120,800	14,462,900	16,294,700
Malawi	483	631	1,350	3,822	18,381	34,396	36,874
Mali	149,900	246,500	522,200	536,100	928,300	1,055,400	1,001,000
Mauritania	14,213	22,890			79,984	99,913	111,297
Mauritius	3,593	6,562	11,118	25,370	44,631	49,325	54,865
Morocco				148,198	211,173	240,991	230,001
Mozambique		64,000	83,000	947,000	20,473,400	30,509,800	36,658,900
Namibia			1,328	3,351	7,189	8,653	10,160
Niger	206,600	381,700	510,222	515,200	648,800	684,500	724,200
Nigeria				157,276	1,619,286	2,445,773	2,502,770
Oman	246	577	1,457	1,861	2,600	2,799	2,901
Qatar		4,509	5,626	7,456	9,497	8,996	9,170
Réunion			2,083	3,314	2,809	3,214	
Rwanda	51,200	90,000	139,800	178,630	338,560	408,600	535,990
Sao Tomé e Príncipe		26,946	40,360		31,101	48,915	117,171
Saudi Arabia				154,265	191,809	227,713	231,400
Senegal	381,400	534,200	998,100	1,185,100	1,763,900	1,878,600	1,951,900
Seychelles	199	416	701	1,125	1,179	1,191	1,466
Sierra Leone	631	1,048	4,002	82,614	566,824	709,799	734,139
Somalia		30,922	66,167			1,636,052	1,660,594
South Africa				176,754	343,037	384,624	431,403
Sudan	2,380	4,505	12,258	93,450		842,755	1,469,601
Swaziland	147	287	636	1,357	2,314	3,073	3,229
Syria	18,078	33,858	54,650	184,389	378,143	489,728	515,411
Tanzania	17,979	32,486	84,040	687,706	2,532,840	3,130,070	3,968,070
Togo	106,127	151,600	235,400	350,100	577,200	647,700	761,500
Tunisia				6,583	10,405	11,316	12,193
Uganda	456		23,215	1,465,720	4,997,980	5,434,500	6,259,303
United Arab Emirates				46,857	69,478	74,663	86,535
Yemen				88,998	413,081	463,969	574,584
Zambia	1,023	1,692	4,295	71,616	1,775,900	2,033,200	3,006,000
Zimbabwe	1,344	2,219	5,619	13,565	40,351	50,438	66,112

Source: Euromonitor from national statistics

Consumer Expenditure

Consumer Expenditure 1977-2002 (continued)

- Million units of national currency/as stated

Africa and Middle East	1998	1999	2000	2001	2002	Total US$ million 2002	US$ per capita 2002
Algeria	1,632,295	1,806,998	1,857,034	2,021,275	2,197,790	27,582.0	900.7
Angola							
Bahrain	1,328	1,378	1,412	1,463	1,338	3,558.4	5,555.3
Benin	1,099,350	1,155,220	1,259,160	1,344,184	1,569,600	2,252.0	338.3
Botswana	6,136	6,937	7,825	9,477	9,308	1,470.9	858.7
Burkina Faso	1,110,700	1,162,900	1,206,600	1,281,200	1,294,600	1,857.4	141.2
Burundi	362,396	386,157	474,498	473,594	505,355	543.0	76.5
Cameroon	3,757,897	4,317,421	4,498,423	4,669,233	5,029,242	7,215.7	435.1
Cape Verde	26,436	30,271	35,341	37,051	41,590	355.0	771.7
Central African Republic	358,540	384,056	428,711	454,084	492,887	707.2	185.4
Chad	426,158	387,708	432,802	544,113	597,683	857.5	104.1
Comoros	80,700	88,213	95,142	104,134	113,620	217.4	284.3
Congo Dem Rep							
Congo-Brazzaville	807,200	597,500	437,300	517,300	781,200	1,120.8	370.1
Côte d'Ivoire	4,297,204	4,515,171	4,620,656	4,717,571	5,275,800	7,569.4	480.1
Djibouti	45,007	46,231	46,253	47,253	48,219	271.3	405.4
Egypt	221,250	238,051	269,464	284,775	310,771	69,065.3	1,072.6
Equatorial Guinea	176,585	361,400	669,621	892,422	1,559,582	2,237.6	4,566.1
Eritrea							
Ethiopia	35,472	39,671	43,448	42,794	45,760	5,341.0	79.5
Gabon	1,408,600	1,419,966	1,833,197	1,757,185	1,911,834	2,743.0	2,070.2
Gambia	2,166	2,256	2,571	3,032	3,407	171.0	119.7
Ghana	13,508,290	15,535,849	21,041,156	28,973,660	37,493,645	4,726.5	215.8
Guinea	2,635,256	2,759,081	3,179,194	3,355,991	3,643,428	1,844.0	240.7
Guinea-Bissau	94,254	107,565	130,995	142,392	124,200	178.2	136.8
Iran	190,745,000	241,647,000	263,936,000	302,632,440	354,422,038	51,313.8	741.1
Iraq							
Israel	222,073	243,332	261,752	265,515	277,700	58,613.5	9,126.9
Jordan	4,379	4,439	5,162	5,466	5,515	7,778.8	1,452.6
Kenya	511,235	536,389	553,305	575,961	693,171	8,802.3	268.6
Kuwait	3,682	3,901	4,064	4,481	5,056	16,635.1	7,099.5
Lebanon	19,622,171	19,946,575	20,556,146	20,612,037	21,024,744	13,946.8	4,026.1
Lesotho	5,544	5,723	6,352	6,442	6,798	644.9	278.7
Liberia	78,804	90,459	105,009				
Libya	8,072	8,514	7,962	7,770	7,699	6,059.3	1,032.1
Madagascar	17,726,000	20,589,600	23,437,600	26,129,122	25,387,000	3,715.9	212.2
Malawi	46,302	69,784	80,064	101,504	132,994	1,734.3	144.0
Mali	1,138,000	1,203,000	1,384,800	1,448,389	1,550,100	2,224.0	183.8
Mauritania	113,422	133,590	150,434	157,937	177,041	651.5	223.5
Mauritius	62,436	68,711	73,938	80,942	88,025	2,937.9	2,480.0
Morocco	247,377	240,914	254,195	273,954	284,902	25,851.8	885.1
Mozambique	38,864,900	41,117,000	46,023,624	51,469,566	47,973,500	2,026.1	94.9
Namibia	11,185	12,235	13,636	15,635	17,515	1,661.6	907.5
Niger	750,900	717,877	765,051	801,400	1,020,600	1,464.3	124.0
Nigeria	2,837,057	2,062,174	2,533,550	3,562,997	4,777,061	39,618.0	318.2
Oman	3,120	3,031	3,012	3,087	3,087	8,028.8	2,853.8
Qatar	10,409	11,074	13,965	14,595	16,435	4,515.1	7,111.1
Réunion							
Rwanda	577,660	572,280	601,240	625,953	645,675	1,355.5	140.7
Sao Tomé e Príncipe	112,389	133,976	154,615	182,291	214,345	23.6	151.0
Saudi Arabia	247,834	248,459	254,342	252,003	261,503	69,827.2	3,057.2
Senegal	2,060,000	2,316,468	2,406,391	2,504,784	2,756,300	3,954.6	384.3
Seychelles	1,604	1,775	1,924	2,000	2,161	394.4	5,048.7
Sierra Leone	887,613	1,040,870	1,142,680	1,221,920	1,364,373	650.0	122.1
Somalia							
South Africa	466,552	505,698	558,425	608,609	682,374	64,737.1	1,458.2
Sudan	1,960,820	2,265,010	2,516,147	2,660,937	2,958,871	11,237.4	351.0
Swaziland	3,732	5,031	5,605	6,254	7,485	710.1	644.1
Syria	542,374	575,866	579,627	631,865	667,780	59,490.4	3,408.6
Tanzania	4,909,250	5,667,440	6,069,580	6,435,845	7,058,975	7,303.0	204.0
Togo	726,400	752,200	820,000	851,290	895,200	1,284.4	256.0
Tunisia	13,314	14,474	15,720	17,013	18,181	12,788.1	1,319.9
Uganda	6,470,102	7,053,392	7,974,033	8,380,059	8,460,420	4,706.6	195.6
United Arab Emirates	90,985	87,570	85,425	88,410	91,403	24,888.5	7,615.1
Yemen	556,931	750,546	953,623	944,990	1,137,005	6,474.1	318.2
Zambia	3,675,597	4,665,992	6,441,407	8,747,048	11,707,952	2,661.8	264.8
Zimbabwe	92,704	135,783	200,042	349,222	546,910	9,937.3	807.5

Source: *Euromonitor from national statistics*

Table 6.2

Consumer Expenditure by Object 2002

- US$ million

	Food and Non-alcoholic Beverages	Alcoholic Beverages and Tobacco	Clothing and Footwear	Housing	Household Goods and Services	Health Goods and Medical Services
Algeria	10,109.1	824.8	1,405.9	5,234.2	1,452.1	1,221.7
Argentina	15,701.6	1,628.7	4,614.7	9,877.4	4,369.5	5,441.6
Australia	25,315.7	10,352.8	9,353.7	48,698.8	13,473.1	12,481.5
Azerbaijan	1,723.7	91.1	140.1	324.9	124.0	139.0
Bolivia	1,802.4	152.5	289.6	714.6	295.8	173.2
Brazil	37,174.6	4,572.6	20,299.6	61,680.2	25,600.7	17,540.0
Canada	39,376.3	14,957.4	21,217.5	92,263.5	26,287.8	17,420.9
Chile	11,874.2	944.2	2,950.8	4,062.6	946.7	4,532.7
China	172,237.5	14,013.7	46,608.5	55,506.0	37,884.6	30,795.7
Colombia	14,701.3	2,468.8	2,875.6	8,727.3	3,211.5	2,374.2
Ecuador	3,787.6	780.6	1,602.1	1,487.5	615.3	356.3
Egypt	27,522.1	623.2	2,045.6	8,894.3	2,243.9	1,651.5
Hong Kong, China	11,235.9	571.2	12,361.6	18,091.0	10,270.7	3,901.8
India	138,078.7	12,022.9	14,121.8	33,002.7	9,271.5	23,824.6
Indonesia	68,623.2	6,547.4	7,035.0	15,954.0	5,762.4	2,386.8
Israel	11,490.8	1,020.2	2,054.2	17,048.3	4,012.6	572.5
Japan	322,934.4	70,595.3	113,474.2	589,147.3	95,765.1	88,056.3
Jordan	3,223.6	359.5	439.9	1,588.0	355.0	202.4
Kazakhstan	6,383.4	652.4	605.4	1,438.4	1,154.6	584.6
Kuwait	4,318.2	285.6	1,748.4	2,821.5	1,605.4	217.3
Malaysia	9,427.2	1,101.2	1,471.2	9,172.3	2,170.0	952.8
Mexico	105,673.0	10,500.0	15,847.8	58,664.4	37,714.7	19,207.0
Morocco	8,581.0	580.5	2,069.9	4,394.1	1,518.2	1,501.6
New Zealand	4,286.4	1,534.1	1,573.9	7,025.7	2,660.7	1,091.0
Nigeria	22,545.8	1,184.7	2,124.5	3,372.0	2,007.4	1,397.5
Pakistan	26,262.4	1,520.0	3,547.5	5,233.8	1,495.4	2,381.4
Peru	12,530.7	1,032.9	2,712.7	2,974.8	3,215.6	2,154.3
Philippines	20,872.3	932.7	1,420.2	11,956.9	2,702.2	897.2
Saudi Arabia	16,523.9	882.8	6,973.0	12,150.1	5,103.9	2,008.0
Singapore	4,516.8	668.0	1,468.0	5,756.8	2,682.5	2,287.3
South Africa	12,469.8	5,597.8	3,165.5	7,481.8	5,986.1	5,164.6
South Korea	38,889.4	6,161.6	11,379.9	47,941.9	12,069.7	21,349.9
Taiwan	40,695.3	3,497.4	6,986.6	31,366.4	5,257.1	16,709.4
Thailand	21,846.9	4,915.6	9,164.1	7,502.0	7,015.8	5,904.4
Tunisia	4,053.5	414.4	1,609.2	2,546.0	594.4	1,148.6
Turkmenistan	1,074.9	52.9	96.9	227.7	67.0	81.2
United Arab Emirates	2,747.4	187.9	2,751.3	3,550.4	1,823.6	812.3
USA	516,399.0	160,520.0	331,720.0	1,267,118.0	361,112.0	1,260,562.0
Venezuela	17,560.5	1,884.3	1,220.1	9,034.3	1,538.1	1,383.2
Vietnam	5,380.4	1,332.0	1,848.0	1,949.2	1,925.2	1,730.8

Source: Euromonitor from national statistics

Consumer Expenditure by Object 2002 (continued)

● US$ million

	Transport	Communi-cations	Leisure and Recreation	Education	Hotels and Catering	Miscellaneous Goods and Services	Total
Algeria	3,100.9	823.3	935.9	319.8	575.0	1,579.3	27,582.0
Argentina	7,125.1	1,752.7	4,602.6	1,906.1	4,563.1	2,628.2	64,211.3
Australia	27,946.4	6,646.9	29,014.5	5,716.2	18,082.0	32,549.3	239,630.9
Azerbaijan	390.4	40.0	48.5	46.1	51.2	134.4	3,253.4
Bolivia	1,153.8	184.4	128.7	335.5	548.7	99.3	5,878.6
Brazil	29,030.5	10,998.5	41,650.3	16,945.9	13,725.3	22,603.3	301,821.5
Canada	59,943.2	9,107.8	43,069.0	5,465.4	31,138.3	37,139.7	397,386.8
Chile	1,912.5	1,517.0	2,171.2	3,076.9	2,246.8	2,181.3	38,417.0
China	16,328.1	79,776.9	24,735.8	38,056.1	28,555.0	39,034.5	583,532.3
Colombia	5,369.0	1,484.1	2,800.7	3,019.9	2,889.5	3,127.8	53,049.6
Ecuador	2,406.4	169.4	268.5	697.2	500.4	205.3	12,876.6
Egypt	10,377.6	2,240.1	2,794.8	1,470.7	1,589.1	7,612.2	69,065.3
Hong Kong, China	7,966.1	1,695.4	5,139.9	2,354.9	9,947.5	7,394.4	90,930.4
India	40,198.6	2,985.2	4,211.2	7,318.6	4,274.6	26,408.7	315,719.2
Indonesia	3,195.1	1,453.2	2,061.8	5,334.5	5,302.8	2,088.0	125,744.2
Israel	1,713.5	1,005.7	4,132.8	2,536.2	2,043.2	10,983.4	58,613.5
Japan	241,746.4	61,416.6	212,506.8	49,889.9	167,047.9	228,603.2	2,241,183.4
Jordan	637.0	146.0	180.1	305.4	61.8	280.3	7,778.8
Kazakhstan	1,822.8	340.5	390.2	285.3	206.0	584.1	14,447.7
Kuwait	1,765.7	818.8	775.3	209.8	416.9	1,652.4	16,635.1
Malaysia	6,666.1	1,267.9	1,755.7	810.1	5,489.5	1,940.8	42,224.7
Mexico	81,615.6	8,377.5	21,450.3	14,418.7	36,744.2	38,307.7	448,521.0
Morocco	3,779.3	844.5	624.8	331.7	531.1	1,094.9	25,851.8
New Zealand	4,977.4	891.2	2,349.5	1,859.7	2,737.0	2,275.9	33,262.6
Nigeria	449.7	1,017.7	1,383.0	423.9	663.0	3,048.7	39,618.0
Pakistan	2,896.7	400.2	535.3	2,070.9	459.2	2,201.4	49,004.3
Peru	4,469.6	631.3	1,860.0	3,021.3	3,711.8	2,676.7	40,991.6
Philippines	4,291.3	439.5	252.5	2,047.0	2,706.5	6,486.0	55,004.2
Saudi Arabia	6,391.5	2,271.3	5,245.4	2,055.3	2,496.4	7,725.8	69,827.2
Singapore	6,570.5	957.7	2,721.2	2,681.4	5,532.2	1,802.6	37,645.0
South Africa	11,116.7	1,288.5	2,979.2	1,555.1	1,684.5	6,247.3	64,737.1
South Korea	32,744.2	13,298.2	23,741.6	13,523.6	19,652.3	37,768.8	278,521.2
Taiwan	16,113.4	5,275.4	34,945.6	890.8	3,926.1	13,656.6	179,319.9
Thailand	7,523.9	1,098.6	2,316.0	1,104.8	6,801.9	1,724.0	76,917.9
Tunisia	889.4	286.2	555.6	270.3	168.2	252.2	12,788.1
Turkmenistan	221.6	19.3	28.9	35.1	27.2	121.4	2,054.3
United Arab Emirates	3,120.8	857.7	2,556.3	464.8	4,210.2	1,805.9	24,888.5
USA	824,502.0	153,710.0	663,101.0	185,715.0	458,853.0	1,131,654.0	7,314,966.0
Venezuela	3,030.5	389.9	2,042.4	845.9	7,819.8	12,940.1	59,689.0
Vietnam	2,672.0	370.8	1,133.4	1,656.3	1,376.5	1,002.8	22,377.4

Source: Euromonitor from national statistics

■ Food and Non-alcoholic Beverages

Table 6.3

Consumer Expenditure on Food and Non-alcoholic Beverages 1990-2002

● Million units of national currency/as stated

	1990	1992	1993	1994	1995	1996	1997
Algeria	153,671	262,264	297,244	377,840	476,555	581,032	599,725
Argentina	15,060	40,994	42,725	46,876	46,106	48,910	52,974
Australia	26,916	29,199	29,743	30,708	33,154	34,484	35,567
Azerbaijan				1,682,967	4,995,759	6,687,227	6,860,431
Bolivia	4,115	5,853	6,380	7,035	8,116	9,346	9,999
Brazil	1	73	1,537	37,341	68,219	85,318	89,916
Canada	41,975	43,427	45,036	45,810	47,418	48,731	50,320
Chile	1,807,206	3,150,331	3,706,530	4,307,902	5,226,289	6,021,409	6,713,631
China	411,422	585,079	697,690	935,788	1,202,688	1,384,127	1,398,512
Colombia	5,190,505	8,751,748	10,617,521	13,336,106	16,716,459	19,143,985	22,442,533
Ecuador	1,830,999	4,251,112	6,052,172	7,862,042	9,134,161	11,252,810	15,252,934
Egypt	33,280	46,447	50,886	55,479	64,989	76,449	86,751
Hong Kong, China	50,351	58,983	64,436	74,179	84,402	92,475	96,492
India	1,750,726	2,298,324	2,542,575	2,960,160	3,406,401	3,904,401	4,691,103
Indonesia	63,711,961	79,024,315	99,952,244	119,397,485	145,619,483	171,858,443	201,624,100
Israel	15,638	22,191	25,250	30,384	33,931	39,221	43,418
Japan	38,290,700	41,713,100	42,300,700	43,062,600	43,424,400	43,478,500	43,214,400
Jordan	785	1,064	1,054	1,102	1,184	1,453	1,599
Kazakhstan			10,886	165,522	367,822	490,090	615,756
Kuwait	760	507	744	674	723	955	945
Malaysia	13,483	17,166	18,310	21,191	24,073	26,836	28,068
Mexico	140,241	204,986	224,388	248,962	309,081	437,916	519,685
Morocco	59,790	70,432	69,140	79,056	77,269	88,983	83,087
New Zealand	5,847	6,187	6,309	6,370	6,789	7,108	7,393
Nigeria	90,974	227,467	301,487	412,509	921,395	1,368,468	1,416,421
Pakistan	339,131	496,918	586,347	675,180	804,393	919,548	1,112,831
Peru	1,339	11,245	16,771	22,605	27,707	31,788	34,617
Philippines	293,607	390,343	430,063	482,708	541,604	612,131	676,315
Saudi Arabia	36,355	43,529	45,893	43,734	45,229	53,382	55,243
Singapore	5,462	6,284	6,534	6,700	6,764	7,184	7,469
South Africa	37,847	51,932	56,921	66,506	73,233	82,546	95,764
South Korea	21,736,160	26,628,202	28,509,875	32,727,475	34,952,256	36,661,211	39,081,547
Taiwan	610,005	749,709	817,019	903,746	977,923	1,060,413	1,112,449
Thailand	324,829	400,030	417,092	464,437	537,245	609,390	677,585
Tunisia	2,374	2,882	3,078	3,285	3,540	3,811	4,066
Turkmenistan			774	11,684	114,156	1,157,366	1,923,532
United Arab Emirates	9,965	10,332	9,985	9,529	10,945	10,810	12,162
USA	342,277	355,625	366,660	381,106	393,297	407,954	415,058
Venezuela	558,311	1,078,683	1,351,040	2,071,633	2,956,770	5,904,743	8,670,551
Vietnam	19,158,285	25,100,063	30,826,736	35,767,739	43,807,920	52,652,340	58,521,839

Source: Euromonitor from national statistics/OECD/Eurostat

Consumer Expenditure on Food and Non-alcoholic Beverages 1990-2002 (continued)

● Million units of national currency/as stated

	1998	1999	2000	2001	2002	Total US$ million 2002	US$ per capita 2002
Algeria	633,626	680,079	692,459	754,037	805,511	10,109.1	330.1
Argentina	54,058	50,360	49,208	45,409	48,098	15,701.6	416.3
Australia	37,523	39,381	40,318	43,449	46,595	25,315.7	1,302.1
Azerbaijan	7,270,242	7,270,031	7,622,122	7,999,631	8,378,467	1,723.7	211.5
Bolivia	11,504	11,867	12,664	12,914	12,923	1,802.4	209.3
Brazil	89,472	94,489	102,744	105,759	108,581	37,174.6	215.2
Canada	52,157	53,968	56,298	59,404	61,794	39,376.3	1,269.1
Chile	7,122,298	6,928,937	7,449,326	7,828,361	8,180,571	11,874.2	766.3
China	1,370,286	1,341,824	1,329,842	1,407,480	1,425,603	172,237.5	133.1
Colombia	26,497,897	27,979,229	31,659,456	34,567,583	36,815,617	14,701.3	366.6
Ecuador	21,704,110	31,708,418	64,662,476	85,450,229	94,689,311	3,787.6	288.9
Egypt	94,173	94,818	106,407	111,497	123,841	27,522.1	427.4
Hong Kong, China	89,502	87,274	88,768	90,875	87,628	11,235.9	1,556.7
India	4,911,271	5,749,378	6,371,270	6,283,780	6,712,046	138,078.7	133.2
Indonesia	363,310,620	453,101,932	482,642,698	554,737,406	638,963,765	68,623.2	317.5
Israel	45,910	49,207	50,427	52,817	54,442	11,490.8	1,789.3
Japan	43,771,500	42,748,600	40,701,900	40,908,800	40,492,100	322,934.4	2,541.9
Jordan	1,816	1,868	2,157	2,269	2,286	3,223.6	601.9
Kazakhstan	611,833	699,550	774,231	913,154	978,441	6,383.4	396.6
Kuwait	1,017	1,046	1,075	1,182	1,312	4,318.2	1,842.9
Malaysia	26,508	28,757	33,429	34,349	35,823	9,427.2	406.9
Mexico	641,542	761,160	891,676	971,822	1,020,374	105,673.0	1,037.6
Morocco	87,991	83,182	86,988	92,542	94,568	8,581.0	293.8
New Zealand	7,755	8,211	8,603	8,673	9,268	4,286.4	1,098.4
Nigeria	1,582,274	1,191,537	1,451,032	2,018,126	2,718,526	22,545.8	181.1
Pakistan	1,136,449	1,307,676	1,361,001	1,457,280	1,568,491	26,262.4	161.3
Peru	37,368	38,505	41,199	42,362	44,064	12,530.7	472.5
Philippines	760,427	829,462	896,164	982,155	1,077,085	20,872.3	263.1
Saudi Arabia	59,083	58,863	60,848	59,839	61,882	16,523.9	723.5
Singapore	7,230	7,426	7,685	7,910	8,088	4,516.8	1,352.0
South Africa	105,249	110,926	118,418	125,508	131,440	12,469.8	280.9
South Korea	39,332,167	43,655,559	44,988,293	46,752,293	48,654,200	38,889.4	807.4
Taiwan	1,222,917	1,291,772	1,361,739	1,379,277	1,406,821	40,695.3	1,803.2
Thailand	725,387	777,837	824,989	880,689	938,544	21,846.9	350.9
Tunisia	4,395	4,726	5,096	5,462	5,763	4,053.5	418.4
Turkmenistan	2,269,512	3,254,708	4,150,270	5,648,875	6,707,137	1,074.9	233.2
United Arab Emirates	12,236	11,079	10,634	10,081	10,090	2,747.4	840.6
USA	431,742	457,421	482,459	499,321	516,399	516,399.0	1,850.5
Venezuela	11,971,686	12,929,560	14,631,243	16,938,244	20,386,836	17,560.5	699.8
Vietnam	66,027,618	69,511,015	72,124,943	75,958,732	82,209,138	5,380.4	65.3

Source: *Euromonitor from national statistics/OECD/Eurostat*

Consumer Expenditure on Alcoholic Beverages and Tobacco 1990-2002

- Million units of national currency/as stated

	1990	1992	1993	1994	1995	1996	1997
Algeria	11,730	17,844	21,267	24,897	34,555	40,715	45,723
Argentina	1,690	4,595	4,614	5,073	4,772	4,630	4,926
Australia	9,080	9,830	10,362	10,424	11,306	12,031	12,605
Azerbaijan				75,934	227,628	303,429	309,425
Bolivia	278	389	444	515	636	737	818
Brazil	0	9	195	3,835	7,069	8,959	9,664
Canada	17,551	19,350	18,988	17,421	17,644	17,417	18,641
Chile	203,212	372,729	435,081	496,350	608,074	660,392	730,398
China	43,796	54,033	61,384	73,106	85,397	98,083	105,168
Colombia	700,138	1,286,200	1,699,125	2,184,748	2,802,570	3,170,561	3,904,374
Ecuador	349,928	836,947	1,273,920	1,646,208	1,906,574	2,401,150	3,161,786
Egypt	1,208	1,683	1,786	1,926	2,035	2,130	2,252
Hong Kong, China	5,960	7,232	6,734	7,062	7,786	8,767	8,196
India	111,927	155,065	189,081	174,762	229,089	246,259	254,722
Indonesia	5,516,733	7,282,054	9,763,675	11,132,207	13,126,184	15,010,631	24,715,083
Israel	941	1,601	1,928	2,506	2,638	3,124	3,667
Japan	7,675,900	8,151,000	8,199,800	8,639,700	8,932,400	8,971,500	8,935,100
Jordan	89	122	121	128	133	161	176
Kazakhstan			1,044	21,631	43,048	45,652	54,019
Kuwait	33	22	33	30	32	40	41
Malaysia	1,397	1,817	2,096	2,309	2,689	2,974	3,304
Mexico	16,109	25,575	28,139	32,302	37,784	49,826	57,331
Morocco	3,197	3,555	3,721	3,813	4,271	4,849	5,120
New Zealand	1,855	2,276	2,404	2,538	2,618	2,834	2,895
Nigeria	4,953	18,637	18,602	21,862	49,452	75,407	73,088
Pakistan	15,398	22,452	26,570	30,538	46,190	41,564	47,301
Peru	91	749	1,170	1,660	2,170	2,509	2,830
Philippines	13,656	18,155	20,003	22,452	25,191	28,471	31,457
Saudi Arabia	1,997	2,236	2,403	2,147	2,349	2,862	2,975
Singapore	698	870	891	918	908	976	994
South Africa	17,027	23,638	25,109	27,923	32,471	34,394	38,392
South Korea	3,243,565	3,672,213	3,911,831	4,377,356	4,612,698	5,344,898	5,854,144
Taiwan	78,561	83,622	88,547	96,995	102,346	109,070	122,066
Thailand	80,094	93,217	101,083	114,982	127,556	151,719	158,962
Tunisia	260	346	374	401	489	497	496
Turkmenistan			34	518	6,555	52,933	84,303
United Arab Emirates	583	613	570	569	587	590	691
USA	89,870	96,861	95,085	97,819	100,865	104,310	107,894
Venezuela	62,051	145,067	178,209	265,856	359,844	671,744	922,441
Vietnam	4,126,401	5,406,166	6,639,606	7,703,822	9,435,552	11,340,504	12,604,705

Source: *Euromonitor from national statistics/OECD/Eurostat*

Consumer Expenditure on Alcoholic Beverages and Tobacco 1990-2002 (continued)

● Million units of national currency/as stated

	1998	1999	2000	2001	2002	Total US$ million 2002	US$ per capita 2002
Algeria	50,005	54,932	56,319	60,946	65,721	824.8	26.9
Argentina	4,962	5,123	5,080	4,770	4,989	1,628.7	43.2
Australia	13,397	14,210	15,971	17,777	19,055	10,352.8	532.5
Azerbaijan	423,741	394,666	416,340	433,255	443,041	91.1	11.2
Bolivia	819	908	1,000	1,046	1,093	152.5	17.7
Brazil	9,843	10,664	11,917	12,617	13,356	4,572.6	26.5
Canada	19,782	20,494	21,269	22,580	23,473	14,957.4	482.1
Chile	739,207	621,279	634,600	648,227	650,516	944.2	60.9
China	104,437	100,980	109,020	114,376	115,991	14,013.7	10.8
Colombia	4,260,258	4,599,933	5,317,229	5,740,723	6,182,359	2,468.8	61.6
Ecuador	4,463,559	6,150,047	12,956,473	17,507,193	19,514,775	780.6	59.5
Egypt	2,341	2,276	2,565	2,692	2,804	623.2	9.7
Hong Kong, China	6,827	6,714	5,232	5,002	4,455	571.2	79.1
India	373,064	357,578	529,080	523,500	584,438	12,022.9	11.6
Indonesia	36,615,562	44,483,365	47,067,123	53,696,894	60,964,116	6,547.4	30.3
Israel	3,719	4,097	4,432	4,520	4,833	1,020.2	158.9
Japan	9,155,100	9,155,400	8,839,100	8,852,400	8,851,800	70,595.3	555.7
Jordan	201	204	238	252	255	359.5	67.1
Kazakhstan	60,754	68,550	74,814	88,888	99,997	652.4	40.5
Kuwait	51	58	61	73	87	285.6	121.9
Malaysia	2,879	3,248	3,805	3,948	4,184	1,101.2	47.5
Mexico	66,607	79,552	87,851	97,747	101,388	10,500.0	103.1
Morocco	5,208	5,256	5,575	6,021	6,398	580.5	19.9
New Zealand	2,900	2,950	2,995	3,023	3,317	1,534.1	393.1
Nigeria	84,941	59,656	76,319	107,181	142,849	1,184.7	9.5
Pakistan	59,225	67,814	71,643	82,678	90,780	1,520.0	9.3
Peru	2,918	2,985	3,284	3,451	3,632	1,032.9	38.9
Philippines	35,369	38,580	41,682	44,782	48,129	932.7	11.8
Saudi Arabia	3,320	3,135	3,241	3,229	3,306	882.8	38.6
Singapore	935	977	1,049	1,119	1,196	668.0	200.0
South Africa	40,690	43,780	48,862	54,166	59,005	5,597.8	126.1
South Korea	5,740,147	6,332,327	6,582,778	7,219,976	7,708,674	6,161.6	127.9
Taiwan	121,287	123,634	127,353	122,582	120,903	3,497.4	155.0
Thailand	168,508	176,720	188,818	200,640	211,174	4,915.6	79.0
Tunisia	495	479	522	565	589	414.4	42.8
Turkmenistan	120,292	161,233	207,174	283,260	330,276	52.9	11.5
United Arab Emirates	703	696	651	677	690	187.9	57.5
USA	116,419	131,104	142,475	149,419	160,520	160,520.0	575.2
Venezuela	1,246,732	1,342,086	1,554,519	1,835,577	2,187,540	1,884.3	75.1
Vietnam	14,331,576	15,545,504	16,727,979	18,197,494	20,352,565	1,332.0	16.2

Source: Euromonitor from national statistics/OECD/Eurostat

Consumer Expenditure on Clothing and Footwear 1990-2002

Table 6.5

● Million units of national currency/as stated

	1990	1992	1993	1994	1995	1996	1997
Algeria	21,274	35,854	43,474	47,743	65,396	73,248	84,603
Argentina	4,437	11,622	12,321	13,041	13,013	13,913	14,695
Australia	11,473	12,125	11,934	12,202	12,652	12,796	12,926
Azerbaijan				138,128	405,061	538,541	563,509
Bolivia	781	1,057	1,068	1,214	1,348	1,379	1,481
Brazil	1	35	694	15,719	26,571	29,182	32,131
Canada	23,668	23,723	24,513	25,358	26,149	26,112	26,992
Chile	752,511	1,308,977	1,470,870	1,578,125	1,777,381	1,905,792	2,004,973
China	142,587	152,917	194,635	252,515	321,288	377,384	368,453
Colombia	1,676,828	2,278,903	2,580,568	2,616,277	3,261,335	3,756,952	4,357,963
Ecuador	566,651	1,242,822	1,789,931	2,312,463	4,701,619	5,729,471	7,731,825
Egypt	4,084	4,959	5,530	5,950	6,697	7,128	7,540
Hong Kong, China	69,772	95,616	115,424	126,536	131,484	151,695	159,997
India	204,492	248,457	275,796	334,967	389,437	468,408	493,512
Indonesia	6,399,869	8,611,435	11,673,959	13,071,219	15,533,118	17,667,380	18,156,849
Israel	3,333	4,935	6,322	7,596	8,891	9,189	9,068
Japan	17,541,900	18,434,700	18,289,800	18,137,000	18,880,200	19,195,900	18,589,000
Jordan	156	218	218	229	206	230	233
Kazakhstan			948	15,085	33,186	56,493	59,720
Kuwait	262	176	258	253	275	361	370
Malaysia	2,018	2,493	2,728	3,156	3,661	3,920	4,293
Mexico	32,032	48,699	50,051	51,941	56,211	71,442	86,290
Morocco	11,441	14,370	14,514	16,281	16,946	19,687	18,859
New Zealand	2,233	2,202	2,242	2,366	2,511	2,523	2,628
Nigeria	8,388	31,476	33,738	43,287	99,365	154,145	140,156
Pakistan	60,018	81,064	94,835	111,159	135,099	166,914	177,214
Peru	309	2,508	3,455	4,774	5,628	5,869	6,454
Philippines	25,061	32,574	35,354	38,198	42,347	46,739	50,625
Saudi Arabia	15,500	18,559	19,567	18,503	19,151	22,610	22,978
Singapore	2,515	2,561	2,782	2,847	2,887	2,887	2,907
South Africa	11,270	14,431	16,803	18,745	21,232	23,534	25,265
South Korea	5,360,208	7,262,022	8,110,128	9,601,808	11,757,326	12,596,802	12,452,557
Taiwan	116,529	143,420	156,005	170,564	191,387	211,106	228,541
Thailand	145,440	195,528	221,346	258,592	301,744	358,249	377,778
Tunisia	672	904	1,000	1,108	1,238	1,367	1,494
Turkmenistan			62	939	9,425	121,841	170,111
United Arab Emirates	4,975	6,585	6,244	7,071	7,835	8,610	10,231
USA	212,231	229,569	238,481	248,103	255,304	266,147	279,561
Venezuela	121,440	243,197	237,258	311,128	448,043	663,159	943,606
Vietnam	6,339,359	8,327,368	10,125,305	11,807,230	14,324,375	17,037,171	18,821,596

Source: Euromonitor from national statistics

Consumer Expenditure on Clothing and Footwear 1990-2002 (continued)

● Million units of national currency/as stated

	1998	1999	2000	2001	2002	Total US$ million 2002	US$ per capita 2002
Algeria	89,788	94,661	96,222	105,564	112,027	1,405.9	45.9
Argentina	15,209	14,934	14,769	13,837	14,136	4,614.7	122.4
Australia	13,959	14,982	15,281	15,985	17,216	9,353.7	481.1
Azerbaijan	614,527	610,595	637,193	660,135	681,118	140.1	17.2
Bolivia	1,580	1,795	1,915	1,994	2,076	289.6	33.6
Brazil	35,842	43,946	49,215	53,330	59,292	20,299.6	117.5
Canada	28,037	29,310	30,757	32,039	33,297	21,217.5	683.8
Chile	2,062,971	1,984,167	2,042,294	2,042,393	2,032,882	2,950.8	190.4
China	335,763	328,843	333,057	365,555	385,776	46,608.5	36.0
Colombia	4,970,613	4,792,989	6,064,198	6,647,944	7,201,153	2,875.6	71.7
Ecuador	10,860,787	13,585,882	27,712,295	37,438,186	40,053,287	1,602.1	122.2
Egypt	7,813	7,513	8,394	8,880	9,205	2,045.6	31.8
Hong Kong, China	129,329	110,245	104,686	101,828	96,407	12,361.6	1,712.6
India	550,676	500,043	618,960	657,390	686,463	14,121.8	13.6
Indonesia	28,628,503	43,243,122	45,667,176	52,917,955	65,504,229	7,035.0	32.5
Israel	8,728	8,898	10,154	10,191	9,733	2,054.2	319.9
Japan	18,319,900	16,882,900	15,940,000	15,001,800	14,228,300	113,474.2	893.2
Jordan	253	253	291	309	312	439.9	82.1
Kazakhstan	66,298	69,939	71,855	86,186	92,792	605.4	37.6
Kuwait	400	417	430	475	531	1,748.4	746.2
Malaysia	3,883	4,346	5,057	5,295	5,591	1,471.2	63.5
Mexico	104,758	117,734	135,321	148,907	153,026	15,847.8	155.6
Morocco	19,941	19,449	20,282	21,981	22,812	2,069.9	70.9
New Zealand	2,680	2,764	2,993	3,162	3,403	1,573.9	403.3
Nigeria	160,752	107,322	141,215	192,453	256,163	2,124.5	17.1
Pakistan	180,426	204,358	206,880	207,302	211,873	3,547.5	21.8
Peru	7,346	8,078	8,606	8,966	9,539	2,712.7	102.3
Philippines	54,320	59,017	63,045	67,976	73,286	1,420.2	17.9
Saudi Arabia	24,531	24,916	25,219	25,146	26,114	6,973.0	305.3
Singapore	2,387	2,636	3,006	2,642	2,629	1,468.0	439.4
South Africa	26,195	25,991	27,849	29,713	33,367	3,165.5	71.3
South Korea	9,685,689	10,466,829	11,901,519	12,374,920	14,237,223	11,379.9	236.3
Taiwan	233,102	241,448	249,409	242,761	241,525	6,986.6	309.6
Thailand	331,463	338,806	356,927	379,299	393,690	9,164.1	147.2
Tunisia	1,656	1,829	1,965	2,141	2,288	1,609.2	166.1
Turkmenistan	185,686	283,765	360,159	496,977	604,909	96.9	21.0
United Arab Emirates	10,587	10,164	9,693	9,978	10,104	2,751.3	841.8
USA	293,115	309,820	322,960	324,836	331,720	331,720.0	1,188.7
Venezuela	1,014,642	997,364	1,196,845	1,199,749	1,416,436	1,220.1	48.6
Vietnam	21,289,510	22,670,265	23,697,754	25,716,816	28,236,855	1,848.0	22.4

Source: *Euromonitor from national statistics*

Table 6.6

◻ Housing

Consumer Expenditure on Housing 1990-2002

● Million units of national currency/as stated

	1990	1992	1993	1994	1995	1996	1997
Algeria	60,548	98,434	113,214	146,257	219,594	259,571	284,781
Argentina	7,857	21,896	23,065	25,243	25,291	25,693	27,481
Australia	47,021	52,564	54,849	57,407	60,500	63,855	67,759
Azerbaijan				441,089	1,264,007	1,623,924	1,627,467
Bolivia	1,394	2,012	2,416	2,696	3,001	3,416	3,652
Brazil	1	46	1,044	27,230	53,254	65,138	85,043
Canada	88,192	100,201	105,081	110,205	113,672	117,777	121,091
Chile	811,474	1,210,771	1,430,699	1,641,106	1,875,768	2,094,597	2,296,038
China	55,690	64,753	90,651	124,949	167,736	215,051	268,180
Colombia	2,202,544	4,171,537	5,627,069	7,401,985	9,224,330	11,423,852	13,862,803
Ecuador	654,250	1,461,566	2,331,972	3,052,321	3,544,651	4,375,852	5,823,128
Egypt	7,948	12,454	15,207	17,191	19,891	22,336	25,260
Hong Kong, China	49,383	69,781	81,285	99,321	115,432	132,445	147,435
India	438,608	530,224	578,456	625,287	695,094	755,213	825,377
Indonesia	12,884,442	16,684,775	23,089,469	27,443,559	34,243,572	42,247,463	49,604,988
Israel	15,442	23,740	28,286	34,524	39,930	47,566	53,873
Japan	47,031,700	54,250,400	57,536,800	60,357,900	62,547,900	64,837,500	67,134,000
Jordan	367	517	529	574	636	697	743
Kazakhstan			2,625	44,631	93,047	113,687	128,565
Kuwait	453	307	449	412	440	557	568
Malaysia	12,315	15,710	17,018	19,892	23,115	25,463	27,705
Mexico	59,797	98,676	116,937	134,304	180,609	234,565	289,217
Morocco	22,372	28,081	29,215	33,106	34,703	38,699	37,973
New Zealand	9,401	10,491	10,560	10,932	11,624	12,604	13,396
Nigeria	20,940	57,268	63,023	72,117	152,795	231,416	249,359
Pakistan	85,310	113,167	128,641	145,565	168,907	176,131	185,608
Peru	302	2,516	3,919	5,342	6,235	7,066	7,449
Philippines	162,356	215,848	237,813	266,924	299,492	338,491	373,983
Saudi Arabia	26,351	31,550	33,264	31,455	32,557	38,341	38,507
Singapore	4,380	5,628	6,819	6,677	7,159	7,645	8,277
South Africa	22,676	28,745	32,043	35,189	40,490	45,577	50,912
South Korea	11,099,355	17,225,192	21,491,000	26,807,406	31,238,321	36,154,729	42,090,263
Taiwan	434,581	574,278	654,485	745,650	830,723	912,523	969,448
Thailand	109,033	129,778	143,243	155,931	182,614	207,413	227,967
Tunisia	1,123	1,420	1,537	1,665	1,825	2,037	2,252
Turkmenistan			181	2,644	25,693	244,790	355,452
United Arab Emirates	6,551	8,288	8,363	8,801	9,764	10,621	11,926
USA	712,918	777,323	814,918	857,381	898,467	939,426	978,885
Venezuela	207,531	474,781	691,336	1,059,637	1,949,726	3,399,884	4,259,740
Vietnam	6,410,588	8,420,933	10,239,072	11,939,896	14,485,323	17,228,600	19,033,075

Source: Euromonitor from national statistics

Consumer Expenditure on Housing 1990-2002 (continued)

● Million units of national currency/as stated

	1998	1999	2000	2001	2002	Total US$ million 2002	US$ per capita 2002
Algeria	310,773	344,781	357,711	384,441	417,069	5,234.2	170.9
Argentina	28,991	28,899	28,733	27,370	30,257	9,877.4	261.9
Australia	71,845	75,820	80,870	85,640	89,633	48,698.8	2,504.8
Azerbaijan	1,678,543	1,402,876	1,485,480	1,562,974	1,579,390	324.9	39.9
Bolivia	4,285	4,463	4,857	5,035	5,124	714.6	83.0
Brazil	95,386	112,989	137,311	157,543	180,157	61,680.2	357.0
Canada	123,919	128,436	134,464	139,795	144,791	92,263.5	2,973.7
Chile	2,441,869	2,438,237	2,605,317	2,705,842	2,798,886	4,062.6	262.2
China	303,098	331,243	355,269	398,707	459,421	55,506.0	42.9
Colombia	16,199,583	17,297,056	18,997,814	20,607,112	21,855,263	8,727.3	217.6
Ecuador	8,697,054	12,046,822	24,985,714	33,585,068	37,187,198	1,487.5	113.4
Egypt	27,799	30,283	34,578	36,828	40,022	8,894.3	138.1
Hong Kong, China	158,656	151,620	145,752	149,263	141,090	18,091.0	2,506.4
India	942,704	1,053,393	1,244,390	1,423,850	1,604,271	33,002.7	31.8
Indonesia	83,543,404	104,263,054	112,034,560	128,736,839	148,550,339	15,954.0	73.8
Israel	59,098	63,766	67,552	70,973	80,772	17,048.3	2,654.6
Japan	68,305,500	69,468,600	70,502,500	71,839,900	73,872,000	589,147.3	4,637.4
Jordan	870	918	1,041	1,110	1,126	1,588.0	296.5
Kazakhstan	132,461	149,522	170,203	203,229	220,472	1,438.4	89.4
Kuwait	621	649	681	760	857	2,821.5	1,204.1
Malaysia	24,818	26,791	31,675	33,119	34,855	9,172.3	395.9
Mexico	366,966	417,177	491,934	544,216	566,461	58,664.4	576.0
Morocco	39,594	39,749	42,245	45,954	48,426	4,394.1	150.4
New Zealand	14,059	14,463	14,651	14,988	15,191	7,025.7	1,800.4
Nigeria	287,791	210,319	235,342	316,118	406,594	3,372.0	27.1
Pakistan	193,262	221,189	234,027	281,946	312,584	5,233.8	32.2
Peru	8,397	8,755	9,484	9,926	10,461	2,974.8	112.2
Philippines	420,494	458,669	495,553	553,905	617,019	11,956.9	150.7
Saudi Arabia	41,658	42,291	43,650	43,537	45,502	12,150.1	532.0
Singapore	8,790	9,020	9,691	10,349	10,308	5,756.8	1,723.2
South Africa	56,293	61,764	67,198	73,682	78,863	7,481.8	168.5
South Korea	44,948,094	45,832,245	51,278,305	56,015,005	59,979,605	47,941.9	995.4
Taiwan	1,023,089	1,060,567	1,098,634	1,083,918	1,084,325	31,366.4	1,389.8
Thailand	243,807	263,283	283,625	302,226	322,286	7,502.0	120.5
Tunisia	2,524	2,822	3,090	3,355	3,620	2,546.0	262.8
Turkmenistan	435,414	626,001	806,640	1,110,464	1,420,721	227.7	49.4
United Arab Emirates	12,499	12,371	12,202	12,609	13,039	3,550.4	1,086.3
USA	1,026,133	1,081,528	1,145,628	1,214,187	1,267,118	1,267,118.0	4,540.8
Venezuela	4,571,095	5,756,761	7,394,848	9,055,206	10,488,344	9,034.3	360.0
Vietnam	21,528,718	23,399,729	24,827,192	26,829,317	29,782,245	1,949.2	23.6

Source: *Euromonitor from national statistics*

Consumer Expenditure on Household Goods and Services 1990-2002

● Million units of national currency/as stated

	1990	1992	1993	1994	1995	1996	1997
Algeria	16,149	25,604	32,341	37,893	54,385	63,552	75,133
Argentina	3,757	10,142	10,921	11,467	11,589	12,814	13,779
Australia	14,454	15,447	16,055	16,946	17,628	18,078	18,578
Azerbaijan				95,359	270,256	360,631	364,891
Bolivia	778	1,183	1,033	1,130	1,262	1,364	1,454
Brazil	1	42	890	21,768	40,030	50,402	53,870
Canada	26,713	26,195	26,849	28,220	28,448	28,837	30,781
Chile	84,022	143,432	180,769	228,531	273,772	327,938	386,274
China	63,322	91,393	121,166	162,381	199,086	213,127	224,151
Colombia	764,533	1,453,766	2,020,745	2,585,514	3,256,767	3,769,698	4,491,048
Ecuador	365,233	859,668	997,034	1,279,206	1,491,113	1,745,528	2,317,826
Egypt	1,783	3,490	4,069	4,610	5,115	5,502	6,107
Hong Kong, China	36,810	58,201	63,790	74,270	82,214	83,673	87,096
India	117,923	140,087	147,362	168,541	190,179	235,008	256,529
Indonesia	6,334,736	8,748,045	11,627,764	13,596,736	16,891,682	20,614,328	22,310,377
Israel	4,333	6,478	7,710	9,112	11,326	13,192	14,337
Japan	12,243,800	13,530,200	13,674,200	13,994,600	14,359,100	14,062,100	14,215,300
Jordan	120	162	159	165	164	176	168
Kazakhstan			1,324	21,478	51,102	58,760	83,363
Kuwait	264	177	260	238	249	312	308
Malaysia	2,809	3,561	4,060	5,160	5,642	6,064	6,342
Mexico	50,359	75,330	82,152	91,135	111,105	141,585	179,994
Morocco	6,476	8,314	8,820	9,981	10,790	12,359	12,647
New Zealand	3,649	3,617	3,851	4,304	4,621	4,782	4,774
Nigeria	3,682	10,078	25,611	30,526	70,956	114,670	111,240
Pakistan	8,052	11,342	13,533	16,131	20,461	25,711	29,679
Peru	324	2,933	4,161	5,617	6,666	7,306	8,087
Philippines	37,934	50,432	55,564	62,365	69,975	79,087	87,379
Saudi Arabia	10,991	13,160	13,875	13,120	13,580	16,025	16,077
Singapore	2,913	3,378	3,720	3,985	4,202	4,537	4,785
South Africa	18,310	22,215	24,806	27,818	31,826	35,319	38,811
South Korea	5,498,653	7,561,516	8,680,160	10,240,321	12,126,699	13,134,184	13,520,437
Taiwan	64,573	85,455	97,754	111,319	127,455	146,186	156,967
Thailand	143,891	176,239	194,945	218,886	250,633	269,667	271,309
Tunisia	325	395	422	450	485	524	562
Turkmenistan			41	608	6,326	69,238	109,312
United Arab Emirates	3,629	4,540	4,450	4,540	5,096	5,367	6,041
USA	210,053	210,019	222,262	242,601	251,092	262,970	278,082
Venezuela	40,747	137,257	170,447	263,853	360,902	639,263	948,694
Vietnam	6,410,588	8,420,933	10,239,072	11,939,896	14,485,323	17,228,600	19,033,075

Source: Euromonitor from national statistics

Consumer Expenditure on Household Goods and Services 1990-2002 (continued)

● Million units of national currency/as stated

	1998	1999	2000	2001	2002	Total US$ million 2002	US$ per capita 2002
Algeria	83,430	93,079	96,207	105,572	115,710	1,452.1	47.4
Argentina	13,760	13,371	13,304	12,533	13,385	4,369.5	115.9
Australia	18,882	19,976	21,298	22,608	24,798	13,473.1	693.0
Azerbaijan	405,955	478,895	507,371	536,840	602,543	124.0	15.2
Bolivia	1,803	1,849	2,012	2,092	2,121	295.8	34.4
Brazil	54,408	58,374	64,826	69,261	74,775	25,600.7	148.2
Canada	32,698	34,770	36,965	39,013	41,254	26,287.8	847.3
Chile	436,461	467,582	533,733	590,697	652,216	946.7	61.1
China	215,593	269,617	292,313	300,637	313,570	37,884.6	29.3
Colombia	5,042,842	5,196,614	6,525,351	7,257,250	8,042,273	3,211.5	80.1
Ecuador	3,653,137	4,994,594	10,354,266	13,942,640	15,382,553	615.3	46.9
Egypt	6,722	7,570	8,633	9,189	10,097	2,243.9	34.8
Hong Kong, China	77,038	74,999	84,151	84,740	80,100	10,270.7	1,422.9
India	283,305	319,481	357,030	407,760	450,689	9,271.5	8.9
Indonesia	33,428,371	38,199,469	41,055,669	47,581,317	53,654,991	5,762.4	26.7
Israel	15,622	18,653	20,340	18,949	19,011	4,012.6	624.8
Japan	13,443,500	13,155,500	12,666,700	12,245,000	12,007,800	95,765.1	753.8
Jordan	188	197	231	246	252	355.0	66.3
Kazakhstan	78,909	105,638	124,479	148,838	176,970	1,154.6	71.7
Kuwait	339	361	379	428	488	1,605.4	685.1
Malaysia	5,861	6,348	7,487	7,835	8,246	2,170.0	93.7
Mexico	227,047	264,574	313,317	346,497	364,172	37,714.7	370.3
Morocco	14,189	13,831	14,694	15,936	16,732	1,518.2	52.0
New Zealand	4,972	5,154	5,465	5,710	5,753	2,660.7	681.8
Nigeria	133,685	93,115	125,409	178,825	242,049	2,007.4	16.1
Pakistan	36,009	41,131	63,894	71,348	89,310	1,495.4	9.2
Peru	8,887	9,403	10,200	10,661	11,308	3,215.6	121.2
Philippines	98,246	107,166	115,783	127,170	139,444	2,702.2	34.1
Saudi Arabia	17,071	17,594	18,112	18,076	19,114	5,103.9	223.5
Singapore	4,574	4,838	5,171	4,734	4,803	2,682.5	802.9
South Africa	41,710	44,986	49,097	54,141	63,098	5,986.1	134.8
South Korea	10,845,178	12,352,482	13,415,685	14,115,484	15,100,283	12,069.7	250.6
Taiwan	169,626	174,317	182,073	181,271	181,736	5,257.1	232.9
Thailand	248,698	249,114	269,137	286,522	301,399	7,015.8	112.7
Tunisia	611	660	722	787	845	594.4	61.4
Turkmenistan	147,091	199,922	257,568	355,684	418,062	67.0	14.5
United Arab Emirates	6,415	6,390	6,274	6,470	6,697	1,823.6	557.9
USA	303,917	323,422	341,839	349,099	361,112	361,112.0	1,294.1
Venezuela	1,002,913	1,017,198	1,297,766	1,505,238	1,785,659	1,538.1	61.3
Vietnam	21,528,718	23,199,729	24,609,100	26,587,084	29,416,319	1,925.2	23.4

Source: *Euromonitor from national statistics*

◫ Health Goods and Medical Services

Table 6.8

Consumer Expenditure on Health Goods and Medical Services 1990-2002

● Million units of national currency/as stated

	1990	1992	1993	1994	1995	1996	1997
Algeria	14,095	22,567	27,006	33,030	36,899	41,509	48,801
Argentina	4,069	11,582	12,549	14,329	14,584	15,458	17,463
Australia	9,187	10,854	11,350	12,158	12,573	13,147	13,324
Azerbaijan				74,544	236,154	365,493	413,421
Bolivia	345	490	585	613	712	815	906
Brazil	0	26	549	13,517	25,037	31,756	34,451
Canada	13,036	14,883	15,864	16,239	17,995	18,617	20,024
Chile	306,606	618,953	811,141	991,501	1,221,281	1,480,528	1,745,769
China	13,406	26,966	36,834	53,620	73,825	102,418	127,094
Colombia	612,091	1,094,769	1,486,087	1,932,894	2,113,648	2,679,259	2,850,825
Ecuador	162,149	356,228	564,892	693,777	840,744	1,041,729	1,444,547
Egypt	1,779	2,727	3,108	3,473	4,140	4,445	4,874
Hong Kong, China	13,240	19,217	20,934	25,305	29,034	31,049	31,745
India	131,154	155,249	168,265	187,041	267,911	319,046	358,819
Indonesia	1,915,373	2,540,595	3,357,469	3,992,083	4,981,793	5,977,685	7,229,083
Israel	1,020	1,602	1,972	2,388	2,991	3,435	3,239
Japan	7,274,600	7,400,700	7,467,600	7,893,400	7,876,500	7,904,300	8,699,600
Jordan	37	51	52	55	60	78	92
Kazakhstan			629	11,041	27,665	38,584	39,848
Kuwait	33	22	32	30	33	42	43
Malaysia	830	1,265	1,574	1,888	2,270	2,531	2,795
Mexico	20,809	34,658	39,973	43,741	58,237	73,343	88,729
Morocco	8,986	10,685	10,617	12,170	12,315	13,931	13,207
New Zealand	1,268	1,545	1,640	1,610	1,646	1,657	1,682
Nigeria	3,775	10,712	22,354	25,416	62,540	95,753	96,965
Pakistan	18,660	28,971	39,514	50,242	70,168	81,665	89,702
Peru	216	1,842	2,916	3,824	4,665	5,344	6,047
Philippines	14,415	19,164	21,114	23,699	26,590	30,053	33,204
Saudi Arabia	4,390	5,330	5,617	5,241	5,388	6,202	5,970
Singapore	1,534	1,918	2,027	2,175	2,511	2,668	2,949
South Africa	8,092	12,186	14,678	18,844	23,304	26,513	30,533
South Korea	6,487,402	8,769,899	9,942,492	11,411,926	13,410,767	15,419,975	17,565,429
Taiwan	153,594	206,166	236,686	264,147	315,543	357,291	397,849
Thailand	119,887	144,165	162,629	176,629	198,944	214,621	222,599
Tunisia	509	666	730	800	888	975	1,060
Turkmenistan			44	740	8,251	87,235	131,157
United Arab Emirates	1,223	1,689	1,777	1,902	2,251	2,426	2,692
USA	582,011	698,256	741,099	782,317	830,555	875,775	925,102
Venezuela	24,036	54,059	69,188	104,317	175,794	383,434	701,469
Vietnam	5,840,758	7,672,407	9,328,933	10,878,572	13,197,739	15,697,169	17,341,246

Source: *Euromonitor from national statistics*

Consumer Expenditure on Health Goods and Medical Services 1990-2002 (continued)

● Million units of national currency/as stated

	1998	1999	2000	2001	2002	Total US$ million 2002	US$ per capita 2002
Algeria	59,816	76,336	78,411	85,588	97,348	1,221.7	39.9
Argentina	17,423	17,469	17,290	16,203	16,669	5,441.6	144.3
Australia	13,869	15,306	16,861	20,152	22,973	12,481.5	642.0
Azerbaijan	514,244	566,789	597,331	628,699	675,483	139.0	17.1
Bolivia	1,008	1,076	1,165	1,209	1,242	173.2	20.1
Brazil	35,333	38,903	44,177	47,574	51,231	17,540.0	101.5
Canada	21,613	22,976	24,339	25,893	27,339	17,420.9	561.5
Chile	2,002,128	2,161,535	2,490,313	2,792,918	3,122,773	4,532.7	292.5
China	179,556	167,425	211,736	235,208	254,895	30,795.7	23.8
Colombia	3,549,557	3,851,533	4,630,608	5,319,243	5,945,452	2,374.2	59.2
Ecuador	2,040,947	2,909,732	5,990,717	8,023,383	8,908,386	356.3	27.2
Egypt	5,359	5,720	6,478	6,855	7,431	1,651.5	25.6
Hong Kong, China	30,962	30,846	31,029	30,880	30,430	3,901.8	540.6
India	441,617	628,287	835,170	981,680	1,158,123	23,824.6	23.0
Indonesia	12,318,055	15,544,373	16,618,706	19,158,819	22,224,274	2,386.8	11.0
Israel	4,681	4,521	4,212	3,284	2,712	572.5	89.1
Japan	9,133,400	9,515,600	9,994,600	10,444,800	11,041,200	88,056.3	693.1
Jordan	112	115	134	142	144	202.4	37.8
Kazakhstan	52,534	58,871	65,905	78,381	89,608	584.6	36.3
Kuwait	47	50	52	58	66	217.3	92.7
Malaysia	2,584	2,816	3,306	3,443	3,621	952.8	41.1
Mexico	106,796	128,565	157,025	172,709	185,462	19,207.0	188.6
Morocco	14,124	13,914	14,688	15,877	16,548	1,501.6	51.4
New Zealand	1,717	1,830	1,939	2,119	2,359	1,091.0	279.6
Nigeria	90,702	60,818	81,456	128,210	168,510	1,397.5	11.2
Pakistan	106,081	121,151	125,368	134,644	142,227	2,381.4	14.6
Peru	6,337	6,476	6,992	7,281	7,576	2,154.3	81.2
Philippines	37,334	40,723	43,998	45,188	46,301	897.2	11.3
Saudi Arabia	6,174	6,880	7,049	6,993	7,520	2,008.0	87.9
Singapore	3,137	3,371	3,592	3,865	4,096	2,287.3	684.7
South Africa	32,771	36,969	41,068	46,185	54,439	5,164.6	116.3
South Korea	17,796,491	19,853,883	20,954,850	24,403,272	26,710,687	21,349.9	443.3
Taiwan	439,533	482,333	525,736	546,896	577,637	16,709.4	740.4
Thailand	218,033	220,880	230,027	245,148	253,655	5,904.4	94.8
Tunisia	1,168	1,282	1,395	1,512	1,633	1,148.6	118.6
Turkmenistan	178,010	231,860	298,033	407,847	506,974	81.2	17.6
United Arab Emirates	2,807	2,805	2,795	2,867	2,983	812.3	248.5
USA	978,159	1,032,226	1,100,489	1,195,247	1,260,562	1,260,562.0	4,517.3
Venezuela	1,085,144	1,083,447	1,185,297	1,337,179	1,605,821	1,383.2	55.1
Vietnam	19,615,054	21,140,581	22,306,834	23,972,931	26,446,459	1,730.8	21.0

Source: Euromonitor from national statistics

□ Transport

Table 6.9

Consumer Expenditure on Transport 1990-2002

- Million units of national currency/as stated

	1990	1992	1993	1994	1995	1996	1997
Algeria	18,008	35,286	51,848	69,936	96,287	130,860	142,322
Argentina	6,419	17,387	17,831	19,947	20,030	21,461	23,117
Australia	30,178	31,240	32,158	33,840	36,649	38,272	40,455
Azerbaijan				309,831	908,775	1,160,635	1,188,234
Bolivia	1,827	2,931	3,486	3,870	4,316	5,241	6,051
Brazil	1	41	885	21,872	40,640	51,708	56,453
Canada	53,799	52,708	54,151	57,989	60,529	65,066	73,077
Chile	432,639	578,896	699,899	804,358	902,593	1,013,965	1,105,690
China	9,224	21,795	33,900	45,170	55,675	68,751	78,768
Colombia	1,421,997	2,713,146	3,964,308	5,037,887	6,100,159	6,836,569	8,441,271
Ecuador	857,583	2,129,332	3,364,769	4,382,122	5,102,687	6,714,310	9,657,030
Egypt	7,887	12,914	15,151	18,704	22,401	25,605	30,841
Hong Kong, China	23,181	38,352	41,435	45,908	45,975	48,088	57,801
India	268,729	426,155	508,245	581,280	688,352	801,167	981,576
Indonesia	3,456,889	4,758,316	6,276,228	7,186,712	8,757,453	10,825,814	12,238,662
Israel	1,875	4,455	4,820	5,818	7,130	7,197	6,999
Japan	25,655,400	27,854,400	28,293,800	28,833,700	28,824,600	29,663,800	29,766,900
Jordan	235	316	313	325	324	338	331
Kazakhstan			2,271	35,180	75,205	98,755	134,958
Kuwait	310	212	303	278	304	384	371
Malaysia	11,077	12,631	14,076	15,168	16,439	18,799	20,377
Mexico	69,395	108,827	114,522	135,947	167,610	245,026	323,771
Morocco	20,953	25,527	25,857	29,481	30,234	34,572	33,042
New Zealand	6,949	6,445	6,338	6,675	7,712	8,699	9,340
Nigeria	7,767	12,697	11,558	17,707	27,790	43,836	35,305
Pakistan	36,294	48,897	55,630	64,287	79,528	99,489	113,565
Peru	258	2,748	4,828	6,654	7,795	9,892	12,450
Philippines	51,590	68,587	75,567	84,817	95,166	107,558	118,836
Saudi Arabia	13,393	15,816	16,999	16,979	18,391	22,496	23,310
Singapore	5,178	6,277	7,789	9,455	9,575	9,513	9,571
South Africa	26,782	34,180	41,085	45,843	53,562	60,961	64,502
South Korea	10,592,924	15,665,698	18,247,074	21,200,891	25,459,041	28,685,308	31,471,379
Taiwan	282,669	345,259	380,840	417,187	440,816	456,117	479,048
Thailand	161,060	208,519	255,222	276,399	316,436	336,080	318,915
Tunisia	426	543	589	640	705	770	833
Turkmenistan			145	2,197	22,676	225,549	395,645
United Arab Emirates	5,708	7,187	6,792	7,323	7,914	8,793	10,163
USA	441,877	439,266	473,394	510,454	537,214	569,944	597,764
Venezuela	32,581	74,510	119,143	197,372	326,519	722,025	1,152,167
Vietnam	9,259,738	12,163,570	14,789,771	17,246,516	20,923,244	24,885,756	27,492,219

Source: Euromonitor from national statistics

Consumer Expenditure on Transport 1990-2002 (continued)

● Million units of national currency/as stated

	1998	1999	2000	2001	2002	Total US$ million 2002	US$ per capita 2002
Algeria	169,124	197,745	204,165	223,086	247,088	3,100.9	101.3
Argentina	23,668	22,724	22,545	21,179	21,826	7,125.1	188.9
Australia	42,706	43,807	46,911	48,621	51,437	27,946.4	1,437.4
Azerbaijan	1,314,952	1,510,281	1,595,495	1,683,320	1,897,556	390.4	47.9
Bolivia	6,755	7,196	7,798	8,083	8,273	1,153.8	134.0
Brazil	58,267	63,917	72,579	78,450	84,793	29,030.5	168.0
Canada	74,588	81,447	87,871	89,059	94,070	59,943.2	1,932.0
Chile	1,167,827	1,165,345	1,238,487	1,280,587	1,317,585	1,912.5	123.4
China	80,139	93,301	110,260	120,242	135,147	16,328.1	12.6
Colombia	9,443,708	9,894,813	11,336,952	12,395,005	13,445,174	5,369.0	133.9
Ecuador	13,696,257	19,449,035	40,186,153	53,951,221	60,160,329	2,406.4	183.5
Egypt	33,099	37,522	42,641	45,256	46,696	10,377.6	161.2
Hong Kong, China	57,229	54,573	59,098	61,565	62,127	7,966.1	1,103.7
India	1,122,905	1,277,203	1,476,300	1,659,540	1,954,067	40,198.6	38.8
Indonesia	17,578,058	21,001,440	22,506,953	26,009,490	29,750,443	3,195.1	14.8
Israel	6,970	7,843	9,785	9,267	8,118	1,713.5	266.8
Japan	27,573,600	27,361,900	28,725,200	29,304,000	30,312,100	241,746.4	1,902.9
Jordan	383	367	428	454	452	637.0	118.9
Kazakhstan	150,816	176,902	197,980	236,271	279,393	1,822.8	113.3
Kuwait	374	448	469	475	537	1,765.7	753.6
Malaysia	18,427	19,699	23,221	24,247	25,331	6,666.1	287.7
Mexico	442,529	530,215	663,245	728,901	788,077	81,615.6	801.4
Morocco	35,580	34,796	36,864	39,911	41,650	3,779.3	129.4
New Zealand	8,754	8,964	9,573	10,113	10,762	4,977.4	1,275.5
Nigeria	28,687	21,735	27,557	52,504	54,229	449.7	3.6
Pakistan	123,709	141,887	144,751	158,991	173,004	2,896.7	17.8
Peru	13,352	13,415	14,515	15,111	15,717	4,469.6	168.5
Philippines	133,615	145,745	157,466	186,738	221,446	4,291.3	54.1
Saudi Arabia	25,621	23,245	23,921	23,802	23,936	6,391.5	279.8
Singapore	8,818	10,056	12,265	12,241	11,765	6,570.5	1,966.7
South Africa	66,578	72,895	87,158	98,054	117,178	11,116.7	250.4
South Korea	29,418,158	32,938,146	35,873,636	38,597,739	40,965,941	32,744.2	679.8
Taiwan	497,729	515,942	549,176	553,549	557,036	16,113.4	714.0
Thailand	290,815	292,636	306,095	315,404	323,227	7,523.9	120.9
Tunisia	913	998	1,088	1,182	1,265	889.4	91.8
Turkmenistan	513,472	674,324	865,688	1,191,226	1,383,051	221.6	48.1
United Arab Emirates	10,800	10,789	10,684	11,002	11,461	3,120.8	954.9
USA	620,264	680,209	748,819	775,376	824,502	824,502.0	2,954.6
Venezuela	1,724,912	2,078,135	2,511,347	2,928,631	3,518,221	3,030.5	120.8
Vietnam	31,097,037	32,695,466	34,582,165	37,254,520	40,827,170	2,672.0	32.4

Source: *Euromonitor from national statistics*

Consumer Expenditure on Communications 1990-2002

● Million units of national currency/as stated

	1990	1992	1993	1994	1995	1996	1997
Algeria	3,995	8,804	11,947	15,111	23,368	29,322	33,125
Argentina	1,582	4,089	4,223	4,615	4,507	4,762	5,194
Australia	3,356	4,227	4,811	5,344	5,992	6,758	7,418
Azerbaijan				27,878	79,897	109,328	109,778
Bolivia	82	155	204	274	364	446	775
Brazil	0	7	164	4,345	8,615	11,650	14,222
Canada	6,483	6,971	7,183	7,387	8,068	8,880	9,649
Chile	108,344	268,773	338,362	439,068	496,212	588,588	684,405
China	35,145	58,738	90,311	130,284	188,489	257,159	317,959
Colombia	123,831	281,504	367,010	514,716	894,428	1,211,698	1,672,098
Ecuador	40,839	85,906	163,097	233,640	274,141	355,543	578,059
Egypt	1,491	2,912	3,273	3,795	4,590	5,368	5,654
Hong Kong, China	4,051	6,178	6,587	7,389	8,166	9,025	10,047
India	21,200	29,484	32,259	40,752	50,305	60,625	72,800
Indonesia	1,067,171	1,490,275	1,940,547	2,384,344	2,911,133	3,522,744	4,213,748
Israel	1,162	1,883	2,409	2,891	2,341	2,758	3,510
Japan	2,880,300	3,251,300	3,768,700	4,013,200	4,429,100	5,262,000	6,437,100
Jordan	25	34	34	35	35	49	54
Kazakhstan			433	7,974	8,216	14,210	15,865
Kuwait	66	42	69	62	75	92	102
Malaysia	1,365	1,640	1,786	2,165	2,456	2,866	3,281
Mexico	5,736	11,968	14,313	17,163	20,016	25,936	31,726
Morocco	3,793	4,739	4,914	5,669	5,863	6,778	6,556
New Zealand	976	1,067	1,118	1,142	1,226	1,402	1,461
Nigeria	813	3,831	6,335	9,238	24,398	42,359	44,362
Pakistan	1,840	2,998	3,661	4,122	5,397	6,363	7,575
Peru	12	145	282	472	658	843	1,596
Philippines	3,811	5,230	5,904	6,921	7,849	9,580	10,983
Saudi Arabia	4,509	5,399	5,692	5,383	5,571	6,569	6,678
Singapore	442	539	764	987	1,033	1,088	1,183
South Africa	3,482	4,614	4,866	5,327	6,156	7,328	8,090
South Korea	1,396,500	2,093,600	2,560,800	3,392,900	4,635,500	5,856,300	7,509,400
Taiwan	35,430	40,183	44,324	45,448	49,615	58,711	63,922
Thailand	11,040	18,091	22,282	26,772	31,678	40,804	46,754
Tunisia	114	150	164	180	200	220	239
Turkmenistan			10	141	1,579	16,352	28,081
United Arab Emirates	1,873	2,070	2,013	2,043	2,425	2,398	3,095
USA	67,173	77,370	81,508	89,952	95,591	105,150	113,232
Venezuela	2,389	7,597	13,974	26,385	40,710	91,312	172,767
Vietnam	854,745	1,122,792	1,365,210	1,591,986	1,931,376	2,297,147	2,537,743

Source: *Euromonitor from national statistics*

Consumer Expenditure on Communications 1990-2002 (continued)

- Million units of national currency/as stated

	1998	1999	2000	2001	2002	Total US$ million 2002	US$ per capita 2002
Algeria	38,836	47,188	51,027	57,154	65,602	823.3	26.9
Argentina	5,301	5,250	5,344	5,151	5,369	1,752.7	46.5
Australia	8,039	8,685	9,986	11,140	12,234	6,646.9	341.9
Azerbaijan	125,653	145,042	160,537	173,780	194,543	40.0	4.9
Bolivia	928	1,027	1,170	1,244	1,322	184.4	21.4
Brazil	16,229	19,504	23,997	27,829	32,125	10,998.5	63.7
Canada	10,529	10,983	12,085	13,274	14,293	9,107.8	293.5
Chile	752,821	791,591	889,006	963,406	1,045,130	1,517.0	97.9
China	408,000	519,041	694,717	679,332	660,310	79,776.9	61.7
Colombia	2,462,517	2,323,525	2,870,616	3,400,719	3,716,570	1,484.1	37.0
Ecuador	819,281	1,227,802	2,657,318	3,658,303	4,235,071	169.4	12.9
Egypt	6,396	7,241	8,626	9,386	10,080	2,240.1	34.8
Hong Kong, China	10,038	11,254	12,047	12,480	13,222	1,695.4	234.9
India	86,035	100,245	114,870	129,310	145,113	2,985.2	2.9
Indonesia	6,773,116	8,516,332	9,562,339	11,337,889	13,531,330	1,453.2	6.7
Israel	3,759	4,237	4,688	4,624	4,765	1,005.7	156.6
Japan	6,847,500	6,860,200	7,089,300	7,398,800	7,700,900	61,416.6	483.4
Jordan	66	73	90	98	104	146.0	27.3
Kazakhstan	19,880	29,040	34,190	41,844	52,192	340.5	21.2
Kuwait	119	147	161	198	249	818.8	349.4
Malaysia	2,957	3,335	4,116	4,405	4,818	1,267.9	54.7
Mexico	38,008	47,730	63,423	71,584	80,893	8,377.5	82.3
Morocco	7,133	7,031	7,801	8,674	9,307	844.5	28.9
New Zealand	1,571	1,550	1,674	1,747	1,927	891.2	228.4
Nigeria	57,442	42,962	55,290	83,243	122,711	1,017.7	8.2
Pakistan	8,876	10,099	15,153	18,700	23,902	400.2	2.5
Peru	1,698	1,714	1,949	2,084	2,220	631.3	23.8
Philippines	13,895	17,184	19,343	20,950	22,679	439.5	5.5
Saudi Arabia	7,245	7,270	7,834	7,987	8,506	2,271.3	99.4
Singapore	1,109	1,355	1,732	1,773	1,715	957.7	286.7
South Africa	8,831	9,900	11,394	12,524	13,582	1,288.5	29.0
South Korea	8,807,400	11,045,000	13,568,700	14,937,700	16,637,300	13,298.2	276.1
Taiwan	89,026	129,989	138,362	149,360	182,367	5,275.4	233.7
Thailand	38,799	41,494	43,454	45,703	47,195	1,098.6	17.6
Tunisia	264	290	331	369	407	286.2	29.5
Turkmenistan	37,442	49,532	66,760	93,970	120,483	19.3	4.2
United Arab Emirates	3,234	2,974	2,747	2,902	3,150	857.7	262.4
USA	121,396	131,130	139,616	145,631	153,710	153,710.0	550.8
Venezuela	209,061	244,822	314,999	371,315	452,656	389.9	15.5
Vietnam	2,870,496	4,039,725	4,476,725	4,948,119	5,665,055	370.8	4.5

Source: *Euromonitor from national statistics*

Table 6.11

□ Leisure and Recreation

Consumer Expenditure on Leisure and Recreation 1990-2002

● Million units of national currency/as stated

	1990	1992	1993	1994	1995	1996	1997
Algeria	7,256	14,828	17,648	21,935	31,737	39,160	45,784
Argentina	4,073	11,736	12,079	13,769	13,654	14,828	16,143
Australia	24,440	27,166	29,361	32,062	35,424	37,909	40,098
Azerbaijan				43,362	125,744	167,497	185,822
Bolivia	503	763	772	822	901	1,008	1,033
Brazil	1	49	1,066	26,635	50,056	64,408	72,110
Canada	34,785	36,757	38,514	42,113	44,456	46,638	49,447
Chile	391,014	739,353	916,268	1,109,000	1,170,699	1,234,151	1,312,234
China	40,440	54,424	63,880	79,142	98,564	122,197	149,080
Colombia	503,075	995,958	1,396,193	1,911,657	2,363,373	3,033,524	3,607,982
Ecuador	236,261	554,169	745,481	931,259	1,064,771	1,291,601	1,719,191
Egypt	2,666	4,236	4,692	5,538	6,319	7,649	8,212
Hong Kong, China	24,547	30,765	39,616	43,657	49,512	56,489	56,336
India	43,773	58,437	67,202	72,106	92,676	109,776	114,773
Indonesia	2,762,297	4,403,125	5,231,933	6,908,166	8,457,253	10,344,388	11,375,619
Israel	3,717	6,369	7,381	9,149	10,772	12,273	14,622
Japan	26,823,200	28,265,300	28,473,500	28,021,000	27,913,900	27,901,100	28,726,500
Jordan	72	96	95	98	98	106	107
Kazakhstan			648	10,121	21,585	33,363	33,679
Kuwait	104	71	104	100	109	134	148
Malaysia	3,181	3,989	4,226	4,824	5,303	5,498	5,484
Mexico	21,902	37,968	40,608	48,917	62,224	73,145	103,456
Morocco	3,639	4,116	4,171	4,565	4,486	5,075	4,900
New Zealand	2,325	2,428	2,538	2,821	3,280	3,552	3,708
Nigeria	1,722	5,633	11,508	17,070	41,093	62,574	64,394
Pakistan	4,204	5,654	6,671	8,398	10,554	12,625	13,656
Peru	238	2,048	2,763	3,635	4,258	4,816	5,160
Philippines	3,793	5,043	5,556	6,237	6,997	7,909	8,738
Saudi Arabia	11,652	13,593	14,451	14,083	14,722	17,703	17,856
Singapore	3,561	4,005	4,783	5,012	4,720	4,989	4,715
South Africa	9,508	13,303	14,718	15,574	16,864	18,546	20,131
South Korea	7,685,553	11,063,415	12,485,759	15,134,584	18,152,134	19,933,930	20,872,092
Taiwan	378,654	495,696	573,469	632,821	705,330	784,044	868,751
Thailand	30,413	40,548	47,743	56,177	69,847	85,957	86,718
Tunisia	341	401	424	448	474	510	545
Turkmenistan			18	287	3,030	32,586	48,433
United Arab Emirates	4,001	5,381	5,513	5,954	6,832	7,595	8,601
USA	307,883	337,026	364,038	393,609	428,282	457,749	487,431
Venezuela	44,949	86,161	102,469	143,483	220,111	525,357	913,861
Vietnam	3,703,895	4,865,429	5,915,908	6,912,797	8,374,536	9,969,757	11,017,370

Source: *Euromonitor from national statistics*

Consumer Expenditure on Leisure and Recreation 1990-2002 (continued)

• Million units of national currency/as stated

	1998	1999	2000	2001	2002	Total US$ million 2002	US$ per capita 2002
Algeria	52,172	60,283	61,922	67,724	74,573	935.9	30.6
Argentina	16,656	15,643	15,239	14,126	14,099	4,602.6	122.0
Australia	42,520	44,729	48,173	50,277	53,403	29,014.5	1,492.4
Azerbaijan	206,831	202,913	214,451	222,708	235,676	48.5	5.9
Bolivia	948	1,003	1,003	953	923	128.7	14.9
Brazil	76,503	86,200	100,107	110,194	121,654	41,650.3	241.1
Canada	52,368	56,225	60,196	63,634	67,589	43,069.0	1,388.1
Chile	1,380,884	1,391,725	1,413,627	1,454,892	1,495,834	2,171.2	140.1
China	156,681	166,149	177,069	179,266	204,738	24,735.8	19.1
Colombia	4,112,792	4,507,177	5,492,645	6,202,558	7,013,609	2,800.7	69.8
Ecuador	1,924,219	2,707,910	5,160,217	6,376,316	6,712,189	268.5	20.5
Egypt	8,663	9,684	10,930	11,530	12,576	2,794.8	43.4
Hong Kong, China	48,820	43,167	45,212	42,529	40,086	5,139.9	712.1
India	135,875	142,637	171,120	187,230	204,710	4,211.2	4.1
Indonesia	16,182,017	17,942,175	17,518,370	18,159,866	19,197,423	2,061.8	9.5
Israel	16,011	18,125	19,690	19,430	19,580	4,132.8	643.5
Japan	28,129,600	27,795,300	27,573,200	26,771,000	26,645,800	212,506.8	1,672.7
Jordan	116	115	129	131	128	180.1	33.6
Kazakhstan	43,399	39,557	43,807	50,970	59,812	390.2	24.2
Kuwait	170	173	184	208	236	775.3	330.9
Malaysia	4,921	5,348	6,189	6,358	6,671	1,755.7	75.8
Mexico	139,697	149,774	183,514	198,255	207,123	21,450.3	210.6
Morocco	5,547	5,767	6,075	6,492	6,886	624.8	21.4
New Zealand	3,944	4,157	4,476	4,964	5,080	2,349.5	602.1
Nigeria	78,013	57,377	76,420	111,826	166,764	1,383.0	11.1
Pakistan	14,242	16,310	19,613	26,150	31,968	535.3	3.3
Peru	5,488	5,620	6,021	6,269	6,541	1,860.0	70.1
Philippines	9,825	10,717	11,578	12,304	13,029	252.5	3.2
Saudi Arabia	19,096	18,966	19,324	19,021	19,644	5,245.4	229.7
Singapore	4,222	4,732	5,253	4,791	4,873	2,721.2	814.5
South Africa	21,816	23,422	25,207	27,405	31,403	2,979.2	67.1
South Korea	18,098,410	20,158,134	23,322,245	26,290,221	29,702,938	23,741.6	492.9
Taiwan	940,410	1,034,617	1,118,477	1,152,150	1,208,057	34,945.6	1,548.4
Thailand	79,132	82,991	89,808	95,441	99,495	2,316.0	37.2
Tunisia	589	634	688	743	790	555.6	57.3
Turkmenistan	57,561	83,741	107,448	149,634	180,421	28.9	6.3
United Arab Emirates	9,389	9,073	8,908	9,151	9,388	2,556.3	782.1
USA	521,125	561,378	601,205	630,741	663,101	663,101.0	2,376.2
Venezuela	1,040,642	1,389,696	1,728,936	1,974,827	2,371,167	2,042.4	81.4
Vietnam	12,465,322	13,428,560	14,179,465	15,246,254	17,317,481	1,133.4	13.7

Source: *Euromonitor from national statistics*

■ Education

Table 6.12

Consumer Expenditure on Education 1990-2002

● Million units of national currency/as stated

	1990	1992	1993	1994	1995	1996	1997
Algeria	1,757	2,915	4,605	5,203	8,543	11,271	14,803
Argentina	1,625	4,715	4,980	5,348	5,120	5,378	7,552
Australia	4,002	4,839	5,266	5,399	5,831	6,414	7,324
Azerbaijan				41,549	116,733	147,165	146,689
Bolivia	470	697	839	883	1,033	1,239	1,431
Brazil	0	17	379	9,594	18,277	23,828	27,266
Canada	1,743	2,164	2,336	2,468	2,744	3,620	4,921
Chile	198,999	387,653	494,410	637,008	804,206	992,958	1,208,354
China	30,703	41,360	61,735	83,051	111,096	145,821	168,071
Colombia	289,746	602,979	846,938	1,222,038	1,480,339	2,468,454	3,722,420
Ecuador	220,544	506,487	810,398	999,484	1,220,091	1,585,708	2,280,906
Egypt	1,192	1,994	2,232	2,665	3,061	3,758	4,184
Hong Kong, China	4,102	5,349	6,335	7,941	9,409	11,170	13,237
India	55,108	78,605	85,977	96,588	108,457	130,495	153,066
Indonesia	3,326,099	4,505,123	6,174,656	7,413,866	9,291,883	11,457,229	13,765,978
Israel	2,135	3,377	4,706	5,775	5,302	6,179	6,675
Japan	5,162,500	5,735,600	5,973,600	6,063,300	6,122,100	6,212,400	6,280,800
Jordan	60	82	81	84	83	113	123
Kazakhstan			393	6,204	13,142	17,827	21,413
Kuwait	34	23	33	31	33	45	44
Malaysia	858	1,170	1,359	1,508	1,656	1,813	1,912
Mexico	11,742	20,505	27,291	32,887	43,345	53,840	66,176
Morocco	1,143	1,666	1,812	2,218	2,424	2,297	2,281
New Zealand	1,713	1,834	1,947	2,198	2,390	2,629	2,996
Nigeria	611	1,610	2,786	3,884	8,078	16,329	15,275
Pakistan	27,279	35,217	39,952	45,398	53,797	64,309	73,470
Peru	286	2,501	3,976	5,219	6,387	7,523	8,711
Philippines	31,864	42,363	46,674	52,387	58,779	66,433	73,399
Saudi Arabia	4,386	5,251	5,534	5,234	5,361	6,293	6,129
Singapore	2,420	2,783	3,317	3,602	3,423	3,756	4,157
South Africa	2,199	2,873	4,186	5,083	6,181	7,078	7,857
South Korea	4,087,261	5,639,785	6,546,158	7,594,056	9,196,170	10,785,071	11,995,334
Taiwan	4,102	5,868	7,143	9,039	11,587	14,542	17,866
Thailand	17,210	21,326	23,801	27,024	32,053	37,506	38,984
Tunisia	118	155	169	185	205	225	244
Turkmenistan			25	374	3,693	38,541	62,727
United Arab Emirates	673	864	878	992	1,153	1,300	1,500
USA	83,669	95,977	101,249	107,176	114,507	122,326	130,518
Venezuela	13,748	33,275	45,845	70,561	118,311	221,833	399,494
Vietnam	5,555,841	7,298,142	8,873,863	10,333,717	12,553,947	14,931,454	16,495,332

Source: *Euromonitor from national statistics*

Consumer Expenditure on Education 1990-2002 (continued)

● Million units of national currency/as stated

	1998	1999	2000	2001	2002	Total US$ million 2002	US$ per capita 2002
Algeria	17,898	19,657	20,958	23,227	25,482	319.8	10.4
Argentina	7,511	7,086	7,160	6,730	5,839	1,906.1	50.5
Australia	8,015	8,544	9,059	9,834	10,521	5,716.2	294.0
Azerbaijan	152,441	178,276	188,365	202,607	224,036	46.1	5.7
Bolivia	1,885	1,920	1,008	1,364	2,406	335.5	39.0
Brazil	29,434	33,706	39,742	44,374	49,496	16,945.9	98.1
Canada	6,129	6,946	7,423	7,900	8,577	5,465.4	176.2
Chile	1,419,757	1,568,898	1,857,823	1,990,940	2,119,778	3,076.9	198.6
China	192,026	220,421	242,081	293,363	314,989	38,056.1	29.4
Colombia	4,728,944	5,504,811	6,005,253	6,857,633	7,562,623	3,019.9	75.3
Ecuador	3,482,024	5,049,809	10,884,334	15,134,664	17,430,177	697.2	53.2
Egypt	4,215	4,893	5,614	5,941	6,618	1,470.7	22.8
Hong Kong, China	14,747	15,801	16,897	17,591	18,366	2,354.9	326.3
India	184,646	224,501	279,590	306,060	355,758	7,318.6	7.1
Indonesia	23,690,253	30,179,234	34,006,386	41,351,287	49,670,526	5,334.5	24.7
Israel	7,790	8,974	9,505	9,398	12,016	2,536.2	394.9
Japan	6,220,600	6,231,700	6,210,900	6,179,800	6,255,600	49,889.9	392.7
Jordan	150	103	189	207	217	305.4	57.0
Kazakhstan	24,769	29,713	33,658	41,295	43,731	285.3	17.7
Kuwait	49	51	52	57	64	209.8	89.5
Malaysia	1,883	2,134	2,629	2,746	3,078	810.1	35.0
Mexico	84,025	99,221	121,746	131,075	139,226	14,418.7	141.6
Morocco	2,763	2,847	3,089	3,402	3,655	331.7	11.4
New Zealand	3,205	3,355	3,566	3,717	4,021	1,859.7	476.6
Nigeria	21,001	16,514	24,708	38,363	51,117	423.9	3.4
Pakistan	82,340	96,142	100,948	113,787	123,680	2,070.9	12.7
Peru	8,840	8,872	9,714	10,145	10,624	3,021.3	113.9
Philippines	82,527	90,019	97,258	101,375	105,630	2,047.0	25.8
Saudi Arabia	6,559	6,939	7,170	7,220	7,697	2,055.3	90.0
Singapore	3,968	4,281	5,059	4,749	4,801	2,681.4	802.6
South Africa	9,073	10,625	12,492	14,140	16,392	1,555.1	35.0
South Korea	12,099,630	12,884,331	13,959,535	15,425,439	16,919,244	13,523.6	280.8
Taiwan	23,877	26,454	27,674	28,492	30,794	890.8	39.5
Thailand	39,878	40,854	43,240	45,769	47,461	1,104.8	17.7
Tunisia	268	294	324	356	384	270.3	27.9
Turkmenistan	79,110	99,860	128,834	174,578	219,260	35.1	7.6
United Arab Emirates	1,590	1,344	1,187	1,636	1,707	464.8	142.2
USA	140,150	152,118	163,989	174,889	185,715	185,715.0	665.5
Venezuela	579,686	615,845	756,953	863,188	982,085	845.9	33.7
Vietnam	18,658,221	20,152,190	21,295,452	22,922,689	25,306,966	1,656.3	20.1

Source: *Euromonitor from national statistics*

◻ Hotels and Catering

Table 6.13

Consumer Expenditure on Hotels and Catering 1990-2002

- Million units of national currency/as stated

	1990	1992	1993	1994	1995	1996	1997
Algeria	4,085	5,817	8,954	9,817	11,478	16,495	21,608
Argentina	4,161	11,468	12,055	13,731	13,643	14,029	15,241
Australia	16,268	17,394	17,744	19,866	21,696	21,932	22,777
Azerbaijan				32,780	97,676	123,442	131,147
Bolivia	1,102	1,607	1,794	1,971	2,271	2,664	2,924
Brazil	0	24	513	12,539	23,034	28,970	30,893
Canada	28,207	29,218	30,282	32,096	33,198	34,237	36,088
Chile	288,180	532,377	668,999	780,965	898,315	1,034,078	1,154,641
China	30,765	43,667	56,414	80,294	113,242	133,956	149,884
Colombia	662,082	1,451,094	2,238,085	3,057,045	3,875,894	4,543,666	4,904,763
Ecuador	231,509	575,290	850,854	1,069,988	1,211,653	1,496,218	2,044,743
Egypt	693	1,190	1,433	1,722	2,260	2,833	3,543
Hong Kong, China	38,531	51,578	58,095	64,665	69,303	74,965	79,289
India	31,751	42,395	48,897	58,784	68,836	89,939	103,693
Indonesia	5,975,505	7,784,264	10,226,774	12,158,743	14,973,366	17,933,055	19,857,818
Israel	3,116	4,773	5,521	6,764	5,821	6,424	6,651
Japan	14,180,500	16,587,800	17,519,600	18,642,300	18,655,600	19,396,100	20,081,500
Jordan	10	14	14	15	15	23	27
Kazakhstan			223	3,689	7,936	14,413	16,204
Kuwait	49	43	64	60	65	85	73
Malaysia	9,784	10,029	11,454	13,956	15,625	16,706	17,542
Mexico	37,964	67,613	78,183	88,766	98,427	126,306	158,026
Morocco	2,412	2,802	3,046	3,588	3,793	4,466	4,407
New Zealand	3,056	2,990	3,074	3,340	3,810	4,077	4,300
Nigeria	1,318	4,282	6,478	8,109	16,120	31,748	28,820
Pakistan	3,374	4,737	5,306	6,353	7,753	11,823	13,078
Peru	370	3,195	4,872	6,539	7,983	9,362	10,468
Philippines	37,934	50,432	55,564	62,365	69,975	79,087	87,379
Saudi Arabia	5,458	6,598	6,956	6,546	6,652	7,830	7,760
Singapore	8,144	8,024	7,967	7,985	8,527	8,835	9,335
South Africa	5,786	7,072	7,552	7,783	9,214	10,331	11,427
South Korea	6,838,419	10,389,513	11,225,101	12,765,998	14,281,318	16,098,235	17,142,026
Taiwan	40,912	56,579	65,503	73,604	85,344	97,595	107,014
Thailand	131,678	156,214	171,037	194,171	224,861	255,219	255,544
Tunisia	101	119	126	133	142	152	162
Turkmenistan			14	225	2,217	28,775	46,339
United Arab Emirates	2,994	4,960	5,750	6,681	8,085	9,469	10,946
USA	256,301	277,932	295,073	309,715	324,416	339,491	358,141
Venezuela	125,664	264,409	396,530	633,321	1,001,762	1,909,806	3,294,748
Vietnam	3,684,285	5,309,628	6,876,733	7,841,389	9,941,028	12,150,541	13,505,040

Source: *Euromonitor from national statistics*

Consumer Expenditure on Hotels and Catering 1990-2002 (continued)

- Million units of national currency/as stated

	1998	1999	2000	2001	2002	Total US$ million 2002	US$ per capita 2002
Algeria	26,197	34,971	35,963	39,210	45,814	575.0	18.8
Argentina	15,204	14,801	14,648	13,726	13,978	4,563.1	121.0
Australia	24,768	27,800	29,671	32,054	33,281	18,082.0	930.0
Azerbaijan	141,987	193,672	204,094	214,797	249,081	51.2	6.3
Bolivia	3,263	3,447	3,731	3,856	3,934	548.7	63.7
Brazil	31,127	33,313	36,743	38,403	40,089	13,725.3	79.4
Canada	38,406	40,949	43,761	46,227	48,866	31,138.3	1,003.6
Chile	1,248,083	1,274,361	1,387,408	1,470,161	1,547,903	2,246.8	145.0
China	164,368	177,317	200,757	225,359	236,348	28,555.0	22.1
Colombia	5,669,687	6,024,333	6,488,044	6,934,820	7,236,031	2,889.5	72.1
Ecuador	2,920,155	4,083,544	8,436,905	11,278,609	12,511,040	500.4	38.2
Egypt	4,249	5,509	6,245	6,612	7,151	1,589.1	24.7
Hong Kong, China	71,900	73,493	76,201	76,471	77,580	9,947.5	1,378.2
India	119,239	140,341	166,760	183,660	207,791	4,274.6	4.1
Indonesia	31,564,759	35,884,350	38,361,779	44,222,157	49,375,775	5,302.8	24.5
Israel	7,278	7,901	8,283	7,845	9,680	2,043.2	318.2
Japan	20,364,900	20,589,900	20,699,700	20,585,700	20,945,800	167,047.9	1,314.9
Jordan	33	34	40	43	44	61.8	11.5
Kazakhstan	17,939	20,673	23,122	27,479	31,578	206.0	12.8
Kuwait	83	91	95	109	127	416.9	177.9
Malaysia	15,849	17,978	19,400	20,173	20,860	5,489.5	236.9
Mexico	201,482	242,140	300,394	329,365	354,801	36,744.2	360.8
Morocco	4,889	4,903	5,171	5,577	5,853	531.1	18.2
New Zealand	4,464	4,589	4,946	5,499	5,918	2,737.0	701.4
Nigeria	28,213	24,169	36,068	56,151	79,942	663.0	5.3
Pakistan	14,562	16,668	19,540	22,491	27,425	459.2	2.8
Peru	10,941	11,146	12,046	12,532	13,052	3,711.8	140.0
Philippines	98,246	107,166	115,783	127,180	139,663	2,706.5	34.1
Saudi Arabia	8,247	8,687	8,918	8,835	9,349	2,496.4	109.3
Singapore	8,540	8,408	9,770	9,643	9,906	5,532.2	1,655.9
South Africa	12,602	13,711	14,569	15,592	17,756	1,684.5	37.9
South Korea	15,679,848	18,983,943	20,436,745	22,629,650	24,586,819	19,652.3	408.0
Taiwan	116,412	123,041	127,283	128,782	135,724	3,926.1	174.0
Thailand	249,428	250,592	264,873	275,678	292,210	6,801.9	109.3
Tunisia	175	189	205	222	239	168.2	17.4
Turkmenistan	59,154	81,904	105,279	144,281	169,888	27.2	5.9
United Arab Emirates	12,061	11,972	12,261	14,134	15,462	4,210.2	1,288.2
USA	378,635	397,292	426,040	441,865	458,853	458,853.0	1,644.3
Venezuela	4,955,673	5,961,420	7,062,401	7,710,651	9,078,372	7,819.8	311.6
Vietnam	15,355,261	16,747,733	17,670,413	18,988,888	21,032,981	1,376.5	16.7

Source: Euromonitor from national statistics

Table 6.14

◻ Miscellaneous Goods and Services

Consumer Expenditure on Miscellaneous Goods and Services 1990-2002

- Million units of national currency/as stated

	1990	1992	1993	1994	1995	1996	1997
Algeria	31,745	50,708	60,246	84,708	95,354	100,565	101,460
Argentina	2,672	6,796	7,472	7,964	6,822	6,595	6,596
Australia	31,422	35,838	36,803	37,092	39,072	41,956	45,961
Azerbaijan				121,595	353,290	479,746	477,021
Bolivia	226	396	445	496	543	625	715
Brazil	0	24	528	13,217	24,902	32,120	36,021
Canada	27,828	31,156	34,815	37,951	38,671	41,781	45,715
Chile	335,350	581,480	693,719	815,154	932,537	1,056,706	1,172,364
China	43,286	58,775	70,506	96,896	118,283	143,997	161,602
Colombia	733,078	1,384,044	1,899,965	2,473,055	3,060,965	3,800,310	4,589,860
Ecuador	105,930	287,930	429,945	562,074	641,350	800,929	1,140,514
Egypt	7,649	11,709	12,223	14,280	16,302	21,569	22,826
Hong Kong, China	23,655	31,263	35,158	39,691	44,051	47,616	59,554
India	318,189	423,487	530,623	602,901	684,823	780,942	967,690
Indonesia	3,768,892	6,163,827	8,754,600	9,667,644	11,960,832	13,790,890	10,481,758
Israel	11,364	16,518	20,145	24,056	28,748	32,675	36,681
Japan	23,534,300	26,055,700	25,970,700	27,969,400	27,305,500	28,355,300	28,541,000
Jordan	136	184	213	221	230	238	222
Kazakhstan			1,072	11,466	27,282	36,194	37,615
Kuwait	263	184	269	256	272	374	400
Malaysia	3,143	4,437	4,725	5,991	6,905	7,125	6,696
Mexico	49,519	75,048	90,512	96,013	111,896	144,469	171,058
Morocco	3,996	5,991	5,591	6,605	8,079	9,295	7,922
New Zealand	2,850	3,065	3,105	3,091	3,194	3,564	3,705
Nigeria	12,333	31,467	48,567	60,042	145,306	209,067	227,384
Pakistan	21,784	29,540	35,491	39,792	50,534	60,291	68,749
Peru	251	2,380	3,774	5,107	6,077	6,973	7,912
Philippines	91,041	121,037	133,353	149,677	167,939	189,808	209,710
Saudi Arabia	19,283	21,227	21,990	21,710	22,858	27,400	27,917
Singapore	3,781	3,569	3,086	2,682	2,216	2,590	3,173
South Africa	13,775	18,978	20,660	23,538	28,504	32,497	39,719
South Korea	7,928,075	11,346,086	13,441,137	16,761,429	21,807,485	26,624,274	29,068,617
Taiwan	159,073	201,684	225,972	303,014	286,669	332,322	412,163
Thailand	27,035	36,598	42,458	49,310	57,389	67,701	70,329
Tunisia	221	229	233	238	214	228	240
Turkmenistan			81	1,154	11,930	131,465	189,424
United Arab Emirates	4,682	5,555	5,467	5,415	6,591	6,684	8,487
USA	525,238	614,429	660,937	696,161	739,398	786,257	857,615
Venezuela	118,005	167,522	384,305	730,305	1,191,671	2,504,554	4,764,143
Vietnam	2,341,232	2,431,271	3,344,163	3,604,669	5,031,637	7,089,961	8,680,760

Source: Euromonitor from national statistics

Consumer Expenditure on Miscellaneous Goods and Services 1990-2002 (continued)

- Million units of national currency/as stated

	1998	1999	2000	2001	2002	Total US$ million 2002	US$ per capita 2002
Algeria	100,631	103,286	105,669	114,726	125,845	1,579.3	51.6
Argentina	6,629	7,630	7,686	7,347	8,051	2,628.2	69.7
Australia	49,203	51,230	54,530	57,429	59,909	32,549.3	1,674.2
Azerbaijan	537,262	543,794	572,265	602,675	653,115	134.4	16.5
Bolivia	663	645	694	716	712	99.3	11.5
Brazil	38,163	44,052	52,323	58,817	66,020	22,603.3	130.8
Canada	48,403	51,224	54,370	55,817	58,284	37,139.7	1,197.0
Chile	1,257,775	1,273,794	1,375,228	1,440,333	1,502,761	2,181.3	140.8
China	210,554	240,674	260,464	300,220	323,087	39,034.5	30.2
Colombia	5,154,246	5,319,137	6,534,657	7,172,249	7,832,831	3,127.8	78.0
Ecuador	1,348,600	1,745,562	3,577,172	4,751,732	5,131,884	205.3	15.7
Egypt	20,420	25,023	28,352	30,108	34,252	7,612.2	118.2
Hong Kong, China	53,251	55,472	57,206	57,288	57,668	7,394.4	1,024.4
India	1,072,132	1,233,472	1,007,040	1,114,310	1,283,737	26,408.7	25.5
Indonesia	13,698,347	14,469,496	15,431,774	17,720,132	19,441,332	2,088.0	9.7
Israel	42,507	47,110	52,683	54,215	52,037	10,983.4	1,710.3
Japan	28,075,600	27,577,500	28,274,500	28,212,600	28,664,100	228,603.2	1,799.4
Jordan	191	191	194	206	199	280.3	52.3
Kazakhstan	59,552	57,293	64,159	76,237	89,536	584.1	36.3
Kuwait	411	409	426	458	502	1,652.4	705.2
Malaysia	6,166	6,291	6,783	6,985	7,375	1,940.8	83.8
Mexico	209,875	278,548	319,470	346,037	369,898	38,307.7	376.1
Morocco	10,418	10,189	10,723	11,587	12,067	1,094.9	37.5
New Zealand	3,925	4,220	4,529	4,696	4,921	2,275.9	583.2
Nigeria	283,557	176,650	202,735	279,997	367,607	3,048.7	24.5
Pakistan	70,128	85,388	91,566	113,917	131,479	2,201.4	13.5
Peru	8,089	8,246	8,808	9,050	9,413	2,676.7	100.9
Philippines	235,791	257,198	277,880	305,427	334,703	6,486.0	81.8
Saudi Arabia	29,229	29,673	29,056	28,318	28,933	7,725.8	338.3
Singapore	2,653	2,967	3,355	2,932	3,228	1,802.6	539.6
South Africa	44,744	50,729	55,113	57,499	65,851	6,247.3	140.7
South Korea	29,407,049	33,726,767	37,396,027	40,462,821	47,252,208	37,768.8	784.2
Taiwan	457,136	437,202	475,357	473,590	472,103	13,656.6	605.1
Thailand	65,731	67,915	70,318	72,186	74,065	1,724.0	27.7
Tunisia	257	273	295	319	358	252.2	26.0
Turkmenistan	244,156	348,284	446,275	610,588	757,447	121.4	26.3
United Arab Emirates	8,664	7,913	7,389	6,903	6,632	1,805.9	552.5
USA	924,981	988,865	1,068,226	1,086,433	1,131,654	1,131,654.0	4,055.3
Venezuela	6,576,165	8,163,302	10,654,388	13,029,621	15,022,862	12,940.1	515.7
Vietnam	10,641,628	12,022,503	12,709,474	13,658,064	15,322,315	1,002.8	12.2

Source: *Euromonitor from national statistics*

Consumer Market Sizes

◘ Fresh Foods

Table 7.1

Per Capita Retail Sales of Meat and Fish 2002

● Kg per capita

	Total Meat	Beef & Veal	Pork	Lamb, Mutton & Goat	Poultry	Fresh Fish	Dried Fish	Shellfish
Argentina	77.86	42.01	2.92	0.75	27.69	2.97	4.44	2.24
Australia	100.79	44.51	5.45	16.11	26.23	4.74	2.04	2.31
Brazil	44.31	20.10	9.28	4.38	8.87	1.71	0.30	0.93
Canada	100.53	32.83	29.09	1.34	36.86	5.38	0.26	2.53
Chile	40.76	19.18	6.20	3.99	9.27	3.62	0.57	0.50
China	24.41	2.09	13.87	1.28	5.52	4.94		0.63
Colombia	53.65	24.44	9.50	3.56	14.14	1.88	0.32	0.38
Egypt	17.11	4.58	0.03	0.78	7.34	13.27	2.00	2.59
Hong Kong, China	93.28	20.65	28.64	2.54	41.45	25.85	0.96	9.93
India	4.78	1.33	0.18	0.72	0.96	0.31	0.60	0.40
Indonesia	5.31	0.93	0.32	0.14	3.85	14.76	2.23	1.27
Israel	32.74	3.58	1.47	0.48	27.20	4.75		
Japan	19.68	4.20	6.68	0.58	4.79	28.62	26.49	4.24
Malaysia	23.85	1.33	9.94	1.73	8.05	20.31	3.79	5.23
Mexico	44.95	20.02	8.28	4.48	8.88	2.53	0.64	0.55
Morocco	6.13	1.46	0.01	0.32	2.32	5.21	0.29	0.77
New Zealand	107.26	39.40	14.93	21.82	28.95	8.49	0.62	0.16
Philippines	15.09	4.04	1.24	1.08	5.56			
Saudi Arabia	38.15	4.84		11.30	20.01	11.08	1.96	1.02
Singapore	32.90	10.36	11.05	1.57	7.42	53.91	11.14	7.20
South Africa	29.62	9.41	5.31	3.92	8.57	2.64	0.12	0.24
South Korea	38.71	9.57	16.17	1.25	10.64	32.12	32.61	12.00
Taiwan	21.88	5.19	7.05	1.69	7.95			
Thailand	23.52	4.68	6.26	0.11	8.43			
USA	88.15	31.99	23.05	0.56	26.62	2.70	0.14	2.07
Venezuela	37.35	21.78	5.24	1.59	5.62	6.01	1.77	1.08
Vietnam	25.85	1.19	18.68	0.49	3.91			

Source: Euromonitor from industry sources/national statistics

◘ Fresh Foods

Table 7.2

Per Capita Retail Sales of Fresh Produce 2002

● Kg per capita/as stated

	Total Vegetables	Potatoes	Fresh Tomatoes	Green Vegetables	Total Fruit	Citrus Fruit	Non-Citrus Fruit	Eggs (units)
Argentina	151.80	62.64	13.19	75.97	158.00	31.75	126.25	140.56
Australia	244.84	65.37	21.55	157.92	110.75	43.36	67.39	118.81
Brazil	135.86	64.20	3.90	67.76	66.84	21.33	45.51	124.60
Canada	144.54	78.45	7.67	58.42	63.75	13.81	49.93	192.07
Chile	89.34	45.82	8.37	35.14				110.63
China	141.68	12.11	8.82	120.76	34.33	5.67	28.66	64.19
Colombia	87.24	37.89	5.52	43.83	146.48	11.92	134.57	97.97
Egypt	37.32	9.23	11.84	16.26	39.25	15.01	24.24	159.85
Hong Kong, China	92.47	15.67	19.17	57.63	90.90	13.55	77.35	138.39
India	77.49	19.63	7.13	50.73	40.16	27.05	13.11	46.34
Indonesia	43.93	10.55	1.58	31.81	33.34	3.32	30.02	37.30
Israel	141.17	24.77	32.91	83.48	95.17	20.96	74.21	137.40
Japan	149.31	61.35	12.96	75.00	39.21	14.65	24.56	258.67
Malaysia	75.38	8.53	15.52	51.33				65.81
Mexico	72.90	36.12	7.71	29.11	27.88	14.05	13.83	79.40
Morocco	51.42	15.93	18.23	17.26	29.68	7.95	21.72	46.45
New Zealand	131.22	52.48	10.70	68.04	71.59	5.97	65.62	258.39
Philippines	39.39	1.70	3.05	34.65	76.07			32.43
Saudi Arabia	119.35	26.05	56.47	36.83	45.12	21.79	23.33	106.53
Singapore	163.77	67.48	23.19	73.10	58.57	23.15	35.42	229.16
South Africa	95.93	26.53	12.36	57.04	45.01	22.07	22.94	37.22
South Korea	87.19	6.39	6.52	74.28	52.91	12.92	39.99	99.36
Taiwan	132.76	40.57	25.33	66.86	99.01	24.20	74.80	62.73
Thailand	65.28	19.01	1.33	44.94	67.14			41.02
USA	93.58	23.95	8.11	61.53	54.23	14.89	39.34	95.65
Venezuela	64.38	37.37	6.74	20.27	61.59	10.67	50.92	105.47
Vietnam	109.82	22.55	12.17	75.10	61.48	6.15	55.33	45.49

Source: Euromonitor from industry sources/national statistics

Per Capita Retail Sales of Dairy Products and Ice Cream 2002

● US$ per capita

	Milk	Cream	Cheese	Yoghurt	Chilled Desserts	Fromage Frais & Quark	Ice Cream
Argentina	12.71	0.29	18.54	5.02	1.09	0.42	3.91
Australia	82.06	1.60	33.68	14.98	3.40	3.42	46.63
Brazil	14.00	0.77	13.40	4.90	0.42	0.80	3.59
Canada	48.37	7.50	58.65	15.78	0.59	4.16	37.61
Chile	8.53	0.69	14.20	9.01	2.35	1.36	16.86
China	1.34			0.21	0.23		2.11
Colombia	32.32	3.78	16.80	19.61	0.78	0.73	16.42
Egypt	0.76	0.21	7.63	1.60			2.32
Hong Kong, China	15.39	0.01	0.99	2.63			13.41
India	0.77		0.06	0.00			0.12
Indonesia	0.56	0.00	0.09	0.00			0.55
Israel	46.99	7.45	54.46	18.57	12.45	10.32	24.15
Japan	50.64	1.53	15.36	23.53	10.18	0.14	30.67
Malaysia	1.90	0.01	0.09	0.52	0.27		4.44
Mexico	24.22	11.17	26.06	7.44	0.65	4.60	7.64
Morocco	16.31	1.29	0.94	2.33			5.62
New Zealand	76.82	1.34	31.85	13.05	3.57	2.53	28.17
Philippines	1.46	0.07	1.66	0.11			1.64
Saudi Arabia	16.89	3.40	21.40	17.74	0.35	0.07	9.85
Singapore	12.43	0.84	5.97	2.32	0.40		13.84
South Africa	8.35	0.91	4.78	2.03	0.00	0.20	6.11
South Korea	18.91	0.00	3.13	12.19			23.56
Taiwan	18.30	0.13	0.76	5.03	2.76		4.74
Thailand	1.41	0.05	0.35	3.30	0.05		1.79
USA	81.82	5.88	47.59	12.74	1.67	4.24	47.11
Venezuela	3.48	0.00	15.95	3.05	0.04		5.70
Vietnam	0.46	0.00	0.00	0.34	0.00		0.52

Source: Euromonitor from industry sources/national statistics

Per Capita Retail Sales of Bakery Products 2002

● US$ per capita

	Bread	Pastries	Cakes	Biscuits	Breakfast Cereals
Argentina	19.21	0.44	4.46	9.85	1.24
Australia	67.28	8.66	13.39	41.05	23.35
Brazil	42.35	0.93	6.38	13.54	0.75
Canada	39.92	18.38	13.40	26.27	23.17
Chile	64.70	1.59	15.16	8.25	3.31
China	0.69	1.70	1.76	1.33	
Colombia	26.89	1.37	0.50	6.78	1.70
Egypt	53.95	0.71	1.10	3.41	0.07
Hong Kong, China	18.77	4.25	14.56	12.63	3.50
India	1.39		0.12	0.54	0.02
Indonesia	0.56	1.94	0.40	1.62	0.08
Israel	108.95	32.04	20.66	25.85	4.71
Japan	24.02	39.21	69.13	20.45	2.23
Malaysia	5.98	3.80	3.42	6.45	1.84
Mexico	45.01	8.10	31.08	14.43	10.88
Morocco	5.66	0.17	0.48	4.28	0.03
New Zealand	53.50	5.37	8.03	41.37	18.27
Philippines	1.86	0.80	1.90	3.17	0.30
Saudi Arabia	28.35	6.83	10.80	9.72	2.53
Singapore	20.21	5.67	7.43	24.99	4.93
South Africa	15.83	0.84	1.61	7.43	2.44
South Korea	14.07	6.11	11.28	14.98	2.81
Taiwan	1.22	16.30	6.45	8.95	2.10
Thailand	3.56	1.80	2.21	1.42	0.24
USA	64.26	41.98	39.21	40.00	33.96
Venezuela	28.62	1.72	2.07	5.72	5.11
Vietnam	1.84	0.02	0.20	1.39	0.00

Source: Euromonitor from industry sources/national statistics

■ Packaged Food

Table 7.5

Per Capita Retail Sales of Confectionery 2002

● US$ per capita

	Total Confectionery	Chocolate Confectionery	Sugar Confectionery	Gum
Argentina	13.57	6.68	4.16	2.73
Australia	75.51	51.58	17.62	6.31
Brazil	17.51	5.93	8.68	2.90
Canada	55.34	34.47	13.61	7.26
Chile	17.55	9.25	6.14	2.16
China	3.12	0.36	2.37	0.39
Colombia	7.51	2.22	3.17	2.12
Egypt	9.71	2.78	4.97	1.96
Hong Kong, China	28.79	13.66	9.99	5.14
India	0.48	0.18	0.24	0.06
Indonesia	2.72	0.85	1.59	0.28
Israel	47.38	23.28	12.28	11.82
Japan	59.64	30.45	18.65	10.54
Malaysia	8.07	3.24	4.35	0.48
Mexico	27.99	8.44	11.27	8.28
Morocco	12.04	2.45	7.29	2.31
New Zealand	54.81	34.22	16.11	4.48
Philippines	6.36	2.64	2.52	1.20
Saudi Arabia	20.21	13.25	4.69	2.28
Singapore	31.16	12.77	18.38	
South Africa	10.73	5.46	4.19	1.08
South Korea	18.41	5.97	5.36	7.08
Taiwan	18.98	5.55	8.36	5.07
Thailand	2.73	0.53	1.58	0.62
USA	91.68	49.05	32.23	10.40
Venezuela	8.19	2.36	3.21	2.62
Vietnam	4.05	1.13	2.44	0.47

Source: Euromonitor from industry sources/national statistics

■ Packaged Food

Table 7.6

Per Capita Retail Sales of Packaged Foods 2002

● US$ per capita

	Canned Food	Frozen Food	Dried Food	Chilled Food	Oils and Fats	Sauces, Dressings & Condiments	Sweet and Savoury Snacks
Argentina	8.65	2.73	13.86	6.53	9.00	9.88	2.35
Australia	39.04	32.51	21.80	12.75	20.63	31.67	41.98
Brazil	4.46	3.40	21.61	1.58	16.41	7.40	3.29
Canada	39.71	67.50	23.96	63.51	26.46	43.21	40.87
Chile	8.05	7.73	15.02	14.43	17.24	11.74	8.94
China	1.81	3.82	3.57	0.93	1.22	5.79	1.13
Colombia	6.14	1.47	22.22	13.13	26.77	7.60	12.85
Egypt	1.65	1.04	9.36	2.12	11.06	2.47	3.64
Hong Kong, China	28.77	30.90	58.20	4.24	11.55	15.89	7.58
India	0.03	0.07	0.41		1.38	0.25	0.12
Indonesia	0.42	0.34	8.41	0.14	1.75	1.10	1.92
Israel	16.98	72.64	22.84	27.48	24.06	24.71	27.68
Japan	43.82	30.00	167.41	350.42	20.31	101.75	57.35
Malaysia	8.17	3.81	19.27	3.92	6.95	10.53	4.75
Mexico	8.36	2.03	18.97	6.26	11.92	14.64	32.31
Morocco	1.16	0.01	3.00		21.31	1.08	0.12
New Zealand	32.54	39.91	17.59	18.27	28.35	20.64	26.20
Philippines	3.37	8.90	3.99	1.83	6.43	2.19	4.30
Saudi Arabia	10.75	7.17	53.24	2.86	11.15	11.43	11.76
Singapore	15.93	11.04	40.46	9.58	10.22	9.85	9.95
South Africa	8.93	4.08	10.77	10.30	16.32	5.64	8.07
South Korea	13.10	7.48	78.70	19.22	15.64	17.78	13.95
Taiwan	5.06	7.30	68.47	5.63	9.86	14.65	21.07
Thailand	2.15	0.08	6.76	0.33	4.50	7.50	4.99
USA	61.89	90.97	35.71	65.82	16.75	51.70	81.73
Venezuela	17.77	3.23	22.99	51.22	22.92	11.96	7.48
Vietnam	0.22	0.27	1.22	0.07	2.65	3.32	0.66

Source: Euromonitor from industry sources/national statistics

Per Capita Retail Sales of Alcoholic Drinks and Tobacco 2002

• Litres per capita/as stated

	Total Alcoholic Drinks	Beer	Wine	Spirits	Total Tobacco (US$)	Cigarettes (units)
Argentina	53.42	24.39	28.40	0.60	78.34	996.9
Australia	93.15	67.02	17.21	1.98	235.45	1,190.7
Brazil	20.70	16.98	1.40	2.12	38.41	630.6
Canada	63.10	49.37	8.32	3.62	252.69	1,334.4
Chile	36.44	20.79	13.09	2.55	53.41	859.8
China	16.34	12.88	0.91	2.55	40.10	1,328.5
Colombia	24.76	22.80	0.74	1.21	13.71	488.0
Egypt	0.49	0.47	0.02	0.00	25.47	985.1
Hong Kong, China	14.40	13.17	0.91	0.18	136.13	698.0
India	1.04	0.50	0.00	0.54	2.61	82.4
Indonesia	0.30	0.25	0.03	0.01	30.07	949.9
Israel	4.69	3.41	0.92	0.29	127.62	1,313.3
Japan	52.63	38.68	6.91	3.80	272.64	2,473.9
Malaysia	1.94	1.62	0.08	0.23	62.72	812.2
Mexico	32.18	30.57	0.12	1.25	37.25	481.1
Morocco	4.65	3.33	1.24	0.08	19.33	503.3
New Zealand	76.29	54.11	16.31	1.33	165.96	933.4
Philippines	14.79	9.78	0.07	4.93	20.36	878.5
Saudi Arabia					39.54	694.3
Singapore	10.53	8.83	1.13	0.51	203.30	1,019.2
South Africa	78.44	66.85	6.03	2.04	38.75	538.3
South Korea	36.98	23.83	4.54	8.61	117.13	1,991.1
Taiwan	16.95	14.17	1.63	1.16	93.13	1,803.4
Thailand	29.97	20.20	0.04	9.53	24.15	562.2
USA	77.34	64.38	5.86	3.70	308.09	1,402.6
Venezuela	79.76	76.53	0.24	2.99	35.32	599.4
Vietnam	2.76	2.48	0.09	0.19	2.29	381.1

Source: Euromonitor from industry sources/national statistics

Per Capita Retail Sales of Hot and Soft Drinks 2002

• US$ per capita/as stated

	Coffee	Tea	Bottled Water (Litres)	Carbonates (Litres)
Argentina	3.64	1.69	12.00	60.56
Australia	17.89	9.51	13.53	86.91
Brazil	7.92	0.63	21.07	48.76
Canada	13.25	5.93	26.70	97.29
Chile	4.53	6.22	6.99	82.61
China	0.03	0.20	4.92	3.79
Colombia	3.35	0.23	6.66	40.58
Egypt	0.53	8.50	13.22	9.02
Hong Kong, China	8.34	21.58	18.69	18.62
India	0.08	0.69	0.82	1.15
Indonesia	1.29	2.28	24.11	3.16
Israel	40.21	12.21	37.18	41.82
Japan	30.44	22.65	9.70	17.48
Malaysia	6.38	2.38	4.71	7.98
Mexico	4.81	0.56	132.87	119.06
Morocco	5.37	6.44	12.82	10.76
New Zealand	12.91	7.88	4.28	68.00
Philippines	2.41	0.38	11.55	28.02
Saudi Arabia	8.47	5.98	31.18	66.36
Singapore	10.12	6.10	7.47	25.88
South Africa	0.79	3.20	1.05	39.67
South Korea	10.11	3.83	21.78	20.05
Taiwan	3.52	5.65	14.39	9.06
Thailand	1.84	0.37	14.44	11.97
USA	21.02	4.86	30.28	163.89
Venezuela	4.04	0.92	7.42	44.10
Vietnam	0.63	1.04	0.83	2.31

Source: Euromonitor from industry sources/national statistics

■ Household Cleaning Products

Table 7.9

Per Capita Retail Sales of Household Cleaning Products 2002

● US$ per capita

	Laundry Detergents	Fabric Softeners	Hand Dishwashing	Automatic Dishwashing	Surface Cleaners	Air Fresheners
Argentina	5.06	0.48	1.10	0.09	1.53	0.97
Australia	15.19	2.08	2.93	2.12	8.41	3.86
Brazil	7.29	1.49	0.94	0.06	2.62	0.17
Canada	13.20	3.76	2.06	2.80	6.35	2.74
Chile	11.95	0.47	2.31	0.02	1.89	0.85
China	1.58	0.06	0.41		0.34	0.04
Colombia	10.00	0.06	1.09	0.04	1.22	0.20
Egypt	9.13	0.04	1.04	0.04	1.06	0.02
Hong Kong, China	7.88	1.35	3.03	0.38	2.50	1.07
India	1.07		0.11		0.09	0.01
Indonesia	1.91	0.05	0.05		0.24	0.01
Israel	19.80	3.53	5.06	2.37	12.27	2.15
Japan	10.67	2.31	5.52	0.38	6.13	5.59
Malaysia	6.48	0.19	0.92	0.04	1.34	0.64
Mexico	11.97	2.66	1.66	0.03	5.33	0.60
Morocco	6.03	0.01	0.55	0.04	0.78	0.01
New Zealand	15.31	1.10	3.06	1.83	5.88	3.01
Philippines	3.20	0.05	0.39		1.34	0.14
Saudi Arabia	5.84	0.88	1.60	0.28	1.79	0.73
Singapore	7.67	1.06	2.80	0.08	3.60	3.41
South Africa	6.62	0.66	0.45	0.06	0.95	0.45
South Korea	6.44	1.86	1.60	0.00	2.72	0.66
Taiwan	5.39	0.70	2.99	0.03	2.63	0.65
Thailand	3.39	1.08	0.57		0.47	0.42
USA	20.02	5.20	3.26	2.45	10.80	5.99
Venezuela	8.79	0.90	1.06	0.03	3.66	0.06
Vietnam	4.12	0.13	0.20		0.47	0.14

Source: Euromonitor from industry sources/national statistics

■ OTC Healthcare

Table 7.10

Per Capita Retail Sales of OTC Healthcare Products 2002

● US$ per capita

	Analgesics	Respiratory Remedies	Digestive Remedies	Medicated Skin Care	Vitamins & Dietary Supplements
Argentina	2.32	1.75	1.33	0.67	0.22
Australia	6.99	9.85	3.27	5.61	13.22
Brazil	2.02	3.24	1.54	1.36	2.11
Canada	8.36	13.46	4.78	7.72	10.97
Chile	2.45	2.14	1.35	1.40	1.31
China	0.09	0.19	0.09	0.10	0.81
Colombia	2.26	1.74	1.09	0.74	1.27
Egypt	1.80	1.77	1.06	1.00	0.22
Hong Kong, China	4.11	7.38	2.84	1.21	16.62
India	0.19	0.19	0.09	0.06	0.23
Indonesia	0.46	0.64	0.22	0.38	1.02
Israel	3.87	3.34	3.47	3.12	9.11
Japan	9.49	21.90	11.34	14.56	84.36
Malaysia	1.49	2.44	0.56	1.09	5.81
Mexico	1.60	2.91	1.55	1.87	3.04
Morocco	1.44	1.67	2.17	1.67	0.80
New Zealand	2.59	5.83	0.60	2.91	8.40
Philippines	1.31	1.37	0.46	0.59	2.15
Saudi Arabia	2.91	4.09	1.77	2.53	2.15
Singapore	3.93	12.02	2.23	3.57	23.14
South Africa	2.35	2.64	0.91	1.28	0.90
South Korea	3.18	3.42	3.33	2.26	24.44
Taiwan	2.36	4.71	2.04	2.77	34.89
Thailand	0.62	1.11	0.45	0.49	2.24
USA	13.55	15.00	11.19	10.78	45.23
Venezuela	1.79	3.05	1.93	1.40	3.33
Vietnam	0.20	0.27	0.26	0.12	0.38

Source: Euromonitor from industry sources/national statistics

Per Capita Retail Sales of Disposable Paper Products 2002

- US$ per capita

	Sanitary Protection	Nappies, Diapers & Pants	Toilet Paper	Tissues	Kitchen Towels
Argentina	1.99	5.06	2.83	0.24	0.58
Australia	6.82	11.61	16.56	5.80	3.01
Brazil	2.59	3.35	3.26	0.06	0.65
Canada	5.46	9.27	13.53	5.32	4.49
Chile	3.59	8.62	6.71	0.79	1.75
China	1.93	0.23	1.85	0.23	0.00
Colombia	4.98	4.16	2.58	0.95	0.30
Egypt	1.48	2.24	3.60	0.27	0.18
Hong Kong, China	9.09	12.21	10.26	2.39	0.27
India	0.05	0.02	0.00	0.00	
Indonesia	0.28	0.07	0.05	0.06	0.00
Israel	12.41	19.69	11.99	3.07	1.50
Japan	7.56	12.71	8.52	6.83	0.94
Malaysia	4.00	3.61	1.48	1.09	0.16
Mexico	4.49	10.09	8.22	0.63	0.49
Morocco	2.26	13.03	1.34	1.42	0.52
New Zealand	6.36	13.06	15.69	3.05	2.58
Philippines	1.30	1.40	0.67	0.45	0.03
Saudi Arabia	5.97	16.29	1.37	5.74	0.09
Singapore	6.29	7.83	3.49	4.03	1.03
South Africa	1.21	1.10	6.23	0.53	0.17
South Korea	6.17	7.87	6.30	1.32	0.27
Taiwan	8.17	8.81	12.14	4.39	0.81
Thailand	1.70	0.95	1.47	0.33	0.04
USA	8.55	17.80	19.82	5.88	11.60
Venezuela	2.85	8.52	11.36	1.22	2.58
Vietnam	1.64	0.06	0.25	0.16	

Source: Euromonitor from industry sources/national statistics

Per Capita Retail Sales of Cosmetics and Toiletries 2002

- US$ per capita

	Baby Care	Bath & Shower Products	Deodorants	Hair Care	Colour Cosmetics
Argentina	0.32	2.33	3.16	6.18	1.42
Australia	1.95	10.67	6.93	24.54	12.46
Brazil	0.93	3.44	3.05	9.62	3.31
Canada	1.66	12.64	4.76	33.01	17.29
Chile	1.21	3.53	5.30	13.89	5.08
China	0.09	0.58	0.01	1.08	0.33
Colombia	0.46	3.12	2.17	4.28	1.09
Egypt	0.31	3.59	0.12	1.01	0.66
Hong Kong, China	2.38	7.76	0.76	12.94	9.94
India	0.09	1.13	0.02	0.60	0.07
Indonesia	0.06	0.70	0.06	1.17	0.28
Israel	2.04	6.00	4.28	14.89	7.81
Japan	1.22	10.91	1.76	34.36	27.48
Malaysia	1.59	5.63	0.78	6.16	3.04
Mexico	0.69	5.90	2.28	8.33	5.80
Morocco	0.23	0.24	0.08	1.16	2.41
New Zealand	0.68	9.75	4.33	15.72	4.40
Philippines	0.94	1.87	0.78	3.94	0.69
Saudi Arabia	2.20	5.00	2.02	10.00	6.65
Singapore	2.68	10.49	2.35	15.48	14.23
South Africa	0.40	2.45	2.62	4.81	4.19
South Korea	1.55	3.84	0.00	9.70	15.68
Taiwan	2.54	5.94	0.29	11.43	11.19
Thailand	0.55	4.55	0.64	3.68	2.40
USA	2.24	15.57	6.64	34.18	27.94
Venezuela	0.54	3.57	2.36	7.74	5.87
Vietnam	0.10	0.59	0.02	0.72	0.11

Cosmetics and Toiletries
Per Capita Retail Sales of Cosmetics and Toiletries 2002 (continued)

- US$ per capita

	Men's Grooming	Oral Hygiene	Fragrances	Skin Care	Sun Care
Argentina	3.81	2.18	2.28	2.45	0.24
Australia	8.53	12.01	7.47	11.21	1.84
Brazil	2.77	3.94	6.33	3.47	0.74
Canada	9.12	10.10	11.24	16.13	1.94
Chile	5.82	6.03	7.45	5.41	0.72
China	0.04	0.84	0.09	1.16	0.01
Colombia	2.52	3.65	2.16	3.57	0.30
Egypt	0.90	0.29	0.75	0.43	0.17
Hong Kong, China	4.13	12.94	7.32	40.08	0.94
India	0.19	0.44	0.01	0.24	0.01
Indonesia	0.08	1.13	0.15	0.34	0.00
Israel	3.84	11.79	12.23	18.72	3.76
Japan	14.96	14.08	4.03	51.37	1.51
Malaysia	1.93	4.53	2.08	6.86	0.10
Mexico	3.17	5.95	8.04	4.97	0.42
Morocco	0.49	0.34	0.58	0.21	0.06
New Zealand	8.08	7.26	12.36	6.81	1.97
Philippines	0.81	3.65	1.45	3.04	0.04
Saudi Arabia	2.52	5.55	7.23	9.46	0.14
Singapore	4.89	9.39	17.85	28.48	1.75
South Africa	3.28	2.36	5.36	2.01	0.29
South Korea	4.30	4.11	4.41	58.62	0.94
Taiwan	1.41	10.47	5.08	34.03	0.92
Thailand	0.42	2.98	0.60	3.66	0.18
USA	12.90	16.14	21.29	23.04	4.16
Venezuela	2.49	7.21	2.25	5.63	0.38
Vietnam	0.16	1.20	0.09	0.29	0.02

Source: Euromonitor from industry sources/national statistics

Clothing
Table 7.13
Per Capita Retail Sales of Clothing and Footwear 2002

- US$ per capita

	Total Clothing	Men's Outerwear	Women's Outerwear	Footwear
Argentina	98.62	34.64	46.87	27.92
Australia	281.12	75.04	144.61	51.15
Brazil	75.81	22.03	38.71	32.61
Canada	428.20	116.62	257.97	59.57
Chile	164.05	66.25	68.03	21.80
China	39.63	13.29	24.09	8.63
Colombia	99.63	33.17	55.06	11.60
Egypt	19.50	4.11	5.60	8.72
Hong Kong, China	69.93	29.26	35.99	45.61
India	32.37	5.27	11.97	1.04
Indonesia		3.82	4.32	3.19
Israel	236.12	63.36	115.56	69.27
Japan	451.28	145.30	244.65	78.82
Malaysia	53.35	15.53	20.62	11.45
Mexico	163.68	67.67	50.37	53.29
Morocco				
New Zealand	267.01	101.45	71.20	38.37
Philippines				22.09
Saudi Arabia	345.90	145.64	170.05	94.15
Singapore	373.50	127.73	182.89	118.27
South Africa	71.15	27.56	30.03	16.22
South Korea	148.42	52.08	62.83	12.72
Taiwan		91.21	97.81	66.12
Thailand			86.46	8.47
USA	660.04	226.13	228.91	160.48
Venezuela	49.38	19.31	13.75	18.21
Vietnam	16.73	4.89	6.61	10.28

Source: Euromonitor from industry sources/national statistics

    Table 7.14

Per Capita Retail Sales of White Goods 2002

● Sales per '000 inhabitants

	Refrigeration Appliances	Fridge-freezers	Freezers	Large Cooking Appliances	Microwaves	Home Laundry Appliances	Dishwashers
Argentina	5.04	3.01	0.50	3.63	1.77	4.79	0.04
Australia	36.47	19.34	7.55	35.85	13.81	49.45	10.62
Brazil	27.07	5.32	3.14	23.82	5.17	7.54	0.27
Canada	30.29	21.03	7.55	19.07	28.23	37.15	15.77
Chile	21.21	17.99	0.83	25.62	12.19	21.68	0.51
China	6.27	6.02	0.08	16.18	4.31	10.01	0.23
Colombia							
Egypt							
Hong Kong, China							
India	3.11	0.57		9.54	0.19	1.28	0.01
Indonesia							
Israel							
Japan	36.57	31.94	1.37	54.97	28.20	35.59	2.69
Malaysia							
Mexico	14.72	6.57	0.64	10.46	7.66	18.75	1.09
Morocco							
New Zealand							
Philippines							
Saudi Arabia							
Singapore							
South Africa	16.42	11.10	4.54	10.22	7.36	7.90	0.85
South Korea							
Taiwan							
Thailand							
USA	50.76	34.92	9.08	43.05	47.70	51.96	22.24
Venezuela							
Vietnam							

Source: Euromonitor from industry sources/national statistics

    Table 7.15

Per Capita Retail Sales of Small Electrical Appliances 2002

● Sales per '000 inhabitants

	Food Preparation Appliances	Small Cooking Appliances	Hair Care Appliances	Irons	Body Shavers	Vacuum Cleaners
Argentina	5.36	3.65	7.53	8.48	2.20	1.37
Australia	62.71	61.95	61.80	25.10	25.49	25.79
Brazil	35.54	13.88	20.67	27.34	2.84	3.80
Canada	111.43	258.02	77.93	55.56	27.86	78.14
Chile	34.62	14.05	17.17	3.90	4.05	10.33
China	4.25	6.19	2.46	2.37	2.26	0.62
Colombia						
Egypt						
Hong Kong, China						
India	3.71	1.82	0.06	5.33	0.03	0.13
Indonesia						
Israel						
Japan	9.39	169.23	47.20	17.21	64.04	42.86
Malaysia						
Mexico	36.48	25.45	17.90	6.69	4.68	10.97
Morocco						
New Zealand						
Philippines						
Saudi Arabia						
Singapore						
South Africa	9.14	26.12	31.94	58.52	2.61	8.37
South Korea						
Taiwan						
Thailand						
USA	81.01	226.65	212.47	63.15	33.74	91.03
Venezuela						
Vietnam						

Source: Euromonitor from industry sources/national statistics

■ Consumer Electronics

Table 7.16

Per Capita Retail Sales of Consumer Electronics 2002

- Sales per '000 inhabitants

	Colour TVs	VCRs	Camcorders	In-home Audio Systems	Personal Stereos	DVD Players	In-car Entertainment	PCs
Argentina	6.85	8.96	2.83	3.90		1.43	4.87	14.70
Australia	48.53	38.16	1.08	35.80	101.29	3.76	29.02	53.63
Brazil	6.00	7.10	4.33	4.79	16.47	0.39	5.96	11.01
Canada	58.49	48.09	11.39	32.26	116.24	25.08	82.71	49.13
Chile	8.27	5.43	3.03	1.96	11.97	2.56	5.71	
China	18.43	2.90	2.69	1.95	10.58		1.04	4.74
Colombia	4.15	0.62	3.51	0.52	1.77	0.23	2.04	
Egypt	4.27	0.61	0.32					
Hong Kong, China	68.36	56.92	27.63	31.00	68.87		34.43	4.27
India	3.25	0.11	0.06	0.40	2.03	0.00	0.56	0.45
Indonesia	8.50	1.19		1.66				2.13
Israel	10.59	7.18	2.15				17.64	15.60
Japan	62.37	54.65	11.89	15.21	78.74	10.77	32.45	15.68
Malaysia	9.40	6.82	2.97	2.85	15.32	2.34	5.29	1.75
Mexico	7.05	2.26	3.14	0.85	4.49	1.07	3.72	11.18
Morocco	3.21	0.46	0.10					
New Zealand	46.32	20.86	5.99	18.47	48.58	4.03	15.50	63.10
Philippines		3.98	0.60	2.88	17.13			3.33
Saudi Arabia								
Singapore	54.85	30.93	16.23	16.77	71.83	9.47	23.73	9.08
South Africa	14.68	9.85	2.27	2.44	29.83		9.49	31.60
South Korea	32.29	24.52	10.14	22.33	12.45	3.67	54.81	42.38
Taiwan	44.42	26.38	4.74	40.50	88.66	5.22	12.39	56.32
Thailand	28.38	3.73	0.72	13.59	78.59			3.67
USA	104.87	101.46	20.43	40.48	285.96	55.22	95.19	61.21
Venezuela	6.02	0.85	2.21	0.51	2.94	0.49	1.76	6.87
Vietnam	13.09	1.67	1.00					

Source: Euromonitor from industry sources/national statistics

■ Personal and Leisure Goods

Table 7.17

Per Capita Retail Sales of Personal and Leisure Goods 2002

- US$ per capita

	Musical Instruments	Toys & Games	CDs	Blank Audio Cassettes	Blank Video Cassettes	Bicycles	Books
Argentina	1.11	4.25	1.55	0.50	0.39	3.26	7.27
Australia	9.96	99.65	14.78	1.15	1.34	5.04	60.89
Brazil	0.35	6.45	3.14	0.93	0.77	1.73	1.00
Canada	12.71	98.11	15.76	0.33	2.00	8.93	53.58
Chile	0.53	5.85	3.92	1.20	0.88	1.85	22.55
China	0.60	0.59	0.08			1.17	2.45
Colombia	0.54	3.90	0.49	0.16	0.11	0.18	15.48
Egypt							
Hong Kong, China	10.88	18.28	14.04				11.91
India	0.12	0.11	0.80			0.47	0.75
Indonesia		0.74	0.16				0.15
Israel		8.37	8.31			1.54	25.38
Japan	17.12	56.50	23.72	6.73	5.67	18.50	150.18
Malaysia	0.58	2.88	4.33	1.32	0.93	0.94	11.40
Mexico	0.41	7.80	3.39	0.94	0.76	1.60	34.03
Morocco							
New Zealand	8.31	47.83	16.72	0.72	1.28	11.04	69.58
Philippines	3.26	4.23					0.99
Saudi Arabia							
Singapore	3.44	44.26	20.33	6.09	5.10	13.69	101.68
South Africa	0.28	0.90	3.47	0.22	0.07	0.40	5.36
South Korea	17.24	11.92		0.58	0.88		15.26
Taiwan	11.05	11.08				0.03	27.45
Thailand	5.65	1.58		0.22			0.99
USA	14.15	116.57	54.59	0.59	2.11	15.52	102.42
Venezuela	0.56	2.31	1.06	0.31	0.19	0.06	25.53
Vietnam						0.10	4.18

Source: Euromonitor from industry sources/national statistics

Consumer Prices and Costs

Index of Consumer Prices

Index of Consumer Prices 1985-2002

Table 8.1

- 1995 = 100

	1985	1990	1995	1997	1998	1999	2000	2001	2002
North America									
Canada		90.0	100.0	103.2	104.4	106.1	108.3	110.2	112.7
USA		87.5	100.0	104.1	105.3	106.9	109.7	116.5	120.0
Latin America									
Anguilla	70.3	85.2	100.0	104.0	106.6	107.3	116.1	119.7	122.8
Antigua	74.8	92.3	100.0	103.3	106.7	107.9	108.8	110.3	112.3
Argentina		24.7	100.0	100.7	101.6	100.4	99.5	98.4	123.9
Aruba	66.3	78.9	100.0	106.3	108.3	110.7	115.2	118.5	120.3
Bahamas	64.7	82.9	100.0	101.9	103.3	104.6	106.3	108.5	110.8
Barbados	71.2	85.5	100.0	110.3	109.0	110.6	113.3	116.3	116.7
Belize	77.4	86.4	100.0	107.5	106.6	105.3	106.0	107.2	109.6
Bermuda	68.0	86.7	100.0	104.6	106.7	109.3	112.2	115.4	118.1
Bolivia		56.7	100.0	118.4	130.7	133.5	136.6	139.4	141.6
Brazil			100.0	123.8	127.7	133.9	143.4	153.2	166.3
British Virgin Islands	68.3	81.0	100.0	111.0	115.9	118.6	121.8	125.6	129.1
Cayman Islands	64.4	83.0	100.0	105.4	108.5	115.9	119.0	120.4	123.3
Chile		52.3	100.0	114.0	119.8	123.8	128.5	133.1	136.4
Colombia		32.9	100.0	142.4	169.0	187.4	204.7	221.0	235.0
Costa Rica	18.9	41.5	100.0	133.1	148.6	163.5	181.4	201.8	220.4
Cuba									
Dominica	71.2	87.3	100.0	104.1	105.2	106.5	107.3	87.3	87.4
Dominican Republic	11.9	50.9	100.0	114.1	119.7	127.4	137.3	149.4	157.3
Ecuador		19.2	100.0	162.5	221.1	336.7	660.1	908.9	1,022.3
El Salvador	18.9	54.5	100.0	114.7	117.7	118.3	120.9	125.4	127.8
French Guiana	76.9	90.2	100.0	101.8	102.3	102.5	104.0	105.6	107.2
Grenada	77.4	87.0	100.0	104.1	105.6				
Guadeloupe	78.3	89.0	100.0	102.6	104.2	104.6	104.6	107.3	109.8
Guatemala	18.1	48.5	100.0	121.3	129.3	136.0	144.2	154.7	167.3
Guyana	29.6	35.9	100.0	110.9	116.0	124.8	132.4	135.9	140.5
Haiti	35.5	43.9	100.0	43.9	48.6	52.8	60.1	68.6	75.4
Honduras	25.9	39.3	100.0	148.8	169.2	188.9	209.9	230.0	247.7
Jamaica	10.2	18.9	100.0	138.6	150.6	159.5	172.6	184.6	196.5
Martinique	73.8	86.5	100.0	102.5	103.8	104.2	105.3	107.4	109.8
Mexico		43.6	100.0	151.9	182.6	208.0	230.3	245.0	257.3
Netherlands Antilles	76.5	88.8	100.0	106.9	108.2	108.6	114.9	117.0	117.4
Nicaragua		1.8	100.0	121.9	137.9	153.3	171.1	183.6	192.1
Panama	92.2	94.4	100.0	102.6	103.2	104.4	106.0	106.3	107.5
Paraguay	12.6	43.2	100.0	117.5	131.0	139.9	152.4	163.5	173.5
Peru		5.5	100.0	121.1	129.9	134.4	139.4	142.2	142.5
Puerto Rico	73.3	84.7	100.0	111.3	117.1	123.8	131.8	141.0	149.7
St Kitts	78.8	87.7	100.0	111.1	114.9	118.8	121.3	126.4	131.9
St Lucia	67.6	81.2	100.0	101.0	103.8	107.5	111.4	113.6	114.9
St Vincent and the Grenadines	73.8	84.9	100.0	104.9	107.1	108.2	108.4	109.3	110.4
Suriname	0.6	1.4	100.0	106.3	126.5	251.6	400.8	555.8	652.8
Trinidad and Tobago	44.8	71.3	100.0	107.1	113.1	117.0	121.1	127.9	132.5
Uruguay	0.5	9.3	100.0	153.8	170.4	180.0	188.6	196.8	224.3
Venezuela		16.0	100.0	296.4	398.5	503.1	585.2	654.8	805.6

Source: *Euromonitor from national statistical offices/UN/OECD/ILO*
Notes: *Some data refer to capital cities or to certain sectors of the population only*

□ Index of Consumer Prices

Index of Consumer Prices 1985-2002

● 1995 = 100

	1985	1990	1995	1997	1998	1999	2000	2001	2002
Asia Pacific									
Afghanistan	6.4	24.0	100.0	117.0	124.8	137.8	148.9	157.7	170.6
American Samoa	70.5	88.2	100.0	106.1	108.0	108.8	110.8	112.4	113.9
Armenia		2.0	100.0	135.2	147.0	147.9	146.7	151.3	153.0
Azerbaijan			100.0	124.1	123.2	112.6	114.6	116.4	119.6
Bangladesh	57.4	90.7	100.0	107.5	116.8	124.3	127.0	128.9	133.4
Bhutan	38.3	59.0	100.0	115.9	128.2	136.9	142.3	147.2	133.2
Brunei	79.5	85.8	100.0	103.7	103.3	103.2	104.5	105.1	104.5
Cambodia		100.0	100.0	115.7	132.8	138.1	137.0	136.2	140.7
China		54.6	100.0	111.4	110.4	108.9	109.2	109.7	108.8
Fiji	59.8	82.6	100.0	106.5	112.6	114.9	116.1	121.2	122.0
French Polynesia	85.8	93.6	100.0	102.4	103.8	104.7	105.7	106.7	109.8
Guam	43.1	61.7	100.0	106.5	106.0	105.7	110.4	109.0	108.7
Hong Kong, China		63.5	100.0	112.5	115.7	111.1	107.0	105.3	102.1
India		60.4	100.0	118.7	126.1	136.8	145.5	149.3	155.8
Indonesia		65.3	100.0	115.2	181.7	218.6	228.5	255.9	285.3
Japan		94.4	100.0	100.6	100.4	99.7	98.5	96.9	96.0
Kazakhstan			100.0	163.5	162.2	189.7	214.7	232.7	246.3
Kiribati	62.0	78.5	100.0	99.4					
Kyrgyzstan			100.0	162.9	179.9	244.5	290.2	310.3	317.0
Laos		62.0	100.0	74.1	140.8	321.6			
Macau	51.0	68.8	100.0	108.5	68.8	68.3	67.2	65.9	64.1
Malaysia		82.6	100.0	106.1	111.7	114.8	116.7	118.3	120.4
Maldives		56.9	100.0	114.3	112.7	116.1	114.7	115.4	122.2
Mongolia (a)	101.0			136.6	149.4	160.7	179.3	193.9	212.4
Myanmar	12.8	30.3	100.0	30.3	37.9	46.0	45.9	55.6	87.4
Nauru									
Nepal	34.6	59.0	100.0	116.6	130.0	139.0	142.3	146.2	151.1
New Caledonia	78.2	87.6	100.0	103.4	104.6	104.8	106.5	108.9	110.9
North Korea									
Pakistan		58.8	100.0	122.9	130.6	136.0	141.9	146.4	151.2
Papua New Guinea	55.1	70.8	100.0	116.1	131.8	151.5	175.1	182.6	190.9
Philippines		59.3	100.0	115.4	126.6	135.1	141.0	149.6	154.2
Singapore		88.1	100.0	103.4	103.1	103.2	104.6	105.6	105.2
Solomon Islands	32.2	59.9	100.0	120.8	135.7	146.9			
South Korea		64.8	100.0	111.2	119.6	120.4	122.9	128.1	132.0
Sri Lanka	34.1	61.3	100.0	127.0	138.9	145.4	154.4	176.3	193.1
Taiwan		83.2	100.0	104.0	105.8	106.0	107.4	107.4	107.2
Tajikistan		0.0	100.0	635.6	9,089.5	11,452.7	14,201.4		
Thailand		79.1	100.0	111.8	120.8	121.2	123.0	125.1	125.8
Tonga	50.7	82.0	100.0	105.3	108.8	113.6	120.8	130.8	144.4
Turkmenistan			100.0	2,006.7	2,343.3	2,893.9	3,125.5	3,488.0	4,011.2
Tuvalu	67.7	91.7	100.0	102.3	103.1				
Uzbekistan		0.0	100.0	208.0	262.0	292.3	296.7	318.0	345.1
Vanuatu	55.4	83.4	100.0	103.8	107.2	109.3	112.1	116.2	119.1
Vietnam		33.5	100.0	109.1	117.0	122.0	120.0	119.5	124.3
Western Samoa	52.2	76.8	100.0	119.0	104.8				
Australasia									
Australia		88.6	100.0	105.4	108.3	112.0	114.7	118.7	122.0
New Zealand		90.3	100.0	103.6	104.8	104.7	107.4	110.2	113.3

Source: *Euromonitor from national statistical offices/UN/OECD/ILO*
Notes: *Some data refer to capital cities or to certain sectors of the population only*
(a) 1978-1986: 1986=100; 1996-2002: 1996=100

Index of Consumer Prices

Index of Consumer Prices 1985-2002

- 1995 = 100

	1985	1990	1995	1997	1998	1999	2000	2001	2002
Africa and Middle East									
Algeria		29.6	100.0	127.6	135.6	138.4	137.5	142.3	145.6
Angola		439.4	100.0	16,300.0	33,800.0	117,650.0	500,000.0	1,263,000.0	2,638,000.0
Bahrain	94.8	93.5	100.0	93.5	93.2	92.0	91.3	90.3	89.8
Benin			100.0	107.5	113.8	114.1	118.9	123.6	126.7
Botswana	33.9	55.1	100.0	119.7	127.6	137.5	149.2	159.0	172.1
Burkina Faso	75.4	73.6	100.0	108.5	114.6	113.3	113.0	118.5	122.1
Burundi	44.2	60.1	100.0	165.9	186.6	193.0	242.4	262.1	288.5
Cameroon	74.0	91.4	100.0	108.9	112.4	114.4	115.8	121.1	126.4
Cape Verde	54.1	75.3	100.0	115.2	120.1	125.3	122.3	121.8	124.4
Central African Republic	78.4	71.9	100.0	104.9	104.3	101.9	105.0	108.8	110.9
Chad	89.5	69.7	100.0	118.3	134.6	113.2	117.1	131.7	137.6
Comoros									
Congo Dem Rep	0.8	15.6	100.0						
Congo-Brazzaville	63.7	65.0	100.0	128.7	126.1	131.3	130.2	130.3	136.0
Côte d'Ivoire	56.7	69.4	100.0	72.3	75.6	76.2	78.1	81.5	84.0
Djibouti	60.2	77.6	100.0	108.5	112.8	114.3	119.0	124.3	129.5
Egypt		52.4	100.0	112.2	116.8	120.4	123.7	126.5	129.9
Equatorial Guinea	88.7	69.2	100.0	114.7	122.8	130.0	139.9	144.4	212.2
Eritrea									
Ethiopia	50.9	54.4	100.0	54.4	54.9	56.9	58.0	53.8	53.2
Gabon	68.1	74.7	100.0	108.0	110.4	109.8	110.3	112.6	114.0
Gambia	27.7	72.6	100.0	103.9	105.1	109.1	110.0	114.9	121.4
Ghana	7.9	30.9	100.0	187.4	222.9	250.6	313.6	416.9	492.1
Guinea		60.8	100.0	105.2	110.6	115.5	123.5	130.1	134.6
Guinea-Bissau			100.0	177.6	204.5	211.6	218.6	227.8	235.5
Iran	11.0	28.3	100.0	151.0	180.3	218.1	249.6	277.8	317.5
Iraq	0.1	0.2	100.0						
Israel		54.7	100.0	121.3	127.9	134.5	136.1	137.6	145.3
Jordan		81.2	100.0	109.7	113.1	113.8	114.6	116.6	118.8
Kenya	23.2	33.7	100.0	120.2	127.2	130.5	138.2	143.1	145.5
Kuwait		87.2	100.0	104.2	104.4	107.5	109.5	111.3	112.8
Lebanon		24.2	100.0	108.3					
Lesotho	28.7	54.0	100.0	118.4	127.6	138.6	147.1	157.3	173.8
Liberia	45.3	62.1	100.0	119.4	128.9	132.9	141.7	148.7	157.3
Libya									
Madagascar	17.3	35.3	100.0	125.2	132.9	146.1	163.5	177.0	188.0
Malawi	10.3	24.7	100.0	150.2	195.0	282.2	365.7	448.7	514.8
Mali		75.1	100.0	105.7	109.9	108.6	107.9	113.4	119.1
Mauritania	50.1	71.0	100.0	109.5	118.2	123.1	127.1	133.1	137.0
Mauritius	49.8	71.0	100.0	113.6	121.4	129.8	135.2	142.5	149.8
Morocco		75.6	100.0	104.1	106.9	107.7	109.7	110.4	113.5
Mozambique	2.7	11.7	100.0	171.2	197.9	11.7	12.8	13.9	15.0
Namibia	31.4	57.4	100.0	117.6	124.8	135.5	148.1	161.8	180.1
Niger	81.6	70.2	100.0	108.4	114.0	111.3	114.6	119.1	122.3
Nigeria		14.4	100.0	139.9	154.3	161.7	185.2	209.2	236.1
Oman		95.5	100.0	100.0	99.5	100.0	98.8	97.8	97.1
Qatar	77.4	89.8	100.0	110.1	113.2	115.7	117.6		
Réunion	75.0	86.6	100.0	103.3	104.6	105.5	107.5	110.0	113.0
Rwanda	30.6	34.1	100.0	120.3	127.8	124.7	129.6	133.9	136.6
Sao Tomé e Príncipe									
Saudi Arabia		89.6	100.0	101.3	101.0	99.4	98.6	98.2	97.7
Senegal	71.4	71.8	100.0	104.5	105.6	106.5	107.3	110.5	112.4
Seychelles	83.6	92.4	100.0	99.6	102.3	108.7	115.4	122.5	122.6
Sierra Leone	0.8	19.3	100.0	141.4	191.8	257.2	254.9	260.4	252.1
Somalia [a]	31.6								
South Africa		57.2	100.0	116.6	124.3	132.9	142.1	150.7	166.7
Sudan	0.4	2.9	100.0						
Swaziland		58.5	100.0	115.7	124.4	131.7	144.8	155.9	174.1
Syria	15.6	60.6	100.0	106.1	107.3	107.3	105.5	106.7	107.9
Tanzania	7.4	29.8	100.0	140.4	158.4	170.9	181.1	190.3	197.9
Togo	58.1	60.5	100.0	113.2	111.3	111.3	113.4	124.4	129.0
Tunisia		75.5	100.0	107.5	110.9	113.9	117.2	119.5	122.8
Uganda		41.1	100.0	115.7	116.5	123.2	127.3	129.7	129.3
United Arab Emirates		78.3	100.0	106.0	108.1	110.4	111.9	114.4	117.6
Yemen		17.8	100.0	133.6	141.6	153.8	160.9		
Zambia	0.2	2.8	100.0	175.1	217.9	274.1	340.7	403.4	489.7
Zimbabwe	16.3	29.8	100.0	144.3	190.1	301.3	469.6	807.5	1,334.1

Source: Euromonitor from national statistical offices/UN/OECD/ILO
Notes: Some data refer to capital cities or to certain sectors of the population only
(a) 1988=100

Index of Food and Non-Alcoholic Beverage Prices 1990-2002

- 1995 = 100

	1990	1995	1996	1997	1998	1999	2000	2001	2002
North America									
Canada	94.9	100.0	101.1	102.6	103.9	105.1	106.5	111.0	114.1
USA	92.0	100.0	103.1	105.0	106.5	108.2	110.6	113.7	115.2
Latin America									
Anguilla	86.5	100.0	102.9	104.0	103.2	105.3	106.5	108.1	109.4
Antigua	87.1	100.0	103.7	102.5	104.0	107.2	109.1	113.1	115.8
Argentina	25.6	100.0	99.5	98.9	100.5	96.9	94.3	92.5	124.5
Aruba	80.2	100.0	103.9	107.2	109.4	111.7	113.7	117.5	120.0
Bahamas	88.2	100.0	102.6	104.3	106.6	106.8	108.6	110.8	113.1
Barbados	90.7	100.0	103.9	118.0	112.9	115.7	118.6	124.8	127.0
Belize	86.8	100.0	106.3	108.2	107.2	105.4	106.1	106.5	107.7
Bermuda	91.3	100.0	103.3	105.9	108.4	110.7	113.2	115.4	117.1
Bolivia	55.3	100.0	114.1	117.8	125.5	123.6	122.2	123.7	123.3
Brazil		100.0	116.1	126.1	129.7	138.8	150.5	162.1	176.1
British Virgin Islands	83.1	100.0	109.6	112.5	116.0	116.9	117.3	122.3	124.0
Cayman Islands	91.2	100.0	104.4	105.9	107.5	109.7	111.5	115.3	117.8
Chile	56.9	100.0	109.8	117.3	123.5	125.7	129.4	131.8	136.8
Colombia	36.0	100.0	116.6	136.4	164.0	178.3	193.5	243.2	261.4
Costa Rica	100.0	100.0	118.7	136.3	155.9	171.0	187.8	208.1	228.8
Cuba									
Dominica	87.7	100.0	101.8	105.5	105.5	105.8	105.5	87.7	89.0
Dominican Republic	53.1	100.0	104.5	112.5	119.8	126.2	126.7	133.6	139.2
Ecuador	21.3	100.0	121.4	158.9	217.6	285.8	530.4	971.6	1,111.5
El Salvador	48.5	100.0	112.8	118.2	120.5	119.4	119.7	124.1	125.4
French Guiana	93.5	100.0	100.6	102.2	103.3	102.3	103.9	106.6	109.4
Grenada	85.0	100.0	104.7	104.8	106.3				
Guadeloupe	89.8	100.0	101.2	102.2	105.2	104.8	103.5	108.9	111.7
Guatemala	48.7	100.0	111.5	119.1	124.6	127.3	132.8	146.1	161.5
Guyana	37.6	100.0	107.5	108.5	112.4	122.3	127.3	128.0	134.7
Haiti	46.2	100.0	110.1	46.2	50.7	51.7	56.7	65.5	72.3
Honduras	35.6	100.0	124.7	149.3	166.8	180.0	191.7	208.3	216.3
Jamaica	18.0	100.0	124.1	133.9	143.3	146.6	156.8	162.2	178.3
Martinique	88.7	100.0	100.8	102.5	105.3	105.1	105.0	109.3	114.9
Mexico	50.6	100.0	139.0	159.2	186.4	210.5	227.8	240.8	249.3
Netherlands Antilles	81.8	100.0	105.2	107.6	109.0	111.1	118.2	122.2	126.7
Nicaragua	2.1	100.0	111.4	121.5	138.8	146.4	153.7	167.0	172.3
Panama	92.3	100.0	100.7	101.5	101.8	101.8	102.5	102.0	101.5
Paraguay	44.7	100.0	106.0	110.7	123.1	126.9	137.4	142.7	148.6
Peru	5.9	100.0	110.5	117.4	126.2	128.1	126.5	126.6	125.8
Puerto Rico	70.4	100.0	110.1	122.3	137.3	151.5	165.2	188.6	211.1
St Kitts	84.4	100.0	103.9	113.4	117.9	119.2	121.9	125.8	129.7
St Lucia	78.0	100.0	99.6	97.0	101.1	104.1	105.5	108.7	111.1
St Vincent and the Grenadines	83.4	100.0	106.6	106.3	103.6	104.1	102.9	104.0	105.3
Suriname	1.3	100.0	92.7	91.9	105.1	200.3	309.5	412.6	490.9
Trinidad and Tobago	53.1	100.0	110.3	121.2	139.4	151.5	163.9	187.0	203.3
Uruguay	11.2	100.0	123.6	146.3	161.6	167.5	177.0	182.4	207.5
Venezuela	19.2	100.0	206.8	265.0	378.2	485.2	577.2	627.9	797.9

Source: *Euromonitor from national statistical offices/OECD/ILO*

Index of Food and Non-Alcoholic Beverage Prices 1990-2002

- 1995 = 100

	1990	1995	1996	1997	1998	1999	2000	2001	2002
Asia Pacific									
Afghanistan [a]	100.0								
American Samoa	91.8	100.0	102.4	103.5	101.9	102.5	102.6	104.2	105.7
Armenia		100.0	114.9	124.5	132.2	124.8	117.3	122.9	125.5
Azerbaijan		100.0	115.7	117.9	107.3	98.5	100.2	100.6	102.6
Bangladesh		100.0	101.4	105.8	116.9	126.5	129.2	130.1	132.8
Bhutan	60.8	100.0	109.3	113.3	126.3	133.6	134.9	136.9	139.7
Brunei	90.8	100.0	103.0	106.8	107.2	107.0	107.0	107.5	108.0
Cambodia		100.0	107.6	114.8	130.9	140.8	136.1	133.3	135.6
China	45.3	100.0	107.6	111.5	112.8	112.5	118.2	119.2	119.3
Fiji	91.4	100.0	102.3	107.1	115.4	117.4	113.6	118.3	118.8
French Polynesia	93.7	100.0	101.5	103.8	104.8	104.8	105.6	108.0	113.4
Guam	44.3	100.0	112.1	44.3	44.9	44.7	47.2	50.0	51.9
Hong Kong, China	71.5	100.0	106.4	112.5	115.7	111.1	107.0	105.3	102.1
India	58.8	100.0	109.3	122.3	129.1	141.2	148.0	150.4	154.1
Indonesia	70.7	100.0	104.4	110.7	189.7	229.7	230.7	254.5	279.8
Japan	95.1	100.0	100.2	101.8	103.2	102.7	100.5	99.4	98.5
Kazakhstan		100.0	127.0	145.8	140.9	167.8	187.1	202.4	206.5
Kiribati	81.5	100.0	98.4	97.5					
Kyrgyzstan		100.0	141.2	176.3	194.8	274.6	325.3	343.9	344.9
Laos [b]		100.0	125.3	241.7	529.0				
Macau	68.6	100.0	104.5	108.2	108.9	104.1	102.5	101.1	98.9
Malaysia	87.5	100.0	102.3	105.8	113.3	115.3	115.5	116.0	116.2
Maldives	56.5	100.0	109.3	130.6	124.4	129.6	123.4	125.9	144.2
Mongolia [b]		100.0	125.5	128.1					
Myanmar [c]			100.0	124.8	152.3	148.4	177.4	298.6	
Nauru									
Nepal	58.4	100.0	110.7	116.5	134.4	144.7	140.8	142.7	148.5
New Caledonia	87.3	100.0	103.1	107.0	108.2	109.2	109.9	112.7	115.4
North Korea									
Pakistan	56.5	100.0	112.9	129.0	137.6	142.3	148.2	152.3	160.3
Papua New Guinea	73.0	100.0	113.8	121.1	137.2	160.6	182.4	190.5	205.9
Philippines	57.0	100.0	106.7	108.0	109.4	116.3	127.6	139.5	141.5
Singapore	90.0	100.0	101.3	102.3	102.4	104.1	107.9	113.6	113.9
Solomon Islands	61.2	100.0	113.1	125.6	141.7	157.6			
South Korea	71.5	100.0	102.7	108.1	119.2	124.3	125.4	130.3	136.5
Sri Lanka	61.7	100.0	119.2	132.1	146.6	152.4	159.2	183.5	203.0
Taiwan	102.7	100.0	103.9	103.1	107.7	106.9	107.3	106.3	106.1
Tajikistan	0.0	100.0	381.4	672.8					
Thailand	75.8	100.0	108.9	116.4	127.6	126.4	127.1	128.2	128.3
Tonga	85.2	100.0	107.3	110.6	117.5	123.9	124.4	139.0	162.4
Turkmenistan		100.0	1,023.7	1,882.1	2,311.1	3,021.3	3,248.1	3,569.0	4,194.8
Tuvalu	91.8	100.0	101.0	100.8	101.0				
Uzbekistan									
Vanuatu	88.2	100.0	98.9	99.6	102.8	104.3	106.4	108.7	110.7
Vietnam	30.1	100.0	106.4	107.4	118.7	119.7	116.9	116.2	122.4
Western Samoa	78.4	100.0	112.6	125.3	96.4				
Australasia									
Australia	88.6	100.0	102.8	105.4	108.3	112.0	114.7	118.7	122.0
New Zealand	97.1	100.0	101.4	103.7	106.9	108.1	109.4	116.2	119.7

Source: Euromonitor from national statistical offices/OECD/ILO
Notes: (a) 1990=100, (b) 1996=100, (c) 1997=100

◻ Index of Consumer Prices
Index of Food and Non-Alcoholic Beverage Prices 1990-2002
- 1995 = 100

	1990	1995	1996	1997	1998	1999	2000	2001	2002
Africa and Middle East									
Algeria	34.2	100.0	120.7	131.2	133.7	132.8	129.6	134.5	132.4
Angola		100.0	3,675.0	7,425.0	16,725.0	64,275.0	250,000.0	627,750.0	1,271,500.0
Bahrain	93.4	100.0	100.5	93.4	94.4	93.5	92.3	91.0	90.1
Benin	62.3	100.0	110.1	117.9	126.5	126.1	127.5	130.5	137.8
Botswana	54.7	100.0	113.2	124.8	132.5	141.6	148.3	152.2	166.3
Burkina Faso	79.4	100.0	115.4	118.3	131.9	123.8	116.7	126.9	133.1
Burundi	58.4	100.0	124.0	167.5	188.5	190.4	246.7	248.2	279.0
Cameroon		100.0	103.0	110.3	113.9	115.0	117.7	125.9	130.0
Cape Verde	71.5	100.0	105.5	116.2	121.5	125.8	131.3	135.7	142.0
Central African Republic	71.8	100.0	105.8	106.5	103.6	100.4	104.3	107.9	111.6
Chad	69.7	100.0	114.4	124.0	128.4	112.1	120.8	144.1	151.9
Comoros									
Congo Dem Rep									
Congo-Brazzaville	67.3	100.0	107.3	133.7	133.2	139.6	132.3	130.1	136.2
Côte d'Ivoire									
Djibouti									
Egypt	63.8	100.0	107.8	121.0	128.5	125.6	126.5	128.7	132.4
Equatorial Guinea									
Eritrea									
Ethiopia	50.4	100.0	95.0	50.4	51.3	56.0	55.4	46.9	46.2
Gabon	84.3	100.0	101.0	107.4	110.7	109.9	110.5	116.0	119.7
Gambia	72.9	100.0	101.1	102.6	106.2	110.4	110.7	109.9	117.6
Ghana	32.6	100.0	135.8	164.2	198.7	216.1	241.6	297.7	357.7
Guinea	60.0	100.0	101.4	101.0	111.2	117.1	121.8	128.2	133.8
Guinea-Bissau	15.1	100.0	150.7	224.8	242.8	237.7	255.0	247.3	268.3
Iran	24.7	100.0	125.0	137.6	170.0	211.3	236.5	252.1	292.8
Iraq [a]	100.0								
Israel	65.6	100.0	112.6	124.6	131.9	138.6	131.3	135.8	138.9
Jordan	79.2	100.0	107.0	114.0	118.6	117.6	116.8	117.1	117.8
Kenya	32.3	100.0	108.2	125.1	129.6	131.9	136.2	139.4	141.4
Kuwait	89.3	100.0	105.8	104.2	103.4	106.2	108.7	109.8	111.3
Lebanon	28.6	100.0	108.5	107.9					
Lesotho	100.0	100.0	109.6	119.8	130.7	140.5	147.0	156.5	186.3
Liberia									
Libya									
Madagascar	34.4	100.0	119.0	123.9	131.3	147.4	168.4	184.3	205.0
Malawi	21.3	100.0	145.3	157.2	200.9	287.3	343.9	404.5	469.1
Mali	74.3	100.0	109.1	107.3	77.3	74.4	71.1	76.8	82.4
Mauritania	74.0	100.0	107.5	112.1	121.8	126.3	131.1	139.7	144.9
Mauritius	111.4	100.0	105.5	110.5	119.7	127.4	129.0	134.2	144.1
Morocco	80.5	100.0	101.8	102.5	103.5	103.2	103.0	100.6	105.1
Mozambique [b]						100.0	107.6	119.0	128.6
Namibia	58.7	100.0	106.7	114.9	118.0	124.5	133.2	148.4	177.4
Niger	69.1	100.0	112.2	118.4	127.0	120.2	123.9	132.8	138.7
Nigeria	15.8	100.0	129.7	136.5	151.2	160.9	187.2	210.1	238.4
Oman	98.7	100.0	102.7	103.2	102.9	102.7	101.4	100.8	99.7
Qatar	96.3	100.0	104.4	103.9	108.1	108.0	108.5		
Réunion	88.8	100.0	101.9	103.5	106.3	105.3	106.1	107.7	114.9
Rwanda	35.8	100.0	104.2	129.2	140.7	119.9	121.0	128.3	126.7
Sao Tomé e Príncipe									
Saudi Arabia	89.5	100.0	102.8	104.9	105.2	101.6	99.8	100.4	99.9
Senegal	70.0	100.0	101.7	102.4	106.2	106.4	105.2	110.4	114.8
Seychelles	100.9	100.0	97.1	99.3	101.8	100.8	102.3	107.3	108.0
Sierra Leone	32.3	100.0	122.4	130.8	172.3	231.2	230.4	242.4	241.3
Somalia									
South Africa	50.3	100.0	109.1	121.9	132.7	139.8	147.3	153.8	161.3
Sudan [a]	100.0								
Swaziland	48.4	100.0	110.6	123.9	129.0	135.4	144.4	153.8	187.5
Syria	67.6	100.0	108.1	112.2	110.1	105.4	103.4	106.8	105.4
Tanzania									
Togo	100.0	100.0	105.8	120.8	109.0	103.5	100.0	95.8	91.2
Tunisia	77.2	100.0	101.2	106.1	109.3	110.4	113.9	117.1	118.5
Uganda	42.0	100.0	106.6	125.9	123.3	131.8	133.1	128.6	123.1
United Arab Emirates	83.3	100.0	101.7	106.2	106.3	107.0	111.7	113.9	117.7
Yemen	15.9	100.0	130.9	134.8	142.2	157.0	165.2		
Zambia	2.7	100.0	142.8	172.4	214.2	262.9	320.3	384.3	473.4
Zimbabwe	23.3	100.0	126.9	149.2	208.1	349.4	520.4	833.6	1,304.1

Source: *Euromonitor from national statistical offices/OECD/ILO*
Notes: *(a) 1990=100, (b) 1999=100*

▣ Costs of Goods and Services

Table 8.3

Costs of Selected Food and Drink Items 2002

● US$

	Apples (Kg)	Beer (33cl)	Butter (250g)	Flour (Kg)	Fresh Chicken (Kg)	Instant Coffee (250g)
North America						
Canada	1.81	0.48	1.17	0.93	3.16	3.77
USA	2.00		2.06	0.69	2.49	6.78
Latin America						
Anguilla	4.45	0.79	1.75	1.58	3.07	11.89
Antigua						
Argentina	1.81	0.89	2.24	0.54	2.49	6.26
Aruba						
Bahamas	2.26	2.26	0.89	1.03	3.34	12.75
Barbados	3.33	1.10	1.45	1.22	6.29	
Belize						
Bermuda	3.96	4.26	1.22	1.13	3.92	7.75
Bolivia	0.91	0.45	1.22	0.44	1.07	6.50
Brazil	1.25	0.42	0.96	0.48	0.85	
British Virgin Islands						
Cayman Islands						
Chile	0.46	0.46	0.97	0.71	1.38	4.17
Colombia	1.23	0.52	1.21	0.46	1.85	3.67
Costa Rica	1.63	0.69	1.76	0.73	2.57	
Cuba						
Dominica		1.05	1.64	0.74	2.20	16.71
Dominican Republic		1.01			1.68	
Ecuador	2.34	0.41			2.24	4.79
El Salvador	1.69	0.56			2.08	5.50
French Guiana						
Grenada						
Guadeloupe						
Guatemala	1.94	0.39			2.44	4.89
Guyana	1.11	0.74	1.05	0.55	1.63	9.74
Haiti						
Honduras			0.90	0.85	2.28	
Jamaica		2.48		1.97	2.47	11.06
Martinique						
Mexico	1.56	0.72	1.27	0.95	1.99	4.91
Netherlands Antilles	2.23	1.53	1.15	2.33	1.71	5.77
Nicaragua		0.60	1.32		1.77	
Panama	1.41	0.43	1.05	0.76	2.02	
Paraguay						
Peru	0.74	0.59	1.97	0.93	1.48	6.90
Puerto Rico						
St Kitts		0.98	3.09	2.63	7.73	2.92
St Lucia	0.96	1.29	3.73	1.43	4.31	7.67
St Vincent and the Grenadines		1.10	1.74	0.62	3.55	8.05
Suriname		0.54	1.56	0.32	2.48	8.99
Trinidad and Tobago						
Uruguay	1.14	0.49	1.66	0.49	1.68	5.72
Venezuela	0.65	0.57		0.96	1.44	6.62

Source: *Euromonitor from International Labour Organisation*

Costs of Goods and Services

Costs of Selected Food and Drink Items 2002 (continued)

● US$

	Milk (Litre)	Potatoes (Kg)	Red Table Wine (Litre)	Soft Drinks (Cola etc.) (33cl)	Sugar (Kg)	Tea (100g)
North America						
Canada	1.02	0.50	7.26	0.14	0.80	1.53
USA		0.93	6.46		0.95	
Latin America						
Anguilla	2.91	1.85		0.62	1.12	3.40
Antigua						
Argentina	1.03	1.04	1.94	0.34	0.65	1.69
Aruba						
Bahamas	1.16	0.97	23.38	1.05	0.76	3.28
Barbados	1.79	1.30	14.13	0.53	1.30	
Belize						
Bermuda	1.98	1.95	11.17	0.73	0.93	
Bolivia	0.45	0.33	2.85	0.45	0.47	0.95
Brazil	0.47	0.43	1.20		0.35	
British Virgin Islands						
Cayman Islands						
Chile	0.66	0.35	1.69	0.43	0.67	0.59
Colombia	0.50	0.33	2.75	0.22	0.67	
Costa Rica	0.46	0.49		0.43	1.44	4.09
Cuba						
Dominica	2.33	2.42	4.81	0.67	0.83	4.63
Dominican Republic	1.07	0.83		0.24	0.71	
Ecuador	0.47	0.49		1.29	0.66	
El Salvador	0.97	0.61		0.26	0.68	
French Guiana						
Grenada						
Guadeloupe						
Guatemala	0.86	0.73		0.35	0.52	
Guyana	1.10	0.74	1.25	0.26		
Haiti						
Honduras	0.90	0.54			0.68	
Jamaica	1.63	1.08			1.57	
Martinique						
Mexico	0.76	0.90	5.60	0.37	0.75	
Netherlands Antilles	0.76	0.85	12.18	0.72	0.93	2.43
Nicaragua	0.47	0.68			0.54	
Panama	0.68	0.68		0.45	0.68	2.13
Paraguay						
Peru	0.69	0.28	6.07	0.29	0.54	1.18
Puerto Rico						
St Kitts		1.21		0.45	1.18	1.64
St Lucia	1.49	0.71	10.44		1.12	
St Vincent and the Grenadines		1.09	6.74	0.30	0.68	
Suriname	0.43	0.26			0.26	1.21
Trinidad and Tobago						
Uruguay	0.47	0.60		0.32	0.79	3.41
Venezuela	1.17	0.84			0.72	5.41

Source: Euromonitor from International Labour Organisation

◻ Costs of Goods and Services

Table 8.4

Costs of Selected Food and Drink Items 2002(continued)

● US$

	Apples (Kg)	Beer (33cl)	Butter (250g)	Flour (Kg)	Fresh Chicken (Kg)	Instant Coffee (250g)
Asia Pacific						
Afghanistan						
American Samoa	1.95	1.29			2.29	
Armenia	0.32	0.31	0.71	0.39	2.74	2.70
Azerbaijan	0.44	0.66	0.63	0.44	2.08	5.35
Bangladesh	0.89			0.26	1.47	
Bhutan						
Brunei						
Cambodia	1.37	0.75				3.75
China	0.54	0.06		0.28	1.63	
Fiji	1.67	0.50	0.62	0.45	2.88	9.85
French Polynesia						
Guam						
Hong Kong, China	1.59	0.73	1.25	1.16	2.06	7.01
India	0.99	0.58		0.33		
Indonesia	1.05	0.50		0.33	1.08	
Japan	3.98	1.55	3.29	1.55		16.04
Kazakhstan	0.57	0.28	0.65	0.29	1.98	4.61
Kiribati						
Kyrgyzstan	0.21	0.47	0.62	0.54	2.26	5.07
Laos						
Macau	1.76	0.58	1.22			8.23
Malaysia	1.00	1.24	0.68	0.39	1.37	4.91
Maldives					1.27	5.17
Mongolia						
Myanmar						
Nauru						
Nepal						
New Caledonia						
North Korea						
Pakistan	0.49		0.81	0.18		7.97
Papua New Guinea	2.67	0.62	0.93	0.62	2.83	6.07
Philippines	1.24	0.33	0.96	1.43	1.84	2.39
Singapore	1.10	1.35	1.08	0.83		3.56
Solomon Islands						
South Korea	2.10	0.61		0.50	2.52	6.86
Sri Lanka	2.09	0.29	0.85	0.23	1.75	5.85
Taiwan						
Tajikistan	0.21	0.78	2.04	1.91	3.45	6.36
Thailand		0.57	0.87		1.27	2.75
Tonga						
Turkmenistan						
Tuvalu						
Uzbekistan						
Vanuatu						
Vietnam						
Western Samoa						
Australasia						
Australia	1.29	0.38	0.73	1.14	2.16	3.38
New Zealand	0.82	1.86	0.44	0.39	1.78	4.79

Source: *Euromonitor from International Labour Organisation*

Costs of Goods and Services

Costs of Selected Food and Drink Items 2002 (continued)

• US$

	Milk (Litre)	Potatoes (Kg)	Red Table Wine (Litre)	Soft Drinks (Cola etc.) (33cl)	Sugar (Kg)	Tea (100g)
Asia Pacific						
Afghanistan						
American Samoa				0.55	0.59	
Armenia	0.51	0.25	1.44	0.25	0.55	0.63
Azerbaijan	0.67	0.34	2.21	0.44	0.64	0.62
Bangladesh	0.39	0.14		0.37	0.57	0.32
Bhutan						
Brunei						
Cambodia		0.72		0.41	0.39	0.31
China	0.41		0.94	0.08	0.62	
Fiji		0.48		0.41	0.25	
French Polynesia						
Guam						
Hong Kong, China	3.02	0.91	12.18	0.52	1.73	3.09
India		0.12			0.35	0.42
Indonesia		0.40	1.08	0.17	0.39	0.15
Japan	1.65	2.14	4.23	1.03	1.63	4.86
Kazakhstan	0.43	0.17	3.08	0.16	0.57	0.47
Kiribati						
Kyrgyzstan	0.30	0.08		0.37	0.52	0.46
Laos						
Macau	1.29	0.81	6.12	0.25	1.17	0.64
Malaysia	0.83	0.51		0.30	0.40	0.93
Maldives		0.40			0.31	0.26
Mongolia						
Myanmar						
Nauru						
Nepal						
New Caledonia						
North Korea						
Pakistan	0.29	0.24			0.40	0.40
Papua New Guinea	1.83	1.78	9.47	0.36	1.03	2.44
Philippines	1.02	0.89		0.20	0.64	2.06
Singapore	1.45	0.64		0.31	0.49	1.38
Solomon Islands						
South Korea	1.48	1.17		0.20	0.83	
Sri Lanka	0.37	0.63	10.10	0.14	0.43	0.30
Taiwan						
Tajikistan	0.34	0.58	0.46	0.48	1.59	0.87
Thailand	4.32			0.19	0.32	2.14
Tonga						
Turkmenistan						
Tuvalu						
Uzbekistan						
Vanuatu						
Vietnam						
Western Samoa						
Australasia						
Australia	0.81	0.56	6.06	0.72	0.55	1.02
New Zealand	0.69	0.43	7.55	0.13	0.60	0.66

Source: *Euromonitor from International Labour Organisation*

◘ Costs of Goods and Services

Costs of Selected Food and Drink Items 2002(continued)

● US$

	Apples (Kg)	Beer (33cl)	Butter (250g)	Flour (Kg)	Fresh Chicken (Kg)	Instant Coffee (250g)
Africa and Middle East						
Algeria	1.41				2.17	
Angola						
Bahrain	1.14		1.13	0.51	2.65	7.34
Benin	1.17	0.57	1.52		7.12	5.55
Botswana						
Burkina Faso		0.26	0.17	0.42	1.21	1.21
Burundi						
Cameroon						
Cape Verde	2.17	0.74	1.23	0.45	3.03	3.72
Central African Republic						
Chad						
Comoros	3.23	1.38	1.28	0.68	3.90	9.56
Congo Dem Rep						
Congo-Brazzaville						
Côte d'Ivoire						
Djibouti						
Egypt	1.93		0.84	0.29		
Equatorial Guinea						
Eritrea		0.42	3.84	0.46	6.40	1.33
Ethiopia		0.44	0.47	0.31		
Gabon						
Gambia						
Ghana						
Guinea						
Guinea-Bissau						
Iran	1.73		3.32	2.15	7.01	
Iraq						
Israel	1.80	0.65	1.57	0.52	3.75	6.47
Jordan	1.25	0.58	1.21	0.18	1.90	
Kenya						
Kuwait	1.41		0.98	0.38	2.95	7.07
Lebanon	1.39	0.81	1.09	0.73	1.86	
Lesotho	0.62	0.38		0.36	1.77	
Liberia						
Libya						
Madagascar	1.03	0.21	0.89	0.56	2.78	
Malawi	1.40	0.40		0.20	2.36	
Mali						
Mauritania						
Mauritius	1.15	0.50	0.87	0.17	1.97	2.70
Morocco	1.33		0.68	0.28	2.68	11.36
Mozambique						
Namibia	1.17	0.66	1.14	0.67	2.54	2.69
Niger						
Nigeria		0.44	1.06	0.56	2.30	
Oman	1.23		0.97	0.30	1.94	7.37
Qatar						
Réunion						
Rwanda						
Sao Tomé e Príncipe						
Saudi Arabia	1.41			0.47	2.37	7.99
Senegal	1.35	0.12	1.22		2.32	4.86
Seychelles	3.11	5.95	1.37	2.35	4.61	3.94
Sierra Leone						
Somalia						
South Africa	0.76	0.39	0.85	0.52	1.70	1.48
Sudan						
Swaziland						
Syria	2.91	1.47	3.99	2.21	6.76	
Tanzania	3.56	0.37	1.70	0.32		7.56
Togo					1.72	3.87
Tunisia						
Uganda						
United Arab Emirates						
Yemen						
Zambia	1.13	0.35	0.74	1.97	2.17	2.08
Zimbabwe	1.08	0.21	0.47	0.78	2.43	

Source: *Euromonitor from International Labour Organisation*

▢ Costs of Goods and Services

Costs of Selected Food and Drink Items 2002 (continued)

● US$

	Milk (Litre)	Potatoes (Kg)	Red Table Wine (Litre)	Soft Drinks (Cola etc.) (33cl)	Sugar (Kg)	Tea (100g)
Africa and Middle East						
Algeria						
Angola						
Bahrain	1.19	0.53		0.25	0.62	1.74
Benin	1.11	0.83	2.06	0.39	0.39	
Botswana				0.44	0.61	0.57
Burkina Faso	0.64	0.64	1.64	0.45	0.76	
Burundi						
Cameroon						
Cape Verde		0.56	5.57	0.44	0.57	
Central African Republic						
Chad						
Comoros	0.71	0.96		0.58	0.44	0.20
Congo Dem Rep						
Congo-Brazzaville						
Côte d'Ivoire						
Djibouti						
Egypt	0.55	0.41		0.20	0.41	0.41
Equatorial Guinea						
Eritrea	1.40	0.60		0.31	0.60	0.49
Ethiopia	0.36	0.15		0.20	0.71	0.23
Gabon						
Gambia						
Ghana						
Guinea						
Guinea-Bissau						
Iran	1.16	0.72		0.41	2.15	0.63
Iraq						
Israel	0.93	1.02	10.08	0.29	0.66	2.00
Jordan	0.69			0.36	0.44	1.42
Kenya						
Kuwait	1.30	0.79			0.69	1.86
Lebanon		0.59		0.59	0.60	0.41
Lesotho	0.63	0.33		0.34	0.46	0.67
Liberia						
Libya						
Madagascar	0.46	0.14	2.98		0.78	
Malawi		0.15			0.49	0.37
Mali						
Mauritania						
Mauritius	0.43	0.50	2.31	0.20	0.14	0.46
Morocco	0.50	0.86		0.16	0.41	2.35
Mozambique						
Namibia	1.02	0.86		0.48	0.78	1.11
Niger						
Nigeria	0.60	0.29	3.55	0.25	1.10	1.18
Oman	1.35	0.61		0.28	0.33	1.13
Qatar						
Réunion						
Rwanda						
Sao Tomé e Príncipe						
Saudi Arabia	0.98	0.78		0.27	0.57	0.64
Senegal		0.66	3.41		0.93	0.52
Seychelles	1.38	1.09		0.65	0.78	
Sierra Leone						
Somalia						
South Africa	0.48	0.42	3.34	0.36	0.53	2.34
Sudan						
Swaziland						
Syria	1.76	1.15	7.60	1.33	2.22	1.69
Tanzania	0.40	0.24		0.26	0.73	
Togo		0.60	0.99		0.80	
Tunisia						
Uganda						
United Arab Emirates						
Yemen						
Zambia	0.40	0.60		0.30	1.24	1.49
Zimbabwe	0.70	1.03		0.34	0.51	0.30

Source: *Euromonitor from International Labour Organisation*

Cultural Indicators

Table 9.1

◘ Book Titles Published

Total Book Titles Published 1995-2002

- Number

	1995	1996	1997	1998	1999	2000	2001	2002
Algeria		670	133					
Argentina	9,113	9,850	10,590	11,991	13,101	13,927	14,420	15,137
Australia								
Azerbaijan	498	542	496	444	437	465	457	478
Bolivia								
Brazil	48,499	35,702	41,947	41,114	41,581	42,076	42,540	43,028
Canada	17,931	19,900	21,669	20,848	22,941	24,063	25,560	26,810
Chile	2,469	2,178	1,969	1,689	1,443	1,369	1,361	1,313
China	30,611	33,431	36,431	40,582	38,255	67,058	68,937	71,773
Colombia			5,302					
Ecuador					1,050			
Egypt	2,215	1,917	2,507	1,410	1,291	1,164	1,063	976
Hong Kong, China								
India	11,643	11,903	12,169	13,840	15,081	15,867	16,349	17,038
Indonesia	3,896	3,818	3,801	3,777	3,774	3,790	3,803	3,823
Israel		4,909						
Japan		58,105	62,336	63,023	63,590	42,062	43,431	43,968
Jordan	465	511	551	589	618	675	730	791
Kazakhstan	1,115	1,226			1,223	1,121	1,079	1,005
Kuwait	465	511		25				
Malaysia	6,465	5,843	5,799	5,816	5,084	5,079	5,113	5,123
Mexico		6,183	6,463	6,734	6,952	7,095	7,179	7,306
Morocco	940	918	1,339	894	386	378	435	474
New Zealand			5,088	5,204	5,405	5,591	5,812	6,014
Nigeria	1,314							
Pakistan								
Peru	1,294	612	1,416	1,942	2,082	2,149	2,215	2,286
Philippines	1,229	927	546	958	1,380	1,432	1,498	1,510
Saudi Arabia		3,900	3,780					
Singapore								
South Africa	5,418	5,684	5,762	5,897	5,954	6,096	6,203	6,310
South Korea	18,553	18,422	19,135	21,819	20,213	19,970	18,734	18,163
Taiwan	26,084	24,876	23,801	30,868	30,871	34,258	36,304	38,350
Thailand	8,010	8,142	8,269	8,396	8,528	8,684	8,892	9,068
Tunisia	563	719			1,260			
Turkmenistan	366	199						
United Arab Emirates								
USA	62,039	67,840	67,154	70,675	74,108	77,476	80,091	85,260
Venezuela	4,225	3,468	3,332	3,270	3,232	3,215	3,223	3,181
Vietnam	8,186	8,263	8,363	8,488	8,616	8,890	8,954	9,018

Source: *Euromonitor from UNESCO/national statistics*

Book Titles Published by Subject 2002

● Number

	General	Philosophy	Religion	Social Sciences	Philology
Algeria					
Argentina	231	1,495	690	4,087	153
Australia					
Azerbaijan	19	3	14	113	5
Bolivia					
Brazil	2,083	2,454	4,385	5,228	420
Canada	715	518	1,086	8,259	639
Chile	2	41	103	344	38
China	2,766	1,607		2,103	7,465
Colombia					
Ecuador					
Egypt	106	7	131	77	182
Hong Kong, China					
India	853	309	418	3,232	859
Indonesia	343	55	316	630	194
Israel	35			409	
Japan	2,293	2,908		16,782	
Jordan	66	6	42	159	41
Kazakhstan	66	6	10	423	63
Kuwait					
Malaysia	206	67	440	1,154	574
Mexico	502	744	499	2,157	374
Morocco	21	3	49	184	7
New Zealand	237	34	125	2,509	384
Nigeria					
Pakistan					
Peru	48	26	67	905	323
Philippines	10	12	60	721	102
Saudi Arabia					
Singapore					
South Africa					
South Korea	355	518	1,169	4,014	1,660
Taiwan					
Thailand	520	222	273	2,622	290
Tunisia					
Turkmenistan					
United Arab Emirates					
USA	5,288	4,437	6,799		
Venezuela	65	200	183	888	43
Vietnam				1,559	

Source: Euromonitor from UNESCO/national statistics

Book Titles Published by Subject 2002 (continued)

● Number

	Pure Sciences	Applied Sciences	Arts	Literature	Geography/ History	Total, including others
Algeria						
Argentina	404	2,282	1,128	3,246	1,421	15,137
Australia						
Azerbaijan	30	33	12	205	44	478
Bolivia						
Brazil	823	20,503	503	5,149	1,480	43,028
Canada	1,300	4,294	1,996	5,513	2,490	26,810
Chile	27	91	35	517	115	1,313
China	2,181	32,945	6,808	10,870	5,028	71,773
Colombia						
Ecuador						
Egypt	251	65	15	97	45	976
Hong Kong, China						
India	1,101	1,528	439	7,716	583	17,038
Indonesia	776	682	133	603	91	3,823
Israel			32	2,378		
Japan			10,527	11,458		43,968
Jordan	102	192	31	81	71	791
Kazakhstan	98	119	9	118	93	1,005
Kuwait						
Malaysia	665	721	403	642	251	5,123
Mexico	281	1,286	520	481	462	7,306
Morocco	2	42	18	89	59	474
New Zealand	452	780	318	674	501	6,014
Nigeria						
Pakistan						
Peru	284	116	76	315	126	2,286
Philippines	76	63	109	248	109	1,510
Saudi Arabia						
Singapore						
South Africa						6,310
South Korea	405	3,537	1,010	4,670	825	18,163
Taiwan						38,350
Thailand	670	2,753	409	816	493	9,068
Tunisia						
Turkmenistan						
United Arab Emirates						
USA	6,190		3,270	5,015		85,260
Venezuela	134	435	253	782	198	3,181
Vietnam				1,475		9,018

Source: Euromonitor from UNESCO/national statistics

Table 9.3

Book Titles Published

Book Titles Published by Subject 2002 (% analysis)

- % of total

	General	Philosophy	Religion	Social Sciences	Philology
Algeria					
Argentina	1.5	9.9	4.6	27.0	1.0
Australia					
Azerbaijan	4.0	0.6	2.9	23.6	1.0
Bolivia					
Brazil	4.8	5.7	10.2	12.2	1.0
Canada	2.7	1.9	4.1	30.8	2.4
Chile	0.2	3.1	7.8	26.2	2.9
China	3.9	2.2		2.9	10.4
Colombia					
Ecuador					
Egypt	10.9	0.7	13.4	7.9	18.6
Hong Kong, China					
India	5.0	1.8	2.5	19.0	5.0
Indonesia	9.0	1.4	8.3	16.5	5.1
Israel					
Japan	5.2	6.6		38.2	
Jordan	8.3	0.8	5.3	20.1	5.2
Kazakhstan	6.6	0.6	1.0	42.1	6.3
Kuwait					
Malaysia	4.0	1.3	8.6	22.5	11.2
Mexico	6.9	10.2	6.8	29.5	5.1
Morocco	4.4	0.6	10.3	38.8	1.5
New Zealand	3.9	0.6	2.1	41.7	6.4
Nigeria					
Pakistan					
Peru	2.1	1.1	2.9	39.6	14.1
Philippines	0.7	0.8	4.0	47.7	6.8
Saudi Arabia					
Singapore					
South Africa					
South Korea	2.0	2.9	6.4	22.1	9.1
Taiwan					
Thailand	5.7	2.4	3.0	28.9	3.2
Tunisia					
Turkmenistan					
United Arab Emirates					
USA	6.2	5.2	8.0		
Venezuela	2.0	6.3	5.8	27.9	1.4
Vietnam				17.3	

Source: *Euromonitor from UNESCO/national statistics*

Book Titles Published by Subject 2002 (% analysis) (continued)

● % of total

	Pure Sciences	Applied Sciences	Arts	Literature	Geography/ History	Total, including others
Algeria						
Argentina	2.7	15.1	7.5	21.4	9.4	100.0
Australia						
Azerbaijan	6.3	6.9	2.5	42.9	9.2	100.0
Bolivia						
Brazil	1.9	47.7	1.2	12.0	3.4	100.0
Canada	4.8	16.0	7.4	20.6	9.3	100.0
Chile	2.1	6.9	2.7	39.4	8.8	100.0
China	3.0	45.9	9.5	15.1	7.0	100.0
Colombia						
Ecuador						
Egypt	25.7	6.7	1.5	9.9	4.6	100.0
Hong Kong, China						
India	6.5	9.0	2.6	45.3	3.4	100.0
Indonesia	20.3	17.8	3.5	15.8	2.4	100.0
Israel						
Japan			23.9	26.1		100.0
Jordan	12.9	24.3	3.9	10.2	9.0	100.0
Kazakhstan	9.8	11.8	0.9	11.7	9.3	100.0
Kuwait						
Malaysia	13.0	14.1	7.9	12.5	4.9	100.0
Mexico	3.8	17.6	7.1	6.6	6.3	100.0
Morocco	0.4	8.9	3.8	18.8	12.4	100.0
New Zealand	7.5	13.0	5.3	11.2	8.3	100.0
Nigeria						
Pakistan						
Peru	12.4	5.1	3.3	13.8	5.5	100.0
Philippines	5.0	4.2	7.2	16.4	7.2	100.0
Saudi Arabia						
Singapore						
South Africa						
South Korea	2.2	19.5	5.6	25.7	4.5	100.0
Taiwan						
Thailand	7.4	30.4	4.5	9.0	5.4	100.0
Tunisia						
Turkmenistan						
United Arab Emirates						
USA	7.3		3.8	5.9		100.0
Venezuela	4.2	13.7	8.0	24.6	6.2	100.0
Vietnam				16.4		100.0

Source: Euromonitor from UNESCO/national statistics

Cinema Attendances 1992-2002

● Million

	1992	1994	1995	1996	1997	1998	1999	2000	2001	2002	Trips per capita 2002
Algeria	0.5	0.5	0.6	0.6	0.6	0.6	0.6	0.9	0.9	0.9	0.0
Argentina	6.6	19.1	19.0	21.4	26.2	32.3	29.8	32.0	34.3	36.6	1.0
Australia	45.2	67.4	69.0	74.2	76.4	79.5	90.3	95.6	102.6	107.9	5.5
Azerbaijan	3.6	2.3	2.3	2.3	2.3	2.4	1.6	1.6	1.6	1.6	0.2
Bolivia	2.0	1.9	2.3	1.2	1.2	1.6	1.5	1.2	0.9	0.8	0.1
Brazil	93.0	86.7	89.5	93.8	50.7	67.5	68.4	77.6	62.5	58.8	0.3
Canada	80.7	87.8	85.8	90.6	97.6	112.8	106.7	111.1	114.3	118.2	3.8
Chile	8.1	8.2	7.6	7.0	6.0	6.8	5.2	4.5	3.8	3.1	0.2
China	1,054.5	1,438.2	1,332.3	1,346.3	1,359.9	1,248.1	1,237.4	1,250.2	1,230.5	1,299.2	1.0
Colombia						17.0					
Ecuador	7.5	9.0	9.2	10.5	10.2	12.2	12.4	13.9	14.6	15.5	1.2
Egypt	10.7	11.1	10.3	9.9	8.4	7.3	6.2	5.0	3.8	2.6	0.0
Hong Kong, China	46.6	34.0	27.4	20.6	19.2	13.9	13.5	13.2	9.9	7.7	1.1
India	4,105.7	3,791.3	3,375.3	3,378.1	3,581.4	2,876.3	2,834.0	2,590.2	2,360.3	2,145.3	2.1
Indonesia	141.4	159.5	167.9	178.5	187.3	198.3	207.4	218.9	227.2	237.8	1.1
Israel	9.1	10.1	6.0	10.7	11.9	7.4	9.0	9.1	9.1	9.0	1.4
Japan	124.5	125.0	125.4	125.9	138.8	151.8	139.3	137.1	137.1	137.2	1.1
Jordan											
Kazakhstan	56.9	13.3	6.6	3.5	1.0	1.0	1.0	0.8	0.8	0.6	0.0
Kuwait	0.3	0.9	0.5	0.8	1.0	1.0	1.3	1.3	1.4	1.6	0.7
Malaysia	26.3	26.2	21.5	16.0	16.2	0.2	15.0	15.4	15.8	15.8	0.7
Mexico	61.3	80.6	62.9	79.7	95.2	113.1	119.8	119.7	128.5	136.5	1.3
Morocco	22.6	2.6	17.5	16.5	14.4	11.6	10.4	9.1	7.8	6.1	0.2
New Zealand	6.7	13.4	14.1	14.4	16.6	16.7	17.1	20.2	21.7	23.4	6.0
Nigeria											
Pakistan	8.8	9.3	9.5	9.8	10.1	10.4	10.7	10.9	11.0	11.4	0.1
Peru						6.5					
Philippines	187.0	153.6	134.7	97.9	108.0	103.1	104.6	103.8	100.5	99.2	1.3
Saudi Arabia											
Singapore	17.2	16.4	16.1	15.2	15.3	14.6	14.0	13.4	12.9	12.2	3.6
South Africa	21.5	26.7	27.6	32.1	36.5	37.1	37.9	43.1	45.7	48.8	1.1
South Korea	48.1	48.7	45.1	42.4	47.8	50.6	55.3	49.7	50.0	50.1	1.0
Taiwan	53.5	43.6	38.4	32.3	30.0	22.4	22.1	21.8	21.7	20.8	0.9
Thailand	6.3	5.2	3.5	4.1	4.2	4.2	1.8	2.5	1.9	1.3	0.0
Tunisia											
Turkmenistan											
United Arab Emirates	4.0	3.8	3.9	4.3	4.0	3.8	3.7	3.8	3.7	3.6	1.1
USA [a]	938.3	1,191.7	1,237.2	1,312.2	1,295.2	1,347.8	1,417.4	1,375.8	1,490.6	1,540.4	5.5
Venezuela	18.4	16.0	13.5	13.2	12.5	14.2	17.1	21.5	25.9	30.6	1.2
Vietnam											

Source: Euromonitor from European Audiovisual Observatory/national statistics
Notes: (a) Data include Canada

Table 9.5

◻ Libraries

Library Statistics 2002

● Number

	Public Libraries	Public Library Book Stocks (million volumes)	National Libraries
Algeria			1
Argentina			3
Australia			
Azerbaijan	4,303	37	1
Bolivia			2
Brazil			1
Canada			1
Chile			1
China	2,877	428	
Colombia			1
Ecuador			1
Egypt		6	1
Hong Kong, China	64		
India			8
Indonesia			1
Israel			1
Japan	2,396	237	1
Jordan	254		1
Kazakhstan	2,465	62	1
Kuwait	25	0	1
Malaysia	14	16	1
Mexico			1
Morocco			
New Zealand			1
Nigeria			1
Pakistan			1
Peru			1
Philippines			1
Saudi Arabia			1
Singapore		6	1
South Africa			2
South Korea	440	25	1
Taiwan	408	20	
Thailand			1
Tunisia	344	4	
Turkmenistan		10	
United Arab Emirates			
USA	10,529		34,871
Venezuela	23		1
Vietnam	630		4

Source: Euromonitor from UNESCO/national statistics

Newspapers 2002

● Number/as stated

	Total Number	Dailies	Non-Dailies	Total Circulation ('000)	Daily Circulation ('000)	Non-daily Circulation ('000)
Algeria						
Argentina		106		2,808	1,071	1,737
Australia	143	48	95	3,387	3,012	375
Azerbaijan	285	25	260		158	
Bolivia						
Brazil	2,684	523	2,161		6,972	
Canada	102	74	28		5,005	
Chile	59	47	12			
China	1,986	980	1,006	181,695	82,863	98,832
Colombia	26	23	3	1,249	1,132	117
Ecuador					746	
Egypt						
Hong Kong, China		53		1,541	1,469	72
India	500	402	98	39,676	31,085	8,591
Indonesia	465	176	289	10,273	4,665	5,608
Israel						
Japan	111	106	5		70,815	
Jordan	41	6	35			
Kazakhstan						
Kuwait	39	8	31			
Malaysia	34	32	2	2,454	2,334	120
Mexico	310	299	11		8,734	
Morocco						
New Zealand	37	26	11	819	751	68
Nigeria						
Pakistan					7,012	
Peru						
Philippines						
Saudi Arabia	32	5	27			
Singapore	10	8	2	1,144	1,045	99
South Africa	128	18	110	2,123	1,137	986
South Korea	4,660	121	4,539			
Taiwan	397	180	217	23	12	11
Thailand		31				
Tunisia						
Turkmenistan	20				928	
United Arab Emirates						
USA	2,382	1,469	913	113,966	55,186	58,780
Venezuela						
Vietnam						

Source: Euromonitor from World Association of Newspapers

Economic Indicators

GDP

Table 10.1

Total Gross Domestic Product 1977-2002 (national currencies)

- Million units of national currency

	1977	1980	1985	1990	1993	1994	1995	1996
North America								
Canada	217,879	309,891	477,988	669,514	729,580	772,827	812,460	839,064
USA	2,031,400	2,795,600	4,213,000	5,803,200	6,642,300	7,054,300	7,400,500	7,813,200
Latin America								
Anguilla			45	120	154	152	167	170
Antigua	179	297	544	1,057	1,233	1,350	1,333	1,459
Argentina	0	0	5	68,922	236,505	257,440	258,032	272,150
Aruba							1,203	1,295
Bahamas	955	1,454	2,195	3,134	3,323	3,425	3,504	3,742
Barbados	890	1,731	2,410	3,440	3,309	3,485	3,742	3,995
Belize	212	389	418	811	1,061	1,105	1,174	1,211
Bermuda		752	1,174	1,649			2,044	2,155
Bolivia	0	0	2,867	15,443	24,459	27,636	32,235	37,537
Brazil (a)	0	0	0	12	14,097	349,205	646,192	778,887
British Virgin Islands			90					552
Cayman Islands			255	596			829	850
Chile	287,770	1,075,270	2,651,940	9,245,500	19,276,500	23,714,700	28,309,200	31,237,300
Colombia	716,030	1,579,130	4,965,880	20,228,100	43,898,200	67,532,900	84,439,100	100,711,000
Costa Rica	26,331	41,405	197,920	522,848	1,370,290	1,658,240	2,105,690	2,459,960
Cuba		9,853	13,952					341,601
Dominica	98	160	266	449	541	582	592	638
Dominican Republic	4,587	6,631	15,702	60,305	121,808	137,566	162,283	183,361
Ecuador	166,376	293,338	1,109,936	8,204,187	27,450,998	36,478,459	46,005,412	60,726,552
El Salvador	7,167	8,917	14,331	36,488	60,359	70,748	83,130	90,261
French Guiana					484	511	533	575
Grenada	134	202	346	597	675	709	746	796
Guadeloupe		995	1,420					
Guatemala	5,481	7,879	11,180	34,317	64,243	74,669	85,157	95,479
Guyana	1,120	1,508	1,964	15,665	59,124	75,412	88,271	99,038
Haiti	4,897	6,919	10,050	13,068	19,894	30,936	35,265	46,647
Honduras	3,339	5,132	7,279	12,537	22,689	28,862	37,507	47,763
Jamaica	2,954	4,773	11,674	32,990	118,342	158,365	200,027	237,382
Martinique		1,036	1,851				2,032	2,162
Mexico	1,849	4,470	47,168	694,872	1,256,200	1,423,360	1,840,430	2,525,580
Netherlands Antilles		2,198	2,584	3,253	3,811	4,095	4,224	4,422
Nicaragua	0	0	0	1,517	10,750	11,972	13,855	16,204
Panama	2,077	3,810	5,402	5,818	7,942	8,469	8,658	9,154
Paraguay	263,610	560,460	1,393,890	6,474,400	11,991,700	14,960,100	17,698,600	19,804,800
Peru	0	0	0	5,443	69,262	98,577	120,858	136,929
Puerto Rico		15,956	21,969					32,262
St Kitts	81	130	211	430	536	599	623	663
St Lucia	219	366	602	1,123	1,344	1,400	1,496	1,543
St Vincent and the Grenadines	97	160	305	535	645	657	713	752
Suriname	1,283	1,590	1,747	3,169	11,002	64,220	228,924	299,609
Trinidad and Tobago	7,533	14,966	18,071	21,539	24,491	28,962	31,697	34,587
Uruguay	20	92	479	10,886	59,125	88,140	122,521	163,546
Venezuela	155,710	254,200	449,030	2,279,260	5,453,900	8,675,170	13,685,700	29,437,700

Source: Euromonitor from International Monetary Fund (IMF), International Financial Statistics
Notes: (a) New series starting 1993

GDP

Total Gross Domestic Product 1977-2002 (national currencies) (continued)

• Million units of national currency

	1997	1998	1999	2000	2001	2002	Total US$ million 2002	US$ per capita 2002
North America								
Canada	885,022	915,865	975,263	1,064,990	1,107,460	1,154,950	735,955.7	23,720
USA	8,318,400	8,781,500	9,274,300	9,824,600	10,082,200	10,445,600	10,445,600.0	37,432
Latin America								
Anguilla	171	174	174	183	190	187	70.0	8,747
Antigua	1,569	1,674	1,758	1,787	1,788	1,722	637.7	9,096
Argentina	292,859	298,948	283,523	284,204	268,697	313,039	102,191.5	2,710
Aruba	1,420	1,482	1,597	1,679	1,753	1,687	942.3	8,062
Bahamas	3,940	4,190	4,573	4,920	4,917	5,058	5,058.0	15,547
Barbados	4,413	4,742	4,965	5,183	5,098	5,006	2,503.1	9,123
Belize	1,235	1,259	1,376	1,546	1,610	1,666	833.1	3,253
Bermuda	2,190	2,328	2,477	2,617	2,758	2,818	2,820.5	42,135
Bolivia	41,644	46,822	48,156	51,884	53,010	55,933	7,801.0	906
Brazil (a)	870,743	914,188	973,846	1,101,250	1,200,060	1,321,490	452,436.5	2,619
British Virgin Islands	573	612	678	737	793	813	813.4	37,059
Cayman Islands	868	924	979	1,035	1,089	1,110	1,362.2	33,063
Chile	34,722,600	36,534,900	37,138,500	40,393,500	43,343,600	45,762,500	66,424.9	4,287
Colombia	121,708,000	140,483,000	151,565,000	174,896,000	187,936,000	203,142,000	81,119.2	2,023
Costa Rica	2,984,020	3,625,330	4,512,760	4,917,760	5,387,530	6,058,180	16,836.8	4,308
Cuba	360,295	410,389	430,722	452,960	474,934	480,158	44,493.3	3,952
Dominica	662	701	723	725	742	716	265.1	3,733
Dominican Republic	214,864	241,977	278,347	321,783	361,569	396,117	21,285.4	2,450
Ecuador	79,040,200	107,421,066	161,350,684	348,015,946	427,962,500	457,558,675	18,302.3	1,396
El Salvador	97,428	105,074	109,066	114,924	120,783	124,984	14,283.9	2,193
French Guiana	601	644	692	738	787	800	752.7	3,680
Grenada	850	947	1,021	1,109	1,173	1,151	426.5	4,498
Guadeloupe	4,386	4,678	5,038	5,494	5,873	5,956	5,605.0	11,564
Guatemala	107,873	124,022	135,287	149,743	164,795	181,945	23,261.7	1,965
Guyana	105,859	108,002	123,665	125,990	122,605	124,812	654.6	743
Haiti	54,005	62,997	69,254	77,580	85,442	92,164	3,150.9	384
Honduras	61,322	70,438	77,096	89,401	99,062	107,870	6,564.1	974
Jamaica	258,026	273,429	294,076	329,171	358,036	366,987	7,579.9	2,834
Martinique	2,259	2,440	2,674	2,908	3,121	3,177	2,989.9	7,349
Mexico	3,174,280	3,846,350	4,593,690	5,491,370	5,828,590	6,152,830	637,205.4	6,257
Netherlands Antilles	4,537	4,624	4,630	4,762	4,877	4,912	2,744.1	12,210
Nicaragua	18,601	21,881	26,144	30,884	34,200	35,937	2,521.7	518
Panama	9,481	10,233	10,553	10,972	11,044	11,099	11,099.1	3,800
Paraguay	20,934,300	23,436,900	24,144,300	26,921,000	28,118,800	31,977,000	5,594.0	980
Peru	157,274	166,514	174,719	186,756	189,943	200,012	56,878.1	2,145
Puerto Rico	32,100	34,100	36,456	38,902	40,911	41,729	41,728.9	10,443
St Kitts	742	775	823	891	928	900	333.2	8,850
St Lucia	1,566	1,704	1,796	1,836	1,757	1,815	672.1	4,190
St Vincent and the Grenadines	793	857	892	905	940	951	352.1	2,987
Suriname	362,109	328,080	567,543	844,091	1,244,966	1,278,581	544.8	1,284
Trinidad and Tobago	35,871	38,065	42,889	51,485	56,700	58,200	9,313.9	7,062
Uruguay	204,926	234,267	237,143	243,027	247,211	261,987	12,324.7	3,733
Venezuela	43,343,700	52,482,500	62,577,000	82,450,700	91,324,800	75,792,369	65,284.8	2,602

Source: Euromonitor from International Monetary Fund (IMF), International Financial Statistics
Notes: (a) New series starting 1993

◘ GDP

Total Gross Domestic Product 1977-2002 (national currencies) (continued)

● Million units of national currency

	1977	1980	1985	1990	1993	1994	1995	1996
Asia Pacific								
Afghanistan	80,160	171,900	250,400					
American Samoa					315	312	297	312
Armenia					853,063	187,065	522,256	661,209
Azerbaijan				1,466	157,100	1,873,400	10,669,000	13,662,333
Bangladesh	105,360	197,990	405,410	1,003,290	1,253,700	1,354,120	1,525,180	1,663,240
Bhutan		1,113	2,392	4,983	7,193	8,589	10,064	11,808
Brunei	4,227	10,554	7,752	7,527			16,092	18,292
Cambodia				724,092	6,544,635	6,811,577	8,110,675	8,885,560
China (a)	264,400	455,130	879,210	1,831,950	3,450,060	4,669,070	5,851,050	6,833,040
Fiji	660	984	1,317	1,952	2,565	2,673	2,800	2,962
French Polynesia		96,832	226,772	297,754			95,561	124,438
Guam					1,001	1,011	1,073	1,133
Hong Kong, China	72,724	142,202	272,886	587,620	912,809	1,029,770	1,096,260	1,210,920
India (b)	960,700	1,360,130	2,622,400	5,686,700	8,592,200	10,127,700	11,880,100	13,682,100
Indonesia (c)	19,010,700	45,445,700	98,406,000	210,866,000	329,776,000	382,220,000	454,514,000	532,568,000
Japan	185,622,000	243,235,000	325,792,000	441,915,000	486,519,000	491,835,000	497,739,000	510,802,000
Kazakhstan					28,232	453,065	1,048,990	1,353,750
Kiribati		25	33	36	48	54	62	64
Kyrgyzstan					5,355	12,019	16,145	23,399
Laos		6,264	84,000	612,621	950,922	1,107,750	1,419,000	1,725,700
Macau			12,683	29,608			45,575	47,524
Malaysia	32,340	53,308	77,547	119,081	172,194	195,461	222,473	253,732
Maldives	142	440	885	2,048	3,499	4,101	4,696	5,301
Mongolia		6,755	9,372	10,465	166,219	283,263	550,254	646,559
Myanmar (d)	29,618	38,609	55,989	151,941	360,321	472,774	604,729	791,980
Nauru					229	252	251	253
Nepal	17,280	23,351	46,587	103,416	171,474	199,272	219,175	248,913
New Caledonia		90,800	139,650					
North Korea					22,996	23,473	23,729	23,530
Pakistan (e)	149,748	234,179	472,157	853,800	1,332,800	1,561,100	1,865,900	2,120,200
Papua New Guinea	1,410	1,855	2,200	3,076	4,867	5,381	5,888	6,881
Philippines	154,226	243,749	571,883	1,077,240	1,474,460	1,692,930	1,905,950	2,171,920
Singapore	16,039	25,091	38,924	66,885	93,179	106,653	117,768	128,244
Solomon Islands	74	147	237	526	901	1,052	1,217	1,387
South Korea	17,945,500	37,788,500	81,312,300	178,797,000	277,496,000	323,407,000	377,350,000	418,479,000
Sri Lanka	36,407	66,527	162,375	321,784	499,565	579,084	667,772	768,128
Taiwan	820,473	1,491,059	2,473,786	4,307,043	5,918,376	6,463,600	7,017,933	7,678,126
Tajikistan					7	20	65	308
Thailand	403,530	662,482	1,056,500	2,183,540	3,165,220	3,629,340	4,186,210	4,611,040
Tonga	31	49	86	147	199	195	199	209
Turkmenistan					9,653	87,200	652,000	7,751,700
Tuvalu					7	8	8	8
Uzbekistan					5,095	64,878	302,787	559,072
Vanuatu		7,385	12,534	17,899	23,826	24,962	25,550	26,711
Vietnam (a, f)		3,000	76,000	41,955,000	140,258,000	178,534,000	228,892,000	272,037,000
Western Samoa		96	195	346	419	499	496	556
Australasia								
Australia	95,975	137,115	238,583	395,083	435,640	460,074	484,853	517,201
New Zealand (b)	14,970	22,992	45,282	73,151	81,388	87,051	92,679	96,910

Source: *Euromonitor from International Monetary Fund (IMF), International Financial Statistics*
Notes: *(a) Net material product/national income, (b) Year beginning 1 April, (c) New series starting 1993, (d) Data derived from net material product, (e) Year ending 30 June, (f) Year ending 15 July*

GDP

Total Gross Domestic Product 1977-2002 (national currencies) (continued)

● Million units of national currency

	1997	1998	1999	2000	2001	2002	Total US$ million 2002	US$ per capita 2002
Asia Pacific								
Afghanistan								
American Samoa	334	350	368	387	405	412	412.0	5,449.7
Armenia	804,336	955,385	987,444	1,031,340	1,175,880	1,356,980	2,366.7	620.4
Azerbaijan	15,791,086	17,172,175	18,875,300	23,590,500	26,578,000	32,511,166	6,688.4	820.7
Bangladesh	1,807,010	2,001,770	2,196,970	2,370,860	2,535,460	2,714,140	46,886.1	356.3
Bhutan	14,314	16,337	19,122	21,698	24,126	25,694	528.6	240.5
Brunei	18,501	19,590	19,588	20,239	21,077	21,942	12,253.9	36,391.8
Cambodia	9,778,049	11,363,740	12,587,206	12,931,658	13,357,118	14,376,910	3,675.0	319.9
China [a]	7,489,420	7,900,330	8,267,310	8,935,670	9,861,810	10,239,800	1,237,145.0	956.1
Fiji	3,060	3,283	3,588	3,432	3,646	3,774	1,725.6	2,085.9
French Polynesia	139,840	153,448	163,201	175,787	183,600	184,518	1,385.7	5,773.5
Guam	1,136	1,197	1,263	1,347	1,393	1,417	1,416.6	8,227.3
Hong Kong, China	1,344,550	1,279,850	1,246,130	1,288,340	1,278,990	1,271,080	162,981.5	22,580.2
India [b]	15,225,500	17,409,400	19,296,400	21,043,000	22,960,500	25,169,507	517,781.3	499.6
Indonesia [c]	627,695,000	955,753,000	1,099,720,000	1,282,020,000	1,490,970,000	1,603,342,918	172,195.3	796.7
Japan	521,862,000	515,835,000	511,837,000	513,534,000	503,304,000	500,529,000	3,991,841.3	31,421.0
Kazakhstan	1,604,760	1,652,550	2,098,570	2,603,860	3,131,630	3,754,903	24,497.2	1,522.1
Kiribati	64	76	83	83	91	98	53.2	618.5
Kyrgyzstan	30,686	34,181	48,744	65,358	73,883	75,240	1,603.0	340.1
Laos	2,200,000	4,240,000	10,329,000	13,671,000	15,670,000	18,259,000	1,815.7	323.9
Macau	47,476	46,001	48,500	50,112	51,677	52,503	6,288.6	12,934.1
Malaysia	281,795	283,243	300,764	342,612	334,309	360,658	94,910.0	4,096.6
Maldives	6,982	6,357	6,935	7,348	7,651	8,185	639.5	2,163.1
Mongolia	832,636	817,393	873,679	986,254	1,067,380	1,235,108	1,112.4	411.3
Myanmar [d]	1,119,510	1,609,780	2,190,300	2,551,788	2,870,348	3,028,217	460,676.0	9,958.3
Nauru	266	281	304	329	345	343	186.0	13,408.9
Nepal	280,513	300,845	342,036	379,521	410,194	428,033	5,496.3	223.3
New Caledonia	278,103	285,890	292,752	306,968	320,305	323,508	2,429.4	11,037.2
North Korea								
Pakistan [e]	2,428,300	2,677,700	2,938,400	3,147,200	3,416,300	3,726,600	62,397.2	383.3
Papua New Guinea	7,064	7,789	8,781	9,414	9,879	9,997	2,566.6	519.6
Philippines	2,426,740	2,665,060	2,976,900	3,354,730	3,673,690	4,022,690	77,953.7	982.6
Singapore	140,279	137,618	140,070	157,700	152,065	155,727	86,969.7	26,032.4
Solomon Islands	1,452	1,561	1,605	1,523	1,447	1,536	227.6	493.8
South Korea	453,276,000	444,366,000	482,744,000	521,959,000	551,557,000	596,381,000	476,689.1	9,897.0
Sri Lanka	890,272	1,017,990	1,105,960	1,257,630	1,400,120	1,564,990	16,359.6	860.0
Taiwan	8,328,780	8,938,967	9,289,929	9,663,388	9,506,624	9,734,351	281,586.5	12,476.8
Tajikistan	632	1,025	1,345	1,807	2,512	3,345	1,210.1	192.1
Thailand	4,732,610	4,626,450	4,637,080	4,916,500	5,123,420	5,433,290	126,472.9	2,031.6
Tonga	208	219	237	261	270	296	134.8	1,362.0
Turkmenistan	11,108,800	13,994,000	20,056,000	25,648,000	33,863,000	34,506,734	5,529.9	1,199.7
Tuvalu	9	9	9	10	10	11	5.8	458.6
Uzbekistan	976,830	1,416,157	2,128,660	3,255,567	4,925,340	7,469,347		
Vanuatu	27,764	29,207	30,214	31,816	31,973	31,752	228.1	1,164.1
Vietnam [a, f]	313,624,000	361,016,000	399,942,000	441,646,000	484,492,000	533,098,000	34,889.8	423.2
Western Samoa	625	659	699	775	850	890	263.6	1,442.4
Australasia								
Australia	545,608	577,393	607,280	650,422	690,796	731,896	397,648.5	20,453.0
New Zealand [b]	99,982	100,627	104,775	110,558	120,002	126,132	58,335.3	14,949.2

Source: Euromonitor from International Monetary Fund (IMF), International Financial Statistics
Notes: (a) Net material product/national income, (b) Year beginning 1 April, (c) New series starting 1993, (d) Data derived from net material product, (e) Year ending 30 June, (f) Year ending 15 July

□ GDP

Total Gross Domestic Product 1977-2002 (national currencies) (continued)

- Million units of national currency

	1977	1980	1985	1990	1993	1994	1995	1996
Africa and Middle East								
Algeria	87,241	162,507	291,597	554,388	1,189,720	1,487,400	2,004,990	2,570,030
Angola			0	0	0	1	14	835
Bahrain	770	1,158	1,373	1,703	1,955	2,093	2,199	2,294
Benin	148,500	245,613	469,878	502,334	596,412	831,053	1,002,910	1,129,530
Botswana	351	772	1,829	6,540	9,119	11,041	12,262	14,204
Burkina Faso	184,900	272,000	663,100	778,500	832,800	993,900	1,144,500	1,228,000
Burundi	49,578	85,607	141,347	196,656	236,676	270,051	249,865	265,414
Cameroon	789,900	1,356,200	3,896,000	3,334,200	3,125,600	3,786,000	4,365,500	4,836,500
Cape Verde	3,172	5,715	12,625	21,573	29,078	33,497	37,705	41,697
Central African Republic	106,900	168,400	316,200	392,300	362,100	472,600	556,700	515,500
Chad	161,300	200,000	390,000	439,000	412,000	655,000	717,800	813,000
Comoros		28,628	51,700	68,074	74,632	77,351	86,812	88,432
Congo Dem Rep				0	0	69	396	2,896
Congo-Brazzaville	181,700	360,400	970,800	762,100	760,200	982,300	1,056,200	1,299,700
Côte d'Ivoire	1,590,400	2,149,900	3,134,800	2,939,700	2,946,200	4,256,000	4,987,700	5,548,200
Djibouti	34,800	54,969	64,988	80,388	82,827	87,384	88,456	87,795
Egypt (a)	8,210	15,470	37,451	96,100	157,300	175,000	204,000	229,400
Equatorial Guinea		6,657	38,067	36,300	45,800	45,800	81,600	142,200
Eritrea							3,648	3,984
Ethiopia	6,826	8,541	13,027	16,826	26,671	28,329	33,885	37,938
Gabon	690,200	904,500	1,576,000	1,477,300	1,530,800	2,326,700	2,475,200	2,912,600
Gambia	355	435	782	2,367	3,229	3,461	3,492	3,880
Ghana	11,163	42,853	343,048	2,031,690	3,872,500	5,205,200	7,752,600	11,339,200
Guinea		126,798	380,292	1,760,500	3,075,145	3,303,937	3,662,011	3,884,446
Guinea-Bissau		29,370	104,686	70,700	65,600	125,800	124,100	135,900
Iran	5,038,000	6,178,700	14,500,800	35,314,900	100,047,000	130,564,000	185,928,000	248,348,000
Iraq	6,042	15,825	15,369					27,388
Israel	14	112	28,437	105,831	186,576	224,838	271,315	316,759
Jordan	625	1,151	2,020	2,668	3,884	4,358	4,715	4,912
Kenya	32,699	44,648	100,831	195,536	333,616	400,700	465,654	528,739
Kuwait	4,052	7,755	6,450	5,328	7,231	7,380	7,925	9,303
Lebanon		14,000	59,329	1,973,000	13,121,600	15,305,000	18,027,607	20,417,346
Lesotho	168	287	551	1,592	2,664	2,965	3,384	4,054
Liberia	706	917	1,057	1,317	1,878	2,112	2,385	2,491
Libya	5,763	10,882	8,227	8,185	9,332	9,967	10,680	12,180
Madagascar	468,100	689,800	1,893,200	4,604,100	6,450,900	9,131,100	13,478,700	16,224,300
Malawi	728	1,005	1,945	5,070	8,969	10,227	21,940	36,454
Mali	204,500	300,500	554,500	673,400	712,100	978,700	1,187,100	1,319,300
Mauritania	24,998	31,728	53,230	84,615	114,544	124,162	137,339	148,318
Mauritius	5,442	8,697	16,618	39,275	56,570	63,043	69,082	77,310
Morocco	49,760	74,090	129,506	212,820	249,220	279,320	281,700	319,340
Mozambique		78,000	111,000	1,341,000	8,011,470	13,319,200	20,678,100	32,718,600
Namibia		2,343	2,854	6,323	9,302	11,549	12,706	15,011
Niger	288,800	536,200	657,000	677,200	647,300	787,100	834,600	1,033,200
Nigeria	33,585	50,270	72,355	260,637	701,473	914,939	1,977,740	2,823,930
Oman	947	2,047	3,591	4,493	4,804	4,967	5,307	5,874
Qatar	14,322	28,663	22,398	26,792	26,050	26,843	29,622	32,976
Réunion		1,435	2,548				4,234	6,775
Rwanda	71,600	108,000	173,700	213,533	281,868	165,792	336,489	426,175
Sao Tomé e Príncipe		1,629	2,319	8,250	20,469	36,295	64,613	98,900
Saudi Arabia (b)	225,401	520,589	313,941	391,993	494,907	503,054	533,504	590,748
Senegal	486,100	631,000	1,158,500	1,551,500	1,521,900	1,864,900	2,222,700	2,349,500
Seychelles	493	942	1,205	1,967	2,432	2,459	2,420	2,500
Sierra Leone	744	1,156	4,365	98,386	436,304	535,019	657,604	867,072
Somalia		17,341	87,290					2,413,179
South Africa	34,261	62,730	127,598	289,816	426,133	482,120	548,100	617,954
Sudan	288	495	1,391	11,011	83,518	168,042	483,218	1,021,710
Swaziland	263	422	803	2,224	3,357	4,068	4,949	5,686
Syria	27,013	51,270	83,225	268,328	413,755	506,101	570,975	690,857
Tanzania	28,868	45,749	115,006	830,693	1,725,535	2,298,866	3,020,501	3,767,641
Togo	168,800	238,400	338,200	442,500	352,300	545,600	553,600	749,700
Tunisia	2,192	3,541	7,018	10,816	14,663	15,814	17,052	19,066
Uganda	486	1,352	25,622	1,602,090	4,024,190	5,171,740	5,977,760	6,636,520
United Arab Emirates	63,300	109,800	99,200	123,541	130,390	134,610	147,030	163,750
Yemen				122,095	227,691	292,279	488,509	702,112
Zambia	1,986	3,064	7,072	113,341	1,482,100	2,240,700	2,998,300	3,969,500
Zimbabwe	2,198	3,441	9,100	21,494	42,481	56,159	61,622	84,759

Source: Euromonitor from International Monetary Fund (IMF), International Financial Statistics
Notes: (a) From 1980, year ending 30 June, (b) Islamic lunar year

□ GDP

Total Gross Domestic Product 1977-2002 (national currencies) (continued)

- Million units of national currency

	1997	1998	1999	2000	2001	2002	Total US$ million 2002	US$ per capita 2002
Africa and Middle East								
Algeria	2,780,170	2,810,120	3,215,130	4,078,680	4,222,000	4,666,855	58,568.6	1,912.6
Angola	1,752	2,532	16,991	88,944	208,921	489,648	11,248.5	793.1
Bahrain	2,387	2,326	2,490	2,863	2,824	2,889	7,682.7	11,993.8
Benin	1,249,760	1,377,100	1,470,000	1,605,400	1,738,400	1,959,000	2,810.7	422.3
Botswana	17,740	20,163	21,524	24,943	28,671	32,000	5,057.0	2,952.3
Burkina Faso	1,334,900	1,466,400	1,518,200	1,560,700	1,706,900	1,833,200	2,630.2	199.9
Burundi	342,818	400,166	455,443	511,039	549,981	580,498	623.7	87.9
Cameroon	5,266,500	5,572,000	6,010,600	6,613,600	7,043,800	7,490,412	10,746.8	648.1
Cape Verde	45,969	51,307	59,819	63,635	67,782	72,478	618.6	1,344.8
Central African Republic	557,500	623,600	659,739	705,500	736,000	750,720	1,077.1	282.4
Chad	889,000	1,003,000	927,000	978,000	1,189,000	1,206,592	1,731.2	210.3
Comoros	92,836	95,304	102,781	108,851	120,676	129,239	247.2	323.4
Congo Dem Rep	7,804	9,990	51,824	334,926	1,556,120	1,602,804	4,625.9	82.4
Congo-Brazzaville	1,355,700	1,150,100	1,449,400	2,292,600	2,190,000	2,225,200	3,192.6	1,054.1
Côte d'Ivoire	6,834,400	7,541,100	7,734,100	7,546,500	7,869,500	8,166,900	11,717.4	743.1
Djibouti	89,336	91,396	95,273	98,242	101,870	105,210	592.0	884.5
Egypt (a)	257,200	287,400	307,600	340,100	358,700	381,700	84,828.4	1,317.4
Equatorial Guinea	322,700	264,800	467,000	891,900	1,305,400	1,509,800	2,166.2	4,420.3
Eritrea	4,414	4,762	5,214	5,691	6,918	7,029		
Ethiopia	45,238	44,840	48,688	52,074	53,011	55,903	6,524.9	97.2
Gabon	3,109,000	2,645,200	2,870,800	3,558,300	3,340,300	3,415,781	4,900.8	3,698.8
Gambia	4,433	4,433	4,922	5,382	6,126	7,103	356.6	249.5
Ghana	14,113,400	17,296,000	20,579,800	27,152,500	38,013,925	39,724,552	5,007.7	228.7
Guinea	4,144,418	4,438,273	4,802,191	5,436,893	5,924,881	6,350,160	3,213.9	419.5
Guinea-Bissau	163,100	121,800	138,200	153,400	145,900	150,900	216.5	166.2
Iran	292,661,000	329,086,000	436,540,000	579,875,000	665,656,000	700,935,768	101,482.5	1,465.8
Iraq	82,164	92,024	102,422					
Israel	356,055	393,107	429,542	468,143	474,043	491,257	103,688.4	16,145.6
Jordan	5,138	5,610	5,767	6,002	6,260	6,889	9,715.8	1,814.3
Kenya	623,235	694,029	743,479	796,343	882,725	969,354	12,309.4	375.7
Kuwait	9,060	7,656	8,884	11,357	10,496	10,738	35,330.7	15,078.4
Lebanon	22,880,199	24,638,603	24,945,000	24,721,000	25,115,000	26,068,000	17,292.2	4,991.8
Lesotho	4,720	4,921	5,565	6,238	6,478	7,542	715.5	309.2
Liberia	2,602	115,231	128,527	142,913				
Libya	14,149	12,742	14,139	17,395	16,894	17,182	13,521.6	2,303.2
Madagascar	18,050,900	20,349,500	23,384,000	26,242,000	29,843,000	30,058,000	4,399.6	251.3
Malawi	42,310	57,319	78,622	97,159	126,039	128,308	1,673.1	138.9
Mali	1,574,600	1,723,500	1,802,700	1,883,100	2,203,800	2,359,300	3,385.0	279.8
Mauritania	160,618	180,568	203,339	215,319	239,049	249,089	916.6	314.4
Mauritius	86,428	99,890	107,444	119,529	131,835	143,510	4,789.7	4,043.2
Morocco	318,340	344,000	345,590	354,070	382,900	407,798	37,003.2	1,266.9
Mozambique	40,603,300	45,719,300	49,148,300	49,885,500	56,370,600	61,049,400	2,578.3	120.8
Namibia	16,754	18,790	20,693	23,264	26,689	27,410	2,600.4	1,420.3
Niger	1,083,000	1,225,000	1,242,600	1,174,800	1,278,100	1,354,900	1,943.9	164.7
Nigeria	2,939,650	2,881,310	3,322,030	4,902,800	5,702,650	5,901,960	48,947.2	393.1
Oman	6,090	5,416	6,041	7,639	7,668	7,814	20,322.8	7,223.6
Qatar	41,124	37,330	44,397	64,646	62,341	63,578	17,466.5	27,508.9
Réunion	7,051	7,406						
Rwanda	563,417	627,342	633,299	681,455	731,051	784,418	1,646.8	170.9
Sao Tomé e Príncipe	200,000	281,000	334,109	369,533	421,990	486,777	53.6	342.8
Saudi Arabia (b)	617,902	546,648	603,588	706,657	686,296	705,854	188,479.0	8,252.0
Senegal	2,509,300	2,716,500	2,893,100	3,114,000	3,379,600	3,551,800	5,095.9	495.2
Seychelles	2,830	3,201	3,330	3,398	3,337	3,257	594.3	7,607.8
Sierra Leone	834,502	1,051,340	1,209,550	1,330,430	1,487,848	1,586,046	755.6	142.0
Somalia	2,449,378							
South Africa	685,730	738,926	800,696	888,057	982,944	1,098,710	104,235.0	2,347.8
Sudan	1,601,200	2,226,148	2,519,063	2,807,800	3,102,738	3,257,875	12,373.0	386.4
Swaziland	6,613	7,449	8,408	9,639	10,971	12,287	1,165.7	1,057.3
Syria	745,569	790,444	819,092	896,634	950,463	976,126	86,960.0	4,982.5
Tanzania	4,703,459	5,571,641	6,432,912	7,267,133	8,186,485	9,068,055	9,381.6	262.1
Togo	874,800	835,600	878,700	859,000	903,600	1,021,400	1,465.4	292.1
Tunisia	20,898	22,561	24,672	26,685	28,800	29,900	21,030.7	2,170.7
Uganda	7,195,220	7,771,980	8,857,680	9,616,360	10,283,500	10,803,800	6,010.3	249.8
United Arab Emirates	181,179	170,666	193,401	238,802	237,481	244,658	66,619.0	20,383.3
Yemen	852,897	797,681	1,046,470	1,483,330	1,359,140	1,417,583	8,071.6	396.8
Zambia	5,155,800	6,045,720	7,500,740	10,103,210	13,184,912	13,580,459	3,087.5	307.2
Zimbabwe	102,074	135,722	214,984	321,165	517,223	451,018	8,195.0	665.9

Source: Euromonitor from International Monetary Fund (IMF), International Financial Statistics
Notes: (a) From 1980, year ending 30 June, (b) Islamic lunar year

□ GDP

Table 10.2

Total Gross Domestic Product 1977-2002 (US$)

• US$ million

	1977	1980	1985	1990	1992	1993	1994	1995
North America								
Canada	204,879	265,041	350,051	573,818	581,105	565,535	565,908	591,982
USA	2,031,400	2,795,600	4,213,000	5,803,200	6,318,900	6,642,300	7,054,300	7,400,500
Latin America								
Anguilla			17	44	53	57	56	62
Antigua	66	110	202	392	424	457	500	494
Argentina	51,345	209,018	88,151	141,353	228,990	236,755	257,696	258,097
Aruba								672
Bahamas	955	1,454	2,195	3,134	3,195	3,323	3,425	3,504
Barbados	445	865	1,205	1,720	1,588	1,654	1,743	1,871
Belize	106	195	209	405	485	531	552	587
Bermuda		752	1,174	1,649				2,044
Bolivia	3,259	5,012	6,515	4,868	5,644	5,735	5,981	6,715
Brazil (a)	68	91	86	180	151	169	546,230	704,168
British Virgin Islands			90					
Cayman Islands			319	718				1,001
Chile	13,362	27,571	16,486	30,323	44,468	47,695	56,440	71,349
Colombia	19,471	33,399	34,894	40,274	44,140	50,863	79,936	92,503
Costa Rica	3,072	4,831	3,923	5,709	8,574	9,638	10,558	11,716
Cuba		13,877	15,855					
Dominica	36	59	99	166	192	200	215	219
Dominican Republic	4,587	6,631	5,045	7,074	8,822	9,609	10,453	11,935
Ecuador	6,655	11,734	15,957	10,686	12,656	14,304	16,606	17,939
El Salvador	2,867	3,567	5,732	5,328	5,961	6,936	8,105	9,496
French Guiana					581	566	608	698
Grenada	50	75	128	221	251	250	263	276
Guadeloupe		1,387	1,084					
Guatemala	5,481	7,879	11,180	7,650	10,441	11,400	12,983	14,656
Guyana	439	591	462	396	374	467	545	622
Haiti	979	1,384	2,010	2,614	1,532	1,551	2,057	2,334
Honduras	1,670	2,566	3,640	3,049	3,419	3,506	3,432	3,960
Jamaica	3,250	2,679	2,100	4,592	3,698	4,743	4,786	5,692
Martinique		1,444	1,413					2,658
Mexico	81,926	194,763	183,623	247,057	334,334	403,194	421,721	286,697
Netherlands Antilles		1,221	1,436	1,817	1,998	2,129	2,288	2,360
Nicaragua	1,429	1,409	2,965	10,763	1,793	1,913	1,781	1,836
Panama	2,077	3,810	5,402	5,818	7,273	7,942	8,469	8,658
Paraguay	2,092	4,448	4,545	5,265	6,446	6,875	7,854	9,016
Peru	12,559	20,806	17,234	28,969	36,083	34,834	44,910	53,635
Puerto Rico		15,956	21,969		35,834			
St Kitts	30	48	78	159	182	198	222	231
St Lucia	81	135	223	416	498	498	518	554
St Vincent and the Grenadines	36	59	113	198	233	239	243	264
Suriname	719	891	978	1,775	2,860	6,164	479	518
Trinidad and Tobago	3,139	6,236	7,376	5,068	5,440	4,577	4,888	5,329
Uruguay	4,286	10,163	4,731	9,309	12,878	15,002	17,475	19,298
Venezuela	36,275	59,220	59,871	48,598	60,423	60,048	58,417	77,389

Source: *Euromonitor from International Monetary Fund (IMF), International Financial Statistics*
Notes: *(a) New series starting 1993*

GDP

Total Gross Domestic Product 1977-2002 (US$) (continued)

- US$ million

	1996	1997	1998	1999	2000	2001	2002	US$ per capita 2002
North America								
Canada	615,389	639,180	617,384	656,420	717,112	715,062	735,956	23,720.1
USA	7,813,200	8,318,400	8,781,500	9,274,300	9,824,600	10,082,200	10,445,600	37,432.1
Latin America								
Anguilla	63	63	65	65	68	71	70	8,747.1
Antigua	540	581	620	651	662	662	638	9,096.0
Argentina	272,242	293,006	299,098	283,665	284,346	268,831	102,191	2,709.5
Aruba	723	793	828	892	938	980	942	8,062.4
Bahamas	3,742	3,940	4,190	4,573	4,920	4,917	5,058	15,547.3
Barbados	1,997	2,206	2,371	2,482	2,591	2,549	2,503	9,123.3
Belize	606	618	630	688	773	805	833	3,252.6
Bermuda	2,155	2,190	2,328	2,477	2,629	2,758	2,821	42,135.2
Bolivia	7,397	7,926	8,497	8,285	8,391	8,023	7,801	906.0
Brazil [a]	774,935	807,747	787,740	536,634	601,730	508,994	452,436	2,618.5
British Virgin Islands	552	573	612	678	737	793	813	37,058.7
Cayman Islands	1,026	1,048	1,116	1,200	1,291	1,324	1,362	33,062.6
Chile	75,770	82,812	79,374	72,996	75,436	68,264	66,425	4,286.7
Colombia	97,147	106,672	98,513	86,301	83,766	81,724	81,119	2,022.7
Costa Rica	11,844	12,829	14,094	15,796	15,957	16,382	16,837	4,308.1
Cuba	17,979	17,211	17,843	18,727	19,694	20,649	44,493	3,952.5
Dominica	236	245	259	268	268	275	265	3,733.3
Dominican Republic	13,312	15,062	15,850	17,361	19,603	21,329	21,285	2,450.0
Ecuador	19,040	19,769	19,723	13,689	13,927	17,119	18,302	1,395.9
El Salvador	10,310	11,127	12,002	12,458	13,127	13,804	14,284	2,193.1
French Guiana	730	682	722	737	680	704	753	3,680.0
Grenada	295	315	351	378	411	434	426	4,498.1
Guadeloupe		4,973	5,244	5,368	5,062	5,256	5,605	11,564.4
Guatemala	15,783	17,785	19,395	18,318	19,289	20,970	23,262	1,964.5
Guyana	706	743	718	695	691	655	655	742.7
Haiti	2,971	3,243	3,757	4,089	3,664	3,498	3,151	383.8
Honduras	4,080	4,716	5,262	5,424	6,025	6,402	6,564	973.6
Jamaica	6,395	7,288	7,481	7,532	7,709	7,784	7,580	2,833.5
Martinique	2,746	2,562	2,735	2,849	2,679	2,793	2,990	7,349.0
Mexico	332,337	400,871	421,008	480,491	580,756	623,890	637,205	6,256.5
Netherlands Antilles	2,470	2,535	2,583	2,587	2,660	2,725	2,744	12,210.3
Nicaragua	1,921	1,969	2,068	2,214	2,435	2,558	2,522	517.5
Panama	9,154	9,481	10,233	10,553	10,972	11,044	11,099	3,800.4
Paraguay	9,629	9,612	8,596	7,741	7,722	6,848	5,594	980.1
Peru	55,814	59,033	56,831	51,641	53,512	54,164	56,878	2,144.7
Puerto Rico	32,262	32,100	34,100	36,456	38,902	40,911	41,729	10,442.9
St Kitts	246	275	287	305	330	344	333	8,850.4
St Lucia	572	580	631	665	680	651	672	4,189.6
St Vincent and the Grenadines	278	294	317	330	335	348	352	2,986.8
Suriname	747	903	818	660	638	571	545	1,283.9
Trinidad and Tobago	5,760	5,738	6,044	6,809	8,172	9,096	9,314	7,061.7
Uruguay	20,515	21,704	22,371	20,913	20,086	18,561	12,325	3,732.9
Venezuela	70,538	88,704	95,849	103,311	121,258	126,197	65,285	2,601.7

Source: Euromonitor from International Monetary Fund (IMF), International Financial Statistics
Notes: (a) New series starting 1993

■ GDP

Total Gross Domestic Product 1977-2002 (US$) (continued)

• US$ million

	1977	1980	1985	1990	1992	1993	1994	1995
Asia Pacific								
Afghanistan	1,781	3,895	4,949					
American Samoa					316	315	312	297
Armenia						93,692	648	1,287
Azerbaijan					445	1,571	1,193	2,417
Bangladesh	6,853	12,811	14,482	29,023	30,691	31,685	33,675	37,866
Bhutan		142	193	285	245	236	274	310
Brunei	1,733	4,929	3,523	4,153				11,353
Cambodia					2,395	2,434	2,676	3,309
China [a]	142,319	303,744	299,391	382,996	469,003	598,765	541,735	700,605
Fiji	719	1,203	1,141	1,318	1,553	1,664	1,826	1,991
French Polynesia		1,260	1,388	3,008				1,378
Guam					994	1,001	1,011	1,073
Hong Kong, China	15,599	28,577	35,027	75,435	102,230	118,001	133,245	141,712
India [b]	109,938	172,980	212,019	324,889	288,744	281,773	322,809	366,363
Indonesia [c]	45,809	72,482	88,608	114,426	139,116	158,007	176,892	202,131
Japan	691,304	1,072,744	1,365,798	3,052,068	3,802,433	4,375,250	4,812,099	5,291,741
Kazakhstan						11,293	12,749	17,211
Kiribati		28	23	28	34	33	39	46
Kyrgyzstan					2	874	1,109	1,492
Laos		626	1,527	866	1,179	1,328	1,544	1,763
Macau			1,587	3,690				5,720
Malaysia	13,140	24,488	31,231	44,025	59,152	66,895	74,482	88,833
Maldives	16	58	125	214	282	319	354	399
Mongolia					1,111	548	686	1,227
Myanmar [d]	4,191	5,905	6,676	24,212	41,271	59,129	79,531	107,783
Nauru					170	156	184	186
Nepal	1,382	1,946	2,553	3,521	3,499	3,528	4,034	4,224
New Caledonia		1,182	855		2,924			
North Korea						10,696	10,918	11,037
Pakistan [e]	15,198	23,766	29,783	39,518	48,276	47,643	51,314	59,247
Papua New Guinea	1,782	2,765	2,200	3,221	4,378	4,976	5,321	4,601
Philippines	20,833	32,450	30,734	44,312	52,976	54,368	64,084	74,120
Singapore	6,575	11,718	17,692	36,901	49,067	57,668	69,825	83,089
Solomon Islands	82	177	160	208	261	283	320	357
South Korea	37,077	62,210	93,460	252,622	314,737	345,716	402,525	489,256
Sri Lanka	4,103	4,024	5,978	8,032	9,703	10,338	11,719	13,029
Taiwan	21,591	41,417	62,093	158,873	210,195	222,245	244,278	264,928
Tajikistan					405	676	817	529
Thailand	19,781	32,353	38,901	85,343	111,453	125,011	144,308	168,018
Tonga	34	56	60	115	137	144	148	157
Turkmenistan							4,542	5,878
Tuvalu					6	5	6	6
Uzbekistan					266	543	6,620	10,169
Vanuatu		108	118	153	190	196	214	228
Vietnam [a, f]				6,472	9,867	13,181	16,281	20,736
Western Samoa		104	87	150	159	163	197	201
Australasia								
Australia	106,423	156,124	166,621	308,403	304,437	296,241	336,373	359,409
New Zealand [b]	14,530	22,395	22,379	43,641	40,416	43,981	51,616	60,818

Source: Euromonitor from International Monetary Fund (IMF), International Financial Statistics
Notes: (a) Net material product/national income, (b) Year beginning 1 April, (c) New series starting 1993, (d) Data derived from net material product, (e) Year ending 30 June, (f) Year ending 15 July

Total Gross Domestic Product 1977-2002 (US$) (continued)

● US$ million

	1996	1997	1998	1999	2000	2001	2002	US$ per capita 2002
Asia Pacific								
Afghanistan								
American Samoa	312	334	350	368	387	405	412	5,449.7
Armenia	1,597	1,639	1,892	1,845	1,912	2,118	2,367	620.4
Azerbaijan	3,176	3,962	4,438	4,581	5,273	5,708	6,688	820.7
Bangladesh	39,796	41,169	42,676	44,758	45,470	45,433	46,886	356.3
Bhutan	333	394	396	444	483	511	529	240.5
Brunei	12,973	12,460	11,705	11,556	11,740	11,764	12,254	36,391.8
Cambodia	3,386	3,319	3,035	3,306	3,367	3,411	3,675	319.9
China [a]	821,855	903,448	954,266	998,678	1,079,383	1,191,461	1,237,145	956.1
Fiji	2,111	2,120	1,652	1,822	1,612	1,602	1,726	2,085.9
French Polynesia	1,742	1,748	1,896	1,917	1,786	1,811	1,386	5,773.5
Guam	1,133	1,136	1,197	1,263	1,347	1,393	1,417	8,227.3
Hong Kong, China	156,566	173,668	165,242	160,636	165,359	163,999	162,982	22,580.2
India [b]	386,138	419,282	421,950	448,176	468,230	486,591	517,781	499.6
Indonesia [c]	227,370	215,749	95,445	140,000	152,227	145,307	172,195	796.7
Japan	4,695,778	4,313,230	3,940,529	4,493,464	4,765,313	4,141,431	3,991,841	31,421.0
Kazakhstan	20,114	21,273	21,104	17,558	18,320	21,342	24,497	1,522.1
Kiribati	50	47	48	54	48	47	53	618.5
Kyrgyzstan	1,827	1,767	1,640	1,250	1,370	1,527	1,603	340.1
Laos	1,874	1,746	1,285	1,454	1,733	1,750	1,816	323.9
Macau	5,966	5,954	5,766	6,070	6,256	6,433	6,289	12,934.1
Malaysia	100,850	100,169	72,175	79,148	90,161	87,976	94,910	4,096.6
Maldives	450	593	540	589	624	625	639	2,163.1
Mongolia	1,179	1,054	972	855	916	972	1,112	411.3
Myanmar [d]	135,129	181,038	256,586	351,949	397,121	429,431	460,676	9,958.3
Nauru	198	197	177	196	190	178	186	13,408.9
Nepal	4,391	4,836	4,560	5,012	5,338	5,473	5,496	223.3
New Caledonia		3,477	3,533	3,439	3,118	3,160	2,429	11,037.2
North Korea	10,944							
Pakistan [e]	59,044	59,346	59,580	59,823	58,664	55,166	62,397	383.3
Papua New Guinea	5,217	4,912	3,756	3,416	3,384	2,915	2,567	519.6
Philippines	82,847	82,344	65,172	76,157	75,912	72,044	77,954	982.6
Singapore	90,951	94,476	82,229	82,639	91,475	84,871	86,970	26,032.4
Solomon Islands	389	391	324	332	299	274	228	493.8
South Korea	520,203	476,486	317,078	406,070	461,519	427,236	476,689	9,897.0
Sri Lanka	13,897	15,091	15,795	15,657	16,332	15,664	16,360	860.0
Taiwan	279,716	272,896	267,401	288,301	288,489	289,393	281,586	12,476.8
Tajikistan	1,042	1,124	1,320	1,087	870	1,059	1,210	192.1
Thailand	181,947	150,892	111,860	122,630	122,570	115,309	126,473	2,031.6
Tonga	170	165	147	148	148	127	135	1,362.0
Turkmenistan	2,380	2,681	2,862	3,857	4,932	6,512	5,530	1,199.7
Tuvalu	6	6	6	6	6	5	6	458.6
Uzbekistan	13,954	15,526	14,987	17,081	13,759	12,192		
Vanuatu	239	240	229	234	231	220	228	1,164.1
Vietnam [a, f]	24,658	26,844	27,210	28,684	31,173	32,902	34,890	423.2
Western Samoa	226	244	224	232	236	244	264	1,442.4
Australasia								
Australia	404,740	404,940	362,723	391,806	377,093	357,289	397,649	20,453.0
New Zealand [b]	66,612	66,107	53,862	55,448	50,227	50,448	58,335	14,949.2

Source: *Euromonitor from International Monetary Fund (IMF), International Financial Statistics*
Notes: *(a) Net material product/national income. (b) Year beginning 1 April. (c) New series starting 1993. (d) Data derived from net material product. (e) Year ending 30 June. (f) Year ending 15 July*

■ GDP

Total Gross Domestic Product 1977-2002 (US$) (continued)

● US$ million

	1977	1980	1985	1990	1992	1993	1994	1995
Africa and Middle East								
Algeria	21,038	42,348	57,997	61,891	49,217	50,962	42,426	42,066
Angola			6,805	10,261	10,514	10,126	16,802	5,090
Bahrain	1,946	3,072	3,652	4,529	4,751	5,201	5,568	5,849
Benin	604	1,163	1,046	1,845	2,152	2,106	1,497	2,009
Botswana	417	993	961	3,515	3,970	3,763	4,113	4,423
Burkina Faso	753	1,287	1,476	2,859	3,070	2,941	1,790	2,293
Burundi	551	951	1,171	1,148	1,084	975	1,069	1,000
Cameroon	3,215	6,419	8,672	12,246	11,992	11,038	6,819	8,746
Cape Verde	93	142	138	308	358	362	409	491
Central African Republic	435	797	704	1,441	1,412	1,279	851	1,115
Chad	657	947	868	1,612	1,666	1,455	1,180	1,438
Comoros		135	115	250	266	264	186	232
Congo Dem Rep				8,352	8,206	10,708	5,807	5,643
Congo-Brazzaville	740	1,706	2,161	2,799	2,930	2,685	1,769	2,116
Côte d'Ivoire	6,473	10,176	6,978	10,797	11,140	10,405	7,666	9,992
Djibouti	196	309	366	452	478	466	492	498
Egypt (a)	20,981	22,100	53,501	62,000	41,876	46,920	51,697	60,138
Equatorial Guinea		32	85	133	160	162	82	163
Eritrea								592
Ethiopia	3,298	4,126	6,293	8,129	7,419	5,334	5,184	5,502
Gabon	2,809	4,281	3,508	5,426	5,593	5,406	4,191	4,959
Gambia	155	253	201	300	332	354	361	366
Ghana	9,707	15,583	6,310	6,226	6,413	5,966	5,441	6,458
Guinea		6,685	15,629	2,667	2,958	3,218	3,383	3,694
Guinea-Bissau		56,463	42,724	2,103	548	423	634	446
Iran	71,343	87,499	159,259	518,605	1,013,774	78,916	74,661	106,370
Iraq	20,460	53,587	49,441					
Israel	13,776	21,781	24,123	52,491	65,772	65,926	74,671	90,099
Jordan	1,897	3,864	5,119	4,020	5,319	5,606	6,237	6,732
Kenya	3,951	6,017	6,136	8,533	8,209	5,752	7,149	9,054
Kuwait	14,140	28,691	21,446	18,471	19,870	23,955	24,859	26,555
Lebanon		4,074	3,614	2,838	5,546	7,535	9,110	11,118
Lesotho	193	368	247	615	822	815	835	933
Liberia	706	917	1,057	1,317	1,671	1,878	2,112	2,385
Libya	19,466	36,756	27,787	28,904	33,887	30,660	28,611	25,541
Madagascar	1,905	3,265	2,858	3,081	3,001	3,371	2,977	3,160
Malawi	806	1,238	1,131	1,858	1,800	2,037	1,171	1,436
Mali	832	1,422	1,234	2,473	2,725	2,515	1,763	2,378
Mauritania	548	691	691	1,050	1,110	948	1,005	1,058
Mauritius	824	1,132	1,076	2,642	3,189	3,205	3,510	3,973
Morocco	11,050	18,821	12,870	25,820	28,451	26,802	30,352	32,985
Mozambique		2,361	2,521	1,415	1,969	2,028	2,163	2,247
Namibia		3,008	1,281	2,444	2,931	2,847	3,253	3,503
Niger	1,176	2,538	1,462	2,487	2,345	2,286	1,418	1,672
Nigeria	52,094	91,938	80,954	32,424	31,784	31,791	41,596	90,327
Oman	2,741	5,927	10,396	11,685	12,452	12,493	12,919	13,803
Qatar	3,618	7,838	6,153	7,360	7,646	7,157	7,374	8,138
Réunion		1,999	1,945					5,539
Rwanda	746	1,255	1,716	2,551	2,008	1,954	1,178	1,283
Sao Tomé e Príncipe		47	52	58	45	48	50	45
Saudi Arabia (b)	63,942	156,486	86,673	104,671	136,304	132,151	134,327	142,458
Senegal	1,979	2,987	2,579	5,698	5,964	5,375	3,359	4,453
Seychelles	65	147	169	369	434	469	486	508
Sierra Leone	649	1,101	857	650	680	769	912	871
Somalia		2,755	2,211					
South Africa	39,400	80,543	57,253	112,014	130,513	130,406	135,778	151,113
Sudan	8,279	9,901	6,039	24,469	4,186	5,242	5,802	8,319
Swaziland	302	542	361	860	982	1,027	1,146	1,364
Syria	6,882	13,062	21,204	23,904	33,107	36,860	45,087	50,866
Tanzania	3,483	5,581	6,582	4,259	4,601	4,258	4,511	5,255
Togo	687	1,128	753	1,625	1,676	1,244	983	1,109
Tunisia	5,110	8,743	8,410	12,314	15,497	14,608	15,633	18,030
Uganda	5,881	18,228	3,813	3,736	3,252	3,367	5,280	6,170
United Arab Emirates	16,217	29,617	27,023	33,653	35,413	35,519	36,668	40,052
Yemen					15,314	18,958	24,336	11,962
Zambia	2,515	3,885	2,252	3,742	3,308	3,273	3,347	3,470
Zimbabwe	3,499	5,355	5,639	8,767	6,746	6,553	6,889	7,111

Source: Euromonitor from International Monetary Fund (IMF), International Financial Statistics
Notes: (a) From 1980, year ending 30 June, (b) Islamic lunar year

■ GDP

Total Gross Domestic Product 1977-2002 (US$) (continued)

● US$ million

	1996	1997	1998	1999	2000	2001	2002	US$ per capita 2002
Africa and Middle East								
Algeria	46,942	48,177	47,841	48,294	54,195	54,678	58,569	1,912.6
Angola	6,522	7,649	6,446	6,088	8,859	9,471	11,248	793.1
Bahrain	6,101	6,349	6,186	6,621	7,614	7,512	7,683	11,993.8
Benin	2,208	2,141	2,334	2,388	2,255	2,371	2,811	422.3
Botswana	4,273	4,859	4,771	4,654	4,889	4,909	5,057	2,952.3
Burkina Faso	2,401	2,287	2,486	2,466	2,192	2,329	2,630	199.9
Burundi	877	973	894	808	709	662	624	87.9
Cameroon	9,455	9,023	9,445	9,762	9,289	9,609	10,747	648.1
Cape Verde	505	493	523	578	532	550	619	1,344.8
Central African Republic	1,008	955	1,057	1,072	991	1,004	1,077	282.4
Chad	1,589	1,523	1,700	1,506	1,374	1,622	1,731	210.3
Comoros	230	212	215	223	204	219	247	323.4
Congo Dem Rep	5,771	5,941	6,218	12,897	15,351	7,531	4,626	82.4
Congo-Brazzaville	2,541	2,323	1,949	2,354	3,220	2,988	3,193	1,054.1
Côte d'Ivoire	10,846	11,709	12,783	12,561	10,599	10,735	11,717	743.1
Djibouti	494	503	514	536	553	573	592	884.5
Egypt [a]	67,640	75,898	84,829	90,597	97,954	90,284	84,828	1,317.4
Equatorial Guinea	278	553	449	758	1,253	1,781	2,166	4,420.3
Eritrea	627	658	642	676	620	724		
Ethiopia	5,973	6,743	6,301	6,130	6,337	6,268	6,525	97.2
Gabon	5,694	5,327	4,484	4,663	4,998	4,557	4,901	3,698.8
Gambia	396	435	417	432	421	391	357	249.5
Ghana	6,926	6,884	7,474	7,710	4,977	5,301	5,008	228.7
Guinea	3,869	3,784	3,588	3,461	3,112	3,038	3,214	419.5
Guinea-Bissau	335	279	206	224	215	199	217	166.2
Iran	141,852	166,956	187,849	249,034	328,647	379,603	101,483	1,465.8
Iraq	88,105	264,315	296,032	329,483				
Israel	99,246	103,224	103,447	103,761	114,816	112,716	103,688	16,145.6
Jordan	6,928	7,246	7,912	8,135	8,466	8,830	9,716	1,814.3
Kenya	9,257	10,612	11,497	10,572	10,454	11,236	12,309	375.7
Kuwait	31,070	29,865	25,123	29,184	37,022	34,223	35,331	15,078.4
Lebanon	12,993	14,863	16,251	16,544	16,399	16,660	17,292	4,991.8
Lesotho	943	1,024	890	911	899	752	716	309.2
Liberia	2,491	2,602	2,776	3,067	3,490			
Libya	27,885	30,701	27,251	30,484	33,962	27,922	13,522	2,303.2
Madagascar	3,995	3,546	3,740	3,721	3,878	4,530	4,400	251.3
Malawi	2,381	2,573	1,845	1,783	1,632	1,746	1,673	138.9
Mali	2,579	2,698	2,921	2,928	2,645	3,006	3,385	279.8
Mauritania	1,081	1,058	958	971	901	935	917	314.4
Mauritius	4,307	4,104	4,163	4,266	4,554	4,526	4,790	4,043.2
Morocco	36,639	33,414	35,817	35,248	33,322	33,876	37,003	1,266.9
Mozambique	2,841	3,449	3,775	3,772	3,229	2,723	2,578	120.8
Namibia	3,491	3,636	3,399	3,387	3,352	3,100	2,600	1,420.3
Niger	2,020	1,856	2,076	2,018	1,650	1,744	1,944	164.7
Nigeria	129,038	134,316	131,651	35,977	48,210	51,269	48,947	393.1
Oman	15,278	15,837	14,085	15,712	19,868	19,944	20,323	7,223.6
Qatar	9,059	11,298	10,255	12,197	17,760	17,127	17,466	27,508.9
Réunion	8,603	7,996	8,302					
Rwanda	1,392	1,870	2,000	1,875	1,732	1,651	1,647	170.9
Sao Tomé e Príncipe	45	44	41	47	46	48	54	342.8
Saudi Arabia [b]	157,743	164,994	145,967	161,172	188,693	183,257	188,479	8,252.0
Senegal	4,593	4,299	4,605	4,699	4,374	4,610	5,096	495.2
Seychelles	503	563	608	623	595	570	594	7,607.8
Sierra Leone	942	850	672	670	636	749	756	142.0
Somalia	921	935						
South Africa	143,732	148,814	133,663	131,058	127,965	114,174	104,235	2,347.8
Sudan	8,169	10,162	11,086	9,975	10,920	11,993	12,373	386.4
Swaziland	1,322	1,435	1,348	1,376	1,389	1,274	1,166	1,057.3
Syria	61,546	66,420	70,418	72,970	79,878	84,674	86,960	4,982.5
Tanzania	6,496	7,684	8,383	8,638	9,079	9,341	9,382	262.1
Togo	1,466	1,499	1,416	1,427	1,207	1,233	1,465	292.1
Tunisia	19,587	18,897	19,813	20,799	19,468	20,018	21,031	2,170.7
Uganda	6,344	6,644	6,266	6,088	5,848	5,857	6,010	249.8
United Arab Emirates	44,606	49,353	46,471	52,662	65,024	64,665	66,619	20,383.3
Yemen	7,457	6,597	5,870	6,720	9,172	8,058	8,072	396.8
Zambia	3,286	3,922	3,247	3,141	3,248	3,651	3,087	307.2
Zimbabwe	8,474	8,428	5,732	5,613	7,231	9,395	8,195	665.9

Source: *Euromonitor from International Monetary Fund (IMF), International Financial Statistics*
Notes: *(a) From 1980, year ending 30 June, (b) Islamic lunar year*

GDP

Origin of Gross Domestic Product: Latest Year

Table 10.3

● Billion units of national currency

	Year	Agriculture, Forestry & Fishing	Mining & Quarrying	Manufacturing	Electricity, Gas & Water	Construction
Algeria	2002	398.8	1,624.7	237.9	57.9	340.1
Argentina	2002	15.8	4.9	35.2	7.2	7.9
Australia	2002	20.4	32.5	81.8	12.1	38.2
Azerbaijan	2002	4,150.2	8,120.7	1,816.8	382.8	3,185.0
Bolivia	2002	7.1	4.2	6.6	1.3	1.6
Brazil	2002	88.0	14.8	225.3	38.6	116.7
Canada	1998	17.2	27.9	127.9	27.4	38.7
Chile	2002	2,166.0	3,049.9	5,979.2	1,077.7	2,960.6
China	1993	688.2		1,414.4		228.5
Colombia	2002	25,733.8	19,932.3	23,747.2	8,855.6	3,290.6
Ecuador	2002	53,197,685.9	75,982,173.4	90,665,474.3	1,263,750.3	18,795,109.0
Egypt	2002	54.1	19.3	68.2	6.5	21.1
Hong Kong, China	2002	0.8	0.2	59.4	41.2	56.0
India	2002	5,541.8	533.3	3,351.1	636.4	1,481.9
Indonesia	2002	281,325.0	191,827.2	402,601.1	29,100.5	92,366.3
Israel	1996	6.7		52.6	5.2	23.1
Japan	2002	5,788.6	505.0	108,704.0	14,565.7	35,205.8
Jordan	2002	0.1	0.2	0.8	0.2	0.1
Kazakhstan	2002	297.5		1,099.0		229.8
Kuwait	1998	0.0	2.4	0.9	0.0	0.2
Malaysia	2002	33.1	36.7	110.9	12.4	14.7
Mexico	2002	172.5	72.5	1,092.3	65.7	302.7
Morocco	2002	64.1	7.3	66.9	27.0	19.3
New Zealand	2002	7.7	1.4	17.3	2.3	4.5
Nigeria	2002	1,796.3	2,304.7	305.0	5.6	40.0
Pakistan	2002	829.4	22.8	537.0	106.6	103.2
Peru	2002	15.5	11.4	28.2	4.8	9.0
Philippines	2002	569.6	21.7	913.4	129.4	183.4
Saudi Arabia	2002	37.0	225.6	56.1	1.0	51.6
Singapore	2002	0.2		41.2	2.8	8.4
South Africa	2002	29.2	78.0	201.1	27.6	30.1
South Korea	1991	16,547.0	1,598.0	62,803.0	4,408.0	27,191.0
Taiwan	2002	162.7	30.7	2,106.8	170.5	239.3
Thailand	2002	437.2	136.0	1,765.3	172.2	97.2
Tunisia	2002	3.1	0.2	5.6	1.4	1.5
Turkmenistan	2002	12,029.8		12,348.7		2,750.9
United Arab Emirates	2002	7.6	76.1	25.3	5.2	18.2
USA	2002	123.2	108.0	1,612.9	219.8	531.7
Venezuela	2002	30.3	5.4	80.8	11.2	31.1
Vietnam	2002	121,066.9	56,531.0	108,826.0	18,645.0	27,420.6

Source: Euromonitor from national statistics

Origin of Gross Domestic Product: Latest Year (continued)

● Billion units of national currency

	Year	Wholesale & Retail Trade, Restaurants & Hotels	Transport, Storage & Communications	Finance, Insurance, Real Estate & Business Services	Community, Social & Personal Services	Other	Total GDP
Algeria	2002	634.0	343.9	128.8	71.8	541.4	4,379.2
Argentina	2002	33.2	20.4	49.9	44.7	14.0	233.3
Australia	2002	63.5	77.4	149.5	71.7	166.8	713.8
Azerbaijan	2002	2,354.3	2,903.1	332.6	732.1	3,320.4	27,298.0
Bolivia	2002	5.7	6.7	8.0	9.4		50.5
Brazil	2002	80.7	66.6	216.7	277.9		1,125.4
Canada	1998	105.6	56.6	159.5	122.4	34.2	717.6
Chile	2002	4,013.1	2,872.2	7,444.9	3,996.0	1,382.1	34,941.8
China	1993	309.1	212.3		178.2	432.7	3,463.4
Colombia	2002	21,155.7	16,068.8	23,074.0	48,656.4		190,514.4
Ecuador	2002	84,605,957.9	46,199,469.6	39,471,579.4	53,592,822.6		463,774,022.4
Egypt	2002	67.4	23.8	21.7	53.9	7.7	343.8
Hong Kong, China	2002	312.4	124.2	251.0	271.2	52.1	1,168.3
India	2002	3,265.3	1,688.8	2,987.9	1,624.3	2,002.7	23,113.6
Indonesia	2002	258,869.2	97,343.5	105,621.7	83,293.5	67,663.6	1,610,011.6
Israel	1996	34.0	20.1	57.7	76.9	27.6	303.8
Japan	2002	68,479.6	31,330.8	98,882.1	128,802.1	24,750.2	517,013.9
Jordan	2002	0.7	0.9	1.0	0.3	2.0	6.1
Kazakhstan	2002	449.9	429.6			1,241.4	3,747.2
Kuwait	1998	0.7	0.5	1.2	2.0	0.2	8.0
Malaysia	2002	50.6	25.9	39.7	27.8	23.9	375.6
Mexico	2002	1,103.0	642.7	608.0	1,414.8		5,474.3
Morocco	2002	54.9	28.7	19.1	59.9	50.5	397.8
New Zealand	2002	17.7	11.4	27.6	13.9	8.8	112.6
Nigeria	2002	795.4	141.7	134.4	60.4	159.7	5,743.2
Pakistan	2002	511.8	393.8	265.8	336.8	321.1	3,428.3
Peru	2002	34.1	16.5	26.2	33.1	1.4	180.0
Philippines	2002	591.7	282.0	540.0	380.9	397.1	4,009.3
Saudi Arabia	2002	41.0	36.3	32.5	16.3	111.4	608.9
Singapore	2002	19.9	17.9	38.1		27.3	155.7
South Africa	2002	134.5	108.6	229.3	31.0	299.5	1,168.9
South Korea	1991	28,202.0	14,307.0	32,883.0	9,181.0	19,390.0	216,511.0
Taiwan	2002	1,638.0	555.8	1,629.2	235.1	1,400.4	8,168.5
Thailand	2002	863.3	418.9	207.9	239.6	766.5	5,104.0
Tunisia	2002	8.2	2.6	1.6	5.0	0.8	30.1
Turkmenistan	2002	2,565.1	2,482.2	440.4	482.3	10,203.8	43,303.3
United Arab Emirates	2002	21.5	23.2	31.2	32.4	3.0	243.6
USA	2002	1,685.4	647.8	2,139.0	2,392.7	1,017.1	10,477.6
Venezuela	2002	61.6	39.3	74.4	40.7	45.7	420.5
Vietnam	2002	72,649.7	21,383.8	9,723.0	43,320.4	52,465.7	532,032.1

Source: *Euromonitor from national statistics*

GDP

Origin of Gross Domestic Product: Latest Year (% Analysis)

Table 10.4

● % of total GDP

	Year	Agriculture, Forestry & Fishing	Mining & Quarrying	Manufacturing	Electricity, Gas & Water	Construction
Algeria	2002	9.1	37.1	5.4	1.3	7.8
Argentina	2002	6.8	2.1	15.1	3.1	3.4
Australia	2002	2.9	4.6	11.5	1.7	5.3
Azerbaijan	2002	15.2	29.7	6.7	1.4	11.7
Bolivia	2002	14.0	8.2	13.0	2.6	3.2
Brazil	2002	7.8	1.3	20.0	3.4	10.4
Canada	1998	2.4	3.9	17.8	3.8	5.4
Chile	2002	6.2	8.7	17.1	3.1	8.5
China	1993	19.9		40.8		6.6
Colombia	2002	13.5	10.5	12.5	4.6	1.7
Ecuador	2002	11.5	16.4	19.5	0.3	4.1
Egypt	2002	15.7	5.6	19.9	1.9	6.1
Hong Kong, China	2002	0.1	0.0	5.1	3.5	4.8
India	2002	24.0	2.3	14.5	2.8	6.4
Indonesia	2002	17.5	11.9	25.0	1.8	5.7
Israel	1996	2.2		17.3	1.7	7.6
Japan	2002	1.1	0.1	21.0	2.8	6.8
Jordan	2002	1.4	2.8	13.0	2.6	1.7
Kazakhstan	2002	7.9		29.3		6.1
Kuwait	1998	0.4	29.5	11.4	0.0	3.0
Malaysia	2002	8.8	9.8	29.5	3.3	3.9
Mexico	2002	3.2	1.3	20.0	1.2	5.5
Morocco	2002	16.1	1.8	16.8	6.8	4.9
New Zealand	2002	6.9	1.2	15.3	2.1	4.0
Nigeria	2002	31.3	40.1	5.3	0.1	0.7
Pakistan	2002	24.2	0.7	15.7	3.1	3.0
Peru	2002	8.6	6.3	15.7	2.7	5.0
Philippines	2002	14.2	0.5	22.8	3.2	4.6
Saudi Arabia	2002	6.1	37.0	9.2	0.2	8.5
Singapore	2002	0.1		26.5	1.8	5.4
South Africa	2002	2.5	6.7	17.2	2.4	2.6
South Korea	1991	7.6	0.7	29.0	2.0	12.6
Taiwan	2002	2.0	0.4	25.8	2.1	2.9
Thailand	2002	8.6	2.7	34.6	3.4	1.9
Tunisia	2002	10.4	0.7	18.6	4.8	5.0
Turkmenistan	2002	27.8		28.5		6.4
United Arab Emirates	2002	3.1	31.2	10.4	2.2	7.5
USA	2002	1.2	1.0	15.4	2.1	5.1
Venezuela	2002	7.2	1.3	19.2	2.7	7.4
Vietnam	2002	22.8	10.6	20.5	3.5	5.2

Source: Euromonitor from national statistics

Origin of Gross Domestic Product: Latest Year (% Analysis) (continued)

● % of total GDP

	Year	Wholesale & Retail Trade, Restaurants & Hotels	Transport, Storage & Communications	Finance, Insurance, Real Estate & Business Services	Community, Social & Personal Services	Other	Total GDP
Algeria	2002	14.5	7.9	2.9	1.6	12.4	100.0
Argentina	2002	14.2	8.8	21.4	19.2	6.0	100.0
Australia	2002	8.9	10.8	20.9	10.0	23.4	100.0
Azerbaijan	2002	8.6	10.6	1.2	2.7	12.2	100.0
Bolivia	2002	11.2	13.3	15.8	18.6		100.0
Brazil	2002	7.2	5.9	19.3	24.7		100.0
Canada	1998	14.7	7.9	22.2	17.1	4.8	100.0
Chile	2002	11.5	8.2	21.3	11.4	4.0	100.0
China	1993	8.9	6.1		5.1	12.5	100.0
Colombia	2002	11.1	8.4	12.1	25.5		100.0
Ecuador	2002	18.2	10.0	8.5	11.6		100.0
Egypt	2002	19.6	6.9	6.3	15.7	2.3	100.0
Hong Kong, China	2002	26.7	10.6	21.5	23.2	4.5	100.0
India	2002	14.1	7.3	12.9	7.0	8.7	100.0
Indonesia	2002	16.1	6.0	6.6	5.2	4.2	100.0
Israel	1996	11.2	6.6	19.0	25.3	9.1	100.0
Japan	2002	13.2	6.1	19.1	24.9	4.8	100.0
Jordan	2002	12.0	14.0	16.0	4.8	31.8	100.0
Kazakhstan	2002	12.0	11.5			33.1	100.0
Kuwait	1998	8.2	5.7	14.8	24.3	2.7	100.0
Malaysia	2002	13.5	6.9	10.6	7.4	6.4	100.0
Mexico	2002	20.1	11.7	11.1	25.8		100.0
Morocco	2002	13.8	7.2	4.8	15.1	12.7	100.0
New Zealand	2002	15.7	10.1	24.5	12.3	7.8	100.0
Nigeria	2002	13.8	2.5	2.3	1.1	2.8	100.0
Pakistan	2002	14.9	11.5	7.8	9.8	9.4	100.0
Peru	2002	18.9	9.2	14.5	18.4	0.8	100.0
Philippines	2002	14.8	7.0	13.5	9.5	9.9	100.0
Saudi Arabia	2002	6.7	6.0	5.3	2.7	18.3	100.0
Singapore	2002	12.8	11.5	24.5		17.5	100.0
South Africa	2002	11.5	9.3	19.6	2.6	25.6	100.0
South Korea	1991	13.0	6.6	15.2	4.2	9.0	100.0
Taiwan	2002	20.1	6.8	19.9	2.9	17.1	100.0
Thailand	2002	16.9	8.2	4.1	4.7	15.0	100.0
Tunisia	2002	27.2	8.7	5.4	16.5	2.7	100.0
Turkmenistan	2002	5.9	5.7	1.0	1.1	23.6	100.0
United Arab Emirates	2002	8.8	9.5	12.8	13.3	1.2	100.0
USA	2002	16.1	6.2	20.4	22.8	9.7	100.0
Venezuela	2002	14.6	9.3	17.7	9.7	10.9	100.0
Vietnam	2002	13.7	4.0	1.8	8.1	9.9	100.0

Source: *Euromonitor from national statistics*

■ GDP

Table 10.5

Usage of Gross Domestic Product: Latest Year

- Billion units of national currency

	Year	Government Final Consumption	Private Final Consumption	Increases in Stocks	Gross Fixed Capital Formation	Exports of Goods & Services	Imports of Goods & Services	Total
Algeria	2000	560.2	1,713.2	15.2	869.3	1,749.0	-828.3	4,078.7
Argentina	2002	38.2	193.3	-3.7	37.5	86.7	-39.0	313.0
Australia	2002	132.1	441.1	-1.5	170.3	151.3	-162.0	731.9
Azerbaijan	2002		15,393.8					32,511.2
Bolivia	2002	8.6	41.8	-0.6	8.9	12.3	-15.1	55.9
Brazil	2002	254.7	783.3	8.4	247.2	208.3	-180.4	1,321.5
Canada	2002	218.9	656.2	2.9	227.2	474.3	-424.0	1,155.0
Chile	2002	5,784.9	28,903.7	367.3	9,657.8	15,619.7	-14,570.9	45,762.5
China	1999	1,038.8	3,933.4	122.6	2,947.6	241.8		8,267.3
Colombia	2001	37,474.7	123,365.0	1,671.1	26,592.5	39,153.4	-40,526.2	187,936.0
Ecuador	2001	41,237.0	291,097.5	4,056.0	73,475.0	142,837.0	-124,741.0	427,962.5
Egypt	2002	45.2	285.5	1.7	67.5	68.0	-86.2	381.7
Hong Kong, China	2002	131.4	708.6	3.8	304.0	1,913.7	-1,790.3	1,271.1
India	2000	2,645.6	13,593.6	138.3	4,597.9	2,901.8	-3,060.9	21,043.0
Indonesia	2001	110,837.0	999,266.0	-56,820.0	310,909.0	612,482.0	-485,700.0	1,490,970.0
Israel	2002	153.1	291.6	1.4	87.2	182.8	-224.9	491.3
Japan	2001	88,312.0	283,652.0	-1,708.0	129,874.0	52,567.0	-49,393.0	503,304.0
Jordan	1999	1.4	4.0	0.1	1.4	2.5	-3.5	5.8
Kazakhstan	1998	186.9	1,270.0	1.5	272.4	525.9	-604.2	1,652.6
Kuwait	1998	2.4	4.4	0.0	1.4	3.5	-4.0	7.7
Malaysia	2002	50.0	159.5	4.4	83.8	411.4	-348.4	360.7
Mexico	2002	723.5	4,304.6	85.0	1,161.7	1,673.5	-1,795.4	6,152.8
Morocco	2001	74.6	259.8	2.1	85.3	105.4	-119.6	382.9
New Zealand	2002	23.1	74.5	1.5	24.2	42.8	-40.2	126.1
Nigeria	1996	143.1	2,368.0	0.4	246.7	852.8	-712.4	2,823.9
Pakistan	2002	425.9	2,793.4	58.0	459.5	661.0	-671.2	3,726.6
Peru	2002	21.7	143.4	2.6	34.4	32.4	-34.4	200.0
Philippines	2002	488.7	2,750.8	2.1	774.1	1,968.5	-1,989.1	4,022.7
Saudi Arabia	2002	181.5	260.9	8.2	130.0	287.9	-162.6	705.9
Singapore	1996	12.2	52.9	-1.8	49.4	20.4		128.2
South Africa	2002	211.4	682.4	7.6	166.4	373.0	-335.6	1,098.7
South Korea	2002	62,968.0	358,834.0	-4,158.5	159,482.0	238,634.0	-230,056.0	596,381.0
Taiwan	1996	1,082.3	4,597.7	23.1	1,565.4	3,630.4		7,678.1
Thailand	2002	609.8	3,067.4	43.7	1,251.6	3,516.9	-3,123.6	5,433.3
Tunisia	2002	4.9	18.7	0.2	7.4	13.4	-14.7	29.9
Turkmenistan	2002		12,584.2					34,506.7
United Arab Emirates	1998	28.6	90.7	2.2	49.2	115.0	-115.0	170.7
USA	1997	1,487.9	5,529.3	62.9	1,173.0	966.4	-1,055.8	8,318.4
Venezuela	2001	7,846.7	61,107.9	3,057.0	14,952.6	20,320.2	-15,959.6	91,324.8
Vietnam	2002		334,629.9		160,840.0			533,098.0

Source: International Monetary Fund (IMF), International Financial Statistics

Usage of Gross Domestic Product: Latest Year (% Analysis)

- % of total GDP

	Year	Government Final Consumption	Private Final Consumption	Increases in Stocks	Gross Fixed Capital Formation	Exports of Goods & Services	Imports of Goods & Services	Total
Algeria	2000	13.7	42.0	0.4	21.3	42.9	-20.3	100.0
Argentina	2002	12.2	61.7	-1.2	12.0	27.7	-12.5	100.0
Australia	2002	18.0	60.3	-0.2	23.3	20.7	-22.1	100.0
Azerbaijan	2002		47.3					100.0
Bolivia	2002	15.4	74.8	-1.1	15.9	21.9	-26.9	100.0
Brazil	2002	19.3	59.3	0.6	18.7	15.8	-13.6	100.0
Canada	2002	19.0	56.8	0.2	19.7	41.1	-36.7	100.0
Chile	2002	12.6	63.2	0.8	21.1	34.1	-31.8	100.0
China	1999	12.6	47.6	1.5	35.7	2.9		100.0
Colombia	2001	19.9	65.6	0.9	14.1	20.8	-21.6	100.0
Ecuador	2001	9.6	68.0	0.9	17.2	33.4	-29.1	100.0
Egypt	2002	11.8	74.8	0.4	17.7	17.8	-22.6	100.0
Hong Kong, China	2002	10.3	55.7	0.3	23.9	150.6	-140.8	100.0
India	2000	12.6	64.6	0.7	21.9	13.8	-14.5	100.0
Indonesia	2001	7.4	67.0	-3.8	20.9	41.1	-32.6	100.0
Israel	2002	31.2	59.4	0.3	17.8	37.2	-45.8	100.0
Japan	2001	17.5	56.4	-0.3	25.8	10.4	-9.8	100.0
Jordan	1999	24.0	68.7	1.7	23.5	43.4	-61.3	100.0
Kazakhstan	1998	11.3	76.9	0.1	16.5	31.8	-36.6	100.0
Kuwait	1998	31.5	56.9	0.1	18.9	45.3	-52.8	100.0
Malaysia	2002	13.9	44.2	1.2	23.2	114.1	-96.6	100.0
Mexico	2002	11.8	70.0	1.4	18.9	27.2	-29.2	100.0
Morocco	2001	19.5	67.9	0.6	22.3	27.5	-31.2	100.0
New Zealand	2002	18.3	59.1	1.2	19.2	34.0	-31.9	100.0
Nigeria	1996	5.1	83.9	0.0	8.7	30.2	-25.2	100.0
Pakistan	2002	11.4	75.0	1.6	12.3	17.7	-18.0	100.0
Peru	2002	10.9	71.7	1.3	17.2	16.2	-17.2	100.0
Philippines	2002	12.1	68.4	0.1	19.2	48.9	-49.4	100.0
Saudi Arabia	2002	25.7	37.0	1.2	18.4	40.8	-23.0	100.0
Singapore	1996	9.5	41.3	-1.4	38.5	15.9		100.0
South Africa	2002	19.2	62.1	0.7	15.1	34.0	-30.5	100.0
South Korea	2002	10.6	60.2	-0.7	26.7	40.0	-38.6	100.0
Taiwan	1996	14.1	59.9	0.3	20.4	47.3		100.0
Thailand	2002	11.2	56.5	0.8	23.0	64.7	-57.5	100.0
Tunisia	2002	16.4	62.5	0.7	24.7	44.8	-49.2	100.0
Turkmenistan	2002		36.5					100.0
United Arab Emirates	1998	16.8	53.1	1.3	28.8	67.4	-67.4	100.0
USA	1997	17.9	66.5	0.8	14.1	11.6	-12.7	100.0
Venezuela	2001	8.6	66.9	3.3	16.4	22.3	-17.5	100.0
Vietnam	2002		62.8		30.2			100.0

Source: *International Monetary Fund (IMF), International Financial Statistics*

Table 10.7

GNP

Total Gross National Product 1977-2002 (national currencies)

• Million units of national currency

	1977	1980	1985	1990	1993	1994	1995	1996
North America								
Canada	213,308	302,064	463,656	645,613	704,411	744,833	783,910	810,734
USA	2,052,100	2,830,800	4,238,400	5,832,200	6,666,700	7,071,100	7,420,900	7,831,200
Latin America								
Anguilla								
Antigua	181	294	537	994	1,171	1,279	1,260	1,388
Argentina	0	0	5	67,906	233,510	253,743	253,363	266,648
Aruba								
Bahamas	880	1,186	1,693	2,909	2,779	2,964	2,972	
Barbados	986	1,680	2,372	3,423	3,301	3,471		
Belize		386	399	790	1,024	1,061	1,129	1,159
Bermuda								
Bolivia	0	0	2,598	15,443	25,638	29,101		
Brazil (a)	0	0	0	11	13,742	343,292	636,038	766,659
British Virgin Islands								
Cayman Islands								
Chile	280,157	1,039,000	2,316,800	8,709,100	17,285,200	20,322,900	24,769,300	30,204,300
Colombia	708,330	1,573,410	4,824,100	19,668,500	44,143,400	66,332,800	82,997,400	98,583,100
Costa Rica	25,705	39,417	183,805	501,368	1,336,250	1,636,400	2,065,210	2,421,600
Cuba								
Dominica								
Dominican Republic	4,464	6,421	15,000	57,597	113,047	128,715	151,878	173,395
Ecuador	161,898	278,800	1,028,187	7,575,100	26,353,081	33,668,622	42,767,743	56,569,078
El Salvador	7,095	8,789	13,977	35,517	59,380	69,944	82,291	89,199
French Guiana								
Grenada				565	653	685	710	754
Guadeloupe								
Guatemala	5,448	7,809	10,849	33,489	63,389	73,813	84,231	94,079
Guyana	1,053	1,425	1,857	11,426	47,212	63,939	76,068	91,719
Haiti (b)	4,834	6,847	9,946	11,617	19,009	32,162		
Honduras	3,215	4,857	6,895	11,401	21,191	27,019	34,975	44,694
Jamaica	2,862	4,455	10,186	29,868	113,653	150,413	191,452	232,530
Martinique								
Mexico	1,806	4,159	45,181	666,037	1,096,928	1,272,807		
Netherlands Antilles								
Nicaragua				1,301	8,157	8,888	11,209	13,751
Panama	2,007	3,111	5,206	5,026	6,914	7,462	7,485	8,607
Paraguay	263,970	565,720	1,380,940	6,618,000	12,034,700	15,039,000	17,857,400	19,949,900
Peru	0	0	0	6,630	78,598	109,680		
Puerto Rico								
St Kitts								
St Lucia								
St Vincent and the Grenadines								
Suriname	1,221	1,559	1,746	3,154	10,748	63,482	227,782	300,635
Trinidad and Tobago	6,340	14,485	16,942	19,830	22,639	26,716	28,748	31,305
Uruguay	20	91	443	10,479	58,167	86,523	120,592	161,281
Venezuela	155,340	255,400	438,420	2,211,560	5,291,460	8,400,590	13,362,800	28,772,000

Source: *International Monetary Fund (IMF), International Financial Statistics*
Notes: *(a) New series starting 1990, (b) Year ending 30 September*

GNP

Total Gross National Product 1977-2002 (national currencies) (continued)

● Million units of national currency

	1997	1998	1999	2000	2001	2002	Total US$ million 2002	US$ per capita 2002
North America								
Canada	857,318	885,830	945,752	1,042,630	1,077,850	1,127,560	718,502.3	23,157.6
USA	8,325,400	8,778,100	9,297,100	9,848,000	10,104,100	10,436,700	10,436,700.0	37,400.2
Latin America								
Anguilla								
Antigua	1,496	1,594	1,677	1,702				
Argentina	286,641	291,542	276,126	276,832	260,484			
Aruba								
Bahamas								
Barbados								
Belize	1,188	1,201	1,293	1,437	1,480			
Bermuda								
Bolivia								
Brazil (a)	853,307	892,947	939,739	1,068,440	1,153,590			
British Virgin Islands								
Cayman Islands								
Chile	33,618,100	35,665,300	36,005,900	38,846,400	41,572,200	44,027,600	63,906.7	4,124.2
Colombia	119,002,000	137,973,000	148,902,000	170,061,000				
Costa Rica	2,926,110	3,504,830	3,991,830	4,532,610	5,125,410	5,809,340	16,145.3	4,131.1
Cuba								
Dominica								
Dominican Republic	203,521	228,427	262,730	304,736	343,130	375,076	20,154.8	2,319.8
Ecuador	73,355,860	98,572,024	140,829,865	292,324,299	380,192,500			
El Salvador	95,999	103,647	106,597	112,709	118,458	122,471	13,996.7	2,149.0
French Guiana								
Grenada	803	882	941	1,018				
Guadeloupe								
Guatemala	106,422	123,043	133,807	147,992	163,850	179,560	22,956.8	1,938.8
Guyana	95,399							
Haiti (b)								
Honduras	58,510	67,593	74,761	87,076	96,715	105,085	6,394.6	948.5
Jamaica	253,371	263,583	281,533	315,111	335,526			
Martinique								
Mexico								
Netherlands Antilles								
Nicaragua	16,525	20,561	24,623	29,236	31,800	33,677	2,363.1	485.0
Panama	8,206	8,736	8,846	9,319				
Paraguay	21,156,000	23,741,400	24,276,500	27,301,700	28,283,000	32,606,300	5,704.1	999.4
Peru								
Puerto Rico								
St Kitts								
St Lucia								
St Vincent and the Grenadines								
Suriname	362,188							
Trinidad and Tobago	34,046	36,022						
Uruguay	202,016	231,099	233,894	239,641	242,134	257,940	12,134.4	3,675.2
Venezuela	42,165,500	51,420,600	61,648,200	81,632,600	90,232,800			

Source: *International Monetary Fund (IMF), International Financial Statistics*
Notes: *(a) New series starting 1990, (b) Year ending 30 September*

◻ GNP

Total Gross National Product 1977-2002 (national currencies) (continued)

● Million units of national currency

	1977	1980	1985	1990	1993	1994	1995	1996
Asia Pacific								
Afghanistan								
American Samoa								
Armenia								
Azerbaijan								
Bangladesh [a]	100,300	140,430	392,240	1,024,200	1,287,820	1,396,460	1,571,690	1,712,780
Bhutan		706	1,964	4,657	6,458	7,954	8,856	10,562
Brunei								
Cambodia								
China	264,400	362,410	881,680	1,837,000	3,442,670	4,660,130	5,752,730	
Fiji	651	698	1,280	1,910	2,337	3,001		
French Polynesia								
Guam								
Hong Kong, China					926,054	1,041,810	1,116,770	1,211,110
India [b]	958,300	1,040,340	2,608,100	5,611,300	8,471,400	9,996,900	11,745,300	13,551,300
Indonesia [c]	18,332,200	21,853,800	94,465,000	201,249,000	296,095,000	348,072,000	413,661,000	489,377,000
Japan	185,530,000	204,474,000	327,005,000	444,685,000	490,680,000	495,646,000	501,573,000	516,271,000
Kazakhstan					29,352	421,297	1,005,080	1,403,470
Kiribati								
Kyrgyzstan					5,286	11,830	15,945	22,914
Laos								
Macau								
Malaysia	31,064	36,186	72,039	114,017	163,928	186,049	212,095	241,931
Maldives	142	170	600	1,164				
Mongolia								
Myanmar [b]	29,557	31,708	55,408	151,988	359,892	472,378	604,040	791,864
Nauru								
Nepal [d]	17,599	20,023	45,078	89,941	171,386	199,408		
New Caledonia								
North Korea								
Pakistan [a]	155,228	188,473	510,468	890,700	1,342,800	1,565,100	1,880,000	2,113,000
Papua New Guinea	1,437	1,554	2,491	2,958	4,537	5,136	5,681	6,574
Philippines	153,255	177,022	551,428	1,071,430	1,509,510	1,736,380	1,958,550	2,261,340
Singapore	15,852	17,787	40,330	68,288	93,494	109,037	121,351	130,130
Solomon Islands								
South Korea	17,788,000	24,119,200	79,170,400	178,628,000	277,107,000	322,811,000	376,316,000	417,108,000
Sri Lanka	31,256	42,428	158,975	315,099	493,586	570,774	660,814	756,875
Taiwan	815,349	977,987	2,515,049	4,326,956	5,894,368	6,433,653	7,214,786	7,577,473
Tajikistan								
Thailand	402,250	484,600	1,038,900	2,156,110	3,119,290	3,573,550	4,118,010	4,508,960
Tonga	31	37	80	158	189	208		
Turkmenistan								
Tuvalu								
Uzbekistan								
Vanuatu			11,344	19,182	21,083	21,941	23,841	
Vietnam								
Western Samoa								
Australasia								
Australia [b]	94,507	104,061	232,117	378,237	423,839	443,162	465,896	497,904
New Zealand [b]	14,634	16,549	42,762	70,379	76,980	81,366	86,680	89,647

Source: International Monetary Fund (IMF), International Financial Statistics
Notes: (a) Year ending 30 June, (b) Year beginning 1 April, (c) New series starting 1993, (d) Year ending 15 April

GNP

Total Gross National Product 1977-2002 (national currencies) (continued)

- Million units of national currency

	1997	1998	1999	2000	2001	2002	Total US$ million 2002	US$ per capita 2002
Asia Pacific								
Afghanistan								
American Samoa								
Armenia								
Azerbaijan								
Bangladesh [a]	1,865,470	2,066,740	2,272,500	2,458,000	2,623,880	2,815,800	48,642.2	369.7
Bhutan	13,173	14,013	16,040	18,240				
Brunei								
Cambodia								
China								
Fiji								
French Polynesia								
Guam								
Hong Kong, China	1,355,020	1,308,610	1,280,910	1,310,110	1,320,170	1,298,500	166,497.4	23,067.3
India [b]	15,093,400	17,259,700	19,142,100	20,868,800	22,833,900			
Indonesia [c]	571,512,000	895,379,000	1,005,070,000	1,189,860,000	1,432,900,000			
Japan	528,617,000	522,773,000	518,914,000	518,256,000				
Kazakhstan	1,648,760	1,709,930	1,953,680	2,437,540	3,066,880			
Kiribati								
Kyrgyzstan	29,682	32,433	45,804	61,510	70,744			
Laos								
Macau								
Malaysia	266,699	267,923	279,878	313,703	308,686	335,597	88,315.0	3,812.0
Maldives								
Mongolia								
Myanmar [b]	1,119,440	1,609,810	2,190,180					
Nauru								
Nepal [d]								
New Caledonia								
North Korea								
Pakistan [a]	2,409,000	2,653,300	2,912,800	3,102,300	3,365,400	3,752,500	62,830.9	386.0
Papua New Guinea	6,754	7,445	8,421					
Philippines	2,528,320	2,802,130	3,136,170	3,566,060	3,918,680	4,290,200	83,137.6	1,047.9
Singapore	149,450	145,873	143,507	160,913	154,645			
Solomon Islands								
South Korea	450,853,000	436,642,000	476,598,000	519,227,000	550,014,000	596,881,000	477,088.8	9,905.3
Sri Lanka	880,828	1,006,370	1,088,150	1,233,520	1,377,110	1,535,490	16,051.2	843.8
Taiwan								
Tajikistan								
Thailand	4,609,230	4,466,400	4,510,640	4,839,630	5,038,350	5,343,750	124,388.7	1,998.1
Tonga								
Turkmenistan								
Tuvalu								
Uzbekistan								
Vanuatu								
Vietnam								
Western Samoa								
Australasia								
Australia [b]	526,891	559,318	589,359	631,567	670,993	710,227	385,875.5	19,847.4
New Zealand [b]	93,231	96,192	99,249	109,519	114,340	123,439	57,089.8	14,630.0

Source: *International Monetary Fund (IMF), International Financial Statistics*
Notes: *(a) Year ending 30 June, (b) Year beginning 1 April, (c) New series starting 1993, (d) Year ending 15 April*

□ GNP

Total Gross National Product 1977-2002 (national currencies) (continued)

- Million units of national currency

	1977	1980	1985	1990	1993	1994	1995	1996
Africa and Middle East								
Algeria				581,097	1,149,200	1,426,100	1,873,100	2,364,442
Angola								
Bahrain	790	1,112	1,263	1,786	1,883	2,002	2,177	2,285
Benin	151,341	245,803	459,078	492,901	594,635	816,577	980,793	
Botswana	291	710	1,829	6,130	8,506	10,346		
Burkina Faso	184,100	273,100	749,300	778,400	818,600	970,600	1,100,600	2,679,800
Burundi	48,347	86,429	139,911	194,106	234,002	267,175	246,713	261,411
Cameroon (a)	627,900	1,410,100	3,838,900	3,347,000	3,171,001	3,439,000		
Cape Verde								
Central African Republic								
Chad								
Comoros								
Congo Dem Rep	0	0	0	0	0	109		
Congo-Brazzaville		327,721	868,406	636,800	662,600	780,900	703,300	836,500
Côte d'Ivoire	1,488,800	2,234,200	3,134,800	2,695,100	2,972,880	3,135,914		
Djibouti								
Egypt (b)	8,643	17,231	35,892	74,478	156,465	174,749	191,910	208,662
Equatorial Guinea								
Eritrea								
Ethiopia (c)	6,820	8,527	13,503	16,696	26,257	27,869	33,508	37,662
Gabon	651,400	854,200	1,553,900	1,310,300	1,347,100	2,000,000	2,082,900	2,459,400
Gambia								
Ghana	11,123	42,671	337,280	1,995,010	3,799,600	5,099,100	7,597,500	11,119,200
Guinea								
Guinea-Bissau								
Iran (d)	4,985,600	6,601,900	14,642,300	35,153,000	98,657,300	128,298,000	184,582,000	246,699,000
Iraq		16,299						
Israel (e)	14	108	27,318	103,335	183,624	221,509	267,472	310,460
Jordan	663	1,184	2,016	2,429	3,777	4,249	4,657	4,870
Kenya	35,623	50,969	97,062	185,357	309,233	377,626	445,821	512,130
Kuwait	4,558	9,065	7,853	7,560	8,386	8,321	9,382	10,854
Lebanon								
Lesotho	308	492	1,065	2,643	3,989	4,311	4,795	5,475
Liberia	626	833	986		1,878	2,112		
Libya	5,304							
Madagascar	467,500	698,800	1,553,400	4,603,900	6,450,899	9,131,101		
Malawi	705	924	1,854	4,952	8,785	9,852	21,215	35,857
Mali								
Mauritania								
Mauritius	5,425	8,519	15,918	38,936	56,633	62,600	68,750	76,521
Morocco	51,150	75,720	132,070	223,270	258,290	289,440	290,400	332,020
Mozambique								
Namibia			2,226	6,408	9,486	11,731	13,275	15,321
Niger								
Nigeria	32,272	49,759	70,732	238,270	627,911	849,231	1,773,650	2,612,840
Oman	817	1,835	3,055	3,632	4,154	4,121	4,594	5,179
Qatar								
Réunion								
Rwanda								
Sao Tomé e Príncipe								
Saudi Arabia (f)	223,620	508,424	327,529	398,517	504,666	505,872	541,709	590,860
Senegal	500,100	640,800	1,193,500	1,614,100	1,617,100	2,201,400	2,320,300	2,669,000
Seychelles	463	908	1,163	1,915	2,400	2,469	2,328	2,427
Sierra Leone (a)	733	1,111	4,704	85,967	400,273	473,474	626,173	773,754
Somalia								
South Africa	32,750	60,140	121,869	278,774	417,433	473,521	537,674	604,576
Sudan								
Swaziland	261	416	820	2,297				
Syria								
Tanzania	28,780	42,006	110,557	793,024	1,664,350	2,236,440	2,957,120	3,730,720
Togo	167,500	238,400	338,200	446,000	473,114	534,800		
Tunisia	2,199	3,510	6,873	10,457	13,789	14,896	16,241	18,062
Uganda								
United Arab Emirates								
Yemen (b)				121,155	223,531	287,244	472,336	630,644
Zambia	2,055	3,202	6,986	100,600	1,104,900	2,309,700	2,893,400	3,956,300
Zimbabwe	2,150	3,394	8,944	20,687	40,877	53,375	58,599	81,855

Source: International Monetary Fund (IMF), International Financial Statistics
Notes: (a) Year ending 30 June, (b) From 1980, year ending 30 June, (c) Year ending 7 July, (d) Year beginning 21 March, (e) Year beginning 1 April, (f) Islamic lunar year

◻ GNP

Total Gross National Product 1977-2002 (national currencies) (continued)

● Million units of national currency

	1997	1998	1999	2000	2001	2002	Total US$ million 2002	US$ per capita 2002
Africa and Middle East								
Algeria	2,715,939							
Angola								
Bahrain	2,299	2,265	2,388	2,779	2,700			
Benin								
Botswana								
Burkina Faso	1,350,300	1,472,700	1,506,800	1,546,400	1,693,000	1,819,400	2,610.4	198.4
Burundi	338,402	396,467	450,128	502,341	538,436	569,592	612.0	86.2
Cameroon (a)								
Cape Verde								
Central African Republic								
Chad								
Comoros								
Congo Dem Rep								
Congo-Brazzaville	1,051,200	968,900	1,116,800	1,718,800	1,692,500	1,625,600	2,332.3	770.1
Côte d'Ivoire								
Djibouti								
Egypt (b)	225,273							
Equatorial Guinea								
Eritrea								
Ethiopia (c)	41,241	44,857						
Gabon	2,711,500	2,311,300						
Gambia								
Ghana	13,839,500							
Guinea								
Guinea-Bissau								
Iran (d)	292,170,000	329,466,000	436,008,000	580,152,000	662,244,000			
Iraq								
Israel (e)	347,481	380,799	414,130	442,928	457,584	477,993	100,888.8	15,709.7
Jordan	5,145	5,637	5,715	6,008				
Kenya	609,730	681,652	760,382	778,777				
Kuwait	10,964	9,444	10,439	13,412	11,999	11,738	38,621.1	16,482.7
Lebanon								
Lesotho	6,258	6,306	7,057	7,761	7,986	9,188	871.7	376.7
Liberia								
Libya								
Madagascar								
Malawi	41,721	56,089	77,436	95,722				
Mali								
Mauritania								
Mauritius	86,054	99,253	106,978	118,746	132,228	143,050	4,774.4	4,030.3
Morocco	329,510	358,410	371,050	415,660	415,660			
Mozambique								
Namibia	17,059	19,274	20,588	22,908	26,691			
Niger								
Nigeria	2,713,960	2,705,420	3,083,790	4,540,390	5,249,570	5,535,140	45,905.1	368.7
Oman	5,363	4,669	5,226	6,808	6,853			
Qatar								
Réunion								
Rwanda								
Sao Tomé e Príncipe								
Saudi Arabia (f)	617,672	551,521	611,556	710,002	692,946	705,854	188,479.0	8,252.0
Senegal	2,785,000	2,989,000	3,164,000	3,353,000	3,681,000			
Seychelles	2,768	3,091	3,202	3,246	3,337			
Sierra Leone (a)	725,680	817,068	1,128,870					
Somalia								
South Africa	670,933	721,595	781,432	866,340	951,097	1,070,430	101,552.1	2,287.4
Sudan								
Swaziland								
Syria								
Tanzania	4,654,390	5,496,320	6,385,720	7,150,480	8,147,540			
Togo								
Tunisia	19,900	21,574	23,602	25,385	27,400	28,600	20,116.3	2,076.3
Uganda								
United Arab Emirates								
Yemen (b)	776,857	748,166	948,530					
Zambia	5,082,900							
Zimbabwe								

Source: *International Monetary Fund (IMF), International Financial Statistics*
Notes: *(a) Year ending 30 June, (b) From 1980, year ending 30 June, (c) Year ending 7 July, (d) Year beginning 21 March, (e) Year beginning 1 April, (f) Islamic lunar year*

□ GNP

Table 10.8

Total Gross National Product 1977-2002 (US$)

● US$ million

	1977	1980	1985	1990	1992	1993	1994	1995
North America								
Canada	200,581	258,347	339,555	553,334	560,093	546,025	545,409	571,180
USA	2,052,100	2,830,800	4,238,400	5,832,200	6,342,300	6,666,700	7,071,100	7,420,900
Latin America								
Anguilla								
Antigua	67	109	199	368	394	434	474	467
Argentina	50,756	152,485	83,083	139,269	226,905	233,756	253,995	253,426
Aruba								
Bahamas	880	1,186	1,693	2,909	2,799	2,779	2,964	2,972
Barbados	493	840	1,186	1,711	1,585	1,651	1,735	
Belize		193	199	395	468	512	530	565
Bermuda								
Bolivia	2,999	4,078	5,904	4,868	5,644	6,011	6,298	
Brazil (a)	67	88	82	171	148	165	536,981	693,103
British Virgin Islands								
Cayman Islands								
Chile	13,009	26,641	14,403	28,564	39,962	42,768	48,367	62,427
Colombia	19,261	33,278	33,898	39,160	44,003	51,147	78,516	90,924
Costa Rica	2,999	4,599	3,643	5,475	8,360	9,399	10,418	11,491
Cuba								
Dominica								
Dominican Republic	4,464	6,421	4,819	6,756	8,504	8,918	9,781	11,170
Ecuador	6,476	11,152	14,782	9,867	12,049	13,732	15,327	16,677
El Salvador	2,838	3,516	5,591	5,186	5,853	6,823	8,013	9,400
French Guiana								
Grenada				209	246	242	254	263
Guadeloupe								
Guatemala	5,448	7,809	10,849	7,466	10,359	11,248	12,834	14,497
Guyana	413	559	437	289	263	373	462	536
Haiti (b)	967	1,369	1,989	2,323	1,517	1,482	2,138	
Honduras	1,608	2,429	3,448	2,773	3,081	3,274	3,213	3,693
Jamaica	3,149	2,501	1,832	4,158	3,400	4,556	4,546	5,448
Martinique								
Mexico	80,007	181,212	175,889	236,805	320,803	352,074	377,114	
Netherlands Antilles								
Nicaragua				9,231	1,306	1,451	1,322	1,486
Panama	2,007	3,111	5,206	5,026	6,194	6,914	7,462	7,485
Paraguay	2,095	4,490	4,503	5,381	6,461	6,899	7,895	9,097
Peru	12,287	16,721	16,248	35,287	40,918	39,530	49,968	
Puerto Rico								
St Kitts								
St Lucia								
St Vincent and the Grenadines								
Suriname	684	874	978	1,767	2,853	6,021	473	515
Trinidad and Tobago	2,642	6,035	6,915	4,666	4,985	4,231	4,509	4,833
Uruguay	4,218	10,062	4,379	8,961	12,647	14,759	17,154	18,994
Venezuela	36,189	59,499	58,456	47,154	58,612	58,259	56,568	75,563

Source: International Monetary Fund (IMF), International Financial Statistics
Notes: (a) New series starting 1990, (b) Year ending 30 September

GNP

Total Gross National Product 1977-2002 (US$) (continued)

- US$ million

	1996	1997	1998	1999	2000	2001	2002	US$ per capita 2002
North America								
Canada	594,611	619,172	597,138	636,557	702,056	695,944	718,502	23,157.6
USA	7,831,200	8,325,400	8,778,100	9,297,100	9,848,000	10,104,100	10,436,700	37,400.2
Latin America								
Anguilla								
Antigua	514	554	590	621	630			
Argentina	266,738	286,784	291,688	276,264	276,970	260,614		
Aruba								
Bahamas								
Barbados								
Belize	579	594	601	646	718	740		
Bermuda								
Bolivia								
Brazil (a)	762,769	791,572	769,437	517,840	583,802	489,284		
British Virgin Islands								
Cayman Islands								
Chile	73,264	80,178	77,485	70,770	72,547	65,474	63,907	4,124.2
Colombia	95,094	104,300	96,753	84,785	81,451			
Costa Rica	11,660	12,580	13,625	13,973	14,707	15,585	16,145	4,131.1
Cuba								
Dominica								
Dominican Republic	12,588	14,267	14,963	16,387	18,564	20,242	20,155	2,319.8
Ecuador	17,736	18,347	18,098	11,948	11,698	15,208		
El Salvador	10,188	10,963	11,839	12,176	12,874	13,538	13,997	2,149.0
French Guiana								
Grenada	279	298	327	348	377			
Guadeloupe								
Guatemala	15,552	17,546	19,242	18,117	19,063	20,850	22,957	1,938.8
Guyana	653	670						
Haiti (b)								
Honduras	3,818	4,500	5,050	5,260	5,868	6,250	6,395	948.5
Jamaica	6,264	7,156	7,212	7,211	7,379	7,295		
Martinique								
Mexico								
Netherlands Antilles								
Nicaragua	1,630	1,749	1,943	2,085	2,305	2,378	2,363	485.0
Panama	8,607	8,206	8,736	8,846	9,319			
Paraguay	9,699	9,714	8,708	7,783	7,831	6,888	5,704	999.4
Peru								
Puerto Rico								
St Kitts								
St Lucia								
St Vincent and the Grenadines								
Suriname	749	903						
Trinidad and Tobago	5,213	5,446	5,719					
Uruguay	20,231	21,396	22,068	20,627	19,806	18,179	12,134	3,675.2
Venezuela	68,943	86,292	93,909	101,777	120,055	124,688		

Source: International Monetary Fund (IMF), International Financial Statistics
Notes: (a) New series starting 1990, (b) Year ending 30 September

▣ GNP

Total Gross National Product 1977-2002 (US$) (continued)

● US$ million

	1977	1980	1985	1990	1992	1993	1994	1995
Asia Pacific								
Afghanistan								
American Samoa								
Armenia								
Azerbaijan								
Bangladesh [a]	6,524	12,366	14,011	29,628	31,436	32,548	34,728	39,021
Bhutan		116	159	266	217	212	254	273
Brunei								
Cambodia								
China	142,319	303,744	300,232	384,052	469,253	597,482	540,697	688,833
Fiji	710	1,185	1,110	1,290	1,442	1,516	2,050	
French Polynesia								
Guam								
Hong Kong, China						119,714	134,802	144,363
India [b]	109,663	173,419	210,863	320,582	284,249	277,812	318,639	362,206
Indonesia [c]	44,174	69,275	85,059	109,208	132,984	141,869	161,089	183,963
Japan	690,961	1,072,832	1,370,883	3,071,199	3,833,922	4,412,669	4,849,386	5,332,502
Kazakhstan						11,741	11,855	16,490
Kiribati								
Kyrgyzstan					2	862	1,091	1,473
Laos								
Macau								
Malaysia	12,621	23,607	29,012	42,152	56,009	63,684	70,896	84,689
Maldives	16	43	85	122				
Mongolia								
Myanmar [b]	4,182	5,881	6,606	24,219	41,246	59,058	79,464	107,660
Nauru								
Nepal [d]	1,408	1,987	2,471	3,062	3,499	3,526	4,037	
New Caledonia								
North Korea								
Pakistan [a]	15,754	25,622	32,199	41,226	48,777	48,000	51,445	59,694
Papua New Guinea	1,816	2,853	2,490	3,098	4,029	4,638	5,078	4,438
Philippines	20,702	32,387	29,635	44,073	53,889	55,661	65,729	76,165
Singapore	6,498	11,297	18,331	37,676	50,615	57,863	71,385	85,617
Solomon Islands								
South Korea	36,752	60,965	90,998	252,384	314,338	345,231	401,783	487,915
Sri Lanka	3,523	4,107	5,853	7,865	9,525	10,214	11,551	12,894
Taiwan	21,457	40,779	63,129	159,607	208,542	221,343	243,146	272,359
Tajikistan								
Thailand	19,718	32,090	38,253	84,271	108,974	123,197	142,089	165,281
Tonga	34	63	56	124	146	137	157	
Turkmenistan								
Tuvalu								
Uzbekistan								
Vanuatu			107	164	171	173	188	213
Vietnam								
Western Samoa								
Australasia								
Australia [b]	104,795	153,435	162,105	295,253	294,338	288,216	324,008	345,356
New Zealand [b]	14,203	21,897	21,134	41,987	38,356	41,599	48,245	56,881

Source: *International Monetary Fund (IMF), International Financial Statistics*
Notes: *(a) Year ending 30 June, (b) Year beginning 1 April, (c) New series starting 1993, (d) Year ending 15 April*

GNP

Total Gross National Product 1977-2002 (US$) (continued)

- US$ million

	1996	1997	1998	1999	2000	2001	2002	US$ per capita 2002
Asia Pacific								
Afghanistan								
American Samoa								
Armenia								
Azerbaijan								
Bangladesh [a]	40,981	42,501	44,062	46,297	47,141	47,017	48,642	369.7
Bhutan	298	363	340	373	406			
Brunei								
Cambodia								
China								
Fiji								
French Polynesia								
Guam								
Hong Kong, China	156,590	175,020	168,955	165,119	168,153	169,280	166,497	23,067.3
India [b]	382,446	415,644	418,322	444,592	464,354	483,908		
Indonesia [c]	208,930	196,438	89,416	127,950	141,284	139,648		
Japan	4,746,054	4,369,061	3,993,530	4,555,594	4,809,131			
Kazakhstan	20,853	21,856	21,837	16,346	17,150	20,901		
Kiribati								
Kyrgyzstan	1,789	1,710	1,556	1,174	1,289	1,462		
Laos								
Macau								
Malaysia	96,159	94,803	68,272	73,652	82,553	81,233	88,315	3,812.0
Maldives								
Mongolia								
Myanmar [b]	135,109	181,027	256,590	351,929				
Nauru								
Nepal [d]								
New Caledonia								
North Korea								
Pakistan [a]	58,844	58,874	59,037	59,302	57,827	54,344	62,831	386.0
Papua New Guinea	4,984	4,697	3,590	3,276				
Philippines	86,258	85,791	68,523	80,232	80,694	76,848	83,138	1,047.9
Singapore	92,288	100,653	87,161	84,667	93,339	86,311		
Solomon Islands								
South Korea	518,499	473,939	311,567	400,900	459,103	426,040	477,089	9,905.3
Sri Lanka	13,694	14,931	15,615	15,405	16,019	15,407	16,051	843.8
Taiwan	276,049							
Tajikistan								
Thailand	177,919	146,958	107,990	119,286	120,654	113,395	124,389	1,998.1
Tonga								
Turkmenistan								
Tuvalu								
Uzbekistan								
Vanuatu								
Vietnam								
Western Samoa								
Australasia								
Australia [b]	389,639	391,049	351,368	380,244	366,162	347,046	385,875	19,847.4
New Zealand [b]	61,619	61,644	51,488	52,524	49,755	48,067	57,090	14,630.0

Source: International Monetary Fund (IMF), International Financial Statistics
Notes: (a) Year ending 30 June, (b) Year beginning 1 April, (c) New series starting 1993, (d) Year ending 15 April

▣ GNP

Total Gross National Product 1977-2002 (US$) (continued)

● US$ million

	1977	1980	1985	1990	1992	1993	1994	1995
Africa and Middle East								
Algeria				64,873	50,046	49,226	40,678	39,299
Angola								
Bahrain	1,996	2,948	3,360	4,751	4,783	5,007	5,326	5,790
Benin	616	1,163	1,022	1,810	2,126	2,100	1,471	1,965
Botswana	346	914	961	3,295	3,662	3,510	3,854	
Burkina Faso	749	1,293	1,668	2,859	3,074	2,891	1,748	2,205
Burundi	537	960	1,159	1,133	1,071	964	1,057	988
Cameroon (a)	2,556	6,674	8,545	12,293	11,991	11,199	6,194	
Cape Verde								
Central African Republic								
Chad								
Comoros								
Congo Dem Rep			6,017	8,352	8,206	10,685	9,091	
Congo-Brazzaville		1,551	1,933	2,339	2,588	2,340	1,407	1,409
Côte d'Ivoire	6,060	10,575	6,978	9,899	11,296	10,499	5,648	
Djibouti								
Egypt (b)	22,088	24,616	51,274	48,050	41,768	46,671	51,622	56,574
Equatorial Guinea								
Eritrea								
Ethiopia (c)	3,295	4,119	6,523	8,066	7,355	5,251	5,100	5,441
Gabon	2,651	4,043	3,459	4,813	4,574	4,757	3,602	4,173
Gambia								
Ghana	9,672	15,517	6,204	6,113	6,306	5,854	5,330	6,329
Guinea								
Guinea-Bissau								
Iran (d)	70,601	93,492	160,813	516,228	1,016,006	77,820	73,366	105,600
Iraq		55,192						
Israel (e)	13,431	21,039	23,173	51,253	64,467	64,883	73,565	88,823
Jordan	2,013	3,973	5,107	3,659	5,093	5,451	6,080	6,649
Kenya	4,304	6,869	5,907	8,089	7,835	5,331	6,737	8,669
Kuwait	15,906	33,537	26,111	26,209	25,116	27,782	28,028	31,437
Lebanon								
Lesotho	354	632	478	1,021	1,248	1,221	1,214	1,322
Liberia	626	833	986		1,671	1,878	2,112	
Libya	17,916				32,410			
Madagascar	1,903	3,307	2,345	3,081	3,001	3,371	2,977	
Malawi	781	1,138	1,078	1,815	1,761	1,995	1,128	1,388
Mali								
Mauritania								
Mauritius	821	1,109	1,031	2,620	3,200	3,209	3,485	3,954
Morocco	11,358	19,235	13,125	27,088	29,849	27,777	31,452	34,004
Mozambique								
Namibia			999	2,477	2,945	2,903	3,304	3,660
Niger								
Nigeria	50,057	91,004	79,139	29,642	28,061	28,457	38,608	81,006
Oman	2,364	5,314	8,844	9,445	10,871	10,803	10,717	11,948
Qatar								
Réunion								
Rwanda								
Sao Tomé e Príncipe								
Saudi Arabia (f)	63,437	152,829	90,424	106,413	137,842	134,757	135,079	144,649
Senegal	2,036	3,033	2,657	5,928	6,353	5,711	3,965	4,649
Seychelles	61	142	163	359	424	463	488	489
Sierra Leone (a)	639	1,058	923	568	572	705	807	829
Somalia								
South Africa	37,663	77,218	54,682	107,746	127,568	127,744	133,356	148,239
Sudan								
Swaziland	300	534	369	888				
Syria								
Tanzania	3,472	5,125	6,328	4,066	4,376	4,107	4,388	5,145
Togo	682	1,128	753	1,638	1,825	1,671	963	
Tunisia	5,126	8,668	8,236	11,905	14,787	13,737	14,726	17,173
Uganda								
United Arab Emirates								
Yemen (b)					14,931	18,612	23,917	11,566
Zambia	2,602	4,060	2,225	3,321	2,802	2,440	3,451	3,348
Zimbabwe	3,423	5,281	5,543	8,438	6,451	6,305	6,548	6,762

Source: *International Monetary Fund (IMF), International Financial Statistics*
Notes: *(a) Year ending 30 June, (b) From 1980, year ending 30 June, (c) Year ending 7 July, (d) Year beginning 21 March, (e) Year beginning 1 April, (f) Islamic lunar year*

GNP

Total Gross National Product 1977-2002 (US$) (continued)

- US$ million

	1996	1997	1998	1999	2000	2001	2002	US$ per capita 2002
Africa and Middle East								
Algeria	43,187	47,064						
Angola								
Bahrain	6,076	6,113	6,024	6,351	7,390	7,180		
Benin								
Botswana								
Burkina Faso	5,239	2,313	2,496	2,447	2,172	2,310	2,610	198.4
Burundi	863	960	885	799	697	648	612	86.2
Cameroon [a]								
Cape Verde								
Central African Republic								
Chad								
Comoros								
Congo Dem Rep								
Congo-Brazzaville	1,635	1,801	1,642	1,814	2,414	2,309	2,332	770.1
Côte d'Ivoire								
Djibouti								
Egypt [b]	61,525	66,477						
Equatorial Guinea								
Eritrea								
Ethiopia [c]	5,929	6,147	6,304					
Gabon	4,808	4,646	3,918					
Gambia								
Ghana	6,791	6,750						
Guinea								
Guinea-Bissau								
Iran [d]	140,910	166,676	188,066	248,731	328,804	377,657		
Iraq								
Israel [e]	97,273	100,738	100,208	100,038	108,632	108,802	100,889	15,709.7
Jordan	6,869	7,257	7,951	8,061	8,474			
Kenya	8,967	10,382	11,292	10,812	10,223			
Kuwait	36,250	36,142	30,990	34,292	43,722	39,124	38,621	16,482.7
Lebanon								
Lesotho	1,273	1,358	1,141	1,155	1,118	928	872	376.7
Liberia								
Libya								
Madagascar								
Malawi	2,342	2,537	1,805	1,756	1,608			
Mali								
Mauritania								
Mauritius	4,263	4,087	4,137	4,248	4,524	4,539	4,774	4,030.3
Morocco	38,094	34,587	37,317	37,845	39,119	36,774		
Mozambique								
Namibia	3,564	3,702	3,486	3,370	3,301	3,100		
Niger								
Nigeria	119,393	124,004	123,614	33,397	44,646	47,195	45,905	368.7
Oman	13,470	13,947	12,142	13,592	17,707	17,824		
Qatar								
Réunion								
Rwanda								
Sao Tomé e Príncipe								
Saudi Arabia [f]	157,773	164,932	147,269	163,299	189,587	185,032	188,479	8,252.0
Senegal	5,217	4,772	5,067	5,139	4,709	5,022		
Seychelles	488	551	587	599	568	570		
Sierra Leone [a]	840	739	523	626				
Somalia								
South Africa	140,620	145,603	130,528	127,905	124,836	110,475	101,552	2,287.4
Sudan								
Swaziland								
Syria								
Tanzania	6,433	7,604	8,269	8,574	8,934	9,296		
Togo								
Tunisia	18,555	17,994	18,945	19,897	18,520	19,045	20,116	2,076.3
Uganda								
United Arab Emirates								
Yemen [b]	6,698	6,009	5,506	6,091				
Zambia	3,275	3,867						
Zimbabwe	8,183							

Source: International Monetary Fund (IMF), International Financial Statistics
Notes: (a) Year ending 30 June, (b) From 1980, year ending 30 June, (c) Year ending 7 July, (d) Year beginning 21 March, (e) Year beginning 1 April, (f) Islamic lunar year

◻ Trends in Money Supply **Table 10.9**

Money Supply 1977-2002

• Billion units of national currency

	1977	1985	1990	1992	1993	1994	1995
North America							
Canada	29.06	70.30	97.06	108.54	117.58	125.32	138.07
USA	376.27	706.38	925.06	1,121.86	1,231.00	1,232.00	1,220.71
Latin America							
Anguilla							
Antigua	0.03	0.07	0.16	0.18	0.18	0.22	0.28
Argentina	0.00	0.00	3.07	11.36	15.12	16.36	16.62
Aruba [a]			0.26	0.33	0.38	0.44	0.44
Bahamas	0.09	0.22	0.34	0.38	0.38	0.42	0.44
Barbados	0.14	0.35	0.53	0.50	0.48	0.52	0.43
Belize	0.02	0.06	0.11	0.13	0.14	0.14	0.16
Bermuda							
Bolivia [b]	0.00	0.20	1.00	1.92	2.50	3.23	3.91
Brazil [c, d]	0.00	0.00	0.00	0.05	1.11	25.54	32.09
British Virgin Islands							
Cayman Islands							
Chile	19.80	200.47	735.39	1,343.95	1,628.94	1,892.33	2,312.90
Colombia [e]	103.50	545.26	2,125.02	4,067.00	5,211.30	6,722.40	8,078.50
Costa Rica	4.50	32.44	66.48	109.52	117.19	161.57	151.90
Cuba							
Dominica	0.01	0.03	0.07	0.09	0.08	0.07	0.09
Dominican Republic	0.52	1.68	9.20	13.23	15.07	16.20	19.00
Ecuador	28.56	105.63	748.76	1,550.47	2,864.89	3,912.79	3,641.45
El Salvador [f]	0.40	0.88	0.49	0.60	0.72	0.75	0.81
French Guiana							
Grenada	0.03	0.05	0.09	0.11	0.12	0.14	0.15
Guadeloupe							
Guatemala	0.59	1.35	3.24	4.19	5.05	7.07	7.77
Guyana	0.28	0.71	4.14	9.00	11.88	13.11	15.31
Haiti	0.63	1.59	2.30	3.15	3.87	5.10	6.70
Honduras	0.42	0.82	1.85	2.52	2.82	3.85	4.68
Jamaica	0.47	1.52	4.02	13.39	16.90	21.25	29.32
Martinique							
Mexico	0.21	3.46	47.44	122.22	143.90	145.43	150.57
Netherlands Antilles	0.31	0.53	0.64	0.74	0.79	0.89	0.96
Nicaragua [g]	0.00	0.00	0.05	0.84	0.81	1.10	1.24
Panama	0.21	0.41	0.43	0.64	0.71	0.80	0.81
Paraguay	28.57	125.20	558.06	905.03	1,054.00	1,370.31	1,699.93
Peru [h]	0.00	0.00	0.71	2.84	4.34	5.59	7.50
Puerto Rico							
St Kitts		0.03	0.06	0.07	0.08	0.07	0.08
St Lucia	0.03	0.07	0.17	0.21	0.23	0.23	0.26
St Vincent and the Grenadines	0.02	0.05	0.07	0.09	0.09	0.11	0.11
Suriname	0.22	0.88	2.25	3.22	6.04	20.88	58.10
Trinidad and Tobago	0.73	2.26	2.58	2.70	3.14	3.75	3.92
Uruguay	0.00	0.04	0.72	2.41	3.80	5.34	7.07
Venezuela [i]	36.98	104.71	214.51	363.53	407.22	974.12	1,343.96

Source: *International Monetary Fund (IMF), International Financial Statistics*
Notes: *(a) Included in Netherlands Antilles, (b) New series starting 1985, (c) New series starting 1986, (d) New series starting 1994, (e) New series starting 1990, (f) New series starting 1982, (g) Currency reform occurred in 1984, (h) Currency reform 1991, (i) New series starting 1987*

Money Supply 1977-2002 (continued)

- Billion units of national currency

	1996	1997	1998	1999	2000	2001	2002
North America							
Canada	155.56	169.92	179.58	199.24	225.19	253.75	268.50
USA	1,237.30	1,280.18	1,324.72	1,461.81	1,436.39	1,599.44	1,646.24
Latin America							
Anguilla							
Antigua	0.26	0.26	0.33	0.33	0.31	0.34	0.34
Argentina	19.04	21.48	21.49	21.84	19.84	15.84	28.26
Aruba (a)	0.45	0.47	0.55	0.59	0.60	0.70	0.84
Bahamas	0.45	0.52	0.59	0.75	0.80	0.77	0.81
Barbados	0.63	0.62	0.77	0.92	1.14	1.16	1.18
Belize	0.16	0.17	0.19	0.25	0.29	0.38	0.33
Bermuda							
Bolivia (b)	3.06	3.64	3.90	3.67	3.99	4.74	4.73
Brazil (c, d)	41.68	51.00	54.82	62.29	74.08	83.55	107.21
British Virgin Islands							
Cayman Islands							
Chile	2,686.75	3,228.14	2,799.44	3,718.86	3,905.39	4,106.56	4,809.01
Colombia (e)	9,965.98	11,697.90	10,772.00	13,376.70	16,837.00	18,450.60	21,576.40
Costa Rica	177.52	354.64	415.44	534.09	639.72	724.19	843.11
Cuba							
Dominica	0.10	0.10	0.10	0.13	0.11	0.11	0.13
Dominican Republic	23.22	27.70	29.42	35.84	35.44	41.26	43.76
Ecuador	4,693.85	6,280.88	7,247.64	16,018.38	34,524.47	48,322.00	
El Salvador (f)	0.93	0.93	1.01	1.16	1.09	1.20	1.09
French Guiana							
Grenada	0.15	0.16	0.18	0.19	0.21	0.21	0.25
Guadeloupe							
Guatemala	8.82	12.00	13.61	15.47	18.83	21.06	22.84
Guyana	17.53	19.28	18.98	23.35	25.79	26.09	28.12
Haiti	5.82	6.63	6.65	8.42	9.22	10.61	13.50
Honduras	6.05	8.29	9.35	11.05	11.95	12.39	14.22
Jamaica	33.55	34.47	36.66	45.04	47.90	54.14	59.42
Martinique							
Mexico	206.18	267.11	308.14	395.48	450.74	527.67	618.68
Netherlands Antilles	0.92	0.92	0.95	0.98	1.00	1.14	1.32
Nicaragua (g)	1.65	2.06	2.55	3.15	3.41	3.27	3.37
Panama	0.84	1.00	1.13	1.14	1.18	1.30	1.32
Paraguay	1,708.85	1,886.18	1,984.45	2,166.89	2,562.25	2,743.15	2,759.53
Peru (h)	8.97	15.18	19.17	22.27	21.07	21.45	22.05
Puerto Rico							
St Kitts	0.09	0.09	0.11	0.11	0.12	0.11	0.13
St Lucia	0.25	0.26	0.28	0.31	0.31	0.31	0.32
St Vincent and the Grenadines	0.12	0.15	0.17	0.21	0.24	0.26	0.26
Suriname	56.97	68.47	92.25	139.78	285.60	394.62	546.20
Trinidad and Tobago	3.69	4.46	4.72	5.31	5.66	6.77	7.83
Uruguay	8.82	10.29	14.42	14.87	14.36	13.76	14.28
Venezuela (i)	2,777.65	4,917.78	5,149.17	6,412.64	8,037.22	9,287.01	10,973.50

Source: International Monetary Fund (IMF), International Financial Statistics
Notes: (a) Included in Netherlands Antilles, (b) New series starting 1985, (c) New series starting 1986, (d) New series starting 1994, (e) New series starting 1990, (f) New series starting 1982, (g) Currency reform occurred in 1984, (h) Currency reform 1991, (i) New series starting 1987

Trends in Money Supply

Money Supply 1977-2002 (continued)

- Billion units of national currency

	1977	1985	1990	1992	1993	1994	1995
Asia Pacific							
Afghanistan	23.75	76.36	351.03				
American Samoa							
Armenia				0.11	1.33	13.41	30.08
Azerbaijan				6.07	65.52	372.38	858.38
Bangladesh	11.67	45.96	65.73	80.44	93.28	115.97	135.34
Bhutan [a]		0.26	0.54	0.84	0.82	1.04	1.32
Brunei							
Cambodia					203.82	201.68	278.49
China [a, b]	58.01	301.73	700.95	1,171.43	1,546.94	1,967.43	2,308.35
Fiji	0.08	0.14	0.27	0.31	0.36	0.34	0.39
French Polynesia							
Guam							
Hong Kong, China				124.55	150.60	150.70	151.19
India [c]	178.50	412.41	853.56	1,120.90	1,330.25	1,695.05	1,883.55
Indonesia	2,006.00	10,123.80	23,819.00	28,426.00	34,661.00	42,887.00	49,572.00
Japan	60,786.00	88,980.00	119,628.00	136,138.00	145,614.00	151,665.00	171,544.00
Kazakhstan					8.20	55.42	115.38
Kiribati		0.00					
Kyrgyzstan							2.48
Laos [d]			25.09	35.14	52.24	61.34	67.18
Macau			8.98	20.11			
Malaysia [e]	6.13	14.13	25.41	35.54	48.08	56.17	63.59
Maldives	0.05	0.16	0.31	0.46	0.69	0.85	0.90
Mongolia				7.64	18.55	33.05	42.64
Myanmar	5.59	11.55	30.59	58.69	73.46	98.29	125.96
Nauru							
Nepal	1.93	5.62	14.21	20.43	25.32	30.52	33.55
New Caledonia							
North Korea							
Pakistan	39.97	123.06	254.62	371.80	378.11	435.39	490.96
Papua New Guinea	0.17	0.24	0.34	0.44	0.59	0.61	0.70
Philippines	14.94	36.76	92.94	117.54	143.71	159.90	194.63
Singapore	4.41	8.79	15.26	18.52	22.88	23.41	25.35
Solomon Islands		0.03	0.06	0.10	0.12	0.16	0.17
South Korea	2,172.57	7,557.85	15,905.20	24,586.40	29,041.30	32,510.60	38,872.80
Sri Lanka	5.33	18.66	39.61	50.07	59.36	70.46	75.22
Taiwan	219.19	751.47	1,931.90	2,425.84	2,797.14	3,139.27	3,163.10
Tajikistan							
Thailand	45.41	85.84	195.41	249.72	296.16	346.43	388.28
Tonga	0.00	0.01	0.02	0.02	0.03	0.03	0.02
Turkmenistan							
Tuvalu							
Uzbekistan							
Vanuatu	1.77	2.64	3.89	5.06	5.68	5.73	6.31
Vietnam				14,811.00	19,088.30		26,736.40
Western Samoa	0.00	0.02	0.05	0.04	0.04	0.05	0.06
Australasia							
Australia	11.39	23.30	46.70	60.29	71.03	78.76	83.90
New Zealand	1.95	4.10	9.50	9.77	10.55	11.03	11.58

Source: *International Monetary Fund (IMF), International Financial Statistics*
Notes: *(a) New series starting 1994, (b) New series starting 1985, (c) New series starting 1991, (d) New series starting 1980, (e) New series starting 1992*

Money Supply 1977-2002 (continued)

● Billion units of national currency

	1996	1997	1998	1999	2000	2001	2002
Asia Pacific							
Afghanistan							
American Samoa	0.06	0.07					
Armenia	39.83	44.05	52.68	52.23	71.39	77.30	115.31
Azerbaijan	1,119.74	1,524.08	1,183.26	1,390.08	1,569.81	1,693.10	1,967.27
Bangladesh	141.68	152.63	163.97	184.93	218.95	242.44	254.72
Bhutan [a]	2.07	2.17	2.63	3.72	3.94	5.06	6.97
Brunei							
Cambodia	328.93	384.76	543.27	531.95	539.64	609.72	813.28
China [a, b]	2,756.38	3,480.65	3,869.05	4,697.64	5,454.10	6,168.85	7,266.54
Fiji	0.46	0.45	0.49	0.69	0.59	0.62	0.71
French Polynesia							
Guam							
Hong Kong, China	174.38	167.78	159.99	184.62	184.56	210.88	240.37
India [c]	2,148.91	2,419.25	2,703.49	3,161.18	3,495.89	3,845.99	4,324.94
Indonesia	54,534.00	72,431.00	90,768.00	116,880.00	160,923.00	175,110.00	188,008.00
Japan	188,146.00	204,282.00	214,403.00	239,537.00	247,858.00	281,785.00	347,979.00
Kazakhstan	139.45	150.91	118.74	205.93	236.16	270.01	381.98
Kiribati							
Kyrgyzstan	2.89	3.12	3.21	4.20	4.61	5.56	7.68
Laos [d]	75.56	79.94	168.98	218.98	344.35	371.84	587.00
Macau							
Malaysia [e]	74.18	82.84	58.52	75.60	80.66	83.88	91.93
Maldives	1.06	1.20	1.38	1.59	1.76	1.66	1.89
Mongolia	60.84	76.11	82.58	114.83	130.75	156.13	187.70
Myanmar	167.97	219.98	282.09	345.76	464.97	701.15	1,009.47
Nauru							
Nepal	35.54	38.60	45.51	55.11	63.03	72.16	
New Caledonia							
North Korea							
Pakistan	528.01	699.81	732.29	795.37	876.01	964.92	1,118.40
Papua New Guinea	1.06	1.01	1.11	1.34	1.37	1.42	1.63
Philippines	233.12	266.33	285.95	395.56	390.55	392.25	474.77
Singapore	27.04	27.51	27.24	31.11	33.26	36.08	35.83
Solomon Islands	0.20	0.21	0.21	0.27	0.25	0.25	0.26
South Korea	39,542.10	35,036.10	35,582.50	44,374.50	46,997.00	53,505.50	63,150.50
Sri Lanka	78.20	85.85	96.27	108.55	118.48	122.21	139.36
Taiwan	3,426.06						
Tajikistan							
Thailand	423.69	430.12	451.02	739.66	684.26	650.56	674.85
Tonga	0.02	0.02	0.02	0.03	0.03	0.04	0.06
Turkmenistan							
Tuvalu							
Uzbekistan							
Vanuatu	6.53	6.64	7.60	7.62	8.08	8.04	11.61
Vietnam	33,439.10	39,971.90	45,206.80	68,360.10	90,989.00	112,408.00	125,329.00
Western Samoa	0.06	0.07	0.07	0.08	0.09	0.09	0.10
Australasia							
Australia	95.64	108.35	114.79	125.95	137.72	167.04	
New Zealand	11.06	11.78	12.38	14.65	15.57	17.75	18.69

Source: International Monetary Fund (IMF), International Financial Statistics
Notes: (a) New series starting 1994, (b) New series starting 1985, (c) New series starting 1991, (d) New series starting 1980, (e) New series starting 1992

Trends in Money Supply

Money Supply 1977-2002 (continued)

● Billion units of national currency

Africa and Middle East

	1977	1985	1990	1992	1993	1994	1995
Algeria	48.55	202.23	270.40	377.24	450.32	485.65	520.29
Angola							0.00
Bahrain	0.15	0.22	0.26	0.35	0.36	0.34	0.33
Benin (a)	29.32	87.09	104.55	128.21	111.34	186.22	161.73
Botswana	0.06	0.19	0.59	0.61	0.70	0.77	0.83
Burkina Faso	30.78	69.54	103.63	109.90	122.61	170.32	213.70
Burundi	6.50	17.67	22.77	27.95	31.30	40.15	38.80
Cameroon (b)	128.42	434.32	418.63	311.33	267.46	361.29	319.24
Cape Verde	1.41	4.84	6.93	9.91	10.60	11.47	11.87
Central African Republic (b, c)	18.23	52.42	54.56	51.05	59.42	103.40	111.24
Chad (b)	22.51	68.34	66.34	62.86	45.47	59.79	85.33
Comoros		7.31	10.92	11.07	11.58	12.71	12.04
Congo Dem Rep (c, d)	0.00	0.00	0.00	0.00	0.00	0.00	0.02
Congo-Brazzaville (b)	30.89	113.92	121.03	119.32	95.76	134.49	134.85
Côte d'Ivoire	383.08	620.18	526.40	489.44	493.98	798.85	944.52
Djibouti		20.53	27.36	34.98	36.40	37.61	37.00
Egypt	2.94	14.70	26.21	30.83	34.57	38.27	41.54
Equatorial Guinea (b)		8.05	3.12	3.57	2.55	6.00	9.51
Eritrea							
Ethiopia	1.18	2.70	5.27	7.14	7.45	9.03	9.28
Gabon (b)	99.53	178.16	180.93	142.35	137.44	195.01	219.09
Gambia	0.04	0.16	0.30	0.44	0.46	0.41	0.47
Ghana (e)	2.39	38.31	206.44	360.69	461.35	693.55	925.33
Guinea				218.44	260.85	252.58	274.13
Guinea-Bissau			5.29	2.44	3.10	4.91	7.21
Iran	822.02		9,729.30	14,080.90	18,305.40	25,922.60	34,341.60
Iraq							
Israel	0.00	1.05	7.02	10.54	13.49	14.52	16.72
Jordan	0.33	0.85	1.43	1.72	1.72	1.74	1.74
Kenya	7.33	12.92	27.53	46.58	59.32	66.79	69.33
Kuwait	0.49	1.02		1.11	1.11	1.13	1.19
Lebanon	5.06	20.15	449.92	1,199.40	1,143.22	1,436.85	1,560.61
Lesotho		0.13	0.26	0.35	0.43	0.49	0.54
Liberia	0.05	0.12		0.27	0.43	0.46	0.65
Libya	1.44	3.49	4.45	4.99	5.21	5.89	6.25
Madagascar	99.98	238.59	574.46	915.32	1,024.42	1,603.51	1,848.01
Malawi	0.10	0.17	0.48	0.76	1.02	1.54	2.21
Mali	40.66	113.77	98.47	108.28	117.79	174.17	198.19
Mauritania (f)	4.09	12.17	17.62	20.20	20.94	19.82	18.20
Mauritius	1.22	2.04	5.58	7.21	7.42	8.86	9.57
Morocco (g)	18.00	40.29	90.66	110.08	115.46	128.28	135.96
Mozambique		92.62	495.79	1,056.60	1,606.10	2,417.90	3,264.00
Namibia			0.61	1.00	1.47	1.68	1.82
Niger	32.33	80.59	77.87	71.57	79.52	91.78	100.24
Nigeria	5.42	13.23	34.54	79.27	124.42	178.44	207.51
Oman	0.11	0.33	0.39	0.43	0.45	0.47	0.47
Qatar (h)	2.09	4.02	4.06	3.99	4.25	3.91	3.72
Réunion							
Rwanda	8.03	14.58	16.72	22.51	24.92	28.81	40.66
Sao Tomé e Príncipe							14.23
Saudi Arabia	38.41	81.83	101.94	123.46	121.51	125.69	125.41
Senegal	109.12	193.49	204.20	217.39	197.75	305.34	316.76
Seychelles	0.08	0.16	0.22	0.29	0.34	0.33	0.34
Sierra Leone	0.08	0.90	14.25	31.39	35.05	38.54	49.90
Somalia	1.33	9.77	143.00				
South Africa (i)	4.65	21.33	50.35	70.81	75.55	94.51	111.84
Sudan (a, i)	0.05	0.41	2.77	8.92	15.70	24.28	40.46
Swaziland (i)	0.03	0.08	0.19	0.25	0.29	0.31	0.36
Syria	10.92	54.98	118.72	156.91	191.43	207.11	225.04
Tanzania (h)	6.38	25.47	113.00	186.12	247.33	329.63	428.28
Togo	36.45	82.74	75.25	57.11	46.57	95.29	131.20
Tunisia	0.58	2.06	2.68	2.89	3.00	3.32	3.64
Uganda (i)	0.06	2.19		206.01	259.39	354.02	408.70
United Arab Emirates	5.21	9.51	10.76	14.98	18.17	19.18	20.82
Yemen			56.50	78.31	103.31	139.59	164.02
Zambia (h)	0.39	1.23	12.76		97.33	140.97	227.06
Zimbabwe	0.37	1.02	2.47	3.21	6.26	7.40	11.27

Source: *International Monetary Fund (IMF), International Financial Statistics*
Notes: *(a) New series starting 1985, (b) New series starting 1988, (c) New series starting 1994, (d) Currency reform in 1992, (e) New series starting 1991, (f) New series starting 1989, (g) New series starting 1990, (h) New series starting 1993, (i) New series starting 1992, (j) Currency reform occurred in 1984*

Money Supply 1977-2002 (continued)

● Billion units of national currency

	1996	1997	1998	1999	2000	2001	2002
Africa and Middle East							
Algeria	589.99	675.96	817.26	889.78	1,044.02	1,237.38	
Angola	0.09	0.19	0.27	1.21	5.33	14.30	33.46
Bahrain	0.34	0.35	0.37	0.43	0.45	0.55	0.65
Benin [a]	189.51	193.35	184.19	270.61	365.40	401.76	367.35
Botswana	0.95	1.04	1.51	1.77	1.90	2.35	2.52
Burkina Faso	228.73	268.86	261.94	256.86	270.41	262.28	243.73
Burundi	43.64	48.20	48.82	69.29	68.57	80.08	100.83
Cameroon [b]	314.14	423.90	485.29	537.73	631.06	711.98	813.63
Cape Verde	13.12	15.96	15.63	18.33	20.43	20.95	22.80
Central African Republic [b, c]	116.64	107.19	87.58	98.64	101.83	99.15	94.74
Chad [b]	113.88	108.47	99.75	96.67	113.82	138.69	176.59
Comoros	13.02	10.60	10.02	11.66	14.12	22.94	25.32
Congo Dem Rep [c, d]		41.06	57.89			41.06	57.89
Congo-Brazzaville [b]	153.18	166.56	143.98	184.03	309.58	238.08	271.24
Côte d'Ivoire	966.44	1,079.97	1,219.33	1,197.99	1,153.99	1,324.81	1,750.48
Djibouti	35.93	32.48	29.26	30.27	27.91	28.65	35.52
Egypt	44.52	48.71	58.58	59.07	62.19	67.08	75.78
Equatorial Guinea [b]	14.28	13.66	14.98	28.45	38.33	48.31	73.28
Eritrea							
Ethiopia	9.11	9.88	9.15	10.27	11.41	11.90	13.66
Gabon [b]	276.00	298.25	283.12	268.61	320.45	332.22	346.69
Gambia	0.45	0.63	0.63	0.72	0.98	1.13	1.76
Ghana [e]	1,218.56	1,779.25	2,151.23	2,490.24	3,441.54	5,034.99	8,048.60
Guinea	273.47	331.67	361.47		499.88	559.99	681.23
Guinea-Bissau	10.89	36.63	32.19	39.42	64.52	69.54	85.07
Iran	45,865.00	54,976.90	67,444.40	81,951.60	102,170.00	125,667.00	162,471.00
Iraq							
Israel	20.13	22.40	25.15	30.26	31.03	37.80	38.36
Jordan	1.53	1.63	1.61	1.77	2.02	2.09	2.27
Kenya	78.99	91.04	94.09	109.51	118.97	126.33	149.71
Kuwait	1.24	1.25	1.14	1.37	1.47	1.64	2.07
Lebanon	1,753.44	1,929.36	2,051.53	2,260.80	2,389.30	2,365.30	2,544.44
Lesotho	0.64	0.79	0.98	0.96	1.04	1.29	1.44
Liberia	0.70	0.69	1.57	1.80	1.60	1.70	2.36
Libya	6.32	6.65	6.68	7.00	7.31	7.40	7.84
Madagascar	2,167.69	2,663.95	2,953.16	3,550.32	4,017.96	5,233.72	5,627.91
Malawi	2.76	3.21	5.04	6.71	9.20	10.01	12.74
Mali	240.39	256.00	267.57	266.02	291.15	377.20	486.06
Mauritania [f]	16.23	17.58	18.50	19.68	24.15	27.72	28.91
Mauritius	9.83	10.61	11.59	12.00	13.30	15.45	18.16
Morocco [g]	143.82	166.84	179.80	200.60	216.50	249.69	272.18
Mozambique	3,917.23	4,901.66	5,612.95	6,994.39	8,557.16	10,066.00	11,688.20
Namibia	2.80	2.90	3.68	4.50	5.77	6.31	6.70
Niger	90.70	73.12	59.61	68.80	76.90	104.04	95.56
Nigeria	235.58	275.10	327.30	400.83	649.68	816.71	946.25
Oman	0.50	0.55	0.51	0.51	0.55	0.70	0.77
Qatar [h]	3.89	4.13	4.22	4.18	4.45	5.22	6.29
Réunion							
Rwanda	45.42	55.75	55.29	59.17	63.11	63.61	
Sao Tomé e Príncipe	23.68	49.20	47.58	50.12	61.88	95.48	108.60
Saudi Arabia	133.11	141.29	140.41	156.82	165.71	179.70	202.57
Senegal	343.62	343.21	397.00	439.76	464.05	532.97	563.95
Seychelles	0.45	0.65	0.78	1.07	1.14	1.29	1.58
Sierra Leone	53.21	83.61	89.74	134.08	139.96	189.44	247.48
Somalia							
South Africa [i]	147.66	173.34	213.53	259.94	266.19	312.36	349.82
Sudan [a, i]	75.36	99.85	129.08	165.01	234.59	271.39	352.26
Swaziland [i]	0.42	0.49	0.50	0.66	0.66	0.75	0.83
Syria	244.50	260.93	281.93	313.32	368.67	419.91	494.68
Tanzania [h]	449.21	493.87	545.52	632.58	695.01	766.02	958.79
Togo	120.96	123.25	131.77	144.77	176.89	161.55	148.41
Tunisia	4.11	4.64	4.99	5.79	6.37	7.01	6.89
Uganda [i]	450.84	512.53	612.44	689.36	805.49	908.80	1,099.44
United Arab Emirates	22.27	25.37	27.78	30.25	34.07	39.46	47.05
Yemen	156.58	166.38	179.93	207.20	247.25	283.15	306.45
Zambia [h]	271.13	355.22	414.94	513.02	775.85	1,041.40	1,339.31
Zimbabwe	13.87	21.32	26.33	35.47	54.40	132.09	356.64

Source: International Monetary Fund (IMF), International Financial Statistics
Notes: (a) New series starting 1985, (b) New series starting 1988, (c) New series starting 1994, (d) Currency reform in 1992, (e) New series starting 1991, (f) New series starting 1989, (g) New series starting 1990, (h) New series starting 1993, (i) New series starting 1992, (j) Currency reform occurred in 1984

Annual Rates of Inflation 1977-2002

- % growth

	1977	1985	1990	1996	1997	1998	1999	2000	2001	2002
North America										
Canada [a]	8.0	4.0	4.8	1.6	1.6	1.0	1.7	2.7	2.5	2.2
USA	6.5	3.6	5.4	2.9	2.3	1.6	2.2	3.4	2.8	1.6
Latin America										
Anguilla				4.0	2.6	2.4	2.1	2.5	2.8	-0.5
Antigua	13.8	1.0	6.6	3.0	0.2	3.4	1.1	0.7	1.0	2.2
Argentina [b, c, d]	176.0	672.2	2,314.0	0.2	0.5	0.9	-1.2	-0.9	-1.1	25.9
Aruba		4.0	5.8	3.2	3.0	1.9	2.3	4.0	2.9	3.3
Bahamas	3.2	4.6	4.7	1.4	0.5	1.3	1.3	1.6	2.0	2.2
Barbados [e]	8.4	3.9	3.1	2.4	7.7	-1.3	1.6	2.4	2.6	0.2
Belize		4.2	3.0	6.4	1.0	-0.9	-1.2	0.6	1.2	2.2
Bermuda				3.0	2.5	2.2	2.0	2.7	2.9	2.9
Bolivia [f]	8.1	11,749.6	17.1	12.4	4.7	7.7	2.2	4.6	1.6	0.9
Brazil [g]		226.0	2,947.7	15.8	6.9	3.2	4.9	7.0	6.8	8.4
British Virgin Islands				3.0	2.7	5.9	6.1	5.4	5.0	5.0
Cayman Islands				2.0	2.2	2.5	2.2	2.7	3.1	3.3
Chile [d]	91.9	29.5	26.0	7.4	6.1	5.1	3.3	3.8	3.6	2.5
Colombia [d]	33.1	24.0	29.1	20.2	18.5	18.7	10.9	9.2	8.0	6.3
Costa Rica	4.2	15.1	19.0	17.5	13.2	11.7	10.0	11.0	11.2	9.2
Cuba				0.5	2.9	2.7	3.2	3.0		
Dominica	9.5	3.7	3.2	1.7	2.4	1.0	1.2	0.9	1.5	0.2
Dominican Republic [h]	12.9	45.3	50.5	5.4	8.3	4.8	6.5	7.7	8.9	5.2
Ecuador [a, f]	13.0	28.0	48.5	24.4	30.6	36.1	52.2	96.1	37.7	12.5
El Salvador	11.8	22.3	24.0	9.8	4.5	2.5	0.5	2.3	3.8	1.9
French Guiana				2.6	4.4	4.6	4.1	4.7	4.9	5.1
Grenada [h]	18.5	2.5	2.7	2.0	1.2	1.4	0.2	2.2	3.2	3.0
Guadeloupe				7.2	9.2	7.0	4.9	5.1	4.2	3.8
Guatemala	12.3	18.7	41.2	11.1	9.2	7.0	4.9	6.0	7.6	8.0
Guyana	8.3	15.0	63.6	7.1	3.6	4.6	7.5	6.1	2.6	5.3
Haiti [a, f]	6.5	10.6	21.3	20.6	20.6	10.6	8.7	13.7	14.2	9.9
Honduras [i]	8.4	3.4	23.3	23.8	20.2	13.7	11.7	11.1	9.7	7.7
Jamaica [d]	11.2	25.7	22.0	26.4	9.7	8.6	6.0	8.2	7.0	7.1
Martinique				4.1	3.8	4.4	5.3	5.8		
Mexico	29.0	57.7	26.7	34.4	20.6	15.9	16.6	9.5	6.4	5.0
Netherlands Antilles [i]	5.4	0.5	3.7	3.6	3.3	1.1	0.4	5.8	1.8	0.4
Nicaragua [d, f, h]	11.4	219.5	7,485.5	11.6	9.2	13.0	11.2	11.5	7.4	4.0
Panama	4.6	1.0	0.8	1.3	1.3	0.6	1.2	1.5	0.3	1.0
Paraguay	9.3	25.2	38.2	9.8	7.0	11.5	6.8	9.0	7.3	10.5
Peru [e]	38.1	163.4	7,481.7	11.5	8.6	7.2	3.5	3.8	2.0	0.2
Puerto Rico				5.1	2.7	2.3	2.6	3.0		
St Kitts	17.7	2.6	4.0	2.1	8.9	3.4	3.9	2.1	2.1	2.1
St Lucia	8.9	1.4	4.7	0.9	0.0	3.2	3.4	3.8	0.1	1.6
St Vincent and the Grenadines [a]	10.2	2.1	7.6	4.4	0.4	2.1	1.0	0.2	0.8	0.8
Suriname [f, h]	9.7	10.9	21.7	-0.7	7.1	19.0	98.9	80.4	4.9	28.3
Trinidad and Tobago	11.7	7.6	11.1	3.4	3.6	5.6	3.4	3.6	5.5	4.2
Uruguay [i]	58.2	72.2	112.5	28.3	19.8	10.8	5.7	4.8	4.4	14.0
Venezuela [c]	7.8	11.4	40.7	99.9	50.0	35.8	23.6	16.2	12.5	22.4

Source: *Euromonitor from International Monetary Fund (IMF), International Financial Statistics and World Economic Outlook/UN/national statistics*
Notes: *(a) New series starting 1981, (b) New series starting 1982, (c) New series starting 1984, (d) New series starting 1988, (e) New series starting 1979, (f) New series starting 1980, (g) New series starting 1989, (h) New series starting 1987, (i) New series starting 1978, (j) New series starting 1986, (k) New series starting 1990, (l) New series staring 1982, (m) New series starting 1991, (n) New series starting 1985*

□ Annual Rates of Inflation

Annual Rates of Inflation 1977-2002

● % growth

	1977	1985	1990	1996	1997	1998	1999	2000	2001	2002
Asia Pacific										
Afghanistan	7.7	112.3	41.9	14.0	14.0	14.0	12.0	15.3		
American Samoa				2.4	2.3	2.2	2.2	2.7	2.9	
Armenia			5.6	18.7	13.9	8.7	0.7	-0.8	3.1	1.1
Azerbaijan			7.8	19.8	3.6	-0.7	-8.6	1.8	1.5	2.8
Bangladesh	4.8	10.5	6.1	4.1	5.2	8.3	6.2	2.4	1.9	3.4
Bhutan		1.9	10.0	8.8	6.5	10.6	6.8	4.0	3.4	2.5
Brunei				3.6	3.7	2.9	1.0	1.6	1.8	
Cambodia			141.8	10.1	3.2	14.8	4.0	-0.8	-0.6	3.2
China		9.3	3.1	8.3	2.8	-0.8	-1.4	0.3	0.5	-0.8
Fiji (e)	7.0	4.4	8.2	3.1	3.4	5.7	2.0	1.1	4.3	0.8
French Polynesia				7.8	6.6	5.5	5.4	5.6	2.8	
Guam				2.1	2.4	2.0	2.0	2.4	2.0	
Hong Kong, China		3.5	10.3	6.3	5.8	2.9	-4.0	-3.7	-1.6	-3.0
India (d)	8.3	5.6	9.0	9.0	7.2	13.2	4.7	4.0	3.7	4.4
Indonesia (e)	11.0	4.7	7.8	8.0	6.7	57.6	20.3	4.5	12.0	11.5
Japan	8.2	2.0	3.1	0.1	1.7	0.7	-0.3	-0.7	-0.7	-0.9
Kazakhstan			5.6	39.3	17.4	7.1	8.3	13.2	8.4	5.8
Kiribati	8.9	4.5	4.0	-1.5	2.2	3.7	1.8	0.4	6.0	3.2
Kyrgyzstan			4.2	31.9	23.4	10.5	35.9	18.7	6.9	2.1
Laos (h)	90.0	114.7	35.6	13.0	27.5	91.0	128.4	25.1	7.8	10.6
Macau (g)			8.0	4.8	3.5	0.2	0.7	1.0	1.1	
Malaysia (f, k)	4.8	0.3	2.6	3.5	2.7	5.3	2.7	1.5	1.4	1.8
Maldives		-9.2	3.6	6.3	7.6	-1.4	3.0	-1.2	0.6	0.9
Mongolia		-1.0	0.0	46.9	36.6	9.4	7.6	11.6	8.0	0.9
Myanmar (g)	-1.2	6.8	17.6	16.3	29.7	51.5	18.4	-0.1	21.1	57.1
Nauru				4.0	6.1	4.0	6.7	7.5	4.0	
Nepal (d)	9.9	8.1	8.2	9.2	4.0	10.0	5.5	0.9	2.5	2.4
New Caledonia				2.5	3.3	2.8	2.4	2.8	2.5	2.8
North Korea				2.3						
Pakistan (l)	10.1	5.6	9.1	10.4	11.4	6.2	4.1	4.4	3.1	3.3
Papua New Guinea	4.5	3.7	7.0	11.6	4.0	13.6	14.9	15.6	9.3	11.8
Philippines (a)	9.9	23.2	13.2	9.0	5.9	9.7	6.7	4.4	6.1	3.1
Singapore (a)	3.2	0.5	3.5	1.4	2.0	-0.3	0.0	1.4	1.0	-0.4
Solomon Islands	8.6	9.6	8.7	11.8	8.1	12.4	8.3	7.3	6.8	9.8
South Korea	10.2	2.5	8.6	5.0	4.4	7.5	0.8	2.2	4.0	2.8
Sri Lanka	1.2	1.5	21.5	15.9	9.6	9.4	4.7	6.2	14.2	9.6
Taiwan	7.0	-0.2	4.1	3.1	0.9	1.7	0.2	1.3	0.0	-0.2
Tajikistan			5.6	418.2	88.0	43.2	27.5	32.9	38.6	12.2
Thailand	7.6	2.4	5.9	5.8	5.6	8.1	0.3	1.5	1.7	0.6
Tonga	17.5	16.8	9.7	3.0	2.1	3.3	4.9	5.9	8.3	10.4
Turkmenistan				992.4	83.7	16.8	23.5	8.0	11.6	15.0
Tuvalu					1.4	0.8	1.0	5.0	1.8	1.5
Uzbekistan			4.0	54.0	70.9	16.7	44.6	50.7	48.9	38.7
Vanuatu	5.7	1.1	4.8	0.9	2.8	3.3	2.0	2.5	3.7	2.2
Vietnam	5.0	91.6	36.0	5.7	3.2	7.7	4.2	-1.6	-0.4	4.0
Western Samoa	14.6	9.1	15.2	5.4	6.9	2.2	0.3	1.0	3.8	8.1
Australasia										
Australia (e)	12.3	6.7	7.3	2.6	0.3	0.9	1.5	4.5	4.4	3.0
New Zealand (b)	14.6	15.4	5.5	2.3	1.2	1.3	-0.1	2.6	2.6	2.7

Source: Euromonitor from International Monetary Fund (IMF), International Financial Statistics and World Economic Outlook/UN/national statistics
Notes: (a) New series starting 1981, (b) New series starting 1982, (c) New series starting 1984, (d) New series starting 1988, (e) New series starting 1979, (f) New series starting 1980, (g) New series starting 1989, (h) New series starting 1987, (i) New series starting 1978, (j) New series starting 1986, (k) New series starting 1990, (l) New series staring 1982, (m) New series starting 1991, (n) New series starting 1985

◻ Annual Rates of Inflation

Annual Rates of Inflation 1977-2002

- % growth

	1977	1985	1990	1996	1997	1998	1999	2000	2001	2002
Africa and Middle East										
Algeria	12.0	10.5	16.6	18.7	5.7	5.0	2.6	0.3	4.2	1.4
Angola		1.8	2.8	4,145.1	219.2	107.3	248.2	325.0	152.6	108.9
Bahrain	17.7	-2.6	0.9	-0.5	2.4	-0.2	-1.4	-0.7	0.2	1.2
Benin		1.2	1.1	4.9	3.5	5.8	0.3	4.2	4.0	2.5
Botswana (a, m)	13.2	8.1	11.4	10.1	8.7	6.7	7.7	8.6	6.6	8.1
Burkina Faso	30.0	6.9	-0.8	6.2	2.3	5.1	-1.1	-0.3	5.0	2.2
Burundi	6.8	3.8	7.0	26.4	31.1	12.5	3.4	24.3	9.2	-1.4
Cameroon	14.7	8.5	1.1	3.9	4.8	3.2	1.5	-2.1	4.5	2.8
Cape Verde	11.2	5.4	10.7	6.0	8.6	4.4	4.4	-2.5	3.3	1.9
Central African Republic		10.4	-0.4	3.7	1.6	-1.9	-1.4	3.2	3.4	3.4
Chad	8.4	5.2	-0.2	12.4	5.6	12.1	-6.8	3.8	12.4	5.2
Comoros	9.4	8.4	-7.4	2.0	3.0	3.5	3.5	4.5	-3.5	3.3
Congo Dem Rep (d)	68.9	23.8	81.3	541.9	175.5	29.1	284.9	513.9	359.9	31.5
Congo-Brazzaville	14.0	3.5	2.9	10.0	13.2	6.2	5.4	-0.9	0.1	4.6
Côte d'Ivoire	27.4	1.9	-0.8	2.5	4.0	4.7	0.8	2.5	4.3	3.1
Djibouti	30.9	2.1	7.8	3.5	2.5	2.2	-20.8	2.4	1.8	0.6
Egypt (c)	12.7	12.1	16.8	7.2	4.6	4.2	3.1	2.7	2.3	2.7
Equatorial Guinea	12.1	63.7	1.1	6.0	4.5	3.7	6.0	6.5	6.0	12.0
Eritrea				10.3	3.7	9.5	8.4	19.9	14.6	18.8
Ethiopia	16.7	19.1	5.2	-5.1	2.4	2.6	7.9	0.7	-8.1	1.6
Gabon	13.9	7.4	7.7	0.7	4.0	1.4	-1.9	0.5	2.1	0.2
Gambia	12.4	18.3	12.2	1.1	2.8	1.1	3.8	0.8	4.5	8.6
Ghana	116.5	10.3	37.3	46.6	27.9	14.6	12.4	25.2	32.9	14.8
Guinea	4.6	19.0	19.4	3.0	1.9	5.1	4.6	6.8	5.4	3.0
Guinea-Bissau	3.0	112.7	33.0	50.7	49.1	6.5	-2.0	8.6	3.2	0.9
Iran	27.3	4.4	7.6	28.9	17.3	17.9	20.1	14.5	11.3	14.3
Iraq				8.1	200.0			100.0	60.0	
Israel (f, i, n)	36.8	304.7	17.2	11.3	9.0	5.4	5.2	1.1	1.1	5.6
Jordan (d, e)	14.6	3.0	16.2	6.5	3.0	3.1	0.6	0.7	1.8	1.8
Kenya (i)	14.8	13.0	17.8	8.9	11.4	6.7	5.7	10.0	5.7	2.0
Kuwait (i)	9.9	1.5	9.8	3.6	0.7	0.2	3.0	1.8	1.7	1.4
Lebanon	6.3	54.5	62.7	8.9	7.7	4.5	0.2	-0.4	-0.4	1.8
Lesotho (f, i)	16.7	13.3	11.6	9.3	8.5	7.8	8.0	6.1	-9.6	33.8
Liberia	6.2	-1.0					3.0	5.0	5.0	5.6
Libya	6.3	9.1	8.5	4.0	3.6	3.7	2.6	-2.9	-8.8	2.8
Madagascar	3.1	10.6	11.8	19.8	4.5	6.2	9.9	12.0	6.9	15.9
Malawi (f)	4.1	10.5	11.8	37.6	9.1	29.7	44.8	29.6	27.2	14.7
Mali	25.7	10.8	0.6	6.8	-0.4	4.0	-1.2	-0.7	5.2	5.0
Mauritania	10.3	10.3	6.6	4.7	4.6	8.0	4.1	3.3	4.7	3.8
Mauritius (a)	9.2	6.7	13.5	6.6	6.8	6.8	6.9	4.2	5.4	6.7
Morocco	12.6	7.7	6.9	3.0	1.0	2.8	0.7	1.9	0.6	2.8
Mozambique	2.0	30.8	47.0	48.5	7.4	1.5	2.9	12.7	9.0	16.8
Namibia	10.2	12.0	12.0	8.0	8.8	6.2	8.6	9.0	9.5	11.3
Niger	23.3	-0.9	-0.8	5.3	2.9	4.5	-2.3	2.9	4.0	2.6
Nigeria	13.8	7.4	7.4	29.3	8.2	10.3	4.8	14.5	13.0	12.9
Oman		-4.0	10.0	0.1	0.1	-0.8	0.4	-1.1	-1.1	-0.7
Qatar	20.0	1.9	3.0	7.4	2.8	2.6	2.2	1.7	1.4	1.0
Réunion				5.3	5.8					
Rwanda	13.7	1.8	4.2	7.4	12.0	6.2	-2.4	4.3	3.0	2.5
Sao Tomé e Príncipe	7.4	0.1	42.2	42.0	69.0	42.1	16.3	11.0	9.5	9.2
Saudi Arabia (a, e, i)	11.4	-3.1	2.1	1.2	0.1	-0.4	-1.6	-0.8	-0.5	-0.5
Senegal	11.3	13.0	0.3	2.8	1.6	1.2	0.8	0.7	3.1	2.2
Seychelles (a)	15.0	0.8	3.9	-1.1	0.6	2.6	6.3	6.3	6.0	0.2
Sierra Leone (e)	8.3	76.6	110.9	23.1	14.9	35.5	34.1	-0.8	2.1	-3.3
Somalia	10.6	37.8								
South Africa (f, h)	11.2	16.3	14.3	7.4	8.6	6.9	5.2	5.3	5.7	9.6
Sudan	17.1	45.4	65.2	132.8	46.7	17.1	16.0	8.0	6.4	8.3
Swaziland (f)	20.8	20.5	13.1	6.4	7.1	8.1	6.1	12.2	5.9	12.0
Syria	12.0	17.3	19.4	8.2	1.9	-0.8	-1.9	-0.5	0.4	1.5
Tanzania (a)	11.6	33.3	35.8	21.0	16.1	12.8	7.9	5.9	5.1	4.6
Togo	22.5	-1.8	1.0	4.7	8.3	1.0	-0.1	1.9	3.9	3.1
Tunisia	6.7	7.3	6.5	3.7	3.7	3.1	2.7	2.9	2.0	2.7
Uganda	74.9	157.7	33.1	7.2	6.9	0.0	6.4	2.8	2.0	-0.3
United Arab Emirates	22.0	3.5	0.6	3.0	2.9	2.0	2.1	1.4	2.2	1.4
Yemen (e)	24.9		33.5	30.2	5.4	7.9	8.0	10.9	11.9	12.2
Zambia (m)	19.8	37.4	107.0	43.1	24.4	24.5	26.8	26.0	21.4	22.2
Zimbabwe (i)	10.3	8.5	17.4	21.4	18.7	31.8	58.5	55.9	76.7	140.1

Source: Euromonitor from International Monetary Fund (IMF), International Financial Statistics and World Economic Outlook/UN/national statistics
Notes: (a) New series starting 1981, (b) New series starting 1982, (c) New series starting 1984, (d) New series starting 1988, (e) New series starting 1979, (f) New series starting 1980, (g) New series starting 1989, (h) New series starting 1987, (i) New series starting 1978, (j) New series starting 1986, (k) New series starting 1990, (l) New series staring 1982, (m) New series starting 1991, (n) New series starting 1985

Public Consumption 1990-2002

● Billion units of national currency

	1990	1994	1995	1996	1997	1998	1999	2000	2001	2002	Total US$ billion 2002
North America											
Canada	135.2	171.7	172.6	171.4	171.9	176.8	183.3	196.0	207.5	218.9	139.5
USA [a]	1,181.4	1,327.9	1,372.0	1,421.9	1,487.9	1,538.5	1,641.0	1,751.0	1,858.0	1,973.3	1,973.3
Latin America											
Anguilla	0.0										
Antigua	0.2	0.3	0.3	0.3	0.3	0.4	0.4	0.4			
Argentina		33.9	34.4	34.0	35.3	37.4	38.9	39.2	38.0	38.2	12.5
Aruba											
Bahamas	0.4	0.5	0.5								
Barbados	0.7	0.7	0.8	0.8	0.9	1.0	1.0	1.1	1.1		
Belize	0.1	0.2	0.2	0.2	0.2	0.2	0.2	0.2	0.3		
Bermuda	0.2										
Bolivia	1.8	3.8	4.4	5.0	5.8	6.7	7.1	7.6	8.1	8.6	1.2
Brazil	0.0	62.4	126.7	144.0	158.5	174.8	185.8	210.0	230.7	254.7	87.2
British Virgin Islands											
Cayman Islands											
Chile	901.9	2,420.1	2,938.5	3,426.1	3,860.5	4,197.1	4,603.8	5,020.4	5,432.6	5,784.9	8.4
Colombia	2,076.5	9,774.3	12,622.3	18,122.5	24,245.7	28,547.9	33,587.7	37,057.1	37,474.7	42,046.2	16.8
Costa Rica	94.9	228.9	284.6	330.5	390.1	469.9	565.2	652.7	770.8	893.1	2.5
Cuba											
Dominica	0.1	0.1	0.1	0.1	0.1	0.2	0.2	0.2			
Dominican Republic	1.8	6.7	8.3	10.4	16.4	19.4	22.5	27.1	32.8	38.2	2.1
Ecuador	706.2	3,427.0	5,789.0	7,146.0	9,147.4	12,523.6	16,720.0	31,861.0	41,237.0		
El Salvador	3.6	5.9	7.2	8.4	8.8	10.2	10.9	11.7	12.6	11.9	1.4
French Guiana											
Grenada	0.1	0.1	0.1	0.1	0.1	0.2	0.1	0.2			
Guadeloupe											
Guatemala	2.3	4.5	4.7	4.9	5.4	7.0	8.6	10.5	12.4	13.0	1.7
Guyana	2.1	11.8	14.1	17.3	21.7						
Haiti											
Honduras	1.6	2.8	3.5	4.6	5.4	7.1	8.7	11.2	13.8	14.9	0.9
Jamaica	4.3	16.5	22.6	32.5	40.1	46.8	48.6	53.6	55.7		
Martinique											
Mexico	61.9	164.2	192.0	243.7	314.6	400.0	506.5	609.7	686.0	723.5	74.9
Netherlands Antilles											
Nicaragua	0.5	2.0	2.2	2.7	3.2	3.7	4.9	5.7	6.9	6.1	0.4
Panama	1.0	1.1	1.2	1.3	1.4	1.5	1.5	1.6			
Paraguay	401.9	1,012.5	1,275.9	1,528.5	1,693.0	1,928.3	2,135.4	2,601.6	2,479.9	2,470.2	0.4
Peru	0.4	8.7	11.8	13.8	15.5	17.6	19.0	20.9	21.3	21.7	6.2
Puerto Rico											
St Kitts	0.1	0.1	0.1	0.1	0.1	0.1	0.2	0.2	0.2		
St Lucia											
St Vincent and the Grenadines	0.1	0.1	0.1	0.2	0.2	0.2	0.2	0.2	0.2		
Suriname	0.8	6.8	45.4	48.1	51.3						
Trinidad and Tobago	3.5	4.4	5.0	5.5	5.6	6.3					
Uruguay	1.4	10.5	14.5	21.0	25.3	29.4	30.9	32.1	33.8	33.6	1.6
Venezuela	191.8	627.0	974.8	1,475.6	2,807.7	3,957.6	4,700.3	5,958.9	7,846.7		

Source: International Monetary Fund (IMF), International Financial Statistics
Notes: (a) General Government Expenditure and Investment

◻ Public and Private Consumption

Public Consumption 1990-2002

● Billion units of national currency

	1990	1994	1995	1996	1997	1998	1999	2000	2001	2002	Total US$ billion 2002
Asia Pacific											
Afghanistan											
American Samoa											
Armenia		21.1	58.3	74.3	90.2	105.6	117.6	121.8	132.7	137.6	0.2
Azerbaijan											
Bangladesh	42.1	66.1	70.6	73.3	78.9	94.7	100.8	108.4	114.3	120.4	2.1
Bhutan	0.8	1.6	2.4	2.5	3.7	3.3	4.3	4.4			
Brunei											
Cambodia											
China	225.2	598.6	669.1	785.2	872.5	948.5	1,038.8	1,170.5	1,302.9		
Fiji	0.3	0.4	0.4	0.5	0.5	0.6	0.6				
French Polynesia											
Guam											
Hong Kong, China	43.1	83.1	93.6	103.5	112.7	116.5	120.0	120.1	128.8	131.4	16.8
India	660.3	1,086.4	1,288.2	1,457.3	1,721.9	2,140.3	2,481.3	2,645.6	2,949.7		
Indonesia	18,953.0	31,014.0	35,584.0	40,299.0	42,952.0	54,415.9	72,631.3	90,779.7	110,837.0		
Japan	58,809.0	71,285.0	74,698.0	77,356.0	79,201.0	80,735.0	82,876.0	85,731.0	88,312.0	89,433.0	713.3
Kazakhstan		45.2	137.7	182.8	207.0	186.9	232.7	314.0	436.0		
Kiribati											
Kyrgyzstan		2.3	3.2	4.3	5.3	6.1	9.3	13.1	12.9	13.6	0.3
Laos											
Macau	2.3										
Malaysia	16.4	24.0	27.5	28.2	30.3	27.7	33.0	35.7	42.1	50.0	13.2
Maldives	0.5										
Mongolia	2.0										
Myanmar											
Nauru											
Nepal	9.0	16.0	20.3	23.0	25.0	28.0	30.5	34.6	41.0	45.4	0.6
New Caledonia											
North Korea											
Pakistan	129.6	189.1	219.1	268.1	288.8	301.6	304.4	351.6	350.4	425.9	7.1
Papua New Guinea	0.8	1.0	1.0	1.4	1.4	1.4	1.5				
Philippines	108.8	182.8	217.0	259.5	319.9	354.4	389.2	438.9	444.8	488.7	9.5
Singapore	6.8	9.0	10.1	12.2	13.2	13.9	14.1	16.8	18.3		
Solomon Islands											
South Korea	18,701.7	32,856.7	36,433.5	42,477.4	45,659.7	48,782.1	50,089.4	52,479.7	57,179.7	62,968.0	50.3
Sri Lanka	31.4	56.0	76.6	81.0	92.2	99.1	99.9	132.2	141.1	143.0	1.5
Taiwan	739.6	960.8	1,002.4	1,082.3							
Tajikistan											
Thailand	205.4	354.4	414.4	469.5	476.7	511.7	533.0	559.8	592.7	609.8	14.2
Tonga											
Turkmenistan											
Tuvalu											
Uzbekistan											
Vanuatu	5.1	6.9	6.9								
Vietnam											
Western Samoa											
Australasia											
Australia	72.6	85.8	89.6	95.5	99.2	104.6	109.5	118.8	124.0	132.1	71.8
New Zealand	14.1	15.3	16.4	17.0	18.6	19.0	20.2	20.3	21.1	23.1	10.7

Source: International Monetary Fund (IMF), International Financial Statistics
Notes: (a) General Government Expenditure and Investment

▫ Public and Private Consumption
Public Consumption 1990-2002

• Billion units of national currency

	1990	1994	1995	1996	1997	1998	1999	2000	2001	2002	Total US$ billion 2002
Africa and Middle East											
Algeria	90.1	263.9	340.2	405.4	459.8	503.6	543.6	560.2			
Angola	0.0										
Bahrain	0.4	0.4	0.5	0.5	0.5	0.5	0.5	0.5	0.5	0.6	1.5
Benin	66.2	90.1	100.1	108.3	113.8	122.5	128.9	136.9	145.9	166.7	0.2
Botswana	1.6	3.0	3.5	4.0	4.7	5.5	6.6	7.5	8.7	10.6	1.7
Burkina Faso	111.8	176.5	183.8	191.9	192.2	165.9	215.7	234.0	252.0	296.2	0.4
Burundi	38.3	32.5	33.6	45.4	42.3	47.7	51.6	56.6	62.5	83.6	0.1
Cameroon	427.6	257.5	299.9	305.0	332.1						
Cape Verde											
Central African Republic	6.0										
Chad											
Comoros											
Congo Dem Rep		0.0	0.0	0.1	0.5	0.6	2.6	15.1	68.9		
Congo-Brazzaville	153.5	200.8	133.6	133.8	257.2	164.1	185.3	219.3	241.4	281.0	0.4
Côte d'Ivoire	499.0	555.0	594.0	714.4	713.2	1,132.0	1,150.0	1,050.0	1,100.5	1,290.6	1.9
Djibouti											
Egypt	10.9	18.0	21.5	23.8	26.1	32.5	35.7	38.1	40.6	45.2	10.0
Equatorial Guinea	6.8										
Eritrea											
Ethiopia	3.2	3.2	3.7	4.2	5.2	6.2	9.1	12.0	9.1		
Gabon	251.3	278.9	291.0	308.8	345.0	425.7					
Gambia											
Ghana	222.0	714.3	935.9	1,365.6	1,743.8						
Guinea											
Guinea-Bissau	10.5	15.6	10.0	10.9	13.5	11.3	14.9	21.4	17.4	23.4	0.0
Iran	4,277.5	21,005.4	29,707.8	35,173.5	38,206.7	47,036.6	55,997.5	80,554.0	97,219.0		
Iraq											
Israel	31.7	62.6	79.3	93.2	102.8	111.8	121.7	130.0	139.0	153.1	32.3
Jordan	0.7	1.0	1.1	1.2	1.3	1.4	1.4	1.5			
Kenya	36.6	60.7	69.1	84.5	100.7	113.6	125.9	139.2	168.7	184.3	2.3
Kuwait	2.1	2.5	2.6	2.6	2.5	2.4	2.5	2.5	2.5	2.8	9.3
Lebanon											
Lesotho	0.2	0.5	0.6	0.7	0.8	1.0	1.1	1.1	1.2		
Liberia											
Libya	2.0	2.3	2.4	2.9	3.3	3.3	3.1	3.6			
Madagascar	383.6	723.9	904.2	731.9	1,097.7	1,621.0	1,741.1	2,063.8	2,639.0	2,585.0	0.4
Malawi	0.8	3.3	4.1	4.6	5.2	6.4	9.7	12.9			
Mali	95.6	187.9	204.4	210.5	290.6	322.9	308.5	310.8	346.8	369.0	0.5
Mauritania		25.9	30.1	31.1	32.5	23.5					
Mauritius	4.6	7.9	8.3	9.5	10.4	12.6	14.2	15.6	16.7	18.0	0.6
Morocco	33.0	47.9	49.0	53.8	56.6	62.0	66.2	67.7	74.6		
Mozambique	271.0	2,060.7	2,011.3	2,874.9	3,648.4	4,411.0	4,852.1	5,385.8	6,349.8	7,283.3	0.3
Namibia	1.9	3.3	3.8	4.6	5.1	5.6	6.3	6.8	7.6		
Niger	110.4	127.4	131.9	137.5	138.8	139.8	199.3	172.3	182.7	200.6	0.3
Nigeria	11.5	88.5	123.2	143.1	171.3	204.3	252.6	260.3	275.5	278.6	2.3
Oman	1.2	1.4	1.5	1.4	1.4	1.4	1.4	1.6	1.8		
Qatar	8.8	9.3	9.4	10.9	11.2						
Réunion											
Rwanda	21.6	13.6	30.9	44.1	49.9	54.5	61.2	60.9	69.6		
Sao Tomé e Príncipe											
Saudi Arabia	120.1	122.6	125.9	144.8	161.8	155.2	154.1	183.8	188.7	181.5	48.5
Senegal	222.3	258.4	276.1	286.0	303.0	324.2	308.6	365.7	493.7		
Seychelles	0.5	0.7	0.7	0.7	0.7	0.8					
Sierra Leone	7.7	54.2	57.9	85.0	86.0	107.2	119.7	134.4			
Somalia											
South Africa	57.0	96.5	100.4	118.0	131.9	140.2	149.1	166.3	185.3	211.4	20.1
Sudan											
Swaziland	0.4	0.9	1.0	1.2	1.6	1.8	1.9	1.9	2.0		
Syria	38.5	68.0	76.7	81.3	85.0	88.5	86.9	98.4			
Tanzania	147.7	393.5	462.3	435.3	413.6	433.8	451.1	473.7	516.3		
Togo	56.3	77.1	77.0	100.6	95.2	103.0	95.4	96.7	88.6	100.8	0.1
Tunisia	1.8	2.6	2.8	3.0	3.3	3.5	3.8	4.2	4.5	4.9	3.4
Uganda	128.3	476.6	577.2	660.6	915.7	1,011.9	1,134.5	1,301.8	1,486.0	1,693.6	0.9
United Arab Emirates	20.1	24.2	25.4	26.2	28.1	28.6					
Yemen	22.1	57.6	74.0	97.5	120.1	124.5	161.2	203.7			
Zambia	21.6	293.6	464.0	676.5	792.3						
Zimbabwe	4.2	9.4	11.1	14.5	17.1	21.2					

Source: International Monetary Fund (IMF), International Financial Statistics
Notes: (a) General Government Expenditure and Investment

Table 10.12

▣ Public and Private Consumption

Private Consumption 1990-2002

● Billion units of national currency

	1990	1994	1995	1996	1997	1998	1999	2000	2001	2002	Total US$ billion 2002
North America											
Canada	394.3	447.7	462.9	482.4	512.9	534.4	561.6	594.1	623.2	656.2	418.1
USA	3,831.5	4,716.4	4,969.0	5,237.5	5,529.3	5,856.0	6,246.5	6,683.8	6,987.0	7,303.8	7,303.8
Latin America											
Anguilla	0.0		0.1	0.1	0.1	0.1	0.1	0.1	0.1		
Antigua	0.5	0.6	0.7	0.8	0.8	0.8	0.7	0.8	0.8		
Argentina	55.3	180.0	176.9	186.5	203.0	206.4	198.9	197.0	185.2	193.3	63.1
Aruba			0.8	0.9	1.0	1.0	1.1	1.1	1.2		
Bahamas	2.0	2.1	2.1	2.2	2.3	2.1	2.2	2.3	2.3		
Barbados	2.2	2.0	2.3	2.4	2.8	3.0	3.2	3.5	3.3		
Belize	0.5	0.7	0.8	0.8	0.8	0.8	0.9	1.1	1.2		
Bermuda	1.1	1.4	1.4	1.5	1.6	1.7	1.8	1.8	1.9		
Bolivia	11.9	21.4	24.4	28.2	31.1	35.1	37.0	39.7	40.5	41.8	5.8
Brazil	0.0	208.3	386.9	486.8	545.7	566.2	606.7	670.7	727.1	783.3	268.2
British Virgin Islands				0.3	0.4	0.4	0.4	0.4	0.5		
Cayman Islands	0.4		0.4	0.4	0.5	0.5	0.5	0.5	0.6		
Chile	5,719.6	14,648.7	17,270.3	19,785.0	21,972.0	23,703.6	23,927.9	25,811.9	27,735.3	28,903.7	42.0
Colombia	13,238.5	44,510.2	55,461.8	65,965.7	79,193.8	92,501.2	97,631.2	110,217.0	123,365.0	133,076.0	53.1
Costa Rica	321.1	1,189.3	1,496.2	1,822.3	2,168.9	2,510.9	2,916.4	3,290.3	3,690.4	4,145.6	11.5
Cuba				284.1	328.4	341.3	375.4	381.6	393.7		
Dominica	0.3	0.4	0.4	0.4	0.4	0.4	0.4	0.4	0.5		
Dominican Republic	49.3	109.0	127.8	147.1	166.2	187.6	209.2	248.9	273.1	300.8	16.2
Ecuador	5,621.9	25,024.7	31,133.7	38,791.0	53,152.6	75,609.8	105,659.1	217,564.0	291,097.5	321,916.0	12.9
El Salvador	32.4	61.7	72.7	79.7	85.2	89.3	93.7	101.1	107.3	110.9	12.7
French Guiana			0.4	0.4	0.4	0.4	0.5	0.5	0.5		
Grenada	0.4	0.4	0.5	0.6	0.6	0.7	0.5	0.8	0.8		
Guadeloupe					3.1	3.2	3.2	3.4	3.7		
Guatemala	28.7	63.9	72.9	83.1	93.8	105.4	114.6	125.7	139.9	156.8	20.0
Guyana	9.5	36.1	40.9	44.2	47.1	48.6	52.9	57.4	56.2		
Haiti	11.7	31.3	38.2	41.7	49.4	57.1	62.2	72.4	82.4	90.4	3.1
Honduras	8.4	18.1	23.8	30.8	39.6	46.9	53.2	63.2	72.3	79.8	4.9
Jamaica	21.4	108.2	139.8	162.3	174.7	181.9	196.6	223.3	246.0		
Martinique			1.4	1.7	1.8	1.9	2.1	2.2	2.3		
Mexico	514.1	1,016.1	1,232.0	1,646.3	2,042.1	2,593.3	3,084.1	3,683.7	4,056.8	4,304.6	445.8
Netherlands Antilles			2.8	3.0	3.0	2.4	2.3	2.5	2.5		
Nicaragua	1.0	10.7	12.1	15.0	17.8	20.4	24.9	28.6	31.4	33.4	2.3
Panama	3.0	4.2	4.1	5.3	4.7	5.3	5.3	5.7	6.0		
Paraguay	4,996.5	13,231.8	15,089.2	16,853.3	17,704.3	20,101.4	19,762.5	22,406.8	24,604.3	27,527.0	4.8
Peru	4.0	71.3	85.9	98.6	110.9	118.6	122.2	131.8	136.9	143.4	40.8
Puerto Rico				20.4	21.3	22.6	24.2	25.5	27.3		
St Kitts	0.3	0.3	0.4	0.4	0.4	0.4	0.6	0.5	0.5		
St Lucia			0.9	0.9	0.9	1.0	1.0	1.0	1.0		
St Vincent and the Grenadines	0.3	0.5	0.5	0.5	0.6	0.6	0.6	0.6	0.6		
Suriname	1.7	18.0	36.6	162.3	212.7	286.8	507.8	767.5	1,163.2		
Trinidad and Tobago	11.6	15.0	17.0	19.5	22.3	23.9	25.4	29.3	32.8		
Uruguay	7.6	64.2	89.3	118.0	148.4	169.4	173.4	181.1	183.8	190.9	9.0
Venezuela	1,415.4	6,077.1	9,507.7	18,618.0	28,524.0	37,684.9	43,236.9	52,295.0	61,107.9	70,567.8	60.8

Source: *International Monetary Fund (IMF), International Financial Statistics*
Notes: *(a) Includes government final consumption expenditure*

Public and Private Consumption

Private Consumption 1990-2002

- Billion units of national currency

	1990	1994	1995	1996	1997	1998	1999	2000	2001	2002	Total US$ billion 2002
Asia Pacific											
Afghanistan											
American Samoa			0.2	0.2	0.2	0.2	0.2	0.2	0.3		
Armenia		176.9	555.1	664.0	832.6	956.3	951.6	1,001.7	1,100.0	1,215.8	2.1
Azerbaijan		3,201.6	8,994.0	11,982.6	12,036.1	13,348.7	13,071.6	13,849.8	14,506.9	15,393.8	3.2
Bangladesh	832.1	1,110.6	1,254.4	1,342.2	1,440.8	1,558.6	1,707.1	1,838.5	1,964.9	2,105.1	36.4
Bhutan	2.8	3.8	3.4	5.2	7.1	9.3	10.1	11.3	12.7		
Brunei				12.0	12.8	13.6	13.6	13.5	14.1		
Cambodia			3,366.5	4,010.1	4,544.9	5,274.3	5,487.8	6,083.4	6,810.9		
China	911.3	2,081.0	2,694.5	3,215.2	3,485.5	3,692.1	3,933.4	4,291.1	4,592.3	4,798.4	579.7
Fiji	1.4	1.7	1.8	1.9	1.9	2.1	2.1	2.2	2.3		
French Polynesia	178.7		46.5	59.4	63.8	68.8	73.0	77.5	84.4		
Guam			0.7	0.7	0.8	0.8	0.8	0.9	0.9		
Hong Kong, China	332.8	606.6	668.4	725.9	806.8	772.3	740.8	744.4	745.5	708.6	90.9
India	3,871.4	6,641.6	7,658.0	9,036.5	9,816.7	11,394.1	12,653.5	13,593.6	14,928.9	15,522.8	319.3
Indonesia	114,693.0	228,119.0	279,876.0	332,094.0	387,108.0	647,824.0	813,183.0	867,997.0	999,266.0	1,151,954.9	123.7
Japan	234,140.0	272,678.0	275,745.0	282,121.0	287,152.0	286,946.0	288,764.0	287,231.0	283,652.0	287,985.0	2,296.8
Kazakhstan		328.8	721.1	952.8	1,179.1	1,270.0	1,460.1	1,595.4	1,875.6	2,140.2	14.0
Kiribati			0.0	0.0	0.0	0.0	0.0	0.0	0.1		
Kyrgyzstan		9.4	12.1	19.2	21.2	30.2	37.8	42.9	47.9	50.8	1.1
Laos			12.1	20.0	21.1	30.2	37.8	50.0	55.8		
Macau	10.2			20.6	21.3	20.6	21.8	23.9	24.9		
Malaysia	61.7	94.1	106.6	116.8	127.8	117.7	125.1	145.4	150.6	159.5	42.0
Maldives	0.5		1.5	1.9	2.2	2.6	2.7	3.1			
Mongolia	5.7		364.7	412.9	518.9	598.8	701.3	757.7	839.5		
Myanmar (a)	134.2	417.2	523.9	701.2	987.5	1,419.7	1,906.1	39.2	40.7		
Nauru			0.2	0.2	0.2	0.2	0.2	0.2	0.2		
Nepal	86.3	154.0	166.4	191.5	216.4	231.4	264.9	287.9	309.1	326.1	4.2
New Caledonia	143.5				172.7	173.7	188.8	195.7	212.1		
North Korea											
Pakistan	608.8	1,109.9	1,351.4	1,545.2	1,818.2	1,929.7	2,224.0	2,342.4	2,567.3	2,793.4	46.8
Papua New Guinea	1.8	2.2	2.5	3.4	4.1	4.6	6.1	5.4	5.8		
Philippines	767.1	1,258.8	1,411.9	1,595.4	1,762.0	1,980.1	2,161.6	2,335.5	2,565.0	2,750.8	53.3
Singapore	30.8	47.2	48.8	52.9	56.3	53.8	57.6	64.2	64.8	66.9	37.4
Solomon Islands			0.8	0.8	0.9	0.5	0.5	0.9	0.9		
South Korea	93,504.9	175,970.0	206,406.0	233,644.0	254,986.0	242,834.0	271,136.0	299,122.0	326,210.0	358,834.0	286.8
Sri Lanka	244.3	434.9	489.1	569.4	643.8	723.5	790.4	906.2	1,024.0	1,175.2	12.3
Taiwan	2,446.6	3,897.2	4,227.1	4,597.7	5,017.1	5,390.2	5,692.6	5,973.7	6,009.7	6,143.6	177.7
Tajikistan			0.1	0.2	0.5	0.8	1.0	1.4	1.9		
Thailand	1,235.0	1,958.7	2,225.7	2,479.8	2,587.0	2,505.3	2,595.1	2,750.5	2,913.7	3,067.4	71.4
Tonga			0.1	0.1	0.1	0.1	0.1	0.2	0.2		
Turkmenistan		19.7	198.9	2,036.2	3,321.1	4,095.7	5,865.5	7,478.1	12,170.8	12,584.2	2.0
Tuvalu			0.0	0.0	0.0	0.0	0.0	0.0	0.0		
Uzbekistan			254.1	455.2	734.1	1,189.8	1,747.5	2,608.3	3,666.0		
Vanuatu	11.3	12.3	12.8	14.3	16.9	17.8	19.0	19.8	21.4		
Vietnam	73,282.1	133,857.0	163,272.2	197,072.2	219,917.0	249,508.4	268,702.8	283,045.0	303,669.4	334,629.9	21.9
Western Samoa			0.2	0.3	0.3	0.3	0.3	0.5	0.5		
Australasia											
Australia	228.0	273.3	292.6	307.5	325.1	344.4	364.8	388.5	414.6	441.1	239.6
New Zealand	44.6	51.2	54.5	57.5	59.5	61.5	63.7	66.1	69.4	74.5	34.5

Source: *International Monetary Fund (IMF), International Financial Statistics*
Notes: *(a) Includes government final consumption expenditure*

■ Public and Private Consumption

Private Consumption 1990-2002

● Billion units of national currency

Africa and Middle East	1990	1994	1995	1996	1997	1998	1999	2000	2001	2002	Total US$ billion 2002
Algeria	313.6	837.5	1,114.8	1,335.0	1,430.3	1,555.4	1,667.2	1,713.2	1,860.2	2,033.3	25.5
Angola	0.0										
Bahrain	1.0	1.1	1.2	1.1	1.2	1.3	1.3	1.3	1.2	1.3	3.6
Benin	404.1	657.8	791.2	913.9	1,028.8	1,117.2	1,215.6	1,305.7	1,400.3	1,569.6	2.3
Botswana	2.1	3.8	4.3	4.7	5.3	6.1	6.9	7.8	8.4	9.3	1.5
Burkina Faso	617.8	776.2	891.1	988.6	959.8	1,080.5	1,162.9	1,206.6	1,281.2	1,294.6	1.9
Burundi	163.2	256.7	228.9	215.2	292.8	375.1	401.0	492.7	553.7	505.4	0.5
Cameroon	2,298.2	2,538.9	3,018.9	3,354.8	3,537.2	3,757.9	4,317.4	4,498.4	4,669.2		
Cape Verde			21.3	23.1	25.0	26.4	30.3	35.3	37.1		
Central African Republic	317.0		292.6	298.4	332.3	358.5	384.1	428.7	454.1		
Chad			273.8	308.0	369.2	426.2	387.7	432.8	544.1		
Comoros			75.9	78.1	80.5	80.7	88.2	95.1	104.1		
Congo Dem Rep	0.0	0.1	0.3	2.0	6.4	8.5	43.0	272.3	1,518.4		
Congo-Brazzaville	403.2	499.9	372.2	671.5	551.3	373.3	506.9	514.4	727.2	781.2	1.1
Côte d'Ivoire	1,761.8	2,749.2	3,379.0	3,502.3	4,535.0	4,916.0	4,868.0	5,076.6	5,241.7	5,275.8	7.6
Djibouti			58.7	65.4	66.5	45.0	46.2	46.3	47.3		
Egypt	68.9	130.5	151.9	176.5	200.5	220.4	230.8	258.0	270.0	285.5	63.4
Equatorial Guinea	23.6		52.4	78.3	168.1	176.6	361.4	669.6	892.4		
Eritrea											
Ethiopia	12.3	23.7	27.9	31.3	41.7	35.1	39.0	40.6	43.4		
Gabon	617.0	959.6	1,119.3	1,169.1	1,348.2	1,408.6	1,420.0	1,833.2	1,757.2		
Gambia			2.0	2.3	2.7	2.2	2.3	2.6	3.0		
Ghana	1,736.1	3,834.9	5,909.9	8,629.0	11,267.0	13,508.3	15,535.8	21,041.2	28,973.7		
Guinea			2,689.4	3,322.1	3,647.3	2,635.3	2,759.1	3,179.2	3,356.0		
Guinea-Bissau	64.2	119.6	117.5	128.8	144.6	127.5	119.2	115.3	121.9	124.2	0.2
Iran	20,655.6	60,138.3	87,496.2	113,239.0	140,807.0	181,172.0	225,770.0	276,612.0	304,570.0		
Iraq	11.8										
Israel	64.7	142.5	159.4	184.8	203.4	222.5	242.7	263.8	276.0	291.6	61.6
Jordan	2.0	2.9	3.0	3.5	3.6	4.1	4.0	4.8	5.1	5.2	7.3
Kenya	121.7	250.1	322.6	359.4	453.2	513.2	540.4	609.9	685.6	693.2	8.8
Kuwait	3.1	3.0	3.3	4.1	4.1	4.4	4.5	5.0	5.4	6.0	19.7
Lebanon			15,222.9	16,686.5	17,660.2	19,622.2	19,946.6	20,556.1	20,612.0		
Lesotho	2.2	3.5	4.1	4.8	5.4	5.5	5.7	6.4	6.6		
Liberia			1.4	1.4	1.7	78.8	90.5	105.0			
Libya	4.0	6.0	6.3	6.8	8.4	8.1	8.5	8.0	7.8		
Madagascar	3,965.1	8,102.8	12,120.8	14,462.9	16,294.7	17,726.0	20,032.0	22,483.0	24,001.0	25,387.0	3.7
Malawi	3.8	7.7	18.4	34.4	36.9	46.3	69.8	80.1	101.5		
Mali	536.1	749.0	928.3	1,055.4	1,051.7	1,191.0	1,324.3	1,393.5	1,509.7	1,550.1	2.2
Mauritania		87.9	80.0	99.9	111.3	113.4	133.6	150.4	157.9		
Mauritius	25.4	40.5	44.6	49.3	54.9	62.4	68.7	73.9	80.1	88.0	2.9
Morocco	138.7	197.2	201.7	227.3	218.6	234.3	229.1	242.0	259.8	269.9	24.5
Mozambique	947.0	12,648.2	20,473.4	30,509.8	36,658.9	38,821.8	40,607.6	39,876.6	40,793.8	47,973.5	2.0
Namibia	3.4	6.4	7.2	8.7	10.2	11.2	12.2	14.1	15.8		
Niger	515.2	604.5	648.8	808.1	853.7	997.1	1,011.1	874.0	926.9	1,020.6	1.5
Nigeria	155.3	694.1	1,543.1	2,368.0	2,434.6	2,757.0	1,969.6	2,446.5	3,465.6	4,599.6	38.1
Oman	1.9	2.3	2.6	2.8	2.9	3.1	3.0	3.0	3.2		
Qatar	7.5	8.0	9.5	9.0	9.2	10.4	11.1	14.0	14.6		
Réunion	3.3		2.8	3.2							
Rwanda	178.6	229.7	338.6	408.6	536.0	577.7	571.1	614.5	661.6		
Sao Tomé e Príncipe			31.1	48.9	117.2	112.4	134.0	154.6	182.3		
Saudi Arabia	155.9	240.5	250.3	259.5	261.4	251.4	252.2	258.1	259.6	260.9	69.7
Senegal	1,185.1	1,450.6	1,763.9	1,769.3	1,871.5	2,029.7	2,224.3	2,384.8	2,620.7	2,756.3	4.0
Seychelles	1.1	1.1	1.2	1.2	1.5	1.6	1.8	1.9	2.0		
Sierra Leone	82.6	436.9	566.8	709.8	734.1	887.6	1,040.9	1,142.7	1,221.9		
Somalia				1,636.1	1,660.6						
South Africa	176.8	298.2	343.0	384.6	431.4	466.6	504.3	556.7	608.6	682.4	64.7
Sudan	93.5			842.8	1,469.6	1,960.8	2,265.0	2,516.1	2,660.9		
Swaziland	1.4	3.1	3.9	4.8	4.8	5.4	6.2	7.3	8.4		
Syria	184.4	348.9	378.1	489.7	515.4	542.4	575.9	579.6	631.9		
Tanzania	687.7	1,932.0	2,532.8	3,130.1	3,968.1	4,909.3	5,667.4	6,069.6	6,917.6		
Togo	350.1	438.1	577.2	647.8	761.5	726.5	762.1	747.1	800.6	895.2	1.3
Tunisia	6.9	9.8	10.7	11.6	12.6	13.7	14.9	16.2	17.5	18.7	13.2
Uganda	1,465.7	4,356.6	4,998.0	5,434.5	5,726.7	6,224.6	7,046.7	7,667.2	8,160.4	8,460.4	4.7
United Arab Emirates	46.7	60.7	69.3	74.4	86.2	90.7	87.3	85.1	88.1	91.0	24.8
Yemen	89.0	230.9	413.1	464.0	574.6	556.9	750.5	856.3	945.0		
Zambia	71.6	1,602.7	1,775.9	2,033.2	3,006.0	3,675.6	4,666.0	6,441.4	8,747.0		
Zimbabwe	13.6	34.7	40.4	50.4	66.1	92.7	135.8	200.0	349.2		

Source: International Monetary Fund (IMF), International Financial Statistics
Notes: (a) Includes government final consumption expenditure

Government Finance and International Liquidity: Latest Year

• Million units of national currency

	Year	Budget Expenditure	Budget Revenue	Budget Surplus/ Deficit	Foreign Debt	Foreign Exchange Reserves (US$ million)	Gold Reserves (million troy oz)
North America							
Canada	2001	212,611.0	226,828.0	14,380.0	28,406	30,484	1.05
USA	2002	2,044,900.0	1,814,380.0	-230,518.0	1,211,900	33,818	262.00
Latin America							
Anguilla	2002						
Antigua	2002					88	
Argentina	1991	8,991.5	8,028.5	-963.0	339	5,812	4.12
Aruba	2002					340	0.10
Bahamas	2002	1,019.1	888.9	-135.2	99	372	
Barbados	1989	1,077.1	1,002.4	-74.6	817	107	0.01
Belize	1996	317.8	288.3	-15.7	330	53	
Bermuda	1989						
Bolivia	1996	9,883.2	9,014.3	-868.9	1,125	904	0.94
Brazil	1992	187.2	173.6	-24.4	3	22,520	2.23
British Virgin Islands	2001						
Cayman Islands	2000						
Chile	2000	8,919,700.0	8,976,100.0	56,400.0	1,477,700	14,686	0.07
Colombia	2002	42,870,200.0	31,497,700.0	-11,372,500.0		10,190	0.33
Costa Rica	2002	1,021,560.0	781,797.0	-239,767.0	796,811	1,469	0.00
Cuba	2002						
Dominica	2002					45	
Dominican Republic	1997	32,691.1	34,729.1	2,038.0	2,418	391	0.02
Ecuador	2002	101,754,500.0	105,133,250.0	3,378,675.0		689	0.85
El Salvador	2000	16,515.9	13,030.6	-2,658.6	19,947	1,890	0.47
French Guiana	2002						
Grenada	1995	209.7	205.0	16.8		37	
Guadeloupe	1993						
Guatemala	2002	22,233.1	20,503.5	-1,351.8	2,956	2,291	0.22
Guyana	1997	45,682.0	36,006.2	-6,611.2	222,436	315	
Haiti	2002	10,376.7	7,722.2	-2,541.8		81	0.00
Honduras	2000	20,975.7	15,872.0	-3,847.6	54,821	1,302	0.02
Jamaica	2002					1,645	
Martinique	2000						
Mexico	2002	987,478.0	875,535.0	-111,943.0	596,878	49,895	0.22
Netherlands Antilles	1993	719.4	587.8	-25.2	171	234	0.55
Nicaragua	1994	3,009.0	2,222.0	-4.0		141	0.10
Panama	2000	2,803.9	2,688.4	30.2	5,552	707	
Paraguay	1993	1,559,380.0	1,688,010.0	138,670.0	1,430,090	519	0.03
Peru	2001	34,754.0	29,788.0	-3,480.0		8,670	1.11
Puerto Rico	1999						
St Kitts	1994	176.5	181.8	6.8		32	
St Lucia	1991	280.2	299.8	19.6		47	
St Vincent and the Grenadines	2001	353.2	294.0	-8.7	376	61	
Suriname	2002					96	0.02
Trinidad and Tobago	1995	8,917.9	8,847.3	62.5		358	0.05
Uruguay	1994	28,717.0	26,409.0	-2,308.0	13,893	946	1.70
Venezuela	2001	22,883,800.0	19,326,500.0	-3,941,090.0		8,825	10.94

Source: *International Monetary Func (IMF), International Financial Statistics*

■ Government Finance

Government Finance and International Liquidity: Latest Year

● Million units of national currency

	Year	Budget Expenditure	Budget Revenue	Budget Surplus/ Deficit	Foreign Debt	Foreign Exchange Reserves (US$ million)	Gold Reserves (million troy oz)
Asia Pacific							
Afghanistan	1991					221	0.96
American Samoa	1997					60	
Armenia	2002					395	0.04
Azerbaijan	1999	3,859,630.0	3,316,970.0	-479,463.0		666	
Bangladesh	1991	73,000.0	80,505.0	7,505.0	179,644	1,207	0.08
Bhutan	1993	2,397.3	1,650.9	312.2	2,802	97	
Brunei	1993						
Cambodia	2002					776	
China	1996	827,500.0	740,800.0	-86,700.0	966,734	105,029	12.70
Fiji	1998	1,245.5	1,138.6	-104.3	394	359	0.00
French Polynesia	1998						
Guam	1998						
Hong Kong, China	1996	182,680.0	208,358.0	25,678.0		63,808	0.07
India	2001	3,953,060.0	3,093,720.0	-1,079,200.0	595,940	45,251	11.50
Indonesia	2001	359,039,000.0	307,876,000.0	-17,340,000.0	612,630,000	27,048	3.10
Japan	1990	67.5	62.1	-6.8	1,186,000	69,487	24.23
Kazakhstan	2002	806,854.0	807,846.0	992.0		2,550	1.71
Kiribati	1994					94	
Kyrgyzstan	2000	11,284.4	10,039.6	-1,244.8		238	0.08
Laos	1991	81,922.0	79,022.0	-2,900.0	18,410	28	0.02
Macau	1997						
Malaysia	1999	68,210.0	58,675.0	-9,488.0	18,369	29,670	1.18
Maldives	2002	3,334.1	2,573.2	-595.5	2,338	131	0.00
Mongolia	2001	413,244.0	358,244.0	-45,824.0	878,920	206	0.18
Myanmar	2000	221,255.0	134,308.0	-86,578.0		223	0.23
Nauru	1993						
Nepal	2002	75,705.0	48,390.0	-16,749.0	207,332	1,010	0.15
New Caledonia	1993						
North Korea	1998						
Pakistan	2000	725,642.0	531,300.0	-172,117.0	1,173,450	1,499	2.09
Papua New Guinea	1999	2,457.9	1,750.6	-241.8	3,588	204	0.06
Philippines	1994	309,942.0	334,488.0	18,114.0	317,068	5,866	2.89
Singapore	1994	20,008.0	33,094.0	13,086.0	5	57,890	
Solomon Islands	1991	231.7	132.4			8	
South Korea	1998	87,995,000.0	95,482,000.0	-16,954,000.0	24,425,000	51,963	0.43
Sri Lanka	2000	322,048.0	211,282.0	-118,995.0	542,040	976	0.06
Taiwan	1996	2,005,897.0	2,023,977.0	18,080.0		88,038	13.57
Tajikistan	1996						
Thailand	1996	819,083.0	853,201.0	43,303.0	120,109	37,192	2.47
Tonga	1991	99.2	51.7	-10.1	7	30	
Turkmenistan	1996						
Tuvalu	1999						
Uzbekistan	1994						
Vanuatu	2002					32	
Vietnam	2001	117,180,000.0	97,750,000.0	-14,130,000.0		3,660	
Western Samoa	1994	317.0	208.0	-108.0		47	
Australasia							
Australia	1997	140,478.0	135,271.0	2,028.0	42,610	16,100	2.56
New Zealand	1991	30,084.0	28,457.0	1,419.0	22,950	2,872	0.00

Source: *International Monetary Func (IMF), International Financial Statistics*

■ Government Finance

Government Finance and International Liquidity: Latest Year

- Million units of national currency

	Year	Budget Expenditure	Budget Revenue	Budget Surplus/ Deficit	Foreign Debt	Foreign Exchange Reserves (US$ million)	Gold Reserves (million troy oz)
Africa and Middle East							
Algeria	2002					23,108	5.58
Angola	2002					375	
Bahrain	2001	826.6	969.3	-30.9	141	1,599	0.15
Benin	1999					397	0.01
Botswana	2000	11,192.3	13,975.1	2,838.0	3,068	6,256	
Burkina Faso	1999	432,100.0	236,500.0	-63,800.0		284	0.01
Burundi	2002	176,744.0	113,550.0	-178.2	1,174,250	58	0.00
Cameroon	1999	859,800.0	867,460.0	7,160.0	4,432,120	1	0.03
Cape Verde	2002					80	
Central African Republic	2002					123	0.01
Chad	2001	141,453.0	96,867.0	3,653.0	795,993	122	0.01
Comoros	1997					40	0.00
Congo Dem Rep	1995	32.9	21.2	0.1	922	147	0.03
Congo-Brazzaville	2000	584,800.0	604,520.0	26,520.0	3,247,900	221	0.01
Côte d'Ivoire	1998	1,526,700.0	1,392,200.0	-84,000.0	6,581,200	855	0.04
Djibouti	2002					71	
Egypt	1993	56,143.0	59,443.0	2,681.0	-1,362	12,761	2.43
Equatorial Guinea	2002					88	
Eritrea	2002						
Ethiopia	1999	10,789.8	7,847.0	-2,524.3	34,785	449	0.30
Gabon	1993	695,140.0	791,770.0	120,690.0		1	0.01
Gambia	1993	695.1	791.8	120.7		103	
Ghana	1998	4,513,200.0	3,276,100.0	-1,048,800.0		293	0.28
Guinea	1999	1,010,060.0	574,901.0	-116,309.0		198	
Guinea-Bissau	1992	8,552.3	2,592.2	-3,655.8		18	
Iran	1994	28,912,400.0	29,244,500.0	332,100.0		5,287,000	4.74
Iraq	2001						
Israel	1997	165,250.0	145,110.0	1,017.0	92,523	20,332	0.01
Jordan	2001	2,027.7	1,578.7	-155.5	4,491	3,061	0.41
Kenya	2002	232,536.0	198,723.0	-26,990.0		1,050	0.00
Kuwait	2002	3,235.1	5,632.3	2,397.2		8,357	2.54
Lebanon	1998	8,385,460.0	4,440,870.0	-3,944,600.0	6,282,600	6,508	9.22
Lesotho	2001	2,968.9	2,864.9	153.6	6,246	381	
Liberia	2002					3	
Libya	2002					13,621	4.62
Madagascar	1995	2,344,200.0	1,149,600.0	-212,800.0	15,072,400	109	
Malawi	2002					162	0.01
Mali	1999	417,500.0	272,700.0	-61,400.0	1,618,000	337	0.02
Mauritania	1996	36,740.0	44,720.0	11,260.0		140	0.01
Mauritius	2001	30,592.0	25,374.0	1,171.0	6,816	796	0.06
Morocco	2000	122,019.0	100,907.0	-20,773.0	118,646	4,612	0.71
Mozambique	2002					819	
Namibia	1993	3,407.5	2,958.5	-402.7	11	134	
Niger	1999					26	0.01
Nigeria	1998	443,563.0	310,174.0	-133,389.0	633,017	7,100	0.69
Oman	2001	2,295.1	2,077.2	-324.1	901	2,277	0.29
Qatar	2002					1,404	0.02
Réunion	2001						
Rwanda	2001	157,500.0	86,206.0	-40,200.0	577,327	200	
Sao Tomé e Príncipe	2002					17	
Saudi Arabia	2002					16,715	4.60
Senegal	1999					399	0.03
Seychelles	2000	1,923.2	1,377.1	-496.5		44	
Sierra Leone	2000	370,697.0	152,174.0	-124,064.0	2,153,630	44	
Somalia	1989	0.0	0.0	0.0	0	0	0.02
South Africa	2000	228,412.0	211,984.0	-16,428.0	31,118	5,793	5.90
Sudan	1997	120,700.0	107,300.0	-13,400.0		82	
Swaziland	2001	3,332.5	2,922.7	-255.3	3,498	260	
Syria	1996	155,596.0	152,231.0	-1,577.0		193	0.83
Tanzania	1997	515,390.0	572,029.0	77,142.6	-31,934	609	
Togo	1999					121	0.01
Tunisia	1999	7,864.8	7,180.2	-646.2	9,572	2,207	0.22
Uganda	2001	2,125,270.0	1,083,490.0	-268,434.0	3,395,190	982	
United Arab Emirates	1999	20,050.0	6,863.0	57.0		10,377	0.40
Yemen	1999	310,702.0	279,418.0	-40,278.0		1,295	0.05
Zambia	1991	127,623.0	41,534.2	-98,416.6	604,975	185	0.02
Zimbabwe	1997	36,202.3	30,669.5	-5,076.8	28,932	160	0.77

Source: *International Monetary Func (IMF), International Financial Statistics*

Government Expenditure by Object 2002

● Million units of national currency

	General Public Services	Defence	Education	Health	Social Security & Welfare	Housing/ Amenities	Other Community/ Social	Economic Services	Other
North America									
Canada	15,667	12,800	4,129	2,375	98,931	2,976	3,362	12,004	63,704
USA	208,371	314,346	38,429	429,100	557,806	51,692	8,001	147,022	235,992
Latin America									
Anguilla									
Antigua									
Argentina	4,473	1,774	3,092	863	23,145	750	62	2,015	13,605
Aruba									
Bahamas	293	37	212	177	75	12		164	115
Barbados									
Belize	15	31	97	8	31	39	6	259	24
Bermuda									
Bolivia	613	1,098	2,837	1,736	2,608	300	39	2,452	2,528
Brazil	54,420	16,306	31,534	12,987	154,925	5,071	696	54,599	91,471
British Virgin Islands									
Cayman Islands									
Chile	368,040	772,504	1,936,130	1,322,283	3,873,257	382,099		1,058,589	600,885
Colombia	1,939,786	4,950,295	7,353,416	3,243,397	4,971,184	2,313,532	343,262	1,042,463	11,699,984
Costa Rica	44,910		305,058	304,419	367,571	7,736	6,241	207,813	124,261
Cuba									
Dominica									
Dominican Republic	13,437	4,209	14,461	10,028	6,970	745	1,051	14,491	9,085
Ecuador									
El Salvador	1,830	1,143	3,870	103	152	344	352	2,305	3,324
French Guiana									
Grenada									
Guadeloupe									
Guatemala									
Guyana									
Haiti									
Honduras									
Jamaica	16,233	2,236	17,951	7,844	1,527	2,215	368	12,300	86,984
Martinique									
Mexico	47,075	23,243	231,868	49,487	191,219	66,603	4,165	40,207	201,682
Netherlands Antilles	126		133	41	405	39	5	51	48
Nicaragua	1,136	516	1,913	1,761	2,296	660	373	1,527	5,078
Panama	228	81	452	476	588	42	32	195	852
Paraguay									
Peru									
Puerto Rico									
St Kitts									
St Lucia									
St Vincent and the Grenadines	132		60	44	36	6		38	52
Suriname									
Trinidad and Tobago									
Uruguay	2,230	3,325	6,256	5,380	46,173	1,399	840	4,515	11,959
Venezuela	2,605,347	1,468,076	5,970,703	1,584,823	2,450,793	1,792,554	192,517	2,549,399	6,900,755

Source: *Euromonitor/International Monetary Fund (IMF), Government Finance Statistics/national statistics*

Government Expenditure by Object 2002

- Million units of national currency

	General Public Services	Defence	Education	Health	Social Security & Welfare	Housing/ Amenities	Other Community/ Social	Economic Services	Other
Asia Pacific									
Afghanistan									
American Samoa									
Armenia									
Azerbaijan	42,512	239,030	116,970	69,200	2,103,565	932	67,072	332,766	3,077,542
Bangladesh									
Bhutan	2,371		1,572	955		466	85	4,219	24
Brunei									
Cambodia									
China	118,678	155,204	23,052	5,858	95,543	2,732	5,349	310,022	578,379
Fiji	466	47	176	106	47	53	24	76	214
French Polynesia									
Guam									
Hong Kong, China	14,597	14,911	51,568	43,251	48,043	99,953	22,951	45,606	7,919
India	235,480	620,266	747,707	100,819		281,276		562,058	1,546,674
Indonesia	17,882,630	6,971,003	19,934,243	9,629,811	20,968,226	39,922,856	3,715,182	9,830,674	362,679,096
Japan		4,789,725	5,403,706			15,745,916			63,308,373
Kazakhstan	35,681	26,897	18,508	13,982	162,981		6,861	107,802	140,198
Kiribati									
Kyrgyzstan	2,076	1,443	2,232	1,083	772	812	458	1,577	2,007
Laos									
Macau									
Malaysia	12,646	7,518			35,518			8,060	33,113
Maldives	873	605	782	376	76	315		275	80
Mongolia	33,985	30,942	19,876	43,453	99,540	2,715	8,749	53,482	131,879
Myanmar	33,199	70,037	38,377	7,442	4,961	617	2,561	66,532	33,763
Nauru									
Nepal	4,138	6,710	12,793	4,365	3,495	3,683		22,074	21,942
New Caledonia									
North Korea									
Pakistan									
Papua New Guinea	405	70	1,218	259	106	57	15	1,110	727
Philippines	32,294	33,083	120,029	11,997	27,439	2,958	4,476	78,873	429,768
Singapore	2,121	7,851	7,158	1,543	4,745	3,366	28	5,315	2,192
Solomon Islands									
South Korea	13,593,585	260,908	27,673,887	4,347,178	6,031,017	23,671,214	22,072	22,513,888	722,548
Sri Lanka	16,204	57,560	27,369	20,723	43,417	9,998		58,173	203,269
Taiwan	166,345	143,037	309,972	16,494	218,092	47,108	21,677	306,300	8,939
Tajikistan	61	20	11	4	74	3	12	36	79
Thailand	105,854	84,005	248,204	87,318	82,445	61,311	5,994	209,436	257,988
Tonga									
Turkmenistan									
Tuvalu									
Uzbekistan									
Vanuatu									
Vietnam	7,702,688		16,114,900	3,844,699	12,612,271			7,949,993	73,829,351
Western Samoa									
Australasia									
Australia	12,002	11,393	12,924	26,895	58,166	2,148	1,788	7,735	41,049
New Zealand	1,628	1,418	6,033	6,621	13,625	58	466	2,384	4,018

Source: Euromonitor/International Monetary Fund (IMF), Government Finance Statistics/national statistics

■ Government Expenditure by Category

Government Expenditure by Object 2002

● Million units of national currency

Africa and Middle East	General Public Services	Defence	Education	Health	Social Security & Welfare	Housing/ Amenities	Other Community/ Social	Economic Services	Other
Algeria									
Angola									
Bahrain	242	136	110	65	60	32	6	36	157
Benin									
Botswana									
Burkina Faso									
Burundi	32,241	24,124	21,892	1,992	5,696		222	4,322	37,162
Cameroon	255,151	64,272	100,420	28,580	508	2,509	17,905	21,038	814,911
Cape Verde									
Central African Republic									
Chad									
Comoros									
Congo Dem Rep									
Congo-Brazzaville									
Côte d'Ivoire									
Djibouti									
Egypt	3,528	11,186	17,265	4,539	579	5,406	8,912	13,864	30,894
Equatorial Guinea									
Eritrea									
Ethiopia	1,140	869	2,087	826	3	595	192	6,474	2,043
Gabon									
Gambia									
Ghana									
Guinea									
Guinea-Bissau									
Iran	7,189,132	17,541,928	32,569,869	12,359,117	39,810,357	6,560,708	5,400,694	48,364,690	38,194,822
Iraq									
Israel	5,273	39,006	31,058	33,575	64,177	5,526	2,031	11,124	36,457
Jordan	134	378	336	220	360	29	31	168	434
Kenya	26,760	11,629	66,646	19,744	5,360	8,683	115	31,267	42,795
Kuwait	444	274	868	382	1,115	288	187	504	552
Lebanon	1,104,846	839,616	772,722	194,205	235,174	183,889	41,691	1,435,897	3,273,716
Lesotho									
Liberia									
Libya									
Madagascar	1,124,430	423,854	927,121	438,967	114,430			907,168	1,844,800
Malawi									
Mali									
Mauritania									
Mauritius	2,812	262	4,543	2,653	6,934	2,159	421	5,374	6,428
Morocco	16,481	19,730	25,739	4,610	14,724	547	973	8,753	43,240
Mozambique									
Namibia									
Niger									
Nigeria	33,214	22,459	4,139	1,522	2,434				902,752
Oman	201	823	367	151	168	145	40	214	223
Qatar									
Réunion									
Rwanda									
Sao Tomé e Príncipe									
Saudi Arabia	8,840	70,720		16,483				7,957	
Senegal									
Seychelles	216	72	114	130	278	15	70	207	1,073
Sierra Leone									
Somalia									
South Africa	14,930	7,824	17,592	13,578	15,203	7,582	3,012	9,814	204,399
Sudan	16,264	97,267	22,517	4,099	121	153	647	6,088	229,096
Swaziland	928	222	667	246	13	116	23	739	375
Syria	8,024	42,105	19,347	2,598	17,499	1,890	3,568	100,722	17,551
Tanzania									
Togo									
Tunisia	845	486	1,725	583	1,962	476	318	1,623	1,705
Uganda	336,116	176,574	446,020	326,108		141,417		726,460	234,586
United Arab Emirates	933	6,229	2,642	1,648	659	527	454	1,509	9,168
Yemen	157,213	70,911	120,659	26,431		7,973	16,590	16,662	63,124
Zambia	1,053,723	17,574	366,625	395,146	43,169	84,298	7,352	632,234	51,761
Zimbabwe									

Source: Euromonitor/International Monetary Fund (IMF), Government Finance Statistics/national statistics

Government Expenditure by Object 2002 (% Analysis)

● % of total expenditure

	General Public Services	Defence	Education	Health	Social Security & Welfare	Housing/ Amenities	Other Community/ Social	Economic Services	Other
North America									
Canada	7.3	5.9	1.9	1.1	45.8	1.4	1.6	5.6	29.5
USA	10.5	15.8	1.9	21.6	28.0	2.6	0.4	7.4	11.9
Latin America									
Anguilla									
Antigua									
Argentina	9.0	3.6	6.2	1.7	46.5	1.5	0.1	4.0	27.3
Aruba									
Bahamas	27.0	3.5	19.5	16.3	6.9	1.1		15.1	10.6
Barbados									
Belize	3.0	6.0	19.1	1.6	6.0	7.6	1.2	50.7	4.7
Bermuda									
Bolivia	4.3	7.7	20.0	12.2	18.3	2.1	0.3	17.3	17.8
Brazil	12.9	3.9	7.5	3.1	36.7	1.2	0.2	12.9	21.7
British Virgin Islands									
Cayman Islands									
Chile	3.6	7.5	18.8	12.8	37.6	3.7		10.3	5.8
Colombia	5.1	13.1	19.4	8.6	13.1	6.1	0.9	2.8	30.9
Costa Rica	3.3		22.3	22.3	26.9	0.6	0.5	15.2	9.1
Cuba									
Dominica									
Dominican Republic	18.0	5.7	19.4	13.5	9.4	1.0	1.4	19.5	12.2
Ecuador									
El Salvador	13.6	8.5	28.8	0.8	1.1	2.6	2.6	17.2	24.8
French Guiana									
Grenada									
Guadeloupe									
Guatemala									
Guyana									
Haiti									
Honduras									
Jamaica	11.0	1.5	12.2	5.3	1.0	1.5	0.2	8.3	58.9
Martinique									
Mexico	5.5	2.7	27.1	5.8	22.4	7.8	0.5	4.7	23.6
Netherlands Antilles	14.9		15.7	4.9	47.7	4.6	0.6	6.0	5.6
Nicaragua	7.4	3.4	12.5	11.5	15.0	4.3	2.4	10.0	33.3
Panama	7.7	2.8	15.3	16.1	20.0	1.4	1.1	6.6	28.9
Paraguay									
Peru									
Puerto Rico									
St Kitts									
St Lucia									
St Vincent and the Grenadines	35.8		16.2	12.1	9.8	1.8		10.2	14.1
Suriname									
Trinidad and Tobago									
Uruguay	2.7	4.1	7.6	6.6	56.3	1.7	1.0	5.5	14.6
Venezuela	10.2	5.8	23.4	6.2	9.6	7.0	0.8	10.0	27.0

Source: Euromonitor/International Monetary Fund (IMF), Government Finance Statistics/national statistics

◻ Government Expenditure by Category

Government Expenditure by Object 2002 (% Analysis)

● % of total expenditure

	General Public Services	Defence	Education	Health	Social Security & Welfare	Housing/ Amenities	Other Community/ Social	Economic Services	Other
Asia Pacific									
Afghanistan									
American Samoa									
Armenia									
Azerbaijan	0.7	4.0	1.9	1.1	34.8	0.0	1.1	5.5	50.9
Bangladesh									
Bhutan	23.6		15.6	9.5		4.6	0.9	42.0	0.2
Brunei									
Cambodia									
China	9.2	12.0	1.8	0.5	7.4	0.2	0.4	23.9	44.7
Fiji	38.5	3.9	14.6	8.8	3.9	4.4	2.0	6.3	17.7
French Polynesia									
Guam									
Hong Kong, China	4.2	4.3	14.8	12.4	13.8	28.7	6.6	13.1	2.3
India	5.8	15.1	18.3	2.5		6.9		13.7	37.8
Indonesia	3.6	1.4	4.1	2.0	4.3	8.1	0.8	2.0	73.8
Japan		5.4	6.1			17.6			70.9
Kazakhstan	7.0	5.2	3.6	2.7	31.8		1.3	21.0	27.3
Kiribati									
Kyrgyzstan	16.7	11.6	17.9	8.7	6.2	6.5	3.7	12.7	16.1
Laos									
Macau									
Malaysia	14.2	8.5			40.0			9.1	37.3
Maldives	25.8	17.9	23.1	11.1	2.3	9.3		8.1	2.4
Mongolia	8.0	7.3	4.7	10.2	23.4	0.6	2.1	12.6	31.1
Myanmar	12.9	27.2	14.9	2.9	1.9	0.2	1.0	25.8	13.1
Nauru									
Nepal	5.5	8.9	16.9	5.8	4.6	4.9		29.2	29.0
New Caledonia									
North Korea									
Pakistan									
Papua New Guinea	10.2	1.8	30.7	6.5	2.7	1.4	0.4	28.0	18.3
Philippines	4.4	4.5	16.2	1.6	3.7	0.4	0.6	10.6	58.0
Singapore	6.2	22.9	20.9	4.5	13.8	9.8	0.1	15.5	6.4
Solomon Islands									
South Korea	13.8	0.3	28.0	4.4	6.1	23.9	0.0	22.8	0.7
Sri Lanka	4.3	15.2	7.2	5.5	11.5	2.6		15.4	53.7
Taiwan	13.4	11.6	25.0	1.3	17.6	3.8	1.8	24.7	0.7
Tajikistan	20.4	6.6	3.7	1.4	24.6	1.0	3.8	12.1	26.3
Thailand	9.3	7.4	21.7	7.6	7.2	5.4	0.5	18.3	22.6
Tonga									
Turkmenistan									
Tuvalu									
Uzbekistan									
Vanuatu									
Vietnam	6.3		13.2	3.2	10.3			6.5	60.5
Western Samoa									
Australasia									
Australia	6.9	6.5	7.4	15.4	33.4	1.2	1.0	4.4	23.6
New Zealand	4.5	3.9	16.6	18.3	37.6	0.2	1.3	6.6	11.1

Source: Euromonitor/International Monetary Fund (IMF), Government Finance Statistics/national statistics

◻ Government Expenditure by Category

Government Expenditure by Object 2002 (% Analysis)

● % of total expenditure

	General Public Services	Defence	Education	Health	Social Security & Welfare	Housing/ Amenities	Other Community/ Social	Economic Services	Other
Africa and Middle East									
Algeria									
Angola									
Bahrain	28.7	16.1	13.1	7.7	7.1	3.7	0.7	4.2	18.6
Benin									
Botswana									
Burkina Faso									
Burundi	25.3	18.9	17.1	1.6	4.5		0.2	3.4	29.1
Cameroon	19.5	4.9	7.7	2.2	0.0	0.2	1.4	1.6	62.4
Cape Verde									
Central African Republic									
Chad									
Comoros									
Congo Dem Rep									
Congo-Brazzaville									
Côte d'Ivoire									
Djibouti									
Egypt	3.7	11.6	18.0	4.7	0.6	5.6	9.3	14.4	32.1
Equatorial Guinea									
Eritrea									
Ethiopia	8.0	6.1	14.7	5.8	0.0	4.2	1.3	45.5	14.4
Gabon									
Gambia									
Ghana									
Guinea									
Guinea-Bissau									
Iran	3.5	8.4	15.7	5.9	19.1	3.2	2.6	23.3	18.4
Iraq									
Israel	2.3	17.1	13.6	14.7	28.1	2.4	0.9	4.9	16.0
Jordan	6.4	18.1	16.1	10.5	17.2	1.4	1.5	8.0	20.8
Kenya	12.6	5.5	31.3	9.3	2.5	4.1	0.1	14.7	20.1
Kuwait	9.6	5.9	18.8	8.3	24.2	6.2	4.1	10.9	12.0
Lebanon	13.7	10.4	9.6	2.4	2.9	2.3	0.5	17.8	40.5
Lesotho									
Liberia									
Libya									
Madagascar	19.5	7.3	16.0	7.6	2.0			15.7	31.9
Malawi									
Mali									
Mauritania									
Mauritius	8.9	0.8	14.4	8.4	22.0	6.8	1.3	17.0	20.4
Morocco	12.2	14.6	19.1	3.4	10.9	0.4	0.7	6.5	32.1
Mozambique									
Namibia									
Niger									
Nigeria	3.4	2.3	0.4	0.2	0.3				93.4
Oman	8.6	35.3	15.7	6.5	7.2	6.2	1.7	9.2	9.6
Qatar									
Réunion									
Rwanda									
Sao Tomé e Príncipe									
Saudi Arabia	8.5	68.0		15.8				7.7	
Senegal									
Seychelles	9.9	3.3	5.2	6.0	12.8	0.7	3.2	9.5	49.3
Sierra Leone									
Somalia									
South Africa	5.1	2.7	6.0	4.6	5.2	2.6	1.0	3.3	69.5
Sudan	4.3	25.9	6.0	1.1	0.0	0.0	0.2	1.6	60.9
Swaziland	27.9	6.7	20.0	7.4	0.4	3.5	0.7	22.2	11.3
Syria	3.8	19.7	9.1	1.2	8.2	0.9	1.7	47.2	8.2
Tanzania									
Togo									
Tunisia	8.7	5.0	17.7	6.0	20.2	4.9	3.3	16.7	17.5
Uganda	14.1	7.4	18.7	13.7		5.9		30.4	9.8
United Arab Emirates	3.9	26.2	11.1	6.9	2.8	2.2	1.9	6.3	38.6
Yemen	32.8	14.8	25.2	5.5		1.7	3.5	3.5	13.2
Zambia	40.0	0.7	13.9	15.0	1.6	3.2	0.3	24.0	2.0
Zimbabwe									

Source: *Euromonitor/International Monetary Fund (IMF), Government Finance Statistics/national statistics*

□ Exchange Rates

Table 10.16

Exchange Rates Against US$ 1977-2002

● Units of national currency per US$

	1977	1980	1985	1990	1992	1993	1994	1995
North America								
Canada	1.06	1.17	1.37	1.17	1.21	1.29	1.37	1.37
USA	1.00	1.00	1.00	1.00	1.00	1.00	1.00	1.00
Latin America								
Anguilla	2.70	2.70	2.70	2.70	2.70	2.70	2.70	2.70
Antigua	2.70	2.70	2.70	2.70	2.70	2.70	2.70	2.70
Argentina (a)	0.00	0.00	0.00	0.49	0.99	1.00	1.00	1.00
Aruba	1.79	1.79	1.79	1.79	1.79	1.79	1.79	1.79
Bahamas (b)	1.00	1.00	1.00	1.00	1.00	1.00	1.00	1.00
Barbados	2.00	2.00	2.00	2.00	2.00	2.00	2.00	2.00
Belize	2.00	2.00	2.00	2.00	2.00	2.00	2.00	2.00
Bermuda	1.00	1.00	1.00	1.00	1.00	1.00	1.00	1.00
Bolivia (c)	0.00	0.00	0.44	3.17	3.90	4.27	4.62	4.80
Brazil (d)	0.00	0.00	0.00	0.06	4.25	83.23	0.64	0.92
British Virgin Islands	1.00	1.00	1.00	1.00	1.00	1.00	1.00	1.00
Cayman Islands	0.80	0.80	0.80	0.83	0.84	0.85	0.83	0.83
Chile (b)	21.54	39.00	160.86	304.90	362.58	404.17	420.18	396.77
Colombia	36.77	47.28	142.31	502.26	759.28	863.07	844.84	912.83
Costa Rica	8.57	8.57	50.45	91.58	134.51	142.17	157.07	179.73
Cuba	0.71	0.71	0.88	0.80	0.80	0.70	1.00	1.00
Dominica	2.70	2.70	2.70	2.70	2.70	2.70	2.70	2.70
Dominican Republic (b)	1.00	1.00	3.11	8.53	12.77	12.68	13.16	13.60
Ecuador (b)	25.00	25.00	69.56	767.75	1,533.96	1,919.10	2,196.73	2,564.49
El Salvador (b)	2.50	2.50	2.50	6.85	8.36	8.70	8.73	8.75
French Guiana (e)	0.88	0.72	1.31	0.78	0.77	0.85	0.84	0.76
Grenada	2.70	2.70	2.70	2.70	2.70	2.70	2.70	2.70
Guadeloupe (e)	0.88	0.72	1.31	0.78	0.77	0.85	0.84	0.76
Guatemala	1.00	1.00	1.00	4.49	5.17	5.64	5.75	5.81
Guyana (b)	2.55	2.55	4.25	39.53	125.00	126.73	138.29	141.99
Haiti (b, f)	5.00	5.00	5.00	5.00	9.80	12.82	15.04	15.11
Honduras (b)	2.00	2.00	2.00	4.11	5.50	6.47	8.41	9.47
Jamaica	0.91	1.78	5.56	7.18	22.96	24.95	33.09	35.14
Martinique (e)	0.88	0.72	1.31	0.78	0.77	0.85	0.84	0.76
Mexico (b, g)	0.02	0.02	0.26	2.81	3.09	3.12	3.38	6.42
Netherlands Antilles	1.80	1.80	1.80	1.79	1.79	1.79	1.79	1.79
Nicaragua (b, h)	0.00	0.00	0.00	0.14	5.00	5.62	6.72	7.55
Panama	1.00	1.00	1.00	1.00	1.00	1.00	1.00	1.00
Paraguay	126.00	126.00	306.67	1,229.81	1,500.26	1,744.35	1,904.76	1,963.02
Peru (i)	0.00	0.00	0.00	0.19	1.25	1.99	2.19	2.25
Puerto Rico	1.00	1.00	1.00	1.00	1.00	1.00	1.00	1.00
St Kitts	2.70	2.70	2.70	2.70	2.70	2.70	2.70	2.70
St Lucia	2.70	2.70	2.70	2.70	2.70	2.70	2.70	2.70
St Vincent and the Grenadines	2.70	2.70	2.70	2.70	2.70	2.70	2.70	2.70
Suriname (f)	1.79	1.79	1.79	1.79	1.79	1.79	134.12	442.23
Trinidad and Tobago	2.40	2.40	2.45	4.25	4.25	5.35	5.92	5.95
Uruguay	0.00	0.01	0.10	1.17	3.02	3.94	5.04	6.35
Venezuela (i)	4.29	4.29	7.50	46.90	68.38	90.83	148.50	176.84

Source: International Monetary Fund (IMF)/Euromonitor research
Notes: Annual average market exchange rates
(a) Units per million US$ from 1977 to 1983; units per thousand US$ from 1984 to 1988; units per US$ from 1989, (b) Principal rate, (c) Bolivianos per million US $ to 1983; per US $ from 1984, (d) Reais per trillion US$ from 1977-1983; per billion US$ in 1984-1986; per million US$ in 1987-89; per thousand US$ in 1990-1992; per US$ from 1993, (e) Data refer to Euro per US$, (f) End of year exchange rate, (g) New pesos per thousand US$ from 1977-1985; per US$ from 1986, (h) Gold córdobas per billion US$ from 1977-1987, per million US$ in 1988, per thousand US$ in 1989-1990, per US$ from 1991, (i) New soles per billion US$ from 1977-1987; per million US$ in 1988-1989; per thousand US$ in 1990-1991; per US$ from 1992, (j) Devalued on 11/12/95

■ Exchange Rates

Exchange Rates Against US$ 1977-2002 (continued)

- Units of national currency per US$

	1996	1997	1998	1999	2000	2001	2002	Oct 2003
North America								
Canada	1.36	1.38	1.48	1.49	1.49	1.55	1.57	1.42
USA	1.00	1.00	1.00	1.00	1.00	1.00	1.00	1.00
Latin America								
Anguilla	2.70	2.70	2.70	2.70	2.70	2.69	2.68	2.67
Antigua	2.70	2.70	2.70	2.70	2.70	2.70	2.70	2.67
Argentina [a]	1.00	1.00	1.00	1.00	1.00	1.00	3.06	3.01
Aruba	1.79	1.79	1.79	1.79	1.79	1.79	1.79	1.78
Bahamas [b]	1.00	1.00	1.00	1.00	1.00	1.00	1.00	1.00
Barbados	2.00	2.00	2.00	2.00	2.00	2.00	2.00	1.99
Belize	2.00	2.00	2.00	2.00	2.00	2.00	2.00	1.97
Bermuda	1.00	1.00	1.00	1.00	1.00	1.00	1.00	1.00
Bolivia [c]	5.07	5.25	5.51	5.81	6.18	6.61	7.17	7.87
Brazil [d]	1.01	1.08	1.16	1.81	1.83	2.36	2.92	3.15
British Virgin Islands	1.00	1.00	1.00	1.00	1.00	1.00	1.00	1.00
Cayman Islands	0.83	0.83	0.83	0.82	0.80	0.82	0.82	0.82
Chile [b]	412.27	419.30	460.29	508.78	535.47	634.94	688.94	727.64
Colombia	1,036.69	1,140.96	1,426.04	1,756.23	2,087.90	2,299.63	2,504.24	2,947.11
Costa Rica	207.69	232.60	257.23	285.69	308.19	328.87	359.82	405.55
Cuba	19.00	20.93	23.00	23.00	23.00	23.00	10.79	2.35
Dominica	2.70	2.70	2.70	2.70	2.70	2.70	2.70	2.67
Dominican Republic [b]	13.77	14.27	15.27	16.03	16.41	16.95	18.61	27.26
Ecuador [b]	3,189.47	3,998.27	5,446.57	11,786.80	24,988.40	25,000.00	25,000.00	25,000.00
El Salvador [b]	8.76	8.76	8.76	8.76	8.76	8.75	8.75	8.73
French Guiana [e]	0.79	0.88	0.89	0.94	1.09	1.12	1.06	0.90
Grenada	2.70	2.70	2.70	2.70	2.70	2.70	2.70	2.67
Guadeloupe [e]	0.79	0.88	0.89	0.94	1.09	1.12	1.06	0.90
Guatemala	6.05	6.07	6.39	7.39	7.76	7.86	7.82	8.13
Guyana [b]	140.38	142.40	150.52	178.00	182.43	187.32	190.66	178.46
Haiti [b, f]	15.70	16.65	16.77	16.94	21.17	24.43	29.25	40.56
Honduras [b]	11.71	13.00	13.39	14.21	14.84	15.47	16.43	17.84
Jamaica	37.12	35.40	36.55	39.04	42.70	46.00	48.42	55.42
Martinique [e]	0.79	0.88	0.89	0.94	1.09	1.12	1.06	0.90
Mexico [b, g]	7.60	7.92	9.14	9.56	9.46	9.34	9.66	10.73
Netherlands Antilles	1.79	1.79	1.79	1.79	1.79	1.79	1.79	1.78
Nicaragua [b, h]	8.44	9.45	10.58	11.81	12.68	13.37	14.25	14.89
Panama	1.00	1.00	1.00	1.00	1.00	1.00	1.00	1.00
Paraguay	2,056.81	2,177.86	2,726.49	3,119.07	3,486.35	4,105.92	5,716.26	6,687.81
Peru [i]	2.45	2.66	2.93	3.38	3.49	3.51	3.52	3.60
Puerto Rico	1.00	1.00	1.00	1.00	1.00	1.00	1.00	1.00
St Kitts	2.70	2.70	2.70	2.70	2.70	2.70	2.70	2.67
St Lucia	2.70	2.70	2.70	2.70	2.70	2.70	2.70	2.67
St Vincent and the Grenadines	2.70	2.70	2.70	2.70	2.70	2.70	2.70	2.67
Suriname [f]	401.26	401.00	401.00	859.44	1,322.47	2,178.50	2,346.75	2,435.44
Trinidad and Tobago	6.01	6.25	6.30	6.30	6.30	6.23	6.25	6.15
Uruguay	7.97	9.44	10.47	11.34	12.10	13.32	21.26	27.96
Venezuela [j]	417.33	488.63	547.56	605.72	679.96	723.67	1,160.95	1,592.25

Source: *International Monetary Fund (IMF)/Euromonitor research*
Notes: *Annual average market exchange rates*
(a) Units per million US$ from 1977 to 1983; units per thousand US$ from 1984 to 1988; units per US$ from 1989, (b) Principal rate, (c) Bolivianos per million US $ to 1983; per US $ from 1984, (d) Reais per trillion US$ from 1977-1983; per billion US$ in 1984-1986; per million US$ in 1987-89; per thousand US$ in 1990-1992; per US$ from 1993, (e) Data refer to Euro per US$, (f) End of year exchange rate, (g) New pesos per thousand US$ from 1977-1985; per US$ from 1986, (h) Gold córdobas per billion US$ from 1977-1987, per million US$ in 1988, per thousand US$ in 1989-1990, per US$ from 1991, (i) New soles per billion US$ from 1977-1987; per million US$ in 1988-1989; per thousand US$ in 1990-1991; per US$ from 1992, (j) Devalued on 11/12/95

Exchange Rates Against US$ 1977-2002 (continued)

- Units of national currency per US$

	1977	1980	1985	1990	1992	1993	1994	1995
Asia Pacific								
Afghanistan [a]	45.00	44.13	50.60	50.60	50.60	50.60	425.10	833.33
American Samoa	1.00	1.00	1.00	1.00	1.00	1.00	1.00	1.00
Armenia						9.11	288.65	405.91
Azerbaijan					54.20	99.98	1,570.22	4,413.54
Bangladesh [a]	15.38	15.45	27.99	34.57	38.95	39.57	40.21	40.28
Bhutan	8.74	7.86	12.37	17.51	25.92	30.49	31.37	32.43
Brunei	2.44	2.14	2.20	1.81	1.63	1.62	1.53	1.42
Cambodia					1,266.58	2,689.00	2,545.25	2,450.83
China [a]	1.86	1.50	2.94	4.78	5.51	5.76	8.62	8.35
Fiji	0.92	0.82	1.15	1.48	1.50	1.54	1.46	1.41
French Polynesia	89.18	76.82	163.35	99.00	96.24	102.96	100.94	69.35
Guam	1.00	1.00	1.00	1.00	1.00	1.00	1.00	1.00
Hong Kong, China	4.66	4.98	7.79	7.79	7.74	7.74	7.73	7.74
India	8.74	7.86	12.37	17.50	25.92	30.49	31.37	32.43
Indonesia	415.00	626.99	1,110.58	1,842.81	2,029.92	2,087.10	2,160.75	2,248.61
Japan	268.51	226.74	238.54	144.79	126.65	111.20	102.21	94.06
Kazakhstan						2.50	35.54	60.95
Kiribati	0.90	0.88	1.43	1.28	1.36	1.47	1.37	1.35
Kyrgyzstan					414.50	6.13	10.84	10.82
Laos [b]	200.00	10.00	55.00	707.75	716.08	716.25	717.67	804.69
Macau		5.33	7.99	8.02	7.96	8.00	7.96	7.97
Malaysia	2.46	2.18	2.48	2.70	2.55	2.57	2.62	2.50
Maldives	8.77	7.55	7.10	9.55	10.57	10.96	11.59	11.77
Mongolia					42.56	303.20	412.72	448.61
Myanmar	7.07	6.54	8.39	6.28	6.04	6.09	5.94	5.61
Nauru	0.90	0.88	1.43	1.28	1.36	1.47	1.37	1.35
Nepal	12.50	12.00	18.25	29.37	42.72	48.61	49.40	51.89
New Caledonia	89.18	76.82	163.35	99.00	96.24	102.96	100.94	69.35
North Korea [c]	0.90	0.76	1.07			2.15	2.15	2.15
Pakistan	9.85	9.85	15.85	21.61	24.96	27.97	30.42	31.49
Papua New Guinea	0.79	0.67	1.00	0.96	0.96	0.98	1.01	1.28
Philippines	7.40	7.51	18.61	24.31	25.51	27.12	26.42	25.71
Singapore	2.44	2.14	2.20	1.81	1.63	1.62	1.53	1.42
Solomon Islands	0.90	0.83	1.48	2.53	2.93	3.19	3.29	3.41
South Korea	484.00	607.43	870.02	707.76	780.65	802.67	803.45	771.27
Sri Lanka	8.87	16.53	27.16	40.06	43.83	48.32	49.42	51.25
Taiwan	38.00	36.00	39.84	27.11	25.40	26.63	26.46	26.49
Tajikistan					0.00	0.01	0.02	0.12
Thailand	20.40	20.48	27.16	25.59	25.40	25.32	25.15	24.92
Tonga	0.90	0.88	1.43	1.28	1.35	1.38	1.32	1.27
Turkmenistan							19.20	110.92
Tuvalu	0.90	0.88	1.43	1.28	1.36	1.47	1.37	1.35
Uzbekistan					1.67	9.39	9.80	29.78
Vanuatu	79.41	68.29	106.03	117.06	113.39	121.58	116.41	112.11
Vietnam				6,482.80	11,202.20	10,641.00	10,965.70	11,038.20
Western Samoa	0.79	0.92	2.25	2.31	2.47	2.57	2.54	2.47
Australasia								
Australia	0.90	0.88	1.43	1.28	1.36	1.47	1.37	1.35
New Zealand	1.03	1.03	2.02	1.68	1.86	1.85	1.69	1.52

Source: *International Monetary Fund (IMF)/Euromonitor research*
Notes: *Annual average market exchange rates*
(a) Principal rate, (b) Devaluation in March 1990, (c) End of year exchange rate

◻ Exchange Rates

Exchange Rates Against US$ 1977-2002 (continued)

• Units of national currency per US$

	1996	1997	1998	1999	2000	2001	2002	Oct 2003
Asia Pacific								
Afghanistan [a]	2,333.33	3,000.00	3,000.00	3,000.00	3,000.00	3,000.00	3,000.00	3,789.60
American Samoa	1.00	1.00	1.00	1.00	1.00	1.00	1.00	1.00
Armenia	414.04	490.85	504.92	535.06	539.53	555.08	573.35	
Azerbaijan	4,301.26	3,985.37	3,869.00	4,120.17	4,474.15	4,656.58	4,860.82	
Bangladesh [a]	41.79	43.89	46.91	49.09	52.14	55.81	57.89	60.04
Bhutan	35.43	36.31	41.26	43.06	44.94	47.19	48.61	47.20
Brunei	1.41	1.48	1.67	1.69	1.72	1.79	1.79	1.76
Cambodia	2,624.08	2,946.25	3,744.42	3,807.83	3,840.75	3,916.33	3,912.08	3,987.67
China [a]	8.31	8.29	8.28	8.28	8.28	8.28	8.28	8.29
Fiji	1.40	1.44	1.99	1.97	2.13	2.28	2.19	1.92
French Polynesia	71.44	79.99	80.92	85.14	98.45	101.36	133.16	
Guam	1.00	1.00	1.00	1.00	1.00	1.00	1.00	1.00
Hong Kong, China	7.73	7.74	7.75	7.76	7.79	7.80	7.80	7.79
India	35.43	36.31	41.26	43.06	44.94	47.19	48.61	46.88
Indonesia	2,342.30	2,909.38	10,013.60	7,855.15	8,421.77	10,260.80	9,311.19	8,649.75
Japan	108.78	120.99	130.91	113.91	107.77	121.53	125.39	117.54
Kazakhstan	67.30	75.44	78.30	119.52	142.13	146.74	153.28	151.35
Kiribati	1.28	1.35	1.59	1.55	1.72	1.93	1.84	1.58
Kyrgyzstan	12.81	17.36	20.84	39.01	47.70	48.38	46.94	
Laos [b]	921.02	1,259.98	3,298.33	7,102.02	7,887.64	8,954.58	10,056.30	7,869.61
Macau	7.97	7.97	7.98	7.99	8.01	8.03	8.35	8.29
Malaysia	2.52	2.81	3.92	3.80	3.80	3.80	3.80	3.80
Maldives	11.77	11.77	11.77	11.77	11.77	12.24	12.80	12.69
Mongolia	548.40	789.99	840.83	1,021.87	1,076.67	1,097.70	1,110.31	1,121.47
Myanmar	5.86	6.18	6.27	6.22	6.43	6.68	6.57	6.45
Nauru	1.28	1.35	1.59	1.55	1.72	1.94	1.84	1.58
Nepal	56.69	58.01	65.98	68.24	71.09	74.95	77.88	78.11
New Caledonia	71.44	79.99	80.92	85.14	98.45	101.36	133.16	
North Korea [c]	2.15	2.15	2.20	2.20	2.20	2.20	2.20	2.20
Pakistan	35.91	40.92	44.94	49.12	53.65	61.93	59.72	60.04
Papua New Guinea	1.32	1.44	2.07	2.57	2.78	3.39	3.90	3.56
Philippines	26.22	29.47	40.89	39.09	44.19	50.99	51.60	53.98
Singapore	1.41	1.48	1.67	1.69	1.72	1.79	1.79	1.75
Solomon Islands	3.57	3.72	4.82	4.84	5.09	5.28	6.75	7.50
South Korea	804.45	951.29	1,401.44	1,188.82	1,130.96	1,290.99	1,251.09	1,196.70
Sri Lanka	55.27	58.99	64.45	70.64	77.01	89.38	95.66	96.67
Taiwan	27.45	30.52	33.43	32.22	33.50	32.85	34.57	34.55
Tajikistan	0.30	0.56	0.78	1.24	2.08	2.37	2.76	
Thailand	25.34	31.36	41.36	37.81	40.11	44.43	42.96	41.93
Tonga	1.23	1.26	1.49	1.60	1.76	2.12	2.20	2.15
Turkmenistan	3,257.67	4,143.42	4,890.17	5,200.00	5,200.00	5,200.00	6,240.00	
Tuvalu	1.28	1.35	1.59	1.55	1.72	1.94	1.84	1.58
Uzbekistan	40.07	62.92	94.49	124.63	236.61	403.98		
Vanuatu	111.72	115.87	127.52	129.07	137.64	145.31	139.20	131.20
Vietnam	11,032.60	11,683.30	13,268.00	13,943.20	14,167.70	14,725.20	15,279.50	16,049.00
Western Samoa	2.46	2.56	2.95	3.01	3.29	3.48	3.38	3.06
Australasia								
Australia	1.28	1.35	1.59	1.55	1.72	1.93	1.84	1.58
New Zealand	1.45	1.51	1.87	1.89	2.20	2.38	2.16	1.76

Source: International Monetary Fund (IMF)/Euromonitor research
Notes: Annual average market exchange rates
(a) Principal rate, (b) Devaluation in March 1990, (c) End of year exchange rate

□ Exchange Rates

Exchange Rates Against US$ 1977-2002 (continued)

● Units of national currency per US$

	1977	1980	1985	1990	1992	1993	1994	1995
Africa and Middle East								
Algeria	4.15	3.84	5.03	8.96	21.84	23.35	35.06	47.66
Angola	0.00	0.00	0.00	0.00	0.00	0.00	0.00	0.00
Bahrain	0.40	0.38	0.38	0.38	0.38	0.38	0.38	0.38
Benin	245.68	211.28	449.26	272.26	264.69	283.16	555.21	499.15
Botswana	0.84	0.78	1.90	1.86	2.11	2.42	2.68	2.77
Burkina Faso	245.68	211.28	449.26	272.26	264.69	283.16	555.21	499.15
Burundi	90.00	90.00	120.69	171.26	208.30	242.78	252.66	249.76
Cameroon	245.68	211.28	449.26	272.26	264.69	283.16	555.21	499.15
Cape Verde	34.05	40.17	91.63	70.03	68.02	80.43	81.89	76.85
Central African Republic	245.68	211.28	449.26	272.26	264.69	283.16	555.21	499.15
Chad	245.68	211.28	449.26	272.26	264.69	283.16	555.21	499.15
Comoros	245.68	211.28	449.26	272.26	264.69	283.16	416.40	374.36
Congo Dem Rep	0.00	0.00	0.00	0.00	0.00	0.00	0.01	0.07
Congo-Brazzaville	245.68	211.28	449.26	272.26	264.69	283.16	555.21	499.15
Côte d'Ivoire	245.68	211.28	449.26	272.26	264.69	283.16	555.21	499.15
Djibouti	177.72	177.72	177.72	177.72	177.72	177.72	177.72	177.72
Egypt (a)	0.39	0.70	0.70	1.55	3.32	3.35	3.39	3.39
Equatorial Guinea	245.68	211.28	449.26	272.26	264.69	283.16	555.21	499.15
Eritrea	2.07	2.07	2.07	2.07	2.80	5.00	5.46	6.16
Ethiopia	2.07	2.07	2.07	2.07	2.80	5.00	5.46	6.16
Gabon	245.68	211.28	449.26	272.26	264.69	283.16	555.21	499.15
Gambia	2.29	1.72	3.89	7.88	8.89	9.13	9.58	9.55
Ghana (a)	1.15	2.75	54.37	326.33	437.09	649.06	956.71	1,200.43
Guinea (b, c)	21.14	18.97	24.33	660.17	902.00	955.49	976.64	991.41
Guinea-Bissau (d)	0.52	0.52	2.45	33.62	106.68	155.11	198.34	278.04
Iran	70.62	70.61	91.05	68.10	65.55	1,267.77	1,748.75	1,747.93
Iraq (a)	0.30	0.30	0.31	0.31	0.31	0.31	0.31	0.31
Israel	0.00	0.01	1.18	2.02	2.46	2.83	3.01	3.01
Jordan	0.33	0.30	0.39	0.66	0.68	0.69	0.70	0.70
Kenya	8.28	7.42	16.43	22.91	32.22	58.00	56.05	51.43
Kuwait	0.29	0.27	0.30	0.29	0.29	0.30	0.30	0.30
Lebanon	3.07	3.44	16.42	695.09	1,712.79	1,741.36	1,680.07	1,621.41
Lesotho (a)	0.87	0.78	2.23	2.59	2.85	3.27	3.55	3.63
Liberia (a)	1.00	1.00	1.00	1.00	1.00	1.00	1.00	1.00
Libya (c)	0.30	0.30	0.30	0.28	0.28	0.30	0.35	0.42
Madagascar	245.68	211.28	662.48	1,494.15	1,863.97	1,913.78	3,067.34	4,265.63
Malawi	0.90	0.81	1.72	2.73	3.60	4.40	8.74	15.28
Mali	245.68	211.28	449.26	272.26	264.69	283.16	555.21	499.15
Mauritania	45.59	45.91	77.09	80.61	87.03	120.81	123.58	129.77
Mauritius	6.61	7.68	15.44	14.86	15.56	17.65	17.96	17.39
Morocco	4.50	3.94	10.06	8.24	8.54	9.30	9.20	8.54
Mozambique (e)	33.13	33.04	44.04	947.52	2,566.48	3,951.11	6,158.40	9,203.39
Namibia	0.87	0.78	2.23	2.59	2.85	3.27	3.55	3.63
Niger	245.68	211.28	449.26	272.26	264.69	283.16	555.21	499.15
Nigeria (a)	0.64	0.55	0.89	8.04	17.30	22.07	22.00	21.90
Oman (c)	0.35	0.35	0.35	0.38	0.38	0.38	0.38	0.38
Qatar	3.96	3.66	3.64	3.64	3.64	3.64	3.64	3.64
Réunion (f)	0.88	0.72	1.31	0.78	0.77	0.85	0.84	0.76
Rwanda	95.94	86.06	101.25	83.70	133.94	144.24	140.70	262.18
Sao Tomé e Príncipe	37.56	34.77	44.60	143.33	321.34	429.85	732.63	1,420.34
Saudi Arabia	3.53	3.33	3.62	3.75	3.75	3.75	3.75	3.75
Senegal	245.68	211.28	449.26	272.26	264.69	283.16	555.21	499.15
Seychelles	7.64	6.39	7.13	5.34	5.12	5.18	5.06	4.76
Sierra Leone	1.15	1.05	5.09	151.45	499.44	567.46	586.74	755.22
Somalia	6.29	6.29	39.49					2,620.00
South Africa (a)	0.87	0.78	2.23	2.59	2.85	3.27	3.55	3.63
Sudan (a)	0.03	0.05	0.23	0.45	9.74	15.93	28.96	58.09
Swaziland	0.87	0.78	2.22	2.59	2.85	3.27	3.55	3.63
Syria (a)	3.93	3.93	3.93	11.23	11.23	11.23	11.23	11.23
Tanzania	8.29	8.20	17.47	195.06	297.71	405.27	509.63	574.76
Togo	245.68	211.28	449.26	272.26	264.69	283.16	555.21	499.15
Tunisia	0.43	0.40	0.83	0.88	0.88	1.00	1.01	0.95
Uganda (a)	0.08	0.07	6.72	428.86	1,133.83	1,195.02	979.45	968.92
United Arab Emirates	3.90	3.71	3.67	3.67	3.67	3.67	3.67	3.67
Yemen					12.01	12.01	12.01	40.84
Zambia	0.79	0.79	3.14	30.29	172.21	452.76	669.37	864.12
Zimbabwe	0.63	0.64	1.61	2.45	5.10	6.48	8.15	8.67

Source: International Monetary Fund (IMF)/Euromonitor research
Notes: Annual average market exchange rates
(a) Principal rate, (b) Syli up to 1985; replaced by franc guinéen, (c) End of year exchange rate, (d) Adopted the CFA franc to replace the Guinean peso from August 1997, (e) Mozambique escudo replaced by metical during 1980, (f) Data refer to Euro per US$

◻ Exchange Rates

Exchange Rates Against US$ 1977-2002 (continued)

● Units of national currency per US$

Notes:	1996	1997	1998	1999	2000	2001	2002	Oct 2003
Africa and Middle East								
Algeria	54.75	57.71	58.74	66.57	75.26	77.22	79.68	81.37
Angola	0.13	0.23	0.39	2.79	10.04	22.06	43.53	55.51
Bahrain	0.38	0.38	0.38	0.38	0.38	0.38	0.38	0.38
Benin	511.55	583.67	589.95	615.70	711.98	733.04	696.99	587.27
Botswana	3.32	3.65	4.23	4.62	5.10	5.84	6.33	5.00
Burkina Faso	511.55	583.67	589.95	615.70	711.98	733.04	696.99	587.27
Burundi	302.75	352.35	447.77	563.56	720.67	830.35	930.75	1,075.91
Cameroon	511.55	583.67	589.95	615.70	711.98	733.04	696.99	601.60
Cape Verde	82.59	93.18	98.16	103.50	119.69	123.23	117.17	98.71
Central African Republic	511.55	583.67	589.95	615.70	711.98	733.04	696.99	601.60
Chad	511.55	583.67	589.95	615.70	711.98	733.04	696.99	601.60
Comoros	383.66	437.75	442.46	461.78	533.98	549.78	522.74	438.81
Congo Dem Rep	0.50	1.31	1.61	4.02	21.82	206.62	346.49	
Congo-Brazzaville	511.55	583.67	589.95	615.70	711.98	733.04	696.99	601.60
Côte d'Ivoire	511.55	583.67	589.95	615.70	711.98	733.04	696.99	587.27
Djibouti	177.72	177.72	177.72	177.72	177.72	177.72	177.72	180.40
Egypt [a]	3.39	3.39	3.39	3.40	3.47	3.97	4.50	5.86
Equatorial Guinea	511.55	583.67	589.95	615.70	711.98	733.04	696.99	601.60
Eritrea	6.35	6.71	7.41	7.71	9.17	9.55		
Ethiopia	6.35	6.71	7.12	7.94	8.22	8.46	8.57	8.78
Gabon	511.55	583.67	589.95	615.70	711.98	733.04	696.99	601.60
Gambia	9.79	10.20	10.64	11.40	12.79	15.69	19.92	26.22
Ghana [a]	1,637.23	2,050.17	2,314.15	2,669.30	5,455.06	7,170.76	7,932.70	8,662.14
Guinea [b, c]	1,004.02	1,095.33	1,236.83	1,387.40	1,746.87	1,950.56	1,975.84	2,038.85
Guinea-Bissau [d]	405.75	583.67	589.95	615.70	711.98	733.04	696.99	587.27
Iran	1,750.76	1,752.92	1,751.86	1,752.93	1,764.43	1,753.56	6,906.96	6,075.77
Iraq [a]	0.31	0.31	0.31	0.31	0.31	0.31	0.31	975.18
Israel	3.19	3.45	3.80	4.14	4.08	4.21	4.74	4.58
Jordan	0.71	0.71	0.71	0.71	0.71	0.71	0.71	0.71
Kenya	57.11	58.73	60.37	70.33	76.18	78.56	78.75	76.21
Kuwait	0.30	0.30	0.30	0.30	0.31	0.31	0.30	0.30
Lebanon	1,571.44	1,539.45	1,516.13	1,507.84	1,507.50	1,507.50	1,507.50	1,552.57
Lesotho [a]	4.30	4.61	5.53	6.11	6.94	8.61	10.54	7.74
Liberia [a]	1.00	1.00	41.51	41.90	40.95	48.58	61.75	0.99
Libya [c]	0.44	0.46	0.47	0.46	0.51	0.61	1.27	1.22
Madagascar	4,061.25	5,090.89	5,441.40	6,283.77	6,767.48	6,588.49	6,831.96	6,136.87
Malawi	15.31	16.44	31.07	44.09	59.54	72.20	76.69	93.67
Mali	511.55	583.67	589.95	615.70	711.98	733.04	696.99	587.27
Mauritania	137.22	151.85	188.48	209.51	238.92	255.63	271.74	273.04
Mauritius	17.95	21.06	23.99	25.19	26.25	29.13	29.96	28.28
Morocco	8.72	9.53	9.60	9.80	10.63	11.30	11.02	9.76
Mozambique [e]	11,517.80	11,772.60	12,110.20	13,028.60	15,447.10	20,703.60	23,678.00	23,422.40
Namibia	4.30	4.61	5.53	6.11	6.94	8.61	10.54	7.85
Niger	511.55	583.67	589.95	615.70	711.98	733.04	696.99	587.27
Nigeria [a]	21.88	21.89	21.89	92.34	101.70	111.23	120.58	131.85
Oman [c]	0.38	0.38	0.38	0.38	0.38	0.38	0.38	0.39
Qatar	3.64	3.64	3.64	3.64	3.64	3.64	3.64	3.64
Réunion [f]	0.79	0.88	0.89	0.94	1.09	1.12	1.06	0.90
Rwanda	306.10	301.32	313.72	337.83	393.44	442.80	476.33	
Sao Tomé e Príncipe	2,203.16	4,552.51	6,883.24	7,118.96	7,978.17	8,842.11	9,088.32	8,883.12
Saudi Arabia	3.75	3.75	3.75	3.75	3.75	3.75	3.75	3.75
Senegal	511.55	583.67	589.95	615.70	711.98	733.04	696.99	587.27
Seychelles	4.97	5.03	5.26	5.34	5.71	5.86	5.48	5.49
Sierra Leone	920.73	981.48	1,563.62	1,804.19	2,092.12	1,986.15	2,099.03	1,930.06
Somalia	2,620.00	2,620.00	2,620.00	2,588.71	2,613.08	2,620.00	2,606.92	2,613.45
South Africa [a]	4.30	4.61	5.53	6.11	6.94	8.61	10.54	7.72
Sudan [a]	125.08	157.57	200.80	252.55	257.12	258.70	263.31	2,582.50
Swaziland	4.30	4.61	5.53	6.11	6.94	8.61	10.54	7.76
Syria [a]	11.23	11.23	11.23	11.23	11.23	11.23	11.23	48.91
Tanzania	579.98	612.12	664.67	744.76	800.41	876.41	966.58	1,055.77
Togo	511.55	583.67	589.95	615.70	711.98	733.04	696.99	587.27
Tunisia	0.97	1.11	1.14	1.19	1.37	1.44	1.42	1.33
Uganda [a]	1,046.08	1,083.01	1,240.31	1,454.83	1,644.48	1,755.66	1,797.55	1,815.58
United Arab Emirates	3.67	3.67	3.67	3.67	3.67	3.67	3.67	3.67
Yemen	94.16	129.28	135.88	155.72	161.72	168.67	175.63	
Zambia	1,207.90	1,314.50	1,862.07	2,388.02	3,110.84	3,610.93	4,398.59	4,916.00
Zimbabwe	10.00	12.11	23.68	38.30	44.42	55.05	55.04	511.91

Source: *International Monetary Fund (IMF)/Euromonitor research*
Notes: *Annual average market exchange rates*
(a) Principal rate, (b) Syli up to 1985; replaced by franc guinéen, (c) End of year exchange rate, (d) Adopted the CFA franc to replace the Guinean peso from August 1997, (e) Mozambique escudo replaced by metical during 1980, (f) Data refer to Euro per US$

Exchange Rates

Table 10.17

Exchange Rates Against ECU/EUR 1990-2002

- Units of national currency per ECU/EUR

	1990	1995	1996	1997	1998	1999	2000	2001	2002	Oct 2003
North America										
Canada	1.49	1.79	1.73	1.57	1.67	1.58	1.37	1.39	1.49	1.57
USA	1.28	1.31	1.27	1.13	1.12	1.07	0.92	0.90	0.95	1.18
Latin America										
Anguilla	3.44	3.53	3.43	3.06	3.03	2.88	2.49	2.42	2.55	3.13
Antigua	3.44	3.53	3.43	3.06	3.03	2.88	2.49	2.42	2.55	3.13
Argentina	0.62	1.29	1.28	1.13	1.12	1.07	0.92	0.90	2.95	3.50
Aruba	2.28	2.34	2.27	2.03	2.01	1.91	1.65	1.60	1.69	2.10
Bahamas	1.28	1.31	1.27	1.13	1.12	1.07	0.92	0.90	0.95	1.17
Barbados	2.55	2.62	2.54	2.27	2.24	2.13	1.85	1.79	1.89	2.33
Belize	2.55	2.62	2.54	2.27	2.24	2.13	1.85	1.79	1.89	2.31
Bermuda	1.28	1.31	1.27	1.13	1.12	1.07	0.92	0.90	0.95	1.17
Bolivia		6.28	6.44	5.96	6.20	6.17	5.67	6.01	7.05	9.40
Brazil		1.19	1.26	1.22	1.30	1.93	1.69	2.13	2.85	3.37
British Virgin Islands	1.28	1.31	1.27	1.13	1.12	1.07	0.92	0.90	0.95	1.18
Cayman Islands						0.88	0.74	0.72	0.77	0.96
Chile	388.82	512.79	520.78	519.75	516.69	541.88	498.13	575.85	666.52	797.47
Colombia	632.78	1,179.50	1,268.82	1,290.91	1,604.55	1,868.15	1,931.49	2,083.05	2,448.05	3,459.85
Costa Rica						302.39	284.25	298.64	352.43	493.80
Cuba		1.31	1.27	1.13	1.12	1.07	0.92	0.90	1.92	2.77
Dominica	3.44	3.53	3.43	3.06	3.03	2.88	2.49	2.42	2.55	3.13
Dominican Republic						17.02	14.68	14.73	17.40	39.11
Ecuador	1,020.84	3,255.10	3,738.26	4,518.94	6,136.19	12,380.30	23,111.23	22,449.74	19,658.28	29,442.50
El Salvador						9.33	8.09	7.85	8.25	10.25
French Guiana	1.00	1.00	1.00	1.00	1.00	1.00	1.00	1.00	1.00	1.00
Grenada	3.44	3.53	3.43	3.06	3.03	2.88	2.49	2.42	2.55	3.13
Guadeloupe	1.00	1.00	1.00	1.00	1.00	1.00	1.00	1.00	1.00	1.00
Guatemala						7.60	7.18	7.11	7.66	9.81
Guyana						179.88	167.36	161.83	169.60	209.75
Haiti						17.90	18.74	21.79	28.24	45.83
Honduras						15.18	13.78	14.04	16.16	21.36
Jamaica						43.23	41.00	39.22	41.55	46.53	65.72
Martinique	1.00	1.00	1.00	1.00	1.00	1.00	1.00	1.00	1.00	1.00
Mexico	3.62	9.03	9.65	8.98	10.30	10.18	8.75	8.38	9.18	13.27
Netherlands Antilles	2.28	2.34	2.27	2.03	2.01	1.91	1.65	1.60	1.69	2.09
Nicaragua						12.49	11.35	11.96	13.44	17.87
Panama	1.28	1.31	1.27	1.13	1.12	1.07	0.92	0.90	0.95	1.18
Paraguay						3,317.14	3,232.07	3,726.80	5,587.91	7,490.64
Peru	0.08	2.91	2.95	3.01	3.29	3.60	3.23	3.18	3.46	4.24
Puerto Rico	1.28	1.31	1.27	1.13	1.12	1.07	0.92	0.90	0.95	1.18
St Kitts	3.44	3.53	3.43	3.06	3.03	2.88	2.49	2.42	2.55	3.13
St Lucia	3.44	3.53	3.43	3.06	3.03	2.88	2.49	2.42	2.55	3.13
St Vincent and the Grenadines	3.44	3.53	3.43	3.06		4.47	2.49	2.39	2.53	3.13
Suriname						653.29	772.94	1,002.09	2,052.77	2,947.08
Trinidad and Tobago						6.61	5.76	5.51	5.78	7.21
Uruguay						12.05	10.54	11.50	20.36	32.89
Venezuela	60.18	226.27	434.84	551.92	615.11	644.73	628.56	649.40	1,108.82	1,884.32

Source: European Central Bank/Euromonitor research
Notes: Annual average market exchange rates

◘ Exchange Rates

Exchange Rates Against ECU/EUR 1990-2002

● Units of national currency per ECU/EUR

	1990	1995	1996	1997	1998	1999	2000	2001	2002	Oct 2003
Asia Pacific										
Afghanistan	64.56	1,090.00	2,962.75	3,402.00	3,362.70	5,025.90	4,468.12	4,258.41	4,468.14	5,038.79
American Samoa	1.28	1.31	1.27	1.13	1.12	1.07	0.92	0.90	0.95	1.18
Armenia										
Azerbaijan	0.77	5,772.95	5,461.52	4,519.58	4,336.76	4,416.16	4,034.79	4,130.73		
Bangladesh	44.10	52.68	53.07	49.77	52.58	52.46	48.35	50.88	56.40	70.78
Bhutan	22.30	41.92	44.34	41.05	46.32	48.88	41.52	42.34	46.07	55.81
Brunei	2.31	1.83	1.77	1.68	1.88	1.81	1.59	1.60	1.69	2.08
Cambodia		3,205.69	3,331.93	3,341.05	4,197.12	4,084.20	3,560.78	3,485.40	3,796.28	4,687.36
China	6.09	10.81	10.41	10.21	9.29	8.82	7.66	7.42	7.84	9.76
Fiji	1.89	1.84	1.78	1.64	2.23	2.10	1.97	2.04	2.05	2.16
French Polynesia	119.25	119.25	119.25	119.25	119.25	119.25	119.25	119.25	119.25	120.02
Guam	1.28	1.31	1.27	1.13	1.12	1.07	0.92	0.90	0.95	1.18
Hong Kong, China	9.93	10.01	9.69	8.78	8.69	8.27	7.20	6.99	7.39	9.07
India	22.30	41.92	44.34	41.05	46.32	48.88	41.52	42.34	46.07	53.41
Indonesia	2,352.92	2,903.59	2,918.32	3,276.53	11,306.46	8,354.37	7,755.83	9,213.46	8,831.88	9,895.62
Japan	184.13	123.01	138.08	137.10	146.40	121.30	99.50	108.70	118.10	129.92
Kazakhstan		79.72	85.45	85.55	88.27	126.80	131.58	132.28	142.72	173.82
Kiribati	1.63	1.77	1.62	1.53	1.79	1.65	1.59	1.73	1.74	1.71
Kyrgyzstan										
Laos	902.95	1,052.54	1,169.47	1,428.82	3,697.10	5,826.34	6,949.62	6,830.41	7,486.32	9,252.25
Macau	10.24	10.42	10.12	9.04	8.96	8.52	7.42	7.20	7.61	9.67
Malaysia	3.45	3.24	3.15	3.18	4.39	4.05	3.51	3.41	3.60	4.48
Maldives						12.18	10.75	10.51	11.32	14.95
Mongolia		586.79	696.33	895.85	942.48	1,054.80	988.55	982.87	1,043.64	1,319.46
Myanmar	8.09	7.41	7.51	7.08	7.11	6.53	4.43	5.98	6.29	7.59
Nauru	1.63	1.77	1.62	1.53	1.79	1.65	1.59	1.73	1.74	1.71
Nepal	37.47	67.87	71.98	65.78	73.95	72.98	65.59	68.13	76.03	90.76
New Caledonia	119.25	119.25	119.25	119.25	119.25	119.25	119.25	119.25	119.25	120.02
North Korea		2.81	2.73	2.44	2.47	2.35	2.03	1.97	2.08	2.59
Pakistan	27.44	41.33	45.16	46.36	54.75	54.72	49.80	56.12	58.85	70.39
Papua New Guinea	1.22	1.67	1.67	1.63	2.32	2.77	2.58	3.01	3.59	3.94
Philippines	29.95	33.27	32.83	33.42	45.82	41.64	40.88	45.86	48.97	64.86
Singapore	2.31	1.83	1.77	1.68	1.88	1.81	1.59	1.60	1.69	2.03
Solomon Islands	3.23	4.45	4.53	4.22	5.40	5.30	4.76	4.76	6.26	9.02
South Korea	904.03	997.16	1,007.54	1,078.03	1,565.61	1,267.95	1,043.50	1,154.83	1,181.55	1,354.56
Sri Lanka	51.11	67.04	70.18	66.90	72.24	75.45	71.03	80.30	90.56	111.38
Taiwan	34.30	34.26	34.38	32.47	37.51	34.37	28.89	30.46	32.70	39.89
Tajikistan										
Thailand	32.50	32.23	31.37	35.47	46.11	40.31	37.09	39.91	40.72	46.41
Tonga	1.63	1.66	1.56	1.43	1.67	1.61	1.62	1.91	2.06	2.49
Turkmenistan		145.08	4,136.43	4,698.64	5,481.39	5,541.65	4,802.79	4,657.00		
Tuvalu	1.63	1.77	1.62	1.53	1.79	1.65	1.59	1.73	1.74	1.71
Uzbekistan										
Vanuatu	149.35	146.64	141.86	131.40	142.93	138.15	127.76	131.72	133.67	156.99
Vietnam	8,270.76	14,524.00	14,075.00	14,651.80	14,903.43	14,862.89	13,106.74	13,474.56	15,085.21	18,972.70
Western Samoa	2.95	3.24	3.13	2.90	3.30	3.23	2.94	2.10	3.21	3.49
Australasia										
Australia	1.63	1.77	1.62	1.53	1.79	1.65	1.59	1.73	1.74	1.71
New Zealand	2.14	1.99	1.85	1.71	2.10	2.01	2.03	2.13	2.04	1.97

Source: *European Central Bank/Euromonitor research*
Notes: *Annual average market exchange rates*

▣ Exchange Rates

Exchange Rates Against ECU/EUR 1990-2002

● Units of national currency per ECU/EUR

Africa and Middle East

	1990	1995	1996	1997	1998	1999	2000	2001	2002	Oct 2003
Algeria	11.43	62.34	69.52	65.44	68.57	70.82	70.89	70.75	77.83	93.23
Angola						2,946,380.00	5.55	10.38	29.84	68.51
Bahrain	0.48	0.49	0.48	0.43	0.42	0.40	0.35	0.34	0.36	0.45
Benin		644.86	638.85	657.61	665.96	665.96	665.96	665.96	665.96	655.96
Botswana						4.93	4.72	5.15	5.94	5.37
Burkina Faso		644.86	638.85	657.61	665.96	665.96	665.96	665.96	665.96	655.96
Burundi						583.58	642.44	738.83	892.08	1,301.71
Cameroon		644.86	638.85	657.61	665.96	665.96	665.96	665.96	665.96	682.51
Cape Verde	110.27	110.27	110.27	110.27	110.27	110.27	110.27	110.27	110.27	110.25
Central African Republic		644.86	638.85	657.61	665.96	665.96	665.96	665.96	665.96	682.51
Chad		644.86	638.85	657.61	665.96	665.96	665.96	665.96	665.96	682.51
Comoros		491.97	491.97	491.97	491.97	491.97	491.97	491.97	491.97	490.22
Congo, Democratic Republic										
Congo-Brazzaville		644.86	638.85	657.61	665.96	665.96	665.96	665.96	665.96	682.51
Côte d'Ivoire		644.86	638.85	657.61	665.96	665.96	665.96	665.96	665.96	655.96
Djibouti	226.74	232.46	225.66	201.53	199.22	189.45	164.21	159.24	168.12	212.13
Egypt	2.55	4.45	4.30	3.84	3.82	3.64	3.28	3.64	4.41	7.29
Equatorial Guinea		644.86	638.85	657.61	665.96	665.96	665.96	665.96	665.96	682.51
Eritrea						8.22	8.45	8.55		
Ethiopia						8.29	7.47	7.55	8.32	10.41
Gabon		644.86	638.85	657.61	665.96	665.96	665.96	665.96	665.96	682.51
Gambia						12.00	12.39	14.77	19.21	35.54
Ghana						2,813.10	5,055.49	6,581.96	7,818.50	10,320.80
Guinea						1,422.58	1,543.48	1,739.30	1,923.00	2,405.92
Guinea-Bissau		363.68	515.19	661.88	665.96	665.96	665.96	665.96	665.96	655.96
Iran						1,872.42	1,623.23	1,573.36	1,649.17	9,303.83
Iraq					0.35	0.33	0.29	0.28	0.29	0.38
Israel	2.57	3.89	4.00	3.90	4.27	4.41	3.78	3.77	4.48	5.24
Jordan	0.85	0.92	0.90	0.80	0.80	0.76	0.66	0.64	0.67	0.84
Kenya						74.83	70.44	70.60	74.98	92.80
Kuwait	0.37	0.39	0.38	0.34	0.34	0.32	0.28	0.28	0.29	0.35
Lebanon						1,600.03	1,398.77	1,366.10	1,480.19	1,829.56
Lesotho		4.75	5.45	5.23	6.23	6.51	6.40	7.69	9.82	8.13
Liberia						1.07	0.39	23.53	0.94	1.17
Libya						0.46	0.46	0.54	1.17	1.44
Madagascar						6,513.34	6,118.33	5,828.26	6,381.41	7,209.53
Malawi						46.60	43.81	59.06	74.58	123.67
Mali		644.86	638.85	657.61	665.96	665.96	665.96	665.96	665.96	655.96
Mauritania						223.88	224.76	234.39	267.63	320.90
Mauritius						27.02	24.29	26.21	28.53	33.98
Morocco	10.52	11.11	11.07	10.80	10.75	10.42	9.83	10.14	10.46	11.13
Mozambique						13,288.20	14,414.34	18,404.07	22,067.07	26,898.70
Namibia		4.75	5.45	5.23	6.23	6.51	6.40	7.69	9.82	8.37
Niger		644.86	638.85	657.61	665.96	665.96	665.96	665.96	665.96	655.96
Nigeria	10.25	28.66	27.79	24.82	96.07	101.31	97.09	104.84	119.88	158.84
Oman	0.49	0.50	0.49	0.44	0.43	0.41	0.36	0.34	0.36	0.45
Qatar	4.64	4.76	4.62	4.13	4.08	3.88	3.36	3.26	3.44	4.29
Réunion	1.00	1.00	1.00	1.00	1.00	1.00	1.00	1.00	1.00	1.00
Rwanda										
Sao Tomé e Príncipe						2,547.30	1,978.09	3,033.99	8,508.84	10,194.80
Saudi Arabia	4.78	4.90	4.76	4.25	4.20	3.99	3.46	3.36	3.54	4.42
Senegal		644.86	638.85	657.61	665.96	665.96	665.96	665.96	665.96	655.96
Seychelles						5.69	5.26	5.30	5.59	6.16
Sierra Leone						1,807.90	625.88	1,694.30	1,887.32	2,273.08
Somalia						2,792.44	2,416.36	2,348.35	2,464.52	3,070.15
South Africa		4.75	5.45	5.23	6.23	6.51	6.40	7.69	9.82	8.03
Sudan						269.07	23.94	1,312.63	2,441.44	3,041.41
Swaziland		4.75	5.45	5.23	6.23	6.51	6.40	7.69	9.82	8.10
Syria	14.32	14.68	14.25	12.73	12.58	11.97	10.37	10.06	10.62	56.18
Tanzania						784.76	743.30	794.96	938.40	1,257.90
Togo		644.86	638.85	657.61	665.96	665.96	665.96	665.96	665.96	655.96
Tunisia	1.12	1.24	1.24	1.25	1.27	1.26	1.27	1.29	1.35	1.50
Uganda						1,538.55	1,525.38	1,602.94	1,643.06	2,350.31
United Arab Emirates	4.68	4.80	4.66	4.16	4.12	3.92	3.40	3.29	3.47	4.33
Yemen										
Zambia						2,589.42	2,663.77	2,594.96	4,204.84	5,806.06
Zimbabwe						40.74	40.83	58.92	54.04	961.75

Source: European Central Bank/Euromonitor research
Notes: Annual average market exchange rates

Energy Resources & Output

Consumption of Refinery Products   **Table 11.1**

Consumption of Motor Gasoline 1977-2002

- '000 metric tonnes

	1977	1980	1985	1990	1995	1997	1998	1999	2000	2001	2002
North America											
Canada	26,072	28,290	24,078	25,464	26,043	26,727	27,464	28,167	28,178	28,526	28,759
USA	308,188	285,052	289,922	310,682	334,458	344,122	354,073	361,767	364,047	369,038	374,777
Latin America											
Anguilla											
Antigua	5	8	111	19	25						
Argentina	4,490	5,445	4,383	4,273	6,223	4,308	4,236	3,836	3,414	3,337	3,039
Aruba				30	47						
Bahamas	89	83	50	100	78						
Barbados	55	51	47	63	61						
Belize	21	22	24	21	26						
Bermuda	39	22	21	22	22						
Bolivia	481	413	340	382	404	446	452	467	426	404	382
Brazil	9,902	7,928	11,712	8,082	13,672	13,355	14,043	13,152	12,727	12,450	12,197
British Virgin Islands	3	3	4	5	6						
Cayman Islands	6	10	10	20	22						
Chile	1,018	1,100	997	1,478	2,083	2,237	2,327	2,374	2,382	2,366	2,357
Colombia	2,879	3,145	3,639	4,521	5,576	5,758	5,730	4,961	4,433	4,029	3,607
Costa Rica	136	129	163	204	405	447	502	543	564	602	631
Cuba	978	1,088	1,156	1,088	957	406	400	389	379	360	346
Dominica	5	5	6	10	13						
Dominican Republic	322	289	297	695	600	591	602	1,065	1,232	1,271	1,309
Ecuador	768	1,264	1,089	1,367	1,236	1,326	1,355	1,251	1,383	1,478	1,567
El Salvador	140	133	135	162	281	307	341	360	350	346	343
French Guiana	28	25	22	32	33						
Grenada	7	7	5	14	19						
Guadeloupe	64	45	59	112	125						
Guatemala	241	254	250	334	426	550	657	694	752	819	884
Guyana	40	37	49	52	72						
Haiti	30	45	42	49	54	85	93	92	99	102	108
Honduras	119	93	130	134	229	248	282	304	305	312	315
Jamaica	286	205	170	237	346	437	466	480	492	521	538
Martinique	81	77	62	94	114						
Mexico	8,395	13,764	13,971	22,045	26,100	21,970	21,364	21,364	22,275	22,677	23,171
Netherlands Antilles	108	150	100	85	61	69	69	100	100	102	104
Nicaragua	185	130	121	74	112	116	133	147	155	156	157
Panama	254	218	186	206	298	340	381	400	390	376	361
Paraguay	96	126	112	145	241	169	220	214	171	162	153
Peru	1,299	1,168	1,129	1,195	774	1,220	1,188	1,176	1,073	1,018	960
Puerto Rico	1,860	1,940	1,700	1,930	2,170						
St Kitts	3	5	5	6	8						
St Lucia	9	20	15	20	24						
St Vincent and the Grenadines	4	5	5	10	15						
Suriname	37	42	48	66	63						
Trinidad and Tobago	243	765	402	344	202	308	315	324	331	340	350
Uruguay	227	221	166	205	297	320	347	346	299	284	269
Venezuela	5,510	6,966	6,652	7,592	10,943	8,559	8,350	8,672	9,026	9,323	9,610

Source: *Euromonitor from OECD*

Consumption of Motor Gasoline 1977-2002

● '000 metric tonnes

	1977	1980	1985	1990	1995	1997	1998	1999	2000	2001	2002
Asia Pacific											
Afghanistan	68	102	95	113	75						
American Samoa	6	9	8	16	17						
Armenia					55	21	22	23	23	23	23
Azerbaijan					900	492	446	245	321	370	437
Bangladesh	57	58	40	72	131	279	284	203	269	260	252
Bhutan		1	1	3	5						
Brunei	54	72	110	213	176	195	188	190	188	185	183
Cambodia	15	12	25	32	36						
China	10,305	9,920	13,996	18,841	28,566	33,111	33,278	33,709	34,947	35,509	36,107
Fiji	39	43	45	49	45						
French Polynesia	30	31	36	40	45						
Guam	97	90	85	90	215						
Hong Kong, China	133	190	195	285	385	344	356	370	398	431	458
India	1,370	1,459	2,238	3,711	4,362	5,005	5,511	5,776	6,436	6,657	7,207
Indonesia	2,112	2,892	3,011	4,498	5,840	8,283	8,489	8,901	9,174	9,258	9,496
Japan	23,127	25,432	26,878	32,663	37,545	39,868	40,796	41,828	43,008	43,958	45,061
Kazakhstan					2,233	1,906	1,919	1,343	1,643	1,714	1,942
Kiribati	1	1	1	1	1						
Kyrgyzstan					211	115	227	230	160	152	144
Laos			14	15	19						
Macau	10	12	14	18	26						
Malaysia	543	1,254	1,955	2,667	4,094	5,317	5,572	6,466	6,079	5,895	5,682
Maldives		1	1	1							
Mongolia	170	220	260	310	185						
Myanmar	219	247	234	141	209	248	299	304	336	338	342
Nauru	5	6	6	6	6						
Nepal	18	13	13	13	22	35	37	39	42	44	46
New Caledonia	54	93	47	55	56						
North Korea	504	700	950	1,900	1,800			1,685	1,702	1,750	1,796
Pakistan	522	578	784	1,070	1,080	1,197	1,223	1,207	1,076	991	907
Papua New Guinea	95	86	84	87	80						
Philippines	1,720	1,552	992	1,508	1,685	2,526	2,654	2,735	2,670	2,537	2,416
Singapore	293	349	695	1,042	1,321	690	718	666	666	630	619
Solomon Islands	4	4	6	8	8						
South Korea	818	769	814	2,787	6,986	8,432	7,206	7,548	7,314	7,352	7,216
Sri Lanka	110	102	123	169	181	195	204	213	224	242	255
Taiwan						6,386	6,707	6,977	7,067	7,077	7,169
Tajikistan					996	996	996	996	673	589	545
Thailand	1,608	1,706	1,547	2,728	4,381	5,384	5,238	5,196	5,001	4,633	4,380
Tonga	3	3	4	10	12						
Turkmenistan					500	347	313	474	478	500	524
Tuvalu											
Uzbekistan					1,635	1,407	1,370	1,600	1,668	1,717	1,775
Vanuatu			5	4	4						
Vietnam	160	250	270	703	1,007	1,469	1,174	1,377	1,545	1,670	1,797
Western Samoa	8	10	14	15							
Australasia											
Australia	10,479	10,915	11,540	12,735	13,054	13,069	13,102	13,306	13,618	13,023	13,085
New Zealand	1,700	1,645	1,624	2,002	2,069	2,130	2,151	2,183	2,162	2,175	2,188

Source: Euromonitor from OECD

◘ Consumption of Refinery Products

Consumption of Motor Gasoline 1977-2002

● '000 metric tonnes

	1977	1980	1985	1990	1995	1997	1998	1999	2000	2001	2002
Africa and Middle East											
Algeria	798	1,214	1,680	2,177	2,023	1,933	1,883	1,891	1,902	1,932	1,958
Angola	86	80	84	71	73	134	105	163	117	110	105
Bahrain	75	110	170	226	301	304	321	336	353	364	375
Benin	31	34	59	59	65	126	110	190	210	224	237
Botswana											
Burkina Faso	31	53	51	54	67						
Burundi	13	16	17	23	25						
Cameroon	138	320	413	53	354	254	287	237	261	254	247
Cape Verde	1	2	3	4	5						
Central African Republic	15	22	15	15	16						
Chad	23	24	25	6	7						
Comoros	3	3	3	4	4						
Congo Dem Rep	154	198	175	204	148	235	222	135	138	148	153
Congo-Brazzaville						53	53	29	40	45	54
Côte d'Ivoire	216	317	272	439	569	163	163	163	168	169	172
Djibouti	10	14	11	16	18						
Egypt	1,531	1,325	1,958	2,172	1,930	2,080	2,150	2,255	2,329	2,424	2,511
Equatorial Guinea	5	2	5	5	5						
Eritrea						15	16	16	14	13	11
Ethiopia	75	160	116	150	127	130	134	135	144	148	155
Gabon	15	30	38	58	28	41	45	46	35	34	33
Gambia	18	22	22	26	28						
Ghana	225	246	280	316	337	389	416	481	549	590	646
Guinea	42	46	65	67	73						
Guinea-Bissau	6	7	7	12	15						
Iran	3,102	3,596	4,457	5,805	7,436	9,414	10,096	10,410	11,364	11,586	12,308
Iraq	580	1,150	1,450	2,300	2,990	2,886	2,988	2,894	3,166	3,398	3,660
Israel	702	750	1,014	1,682	2,003	2,005	2,002	2,206	2,085	2,089	2,018
Jordan	215	270	332	400	486	533	530	550	604	637	681
Kenya	280	313	239	298	339	391	396	419	469	501	548
Kuwait	605	892	1,127	1,080	1,473	1,693	1,782	1,687	1,554	1,478	1,363
Lebanon	400	500	739	1,000	1,279	1,310	1,412	1,344	1,264	1,228	1,163
Lesotho											
Liberia	67	69	49	29	27						
Libya	575	818	983	1,400	1,600	1,716	1,788	1,874	1,917	1,991	2,036
Madagascar	100	95	48	60	78						
Malawi	36	55	46	61	68						
Mali	45	54	51	55	61						
Mauritania	26	31	32	233	266						
Mauritius	56	33	32	56	84						
Morocco	366	378	332	398	369	380	385	409	405	411	416
Mozambique	79	93	40	39	39	43	49	49	50	50	50
Namibia											
Niger	25	35	42	44	47						
Nigeria	982	2,955	2,979	4,735	3,108	3,308	3,265	4,469	4,745	4,923	5,106
Oman	139	200	397	483	631	678	700	717	738	746	752
Qatar	110	170	247	304	438	414	439	457	477	493	507
Réunion	72	98	69	125	133						
Rwanda	18	23	21	35	33						
Sao Tomé e Príncipe	3	5	5	5	5						
Saudi Arabia	1,958	3,240	6,100	6,673	9,805	9,643	9,728	9,653	9,778	9,824	9,903
Senegal	86	130	108	174	179	78	84	86	98	105	116
Seychelles	6	6	5	6	7						
Sierra Leone	42	20	30	23	30						
Somalia											
South Africa	3,559	3,680	4,400	4,350	7,500	7,898	8,024	7,843	7,510	7,055	6,661
Sudan	225	152	194	200	194	242	223	240	275	295	324
Swaziland											
Syria	482	600	845	989	1,023	1,142	1,176	1,218	1,247	1,276	1,309
Tanzania	99	87	87	103	110	98	98	102	107	114	120
Togo	39	50	34	59	64	98	109	122	128	133	139
Tunisia	141	154	220	259	311	340	346	366	389	415	441
Uganda	95	88	79	86	94						
United Arab Emirates	371	585	770	850	1,158	1,551	1,680	1,477	1,404	1,358	1,311
Yemen	196	256	379	495	1,140	1,032	1,032	1,069	1,081	1,119	1,163
Zambia	174	170	110	106	107	110	110	126	133	137	141
Zimbabwe	200	180	184	171	300	435	435	477	349	307	265

Source: Euromonitor from OECD

Energy Production: Selected Materials 2002

● Million tonnes of oil equivalent/as stated

	Coal	Crude Oil	Natural Gas	Electricity (GWh)
Algeria		70.2	72.3	26,655
Argentina		39.4	32.5	97,575
Australia	183.6	31.5	31.0	221,877
Azerbaijan		15.3	4.3	20,590
Bolivia			4.9	4,171
Brazil	2.2	74.4	8.2	368,540
Canada	35.5	135.6	165.2	562,581
Chile				47,324
China	703.0	168.9	29.3	1,581,062
Colombia	25.7	29.7	5.5	40,887
Ecuador		20.8		12,184
Egypt		37.0	20.4	91,153
Hong Kong, China				34,985
India	168.4	36.7	24.4	566,427
Indonesia	63.3	62.4	63.5	96,935
Israel				51,065
Japan	1.7			998,286
Jordan				8,100
Kazakhstan	37.6	47.2	11.0	57,996
Kuwait		91.8	7.8	34,150
Malaysia		37.0	45.2	74,511
Mexico	5.7	178.4	31.3	213,145
Morocco	0.1	0.0		15,137
New Zealand	2.6		5.7	42,569
Nigeria		98.6	16.0	16,937
Pakistan	1.6		18.8	71,926
Peru		4.8		21,729
Philippines				52,542
Saudi Arabia		418.1	50.7	145,655
Singapore				34,759
South Africa	126.8			217,509
South Korea	1.5			320,561
Taiwan	0.1			216,897
Thailand		7.9	17.0	105,651
Tunisia		3.6		11,911
Turkmenistan		9.0	44.9	11,368
United Arab Emirates		105.6	41.4	41,730
USA	571.7	350.4	492.9	3,663,560
Venezuela	5.8	151.4	24.6	95,074
Vietnam		17.3		31,986

Source: Euromonitor from Organisation for Economic Co-operation and Development (OECD)

Production of Coal 1984-2002

● Million tonnes of oil equivalent

	1984	1985	1990	1995	1996	1997	1998	1999	2000	2001	2002
Algeria											
Argentina											
Australia	73.0	88.4	108.6	128.5	133.9	141.4	149.2	153.0	162.0	174.1	183.6
Azerbaijan											
Bolivia											
Brazil	3.4	3.5	1.9	2.0	1.8	2.1	2.0	2.1	2.1	2.1	2.2
Canada	31.7	33.7	37.9	40.8	41.6	43.0	40.8	39.2	37.1	37.6	35.5
Chile											
China	397.6	439.8	542.3	650.9	691.5	665.5	619.7	523.9	501.8	547.8	703.0
Colombia	4.3	5.8	13.3	16.7	19.5	21.0	19.6	21.3	24.8	28.5	25.7
Ecuador											
Egypt											
Hong Kong, China											
India	71.9	74.2	104.9	135.2	145.7	149.6	150.3	147.4	157.0	160.3	168.4
Indonesia	0.9	1.2	6.6	25.7	31.0	33.7	38.3	45.3	47.4	56.9	63.3
Israel											
Japan	9.9	9.6	4.6	3.4	3.6	2.4	2.0	2.2	1.7	1.8	1.7
Jordan											
Kazakhstan		68.0	67.7	42.6	39.3	37.3	36.0	30.0	38.5	40.6	37.6
Kuwait											
Malaysia											
Mexico	2.8	2.9	3.4	4.1	4.6	4.5	4.8	4.9	5.4	5.5	5.7
Morocco			0.4	0.3	0.2	0.2	0.1	0.1	0.1	0.1	0.1
New Zealand	1.4	1.3	1.5	2.1	2.2	2.0	2.0	2.2	2.2	2.4	2.6
Nigeria											
Pakistan	1.0	1.0	1.3	1.4	1.5	1.4	1.5	1.5	1.4	1.5	1.6
Peru											
Philippines											
Saudi Arabia											
Singapore											
South Africa	93.7	99.8	100.1	116.9	116.9	124.6	127.1	125.6	126.5	126.3	126.8
South Korea	9.8	10.4	7.7	2.6	2.2	2.0	2.0	1.9	1.9	1.7	1.5
Taiwan						0.1	0.1	0.1	0.1	0.1	0.1
Thailand											
Tunisia											
Turkmenistan											
United Arab Emirates											
USA	493.0	483.1	561.4	550.7	567.1	580.3	598.4	579.7	565.6	589.4	571.7
Venezuela			1.6	3.2	3.1	3.9	4.7	4.8	5.6	5.5	5.8
Vietnam											

Source: *BP Amoco, BP Statistical Review of World Energy*
Notes: *Million tonnes of oil equivalent = the amount of oil required to fuel an oil-fired plant in order to generate the same amount of electricity*

Production of Crude Oil 1982-2002

● Million metric tonnes

	1982	1985	1990	1995	1996	1997	1998	1999	2000	2001	2002
Algeria	46.8	50.0	57.5	56.6	59.3	60.3	61.8	63.9	66.8	65.8	70.2
Argentina	25.6	24.2	25.4	37.5	40.8	43.4	44.0	41.8	40.4	40.8	39.4
Australia	19.8	28.8	28.4	25.4	26.6	28.8	27.4	24.5	35.4	31.8	31.5
Azerbaijan		13.2	12.5	9.2	9.1	9.2	11.4	13.8	14.0	14.9	15.3
Bolivia											
Brazil	13.3	27.8	32.3	35.5	40.2	43.1	49.8	56.3	63.2	66.3	74.4
Canada	74.6	85.6	92.6	111.9	115.5	120.7	125.1	121.0	126.9	127.5	135.6
Chile											
China	101.7	124.9	138.3	149.0	158.5	160.1	160.2	160.2	162.6	164.8	168.9
Colombia	7.3	9.1	22.3	29.5	31.8	33.2	38.5	41.6	35.3	31.0	29.7
Ecuador	10.9	14.6	14.9	20.1	20.0	20.2	19.5	19.4	20.9	21.2	20.8
Egypt	33.3	45.1	45.5	46.6	45.1	43.8	43.0	41.4	38.8	37.3	37.0
Hong Kong, China											
India	19.9	30.2	34.8	37.8	36.3	37.3	36.7	36.5	36.1	36.0	36.7
Indonesia	66.6	66.3	74.4	76.5	76.7	75.7	74.2	68.6	71.5	68.0	62.4
Israel											
Japan											
Jordan											
Kazakhstan		22.7	25.8	20.6	23.0	25.8	25.9	30.1	35.3	40.1	47.2
Kuwait	42.7	55.5	46.8	104.9	105.1	105.1	107.2	98.3	104.0	101.9	91.8
Malaysia	14.5	21.6	29.9	34.0	34.4	35.1	36.9	35.6	35.5	35.0	37.0
Mexico	151.0	145.9	146.3	150.5	162.6	169.7	173.5	165.2	171.2	176.6	178.4
Morocco				0.0	0.0	0.0	0.0	0.0	0.0	0.0	0.0
New Zealand											
Nigeria	63.5	73.8	89.2	97.5	104.7	112.7	105.9	99.2	103.3	107.8	98.6
Pakistan											
Peru	9.7	9.3	6.4	6.1	6.0	5.9	5.8	5.4	5.1	4.8	4.8
Philippines											
Saudi Arabia	340.2	172.1	342.6	435.4	443.5	451.3	452.0	419.1	450.6	434.1	418.1
Singapore											
South Africa											
South Korea											
Taiwan											
Thailand	0.2	2.0	2.5	3.4	3.8	4.5	4.7	5.2	6.6	7.0	7.9
Tunisia	5.1	5.4	4.6	4.3	4.2	3.8	4.0	4.1	3.8	3.5	3.6
Turkmenistan		6.8	5.7	4.1	4.4	5.4	6.4	7.1	7.2	8.0	9.0
United Arab Emirates	65.5	59.3	108.4	114.0	117.9	117.0	119.9	107.6	117.0	113.5	105.6
USA	480.7	498.7	416.6	383.6	382.1	380.0	368.1	352.6	352.6	349.2	350.4
Venezuela	101.6	90.5	115.9	152.4	162.2	171.4	181.0	167.1	171.6	165.2	151.4
Vietnam		2.7	7.7	8.9	10.1	12.1	14.6	16.2	17.1	17.3

Source: BP Amoco, BP Statistical Review of World Energy
Notes: Million tonnes of oil equivalent = the amount of oil required to fuel an oil-fired plant in order to generate the same amount of electricity

■ Energy Production

Electricity Production 2002

Table 11.5

● GWh/% shares

	Net Total Production	% Fossil Fuels	% Combustible Renewables and Waste	% Geothermal	% Hydroelectric	% Nuclear	% Wind Powered	% Other Sources
North America								
Canada	562,581	29.27	1.26		56.70	12.69	0.08	
USA	3,663,560	71.89	1.86	0.35	4.56	21.14	0.17	
Latin America								
Anguilla								
Antigua								
Argentina	97,575	68.42	0.26		25.83	5.39	0.10	
Aruba								
Bahamas								
Barbados								
Belize								
Bermuda								
Bolivia	4,171	46.94	1.58		51.47			
Brazil	368,540	9.77	2.87		85.19	2.17	0.00	
British Virgin Islands								
Cayman Islands								
Chile	47,324	58.30	1.93		39.77			
Colombia	40,887	24.98	1.30		73.72			
Costa Rica	7,557	0.64	0.29	14.73	80.91		3.44	
Cuba	15,494	94.44	4.84		0.72			
Dominica								
Dominican Republic	10,664	90.94	0.27		8.79			
Ecuador	12,184	23.10			76.90			
El Salvador	3,690	46.59	0.68	22.47	30.27			
French Guiana								
Grenada								
Guadeloupe								
Guatemala	8,619	48.87	14.45		36.68			
Guyana								
Haiti	385	55.83			44.15			
Honduras	4,277	37.57	0.07		62.36			
Jamaica	6,763	97.28	1.04		1.69			
Martinique								
Mexico	213,145	81.63	0.21	2.55	12.16	3.42	0.01	0.01
Netherlands Antilles	1,158	100.00						
Nicaragua	2,776	82.49	3.10	4.79	9.62			
Panama	4,814	27.09	1.52		71.40			
Paraguay	55,014	0.03	0.08		99.89			
Peru	21,729	17.14	0.75		82.11		0.00	
Puerto Rico								
St Kitts								
St Lucia								
St Vincent and the Grenadines								
Suriname								
Trinidad and Tobago	5,750	99.88	0.12					
Uruguay	8,769	9.45	0.34		90.20			
Venezuela	95,074	25.92			74.08			

Source: *Euromonitor from OECD*

◫ Energy Production

Electricity Production 2002

● GWh/% shares

	Net Total Production	% Fossil Fuels	% Combustible Renewables and Waste	% Geothermal	% Hydroelectric	% Nuclear	% Wind Powered	% Other Sources
Asia Pacific								
Afghanistan								
American Samoa								
Armenia	6,233	43.88			20.97	35.15		
Azerbaijan	20,590	92.81			7.19			
Bangladesh	16,466	94.64			5.36			
Bhutan								
Brunei	2,415	100.00						
Cambodia								
China	1,581,062	83.30	0.16		15.42	1.13		
Fiji								
French Polynesia								
Guam								
Hong Kong, China	34,985	100.00						
India	566,427	84.85			11.30	3.48	0.37	
Indonesia	96,935	89.30		2.80	7.90			
Japan	998,286	60.06	1.04	0.32	8.64	29.91	0.03	
Kazakhstan	57,996	85.46			14.54			
Kiribati								
Kyrgyzstan	17,165	6.55			93.45			
Laos								
Macau								
Malaysia	74,511	93.51			6.49			
Maldives								
Mongolia								
Myanmar	5,519	62.44			37.56			
Nauru								
Nepal	1,767	1.98			98.02			
New Caledonia								
North Korea	30,340	31.73			68.27			
Pakistan	71,926	75.72			20.43	3.85		
Papua New Guinea								
Philippines	52,542	60.36		25.91	13.73			
Singapore	34,759	97.87						2.13
Solomon Islands								
South Korea	320,561	60.48	0.10		1.81	37.57	0.00	0.03
Sri Lanka	8,067	69.42			30.58			
Taiwan	216,897	78.46			4.21	17.33		
Tajikistan	14,747	2.58			97.42			
Thailand	105,651	91.80	2.05		6.15			0.00
Tonga								
Turkmenistan	11,368	99.94			0.06			
Tuvalu								
Uzbekistan	50,062	88.47			11.53			
Vanuatu								
Vietnam	31,986	51.38			48.62			
Western Samoa								
Australasia								
Australia	221,877	91.55	0.60		7.73		0.11	
New Zealand	42,569	36.94	0.98	9.67	50.22		2.19	

Source: Euromonitor from OECD

■ Energy Production

Electricity Production 2002

● GWh/% shares

	Net Total Production	% Fossil Fuels	% Combustible Renewables and Waste	% Geothermal	% Hydroelectric	% Nuclear	% Wind Powered	% Other Sources
Africa and Middle East								
Algeria	26,655	99.69			0.31			
Angola	1,505	50.17			49.83			
Bahrain	7,363	100.00						
Benin	81	96.30			6.17			
Botswana								
Burkina Faso								
Burundi								
Cameroon	3,636	0.99			99.01			
Cape Verde								
Central African Republic								
Chad								
Comoros								
Congo Dem Rep	4,964	0.38			99.62			
Congo-Brazzaville	481	0.83			99.58			
Côte d'Ivoire	3,981	66.26			33.74			
Djibouti								
Egypt	91,153	81.84			18.16			
Equatorial Guinea								
Eritrea	208	100.00						
Ethiopia	1,810	1.22		1.77	97.02			
Gabon	1,187	30.92			69.09			
Gambia								
Ghana	8,406	8.86			91.14			
Guinea								
Guinea-Bissau								
Iran	144,054	97.17			2.83			
Iraq	37,711	98.25			1.74			
Israel	51,065	99.93			0.07			
Jordan	8,100	99.32			0.64		0.04	
Kenya	3,593	44.98		12.25	42.78			
Kuwait	34,150	100.00						
Lebanon	6,935	96.61			3.39			
Lesotho								
Liberia								
Libya	22,097	100.00						
Madagascar								
Malawi								
Mali								
Mauritania								
Mauritius								
Morocco	15,137	93.60			5.58		0.82	
Mozambique	7,570	0.42			99.58			
Namibia								
Niger								
Nigeria	16,937	63.05			36.95			
Oman	10,486	100.00						
Qatar	10,658	100.00						
Réunion								
Rwanda								
Sao Tomé e Príncipe								
Saudi Arabia	145,655	100.00						
Senegal	1,756	100.00						
Seychelles								
Sierra Leone								
Somalia								
South Africa	217,509	90.99			2.34	6.67		
Sudan	2,620	55.23			44.77			
Swaziland								
Syria	26,266	61.08			38.92			
Tanzania	2,861	2.83			97.17			
Togo	53	98.11			1.89			
Tunisia	11,911	98.97			0.71		0.32	
Uganda								
United Arab Emirates	41,730	100.00						
Yemen	3,432	100.00						
Zambia	7,001	0.70			99.30			
Zimbabwe	7,026	49.32			50.68			

Source: Euromonitor from OECD

Table 11.6

Production of Natural Gas 1984-2002

- Million tonnes of oil equivalent

	1984	1985	1990	1995	1996	1997	1998	1999	2000	2001	2002
Algeria	28.3	30.8	44.3	52.8	56.1	64.6	68.9	77.4	76.0	70.4	72.3
Argentina	12.1	12.5	16.1	22.5	23.9	24.6	26.6	31.1	33.7	33.4	32.5
Australia	11.4	12.1	18.6	26.8	27.5	27.0	27.3	27.5	28.0	30.2	31.0
Azerbaijan		11.8	8.3	5.5	5.3	5.0	4.7	5.0	4.7	4.7	4.3
Bolivia	2.2	2.2	2.7	2.8	2.9	2.9	2.8	2.3	3.1	4.6	4.9
Brazil	1.9	2.4	3.4	4.3	5.0	5.4	5.6	6.1	6.1	6.8	8.2
Canada	64.4	68.9	89.4	133.4	138.2	140.6	144.5	146.0	151.0	168.1	165.2
Chile											
China	10.6	10.8	12.8	15.8	17.9	20.0	20.1	21.9	24.5	27.3	29.3
Colombia	3.5	3.6	3.7	4.0	4.2	5.3	5.6	4.7	5.3	5.5	5.5
Ecuador											
Egypt	3.0	3.7	6.1	9.9	10.4	10.5	11.0	13.2	16.5	19.3	20.4
Hong Kong, China											
India	3.6	4.3	11.1	16.9	18.4	18.6	22.2	22.4	23.5	23.7	24.4
Indonesia	27.8	27.7	40.8	57.4	60.4	60.8	58.2	64.3	60.5	59.7	63.5
Israel											
Japan											
Jordan											
Kazakhstan		4.6	6.0	5.0	5.5	6.8	6.7	8.4	9.7	9.7	11.0
Kuwait	3.9	3.8	3.8	8.4	8.4	8.3	8.5	7.8	8.6	8.6	7.8
Malaysia	6.8	9.2	16.0	26.0	30.3	34.8	34.6	36.8	40.7	42.6	45.2
Mexico	28.7	26.8	24.1	25.3	28.1	30.4	32.9	34.6	33.4	31.8	31.3
Morocco											
New Zealand	2.6	3.2	4.1	3.7	4.4	4.6	4.0	4.7	4.9	5.2	5.7
Nigeria	2.5	2.4	3.6	4.4	4.9	4.6	4.6	5.4	9.8	16.6	16.0
Pakistan	7.0	7.3	10.1	13.1	13.8	14.0	14.4	15.6	17.0	17.9	18.8
Peru											
Philippines											
Saudi Arabia	16.4	16.9	30.2	38.6	40.0	40.8	42.1	41.6	44.8	48.3	50.7
Singapore											
South Africa											
South Korea											
Taiwan											
Thailand	2.1	2.8	4.9	9.1	10.6	12.7	13.9	15.3	16.1	16.2	17.0
Tunisia											
Turkmenistan		69.8	73.7	27.1	29.6	14.5	11.2	19.1	39.5	43.1	44.9
United Arab Emirates	9.9	11.9	18.1	28.2	30.4	32.7	33.4	34.2	35.9	40.5	41.4
USA	453.8	427.9	462.8	481.4	488.0	488.8	494.3	487.4	490.4	501.9	492.9
Venezuela	15.6	15.6	19.8	24.8	26.8	27.7	29.1	24.7	25.1	26.2	24.6
Vietnam											

Source: BP Amoco, BP Statistical Review of World Energy
Notes: Million tonnes of oil equivalent = the amount of oil required to fuel an oil-fired plant in order to generate the same amount of electricity

Energy Production

Refinery Output 1992-2002

Table 11.7

- '000 tonnes of oil per year

	1992	1994	1995	1997	1998	1999	2000	2001	2002
North America									
Canada	79,888	83,756	83,683	89,907	90,672	91,583	93,712	96,413	100,219
USA	732,835	754,572	758,614	794,543	808,363	807,518	822,834	819,874	821,696
Latin America									
Anguilla									
Antigua									
Argentina	24,050	23,770	22,393	25,393	27,257	28,232	26,430	25,512	23,179
Aruba									
Bahamas									
Barbados	233	251	270						
Belize									
Bermuda									
Bolivia	1,276	1,384	1,496	1,582	1,590	1,607	1,549	1,501	1,410
Brazil	59,133	63,308	62,089	71,974	77,502	80,182	81,265	83,472	84,946
British Virgin Islands									
Cayman Islands									
Chile	6,249	7,078	7,677	8,369	9,101	9,079	9,138	8,968	8,779
Colombia	11,757	12,607	13,723	14,597	14,478	15,058	15,126	15,577	15,804
Costa Rica	530	563	738	613	47	48	48	49	49
Cuba	1,715	1,562	1,611	1,661	1,413	1,153	2,320	2,808	3,266
Dominica									
Dominican Republic	1,408	1,569	1,571	1,531	1,562	1,666	1,625	1,592	1,465
Ecuador	5,807	6,329	6,683	7,219	6,961	6,039	7,641	8,494	11,259
El Salvador	803	832	732	766	900	1,003	943	931	825
French Guiana									
Grenada									
Guadeloupe									
Guatemala	744	752	764	750	747	925	840	864	733
Guyana									
Haiti									
Honduras	288								
Jamaica	1,222	879	697	682	681	474	957	1,070	1,218
Martinique	714	724	732						
Mexico	67,308	71,718	68,603	63,874	66,816	67,718	64,176	63,886	61,812
Netherlands Antilles	11,592	12,354	12,380	12,435	12,842	11,387	11,808	11,561	12,254
Nicaragua	642	653	568	760	852	823	833	837	863
Panama	1,659	1,151	1,329	2,110	2,330	2,370	2,131	1,981	1,705
Paraguay	299	254	200	140	127	113	102	99	99
Peru	7,634	7,524	7,240	7,689	8,260	7,463	7,454	7,328	7,631
Puerto Rico	7,340	8,026	7,944						
St Kitts									
St Lucia									
St Vincent and the Grenadines									
Suriname									
Trinidad and Tobago	5,143	5,131	4,773	5,103	7,070	7,477	7,537	7,736	7,732
Uruguay	1,143		1,313	1,397	1,826	1,578	1,906	1,962	2,325
Venezuela	45,598	48,273	49,711	53,612	54,681	52,552	53,718	52,789	53,333

Source: Euromonitor from OECD

Energy Production
Refinery Output 1992-2002

• '000 tonnes of oil per year

	1992	1994	1995	1997	1998	1999	2000	2001	2002
Asia Pacific									
Afghanistan									
American Samoa									
Armenia									
Azerbaijan	11,015	8,939	8,629	8,298	8,214	7,598	8,367	8,948	10,525
Bangladesh	1,020	1,231	1,408	1,371	1,271	1,033	1,370	1,451	1,904
Bhutan									
Brunei	366	392	451	473	474	489	467	437	383
Cambodia									
China	120,259	128,359	139,338	162,257	162,665	175,868	195,835	211,161	229,760
Fiji									
French Polynesia									
Guam									
Hong Kong, China									
India	53,834	55,965	57,596	64,149	66,383	77,973	101,427	108,012	115,619
Indonesia	39,607	39,344	39,987	42,439	44,729	45,739	46,918	49,269	52,242
Japan	195,022	209,870	210,747	215,326	212,110	208,255	206,162	200,406	194,702
Kazakhstan	17,659	11,795	10,753	9,472	8,807	6,517	6,638	6,364	7,156
Kiribati									
Kyrgyzstan				231	130	174	133	143	113
Laos									
Macau									
Malaysia	9,309	13,674	13,574	16,246	16,414	17,345	20,474	21,699	23,914
Maldives									
Mongolia									
Myanmar	714	821	907	966	952	920	895	810	718
Nauru									
Nepal									
New Caledonia									
North Korea	2,885	2,835	2,810	2,735	2,600	2,627	2,654	2,719	2,798
Pakistan	6,330	6,309	5,931	6,302	6,390	6,611	8,822	9,915	11,246
Papua New Guinea									
Philippines	11,670	11,751	15,774	17,380	16,667	16,157	15,195	14,082	12,714
Singapore	44,063	47,612	46,729	48,068	48,340	40,494	35,225	32,280	30,774
Solomon Islands									
South Korea	70,811	79,548	89,464	120,972	113,963	120,349	122,001	119,210	111,665
Sri Lanka	1,533	1,907	1,821	1,776	2,090	1,807	2,209	2,453	3,217
Taiwan	23,876	27,138	31,181	33,988	34,761	41,933	46,390	50,701	51,805
Tajikistan	56	30	24	25	14	12	12	11	11
Thailand	14,431	19,291	22,064	34,816	32,582	33,064	32,639	31,847	30,366
Tonga									
Turkmenistan	4,770	3,499	3,200	4,136	5,956	6,092	6,113	6,285	6,432
Tuvalu									
Uzbekistan	6,465	5,898	6,607	6,767	7,244	7,133	6,826	6,449	5,974
Vanuatu									
Vietnam	42	1							
Western Samoa									
Australasia									
Australia	31,990	33,997	34,894	36,652	37,144	36,399	36,708	35,403	34,298
New Zealand	4,742	5,079	4,708	4,952	5,145	4,877	5,060	4,981	5,112

Source: Euromonitor from OECD

◻ Energy Production

Refinery Output 1992-2002

- '000 tonnes of oil per year

	1992	1994	1995	1997	1998	1999	2000	2001	2002
Africa and Middle East									
Algeria	20,669	19,235	19,850	20,063	18,860	20,390	20,033	19,833	18,380
Angola	1,704	1,743	1,785	1,864	1,743	1,937	1,774	1,700	1,705
Bahrain	12,851	12,067	12,539	12,508	12,384	13,029	12,720	12,980	12,780
Benin									
Botswana									
Burkina Faso									
Burundi									
Cameroon	1,040	1,403	1,220	1,585	1,635	1,364	1,543	1,591	1,506
Cape Verde									
Central African Republic									
Chad									
Comoros									
Congo Dem Rep	162	65	63	64	66	66	66	65	64
Congo-Brazzaville	475	259	427	189	223	289	379	407	409
Côte d'Ivoire	2,878	2,806	2,877	2,972	3,023	2,951	2,948	3,031	3,191
Djibouti									
Egypt	23,600	25,919	26,667	27,921	28,790	28,060	26,233	24,094	21,358
Equatorial Guinea									
Eritrea	646	718	604	402	467	425	383	402	439
Ethiopia	431	641	622	340	340	340	340	349	361
Gabon	625	666	681	687	764	815	767	766	715
Gambia									
Ghana	889	1,017	862	11	725	1,307	1,062	1,145	1,159
Guinea									
Guinea-Bissau									
Iran	43,362	54,585	54,628	60,780	64,457	67,582	68,473	68,678	67,034
Iraq	17,520	22,120	21,673	21,515	22,220	21,434	21,827	21,307	21,261
Israel	10,063	11,330	10,901	10,617	11,307	10,532	10,566	9,939	9,617
Jordan	2,910	2,956	3,128	3,443	3,454	3,462	3,821	4,082	4,588
Kenya	2,217	2,058	1,809	1,624	1,698	1,677	1,986	2,043	2,263
Kuwait	17,750	40,121	43,996	47,010	46,941	47,128	36,815	34,510	29,020
Lebanon	429								
Lesotho									
Liberia									
Libya	13,463	14,230	14,522	14,889	13,952	15,284	14,848	15,053	14,228
Madagascar	184	197	199						
Malawi									
Mali									
Mauritania	920	921	926						
Mauritius									
Morocco	5,976	6,410	6,028	5,730	5,870	6,999	6,579	6,827	6,158
Mozambique				4	4	4	4	4	4
Namibia									
Niger									
Nigeria	13,140	8,219	11,200	13,367	7,570	7,865	4,826	4,511	3,860
Oman	2,923	3,632	3,638	3,247	3,905	3,911	3,939	4,186	4,541
Qatar	2,690	2,819	2,646	2,621	2,842	2,803	2,565	2,461	2,280
Réunion									
Rwanda									
Sao Tomé e Príncipe									
Saudi Arabia	74,178	75,143	72,080	77,121	77,991	76,493	79,133	83,378	91,368
Senegal	601	171	679	798	817	820	881	904	955
Seychelles									
Sierra Leone	193	204	208						
Somalia									
South Africa	17,838	21,059	23,230	28,768	23,353	25,162	25,307	23,217	21,905
Sudan	724	617	710	896	580	417	1,959	2,257	3,250
Swaziland									
Syria	11,587	11,630	11,704	12,057	12,081	12,086	12,124	12,193	12,294
Tanzania	589	592	598	599	599	621	648	688	737
Togo									
Tunisia	1,590	1,669	1,800	2,009	1,808	1,811	1,905	1,904	1,933
Uganda									
United Arab Emirates	20,412	21,975	21,985	22,540	22,110	18,294	19,609	19,071	21,024
Yemen	5,180	3,504	3,457	4,296	4,333	4,375	4,439	4,491	4,554
Zambia	597	528	564	531	522	196	23	19	17
Zimbabwe									

Source: Euromonitor from OECD

Table 11.8

Proven Coal Reserves at End 2002

● As stated

	Reserves (million tonnes)	Reserves/ Production Ratio (years)	Share of World Coal Reserves (% of total)
Algeria			
Argentina			
Australia	82,090	243	8.3
Azerbaijan			
Bolivia			
Brazil	11,929	500	1.2
Canada	6,578	97	0.7
Chile			
China	114,500	82	11.6
Colombia	6,648	168	0.7
Ecuador			
Egypt			
Hong Kong, China			
India	84,396	235	8.6
Indonesia	5,370	52	0.5
Israel			
Japan	773	500	0.1
Jordan			
Kazakhstan	34,000	464	3.5
Kuwait			
Malaysia			
Mexico	1,211	101	0.1
Morocco			
New Zealand	572	134	0.1
Nigeria			
Pakistan	2,265	500	0.2
Peru			
Philippines			
Saudi Arabia			
Singapore			
South Africa	49,520	221	5.0
South Korea	78	23	0.1
Taiwan	99	500	
Thailand	1,268	64	0.1
Tunisia			
Turkmenistan			
United Arab Emirates			
USA	249,994	252	25.4
Venezuela	479	60	0.1
Vietnam	150	10	0.1

Source: Euromonitor from industry sources/national statistics

Proven Oil Reserves at End 2002

● As stated

	Reserves (billion barrels)	Reserves (billion tonnes of oil equivalent)	Reserves/ Production Ratio (years)
Algeria	9.2	1.2	16.5
Argentina	2.9	0.4	10.1
Australia	3.5	0.4	14.1
Azerbaijan	7.0	1.0	62.5
Bolivia			
Brazil	8.3	1.1	15.4
Canada	6.9	0.9	9.0
Chile			
China	18.3	2.5	14.8
Colombia	1.8	0.3	8.5
Ecuador	4.6	0.7	31.2
Egypt	3.7	0.5	14.1
Hong Kong, China			
India	5.4	0.7	19.4
Indonesia	5.0	0.7	11.1
Israel			
Japan			
Jordan			
Kazakhstan	9.0	1.2	26.1
Kuwait	96.5	13.3	100.0
Malaysia	3.0	0.4	10.6
Mexico	12.6	1.8	10.1
Morocco			
New Zealand			
Nigeria	24.0	3.2	32.8
Pakistan			
Peru	0.3	0.1	9.2
Philippines			
Saudi Arabia	261.8	36.0	86.0
Singapore			
South Africa			
South Korea			
Taiwan			
Thailand	0.6	0.1	9.6
Tunisia	0.3	0.1	11.2
Turkmenistan	0.5	0.1	8.3
United Arab Emirates	97.8	13.0	100.0
USA	30.4	3.8	10.8
Venezuela	77.8	11.2	74.0
Vietnam	0.6	0.1	4.7

Source: Euromonitor from industry sources/national statistics

Proven Natural Gas Reserves at End 2002

- Trillion cubic metres

	Reserves (trillion cu m)	Reserves/ Production Ratio (years)
Algeria	4.5	56.3
Argentina	0.8	21.1
Australia	2.6	73.9
Azerbaijan	0.8	100.0
Bolivia	0.7	100.0
Brazil	0.2	25.2
Canada	1.7	9.3
Chile		
China	1.5	46.3
Colombia	0.1	20.7
Ecuador	0.1	100.0
Egypt	1.7	73.1
Hong Kong, China		
India	0.8	26.9
Indonesia	2.6	37.1
Israel		
Japan		
Jordan		
Kazakhstan	1.8	100.0
Kuwait	1.5	100.0
Malaysia	2.1	42.2
Mexico	0.3	7.1
Morocco		
New Zealand		
Nigeria	3.5	100.0
Pakistan	0.8	35.8
Peru	0.3	100.0
Philippines		
Saudi Arabia	6.4	100.0
Singapore		
South Africa		
South Korea		
Taiwan		
Thailand	0.4	20.0
Tunisia		
Turkmenistan	2.0	38.2
United Arab Emirates	6.0	100.0
USA	5.2	9.6
Venezuela	4.2	100.0
Vietnam	0.2	80.2

Source: *Euromonitor from industry sources/national statistics*

Primary Energy Consumption: Selected Materials 2002

● Million tonnes of oil equivalent

	Crude Oil	Hydroelectricity	Natural Gas	Nuclear Energy	Coal	Total
Algeria	8.7	0.1	19.2		0.5	34.0
Argentina	16.8	7.6	27.2	1.3	0.6	53.5
Australia	38.0	3.8	21.6		49.5	112.9
Azerbaijan	3.6	0.5	7.1			11.2
Bolivia						
Brazil	85.4	64.4	12.3	3.4	12.0	177.5
Canada	89.7	78.6	72.6	17.0	30.7	288.7
Chile	10.8	5.2	5.9		2.0	23.9
China	245.7	55.8	27.0	5.9	663.4	997.8
Colombia	10.0	7.6	5.5		2.0	25.2
Ecuador	5.9	1.7	0.1			7.7
Egypt	26.1	3.1	20.4		0.8	50.3
Hong Kong, China	13.1		2.1		5.4	20.6
India	97.7	16.9	25.4	4.4	180.8	325.1
Indonesia	51.2	2.1	31.3		17.8	102.4
Israel						
Japan	242.6	20.5	69.7	71.3	105.3	509.4
Jordan						
Kazakhstan	6.5	2.0	8.7	0.1	21.7	38.9
Kuwait	10.7		7.8			18.6
Malaysia	22.5	1.7	24.3		3.3	51.8
Mexico	80.9	5.6	37.9	2.2	7.0	133.7
Morocco					2.5	
New Zealand	6.8	5.4	5.0		1.3	18.4
Nigeria						
Pakistan	17.9	4.6	18.8	0.4	2.1	43.8
Peru	7.0	4.1	0.4		0.4	11.8
Philippines	15.6	1.6	1.6		3.5	22.3
Saudi Arabia	63.4		50.8			114.2
Singapore	35.5		1.6			37.1
South Africa	23.6	0.9		2.9	81.8	109.2
South Korea	105.0	1.2	23.6	27.0	49.1	205.8
Taiwan	38.8	1.4	7.7	9.0	32.5	89.3
Thailand	35.3	1.6	23.3		8.6	68.9
Tunisia						
Turkmenistan	2.6		11.9			14.5
United Arab Emirates	12.4		35.4			47.8
USA	984.3	58.2	600.7	183.5	553.8	2,293.0
Venezuela	22.9	14.0	24.6			61.5
Vietnam						

Source: *BP Amoco, BP Statistical Review of World Energy*

Consumption of Coal 1984-2002

• Million tonnes of oil equivalent

	1984	1985	1990	1995	1996	1997	1998	1999	2000	2001	2002
Algeria	0.8	0.8	0.6	0.6	0.5	0.3	0.5	0.5	0.6	0.6	0.5
Argentina	0.7	0.9	1.0	0.9	0.9	0.8	0.7	0.7	0.7	0.7	0.6
Australia	32.6	35.3	39.5	41.2	43.9	45.4	45.9	45.5	47.5	49.3	49.5
Azerbaijan		0.1	0.1								
Bolivia											
Brazil	8.3	9.9	9.5	10.7	11.2	11.4	11.2	11.7	12.8	12.2	12.0
Canada	32.3	29.3	24.4	25.2	25.7	26.8	28.1	27.8	29.4	30.3	30.7
Chile	1.2	1.2	2.4	2.4	3.2	4.2	3.7	3.5	3.9	2.1	2.0
China	394.9	436.5	533.6	635.7	676.9	649.3	616.8	512.7	493.7	518.7	663.4
Colombia	3.0	2.9	3.5	3.4	3.2	3.1	2.8	2.1	2.2	3.3	2.0
Ecuador											
Egypt	0.7	0.7	0.8	0.7	0.9	0.9	0.9	0.9	0.9	0.8	0.8
Hong Kong, China	2.7	3.4	5.5	5.6	4.2	3.5	4.4	3.9	3.7	4.9	5.4
India	70.4	77.4	107.8	142.8	154.4	160.2	159.9	157.1	171.4	172.5	180.8
Indonesia	0.3	0.9	4.0	5.7	6.9	8.2	9.3	11.6	13.7	16.7	17.8
Israel											
Japan	69.9	73.7	76.0	86.2	88.3	89.8	88.4	91.5	98.9	103.0	105.3
Jordan											
Kazakhstan		38.1	40.2	27.5	25.9	22.4	22.9	19.8	23.2	22.5	21.7
Kuwait											
Malaysia	0.2	0.3	1.3	1.5	1.5	1.1	1.7	1.8	1.9	2.6	3.3
Mexico	2.9	3.1	3.4	4.9	5.7	5.8	5.9	6.0	6.2	6.8	7.0
Morocco				2.5	2.5	2.5	2.5	2.5	2.5	2.5	2.5
New Zealand	1.3	0.9	1.3	1.2	1.2	1.2	1.1	1.2	1.1	1.3	1.3
Nigeria											
Pakistan	1.2	1.3	2.1	2.2	2.2	2.1	2.1	2.1	2.0	2.1	2.1
Peru	0.1	0.2	0.2	0.4	0.3	0.4	0.4	0.5	0.5	0.4	0.4
Philippines	0.8	1.2	1.0	1.4	2.0	2.4	2.7	2.9	4.3	4.5	3.5
Saudi Arabia											
Singapore											
South Africa	64.3	66.2	71.3	77.4	81.7	84.3	83.4	82.3	81.9	80.7	81.8
South Korea	19.9	22.0	24.4	28.1	32.2	34.8	36.1	38.2	43.0	45.7	49.1
Taiwan	6.7	7.1	11.2	17.1	19.4	21.9	23.8	24.9	28.9	30.8	32.5
Thailand	0.8	1.6	3.7	7.1	8.7	8.7	7.3	7.9	7.8	8.8	8.6
Tunisia											
Turkmenistan		0.3	0.4								
United Arab Emirates											
USA	430.2	440.5	485.2	504.7	528.2	540.9	546.0	546.3	565.3	545.9	553.8
Venezuela	0.3	0.2	0.2	0.2	0.2	0.3	0.3	0.3	0.0		
Vietnam											

Source: BP Amoco, BP Statistical Review of World Energy
Notes: Million tonnes of oil equivalent = the amount of oil required to fuel an oil-fired plant in order to generate the same amount of electricity

| ◻ Primary Energy Consumption | | | | | | | | | | **Table 11.13** |

Consumption of Crude Oil 1982-2002

● Million metric tonnes

	1982	1985	1990	1995	1996	1997	1998	1999	2000	2001	2002
Algeria	6.2	8.0	9.2	8.4	8.1	8.0	8.2	8.1	8.5	8.8	8.7
Argentina	20.9	19.0	18.3	19.5	20.4	21.2	22.1	20.8	20.3	19.0	16.8
Australia	28.4	27.0	31.6	35.3	35.9	37.0	37.0	38.0	37.7	38.1	38.0
Azerbaijan		8.2	8.5	8.5	7.0	6.0	7.5	7.4	6.2	3.7	3.6
Bolivia											
Brazil	52.8	51.7	58.4	69.2	74.1	79.9	83.2	83.2	85.4	87.5	85.4
Canada	75.4	71.2	75.3	79.8	82.1	82.1	86.7	87.2	88.1	88.7	89.7
Chile	4.9	4.6	6.6	9.7	10.6	11.4	11.4	11.7	11.8	10.6	10.8
China	82.4	90.3	110.3	160.7	174.4	185.6	190.3	207.2	230.1	323.2	245.7
Colombia	7.7	7.7	9.5	11.8	12.2	12.3	12.0	10.6	10.5	11.1	10.0
Ecuador	3.6	4.1	4.2	5.1	5.7	6.5	6.6	6.0	5.8	5.9	5.9
Egypt	17.2	20.8	23.8	23.3	24.6	26.0	27.3	27.8	27.2	26.1	26.1
Hong Kong, China	6.7	5.2	6.3	9.5	9.3	9.2	8.8	9.3	9.7	11.7	13.1
India	35.4	43.3	57.9	73.0	79.4	83.3	86.8	95.2	97.5	96.7	97.7
Indonesia	22.2	22.0	29.8	39.1	42.4	45.9	43.5	46.8	50.4	52.1	51.2
Israel											
Japan	207.8	206.3	247.7	267.6	268.8	265.0	253.6	257.3	255.4	247.5	242.6
Jordan											
Kazakhstan		20.5	21.5	12.0	10.2	10.3	8.2	6.6	7.0	6.8	6.5
Kuwait	6.6	8.0	5.5	6.5	6.3	6.9	9.1	10.3	10.4	10.5	10.7
Malaysia	9.0	9.4	13.0	17.9	19.0	20.2	19.0	20.3	20.4	20.6	22.5
Mexico	53.7	57.8	67.7	71.4	73.8	77.3	81.2	80.8	84.1	83.4	80.9
Morocco											
New Zealand	3.9	3.8	4.9	5.8	5.9	6.1	6.1	6.3	6.3	6.4	6.8
Nigeria											
Pakistan	6.0	7.7	10.7	15.8	16.6	17.0	17.6	18.2	18.8	18.4	17.9
Peru	6.5	5.6	5.7	7.1	7.3	7.2	7.3	7.4	7.3	7.0	7.0
Philippines	9.8	7.4	11.5	16.8	17.5	18.8	19.1	18.0	16.6	16.5	15.6
Saudi Arabia	40.3	47.2	51.2	51.4	53.7	55.3	58.8	60.9	62.4	62.7	63.4
Singapore	10.7	12.0	23.3	32.0	30.3	32.4	33.3	31.6	33.5	36.4	35.5
South Africa	13.1	14.1	16.6	20.1	20.7	21.0	21.3	21.8	22.5	23.0	23.6
South Korea	23.7	26.1	49.5	94.8	101.4	111.4	93.9	100.7	103.2	103.1	105.0
Taiwan	17.4	16.8	26.8	34.7	34.8	36.0	37.2	39.9	39.8	39.2	38.8
Thailand	10.0	11.0	19.6	34.7	37.5	37.8	35.4	35.4	34.8	33.1	35.3
Tunisia											
Turkmenistan		4.8	4.4	3.9	3.0	3.0	2.8	2.5	2.3	2.4	2.6
United Arab Emirates	6.4	7.4	12.7	18.0	17.8	16.3	11.9	13.0	14.2	12.3	12.4
USA	705.5	720.2	781.8	807.7	836.5	848.0	863.8	888.9	897.6	896.1	984.3
Venezuela	19.2	17.2	18.4	20.0	19.0	20.4	21.6	21.3	22.5	22.2	22.9
Vietnam											

Source: *BP Amoco, BP Statistical Review of World Energy*

Consumption of Natural Gas 1982-2002

- Million tonnes of oil equivalent

	1982	1985	1990	1995	1996	1997	1998	1999	2000	2001	2002
Algeria	9.9	11.3	14.5	18.9	19.3	18.1	18.8	19.1	18.9	19.4	19.2
Argentina	12.3	14.4	18.3	24.3	25.7	25.7	27.5	29.1	29.9	28.1	27.2
Australia	10.9	12.4	16.5	17.6	17.9	17.6	18.3	17.8	19.1	21.4	21.6
Azerbaijan		12.2	14.2	7.2	5.3	5.0	4.7	5.0	4.9	7.0	7.1
Bolivia											
Brazil	1.1	2.4	3.4	4.3	5.0	5.4	5.6	6.4	8.2	10.5	12.3
Canada	48.9	44.8	55.6	63.8	66.9	67.3	63.3	65.4	69.8	74.5	72.6
Chile	0.6	0.7	1.5	1.5	1.5	2.5	2.9	4.1	4.7	5.7	5.9
China	9.5	11.5	13.2	15.9	15.9	17.4	17.4	19.3	22.1	25.0	27.0
Colombia	3.2	3.6	3.7	4.0	4.2	5.3	5.6	4.7	5.3	5.5	5.5
Ecuador	0.1	0.1	0.1	0.1	0.1	0.1	0.1	0.1	0.1	0.1	0.1
Egypt	2.0	3.7	6.1	9.9	10.2	10.4	10.8	12.9	16.5	19.3	20.4
Hong Kong, China					1.5	2.4	2.2	2.4	2.2	2.2	2.1
India	2.1	3.5	11.2	17.7	18.5	19.1	21.8	22.3	23.4	24.5	25.4
Indonesia	6.1	12.3	18.0	27.0	28.2	28.7	25.0	28.7	27.5	30.1	31.3
Israel											
Japan	24.7	35.9	46.1	55.0	59.5	58.6	62.5	67.1	68.6	71.1	69.7
Jordan											
Kazakhstan		7.8	11.3	9.7	8.1	6.4	6.5	7.1	8.7	9.1	8.7
Kuwait	3.3	3.8	5.6	8.4	8.4	8.3	8.5	7.8	8.6	8.6	7.8
Malaysia	0.8	2.4	6.8	12.4	14.3	15.0	15.7	16.7	18.3	23.2	24.3
Mexico	26.1	26.6	25.0	26.7	27.9	28.5	30.9	30.4	31.4	35.1	37.9
Morocco											
New Zealand	1.6	2.9	3.8	3.7	4.3	4.6	4.0	4.7	4.9	5.2	5.0
Nigeria					3.1						
Pakistan	7.0	7.3	10.1	13.1	13.8	14.0	14.4	15.6	17.0	17.9	18.8
Peru	0.7	0.5	0.4	0.4	0.4	0.2	0.4	0.4	0.3	0.3	0.4
Philippines										0.1	1.6
Saudi Arabia	10.8	16.9	30.2	38.6	40.1	41.3	42.0	41.6	44.8	48.3	50.8
Singapore				1.4	1.4	1.4	1.4	1.4	1.4	1.1	1.6
South Africa											
South Korea			3.0	9.2	12.2	14.8	13.8	16.8	18.9	20.8	23.6
Taiwan	1.1	1.0	1.7	3.9	4.0	4.6	5.7	5.6	6.2	6.7	7.7
Thailand	1.2	2.8	4.9	9.0	10.7	13.1	14.3	15.6	18.4	20.3	23.3
Tunisia					0.6						
Turkmenistan		7.8	8.8	7.2	9.0	9.1	9.2	10.2	11.3	11.6	11.9
United Arab Emirates	5.9	9.1	15.2	22.3	24.4	26.1	27.4	28.3	29.6	34.3	35.4
USA	462.6	449.4	486.3	558.5	568.5	567.8	552.8	559.6	582.4	578.2	600.7
Venezuela	14.3	15.6	19.8	24.8	26.8	27.7	29.1	24.7	25.1	26.2	24.6
Vietnam											

Source: BP Amoco, BP Statistical Review of World Energy
Notes: Million tonnes of oil equivalent = the amount of oil required to fuel an oil-fired plant in order to generate the same amount of electricity

Residential Consumption of Electricity 1984-2002

- '000 GWh

	1984	1985	1990	1995	1996	1997	1998	1999	2000	2001	2002
North America											
Canada					146.8	134.5	129.3	133.3	138.2	140.2	144.1
USA						1,075.8	1,127.7	1,144.9	1,193.4	1,156.7	1,175.7
Latin America											
Anguilla											
Antigua											
Argentina	9.6	9.7	11.1	16.6	17.6	18.5	19.2	20.6	21.4	22.5	23.2
Aruba											
Bahamas											
Barbados											
Belize											
Bermuda											
Bolivia	0.7	0.7	1.1	1.0	1.2	1.2	1.3	1.3	1.4	1.5	1.6
Brazil	30.9	32.6	48.7	63.5	69.1	74.1	79.4	81.3	83.5	84.7	86.7
British Virgin Islands											
Cayman Islands											
Chile	1.6	1.8	2.8	7.6	8.2	5.2	5.7	6.0	6.2	6.5	6.7
Colombia	8.8	9.3	12.6	14.6	14.7	14.7	14.7	11.6	11.1	10.8	10.3
Costa Rica	2.4	2.6	3.3	4.6	2.0	2.1	2.3	2.4	2.3	2.3	2.1
Cuba		3.4	4.1	3.2	3.4	3.7	3.9	4.1	4.5	4.9	5.3
Dominica											
Dominican Republic	2.8	3.2	3.3	4.9	3.6	3.6	4.0	4.5	4.7	4.8	4.9
Ecuador	1.3	1.4	1.8	2.6	2.7	2.7	2.9	2.9	2.8	2.7	2.6
El Salvador		0.5	0.7	1.0	1.1	1.2	1.2	1.4	1.3	1.3	1.2
French Guiana											
Grenada											
Guadeloupe											
Guatemala		0.5	0.7	1.1	1.2	1.1	1.1	1.3	1.4	1.4	1.5
Guyana											
Haiti	0.3	0.3	0.4	0.2	0.1	0.1	0.1	0.1	0.1	0.1	0.1
Honduras		0.4	0.6	0.9	0.9	1.0	1.1	1.2	1.3	1.4	1.5
Jamaica		0.2	0.2	0.7	0.8	0.8	0.9	0.9	0.9	0.9	0.9
Martinique											
Mexico						29.6	31.7	33.4	36.1	38.1	40.2
Netherlands Antilles											
Nicaragua		0.3	0.3	0.4	0.4	0.5	0.5	0.5	0.4	0.4	0.3
Panama	2.1	2.0	2.2	2.9	2.3	2.5	2.7	1.0	1.1	1.0	1.0
Paraguay	1.1	1.1	2.1	3.7	2.2	1.7	1.8	1.9	2.0	2.1	2.3
Peru	2.9	3.2	3.8	4.8	4.4	5.0	5.3	5.9	6.3	6.5	6.9
Puerto Rico											
St Kitts											
St Lucia											
St Vincent and the Grenadines											
Suriname											
Trinidad and Tobago		0.8	0.8	1.0	1.0	1.0	1.1	1.6	1.8	1.9	2.1
Uruguay		1.5	1.8	2.2	2.4	2.5	2.6	2.9	2.9	3.0	3.0
Venezuela	8.1	7.8	9.5	12.4	12.8	13.7	14.5	15.2	15.2	15.0	15.0

Source: Euromonitor from OECD

◻ Residential Consumption of Electricity

Residential Consumption of Electricity 1984-2002

• '000 GWh

	1984	1985	1990	1995	1996	1997	1998	1999	2000	2001	2002
Asia Pacific											
Afghanistan											
American Samoa											
Armenia				1.3	1.1	2.4	2.2	1.6	1.6	1.6	1.6
Azerbaijan					3.3	0.4	0.4	9.8	11.3	11.7	12.8
Bangladesh		0.3	0.6	1.1	1.3	1.3	1.4	1.5	1.7	1.8	2.0
Bhutan											
Brunei			0.3	0.5	0.5	0.5	0.5	0.5	0.5	0.5	0.5
Cambodia											
China	15.9	22.3	48.1	100.6	113.2	125.3	132.5	148.1	167.2	173.0	187.3
Fiji											
French Polynesia											
Guam											
Hong Kong, China	3.0	3.2	5.3	7.5	8.1	8.0	9.0	8.7	9.0	9.2	9.5
India	16.7	18.6	32.0	51.4	53.5	57.6	61.4	69.1	70.3	73.2	75.6
Indonesia	4.6	5.0	9.0	17.6	20.5	22.7	24.9	26.9	30.6	31.3	33.9
Japan						243.5	251.7	259.0	257.9	257.2	255.2
Kazakhstan					6.1	5.4	5.4	5.5	5.9	6.1	6.4
Kiribati											
Kyrgyzstan					1.7	1.6	1.6	1.9	2.4	2.8	3.3
Laos											
Macau											
Malaysia	2.4	2.6	4.0	7.0	8.6	10.2	10.2	10.3	11.3	11.4	12.2
Maldives											
Mongolia											
Myanmar	1.3	1.6	1.8	2.5	1.1	1.2	1.3	1.1	1.3	1.4	1.6
Nauru											
Nepal		0.3	0.2	0.2	0.3	0.4	0.4	0.5	0.5	0.5	0.5
New Caledonia											
North Korea								34.6	37.1	39.1	41.5
Pakistan	4.5	5.1	9.4	15.6	17.1	17.7	18.7	21.5	22.8	23.4	24.4
Papua New Guinea											
Philippines	4.2	4.5	5.7	6.9	9.1	10.1	11.5	12.4	12.9	13.2	13.7
Singapore	1.3	1.5	2.4	3.4	4.6	5.2	5.5	5.5	5.9	5.9	6.2
Solomon Islands											
South Korea	8.8	9.6	17.7	28.3	30.6	32.5	32.9	33.7	31.1	39.2	40.0
Sri Lanka		0.8	1.0	1.5	1.6	1.5	1.7	1.8	1.7	1.8	1.7
Taiwan						27.8	31.5	32.5	34.5	35.9	37.6
Tajikistan					0.3	2.4	2.6	3.0	2.9	2.7	2.6
Thailand	4.7	5.2	8.1	14.6	16.0	17.7	18.9	18.2	19.5	20.2	21.4
Tonga											
Turkmenistan					1.0	0.8	0.9	1.0	1.2	1.3	1.5
Tuvalu											
Uzbekistan				7.1	7.1	7.1	7.0	7.1	7.2	7.4	7.5
Vanuatu											
Vietnam		2.1	4.3	5.2	6.1	7.2	8.5	10.0	11.0	12.3	13.7
Western Samoa											
Australasia											
Australia						44.8	46.2	47.3	48.8	49.6	51.1
New Zealand						11.0	11.1	11.2	11.3	11.5	11.7

Source: Euromonitor from OECD

Residential Consumption of Electricity 1984-2002

● '000 GWh

	1984	1985	1990	1995	1996	1997	1998	1999	2000	2001	2002
Africa and Middle East											
Algeria	2.0	2.3	5.6	8.0	8.4	8.5	9.6	10.6	11.3	11.8	12.4
Angola					0.5	0.5	0.5	0.7	0.8	0.8	0.9
Bahrain					2.4	2.7	2.7	3.1	3.1	3.1	3.1
Benin			0.1	0.1	0.1	0.1	0.1	0.2	0.2	0.2	0.2
Botswana											
Burkina Faso											
Burundi											
Cameroon		0.4	0.4	0.4	0.4	0.4	0.5	0.4	0.4	0.4	0.4
Cape Verde											
Central African Republic											
Chad											
Comoros											
Congo Dem Rep		1.4	1.6	2.1	2.0	1.9	1.8	1.1	1.0	0.9	0.8
Congo-Brazzaville						0.1	0.1	0.1	0.1	0.1	0.1
Côte d'Ivoire	2.0	1.9	2.2		1.2	1.1	1.2	1.3	1.4	1.5	1.6
Djibouti											
Egypt	7.8	8.8	13.3	19.4	17.7	17.7	18.5	20.2	22.4	21.4	22.7
Equatorial Guinea											
Eritrea						0.1	0.1	0.1	0.1	0.1	0.1
Ethiopia		0.3	0.3	0.4	0.4	0.6	0.5	0.5	0.5	0.5	0.5
Gabon		0.2	0.2	0.2	0.2	0.3	0.3	0.2	0.2	0.2	0.2
Gambia											
Ghana		0.4	1.0	1.3	1.4	1.5	1.6	1.4	1.6	1.7	1.9
Guinea											
Guinea-Bissau											
Iran					22.2	26.5	28.7	29.8	31.3	32.4	33.8
Iraq											
Israel	3.3	3.5	5.3	6.9	8.6	9.5	10.2	10.2	11.7	12.8	14.1
Jordan	0.6	0.7	0.9	1.4	1.6	1.6	1.8	1.8	1.9	2.0	2.1
Kenya		0.6	0.8	1.1	1.1	1.1	1.2	0.9	0.8	0.8	0.7
Kuwait		7.3	10.1	20.8	21.7	18.2	20.4	21.5	22.1	22.9	23.6
Lebanon						3.7	3.0	2.9	2.9	3.0	3.1	3.2
Lesotho											
Liberia											
Libya											
Madagascar											
Malawi											
Mali											
Mauritania											
Mauritius											
Morocco	1.3	1.5	2.1	3.3	3.4	3.6	3.9	4.0	4.1	4.3	4.4
Mozambique					0.3	0.3	0.3	0.3	0.3	0.3	0.3
Namibia											
Niger											
Nigeria	2.9	3.3	3.7	5.0	5.1	5.3	5.4	5.2	5.4	5.6	5.8
Oman					5.5	3.3	3.7	3.8	4.0	4.3	4.6
Qatar	3.3	3.7	4.6	5.6	6.2						
Réunion											
Rwanda											
Sao Tomé e Príncipe											
Saudi Arabia	16.9	19.5	26.8	40.5	42.1	47.7	48.6	50.0	53.5	54.5	57.4
Senegal		0.2	0.2	0.2	0.2	0.2	0.2	0.3	0.4	0.4	0.5
Seychelles											
Sierra Leone											
Somalia											
South Africa					29.6	30.7	30.2	29.5	28.7	27.1	25.8
Sudan		0.6	0.6	0.8	0.8	0.7	0.6	1.0	1.0	1.1	1.1
Swaziland											
Syria					5.8	6.7	6.9	7.3	7.8	8.0	8.4
Tanzania					0.7	0.7	0.7	0.7	0.7	0.7	0.7
Togo						0.2	0.2	0.2	0.2	0.2	0.2
Tunisia	0.7	0.8	1.1	1.8	1.7	2.0	2.1	2.1	2.3	2.3	2.4
Uganda											
United Arab Emirates						11.5	12.2	11.8	12.5	12.6	13.1
Yemen											
Zambia		0.7	0.5	0.6	0.6	0.6	0.6	1.1	1.1	1.2	1.2
Zimbabwe		1.7	1.9	1.8	1.8	2.0	2.0	2.2	2.3	2.3	2.4

Source: Euromonitor from OECD

Environmental Data

☒ Air and Water Pollution

Table 12.1

Carbon Dioxide Emissions 2002

● '000 metric tonnes

	Fossil Fuels	Natural Gases	Coal	Petroleum
North America				
Canada	164,442.0	57,952.2	36,868.5	73,818.4
USA	1,618,303.4	366,635.8	584,455.7	667,716.4
Latin America				
Anguilla				
Antigua				110.3
Argentina	36,421.5	18,315.1	1,079.0	16,574.3
Aruba	98.4			143.4
Bahamas				1,115.8
Barbados	374.1	15.5		359.7
Belize	75.8			58.9
Bermuda				159.1
Bolivia	2,925.1	689.6		1,972.2
Brazil	101,004.9	9,247.4	14,922.3	76,011.5
British Virgin Islands				
Cayman Islands	93.5			91.7
Chile	14,991.6	4,118.8	2,825.5	8,994.5
Colombia	16,472.5	2,975.1	2,855.2	9,393.7
Costa Rica	1,411.7		0.3	1,379.5
Cuba	8,249.1	365.1	35.9	7,987.8
Dominica				22.6
Dominican Republic	3,829.8		40.5	3,568.2
Ecuador	5,746.5	558.9		5,007.5
El Salvador	1,494.0		0.8	1,493.2
French Guiana				236.8
Grenada	34.4			29.8
Guadeloupe	492.7			
Guatemala	2,760.9		201.3	2,370.7
Guyana				405.6
Haiti	427.1			
Honduras	1,518.8		129.0	1,322.7
Jamaica	3,205.0		47.7	3,133.0
Martinique	533.9			537.5
Mexico	102,775.2	18,926.4	5,991.3	78,947.8
Netherlands Antilles	3,230.7			
Nicaragua	1,071.9			
Panama	2,381.5		37.3	2,456.6
Paraguay	1,160.6		38.2	1,156.6
Peru	7,620.4	266.1	963.4	6,929.5
Puerto Rico	7,646.6		111.5	6,521.9
St Kitts				26.7
St Lucia	53.8			
St Vincent and the Grenadines	37.6			34.8
Suriname				423.0
Trinidad and Tobago	7,629.0	6,619.2		901.9
Uruguay	1,740.9	33.0	1.1	1,571.4
Venezuela	30,033.5	19,387.2	168.4	16,997.2

Source: *Energy Information Administration of the US Government, International Energy Annual*

□ Air and Water Pollution

Carbon Dioxide Emissions 2002

● '000 metric tonnes

	Fossil Fuels	Natural Gases	Coal	Petroleum
Asia Pacific				
Afghanistan	297.9	122.4	0.6	186.8
American Samoa				165.0
Armenia	1,028.8	804.0	1.2	208.2
Azerbaijan	14,724.1	6,857.6	0.5	6,226.6
Bangladesh	8,758.9	5,327.6	37.3	3,033.8
Bhutan	82.2		45.0	37.0
Brunei	1,203.4	645.1		460.8
Cambodia				141.1
China	718,995.8	18,660.8	491,053.1	185,199.7
Fiji	263.8		14.0	254.8
French Polynesia				200.5
Guam				918.5
Hong Kong, China	17,495.2	372.7	3,734.6	11,947.7
India	278,778.4	15,014.9	195,593.1	73,573.5
Indonesia	70,717.8	19,960.1	6,354.2	45,246.0
Japan	321,579.4	42,672.5	98,897.8	177,589.2
Kazakhstan	44,356.4	7,714.9	20,169.3	6,027.6
Kiribati				6.2
Kyrgyzstan	2,078.3	1,012.1	779.7	499.0
Laos	74.4		0.7	60.3
Macau				528.9
Malaysia	31,421.0	12,068.8	2,462.5	17,136.8
Maldives	86.7			80.5
Mongolia	1,579.3		1,169.5	374.8
Myanmar				
Nauru	46.4			46.4
Nepal	913.5		259.6	636.2
New Caledonia	547.7		109.6	402.5
North Korea	69,655.3		64,889.2	3,463.8
Pakistan	31,021.4	14,010.0	2,175.4	16,120.0
Papua New Guinea	824.0	58.6		720.9
Philippines	20,422.5	5.0	6,618.8	13,323.1
Singapore	33,350.5	798.5	1.1	34,110.9
Solomon Islands	30.7			
South Korea	130,644.9	11,272.8	57,368.3	66,034.3
Sri Lanka	2,632.0		0.4	2,471.8
Taiwan	76,268.3	3,942.8	36,438.3	34,027.2
Tajikistan	1,880.3	724.3	52.8	1,143.0
Thailand	46,401.8	9,310.3	9,738.0	24,259.2
Tonga	41.9			39.4
Turkmenistan	6,700.2	5,755.6	12.1	1,717.0
Tuvalu				
Uzbekistan	30,598.2	23,898.4	1,223.8	5,832.1
Vanuatu				15.4
Vietnam	11,855.9	945.8	4,012.1	6,982.1
Western Samoa	41.0			42.1
Australasia				
Australia	100,204.2	11,967.3	54,038.8	32,239.8
New Zealand	10,964.6	3,255.5	920.4	5,622.4

Source: *Energy Information Administration of the US Government, International Energy Annual*

□ Air and Water Pollution

Carbon Dioxide Emissions 2002

● '000 metric tonnes

Africa and Middle East	Fossil Fuels	Natural Gases	Coal	Petroleum
Algeria	22,284.9	15,713.0	484.1	7,460.4
Angola	3,714.2	2,404.6		1,216.5
Bahrain	5,972.5	4,516.1		1,304.3
Benin				163.5
Botswana	1,032.3		674.8	318.4
Burkina Faso	222.3			
Burundi	96.3			93.8
Cameroon	1,911.6	1,181.5	0.6	734.7
Cape Verde	40.3			37.2
Central African Republic	76.0			76.0
Chad				45.4
Comoros	25.9			
Congo Dem Rep	874.5	646.6		177.8
Congo-Brazzaville	1,096.0		177.7	817.1
Côte d'Ivoire	2,056.4	765.5		1,308.6
Djibouti	476.7			
Egypt	34,283.4	12,175.8	1,150.1	21,099.1
Equatorial Guinea	523.0	497.8		40.6
Eritrea				416.0
Ethiopia				966.8
Gabon	1,705.0	937.0		769.9
Gambia				57.9
Ghana	1,478.8		1.9	1,235.8
Guinea				343.4
Guinea-Bissau	78.3			82.7
Iran	81,833.1	40,056.7	1,247.2	39,231.6
Iraq	21,055.1	2,403.4		19,368.3
Israel	17,701.3	5.3	6,127.0	11,355.5
Jordan	4,116.8	165.1		4,000.6
Kenya	2,303.6		47.8	2,217.4
Kuwait	18,801.6	5,474.4		14,389.5
Lebanon	4,463.8		139.3	4,220.0
Lesotho	49.2			
Liberia	135.6			127.3
Libya	10,832.3	3,312.0	3.2	7,244.8
Madagascar	402.1		8.9	371.1
Malawi	213.6		40.7	190.5
Mali				162.7
Mauritania	762.5		1.7	842.5
Mauritius	641.3		38.2	620.9
Morocco	7,652.2	26.6	1,787.6	5,858.2
Mozambique	398.5	32.0	21.3	294.5
Namibia	251.4		4.2	302.7
Niger	315.9		97.3	209.9
Nigeria	20,843.5	10,460.0	43.3	11,453.6
Oman	6,275.4	4,092.7		2,187.9
Qatar	9,853.7	8,731.4		1,456.2
Réunion				458.0
Rwanda				204.7
Sao Tomé e Príncipe				19.8
Saudi Arabia	79,231.5	30,505.3		50,143.5
Senegal	1,321.5	18.3		1,421.6
Seychelles				136.9
Sierra Leone				253.0
Somalia				165.6
South Africa	101,385.0	808.0	85,196.3	21,343.5
Sudan				1,468.6
Swaziland	339.0		211.0	134.7
Syria	13,742.7	3,223.9	1.6	10,525.9
Tanzania	705.9		3.2	678.1
Togo	298.9			
Tunisia	5,323.1	2,093.6	106.4	3,152.9
Uganda				262.2
United Arab Emirates	30,636.6	18,698.6		15,223.2
Yemen	2,493.9			
Zambia	632.8		107.4	520.5
Zimbabwe	4,162.1		2,614.3	1,294.9

Source: Energy Information Administration of the US Government, International Energy Annual

Protection of Natural Areas 2002

- '000 hectares, number

	National Systems, Sites	Biosphere Reserves, Sites	Wetlands, Sites
North America			
Canada	937	6	36
USA	2,341	47	18
Latin America			
Anguilla			
Antigua			
Argentina	112	9	11
Aruba			
Bahamas			1
Barbados			
Belize	53		1
Bermuda			
Bolivia	31	3	7
Brazil	321	2	7
British Virgin Islands			
Cayman Islands			
Chile	87	7	7
Colombia	79	3	2
Costa Rica	130	2	10
Cuba		6	1
Dominica			
Dominican Republic	61		1
Ecuador	27	2	8
El Salvador	3		1
French Guiana			
Grenada			
Guadeloupe			
Guatemala	42	2	4
Guyana	1		
Haiti	8		
Honduras	72	1	4
Jamaica	143		1
Martinique			
Mexico	69	11	6
Netherlands Antilles			
Nicaragua	73	1	8
Panama	33	2	3
Paraguay	20	1	4
Peru	36	3	8
Puerto Rico			
St Kitts			
St Lucia			2
St Vincent and the Grenadines			
Suriname	18		1
Trinidad and Tobago	25		1
Uruguay	13	1	1
Venezuela	195	1	5

Source: Euromonitor from national statistics/World Resources Institute

	National Systems, Sites	Biosphere Reserves, Sites	Wetlands, Sites

▣ Conservation
Protection of Natural Areas 2002

● '000 hectares, number

	National Systems, Sites	Biosphere Reserves, Sites	Wetlands, Sites
Asia Pacific			
Afghanistan	7		
American Samoa			
Armenia	5		2
Azerbaijan	35		2
Bangladesh	10		2
Bhutan	10		
Brunei			
Cambodia	23	1	3
China	265	12	21
Fiji	15		
French Polynesia			
Guam			
Hong Kong, China			
India	345	3	6
Indonesia	170	6	3
Japan	65	4	13
Kazakhstan	73		
Kiribati			
Kyrgyzstan	78	2	
Laos	20		
Macau			
Malaysia	190		1
Maldives			
Mongolia	42	3	6
Myanmar	4		
Nauru			
Nepal	27		1
New Caledonia			
North Korea			
Pakistan	55	1	16
Papua New Guinea			2
Philippines	17	2	4
Singapore	5		
Solomon Islands			
South Korea	25	1	2
Sri Lanka	110	2	2
Taiwan			
Tajikistan	19		5
Thailand	112	3	6
Tonga			
Turkmenistan	23	1	
Tuvalu			
Uzbekistan	11	1	1
Vanuatu			
Vietnam	52	2	1
Western Samoa			
Australasia			
Australia	966	12	57
New Zealand	218		5

Source: *Euromonitor from national statistics/World Resources Institute*

◻ Conservation

Protection of Natural Areas 2002

- '000 hectares, number

	National Systems, Sites	Biosphere Reserves, Sites	Wetlands, Sites
Africa and Middle East			
Algeria	19	3	13
Angola	14		
Bahrain			2
Benin	5	1	2
Botswana	12		1
Burkina Faso	13	1	3
Burundi	13		1
Cameroon	18	3	
Cape Verde			
Central African Republic	14	2	
Chad	9		2
Comoros			1
Congo Dem Rep	43	3	2
Congo-Brazzaville	12	2	1
Côte d'Ivoire	12	2	1
Djibouti			
Egypt	13		2
Equatorial Guinea			
Eritrea	3		
Ethiopia	39		
Gabon	3	1	3
Gambia	6		1
Ghana	16	1	6
Guinea		2	12
Guinea-Bissau		1	1
Iran	78	9	
Iraq			
Israel	15	1	2
Jordan	11	1	1
Kenya	68	5	4
Kuwait	2		
Lebanon	3		4
Lesotho	1		
Liberia	2		
Libya	8		2
Madagascar	62	2	2
Malawi	9	1	1
Mali	13	1	3
Mauritania	9		2
Mauritius		1	1
Morocco	7	2	4
Mozambique	12		
Namibia	21		4
Niger	6	2	4
Nigeria	21	1	1
Oman	6		
Qatar			
Réunion			
Rwanda	6	1	
Sao Tomé e Príncipe			
Saudi Arabia	19		
Senegal	14	3	4
Seychelles			
Sierra Leone	6		1
Somalia	10		
South Africa	232	4	17
Sudan	27	2	
Swaziland		2	
Syria			1
Tanzania	98	3	3
Togo	9		2
Tunisia	6	4	1
Uganda	54	1	1
United Arab Emirates	2		
Yemen			
Zambia	77		2
Zimbabwe	68		

Source: *Euromonitor from national statistics/World Resources Institute*

Coastal Areas and Fresh Water Availability 2002

● As stated

	Length of Marine Coastline 2001 (km)	Extent of Territorial Sea 2001 (nautical miles)	Fresh Water Resources 2001 (cu m per capita)
North America			
Canada	243,791	12	89,903
USA	19,924	12	8,622
Latin America			
Anguilla	61	3	
Antigua	153		1,471
Argentina	4,989	12	25,510
Aruba	69	12	
Bahamas	3,542	12	
Barbados	97	12	375
Belize	386	12	66,666
Bermuda	103	12	
Bolivia			39,090
Brazil	4,791	12	43,438
British Virgin Islands	80	3	
Cayman Islands	160	12	
Chile	6,435	12	31,047
Colombia	3,208	12	53,635
Costa Rica	1,290	12	30,338
Cuba	3,735	12	3,542
Dominica	148	12	
Dominican Republic	1,288	6	2,551
Ecuador	2,237	200	36,634
El Salvador	307	200	2,662
French Guiana	378	12	
Grenada	121	12	
Guadeloupe	306	12	
Guatemala	400	12	12,235
Guyana	459	12	316,688
Haiti	1,771	12	1,540
Honduras	820	12	17,147
Jamaica	1,022	12	3,842
Martinique	350	12	
Mexico	9,330	12	4,634
Netherlands Antilles	364	12	
Nicaragua	910	200	37,560
Panama	2,490	200	50,602
Paraguay			16,168
Peru	2,414	200	73,652
Puerto Rico	501	12	
St Kitts			
St Lucia			
St Vincent and the Grenadines			
Suriname	386	12	479,616
Trinidad and Tobago	362	12	4,071
Uruguay	660	200	41,446
Venezuela	2,800	12	29,822

Source: Euromonitor from industry sources/national statistics

■ Conservation

Coastal Areas and Fresh Water Availability 2002

● As stated

	Length of Marine Coastline 2001 (km)	Extent of Territorial Sea 2001 (nautical miles)	Fresh Water Resources 2001 (cu m per capita)
Asia Pacific			
Afghanistan			
American Samoa	116	12	
Armenia			2,787
Azerbaijan			3,449
Bangladesh	580	12	8,681
Bhutan			118,012
Brunei	161	12	25,147
Cambodia	443	12	38,580
China	14,500	12	2,225
Fiji	1,129	12	
French Polynesia	2,525	12	
Guam	126	12	
Hong Kong, China	733	3	
India	7,000	12	1,844
Indonesia	54,716	12	13,758
Japan	29,751	12	3,372
Kazakhstan			7,644
Kiribati	1,143	12	
Kyrgyzstan			9,076
Laos			68,378
Macau	40		
Malaysia	4,675	12	25,898
Maldives	644	12	
Mongolia			17,609
Myanmar	1,930	12	20,880
Nauru	30	12	
Nepal			9,098
New Caledonia	2,254	12	
North Korea	2,495		3,520
Pakistan	1,046	12	1,783
Papua New Guinea	5,152	12	149,838
Philippines	36,289	100	6,561
Singapore	193	3	
Solomon Islands	5,313	12	
South Korea	2,413	12	1,463
Sri Lanka	1,340	12	2,733
Taiwan	1,448	12	
Tajikistan			12,851
Thailand	3,219	12	6,862
Tonga	419	12	
Turkmenistan			13,161
Tuvalu	24	12	
Uzbekistan			4,302
Vanuatu	2,528	12	
Vietnam	3,444	12	11,117
Western Samoa			
Australasia			
Australia	25,760	12	18,027
New Zealand	15,134	12	86,071

Source: *Euromonitor from industry sources/national statistics*

□ Conservation

Coastal Areas and Fresh Water Availability 2002

● As stated

	Length of Marine Coastline 2001 (km)	Extent of Territorial Sea 2001 (nautical miles)	Fresh Water Resources 2001 (cu m per capita)
Africa and Middle East			
Algeria	998	12	478
Angola	1,600	12	13,305
Bahrain	161	12	
Benin	121	200	3,799
Botswana			9,033
Burkina Faso			1,740
Burundi			524
Cameroon	402	50	17,535
Cape Verde	965	12	680
Central African Republic			36,419
Chad			5,379
Comoros	340	12	1,792
Congo Dem Rep	37	12	25,715
Congo-Brazzaville	169	200	263,043
Côte d'Ivoire	515	12	4,382
Djibouti	314	12	3,639
Egypt	2,450	12	1,159
Equatorial Guinea	296	12	65,645
Eritrea	2,234		2,046
Ethiopia			1,639
Gabon	885	12	130,029
Gambia	80	12	5,875
Ghana	539	12	2,661
Guinea	320	12	29,246
Guinea-Bissau	350	12	21,402
Iran	2,440	12	2,443
Iraq	58	12	5,084
Israel	273	12	707
Jordan	26	3	119
Kenya	536	12	981
Kuwait	499	12	
Lebanon	225	12	1,087
Lesotho			2,592
Liberia	579	200	74,121
Libya	1,770	12	151
Madagascar	4,828	12	21,346
Malawi			1,840
Mali			9,057
Mauritania	754	12	4,118
Mauritius	177	12	1,817
Morocco	1,835	12	1,020
Mozambique	2,470	12	11,445
Namibia	1,572	12	25,266
Niger			2,819
Nigeria	853	30	2,124
Oman	2,092	12	409
Qatar	563	12	170
Réunion	201	12	
Rwanda			708
Sao Tomé e Príncipe	209	12	14,864
Saudi Arabia	2,640	12	112
Senegal	531	12	3,955
Seychelles	491	12	
Sierra Leone	402	200	31,178
Somalia	3,025	200	1,788
South Africa	2,798	12	1,139
Sudan	853	12	4,599
Swaziland			4,306
Syria	193	35	2,630
Tanzania	1,424	12	2,538
Togo	56	30	2,605
Tunisia	1,148	12	391
Uganda			2,863
United Arab Emirates	1,318	12	65
Yemen	1,906	12	226
Zambia			11,079
Zimbabwe			876

Source: Euromonitor from industry sources/national statistics

Table 12.4

▣ Deforestation

World Forest Statistics 2000

● '000 hectares, unless otherwise stated

	Total Land Area 2000	Total Forest Land 1995	Total Forest Land 2000	Total % Increase/ Decrease 1995-2000	Annual Average % Increase/ Decrease 1995-2000	Forest as % of Land Area 2000
North America						
Canada	922,097	244,356	244,356	0.00	0.00	26.5
USA	915,896	224,395	226,226	0.82	0.16	24.7
Latin America						
Anguilla						
Antigua	44	9	9	0.00	0.00	20.5
Argentina	273,669	36,124	34,756	-3.79	-0.76	12.7
Aruba	19					
Bahamas	1,001	842	842	0.00	0.00	84.1
Barbados	43	2	2	0.00	0.00	4.7
Belize	2,280	1,525	1,347	-11.66	-2.33	59.1
Bermuda	5					
Bolivia	108,438	53,839	53,026	-1.51	-0.30	48.9
Brazil	845,651	543,754	532,760	-2.02	-0.40	63.0
British Virgin Islands	34	6	6	0.00	0.00	17.6
Cayman Islands	26	13	13	0.00	0.00	50.0
Chile	74,880	15,613	15,500	-0.72	-0.14	20.7
Colombia	103,870	50,585	49,650	-1.85	-0.37	47.8
Costa Rica	5,106	2,045	1,966	-3.87	-0.77	38.5
Cuba	10,982	2,213	2,350	6.20	1.24	21.4
Dominica	75	48	46	-4.17	-0.83	61.3
Dominican Republic	4,838	1,374	1,374	0.00	0.00	28.4
Ecuador	27,684	11,240	10,548	-6.16	-1.23	38.1
El Salvador	2,072	156	120	-23.15	-4.63	5.8
French Guiana	8,815	7,954	7,926	-0.35	-0.07	89.9
Grenada	34	5	5	0.00	0.00	14.7
Guadeloupe	169	83	82	-1.20	-0.24	48.5
Guatemala	10,843	3,117	2,852	-8.52	-1.70	26.3
Guyana	19,685	17,116	16,870	-1.44	-0.29	85.7
Haiti	2,756	123	88	-28.06	-5.61	3.2
Honduras	11,189	5,678	5,382	-5.22	-1.04	48.1
Jamaica	1,083	352	325	-7.70	-1.54	30.0
Martinique	106		47			44.3
Mexico	190,869	58,311	55,161	-5.40	-1.08	28.9
Netherlands Antilles	80	1	1	0.00	0.00	1.3
Nicaragua	12,140	3,867	3,278	-15.23	-3.05	27.0
Panama	7,443	3,134	2,873	-8.31	-1.66	38.6
Paraguay	39,730	23,977	23,361	-2.57	-0.51	58.8
Peru	128,000	66,496	65,152	-2.02	-0.40	50.9
Puerto Rico	887	232	229	-1.17	-0.23	25.8
St Kitts	36	4	4	0.00	0.00	11.1
St Lucia	61	12	9	-21.74	-4.35	14.8
St Vincent and the Grenadines	39	7	6	-7.69	-1.54	15.4
Suriname	15,600	14,118	14,118	0.00	0.00	90.5
Trinidad and Tobago	513	270	259	-4.07	-0.81	50.5
Uruguay	17,502	1,041	1,295	24.36	4.87	7.4
Venezuela	88,205	50,586	49,483	-2.18	-0.44	56.1

Source: *UN Food and Agriculture Organisation*

¤ Deforestation
World Forest Statistics 2000

● '000 hectares, unless otherwise stated

Asia Pacific	Total Land Area 2000	Total Forest Land 1995	Total Forest Land 2000	Total % Increase/ Decrease 1995-2000	Annual Average % Increase/ Decrease 1995-2000	Forest as % of Land Area 2000
Afghanistan	65,209	1,369	1,351	-1.34	-0.27	2.1
American Samoa	20	12	12	0.00	0.00	60.0
Armenia	2,820	330	351	6.38	1.28	12.4
Azerbaijan	8,660	1,026	1,094	6.61	1.32	12.6
Bangladesh	13,017	1,250	1,334	6.75	1.35	10.2
Bhutan	4,700	3,017	3,016	-0.05	-0.01	64.2
Brunei	527	447	442	-1.15	-0.23	83.9
Cambodia	17,652	9,620	9,335	-2.97	-0.59	52.9
China	932,742	154,369	163,480	5.90	1.18	17.5
Fiji	1,827	823	815	-1.01	-0.20	44.6
French Polynesia	366	105	105	0.00	0.00	28.7
Guam	55	21	21	0.00	0.00	38.2
Hong Kong, China	99					
India	297,319	63,924	64,113	0.30	0.06	21.6
Indonesia	181,157	111,593	104,986	-5.92	-1.18	58.0
Japan	36,450	24,079	24,081	0.01	0.00	66.1
Kazakhstan	269,970	10,934	12,148	11.11	2.22	4.5
Kiribati	73	28	28	0.00	0.00	38.4
Kyrgyzstan	19,180	882	1,003	13.68	2.74	5.2
Laos	23,080	12,821	12,561	-2.03	-0.41	54.4
Macau	2					
Malaysia	32,855	20,469	19,292	-5.75	-1.15	58.7
Maldives	30	1	1	0.00	0.00	3.3
Mongolia	156,650	10,966	10,652	-2.86	-0.57	6.8
Myanmar	65,755	36,987	34,390	-7.02	-1.40	52.3
Nauru	2					
Nepal	14,300	4,290	3,904	-9.00	-1.80	27.3
New Caledonia	1,828	373	373	0.00	0.00	20.4
North Korea	12,041	8,212	8,212	0.00	0.00	68.2
Pakistan	77,088	2,621	2,467	-5.88	-1.18	3.2
Papua New Guinea	45,286	31,179	30,613	-1.82	-0.36	67.6
Philippines	29,817	6,232	5,785	-7.18	-1.44	19.4
Singapore	61	2	2	0.00	0.00	3.3
Solomon Islands	2,799	2,558	2,536	-0.88	-0.18	90.6
South Korea	9,873	6,274	6,250	-0.39	-0.08	63.3
Sri Lanka	6,463	2,113	1,939	-8.26	-1.65	30.0
Taiwan						
Tajikistan	14,060	387	394	1.81	0.36	2.8
Thailand	51,089	15,327	14,765	-3.67	-0.73	28.9
Tonga	72	4	4	0.00	0.00	5.6
Turkmenistan	46,993	3,759	3,759	0.00	0.00	8.0
Tuvalu	3					
Uzbekistan	41,424	1,947	1,988	2.13	0.43	4.8
Vanuatu	1,219	444	447	0.70	0.14	36.7
Vietnam	32,549	9,569	9,830	2.72	0.54	30.2
Western Samoa	283	117	105	-10.56	-2.11	37.1
Australasia						
Australia	768,230	158,255	158,255	0.00	0.00	20.6
New Zealand	26,799	7,758	7,959	2.59	0.52	29.7

Source: UN Food and Agriculture Organisation

⬛ Deforestation

World Forest Statistics 2000

● '000 hectares, unless otherwise stated

Africa and Middle East	Total Land Area 2000	Total Forest Land 1995	Total Forest Land 2000	Total % Increase/ Decrease 1995-2000	Annual Average % Increase/ Decrease 1995-2000	Forest as % of Land Area 2000
Algeria	238,174	2,024	2,145	5.95	1.19	0.9
Angola	124,670	70,376	69,756	-0.88	-0.18	56.0
Bahrain	71					
Benin	11,062	3,003	2,650	-11.76	-2.35	24.0
Botswana	56,673	13,006	12,427	-4.46	-0.89	21.9
Burkina Faso	27,360	7,168	7,089	-1.11	-0.22	25.9
Burundi	2,568	168	94	-44.12	-8.82	3.7
Cameroon	46,540	24,969	23,858	-4.45	-0.89	51.3
Cape Verde	403	60	85	41.67	8.33	21.1
Central African Republic	62,298	23,081	22,907	-0.76	-0.15	36.8
Chad	125,920	13,096	12,692	-3.08	-0.62	10.1
Comoros	223	10	8	-20.00	-4.00	3.6
Congo Dem Rep	226,705	137,837	135,207	-1.91	-0.38	59.6
Congo-Brazzaville	34,150	22,146	22,060	-0.39	-0.08	64.6
Côte d'Ivoire	31,800	8,443	7,117	-15.70	-3.14	22.4
Djibouti	2,318	7	6	-14.29	-2.86	0.3
Egypt	99,545	100	72	-27.64	-5.53	0.1
Equatorial Guinea	2,805	1,805	1,752	-2.94	-0.59	62.5
Eritrea	10,100	1,611	1,586	-1.57	-0.31	15.7
Ethiopia	100,000	4,800	4,593	-4.31	-0.86	4.6
Gabon	25,767	21,876	21,826	-0.23	-0.05	84.7
Gambia	1,000	459	481	4.91	0.98	48.1
Ghana	22,754	6,929	6,335	-8.57	-1.71	27.8
Guinea	24,572	7,101	6,929	-2.42	-0.48	28.2
Guinea-Bissau	2,812	2,296	2,188	-4.72	-0.94	77.8
Iran	163,620	7,299	7,299	0.00	0.00	4.5
Iraq	43,737	787	799	1.49	0.30	1.8
Israel	2,062	107	132	23.13	4.63	6.4
Jordan	8,893	89	86	-3.26	-0.65	1.0
Kenya	56,914	17,558	17,096	-2.63	-0.53	30.0
Kuwait	1,782	5	5	11.11	2.22	0.3
Lebanon	1,023	36	36	-0.83	-0.17	3.5
Lesotho	3,035	15	15	0.00	0.00	0.5
Liberia	9,632	3,858	3,481	-9.76	-1.95	36.1
Libya	175,954	352	358	1.73	0.35	0.2
Madagascar	58,154	12,329	11,747	-4.72	-0.94	20.2
Malawi	9,408	2,954	2,562	-13.27	-2.65	27.2
Mali	122,019	13,666	13,186	-3.51	-0.70	10.8
Mauritania	102,522	359	317	-11.65	-2.33	0.3
Mauritius	203	17	16	-3.03	-0.61	7.9
Morocco	44,630	3,035	3,025	-0.32	-0.06	6.8
Mozambique	78,409	30,893	30,601	-0.95	-0.19	39.0
Namibia	82,329	8,439	8,040	-4.72	-0.94	9.8
Niger	126,670	1,583	1,328	-16.13	-3.23	1.0
Nigeria	91,077	15,483	13,517	-12.70	-2.54	14.8
Oman	30,950	1	1	0.00	0.00	0.0
Qatar	1,100	1	1	66.67	13.33	0.1
Réunion	250	85	71	-15.98	-3.20	28.4
Rwanda	2,467	381	307	-19.46	-3.89	12.4
Sao Tomé e Príncipe	96	27	27	0.00	0.00	28.1
Saudi Arabia	214,969	1,505	1,504	-0.05	-0.01	0.7
Senegal	19,253	6,431	6,205	-3.51	-0.70	32.2
Seychelles	45	30	30	0.00	0.00	66.7
Sierra Leone	7,162	1,235	1,055	-14.60	-2.92	14.7
Somalia	62,734	7,905	7,515	-4.93	-0.99	12.0
South Africa	122,104	8,975	8,917	-0.64	-0.13	7.3
Sudan	237,600	66,409	61,627	-7.20	-1.44	25.9
Swaziland	1,720	493	522	5.93	1.19	30.3
Syria	18,378	460	461	0.33	0.07	2.5
Tanzania	88,359	39,276	38,811	-1.18	-0.24	43.9
Togo	5,439	615	510	-17.02	-3.40	9.4
Tunisia	15,536	505	510	1.01	0.20	3.3
Uganda	19,710	4,652	4,190	-9.92	-1.98	21.3
United Arab Emirates	8,360	280	321	14.60	2.92	3.8
Yemen	52,797	502	449	-10.49	-2.10	0.9
Zambia	74,339	35,497	31,246	-11.98	-2.40	42.0
Zimbabwe	38,685	20,638	19,040	-7.74	-1.55	49.2

Source: *UN Food and Agriculture Organisation*

Foreign Trade

■ Imports

Table 13.1

Total Imports (cif) 1977-2002 (US$)

- US$ million

	1977	1980	1985	1990	1991	1992	1993	1994
North America								
Canada	42,083	62,544	80,640	123,244	124,782	129,262	139,035	155,072
USA	160,411	256,984	352,463	516,987	508,363	553,923	603,438	689,215
Latin America								
Anguilla								
Antigua	34	88	166	255	295	312	323	342
Argentina	4,162	10,541	3,814	4,076	8,275	14,872	16,784	21,527
Aruba				536	481			
Bahamas	3,568	7,546	3,078	1,112	1,091	1,038	954	1,056
Barbados	273	525	611	704	699	524	577	614
Belize	90	150	128	211	256	274	281	260
Bermuda	204	343			510	562	534	551
Bolivia	618	665	691	687	970	1,090	1,206	1,209
Brazil	13,257	24,961	14,332	22,524	22,950	23,068	27,740	35,997
British Virgin Islands								
Cayman Islands	43	103	36	288	268	69	59	53
Chile	2,539	5,797	3,072	7,742	8,207	10,183	11,134	11,820
Colombia	1,880	4,739	4,141	5,590	4,906	6,516	9,832	11,883
Costa Rica	1,021	1,540	1,098	1,990	1,877	2,441	3,515	3,789
Cuba								
Dominica	22	48	55	118	110	105	94	96
Dominican Republic	975	1,640	1,487	2,062	1,988	2,501	2,436	3,440
Ecuador	1,189	2,253	1,767	1,865	2,399	2,431	2,562	3,622
El Salvador	929	966	961	1,263	1,406	1,699	1,912	2,249
French Guiana	144	255	257	786	770	671	522	676
Grenada	32	50	69	106	124	107	118	119
Guadeloupe	375	679	646	1,677	1,644	1,518	1,394	1,480
Guatemala	1,053	1,598	1,175	1,649	1,851	2,532	2,599	2,781
Guyana	314	396	226	311	307	443	484	506
Haiti	213	375	442	332	400	278	355	252
Honduras	575	1,009	888	935	955	1,037	1,130	1,056
Jamaica	860	1,171	1,111	1,928	1,823	1,676	2,132	2,224
Martinique	428	843	682	1,710	1,602	1,750	1,557	1,629
Mexico	5,489	22,144	19,116	43,548	52,315	65,050	68,439	83,075
Netherlands Antilles	3,128	5,676	1,388	2,141	2,139	1,868	1,947	1,758
Nicaragua	762	887	964	637	751	855	744	870
Panama	861	1,449	1,392	1,539	1,695	2,024	2,188	2,404
Paraguay	308	615	502	1,352	1,460	1,422	1,689	2,140
Peru	1,911	2,499	1,835	3,470	4,195	4,861	4,859	6,691
Puerto Rico								
St Kitts	22	45	51	110	110	95	118	128
St Lucia	59	124	125	271	295	306	300	303
St Vincent and the Grenadines	30	57	79	136	140	132	134	130
Suriname	398	504	299	472	509	542	986	423
Trinidad and Tobago	1,819	3,178	1,534	1,109	1,667	1,104	1,463	1,131
Uruguay	730	1,680	708	1,343	1,637	2,045	2,326	2,786
Venezuela	10,938	11,827	8,106	7,335	11,147	14,066	12,511	9,187

Source: *Euromonitor from International Monetary Fund (IMF), International Financial Statistics*

Imports

Total Imports (cif) 1977-2002 (US$) (continued)

• US$ million

	1995	1996	1997	1998	1999	2000	2001	2002
North America								
Canada	168,041	174,959	200,873	206,066	220,183	244,786	227,291	227,499
USA	770,852	822,025	899,019	944,353	1,059,440	1,259,300	1,179,180	1,202,430
Latin America								
Anguilla								
Antigua	346	365	370	385	414	436	419	434
Argentina	20,122	23,762	30,450	31,404	25,508	25,280	20,320	8,990
Aruba	567	578	614	815	782	835	841	841
Bahamas	1,243	1,366	1,666	1,873	1,772	1,764	1,742	1,614
Barbados	771	834	996	1,010	1,108	1,156	1,087	1,039
Belize	257	255	286	295	370	452	434	532
Bermuda	550	569	619	629	712	719	772	787
Bolivia	1,424	1,635	1,851	1,983	1,755	1,830	1,708	1,770
Brazil	53,783	56,947	64,996	60,652	51,759	58,631	58,351	49,577
British Virgin Islands								
Cayman Islands	63	57	55	47	80	72	105	115
Chile	15,900	19,123	20,825	19,880	15,988	18,507	17,814	17,093
Colombia	13,853	13,684	15,378	14,635	10,659	11,539	12,834	12,738
Costa Rica	4,036	4,300	4,924	6,230	6,320	6,372	6,564	7,188
Cuba	2,825	3,205	3,987	4,181	4,301	4,900	4,959	5,256
Dominica	117	130	125	132	138	148	131	115
Dominican Republic	3,639	4,118	4,821	5,631	5,988	7,379	7,506	8,424
Ecuador	4,153	3,935	4,955	5,576	3,017	3,721	5,363	6,431
El Salvador	2,853	2,671	2,981	3,121	3,140	3,795	3,866	3,907
French Guiana								
Grenada	124	152	173	200	210	206	221	235
Guadeloupe	1,887							
Guatemala	3,293	3,146	3,852	4,651	4,382	4,791	5,607	6,078
Guyana	528	598	630	548	520	587	583	563
Haiti	653	665	648	797	1,025	1,036	1,013	1,130
Honduras	1,643	1,840	2,149	2,535	2,676	2,855	2,918	2,979
Jamaica	2,818	2,965	3,131	3,035	2,899	3,326	3,360	3,533
Martinique	1,958							
Mexico	75,858	93,674	114,847	130,948	148,648	182,702	176,185	176,607
Netherlands Antilles	1,522	1,269	1,488	1,169	1,360	1,290	1,362	1,347
Nicaragua	993	1,154	1,450	1,492	1,862	1,805	1,779	1,795
Panama	2,511	2,780	3,002	3,398	3,516	3,379	2,964	2,982
Paraguay	2,782	2,850	3,099	2,471	1,725	2,050	1,989	2,048
Peru	9,224	9,473	10,264	9,867	8,075	8,797	7,647	7,161
Puerto Rico	18,817	22,696	21,423	21,854	23,364	28,029	28,143	30,219
St Kitts	133	149	149	155	170	178	180	189
St Lucia	306	313	332	335	355	355	355	267
St Vincent and the Grenadines	136	132	188	193	201	163	186	174
Suriname	585	501	658	552	298	246	213	163
Trinidad and Tobago	1,714	2,144	2,990	2,999	2,741	3,308	3,569	3,643
Uruguay	2,867	3,323	3,727	3,811	3,357	3,466	3,061	2,924
Venezuela	12,650	9,880	14,607	15,818	14,064	16,213	18,022	11,840

Source: Euromonitor from International Monetary Fund (IMF), International Financial Statistics

Imports

Total Imports (cif) 1977-2002 (US$) (continued)

- US$ million

	1977	1980	1985	1990	1991	1992	1993	1994
Asia Pacific								
Afghanistan	328	841	1,194	936	634	426	740	142
American Samoa	55	95	296	360	372	418	460	492
Armenia						206	254	394
Azerbaijan						998	636	778
Bangladesh	1,163	2,599	2,542	3,618	3,412	3,732	3,994	4,602
Bhutan		50	84	81	83	125	90	92
Brunei								
Cambodia								
China	7,148	19,941	42,252	53,345	63,791	80,585	103,959	115,614
Fiji	307	562	442	754	652	630	720	829
French Polynesia	327	547	549	928	914	894	918	871
Guam	269	400	350	410	420	680	583	667
Hong Kong, China	10,446	22,447	29,703	82,490	100,240	123,407	138,650	161,841
India	6,647	14,864	15,928	23,580	20,448	23,579	22,788	26,843
Indonesia	6,230	10,834	10,259	21,837	25,869	27,280	28,328	31,983
Japan	71,340	141,296	130,488	235,368	236,999	233,246	241,624	275,235
Kazakhstan							3,887	3,561
Kiribati	11	16	31	44	43	69	28	26
Kyrgyzstan						418	430	316
Laos	14	92	193	185	170	270	432	564
Macau	198	544	773	1,539	1,852	1,968	2,025	2,001
Malaysia	4,542	10,779	12,253	29,258	36,649	39,855	45,650	59,600
Maldives	10	29	53	137	161	189	191	222
Mongolia		548	1,096	924	361	418	379	258
Myanmar	242	357	286	273	652	658	822	891
Nauru	10				21	20	20	20
Nepal	168	342	453	672	737	776	890	1,155
New Caledonia	292	456	342	883	865	915	919	865
North Korea					2,760	1,710	1,640	1,620
Pakistan	2,458	5,376	5,918	7,411	8,479	9,423	9,545	8,931
Papua New Guinea	642	1,176	1,008	1,193	1,614	1,485	1,299	1,522
Philippines	4,270	8,291	5,455	13,004	12,862	15,497	18,688	22,641
Singapore	10,471	24,007	26,285	60,774	66,095	72,171	85,234	102,670
Solomon Islands	33	89	83	91	112	112	137	139
South Korea	10,811	22,292	31,136	69,844	81,525	81,775	83,800	102,348
Sri Lanka	701	2,057	1,988	2,688	3,055	3,500	4,005	4,767
Taiwan	8,522	19,764	20,124	54,831	63,078	72,181	77,099	85,507
Tajikistan								
Thailand	4,617	9,214	9,242	33,045	37,569	40,686	46,077	54,459
Tonga	20	38	41	62	59	63	61	69
Turkmenistan								
Tuvalu								
Uzbekistan								
Vanuatu	40	73	70	96	83	82	79	89
Vietnam								
Western Samoa	41	63	51	81	94	110	105	81
Australasia								
Australia	13,511	22,399	25,890	41,985	41,648	43,807	45,577	53,425
New Zealand	3,361	5,472	5,992	9,501	8,381	9,201	9,636	11,913

Source: Euromonitor from International Monetary Fund (IMF), International Financial Statistics

Total Imports (cif) 1977-2002 (US$) (continued)

• US$ million

	1995	1996	1997	1998	1999	2000	2001	2002
Asia Pacific								
Afghanistan	50	500	436	373	411	550	551	700
American Samoa	200	228	271	247	188	222	239	285
Armenia	674	856	892	902	800	882	874	991
Azerbaijan	668	961	794	1,077	1,036	1,059	1,314	1,508
Bangladesh	6,502	6,621	6,898	6,974	7,694	8,360	8,350	7,914
Bhutan	112	128	137	134	182	188	156	164
Brunei	2,078				1,034	1,111	1,030	1,033
Cambodia	631		1,116	1,129	1,243	1,424	1,456	1,561
China	132,084	138,833	142,370	140,237	165,699	225,094	243,553	295,171
Fiji	892	987	965	722	903	825	794	772
French Polynesia	1,008	1,020	935	1,018	926	976	1,057	1,276
Guam	516	506	443	659	459	554	673	389
Hong Kong, China	192,751	198,550	208,614	184,518	179,520	212,805	201,076	207,644
India	34,707	37,942	41,432	42,980	46,979	51,523	50,392	56,517
Indonesia	40,630	42,929	41,694	27,337	24,003	33,515	31,010	25,388
Japan	335,882	349,152	338,754	280,484	311,262	379,511	349,089	337,194
Kazakhstan	3,807	4,241	4,301	4,314	3,655	5,040	6,446	6,584
Kiribati	35	38	39	32	33	37	31	73
Kyrgyzstan	522	838	709	842	615	559	472	592
Laos	589	690	706	553	525	535	528	431
Macau	2,042	2,000	2,082	1,955	2,040	2,255	2,386	2,530
Malaysia	77,691	78,418	79,030	58,272	65,389	81,963	73,866	79,869
Maldives	268	302	349	354	402	389	393	392
Mongolia	415	451	468	503	513	615	630	626
Myanmar	1,348	1,371	2,056	2,695	2,323	2,401	2,877	2,348
Nauru	28	26	15	11	13	27	21	25
Nepal	1,333	1,398	1,693	1,246	1,422	1,573	1,473	1,419
New Caledonia	951	990		928	1,009	925	983	1,005
North Korea	1,270	1,423	1,473	1,170	1,212	1,686	1,847	1,782
Pakistan	11,515	12,189	11,650	9,330	10,297	10,864	10,191	11,233
Papua New Guinea	1,452	1,741	1,711	1,240	1,233	1,151	1,073	1,103
Philippines	28,341	34,126	38,622	31,496	32,568	37,027	34,921	37,180
Singapore	124,507	131,338	132,437	104,719	111,060	134,545	116,000	116,448
Solomon Islands	154	151	151	130	110	125	108	100
South Korea	135,119	150,339	144,616	93,282	119,725	160,481	141,098	152,126
Sri Lanka	5,306	5,442	5,864	5,905	5,961	7,177	5,973	6,105
Taiwan	103,698	101,287	113,924	104,946	110,957	139,927	107,274	112,758
Tajikistan	628	770	750	711	663	674	775	785
Thailand	70,786	72,332	62,854	42,971	50,342	61,924	62,058	64,658
Tonga	77	75	73	69	73	69	73	68
Turkmenistan	1,364	1,011	1,183	1,008	1,478	1,785	2,105	2,479
Tuvalu								
Uzbekistan	2,748	4,712	4,186	3,125	2,841	2,810	2,715	2,456
Vanuatu	95	98	94	88	96	57	80	80
Vietnam	11,803	13,520	14,165	17,083	11,636	15,636	16,000	17,019
Western Samoa	95	100	97	97	115	106	130	113
Australasia								
Australia	61,283	65,427	65,892	64,630	69,158	71,529	63,888	72,690
New Zealand	13,957	14,724	14,519	12,495	14,299	13,906	13,347	15,077

Source: Euromonitor from International Monetary Fund (IMF), International Financial Statistics

◻ Imports

Total Imports (cif) 1977-2002 (US$) (continued)

- US$ million

	1977	1980	1985	1990	1991	1992	1993	1994
Africa and Middle East								
Algeria	7,125	10,559	9,841	9,770	7,770	8,310	7,990	9,154
Angola						626	214	138
Bahrain	2,029	3,483	3,107	3,712	4,115	4,263	3,858	3,748
Benin	268	331	331	265	241	578	571	431
Botswana	286	693	672	1,947	1,941	1,888	1,766	1,640
Burkina Faso	209	359	332	536	533	466	509	349
Burundi	74	168	186	231	255	221	196	225
Cameroon	735	1,602	1,151	1,400	1,173	1,163	885	717
Cape Verde	38	68	86	136	147	180	154	209
Central African Republic	63	81	113	154	93	145	126	139
Chad	189	74	166	286	250	243	201	177
Comoros	16	29	36	52	58	69	59	53
Congo Dem Rep	203	278	792	888	711	420	372	382
Congo-Brazzaville	208	562	598	621	594	451	582	631
Côte d'Ivoire	1,756	2,991	1,749	2,098	2,103	2,352	2,115	1,917
Djibouti	107	213	201	215	214	219	211	196
Egypt	4,815	4,860	11,104	16,783	8,052	8,325	8,214	10,219
Equatorial Guinea	10	26	20	61	67	56	60	37
Eritrea								
Ethiopia	352	722	993	1,081	472	839	787	1,033
Gabon	716	674	855	918	834	700	845	756
Gambia	78	165	93	188	202	218	260	212
Ghana	1,038	1,129	866		1,055	2,169	3,942	2,109
Guinea	247			699				
Guinea-Bissau	37	55		86	76	96	61	164
Iran	14,070	12,246	11,635	20,322	27,927	25,860	21,427	13,774
Iraq	4,481	7,477	10,556		540	870	700	620
Israel	5,787	9,784	9,875	16,794	18,658	15,535	22,624	25,237
Jordan	1,381	2,402	2,733	2,600	2,508	3,255	3,539	3,382
Kenya	1,289	2,125	1,436	2,223	1,935	1,841	1,774	2,091
Kuwait	4,846	6,533	6,005	3,972	4,761	7,257	7,038	6,697
Lebanon	1,539	3,650	2,203	2,525	3,743	4,202	2,215	2,598
Lesotho	234	427	339	673	810	899	870	848
Liberia	464	535	284		220	259	314	323
Libya	3,773	6,777	4,101	5,336	5,363	5,051	5,622	4,271
Madagascar	347	600	402	651	436	448	468	441
Malawi	235	439	294	575	703	735	546	491
Mali	159	439	299	602	460	608	634	589
Mauritania	206	286	234	220				403
Mauritius	447	614	529	1,618	1,558	1,625	1,715	1,930
Morocco	3,199	4,255	3,850	6,922	6,873	7,348	6,732	8,272
Mozambique								524
Namibia				1,163	1,149	1,283	1,326	1,412
Niger	197	594	369	389	355	479	375	328
Nigeria	11,095	16,660	8,877	5,627	8,986	8,275	5,537	6,613
Oman	875	1,732	3,153	2,681	3,194	3,769	4,114	3,915
Qatar	1,225	1,423	1,139	1,695	1,720	2,015	1,891	1,927
Réunion	492	887	840	2,133	2,130	2,320	2,057	2,359
Rwanda	119	262	298	287	306	286	332	121
Sao Tomé e Príncipe	14	19	10	21	31	29	32	30
Saudi Arabia	14,656	30,171	23,622	24,069	29,079	33,271	28,198	23,338
Senegal	764	1,052	826	1,220	1,173	1,034	1,087	1,022
Seychelles	46	99	99	187	173	191	238	207
Sierra Leone	181	427	151	149	163	146	147	151
Somalia								
South Africa	6,270	19,700	11,440	18,399	18,829	19,738	19,991	23,363
Sudan	1,081	1,576	771	619	890	821	945	1,227
Swaziland	182	625	316	664	715	866	786	841
Syria	2,702	4,124	3,967	2,400	2,768	3,490	4,140	5,467
Tanzania	744	1,258	845	1,364	1,546	1,510	1,497	1,505
Togo	284	551	288	581	444	395	179	222
Tunisia	1,825	3,526	2,757	5,513	5,189	6,431	6,153	6,581
Uganda	241	293	327	288	196	505	613	875
United Arab Emirates	5,055	8,746	6,549	11,199	13,746	17,410	19,520	21,024
Yemen					2,025	2,587	2,821	2,087
Zambia	671	1,088	722	1,220	818	795	809	594
Zimbabwe	710	1,449	896	1,839	2,037	2,201	1,817	2,241

Source: Euromonitor from International Monetary Fund (IMF), International Financial Statistics

Imports

Total Imports (cif) 1977-2002 (US$) (continued)

- US$ million

	1995	1996	1997	1998	1999	2000	2001	2002
Africa and Middle East								
Algeria	10,100	9,090	9,130	9,018	8,677	10,681	12,435	10,791
Angola	427	2,040	2,477	2,079	3,267	3,516	3,863	4,433
Bahrain	3,716	4,273	4,026	3,566	3,698	4,634	4,306	4,985
Benin	746	654	682	736	749	613	602	658
Botswana	1,911	1,723	2,258	2,387	2,215	2,469	1,809	1,736
Burkina Faso	455	647	587	732	678	611	656	739
Burundi	234	127	121	158	118	148	139	129
Cameroon	1,199	1,227	1,359	1,495	1,318	1,205	1,399	1,423
Cape Verde	252	234	235	228	246	230	233	253
Central African Republic	174	141	141	146	131	117	107	100
Chad	365	332	334	356	316	317	620	997
Comoros	63	57	55	47	80	72	105	115
Congo Dem Rep	397	424	318	322	370	320	290	285
Congo-Brazzaville	670	1,551	926	680	821	465	1,135	1,409
Côte d'Ivoire	2,931	2,902	2,781	3,346	3,208	2,785	2,633	3,783
Djibouti	177	179	148	158	153	163	174	182
Egypt	11,760	13,038	13,211	16,166	16,022	14,010	12,756	12,552
Equatorial Guinea	50	292	330	317	425	451	240	234
Eritrea								
Ethiopia	1,145	1,401	1,314	1,517	1,538	1,262	1,815	1,666
Gabon	882	957	1,104	1,103	841	994	859	840
Gambia	182	258	174	245	192	220	207	222
Ghana	1,907	2,108	2,326	2,563	3,480	2,973	2,949	3,187
Guinea	767	766	811	749	773	707	701	679
Guinea-Bissau	133	87	89	63	51	59	74	104
Iran	13,882	16,274	14,196	14,323	12,683	14,296	17,938	22,190
Iraq	665	950	4,000	4,400	6,900	11,153	11,000	9,430
Israel	29,579	31,620	30,782	29,342	33,166	31,404	35,449	35,517
Jordan	3,698	4,293	4,102	3,828	3,717	4,597	4,844	5,081
Kenya	2,991	2,949	3,279	3,197	2,832	3,105	3,192	3,245
Kuwait	7,790	8,373	8,246	8,619	7,617	7,157	7,869	8,950
Lebanon	5,480	7,540	7,467	7,070	6,207	6,230	7,293	6,447
Lesotho	985	999	1,025	863	781	728	681	779
Liberia	280	350	405	400	270	280	290	240
Libya	4,134	4,384	4,640	4,713	4,158	3,732	4,397	4,292
Madagascar	543	507	470	514	378	551	670	757
Malawi	475	623	781	515	673	532	563	669
Mali	772	772	739	761	824	806	709	750
Mauritania	494	463	438	359	305	340	377	368
Mauritius	1,976	2,289	2,189	2,073	2,247	2,093	1,993	1,955
Morocco	10,023	9,704	9,525	10,290	9,925	11,534	11,038	11,647
Mozambique	704	759	739	790	1,139	1,158	1,048	1,163
Namibia	1,616	1,670	1,753	1,648	1,610	1,550	1,547	1,500
Niger	374	448	374	471	394	393	370	400
Nigeria	8,222	6,438	9,501	9,211	8,588	8,721	11,586	7,547
Oman	4,248	4,578	5,026	5,682	4,674	5,040	5,798	6,005
Qatar	3,398	2,868	3,322	3,409	2,500	4,531	4,672	5,386
Réunion								
Rwanda	238	257	297	284	250	211	250	203
Sao Tomé e Príncipe	29	22	16	28	32	27	28	34
Saudi Arabia	28,091	27,744	28,732	30,013	28,011	30,238	31,223	32,312
Senegal	1,412	1,436	1,335	1,455	1,564	1,519	1,475	1,518
Seychelles	233	379	340	384	434	342	523	599
Sierra Leone	133	211	93	95	81	149	182	264
Somalia								
South Africa	30,546	30,182	32,998	29,242	26,696	29,695	28,248	29,267
Sudan	1,219	1,548	1,580	1,915	1,415	1,553	1,586	1,615
Swaziland	1,008	1,062	1,066	1,083	1,068	1,046	1,129	983
Syria	4,709	5,380	4,028	3,895	3,832	16,707	19,599	18,664
Tanzania	1,675	1,388	1,337	1,453	1,556	1,524	1,712	1,687
Togo	594	664	645	588	576	562	553	591
Tunisia	7,903	7,701	7,948	8,350	8,475	8,567	9,529	9,526
Uganda	1,056	1,191	1,316	1,416	1,342	1,536	1,594	1,111
United Arab Emirates	20,984	22,638	29,952	24,728	33,231	38,139	40,259	44,043
Yemen	1,582	2,038	2,014	2,167	2,008	2,324	2,310	2,404
Zambia	700	835	819	749	812	731	791	788
Zimbabwe	2,661	2,803	2,684	1,808	1,685	2,365	2,777	2,908

Source: *Euromonitor from International Monetary Fund (IMF), International Financial Statistics*

Imports

Imports (cif) by Country of Origin 2002

Table 13.2

- US$ million

	Africa & Middle East	Asia/ Pacific	of which: Japan	Australasia	Europe	of which: Total EU	Latin America	North America	of which: USA	Total, including Others
North America										
Canada	4,062	32,604	10,799	1,585	32,444	27,181	13,693	152,969	152,969	244,179
USA	59,134	408,383	124,633	9,295	268,083	232,183	209,878	213,954		1,202,360
Latin America										
Anguilla										
Antigua	1	103		1	422	328	55	96	90	679
Argentina	443	829	207	43	2,619	2,392	7,381	1,780	1,750	13,763
Aruba	5	36	20		197	189	136	466	460	842
Bahamas	28	1,833	528	5	1,995	843	197	1,098	1,073	5,305
Barbados	3	93	45	14	187	186	288	478	440	1,071
Belize		52	25	1	59	56	147	154	151	419
Bermuda	2	1,940	24	3	1,954	1,906	290	535	457	4,723
Bolivia	6	215	98	2	150	160	1,041	291	277	1,770
Brazil	5,635	7,531	1,997	280	17,925	15,685	11,683	14,167	13,650	58,191
British Virgin Islands										
Cayman Islands										
Chile	303	2,574	540	115	3,310	3,107	6,072	2,848	2,528	17,014
Colombia	135	1,577	644	24	2,220	1,999	3,513	4,187	3,948	12,129
Costa Rica	27	861	416	5	911	837	1,488	3,498	3,445	9,348
Cuba	37	442	29	48	1,291	1,208	674	335	159	2,850
Dominica		79	9		28	25	49	51	50	209
Dominican Republic	51	812	339	28	1,148	1,042	2,174	4,775	4,688	9,121
Ecuador	132	882	374	8	1,067	980	2,106	1,858	1,767	6,179
El Salvador	5	440	114	28	517	489	1,679	1,854	1,831	4,658
French Guiana										
Grenada		8	6	3	28	25	77	65	62	203
Guadeloupe										
Guatemala	18	1,198	210	26	744	660	2,261	2,324	2,246	6,761
Guyana	1	50	13	6	111	106	277	149	141	596
Haiti	7	110	30		134	113	272	665	641	1,203
Honduras	4	478	94	7	267	217	873	2,832	2,821	5,103
Jamaica	9	306	164	32	544	472	794	1,672	1,562	3,482
Martinique										
Mexico	891	14,994	4,143	483	17,214	16,193	5,926	108,944	107,284	153,134
Netherlands Antilles	218	230	54	3	539	522	6,400	829	816	8,287
Nicaragua		238	54	4	140	104	919	489	481	2,000
Panama	6	306	165	16	327	1,473	955	1,063	1,043	3,036
Paraguay	7	289	24	1	208	196	1,607	483	477	2,631
Peru	44	974	277	55	1,381	1,269	2,632	1,967	1,881	7,191
Puerto Rico										
St Kitts		10	7		29	27	49	94	76	184
St Lucia	1	16	7	3	57	41	310	114	108	501
St Vincent and the Grenadines		56	6	2	215	199	65	47	44	391
Suriname	1	127	36	1	200	195	148	140	137	620
Trinidad and Tobago	269	241	119	29	465	436	407	1,221	1,120	2,670
Uruguay	105	251	34	17	582	471	1,763	237	230	2,986
Venezuela		1,325	457	102	3,445	3,324	4,403	5,268	4,891	17,735

Source: International Monetary Fund (IMF), Direction of Trade Statistics
Notes: US$ totals in this table may differ from the totals given for Imports (cif) by Commodity and Trends in Total Imports (cif)

◻ Imports

Imports (cif) by Country of Origin 2002

● US$ million

	Africa & Middle East	Asia/ Pacific	of which: Japan	Australasia	Europe	of which: Total EU	Latin America	North America	of which: USA	Total, including Others
Asia Pacific										
Afghanistan	62	629	92	2	196	117		89	88	978
American Samoa		31	4	70	4	3		1		105
Armenia	176	19	1		449	250	4	125	123	805
Azerbaijan	93	315	33	6	1,201	516	12	79	77	1,712
Bangladesh	435	5,005	595	186	985	820	80	286	234	7,819
Bhutan										
Brunei	5	1,350	351	33	180	177		52	51	1,636
Cambodia	1	1,943	77	9	130	121	1	33	32	2,207
China	14,856	129,200	53,489	6,655	52,312	37,179	8,314	30,879	27,251	295,440
Fiji	1	308	35	456	26	25	1	23	19	838
French Polynesia	3	81	26	250	875	872	3	92	87	1,305
Guam		417	96	15	10		2	1		447
Hong Kong, China	2,927	142,213	25,631	2,241	22,625	19,029	1,405	13,853	12,898	201,368
India	7,998	15,627	2,056	1,587	17,181	13,917	1,317	4,903	4,508	63,483
Indonesia	3,900	16,311	4,409	1,743	4,472	4,687	533	3,056	2,644	31,285
Japan	46,407	133,908		15,884	52,975	43,447	8,594	65,742	58,589	337,149
Kazakhstan	86	1,146	100	6	5,023	1,657	111	691	665	7,147
Kiribati		24	8	27	32	28		4	4	88
Kyrgyzstan	12	271	6		241	95	6	56	47	587
Laos		671	20	13	51	35		5	5	755
Macau	19	1,874	171	36	318	281	7	107	105	2,530
Malaysia	1,611	49,101	13,815	1,719	10,488	9,005	791	13,038	12,703	81,964
Maldives	61	256	4	18	45	42	1	7	5	401
Mongolia	1	348	34	11	358	71	1	75	73	795
Myanmar	8	2,522	127	19	222	94	1	12	12	2,961
Nauru		4		19	5	4		3	3	32
Nepal	184	522	18	20	104	92		24	22	890
New Caledonia	2	174	21	195	753	745	2	41	40	1,179
North Korea	102	1,203	146	3	421	309	265	42	28	2,055
Pakistan	4,117	3,423	675	287	2,361	1,980	86	802	723	11,238
Papua New Guinea	13	433	51	642	55	47	1	27	26	1,196
Philippines	3,171	24,387	9,303	919	3,737	3,268	327	8,209	7,997	42,711
Singapore	10,584	62,447	14,576	2,354	17,257	13,791	1,084	17,181	16,605	116,482
Solomon Islands	1	40	2	37	2	2		2	2	101
South Korea	22,547	67,596	29,856	6,726	21,794	16,849	3,639	24,957	23,111	152,123
Sri Lanka	570	3,248	314	246	1,027	903	30	203	189	5,935
Taiwan										
Tajikistan	29	343	1	1	340	28		7	6	721
Thailand	6,567	35,224	14,902	1,695	9,015	7,109	999	6,611	6,197	64,721
Tonga		29	2	38	6	4		13	12	86
Turkmenistan	267	258	8		1,141	341	1	145	137	1,819
Tuvalu		20	10	4	55	2				79
Uzbekistan	22	673	19	1	1,349	433		155	152	2,203
Vanuatu		65	26	43	6	5		1	1	125
Vietnam	273	12,948	2,349	370	2,534	1,863	195	686	638	19,160
Western Samoa		84	24	71	6	6	3	8	8	186
Australasia										
Australia	2,389	33,992	9,438	2,926	18,943	17,584	855	15,082	14,024	76,506
New Zealand	693	4,910	1,813	3,336	3,114	2,912	176	2,235	2,061	15,097

Source: International Monetary Fund (IMF), Direction of Trade Statistics
Notes: US$ totals in this table may differ from the totals given for Imports (cif) by Commodity and Trends in Total Imports (cif)

Imports

Imports (cif) by Country of Origin 2002

● US$ million

	Africa & Middle East	Asia/ Pacific	of which: Japan	Australasia	Europe	of which: Total EU	Latin America	North America	of which: USA	Total, including Others
Africa and Middle East										
Algeria	418	1,140	212	118	9,720	8,367	269	1,375	1,083	13,068
Angola	434	276	38	4	1,623	1,464	193	414	410	2,948
Bahrain	1,447	755	282	67	1,078	970	88	471	461	3,943
Benin	180	643	9	1	617	579	14	42	39	1,511
Botswana										
Burkina Faso	247	37	9		291	283	2	22	20	637
Burundi	51	15	1		48	45		2	2	131
Cameroon	489	164	20	2	1,193	1,165	19	181	171	2,151
Cape Verde	12	14			261	254	6	11	11	313
Central African Republic	22	7	3	1	66	64	1	7	7	139
Chad	51	9	1	4	240	226	1	141	140	445
Comoros	28	18	5		42	41				89
Congo Dem Rep	358	85	14	3	393	378	7	38	31	921
Congo-Brazzaville	130	178	8	2	585	550	11	60	58	1,112
Côte d'Ivoire	667	478	34	3	1,352	1,301	47	98	84	3,056
Djibouti	223	147	17	1	184	165	2	62	62	659
Egypt	1,452	3,067	559	467	8,367	6,569	584	3,276	3,153	18,512
Equatorial Guinea	22	7	2		259	226	2	121	120	410
Eritrea										
Ethiopia	608	321	59	5	519	396	16	71	66	1,758
Gabon	98	78	30	1	855	833	20	76	72	1,149
Gambia	80	154	7		133	125	32	11	10	411
Ghana	1,110	567	52	36	1,143	1,048	72	260	212	3,229
Guinea	145	141	22	4	474	446	3	74	69	846
Guinea-Bissau	24	28	2		43	42	4	3	3	111
Iran	1,083	5,778	857	417	10,299	8,082	1,074	133	30	20,937
Iraq	975	1,607	311	399	2,429	1,856	67	44	35	5,522
Israel	505	4,482	849	155	17,894	13,554	398	8,013	7,743	35,440
Jordan	1,363	1,043	167	83	1,929	1,563	145	433	416	5,226
Kenya	1,290	870	184	50	1,014	959	65	313	298	3,660
Kuwait	1,356	2,115	952	336	3,377	2,964	124	1,168	1,116	8,550
Lebanon	892	887	145	20	3,893	3,096	88	376	350	6,329
Lesotho										
Liberia	67	3,026	987		2,020	1,400	15	32	31	5,172
Libya	620	954	344	54	3,646	3,253	74	52	20	5,419
Madagascar	434	226	11	4	294	287	14	17	17	1,076
Malawi	385	61	17	12	75	74	1	37	33	594
Mali	390	92	6	4	408	392	5	14	12	1,419
Mauritania	99	136	31	2	472	413	10	27	25	815
Mauritius	528	665	58	95	826	811	37	33	30	2,219
Morocco	1,992	995	151	58	8,701	7,852	487	745	622	13,517
Mozambique	460	248	93	107	331	327	14	117	108	1,534
Namibia										
Niger	156	90	18		117	210	10	21	21	395
Nigeria	618	3,885	286	38	5,949	5,390	600	1,219	1,163	12,497
Oman	1,927	1,573	945	125	1,578	1,425	78	408	392	5,709
Qatar	551	925	407	53	2,088	1,933	50	366	346	4,055
Réunion										
Rwanda	125	18	6		94	80		12	11	320
Sao Tomé e Príncipe	2	2	1		53	51		2	2	59
Saudi Arabia	1,880	10,834	4,142	1,552	16,884	15,114	903	5,497	5,256	46,998
Senegal	361	333	51	3	1,016	1,225	64	117	106	1,958
Seychelles	105	55	3	5	183	165	1	10	9	375
Sierra Leone	61	53	6	1	324	304	4	31	28	489
Somalia	187	42		1	35	31	37	7	7	351
South Africa	4,584	5,586	1,714	840	13,864	12,970	1,244	2,952	2,778	29,142
Sudan	390	892	54	88	730	552	18	48	12	2,177
Swaziland										
Syria	508	1,401	199	19	3,192	2,130	214	314	302	6,958
Tanzania	572	528	76	69	419	395	13	80	68	1,688
Togo	84	301	21	1	465	442	4	25	15	897
Tunisia	666	572	159	15	7,452	6,778	243	389	300	9,528
Uganda	596	159	33	2	221	212	1	28	25	1,019
United Arab Emirates	5,617	19,625	3,246	829	16,796	14,519	823	4,146	3,958	49,503
Yemen	1,015	865	81	86	1,207	769	170	436	403	3,871
Zambia	775	96	21	3	117	118	3	45	39	1,053
Zimbabwe	1,190	116	17	4	215	197	17	58	54	1,835

Source: International Monetary Fund (IMF), Direction of Trade Statistics
Notes: US$ totals in this table may differ from the totals given for Imports (cif) by Commodity and Trends in Total Imports (cif)

Imports (cif) by Country of Origin 2002 (% Analysis)

- % of total imports

	Africa & Middle East	Asia/ Pacific	of which: Japan	Australasia	Europe	of which: Total EU	Latin America	North America	of which: USA	Total, including Others
North America										
Canada	1.7	13.4	4.4	0.6	13.3	11.1	5.6	62.6	62.6	100.0
USA	4.9	34.0	10.4	0.8	22.3	19.3	17.5	17.8		100.0
Latin America										
Anguilla										
Antigua	0.1	15.2		0.2	62.2	48.3	8.1	14.1	13.2	100.0
Argentina	3.2	6.0	1.5	0.3	19.0	17.4	53.6	12.9	12.7	100.0
Aruba	0.6	4.3	2.4	0.1	23.4	22.4	16.2	55.3	54.7	100.0
Bahamas	0.5	34.5	10.0	0.1	37.6	15.9	3.7	20.7	20.2	100.0
Barbados	0.3	8.7	4.2	1.3	17.5	17.3	26.9	44.6	41.1	100.0
Belize		12.4	6.0	0.3	14.1	13.3	35.0	36.8	36.0	100.0
Bermuda		41.1	0.5	0.1	41.4	40.4	6.1	11.3	9.7	100.0
Bolivia	0.3	12.2	5.5	0.1	8.5	9.0	58.8	16.4	15.6	100.0
Brazil	9.7	12.9	3.4	0.5	30.8	27.0	20.1	24.3	23.5	100.0
British Virgin Islands										
Cayman Islands										
Chile	1.8	15.1	3.2	0.7	19.5	18.3	35.7	16.7	14.9	100.0
Colombia	1.1	13.0	5.3	0.2	18.3	16.5	29.0	34.5	32.5	100.0
Costa Rica	0.3	9.2	4.5	0.1	9.7	9.0	15.9	37.4	36.9	100.0
Cuba	1.3	15.5	1.0	1.7	45.3	42.4	23.7	11.8	5.6	100.0
Dominica		37.7	4.6	0.1	13.2	12.0	23.3	24.6	23.7	100.0
Dominican Republic	0.6	8.9	3.7	0.3	12.6	11.4	23.8	52.4	51.4	100.0
Ecuador	2.1	14.3	6.0	0.1	17.3	15.9	34.1	30.1	28.6	100.0
El Salvador	0.1	9.4	2.5	0.6	11.1	10.5	36.0	39.8	39.3	100.0
French Guiana										
Grenada		3.8	2.9	1.5	13.8	12.4	37.7	32.0	30.6	100.0
Guadeloupe										
Guatemala	0.3	17.7	3.1	0.4	11.0	9.8	33.4	34.4	33.2	100.0
Guyana	0.1	8.5	2.3	1.0	18.6	17.7	46.5	24.9	23.7	100.0
Haiti	0.6	9.1	2.5		11.1	9.4	22.6	55.3	53.3	100.0
Honduras	0.1	9.4	1.8	0.1	5.2	4.3	17.1	55.5	55.3	100.0
Jamaica	0.3	8.8	4.7	0.9	15.6	13.6	22.8	48.0	44.9	100.0
Martinique										
Mexico	0.6	9.8	2.7	0.3	11.2	10.6	3.9	71.1	70.1	100.0
Netherlands Antilles	2.6	2.8	0.7		6.5	6.3	77.2	10.0	9.9	100.0
Nicaragua		11.9	2.7	0.2	7.0	5.2	45.9	24.4	24.1	100.0
Panama	0.2	10.1	5.4	0.5	10.8	48.5	31.5	35.0	34.3	100.0
Paraguay	0.3	11.0	0.9		7.9	7.4	61.1	18.4	18.1	100.0
Peru	0.6	13.5	3.9	0.8	19.2	17.6	36.6	27.3	26.2	100.0
Puerto Rico										
St Kitts	0.3	5.2	4.0	0.1	15.6	14.8	26.6	51.3	41.5	100.0
St Lucia	0.2	3.2	1.4	0.6	11.5	8.3	61.8	22.8	21.5	100.0
St Vincent and the Grenadines	0.1	14.2	1.5	0.4	55.1	50.8	16.7	12.1	11.4	100.0
Suriname	0.1	20.4	5.7	0.1	32.3	31.4	23.9	22.6	22.1	100.0
Trinidad and Tobago	10.1	9.0	4.5	1.1	17.4	16.3	15.3	45.7	41.9	100.0
Uruguay	3.5	8.4	1.1	0.6	19.5	15.8	59.0	8.0	7.7	100.0
Venezuela		7.5	2.6	0.6	19.4	18.7	24.8	29.7	27.6	100.0

Source: International Monetary Fund (IMF), Direction of Trade Statistics

◻ Imports

Imports (cif) by Country of Origin 2002 (% Analysis)

● % of total imports

	Africa & Middle East	Asia/ Pacific	of which: Japan	Australasia	Europe	of which: Total EU	Latin America	North America	of which: USA	Total, including Others
Asia Pacific										
Afghanistan	6.3	64.3	9.4	0.2	20.0	11.9		9.1	9.0	100.0
American Samoa		29.2	4.1	66.6	3.4	3.1		0.8		100.0
Armenia	21.9	2.4	0.1		55.8	31.1	0.5	15.5	15.3	100.0
Azerbaijan	5.4	18.4	1.9	0.3	70.2	30.1	0.7	4.6	4.5	100.0
Bangladesh	5.6	64.0	7.6	2.4	12.6	10.5	1.0	3.7	3.0	100.0
Bhutan										
Brunei	0.3	82.5	21.5	2.0	11.0	10.8		3.2	3.1	100.0
Cambodia		88.0	3.5	0.4	5.9	5.5		1.5	1.5	100.0
China	5.0	43.7	18.1	2.3	17.7	12.6	2.8	10.5	9.2	100.0
Fiji	0.2	36.7	4.2	54.5	3.1	3.0	0.1	2.8	2.2	100.0
French Polynesia	0.2	6.2	2.0	19.1	67.1	66.9	0.2	7.1	6.6	100.0
Guam		93.5	21.6	3.4	2.2		0.5	0.3		100.0
Hong Kong, China	1.5	70.6	12.7	1.1	11.2	9.4	0.7	6.9	6.4	100.0
India	12.6	24.6	3.2	2.5	27.1	21.9	2.1	7.7	7.1	100.0
Indonesia	12.5	52.1	14.1	5.6	14.3	15.0	1.7	9.8	8.5	100.0
Japan	13.8	39.7		4.7	15.7	12.9	2.5	19.5	17.4	100.0
Kazakhstan	1.2	16.0	1.4	0.1	70.3	23.2	1.6	9.7	9.3	100.0
Kiribati		27.1	9.5	30.2	36.8	31.4	0.1	4.6	4.6	100.0
Kyrgyzstan	2.1	46.2	1.1	0.1	41.1	16.2	0.9	9.6	8.1	100.0
Laos		88.9	2.6	1.7	6.8	4.6		0.6	0.6	100.0
Macau	0.8	74.1	6.7	1.4	12.6	11.1	0.3	4.2	4.1	100.0
Malaysia	2.0	59.9	16.9	2.1	12.8	11.0	1.0	15.9	15.5	100.0
Maldives	15.2	63.9	1.0	4.4	11.3	10.5	0.2	1.8	1.2	100.0
Mongolia	0.1	43.7	4.3	1.4	45.0	9.0	0.1	9.4	9.2	100.0
Myanmar	0.3	85.2	4.3	0.6	7.5	3.2		0.4	0.4	100.0
Nauru	0.1	13.9	0.7	59.5	16.3	13.6		10.1	10.1	100.0
Nepal	20.6	58.6	2.1	2.2	11.7	10.3		2.7	2.5	100.0
New Caledonia	0.1	14.8	1.8	16.5	63.9	63.2	0.2	3.5	3.4	100.0
North Korea	5.0	58.6	7.1	0.1	20.5	15.1	12.9	2.1	1.3	100.0
Pakistan	36.6	30.5	6.0	2.5	21.0	17.6	0.8	7.1	6.4	100.0
Papua New Guinea	1.1	36.2	4.2	53.7	4.6	4.0	0.1	2.2	2.1	100.0
Philippines	7.4	57.1	21.8	2.2	8.8	7.7	0.8	19.2	18.7	100.0
Singapore	9.1	53.6	12.5	2.0	14.8	11.8	0.9	14.7	14.3	100.0
Solomon Islands	0.7	40.2	2.3	36.3	2.1	2.2		2.1	2.0	100.0
South Korea	14.8	44.4	19.6	4.4	14.3	11.1	2.4	16.4	15.2	100.0
Sri Lanka	9.6	54.7	5.3	4.1	17.3	15.2	0.5	3.4	3.2	100.0
Taiwan										
Tajikistan	4.0	47.7	0.1	0.1	47.2	3.9		1.0	0.8	100.0
Thailand	10.1	54.4	23.0	2.6	13.9	11.0	1.5	10.2	9.6	100.0
Tonga	0.2	33.5	2.2	44.0	6.4	5.2	0.1	15.1	14.3	100.0
Turkmenistan	14.7	14.2	0.5		62.7	18.7		8.0	7.5	100.0
Tuvalu		25.8	12.8	4.6	69.5	1.9	0.1			100.0
Uzbekistan	1.0	30.6	0.9		61.2	19.6		7.0	6.9	100.0
Vanuatu		51.9	20.4	34.2	4.6	4.1		0.8	0.5	100.0
Vietnam	1.4	67.6	12.3	1.9	13.2	9.7	1.0	3.6	3.3	100.0
Western Samoa	0.2	44.9	12.8	38.1	3.3	3.1	1.8	4.2	4.1	100.0
Australasia										
Australia	3.1	44.4	12.3	3.8	24.8	23.0	1.1	19.7	18.3	100.0
New Zealand	4.6	32.5	12.0	22.1	20.6	19.3	1.2	14.8	13.6	100.0

Source: International Monetary Fund (IMF), Direction of Trade Statistics

◻ Imports

Imports (cif) by Country of Origin 2002 (% Analysis)

● % of total imports

	Africa & Middle East	Asia/ Pacific	of which: Japan	Australasia	Europe	of which: Total EU	Latin America	North America	of which: USA	Total, including Others
Africa and Middle East										
Algeria	3.2	8.7	1.6	0.9	74.4	64.0	2.1	10.5	8.3	100.0
Angola	14.7	9.4	1.3	0.1	55.1	49.7	6.6	14.1	13.9	100.0
Bahrain	36.7	19.1	7.1	1.7	27.3	24.6	2.2	11.9	11.7	100.0
Benin	11.9	42.6	0.6	0.1	40.8	38.3	0.9	2.8	2.6	100.0
Botswana										
Burkina Faso	38.8	5.8	1.5	0.1	45.8	44.5	0.3	3.4	3.2	100.0
Burundi	38.5	11.7	1.1		36.3	34.3		1.7	1.3	100.0
Cameroon	22.7	7.6	0.9	0.1	55.5	54.2	0.9	8.4	8.0	100.0
Cape Verde	3.8	4.3			83.2	81.1	2.1	3.4	3.4	100.0
Central African Republic	16.1	5.4	1.9	0.5	47.7	46.2	0.4	5.3	5.1	100.0
Chad	11.4	2.0	0.2	0.9	53.8	50.8	0.1	31.7	31.5	100.0
Comoros	31.3	20.0	6.1	0.2	46.9	46.4	0.3	0.1	0.1	100.0
Congo Dem Rep	38.8	9.2	1.5	0.4	42.7	41.0	0.8	4.2	3.4	100.0
Congo-Brazzaville	11.7	16.0	0.7	0.2	52.6	49.4	1.0	5.4	5.2	100.0
Côte d'Ivoire	21.8	15.7	1.1	0.1	44.2	42.6	1.5	3.2	2.7	100.0
Djibouti	33.8	22.4	2.6	0.2	27.9	25.0	0.4	9.5	9.4	100.0
Egypt	7.8	16.6	3.0	2.5	45.2	35.5	3.2	17.7	17.0	100.0
Equatorial Guinea	5.3	1.7	0.4		63.1	55.1	0.4	29.5	29.1	100.0
Eritrea										
Ethiopia	34.6	18.3	3.4	0.3	29.5	22.5	0.9	4.0	3.8	100.0
Gabon	8.5	6.8	2.7	0.1	74.4	72.5	1.7	6.7	6.3	100.0
Gambia	19.5	37.4	1.6	0.1	32.3	30.3	7.9	2.6	2.5	100.0
Ghana	34.4	17.6	1.6	1.1	35.4	32.4	2.2	8.0	6.6	100.0
Guinea	17.1	16.6	2.6	0.5	56.1	52.8	0.4	8.7	8.2	100.0
Guinea-Bissau	21.8	24.8	1.4		38.9	38.1	3.4	2.4	2.4	100.0
Iran	5.2	27.6	4.1	2.0	49.2	38.6	5.1	0.6	0.1	100.0
Iraq	17.7	29.1	5.6	7.2	44.0	33.6	1.2	0.8	0.6	100.0
Israel	1.4	12.6	2.4	0.4	50.5	38.2	1.1	22.6	21.8	100.0
Jordan	26.1	20.0	3.2	1.6	36.9	29.9	2.8	8.3	8.0	100.0
Kenya	35.2	23.8	5.0	1.4	27.7	26.2	1.8	8.6	8.2	100.0
Kuwait	15.9	24.7	11.1	3.9	39.5	34.7	1.4	13.7	13.1	100.0
Lebanon	14.1	14.0	2.3	0.3	61.5	48.9	1.4	5.9	5.5	100.0
Lesotho										
Liberia	1.3	58.5	19.1		39.0	27.1	0.3	0.6	0.6	100.0
Libya	11.4	17.6	6.3	1.0	67.3	60.0	1.4	1.0	0.4	100.0
Madagascar	40.3	21.0	1.0	0.3	27.3	26.7	1.3	1.6	1.6	100.0
Malawi	64.8	10.3	2.8	2.1	12.6	12.5	0.2	6.3	5.6	100.0
Mali	27.5	6.5	0.4	0.3	28.7	27.6	0.3	1.0	0.9	100.0
Mauritania	12.2	16.7	3.7	0.3	57.9	50.7	1.2	3.3	3.1	100.0
Mauritius	23.8	29.9	2.6	4.3	37.2	36.5	1.7	1.5	1.4	100.0
Morocco	14.7	7.4	1.1	0.4	64.4	58.1	3.6	5.5	4.6	100.0
Mozambique	30.0	16.2	6.0	7.0	21.6	21.3	0.9	7.6	7.0	100.0
Namibia										
Niger	39.4	22.7	4.6		29.6	53.2	2.7	5.3	5.2	100.0
Nigeria	4.9	31.1	2.3	0.3	47.6	43.1	4.8	9.8	9.3	100.0
Oman	33.8	27.5	16.6	2.2	27.6	25.0	1.4	7.1	6.9	100.0
Qatar	13.6	22.8	10.0	1.3	51.5	47.7	1.2	9.0	8.5	100.0
Réunion										
Rwanda	39.2	5.6	1.9	0.1	29.5	24.9	0.1	3.9	3.5	100.0
Sao Tomé e Príncipe	2.7	3.6	1.6	0.2	89.3	85.7	0.6	3.6	3.5	100.0
Saudi Arabia	4.0	23.1	8.8	3.3	35.9	32.2	1.9	11.7	11.2	100.0
Senegal	18.4	17.0	2.6	0.1	51.9	62.6	3.3	6.0	5.4	100.0
Seychelles	28.1	14.8	0.9	1.2	48.7	43.8	0.3	2.7	2.4	100.0
Sierra Leone	12.5	10.8	1.2	0.2	66.3	62.2	0.7	6.4	5.7	100.0
Somalia	53.3	11.8	0.1	0.2	9.9	8.7	10.5	2.0	1.9	100.0
South Africa	15.7	19.2	5.9	2.9	47.6	44.5	4.3	10.1	9.5	100.0
Sudan	17.9	41.0	2.5	4.1	33.5	25.3	0.8	2.2	0.5	100.0
Swaziland										
Syria	7.3	20.1	2.9	0.3	45.9	30.6	3.1	4.5	4.3	100.0
Tanzania	33.9	31.3	4.5	4.1	24.8	23.4	0.8	4.8	4.1	100.0
Togo	9.3	33.5	2.4	0.1	51.8	49.2	0.5	2.8	1.7	100.0
Tunisia	7.0	6.0	1.7	0.2	78.2	71.1	2.5	4.1	3.2	100.0
Uganda	58.5	15.6	3.3	0.1	21.7	20.8	0.1	2.8	2.5	100.0
United Arab Emirates	11.3	39.6	6.6	1.7	33.9	29.3	1.7	8.4	8.0	100.0
Yemen	26.2	22.3	2.1	2.2	31.2	19.9	4.4	11.3	10.4	100.0
Zambia	73.6	9.1	2.0	0.3	11.1	11.2	0.3	4.2	3.7	100.0
Zimbabwe	64.8	6.3	0.9	0.2	11.7	10.7	0.9	3.2	3.0	100.0

Source: *International Monetary Fund (IMF), Direction of Trade Statistics*

Imports

Imports (cif) by Commodity: SITC Classification 2002 | Table 13.4

- US$ million

	0	1	2	3	4	5	6	7	8	9	Total
North America											
Canada	11,169	1,383	6,040	12,330	253	20,580	27,984	110,354	26,432	5,384	221,911
USA	41,516	11,075	21,706	130,799	1,182	91,374	125,285	482,101	192,204	50,945	1,148,189
Latin America											
Anguilla											
Antigua											
Argentina	918	69	593	811	36	3,972	2,849	7,591	2,033	51	18,924
Aruba											
Bahamas	269	62	48	305	3	139	287	492	285	27	1,916
Barbados	146	32	35	63	6	119	165	271	158	3	997
Belize											
Bermuda											
Bolivia	202	11	74	119	4	306	339	459	202	14	1,728
Brazil	2,773	183	1,455	8,209	148	10,889	5,642	25,279	3,699	37	58,313
British Virgin Islands											
Cayman Islands											
Chile	1,076	41	262	2,746	56	2,260	2,375	5,214	1,721	40	15,790
Colombia	1,257	104	417	175	90	2,811	2,090	4,754	1,076	167	12,942
Costa Rica	380	38	122	424	14	961	994	2,577	829	19	6,359
Cuba											
Dominica	22	4	2	11	2	14	20	25	15		116
Dominican Republic											
Ecuador	383	23	144	308	33	1,014	949	2,139	493	193	5,676
El Salvador	554	32	113	497	65	617	726	910	365	10	3,889
French Guiana											
Grenada	37	4	4	17	1	24	36	58	26		208
Guadeloupe											
Guatemala	717	51	103	775	69	1,036	923	1,577	565	4	5,820
Guyana											
Haiti											
Honduras	551	30	24	410	11	546	538	737	252	11	3,110
Jamaica	500	33	60	677	24	375	504	830	513	105	3,620
Martinique											
Mexico	8,727	340	4,597	5,736	391	15,154	30,829	107,283	24,407	1,234	198,698
Netherlands Antilles											
Nicaragua	242	22	14	313	39	297	276	386	189	2	1,779
Panama	359	29	20	521	19	384	450	821	432	1	3,035
Paraguay	127	170	33	362	4	370	304	586	248		2,205
Peru	834	30	179	955	105	1,249	1,063	2,111	646	1	7,172
Puerto Rico											
St Kitts	27	5	6	15	1	16	44	51	26		190
St Lucia	60	10	8	29		21	47	54	31		261
St Vincent and the Grenadines	39	4	6	15	1	17	33	41	21		178
Suriname	76	18	9	38	7	57	100	206	54	4	568
Trinidad and Tobago	298	23	59	886	9	299	487	1,624	235	42	3,962
Uruguay	274	44	111	350	15	559	464	788	309		2,914
Venezuela	1,575	251	320	747	100	2,656	2,440	7,056	1,983	10	17,137

Source: *United Nations, UN Trade Statistics*
Notes: *SITC Classification: 0 Food and live animals; 1 Beverages and tobacco; 2 Crude materials excl. fuels; 3 Mineral fuels etc;4 Oils and fats; 5 Chemicals; 6 Basic manufactures; 7 Machinery and transport equipment; 8 Miscellaneous manufactured goods; 9 Others*

Imports

Imports (cif) by Commodity: SITC Classification 2002

US$ million

	0	1	2	3	4	5	6	7	8	9	Total
Asia Pacific											
Afghanistan											
American Samoa											
Armenia	190	23	10	188	16	101	206	147	55	14	950
Azerbaijan	199	23	41	293	14	94	358	534	104	6	1,666
Bangladesh	782	26	723	404	476	914	2,582	1,913	518	11	8,349
Bhutan											
Brunei											
Cambodia											
China	5,119	457	22,264	16,360	708	32,237	43,869	112,579	16,556	1,666	251,815
Fiji	140	6	6	85	8	63	185	178	79	2	751
French Polynesia											
Guam											
Hong Kong, China	6,830	1,263	2,510	3,957	425	11,374	32,549	85,047	52,813	1,027	197,794
India	1,353	15	4,012	20,927	1,477	5,283	9,121	8,933	2,847	4,333	58,302
Indonesia	2,496	323	3,543	7,395	40	5,830	4,360	9,637	717	24	34,365
Japan	37,441	4,378	22,381	69,945	497	24,964	30,682	94,228	49,712	6,698	340,924
Kazakhstan	449	80	187	699	50	701	1,264	2,330	424	17	6,201
Kiribati											
Kyrgyzstan	53	19	24	152	4	79	77	123	48		579
Laos											
Macau	136	198	22	198	3	84	972	432	370	4	2,419
Malaysia	3,447	251	1,752	3,884	212	5,200	7,681	43,100	4,198	2,293	72,019
Maldives	72	14	15	51	3	21	79	88	48		392
Mongolia	115	17	7	143	6	37	112	180	42		660
Myanmar											
Nauru											
Nepal	120	12	122	288	52	189	289	304	57	380	1,814
New Caledonia	127	31	13	164	3	95	146	358	148	2	1,087
North Korea											
Pakistan	643	2	832	2,850	382	1,825	983	2,018	253	292	10,080
Papua New Guinea											
Philippines	2,370	214	1,013	3,351	49	2,707	3,674	16,134	1,254	26	30,792
Singapore	2,907	1,085	728	14,236	181	6,556	8,328	68,038	10,270	1,687	114,017
Solomon Islands											
South Korea	7,045	601	8,715	33,535	262	12,293	15,720	46,902	10,750	1,706	137,530
Sri Lanka	677	62	105	583	23	502	2,108	897	413	85	5,455
Taiwan											
Tajikistan											
Thailand	2,609	208	2,488	7,448	68	6,215	9,952	28,326	3,488	1,246	62,049
Tonga											
Turkmenistan	226	34	19	27	5	194	492	942	137	130	2,207
Tuvalu											
Uzbekistan											
Vanuatu											
Vietnam											
Western Samoa											
Australasia											
Australia	2,207	484	894	5,202	142	7,645	7,046	26,849	8,738	1,239	60,444
New Zealand	918	152	391	1,347	41	1,700	1,924	5,020	1,780	33	13,306

Source: United Nations, UN Trade Statistics
Notes: SITC Classification: 0 Food and live animals; 1 Beverages and tobacco; 2 Crude materials excl. fuels; 3 Mineral fuels etc;4 Oils and fats; 5 Chemicals; 6 Basic manufactures; 7 Machinery and transport equipment; 8 Miscellaneous manufactured goods; 9 Others

□ Imports

Imports (cif) by Commodity: SITC Classification 2002

● US$ million

	0	1	2	3	4	5	6	7	8	9	Total
Africa and Middle East											
Algeria	2,546	42	274	139	181	1,084	1,674	3,275	411		9,627
Angola											
Bahrain	426	69	340	1,745	9	218	552	867	280		4,507
Benin	110	8	35	99	2	70	147	99	27		596
Botswana	487	51	98	268	24	277	727	1,191	612	217	3,952
Burkina Faso	85	17	8	204	10	73	106	276	29		809
Burundi	15		6	16	1	27	29	31	11	1	137
Cameroon	292	10	78	332	5	211	459	511	86		1,983
Cape Verde											
Central African Republic											
Chad											
Comoros											
Congo Dem Rep											
Congo-Brazzaville											
Côte d'Ivoire											
Djibouti											
Egypt	1,110	50	797	505	181	1,512	1,897	2,498	578	1,259	10,387
Equatorial Guinea											
Eritrea											
Ethiopia	152	9	27	198	19	205	303	514	161	6	1,594
Gabon											
Gambia											
Ghana	497	187	125	791	11	302	481	814	137	3	3,348
Guinea	117	21	8	112	8	71	85	151	36	2	610
Guinea-Bissau											
Iran	2,277	21	701	849	338	2,457	3,620	6,632	529		17,424
Iraq											
Israel	1,539	216	612	3,976	54	3,259	9,727	12,956	3,498	172	36,008
Jordan	743	48	154	738	52	546	1,104	1,426	310	95	5,216
Kenya	304	21	89	703	111	445	397	890	172	10	3,142
Kuwait											
Lebanon	986	198	208	1,349	39	722	1,186	1,728	787	250	7,453
Lesotho											
Liberia											
Libya											
Madagascar											
Malawi	29	21	11	93	13	73	109	153	41	1	545
Mali											
Mauritania											
Mauritius	290	12	58	218	15	160	568	418	172	5	1,915
Morocco	1,313	78	510	1,858	161	1,049	2,564	2,632	785	12	10,961
Mozambique											
Namibia	167	21	35	168	8	167	310	525	181	5	1,587
Niger	102	15	9	40	21	29	33	47	15	1	312
Nigeria	1,000	40	79	98	25	1,371	1,166	2,193	224	1	6,198
Oman	735	527	132	177	70	359	881	2,348	439	263	5,930
Qatar	389	38	89	18	12	299	698	2,012	420	12	3,987
Réunion											
Rwanda	47	2	12	40	9	25	38	61	47		281
Sao Tomé e Príncipe											
Saudi Arabia	4,344	324	638	81	140	3,107	5,237	13,835	3,201	1,310	32,217
Senegal	432	36	61	285	41	225	261	525	88		1,953
Seychelles											
Sierra Leone											
Somalia											
South Africa	769	154	696	3,548	183	2,883	2,469	8,368	2,129	2,107	23,306
Sudan											
Swaziland	122	18	30	86	10	106	138	174	92	5	781
Syria	537	10	205	132	80	451	1,080	748	61	270	3,573
Tanzania	189	12	44	212	65	223	296	612	97	1	1,750
Togo	66	8	10	54	7	37	98	53	22		355
Tunisia	685	57	408	998	53	882	2,573	3,107	1,101	72	9,935
Uganda	82	2	35	164	31	130	195	285	74		999
United Arab Emirates											
Yemen											
Zambia	76	2	38	111	21	213	193	476	217	6	1,352
Zimbabwe											

Source: United Nations, UN Trade Statistics
Notes: SITC Classification: 0 Food and live animals; 1 Beverages and tobacco; 2 Crude materials excl. fuels; 3 Mineral fuels etc;4 Oils and fats; 5 Chemicals; 6 Basic manufactures; 7 Machinery and transport equipment; 8 Miscellaneous manufactured goods; 9 Others

Imports (cif) by Commodity: SITC Classification 2002 (% Analysis)

- % of total imports

	0	1	2	3	4	5	6	7	8	9	Total
North America											
Canada	5.0	0.6	2.7	5.6	0.1	9.3	12.6	49.7	11.9	2.4	100.0
USA	3.6	1.0	1.9	11.4	0.1	8.0	10.9	42.0	16.7	4.4	100.0
Latin America											
Anguilla											
Antigua											
Argentina	4.9	0.4	3.1	4.3	0.2	21.0	15.1	40.1	10.7	0.3	100.0
Aruba											
Bahamas	14.0	3.3	2.5	15.9	0.2	7.2	15.0	25.7	14.9	1.4	100.0
Barbados	14.6	3.2	3.5	6.3	0.6	11.9	16.5	27.2	15.9	0.3	100.0
Belize											
Bermuda											
Bolivia	11.7	0.6	4.3	6.9	0.2	17.7	19.6	26.5	11.7	0.8	100.0
Brazil	4.8	0.3	2.5	14.1	0.3	18.7	9.7	43.4	6.3	0.1	100.0
British Virgin Islands											
Cayman Islands											
Chile	6.8	0.3	1.7	17.4	0.4	14.3	15.0	33.0	10.9	0.3	100.0
Colombia	9.7	0.8	3.2	1.3	0.7	21.7	16.1	36.7	8.3	1.3	100.0
Costa Rica	6.0	0.6	1.9	6.7	0.2	15.1	15.6	40.5	13.0	0.3	100.0
Cuba											
Dominica	19.0	3.2	2.0	9.5	2.1	12.5	17.0	22.0	12.8		100.0
Dominican Republic											
Ecuador	6.7	0.4	2.5	5.4	0.6	17.9	16.7	37.7	8.7	3.4	100.0
El Salvador	14.3	0.8	2.9	12.8	1.7	15.9	18.7	23.4	9.4	0.3	100.0
French Guiana											
Grenada	17.9	2.0	2.0	8.3	0.2	11.5	17.3	27.9	12.7		100.0
Guadeloupe											
Guatemala	12.3	0.9	1.8	13.3	1.2	17.8	15.9	27.1	9.7	0.1	100.0
Guyana											
Haiti											
Honduras	17.7	1.0	0.8	13.2	0.4	17.5	17.3	23.7	8.1	0.4	100.0
Jamaica	13.8	0.9	1.7	18.7	0.7	10.4	13.9	22.9	14.2	2.9	100.0
Martinique											
Mexico	4.4	0.2	2.3	2.9	0.2	7.6	15.5	54.0	12.3	0.6	100.0
Netherlands Antilles											
Nicaragua	13.6	1.2	0.8	17.6	2.2	16.7	15.5	21.7	10.6	0.1	100.0
Panama	11.8	1.0	0.7	17.2	0.6	12.6	14.8	27.1	14.2		100.0
Paraguay	5.8	7.7	1.5	16.4	0.2	16.8	13.8	26.6	11.2		100.0
Peru	11.6	0.4	2.5	13.3	1.5	17.4	14.8	29.4	9.0		100.0
Puerto Rico											
St Kitts	14.3	2.5	2.9	7.8	0.4	8.2	23.3	26.7	13.9		100.0
St Lucia	23.1	3.9	3.0	11.3	0.2	8.2	17.9	20.5	12.0		100.0
St Vincent and the Grenadines	22.0	2.4	3.4	8.7	0.4	9.6	18.6	23.2	11.7		100.0
Suriname	13.3	3.2	1.5	6.7	1.2	10.0	17.7	36.2	9.4	0.7	100.0
Trinidad and Tobago	7.5	0.6	1.5	22.4	0.2	7.6	12.3	41.0	5.9	1.1	100.0
Uruguay	9.4	1.5	3.8	12.0	0.5	19.2	15.9	27.0	10.6		100.0
Venezuela	9.2	1.5	1.9	4.4	0.6	15.5	14.2	41.2	11.6	0.1	100.0

Source: United Nations, UN Trade Statistics
Notes: SITC Classification: 0 Food and live animals; 1 Beverages and tobacco; 2 Crude materials excl. fuels; 3 Mineral fuels etc;4 Oils and fats; 5 Chemicals; 6 Basic manufactures; 7 Machinery and transport equipment; 8 Miscellaneous manufactured goods; 9 Others

■ Imports

Imports (cif) by Commodity: SITC Classification 2002 (% Analysis)

● % of total imports

	0	1	2	3	4	5	6	7	8	9	Total
Asia Pacific											
Afghanistan											
American Samoa											
Armenia	20.0	2.4	1.1	19.7	1.7	10.6	21.7	15.4	5.8	1.5	100.0
Azerbaijan	11.9	1.4	2.5	17.6	0.8	5.7	21.5	32.1	6.2	0.3	100.0
Bangladesh	9.4	0.3	8.7	4.8	5.7	10.9	30.9	22.9	6.2	0.1	100.0
Bhutan											
Brunei											
Cambodia											
China	2.0	0.2	8.8	6.5	0.3	12.8	17.4	44.7	6.6	0.7	100.0
Fiji	18.7	0.8	0.8	11.3	1.1	8.3	24.6	23.7	10.5	0.3	100.0
French Polynesia											
Guam											
Hong Kong, China	3.5	0.6	1.3	2.0	0.2	5.8	16.5	43.0	26.7	0.5	100.0
India	2.3		6.9	35.9	2.5	9.1	15.6	15.3	4.9	7.4	100.0
Indonesia	7.3	0.9	10.3	21.5	0.1	17.0	12.7	28.0	2.1	0.1	100.0
Japan	11.0	1.3	6.6	20.5	0.1	7.3	9.0	27.6	14.6	2.0	100.0
Kazakhstan	7.2	1.3	3.0	11.3	0.8	11.3	20.4	37.6	6.8	0.3	100.0
Kiribati											
Kyrgyzstan	9.2	3.3	4.1	26.3	0.7	13.6	13.4	21.2	8.2		100.0
Laos											
Macau	5.6	8.2	0.9	8.2	0.1	3.5	40.2	17.8	15.3	0.2	100.0
Malaysia	4.8	0.3	2.4	5.4	0.3	7.2	10.7	59.8	5.8	3.2	100.0
Maldives	18.5	3.5	3.9	13.1	0.7	5.4	20.2	22.6	12.2		100.0
Mongolia	17.5	2.6	1.1	21.6	0.8	5.6	17.0	27.3	6.4		100.0
Myanmar											
Nauru											
Nepal	6.6	0.6	6.7	15.9	2.9	10.4	15.9	16.7	3.2	21.0	100.0
New Caledonia	11.7	2.9	1.2	15.1	0.3	8.7	13.4	33.0	13.6	0.2	100.0
North Korea											
Pakistan	6.4		8.2	28.3	3.8	18.1	9.8	20.0	2.5	2.9	100.0
Papua New Guinea											
Philippines	7.7	0.7	3.3	10.9	0.2	8.8	11.9	52.4	4.1	0.1	100.0
Singapore	2.5	1.0	0.6	12.5	0.2	5.8	7.3	59.7	9.0	1.5	100.0
Solomon Islands											
South Korea	5.1	0.4	6.3	24.4	0.2	8.9	11.4	34.1	7.8	1.2	100.0
Sri Lanka	12.4	1.1	1.9	10.7	0.4	9.2	38.6	16.4	7.6	1.6	100.0
Taiwan											
Tajikistan											
Thailand	4.2	0.3	4.0	12.0	0.1	10.0	16.0	45.7	5.6	2.0	100.0
Tonga											
Turkmenistan	10.3	1.5	0.9	1.2	0.2	8.8	22.3	42.7	6.2	5.9	100.0
Tuvalu											
Uzbekistan											
Vanuatu											
Vietnam											
Western Samoa											
Australasia											
Australia	3.7	0.8	1.5	8.6	0.2	12.6	11.7	44.4	14.5	2.1	100.0
New Zealand	6.9	1.1	2.9	10.1	0.3	12.8	14.5	37.7	13.4	0.2	100.0

Source: United Nations, UN Trade Statistics
Notes: SITC Classification: 0 Food and live animals; 1 Beverages and tobacco; 2 Crude materials excl. fuels; 3 Mineral fuels etc;4 Oils and fats; 5 Chemicals; 6 Basic manufactures; 7 Machinery and transport equipment; 8 Miscellaneous manufactured goods; 9 Others

▫ Imports

Imports (cif) by Commodity: SITC Classification 2002 (% Analysis)

● % of total imports

	0	1	2	3	4	5	6	7	8	9	Total
Africa and Middle East											
Algeria	26.4	0.4	2.9	1.4	1.9	11.3	17.4	34.0	4.3		100.0
Angola											
Bahrain	9.5	1.5	7.5	38.7	0.2	4.8	12.3	19.2	6.2		100.0
Benin	18.4	1.3	5.8	16.7	0.4	11.7	24.7	16.6	4.5		100.0
Botswana	12.3	1.3	2.5	6.8	0.6	7.0	18.4	30.1	15.5	5.5	100.0
Burkina Faso	10.5	2.1	1.0	25.2	1.2	9.1	13.1	34.1	3.6	0.1	100.0
Burundi	11.3	0.2	4.1	11.7	1.1	19.3	21.0	22.6	8.3	0.4	100.0
Cameroon	14.7	0.5	4.0	16.7	0.2	10.6	23.1	25.7	4.3		100.0
Cape Verde											
Central African Republic											
Chad											
Comoros											
Congo Dem Rep											
Congo-Brazzaville											
Côte d'Ivoire											
Djibouti											
Egypt	10.7	0.5	7.7	4.9	1.7	14.6	18.3	24.0	5.6	12.1	100.0
Equatorial Guinea											
Eritrea											
Ethiopia	9.5	0.6	1.7	12.4	1.2	12.9	19.0	32.3	10.1	0.4	100.0
Gabon											
Gambia											
Ghana	14.8	5.6	3.7	23.6	0.3	9.0	14.4	24.3	4.1	0.1	100.0
Guinea	19.2	3.4	1.3	18.3	1.3	11.7	13.9	24.7	5.8	0.3	100.0
Guinea-Bissau											
Iran	13.1	0.1	4.0	4.9	1.9	14.1	20.8	38.1	3.0		100.0
Iraq											
Israel	4.3	0.6	1.7	11.0	0.1	9.1	27.0	36.0	9.7	0.5	100.0
Jordan	14.2	0.9	3.0	14.1	1.0	10.5	21.2	27.3	5.9	1.8	100.0
Kenya	9.7	0.7	2.8	22.4	3.5	14.2	12.6	28.3	5.5	0.3	100.0
Kuwait											
Lebanon	13.2	2.7	2.8	18.1	0.5	9.7	15.9	23.2	10.6	3.4	100.0
Lesotho											
Liberia											
Libya											
Madagascar											
Malawi	5.4	3.9	2.1	17.0	2.3	13.4	20.0	28.1	7.5	0.3	100.0
Mali											
Mauritania											
Mauritius	15.1	0.6	3.0	11.4	0.8	8.3	29.7	21.8	9.0	0.2	100.0
Morocco	12.0	0.7	4.7	16.9	1.5	9.6	23.4	24.0	7.2	0.1	100.0
Mozambique											
Namibia	10.5	1.3	2.2	10.6	0.5	10.5	19.5	33.1	11.4	0.3	100.0
Niger	32.6	4.8	3.0	12.7	6.9	9.2	10.7	15.1	4.7	0.4	100.0
Nigeria	16.1	0.6	1.3	1.6	0.4	22.1	18.8	35.4	3.6		100.0
Oman	12.4	8.9	2.2	3.0	1.2	6.1	14.9	39.6	7.4	4.4	100.0
Qatar	9.7	1.0	2.2	0.5	0.3	7.5	17.5	50.5	10.5	0.3	100.0
Réunion											
Rwanda	16.8	0.8	4.2	14.4	3.3	8.8	13.5	21.6	16.6		100.0
Sao Tomé e Príncipe											
Saudi Arabia	13.5	1.0	2.0	0.3	0.4	9.6	16.3	42.9	9.9	4.1	100.0
Senegal	22.1	1.8	3.1	14.6	2.1	11.5	13.3	26.9	4.5		100.0
Seychelles											
Sierra Leone											
Somalia											
South Africa	3.3	0.7	3.0	15.2	0.8	12.4	10.6	35.9	9.1	9.0	100.0
Sudan											
Swaziland	15.6	2.3	3.8	11.0	1.3	13.6	17.7	22.2	11.7	0.7	100.0
Syria	15.0	0.3	5.7	3.7	2.2	12.6	30.2	20.9	1.7	7.5	100.0
Tanzania	10.8	0.7	2.5	12.1	3.7	12.8	16.9	34.9	5.5	0.1	100.0
Togo	18.7	2.3	2.7	15.3	2.0	10.4	27.5	15.0	6.2		100.0
Tunisia	6.9	0.6	4.1	10.0	0.5	8.9	25.9	31.3	11.1	0.7	100.0
Uganda	8.2	0.2	3.5	16.5	3.1	13.0	19.5	28.6	7.4		100.0
United Arab Emirates											
Yemen											
Zambia	5.6	0.2	2.8	8.2	1.5	15.7	14.3	35.2	16.0	0.4	100.0
Zimbabwe											

Source: United Nations, UN Trade Statistics
Notes: SITC Classification: 0 Food and live animals; 1 Beverages and tobacco; 2 Crude materials excl. fuels; 3 Mineral fuels etc;4 Oils and fats; 5 Chemicals; 6 Basic manufactures; 7 Machinery and transport equipment; 8 Miscellaneous manufactured goods; 9 Others

□ Exports

Total Exports (fob) 1977-2002 (US$)

Table 13.6

● US$ million

	1977	1980	1985	1990	1991	1992	1993	1994
North America								
Canada	43,545	67,734	90,950	127,629	127,163	134,435	145,178	165,376
USA	123,182	225,566	218,815	393,592	421,730	448,163	464,773	512,627
Latin America								
Anguilla								
Antigua	7	26	17	21	50	65	62	44
Argentina	5,652	8,021	8,396	12,353	11,978	12,235	13,118	15,659
Aruba				28	26			
Bahamas	3,261	5,009	2,728	238	225	192	162	167
Barbados	97	228	357	215	207	190	187	182
Belize	62	111	90	108	99	116	119	127
Bermuda	39	37	23		49	84	35	32
Bolivia	632	942	623	926	849	710	728	1,032
Brazil	12,120	20,132	25,639	31,414	31,620	35,793	38,555	43,545
British Virgin Islands								
Cayman Islands	9	11	16	18	25	22	22	11
Chile	2,190	4,705	3,804	8,373	8,942	10,007	9,199	11,604
Colombia	2,403	3,924	3,552	6,766	7,232	6,917	7,116	8,419
Costa Rica	828	1,002	976	1,448	1,598	1,841	2,625	2,869
Cuba								
Dominica	12	10	28	55	54	53	49	47
Dominican Republic	780	962	735	735	658	562	511	644
Ecuador	1,436	2,481	2,905	2,714	2,852	3,007	2,904	3,820
El Salvador	972	967	679	582	588	598	732	844
French Guiana	7	25	37	93	70	96	96	136
Grenada	14	17	22	28	22	20	20	24
Guadeloupe	79	107	75	118	147	130	128	152
Guatemala	1,160	1,520	1,057	1,163	1,202	1,295	1,340	1,522
Guyana	259	389	166	257	246	292	414	456
Haiti	149	226	168	160	167	73	80	82
Honduras	513	829	780	831	792	802	814	842
Jamaica	768	963	566	1,158	1,105	1,047	1,071	1,212
Martinique	128	117	162	272	194	242	191	182
Mexico	4,167	18,031	26,757	40,711	42,688	46,196	51,886	60,882
Netherlands Antilles	2,647	5,162	1,031	1,790	1,599	1,559	1,283	1,375
Nicaragua	637	451	302	331	272	223	267	335
Panama	251	361	336	340	358	502	553	583
Paraguay	279	310	304	959	737	657	725	817
Peru	1,726	3,898	2,979	3,231	3,329	3,484	3,515	4,555
Puerto Rico								
St Kitts	15	24	20	28	27	26	27	22
St Lucia	25	58	52	127	110	124	120	94
St Vincent and the Grenadines	10	15	63	83	67	78	58	50
Suriname	310	514	329	472	359	391	1,190	449
Trinidad and Tobago	2,180	4,077	2,139	1,960	1,985	1,691	1,662	1,867
Uruguay	608	1,059	909	1,693	1,605	1,703	1,645	1,913
Venezuela	9,551	19,221	14,438	17,497	15,155	14,185	14,686	16,089

Source: *Euromonitor from International Monetary Fund (IMF), International Financial Statistics*

□ Exports

Total Exports (fob) 1977-2002 (US$) (continued)

- US$ million

	1995	1996	1997	1998	1999	2000	2001	2002
North America								
Canada	192,197	201,633	214,422	214,327	238,446	276,635	259,858	252,394
USA	584,743	625,073	688,696	682,138	702,098	781,125	730,803	693,860
Latin America								
Anguilla								
Antigua	53	38	38	36	38	48	52	57
Argentina	20,967	23,811	26,370	26,441	23,333	26,341	26,543	25,709
Aruba	15	12	24	29	29	173	149	128
Bahamas	176	180	181	300	532	805	649	617
Barbados	239	281	283	252	264	272	259	206
Belize	143	154	159	156	170	170	161	160
Bermuda	56	68	77	77	84	85	90	94
Bolivia	1,101	1,137	1,167	1,104	1,051	1,230	1,285	1,299
Brazil	46,506	47,747	52,994	51,140	48,011	55,086	58,223	60,362
British Virgin Islands								
Cayman Islands	11	6	6	4	5	7	10	10
Chile	16,024	15,657	17,902	16,323	17,162	19,210	18,466	18,340
Colombia	10,056	10,587	11,522	10,852	11,576	13,040	12,257	12,001
Costa Rica	3,453	3,730	4,268	5,511	6,577	5,865	5,010	5,253
Cuba	1,600	2,015	1,812	1,540	1,466	1,635	1,753	1,753
Dominica	45	51	53	62	56	54	43	42
Dominican Republic	872	945	1,017	880	805	966	805	834
Ecuador	4,307	4,900	5,264	4,203	4,451	4,927	4,678	5,030
El Salvador	998	1,024	1,371	1,256	1,177	1,332	1,214	1,234
French Guiana								
Grenada	22	20	23	27	26	28	32	35
Guadeloupe	157							
Guatemala	2,156	2,031	2,344	2,582	2,398	2,696	2,466	2,232
Guyana	455	517	644	484	523	498	477	493
Haiti	110	90	212	320	334	318	274	280
Honduras	1,220	1,316	1,446	1,533	1,164	1,370	1,318	1,284
Jamaica	1,427	1,383	1,383	1,312	1,240	1,304	1,220	1,114
Martinique	223	255	279	267	304	282	307	316
Mexico	79,542	96,000	110,431	117,460	136,391	166,367	158,547	160,682
Netherlands Antilles	1,522	1,269	1,488	1,169	1,451	1,851	1,652	1,697
Nicaragua	457	466	577	573	545	645	592	596
Panama	625	666	723	784	822	859	911	846
Paraguay	919	1,044	1,089	1,014	741	869	990	721
Peru	5,575	5,897	6,841	5,757	6,113	7,028	7,100	7,669
Puerto Rico	23,811	24,478	23,875	30,327	30,153	31,532	32,699	35,655
St Kitts	19	22	22	22	24	26	28	30
St Lucia	109	80	61	62	56	43	44	116
St Vincent and the Grenadines	43	46	46	50	49	47	41	38
Suriname	477	433	701	436	342	399	369	324
Trinidad and Tobago	2,455	2,500	2,542	2,258	2,804	4,274	4,280	3,880
Uruguay	2,106	2,397	2,726	2,771	2,237	2,295	2,060	1,937
Venezuela	18,457	23,060	21,624	17,193	20,190	31,802	27,409	24,482

Source: *Euromonitor from International Monetary Fund (IMF), International Financial Statistics*

□ Exports

Total Exports (fob) 1977-2002 (US$) (continued)

● US$ million

	1977	1980	1985	1990	1991	1992	1993	1994
Asia Pacific								
Afghanistan	306	670	567	235	286	91	180	24
American Samoa	81	127	201	311	327	318	481	248
Armenia						83	156	216
Azerbaijan						1,571	993	638
Bangladesh	476	759	999	1,671	1,689	2,098	2,278	2,661
Bhutan		17	22	70	63	66	65	66
Brunei								
Cambodia								
China	7,520	18,099	27,350	62,091	71,910	84,940	91,744	121,006
Fiji	224	470	307	497	450	443	450	567
French Polynesia	16	30	41	111	128	106	159	224
Guam	31	35	58	60	62	77	106	85
Hong Kong, China	9,616	19,752	30,187	82,160	98,577	119,487	135,244	151,399
India	6,378	8,586	9,140	17,969	17,727	19,628	21,572	25,022
Indonesia	10,853	21,909	18,587	25,675	29,142	33,967	36,823	40,055
Japan	81,083	130,441	177,164	287,581	314,786	339,885	362,244	397,005
Kazakhstan							3,277	3,231
Kiribati	20	3	4	3	3	5	3	5
Kyrgyzstan							340	340
Laos	4	28	54	79	97	133	241	301
Macau	219	538	901	1,701	1,665	1,766	1,787	1,866
Malaysia	6,079	12,945	15,316	29,452	34,350	40,772	47,131	58,845
Maldives	3	8	23	53	54	40	35	48
Mongolia		403	689	661	348	388	383	356
Myanmar	215	477	306	328	423	537	592	803
Nauru	35	65			33	35	41	40
Nepal	81	80	160	204	257	368	384	362
New Caledonia	315	409	268	480	446	410	365	558
North Korea					1,960	1,010	1,020	1,020
Pakistan	1,194	2,631	2,753	5,615	6,559	7,351	6,720	7,400
Papua New Guinea	683	1,031	928	1,177	1,460	1,927	2,585	2,632
Philippines	3,127	5,741	4,611	8,117	8,801	9,751	11,129	13,304
Singapore	8,241	19,375	22,812	52,730	58,966	63,472	74,012	96,825
Solomon Islands	33	74	70	70	84	102	129	142
South Korea	10,048	17,512	30,282	65,016	71,870	76,632	82,236	96,013
Sri Lanka	761	1,062	1,333	1,912	1,987	2,455	2,859	3,208
Taiwan	9,349	19,786	30,696	67,079	76,163	81,387	84,641	92,876
Tajikistan								
Thailand	3,490	6,505	7,121	23,068	28,428	32,472	36,969	45,261
Tonga	7	7	5	11	13	12	16	14
Turkmenistan								
Tuvalu								
Uzbekistan								
Vanuatu	32	36	31	19	18	24	23	25
Vietnam								
Western Samoa	15	17	16	9	6	6	6	4
Australasia								
Australia	13,367	21,944	22,604	39,752	41,854	42,824	42,723	47,528
New Zealand	3,196	5,421	5,720	9,394	9,619	9,785	10,542	12,185

Source: Euromonitor from International Monetary Fund (IMF), International Financial Statistics

Exports

Total Exports (fob) 1977-2002 (US$) (continued)

- US$ million

	1995	1996	1997	1998	1999	2000	2001	2002
Asia Pacific								
Afghanistan	26	173	201	209	167	186	113	79
American Samoa	272	313	424	415	345	346	383	376
Armenia	271	290	233	221	232	294	343	507
Azerbaijan	637	631	781	606	929	897	927	1,002
Bangladesh	3,173	3,297	3,778	3,831	3,922	4,787	4,826	4,566
Bhutan	103	100	118	108	116	123	123	125
Brunei	2,389				2,216	3,552	3,727	4,958
Cambodia	342		626	933	1,040	1,123	1,296	1,572
China	148,780	151,048	182,792	183,712	194,931	249,203	266,098	325,591
Fiji	619	748	620	510	610	584	538	525
French Polynesia	194	253	224	247	253	222	195	184
Guam	85	73	66	86	76	74	61	37
Hong Kong, China	173,750	180,750	188,059	174,002	173,885	201,860	189,894	200,092
India	30,630	33,105	35,008	33,437	35,667	42,379	43,347	49,312
Indonesia	45,417	49,814	53,443	48,848	48,666	62,124	56,447	58,120
Japan	443,116	410,901	420,957	387,927	419,367	479,249	403,496	416,726
Kazakhstan	5,250	5,911	6,497	5,334	5,872	8,812	8,639	9,670
Kiribati	7	5	6	6	6	17	28	24
Kyrgyzstan	409	505	604	514	463	511	480	488
Laos	311	323	359	370	311	330	331	298
Macau	1,997	1,996	2,148	2,141	2,200	2,539	2,300	2,356
Malaysia	73,914	78,327	78,742	73,255	84,621	98,229	88,005	93,265
Maldives	50	59	73	74	64	76	76	90
Mongolia	473	424	452	345	358	466	448	494
Myanmar	860	754	874	1,077	1,136	1,646	2,381	3,046
Nauru	28	30	25	20	36	28	13	17
Nepal	345	385	406	474	602	804	737	568
New Caledonia	471	535	527	374	558	606	554	598
North Korea	840	848	1,025	644	597	708	826	713
Pakistan	8,029	9,365	8,758	8,514	8,491	9,028	9,238	9,913
Papua New Guinea	2,654	2,529	2,163	1,772	1,924	2,096	1,813	1,549
Philippines	17,502	20,408	24,882	29,414	36,576	39,783	32,664	36,502
Singapore	118,268	125,014	124,985	109,895	114,680	137,804	121,751	125,177
Solomon Islands	168	162	175	126	146	93	84	72
South Korea	125,058	129,715	136,164	132,313	143,685	172,267	150,439	162,470
Sri Lanka	3,798	4,095	4,639	4,809	4,594	5,430	4,816	4,699
Taiwan	111,563	115,730	121,081	110,518	121,496	147,777	122,506	130,457
Tajikistan	458	755	746	586	666	792	580	558
Thailand	56,439	55,721	57,374	54,456	58,440	69,057	65,113	68,768
Tonga	14	11	10	8	12	9	7	6
Turkmenistan	1,881	1,682	751	594	1,340	2,700	2,560	3,859
Tuvalu								
Uzbekistan	2,708	2,777	2,881	2,272	2,710	2,324	2,655	2,648
Vanuatu	28	30	35	34	26	30	15	13
Vietnam	5,723	7,408	8,722	9,602	11,540	14,448	15,100	17,374
Western Samoa	9	10	15	15	20	14	16	14
Australasia								
Australia	53,111	60,301	62,910	55,893	56,080	63,870	63,387	65,033
New Zealand	13,645	14,360	14,216	12,069	12,454	13,272	13,723	14,364

Source: *Euromonitor from International Monetary Fund (IMF), International Financial Statistics*

■ Exports

Total Exports (fob) 1977-2002 (US$) (continued)

● US$ million

	1977	1980	1985	1990	1991	1992	1993	1994
Africa and Middle East								
Algeria	5,944	13,871	12,841	12,880	12,440	11,510	10,410	8,892
Angola		56,327	2,260	3,883	3,449	3,833	2,901	3,017
Bahrain	1,845	3,594	2,897	3,761	3,513	3,464	3,726	3,617
Benin	31	63	150	122	21	335	384	398
Botswana	186	504	839	1,785	1,843	1,746	1,757	1,848
Burkina Faso	55	90	71	152	106	64	69	107
Burundi	90	65	112	75	91	73	62	121
Cameroon	704	1,384	722	2,002	1,834	1,840	1,429	1,364
Cape Verde	2	4	6	6	4	4	4	4
Central African Republic	82	116	92	120	47	107	110	151
Chad	107	71	62	188	194	182	132	148
Comoros	9	11	16	18	25	22	22	11
Congo Dem Rep	989	1,627	950	999	830	426	368	419
Congo-Brazzaville	267	911	1,087	981	1,030	1,179	1,069	959
Côte d'Ivoire	2,157	3,135	2,969	3,072	2,686	2,875	2,519	2,742
Djibouti	19	12	14	25	17	16	12	12
Egypt	1,708	3,046	3,714	4,957	3,705	3,063	2,252	3,476
Equatorial Guinea	14	14	17	62	37	50	57	62
Eritrea								
Ethiopia	333	425	333	298	189	169	199	372
Gabon	1,343	2,173	1,951	2,204	2,243	2,082	2,295	2,350
Gambia	47	31	43	31	38	57	67	35
Ghana	1,014	1,257	617		617	1,252	974	1,425
Guinea	314	401	493	671				
Guinea-Bissau	13	11	12	19	20	6	28	86
Iran	9,216	7,109	13,328	19,305	18,661	19,868	18,080	19,434
Iraq	19,012				370	560	550	510
Israel	3,082	5,538	6,260	11,576	11,921	10,019	14,826	16,884
Jordan	249	574	789	1,064	1,130	1,219	1,246	1,424
Kenya	1,186	1,245	958	1,032	1,108	1,339	1,374	1,587
Kuwait	9,754	19,842	10,597	7,042	1,088	6,572	10,246	11,260
Lebanon	760	955	288	494	539	560	452	470
Lesotho	14	58	22	62	67	109	132	143
Liberia	447	600	436					
Libya	11,411	21,910	12,314	13,225	11,234	10,793	8,140	9,120
Madagascar	338	401	274	319	305	278	260	369
Malawi	200	295	246	417	469	396	320	342
Mali	125	205	124	359	312	343	478	335
Mauritania	157	194	374	447				487
Mauritius	309	435	440	1,194	1,194	1,302	1,299	1,347
Morocco	1,302	2,441	2,165	4,265	4,284	3,973	3,055	5,556
Mozambique								157
Namibia				1,086	1,214	1,342	1,240	1,308
Niger	161	566	259	283	307	333	287	225
Nigeria	11,839	25,946	12,537	13,596	12,264	11,886	9,908	9,415
Oman	1,139	2,387	3,938	5,508	4,874	5,553	5,370	5,545
Qatar	2,072	5,680						3,146
Réunion	114	130	137	190	148	213	168	171
Rwanda	89	121	131	109	93	66	65	29
Sao Tomé e Príncipe	23	17	6	4	6	5	5	6
Saudi Arabia	44,729	109,116	27,481	44,417	47,797	50,286	42,395	42,614
Senegal	624	477	562	762	701	673	707	791
Seychelles	11	21	28	57	49	48	51	52
Sierra Leone	136	224	130	138	145	149	118	116
Somalia								
South Africa	9,904	25,540	16,330	23,568	23,279	23,440	24,222	25,308
Sudan	661	543	374	374	305	319	417	503
Swaziland	165	373	179	557	591	639	681	789
Syria	1,070	2,108	1,637	4,212	3,430	3,093	3,146	3,047
Tanzania	507	511	246	331	342	416	450	519
Togo	159	338	190	268	253	275	136	328
Tunisia	929	2,231	1,738	3,527	3,699	4,019	3,747	4,657
Uganda	59	345		152	200	143	179	409
United Arab Emirates	9,636	20,676	14,043	23,544	24,436	24,756		
Yemen					659	619	611	934
Zambia	896	1,305	482	1,309	1,083	756	826	927
Zimbabwe	877	1,409	1,108	1,725	1,530	1,442	1,565	1,881

Source: Euromonitor from International Monetary Fund (IMF), International Financial Statistics

Exports

Total Exports (fob) 1977-2002 (US$) (continued)

- US$ million

	1995	1996	1997	1998	1999	2000	2001	2002
Africa and Middle East								
Algeria	10,258	13,220	13,004	13,430	12,010	14,159	13,958	18,635
Angola	3,723	5,095	5,007	3,543	5,397	7,702	6,380	7,510
Bahrain	4,113	4,702	4,384	3,270	4,363	6,195	5,577	5,369
Benin	420	654	417	407	422	392	374	375
Botswana	2,142	2,537	2,842	1,948	2,162	2,506	2,291	2,222
Burkina Faso	276	233	232	319	255	209	234	237
Burundi	106	40	87	65	54	50	39	30
Cameroon	1,651	1,769	1,860	1,671	1,601	1,635	1,773	1,760
Cape Verde	8	13	14	10	11	11	10	9
Central African Republic	171	147	163	151	146	161	142	138
Chad	243	238	237	262	202	183	189	189
Comoros	11	6	6	4	5	7	10	10
Congo Dem Rep	438	592	530	500	490	450	359	327
Congo-Brazzaville	1,173	1,345	1,668	1,368	1,560	2,489	1,854	1,995
Côte d'Ivoire	3,806	4,446	4,451	4,606	4,662	3,888	3,946	5,167
Djibouti	14	14	11	12	12	12	13	14
Egypt	3,450	3,539	3,921	3,130	3,559	4,689	4,128	4,708
Equatorial Guinea	86	175	495	439	709	1,097	1,166	1,491
Eritrea								
Ethiopia	423	417	587	561	467	486	455	480
Gabon	2,713	3,184	3,024	1,916	2,394	2,462	2,649	2,667
Gambia	16	21	15	27	7	18	18	26
Ghana	1,724	1,669	1,635	1,795	1,851	1,326	1,432	1,407
Guinea	703	816	955	980	963	868	877	861
Guinea-Bissau	44	28	48	26	51	62	63	54
Iran	18,360	22,391	18,381	13,118	21,030	28,345	23,716	24,440
Iraq	496	731	4,600	5,500	12,800	20,603	15,905	13,520
Israel	19,046	20,610	22,503	22,993	25,794	31,404	29,048	29,347
Jordan	1,769	1,817	1,836	1,802	1,832	1,899	2,293	2,433
Kenya	1,879	2,068	2,054	2,008	1,747	1,734	1,944	2,116
Kuwait	12,785	14,889	14,224	9,554	12,164	19,436	16,203	15,425
Lebanon	656	736	643	662	677	715	870	1,046
Lesotho	160	187	196	194	175	173	154	145
Liberia	400	512	500	610	500	500	479	479
Libya	7,706	8,193	7,498	5,077	7,939	10,195	8,915	9,413
Madagascar	369	299	223	243	220	298	373	430
Malawi	405	481	537	431	453	379	449	447
Mali	442	433	561	561	566	545	725	916
Mauritania	499	491	406	350	373	300	300	281
Mauritius	1,538	1,802	1,592	1,645	1,554	1,557	1,615	1,629
Morocco	6,881	6,881	7,032	7,153	7,367	6,961	7,144	7,772
Mozambique	168	217	222	230	263	364	361	412
Namibia	1,409	1,418	1,338	1,232	1,234	1,320	1,179	1,147
Niger	288	325	272	334	287	283	272	280
Nigeria	12,342	16,154	15,207	9,855	13,856	20,975	17,261	15,107
Oman	6,068	7,346	7,630	5,508	4,971	8,363	7,439	11,172
Qatar	3,481	3,752	3,791	4,880	7,061	8,669	8,427	10,399
Réunion								
Rwanda	52	61	87	60	60	52	85	56
Sao Tomé e Príncipe	5	5	5	9	9	7	8	9
Saudi Arabia	50,040	60,729	60,732	38,822	50,761	77,583	68,064	74,112
Senegal	993	988	905	968	1,027	920	1,003	1,109
Seychelles	53	140	113	122	145	193	216	256
Sierra Leone	42	47	17	7	6	13	29	49
Somalia								
South Africa	27,853	29,221	31,027	26,362	26,707	29,983	29,258	29,723
Sudan	556	620	594	596	780	1,807	1,699	1,800
Swaziland	866	856	962	973	937	910	1,054	937
Syria	3,563	3,999	3,916	2,890	3,464	19,260	21,648	19,256
Tanzania	682	784	753	589	543	663	776	875
Togo	378	441	424	968	391	363	357	250
Tunisia	5,475	5,517	5,560	5,738	5,872	5,850	6,609	6,874
Uganda	461	587	555	501	519	460	456	443
United Arab Emirates	24,104	27,304	30,718	34,064	35,527	45,934	46,447	51,793
Yemen	1,945	2,674	2,504	1,497	2,440	4,079	3,215	3,780
Zambia	1,040	1,037	915	729	693	819	889	894
Zimbabwe	2,114	2,406	2,312	1,548	1,419	1,989	1,873	1,845

Source: *Euromonitor from International Monetary Fund (IMF), International Financial Statistics*

□ Exports

Table 13.7

Exports (fob) by Country of Destination 2002

● US$ million

	Africa & Middle East	Asia/ Pacific	of which: Japan	Australasia	Europe	of which: Total EU	Latin America	North America	of which: USA	Total including Others
North America										
Canada	1,937	11,716	5,152	840	12,125	10,540	3,757	221,292	221,292	252,381
USA	29,593	157,377	51,440	14,898	162,946	144,085	148,497	160,799		693,123
Latin America										
Anguilla										
Antigua		1			677	672	9	4	3	690
Argentina	2,492	3,386	403	104	5,902	5,402	12,917	3,326	3,120	28,565
Aruba					38	38	72	16	16	128
Bahamas	3	49	2	1	547	436	63	445	434	1,110
Barbados	1	1		1	39	38	115	40	36	241
Belize		13	7		58	58	36	80	76	188
Bermuda	1	9	4		765	743	22	24	21	880
Bolivia	2	32	6	2	312	96	816	201	193	1,371
Brazil	4,269	8,589	2,425	291	17,040	14,484	14,396	16,417	15,202	62,608
British Virgin Islands										
Cayman Islands										
Chile	320	4,362	1,928	69	4,598	4,238	3,554	3,747	3,484	18,285
Colombia	140	320	193	15	1,885	1,631	3,874	5,493	5,328	11,896
Costa Rica	8	457	122	8	2,090	2,023	937	3,193	3,036	9,624
Cuba	48	165	25	6	878	536	146	208		1,450
Dominica		2	1		24	24	28	5	5	61
Dominican Republic	2	78	32	3	357	342	165	3,958	3,883	4,566
Ecuador	21	490	165	32	1,406	982	1,298	2,276	2,174	5,578
El Salvador	1	33	11	1	112	98	891	1,888	1,853	2,927
French Guiana										
Grenada		5			19	16	15	7	7	49
Guadeloupe										
Guatemala	96	198	67	3	288	228	1,018	2,797	2,706	4,613
Guyana	3	22	3		198	163	190	265	122	681
Haiti	2	2			14	12	21	247	240	286
Honduras	2	54	41	3	314	256	351	3,169	3,088	4,443
Jamaica	30	77	31	7	599	439	90	549	383	1,359
Martinique										
Mexico	154	3,840	1,628	327	6,009	5,320	6,752	131,834	123,767	149,673
Netherlands Antilles	1	93	3	3	131	112	886	348	347	1,663
Nicaragua		7	6	1	91	70	234	672	643	1,083
Panama		21	10		165	167	188	366	361	756
Paraguay	7	57	22		193	132	851	51	44	1,306
Peru	51	1,493	396	37	2,071	1,466	1,281	2,145	1,990	7,079
Puerto Rico										
St Kitts		1			12	12	3	51	46	69
St Lucia					33	33	14	19	18	66
St Vincent and the Grenadines	1	7			157	152	26	16	15	210
Suriname	11	25	17		234	101	74	157	127	502
Trinidad and Tobago	12	22	2	1	443	437	1,199	2,528	2,422	4,258
Uruguay	124	301	48	5	528	474	1,173	215	185	2,283
Venezuela	3	337	107	4	2,382	2,265	7,399	15,172	14,390	26,944

Source: International Monetary Fund (IMF), Direction of Trade Statistics
Notes: US$ totals in this table may differ from the totals given for Exports (fob) by Commodity and Trends in Total Exports (fob)

Exports (fob) by Country of Destination 2002

● US$ million

	Africa & Middle East	Asia/ Pacific	of which: Japan	Australasia	Europe	of which: Total EU	Latin America	North America	of which: USA	Total including Others
Asia Pacific										
Afghanistan	10	58	2		28	20	3	5	4	104
American Samoa		27	2	2						30
Armenia	77	18	3		219	111	1	30	29	352
Azerbaijan	241	80	1		1,304	1,011	18	34	33	1,677
Bangladesh	167	328	56	16	2,422	2,334	44	1,587	1,504	5,442
Bhutan										
Brunei	6	2,662	1,377	386	64	64		282	278	3,418
Cambodia	5	237	68	2	425	415	1	1,055	1,042	1,730
China	16,435	154,097	48,483	5,185	59,522	48,234	9,429	74,369	70,064	325,711
Fiji		151	39	143	80	80	3	159	155	617
French Polynesia		90	84	5	98	97		43	42	237
Guam		36	31		1	1		1		38
Hong Kong, China	3,985	68,565	6,387	1,828	23,375	20,845	3,504	27,985	26,115	133,678
India	7,248	13,160	1,900	592	13,079	11,293	1,533	12,163	11,318	50,072
Indonesia	3,010	32,306	12,045	2,075	8,731	7,924	952	7,948	7,570	57,144
Japan	16,263	153,866		9,764	68,072	61,300	14,650	127,524	120,198	416,632
Kazakhstan	601	1,930	90	2	6,207	2,964	1,330	323	317	10,911
Kiribati		31	19		2	2		1	1	34
Kyrgyzstan	74	137			233	19		41	36	486
Laos	2	216	6		122	113		5	3	448
Macau	5	554	14	3	553	546	11	1,188	1,145	2,359
Malaysia	2,871	52,445	10,511	2,452	13,158	12,083	1,045	21,124	20,330	96,755
Maldives	1	79	16		21	21		112	111	214
Mongolia	3	223	7		73	21	2	162	156	464
Myanmar	29	1,582	100	11	388	361	3	375	345	2,648
Nauru		12		3	1	1		1	1	18
Nepal		282	6	2	91	83	1	156	151	545
New Caledonia	55	136	100	27	178	178	1	9	9	489
North Korea	66	611	209	10	118	79	239			1,049
Pakistan	2,028	1,922	142	143	2,935	2,692	177	2,611	2,419	9,886
Papua New Guinea		617	252	681	231	227		89	88	2,719
Philippines	266	18,088	5,907	458	6,920	6,401	286	11,101	10,392	39,736
Singapore	3,701	71,571	8,935	3,790	17,619	15,675	2,522	19,475	19,106	125,087
Solomon Islands		81	19	1	2	2	1	1	1	88
South Korea	10,351	70,843	15,143	2,662	27,026	21,730	8,676	35,283	32,943	161,480
Sri Lanka	480	496	150	56	1,433	1,271	65	1,819	1,749	4,477
Taiwan										
Tajikistan	30	106			601	239		1	1	737
Thailand	3,743	33,527	10,001	1,845	11,528	10,207	1,117	14,329	13,522	68,851
Tonga		12	11	1	2	1		10	10	25
Turkmenistan	377	97			2,164	520	18	52	49	2,710
Tuvalu					1	1				1
Uzbekistan	8	550	67		1,108	324	4	79	74	1,757
Vanuatu	1	68	4	3	4	4	1	3	3	79
Vietnam	573	6,181	2,299	1,203	4,309	3,791	109	2,531	2,350	15,440
Western Samoa		6	3	49	3	3		7	7	71
Australasia										
Australia	5,130	35,089	12,051	4,239	8,724	8,029	784	7,247	6,248	65,159
New Zealand	584	4,906	1,627	2,875	2,263	2,118	496	2,496	2,199	14,159

Source: International Monetary Fund (IMF), Direction of Trade Statistics
Notes: US$ totals in this table may differ from the totals given for Exports (fob) by Commodity and Trends in Total Exports (fob)

□ Exports

Exports (fob) by Country of Destination 2002

- US$ million

	Africa & Middle East	Asia/ Pacific	of which: Japan	Australasia	Europe	of which: Total EU	Latin America	North America	of which: USA	Total including Others
Africa and Middle East										
Algeria	398	459	37	30	13,612	12,275	1,305	3,426	2,327	19,253
Angola	26	1,680	356		1,941	1,940	247	2,978	2,978	7,232
Bahrain	855	889	146	37	381	337	6	389	381	8,419
Benin	28	106			69	55	14	1	1	222
Botswana										
Burkina Faso	31	64	8		50	47	18	3	3	175
Burundi	7	2			27	16		1	1	37
Cameroon	164	155	4		1,356	1,336	6	174	167	1,999
Cape Verde					19	19		2	2	21
Central African Republic	6	17	1		154	150		2	2	181
Chad	11	3			50	39		6	6	71
Comoros		4	1		18	18		5	5	28
Congo Dem Rep	110	42	28		1,070	1,069		190	190	1,416
Congo-Brazzaville	60	824	74		442	437	87	192	191	2,276
Côte d'Ivoire	1,074	170	11	11	2,535	2,366	149	408	363	4,761
Djibouti	153	10			4	4		2	2	170
Egypt	982	723	63	16	3,018	2,796	38	1,325	1,288	6,985
Equatorial Guinea	43	356	46		648	648	22	692	503	1,781
Eritrea										
Ethiopia	156	63	39	1	246	227		30	26	592
Gabon	143	392	33	31	534	512	371	1,516	1,514	3,281
Gambia	3	5			21	21				29
Ghana	190	151	63	3	1,002	872	16	143	117	1,662
Guinea	87	166	1		448	373		103	77	804
Guinea-Bissau	3	84			7	7	23			117
Iran	3,448	10,442	4,311	56	5,872	4,836	17	183	148	24,744
Iraq	1,102	407	96	21	2,462	2,403	28	4,148	3,453	8,440
Israel	460	4,329	684	324	8,990	7,260	1,119	11,895	11,494	29,213
Jordan	1,284	468	73	1	219	172	6	401	398	2,747
Kenya	1,003	288	25	14	759	721	8	192	184	2,294
Kuwait	623	10,255	3,825	103	1,652	1,602	82	1,881	1,866	15,662
Lebanon	397	83	5	4	313	164	4	65	60	877
Lesotho										
Liberia	21	85			889	751	1	44	43	1,040
Libya	432	41	6		9,366	8,112	37			9,877
Madagascar	40	78	32	1	481	475	1	208	205	832
Malawi	84	33	24	6	197	137	5	70	69	402
Mali	19	57		1	68	61	10	4	2	172
Mauritania	75	60	38		394	358		1	1	538
Mauritius	154	42	13	4	1,184	1,159	1	283	274	1,669
Morocco	484	992	292	71	5,750	5,492	172	441	386	8,039
Mozambique	174	69	18		563	556		8	8	1,277
Namibia										
Niger	62	27	27		67	67				156
Nigeria	1,938	2,741	681	26	4,764	4,325	1,728	5,783	5,654	17,334
Oman	1,296	6,916	1,910	125	397	390		386	384	9,290
Qatar	748	8,707	4,773	156	410	403	8	487	486	11,812
Réunion										
Rwanda	12	77			41	39		4	3	174
Sao Tomé e Príncipe		1			7	6		1		9
Saudi Arabia	8,719	30,069	10,580	789	11,293	10,483	1,090	13,106	12,629	67,518
Senegal	311	210	1		331	344	1	4	2	949
Seychelles	9	41	20	1	219	216		25	25	296
Sierra Leone	4	4	1		82	81		5	4	99
Somalia	88	8			3	2				99
South Africa	5,257	5,883	2,647	585	12,815	12,132	625	4,115	3,802	29,703
Sudan	257	1,442	264		200	180	10	2	1	1,902
Swaziland										
Syria	950	217	20	1	4,371	3,477	19	177	145	5,909
Tanzania	160	273	96	4	298	277	2	26	24	775
Togo	157	42		19	69	59	6	3	3	303
Tunisia	720	165	7	6	5,577	5,395	55	58	54	6,799
Uganda	30	42	13	8	238	210	1	16	16	340
United Arab Emirates	4,544	22,021	10,552	297	2,790	2,555	146	927	907	37,649
Yemen	242	2,675	68		97	96	42	235	234	3,491
Zambia	233	202	60		107	102		8	7	669
Zimbabwe	239	339	113	9	606	524	15	105	99	2,427

Source: *International Monetary Fund (IMF), Direction of Trade Statistics*
Notes: *US$ totals in this table may differ from the totals given for Exports (fob) by Commodity and Trends in Total Exports (fob)*

Table 13.8

□ Exports

Exports (fob) by Country of Destination 2002 (% Analysis)

• % of total exports

	Africa & Middle East	Asia/ Pacific	of which: Japan	Australasia	Europe	of which: Total EU	Latin America	North America	of which: USA	Total including Others
North America										
Canada	0.8	4.6	2.0	0.3	4.8	4.2	1.5	87.7	87.7	100.0
USA	4.3	22.7	7.4	2.1	23.5	20.8	21.4	23.2		100.0
Latin America										
Anguilla										
Antigua		0.1			98.0	97.3	1.3	0.5	0.5	100.0
Argentina	8.7	11.9	1.4	0.4	20.7	18.9	45.2	11.6	10.9	100.0
Aruba	0.1	0.3		0.4	29.7	29.7	56.1	12.2	12.2	100.0
Bahamas	0.2	4.4	0.2	0.1	49.2	39.3	5.7	40.1	39.1	100.0
Barbados	0.5	0.4	0.1	0.3	16.3	15.6	47.7	16.6	14.7	100.0
Belize	0.1	6.9	3.8		31.0	30.6	19.0	42.7	40.4	100.0
Bermuda	0.1	1.0	0.4		86.9	84.4	2.5	2.7	2.4	100.0
Bolivia	0.2	2.3	0.4	0.2	22.8	7.0	59.5	14.6	14.1	100.0
Brazil	6.8	13.7	3.9	0.5	27.2	23.1	23.0	26.2	24.3	100.0
British Virgin Islands										
Cayman Islands										
Chile	1.7	23.9	10.5	0.4	25.1	23.2	19.4	20.5	19.1	100.0
Colombia	1.2	2.7	1.6	0.1	15.8	13.7	32.6	46.2	44.8	100.0
Costa Rica	0.1	4.7	1.3	0.1	21.7	21.0	9.7	33.2	31.5	100.0
Cuba	3.3	11.4	1.8	0.4	60.5	37.0	10.1	14.3		100.0
Dominica		3.7	1.8	0.2	39.0	39.0	45.5	8.6	7.6	100.0
Dominican Republic		1.7	0.7	0.1	7.8	7.5	3.6	86.7	85.0	100.0
Ecuador	0.4	8.8	3.0	0.6	25.2	17.6	23.3	40.8	39.0	100.0
El Salvador		1.1	0.4		3.8	3.3	30.4	64.5	63.3	100.0
French Guiana										
Grenada		10.5	0.4		38.6	33.8	29.9	15.4	13.7	100.0
Guadeloupe										
Guatemala	2.1	4.3	1.4	0.1	6.2	4.9	22.1	60.6	58.7	100.0
Guyana	0.4	3.3	0.4	0.1	29.0	23.9	27.8	38.9	17.9	100.0
Haiti	0.8	0.6	0.1		4.7	4.3	7.3	86.3	83.9	100.0
Honduras		1.2	0.9	0.1	7.1	5.8	7.9	71.3	69.5	100.0
Jamaica	2.2	5.6	2.3	0.5	44.1	32.3	6.6	40.4	28.2	100.0
Martinique										
Mexico	0.1	2.6	1.1	0.2	4.0	3.6	4.5	88.1	82.7	100.0
Netherlands Antilles	0.1	5.6	0.2	0.2	7.9	6.7	53.3	20.9	20.9	100.0
Nicaragua		0.6	0.6	0.1	8.4	6.4	21.6	62.0	59.4	100.0
Panama		2.7	1.3		21.9	22.1	24.9	48.5	47.8	100.0
Paraguay	0.5	4.4	1.7		14.8	10.1	65.2	3.9	3.4	100.0
Peru	0.7	21.1	5.6	0.5	29.3	20.7	18.1	30.3	28.1	100.0
Puerto Rico										
St Kitts		1.5			17.7	17.5	4.4	73.4	66.6	100.0
St Lucia		0.4	0.2		49.8	49.8	21.2	28.2	27.8	100.0
St Vincent and the Grenadines	0.4	3.5			75.1	72.4	12.4	7.4	7.2	100.0
Suriname	2.2	5.0	3.4		46.7	20.1	14.8	31.2	25.3	100.0
Trinidad and Tobago	0.3	0.5	0.1		10.4	10.3	28.2	59.4	56.9	100.0
Uruguay	5.4	13.2	2.1	0.2	23.1	20.8	51.4	9.4	8.1	100.0
Venezuela		1.3	0.4		8.8	8.4	27.5	56.3	53.4	100.0

Source: *International Monetary Fund (IMF), Direction of Trade Statistics*

□ Exports

Exports (fob) by Country of Destination 2002 (% Analysis)

● % of total exports

	Africa & Middle East	Asia/ Pacific	of which: Japan	Australasia	Europe	of which: Total EU	Latin America	North America	of which: USA	Total including Others
Asia Pacific										
Afghanistan	9.3	56.1	1.5	0.2	27.1	19.0	3.0	4.3	4.1	100.0
American Samoa	0.6	89.8	7.6	8.2	0.9	0.5	0.1	0.9		100.0
Armenia	21.9	5.2	0.7	0.1	62.3	31.6	0.4	8.7	8.2	100.0
Azerbaijan	14.3	4.8			77.7	60.3	1.1	2.0	2.0	100.0
Bangladesh	3.1	6.0	1.0	0.3	44.5	42.9	0.8	29.2	27.6	100.0
Bhutan										
Brunei	0.2	77.9	40.3	11.3	1.9	1.9		8.3	8.1	100.0
Cambodia	0.3	13.7	3.9	0.1	24.5	24.0	0.1	61.0	60.2	100.0
China	5.0	47.3	14.9	1.6	18.3	14.8	2.9	22.8	21.5	100.0
Fiji		24.5	6.3	23.2	13.0	12.9	0.5	25.7	25.1	100.0
French Polynesia	0.1	37.8	35.5	2.3	41.4	40.9		18.2	17.5	100.0
Guam		94.5	81.7	1.3	1.9	1.4	0.8	2.2		100.0
Hong Kong, China	3.0	51.3	4.8	1.4	17.5	15.6	2.6	20.9	19.5	100.0
India	14.5	26.3	3.8	1.2	26.1	22.6	3.1	24.3	22.6	100.0
Indonesia	5.3	56.5	21.1	3.6	15.3	13.9	1.7	13.9	13.2	100.0
Japan	3.9	36.9		2.3	16.3	14.7	3.5	30.6	28.8	100.0
Kazakhstan	5.5	17.7	0.8		56.9	27.2	12.2	3.0	2.9	100.0
Kiribati		90.1	56.6	0.4	6.0	4.5	0.1	3.4	3.4	100.0
Kyrgyzstan	15.3	28.3			48.0	3.9		8.4	7.4	100.0
Laos	0.6	48.2	1.4	0.1	27.2	25.3		1.1	0.6	100.0
Macau	0.2	23.5	0.6	0.1	23.5	23.1	0.5	50.4	48.6	100.0
Malaysia	3.0	54.2	10.9	2.5	13.6	12.5	1.1	21.8	21.0	100.0
Maldives	0.5	37.1	7.6		9.8	9.7		52.5	51.7	100.0
Mongolia	0.7	48.2	1.5		15.7	4.6	0.5	35.0	33.7	100.0
Myanmar	1.1	59.7	3.8	0.4	14.6	13.6	0.1	14.2	13.0	100.0
Nauru	2.2	67.2	0.8	18.6	6.8	6.6	0.3	4.8	3.0	100.0
Nepal	0.1	51.7	1.1	0.3	16.8	15.2	0.1	28.7	27.6	100.0
New Caledonia	11.2	27.9	20.5	5.4	36.4	36.3	0.3	1.9	1.8	100.0
North Korea	6.3	58.3	19.9	1.0	11.2	7.5	22.8			100.0
Pakistan	20.5	19.4	1.4	1.4	29.7	27.2	1.8	26.4	24.5	100.0
Papua New Guinea		22.7	9.3	25.1	8.5	8.3		3.3	3.2	100.0
Philippines	0.7	45.5	14.9	1.2	17.4	16.1	0.7	27.9	26.2	100.0
Singapore	3.0	57.2	7.1	3.0	14.1	12.5	2.0	15.6	15.3	100.0
Solomon Islands		91.1	21.2	1.1	2.3	2.0	1.6	0.9	0.8	100.0
South Korea	6.4	43.9	9.4	1.6	16.7	13.5	5.4	21.8	20.4	100.0
Sri Lanka	10.7	11.1	3.3	1.3	32.0	28.4	1.4	40.6	39.1	100.0
Taiwan										
Tajikistan	4.1	14.4			81.5	32.5		0.1	0.1	100.0
Thailand	5.4	48.7	14.5	2.7	16.7	14.8	1.6	20.8	19.6	100.0
Tonga	0.2	46.6	43.3	5.0	6.2	5.9		41.1	41.0	100.0
Turkmenistan	13.9	3.6			79.8	19.2	0.7	1.9	1.8	100.0
Tuvalu	1.6	10.7		0.9	85.3	84.4	1.5			100.0
Uzbekistan	0.5	31.3	3.8		63.1	18.5	0.2	4.5	4.2	100.0
Vanuatu	1.0	85.5	4.9	3.9	4.9	4.7	1.1	3.2	3.2	100.0
Vietnam	3.7	40.0	14.9	7.8	27.9	24.6	0.7	16.4	15.2	100.0
Western Samoa	0.5	8.0	3.6	68.5	4.5	3.8		10.1	10.0	100.0
Australasia										
Australia	7.9	53.9	18.5	6.5	13.4	12.3	1.2	11.1	9.6	100.0
New Zealand	4.1	34.6	11.5	20.3	16.0	15.0	3.5	17.6	15.5	100.0

Source: *International Monetary Fund (IMF), Direction of Trade Statistics*

Exports (fob) by Country of Destination 2002 (% Analysis)

● % of total exports

	Africa & Middle East	Asia/ Pacific	of which: Japan	Australasia	Europe	of which: Total EU	Latin America	North America	of which: USA	Total including Others
Africa and Middle East										
Algeria	2.1	2.4	0.2	0.2	70.7	63.8	6.8	17.8	12.1	100.0
Angola	0.4	23.2	4.9		26.8	26.8	3.4	41.2	41.2	100.0
Bahrain	10.2	10.6	1.7	0.4	4.5	4.0	0.1	4.6	4.5	100.0
Benin	12.8	47.6	0.1		31.0	24.6	6.3	0.3	0.3	100.0
Botswana										
Burkina Faso	17.6	36.6	4.4		28.4	26.9	10.3	1.5	1.5	100.0
Burundi	17.7	4.0	0.6	0.2	72.7	43.2		2.7	2.0	100.0
Cameroon	8.2	7.8	0.2		67.8	66.8	0.3	8.7	8.3	100.0
Cape Verde	0.6	1.1			89.7	89.7		8.4	8.3	100.0
Central African Republic	3.1	9.2	0.5		85.1	83.0	0.1	1.2	1.1	100.0
Chad	15.0	4.2	0.1		70.5	55.1	0.6	7.9	7.9	100.0
Comoros	0.2	14.9	3.2		65.8	64.3	0.1	18.1	17.6	100.0
Congo Dem Rep	7.8	3.0	2.0		75.6	75.5		13.4	13.4	100.0
Congo-Brazzaville	2.6	36.2	3.2		19.4	19.2	3.8	8.4	8.4	100.0
Côte d'Ivoire	22.6	3.6	0.2	0.2	53.3	49.7	3.1	8.6	7.6	100.0
Djibouti	90.1	6.0			2.6	2.4		1.3	1.1	100.0
Egypt	14.1	10.4	0.9	0.2	43.2	40.0	0.5	19.0	18.4	100.0
Equatorial Guinea	2.4	20.0	2.6		36.4	36.4	1.2	38.8	28.3	100.0
Eritrea										
Ethiopia	26.3	10.6	6.6	0.2	41.6	38.4		5.0	4.3	100.0
Gabon	4.4	11.9	1.0	0.9	16.3	15.6	11.3	46.2	46.1	100.0
Gambia	9.5	16.2	0.5		73.0	72.1	0.1	1.0	0.9	100.0
Ghana	11.4	9.1	3.8	0.2	60.3	52.5	1.0	8.6	7.0	100.0
Guinea	10.9	20.7	0.1		55.7	46.4		12.8	9.6	100.0
Guinea-Bissau	2.4	72.3			5.8	5.8	19.5			100.0
Iran	13.9	42.2	17.4	0.2	23.7	19.5	0.1	0.7	0.6	100.0
Iraq	13.1	4.8	1.1	0.2	29.2	28.5	0.3	49.1	40.9	100.0
Israel	1.6	14.8	2.3	1.1	30.8	24.9	3.8	40.7	39.3	100.0
Jordan	46.7	17.0	2.7		8.0	6.3	0.2	14.6	14.5	100.0
Kenya	43.7	12.5	1.1	0.6	33.1	31.4	0.4	8.3	8.0	100.0
Kuwait	4.0	65.5	24.4	0.7	10.5	10.2	0.5	12.0	11.9	100.0
Lebanon	45.3	9.5	0.5	0.5	35.7	18.7	0.4	7.4	6.8	100.0
Lesotho										
Liberia	2.1	8.1			85.5	72.2		4.3	4.2	100.0
Libya	4.4	0.4	0.1		94.8	82.1	0.4			100.0
Madagascar	4.8	9.4	3.9	0.1	57.9	57.1	0.1	25.0	24.7	100.0
Malawi	20.9	8.1	5.9	1.6	49.1	34.2	1.2	17.5	17.3	100.0
Mali	11.1	33.2	0.3	0.4	39.8	35.7	5.6	2.6	1.4	100.0
Mauritania	13.9	11.2	7.1		73.2	66.6		0.2	0.2	100.0
Mauritius	9.2	2.5	0.8	0.2	71.0	69.5	0.1	16.9	16.4	100.0
Morocco	6.0	12.3	3.6	0.9	71.5	68.3	2.1	5.5	4.8	100.0
Mozambique	13.7	5.4	1.4		44.1	43.5		0.7	0.7	100.0
Namibia										
Niger	39.8	17.6	17.1		43.0	42.9				100.0
Nigeria	11.2	15.8	3.9	0.1	27.5	24.9	10.0	33.4	32.6	100.0
Oman	13.9	74.4	20.6	1.3	4.3	4.2		4.2	4.1	100.0
Qatar	6.3	73.7	40.4	1.3	3.5	3.4	0.1	4.1	4.1	100.0
Réunion										
Rwanda	6.8	44.4			23.6	22.6		2.0	1.7	100.0
Sao Tomé e Príncipe	0.6	12.7	2.3		73.4	60.0	1.1	12.2	2.9	100.0
Saudi Arabia	12.9	44.5	15.7	1.2	16.7	15.5	1.6	19.4	18.7	100.0
Senegal	32.8	22.1	0.1		34.9	36.3	0.1	0.4	0.3	100.0
Seychelles	3.2	13.9	6.7	0.3	74.0	73.2		8.6	8.4	100.0
Sierra Leone	3.9	3.6	0.8		83.2	81.9	0.1	5.3	3.7	100.0
Somalia	88.6	8.2	0.1		2.7	2.1	0.1	0.5	0.3	100.0
South Africa	17.7	19.8	8.9	2.0	43.1	40.8	2.1	13.9	12.8	100.0
Sudan	13.5	75.8	13.9		10.5	9.4	0.5	0.1	0.1	100.0
Swaziland										
Syria	16.1	3.7	0.3		74.0	58.8	0.3	3.0	2.5	100.0
Tanzania	20.7	35.2	12.4	0.5	38.5	35.8	0.3	3.4	3.1	100.0
Togo	51.7	13.8		6.1	22.8	19.4	1.8	1.1	1.0	100.0
Tunisia	10.6	2.4	0.1	0.1	82.0	79.3	0.8	0.8	0.8	100.0
Uganda	8.8	12.5	3.9	2.3	70.2	61.9	0.4	4.7	4.6	100.0
United Arab Emirates	12.1	58.5	28.0	0.8	7.4	6.8	0.4	2.5	2.4	100.0
Yemen	6.9	76.6	2.0		2.8	2.8	1.2	6.7	6.7	100.0
Zambia	34.7	30.2	9.0	0.1	16.0	15.2		1.2	1.1	100.0
Zimbabwe	9.9	14.0	4.7	0.4	25.0	21.6	0.6	4.3	4.1	100.0

Source: *International Monetary Fund (IMF), Direction of Trade Statistics*

Table 13.9

◘ Exports

Exports (fob) by Commodity: SITC Classification 2002

● US$ million

	0	1	2	3	4	5	6	7	8	9	Total
North America											
Canada	17,688	1,106	19,047	38,313	389	15,149	36,086	94,148	16,209	16,911	255,046
USA	42,188	5,084	28,990	13,124	1,259	79,845	66,648	371,585	83,871	30,892	723,486
Latin America											
Anguilla											
Antigua											
Argentina	8,505	358	2,265	4,550	1,665	2,102	2,771	3,631	762	434	27,042
Aruba											
Bahamas	85	67	27	65		94	9	46	6		400
Barbados	49	23	1	26	1	31	33	27	18	5	215
Belize											
Bermuda											
Bolivia	285	4	246	312	105	12	117	93	113	95	1,381
Brazil	12,242	1,026	9,207	2,243	636	3,141	10,133	15,985	3,574	1,650	59,838
British Virgin Islands											
Cayman Islands											
Chile	4,439	724	4,708	301	16	1,253	5,905	529	337	659	18,871
Colombia	2,050	55	717	4,221	39	1,358	1,681	842	1,218	13	12,193
Costa Rica	1,331	10	159	43	27	357	410	1,382	1,002	6	4,727
Cuba											
Dominica	16		2			22		2			42
Dominican Republic											
Ecuador	2,036	13	311	1,954	26	97	213	146	114	6	4,916
El Salvador	382	29	17	78	6	178	300	61	176	12	1,239
French Guiana											
Grenada	29					2	3	22	1		57
Guadeloupe											
Guatemala	1,092	60	132	127	33	382	325	88	163		2,401
Guyana											
Haiti											
Honduras	815	56	111	2	27	78	89	21	172	24	1,396
Jamaica	239	58	781	4		66	7	23	145		1,323
Martinique											
Mexico	6,532	1,846	1,610	12,199	38	5,779	13,176	95,186	21,752	151	158,270
Netherlands Antilles											
Nicaragua	362	10	52	9	5	14	27	7	16	32	534
Panama	585	7	16	47	6	33	44	21	38	2	799
Paraguay	163	115	519		52	31	95	6	32		1,013
Peru	1,615	13	1,089	422	99	178	1,504	135	687	1,255	6,998
Puerto Rico											
St Kitts	6						1	20	2		30
St Lucia	22	10				1	2	5	5		45
St Vincent and the Grenadines	32	1					3	2	2		39
Suriname	110	5	540	42	1	5	3	5	2	105	818
Trinidad and Tobago	161	104	10	2,612	6	886	463	847	91	4	5,185
Uruguay	785	56	113	41	7	126	564	127	150	17	1,985
Venezuela	259	101	338	20,498	11	955	2,040	383	91	78	24,755

Source: United Nations, UN Trade Statistics/Comtrade
Notes: SITC Classification: 0 Food and live animals; 1 Beverages and tobacco; 2 Crude materials excl. fuels; 3 Mineral fuels etc;4 Oils and fats; 5 Chemicals; 6 Basic manufactures; 7 Machinery and transport equipment; 8 Miscellaneous manufactured goods; 9 Others

▣ Exports

Exports (fob) by Commodity: SITC Classification 2002

● US$ million

	0	1	2	3	4	5	6	7	8	9	Total
Asia Pacific											
Afghanistan											
American Samoa											
Armenia	4	24	37	20		3	99	29	24	9	250
Azerbaijan	40	22	45	1,927	4	41	25	36	11	18	2,167
Bangladesh	406	3	61	10		78	809	47	4,504	5	5,923
Bhutan											
Brunei											
Cambodia											
China	13,641	885	4,003	10,277	104	14,448	45,480	108,142	93,525	630	291,134
Fiji	196	13	24		1	4	28	1	155	39	461
French Polynesia											
Guam											
Hong Kong, China	2,232	813	2,027	471	82	9,180	26,779	73,454	70,860	1,325	187,223
India	5,263	191	1,795	16,552	198	5,535	18,072	4,525	9,086	1,523	62,740
Indonesia	3,119	309	4,013	14,150	1,441	3,151	12,297	12,234	10,512	228	61,455
Japan	3,099	384	3,530	1,717	72	28,446	39,398	263,898	35,403	16,320	392,267
Kazakhstan	823	28	953	6,902	2	319	3,240	272	67	245	12,850
Kiribati											
Kyrgyzstan	31	21	82	58		8	36	48	14	163	460
Laos											
Macau	8	20	13	13		25	321	96	1,840		2,336
Malaysia	1,793	390	1,910	7,946	2,956	3,916	6,291	51,804	7,677	1,015	85,697
Maldives	56								35		91
Mongolia	21		265	4		3	47	5	102	1	448
Myanmar											
Nauru											
Nepal	93		7			82	253	5	292	210	942
New Caledonia	46	1	416	11		2	716	22	6	1	1,221
North Korea											
Pakistan	911	10	186	218	12	165	4,970	114	2,650	21	9,256
Papua New Guinea											
Philippines	1,322	57	408	266	396	326	1,231	22,256	4,031	76	30,370
Singapore	1,513	993	861	9,075	186	10,024	4,589	77,643	10,377	5,322	120,583
Solomon Islands											
South Korea	2,150	316	1,505	8,021	18	11,874	26,857	85,581	10,993	1,029	148,344
Sri Lanka	962	39	87	20	2	33	564	308	2,767	60	4,842
Taiwan											
Tajikistan											
Thailand	9,813	167	2,335	1,732	112	3,508	7,573	26,688	9,655	2,429	64,012
Tonga											
Turkmenistan	3		273	2,348	3	12	111	14	45	34	2,844
Tuvalu											
Uzbekistan											
Vanuatu											
Vietnam											
Western Samoa											
Australasia											
Australia	11,686	1,169	12,420	12,963	150	2,830	7,491	7,287	2,313	3,835	62,143
New Zealand	6,618	178	1,734	283	62	1,146	1,662	1,235	596	572	14,086

Source: United Nations, UN Trade Statistics/Comtrade
Notes: SITC Classification: 0 Food and live animals; 1 Beverages and tobacco; 2 Crude materials excl. fuels; 3 Mineral fuels etc;4 Oils and fats; 5 Chemicals; 6 Basic manufactures; 7 Machinery and transport equipment; 8 Miscellaneous manufactured goods; 9 Others

□ Exports

Exports (fob) by Commodity: SITC Classification 2002

● US$ million

	0	1	2	3	4	5	6	7	8	9	Total
Africa and Middle East											
Algeria	28	14	59	28,681	5	211	161	64	20		29,244
Angola											
Bahrain	24	5	281	3,434		143	958	36	496	84	5,462
Benin	32	3	121		1	2	7	2	1	12	179
Botswana	170	1	314	4	1	69	4,673	149	106	17	5,504
Burkina Faso	23	4	115	5	5	2	22	12	2	1	192
Burundi	28	2	4							6	41
Cameroon	293	8	337	898	4	11	155	5	3		1,713
Cape Verde											
Central African Republic											
Chad											
Comoros											
Congo Dem Rep											
Congo-Brazzaville											
Côte d'Ivoire											
Djibouti											
Egypt	88	2	104	1,572	15	304	998	67	399	461	4,009
Equatorial Guinea											
Eritrea											
Ethiopia	244		107		1		57		1	4	415
Gabon											
Gambia											
Ghana	293	17	81	89	9	28	138	8	37	302	1,002
Guinea	9	1	316	4	1	101	2	13	15	130	592
Guinea-Bissau											
Iran	869	4	304	25,567	70	598	1,525	258	501		29,696
Iraq											
Israel	694	10	539	99	10	4,273	11,685	11,010	3,324	59	31,704
Jordan	228	45	413	1	89	601	355	426	505	13	2,676
Kenya	794	28	171	121	15	79	149	8	71	7	1,443
Kuwait											
Lebanon	102	50	89	1	9	97	162	125	220	65	920
Lesotho											
Liberia											
Libya											
Madagascar											
Malawi	187	281	12	1		3	4	3	37		528
Mali											
Mauritania											
Mauritius	369	5	11		1	12	150	28	912	10	1,497
Morocco	1,476	10	569	343	12	865	459	732	2,585	13	7,063
Mozambique											
Namibia	626	70	126	8	2	7	434	56	183	38	1,550
Niger	57		75				1	2	1	3	139
Nigeria	7		31	27,188	2	3	27	29	2	1	27,291
Oman	265	413	26	8,792	20	111	315	826	161	50	10,978
Qatar	2		11	13,228		474	199		155	2	14,072
Réunion											
Rwanda	30		26				1			2	59
Sao Tomé e Príncipe											
Saudi Arabia	387	18	184	63,482	30	5,877	1,185	1,005	218	64	72,450
Senegal	46	11	64	158	54	265	42	24	24	1	687
Seychelles											
Sierra Leone											
Somalia											
South Africa	1,865	503	2,316	2,266	30	2,006	10,355	4,158	1,014	3,466	27,980
Sudan											
Swaziland	244	3	85	6	3	136	26	28	105	2	639
Syria	418	2	260	3,822	13	16	214	4	162	88	4,998
Tanzania	290	35	135	1	1	6	70	4	6	224	773
Togo	32	2	71	1	3	6	100	5	5		224
Tunisia	331	59	137	572	141	672	689	1,142	3,147	3	6,894
Uganda	245	36	82	22	3	7	10	9	3	54	472
United Arab Emirates											
Yemen											
Zambia	91	13	30	13		10	807	38	4	20	1,027
Zimbabwe	258	597	355	20	3	50	395	43	116	6	1,844

Source: United Nations, UN Trade Statistics/Comtrade
Notes: SITC Classification: 0 Food and live animals; 1 Beverages and tobacco; 2 Crude materials excl. fuels; 3 Mineral fuels etc;4 Oils and fats; 5 Chemicals; 6 Basic manufactures; 7 Machinery and transport equipment; 8 Miscellaneous manufactured goods; 9 Others

Table 13.10

◻ Exports

Exports (fob) by Commodity: SITC Classification 2002 (% Analysis)

● % of total exports

	0	1	2	3	4	5	6	7	8	9	Total
North America											
Canada	6.9	0.4	7.5	15.0	0.2	5.9	14.1	36.9	6.4	6.6	100.0
USA	5.8	0.7	4.0	1.8	0.2	11.0	9.2	51.4	11.6	4.3	100.0
Latin America											
Anguilla											
Antigua											
Argentina	31.5	1.3	8.4	16.8	6.2	7.8	10.2	13.4	2.8	1.6	100.0
Aruba											
Bahamas	21.4	16.8	6.8	16.2		23.6	2.2	11.4	1.5		100.0
Barbados	22.8	10.8	0.7	12.2	0.4	14.4	15.3	12.4	8.5	2.4	100.0
Belize											
Bermuda											
Bolivia	20.6	0.3	17.8	22.6	7.6	0.9	8.5	6.7	8.1	6.9	100.0
Brazil	20.5	1.7	15.4	3.7	1.1	5.2	16.9	26.7	6.0	2.8	100.0
British Virgin Islands											
Cayman Islands											
Chile	23.5	3.8	24.9	1.6	0.1	6.6	31.3	2.8	1.8	3.5	100.0
Colombia	16.8	0.5	5.9	34.6	0.3	11.1	13.8	6.9	10.0	0.1	100.0
Costa Rica	28.2	0.2	3.4	0.9	0.6	7.6	8.7	29.2	21.2	0.1	100.0
Cuba											
Dominica	37.9	1.1	3.6			51.4	0.3	4.6	1.1		100.0
Dominican Republic											
Ecuador	41.4	0.3	6.3	39.7	0.5	2.0	4.3	3.0	2.3	0.1	100.0
El Salvador	30.8	2.3	1.4	6.3	0.5	14.4	24.2	4.9	14.2	1.0	100.0
French Guiana											
Grenada	51.0	0.3				2.7	4.8	38.6	2.5		100.0
Guadeloupe											
Guatemala	45.5	2.5	5.5	5.3	1.4	15.9	13.5	3.7	6.8		100.0
Guyana											
Haiti											
Honduras	58.4	4.0	8.0	0.1	1.9	5.6	6.4	1.5	12.3	1.7	100.0
Jamaica	18.1	4.4	59.0	0.3		5.0	0.5	1.7	11.0		100.0
Martinique											
Mexico	4.1	1.2	1.0	7.7		3.7	8.3	60.1	13.7	0.1	100.0
Netherlands Antilles											
Nicaragua	67.8	1.9	9.8	1.6	1.0	2.7	5.1	1.3	3.0	5.9	100.0
Panama	73.3	0.9	2.0	5.9	0.7	4.1	5.5	2.6	4.8	0.3	100.0
Paraguay	16.1	11.4	51.2		5.1	3.1	9.3	0.6	3.2		100.0
Peru	23.1	0.2	15.6	6.0	1.4	2.5	21.5	1.9	9.8	17.9	100.0
Puerto Rico											
St Kitts	20.9	1.7	0.1	0.1		0.2	3.4	67.0	6.5	0.1	100.0
St Lucia	48.6	21.6	0.5			2.6	4.8	10.1	11.7		100.0
St Vincent and the Grenadines	80.7	3.3	0.2			0.3	6.8	4.6	4.1		100.0
Suriname	13.4	0.7	66.0	5.1	0.1	0.6	0.3	0.6	0.2	12.9	100.0
Trinidad and Tobago	3.1	2.0	0.2	50.4	0.1	17.1	8.9	16.3	1.7	0.1	100.0
Uruguay	39.5	2.8	5.7	2.1	0.3	6.3	28.4	6.4	7.6	0.9	100.0
Venezuela	1.0	0.4	1.4	82.8		3.9	8.2	1.5	0.4	0.3	100.0

Source: *United Nations, UN Trade Statistics/Comtrade*
Notes: *SITC Classification: 0 Food and live animals; 1 Beverages and tobacco; 2 Crude materials excl. fuels; 3 Mineral fuels etc;4 Oils and fats; 5 Chemicals; 6 Basic manufactures; 7 Machinery and transport equipment; 8 Miscellaneous manufactured goods; 9 Others*

Exports

Exports (fob) by Commodity: SITC Classification 2002 (% Analysis)

● % of total exports

	0	1	2	3	4	5	6	7	8	9	Total
Asia Pacific											
Afghanistan											
American Samoa											
Armenia	1.5	9.7	14.8	8.0		1.3	39.8	11.7	9.6	3.5	100.0
Azerbaijan	1.8	1.0	2.1	88.9	0.2	1.9	1.1	1.6	0.5	0.8	100.0
Bangladesh	6.9	0.1	1.0	0.2		1.3	13.7	0.8	76.0	0.1	100.0
Bhutan											
Brunei											
Cambodia											
China	4.7	0.3	1.4	3.5		5.0	15.6	37.1	32.1	0.2	100.0
Fiji	42.5	2.9	5.3		0.3	0.8	6.0	0.2	33.7	8.5	100.0
French Polynesia											
Guam											
Hong Kong, China	1.2	0.4	1.1	0.3		4.9	14.3	39.2	37.8	0.7	100.0
India	8.4	0.3	2.9	26.4	0.3	8.8	28.8	7.2	14.5	2.4	100.0
Indonesia	5.1	0.5	6.5	23.0	2.3	5.1	20.0	19.9	17.1	0.4	100.0
Japan	0.8	0.1	0.9	0.4		7.3	10.0	67.3	9.0	4.2	100.0
Kazakhstan	6.4	0.2	7.4	53.7		2.5	25.2	2.1	0.5	1.9	100.0
Kiribati											
Kyrgyzstan	6.8	4.6	17.8	12.6		1.6	7.8	10.4	2.9	35.4	100.0
Laos											
Macau	0.3	0.9	0.5	0.5		1.1	13.7	4.1	78.8		100.0
Malaysia	2.1	0.5	2.2	9.3	3.4	4.6	7.3	60.5	9.0	1.2	100.0
Maldives	61.6		0.2						38.2		100.0
Mongolia	4.8		59.1	0.9		0.7	10.5	1.1	22.7	0.3	100.0
Myanmar											
Nauru											
Nepal	9.9		0.7			8.7	26.9	0.5	31.0	22.3	100.0
New Caledonia	3.8	0.1	34.1	0.9		0.1	58.7	1.8	0.5	0.1	100.0
North Korea											
Pakistan	9.8	0.1	2.0	2.4	0.1	1.8	53.7	1.2	28.6	0.2	100.0
Papua New Guinea											
Philippines	4.4	0.2	1.3	0.9	1.3	1.1	4.1	73.3	13.3	0.3	100.0
Singapore	1.3	0.8	0.7	7.5	0.2	8.3	3.8	64.4	8.6	4.4	100.0
Solomon Islands											
South Korea	1.4	0.2	1.0	5.4		8.0	18.1	57.7	7.4	0.7	100.0
Sri Lanka	19.9	0.8	1.8	0.4		0.7	11.7	6.4	57.2	1.2	100.0
Taiwan											
Tajikistan											
Thailand	15.3	0.3	3.6	2.7	0.2	5.5	11.8	41.7	15.1	3.8	100.0
Tonga											
Turkmenistan	0.1		9.6	82.6	0.1	0.4	3.9	0.5	1.6	1.2	100.0
Tuvalu											
Uzbekistan											
Vanuatu											
Vietnam											
Western Samoa											
Australasia											
Australia	18.8	1.9	20.0	20.9	0.2	4.6	12.1	11.7	3.7	6.2	100.0
New Zealand	47.0	1.3	12.3	2.0	0.4	8.1	11.8	8.8	4.2	4.1	100.0

Source: *United Nations, UN Trade Statistics/Comtrade*
Notes: *SITC Classification: 0 Food and live animals; 1 Beverages and tobacco; 2 Crude materials excl. fuels; 3 Mineral fuels etc;4 Oils and fats; 5 Chemicals; 6 Basic manufactures; 7 Machinery and transport equipment; 8 Miscellaneous manufactured goods; 9 Others*

Exports

Exports (fob) by Commodity: SITC Classification 2002 (% Analysis)

● % of total exports

	0	1	2	3	4	5	6	7	8	9	Total
Africa and Middle East											
Algeria	0.1		0.2	98.1		0.7	0.6	0.2	0.1		100.0
Angola											
Bahrain	0.4	0.1	5.1	62.9		2.6	17.5	0.7	9.1	1.5	100.0
Benin	17.6	1.7	67.5		0.3	1.0	4.0	1.0	0.4	6.5	100.0
Botswana	3.1		5.7	0.1		1.3	84.9	2.7	1.9	0.3	100.0
Burkina Faso	12.1	2.1	60.1	2.7	2.7	1.1	11.5	6.0	1.3	0.4	100.0
Burundi	68.0	5.7	10.0				0.3		0.4	15.6	100.0
Cameroon	17.1	0.4	19.7	52.4	0.2	0.6	9.0	0.3	0.2		100.0
Cape Verde											
Central African Republic											
Chad											
Comoros											
Congo Dem Rep											
Congo-Brazzaville											
Côte d'Ivoire											
Djibouti											
Egypt	2.2	0.1	2.6	39.2	0.4	7.6	24.9	1.7	9.9	11.5	100.0
Equatorial Guinea											
Eritrea											
Ethiopia	58.8		25.9		0.2	0.1	13.8	0.1	0.3	0.9	100.0
Gabon											
Gambia											
Ghana	29.3	1.7	8.0	8.9	0.9	2.8	13.7	0.8	3.7	30.2	100.0
Guinea	1.5	0.2	53.4	0.7	0.1	17.0	0.4	2.2	2.5	21.9	100.0
Guinea-Bissau											
Iran	2.9		1.0	86.1	0.2	2.0	5.1	0.9	1.7		100.0
Iraq											
Israel	2.2		1.7	0.3		13.5	36.9	34.7	10.5	0.2	100.0
Jordan	8.5	1.7	15.4		3.3	22.4	13.3	15.9	18.9	0.5	100.0
Kenya	55.0	1.9	11.9	8.4	1.0	5.5	10.3	0.5	4.9	0.5	100.0
Kuwait											
Lebanon	11.1	5.5	9.7	0.2	1.0	10.5	17.6	13.6	23.9	7.0	100.0
Lesotho											
Liberia											
Libya											
Madagascar											
Malawi	35.5	53.3	2.3	0.1		0.5	0.7	0.5	7.0		100.0
Mali											
Mauritania											
Mauritius	24.6	0.3	0.7		0.1	0.8	10.0	1.9	60.9	0.7	100.0
Morocco	20.9	0.1	8.1	4.9	0.2	12.2	6.5	10.4	36.6	0.2	100.0
Mozambique											
Namibia	40.4	4.5	8.1	0.5	0.1	0.4	28.0	3.6	11.8	2.4	100.0
Niger	41.2	0.1	53.8			0.2	1.1	1.2	0.4	2.0	100.0
Nigeria			0.1	99.6			0.1	0.1			100.0
Oman	2.4	3.8	0.2	80.1	0.2	1.0	2.9	7.5	1.5	0.5	100.0
Qatar			0.1	94.0		3.4	1.4		1.1		100.0
Réunion											
Rwanda	51.2	0.1	43.3			0.4	1.3		0.2	3.6	100.0
Sao Tomé e Príncipe											
Saudi Arabia	0.5		0.3	87.6		8.1	1.6	1.4	0.3	0.1	100.0
Senegal	6.7	1.6	9.3	23.0	7.8	38.6	6.1	3.4	3.5	0.1	100.0
Seychelles											
Sierra Leone											
Somalia											
South Africa	6.7	1.8	8.3	8.1	0.1	7.2	37.0	14.9	3.6	12.4	100.0
Sudan											
Swaziland	38.2	0.5	13.2	1.0	0.5	21.3	4.1	4.4	16.4	0.3	100.0
Syria	8.4		5.2	76.5	0.3	0.3	4.3	0.1	3.2	1.8	100.0
Tanzania	37.5	4.5	17.5	0.1	0.2	0.8	9.0	0.6	0.8	29.0	100.0
Togo	14.1	0.9	31.7	0.4	1.5	2.6	44.6	2.3	2.1		100.0
Tunisia	4.8	0.9	2.0	8.3	2.0	9.8	10.0	16.6	45.6		100.0
Uganda	52.0	7.7	17.5	4.7	0.7	1.4	2.1	2.0	0.6	11.4	100.0
United Arab Emirates											
Yemen											
Zambia	8.9	1.3	3.0	1.3		1.0	78.6	3.7	0.4	2.0	100.0
Zimbabwe	14.0	32.4	19.3	1.1	0.2	2.7	21.4	2.3	6.3	0.3	100.0

Source: United Nations, UN Trade Statistics/Comtrade
Notes: SITC Classification: 0 Food and live animals; 1 Beverages and tobacco; 2 Crude materials excl. fuels; 3 Mineral fuels etc;4 Oils and fats; 5 Chemicals; 6 Basic manufactures; 7 Machinery and transport equipment; 8 Miscellaneous manufactured goods; 9 Others

Trade Balance

Trade Balance 1977-2002

Table 13.11

- US$ million

	1977	1980	1985	1990	1991	1992	1993	1994
North America								
Canada	1,462	5,190	10,311	4,385	2,381	5,173	6,143	10,304
USA	-37,229	-31,418	-133,648	-123,395	-86,633	-105,760	-138,665	-176,588
Latin America								
Anguilla								
Antigua	-28	-61	-150	-234	-246	-248	-261	-297
Argentina	1,490	-2,519	4,582	8,277	3,703	-2,637	-3,666	-5,868
Aruba				-508	-455			
Bahamas	-307	-2,536	-349	-874	-866	-845	-792	-889
Barbados	-176	-297	-254	-489	-491	-334	-390	-433
Belize	-28	-39	-38	-103	-158	-158	-162	-132
Bermuda	-165	-306			-461	-478	-499	-519
Bolivia	14	277	-68	239	-121	-380	-478	-177
Brazil	-1,137	-4,829	11,307	8,890	8,670	12,725	10,815	7,548
British Virgin Islands								
Cayman Islands	-34	-92	-20	-270	-243	-47	-37	-42
Chile	-348	-1,092	733	630	734	-175	-1,936	-216
Colombia	523	-814	-589	1,176	2,326	400	-2,716	-3,464
Costa Rica	-193	-539	-122	-542	-279	-600	-890	-920
Cuba								
Dominica	-10	-38	-27	-63	-55	-52	-45	-49
Dominican Republic	-195	-678	-752	-1,327	-1,330	-1,938	-1,925	-2,796
Ecuador	248	228	1,138	849	453	576	342	198
El Salvador	43	1	-282	-681	-818	-1,101	-1,181	-1,405
French Guiana	-137	-230	-220	-693	-700	-574	-427	-540
Grenada	-18	-33	-47	-78	-102	-87	-98	-95
Guadeloupe	-297	-573	-571	-1,559	-1,497	-1,389	-1,265	-1,328
Guatemala	108	-78	-118	-486	-649	-1,236	-1,259	-1,260
Guyana	-55	-7	-59	-54	-60	-150	-70	-50
Haiti	-64	-149	-273	-172	-234	-205	-275	-169
Honduras	-61	-179	-108	-104	-163	-235	-316	-214
Jamaica	-91	-209	-545	-770	-718	-629	-1,061	-1,012
Martinique	-299	-727	-520	-1,438	-1,407	-1,508	-1,366	-1,447
Mexico	-1,322	-4,113	7,641	-2,838	-9,627	-18,854	-16,553	-22,193
Netherlands Antilles	-482	-513	-357	-351	-540	-310	-664	-382
Nicaragua	-125	-437	-663	-307	-479	-632	-477	-536
Panama	-610	-1,089	-1,056	-1,198	-1,337	-1,522	-1,635	-1,821
Paraguay	-29	-304	-198	-393	-723	-765	-964	-1,324
Peru	-185	1,399	1,144	-239	-866	-1,377	-1,345	-2,136
Puerto Rico								
St Kitts	-7	-21	-31	-83	-82	-69	-91	-105
St Lucia	-35	-65	-73	-144	-185	-182	-181	-208
St Vincent and the Grenadines	-20	-42	-16	-53	-73	-54	-76	-80
Suriname	-88	10	30	0	-150	-150	204	26
Trinidad and Tobago	361	899	605	851	318	587	199	736
Uruguay	-122	-622	201	350	-32	-343	-680	-873
Venezuela	-1,387	7,395	6,332	10,162	4,008	119	2,175	6,902

Source: Euromonitor from International Monetary Fund (IMF), International Financial Statistics

▣ Trade Balance

Trade Balance 1977-2002 (continued)

● US$ million

	1995	1996	1997	1998	1999	2000	2001	2002
North America								
Canada	24,156	26,674	13,549	8,261	18,263	31,849	32,567	24,895
USA	-186,109	-196,952	-210,323	-262,215	-357,342	-478,175	-448,377	-508,570
Latin America								
Anguilla								
Antigua	-293	-328	-333	-349	-376	-388	-367	-377
Argentina	846	49	-4,080	-4,963	-2,175	1,061	6,223	16,720
Aruba	-552	-566	-590	-786	-753	-662	-693	-713
Bahamas	-1,067	-1,186	-1,484	-1,573	-1,240	-959	-1,093	-997
Barbados	-532	-553	-713	-758	-844	-884	-827	-833
Belize	-114	-102	-127	-139	-200	-283	-273	-372
Bermuda	-494	-501	-542	-552	-628	-634	-682	-693
Bolivia	-323	-498	-684	-879	-704	-600	-423	-471
Brazil	-7,277	-9,200	-12,001	-9,512	-3,748	-3,545	-128	10,785
British Virgin Islands								
Cayman Islands	-52	-51	-49	-43	-75	-65	-95	-105
Chile	124	-3,466	-2,923	-3,557	1,174	703	652	1,247
Colombia	-3,797	-3,097	-3,855	-3,782	918	1,502	-577	-737
Costa Rica	-583	-569	-656	-719	257	-508	-1,555	-1,935
Cuba	-1,225	-1,190	-2,175	-2,641	-2,835	-3,265	-3,206	-3,504
Dominica	-72	-79	-72	-70	-83	-95	-88	-73
Dominican Republic	-2,767	-3,172	-3,803	-4,751	-5,183	-6,412	-6,701	-7,590
Ecuador	155	965	310	-1,373	1,434	1,205	-685	-1,401
El Salvador	-1,855	-1,647	-1,609	-1,865	-1,963	-2,462	-2,653	-2,674
French Guiana								
Grenada	-102	-132	-151	-173	-184	-178	-189	-200
Guadeloupe	-1,729							
Guatemala	-1,137	-1,115	-1,508	-2,070	-1,984	-2,095	-3,141	-3,846
Guyana	-73	-81	14	-63	2	-89	-106	-70
Haiti	-543	-575	-436	-477	-691	-718	-739	-850
Honduras	-423	-524	-703	-1,002	-1,512	-1,485	-1,600	-1,694
Jamaica	-1,391	-1,582	-1,748	-1,723	-1,659	-2,022	-2,140	-2,419
Martinique	-1,735							
Mexico	3,683	2,326	-4,416	-13,488	-12,257	-16,335	-17,638	-15,925
Netherlands Antilles	0	0	0	0	91	561	290	350
Nicaragua	-536	-687	-873	-918	-1,317	-1,160	-1,187	-1,199
Panama	-1,886	-2,114	-2,279	-2,614	-2,694	-2,519	-2,053	-2,136
Paraguay	-1,863	-1,807	-2,011	-1,457	-984	-1,181	-999	-1,326
Peru	-3,649	-3,575	-3,423	-4,110	-1,962	-1,769	-547	508
Puerto Rico	4,994	1,782	2,452	8,473	6,789	3,503	4,555	5,436
St Kitts	-114	-127	-127	-132	-146	-152	-152	-159
St Lucia	-197	-234	-271	-273	-299	-312	-311	-152
St Vincent and the Grenadines	-93	-85	-142	-143	-152	-115	-144	-136
Suriname	-108	-68	43	-116	44	153	156	160
Trinidad and Tobago	742	356	-448	-741	63	965	711	237
Uruguay	-761	-926	-1,001	-1,040	-1,120	-1,171	-1,000	-987
Venezuela	5,807	13,180	7,018	1,376	6,126	15,589	9,387	12,642

Source: Euromonitor from International Monetary Fund (IMF), International Financial Statistics

□ Trade Balance

Trade Balance 1977-2002 (continued)

- US$ million

	1977	1980	1985	1990	1991	1992	1993	1994
Asia Pacific								
Afghanistan	-22	-171	-627	-701	-348	-335	-560	-118
American Samoa	26	32	-95	-49	-45	-100	21	-244
Armenia						-123	-98	-178
Azerbaijan						573	358	-140
Bangladesh	-687	-1,840	-1,544	-1,947	-1,723	-1,634	-1,716	-1,942
Bhutan		-33	-62	-12	-20	-59	-25	-25
Brunei								
Cambodia								
China	371	-1,842	-14,902	8,746	8,119	4,355	-12,215	5,392
Fiji	-83	-92	-135	-257	-201	-187	-270	-262
French Polynesia	-311	-517	-508	-817	-787	-788	-759	-647
Guam	-238	-365	-292	-350	-358	-603	-477	-582
Hong Kong, China	-830	-2,696	484	-330	-1,663	-3,920	-3,406	-10,442
India	-268	-6,279	-6,788	-5,611	-2,721	-3,951	-1,217	-1,821
Indonesia	4,623	11,075	8,328	3,838	3,273	6,687	8,495	8,072
Japan	9,744	-10,855	46,676	52,213	77,787	106,639	120,620	121,770
Kazakhstan							-610	-330
Kiribati	10	-13	-27	-41	-40	-64	-25	-21
Kyrgyzstan							-90	24
Laos	-10	-64	-139	-106	-73	-137	-191	-264
Macau	21	-6	129	162	-186	-201	-239	-135
Malaysia	1,537	2,165	3,063	195	-2,299	918	1,481	-755
Maldives	-7	-21	-30	-84	-107	-150	-157	-174
Mongolia		-145	-406	-263	-13	-30	4	98
Myanmar	-27	120	20	55	-229	-121	-230	-88
Nauru	25				12	15	21	20
Nepal	-88	-262	-293	-468	-480	-409	-506	-793
New Caledonia	23	-46	-74	-403	-418	-506	-553	-306
North Korea					-800	-700	-620	-600
Pakistan	-1,264	-2,745	-3,165	-1,796	-1,920	-2,072	-2,825	-1,531
Papua New Guinea	41	-145	-80	-15	-154	442	1,285	1,110
Philippines	-1,142	-2,550	-843	-4,887	-4,060	-5,746	-7,559	-9,337
Singapore	-2,230	-4,632	-3,473	-8,044	-7,129	-8,700	-11,222	-5,845
Solomon Islands	0	-15	-13	-21	-28	-9	-8	3
South Korea	-763	-4,780	-854	-4,828	-9,655	-5,144	-1,564	-6,335
Sri Lanka	60	-995	-655	-776	-1,069	-1,044	-1,146	-1,559
Taiwan	827	23	10,572	12,249	13,085	9,206	7,542	7,368
Tajikistan								
Thailand	-1,126	-2,708	-2,121	-9,977	-9,141	-8,214	-9,107	-9,198
Tonga	-13	-30	-36	-51	-46	-50	-46	-56
Turkmenistan								
Tuvalu								
Uzbekistan								
Vanuatu	-8	-37	-39	-77	-64	-58	-56	-64
Vietnam								
Western Samoa	-26	-45	-35	-72	-88	-104	-98	-78
Australasia								
Australia	-144	-454	-3,286	-2,233	206	-983	-2,854	-5,897
New Zealand	-165	-52	-272	-107	1,238	584	905	271

Source: Euromonitor from International Monetary Fund (IMF), International Financial Statistics

◻ Trade Balance

Trade Balance 1977-2002 (continued)

● US$ million

	1995	1996	1997	1998	1999	2000	2001	2002
Asia Pacific								
Afghanistan	-24	-327	-235	-164	-244	-364	-438	-621
American Samoa	72	85	153	168	157	124	144	91
Armenia	-403	-566	-660	-682	-568	-588	-532	-484
Azerbaijan	-30	-329	-13	-471	-107	-161	-387	-506
Bangladesh	-3,328	-3,324	-3,120	-3,143	-3,772	-3,573	-3,524	-3,348
Bhutan	-9	-27	-19	-26	-66	-65	-33	-40
Brunei	311				1,182	2,441	2,697	3,925
Cambodia	-289		-491	-195	-203	-302	-160	11
China	16,696	12,215	40,422	43,475	29,232	24,109	22,545	30,420
Fiji	-273	-239	-345	-212	-294	-241	-256	-247
French Polynesia	-814	-767	-711	-771	-673	-754	-862	-1,092
Guam	-431	-433	-377	-573	-383	-480	-612	-352
Hong Kong, China	-19,001	-17,800	-20,555	-10,516	-5,635	-10,945	-11,182	-7,552
India	-4,077	-4,837	-6,424	-9,543	-11,313	-9,144	-7,045	-7,205
Indonesia	4,787	6,885	11,749	21,511	24,662	28,609	25,437	32,732
Japan	107,234	61,749	82,203	107,443	108,105	99,738	54,407	79,532
Kazakhstan	1,444	1,670	2,196	1,020	2,217	3,772	2,193	3,086
Kiribati	-28	-33	-33	-26	-27	-20	-3	-49
Kyrgyzstan	-113	-332	-105	-328	-152	-48	9	-104
Laos	-278	-367	-347	-183	-214	-205	-197	-133
Macau	-44	-4	66	186	160	284	-87	-174
Malaysia	-3,777	-91	-289	14,983	19,232	16,266	14,139	13,396
Maldives	-218	-243	-276	-280	-338	-313	-317	-301
Mongolia	58	-27	-17	-158	-154	-148	-182	-132
Myanmar	-488	-618	-1,182	-1,617	-1,187	-756	-496	698
Nauru	0	4	10	9	23	1	-8	-8
Nepal	-988	-1,013	-1,287	-772	-820	-769	-736	-852
New Caledonia	-480	-455		-554	-451	-319	-429	-407
North Korea	-430	-575	-448	-526	-615	-978	-1,021	-1,069
Pakistan	-3,486	-2,824	-2,892	-816	-1,805	-1,836	-953	-1,320
Papua New Guinea	1,202	789	453	532	691	945	740	446
Philippines	-10,839	-13,719	-13,740	-2,082	4,008	2,756	-2,257	-678
Singapore	-6,239	-6,324	-7,452	5,176	3,620	3,259	5,751	8,729
Solomon Islands	14	11	24	-4	36	-32	-24	-28
South Korea	-10,061	-20,624	-8,452	39,031	23,960	11,786	9,341	10,344
Sri Lanka	-1,508	-1,346	-1,225	-1,096	-1,367	-1,747	-1,157	-1,406
Taiwan	7,865	14,443	7,157	5,572	10,539	7,850	15,232	17,699
Tajikistan	-170	-15	-4	-125	3	118	-195	-227
Thailand	-14,347	-16,611	-5,480	11,485	8,098	7,133	3,055	4,110
Tonga	-63	-63	-63	-61	-60	-61	-66	-62
Turkmenistan	517	671	-432	-414	-138	915	455	1,380
Tuvalu								
Uzbekistan	-40	-1,935	-1,305	-853	-131	-486	-60	193
Vanuatu	-67	-67	-58	-54	-70	-27	-65	-68
Vietnam	-6,080	-6,111	-5,443	-7,481	-96	-1,188	-900	355
Western Samoa	-86	-90	-82	-82	-95	-91	-115	-99
Australasia								
Australia	-8,171	-5,127	-2,982	-8,737	-13,078	-7,658	-501	-7,656
New Zealand	-312	-364	-303	-427	-1,844	-634	376	-713

Source: Euromonitor from International Monetary Fund (IMF), International Financial Statistics

☐ Trade Balance

Trade Balance 1977-2002 (continued)

● US$ million

	1977	1980	1985	1990	1991	1992	1993	1994
Africa and Middle East								
Algeria	-1,181	3,312	3,000	3,110	4,670	3,200	2,420	-262
Angola						3,207	2,687	2,879
Bahrain	-183	112	-210	49	-602	-799	-132	-131
Benin	-237	-268	-181	-143	-220	-243	-188	-33
Botswana	-99	-188	167	-163	-98	-142	-9	207
Burkina Faso	-154	-269	-261	-384	-427	-402	-439	-242
Burundi	16	-103	-74	-156	-164	-148	-134	-104
Cameroon	-31	-218	-429	602	661	678	545	646
Cape Verde	-36	-64	-80	-130	-142	-175	-150	-205
Central African Republic	18	35	-21	-34	-46	-38	-16	12
Chad	-83	-3	-104	-97	-56	-61	-69	-29
Comoros	-8	-18	-20	-34	-33	-46	-38	-41
Congo Dem Rep	786	1,348	158	111	119	7	-4	37
Congo-Brazzaville	59	349	489	360	435	727	487	328
Côte d'Ivoire	401	144	1,220	975	583	523	403	825
Djibouti	-88	-201	-187	-190	-197	-203	-199	-184
Egypt	-3,107	-1,814	-7,390	-11,826	-4,347	-5,262	-5,962	-6,743
Equatorial Guinea	5	-13	-3	2	-30	-6	-3	25
Eritrea								
Ethiopia	-19	-298	-660	-784	-283	-670	-589	-661
Gabon	627	1,499	1,097	1,286	1,408	1,382	1,450	1,594
Gambia	-30	-134	-50	-157	-164	-161	-194	-177
Ghana	-24	129	-249		-438	-917	-2,968	-684
Guinea	67			-27				
Guinea-Bissau	-24	-44		-66	-55	-91	-33	-78
Iran	-4,855	-5,137	1,693	-1,017	-9,266	-5,992	-3,347	5,660
Iraq	14,531				-170	-310	-150	-110
Israel	-2,706	-4,247	-3,615	-5,218	-6,737	-5,517	-7,798	-8,353
Jordan	-1,132	-1,828	-1,944	-1,536	-1,378	-2,035	-2,293	-1,958
Kenya	-103	-879	-479	-1,191	-827	-502	-400	-504
Kuwait	4,908	13,309	4,592	3,071	-3,672	-686	3,208	4,563
Lebanon	-779	-2,695	-1,915	-2,031	-3,204	-3,643	-1,763	-2,128
Lesotho	-220	-369	-317	-611	-743	-790	-738	-705
Liberia	-16	66	151					
Libya	7,638	15,133	8,213	7,889	5,871	5,742	2,518	4,849
Madagascar	-9	-198	-128	-332	-131	-170	-208	-72
Malawi	-35	-144	-48	-159	-234	-339	-226	-149
Mali	-34	-233	-176	-244	-148	-265	-156	-254
Mauritania	-49	-92	141	227				84
Mauritius	-137	-179	-89	-424	-364	-322	-417	-583
Morocco	-1,897	-1,814	-1,685	-2,657	-2,589	-3,375	-3,677	-2,716
Mozambique								-367
Namibia				-78	65	59	-86	-104
Niger	-36	-28	-110	-106	-48	-145	-88	-103
Nigeria	744	9,285	3,660	7,970	3,278	3,611	4,372	2,803
Oman	264	655	785	2,827	1,680	1,784	1,256	1,630
Qatar	847	4,257						1,219
Réunion	-378	-757	-704	-1,943	-1,982	-2,107	-1,889	-2,188
Rwanda	-30	-142	-167	-178	-213	-220	-267	-92
Sao Tomé e Príncipe	9	-2	-4	-17	-25	-24	-27	-25
Saudi Arabia	30,073	78,945	3,859	20,347	18,718	17,015	14,198	19,276
Senegal	-140	-575	-264	-458	-472	-361	-380	-231
Seychelles	-35	-78	-71	-130	-124	-144	-187	-155
Sierra Leone	-45	-203	-21	-11	-18	3	-29	-35
Somalia								
South Africa	3,633	5,840	4,890	5,169	4,451	3,702	4,230	1,945
Sudan	-420	-1,034	-397	-244	-585	-502	-528	-725
Swaziland	-17	-252	-137	-107	-124	-227	-105	-52
Syria	-1,632	-2,016	-2,329	1,812	662	-397	-993	-2,420
Tanzania	-237	-746	-598	-1,033	-1,204	-1,093	-1,047	-985
Togo	-125	-213	-98	-313	-191	-120	-43	106
Tunisia	-895	-1,294	-1,019	-1,986	-1,490	-2,412	-2,406	-1,924
Uganda	-183	52		-135	4	-362	-434	-466
United Arab Emirates	4,580	11,930	7,494	12,345	10,690	7,346		
Yemen					-1,365	-1,968	-2,211	-1,154
Zambia	225	217	-239	89	266	-40	17	333
Zimbabwe	166	-40	212	-115	-506	-760	-253	-360

Source: *Euromonitor from International Monetary Fund (IMF), International Financial Statistics*

◻ Trade Balance

Trade Balance 1977-2002 (continued)

● US$ million

	1995	1996	1997	1998	1999	2000	2001	2002
Africa and Middle East								
Algeria	158	4,130	3,875	4,412	3,333	3,478	1,522	7,844
Angola	3,296	3,055	2,530	1,464	2,130	4,186	2,517	3,077
Bahrain	397	429	358	-296	665	1,561	1,271	384
Benin	-326	0	-265	-328	-327	-221	-228	-283
Botswana	231	814	583	-440	-52	37	481	486
Burkina Faso	-178	-414	-355	-412	-423	-401	-422	-502
Burundi	-129	-87	-35	-93	-64	-98	-101	-99
Cameroon	452	542	501	176	283	430	374	337
Cape Verde	-244	-222	-221	-218	-235	-219	-223	-244
Central African Republic	-3	5	22	5	15	44	35	38
Chad	-122	-94	-97	-95	-114	-134	-431	-807
Comoros	-51	-51	-49	-43	-75	-65	-95	-105
Congo Dem Rep	41	167	212	178	120	130	70	43
Congo-Brazzaville	503	-206	742	688	739	2,024	718	586
Côte d'Ivoire	875	1,544	1,670	1,261	1,454	1,103	1,313	1,384
Djibouti	-163	-165	-137	-146	-140	-151	-161	-168
Egypt	-8,310	-9,499	-9,291	-13,036	-12,463	-9,321	-8,628	-7,844
Equatorial Guinea	36	-117	165	122	284	646	926	1,256
Eritrea								
Ethiopia	-723	-984	-727	-956	-1,071	-776	-1,359	-1,185
Gabon	1,832	2,227	1,920	813	1,552	1,468	1,790	1,827
Gambia	-166	-237	-159	-218	-185	-201	-189	-196
Ghana	-183	-439	-691	-768	-1,628	-1,647	-1,518	-1,779
Guinea	-64	50	144	231	191	161	176	182
Guinea-Bissau	-89	-59	-40	-37	0	3	-11	-50
Iran	4,478	6,117	4,185	-1,205	8,347	14,049	5,778	2,250
Iraq	-169	-219	600	1,100	5,900	9,450	4,905	4,090
Israel	-10,533	-11,010	-8,279	-6,349	-7,371	0	-6,401	-6,170
Jordan	-1,928	-2,476	-2,266	-2,026	-1,885	-2,698	-2,551	-2,649
Kenya	-1,112	-881	-1,225	-1,189	-1,085	-1,372	-1,248	-1,129
Kuwait	4,995	6,515	5,978	935	4,547	12,279	8,334	6,475
Lebanon	-4,825	-6,804	-6,824	-6,408	-5,530	-5,515	-6,423	-5,401
Lesotho	-825	-812	-829	-670	-606	-555	-527	-633
Liberia	120	162	95	210	230	220	189	239
Libya	3,572	3,809	2,858	364	3,781	6,463	4,518	5,121
Madagascar	-173	-208	-247	-271	-158	-253	-298	-327
Malawi	-69	-143	-244	-84	-221	-153	-113	-222
Mali	-330	-340	-177	-200	-258	-260	16	166
Mauritania	5	28	-32	-9	68	-40	-77	-87
Mauritius	-438	-487	-597	-428	-693	-535	-377	-326
Morocco	-3,142	-2,823	-2,493	-3,137	-2,558	-4,573	-3,894	-3,874
Mozambique	-536	-542	-517	-560	-876	-794	-687	-751
Namibia	-206	-253	-415	-416	-376	-229	-368	-353
Niger	-86	-123	-102	-137	-107	-110	-97	-120
Nigeria	4,121	9,715	5,706	644	5,268	12,254	5,675	7,560
Oman	1,821	2,768	2,604	-173	296	3,323	1,641	5,167
Qatar	83	884	470	1,471	4,562	4,138	3,755	5,013
Réunion								
Rwanda	-186	-197	-210	-224	-190	-159	-165	-147
Sao Tomé e Príncipe	-24	-18	-11	-19	-23	-20	-21	-26
Saudi Arabia	21,949	32,985	32,000	8,809	22,750	47,346	36,841	41,800
Senegal	-419	-448	-430	-487	-536	-599	-472	-410
Seychelles	-180	-239	-227	-261	-289	-149	-307	-344
Sierra Leone	-91	-164	-75	-88	-75	-136	-153	-216
Somalia								
South Africa	-2,693	-960	-1,971	-2,880	11	287	1,011	456
Sudan	-663	-927	-985	-1,319	-635	254	113	185
Swaziland	-142	-205	-104	-111	-131	-137	-75	-45
Syria	-1,146	-1,381	-111	-1,005	-368	2,553	2,049	591
Tanzania	-993	-604	-584	-863	-1,013	-860	-936	-812
Togo	-215	-224	-221	380	-184	-199	-196	-341
Tunisia	-2,428	-2,185	-2,388	-2,613	-2,603	-2,717	-2,921	-2,652
Uganda	-595	-604	-762	-914	-823	-1,076	-1,138	-669
United Arab Emirates	3,120	4,666	767	9,336	2,296	7,795	6,188	7,750
Yemen	363	637	490	-670	432	1,755	905	1,376
Zambia	340	202	96	-20	-119	88	98	106
Zimbabwe	-547	-397	-371	-260	-265	-376	-904	-1,064

Source: *Euromonitor from International Monetary Fund (IMF), International Financial Statistics*

Health

Hospitals and Beds 2002

● As stated

	In-patient Beds ('000)	Hospitals and Clinics	Beds per '000 inhabitants
Algeria	55	237	1.8
Argentina	141		3.7
Australia	74	1,257	3.8
Azerbaijan	63	735	7.7
Bolivia	12	2,437	1.4
Brazil	486	6,895	2.8
Canada	97	1,066	3.1
Chile	44		2.8
China	3,231	64,548	2.5
Colombia	45		1.1
Ecuador	18	3,496	1.4
Egypt	137	339	2.1
Hong Kong, China	37	107	5.1
India	1,514	15,741	1.5
Indonesia	129	1,162	0.6
Israel	39	367	6.1
Japan	2,180	21,020	17.2
Jordan	10	102	1.9
Kazakhstan	104	894	6.5
Kuwait	5	86	2.1
Malaysia	36	323	1.6
Mexico	104	820	1.0
Morocco	28	152	1.0
New Zealand	23	447	5.9
Nigeria			
Pakistan	103	910	0.6
Peru	44	470	1.7
Philippines	81	1,741	1.0
Saudi Arabia	5	55	0.2
Singapore	12	28	3.6
South Africa			
South Korea	283	41,454	5.9
Taiwan	115	17,847	5.1
Thailand	432	3,658	6.9
Tunisia	17	167	1.8
Turkmenistan	32	270	6.9
United Arab Emirates	3	71	0.9
USA	836	5,845	3.0
Venezuela	49	567	1.9
Vietnam	214	1,964	2.6

Source: Euromonitor from OECD/World Health Organisation/National Statistics

Health Personnel 2002

- Number

	Active Pharmacists	Dentists	Doctors	Midwives	Nurses
Algeria	4,200	7,979	29,691		
Argentina			110,400		
Australia	12,000	9,150	47,559		202,000
Azerbaijan	2,706	2,304	27,944		58,896
Bolivia		534	4,472		7,869
Brazil		8,095	479,832		
Canada	19,141	18,085	65,898		308,121
Chile			7,865		
China	399,071		2,140,375	37,894	1,307,407
Colombia			40,486		
Ecuador			18,227		
Egypt					
Hong Kong, China	1,372	2,060	10,052	12,395	44,659
India			462,294		596,776
Indonesia			27,391		153,291
Israel					
Japan				25,252	
Jordan					
Kazakhstan	11,234		52,962		87,934
Kuwait	1,212	424	1,079		7,680
Malaysia		1,967	20,671		25,699
Mexico		9,568	163,818		223,283
Morocco	5,956	2,372	12,496		
New Zealand	3,927	1,581	8,783		37,279
Nigeria	7,396	1,818	22,568	78,122	114,955
Pakistan		5,026	100,738	22,926	41,797
Peru			25,781		
Philippines		2,533	2,960	17,409	5,632
Saudi Arabia	581	268	3,467		8,082
Singapore	1,186	1,181	6,368	410	13,495
South Africa	10,003	5,100	31,614		175,314
South Korea	52,443	19,873	79,282	8,867	179,602
Taiwan	28,315	9,227	36,622	1,006	90,522
Thailand	7,518	3,537	17,728		53,834
Tunisia	2,110	1,458	9,361		
Turkmenistan		924	12,025	3,260	21,873
United Arab Emirates	151	145	1,426		
USA	205,244	172,033	804,923		2,868,451
Venezuela					
Vietnam	13,705		42,016	14,590	46,423

Source: Euromonitor from OECD/World Health Organisation

Table 14.3

□ Medical Services

Access to Health Amenities and Medical Services 2000

● % of population	Improved Sanitary Facilities	Polio Immunisation	Improved Drinking Water
North America			
Canada	100		100
USA	100	90	100
Latin America			
Anguilla		99	
Antigua	96	99	91
Argentina	85	85	79
Aruba			100
Bahamas	93	91	96
Barbados	100	56	100
Belize	42	89	76
Bermuda			
Bolivia	66	89	79
Brazil	77	95	87
British Virgin Islands		99	
Cayman Islands		92	
Chile	97	98	94
Colombia	85	78	91
Costa Rica	96	80	98
Cuba	95	99	95
Dominica		99	
Dominican Republic	71	67	79
Ecuador	59	83	71
El Salvador	83	98	74
French Guiana			
Grenada	97	97	94
Guadeloupe			
Guatemala	85	95	92
Guyana	87	78	94
Haiti	28	58	46
Honduras	77	86	90
Jamaica	84	86	71
Martinique			
Mexico	73	89	86
Netherlands Antilles			
Nicaragua	84	93	79
Panama	94	100	87
Paraguay	95	72	79
Peru	76	96	77
Puerto Rico			
St Kitts	96	99	98
St Lucia		70	98
St Vincent and the Grenadines	96	100	93
Suriname	83	80	95
Trinidad and Tobago	88	90	86
Uruguay	95	90	98
Venezuela	74	86	84

Source: *Euromonitor from World Health Organisation/ World Bank*

Access to Health Amenities and Medical Services 2000

• % of population	Improved Sanitary Facilities	Polio Immunisation	Improved Drinking Water
Asia Pacific			
Afghanistan	12	32	13
American Samoa		95	100
Armenia		96	
Azerbaijan		99	
Bangladesh	53	68	97
Bhutan	69	98	62
Brunei		99	
Cambodia	18	62	30
China	38	90	75
Fiji	43	92	47
French Polynesia	98	97	100
Guam		90	
Hong Kong, China			
India	31	95	88
Indonesia	66	74	76
Japan		99	
Kazakhstan	99	97	91
Kiribati	48	90	47
Kyrgyzstan	100	99	77
Laos	46	57	90
Macau			
Malaysia		95	
Maldives	56	97	100
Mongolia	30	94	60
Myanmar	46	86	68
Nauru		27	
Nepal	27	80	81
New Caledonia			
North Korea		98	
Pakistan	61	74	88
Papua New Guinea	82	46	42
Philippines	83	75	87
Singapore	100	96	100
Solomon Islands	34	90	71
South Korea	63	99	92
Sri Lanka	83	99	83
Taiwan			
Tajikistan		97	
Thailand	96	97	80
Tonga		95	100
Turkmenistan	100	98	58
Tuvalu		80	
Uzbekistan	100	96	85
Vanuatu	100	87	88
Vietnam	73	96	56
Western Samoa			
Australasia			
Australia	100	91	100
New Zealand		82	

Source: Euromonitor from World Health Organisation/ World Bank

◻ Medical Services

Access to Health Amenities and Medical Services 2000

● % of population

Africa and Middle East	Improved Sanitary Facilities	Polio Immunisation	Improved Drinking Water
Algeria	73	86	94
Angola	44	33	38
Bahrain		97	
Benin	23	88	63
Botswana		85	
Burkina Faso	29	57	
Burundi		64	
Cameroon	92	49	62
Cape Verde	71	86	74
Central African Republic	31	31	60
Chad	29	29	27
Comoros	98	70	96
Congo, Democratic Republic	20	42	45
Congo-Brazzaville		36	51
Côte d'Ivoire		72	77
Djibouti	91	46	100
Egypt	94	98	95
Equatorial Guinea	53	32	43
Eritrea	13	52	46
Ethiopia	15	42	24
Gabon	21	52	70
Gambia	37	89	62
Ghana	63	83	64
Guinea	58	57	48
Guinea-Bissau	47		49
Iran	81	100	95
Iraq	79	86	85
Israel		92	
Jordan	99	94	96
Kenya	86	62	49
Kuwait		94	
Lebanon	99	90	100
Lesotho	92	67	91
Liberia		52	
Libya	97	96	72
Madagascar	42	81	47
Malawi	77	73	57
Mali	69	32	65
Mauritania	33	31	37
Mauritius	99	88	
Morocco	75	95	82
Mozambique	43	87	60
Namibia	41	80	77
Niger	20	36	59
Nigeria	63	38	57
Oman	92	100	39
Qatar		90	
Réunion			
Rwanda	8	90	41
Sao Tomé e Príncipe		87	
Saudi Arabia	100	90	95
Senegal	70	49	78
Seychelles		99	
Sierra Leone	28	26	28
Somalia		37	
South Africa	86	96	86
Sudan	62	65	75
Swaziland		97	
Syria	90	97	80
Tanzania	90	64	54
Togo	34	50	54
Tunisia		96	
Uganda	75	53	50
United Arab Emirates		94	
Yemen	45	76	69
Zambia	78	79	64
Zimbabwe	68	70	85

Source: Euromonitor from World Health Organisation/ World Bank

Major Causes of Death 2002

● Death rate per
100,000 inhabitants

	Infectious/ Parasitic Diseases	Malignant Neoplasms	Circulatory Diseases	Respiratory Diseases	Digestive Diseases	Other Diseases	Motor Traffic Accidents	Injury and Poisoning	Suicide/ Self- Inflicted Injury
Algeria									
Argentina			230.4		35.0	336.2	31.9		
Australia	6.5	158.5	195.3	37.5	19.6	82.8	11.9	41.3	13.0
Azerbaijan		61.6	264.3	51.1	45.0				23.3
Bolivia					30.8				6.7
Brazil					40.4				
Canada			198.0		19.4				
Chile					25.4				6.7
China	30.0	230.3	221.6	139.6	31.5	338.9	10.4	62.3	14.6
Colombia					30.3				
Ecuador					34.0				
Egypt									
Hong Kong, China	11.0	172.9	140.5	70.2	20.9	56.5	144.4	31.3	
India					25.8				11.6
Indonesia					28.8				
Israel					14.0				
Japan	11.0	153.4	142.8	75.6	16.9	79.3	7.6	50.2	24.9
Jordan									0.1
Kazakhstan		129.7	498.0	65.7	36.5	124.4		138.1	30.3
Kuwait									
Malaysia	17.9	20.8	64.7		18.6		15.6		2.4
Mexico					89.6				
Morocco	5.3	9.9	39.3	7.1		97.9		11.2	
New Zealand	3.3	174.0	200.0	29.0	9.0	58.0	14.0	39.2	16.5
Nigeria									
Pakistan					27.5				
Peru					31.8				
Philippines					32.0				
Saudi Arabia									
Singapore	6.6	104.3	137.9	57.8	32.5		4.6		7.7
South Africa									
South Korea	13.0	162.3	170.7	36.1	13.1		33.2	65.6	16.1
Taiwan	24.0	136.4	52.7	7.5	18.5		9.7		10.6
Thailand					15.5				
Tunisia									
Turkmenistan					30.0				
United Arab Emirates									
USA	16.0	169.6	243.4	63.1	25.1	96.7	16.5	50.5	9.1
Venezuela					33.3				0.2
Vietnam					18.3				

Source: *Euromonitor from World Health Organisation*

Table 14.5

▣ Illness

Reported AIDS Cases by Date of Report 1985-2002

● Number

	1985	1990	1994	1995	1996	1997	1998	1999	2000	2001	2002
North America											
Canada	380	1,476	1,855	1,727	1,184	793	734	584	644	571	570
USA	12,026	49,446	72,737	69,892	61,109	50,000	43,894	46,143	42,156	43,265	42,786
Latin America											
Anguilla		1									
Antigua		3	6	5	13						
Argentina	28	492	2,181	2,184	2,622	2,297	1,899	1,401	528	1,490	1,464
Aruba				6							
Bahamas	37	169	317	388	375	387	323	314			
Barbados	9	61	119	95	130	113	168	133	23	129	141
Belize		19	45	28	38	30	37	90	46	63	75
Bermuda		33	44	49							
Bolivia	1	12	20	15	8	16	42	34	43	73	79
Brazil	573	8,993	18,341	20,357	22,943	23,546	24,017	20,009	15,013	3,024	15,458
British Virgin Islands		2	1	3							
Cayman Islands		2	3								
Chile	10	147	316	351	427	553	490	541	511	474	479
Colombia	16	781	1,361	910	1,095	589					
Costa Rica	6	79	173	214	214	250	281	215	177	152	137
Cuba		28	102	116	99	129	150	176	247	268	320
Dominica		2	5		14						
Dominican Republic	53	279	433	505	450	427	414	495	438	320	372
Ecuador	1	48	116	70	65	128	186	325	313	299	325
El Salvador	1	54	384	383	418	414	352	425			
French Guiana		41	55	61							
Grenada		5	7	13	18						
Guadeloupe		6	110	83							
Guatemala	5	92	110	141	835	649	397	730	519	303	379
Guyana		61	105	192	144	115	222	338	248	425	480
Haiti	110	1,216	0	0	0	3,932	0				
Honduras	4	739	1,123	1,221	1,086	1,261	1,492	1,136	369	1,065	1,234
Jamaica	3	70	335	511	491	609	643	892	903	445	709
Martinique		45	48	36							
Mexico	29	2,587	4,111	4,310	4,216	3,670	4,758	4,372	4,855	4,297	4,854
Netherlands Antilles		31									
Nicaragua		9	38	21	28	20	30	36	36	37	42
Panama	6	73	289	344	380	463	563	534	263	453	377
Paraguay	0	11	35	50	78	96	27	49			
Peru	4	410	840	1,090	1,177	1,078	1,031	1,009	615	775	893
Puerto Rico											
St Kitts		8	5	5	6						
St Lucia		15	13	10	14						
St Vincent and the Grenadines		4	8	6	19						
Suriname	0	33	26	20		120	112	103			
Trinidad and Tobago	41	176	247	324	323	291	355	397			
Uruguay	3	76	119	127	156	173	180				
Venezuela	55	625	1,101	972	667	46	0				

Source: UNAIDS/World Health Organisation

Illness

Reported AIDS Cases by Date of Report 1985-2002

- Number

	1985	1990	1994	1995	1996	1997	1998	1999	2000	2001	2002
Asia Pacific											
Afghanistan											
American Samoa											
Armenia	0	1	0	0	7	2	2	8	3	4	6
Azerbaijan	0	0	1	1	2	5	3	8	19	17	23
Bangladesh	0	1	0	6	0	3	0				
Bhutan						1	1	1			
Brunei		2	2	4	2	2	0	2	3	0	1
Cambodia			14	91	300	572	1,494	2,256	3,684	3,273	4,111
China	1	2	38	52	38	126	136	230	233	231	292
Fiji	0	2	2	0	0	0	0	4	3	0	2
French Polynesia		9	3	5							
Guam		2	11	3							
Hong Kong, China	3	13	37	45	70	64	63	61	67	24	35
India	0	57	523	1,091	888	2,108	1,148	952	2,098	2,399	2,514
Indonesia	0	5	15	20	31	34	75	57	166	185	232
Japan	6	31	136	169	234	250	231	300	327	155	232
Kazakhstan			1	2	2	8	9	5	8	10	9
Kiribati											
Kyrgyzstan		4	0	2	2	2	6				
Laos	0	0	4	4	16	48	27				
Macau			2								
Malaysia	0	18	105	233	347	568	875	1,200	1,168	482	937
Maldives			1	4	1	2	0	0	1	0	
Mongolia	0	0	0	0	0	0	0	1	0	1	1
Myanmar	0	0	286	618	890	554	231	802	816	668	891
Nauru											
Nepal		2	11	15	32	101	42				
New Caledonia		3	7	4							
North Korea											
Pakistan		5	9	19	20	19	23	17	15	8	10
Papua New Guinea		17	26	44	69	120	220	207	259	132	214
Philippines	4	19	56	52	52	23	42	77	42	24	45
Singapore		8	48	56	92	88	125	140	143	59	150
Solomon Islands											
South Korea		2	11	14	22	33	35	34	32	43	41
Sri Lanka	0	2	14	11	11	9	15	12	14	13	15
Taiwan		7	66	100	161	133	151	175	221	236	267
Tajikistan											
Thailand	2	166	13,923	20,686	24,709	26,713	27,128	26,003	23,352	9,345	19,260
Tonga			1		1						
Turkmenistan											
Tuvalu											
Uzbekistan	0	0	0	0	2	1	2	1	3	0	1
Vanuatu											
Vietnam			118	201	390	688	953	970	1,164	742	1,020
Western Samoa		2	1	2							
Australasia											
Australia	128	674	954	805	658	371	301	181	212	27	182
New Zealand	11	72	44	49	76	43	29	33	27	26	22

Source: UNAIDS/World Health Organisation

□ Illness

Reported AIDS Cases by Date of Report 1985-2002

● Number

	1985	1990	1994	1995	1996	1997	1998	1999	2000	2001	2002
Africa and Middle East											
Algeria		27	53	32	48	39	49	40	58	17	58
Angola	4	214	361	427	465	1,121	1,186	453	1,271	1,389	1,392
Bahrain	0	2	5	10	9	14	11	8	8	4	7
Benin	1	50	324	214	503	1,030	725	650	769	935	790
Botswana		132	575	1,172	1,368	2,224	2,992				
Burkina Faso		202	1,892	1,684	1,838	2,216	2,166	2,031	1,532	1,063	1,436
Burundi		841	443	1,358	2,239	3,510	4,092	4,395	1,762	3,988	4,275
Cameroon		183	1,761	2,766	1,485	3,950	5,410				
Cape Verde		4	14		36						
Central African Republic		1,312	50	649	2,077	0					
Chad		38	1,268	1,132	1,242	2,748	2,030	1,664	1,704	1,661	1,682
Comoros	0	1	3	2	2	3	2	1	4	2	3
Congo Dem Rep		3,916	2,637	8,329	11,572	9,642	5,809	9,953	9,848	10,784	11,109
Congo-Brazzaville		2,405	7,773	10,223							
Côte d'Ivoire	0	3,189	6,566	6,727	5,935	5,949	5,685	6,427			
Djibouti		51	196	231	358	434	111				
Egypt		7	22	16	14	25	23	34	44	35	46
Equatorial Guinea		2	16	98	74	111	189	122	222	220	246
Eritrea	0	56	625	727	896	1,260	1,610	1,086			
Ethiopia		448	6,927	3,793	832	7,631	9,416	11,964	13,347	5,872	15,219
Gabon		61	204	334	601	559	708	594	794	1,238	1,264
Gambia	0	46	53	32	78	74	126				
Ghana		2,013	2,330	2,578	3,295	3,833	4,854	7,752	6,289	3,857	7,232
Guinea	0	112	543	610	922	1,005	1,648	1,069	1,646	1,762	1,829
Guinea-Bissau	0	19	254	77	37	217		120			
Iran	0	10	19	16	27	40	21	27	67	60	71
Iraq	0	0	37	16	15	2	4	0			
Israel	0	38	32	45	67	45	36	137	50	64	85
Jordan		1	6	2	4	12	11	3	14	7	8
Kenya		7,672	8,588	9,133	6,844	4,885	2,565				
Kuwait	0	1	5	4	5	2	19	4	12	5	9
Lebanon	2	10	12	18	5	8	37	32	19	21	27
Lesotho	0	10	238	341	936	2,203	3,242	3,563	3,760	4,040	4,344
Liberia			13	11	8	59	114	79	81	52	68
Libya		5	3	2	3	7	33	4	5	6	8
Madagascar	0	0	9	6	1	6	2	0	2	6	4
Malawi	17	5,859	4,732	5,209	5,406	3,705	1,878	1,711			
Mali	1	242	609	454	594	711	620	290			
Mauritania	0	12	56	103	98						
Mauritius		2	6	6	4	6	2	7	8	7	9
Morocco	0	26	77	57	66	92	93	165	112	129	149
Mozambique	0	98	534	1,380	2,086	1,661	4,376	6,361	7,800	6,991	8,110
Namibia			452	1,836	2,687	3,797	5,158	6,878	4,503	6,805	6,839
Niger		213	467	621	652	217	425	940	1,014	883	1,017
Nigeria		163	1,114	2,829	2,980	3,815	18,490	16,188	9,715	3,661	11,989
Oman	1	23	60	41	27	43	28	36	32	23	23
Qatar	0	10	8	6	2	4	3	9	3	2	3
Réunion	0	12	23	30	0	0					
Rwanda	161	2,204	0	2,072	3,847	1,350	3,948	671			
Sao Tomé e Príncipe		2	1	4	6						
Saudi Arabia	0	5	38	37	100	112	39	24	24	39	48
Senegal	0	156	534	396	327	225	311	208			
Seychelles		0	3	6	6	5	5	8	4	7	6
Sierra Leone	0	7	22	29	62	67	26				
Somalia	0	5									
South Africa	8	345	3,816	4,219	738						
Sudan	0	130	201	257	221	270	511	517	652	492	694
Swaziland	0	20	120	154	613	1,466	733	1,259			
Syria		1	4	6	9	8	8	7	7	12	11
Tanzania	292	11,106	6,096	4,722	8,426	10,592	8,675	8,850	11,673	8,179	10,381
Togo	0	458	1,284	1,710	1,527	1,211	1,623	998	262	941	977
Tunisia	0	36	50	65	54	62	44	42			
Uganda	440	6,616	4,927	2,192	3,032	1,962	1,406	1,149			
United Arab Emirates	0	8	2	1	2	1	1	2			
Yemen	0	1	3	11	60	48	34				
Zambia	3	4,702	1,963	5,950	4,552	1,676					
Zimbabwe	0	4,362	10,647	13,356	12,029	6,732	4,113				

Source: UNAIDS/World Health Organisation

Food Supply: Average Consumption of Calories, Protein and Fat 2002

● Daily averages, calories/grams per inhabitant	Calories (number)	Protein (grams)	Fat (grams)
North America			
Canada	3,192	103.5	129.2
USA	3,797	114.7	155.6
Latin America			
Anguilla			
Antigua	2,409	81.9	89.7
Argentina	3,172	101.7	115.7
Aruba			
Bahamas	2,791	91.5	99.4
Barbados	3,047	90.8	98.1
Belize	2,914	74.8	74.6
Bermuda	2,916	90.4	121.7
Bolivia	2,280	60.2	50.9
Brazil	3,016	80.9	89.4
British Virgin Islands			
Cayman Islands			
Chile	2,900	78.8	85.8
Colombia	2,610	59.4	65.2
Costa Rica	2,769	71.0	76.2
Cuba	2,719	61.7	54.7
Dominica	3,028	88.8	85.3
Dominican Republic	2,347	50.4	82.2
Ecuador	2,821	58.6	94.0
El Salvador	2,577	65.7	56.7
French Guiana			
Grenada	2,768	71.5	100.6
Guadeloupe			
Guatemala	2,204	56.2	51.3
Guyana	2,573	73.1	46.4
Haiti	2,081	44.8	43.2
Honduras	2,418	60.5	67.0
Jamaica	2,718	70.3	81.4
Martinique			
Mexico	3,176	91.5	86.8
Netherlands Antilles	2,560	80.1	79.9
Nicaragua	2,246	60.5	49.9
Panama	2,400	65.2	76.1
Paraguay	2,584	72.5	97.8
Peru	2,637	64.2	53.4
Puerto Rico			
St Kitts	3,012	87.3	92.0
St Lucia	2,841	94.3	71.0
St Vincent and the Grenadines	2,595	65.1	71.8
Suriname	2,659	60.7	68.6
Trinidad and Tobago	2,821	64.4	80.8
Uruguay	2,872	94.0	105.2
Venezuela	2,388	63.5	64.2

Source: *Euromonitor from FAO/National Statistics*

■ Nutrition

Food Supply: Average Consumption of Calories, Protein and Fat 2002

● Daily averages, calories/grams per inhabitant

	Calories (number)	Protein (grams)	Fat (grams)
Asia Pacific			
Afghanistan	1,781	57.0	48.5
American Samoa			
Armenia	1,808	53.4	37.5
Azerbaijan	2,640	76.7	40.4
Bangladesh	2,189	47.0	27.1
Bhutan			
Brunei	2,862	84.9	71.5
Cambodia	2,063	51.1	32.9
China	2,988	88.0	86.7
Fiji	2,817	72.7	102.3
French Polynesia	2,903	96.8	117.3
Guam			
Hong Kong, China			
India	2,513	58.3	52.7
Indonesia	2,923	64.4	60.8
Japan	2,757	90.8	84.0
Kazakhstan	2,700	86.2	77.2
Kiribati	2,947	72.9	108.6
Kyrgyzstan	2,946	96.5	51.0
Laos	2,339	62.0	30.1
Macau			
Malaysia	2,942	76.7	82.3
Maldives	2,628	113.3	65.3
Mongolia	1,967	70.3	73.0
Myanmar	2,832	75.7	49.9
Nauru			
Nepal	2,508	63.8	39.3
New Caledonia	2,784	81.7	102.5
North Korea	2,203	63.3	35.8
Pakistan	2,468	62.2	68.0
Papua New Guinea	2,214	44.3	47.4
Philippines	2,404	55.9	50.1
Singapore			
Solomon Islands	2,290	52.5	44.0
South Korea	3,123	92.2	77.7
Sri Lanka	2,330	53.9	46.2
Taiwan			
Tajikistan	1,601	41.1	32.0
Thailand	2,503	55.8	49.2
Tonga			
Turkmenistan	2,687	78.4	64.6
Tuvalu			
Uzbekistan	2,168	66.5	55.7
Vanuatu	2,564	61.5	92.9
Vietnam	2,617	62.9	41.5
Western Samoa			
Australasia			
Australia	3,159	107.8	141.7
New Zealand	3,289	104.6	119.2

Source: Euromonitor from FAO/National Statistics

Food Supply: Average Consumption of Calories, Protein and Fat 2002

● Daily averages, calories/grams per inhabitant	Calories (number)	Protein (grams)	Fat (grams)
Africa and Middle East			
Algeria	2,997	79.6	70.3
Angola	1,964	41.0	39.5
Bahrain			
Benin	2,504	58.3	42.7
Botswana	2,298	75.1	53.0
Burkina Faso	2,443	71.9	56.6
Burundi	1,620	42.1	10.0
Cameroon	2,280	59.1	48.1
Cape Verde	3,324	77.5	98.8
Central African Republic	1,948	44.9	59.2
Chad	2,256	69.3	70.1
Comoros	1,737	43.1	44.4
Congo, Democratic Republic	1,452	22.6	22.5
Congo-Brazzaville	2,281	43.2	54.1
Côte d'Ivoire	2,607	51.1	56.5
Djibouti	2,247	50.1	71.7
Egypt	3,394	96.8	63.1
Equatorial Guinea			
Eritrea	1,698	50.1	36.7
Ethiopia	2,175	63.9	22.9
Gabon	2,606	73.2	65.4
Gambia	2,412	52.8	84.3
Ghana	2,765	55.9	36.9
Guinea	2,438	51.8	57.1
Guinea-Bissau	2,513	48.7	61.0
Iran	2,946	79.5	57.2
Iraq	2,291	55.7	46.3
Israel	3,506	114.1	125.7
Jordan	2,811	75.6	86.3
Kenya	2,068	53.9	48.4
Kuwait	3,186	94.5	103.5
Lebanon	3,200	84.9	113.5
Lesotho	2,320	63.0	33.6
Liberia	1,870	31.5	48.6
Libya	3,335	91.9	107.2
Madagascar	2,079	48.2	30.4
Malawi	2,203	54.5	28.2
Mali	2,417	69.0	49.3
Mauritania	2,778	76.4	69.5
Mauritius	3,010	80.2	83.6
Morocco	3,061	83.8	58.2
Mozambique	1,996	38.0	31.4
Namibia	2,784	78.8	52.6
Niger	2,114	57.0	38.8
Nigeria	2,770	62.1	62.5
Oman			
Qatar			
Réunion			
Rwanda	2,211	54.1	20.1
Sao Tomé e Príncipe	2,603	49.9	80.8
Saudi Arabia	2,887	77.4	72.9
Senegal	2,284	57.1	69.6
Seychelles	2,463	81.9	84.2
Sierra Leone	1,825	41.2	41.4
Somalia	1,668	47.8	55.0
South Africa	2,941	75.5	79.0
Sudan	2,271	71.7	72.5
Swaziland	2,682	67.1	51.6
Syria	3,040	75.0	100.4
Tanzania	2,007	48.9	31.5
Togo	2,280	53.7	49.7
Tunisia	3,268	92.6	93.5
Uganda	2,436	60.2	30.5
United Arab Emirates	3,357	105.2	98.7
Yemen	2,041	58.1	38.3
Zambia	1,899	45.9	34.4
Zimbabwe	2,176	51.4	64.5

Source: *Euromonitor from FAO/National Statistics*

Share of Total Health Expenditure in GDP 1990-2002

- % of total central government expenditure

	1990	1994	1995	1996	1997	1998	1999	2000	2001	2002
North America										
Canada	9.1	9.8	9.1	8.9	8.9	9.1	9.2	9.1	9.4	9.6
USA	12.0	13.3	13.3	13.2	13.0	12.9	13.0	13.0	13.4	13.6
Latin America										
Anguilla										
Antigua	4.5	4.5	5.7	5.7	5.4	5.3	5.3	5.5	5.8	5.9
Argentina	4.4	4.8	8.2	7.9	7.8	8.0	8.5	8.6	8.8	9.0
Aruba										
Bahamas	5.0	3.9	5.8	6.6	6.7	7.3	7.7	8.0	8.9	9.5
Barbados	7.2	7.1	6.2	6.1	5.9	5.6	5.8	6.4	7.1	7.9
Belize	2.7	4.7	3.8	3.7	4.0	4.3	4.7	4.6	5.0	5.3
Bermuda	3.5	4.6			3.9					
Bolivia	0.4	2.4	4.4	4.6	4.5	5.0	5.2	6.7	7.4	8.0
Brazil	2.9	3.4	7.2	7.4	7.5	7.5	7.9	8.3	8.5	8.6
British Virgin Islands										
Cayman Islands		3.9			4.1					
Chile	2.0	2.5	6.7	6.9	7.2	7.5	7.3	7.2	6.8	6.6
Colombia	1.3	1.5	7.4	8.8	9.3	9.3	9.9	9.6	9.9	10.2
Costa Rica	8.3	6.5	6.3	6.2	6.3	6.5	6.4	6.4	6.7	6.6
Cuba	6.6	9.1	5.7	5.8	6.3	6.4	6.9	6.8	7.0	7.4
Dominica	6.1	6.1	6.1	6.2	6.3	6.1	6.4	6.1	6.2	6.5
Dominican Republic	4.5	5.0	4.9	5.1	6.4	6.5	6.4	6.3	6.2	6.2
Ecuador	1.6	1.8	4.6	5.1	4.6	4.3	3.9	2.4	2.4	2.6
El Salvador	4.8	5.7	6.6	7.6	8.1	8.3	8.5	8.8	8.9	9.2
French Guiana										
Grenada	5.9	5.3	4.4	4.8	4.7	4.8	4.8	4.8	4.9	5.3
Guadeloupe										
Guatemala	3.5	3.0	4.1	4.1	4.3	4.5	4.7	4.7	4.7	4.7
Guyana	3.8	5.2	4.7	4.5	4.8	4.8	5.0	5.1	5.8	6.2
Haiti	3.6	4.4	5.8	5.1	4.9	5.1	4.9	4.9	4.7	4.7
Honduras	8.1	8.0	6.8	6.8	6.1	6.6	6.3	6.8	6.7	6.8
Jamaica	4.5	4.2	4.5	4.5	4.9	5.3	5.8	5.5	5.6	6.0
Martinique										
Mexico	2.9	3.8	5.6	5.3	5.3	5.3	5.4	5.4	5.9	6.3
Netherlands Antilles										
Nicaragua	9.5	12.2	6.4	6.0	5.2	4.8	4.7	4.4	4.4	4.7
Panama	6.6	6.5	7.8	8.0	7.4	7.4	7.6	7.6	7.9	8.2
Paraguay	4.2	5.2	7.8	7.2	7.6	7.3	7.9	7.9	8.3	9.4
Peru	1.0	1.0	4.6	4.5	4.5	4.7	4.9	4.8	5.0	5.1
Puerto Rico										
St Kitts	4.9	5.3	4.7	5.1	4.7	4.7	4.9	5.2	5.5	6.2
St Lucia	3.5	3.8	3.8	4.0	4.2	4.3	4.1	4.3	4.5	4.6
St Vincent and the Grenadines	6.3	5.6	5.8	5.7	6.1	5.9	6.1	6.3	6.4	6.7
Suriname	5.9	6.3	8.3	8.8	9.1	9.9	9.7	9.8	8.6	10.3
Trinidad and Tobago	4.1	3.7	4.5	4.6	4.8	5.3	5.3	5.2	5.3	5.7
Uruguay	6.7	9.1	9.2	9.6	10.0	10.2	10.8	10.9	11.3	11.2
Venezuela	1.5	1.2	4.6	3.9	4.3	5.0	4.6	4.7	4.8	6.6

Source: Euromonitor from WHO

☐ Health Expenditure

Share of Total Health Expenditure in GDP 1990-2002

- % of total central government expenditure

	1990	1994	1995	1996	1997	1998	1999	2000	2001	2002
Asia Pacific										
Afghanistan			1.3	1.3	1.4	1.6	1.5	1.0	1.0	0.9
American Samoa										
Armenia			7.8	7.8	7.8	7.3	7.6	7.5	7.6	7.7
Azerbaijan	3.3	1.9	2.7	2.2	2.2	2.3	2.4	2.1	2.1	1.8
Bangladesh	2.8	3.3	3.5	4.0	3.9	3.8	4.0	3.8	3.9	3.9
Bhutan	4.7	5.6	2.9	3.4	3.6	3.8	3.7	4.1	4.2	4.4
Brunei			2.6	2.6	2.8	3.0	3.2	3.1	3.1	3.1
Cambodia		7.2	6.7	7.5	8.3	8.4	8.1	8.1	8.2	8.0
China	3.5	3.8	3.9	4.2	4.5	4.7	5.1	5.3	5.3	5.6
Fiji		3.9	3.8	3.9	3.9	4.1	3.7	3.9	3.6	3.5
French Polynesia										
Guam										
Hong Kong, China	3.7	4.4	5.0	5.3	5.7	6.2	6.6	7.0	7.4	7.9
India	4.2	5.0	5.0	5.2	5.3	5.0	5.1	4.9	4.9	4.8
Indonesia	1.6	1.8	1.7	2.3	2.4	2.5	2.6	2.7	2.7	2.8
Japan	5.9	6.7	7.0	7.0	7.2	7.1	7.4	7.8	8.3	8.7
Kazakhstan			6.0	6.0	6.2	5.1	4.2	3.7	3.2	2.9
Kiribati			9.0	8.8	9.0	8.4	8.3	8.1	7.7	7.3
Kyrgyzstan	5.8	4.9	7.8	6.7	6.4	6.8	6.1	6.0	6.3	7.3
Laos		3.2	2.8	2.9	3.5	3.3	3.4	3.4	4.1	4.4
Macau										
Malaysia	2.5	2.2	2.2	2.3	2.3	2.5	2.5	2.5	2.8	2.8
Maldives	5.9	5.8	5.9	6.4	6.5	6.4	6.8	7.6	8.2	8.6
Mongolia	7.2		4.2	5.2	5.0	6.2	6.1	6.6	6.6	6.3
Myanmar	2.6	2.3	2.1	2.2	2.1	2.0	2.0	2.2	2.4	2.6
Nauru			10.0	10.6	11.7	11.8	11.4	11.3	11.3	11.9
Nepal	4.5	4.2	5.1	5.2	5.5	5.7	5.5	5.4	5.4	5.6
New Caledonia										
North Korea			3.1	3.0	3.0	3.0	2.6	2.1	1.7	1.2
Pakistan	4.4	4.2	4.2	4.0	4.0	4.0	4.1	4.1	4.1	4.1
Papua New Guinea	3.8	3.5	2.9	2.7	3.2	3.9	4.2	4.1	4.4	4.8
Philippines	2.9	3.2	3.4	3.5	3.6	3.6	3.6	3.4	3.4	3.3
Singapore	3.3	3.1	3.7	3.7	3.6	4.1	4.0	3.5	3.6	3.5
Solomon Islands			4.3	4.2	4.6	5.3	5.6	5.9	6.5	6.4
South Korea	4.5	4.7	4.7	4.9	5.0	5.1	5.6	6.0	6.5	6.7
Sri Lanka	3.3	3.3	3.4	3.3	3.2	3.4	3.6	3.6	3.6	3.6
Taiwan			0.4	0.3	0.3	0.4	0.4	0.4	0.5
Tajikistan	5.4	7.2	2.0	2.9	3.0	2.5	2.8	2.5	2.2	2.0
Thailand	5.5	5.3	3.4	3.6	3.7	3.9	3.7	3.7	3.5	3.3
Tonga			7.5	7.3	7.9	7.7	7.8	7.5	7.8	7.6
Turkmenistan	4.6	1.9	2.4	2.8	4.0	5.0	5.3	5.4	5.1	6.0
Tuvalu			8.9	8.3	8.4	8.6	8.8	7.8	7.3	6.9
Uzbekistan	5.2	4.2	4.8	4.8	4.5	3.9	3.9	3.7	3.1	2.5
Vanuatu			3.3	2.8	3.3	3.5	3.9	3.9	4.3	4.6
Vietnam	2.9	5.0	3.9	4.6	4.5	4.7	5.5	5.2	5.5	5.6
Western Samoa										
Australasia										
Australia	7.8	8.5	8.2	8.3	8.4	8.5	8.4	8.3	8.2	8.1
New Zealand	7.0	7.3	7.2	7.2	7.5	7.9	7.9	8.0	7.7	7.7

Source: *Euronmonitor from WHO*

■ Health Expenditure

Share of Total Health Expenditure in GDP 1990-2002

● % of total central government expenditure

	1990	1994	1995	1996	1997	1998	1999	2000	2001	2002
Africa and Middle East										
Algeria	4.2	4.6	4.8	4.4	4.1	4.4	4.2	3.6	3.6	3.5
Angola			4.8	3.9	3.9	3.5	3.3	3.6	3.5	3.4
Bahrain	7.0		4.5	4.4	4.8	5.0	4.8	4.1	4.2	4.1
Benin	2.8	3.0	3.1	3.2	3.1	3.3	3.2	3.2	3.1	2.9
Botswana	3.0	3.7	5.4	5.6	5.4	5.3	5.8	6.0	5.9	6.0
Burkina Faso	4.1	4.2	3.1	3.7	3.9	3.9	4.3	4.2	3.9	4.1
Burundi	3.1	4.2	3.5	3.2	2.5	2.8	2.6	3.1	3.2	3.4
Cameroon	1.7	2.7	4.1	4.1	4.1	4.2	4.3	4.3	4.4	4.5
Cape Verde		3.3	2.4	2.5	2.4	2.6	2.6	2.6	2.7	2.8
Central African Republic		2.5	2.1	2.0	2.4	2.5	2.8	2.9	3.1	3.4
Chad			3.0	3.1	3.1	2.9	2.9	3.1	2.5	2.5
Comoros			4.8	4.6	4.5	4.5	4.4	4.4	4.2	4.1
Congo Dem Rep			1.8	1.7	1.6	1.7	1.6	1.5	1.1	0.8
Congo-Brazzaville			3.3	2.8	2.8	3.5	2.9	2.2	2.5	2.7
Côte d'Ivoire	3.1	3.6	2.9	2.9	2.8	2.7	2.6	2.7	2.6	2.5
Djibouti			4.8	5.0	4.6	4.9	5.0	5.0	5.1	5.1
Egypt	4.3		3.7	3.8	3.9	4.0	3.9	3.8	3.7	3.6
Equatorial Guinea	6.3	4.2	4.2	4.7	3.6	4.2	3.4	3.4	2.9	3.2
Eritrea		2.0	3.4	3.9	4.4	5.4	4.1	4.3	3.3	3.1
Ethiopia	2.4	3.8	3.8	3.8	4.4	4.9	4.6	4.6	4.7	4.6
Gabon	2.9	3.1	3.1	3.0	2.9	3.2	3.3	3.0	3.5	3.8
Gambia	4.8	4.2	3.9	3.6	3.5	3.8	4.2	4.1	4.1	3.9
Ghana	4.0	3.9	4.2	4.1	3.9	4.1	4.2	4.2	3.5	3.9
Guinea	3.4	3.4	3.5	3.5	3.6	3.6	3.8	3.4	3.4	3.4
Guinea-Bissau			3.6	4.3	3.9	4.0	3.9	3.9	4.5	4.7
Iran	4.2	4.8	5.6	5.4	5.7	5.6	5.4	5.5	5.7	6.4
Iraq	5.6		4.9	4.6	5.0	4.4	3.7	3.7	3.2	2.8
Israel	7.9	8.0	9.9	10.2	10.1	10.0	10.9	10.9	12.2	12.9
Jordan	6.9	7.5	9.6	9.9	8.8	8.8	8.0	8.1	7.6	6.8
Kenya	7.9	7.7	8.1	8.1	8.3	8.4	8.4	8.3	7.8	8.2
Kuwait			3.6	3.1	3.3	3.9	3.5	3.0	3.4	3.5
Lebanon			10.8	10.9	11.3	11.6	11.7	11.8	11.8	11.5
Lesotho			6.2	5.6	5.3	5.9	6.4	6.3	6.9	6.6
Liberia			2.9	3.0	3.2	3.5	3.9	4.0	4.4	4.6
Libya			3.6	3.6	3.5	3.7	3.3	3.3	3.6	3.8
Madagascar		2.0	2.7	2.7	2.0	2.8	3.0	3.5	3.6	4.2
Malawi			6.1	6.5	7.3	6.8	6.9	7.6	7.2	8.4
Mali	3.2	3.5	3.2	3.3	4.2	4.5	4.7	4.9	4.5	4.5
Mauritania		5.4	3.2	3.2	3.3	3.8	4.2	4.3	4.4	4.7
Mauritius		3.9	3.6	3.6	3.5	3.4	3.6	3.4	3.4	3.3
Morocco	2.5		4.6	4.5	4.4	4.3	4.4	4.5	4.3	4.2
Mozambique	4.7	3.6	4.9	5.0	4.6	4.3	4.1	4.3	3.0	3.8
Namibia	5.2	7.3	8.2	7.4	7.4	7.6	7.3	7.1	6.6	6.8
Niger		3.9	3.8	3.8	3.8	3.9	3.8	3.9	3.5	3.2
Nigeria	2.7	2.2	2.8	2.6	2.4	2.5	2.4	2.2	2.1	2.4
Oman			3.0	2.9	2.7	3.1	2.9	2.8	3.0	3.3
Qatar			4.8	4.8	4.0	4.5	4.1	3.2	3.8	3.8
Réunion										
Rwanda	3.4	4.6	6.2	6.1	5.5	5.0	5.4	5.2	5.2	5.1
Sao Tomé e Príncipe			3.3	3.5	3.0	2.9	2.3	2.3	2.0	1.8
Saudi Arabia	7.9	8.9	5.3	5.1	5.1	5.7	5.4	5.3	5.8	6.1
Senegal	2.6	4.3	4.7	4.9	4.9	4.7	4.7	4.6	4.5	4.5
Seychelles			6.2	6.4	6.6	6.7	6.5	6.2	6.3	6.4
Sierra Leone		4.5	2.8	2.6	2.8	3.0	3.5	4.3	4.7	5.2
Somalia			2.6	2.3	2.4	2.0	1.6	1.3	0.9	0.6
South Africa		6.9	8.4	9.2	9.0	8.7	8.8	8.8	8.6	8.4
Sudan	2.4	2.5	3.8	3.5	3.3	4.2	4.2	4.7	4.8	5.2
Swaziland	3.1	3.7	3.3	3.9	3.3	3.7	4.0	4.2	4.3	4.3
Syria	2.1	2.4	2.0	2.0	2.1	2.3	2.5	2.5	2.6	2.7
Tanzania	3.2	4.5	5.3	5.1	5.2	5.0	5.5	5.9	6.2	6.4
Togo	2.8	3.1	2.9	2.6	3.1	2.7	2.7	2.8	2.8	2.5
Tunisia	5.6	5.1	6.8	6.6	6.4	6.8	7.0	7.0	7.1	7.4
Uganda		3.9	3.5	3.4	3.4	3.7	4.0	3.9	4.1	4.4
United Arab Emirates		7.5	3.4	3.2	3.7	4.1	3.7	3.2	3.3	3.4
Yemen	2.5	2.2	5.1	4.4	4.6	5.2	5.0	5.0	6.5	7.4
Zambia	3.3	4.5	5.2	5.8	6.0	5.6	5.2	5.6	5.0	5.7
Zimbabwe	6.1	6.5	7.1	7.5	9.3	11.4	8.1	7.3	5.2	6.8

Source: *Euronmonitor from WHO*

Household Profiles

□ Average Number of Occupants per Household

Table 15.1

Average Number of Occupants per Household at Jan 1st 1978-2002

● Persons

	1978	1980	1985	1990	1991	1992	1993	1994
North America								
Canada	3.44	3.31	3.00	2.86	2.82	2.80	2.79	2.78
USA	3.02	2.93	2.80	2.70	2.71	2.71	2.71	2.67
Latin America								
Anguilla								
Antigua								
Argentina	3.80	3.78	3.71	3.66	3.67	3.66	3.65	3.64
Aruba								
Bahamas								
Barbados								
Belize								
Bermuda								
Bolivia	5.91	5.79	5.62	5.00	4.86	4.71	4.59	4.47
Brazil	3.79	3.87	4.08	3.86	3.84	3.82	3.79	3.75
British Virgin Islands								
Cayman Islands								
Chile	3.53	3.60	3.88	4.09	4.10	4.08	4.02	3.93
Colombia	4.34	4.33	4.69	5.07	4.98	4.91	4.82	4.76
Costa Rica								
Cuba								
Dominica								
Dominican Republic								
Ecuador	3.83	4.03	4.55	5.01	5.00	4.98	4.97	4.95
El Salvador								
French Guiana								
Grenada								
Guadeloupe								
Guatemala								
Guyana								
Haiti								
Honduras								
Jamaica								
Martinique								
Mexico	5.80	5.71	5.55	5.14	4.99	4.85	4.72	4.61
Netherlands Antilles								
Nicaragua								
Panama								
Paraguay								
Peru	3.96	4.11	4.43	4.72	4.75	4.77	4.77	4.77
Puerto Rico								
St Kitts								
St Lucia								
St Vincent and the Grenadines								
Suriname								
Trinidad and Tobago								
Uruguay								
Venezuela	5.51	5.48	5.40	5.47	5.43	5.35	5.24	5.11

Source: *National statistics/UN//Euromonitor*

Average Number of Occupants per Household

Average Number of Occupants per Household at Jan 1st 1978-2002 (continued)

- Persons

	1995	1996	1997	1998	1999	2000	2001	2002
North America								
Canada	2.60	2.59	2.58	2.58	2.59	2.57	2.57	2.58
USA	2.68	2.68	2.68	2.67	2.64	2.64	2.63	2.63
Latin America								
Anguilla		6.25	5.57	6.23	6.02	5.83	5.89	5.96
Antigua		3.31	3.25	3.26	3.28	3.32	3.36	3.41
Argentina	3.64	3.64	3.61	3.61	3.62	3.63	3.63	3.64
Aruba		5.54	5.43	4.96	5.00	5.01	5.02	5.03
Bahamas		4.85	4.82	4.80	4.83	4.89	4.90	4.91
Barbados		4.78	4.78	4.67	4.74	4.66	4.71	4.77
Belize		2.72	2.65	2.70	2.70	2.72	2.70	2.68
Bermuda		4.38	4.67	4.42	4.51	4.46	4.40	4.35
Bolivia	4.36	4.26	4.21	4.19	4.16	4.15	4.16	4.17
Brazil	3.71	3.66	3.61	3.56	3.52	3.49	3.48	3.46
British Virgin Islands		4.42	4.52	4.27	4.33	4.54	4.66	4.79
Cayman Islands		4.71	4.75	4.46	4.67	4.65	4.71	4.76
Chile	3.95	3.99	3.97	3.93	3.89	3.84	3.85	3.87
Colombia	4.74	4.50	4.48	4.47	4.45	4.27	4.28	4.29
Costa Rica		4.25	4.12	3.89	4.07	4.02	3.98	3.93
Cuba		3.97	4.00	3.99	3.99	3.97	3.94	3.92
Dominica		4.30	4.29	4.26	4.28	4.30	4.33	4.35
Dominican Republic		4.67	4.75	4.73	4.73	4.69	4.63	4.57
Ecuador	4.93	4.93	4.93	4.91	4.91	4.91	4.92	4.94
El Salvador		4.32	4.33	4.34	4.36	4.38	4.32	4.27
French Guiana		5.49	5.48	5.48	5.49	5.62	5.56	5.50
Grenada		4.94	5.34	5.35	5.22	5.27	5.33	5.39
Guadeloupe		4.69	4.83	4.73	4.76	4.83	4.88	4.92
Guatemala		4.70	4.71	4.69	4.71	4.77	4.85	4.94
Guyana		4.61	4.57	4.59	4.59	4.67	4.76	4.84
Haiti		5.01	5.04	4.86	5.02	5.06	5.12	5.19
Honduras		4.69	4.67	4.93	4.78	4.74	4.68	4.62
Jamaica		4.78	4.75	4.80	4.78	4.86	4.93	5.00
Martinique		4.56	4.53	4.55	4.55	4.56	4.55	4.54
Mexico	4.59	4.53	4.46	4.32	4.35	4.37	4.40	4.43
Netherlands Antilles		5.07	5.20	4.86	5.05	4.98	4.89	4.80
Nicaragua		3.57	3.55	3.29	3.47	3.51	3.56	3.60
Panama		4.94	4.92	4.92	4.93	4.97	4.90	4.83
Paraguay		4.61	4.61	4.59	4.62	4.64	4.67	4.69
Peru	4.77	4.77	4.76	4.75	4.74	4.72	4.72	4.73
Puerto Rico		4.94	4.89	4.88	4.91	4.91	4.87	4.84
St Kitts		4.46	4.38	4.54	4.44	4.48	4.55	4.62
St Lucia		4.89	4.87	4.80	4.86	4.87	4.83	4.80
St Vincent and the Grenadines		4.22	4.21	4.27	4.23	4.21	4.27	4.32
Suriname		4.80	4.77	5.08	4.89	4.94	4.98	5.03
Trinidad and Tobago		4.82	4.64	4.75	4.74	4.79	4.85	4.91
Uruguay		2.61	2.56	2.56	2.57	2.60	2.57	2.54
Venezuela	4.97	4.86	4.77	4.74	4.73	4.72	4.75	4.77

Source: National statistics/UN//Euromonitor

■ Average Number of Occupants per Household

Average Number of Occupants per Household at Jan 1st 1978-2002 (continued)

● Persons

	1978	1980	1985	1990	1991	1992	1993	1994
Asia Pacific								
Afghanistan								
American Samoa								
Armenia								
Azerbaijan				4.80	4.83	4.87	4.98	5.02
Bangladesh								
Bhutan								
Brunei								
Cambodia								
China	5.27	5.21	4.46	4.10	4.02	3.96	3.89	3.84
Fiji								
French Polynesia								
Guam								
Hong Kong, China	4.28	4.29	3.88	3.64	3.59	3.54	3.49	3.47
India	5.70	5.70	5.39	5.54	5.70	5.75	5.77	5.81
Indonesia	4.57	4.51	4.69	4.53	4.49	4.45	4.41	4.36
Japan	3.34	3.28	3.10	3.00	2.98	2.94	2.90	2.87
Kazakhstan				3.04	3.14	3.24	3.35	3.45
Kiribati								
Kyrgyzstan								
Laos								
Macau								
Malaysia	5.16	5.15	5.31	5.18	5.13	5.08	5.02	4.95
Maldives								
Mongolia								
Myanmar								
Nauru								
Nepal								
New Caledonia								
North Korea								
Pakistan	6.59	6.59	6.69	6.90	6.96	7.07	7.18	7.29
Papua New Guinea								
Philippines	5.56	5.49	5.59	5.32	5.19	5.12	5.14	5.13
Singapore	5.72	5.14	4.32	4.05	4.04	4.01	4.00	3.95
Solomon Islands								
South Korea	5.32	5.07	4.66	3.77	3.73	3.65	3.58	3.51
Sri Lanka			5.17	5.55	5.49	5.50	5.50	5.46
Taiwan			4.54	4.06	3.99	3.93	3.87	3.80
Tajikistan								
Thailand	5.28	5.41	5.12	4.51	4.36	4.24	4.13	4.05
Tonga								
Turkmenistan				4.42	4.52	4.62	4.72	4.81
Tuvalu								
Uzbekistan								
Vanuatu								
Vietnam	5.53	5.38	5.04	5.11	5.18	5.19	5.19	5.18
Western Samoa								
Australasia								
Australia	3.31	3.23	3.11	2.80	2.79	2.76	2.73	2.70
New Zealand	3.30	3.20	3.18	3.00	2.97	2.97	2.96	2.96

Source: *National statistics/UN//Euromonitor*

■ Average Number of Occupants per Household

Average Number of Occupants per Household at Jan 1st 1978-2002 (continued)

● Persons

	1995	1996	1997	1998	1999	2000	2001	2002
Asia Pacific								
Afghanistan		5.03	4.92	5.24	5.04	4.95	5.07	5.20
American Samoa		4.11	4.24	4.16	4.15	4.15	4.20	4.25
Armenia		4.80	4.97	5.11	5.01	4.93	4.83	4.74
Azerbaijan	5.05	5.06	5.05	5.10	5.12	5.14	5.18	5.23
Bangladesh		5.34	5.36	5.36	5.36	5.37	5.37	5.38
Bhutan		4.67	4.65	4.42	4.59	4.60	4.61	4.62
Brunei		4.59	4.58	4.55	4.59	4.64	4.69	4.75
Cambodia		4.30	4.30	4.35	4.33	4.47	4.64	4.82
China	3.82	3.80	3.78	3.75	3.70	3.63	3.63	3.63
Fiji		5.23	5.20	5.33	5.26	5.28	5.32	5.37
French Polynesia		5.70	5.65	5.82	5.73	5.68	5.79	5.91
Guam		6.15	6.09	6.09	6.12	6.18	6.04	5.90
Hong Kong, China	3.42	3.30	3.26	3.28	3.30	3.31	3.32	3.32
India	5.83	5.85	5.86	5.89	5.93	5.93	5.94	5.94
Indonesia	4.28	4.20	4.17	4.14	4.05	4.02	3.99	3.96
Japan	2.84	2.82	2.79	2.77	2.74	2.70	2.66	2.63
Kazakhstan	3.46	3.49	3.63	3.78	3.92	4.04	4.11	4.19
Kiribati		5.69	5.69	5.78	5.72	5.82	5.90	5.99
Kyrgyzstan		5.20	5.13	5.15	5.16	5.11	5.06	5.02
Laos		5.26	5.24	5.41	5.32	5.37	5.45	5.54
Macau		3.29	3.10	3.14	3.20	3.24	3.30	3.35
Malaysia	4.90	4.82	4.76	4.69	4.61	4.54	4.55	4.56
Maldives		5.59	5.55	5.76	5.65	5.57	5.41	5.26
Mongolia		5.02	5.04	4.76	4.95	5.02	5.12	5.22
Myanmar		3.01	3.04	3.18	3.08	3.13	3.22	3.31
Nauru		6.37	6.38	6.38	6.38	6.36	6.21	6.07
Nepal		4.41	4.22	4.27	4.31	4.36	4.44	4.51
New Caledonia		5.18	5.19	4.85	5.08	5.15	5.22	5.28
North Korea		6.00	6.01	5.98	6.01	6.05	6.09	6.14
Pakistan	7.37	7.39	7.46	7.52	7.55	7.55	7.57	7.59
Papua New Guinea		5.75	5.75	5.77	5.77	5.83	5.91	5.99
Philippines	5.10	5.07	5.04	5.03	5.01	5.00	4.93	4.86
Singapore	3.89	3.82	3.75	3.68	3.59	3.52	3.46	3.40
Solomon Islands		6.42	6.44	6.44	6.45	6.44	6.43	6.41
South Korea	3.48	3.44	3.41	3.39	3.38	3.34	3.30	3.26
Sri Lanka	5.40	5.37	5.38	5.46	5.40	5.45	5.53	5.60
Taiwan	3.73	3.64	3.56	3.50	3.44	3.39	3.32	3.26
Tajikistan		4.48	4.44	4.52	4.49	4.54	4.63	4.72
Thailand	3.99	3.94	3.93	3.93	3.93	3.92	3.93	3.93
Tonga		4.81	4.88	4.93	4.88	4.91	4.94	4.98
Turkmenistan	4.91	5.00	5.09	5.09	5.08	5.09	5.01	4.94
Tuvalu		8.05	8.43	7.64	8.17	7.99	7.75	7.52
Uzbekistan		5.77	5.73	5.79	5.77	5.69	5.60	5.52
Vanuatu		5.81	5.83	5.82	5.84	5.78	5.64	5.50
Vietnam	5.20	5.18	5.16	5.12	5.15	5.17	5.11	5.05
Western Samoa		4.88	4.98	4.88	4.92	4.96	4.98	5.00
Australasia								
Australia	2.68	2.65	2.65	2.66	2.61	2.62	2.62	2.62
New Zealand	2.95	2.93	2.93	2.92	2.90	2.88	2.86	2.84

Source: *National statistics/UN///Euromonitor*

◙ Average Number of Occupants per Household

Average Number of Occupants per Household at Jan 1st 1978-2002 (continued)

● Persons

	1978	1980	1985	1990	1991	1992	1993	1994
Africa and Middle East								
Algeria	6.52	6.53	6.82	6.86	6.84	6.78	6.76	6.75
Angola								
Bahrain								
Benin								
Botswana								
Burkina Faso								
Burundi								
Cameroon								
Cape Verde								
Central African Republic								
Chad								
Comoros								
Congo Dem Rep								
Congo-Brazzaville								
Côte d'Ivoire								
Djibouti								
Egypt	4.85	4.86	4.77	4.82	4.74	4.70	4.67	4.65
Equatorial Guinea								
Eritrea								
Ethiopia								
Gabon								
Gambia								
Ghana								
Guinea								
Guinea-Bissau								
Iran								
Iraq								
Israel	3.61	3.61	3.43	3.68	3.72	3.72	3.70	3.67
Jordan	5.68	5.74	5.53	5.89	6.09	6.12	6.16	6.15
Kenya								
Kuwait	9.26	9.78	10.60	9.54	6.74	6.98	7.08	7.57
Lebanon								
Lesotho								
Liberia								
Libya								
Madagascar								
Malawi								
Mali								
Mauritania								
Mauritius								
Morocco	6.75	6.63	6.13	5.88	5.81	5.74	5.67	5.61
Mozambique								
Namibia								
Niger								
Nigeria	5.67	5.38	5.20	4.96	4.97	5.12	5.13	5.17
Oman								
Qatar								
Réunion								
Rwanda								
Sao Tomé e Príncipe								
Saudi Arabia	6.16	6.35	6.12	6.88	7.01	7.05	7.05	7.06
Senegal								
Seychelles								
Sierra Leone								
Somalia								
South Africa	5.42	5.27	5.13	4.39	4.37	4.37	4.39	4.40
Sudan								
Swaziland								
Syria								
Tanzania								
Togo								
Tunisia	6.93	6.51	5.86	5.40	5.33	5.25	5.18	5.12
Uganda								
United Arab Emirates	2.97	3.51	4.27	4.75	4.91	5.06	5.21	5.35
Yemen								
Zambia								
Zimbabwe								

Source: *National statistics/UN//Euromonitor*

◘ Average Number of Occupants per Household

Average Number of Occupants per Household at Jan 1st 1978-2002 (continued)

• Persons

	1995	1996	1997	1998	1999	2000	2001	2002
Africa and Middle East								
Algeria	6.74	6.72	6.64	6.58	6.46	6.45	6.37	6.30
Angola		4.37	4.38	4.34	4.38	4.55	4.64	4.72
Bahrain		3.80	3.80	3.93	3.69	3.81	3.73	3.65
Benin		3.75	4.06	4.13	3.99	4.13	4.20	4.26
Botswana		3.81	3.82	3.76	3.81	3.98	4.15	4.33
Burkina Faso		4.30	4.33	4.37	4.34	4.52	4.64	4.75
Burundi		5.91	5.87	5.73	5.83	5.86	5.98	6.10
Cameroon		3.67	3.65	3.63	3.66	3.81	3.90	4.00
Cape Verde		3.96	4.01	4.05	4.02	4.31	4.40	4.48
Central African Republic		5.29	5.54	5.25	5.37	5.45	5.47	5.49
Chad		5.23	5.25	4.98	5.16	5.32	5.39	5.46
Comoros		5.80	5.79	5.90	5.85	5.92	5.87	5.82
Congo Dem Rep		3.71	3.74	3.78	3.74	3.79	3.84	3.89
Congo-Brazzaville		5.96	6.04	6.11	6.09	6.04	6.12	6.19
Côte d'Ivoire		4.31	4.54	4.60	4.49	4.55	4.56	4.57
Djibouti		4.91	4.86	5.00	4.91	4.99	5.03	5.06
Egypt	4.60	4.59	4.59	4.58	4.59	4.58	4.55	4.53
Equatorial Guinea		4.04	4.07	4.08	4.07	4.18	4.25	4.31
Eritrea								
Ethiopia		4.56	4.55	4.71	4.62	4.73	4.78	4.82
Gabon		7.09	7.06	7.05	7.09	7.12	6.99	6.87
Gambia		5.26	5.30	5.20	5.28	5.34	5.40	5.47
Ghana		5.77	5.76	5.64	5.74	5.83	5.80	5.77
Guinea		5.29	5.31	5.56	5.36	5.43	5.51	5.58
Guinea-Bissau		5.30	5.33	5.23	5.30	5.30	5.21	5.12
Iran		5.21	5.36	5.05	5.23	5.31	5.41	5.52
Iraq		5.16	5.17	5.19	5.19	5.36	5.44	5.53
Israel	3.63	3.63	3.62	3.57	3.55	3.53	3.54	3.55
Jordan	6.15	6.12	6.10	6.09	6.06	6.07	6.10	6.12
Kenya		4.23	4.14	4.27	4.42	4.50	4.55	4.59
Kuwait	7.83	7.94	8.04	8.02	8.18	8.30	8.31	8.33
Lebanon		4.47	4.47	4.45	4.46	4.46	4.42	4.38
Lesotho		5.43	5.41	5.72	5.53	5.61	5.60	5.60
Liberia		4.09	4.30	4.26	4.67	5.03	5.11	5.19
Libya		4.68	4.64	5.15	4.82	4.75	4.81	4.87
Madagascar		4.93	4.93	5.16	5.09	5.23	5.29	5.34
Malawi		5.70	5.63	5.81	5.74	5.95	5.86	5.78
Mali		3.19	3.19	3.08	3.15	3.18	3.14	3.09
Mauritania		4.00	4.05	3.94	4.01	4.11	4.15	4.19
Mauritius		5.05	4.99	5.05	5.03	5.11	5.18	5.26
Morocco	5.56	5.52	5.47	5.43	5.39	5.35	5.31	5.27
Mozambique		5.52	5.55	5.52	5.54	5.64	5.57	5.50
Namibia		4.75	4.75	4.71	4.75	4.76	4.71	4.66
Niger		5.72	5.73	5.76	5.76	6.00	5.91	5.83
Nigeria	5.18	5.16	5.19	5.17	5.19	5.20	5.21	5.23
Oman		3.67	3.62	3.76	3.69	3.72	3.63	3.54
Qatar		4.70	4.70	4.70	4.71	4.71	4.63	4.56
Réunion		5.79	5.72	5.77	5.77	5.87	5.92	5.97
Rwanda		5.70	5.59	5.49	5.81	6.13	6.09	6.04
Sao Tomé e Príncipe		5.37	5.54	5.54	5.48	5.44	5.34	5.24
Saudi Arabia	7.05	7.07	7.21	7.36	7.54	7.67	7.93	8.21
Senegal		5.70	5.71	5.74	5.73	5.77	5.68	5.68
Seychelles		5.59	6.05	6.05	5.90	5.91	5.88	5.84
Sierra Leone		5.64	5.62	5.61	5.66	5.86	5.95	6.04
Somalia		4.45	4.45	5.15	4.73			
South Africa	4.42	4.43	4.40	4.38	4.41	4.42	4.34	4.27
Sudan		6.03	6.03	6.08	6.06	6.11	6.07	6.02
Swaziland		5.90	6.29	6.15	6.13	6.23	6.18	6.13
Syria		4.77	4.79	4.77	4.79	4.93	4.99	5.06
Tanzania		5.28	5.29	5.29	5.30	5.36	5.34	5.31
Togo		5.97	5.97	6.05	6.01	6.03	5.90	5.77
Tunisia	5.07	5.00	4.92	4.87	4.83	4.79	4.79	4.78
Uganda		5.27	5.24	5.34	5.29	5.34	5.26	5.18
United Arab Emirates	5.49	5.62	5.74	5.89	6.11	6.34	6.49	6.65
Yemen		5.51	5.54	5.59	5.56	5.63	5.55	5.46
Zambia		4.35	3.99	3.94	4.04	4.17	4.21	4.25
Zimbabwe		3.59	3.40	3.72	3.56	3.66	3.72	3.78

Source: National statistics/UN//Euromonitor

Table 15.2

Household Facilities: Latest Year

● % of total households

	Year	Bath or Shower	Flush Toilet	Kitchen	Central Heating	Electric Lighting	Water Supply
Algeria	1996					87.9	74.5
Argentina	1990		38.6				92.5
Australia	1990						
Azerbaijan	2002	74.5	89.3		77.6		93.6
Bolivia	2002		33.7			72.2	73.8
Brazil	1991	77.6	35.3			86.9	74.0
Canada	1991		99.8				100.0
Chile	1992		69.9			88.1	88.2
China	2002						98.5
Colombia	1993		63.8			87.3	76.3
Ecuador	1990		59.9	37.5		73.8	59.6
Egypt	1995		28.7			95.5	73.2
Hong Kong, China	1995						
India	2001			64.0		55.8	
Indonesia	2002		55.0			92.7	18.9
Israel	1991		71.5			99.0	94.0
Japan	2002		83.7				
Jordan	1989					30.8	
Kazakhstan	2002	79.3	90.6		92.9		96.0
Kuwait	2002						
Malaysia	1990						
Mexico	1990		52.1			87.5	79.3
Morocco	1994	22.3	66.0	87.0		53.7	52.6
New Zealand	1991		99.0			99.0	99.0
Nigeria	1990						
Pakistan	1990						
Peru	1993		36.0			49.5	42.1
Philippines	1990					55.1	41.6
Saudi Arabia	1993					92.3	
Singapore	1993						
South Africa	1995		59.7			65.5	82.7
South Korea	2002						
Taiwan	2002						
Thailand	1990		20.0			89.3	29.6
Tunisia	2002					77.7	99.0
Turkmenistan	2002	66.9	79.3		76.7		88.1
United Arab Emirates	2002						
USA	1995	98.9		96.7	52.8		96.8
Venezuela	1990		62.8			92.6	81.0
Vietnam	1990		22.0			47.0	34.0

Source: Euromonitor from national statistics/trade sources

Number of Households 1977-2002

• '000

	1977	1980	1985	1990	1991	1992	1993	1994
North America								
Canada	7,119	7,539	8,735	9,624	9,873	10,056	10,247	10,387
USA	73,107	76,944	84,515	91,994	92,718	93,649	94,723	97,107
Latin America								
Anguilla								
Antigua								
Argentina	6,988	7,411	8,117	8,823	8,927	9,071	9,215	9,376
Aruba								
Bahamas								
Barbados								
Belize								
Bermuda								
Bolivia	848	952	1,125	1,299	1,369	1,445	1,522	1,601
Brazil	28,174	30,553	32,745	37,062	37,832	38,634	39,523	40,495
British Virgin Islands								
Cayman Islands								
Chile	2,992	3,049	3,082	3,173	3,224	3,294	3,397	3,537
Colombia	5,703	6,016	6,152	6,436	6,669	6,899	7,160	7,394
Costa Rica								
Cuba								
Dominica								
Dominican Republic								
Ecuador	1,994	2,012	2,025	2,049	2,102	2,155	2,208	2,268
El Salvador								
French Guiana								
Grenada								
Guadeloupe								
Guatemala								
Guyana								
Haiti								
Honduras								
Jamaica								
Martinique								
Mexico	10,197	11,723	13,601	16,203	17,011	17,819	18,621	19,440
Netherlands Antilles								
Nicaragua								
Panama								
Paraguay								
Peru	4,112	4,222	4,403	4,569	4,627	4,691	4,763	4,846
Puerto Rico								
St Kitts								
St Lucia								
St Vincent and the Grenadines								
Suriname								
Trinidad and Tobago								
Uruguay								
Venezuela	2,558	2,758	3,231	3,564	3,679	3,821	3,991	4,184

Source: *National statistical offices/Euromonitor*

■ Households

Number of Households 1977-2002 (continued)

● '000

	1995	1996	1997	1998	1999	2000	2001	2002
North America								
Canada	11,244	11,413	11,580	11,701	11,790	11,900	11,964	12,098
USA	97,693	98,534	99,487	100,928	102,803	103,794	105,000	106,481
Latin America								
Anguilla		1	1	1	1	1	1	1
Antigua		20	20	20	20	20	21	21
Argentina	9,487	9,626	9,809	9,933	10,028	10,143	10,258	10,404
Aruba		16	16	19	19	21	22	23
Bahamas		58	60	61	62	63	65	66
Barbados		55	56	57	57	58	58	58
Belize		79	84	84	86	89	92	96
Bermuda		14	13	14	14	15	15	15
Bolivia	1,681	1,761	1,823	1,878	1,934	1,985	2,024	2,096
Brazil	41,585	42,718	43,967	45,187	46,306	47,279	48,583	50,553
British Virgin Islands		4	4	5	5	5	5	5
Cayman Islands		7	7	8	8	8	8	9
Chile	3,570	3,588	3,658	3,743	3,835	3,938	3,971	4,012
Colombia	7,555	8,093	8,273	8,424	8,603	9,114	9,234	9,535
Costa Rica		815	858	928	907	935	965	995
Cuba		2,768	2,764	2,778	2,792	2,818	2,845	2,872
Dominica		17	17	17	17	17	16	16
Dominican Republic		1,689	1,691	1,726	1,756	1,798	1,849	1,900
Ecuador	2,323	2,373	2,424	2,478	2,525	2,575	2,616	2,671
El Salvador		1,325	1,353	1,380	1,405	1,428	1,477	1,527
French Guiana		27	29	30	31	32	35	37
Grenada		19	17	17	18	18	18	18
Guadeloupe		91	90	93	94	94	97	99
Guatemala		2,153	2,203	2,271	2,322	2,357	2,378	2,398
Guyana		181	184	184	186	184	183	182
Haiti		1,447	1,469	1,554	1,538	1,555	1,569	1,583
Honduras		1,223	1,263	1,229	1,304	1,352	1,404	1,458
Jamaica		519	528	527	533	531	535	536
Martinique		83	85	85	86	87	88	90
Mexico	19,848	20,467	21,143	22,164	22,407	22,640	22,831	23,263
Netherlands Antilles		41	40	44	42	44	45	47
Nicaragua		1,172	1,208	1,338	1,302	1,321	1,337	1,353
Panama		538	549	558	565	571	588	605
Paraguay		1,061	1,090	1,123	1,146	1,170	1,193	1,216
Peru	4,934	5,025	5,120	5,220	5,326	5,436	5,523	5,628
Puerto Rico		755	770	778	779	789	808	826
St Kitts		9	9	9	9	8	8	8
St Lucia		30	30	31	31	32	33	33
St Vincent and the Grenadines		26	27	26	27	27	27	27
Suriname		85	86	81	85	84	84	84
Trinidad and Tobago		263	275	270	272	270	269	269
Uruguay		1,225	1,255	1,264	1,265	1,256	1,278	1,299
Venezuela	4,399	4,591	4,775	4,906	5,011	5,117	5,190	5,352

Source: National statistical offices/Euromonitor

◻ Households

Number of Households 1977-2002 (continued)

● '000

	1977	1980	1985	1990	1991	1992	1993	1994
Asia Pacific								
Afghanistan								
American Samoa								
Armenia								
Azerbaijan	1,325	1,357	1,409	1,462	1,473	1,484	1,495	1,505
Bangladesh								
Bhutan								
Brunei								
Cambodia								
China	178,790	189,907	238,043	278,620	288,237	296,231	305,042	312,132
Fiji								
French Polynesia								
Guam								
Hong Kong, China	1,051	1,158	1,393	1,559	1,595	1,633	1,678	1,721
India	109,299	117,396	138,056	150,634	152,009	153,616	155,885	157,746
Indonesia	29,613	32,113	34,694	39,695	40,759	41,844	42,913	44,060
Japan	33,944	35,434	38,832	41,036	41,689	42,281	42,949	43,549
Kazakhstan	5,260	5,318	5,415	5,511	5,341	5,162	4,973	4,806
Kiribati								
Kyrgyzstan								
Laos								
Macau								
Malaysia	2,426	2,675	2,953	3,443	3,567	3,691	3,823	3,969
Maldives								
Mongolia								
Myanmar								
Nauru								
Nepal								
New Caledonia								
North Korea								
Pakistan	12,130	13,306	15,267	17,265	17,623	17,802	17,989	18,184
Papua New Guinea								
Philippines	7,782	8,671	9,645	11,407	11,975	12,413	12,686	13,025
Singapore	419	466	579	662	677	696	711	734
Solomon Islands								
South Korea	6,699	7,488	8,762	11,355	11,618	11,972	12,355	12,702
Sri Lanka			3,050	3,055	3,119	3,147	3,179	3,234
Taiwan	3,245	3,675	4,287	5,026	5,160	5,287	5,419	5,567
Tajikistan								
Thailand	8,397	8,607	10,025	12,317	12,908	13,437	13,921	14,352
Tonga								
Turkmenistan	855	849	840	830	831	831	831	831
Tuvalu								
Uzbekistan								
Vanuatu								
Vietnam	9,032	10,120	11,935	13,051	13,144	13,419	13,693	13,994
Western Samoa								
Australasia								
Australia	4,190	4,566	5,083	6,067	6,173	6,302	6,446	6,579
New Zealand	936	999	1,047	1,152	1,178	1,191	1,209	1,228

Source: *National statistical offices/Euromonitor*

■ Households

Number of Households 1977-2002 (continued)

- '000

	1995	1996	1997	1998	1999	2000	2001	2002
Asia Pacific								
Afghanistan		3,976	4,193	4,028	4,290	4,479	4,464	4,488
American Samoa		14	14	15	16	16	17	18
Armenia		787	760	741	758	773	788	804
Azerbaijan	1,513	1,528	1,544	1,543	1,553	1,561	1,556	1,579
Bangladesh		22,378	22,704	23,093	23,480	23,853	24,135	24,449
Bhutan		401	413	447	443	455	464	475
Brunei		65	67	68	69	70	70	71
Cambodia		2,353	2,408	2,435	2,500	2,472	2,424	2,384
China	316,760	321,730	326,930	332,970	341,530	351,420	353,289	358,426
Fiji		148	150	148	152	154	154	154
French Polynesia		38	39	39	40	41	41	41
Guam		25	26	26	27	27	28	29
Hong Kong, China	1,783	1,890	1,964	2,008	2,051	2,093	2,130	2,193
India	159,854	162,242	164,614	166,543	168,212	169,857	171,311	174,863
Indonesia	45,653	47,195	48,281	49,383	51,204	52,349	53,208	54,596
Japan	44,108	44,627	45,141	45,673	46,207	47,031	47,690	48,233
Kazakhstan	4,772	4,708	4,509	4,312	4,153	4,011	3,931	3,889
Kiribati		14	14	14	14	14	14	14
Kyrgyzstan		882	898	899	903	915	928	940
Laos		920	948	942	984	999	1,004	1,012
Macau		132	144	145	145	145	145	145
Malaysia	4,107	4,261	4,406	4,568	4,733	4,911	4,965	5,117
Maldives		45	47	46	49	51	53	56
Mongolia		493	499	537	525	526	522	518
Myanmar		14,321	14,366	13,907	14,535	14,469	14,225	13,996
Nauru		2	2	2	2	2	2	2
Nepal		4,878	5,232	5,290	5,363	5,424	5,431	5,454
New Caledonia		38	39	42	41	41	41	42
North Korea		3,738	3,793	3,871	3,913	3,948	3,969	4,000
Pakistan	18,497	18,949	19,296	19,701	20,189	20,565	20,842	21,555
Papua New Guinea		757	774	788	806	815	819	825
Philippines	13,408	13,804	14,192	14,536	14,912	15,272	15,690	16,138
Singapore	761	789	820	852	888	923	952	969
Solomon Islands		60	62	64	66	68	70	72
South Korea	12,958	13,236	13,492	13,697	13,869	14,138	14,413	14,589
Sri Lanka	3,301	3,353	3,383	3,366	3,432	3,437	3,415	3,396
Taiwan	5,731	5,908	6,104	6,273	6,431	6,576	6,733	6,875
Tajikistan		1,292	1,324	1,320	1,349	1,354	1,343	1,334
Thailand	14,697	15,002	15,182	15,353	15,504	15,662	15,709	15,938
Tonga		20	20	20	20	20	20	20
Turkmenistan	831	832	832	847	863	878	901	914
Tuvalu		1	1	1	1	2	2	2
Uzbekistan		3,929	4,018	4,041	4,117	4,237	4,356	4,484
Vanuatu		29	30	31	31	33	34	36
Vietnam	14,206	14,509	14,808	15,162	15,272	15,544	15,867	16,135
Western Samoa		35	34	36	36	36	36	37
Australasia								
Australia	6,690	6,859	6,959	7,012	7,216	7,286	7,347	7,471
New Zealand	1,249	1,276	1,291	1,305	1,321	1,338	1,354	1,373

Source: *National statistical offices/Euromonitor*

Households

Number of Households 1977-2002 (continued)

• '000

	1977	1980	1985	1990	1991	1992	1993	1994
Africa and Middle East								
Algeria	2,579	2,812	3,200	3,589	3,697	3,825	3,932	4,035
Angola								
Bahrain								
Benin								
Botswana								
Burkina Faso								
Burundi								
Cameroon								
Cape Verde								
Central African Republic								
Chad								
Comoros								
Congo Dem Rep								
Congo-Brazzaville								
Côte d'Ivoire								
Djibouti								
Egypt	7,833	8,472	9,537	10,674	11,006	11,338	11,670	11,957
Equatorial Guinea								
Eritrea								
Ethiopia								
Gabon								
Gambia								
Ghana								
Guinea								
Guinea-Bissau								
Iran								
Iraq								
Israel	975	1,014	1,167	1,228	1,291	1,355	1,404	1,453
Jordan	330	389	488	589	608	628	649	672
Kenya								
Kuwait	151	167	195	225	203	214	217	228
Lebanon								
Lesotho								
Liberia								
Libya								
Madagascar								
Malawi								
Mali								
Mauritania								
Mauritius								
Morocco	2,706	3,044	3,608	4,166	4,267	4,372	4,480	4,591
Mozambique								
Namibia								
Niger								
Nigeria	10,459	12,140	14,929	17,464	17,910	17,996	18,560	18,983
Oman								
Qatar								
Réunion								
Rwanda								
Sao Tomé e Príncipe								
Saudi Arabia	1,000	1,118	1,529	1,940	1,996	2,074	2,154	2,235
Senegal								
Seychelles								
Sierra Leone								
Somalia								
South Africa	4,683	5,228	6,252	8,105	8,282	8,457	8,620	8,779
Sudan								
Swaziland								
Syria								
Tanzania								
Togo								
Tunisia	852	1,010	1,273	1,536	1,578	1,626	1,671	1,715
Uganda								
United Arab Emirates	261	290	337	385	394	403	412	421
Yemen								
Zambia								
Zimbabwe								

Source: National statistical offices/Euromonitor

■ Households

Number of Households 1977-2002 (continued)

● '000

	1995	1996	1997	1998	1999	2000	2001	2002
Africa and Middle East								
Algeria	4,137	4,249	4,352	4,446	4,542	4,639	4,732	4,845
Angola		2,552	2,629	2,742	2,806	2,829	2,928	3,005
Bahrain		155	160	155	163	162	170	175
Benin		1,442	1,368	1,380	1,468	1,476	1,527	1,561
Botswana		391	399	413	416	407	402	396
Burkina Faso		2,456	2,508	2,552	2,638	2,639	2,726	2,769
Burundi		1,051	1,075	1,119	1,116	1,142	1,157	1,164
Cameroon		3,642	3,767	3,887	3,962	3,961	4,080	4,146
Cape Verde		97	98	100	103	99	101	103
Central African Republic		628	611	658	655	663	680	695
Chad		1,300	1,332	1,442	1,426	1,439	1,477	1,508
Comoros		106	109	110	114	117	125	131
Congo Dem Rep		12,421	12,675	12,864	13,287	13,635	14,093	14,429
Congo-Brazzaville		441	454	462	477	487	485	489
Côte d'Ivoire		3,170	3,069	3,080	3,212	3,251	3,365	3,453
Djibouti		123	126	124	127	128	130	132
Egypt	12,373	12,723	13,004	13,242	13,478	13,718	13,956	14,222
Equatorial Guinea		100	102	104	107	108	111	114
Eritrea								
Ethiopia		12,296	12,636	12,505	13,073	13,230	13,623	13,923
Gabon		154	159	163	167	172	183	193
Gambia		215	221	232	236	245	254	261
Ghana		3,103	3,195	3,350	3,385	3,468	3,638	3,796
Guinea		1,364	1,374	1,320	1,372	1,367	1,376	1,373
Guinea-Bissau		207	211	219	222	229	242	254
Iran		12,066	11,938	12,905	12,674	12,693	12,609	12,546
Iraq		3,946	4,041	4,144	4,264	4,313	4,471	4,589
Israel	1,509	1,548	1,590	1,651	1,699	1,746	1,773	1,824
Jordan	697	725	754	781	809	835	855	895
Kenya		6,514	6,791	6,720	6,631	6,687	6,988	7,134
Kuwait	230	239	246	253	258	264	270	282
Lebanon		681	697	712	720	736	767	792
Lesotho		358	369	357	377	384	400	413
Liberia		524	535	595	599	627	701	775
Libya		1,175	1,226	1,081	1,121	1,179	1,211	1,204
Madagascar		2,830	2,920	2,875	3,003	3,049	3,179	3,277
Malawi		1,710	1,766	1,757	1,827	1,838	1,973	2,082
Mali		3,157	3,236	3,430	3,434	3,536	3,736	3,909
Mauritania		590	599	634	640	649	676	696
Mauritius		222	226	225	228	227	226	225
Morocco	4,706	4,825	4,947	5,072	5,193	5,322	5,429	5,544
Mozambique		3,199	3,279	3,384	3,445	3,490	3,700	3,878
Namibia		329	337	349	353	362	378	393
Niger		1,626	1,676	1,723	1,779	1,790	1,912	2,024
Nigeria	19,457	20,022	20,590	21,314	21,934	22,580	23,197	23,771
Oman		597	627	624	655	683	740	794
Qatar		118	120	122	124	127	134	139
Réunion		114	117	117	119	119	121	122
Rwanda		942	1,023	1,145	1,191	1,262	1,424	1,594
Sao Tomé e Príncipe		25	25	25	26	27	28	30
Saudi Arabia	2,317	2,396	2,479	2,557	2,640	2,720	2,756	2,813
Senegal		1,480	1,517	1,550	1,592	1,644	1,747	1,811
Seychelles		13	12	12	13	13	13	13
Sierra Leone		751	775	801	821	829	857	881
Somalia		1,872	1,942	1,753	2,000			
South Africa	8,923	9,060	9,227	9,405	9,558	9,750	10,015	10,180
Sudan		4,456	4,551	4,608	4,719	4,825	5,103	5,316
Swaziland		150	145	153	157	162	171	180
Syria		3,014	3,083	3,175	3,243	3,272	3,371	3,451
Tanzania		5,741	5,867	6,000	6,128	6,255	6,516	6,737
Togo		690	708	717	741	768	821	869
Tunisia	1,758	1,805	1,862	1,906	1,945	1,981	2,002	2,049
Uganda		3,640	3,764	3,799	3,938	4,078	4,383	4,643
United Arab Emirates	430	439	448	457	466	475	482	497
Yemen		2,783	2,886	2,968	3,089	3,217	3,494	3,725
Zambia		2,018	2,078	2,152	2,173	2,197	2,296	2,365
Zimbabwe		3,117	3,226	2,994	3,194	3,190	3,230	3,255

Source: National statistical offices/Euromonitor

Table 15.4

■ Households

Household by Number of Persons 2002

● % of total households

	One Person	Two Persons	Three Persons	Four Persons	Five or More Persons
Algeria					
Argentina	15.3	18.1	20.2	20.0	26.4
Australia	24.9	33.5	15.8	15.1	10.7
Azerbaijan	6.6	34.8	19.4	25.1	14.1
Bolivia	10.1	14.1	16.1	16.5	43.1
Brazil	8.8	14.3	15.0	21.5	40.5
Canada	31.0	32.2	16.0	14.9	5.8
Chile	7.3	17.2	25.1	26.3	24.1
China	7.4	16.7	31.5	24.4	20.0
Colombia	8.1	13.8	19.2	21.4	37.6
Ecuador	12.6	14.1	13.2	15.9	44.1
Egypt	6.1	9.5	12.7	15.1	56.7
Hong Kong, China	13.1	20.2	23.3	25.5	17.9
India	3.5	8.0	12.0	19.4	57.1
Indonesia	3.8	11.7	21.3	23.2	40.0
Israel	17.6	22.7	16.3	17.8	25.5
Japan	24.1	26.2	20.1	16.5	13.0
Jordan	3.5	8.7	11.1	17.2	59.5
Kazakhstan	11.1	19.1	27.9	25.6	16.4
Kuwait	11.9	12.4	12.0	12.3	51.4
Malaysia	8.2	11.1	12.9	16.5	51.3
Mexico	6.3	13.7	19.0	22.6	38.4
Morocco	6.4	9.4	10.5	11.8	61.9
New Zealand	21.6	34.0	16.8	15.0	12.7
Nigeria	9.9	10.9	13.0	14.6	51.7
Pakistan	3.3	8.3	8.7	10.6	69.0
Peru	6.1	7.2	16.5	22.9	47.3
Philippines	3.6	8.7	14.1	18.9	54.7
Saudi Arabia					
Singapore	13.0	17.5	20.2	30.5	18.9
South Africa	21.1	22.7	19.7	16.6	20.0
South Korea	16.1	19.2	21.4	31.0	12.3
Taiwan	11.9	19.8	18.0	22.3	28.0
Thailand	9.1	18.5	22.4	24.9	25.1
Tunisia	4.8	8.0	11.4	12.9	62.9
Turkmenistan	6.3	33.0	20.0	23.7	16.9
United Arab Emirates					
USA	26.8	33.5	15.9	14.4	9.5
Venezuela	7.9	14.4	19.9	33.0	24.9
Vietnam	5.8	7.8	14.9	22.0	49.5

Source: *National statistical offices/Euromonitor*

Household by Number of Rooms 2002

● % of total households

	One Room	Two Rooms	Three Rooms	Four Rooms	Five or More Rooms
Algeria	13.0	23.8	31.2	19.5	12.6
Argentina	14.3	30.3	36.6	15.2	3.7
Australia	1.6	3.1	8.6	16.6	70.1
Azerbaijan	5.4	28.9	33.8	19.3	12.6
Bolivia	32.1	34.7	15.2	9.8	8.2
Brazil	2.1	9.4	7.4	14.7	66.4
Canada	1.2	2.7	8.0	13.6	74.5
Chile	23.6	24.6	23.0	18.8	10.0
China	15.4	42.5	27.9	9.0	5.1
Colombia	18.4	16.7	17.3	16.1	31.5
Ecuador	22.3	30.2	23.3	12.3	11.9
Egypt	3.7	18.7	35.5	20.8	21.2
Hong Kong, China	3.5	3.8	24.8	36.2	31.7
India	9.9	24.7	25.4	21.3	18.7
Indonesia	15.7	43.6	30.6	6.4	3.8
Israel	3.7	15.5	38.7	17.9	24.2
Japan	3.0	4.9	24.3	37.0	30.8
Jordan	30.0	42.3	22.9	3.6	1.2
Kazakhstan	12.4	37.4	41.4	7.3	1.5
Kuwait					
Malaysia	8.3	23.2	36.9	25.9	5.6
Mexico	23.8	24.9	22.9	15.7	12.7
Morocco					
New Zealand	2.3	2.0	7.0	15.1	73.6
Nigeria					
Pakistan	38.1	31.9	15.6	8.2	6.2
Peru	27.4	22.4	12.2	14.0	24.0
Philippines	17.4	42.1	29.0	7.1	4.4
Saudi Arabia					
Singapore	2.6	3.6	25.7	36.9	31.1
South Africa	20.4	18.6	14.8	21.9	24.4
South Korea	10.6	22.7	37.2	25.4	4.0
Taiwan	1.2	5.2	16.1	26.9	50.5
Thailand	7.5	21.1	36.0	28.5	6.9
Tunisia	21.1	35.2	25.5	12.7	5.5
Turkmenistan	6.1	25.8	33.8	21.5	12.7
United Arab Emirates	19.2	23.4	25.3	12.6	19.4
USA	0.5	1.1	8.4	18.6	71.5
Venezuela	24.4	35.2	30.7	7.4	2.3
Vietnam	15.4	42.2	29.6	8.7	4.1

Source: National statistical offices/Euromonitor

Total Housing Stock 1977-2002

● '000 units

	1977	1980	1985	1990	1995	1996	1997	1998	1999	2000	2001	2002
Algeria												
Argentina	7,623	8,310	8,820	8,515	9,546	9,656	9,752	9,821	9,905	10,029	10,272	10,516
Australia	3,930	5,066	5,690	6,162	6,530	6,720	6,880	7,012	7,146	7,281	7,656	7,838
Azerbaijan												
Bolivia												
Brazil	21,453	25,211	31,056	31,900	36,970	39,745	42,352	44,243	45,791	47,347	48,869	48,110
Canada	7,278	8,063	8,906	9,619	10,993	11,227	11,580	11,630	11,702	11,803	12,116	12,199
Chile												
China	180,000	205,000	260,100	275,100	278,343	278,864	279,349	289,684	300,546	307,493	311,955	282,093
Colombia	5,258	5,397	5,898	6,500	7,430	7,450	7,468	7,491	7,520	7,550	7,890	8,078
Ecuador				2,111								
Egypt						18,791						
Hong Kong, China	979	1,195	1,348	1,711	1,999	2,005	2,049	2,082	2,160	2,249	2,284	2,291
India	106,790	110,100	115,100	119,000	123,389	124,282	125,182	126,089	126,972	127,890	128,819	129,758
Indonesia	29,978	36,700	40,920	43,950	46,002	46,321	47,670	49,240	51,200	52,960	54,697	48,797
Israel	1,030	1,150	1,323	1,410	1,561	1,587	1,613	1,639	1,665	1,704	1,734	1,745
Japan	33,825	36,970	40,400	46,796	49,328	49,915	50,509	51,111	51,140	51,171	52,051	52,480
Jordan												
Kazakhstan					4,459	4,460	4,462	4,473	4,486	4,492	4,492	4,537
Kuwait					252							
Malaysia	2,460	2,540	2,850	3,200	3,671	3,767	3,890	3,956	4,050	4,146	4,185	4,210
Mexico	11,896	12,216	14,197	15,035	15,192	15,230	15,290	15,360	15,436	15,513	15,980	16,287
Morocco	2,710	2,926	3,278	3,754	4,207	4,301	4,396	4,494	4,597	4,698	4,801	4,915
New Zealand	1,018	1,101	1,250	1,370	1,103	1,269	1,302	1,335	1,358	1,381	1,418	1,446
Nigeria	16,567	20,134	24,100	25,420	25,975	26,081	26,187	26,294	26,399	26,509	26,626	26,735
Pakistan												
Peru			4,906									
Philippines	7,389	8,501	9,872	10,450	10,830	10,959	11,090	11,231	11,353	11,462	11,570	11,658
Saudi Arabia												
Singapore	297	373	552	686	700	725	755	791	824	847	882	903
South Africa	5,250	6,258	8,100	8,596	8,685	8,698	8,685	8,672	8,683	8,694	8,846	8,865
South Korea	2,890	5,463	6,104	7,270	10,135	10,588	11,373	11,695	11,957	12,225	13,294	13,659
Taiwan	2,997	3,677	4,500	5,088	5,790	5,999	6,239	6,489	6,814	7,154	7,325	7,576
Thailand	6,399	8,311	9,016	10,950	11,609	11,777	11,851	11,921	12,043	12,167	12,307	12,425
Tunisia												
Turkmenistan												
United Arab Emirates												
USA												
Venezuela	2,510	2,650	3,050	3,866	3,943	4,008	4,070	4,130	4,190	4,249	4,325	4,266
Vietnam												

Source: *National statistical offices/Euromonitor*

New Dwellings Completed

New Dwellings Completed 1977-2002

Table 15.7

● '000 units

	1977	1980	1985	1990	1995	1996	1997	1998	1999	2000	2001	2002
Algeria				0.5	0.7	0.7	0.8	0.8	0.8	0.9	0.9	0.8
Argentina	54.0	33.0		85.4	121.5	96.3	69.0	88.9	107.2	103.0	105.5	108.0
Australia	45.4	78.5	111.6	160.0	170.2	135.9	119.0	131.6	145.5	160.9	169.7	171.4
Azerbaijan				33.3	6.6	5.5	5.4	5.5	5.3	5.3	5.8	6.7
Bolivia				9.6	13.9	16.5	14.1	14.7	14.9	15.1	15.5	16.2
Brazil	106.0	148.0	136.0	110.0	159.3	227.8	334.9	485.0	498.0	502.0	478.4	450.8
Canada	254.0	176.0	166.0	181.6	110.9	147.1	49.0	150.1	146.1	139.0	130.1	123.8
Chile			61.0	79.0	135.6	141.1	147.5	152.4	155.8	156.0	163.1	166.1
China			911.0	400.0	687.5	563.1	503.1	450.0	402.0	359.4	424.1	485.7
Colombia				5.3	9.1	6.1	5.0	6.5	5.2	5.0	4.7	4.5
Ecuador					12.5							
Egypt												
Hong Kong, China	34.5	57.3	68.9	32.9	61.3	46.3	53.5	54.7	83.3	85.3	81.3	74.1
India	75.4	97.9		175.9	221.4	230.5	239.6	248.7	257.8	266.9	275.3	294.6
Indonesia	11.5	26.2	60.5	210.0	314.0	328.0	345.4	361.0	378.0	395.8	405.7	427.0
Israel			19.9	19.9								
Japan	1,702.4	1,482.6	1,236.0	1,707.6	1,470.0	1,643.0	1,387.0	1,198.0	1,009.0	820.0	748.0	666.1
Jordan												
Kazakhstan				0.1	20.4	15.7	13.9	10.5	8.8	9.0	10.0	11.4
Kuwait												
Malaysia			112.0		99.7	112.6	66.2	94.0	90.6	87.3	82.6	79.5
Mexico				27.0	38.0	61.0	70.0	76.0	112.0	89.0	92.0	93.0
Morocco												
New Zealand	24.3	14.4	22.0	22.8	23.7	21.3	22.4	22.6	20.7	20.6	21.2	20.6
Nigeria		24.6		104.2	152.1	162.0	171.1	181.0	190.1	200.0	213.4	202.5
Pakistan												
Peru												
Philippines	23.2	22.0	26.0	70.0	96.0	111.0	42.0	54.0	54.8	57.8	59.4	55.2
Saudi Arabia												
Singapore	35.5	23.9	59.6	32.0	26.2	27.5	31.3	36.6	34.8	27.7	23.3	22.2
South Africa		24.0	20.0	36.0	46.9	53.8	52.9	50.0	49.2	48.4	45.7	44.0
South Korea				619.7	452.2	784.3	321.1	261.4	235.9	212.9	201.4	207.5
Taiwan				105.0	210.0	246.0	255.0	129.0	272.0	255.0	261.1	270.1
Thailand												
Tunisia												
Turkmenistan					10.0	7.7	8.1	7.9	9.3	10.1	11.2	12.2
United Arab Emirates												
USA	1,690.0	1,191.0	1,733.0	1,111.0	1,333.0	1,426.0	1,442.0	1,467.0	1,575.7	1,632.0	1,630.4	1,629.0
Venezuela		83.0	45.0	44.0	63.0	57.4	58.6	59.8	60.7	61.6	61.1	58.9
Vietnam												

Source: *National statistical offices/Euromonitor*

Income and Deductions

Annual Gross Income 1990-2002

- Million units of national currency/as stated

	1990	1995	1996	1997	1998	1999	2000	2001	2002	US$ per capita 2002
Algeria	454,598	1,482,555	1,849,981	1,964,338	1,993,000	2,283,463	2,790,163	3,146,121	3,295,581	1,351
Argentina	49,500	181,092	186,924	203,244	210,519	200,689	207,537	192,231	212,477	1,839
Australia	295,334	354,941	378,879	400,637	415,195	442,358	469,385	501,199	525,921	14,697
Azerbaijan		4,061,116	4,991,468	5,530,808	6,922,017	7,559,096	9,162,380	10,124,960	11,254,742	284
Bolivia	12,209	24,317	28,568	33,561	37,199	37,808	41,517	42,683	43,384	703
Brazil	7	449,374	533,825	585,856	634,463	650,749	715,763	779,210	869,997	1,724
Canada	535,671	619,485	636,101	658,449	687,598	723,741	777,458	805,921	840,150	17,255
Chile	7,204,308	20,322,390	23,222,558	26,674,555	28,319,946	28,653,713	31,357,709	32,874,011	33,860,738	3,172
China	1,299,121	3,533,203	4,187,923	4,537,633	4,695,870	4,930,545	5,317,788	5,758,430	6,159,894	575
Colombia	11,302,491	49,265,401	61,851,366	75,133,041	86,854,755	94,162,814	112,557,838	122,505,047	133,221,533	1,327
Ecuador	7,198,436	41,057,070	55,938,263	72,594,472	96,021,543	148,061,842	321,483,210	397,568,603	455,124,214	1,388
Egypt	78,802	144,951	165,129	181,725	194,154	214,559	243,256	264,315	274,743	948
Hong Kong, China	485,635	909,554	1,011,168	1,133,921	1,052,712	1,050,086	1,080,119	1,073,946	1,065,001	18,919
India	4,076,511	8,958,189	10,594,050	11,717,164	13,518,680	14,913,705	15,673,256	16,384,611	18,254,342	362
Indonesia	180,721,714	356,297,209	404,749,655	475,825,285	715,751,884	857,398,687	970,376,352	1,108,273,426	1,235,270,377	614
Israel	91,829	197,054	212,212	249,686	288,703	304,025	325,936	348,266	385,113	12,657
Japan	374,131,653	427,903,851	428,019,535	442,332,868	442,833,864	437,743,129	435,603,343	433,992,852	428,679,228	26,911
Jordan	2,159	3,350	3,536	3,630	3,916	4,096	4,311	4,573	4,882	1,286
Kazakhstan		600,130	826,237	1,034,044	1,080,290	1,314,943	1,534,415	1,960,014	2,231,582	905
Kuwait	3,074	3,717	4,944	5,321	5,567	6,013	6,553	6,802	7,278	10,221
Malaysia	81,422	152,263	175,329	200,638	202,519	213,080	240,073	249,337	268,172	3,046
Mexico	513,542	1,360,959	1,884,272	2,321,748	2,971,288	3,528,680	4,119,608	4,304,466	4,617,814	4,696
Morocco	174,512	228,397	239,520	249,659	265,522	276,604	288,888	303,597	318,081	988
New Zealand	60,221	71,007	75,521	77,650	79,740	82,816	85,546	89,890	95,477	11,316
Nigeria	181,747	1,451,158	1,908,171	1,951,257	1,850,327	2,121,438	2,854,495	3,234,789	4,061,993	271
Pakistan	762,804	1,434,400	1,698,887	1,934,495	2,096,682	2,289,225	2,457,293	2,689,509	2,956,119	304
Peru	3,979	90,545	103,056	117,798	125,052	132,153	142,336	144,802	150,883	1,618
Philippines	735,213	1,357,555	1,556,352	1,748,057	1,879,745	2,037,783	2,199,698	2,391,453	2,599,020	635
Saudi Arabia	184,742	224,585	249,631	278,674	298,407	294,173	293,958	293,079	301,707	3,527
Singapore	39,468	60,816	69,111	75,681	77,641	79,691	86,547	91,819	95,917	16,034
South Africa	190,414	363,689	409,646	461,877	491,369	536,716	590,418	645,729	715,163	1,528
South Korea	134,278,271	297,172,557	339,573,734	370,862,681	386,319,164	386,774,249	404,044,723	448,302,527	483,482,677	8,023
Taiwan	3,212,193	5,658,816	5,849,205	6,388,819	6,728,994	7,022,652	7,958,051	7,257,181	7,780,737	9,973
Thailand	1,358,328	2,464,078	2,654,014	2,736,246	2,786,973	2,802,068	3,005,619	3,151,200	3,292,708	1,231
Tunisia	9,206	13,384	16,101	16,972	17,530	18,732	19,881	20,400	21,076	1,530
Turkmenistan		474,674	5,782,768	8,383,915	10,247,310	12,649,000	16,505,713	20,891,044	25,139,194	874
United Arab Emirates	56,799	85,999	94,056	100,554	106,526	117,456	126,578	133,172	140,191	11,680
USA	4,465,817	5,647,830	5,978,778	6,357,728	6,747,321	7,226,782	7,633,036	7,882,297	8,139,890	29,170
Venezuela	1,746,526	10,392,486	23,575,091	31,793,550	41,326,385	53,168,811	67,668,762	73,764,526	89,477,916	3,071
Vietnam	41,158,147	182,684,696	204,463,883	236,484,680	272,892,034	305,319,999	339,978,298	364,956,280	391,690,094	311

Source: Euromonitor from national statistics

Annual Gross Earnings 1990-2002

• Million units of national currency/as stated

	1990	1995	1996	1997	1998	1999	2000	2001	2002	US$ per capita 2002
Algeria	367,085	995,821	1,271,544	1,507,386	1,643,257	1,862,064	2,115,322	2,423,466	2,598,383	1,065
Argentina	35,154	114,935	117,210	127,276	132,711	126,316	133,895	125,183	139,169	1,205
Australia	228,069	296,614	317,397	327,364	342,296	369,872	383,221	409,068	430,706	12,036
Azerbaijan		2,111,780	2,550,640	2,942,390	3,772,499	3,900,493	4,947,685	5,577,396	6,205,190	157
Bolivia	10,438	19,993	18,947	25,518	30,578	33,066	31,838	33,380	35,235	571
Brazil	5	320,998	383,032	421,710	441,540	453,467	505,677	536,093	605,024	1,199
Canada	431,912	466,472	480,910	502,499	533,819	559,041	593,293	614,501	646,164	13,271
Chile	3,878,240	10,895,537	13,309,900	14,930,069	15,927,435	16,481,687	17,611,487	18,389,979	18,587,753	1,741
China	1,013,314	2,849,175	3,372,116	3,593,351	3,644,464	3,765,457	3,973,983	4,326,683	4,691,154	438
Colombia	8,654,632	37,400,407	47,256,274	57,343,313	63,920,264	65,194,532	77,125,370	85,021,718	84,778,820	844
Ecuador	5,134,498	28,681,040	38,692,713	50,284,517	64,422,176	99,983,789	214,149,343	268,388,979	306,344,109	935
Egypt	59,294	106,832	122,243	135,544	145,928	165,902	194,307	215,947	206,842	714
Hong Kong, China	388,800	702,798	762,115	882,013	803,909	771,124	808,165	789,920	770,550	13,689
India	3,263,898	7,190,406	8,526,176	9,262,717	10,644,026	11,778,696	12,419,809	12,942,741	14,262,763	283
Indonesia	116,837,651	228,747,832	257,262,499	301,489,716	449,874,901	531,399,883	600,393,460	686,178,116	625,042,878	311
Israel	83,013	173,999	187,171	220,723	247,707	263,590	285,474	305,236	340,560	11,193
Japan	276,944,329	327,017,849	327,050,284	342,202,464	339,108,222	331,664,236	330,607,619	330,227,299	329,424,812	20,680
Jordan	1,407	2,115	2,168	2,250	2,405	2,619	2,666	2,838	3,014	794
Kazakhstan		492,107	660,990	837,576	864,232	1,078,253	1,242,876	1,605,251	1,832,919	743
Kuwait	2,773	3,369	4,498	4,867	5,053	5,425	5,787	6,071	5,948	8,352
Malaysia	73,154	135,393	157,916	178,990	180,629	189,896	210,242	222,522	239,240	2,717
Mexico	328,889	841,028	1,173,010	1,462,748	1,938,498	2,253,533	2,653,331	2,725,897	2,916,196	2,965
Morocco	151,613	168,786	203,592	209,279	218,589	225,200	225,704	246,516	265,986	826
New Zealand	43,093	53,312	59,662	60,008	60,350	62,831	65,960	68,393	72,999	8,652
Nigeria	135,693	1,049,044	1,369,685	1,415,637	1,357,030	1,534,861	2,020,201	2,313,683	2,920,528	195
Pakistan	586,825	1,118,223	1,335,155	1,471,114	1,597,285	1,725,713	1,877,110	2,049,472	2,267,639	233
Peru	2,266	50,427	51,636	62,457	71,309	79,374	86,716	90,409	98,124	1,052
Philippines	531,896	971,350	1,114,892	1,255,105	1,360,318	1,475,809	1,582,054	1,732,656	1,879,871	459
Saudi Arabia	132,102	156,135	177,169	199,718	213,104	206,760	207,437	204,061	212,583	2,485
Singapore	34,191	48,876	58,769	62,891	64,209	62,830	70,497	76,499	83,743	13,999
South Africa	130,320	249,589	279,373	308,486	334,361	359,077	398,799	434,048	487,026	1,041
South Korea	118,717,822	265,171,033	301,399,886	327,149,754	342,891,762	341,226,401	357,438,164	397,529,306	429,543,125	7,128
Taiwan	2,583,919	4,538,470	4,974,309	5,934,841	6,166,679	6,448,426	7,114,497	6,435,125	6,982,584	8,950
Thailand	1,229,287	2,223,714	2,380,651	2,433,839	2,463,685	2,465,820	2,671,995	2,803,661	2,978,539	1,114
Tunisia	7,903	11,713	14,132	14,886	14,769	16,005	17,393	17,573	18,303	1,329
Turkmenistan		321,774	3,808,028	5,559,314	6,674,335	8,144,153	10,598,594	13,563,748	16,122,763	561
United Arab Emirates	41,213	62,100	66,984	71,837	76,732	86,505	94,993	100,472	105,358	8,778
USA	3,153,030	3,967,127	4,261,660	4,530,912	4,840,395	5,179,512	5,510,706	5,712,133	5,929,503	21,249
Venezuela	899,071	5,200,266	13,532,482	18,149,811	26,196,714	29,054,788	35,954,645	38,088,693	47,870,900	1,643
Vietnam	39,093,893	172,365,955	194,320,740	225,624,630	261,005,089	292,521,491	326,396,135	350,173,472	373,809,441	297

Source: Euromonitor from national statistics

■ Annual Gross Income   **Table 16.3**

Gross Income by Source 2002

● % of gross income

	Benefits	Employment	Investments	Other Sources	Total
Algeria	6.21	78.84	3.40	11.54	100.00
Argentina	17.79	65.50	11.87	4.84	100.00
Australia	12.36	81.90	3.60	2.14	100.00
Azerbaijan	7.59	55.13	4.23	33.05	100.00
Bolivia	6.40	81.22	2.12	10.27	100.00
Brazil	21.85	69.54	7.05	1.56	100.00
Canada	13.22	76.91	6.37	3.50	100.00
Chile	20.58	54.89	8.69	15.84	100.00
China	19.32	76.16	2.09	2.44	100.00
Colombia	10.33	63.64	11.39	14.64	100.00
Ecuador	6.08	67.31	8.43	18.18	100.00
Egypt	7.96	75.29	10.25	6.51	100.00
Hong Kong, China	12.15	72.35	10.11	5.39	100.00
India	4.26	78.13	3.72	13.89	100.00
Indonesia	18.14	50.60	4.90	26.35	100.00
Israel	5.09	88.43	2.79	3.69	100.00
Japan	15.02	76.85	3.41	4.73	100.00
Jordan	11.29	61.74	22.40	4.57	100.00
Kazakhstan	10.60	82.14	3.29	3.97	100.00
Kuwait	1.63	81.72	6.63	10.02	100.00
Malaysia	5.47	89.21	4.17	1.14	100.00
Mexico	6.51	63.15	6.43	23.91	100.00
Morocco	3.72	83.62	1.51	11.15	100.00
New Zealand	12.57	76.46	5.49	5.48	100.00
Nigeria	8.53	71.90	3.38	15.90	100.00
Pakistan	0.94	76.71	13.42	8.93	100.00
Peru	15.08	65.03	7.85	12.04	100.00
Philippines	6.15	72.33	1.76	19.76	100.00
Saudi Arabia	10.88	70.46	8.92	9.75	100.00
Singapore	1.24	87.31	10.99	0.46	100.00
South Africa	12.79	68.10	8.45	10.67	100.00
South Korea	4.27	88.84	2.93	3.95	100.00
Taiwan	3.43	89.74	5.08	1.75	100.00
Thailand	7.12	90.46	1.07	1.35	100.00
Tunisia	5.65	86.84	3.33	4.19	100.00
Turkmenistan	8.46	64.13	3.56	23.84	100.00
United Arab Emirates	11.47	75.15	5.69	7.69	100.00
USA	6.86	72.84	16.57	3.72	100.00
Venezuela	14.45	53.50	17.19	14.86	100.00
Vietnam	1.91	95.44	0.93	1.72	100.00

Source: *Euromonitor from national statistics*

Annual Disposable Income 1990-2002

- Million units of national currency/as stated

	1990	1995	1996	1997	1998	1999	2000	2001	2002	US$ per capita 2002
Algeria	382,041	1,192,151	1,554,294	1,643,618	1,657,971	1,892,569	2,288,343	2,626,223	2,731,441	1,119
Argentina	39,603	148,358	153,608	164,880	169,969	164,800	170,533	158,057	176,374	1,527
Australia	220,454	268,513	281,386	296,236	307,144	326,922	346,905	370,047	387,911	10,840
Azerbaijan		3,540,028	4,367,491	4,824,516	6,191,316	6,805,106	8,308,426	9,218,639	10,177,867	257
Bolivia	11,162	21,568	25,024	28,905	32,374	32,842	36,038	37,076	37,846	613
Brazil	6	341,702	416,436	465,867	511,255	551,919	607,944	665,696	749,276	1,485
Canada	420,951	482,850	492,316	506,690	526,337	555,057	594,764	618,607	644,328	13,233
Chile	6,602,203	18,596,927	20,686,338	23,353,151	25,061,005	25,774,609	27,598,565	29,323,301	30,598,496	2,866
China	1,096,632	3,015,267	3,518,823	3,847,761	3,944,469	4,126,665	4,467,868	4,750,240	5,087,787	475
Colombia	10,964,117	47,839,960	60,394,246	73,298,398	84,980,737	91,322,373	107,614,015	119,963,247	131,500,539	1,309
Ecuador	5,233,886	28,521,035	38,894,013	51,130,342	68,270,244	103,986,658	220,689,041	271,648,441	315,216,825	962
Egypt	72,022	134,603	151,776	166,816	178,181	190,331	212,595	232,983	239,373	826
Hong Kong, China	450,527	838,643	943,305	1,058,494	986,153	985,747	1,020,686	1,013,171	1,006,297	17,876
India	3,926,701	8,690,252	10,154,572	11,332,606	12,931,251	14,237,622	14,965,546	15,735,605	17,393,501	345
Indonesia	149,470,725	296,092,425	344,642,044	407,303,598	617,897,167	736,718,558	837,945,156	967,709,809	1,083,065,296	538
Israel	71,200	152,940	165,752	193,124	224,866	234,638	250,421	267,859	298,514	9,811
Japan	268,509,376	307,235,935	306,729,655	313,966,163	316,948,805	313,314,000	312,091,165	311,041,242	306,312,758	19,229
Jordan	2,052	3,160	3,322	3,407	3,668	3,828	3,970	4,260	4,561	1,201
Kazakhstan		520,600	715,042	933,800	973,079	1,168,808	1,301,321	1,650,012	1,876,843	761
Kuwait	2,980	3,606	4,793	5,154	5,386	5,830	6,325	6,588	7,060	9,914
Malaysia	64,376	119,786	139,299	155,269	160,032	169,989	192,171	199,538	215,784	2,451
Mexico	459,216	1,255,795	1,725,654	2,152,928	2,753,289	3,274,837	3,821,000	3,983,519	4,264,249	4,336
Morocco	154,019	190,773	201,642	202,775	214,602	222,906	233,163	245,654	258,064	802
New Zealand	42,274	49,147	53,161	55,148	58,404	60,309	62,104	65,641	69,330	8,217
Nigeria	160,226	1,282,716	1,732,038	1,801,714	1,684,007	1,937,221	2,606,617	2,953,894	3,716,306	248
Pakistan	681,815	1,316,055	1,563,030	1,785,766	1,943,441	2,150,168	2,316,352	2,520,005	2,766,823	285
Peru	3,430	81,647	93,381	106,254	114,798	121,889	131,812	134,958	139,654	1,497
Philippines	592,099	1,094,325	1,264,613	1,416,121	1,529,254	1,674,415	1,798,548	1,960,119	2,135,573	522
Saudi Arabia	178,698	217,308	242,207	270,016	289,883	284,894	285,616	283,454	292,746	3,422
Singapore	37,903	58,699	66,471	72,942	74,645	76,495	82,530	87,381	91,289	15,261
South Africa	164,644	314,807	349,665	399,038	428,276	463,243	507,164	548,835	601,719	1,286
South Korea	111,639,217	246,146,339	276,071,489	299,294,622	319,979,358	324,414,786	341,144,838	359,343,451	391,808,263	6,502
Taiwan	2,614,259	4,649,778	4,882,241	5,270,358	5,477,427	5,717,500	5,862,142	6,107,923	6,471,094	8,294
Thailand	1,315,072	2,370,942	2,541,482	2,589,891	2,641,703	2,654,210	2,830,029	2,932,772	3,063,277	1,145
Tunisia	7,117	10,420	12,312	13,096	13,649	14,584	15,310	15,914	16,426	1,192
Turkmenistan		389,404	4,720,378	6,864,162	8,414,848	10,294,225	13,476,980	16,960,707	20,397,707	709
United Arab Emirates	53,690	81,959	89,964	95,762	101,894	111,988	120,387	127,555	134,137	11,175
USA	3,785,838	4,761,464	4,955,691	5,186,144	5,462,679	5,770,318	6,113,848	6,341,148	6,743,754	24,166
Venezuela	1,622,752	9,824,106	22,411,029	30,383,742	39,490,469	50,927,129	64,815,847	70,654,890	85,625,853	2,939
Vietnam	34,718,673	153,241,456	171,510,497	197,333,101	230,804,981	251,644,629	276,767,778	303,924,600	325,517,033	258

Source: Euromonitor from national statistics

Table 16.5

□ Income and Deductions

Tax and Social Security Contributions 1990-2002

● Million units of national currency/as stated

	1990	1995	1996	1997	1998	1999	2000	2001	2002	US$ per capita 2002
Algeria	72,557	290,405	295,687	320,721	335,029	390,894	501,820	519,899	564,139	231
Argentina	9,897	32,734	33,315	38,365	40,550	35,888	37,004	34,174	36,103	312
Australia	74,880	86,428	97,493	104,401	108,051	115,436	122,480	131,152	138,010	3,857
Azerbaijan		521,088	623,977	706,292	730,701	753,990	853,954	906,321	1,076,875	27
Bolivia	1,048	2,749	3,544	4,655	4,825	4,966	5,479	5,608	5,539	90
Brazil	2	107,672	117,389	119,989	123,208	98,830	107,818	113,514	120,721	239
Canada	114,721	136,635	143,785	151,759	161,261	168,683	182,694	187,314	195,822	4,022
Chile	602,104	1,725,463	2,536,220	3,321,404	3,258,940	2,879,104	3,759,144	3,550,710	3,262,242	306
China	202,489	517,936	669,100	689,871	751,400	803,879	849,920	1,008,190	1,072,107	100
Colombia	338,374	1,425,441	1,457,120	1,834,643	1,874,018	2,840,441	4,943,823	2,541,800	1,720,994	17
Ecuador	1,964,550	12,536,035	17,044,251	21,464,130	27,751,298	44,075,183	100,794,169	125,920,162	139,907,390	427
Egypt	6,780	10,348	13,353	14,910	15,973	24,227	30,661	31,332	35,370	122
Hong Kong, China	35,108	70,911	67,862	75,426	66,559	64,340	59,432	60,775	58,705	1,043
India	149,810	267,938	439,478	384,558	587,429	676,083	707,709	649,006	860,841	17
Indonesia	31,250,989	60,204,784	60,107,612	68,521,686	97,854,717	120,680,129	132,431,196	140,563,617	152,205,081	76
Israel	20,628	44,114	46,461	56,563	63,836	69,386	75,515	80,407	86,599	2,846
Japan	105,622,277	120,667,916	121,289,880	128,366,705	125,885,058	124,429,130	123,512,178	122,951,610	122,366,470	7,682
Jordan	107	190	214	223	248	269	341	314	320	84
Kazakhstan		79,530	111,195	100,244	107,212	146,135	233,094	310,001	354,740	144
Kuwait	94	111	152	167	181	183	228	214	219	307
Malaysia	17,045	32,478	36,030	45,369	42,486	43,091	47,902	49,800	52,388	595
Mexico	54,326	105,164	158,618	168,820	217,999	253,843	298,608	320,947	353,565	360
Morocco	20,494	37,624	37,878	46,884	50,920	53,698	55,725	57,943	60,017	186
New Zealand	17,947	21,861	22,361	22,502	21,335	22,507	23,442	24,250	26,146	3,099
Nigeria	21,521	168,442	176,132	149,542	166,320	184,217	247,878	280,894	345,687	23
Pakistan	80,988	118,345	135,857	148,730	153,241	139,057	140,941	169,505	189,296	19
Peru	549	8,898	9,675	11,544	10,254	10,264	10,524	9,844	11,229	120
Philippines	143,114	263,230	291,740	331,936	350,492	363,368	401,150	431,333	463,447	113
Saudi Arabia	6,044	7,277	7,424	8,658	8,524	9,279	8,343	9,625	8,960	105
Singapore	1,565	2,117	2,640	2,739	2,995	3,196	4,017	4,439	4,627	774
South Africa	25,770	48,882	59,982	62,839	63,093	73,473	83,254	96,893	113,443	242
South Korea	22,639,054	51,026,218	63,502,245	71,568,059	66,339,807	62,359,463	62,899,885	88,959,076	91,674,414	1,521
Taiwan	597,935	1,009,038	966,963	1,118,460	1,251,567	1,305,152	2,095,909	1,149,258	1,309,642	1,679
Thailand	43,256	93,136	112,532	146,355	145,271	147,858	175,589	218,428	229,430	86
Tunisia	2,088	2,964	3,789	3,876	3,882	4,148	4,571	4,486	4,651	338
Turkmenistan		85,270	1,062,390	1,519,753	1,832,462	2,354,775	3,028,733	3,930,337	4,741,487	165
United Arab Emirates	3,109	4,039	4,092	4,793	4,631	5,468	6,191	5,617	6,054	504
USA	679,979	886,365	1,023,086	1,171,584	1,284,643	1,456,464	1,519,188	1,541,149	1,396,136	5,003
Venezuela	123,774	568,380	1,164,062	1,409,808	1,835,916	2,241,682	2,852,915	3,109,636	3,852,063	132
Vietnam	6,439,474	29,443,240	32,953,385	39,151,579	42,087,053	53,675,370	63,210,520	61,031,680	66,173,060	53

Source: *Euromonitor from national statistics*

Industrial Markets

Table 17.1

□ Industrial Output

Indices of General Industrial Production 1977-2002

● 1995 = 100

	1977	1980	1985	1990	1995	1997	1998	1999	2000	2001	2002
North America											
Canada	64.2	69.0	79.4	88.3	100.0	106.2	109.9	115.4	121.9	118.0	120.0
USA	64.5	68.6	76.8	86.4	100.0	112.0	118.3	123.3	129.1	124.6	123.7
Latin America											
Anguilla											
Antigua											
Argentina	85.4	82.1	70.6	81.3	100.0						
Aruba											
Bahamas											
Barbados	85.0	91.4	88.7	98.9	100.0	104.3	112.1	112.9	111.1	104.3	99.3
Belize											
Bermuda											
Bolivia	84.8	85.6	57.4	74.3	100.0	104.8	109.8	104.6	104.1	102.2	102.6
Brazil	73.4	90.6	89.7	90.6	100.0	105.7	103.4	102.9	109.7	111.5	114.0
British Virgin Islands											
Cayman Islands											
Chile				73.3	100.0	115.6	118.8	124.8	130.1	132.2	132.9
Colombia	47.2	54.9	60.4	84.7	100.0						
Costa Rica				78.0	100.0	108.2	120.1	146.3	143.9	134.4	134.6
Cuba											
Dominica											
Dominican Republic											
Ecuador											
El Salvador					100.0	110.2	117.5	121.7	126.4	131.8	137.5
French Guiana											
Grenada											
Guadeloupe											
Guatemala											
Guyana											
Haiti											
Honduras											
Jamaica											
Martinique											
Mexico	55.9	75.5	81.6	97.0	100.0	120.3	127.8	133.3	141.5	136.4	136.3
Netherlands Antilles											
Nicaragua											
Panama					100.0	110.2	115.6	112.2	110.3	106.8	101.2
Paraguay											
Peru				77.4	100.0	109.4	108.8	109.9	113.3	113.9	119.9
Puerto Rico											
St Kitts											
St Lucia											
St Vincent and the Grenadines											
Suriname											
Trinidad and Tobago		58.2	57.6	71.1	100.0	112.4	125.0	139.0	146.4	157.6	171.1
Uruguay			89.4	116.1	100.0						
Venezuela											

Source: *United Nations/Euromonitor*
Notes: *Indices based on value of production (or contribution to GDP) at constant prices*

Industrial Output
Indices of General Industrial Production 1977-2002

- 1995 = 100

	1977	1980	1985	1990	1995	1997	1998	1999	2000	2001	2002
Asia Pacific											
Afghanistan											
American Samoa											
Armenia											
Azerbaijan				111.1	100.0						
Bangladesh	32.4	31.4	34.5	66.7	100.0	110.3	112.5	121.4	131.5	140.9	146.0
Bhutan											
Brunei											
Cambodia											
China				97.3	100.0						
Fiji	53.5	60.9	62.7	83.8	100.0	90.9	92.5	98.7	91.8	97.3	103.5
French Polynesia											
Guam											
Hong Kong, China	36.9	78.4	111.1	97.3	100.0	96.6	90.2	84.7	85.1	82.4	76.4
India	33.7	36.7	51.3	74.9	100.0	113.1	117.8	125.6	131.9	135.4	139.8
Indonesia											
Japan	59.5	70.9	83.6	104.8	100.0	106.0	99.0	99.9	105.5	97.7	96.2
Kazakhstan				208.3	100.0						
Kiribati											
Kyrgyzstan											
Laos											
Macau											
Malaysia	19.9	25.2	34.8	59.4	100.0	122.8	114.0	124.3	148.1	142.0	147.8
Maldives											
Mongolia				145.8	100.0	101.9	104.7	106.6	110.2	121.9	133.5
Myanmar											
Nauru											
Nepal											
New Caledonia											
North Korea											
Pakistan					100.0	104.8	107.4	108.0	115.2	122.9	132.3
Papua New Guinea											
Philippines	12.3	14.8	34.2	65.7	100.0						
Singapore											
Solomon Islands											
South Korea	16.3	22.0	36.0	66.4	100.0	113.6	106.2	131.9	154.1	156.1	167.5
Sri Lanka											
Taiwan											
Tajikistan											
Thailand											
Tonga											
Turkmenistan				152.9	100.0						
Tuvalu											
Uzbekistan											
Vanuatu											
Vietnam											
Western Samoa											
Australasia											
Australia	65.4	71.8	81.9	92.3	100.0	104.9	108.3	110.1	115.0	117.1	119.8
New Zealand				89.9	100.0	104.0	103.6	100.8	104.2	106.7	107.1

Source: United Nations/Euromonitor
Notes: Indices based on value of production (or contribution to GDP) at constant prices

◻ Industrial Output

Indices of General Industrial Production 1977-2002

● 1995 = 100

	1977	1980	1985	1990	1995	1997	1998	1999	2000	2001	2002
Africa and Middle East											
Algeria	52.8	70.3	110.4	116.3	100.0	89.6	95.7	96.0	97.3	97.0	98.5
Angola											
Bahrain											
Benin											
Botswana											
Burkina Faso											
Burundi											
Cameroon				93.7	100.0	117.1	121.1	128.5	130.1	128.2	122.3
Cape Verde											
Central African Republic				119.2	100.0						
Chad											
Comoros											
Congo Dem Rep											
Congo-Brazzaville											
Côte d'Ivoire					100.0	125.0	138.8	143.2	132.0	126.5	113.3
Djibouti											
Egypt											
Equatorial Guinea											
Eritrea											
Ethiopia											
Gabon											
Gambia											
Ghana											
Guinea											
Guinea-Bissau											
Iran											
Iraq											
Israel	49.1	52.8	63.3	69.6	100.0	107.2	110.2	111.8	123.1	116.4	113.6
Jordan	25.6	44.8	69.5	75.8	100.0	99.6	102.1	102.5	106.5	117.2	129.6
Kenya											
Kuwait											
Lebanon											
Lesotho											
Liberia											
Libya											
Madagascar											
Malawi				105.8	100.0	102.7	99.4	90.4	91.2	81.8	81.9
Mali				93.2	100.0						
Mauritania											
Mauritius											
Morocco	53.8	62.5	73.2	89.0	100.0	108.3	110.4	111.8	114.9	119.7	123.8
Mozambique											
Namibia											
Niger											
Nigeria	53.4	72.2	67.9	101.5	100.0						
Oman											
Qatar											
Réunion											
Rwanda											
Sao Tomé e Príncipe											
Saudi Arabia											
Senegal	98.4	82.0	96.8	96.7	100.0	98.0	102.9	104.4	99.7	100.5	124.9
Seychelles											
Sierra Leone											
Somalia											
South Africa	79.2	90.0	94.5	97.2	100.0	105.7	102.8	101.8	104.5	106.7	111.2
Sudan											
Swaziland											
Syria											
Tanzania											
Togo											
Tunisia	52.7	69.3	75.6	82.4	100.0	107.2	114.6	120.7	128.3	136.0	135.8
Uganda											
United Arab Emirates											
Yemen											
Zambia	145.1	138.2	121.6	132.6	100.0	105.9	108.6	93.4	95.8	90.0	82.9
Zimbabwe	70.8	83.3	94.2	112.0	100.0	106.8	109.9	103.2	96.6	87.8	76.2

Source: United Nations/Euromonitor
Notes: Indices based on value of production (or contribution to GDP) at constant prices

Indices of Manufacturing Production 1977-2002

Table 17.2

- 1995 = 100

	1977	1980	1985	1990	1995	1997	1998	1999	2000	2001	2002
North America											
Canada	69.0	74.2	83.1	89.8	100.0	107.7	113.0	120.9	127.4	121.7	124.6
USA	56.1	63.0	73.1	85.0	100.0	113.5	120.9	126.9	133.2	127.8	126.5
Latin America											
Anguilla											
Antigua											
Argentina	80.1	92.1	78.3	79.9	100.0	116.3	115.8	103.7	101.8	90.4	77.3
Aruba											
Bahamas											
Barbados	76.5	103.4	90.0	101.3	100.0	104.3	109.1	107.2	106.5	98.3	92.2
Belize											
Bermuda											
Bolivia	113.1	96.7	61.9	78.2	100.0	108.4	112.0	113.4	113.8	113.0	113.2
Brazil	69.7	91.8	89.0	90.1	100.0	104.7	101.4	99.7	105.8	107.2	108.6
British Virgin Islands											
Cayman Islands											
Chile	55.8	59.4	58.2	75.9	100.0	108.0	109.0	108.7	112.3	113.6	116.5
Colombia	58.4	64.9	67.5	86.3	100.0	99.1	97.5	84.2	93.2	93.9	94.8
Costa Rica	69.0	78.4	79.2	78.4	100.0	108.2	120.5	150.3	145.9	133.7	132.7
Cuba											
Dominica											
Dominican Republic											
Ecuador											
El Salvador					100.0	109.9	117.2	121.5	126.5	131.8	137.7
French Guiana											
Grenada											
Guadeloupe											
Guatemala											
Guyana											
Haiti				255.1	100.0	102.0	107.4	110.9	118.2	120.9	127.8
Honduras											
Jamaica											
Martinique											
Mexico	47.7	77.0	83.1	95.6	100.0	121.8	130.8	136.3	145.8	140.3	139.5
Netherlands Antilles											
Nicaragua											
Panama		69.7	76.7	76.9	100.0	105.6	109.9	105.3	100.0	93.4	85.6
Paraguay											
Peru		84.2	74.9	69.3	100.0	106.9	103.4	102.9	109.8	108.9	113.5
Puerto Rico											
St Kitts											
St Lucia											
St Vincent and the Grenadines											
Suriname											
Trinidad and Tobago		60.4	59.7	70.8	100.0	113.0	125.4	140.1	148.7	162.2	178.2
Uruguay		118.8	89.1	116.1	100.0	110.0	116.1	106.1	108.2	102.3	84.9
Venezuela					100.0	98.9	99.3	86.8	90.8	94.9	97.7

Source: *United Nations/Euromonitor*
Notes: *Indices based on value of production (or contribution to GDP) at constant prices*

◘ Industrial Output

Indices of Manufacturing Production 1977-2002

● 1995 = 100

	1977	1980	1985	1990	1995	1997	1998	1999	2000	2001	2002
Asia Pacific											
Afghanistan											
American Samoa											
Armenia											
Azerbaijan				344.8	100.0						
Bangladesh	28.1	36.5	46.0	66.3	100.0	109.8	120.0	123.8	132.8	139.9	144.6
Bhutan											
Brunei											
Cambodia											
China				97.3	100.0						
Fiji	66.0	67.3	66.0	84.2	100.0	78.4	81.1	84.3	76.5	81.2	88.5
French Polynesia											
Guam											
Hong Kong, China	32.9	52.3	69.0	97.3	100.0	95.5	87.2	81.7	81.2	77.7	70.1
India	37.1	38.3	51.7	75.3	100.0	114.5	119.5	128.0	134.9	138.7	143.2
Indonesia	25.0	23.6	30.7	55.8	100.0	106.0	86.7	88.3	91.5	90.5	89.9
Japan	74.6	71.1	84.6	105.2	100.0	106.0	98.5	99.3	105.2	96.9	95.4
Kazakhstan											
Kiribati											
Kyrgyzstan											
Laos											
Macau											
Malaysia	22.7	23.9	29.2	53.7	100.0	126.2	113.3	127.9	159.8	149.2	156.0
Maldives											
Mongolia				245.1	100.0	82.1	73.3	71.1	67.6	81.1	92.5
Myanmar											
Nauru											
Nepal											
New Caledonia											
North Korea											
Pakistan	32.7	40.4	62.2	81.6	100.0	105.3	109.1	109.1	118.4	124.6	133.8
Papua New Guinea											
Philippines				62.7	100.0						
Singapore		34.5	37.0	67.6	100.0	108.2	107.7	122.6	141.4	125.1	135.5
Solomon Islands											
South Korea	21.0	21.2	35.4	66.4	100.0	113.1	105.6	132.0	154.6	156.0	167.4
Sri Lanka											
Taiwan											
Tajikistan											
Thailand	21.7	28.6	37.4	66.3	100.0	107.8	96.5	108.6	111.9	113.5	123.0
Tonga											
Turkmenistan				120.9	100.0						
Tuvalu											
Uzbekistan											
Vanuatu											
Vietnam											
Western Samoa											
Australasia											
Australia	54.7	84.1	87.5	96.7	100.0	104.3	107.7	109.9	110.9	113.9	118.5
New Zealand		81.8	161.1	89.8	100.0	103.5	102.9	99.0	103.3	105.3	106.7

Source: United Nations/Euromonitor
Notes: Indices based on value of production (or contribution to GDP) at constant prices

Industrial Output

Indices of Manufacturing Production 1977-2002

- 1995 = 100

	1977	1980	1985	1990	1995	1997	1998	1999	2000	2001	2002
Africa and Middle East											
Algeria	58.1	73.5	131.6	127.7	100.0	82.3	89.7	88.3	86.8	86.0	85.2
Angola											
Bahrain											
Benin											
Botswana											
Burkina Faso											
Burundi											
Cameroon				94.3	100.0	117.5	121.1	120.4	113.2	129.4	129.9
Cape Verde											
Central African Republic				107.3	100.0						
Chad											
Comoros											
Congo Dem Rep											
Congo-Brazzaville											
Côte d'Ivoire		98.2	113.9	98.2	100.0	119.2	139.5	139.6	126.9	121.5	109.7
Djibouti											
Egypt											
Equatorial Guinea											
Eritrea											
Ethiopia											
Gabon											
Gambia											
Ghana											
Guinea											
Guinea-Bissau											
Iran											
Iraq											
Israel	41.2	52.9	63.4	69.7	100.0	107.3	110.3	112.0	123.6	116.7	113.6
Jordan	23.6	44.5	60.2	73.1	100.0	100.9	104.1	102.0	107.3	120.7	134.9
Kenya	59.9	62.4	68.1	89.3	100.0						
Kuwait											
Lebanon											
Lesotho											
Liberia											
Libya											
Madagascar											
Malawi		89.3	86.6	111.6	100.0	100.2	94.4	81.2	80.2	68.1	68.0
Mali				96.7	100.0						
Mauritania											
Mauritius											
Morocco	46.3	60.2	69.8	89.6	100.0	107.5	110.2	112.7	116.6	120.4	124.0
Mozambique											
Namibia											
Niger											
Nigeria	88.4	86.6	72.8	119.5	100.0						
Oman											
Qatar											
Réunion											
Rwanda											
Sao Tomé e Príncipe											
Saudi Arabia											
Senegal	94.4	78.6	104.6	91.7	100.0	94.5	100.1	99.6	91.7	90.0	123.1
Seychelles											
Sierra Leone											
Somalia											
South Africa	82.8	87.2	86.3	97.7	100.0	106.4	102.8	102.2	106.0	109.0	114.8
Sudan											
Swaziland											
Syria											
Tanzania				109.6	100.0						
Togo											
Tunisia	41.3	54.3	66.8	76.9	100.0	108.2	115.9	122.5	133.2	144.1	143.0
Uganda				47.0	100.0	137.9	153.5	165.1	164.4	168.2	193.9
United Arab Emirates											
Yemen											
Zambia	109.9	101.8	117.1	128.0	100.0	94.8	82.0	94.2	95.4	103.8	116.1
Zimbabwe	95.4	88.4	99.0	123.2	100.0	112.9	112.0	103.7	97.4	88.6	75.1

Source: United Nations/Euromonitor
Notes: Indices based on value of production (or contribution to GDP) at constant prices

Industrial Output

Table 17.3

Indices of Mining Production 1990-2002

• 1995 = 100

	1990	1991	1992	1993	1995	1997	1998	1999	2000	2001	2002
North America											
Canada	81.6	85.1	87.6	90.9	100.0	104.1	105.7	104.0	111.8	113.7	111.9
USA	102.8	100.6	98.0	97.9	100.0	103.7	101.8	97.5	99.6	100.2	97.2
Latin America											
Anguilla											
Antigua											
Argentina											
Aruba											
Bahamas											
Barbados	89.3	85.5	94.4	91.4	100.0	92.9	141.4	164.8	140.4	122.0	116.2
Belize											
Bermuda											
Bolivia	72.0	73.3	73.9	88.0	100.0	100.6	106.7	95.1	93.6	90.5	90.7
Brazil	90.3	91.1	91.9	92.4	100.0	117.7	132.4	144.4	161.6	167.2	185.1
British Virgin Islands											
Cayman Islands											
Chile	68.4	76.5	81.1	84.3	100.0	134.8	142.5	164.6	173.7	176.4	170.0
Colombia	82.9	81.5	83.6	82.6	100.0						
Costa Rica											
Cuba											
Dominica											
Dominican Republic											
Ecuador											
El Salvador					100.0	107.5	113.2	113.7	108.4	121.3	127.4
French Guiana											
Grenada											
Guadeloupe											
Guatemala											
Guyana											
Haiti											
Honduras											
Jamaica											
Martinique											
Mexico	97.3	98.0	99.5	100.3	100.0	112.9	116.0	113.6	117.9	118.9	118.5
Netherlands Antilles											
Nicaragua											
Panama					100.0	160.5	202.2	230.5	228.6	137.1	98.2
Paraguay											
Peru	86.3	83.6	81.4	89.6	100.0	114.6	118.9	134.3	137.5	154.6	171.9
Puerto Rico											
St Kitts											
St Lucia											
St Vincent and the Grenadines											
Suriname											
Trinidad and Tobago											
Uruguay											
Venezuela											

Source: United Nations/Euromonitor
Notes: Indices based on value of production (or contribution to GDP) at constant prices

◻ Industrial Output

Indices of Mining Production 1990-2002

● 1995 = 100

	1990	1991	1992	1993	1995	1997	1998	1999	2000	2001	2002
Asia Pacific											
Afghanistan											
American Samoa											
Armenia											
Azerbaijan											
Bangladesh	68.1	70.0	76.2	85.2	100.0	106.4	113.5	114.6	134.5	150.8	156.4
Bhutan											
Brunei											
Cambodia											
China											
Fiji	107.8	101.2	96.6	99.1	100.0	133.7	106.6	126.8	108.6	110.6	97.8
French Polynesia											
Guam											
Hong Kong, China											
India	80.4	80.9	83.0	84.9	100.0	104.9	104.1	105.1	108.0	109.5	111.9
Indonesia	92.0	101.2	82.0	97.9	100.0	103.3	103.8	96.9	117.7	124.6	138.8
Japan	104.0	107.5	106.5	103.8	100.0	92.8	86.4	86.1	85.8	85.6	78.5
Kazakhstan											
Kiribati											
Kyrgyzstan											
Laos											
Macau											
Malaysia	81.1	85.2	87.6	88.6	100.0	108.4	109.6	106.1	105.9	108.8	110.7
Maldives											
Mongolia						100.0	125.5	116.5	121.0	128.1	141.1	148.7
Myanmar											
Nauru											
Nepal											
New Caledonia											
North Korea											
Pakistan						100.0	96.1	101.0	104.1	113.1	112.7	118.4
Papua New Guinea											
Philippines	96.4	120.1	161.3	120.9	100.0						
Singapore											
Solomon Islands											
South Korea	135.9	135.6	116.6	108.6	100.0	94.0	72.7	78.6	77.5	76.7	79.9
Sri Lanka											
Taiwan											
Tajikistan											
Thailand											
Tonga											
Turkmenistan											
Tuvalu											
Uzbekistan											
Vanuatu											
Vietnam											
Western Samoa											
Australasia											
Australia	81.7	87.6	92.1	92.2	100.0	109.1	112.6	113.2	121.8	129.5	129.3
New Zealand	88.1	91.5	97.6	99.6	100.0	112.6	113.9	112.7	116.3	119.0	120.3

Source: United Nations/Euromonitor
Notes: Indices based on value of production (or contribution to GDP) at constant prices

◻ Industrial Output

Indices of Mining Production 1990-2002

● 1995 = 100

Africa and Middle East	1990	1991	1992	1993	1995	1997	1998	1999	2000	2001	2002
Algeria	125.5	113.8	116.8	104.1	100.0	84.1	87.3	93.0	98.2	95.3	102.6
Angola											
Bahrain											
Benin											
Botswana											
Burkina Faso											
Burundi											
Cameroon											
Cape Verde											
Central African Republic											
Chad											
Comoros											
Congo Dem Rep											
Congo-Brazzaville											
Côte d'Ivoire					100.0	220.0	165.5	169.5	146.5	99.1	25.7
Djibouti											
Egypt											
Equatorial Guinea											
Eritrea											
Ethiopia											
Gabon											
Gambia											
Ghana											
Guinea											
Guinea-Bissau											
Iran											
Iraq											
Israel	67.2	73.0	76.5	83.5	100.0	104.9	109.2	108.2	105.6	107.8	116.1
Jordan	92.2	81.8	79.6	80.1	100.0	104.0	99.4	106.6	108.0	111.4	120.5
Kenya											
Kuwait											
Lebanon											
Lesotho											
Liberia											
Libya											
Madagascar											
Malawi											
Mali											
Mauritania											
Mauritius											
Morocco	103.2	90.3	94.6	93.0	100.0	111.6	111.1	107.5	103.8	106.3	109.0
Mozambique											
Namibia											
Niger											
Nigeria	92.5	96.5	96.4	100.1	100.0						
Oman											
Qatar											
Réunion											
Rwanda											
Sao Tomé e Príncipe											
Saudi Arabia											
Senegal	132.6	133.8	135.7	104.5	100.0	105.6	104.5	122.4	123.7	107.8	120.0
Seychelles											
Sierra Leone											
Somalia											
South Africa	99.9	99.0	99.4	102.3	100.0	100.3	99.2	97.2	95.8	97.1	98.3
Sudan											
Swaziland											
Syria											
Tanzania											
Togo											
Tunisia	102.5	115.3	114.7	102.9	100.0	102.6	109.8	112.9	109.6	106.1	106.9
Uganda											
United Arab Emirates											
Yemen											
Zambia	144.7	133.6	147.6	134.9	100.0	114.5	129.5	92.8	96.1	82.2	66.2
Zimbabwe	86.4	86.2	85.8	83.8	100.0	90.9	108.6	103.4	95.0	81.7	72.2

Source: *United Nations/Euromonitor*
Notes: *Indices based on value of production (or contribution to GDP) at constant prices*

Production of Selected Metals 2002

'000 tonnes	Alumin-ium	Crude Steel	Pig Iron	Refined Copper	Refined Lead	Refined Tin	Slab Zinc	Smelter Copper
North America								
Canada	2,447.2	17,112.0	9,380.4	474.8	174.6		831.2	593.5
USA	4,032.5	119,214.4	44,364.0	1,340.8	1,273.9	0.7	398.8	1,337.2
Latin America								
Anguilla								
Antigua								
Argentina	216.0	4,584.0	2,181.6	16.0	32.8	0.1	40.5	
Aruba								
Bahamas								
Barbados								
Belize								
Bermuda								
Bolivia						7.5		
Brazil	1,237.3	29,388.0	29,496.0	196.8	23.8	9.6	174.1	163.2
British Virgin Islands								
Cayman Islands								
Chile		1,331.2	1,086.0	2,627.1				2,532.6
Colombia		300.0	160.6					
Costa Rica								
Cuba								
Dominica								
Dominican Republic								
Ecuador								
El Salvador								
French Guiana								
Grenada								
Guadeloupe								
Guatemala								
Guyana								
Haiti								
Honduras								
Jamaica								
Martinique								
Mexico	225.5	11,816.0	3,876.0	549.0	131.7	3.4	433.1	308.0
Netherlands Antilles								
Nicaragua								
Panama								
Paraguay								
Peru		690.2	325.0	492.1	134.5	21.7	200.7	199.1
Puerto Rico								
St Kitts								
St Lucia								
St Vincent and the Grenadines								
Suriname								
Trinidad and Tobago								
Uruguay								
Venezuela	536.7	3,013.6			6.0			

Source: Euromonitor from industry sources/national statistics

◻ Metal Production

Production of Selected Metals 2002

● '000 tonnes	Alumin-ium	Crude Steel	Pig Iron	Refined Copper	Refined Lead	Refined Tin	Slab Zinc	Smelter Copper
Asia Pacific								
Afghanistan								
American Samoa								
Armenia								
Azerbaijan								
Bangladesh								
Bhutan								
Brunei								
Cambodia								
China	3,352.8	177,912.0	171,924.0	959.8	755.7	130.1	2,077.8	825.5
Fiji								
French Polynesia								
Guam								
Hong Kong, China								
India	602.6	17,136.0	5,124.0	214.2	74.4	3.6	185.6	217.2
Indonesia						51.0		
Japan	480.1	106,884.0	81,708.0	1,524.7	127.8	0.5	667.8	1,945.2
Kazakhstan	801.7	5,549.3	4,064.2	309.9	64.9	2.8	290.0	453.7
Kiribati								
Kyrgyzstan								
Laos								
Macau								
Malaysia			552,873.0		29.7	21.4		
Maldives								
Mongolia								
Myanmar								
Nauru								
Nepal								
New Caledonia								
North Korea								
Pakistan			10,650.0					10.0
Papua New Guinea								
Philippines				149.4	14.8			220.9
Singapore								
Solomon Islands								
South Korea		501,312.0	27,108.0	546.5	188.5	0.3	548.9	615.3
Sri Lanka								
Taiwan			10,088.9		40.5	23.0		
Tajikistan								
Thailand		1,152.0			35.1	21.3	103.5	
Tonga								
Turkmenistan								
Tuvalu								
Uzbekistan								
Vanuatu								
Vietnam			116.4			2.4		
Western Samoa								
Australasia								
Australia	1,911.8	6,841.1	6,888.0	559.7	144.1	0.7	530.7	451.5
New Zealand	334.7		40,302.2		6.0			

Source: Euromonitor from industry sources/national statistics

Metal Production

Production of Selected Metals 2002

● '000 tonnes	Alumin-ium	Crude Steel	Pig Iron	Refined Copper	Refined Lead	Refined Tin	Slab Zinc	Smelter Copper
Africa and Middle East								
Algeria			872.1		5.4		29.3	
Angola								
Bahrain								
Benin								
Botswana								
Burkina Faso								
Burundi								
Cameroon								
Cape Verde								
Central African Republic								
Chad								
Comoros								
Congo Dem Rep								
Congo-Brazzaville								
Côte d'Ivoire								
Djibouti								
Egypt	190.4		1,419.3	4.0				
Equatorial Guinea								
Eritrea								
Ethiopia								
Gabon								
Gambia								
Ghana								
Guinea								
Guinea-Bissau								
Iran								
Iraq								
Israel								
Jordan								
Kenya								
Kuwait								
Lebanon								
Lesotho								
Liberia								
Libya								
Madagascar								
Malawi								
Mali								
Mauritania								
Mauritius								
Morocco					64.8			
Mozambique								
Namibia								
Niger								
Nigeria	23.8				5.0	0.3		
Oman								
Qatar								
Réunion								
Rwanda								
Sao Tomé e Príncipe								
Saudi Arabia								
Senegal								
Seychelles								
Sierra Leone								
Somalia								
South Africa	781.1	8,587.5	6,435.6	106.3	36.9		14.7	122.1
Sudan								
Swaziland								
Syria								
Tanzania								
Togo								
Tunisia		204.0	180.0					
Uganda								
United Arab Emirates								
Yemen								
Zambia								
Zimbabwe								

Source: Euromonitor from industry sources/national statistics

Mineral Production

Table 17.5

Production of Selected Minerals 2002

● '000 tonnes

	Bauxite	Copper Ore	Gold (tonnes)	Iron Ore	Lead Ore	Silver (tonnes)	Tin Ore	Zinc Ore
North America								
Canada		655.1	145.3	33,527.0	153.5	1,349.6		823.2
USA	99.6	1,195.9	304.6	51,492.0	478.1	1,616.7	0.5	958.1
Latin America								
Anguilla								
Antigua								
Argentina		0.3	4.5	5.4	14.5	31.4		42.5
Aruba								
Bahamas								
Barbados								
Belize								
Bermuda								
Bolivia		0.1	9.0		4.2	470.8	10.5	147.8
Brazil	12,562.3	24.0	68.2	212,866.1	7.4	126.4	20.2	153.5
British Virgin Islands								
Cayman Islands								
Chile		5,519.0	42.1	7,308.0	1.0	1,729.1		34.4
Colombia		3.7	18.0	598.8		4.8		
Costa Rica								
Cuba								
Dominica								
Dominican Republic								
Ecuador			5.8					0.1
El Salvador								
French Guiana								
Grenada								
Guadeloupe								
Guatemala								
Guyana								
Haiti								
Honduras								
Jamaica								
Martinique								
Mexico		234.8	20.5	5,772.0	53.0	1,855.8		316.6
Netherlands Antilles								
Nicaragua								
Panama								
Paraguay								
Peru		577.3	179.8	3,096.0	274.3	2,581.3	40.3	908.4
Puerto Rico								
St Kitts								
St Lucia								
St Vincent and the Grenadines								
Suriname								
Trinidad and Tobago								
Uruguay								
Venezuela	3,924.4		3.8	18,512.4				

Source: *Euromonitor from industry sources/national statistics*

◻ Mineral Production

Production of Selected Minerals 2002

● '000 tonnes

	Bauxite	Copper Ore	Gold (tonnes)	Iron Ore	Lead Ore	Silver (tonnes)	Tin Ore	Zinc Ore
Asia Pacific								
Afghanistan								
American Samoa								
Armenia								
Azerbaijan				1.7				
Bangladesh								
Bhutan								
Brunei								
Cambodia								
China	9,000.0	514.0		228,372.0	711.9	918.0	139.3	1,592.3
Fiji								
French Polynesia								
Guam								
Hong Kong, China								
India	8,627.9	27.6	2.4	89,292.0	43.4	60.2		264.5
Indonesia	883.4	1,036.5	0.2	408.0		850.1	52.5	
Japan		2.0	7.0	38.9	14.3	242.9	6.0	60.0
Kazakhstan	5,194.8	443.6	10.5	33,271.5	34.1	411.6	0.5	
Kiribati								
Kyrgyzstan								
Laos								
Macau								
Malaysia	66.4	6.3	4.1	408.0		6.2	6.5	
Maldives								
Mongolia								
Myanmar								
Nauru								
Nepal								
New Caledonia								
North Korea								
Pakistan	4.9							
Papua New Guinea								
Philippines		44.0	4.4			14.0		
Singapore								
Solomon Islands								
South Korea			0.3	324.0	1.5			11.4
Sri Lanka								
Taiwan								
Tajikistan								
Thailand				144.0	8.8		3.3	16.6
Tonga								
Turkmenistan								
Tuvalu								
Uzbekistan								
Vanuatu								
Vietnam							2.3	27.4
Western Samoa								
Australasia								
Australia	53,495.4	476.6	306.3	187,116.0	756.5	2,483.6	9.0	1,580.5
New Zealand			5.8					

Source: Euromonitor from industry sources/national statistics

□ Mineral Production

Production of Selected Minerals 2002

● '000 tonnes

	Bauxite	Copper Ore	Gold (tonnes)	Iron Ore	Lead Ore	Silver (tonnes)	Tin Ore	Zinc Ore
Africa and Middle East								
Algeria				1,952.2	0.7	1.5		4.7
Angola								
Bahrain								
Benin								
Botswana								
Burkina Faso								
Burundi								
Cameroon								
Cape Verde								
Central African Republic								
Chad								
Comoros								
Congo Dem Rep								
Congo-Brazzaville								
Côte d'Ivoire								
Djibouti								
Egypt				2,994.3				
Equatorial Guinea								
Eritrea								
Ethiopia								
Gabon								
Gambia								
Ghana								
Guinea								
Guinea-Bissau								
Iran								
Iraq								
Israel								
Jordan								
Kenya								
Kuwait								
Lebanon								
Lesotho								
Liberia								
Libya								
Madagascar								
Malawi								
Mali								
Mauritania								
Mauritius								
Morocco		10.4		24.0	107.3	291.9	2.2	192.6
Mozambique								
Namibia								
Niger								
Nigeria							2.3	
Oman								
Qatar								
Réunion								
Rwanda								
Sao Tomé e Príncipe								
Saudi Arabia		0.8				6.4		
Senegal								
Seychelles								
Sierra Leone								
Somalia								
South Africa		119.2	406.1	36,444.0	102.0	103.8		70.1
Sudan								
Swaziland								
Syria								
Tanzania								
Togo								
Tunisia				216.0	8.0	0.1		30.9
Uganda								
United Arab Emirates								
Yemen								
Zambia								
Zimbabwe				300.0				

Source: Euromonitor from industry sources/national statistics

     Table 17.6

Production of Selected Textiles

- '000 tonnes/as stated

	Cotton Yarn	Rayon/ Acetate Fibres/ Filaments	Rayon and Acetate Fabrics	Synth- etic Fibre	Wool Yarn	Woven Cotton Fabric (mn sq m)	Woven Woollen Fabric (mn sq m)
Algeria							
Argentina		1.1		101.8			
Australia	61.9				17.8	99.0	5.5
Azerbaijan						7.6	0.0
Bolivia				5.0			
Brazil				296.1			
Canada				140.2			
Chile				14.9			
China	7,373.6			4,450.3	43.0	22,194.0	569.7
Colombia				49.2			
Ecuador				4.8			
Egypt	231.6						
Hong Kong, China	99.6						
India	2,197.2	2,016.1				19,732.8	
Indonesia							
Israel							
Japan	134.8	187.0	192.9	905.3	23.7	485.4	153.9
Jordan							
Kazakhstan	174.0					3.2	0.8
Kuwait							
Malaysia	76.8						
Mexico	14.4	24.3		470.2		134.4	
Morocco							
New Zealand							
Nigeria							
Pakistan	1,786.0					547.8	
Peru	42.0			36.4			
Philippines							
Saudi Arabia							
Singapore							
South Africa	43.1			165.4		197.6	
South Korea	306.5				12.1	225.0	2.1
Taiwan							
Thailand							
Tunisia							
Turkmenistan						37.6	
United Arab Emirates							
USA	1,827.4	194.4		3,157.2			
Venezuela				40.0			
Vietnam							

Source: Euromonitor from industry sources/national statistics

IT and Telecommunications

Table 18.1

▣ Internet

Internet Hosts 1994-2002

● Number

	1994	1995	1996	1997	1998	1999	2000	2001	2002
North America									
Canada	187,000	373,000	603,000	839,000	1,119,000	1,670,000	2,364,000	2,890,000	2,870,832
USA	3,179,000	6,055,000	10,113,000	20,624,000	30,489,000	53,176,000	80,567,000	106,193,000	113,809,039
Latin America									
Anguilla									
Antigua									
Argentina	1,000	5,000	13,000	20,000	66,000	142,000	270,000	465,000	504,891
Aruba									
Bahamas									
Barbados		2	21	23	44	68	100	130	151
Belize		1	12	257	252	276	293	333	349
Bermuda									
Bolivia	38	66	430	550	626	948	1,324	1,522	1,830
Brazil	5,896	20,113	77,148	117,200	215,100	446,400	876,600	1,645,000	2,039,578
British Virgin Islands									
Cayman Islands									
Chile	3,000	9,000	16,000	18,000	30,000	40,000	75,000	123,000	191,235
Colombia	1,127	2,262	9,054	10,173	16,200	40,565	46,819	57,419	51,020
Costa Rica	798	1,495	3,491	2,965	3,261	7,471	7,357	8,551	9,547
Cuba	1	1	24	51	80	169	660	878	1,041
Dominica									
Dominican Republic									
Ecuador	325	504	590	1,036	1,548	1,922	2,636	3,383	4,120
El Salvador	15	23	132	195	815	975	577	510	580
French Guiana									
Grenada									
Guadeloupe									
Guatemala	15	27	274	665	913	1,772	5,603	6,630	7,800
Guyana	26	40	52	67	69	16	59	20	30
Haiti									
Honduras			408	74	99	119	128	322	362
Jamaica	76	164	249	266	322	367	1,472	1,436	1,603
Martinique									
Mexico	6,656	13,787	29,840	41,659	113,000	405,000	559,000	918,000	1,055,062
Netherlands Antilles									
Nicaragua	49	141	531	505	715	1,047	1,400	2,194	2,603
Panama	17	148	751	1,019	742	1,235	15,084	7,825	10,927
Paraguay	78	108	187	298	1,147	1,660	1,296	2,704	3,736
Peru	171	813	5,192	3,415	4,790	9,230	10,710	13,500	16,438
Puerto Rico	82	82	82	259	1,571	1,310	1,513	1,584	1,718
St Kitts									
St Lucia									
St Vincent and the Grenadines									
Suriname		1	1	1	1	1	10	59	84
Trinidad and Tobago		55	141	919	1,944	4,852	6,596	6,872	7,377
Uruguay	200	600	1,800	10,300	15,400	25,400	54,100	70,900	89,133
Venezuela	530	1,170	2,420	3,870	7,910	14,280	16,150	22,610	27,491

Source: *International Telecommunications Union/World Bank/Trade Sources/Euromonitor*

Internet
Internet Hosts 1994-2002

- Number

	1994	1995	1996	1997	1998	1999	2000	2001	2002
Asia Pacific									
Afghanistan									
American Samoa									
Armenia	152	173	176	442	951	2,313	2,663	2,361	2,109
Azerbaijan	9	16	30	347	435	603	1,542	1,314	1,375
Bangladesh				300	1,000	3,000	3,500	3,000	3,100
Bhutan				2	36	542	794	1,136	1,276
Brunei	123	156	206	339	1,195	1,399	4,636	8,707	10,338
Cambodia	15	22	36	48	60	155	479	623	953
China	1,000	2,000	20,000	16,000	17,000	72,000	70,000	89,000	80,676
Fiji	5	52	75	92	214	359	555	668	865
French Polynesia	10	17	25	189	281	867	1,508	1,726	2,156
Guam									
Hong Kong, China	12,437	17,693	49,162	67,914	83,000	115,000	229,000	388,000	392,006
India	359	1,000	3,000	7,175	13,253	23,445	35,810	83,000	90,505
Indonesia	177	2,000	10,000	10,000	15,000	21,052	26,727	46,000	60,674
Japan	97,000	269,000	734,000	1,169,000	1,688,000	2,637,000	4,641,000	7,118,000	8,617,946
Kazakhstan	7	187	807	1,209	1,480	5,715	7,383	10,947	13,010
Kiribati									
Kyrgyzstan	24	52	85	147	217	3,535	4,115	4,558	5,117
Laos							3	165	243
Macau	12	65	179	151	142	162	180	189	215
Malaysia	2,000	4,194	25,200	32,269	47,852	59,012	68,000	74,000	85,905
Maldives	8	19	33	52	109	228	265	359	405
Mongolia	3	7	10	13	20	50	171	151	181
Myanmar					1	4	4	2	2
Nauru									
Nepal	10	19	60	139	153	290	1,101	1,513	2,143
New Caledonia		1	23	82	113	157	178	4,711	5,225
North Korea									
Pakistan	11	17	511	1,291	3,096	4,735	6,467	11,319	12,700
Papua New Guinea			1	53	118	337	444	439	547
Philippines	334	1,771	3,628	4,313	9,200	12,390	19,450	30,850	43,246
Singapore	5,252	22,769	28,892	57,605	67,100	148,200	175,800	198,000	275,116
Solomon Islands	7	9	5	17	20	210	364	390	475
South Korea	18,000	29,000	66,000	131,000	203,000	461,000	398,000	440,000	480,827
Sri Lanka		6	349	680	539	1,209	2,155	2,286	2,539
Taiwan	15,000	26,000	35,000	177,000	309,000	597,000	1,096,000	1,713,000	1,734,269
Tajikistan				11	74	511	273	299	332
Thailand	2,000	4,055	9,245	14,378	20,527	40,176	63,447	72,000	83,965
Tonga									
Turkmenistan				3	263	852	1,231	1,620	2,170
Tuvalu									
Uzbekistan		35	122	98	236	200	275	213	237
Vanuatu									
Vietnam			5	5	34	126	179	487	613
Western Samoa									
Australasia									
Australia	161,000	310,000	515,000	665,000	792,000	1,090,000	1,616,000	2,289,000	2,489,152
New Zealand	31,000	54,000	85,000	169,000	137,000	271,000	345,000	408,000	436,833

Source: *International Telecommunications Union/World Bank/Trade Sources/Euromonitor*

◻ Internet

Internet Hosts 1994-2002

● Number

	1994	1995	1996	1997	1998	1999	2000	2001	2002
Africa and Middle East									
Algeria	10	16	28	49	88	200	34	665	1,120
Angola		2	4	6	6	8	8	10	
Bahrain	74	142	841	338	577	1,117	1,121	1,718	1,920
Benin	1	4	9	13	12	27	294	500	672
Botswana	18	24	24	550	658	2,226	2,356	1,273	1,834
Burkina Faso			1	45	176	211	380	704	915
Burundi			1	3	15	1	2	1	2
Cameroon				2	3	233	313	390	461
Cape Verde				1	1	17	27	34	43
Central African Republic	4	4	6	6	6	7	7	7	8
Chad				2	2	5	6	1	2
Comoros									
Congo Dem Rep									
Congo-Brazzaville									
Côte d'Ivoire		3	202	253	237	267	607	3,131	5,225
Djibouti		2	4	4	4	39	42	13	19
Egypt	153	561	1,976	1,805	2,420	2,355	2,240	1,802	2,686
Equatorial Guinea									
Eritrea						4	228	254	279
Ethiopia		1	1	78	78	81	84	43	53
Gabon				5	10	22	34	69	128
Gambia				10	10	12	15	120	157
Ghana	4	6	203	252	192	353	17	235	267
Guinea	2	2	2	3	3	227	200	245	368
Guinea-Bissau		3	7	11	15	15	20	20	31
Iran	18	271	285	203	244	1,167	1,690	2,466	2,826
Iraq									
Israel	12,636	27,613	49,238	86,761	114,584	149,490	102,937	143,678	206,219
Jordan	11	19	140	249	370	978	907	2,185	2,277
Kenya	9	17	273	458	686	3,365	4,777	2,702	2,835
Kuwait	220	1,233	2,920	4,057	6,231	4,069	3,360	3,437	3,838
Lebanon	58	88	601	1,134	2,358	3,889	5,611	7,101	9,693
Lesotho			1	19	19	50	102	60	98
Liberia	96	288	623	1,000	1,100	1,350	1,510	1,642	1,830
Libya									
Madagascar	8	19	27	17	61	337	548	234	298
Malawi					1	2	13	22	33
Mali			15	1	1	11	86	87	90
Mauritania			3	8	15	59	120	113	119
Mauritius	71	101	122	201	575	823	3,275	3,126	3,305
Morocco	142	229	468	1,405	2,045	2,034	1,858	2,454	3,332
Mozambique	15	23	31	69	141	162	112	16	18
Namibia	6	11	262	640	2,654	2,043	3,251	4,632	5,580
Niger			5	2	18	32	168	176	211
Nigeria			4	49	410	597	690	723	1,012
Oman	210	360	540	670	664	678	714	4,678	5,073
Qatar		21	189	13	1,069	2,255	127	148	
Réunion									
Rwanda									
Sao Tomé e Príncipe									
Saudi Arabia	2	27	275	37	319	4,160	3,745	11,422	15,677
Senegal	8	14	69	117	194	306	705	730	761
Seychelles			1	1	7	2	9	262	318
Sierra Leone					13	77	210	278	315
Somalia									
South Africa	27,000	48,000	99,000	122,000	144,000	168,000	188,000	238,000	270,588
Sudan			146	266	600	850	1,078	1,282	
Swaziland		1	226	330	278	661	981	1,142	1,432
Syria					1	6	9	9	13
Tanzania			3	25	129	218	816	1,478	1,966
Togo			5	37	110	120	159	220	254
Tunisia	54	79	41	51	15	33	26	218	269
Uganda		58	17	30	113	180	186	293	342
United Arab Emirates		365	1,802	1,940	17,900	24,000	43,000	77,000	86,440
Yemen		2	10	20	30	53	80	110	
Zambia	69	69	173	181	303	537	892	1,095	1,169
Zimbabwe	19	93	176	599	1,031	2,073	2,918	3,494	3,936

Source: International Telecommunications Union/World Bank/Trade Sources/Euromonitor

Internet Users 1994-2002

- '000

	1994	1995	1996	1997	1998	1999	2000	2001	2002
North America									
Canada	690.0	1,220.0	2,000.0	4,500.0	7,500.0	11,000.0	12,700.0	13,500.0	15,526.5
USA	8,500.0	20,000.0	30,000.0	40,000.0	60,000.0	74,100.0	95,354.0	142,823.0	183,127.5
Latin America									
Anguilla									
Antigua									
Argentina	15.0	30.0	50.0	100.0	300.0	1,200.0	2,600.0	3,650.0	5,413.0
Aruba									
Bahamas									
Barbados		0.0	1.0	2.0	5.0	6.0	10.0	15.0	18.9
Belize		0.1	2.0	3.0	5.0	10.0	15.0	18.0	21.2
Bermuda									
Bolivia		5.0	15.0	35.0	50.0	80.0	120.0	180.0	586.2
Brazil	60.0	170.0	740.0	1,310.0	2,500.0	3,500.0	5,000.0	8,000.0	13,375.7
British Virgin Islands									
Cayman Islands									
Chile	20.0	50.0	100.0	157.0	250.0	625.0	2,537.0	3,102.0	5,816.1
Colombia	38.4	68.6	122.5	208.0	433.0	664.0	878.0	1,154.0	1,326.9
Costa Rica	9.5	14.5	30.0	60.0	100.0	150.0	250.0	384.0	457.5
Cuba		0.0	3.5	7.5	25.0	34.8	60.0	120.0	175.0
Dominica									
Dominican Republic					18.0	48.0	74.9	103.1	133.1
Ecuador	3.9	5.0	10.0	13.0	15.0	100.0	180.0	333.0	439.3
El Salvador	0.9	1.7	2.6	10.0	30.0	40.0	50.0	100.0	173.0
French Guiana									
Grenada									
Guadeloupe									
Guatemala	0.1	0.3	2.0	10.0	50.0	65.0	80.0	200.0	278.5
Guyana			0.5	1.0	2.0	28.0	52.0	95.0	103.2
Haiti					1.5	4.0	6.5	9.3	12.8
Honduras	1.8	2.1	2.5	10.0	18.0	35.0	55.0	90.0	111.5
Jamaica	0.9	2.7	14.7	20.0	50.0	60.0	80.0	100.0	125.1
Martinique									
Mexico	39.0	94.0	187.0	596.0	1,222.0	1,822.0	2,712.0	3,636.0	8,689.5
Netherlands Antilles									
Nicaragua	0.6	1.4	4.0	10.0	15.0	20.0	50.0	75.0	104.8
Panama	0.2	1.5	6.0	15.0	30.0	45.0	90.0	120.0	143.2
Paraguay			1.0	5.0	10.0	20.0	40.0	60.0	121.2
Peru	2.0	8.0	60.0	100.0	300.0	500.0	800.0	2,000.0	2,454.1
Puerto Rico	1.0	5.0	10.0	50.0	100.0	200.0	400.0	600.0	1,184.4
St Kitts									
St Lucia									
St Vincent and the Grenadines									
Suriname	0.2	0.5	1.0	4.5	7.6	8.7	11.7	14.5	18.0
Trinidad and Tobago	1.0	2.0	5.0	15.0	35.0	75.0	100.0	120.0	132.3
Uruguay	2.0	10.0	60.0	110.0	230.0	330.0	370.0	400.0	451.8
Venezuela	12.0	27.0	56.0	90.0	322.0	680.0	820.0	1,153.0	1,707.0

Source: *International Telecommunications Union/World Bank/Trade Sources/Euromonitor*

Internet

Internet Users 1994-2002

● '000

	1994	1995	1996	1997	1998	1999	2000	2001	2002
Asia Pacific									
Afghanistan									
American Samoa									
Armenia	0.3	1.7	3.0	3.5	4.0	30.0	50.0	70.0	83.1
Azerbaijan	0.1	0.2	0.5	2.0	3.0	8.0	12.0	25.0	130.9
Bangladesh				1.0	5.0	50.0	100.0	160.0	235.3
Bhutan	0.3					0.8	2.3	3.0	5.3
Brunei		3.0	10.0	15.0	20.0	25.0	30.0	35.0	39.4
Cambodia				0.7	2.0	4.0	6.0	10.0	14.2
China	14.0	60.0	160.0	400.0	2,100.0	8,900.0	22,500.0	33,700.0	77,907.8
Fiji	0.1	0.1	0.5	1.8	5.0	7.5	12.0	38.0	49.0
French Polynesia			0.2	0.5	3.0	8.0	15.0	20.0	34.0
Guam									
Hong Kong, China	170.0	200.0	300.0	675.0	947.0	1,400.0	1,855.0	2,601.0	3,372.2
India	10.0	250.0	450.0	700.0	1,400.0	2,800.0	5,000.0	7,000.0	20,442.3
Indonesia	2.0	50.0	110.0	384.0	510.0	900.0	2,000.0	4,000.0	4,954.4
Japan	1,000.0	2,000.0	5,500.0	11,550.0	16,940.0	27,060.0	47,080.0	55,930.0	75,360.6
Kazakhstan	0.1	1.8	5.0	10.0	20.0	70.0	100.0	150.0	175.7
Kiribati									
Kyrgyzstan					3.5	10.0	51.6	150.6	215.2
Laos					0.5	2.0	6.0	10.0	13.9
Macau	0.1	1.2	3.0	10.0	30.0	40.0	60.0	101.0	124.4
Malaysia	20.0	30.0	180.0	500.0	1,500.0	2,800.0	4,000.0	6,500.0	7,333.5
Maldives			0.6	0.8	1.5	3.0	6.0	10.0	12.1
Mongolia	0.1	0.2	0.4	2.6	3.4	12.0	30.0	40.0	50.1
Myanmar						0.5	7.0	10.0	14.0
Nauru									
Nepal	0.1	0.2	1.0	5.0	15.0	35.0	50.0	60.0	71.9
New Caledonia		0.0	0.5	2.0	4.0	12.0	20.0	24.9	41.2
North Korea									
Pakistan	0.0	0.2	4.0	37.8	61.9	80.0	300.0	500.0	2,244.0
Papua New Guinea			1.0	5.0	12.0	35.0	45.0	50.0	61.0
Philippines	4.0	20.0	40.0	100.0	823.0	1,090.0	1,540.0	2,000.0	4,559.1
Singapore	40.0	100.0	300.0	500.0	750.0	950.0	1,300.0	1,500.0	2,332.4
Solomon Islands	0.0	0.1	1.0	1.5	2.0	2.0	2.0	2.0	2.3
South Korea	138.0	366.0	731.0	1,634.0	3,103.0	10,860.0	19,040.0	24,380.0	29,754.2
Sri Lanka	0.5	1.0	10.0	30.0	55.0	65.0	121.5	150.0	215.2
Taiwan	180.0	250.0	603.0	1,500.0	3,011.0	4,540.0	6,260.0	7,820.0	8,360.6
Tajikistan						2.0	3.0	3.2	5.3
Thailand	30.0	55.0	135.0	375.0	500.0	1,300.0	2,300.0	3,536.0	4,254.9
Tonga									
Turkmenistan						2.0	6.0	8.0	64.2
Tuvalu									
Uzbekistan	0.1	0.4	·1.0	2.5	5.0	7.5	120.0	150.0	257.2
Vanuatu									
Vietnam			0.1	3.0	10.0	100.0	200.0	1,010.0	1,452.1
Western Samoa									
Australasia									
Australia	400.0	500.0	600.0	1,600.0	4,200.0	5,600.0	6,600.0	7,200.0	7,531.3
New Zealand	115.0	180.0	300.0	550.0	750.0	1,113.0	1,515.0	1,762.0	2,002.3

Source: International Telecommunications Union/World Bank/Trade Sources/Euromonitor

Internet

Internet Users 1994-2002

● '000

	1994	1995	1996	1997	1998	1999	2000	2001	2002
Africa and Middle East									
Algeria	0.1	0.5	0.5	3.0	6.0	60.0	150.0	200.0	268.3
Angola			0.1	0.8	2.5	10.0	15.0	20.0	28.7
Bahrain	1.2	2.0	5.0	10.0	20.0	30.0	40.0	140.0	241.2
Benin			0.1	1.5	3.0	10.0	15.0	25.0	37.0
Botswana	0.4	1.0	2.5	5.0	10.0	19.0	25.0	50.0	61.0
Burkina Faso			0.1	2.0	5.0	7.0	9.0	19.0	26.0
Burundi			0.1	0.5	1.0	2.5	5.0	6.0	8.0
Cameroon		0.3	0.6	1.0	2.0	20.0	40.0	45.0	51.2
Cape Verde				1.0	2.0	5.0	8.0	12.0	17.7
Central African Republic			0.1	0.2	0.2	1.0	3.0	2.0	2.3
Chad				0.1	0.3	1.0	3.0	4.0	6.2
Comoros					0.2	0.8	1.2	1.5	1.7
Congo Dem Rep				0.1	0.2	2.1	3.3	4.5	5.5
Congo-Brazzaville									
Côte d'Ivoire		0.0	1.3	3.0	10.0	20.0	40.0	70.0	134.5
Djibouti	0.1	0.1	0.2	0.6	0.7	0.8	1.4	3.3	3.7
Egypt	4.0	20.0	40.0	60.0	100.0	200.0	450.0	600.0	939.3
Equatorial Guinea				0.2	0.2	1.0	2.0	3.3	4.7
Eritrea				0.3	0.3	0.9	5.0	15.0	29.5
Ethiopia		0.0	1.0	3.0	6.0	8.0	10.0	25.0	31.0
Gabon				0.6	2.0	3.0	15.0	41.5	63.2
Gambia	0.1	0.1	0.4	0.6	2.5	9.0	12.0	18.0	23.2
Ghana		0.1	1.0	5.0	6.0	20.0	30.0	40.5	49.8
Guinea	0.0	0.1	0.1	0.3	0.5	5.0	8.0	15.0	23.5
Guinea-Bissau				0.2	0.3	1.5	3.0	4.0	6.2
Iran	0.3	3.0	10.0	30.0	65.0	250.0	625.0	1,005.0	3,158.0
Iraq									
Israel	30.0	50.0	120.0	250.0	600.0	800.0	1,270.0	1,800.0	2,889.1
Jordan	0.6	1.0	2.0	27.4	60.8	120.0	127.3	234.0	461.8
Kenya	0.1	0.2	2.5	10.0	15.0	35.0	200.0	500.0	965.1
Kuwait	2.6	3.5	15.0	40.0	60.0	100.0	150.0	200.0	322.1
Lebanon	1.8	2.5	5.0	45.0	100.0	200.0	300.0	420.0	515.2
Lesotho			0.1	0.1	0.2	1.0	4.0	5.0	6.7
Liberia					0.1	0.4	0.6	0.8	1.2
Libya						6.8	7.4	8.6	10.5
Madagascar			0.5	2.0	9.0	25.0	30.0	35.0	39.4
Malawi				0.5	2.0	10.0	15.0	20.0	24.0
Mali			0.2	1.0	2.0	7.0	18.8	30.0	61.6
Mauritania				0.1	1.0	3.0	5.0	7.0	9.2
Mauritius	0.4	0.9	2.1	5.5	30.0	55.0	87.0	158.0	234.2
Morocco	0.6	1.0	1.6	6.0	40.0	50.0	200.0	400.0	1,105.1
Mozambique			0.5	2.0	3.5	10.0	20.0	30.0	56.6
Namibia	0.1	0.1	0.1	1.0	5.0	6.0	30.0	45.0	73.2
Niger			0.1	0.2	0.3	3.0	4.0	12.0	21.2
Nigeria			10.0	20.0	30.0	50.0	80.0	115.0	150.5
Oman				10.0	20.0	50.0	90.0	120.0	182.4
Qatar	0.6	1.0	5.0	17.0	20.0	24.0	30.0	40.0	47.4
Réunion					0.5	1.9	2.9	3.6	4.1
Rwanda				0.1	0.1	0.5	0.8	1.0	1.1
Sao Tomé e Príncipe									
Saudi Arabia	1.3	2.0	5.0	10.0	20.0	100.0	200.0	300.0	490.7
Senegal		0.1	1.0	2.5	7.5	30.0	40.0	100.0	153.2
Seychelles			0.5	1.0	2.0	5.0	6.0	9.0	12.2
Sierra Leone			0.1	0.2	0.6	2.0	5.0	7.0	10.5
Somalia									
South Africa	330.0	460.0	618.0	800.0	1,266.0	1,820.0	2,400.0	2,890.0	5,372.4
Sudan				0.7	2.0	5.0	30.0	56.0	100.7
Swaziland		0.0	0.5	0.9	1.0	5.0	10.0	14.0	21.2
Syria				5.0	10.0	20.0	30.0	60.0	72.2
Tanzania			0.5	2.5	3.0	25.0	40.0	100.0	216.2
Togo			0.5	5.0	7.5	15.0	100.0	150.0	210.2
Tunisia	0.7	1.0	2.5	4.0	10.0	150.0	250.0	400.0	784.7
Uganda	0.3	0.6	1.0	2.3	15.0	25.0	40.0	60.0	77.1
United Arab Emirates	1.0	3.0	10.0	90.0	200.0	400.0	735.0	976.0	1,568.0
Yemen			0.1	2.5	4.0	10.0	15.0	17.0	24.5
Zambia	0.6	0.8	0.8	0.9	3.0	15.0	20.0	25.0	28.5
Zimbabwe	0.2	0.9	2.0	4.0	10.0	20.0	50.0	100.0	127.2

Source: International Telecommunications Union/World Bank/Trade Sources/Euromonitor

ISDN Subscribers 1994-2002

● Number

	1994	1995	1996	1997	1998	1999	2000	2001	2002
North America									
Canada	1,500	3,100	11,100	61,900	90,500	105,500	114,800	110,300	109,940
USA	352,000	539,000	878,000	1,175,000	1,554,000	2,017,000	2,071,000	2,031,000	1,995,071
Latin America									
Anguilla									
Antigua									
Argentina									
Aruba									
Bahamas									
Barbados			20	67	103	390	420	458	491
Belize									
Bermuda									
Bolivia									
Brazil									
British Virgin Islands									
Cayman Islands									
Chile									
Colombia	114	505	11,680	15,117	39,427	44,540	66,777	88,729	107,405
Costa Rica		123	250	392	655	845	1,855	1,758	1,712
Cuba									
Dominica									
Dominican Republic									
Ecuador		25	50	50	50	97	124	152	179
El Salvador						30	105	167	239
French Guiana	70								
Grenada									
Guadeloupe	340								
Guatemala						100	140	185	225
Guyana									
Haiti									
Honduras									
Jamaica			25			120	180	255	328
Martinique	280								
Mexico									
Netherlands Antilles									
Nicaragua									
Panama						237	360	492	640
Paraguay									
Peru									
Puerto Rico			38	163	329	556	934	1,108	1,418
St Kitts									
St Lucia									
St Vincent and the Grenadines									
Suriname									
Trinidad and Tobago					39	36	53	158	194
Uruguay					456	456	641	1,911	2,105
Venezuela									

Source: *Euromonitor from International Telecommunications Union/national statistics*

ISDN Subscribers 1994-2002

● Number

	1994	1995	1996	1997	1998	1999	2000	2001	2002
Asia Pacific									
Afghanistan									
American Samoa									
Armenia									
Azerbaijan									
Bangladesh									
Bhutan									
Brunei		2	17	38	25	40	50	60	69
Cambodia									
China	1,600	2,100	2,400	4,900	102,000	170,800	689,300	1,088,200	1,563,198
Fiji									
French Polynesia	157	252	341	516	735	1,112	1,760	2,261	2,416
Guam									
Hong Kong, China	350	628	1,002	4,227	8,764	11,479	13,513	12,915	14,072
India			293	1,378	5,258	14,258	16,385	29,227	26,838
Indonesia						5,714	8,500	4,290	5,350
Japan	344,000	521,000	924,000	2,398,000	4,068,000	6,738,000	9,699,000	10,317,000	14,645,522
Kazakhstan									
Kiribati									
Kyrgyzstan						59	100	141	177
Laos									
Macau				64	167	255	236	237	229
Malaysia	68	324	1,941	4,576	8,866	18,089	34,512	29,020	27,528
Maldives									
Mongolia							25		
Myanmar									
Nauru									
Nepal									
New Caledonia	228	348	484	639	879	1,269	1,899	1,645	1,459
North Korea									
Pakistan			64	238	800	2,000	3,034	4,028	4,897
Papua New Guinea									
Philippines						91	177	951	1,281
Singapore	1,626	2,750	5,366	8,901	12,452	23,161	30,207	37,135	54,938
Solomon Islands									
South Korea	4,309	5,788	8,605	21,110	36,242	178,144	174,952	134,764	182,189
Sri Lanka						318	856	1,341	1,803
Taiwan		636	2,566	5,169	15,314	28,366	38,068	37,665	43,640
Tajikistan									
Thailand	45	327	587	1,010	1,396	2,112	4,329	8,379	10,392
Tonga									
Turkmenistan									
Tuvalu									
Uzbekistan									
Vanuatu									
Vietnam									
Western Samoa									
Australasia									
Australia	18,000	28,000	45,000	61,000	114,000	171,000	231,500	292,070	335,868
New Zealand	400								

Source: Euromonitor from International Telecommunications Union/national statistics

◘ Internet

ISDN Subscribers 1994-2002

● Number

	1994	1995	1996	1997	1998	1999	2000	2001	2002
Africa and Middle East									
Algeria									
Angola									
Bahrain			70	173	381	684	1,088	1,533	2,051
Benin									
Botswana									
Burkina Faso									
Burundi									
Cameroon									
Cape Verde					36	103	344	573	904
Central African Republic									
Chad									
Comoros									
Congo Dem Rep									
Congo-Brazzaville									
Côte d'Ivoire						204	705	1,552	2,014
Djibouti									
Egypt									
Equatorial Guinea									
Eritrea									
Ethiopia									
Gabon									
Gambia									
Ghana									
Guinea	10								
Guinea-Bissau									
Iran									
Iraq									
Israel		586	1,700	3,900	25,000	37,000	53,000	56,800	61,090
Jordan						661	1,175	1,826	2,015
Kenya									
Kuwait									
Lebanon									
Lesotho									
Liberia									
Libya									
Madagascar						32	135	300	548
Malawi									
Mali									
Mauritania									
Mauritius	9	29	56	146	242	557	927	1,412	1,712
Morocco			38	216	612	2,397	6,728	10,000	11,836
Mozambique									
Namibia						606	982	2,227	2,784
Niger									
Nigeria									
Oman									
Qatar	84	96	92	79	169	420	651	968	1,185
Réunion									
Rwanda									
Sao Tomé e Príncipe									
Saudi Arabia									
Senegal			3	90	203	533	1,242	1,708	2,016
Seychelles		6	6	10	15	51	153	170	243
Sierra Leone									
Somalia									
South Africa	104	930	3,452	5,700	9,200	14,300	19,290	24,112	26,317
Sudan							215	250	264
Swaziland									
Syria			50	62	65	199	235	977	1,205
Tanzania									
Togo					18	61	61	108	115
Tunisia				32	75	223	368	640	874
Uganda									
United Arab Emirates	439	703	916	2,531	9,309	14,072	19,029	21,983	25,089
Yemen						22	110	250	432
Zambia									
Zimbabwe									

Source: *Euromonitor from International Telecommunications Union/national statistics*

□ Telecommunications								Table 18.4	

Availability of Digital Main Lines 1990-2002

• % of lines connected to digital exchanges

	1990	1995	1996	1997	1998	1999	2000	2001	2002
North America									
Canada	60.2	94.6	95.0	99.4	99.5	99.6	99.7	99.8	99.9
USA	43.0	76.2	80.5	83.9	87.8	91.6	95.4	96.9	97.5
Latin America									
Anguilla	100.0	100.0	100.0	100.0	100.0	100.0	100.0	100.0	100.0
Antigua	100.0	100.0	100.0	100.0	100.0	100.0	100.0	100.0	100.0
Argentina	13.2	77.5	85.2	94.4	100.0	100.0	100.0	100.0	100.0
Aruba									
Bahamas	98.0	100.0	100.0	100.0	100.0	100.0	100.0	100.0	100.0
Barbados	100.0	100.0	100.0	100.0	100.0	100.0	100.0	100.0	100.0
Belize	90.0	95.4	99.5	99.5	99.6	100.0	100.0	100.0	100.0
Bermuda									
Bolivia	12.0	59.0	69.0	60.0	75.0	85.0	98.0	99.3	100.0
Brazil	14.0	46.7	57.1	67.8	73.2	84.6	92.5	97.2	99.7
British Virgin Islands									
Cayman Islands		100.0	100.0	100.0	100.0	100.0	100.0	100.0	100.0
Chile	64.0	100.0	100.0	100.0	100.0	100.0	100.0	100.0	100.0
Colombia	22.4	69.9	75.0	78.5	83.0	92.0	94.0	96.3	99.8
Costa Rica	21.7	56.0	61.0	77.1	76.9	82.2	85.1	88.0	90.3
Cuba	1.0	3.0	11.0	18.0	37.0	40.0	51.7	69.2	73.1
Dominica		100.0	100.0	100.0	100.0	100.0	100.0	100.0	100.0
Dominican Republic		40.0	45.0	50.0	55.0	60.0	63.8	67.5	70.6
Ecuador	33.0	66.5	69.6	89.0	86.8	86.9	89.8	94.5	98.4
El Salvador	49.0	79.0	82.0	84.0	95.7	100.0	100.0	100.0	100.0
French Guiana		100.0	100.0	100.0	100.0	100.0	100.0	100.0	100.0
Grenada	100.0	100.0	100.0	100.0	100.0	100.0	100.0	100.0	100.0
Guadeloupe		100.0	100.0	100.0	100.0	100.0	100.0	100.0	100.0
Guatemala	50.0	64.0	68.4	87.0	92.0	98.4	100.0	100.0	100.0
Guyana	75.0	92.9	95.0	95.0	100.0	100.0	100.0	100.0	100.0
Haiti									
Honduras	45.9	78.5	82.5	89.9	92.5	93.2	94.0	96.2	97.8
Jamaica	100.0	100.0	100.0	100.0	100.0	100.0	100.0	100.0	100.0
Martinique									
Mexico	28.7	88.0	89.8	90.1	97.7	99.6	100.0	100.0	100.0
Netherlands Antilles									
Nicaragua	23.0	77.1	88.0	95.3	98.6	98.6	98.8	99.7	100.0
Panama	48.2	65.1	68.6	73.0	100.0	100.0	100.0	100.0	100.0
Paraguay	24.0	58.0	76.9	87.4	88.0	89.6	89.1	87.9	94.8
Peru	1.0	77.0	84.9	88.0	90.0	95.0	96.0	96.0	97.2
Puerto Rico	95.0	100.0	100.0	100.0	100.0	100.0	100.0	100.0	100.0
St Kitts		100.0	100.0	100.0	100.0	100.0	100.0	100.0	100.0
St Lucia		100.0	100.0	100.0	100.0	100.0	100.0	100.0	100.0
St Vincent and the Grenadines	100.0	100.0	100.0	100.0	100.0	100.0	100.0	100.0	100.0
Suriname	5.6	28.4	35.2	44.0	50.0	54.0	56.0	57.3	59.9
Trinidad and Tobago	82.0	100.0	100.0	100.0	100.0	100.0	100.0	100.0	100.0
Uruguay	58.0	84.0	89.0	100.0	100.0	100.0	100.0	100.0	100.0
Venezuela	19.5	55.0	59.0	64.3	66.1	68.5	80.0	80.0	81.2

Source: Euromonitor from International Telecommunications Union/national statistics

□ Telecommunications

Availability of Digital Main Lines 1990-2002

● % of lines connected to digital exchanges

	1990	1995	1996	1997	1998	1999	2000	2001	2002
Asia Pacific									
Afghanistan									
American Samoa									
Armenia				9.5	11.7	16.3	20.9	21.6	23.2
Azerbaijan		4.0	7.0	7.3	20.9	24.3	30.4	35.4	42.0
Bangladesh	10.8	21.7	39.5	55.0	61.2	61.6	66.4	81.3	87.2
Bhutan	48.6	75.5	78.9	92.0	100.0	100.0	100.0	100.0	100.0
Brunei	43.4	53.0	100.0	100.0	100.0	100.0	100.0	100.0	100.0
Cambodia	43.0	85.0	94.0	100.0	100.0	100.0	100.0	100.0	100.0
China	29.0	99.2	99.5	99.7	99.9	99.9	100.0	100.0	100.0
Fiji	42.3	85.6	84.0	99.3	99.7	99.8	99.9	100.0	100.0
French Polynesia	100.0	100.0	100.0	100.0	100.0	100.0	100.0	100.0	100.0
Guam	91.0	100.0	100.0	100.0	100.0	100.0	100.0	100.0	100.0
Hong Kong, China	78.1	100.0	100.0	100.0	100.0	100.0	100.0	100.0	100.0
India	25.0	87.0	98.7	99.0	99.5	99.8	100.0	100.0	100.0
Indonesia	35.9	93.0	96.0	99.0	99.2	100.0	100.0	100.0	100.0
Japan	39.0	90.4	97.0	100.0	100.0	100.0	100.0	100.0	100.0
Kazakhstan	1.3	11.4	14.0	17.0	20.1	23.9	29.3	34.0	38.7
Kiribati	86.0								
Kyrgyzstan				6.0	13.0	19.0	31.0	33.0	35.2
Laos	11.0	92.0	96.0	98.0	99.0	99.5	100.0	100.0	100.0
Macau	93.7	100.0	100.0	100.0	100.0	100.0	100.0	100.0	100.0
Malaysia	75.0	95.0	96.0	97.0	100.0	100.0	100.0	100.0	100.0
Maldives	100.0	100.0	100.0	100.0	100.0	100.0	100.0	100.0	100.0
Mongolia	6.0	42.2	44.8	55.0	61.5	63.9	85.0	87.7	92.1
Myanmar	18.0	46.0	55.9	61.3	62.7	64.2	76.6	77.7	82.2
Nauru									
Nepal	89.5	99.2	99.8	99.3	100.0	100.0	100.0	100.0	100.0
New Caledonia	80.0	100.0	100.0	100.0	100.0	100.0	100.0	100.0	100.0
North Korea									
Pakistan	14.4	72.9	78.0	80.0	92.6	94.0	94.0	94.0	95.1
Papua New Guinea		58.0	61.0	65.0	70.0	77.0	81.3	84.5	86.3
Philippines	7.0	70.0	85.0	92.0	89.0	99.0	99.9	99.9	100.0
Singapore	48.5	100.0	100.0	100.0	100.0	100.0	100.0	100.0	100.0
Solomon Islands		100.0	100.0	100.0	100.0	100.0	100.0	100.0	100.0
South Korea	45.0	63.4	65.2	66.7	68.2	73.9	80.9	87.5	89.2
Sri Lanka	65.0	90.8	94.7	96.9	100.0	100.0	100.0	100.0	100.0
Taiwan	24.5	91.5	97.6	99.0	100.0	100.0	100.0	100.0	100.0
Tajikistan		3.2	3.2	7.0	7.5	7.3	7.5	7.5	8.2
Thailand	67.0	86.9	89.4	100.0	100.0	100.0	100.0	100.0	100.0
Tonga	45.0								
Turkmenistan		3.0	3.0	16.6	20.4	25.0	30.2	35.3	40.1
Tuvalu									
Uzbekistan		2.8	1.6	1.1	0.2	31.6	33.8	33.3	34.2
Vanuatu		100.0	100.0	100.0	100.0	100.0	100.0	100.0	100.0
Vietnam	15.0	100.0	100.0	100.0	100.0	100.0	100.0	100.0	100.0
Western Samoa		100.0	100.0	100.0	100.0	100.0	100.0	100.0	100.0
Australasia									
Australia	24.0	62.0	74.0	84.0	95.0	100.0	100.0	100.0	100.0
New Zealand	72.0	98.8	99.0	99.0	99.9	100.0	100.0	100.0	100.0

Source: *Euromonitor from International Telecommunications Union/national statistics*

◻ Telecommunications
Availability of Digital Main Lines 1990-2002

- % of lines connected to digital exchanges

	1990	1995	1996	1997	1998	1999	2000	2001	2002
Africa and Middle East									
Algeria	22.0	33.9	45.9	51.3	57.9	70.0	92.0	97.0	98.0
Angola					65.0	81.0	91.4	97.9	100.0
Bahrain	76.0	100.0	100.0	100.0	100.0	100.0	100.0	100.0	100.0
Benin	45.0	70.0	78.3	78.0	77.6	78.7	82.2	83.0	84.2
Botswana	97.7	100.0	100.0	100.0	100.0	100.0	100.0	100.0	100.0
Burkina Faso	58.0	85.1	86.3	87.1	89.5	91.8	95.6	95.6	96.2
Burundi	80.0	99.0	78.7	88.8	89.6	91.9	93.0	93.7	94.8
Cameroon	52.0	68.0	68.3	68.0	68.0	68.0	68.0	68.5	69.3
Cape Verde	10.0	56.0	63.0	76.0	86.6	88.8	100.0	100.0	100.0
Central African Republic	97.2	97.5	97.8	97.7	98.6	96.9	97.0	97.3	97.4
Chad	10.6	17.8	100.0	100.0	100.0	100.0	100.0	100.0	100.0
Comoros									
Congo Dem Rep									
Congo-Brazzaville									
Côte d'Ivoire	63.1	84.0	90.0	90.2	93.8	100.0	100.0	100.0	100.0
Djibouti	100.0	100.0	100.0	100.0	100.0	100.0	100.0	100.0	100.0
Egypt	30.0	67.0	72.0	75.0	82.0	86.0	96.0	99.0	100.0
Equatorial Guinea									
Eritrea	42.0	54.0	55.4	71.2	73.9	74.3	77.4	78.5	79.8
Ethiopia	26.3	38.9	38.1	42.3	40.2	52.2	62.2	74.3	83.6
Gabon	97.0	96.0	96.0	97.6	97.6	97.2	97.2	97.9	99.4
Gambia		100.0	100.0	100.0	100.0	100.0	100.0	100.0	100.0
Ghana	30.0	89.5	90.9	93.8	95.0	100.0	100.0	100.0	100.0
Guinea	1.0	32.5	79.6	92.6	98.8	99.0	99.0	99.0	100.0
Guinea-Bissau	22.0	40.0	46.0	53.0	94.0	100.0	100.0	100.0	100.0
Iran	11.5	27.4	35.2	40.4	45.7	65.4	78.1	82.7	85.1
Iraq									
Israel	44.0	92.0	100.0	100.0	100.0	100.0	100.0	100.0	100.0
Jordan	62.0	70.6	74.0	85.0	93.0	93.9	100.0	100.0	100.0
Kenya	21.0	56.0	58.0	56.0	60.3	64.7	66.9	67.9	70.8
Kuwait	25.0	84.8	92.3	93.0	94.0	97.0	100.0	100.0	100.0
Lebanon	65.0	99.0	99.0	99.0	100.0	100.0	100.0	100.0	100.0
Lesotho	80.4	95.3	97.0	99.0	99.0	99.0	99.0	99.4	99.9
Liberia	29.0	29.0	29.0	29.0	29.0	29.0	29.0	29.0	29.0
Libya									
Madagascar	6.0	10.0	80.0	96.8	98.0	98.7	98.9	80.2	81.3
Malawi	29.0	54.0	55.4	57.5	64.0	65.0	92.0	92.0	94.1
Mali	70.0	83.3	84.0	88.0	93.0	98.0	98.0	100.0	100.0
Mauritania	88.0	99.0	99.0	99.0	100.0	100.0	100.0	100.0	100.0
Mauritius	100.0	100.0	100.0	100.0	100.0	100.0	100.0	100.0	100.0
Morocco	70.1	95.0	98.3	99.3	99.5	100.0	100.0	100.0	100.0
Mozambique	62.0	72.0	91.0	95.0	99.0	99.0	100.0	100.0	100.0
Namibia	29.3	76.0	89.1	93.0	98.0	100.0	100.0	100.0	100.0
Niger	53.0	74.1	57.5	73.0	76.8	79.8	83.1	79.7	81.2
Nigeria	16.5	42.5	45.0	52.1	52.2	63.6	70.6	78.8	83.5
Oman	90.1	99.0	99.0	100.0	100.0	100.0	100.0	100.0	100.0
Qatar	90.0	100.0	100.0	100.0	100.0	100.0	100.0	100.0	100.0
Réunion		100.0	100.0	100.0	100.0	100.0	100.0	100.0	100.0
Rwanda	100.0	100.0	100.0	100.0	100.0	100.0	100.0	100.0	100.0
Sao Tomé e Príncipe	68.0	94.3	98.0	99.2	99.6	100.0	100.0	100.0	100.0
Saudi Arabia	46.0	53.6	54.5	55.5	63.6	93.0	100.0	100.0	100.0
Senegal	59.0	93.2	94.0	100.0	100.0	100.0	100.0	100.0	100.0
Seychelles	65.0	100.0	100.0	100.0	100.0	100.0	100.0	100.0	100.0
Sierra Leone	40.0	85.9	88.0	88.3	88.9	90.0	90.9	89.0	92.2
Somalia									
South Africa	47.6	70.0	74.0	82.0	92.5	99.0	99.6	99.8	100.0
Sudan	2.5	25.0	50.0	89.0	90.0	95.0	100.0	100.0	100.0
Swaziland	8.9	96.0	95.0	99.0	100.0	100.0	100.0	100.0	100.0
Syria	32.0	71.0	77.0	82.0	87.0	87.0	99.0	99.0	100.0
Tanzania	8.8	42.8	64.7	72.5	82.3	91.0	95.0	96.0	98.5
Togo	98.0	99.0	100.0	100.0	100.0	100.0	100.0	100.0	100.0
Tunisia	66.0	80.8	86.0	90.2	99.7	100.0	100.0	100.0	100.0
Uganda	58.0	64.2	75.2	75.6	90.6	90.9	91.3	91.8	92.9
United Arab Emirates	100.0	100.0	100.0	100.0	100.0	100.0	100.0	100.0	100.0
Yemen	60.0	92.8	95.7	100.0	100.0	100.0	100.0	100.0	100.0
Zambia	39.3	70.9	70.9	70.9	73.1	75.7	75.8	80.0	82.7
Zimbabwe	0.5	44.0	48.0	50.0	55.0	60.5	90.0	96.7	100.0

Source: Euromonitor from International Telecommunications Union/national statistics

▨ Telecommunications

Table 18.5

Capital Investment in Telecommunications 1990-2002

● Million units of national currency/as stated

	1990	1995	1996	1997	1998	1999	2000	2001	2002	US$ million 2002
North America										
Canada	4,277	3,598	4,111	5,770	6,449	5,982	6,002	7,721	6,588	4,198.3
USA	20,600	24,000	22,000	23,000	24,000	26,000	29,000	30,000	34,605	34,604.6
Latin America										
Anguilla										
Antigua										
Argentina	300	2,061	1,710	1,347	1,456	1,733	1,904	869	1,025	334.6
Aruba										
Bahamas	19	16	18	18	19	20	20	21	22	22.3
Barbados	50	76	58	51	51	56	54	54	60	30.0
Belize	13	16	12	20	24	35	15	22	28	14.1
Bermuda										
Bolivia	73	44	800	718	604	374	813	1,069	1,089	151.9
Brazil	0	4,043	6,834	7,471	12,300	12,000	16,200	15,400	14,766	5,055.4
British Virgin Islands										
Cayman Islands										
Chile	122,610	259,350	337,830	388,480	481,000	512,000	590,000	626,000	657,669	954.6
Colombia	106,000	563,000	598,000	1,866,000	1,605,000	2,031,000	2,269,696	3,519,000	3,967,461	1,584.3
Costa Rica	3,040	18,416	24,009	28,500	34,300	41,650	48,014	76,647	80,446	223.6
Cuba	58	22	33	94	74	100	107	144	157	14.5
Dominica										
Dominican Republic										
Ecuador	35,700	231,660	322,000	347,230	385,207	525,000	295,753	356,644	467,631	18.7
El Salvador	272	635	688	757	4,176	6,220	7,670	1,427	2,481	283.6
French Guiana										
Grenada	50									
Guadeloupe										
Guatemala	50									
Guyana	556	775	10,534	7,633	9,994	8,959	9,437	9,875	9,345	49.0
Haiti										
Honduras	290	2,036	1,348	2,326	863	1,509	1,204	401	648	39.4
Jamaica	992	5,235	5,350	4,741	4,793	5,357	6,584	6,319	6,819	140.8
Martinique										
Mexico	3,927	9,575	13,527	15,101	28,897	37,909	48,078	59,680	71,191	7,372.8
Netherlands Antilles										
Nicaragua	1	276	343	187	7	15	18	21	23	1.6
Panama	13	44	49	53	57	61	64	67	70	69.7
Paraguay	31	127	147	179	195	258	297	335	250	0.0
Peru	11	1,331	1,823	1,875	2,165	1,453	1,097	612	636	181.0
Puerto Rico	263	378	384	355	369	387	401	413	423	423.3
St Kitts										
St Lucia										
St Vincent and the Grenadines										
Suriname	22	5,386	5,804	6,972	4,508	13,639	25,114	44,000	58,945	25.1
Trinidad and Tobago	19	217	193	215	439	435	601	686	734	117.5
Uruguay	56	761	1,136	1,097	1,020	1,439	1,267	1,134	1,248	58.7
Venezuela	4,570	88,000	178,000	389,000	613,000	615,000	692,000	669	606	0.5

Source: *Euromonitor from International Telecommunications Union/national statistics*

Telecommunications

Capital Investment in Telecommunications 1990-2002

• Million units of national currency/as stated

	1990	1995	1996	1997	1998	1999	2000	2001	2002	US$ million 2002
Asia Pacific										
Afghanistan										
American Samoa										
Armenia	15	777	12,714	11,490	13,089	14,325	31,399	10,070	12,546	21.9
Azerbaijan		6,059	18,183	36,892	52,640	77,306	103,000	124,700	124,920	25.7
Bangladesh	1,115	4,457	2,826	2,039	1,619	2,644	4,677	3,904	4,159	71.8
Bhutan								198	215	4.4
Brunei										
Cambodia										
China	5,980	99,520	91,082	105,595	150,074	160,522	222,381	264,183	272,124	32,877.3
Fiji	16	23	34	39	22	22	22	23	24	11.0
French Polynesia	1,150	2,532	914	1,122	1,330	1,538	2,661	4,214	3,945	29.6
Guam										
Hong Kong, China	3,018	8,956	15,160	14,503	13,954	8,711	7,008	7,174	7,108	911.5
India	27,722	82,153	84,155	86,461	94,503	125,330	157,840	165,710	191,233	3,934.0
Indonesia	1,059,000	3,712,000	4,909,000	4,368,000	4,892,000	2,072,000	2,253,000	17,477,000	24,765,982	2,659.8
Japan	2,266,400	3,303,000	4,112,000	3,965,000	3,710,000	3,398,000	3,522,000	2,992,000	2,808,791	22,400.8
Kazakhstan		10,080	6,698	1,572	3,135	7,113	10,248	13,689	16,896	110.2
Kiribati										
Kyrgyzstan		17	153	311	31	104	106	83	93	2.0
Laos	4,550	4,932	17,972	12,000	25,000	42,049	63,739	91,093	75,153	7.5
Macau	169	287	293	247	290	204	220	412	476	57.1
Malaysia	802	4,313	3,352	5,419	5,123	41,143	4,096	4,485	4,010	1,055.4
Maldives		110	176	173	131	100	135	88	115	8.9
Mongolia	81	1,532	11,035	13,834	2,840	1,086	2,410	2,724	3,120	2.8
Myanmar	110	1,615	2,179	3,441	2,583	2,625	1,421	2,633	3,042	462.8
Nauru										
Nepal	1,206	879	1,703	1,163	1,475	1,384	1,325	1,563	1,618	20.8
New Caledonia	2,250	2,154	2,386	2,262	2,807	3,918	4,272	4,732	4,159	31.2
North Korea										
Pakistan	2,993	13,007	13,956	12,009	11,530	11,212	13,458	8,657	8,554	143.2
Papua New Guinea	24									
Philippines	9,000	29,700	44,000	50,500	46,600	37,100	43,260	42,276	47,328	917.1
Singapore	454	618	513	1,116	868	787	800	663	689	384.8
Solomon Islands	3	12	10	18	25	114	112	116	124	18.4
South Korea	2,100,000	3,370,000	4,698,000	7,702,000	6,277,000	8,367,000	8,783,000	8,574,000	8,984,807	7,181.6
Sri Lanka	592	1,236	3,432	8,988	13,393	15,311	8,691	4,461	4,815	50.3
Taiwan	41,594	43,048	49,176	48,880	76,972	104,195	116,000	113,859	126,981	3,673.2
Tajikistan		20	79	107	324	246	127	2	15	5.5
Thailand	9,802	33,924	47,851	61,655	26,862	30,829	34,967	57,550	67,691	1,575.7
Tonga										
Turkmenistan	16	315	43,870	70,950	34,150	23,027	21,686	19,908	21,518	3.4
Tuvalu										
Uzbekistan		406	4,315	8,405	8,803	6,507	13,535	17,158	20,184	
Vanuatu										
Vietnam				4,000,000	4,500,000	4,500,000	4,657,657	4,810,084	5,045,911	330.2
Western Samoa		3	3	3	3	3	3	3	4	1.0
Australasia										
Australia	2,964	3,805	4,775	5,014	3,824	5,320	6,311	9,000	7,746	4,208.8
New Zealand	749	569	696	587	564	589	643	833	1,004	464.1

Source: Euromonitor from International Telecommunications Union/national statistics

■ Telecommunications

Capital Investment in Telecommunications 1990-2002

● Million units of national currency/as stated

	1990	1995	1996	1997	1998	1999	2000	2001	2002	US$ million 2002
Africa and Middle East										
Algeria	1,943	3,692	7,035	5,692	8,594	7,620	7,373	7,449	8,943	112.2
Angola										
Bahrain	21	18	23	20	27	33	32	43	37	99.7
Benin	423	8,637	5,761	6,250	13,990	19,652	20,989	19,370	21,064	30.2
Botswana	52	49	69	134	174	220	132	145	210	33.2
Burkina Faso	3,765	5,933	10,800	14,848	9,034	9,654	9,839	10,652	10,549	15.1
Burundi	1,336	584	1,026	203	1,050	6,007	17,157	24,950	25,184	27.1
Cameroon	14,339	16,500	18,000	20,800	26,400	28,659	30,493	32,079	31,549	45.3
Cape Verde	180	364	1,281	1,490	1,131	1,620	1,572	1,430	1,527	13.0
Central African Republic		585	43	1,668	49	60	90	68	72	0.1
Chad	1,819	4,228	7,000	1,106	1,185	1,264	1,320	1,397	1,543	2.2
Comoros										
Congo Dem Rep										
Congo-Brazzaville										
Côte d'Ivoire	18,550	22,042	28,518	29,783	35,256	92,832	61,200	82,732	83,713	120.1
Djibouti	1,726	752	384	371	375	382	382	386	397	2.2
Egypt	465	1,076	1,148	1,220	1,292	2,424	1,781	2,412	2,396	532.4
Equatorial Guinea										
Eritrea		20	87	92	130	73	219	15	34	
Ethiopia	37	47	77	159	134	237	272	292	307	35.9
Gabon	12	20,472	14,665	22,886	11,816	12,142	14,198	12,968	12,534	18.0
Gambia	70	90	27	43	132	170	81	104	122	6.1
Ghana	2,018	7,723	11,987	84,648	55,448	231,630	248,614	269,236	345,981	43.6
Guinea		34,266	40,127	41,547	32,328	12,212	8,618	1,603	1,501	0.8
Guinea-Bissau				1,347	1,683	1,978	2,544	3,508	4,120	5.9
Iran	98,169	128,888	104,879	153,032	115,500	149,551	399,000	412,598	210,598	30.5
Iraq										
Israel	763	1,658	3,150	2,983	3,975	2,175	1,726	1,864	1,344	283.7
Jordan	1	9	35	68	104	88	154	188	143	202.1
Kenya	1,781	2,831	4,121	4,163	4,584	4,487	3,960	3,976	4,018	51.0
Kuwait		14	76	13	58	1	1	1	1	3.5
Lebanon										
Lesotho	8	21	13	9	5	8	8	8	8	0.8
Liberia		2	2	3	4	4	5	6	5	0.1
Libya										
Madagascar	7,999	75,933	158,027	142,125	326,485	180,861	75,595	55,086	78,167	11.4
Malawi	34									
Mali	2,420	8,949	15,086	25,050	13,569	9,997	11,924	13,000	12,498	17.9
Mauritania	364	1,608	2,392	1,926	1,049	858	804	772	814	3.0
Mauritius	624	885	1,376	816	1,034	1,249	1,430	1,932	1,834	61.2
Morocco	2,024	2,668	1,723	1,362	1,264	2,326	2,350	2,242	2,242	203.5
Mozambique	18,440	200,000	284,000	486,000	234,000	447,000	839,000	982,000	1,024,681	43.3
Namibia		158	178	225	271	128	250	335	371	35.2
Niger	962	1,228	1,501	1,740	1,978	2,100	2,185	2,253	2,315	3.3
Nigeria	356	4,227	5,557	6,083	14,039	18,625	13,445	20,045	22,877	189.7
Oman	8	16	30	22	26	30	34	38	42	109.7
Qatar		79	93	161	228	166	135	191	186	51.1
Réunion										
Rwanda										
Sao Tomé e Príncipe										
Saudi Arabia	524	374	1,520	3,481	6,481	8,316	5,742	5,230	5,179	1,382.8
Senegal	7,190	16,960	27,960	21,365	40,335	56,530	56,009	48,629	52,165	74.8
Seychelles	41	46	43	24	33	38	24	34	37	6.8
Sierra Leone	17	4,467	7,972	11,291	16,657	21,522	24,584	27,476	31,932	15.2
Somalia										
South Africa	1,515	3,209	3,681	7,031	16,800	11,900	12,100	12,000	9,313	883.5
Sudan		27,958	96,567	111,960	172,213	238,971	279,074	310,598		1,179.6
Swaziland	13	31	42	65	79	79	107	133	141	13.3
Syria	198	3,200	3,564	4,099	4,545	6,465	10,377	8,190	10,338	921.0
Tanzania	2,172	2,856	116,533	117,945	169,317	140,353	17,459	8,269	8,336	8.6
Togo	2,167	2,900	7,300	10,500	10,437	7,441	12,533	16,591	1,702	2.4
Tunisia	40	128	193	154	178	124	218	306	340	239.3
Uganda	3,017	22,430	30,432	26,608	22,300	80,300	88,554	95,476	98,913	55.0
United Arab Emirates	516	593	875	1,280	2,073	2,302	2,003	1,842	2,032	553.3
Yemen	179	1,656	2,350	2,650	7,029	6,117	7,734	8,222	8,519	48.5
Zambia	817	9,079	13,613	17,600	20,150	11,064	24,600	17,448	19,048	4.3
Zimbabwe	86	384	1,317	1,575	2,205	3,600	5,238	4,815	5,239	95.2

Source: *Euromonitor from International Telecommunications Union/national statistics*

Facsimile Machines in Use 1990-2002

● Number

	1990	1995	1996	1997	1998	1999	2000	2001	2002
North America									
Canada	300,000	700,000	800,000	1,000,000	1,075,000	1,128,750	1,178,650	1,223,014	1,255,362
USA	5,084,000	17,000,000	19,000,000	21,000,000	23,773,200	26,150,520	28,459,600	31,077,513	33,547,865
Latin America									
Anguilla									
Antigua	350								
Argentina	15,000	50,000	60,000	75,000	87,000	94,000	101,000	104,551	112,512
Aruba	1,300								
Bahamas	522								
Barbados	1,300	1,781	1,910	2,005	2,102	2,317	2,482	2,639	2,790
Belize	214								
Bermuda									
Bolivia									
Brazil	90,000	270,000	350,000	500,000	522,000	549,000	577,000	609,854	647,266
British Virgin Islands									
Cayman Islands									
Chile	5,700	25,000	32,000	40,000	45,100	49,500	54,113	58,996	64,077
Colombia	35,000	100,000	141,000	173,000	203,000	242,000	271,258	302,755	335,217
Costa Rica	1,707	6,000	7,500	8,500	9,250	10,000	10,700	11,379	12,245
Cuba	207								
Dominica									
Dominican Republic									
Ecuador	15,000	38,000	41,000	45,000	48,700	51,560	53,900	56,172	58,332
El Salvador	3,500								
French Guiana	185								
Grenada									
Guadeloupe	291								
Guatemala	1,000								
Guyana	195								
Haiti									
Honduras									
Jamaica									
Martinique	690								
Mexico	60,000	220,000	250,000	285,000	280,000	280,000	288,000	294,668	300,241
Netherlands Antilles									
Nicaragua									
Panama									
Paraguay	1,189								
Peru	1,814	15,000	21,000	26,000	31,600	37,500	44,000	49,507	55,209
Puerto Rico									
St Kitts									
St Lucia	122								
St Vincent and the Grenadines	148								
Suriname	200	700	800	900	990	1,074	1,155	1,228	1,297
Trinidad and Tobago	1,806	2,023	2,100	2,400	5,024	5,526	6,599	7,678	8,464
Uruguay	5,500	11,000	12,500	13,850	14,750	15,250	15,750	16,162	16,488
Venezuela	9,700	35,000	50,000	70,000	77,500	85,000	93,000	102,641	111,514

Source: *Euromonitor from International Telecommunications Union/national statistics*

■ Telecommunications

Facsimile Machines in Use 1990-2002

• Number

	1990	1995	1996	1997	1998	1999	2000	2001	2002
Asia Pacific									
Afghanistan									
American Samoa									
Armenia	120	350	350	380	410	1,000	1,150	1,377	1,506
Azerbaijan									
Bangladesh	1,160	4,000	5,000	5,500	5,760	5,890	6,020	6,141	6,228
Bhutan	110	700	1,000	1,000	1,500	1,650	1,790	1,912	2,011
Brunei	1,145	2,000	2,400	2,650	2,820	2,980	3,120	3,305	3,408
Cambodia	175	884	1,470	2,995	3,850	4,500	5,000	5,384	5,615
China	39,000	270,000	1,500,000	2,000,000	2,326,800	2,500,000	2,621,500	2,731,224	2,836,422
Fiji	1,513	3,000	3,500	3,800	3,381	2,815	2,453	2,186	1,992
French Polynesia	800	1,993	2,280	2,974	3,000	3,239	3,653	4,051	4,360
Guam									
Hong Kong, China	111,000	285,000	314,000	346,000	363,000	390,000	406,249	407,334	408,959
India	5,000	70,000	100,000	150,000	161,000	172,000	183,000	212,966	230,423
Indonesia	15,000	85,000	125,000	185,000	204,000	224,400	246,000	275,165	313,590
Japan	6,800,000	12,800,000	14,300,000	16,000,000	17,500,000	18,600,000	19,669,000	20,911,884	21,898,191
Kazakhstan	950	2,917	2,646	1,620	1,636	2,045	2,354	2,674	2,992
Kiribati	38								
Kyrgyzstan									
Laos	120	800	1,000	1,250	1,600	1,900	2,194	2,490	2,744
Macau	3,548	7,301	7,380	7,313	6,751	6,290	5,983	5,585	5,465
Malaysia	40,000	100,000	125,000	150,000	175,000	200,000	225,000	250,680	275,226
Maldives	235	3,500	3,850	4,100	4,300	4,450	4,627	4,870	5,255
Mongolia		2,150	5,300	3,630	5,381	7,963	10,540	11,316	12,500
Myanmar	159	1,339	1,599	2,029	2,278	2,540	2,881	3,355	3,960
Nauru	140								
Nepal	500	1,100	2,000	3,500	5,000	8,000	8,900	11,000	11,509
New Caledonia	1,000	2,600	2,950	3,200	3,420	3,690	3,982	4,307	4,636
North Korea									
Pakistan	2,300	159,000	180,000	206,000	268,000	300,000	341,000	404,985	456,284
Papua New Guinea	629								
Philippines	10,000	50,000	64,000	71,000	83,300	90,000	105,600	119,142	131,993
Singapore	33,269	70,000	80,000	90,000	100,000	110,000	121,000	132,851	145,228
Solomon Islands	126	789	859	938	748	764	803	841	888
South Korea	230,000	400,000	650,000	800,000	867,500	900,000	943,600	1,003,894	1,038,177
Sri Lanka	4,000	13,200	15,700	16,500	18,300	19,500	20,770	22,214	23,857
Taiwan	210,000	585,000	720,000	955,000	1,088,000	1,196,800	1,295,300	1,394,152	1,476,920
Tajikistan	400	1,300	1,500	1,800	2,000	2,100	2,200	2,340	2,524
Thailand	6,324	100,000	125,000	150,000	175,000	200,000	225,400	256,324	283,271
Tonga	83	231	289	350	374	395	412	428	442
Turkmenistan									
Tuvalu	4								
Uzbekistan	167	1,037	1,342	1,658	1,799	2,245	2,720	3,325	3,615
Vanuatu									
Vietnam	500	14,900	19,800	23,500	27,900	31,000	34,000	37,000	40,746
Western Samoa	120	430	450	490	520	550	574	594	621
Australasia									
Australia	280,000	700,000	800,000	900,000	1,000,000	1,100,000	1,198,000	1,290,145	1,359,748
New Zealand	28,000	65,000	72,000	78,000	88,400	97,240	110,240	126,761	140,788

Source: Euromonitor from International Telecommunications Union/national statistics

◻ Telecommunications

Facsimile Machines in Use 1990-2002

• Number

	1990	1995	1996	1997	1998	1999	2000	2001	2002
Africa and Middle East									
Algeria	1,600	5,200	6,200	7,000	7,933	8,726	9,190	9,525	9,706
Angola									
Bahrain	2,800	6,299	6,341	6,620	6,687	6,928	4,797	4,614	4,405
Benin	144	800	1,064	1,290	1,520	1,685	1,823	1,945	2,026
Botswana	820	3,149	3,413	3,529	3,650	3,760	3,886	4,029	4,199
Burkina Faso									
Burundi	600	3,000	4,000	4,700	4,990	5,200	5,420	5,656	5,913
Cameroon									
Cape Verde	250	500	1,000	1,250	1,450	1,620	1,762	1,875	1,954
Central African Republic	30	136	222	281	316	316	318	322	323
Chad	72	174	175	185	192	182	186	193	202
Comoros	27								
Congo Dem Rep									
Congo-Brazzaville	110								
Côte d'Ivoire									
Djibouti	101	94	70	345	379	69	66	68	72
Egypt	7,620	27,332	31,394	30,720	33,068	34,194	35,199	35,955	37,261
Equatorial Guinea									
Eritrea	110	777	1,101	1,388	1,615	1,660	1,771	1,943	2,167
Ethiopia	245	1,445	1,604	2,012	2,502	3,090	3,594	4,217	4,860
Gabon	191	360	503	501	533	548	552	574	582
Gambia	190	1,030	1,096	1,149	1,185	1,200	1,214	1,225	1,233
Ghana	1,921	5,000	5,500	5,850	6,120	6,300	6,444	6,579	6,694
Guinea	800	900	1,000	2,018	2,812	3,186	3,578	3,998	4,578
Guinea-Bissau	250	500	500	480	500	550	550	600	625
Iran	13,000	33,000	35,600	38,900	42,000	43,500	45,000	46,413	48,260
Iraq	35,000	142,000	145,000	147,000	148,000	150,000	152,000	153,591	154,539
Israel	35,000	140,000	190,000	250,000	280,000	310,000	339,000	364,879	387,926
Jordan	24,000	32,000	35,000	42,067	51,604	56,764	62,571	69,964	83,442
Kenya	2,000	3,800	4,100	4,350	4,595	4,785	4,969	5,131	5,234
Kuwait	12,000	35,000	40,000	42,000	50,000	60,000	69,000	77,843	86,130
Lebanon	1,700								
Lesotho	250	569	635	695	745	789	824	853	875
Liberia									
Libya									
Madagascar	306								
Malawi	342	1,086	1,192	1,250	1,271	1,299	1,326	1,352	1,387
Mali									
Mauritania	300	302	2,700	2,200	2,600	3,300	4,000	4,763	5,158
Mauritius	800	20,000	25,000	28,000	30,000	32,000	34,000	36,057	38,124
Morocco	1,600	13,000	15,000	18,000	20,500	22,550	24,500	27,134	29,167
Mozambique	840	8,300	9,100	9,600	10,200	10,500	10,900	11,428	11,714
Namibia									
Niger	150	327	345	360	370	380	388	395	401
Nigeria	6,845	7,658	7,956	8,566	8,787	9,094	9,407	9,750	10,168
Oman	1,380	2,889	5,778	6,356	6,991	7,550	8,172	8,902	9,734
Qatar	950	9,400	10,400	11,300	12,000	12,600	13,100	13,499	13,811
Réunion									
Rwanda	300								
Sao Tomé e Príncipe		163	195	210	236	258	279	299	316
Saudi Arabia	27,000	150,000	215,000	284,000	324,700	360,000	405,250	473,112	539,808
Senegal									
Seychelles	275	600	650	684	572	581	605	610	617
Sierra Leone	35	1,000	1,700	1,900	2,500	3,000	3,500	4,007	4,452
Somalia									
South Africa	30,000	100,000	125,000	150,000	171,000	188,100	209,400	236,203	270,899
Sudan	245	5,800	7,000	12,000	18,000	25,000	31,400	38,013	44,538
Swaziland	341	1,100	1,201	1,300	1,400	1,490	1,572	1,640	1,703
Syria	200	5,000	21,000	21,000	21,000	22,000	22,954	23,896	25,421
Tanzania	600								
Togo	335	10,000	16,000	17,000	18,000	18,500	18,900	19,240	19,483
Tunisia	2,500	25,000	28,000	31,000	35,800	40,000	44,900	50,935	58,149
Uganda	698	2,500	3,000	3,500	3,900	4,250	4,595	4,941	5,255
United Arab Emirates	15,562	24,978	22,912	21,095	19,816	18,320	17,105	16,225	15,748
Yemen	778	2,784	3,480	4,106	4,619	5,034	5,455	5,871	6,271
Zambia	460	600	650	855	1,005	1,020	1,050	1,089	1,184
Zimbabwe	1,487	4,100	4,510	4,850	5,200	5,460	5,750	6,136	6,623

Source: Euromonitor from International Telecommunications Union/national statistics

Mobile Telephone Users 1990-2002

● '000

	1990	1995	1996	1997	1998	1999	2000	2001	2002
North America									
Canada	584.0	2,590.0	3,498	4,266.0	5,365.0	6,911.0	8,751.0	10,862.0	13,503.4
USA	5,283.0	33,786.0	44,043	55,312.0	69,209.0	86,047.0	109,478.0	128,375.0	154,889.1
Latin America									
Anguilla		0.2	00	0.7	0.8	1.5	2.2	2.6	3.1
Antigua			01	1.4	1.5	8.5	22.0	36.0	53.8
Argentina	12.0	340.7	568	1,588.0	2,530.0	4,434.0	6,050.0	6,975.0	8,040.9
Aruba		1.7	03	3.4	5.4	12.0	15.0	17.9	20.6
Bahamas	1.9	4.1	05	6.2	8.1	15.9	31.5	55.6	82.5
Barbados		4.6	06	8.0	12.0	20.3	28.5	53.1	89.9
Belize		1.5	02	2.5	3.5	6.6	16.8	38.2	45.1
Bermuda	1.1	6.3	08	10.2	12.6	15.0	18.2	21.1	25.1
Bolivia		10.0	20	118.4	239.3	420.3	582.6	779.9	1,064.7
Brazil	1.0	1,286.0	2,498	4,550.0	7,368.0	15,033.0	23,188.0	28,746.0	38,071.1
British Virgin Islands		1.1	01	1.3	1.3	1.4	1.5	1.6	1.7
Cayman Islands		2.5	03	4.1	5.2	8.4	10.7	12.9	15.2
Chile	13.9	197.3	319	409.7	964.2	2,260.7	3,401.5	5,271.6	6,554.0
Colombia	3.4	275.0	523	1,265.0	1,800.0	1,967.0	2,257.0	3,265.0	4,550.8
Costa Rica		18.8	47	64.4	108.8	138.7	209.1	311.3	410.6
Cuba		1.9	02	3.0	4.1	5.1	6.5	8.1	9.5
Dominica			00	0.6	0.7	0.8	1.2	1.6	2.0
Dominican Republic	3.2	56.0	83	141.6	209.4	424.4	705.4	914.6	1,246.0
Ecuador		54.4	60	126.5	242.8	383.2	482.2	859.2	1,085.2
El Salvador		13.5	23	40.2	137.1	511.4	743.6	857.8	1,059.5
French Guiana					4.0	18.0	39.8	63.6	74.7
Grenada	0.1	0.4	01	1.0	1.4	2.0	4.3	8.0	10.6
Guadeloupe					14.2	88.1	0.2	0.2	0.2
Guatemala	0.3	30.0	43	64.2	111.4	337.8	843.1	1,134.0	1,549.0
Guyana		1.2	01	1.4	1.5	2.8	39.8	753.5	95.4
Haiti					10.0	25.0	67.0	131.6	225.9
Honduras			02	14.4	34.9	78.6	155.3	237.6	345.0
Jamaica	2.0	45.1	55	66.0	78.6	144.4	367.0	635.0	761.1
Martinique				15.0	55.0	102.0	162.1	214.7	249.4
Mexico	64.0	689.0	1,022	1,741.0	3,349.0	7,732.0	14,078.0	21,757.0	28,432.0
Netherlands Antilles	1.4	11.7	14	14.5	16.0	23.1	29.6	35.2	40.2
Nicaragua		4.4	05	7.9	18.3	44.2	90.3	154.5	193.7
Panama		3.2	07	18.5	85.9	232.9	410.4	475.4	541.3
Paraguay		15.8	33	84.2	231.5	435.6	820.8	1,150.0	1,260.5
Peru	1.7	73.5	201	421.8	742.6	1,013.3	1,273.9	1,545.0	2,224.5
Puerto Rico	20.4	171.2	169	367.0	580.0	814.0	926.0	1,211.0	1,334.1
St Kitts			00	0.2	0.4	0.7	1.2	1.8	2.7
St Lucia		1.0	01	1.6	1.9	2.3	2.5	2.7	2.9
St Vincent and the Grenadines		0.2	00	0.3	0.8	1.4	2.4	3.7	5.3
Suriname	0.5	1.7	02	2.3	6.0	17.5	41.0	87.0	138.5
Trinidad and Tobago		6.4	10	17.1	26.3	38.7	133.2	256.1	408.1
Uruguay		39.9	80	99.3	154.5	316.1	440.2	520.0	571.6
Venezuela	7.4	404.0	582	1,072.0	2,010.0	3,785.0	5,256.0	6,490.0	7,062.3

Source: *International Telecommunications Union/World Bank/Trade Sources/Euromonitor*

◘ Telecommunications

Mobile Telephone Users 1990-2002

● '000

	1990	1995	1996	1997	1998	1999	2000	2001	2002
Asia Pacific									
Afghanistan									
American Samoa		2.0	03	2.6	2.6	2.4	2.6	2.7	2.8
Armenia			00	5.0	7.8	8.2	17.5	25.5	34.2
Azerbaijan		6.0	17	40.0	65.0	370.0	430.0	621.0	657.8
Bangladesh		2.5	04	26.0	75.0	149.0	279.0	520.0	671.6
Bhutan									
Brunei	1.8	35.9	44	45.0	49.1	66.0	95.0	137.0	138.5
Cambodia		14.1	23	33.6	61.3	89.1	130.5	223.5	278.2
China	18.0	3,629.0	6,853	13,233.0	23,863.0	43,296.0	85,260.0	144,820.0	228,406.5
Fiji		2.2	04	5.2	8.0	23.4	55.0	80.9	100.0
French Polynesia		1.2	03	5.4	11.1	21.9	39.9	67.3	81.4
Guam		5.0	06	5.7	12.8	20.0	27.2	32.6	36.4
Hong Kong, China	134.0	798.0	1,362	2,230.0	3,174.0	4,275.0	5,447.0	5,776.0	5,940.2
India	5.4	77.0	328	882.0	1,195.0	1,884.0	3,577.0	6,432.0	20,783.0
Indonesia	18.1	210.6	563	916.2	1,065.8	2,221.0	3,669.0	6,521.0	11,046.4
Japan	868.0	11,712.0	26,907	38,254.0	47,308.0	56,846.0	66,784.0	74,819.0	85,555.3
Kazakhstan		4.6	10	11.2	29.7	49.5	197.3	582.0	1,134.2
Kiribati					0.0	0.2	0.4	0.6	1.0
Kyrgyzstan					1.4	2.6	9.0	27.0	38.1
Laos		1.5	04	4.9	6.5	12.1	12.7	29.5	42.4
Macau	2.2	35.9	45	50.6	82.1	118.1	132.0	194.5	209.3
Malaysia	87.0	1,005.0	1,520	2,000.0	2,200.0	2,990.0	4,961.0	7,477.0	8,690.1
Maldives			00	1.3	1.6	2.9	7.6	18.9	25.2
Mongolia		0.6	01	2.0	9.0	34.6	154.6	195.0	320.6
Myanmar		2.8	07	8.5	8.5	11.4	13.4	13.8	14.2
Nauru		0.5	01	0.8	0.8	1.0	1.2	1.4	1.6
Nepal						5.5	10.2	17.3	22.7
New Caledonia		0.8	02	5.2	13.0	25.4	49.9	67.9	96.4
North Korea									
Pakistan	2.0	43.0	65	110.0	206.9	278.8	349.5	812.0	1,202.6
Papua New Guinea			02	3.9	5.6	7.1	8.6	10.7	12.5
Philippines	25.7	493.9	959	1,343.6	1,733.7	2,850.0	6,454.0	11,700.0	17,333.0
Singapore	51.7	306.0	431	848.6	1,095.0	1,631.0	2,747.0	2,992.0	3,077.1
Solomon Islands		0.2	00	0.7	0.7	1.1	1.2	1.0	1.0
South Korea	80.0	1,641.3	3,181	6,879.0	14,019.0	23,443.0	26,816.0	29,046.0	31,591.8
Sri Lanka	1.0	53.1	71	114.9	174.2	227.9	276.6	667.7	756.5
Taiwan	83.0	772.0	970	1,492.0	4,727.0	11,541.0	17,874.0	21,706.0	21,955.3
Tajikistan			00	0.3	0.4	0.6	1.2	1.6	2.4
Thailand	63.0	1,298.0	1,845	2,204.0	1,977.0	2,339.0	3,056.0	7,550.0	8,918.0
Tonga		0.3	00	0.1	0.1	0.1	0.1	0.2	0.2
Turkmenistan		1.5	02	2.5	3.0	4.0	9.5	8.1	10.9
Tuvalu									
Uzbekistan		3.7	10	17.2	26.8	40.4	53.1	62.8	74.5
Vanuatu		0.1	00	0.2	0.2	0.3	0.4	0.4	0.5
Vietnam		23.5	69	160.5	222.7	328.7	788.6	1,251.0	1,820.8
Western Samoa		2.0	25	2.6	2.6	2.9	3.1	3.4	3.6
Australasia									
Australia	185.0	2,242.0	3,990	4,578.0	4,918.0	6,315.0	8,562.0	11,169.0	13,396.8
New Zealand	54.1	365.0	493	566.0	790.0	1,395.0	1,542.0	2,288.0	2,610.8

Source: *International Telecommunications Union/World Bank/Trade Sources/Euromonitor*

◪ Telecommunications

Mobile Telephone Users 1990-2002

● '000

	1990	1995	1996	1997	1998	1999	2000	2001	2002
Africa and Middle East									
Algeria	0.5	4.7	12	17.4	18.0	72.0	86.0	100.0	300.4
Angola		2.0	03	7.1	9.8	24.0	25.8	86.5	121.0
Bahrain	5.1	27.6	40	58.5	92.1	133.5	205.7	299.6	460.5
Benin		1.1	03	4.3	6.3	7.3	55.5	125.0	173.1
Botswana		4.2	07	15.6	15.2	92.0	200.0	316.0	351.0
Burkina Faso			01	1.5	2.7	5.0	25.2	75.0	87.2
Burundi		0.6	01	0.6	0.6	0.8	16.3	30.7	41.8
Cameroon		2.8	04	4.2	5.0	6.0	148.0	310.0	475.0
Cape Verde				0.0	1.0	8.1	19.7	31.5	47.5
Central African Republic		0.0	01	1.4	1.6	4.2	11.0	6.8	8.2
Chad							6.0	22.0	27.2
Comoros									
Congo Dem Rep		8.5	07	8.9	10.0	12.0	15.0	127.9	26.5
Congo-Brazzaville			01	1.8	3.4	5.3	7.4	10.0	13.1
Côte d'Ivoire			14	36.0	91.2	257.1	450.0	728.5	994.0
Djibouti			00	0.2	0.2	0.3	0.2	3.0	4.5
Egypt	4.0	7.4	07	65.4	90.8	481.0	1,359.9	2,793.8	5,801.5
Equatorial Guinea			00	0.3	0.3	0.3	0.3	0.4	0.4
Eritrea									
Ethiopia						6.7	17.8	27.5	41.1
Gabon		4.0	07	9.5	9.7	8.9	120.0	207.8	215.3
Gambia		1.4	03	4.7	5.0	5.3	5.6	55.1	68.0
Ghana		6.2	13	21.9	41.8	70.0	130.0	193.8	324.6
Guinea		1.0	01	2.9	21.6	25.2	42.1	55.7	74.0
Guinea-Bissau									
Iran	2.7	15.9	60	238.9	390.0	490.5	962.6	2,087.0	3,211.4
Iraq									
Israel	15.0	445.0	1,048	1,672.0	2,147.0	2,880.0	4,400.0	5,900.0	6,110.6
Jordan	1.4	12.4	16	45.0	82.4	118.4	388.9	866.0	1,271.6
Kenya	0.5	2.3	03	6.8	10.8	23.8	127.4	600.0	780.2
Kuwait	20.7	118.0	151	210.0	250.0	300.0	476.0	878.0	1,212.1
Lebanon	20.0	120.0	200	425.0	500.0	627.0	743.0	800.0	932.0
Lesotho		0.6	01	3.5	9.8	15.7	21.6	57.0	80.2
Liberia									
Libya				10.0	20.0	30.0	40.0	50.0	60.0
Madagascar		1.3	02	4.1	12.8	35.8	63.1	147.5	177.6
Malawi		0.4	04	7.0	10.5	22.5	49.0	55.7	68.2
Mali		0.8	01	2.8	4.5	6.4	10.4	45.3	60.2
Mauritania									
Mauritius	2.2	11.7	21	37.0	60.5	102.1	180.0	272.4	402.1
Morocco	0.9	30.0	43	74.0	117.0	369.0	2,342.0	4,772.0	7,370.5
Mozambique		1.3	02	2.5	6.7	12.2	51.1	152.7	195.5
Namibia		3.5	07	12.5	19.5	30.0	82.0	100.0	115.1
Niger				0.1	1.3	2.2	2.1	2.1	2.6
Nigeria	2.4	13.0	14	15.0	20.0	25.0	30.0	500.0	1,772.4
Oman	2.7	8.1	13	59.8	103.0	124.1	164.3	324.5	382.9
Qatar	3.8	18.5	29	43.5	65.8	84.4	120.9	178.8	226.7
Réunion	1.7	5.5	14	26.7	50.3	111.0	276.1	542.5	939.4
Rwanda					5.0	11.0	39.0	68.6	100.3
Sao Tomé e Príncipe									
Saudi Arabia	14.9	16.0	191	332.1	627.3	837.0	1,376.0	2,529.0	3,777.6
Senegal		0.1	01	6.9	27.5	87.9	250.3	301.8	493.4
Seychelles		0.1	01	2.2	5.2	16.3	26.0	44.1	53.4
Sierra Leone									
Somalia									
South Africa	5.7	535.0	953	1,600.0	2,500.0	5,269.0	8,308.0	10,789.0	13,953.8
Sudan		1.7	02	3.8	8.6	13.0	23.0	103.8	137.6
Swaziland					4.7	14.0	33.0	55.0	83.8
Syria						0.0	0.0	0.2	0.4
Tanzania		3.5	09	20.2	37.9	51.0	180.2	427.0	707.6
Togo		1.0	02	3.0	7.5	17.0	50.0	120.0	195.0
Tunisia	1.0	3.2	05	7.7	39.0	55.3	119.1	389.2	816.2
Uganda		1.7	04	5.0	30.0	56.4	188.6	276.0	422.2
United Arab Emirates	33.6	129.0	194	309.4	493.3	832.3	1,428.1	1,909.3	2,430.2
Yemen		8.3	09	12.2	16.1	27.7	32.0	152.0	182.0
Zambia		1.5	03	4.5	8.3	28.2	98.9	121.2	222.0
Zimbabwe		5.1	08	5.7	19.0	174.0	309.0	328.7	370.2

Source: International Telecommunications Union/World Bank/Trade Sources/Euromonitor

| ¤ Telecommunications | | | | | | | | Table 18.8 |

Telephone Lines in Use 1990-2002

• '000

	1990	1995	1996	1997	1998	1999	2000	2001	2002
North America									
Canada	15,296	17,567	17,974	18,660	19,294	20,051	20,803	20,278	20,310
USA	136,114	159,735	165,047	172,452	179,822	183,521	187,002	190,000	198,585
Latin America									
Anguilla	3	4	4	5	6	6	6	6	7
Antigua	16	26	28	31	34	37	38	40	41
Argentina	3,027	5,622	6,227	6,852	7,323	7,357	7,894	8,108	8,464
Aruba	19	27	34	33	35	37	38	40	41
Bahamas	70	84	89	98	106	111	114	118	124
Barbados	72	90	97	108	113	115	124	129	133
Belize	17	29	30	31	32	36	36	35	36
Bermuda	37	46	49	52	54	55	56	57	59
Bolivia	183	247	349	384	452	503	511	524	543
Brazil	9,409	13,263	15,106	17,039	19,987	24,985	30,926	37,431	41,283
British Virgin Islands	7	9	10	10	10	10	10	11	11
Cayman Islands	12	19	19	19	28	32	35	38	41
Chile	860	1,818	2,151	2,693	3,047	3,109	3,388	3,581	3,803
Colombia	2,415	3,873	4,645	5,395	6,367	6,665	7,159	7,300	8,089
Costa Rica	281	479	526	685	742	803	1,003	945	953
Cuba	337	353	356	371	388	434	489	573	598
Dominica	12	18	19	19	20	21	23	24	26
Dominican Republic	341	583	619	704	772	827	894	951	1,023
Ecuador	491	698	750	819	991	1,130	1,224	1,336	1,572
El Salvador	125	285	325	360	387	493	626	650	671
French Guiana	30	42	44	47	46	49	51	54	57
Grenada	15	23	24	27	27	29	31	33	35
Guadeloupe	118	165	171	180	197	201	205	208	213
Guatemala	190	286	338	430	517	599	650	756	781
Guyana	16	45	50	55	60	64	68	80	83
Haiti	45	60	60	60	65	70	73	75	77
Honduras	88	161	190	234	250	279	299	310	351
Jamaica	105	290	357	416	463	487	512	532	559
Martinique	122	161	163	170	172	172	172	174	177
Mexico	5,355	8,801	8,826	9,254	9,927	10,927	12,332	13,773	14,066
Netherlands Antilles	47	76	76	77	78	79	80	82	84
Nicaragua	46	97	111	123	141	150	159	154	156
Panama	216	304	325	366	419	462	429	376	402
Paraguay	112	167	176	218	261	268	300	289	274
Peru	565	1,109	1,435	1,646	1,555	1,689	1,717	2,022	2,207
Puerto Rico	982	1,196	1,254	1,322	1,262	1,295	1,332	1,330	1,344
St Kitts	10	14	16	17	18	20	22	24	26
St Lucia	17	31	34	37	40	44	49	54	59
St Vincent and the Grenadines	13	18	19	21	21	24	25	27	29
Suriname	37	54	57	64	67	71	75	77	83
Trinidad and Tobago	165	209	220	243	264	279	299	312	344
Uruguay	415	622	669	761	824	897	929	951	996
Venezuela	1,488	2,463	2,667	2,804	2,592	2,551	2,606	2,693	2,769

Source: *Euromonitor from International Telecommunications Union/national statistics*

■ Telecommunications

Telephone Lines in Use 1990-2002

● '000

	1990	1995	1996	1997	1998	1999	2000	2001	2002
Asia Pacific									
Afghanistan	36	29	29	29	29	29	29	29	29
American Samoa	6	10	13	13	14	14	14	15	15
Armenia	560	583	580	568	557	547	533	531	527
Azerbaijan	620	640	645	658	680	730	801	866	934
Bangladesh	242	287	316	368	413	433	472	565	672
Bhutan	2	5	6	6	10	12	14	18	20
Brunei	35	68	79	77	78	79	81	88	92
Cambodia	3	9	15	20	24	28	31	33	35
China	6,850	40,706	54,947	70,310	87,421	108,716	144,829	180,368	185,109
Fiji	42	65	70	72	77	82	86	92	96
French Polynesia	38	49	51	52	53	52	52	53	53
Guam	39	69	70	71	75	78	80	83	85
Hong Kong, China	2,475	3,278	3,451	3,647	3,729	3,869	3,926	3,898	4,187
India	5,075	11,978	14,543	17,802	21,594	26,511	32,436	38,536	41,550
Indonesia	1,066	3,291	4,186	4,983	5,572	6,080	6,663	7,219	7,631
Japan	54,528	62,292	64,037	65,735	67,488	70,530	74,344	74,567	75,291
Kazakhstan	1,333	1,963	1,917	1,805	1,775	1,760	1,834	1,940	1,950
Kiribati	1	2	2	2	3	3	3	4	4
Kyrgyzstan	314	357	342	351	368	371	376	388	397
Laos	7	17	19	25	28	35	41	53	61
Macau	93	153	161	170	174	178	177	176	185
Malaysia	1,586	3,332	3,771	4,223	4,384	4,431	4,634	4,710	4,913
Maldives	6	14	15	18	20	22	24	27	29
Mongolia	66	78	84	87	103	103	118	124	137
Myanmar	70	158	179	214	229	249	271	295	304
Nauru	1	2	2	2	2	2	2	2	2
Nepal	57	83	113	140	208	253	267	298	307
New Caledonia	28	44	46	47	49	51	51	51	53
North Korea	780	1,100	1,100	1,100	1,100	1,100	1,100	1,100	1,100
Pakistan	843	2,127	2,377	2,558	2,757	2,986	3,053	3,381	3,562
Papua New Guinea	30	44	47	54	57	60	65	62	69
Philippines	610	1,410	1,787	2,078	2,492	2,892	3,061	3,315	3,577
Singapore	1,054	1,429	1,563	1,685	1,778	1,877	1,947	1,948	2,037
Solomon Islands	4	7	7	8	8	8	8	7	8
South Korea	13,276	18,600	19,601	20,422	20,089	20,518	21,932	22,725	22,866
Sri Lanka	121	206	257	342	524	672	767	829	862
Taiwan	6,301	9,175	10,011	10,862	11,500	12,044	12,642	12,847	12,687
Tajikistan	240	263	247	226	221	213	219	223	231
Thailand	1,325	3,482	4,160	4,827	5,038	5,216	5,591	6,042	6,210
Tonga	4	7	8	7	9	9	10	10	11
Turkmenistan	220	320	338	354	354	359	364	388	397
Tuvalu	0	1	1	1	1	1	1	1	1
Uzbekistan	1,403	1,544	1,531	1,541	1,537	1,599	1,655	1,663	1,683
Vanuatu	3	4	4	5	5	6	7	8	8
Vietnam	90	775	1,186	1,333	1,744	2,106	2,543	3,050	3,214
Western Samoa	4	8	8	8	8	9	9	10	10
Australasia									
Australia	7,787	8,900	9,170	9,498	9,540	9,760	10,050	10,060	10,312
New Zealand	1,469	1,719	1,727	1,776	1,809	1,833	1,831	1,823	2,003

Source: *Euromonitor from International Telecommunications Union/national statistics*

◘ Telecommunications

Telephone Lines in Use 1990-2002

● '000

	1990	1995	1996	1997	1998	1999	2000	2001	2002
Africa and Middle East									
Algeria	812	1,176	1,278	1,400	1,477	1,600	1,761	1,880	2,035
Angola	70	53	53	62	65	67	70	80	93
Bahrain	94	141	144	152	158	165	171	174	178
Benin	15	28	33	36	38	44	52	59	67
Botswana	26	60	72	86	102	124	136	150	178
Burkina Faso	16	30	34	36	41	47	53	58	65
Burundi	8	17	15	16	18	19	20	20	22
Cameroon	40	66	71	75	94	95	95	101	103
Cape Verde	8	22	25	33	40	47	55	62	70
Central African Republic	5	8	10	10	10	10	9	9	9
Chad	4	5	6	7	9	10	10	11	12
Comoros	3	4	5	6	6	7	7	8	8
Congo Dem Rep	16	36	36	21	20	20	20	22	22
Congo-Brazzaville	16	21	22	22	22	22	22	22	22
Côte d'Ivoire	73	116	130	142	170	219	264	294	349
Djibouti	6	8	8	8	8	9	10	10	11
Egypt	1,602	2,716	3,025	3,453	3,972	4,686	5,484	6,688	6,836
Equatorial Guinea	1	3	4	4	6	6	6	7	7
Eritrea	12	18	19	22	24	27	31	31	35
Ethiopia	125	142	149	157	164	194	232	284	359
Gabon	21	32	35	37	39	38	39	41	43
Gambia	6	19	21	25	26	29	33	35	41
Ghana	44	63	78	106	144	159	237	242	264
Guinea	11	11	16	20	15	21	24	25	27
Guinea-Bissau	6	7	8	8	8	6	11	12	14
Iran	2,199	5,090	5,825	6,503	7,355	8,371	9,486	10,897	12,021
Iraq	675	639	640	651	650	675	675	670	687
Israel	1,626	2,343	2,539	2,656	2,819	2,877	3,021	3,100	3,187
Jordan	246	317	346	416	511	565	614	668	793
Kenya	175	256	267	272	288	305	321	326	357
Kuwait	331	382	392	412	427	456	467	472	513
Lebanon	300	330	461	562	620	650	682	741	831
Lesotho	12	18	16	20	21	22	22	22	23
Liberia	9	5	5	6	7	7	7	7	7
Libya	220	318	380	400	500	550	605	677	736
Madagascar	32	37	39	43	47	50	55	58	67
Malawi	27	34	35	37	37	41	45	54	60
Mali	11	17	21	24	27	34	39	50	56
Mauritania	6	9	10	13	15	17	19	25	31
Mauritius	56	148	184	223	245	257	281	307	339
Morocco	403	1,128	1,208	1,301	1,393	1,471	1,425	1,191	1,303
Mozambique	47	61	61	66	75	78	86	89	93
Namibia	53	79	86	100	106	108	110	117	123
Niger	9	14	15	16	18	19	20	22	22
Nigeria	289	405	413	400	407	450	497	541	517
Oman	105	170	198	201	220	220	225	235	238
Qatar	92	123	134	142	151	155	160	167	173
Réunion	162	219	226	236	243	268	255	264	274
Rwanda	10	7	10	12	11	13	18	22	25
Sao Tomé e Príncipe	2	3	3	4	4	5	5	5	5
Saudi Arabia	1,234	1,719	2,004	1,877	2,878	2,706	2,955	3,233	3,466
Senegal	44	82	95	116	140	166	206	237	294
Seychelles	9	13	16	18	19	20	19	21	23
Sierra Leone	13	17	17	17	17	18	19	23	23
Somalia	15	15	15	15	15	15	15	15	15
South Africa	3,315	4,002	4,259	4,645	5,075	5,493	4,962	4,924	5,183
Sudan	62	75	99	113	162	251	387	453	547
Swaziland	14	21	23	25	29	31	32	32	35
Syria	496	959	1,199	1,313	1,463	1,600	1,675	1,710	1,843
Tanzania	73	90	93	105	122	150	174	148	153
Togo	11	22	24	25	31	38	43	48	55
Tunisia	303	522	585	654	752	850	955	1,056	1,183
Uganda	28	39	48	54	57	57	62	56	60
United Arab Emirates	396	672	738	835	915	975	1,020	1,053	1,159
Yemen	125	187	205	220	250	284	347	423	467
Zambia	65	77	78	77	78	83	83	86	87
Zimbabwe	124	152	175	212	237	239	249	254	274

Source: Euromonitor from International Telecommunications Union/national statistics

Table 18.9

◻ Telecommunications

International Outgoing Telephone Calls 1990-2002

● Million calls

	1990	1995	1996	1997	1998	1999	2000	2001	2002
North America									
Canada [a]	1,863	2,959	3,760	4,286	6,213	5,310	7,224	9,408	11,466
USA	1,004	2,821	3,485	4,233	4,439	5,249	6,627	6,244	7,559
Latin America									
Anguilla									
Antigua									
Argentina [a]	79	166	179	216	329	458	443	469	572
Aruba									
Bahamas									
Barbados [a]	45	32	34	33	39	45	56	81	91
Belize	1	2	2	2	2	2	2	3	3
Bermuda									
Bolivia [a]	8	21	21	29	35	32	36	35	35
Brazil [a]	165	286	356	477	533	591	650	772	845
British Virgin Islands									
Cayman Islands									
Chile	10	31	45	57	71	92	47	59	60
Colombia	14	29	32	35	43	45	47	51	52
Costa Rica	6	13	14	15	18	21	26	26	28
Cuba [a]	1	11	29	28	29	33	36	37	45
Dominica									
Dominican Republic									
Ecuador [a]	21	37	42	52	62	59	56	64	85
El Salvador		64	29	34	39	54	139	158	207
French Guiana									
Grenada									
Guadeloupe									
Guatemala [a]	19	37	35	48	60	86	125	156	203
Guyana [a]	6	21	30	24	16	16	19	19	20
Haiti									
Honduras	4	6	8	1	2	2	2	2	2
Jamaica [a]	7	62	64	58	60	70	74	96	98
Martinique									
Mexico	71	212	244	292	329	384	442	505	564
Netherlands Antilles									
Nicaragua [a, b]	9	29	32	34	48	51	57	60	69
Panama	6	40	41	41	50	54	52	45	47
Paraguay	11	22	22	30	38	35	33	33	35
Peru [a]	25	63	71	87	99	111	99	102	110
Puerto Rico	88	120	125	129	133	135	137	140	144
St Kitts									
St Lucia									
St Vincent and the Grenadines									
Suriname	5	6	5	4	11	12	18	23	21
Trinidad and Tobago	5	11	12	14	15	16	16	15	18
Uruguay	7	16	18	17	22	21	21	22	25
Venezuela [a]	17	129	138	159	167	163	195	281	315

Source: *Euromonitor from International Telecommunications Union/national statistics*
Notes: *(a) Million minutes, (b) Total traffic, (c) From 1994, including traffic with the CIS, (d) 1994-95: decrease due to privatization and interruption of service for two months*

■ Telecommunications

International Outgoing Telephone Calls 1990-2002

● Million calls

	1990	1995	1996	1997	1998	1999	2000	2001	2002
Asia Pacific									
Afghanistan									
American Samoa									
Armenia [a]	50	53	48	49	57	34	31	33	36
Azerbaijan		10	27	43	40	32	29	15	17
Bangladesh [a]	8	33	38	47	44	45	44	44	46
Bhutan	0	1	1	2	2	2	2	2	3
Brunei [a]		31	35	32	30	23	24	26	29
Cambodia [a]	5	5	7	8	7	7	10	11	14
China	100	444	495	573	610	570	547	478	481
Fiji	2	4	5	5	5	6	6	7	7
French Polynesia	2	2	2	3	3	4	5	6	7
Guam									
Hong Kong, China [a]	729	1,692	1,739	1,718	1,880	2,720	3,142	3,632	3,957
India [a]	147	342	384	420	436	473	540	548	726
Indonesia [a]	78	206	262	290	310	322	314	316	324
Japan	206	358	386	406	413	404	445	430	461
Kazakhstan		28	29	30	28	28	28	29	29
Kiribati									
Kyrgyzstan [a, c]	1	27	26	29	30	22	23	25	27
Laos [a]	1	5	6	6	8	8	8	7	12
Macau	21	47	50	58	64	64	72	73	115
Malaysia [a]	140	369	571	589	685	690	895	1,025	1,135
Maldives	0	3	4	4	5	6	6	7	6
Mongolia	0	1	1	1	1	2	2	2	2
Myanmar	0	3	4	5	5	5	5	4	5
Nauru									
Nepal [a]	7	15	17	17	19	25	26	32	37
New Caledonia [a]	5	9	10	10	13	16	18	19	25
North Korea									
Pakistan [a]	30	66	72	77	84	87	99	180	194
Papua New Guinea [a]	19	24	27	23	25	25	24	25	28
Philippines	107	180	227	250	174	129	136	163	157
Singapore [a]	325	773	942	1,161	1,235	1,350	1,515	1,871	1,952
Solomon Islands [a]	1	3	3	4	2	2	3	6	5
South Korea	59	147	171	222	231	333	191	262	258
Sri Lanka [a]	13	28	30	34	39	45	47	48	52
Taiwan [a]		593	701	789	861	958	1,058	1,522	1,704
Tajikistan		0	0	0	0	0	0	0	0
Thailand	26	70	80	90	96	95	96	105	108
Tonga									
Turkmenistan [a]	20	14	14	12	15	17	16	19	21
Tuvalu									
Uzbekistan	3	15	13	15	15	16	15	15	15
Vanuatu									
Vietnam [a]	6	39	52	55	50	47	48	55	57
Western Samoa [a]	3	7	7	7	7	8	8	8	9
Australasia									
Australia [a]	537	925	984	1,300	1,440	1,465	2,000	2,250	2,750
New Zealand [a]	146	312	350	405	585	610	815	950	1,128

Source: Euromonitor from International Telecommunications Union/national statistics
Notes: (a) Million minutes, (b) Total traffic, (c) From 1994, including traffic with the CIS, (d) 1994-95: decrease due to privatization and interruption of service for two months

■ Telecommunications

International Outgoing Telephone Calls 1990-2002

● Million calls

	1990	1995	1996	1997	1998	1999	2000	2001	2002
Africa and Middle East									
Algeria [a]	92	84	93	100	121	143	152	209	226
Angola [a]	7	18	18	22	28	35	35	36	36
Bahrain [a]	53	89	92	107	124	134	140	170	192
Benin [a]	3	6	7	9	11	11	16	17	18
Botswana [a]	22	30	31	37	40	40	42	59	62
Burkina Faso [a]	2	6	7	8	9	10	11	15	16
Burundi [a]	1	3	2	2	2	2	3	4	4
Cameroon [a]	15	24	25	25	24	28	27	22	23
Cape Verde [a]	2	4	5	5	6	7	7	8	9
Central African Republic	1	2	3	3	3	4	5	5	5
Chad [a]	1	2	2	3	3	3	3	4	4
Comoros									
Congo Dem Rep									
Congo-Brazzaville									
Côte d'Ivoire [a]	23	34	38	40	57	71	43	62	67
Djibouti	1	2	2	2	2	2	2	2	2
Egypt [a]	48	100	113	119	127	149	187	223	239
Equatorial Guinea									
Eritrea	0	0	1	1	1	1	1	1	1
Ethiopia	1	3	3	4	4	4	4	5	5
Gabon [a]	16	16	18	18	19	19	22	27	32
Gambia [a]	2	5	6	5	6	6	7	7	7
Ghana [a]	5	17	21	22	29	30	44	47	50
Guinea [a, d]	8	4	2	6	16	12	18	19	23
Guinea-Bissau [a]	1	2	2	3	2	2	3	4	5
Iran	16	36	37	45	46	56	58	68	75
Iraq									
Israel [a]	118	266	320	459	661	804	1,022	1,120	1,355
Jordan [a]	39	72	75	92	122	146	171	190	248
Kenya [a]	21	25	26	29	29	28	24	24	24
Kuwait	17	36	43	50	56	64	67	73	85
Lebanon [a]	6	34	39	60	70	81	85	93	101
Lesotho [a]	9	22	24	33	34	36	37	38	39
Liberia [a]	2	2	2	5	6	7	8	9	10
Libya									
Madagascar [a]		5	6	8	9	10	9	10	10
Malawi [a]	4	7	8	10	11	10	15	24	24
Mali [a]	5	7	9	11	12	13	14	15,326	18
Mauritania [a]	3	4	5	5	6	8	9	10	12
Mauritius	4	6	6	7	8	10	11	13	16
Morocco [a]	85	130	129	150	181	220	245	270	271
Mozambique [a]	6	22	13	16	19	21	22	22	27
Namibia [a]	33	51	45	48	62	62	62	60	63
Niger [a]	3	4	4	5	6	6	6	6	7
Nigeria [a]	45	94	40	53	55	58	58	61	68
Oman	25	54	63	74	93	102	117	159	145
Qatar	9	19	22	28	33	38	44	58	67
Réunion									
Rwanda									
Sao Tomé e Príncipe									
Saudi Arabia	81	197	212	252	277	258	295	348	387
Senegal	13,578	20	24	28	32	36	42	70	78
Seychelles [a]	1	2	3	4	5	6	7	8	9
Sierra Leone [a]	1	2	4	4	4	4	5	8	7
Somalia									
South Africa [a]	156	305	353	369	405	462	495	510	630
Sudan	6	3	4	8	9	12	11	12	12
Swaziland [a]	13	25	25	20	28	29	27	26	27
Syria [a]	21	68	84	90	103	122	169	163	105
Tanzania	3	5	6	10	11	12	13	9	9
Togo [a]	6	8	9	8	8	8	10	14	16
Tunisia [a]	65	88	94	98	115	140	146	174	201
Uganda [a]	4	5	6	6	6	6	7	7	9
United Arab Emirates [a]	229	504	589	738	875	963	1,124	1,396	1,520
Yemen [a]	20	23	24	26	28	32	36	43	52
Zambia	2	3	4	4	4	4	4	5	4
Zimbabwe [a]	16	56	49	50	53	66	72	78	79

Source: Euromonitor from International Telecommunications Union/national statistics
Notes: (a) Million minutes, (b) Total traffic, (c) From 1994, including traffic with the CIS, (d) 1994-95: decrease due to privatization and interruption of service for two months

▫ Telecommunications								**Table 18.10**

National Telephone Calls 1990-2002

● Million calls

	1990	1995	1996	1997	1998	1999	2000	2001	2002
North America									
Canada	3,094	3,722	3,851	3,900	3,950	4,005	4,050	4,092	4,169
USA	467,859	578,225	599,038	618,361	618,762	656,099	642,502	653,527	677,183
Latin America									
Anguilla									
Antigua									
Argentina									
Aruba									
Bahamas [a]									
Barbados [b]						53	53	56	63
Belize									
Bermuda									
Bolivia [b]	55	164	200	227	312	279	357	401	420
Brazil [a, b]	11,100	20,354	22,975	25,400	39,547	41,288	37,036	40,986	43,424
British Virgin Islands									
Cayman Islands									
Chile	2,086	5,079	5,946	6,714	7,535	7,678	7,813	8,304	8,727
Colombia [a]	413	821	888	1,033	1,289	1,372	1,449	1,566	1,674
Costa Rica [c]	1,813	3,010	3,397	3,759	4,040	4,275	4,412	4,752	5,080
Cuba	159								
Dominica									
Dominican Republic									
Ecuador [b]						5,045			
El Salvador [c, d]	11	12	24	41	55	2,801	3,376	4,006	5,394
French Guiana									
Grenada									
Guadeloupe	246								
Guatemala [a]	47								
Guyana									
Haiti									
Honduras	185	392	607	550	634	698	769	877	1,006
Jamaica									
Martinique	257								
Mexico [a, b]	4,314	7,294	7,867	9,143	11,717	14,426	16,811	19,496	23,124
Netherlands Antilles									
Nicaragua [c]	290	1,869	2,422	3,150	4,098	3,639	5,970	7,124	8,622
Panama [b]	6,824	11,031	12,539	14,605	16,284	17,503	18,945	21,270	23,660
Paraguay [c]	545								
Peru [b]			5,885	6,362	7,735	7,796	7,568	8,188	8,743
Puerto Rico [e]	2,383	3,230	4,816	5,199	5,827	5,985	6,174	6,817	7,555
St Kitts									
St Lucia									
St Vincent and the Grenadines									
Suriname [c]	162	1,102	1,456	1,168	644	647	974	1,130	1,514
Trinidad and Tobago	762	891	942	1,042	1,131	1,232	1,343	1,464	1,592
Uruguay [a, f]	78	190	240	122	148	157	141	191	251
Venezuela [b]				13,365	15,674	15,824	16,183	17,510	18,695

Source: Euromonitor from International Telecommunications Union/national statistics
Notes: (a) Trunk calls only, (b) Million minutes, (c) Million pulses, (d) National automatic traffic, (e) Local and trunk calls, (f) 1997: the decrease is due to a different definition of the metropolitan area in Montevideo, (g) Long distance calls

◻ Telecommunications
National Telephone Calls 1990-2002

● Million calls

	1990	1995	1996	1997	1998	1999	2000	2001	2002
Asia Pacific									
Afghanistan									
American Samoa									
Armenia		24	35	32	41	46	54	64	72
Azerbaijan (g)	28	17	17	17	16	16	17	18	19
Bangladesh									
Bhutan		4	5	7	9	11	12	14	16
Brunei									
Cambodia									
China	15,429	125,180	170,552	192,214	227,854	247,714	453,156	644,804	640,110
Fiji (c)	192	370	457	484	510	536	567	603	638
French Polynesia (c)	76					56	58	61	66
Guam									
Hong Kong, China									
India (a)	224	76	67	56	49	39	34	35	39
Indonesia (c)	10,295	28,256	35,347	42,144	45,905	47,258	52,859	58,389	66,697
Japan (a)	75,062	32,518	35,572	36,372	38,472	32,520	32,189	32,167	31,049
Kazakhstan (a)	101	130	135	143	167	197	283	364	388
Kiribati	3								
Kyrgyzstan (b)	29	23	23	26	30	34	40	44	52
Laos (b)		50	61	74	117	152	227	300	359
Macau	246	399	436	450	457	461	462	476	468
Malaysia									
Maldives (b)	109	135	141	168	192	214	226	222	251
Mongolia (a)	3	4	4	4	5	6	8	11	12
Myanmar									
Nauru									
Nepal (e)	167	372	497	596	673	737	805	891	1,038
New Caledonia (c)	46	81	97	123	222	252	310	361	439
North Korea									
Pakistan (b)	5,069	9,178	10,816	12,000	13,487	14,898	16,309	18,179	20,713
Papua New Guinea	256								
Philippines (a, b)	278	1,205	1,508	2,235	2,451	2,836	3,255	2,756	3,050
Singapore	4,573	6,084	6,124	6,219	6,243	6,305	6,395	6,503	6,574
Solomon Islands (a)	0	0	0	1	1	1	1	1	1
South Korea	82,757	108,706	87,638	83,425	94,379	99,098	104,370	108,747	115,779
Sri Lanka									
Taiwan	17,516	24,845	26,372	27,915	29,458	30,931	32,313	33,660	34,937
Tajikistan (a)		3	4	4	4	5	7	12	13
Thailand (a)	2,738	629	678	668	601	584	680	768	834
Tonga									
Turkmenistan	10	12	12	13	13	14	15	15	16
Tuvalu									
Uzbekistan	132								
Vanuatu									
Vietnam (a, b)		500	750	1,003	1,232	1,359	1,523	1,654	1,849
Western Samoa									
Australasia									
Australia (b)	7,000	9,874	11,747	12,540	14,332	15,362	15,760	16,303	16,987
New Zealand (a, b)	314	1,885	2,258	2,419	2,544	2,154	2,885	3,000	2,760

Source: *Euromonitor from International Telecommunications Union/national statistics*
Notes: *(a) Trunk calls only, (b) Million minutes, (c) Million pulses, (d) National automatic traffic, (e) Local and trunk calls, (f) 1997: the decrease is due to a different definition of the metropolitan area in Montevideo, (g) Long distance calls*

■ Telecommunications

National Telephone Calls 1990-2002

- Million calls

	1990	1995	1996	1997	1998	1999	2000	2001	2002
Africa and Middle East									
Algeria (c)	4,448	8,889	9,672	11,000	13,000	15,160	17,852	22,529	30,879
Angola (b)			124	143	120	159	241	337	421
Bahrain (c)	311	519	551	623	690	1,052	1,363	1,727	2,309
Benin (c)	21	24	23	24	25	24	83	105	108
Botswana (c)	241	478	573	695	847	1,036	1,276	1,592	2,013
Burkina Faso									
Burundi (b)		165	189	200	221	238	261	290	317
Cameroon (b)	234	294	316	348	390	415	439	460	479
Cape Verde									
Central African Republic									
Chad									
Comoros									
Congo Dem Rep									
Congo-Brazzaville									
Côte d'Ivoire									
Djibouti (c)	9	47	47	14	30	37	49	65	91
Egypt (a)	146	314	371	428	563	791	1,030	1,262	1,493
Equatorial Guinea									
Eritrea (b)	39	110	152	230	185	203	231	248	294
Ethiopia (c)	363	540	568	619	704	786	1,010	1,342	1,838
Gabon	0								
Gambia (c)	33								
Ghana (c)	225	261	258	990	749	658	503	954	1,043
Guinea	1								
Guinea-Bissau									
Iran	25,403	42,140	45,820	47,563	50,794	54,182	57,974	62,368	67,414
Iraq									
Israel	3,840	6,620	7,241	7,515	7,935	8,207	8,611	8,965	9,458
Jordan (a)	805	96	104	119	143	157	152	160	176
Kenya		5	4	4	4	5	5	5	
Kuwait									
Lebanon									
Lesotho (a)	0								
Liberia									
Libya									
Madagascar		60	63	155	186	220	170	156	204
Malawi	52								
Mali									
Mauritania (a)									
Mauritius	105	333	418	527	602	631	670	736	824
Morocco (c)	1,399	3,308	3,543	3,855	3,932	4,030	4,133	4,254	4,403
Mozambique (c)	250	467	422	556	592	601	640	775	827
Namibia					670	704	757	831	815
Niger (a, b)	3	5	4	5	6	7	7	8	9
Nigeria	1,072								
Oman (c)	720								
Qatar	289	635	713	784	788	820	831	820	834
Réunion	297								
Rwanda	20								
Sao Tomé e Príncipe									
Saudi Arabia (a)	5,529	838	1,043	1,338	1,365	1,663	1,758	1,829	1,955
Senegal (c)			525	609	552	758	909	962	
Seychelles (a)				115	150	189	213	254	
Sierra Leone	22	55	63	59	66	71	79	84	91
Somalia									
South Africa (c)	13,524	30,289	31,100	32,600	33,248	33,780	34,297	37,006	41,113
Sudan			76	199	379	358	477	483	
Swaziland (a, b)	12	23	24	26	28	30	31	32	34
Syria	871	1,539	2,603	3,263	4,145	5,020	5,606	5,898	6,323
Tanzania (a)	13	7	7	7	8	7	6	6	6
Togo	9	60	90	150	250	350	400	500	510
Tunisia (c)	1,252	2,100	2,200	2,300	2,497	2,735	3,028	3,407	3,740
Uganda	166	95	91	103	113	123	133	143	152
United Arab Emirates (b)	954	1,996	2,361	2,727	3,480	4,219	5,916	7,364	8,696
Yemen									
Zambia (a)	0	0	0	0	0	0	0	0	0
Zimbabwe (c)	955	1,177	1,447	1,608	4,273	4,694	3,660	4,273	4,738

Source: *Euromonitor from International Telecommunications Union/national statistics*
Notes: *(a) Trunk calls only, (b) Million minutes, (c) Million pulses, (d) National automatic traffic, (e) Local and trunk calls, (f) 1997: the decrease is due to a different definition of the metropolitan area in Montevideo, (g) Long distance calls*

Labour

▫ Total Employment									Table 19.1	
General Level of Employment 1977-2002										

● '000

	1977	1985	1990	1996	1997	1998	1999	2000	2001	2002
North America										
Canada [a]	10,376	11,158	12,514	13,677	13,941	14,317	14,531	14,910	15,077	15,370
USA [b]	92,017	107,150	118,138	126,710	129,875	131,466	133,491	135,207	135,075	136,492
Latin America										
Anguilla										
Antigua										
Argentina [c]			7,110	7,369	7,858	8,279	8,285	8,262	7,943	7,236
Aruba										
Bahamas	74		113	130	135	144	146	152	158	162
Barbados	87	92	105	114	116	120	122	126	127	127
Belize				64	66	69	73	76	80	85
Bermuda	28	32	36	35	35	36	38	39	42	44
Bolivia [d, e]			921	1,849	1,878	1,950	2,017	2,096	2,151	2,199
Brazil [f]	40,179	53,761	62,101	67,920	69,331	69,965	71,679	74,529	77,848	80,657
British Virgin Islands		5								
Cayman Islands										
Chile	2,821	3,721	4,459	5,298	5,380	5,432	5,405	5,381	5,479	5,536
Colombia [g, h]	2,530	3,100	4,324	5,455	5,706	5,655	5,641	5,910	5,928	6,179
Costa Rica	659	827	1,017	1,145	1,227	1,300	1,300	1,319	1,355	1,362
Cuba	2,487	3,164	3,582	3,627	3,705	3,754	3,821	3,843	3,891	3,924
Dominica										
Dominican Republic			2,184	2,471	2,652	2,703	2,723	2,750	2,780	2,797
Ecuador			2,348	2,886	3,062	3,152	3,121	3,437	3,673	3,869
El Salvador	1,359	1,373	885	2,056	2,076	2,228	2,275	2,300	2,331	2,290
French Guiana	13									
Grenada										
Guadeloupe										
Guatemala	709	632	786	831	804	786	779	766	761	758
Guyana										
Haiti	1,894		2,340							
Honduras		281	1,213	1,985	2,088	2,135	2,299	2,367	2,429	2,503
Jamaica	676	782	896	960	956	954	954	952	949	946
Martinique										
Mexico			29,283	35,226	37,360	38,618	39,069	38,983	39,004	39,747
Netherlands Antilles			48	57	56	54	53	52	54	57
Nicaragua			1,122	1,292	1,370	1,442	1,544	1,637	1,726	1,827
Panama		627	694	867	909	937	961	942	922	879
Paraguay		407	486	1,190	1,222	1,250	1,269	1,291	1,321	1,347
Peru [d]			5,092	6,099	6,747	6,929	7,211	7,128	7,620	7,905
Puerto Rico	700	776	971	1,112	1,132	1,136	1,149	1,174	1,193	1,222
St Kitts	22									
St Lucia										
St Vincent and the Grenadines										
Suriname	98		82	87	83	88	73	72	72	69
Trinidad and Tobago	371	400	374	444	460	479	489	494	500	498
Uruguay		967	1,136	1,237	1,196	1,104	1,082	1,068	1,052	1,070
Venezuela	4,154	5,106	6,479	8,026	8,583	8,746	8,953	9,192	9,373	9,608

Source: International Labour Organisation/Euromonitor
Notes: (a) Excluding indigenous populations living on reserves and full-time members of the armed forces, (b) Civilian labour force, (c) Data refer to 28 urban agglomerations, (d) Urban areas, (e) Prior 1996: main towns, (f) Excl. rural population of Rondonia, Acre,Amazonas, Roraima, Para and Amapa., (g) 7 main cities, (h) Excluding armed forces and conscripts, (i) Including armed forces, (j) Including conscripts, (k) Excluding armed forces, (l) Including self-defence forces, (m) Including workers from the Judea, Samaria and Gaza areas

Total Employment

General Level of Employment 1977-2002

• '000

	1977	1985	1990	1996	1997	1998	1999	2000	2001	2002
Asia Pacific										
Afghanistan										
American Samoa	8	10								
Armenia					1,372	1,353	1,347	1,336	1,330	1,327
Azerbaijan		2,619	3,703	3,687	3,694	3,702	3,703	3,705	3,715	3,724
Bangladesh		30,585	50,159	54,597	54,937	55,730	56,003	56,500	56,850	57,044
Bhutan										
Brunei	22	33								
Cambodia										
China (i, j)	393,770	498,730	644,118	679,991	687,891	690,926	706,080	711,724	718,427	729,036
Fiji	72	81	92	110	112	114	118	122	126	130
French Polynesia	25	40	41	45	45	45	45	45	45	46
Guam	26	32	44	45	44	44	44	44	44	43
Hong Kong, China (k)	1,847	2,543	2,741	3,006	3,145	3,205	3,174	3,216	3,249	3,321
India	206,562	249,367	270,862	315,098	321,585	328,985	337,219	340,700	345,156	352,251
Indonesia	48,315	62,457	75,349	86,485	87,128	89,363	91,407	92,103	92,899	95,127
Japan (l)	53,420	58,070	62,510	64,830	65,580	65,160	64,610	64,460	64,140	64,131
Kazakhstan		7,136	7,563	6,361	6,308	6,127	6,064	6,017	5,997	6,012
Kiribati										
Kyrgyzstan		1,614	1,748	1,652	1,689	1,705	1,764	1,741	1,714	1,667
Laos		2,014								
Macau			163	198	201	201	203	200	199	196
Malaysia	3,734	5,653	6,600	8,400	8,569	8,600	8,838	9,322	9,462	9,789
Maldives								86		
Mongolia						793				
Myanmar	12,210	14,792	15,221	17,597	17,964	18,359	18,271	18,406	18,745	18,954
Nauru										
Nepal		7,540								
New Caledonia		33	47	52	53	55	58	60	60	60
North Korea		8,234								
Pakistan (b)	21,649	26,521	29,844	32,413	34,153	35,895	36,808	36,847	37,242	37,871
Papua New Guinea	101									
Philippines	14,323	20,327	22,532	27,442	27,888	28,261	29,071	27,776	30,086	30,779
Singapore	976	1,327	1,504	1,748	1,830	1,869	1,973	2,095	2,047	2,121
Solomon Islands	16	24	26	34	34	35	35	35	36	36
South Korea (b)	12,929	14,970	18,034	20,761	21,045	19,929	20,281	21,062	21,359	21,708
Sri Lanka		5,132	5,964	5,587	5,569	5,946	6,159	6,308	6,500	6,556
Taiwan	5,980	7,428	8,283	9,068	9,176	9,261	9,432	9,570	9,651	9,726
Tajikistan			1,400	1,731	1,143	1,084	1,057	1,016	981	953
Thailand (b)	18,138	25,853	31,039	32,396	33,267	32,215	32,225	33,161	32,867	33,140
Tonga										
Turkmenistan										
Tuvalu										
Uzbekistan				8,561	8,680	8,800	8,885	8,605	8,455	8,117
Vanuatu										
Vietnam			30,286	35,792	36,994	37,718	38,361	39,493	40,525	41,579
Western Samoa										
Australasia										
Australia (b)	5,980	6,698	7,874	8,358	8,451	8,615	8,809	9,066	9,130	9,322
New Zealand (b)	1,471	1,514	1,461	1,686	1,736	1,725	1,751	1,779	1,824	1,863

Source: International Labour Organisation/Euromonitor
Notes: (a) Excluding indigenous populations living on reserves and full-time members of the armed forces, (b) Civilian labour force, (c) Data refer to 28 urban agglomerations, (d) Urban areas, (e) Prior 1996: main towns, (f) Excl. rural population of Rondonia, Acre,Amazonas, Roraima, Para and Amapa., (g) 7 main cities, (h) Excluding armed forces and conscripts, (i) Including armed forces, (j) Including conscripts, (k) Excluding armed forces, (l) Including self-defence forces, (m) Including workers from the Judea, Samaria and Gaza areas

■ Total Employment

General Level of Employment 1977-2002

● '000

	1977	1985	1990	1996	1997	1998	1999	2000	2001	2002
Africa and Middle East										
Algeria	2,337	3,884	4,009	5,389	5,746	5,993	6,068	5,670	5,699	5,529
Angola		377		475						
Bahrain		112	92	123	124	138	148	149	152	148
Benin	47	81	51							
Botswana	63	117	209	238	230	242	257	262	270	275
Burkina Faso			152							
Burundi	34	45	47							
Cameroon	213	3,989	3,844							
Cape Verde										
Central African Republic	21	19	15	14	14	14	14	14	14	14
Chad			10							
Comoros										
Congo Dem Rep										
Congo-Brazzaville										
Côte d'Ivoire		406	385							
Djibouti										
Egypt [b]	9,198	11,937	14,955	16,355	16,566	16,931	17,494	17,445	17,598	17,868
Equatorial Guinea		111								
Eritrea				58						
Ethiopia										
Gabon				58						
Gambia	27	24								
Ghana	475	464	230							
Guinea										
Guinea-Bissau										
Iran										
Iraq										
Israel [b, m]	1,160	1,349	1,491	2,013	2,040	2,072	2,137	2,221	2,270	2,342
Jordan										
Kenya	903	1,174	1,409	1,607	1,647	1,682	1,707	1,734	1,763	1,787
Kuwait [i]				741	778	870	907	941	969	1,024
Lebanon										
Lesotho										
Liberia	40									
Libya	765									
Madagascar	99		281	352	364	374	379	386	390	394
Malawi	322	415	468	724	737	741	737	738	737	735
Mali										
Mauritania										
Mauritius	194	204	283	287	286	293	298	297	300	300
Morocco			3,294	4,034	4,234	4,168	4,175	4,377	4,446	4,598
Mozambique										
Namibia										
Niger	31	23	25							
Nigeria		36,568								
Oman				78	79	81	81	82	83	83
Qatar										
Réunion										
Rwanda										
Sao Tomé e Príncipe										
Saudi Arabia			3,267	2,496	2,526	2,597	2,592	2,531	2,588	2,586
Senegal	107	85								
Seychelles		18	24	26	28	29	31	32	34	36
Sierra Leone	61	69								
Somalia										
South Africa			9,277	9,287	9,247	9,389	10,361	10,467	10,584	10,900
Sudan	5,012	6,991								
Swaziland	66	73	92	90	91	93	93	94	95	95
Syria	1,894	2,408	2,983							
Tanzania	484									
Togo	38	61	57	50	49	48	48	48	47	47
Tunisia			2,498	2,841	2,952	2,900	2,952	3,035	3,172	3,268
Uganda		7,054								
United Arab Emirates										
Yemen		565								
Zambia	370	362								
Zimbabwe	1,012	1,055	1,192	1,273	1,323	1,349	1,316	1,300	1,209	1,105

Source: International Labour Organisation/Euromonitor
Notes: (a) Excluding indigenous populations living on reserves and full-time members of the armed forces, (b) Civilian labour force, (c) Data refer to 28 urban agglomerations, (d) Urban areas, (e) Prior 1996: main towns, (f) Excl. rural population of Rondonia, Acre,Amazonas, Roraima, Para and Amapa., (g) 7 main cities, (h) Excluding armed forces and conscripts, (i) Including armed forces, (j) Including conscripts, (k) Excluding armed forces, (l) Including self-defence forces, (m) Including workers from the Judea, Samaria and Gaza areas

Employment by Activity 2002

• % of total employed population

	A	B	C	D	E	F	G	H	I	J	Total
Algeria	15.7	48.3	11.9				12.7		11.4		100.0
Argentina	0.7	28.1	8.5	0.5	10.4	14.2	0.2	10.0	27.1	0.3	100.0
Australia	4.7	26.8	7.7	0.7	16.1	12.1	0.7	6.7	24.5		100.0
Azerbaijan	38.7	24.0	4.2	1.1	2.9	4.3	1.0	4.5	19.2		100.0
Bolivia	4.9	20.2	12.0	1.0	6.6	14.5	1.4	6.0	33.5		100.0
Brazil	22.4	42.5	6.3		1.8	9.8	1.0	3.6	12.7		100.0
Canada	2.9	26.6	5.6	0.8	16.0	15.1	1.2	7.7	24.0		100.0
Chile	13.2	28.4	8.0	0.5	7.8	14.0	1.3	8.3	18.4		100.0
China	47.4	24.9	5.2	0.5	0.6	11.0	0.8	2.9	6.7		100.0
Colombia	1.2	35.0	4.2	0.6	7.2	18.5	0.2	6.7	26.5		100.0
Ecuador	7.0	20.9	5.8	0.8	5.6	21.0	0.5	6.5	31.9		100.0
Egypt	29.5	27.4	7.9	1.2	3.1	10.3	0.3	7.3	13.0	0.0	100.0
Hong Kong, China	0.2	24.6	8.9	0.4	14.8	9.2	0.0	10.8	30.1		100.0
India											
Indonesia	43.9	12.6	4.3		1.2	13.2		5.0	19.7		100.0
Israel	1.8	34.2	4.9	0.8	16.3	16.6	0.1	6.9	17.7	0.8	100.0
Japan	4.8	26.2	9.7	0.5	10.0	19.4	0.1	6.4	22.9		100.0
Jordan											
Kazakhstan	23.2	23.9	3.2	1.8	2.8	13.3	1.6	8.8	21.3		100.0
Kuwait											
Malaysia	18.4	20.5	9.1	0.4	5.1	22.9	0.3	4.7	18.6		100.0
Mexico	16.2	20.0	6.5	0.5	3.8	18.7	0.3	4.5	28.8	0.6	100.0
Morocco	5.0	32.9	8.7	0.8	2.4	17.8	0.7	5.8	25.8	0.1	100.0
New Zealand	8.7	28.3	6.2	0.5	12.7	15.3	0.2	6.2	21.6	0.3	100.0
Nigeria											
Pakistan	49.4	12.6	5.4	0.7	0.8	12.7	0.1	4.9	13.3	0.0	100.0
Peru	9.2	23.9	3.8	0.3	5.2	11.4	0.5	8.5	37.2		100.0
Philippines	35.1	17.0	5.6	0.4	2.8	11.9	0.3	7.1	19.8		100.0
Saudi Arabia											
Singapore	0.3	24.1	7.9	0.6	17.3	18.8	0.0	10.5	20.4		100.0
South Africa											
South Korea	10.0	17.8	7.6	0.3	10.6	18.3	0.1	6.3	29.1		100.0
Taiwan											
Thailand	45.2	12.9	4.2	0.3		14.4	0.1	2.9	20.1		100.0
Tunisia											
Turkmenistan											
United Arab Emirates	7.9	30.6	19.0	1.0	3.8	11.0	2.3	7.1	17.3		100.0
USA	2.4	36.3	7.3	1.0	12.5	13.7	0.4	6.3	20.2		100.0
Venezuela	11.5	29.3	7.9	0.8	5.7	11.9	1.0	6.8	25.0	0.2	100.0
Vietnam											

Source: *International Labour Organisation/Euromonitor* **Notes:** *A: Agriculture, forestry and fishing; B: Community, social and personal services; C: Construction; D: Electricity, gas and water supply; E: Finance, insurance, real estate and business services; F: Manufacturing; G: Mining and quarrying; H: Transport, storage and communications; I: Wholesale, retail trade and restaurants and hotels; J: Undefined sectors*

◘ Total Employment | Table 19.3

Level of Paid Employment in Manufacturing 1977-2002

● '000

	1977	1985	1990	1996	1997	1998	1999	2000	2001	2002
North America										
Canada		1,798.1	1,910.5	1,867.3	1,950.7	2,026.6	2,120.1	2,187.5	2,173.8	2,271.0
USA	19,682.0	19,248.0	19,076.0	18,495.0	18,675.0	18,805.0	18,511.0	18,465.0	17,687.0	17,600.7
Latin America										
Anguilla										
Antigua										
Argentina [a]		151.2		952.6	1,033.9	1,014.4	939.3	892.0	794.7	671.2
Aruba										
Bahamas	3.2	4.6								
Barbados	9.6	10.0	6.7	4.8	4.4	4.3	4.3	4.3	4.3	4.4
Belize										
Bermuda	1.2	1.2	1.1	0.9	0.9	0.9	1.2	1.2	1.3	1.5
Bolivia	160.5	28.0								
Brazil [b]			3,597.4	2,417.7	2,306.7	2,214.8	2,140.0	2,100.2	2,060.8	1,997.4
British Virgin Islands		0.2								
Cayman Islands										
Chile		494.7	725.7	674.8	687.9	670.0	591.4	687.3	644.5	663.2
Colombia [c, d]	479.7	439.9	488.8	554.3	545.5	513.0	458.7	399.8	406.8	430.1
Costa Rica	104.1	100.0	137.4	147.0	145.6	150.9	151.0	145.4	147.7	145.0
Cuba	550.5	695.1								
Dominica										
Dominican Republic		140.8								
Ecuador [d]	86.5	96.9	111.7	123.7	132.8	125.8	123.4	135.0	138.5	140.7
El Salvador	57.9	49.0	50.1	66.0	65.2	63.8	62.2	60.8	58.4	53.4
French Guiana	1.0									
Grenada										
Guadeloupe										
Guatemala	84.5	78.2	103.3	147.2	147.0	146.5	146.8	146.7	146.8	148.2
Guyana										
Haiti	116.6									
Honduras	111.6									
Jamaica	73.6	98.6	136.1	97.1	95.3	92.7	92.0	90.4	88.8	87.1
Martinique										
Mexico				4,343.8	4,697.9	5,333.3	5,603.7	5,791.7	5,954.8	6,258.7
Netherlands Antilles	11.1	5.6								
Nicaragua	30.5	57.0	45.4	27.8	27.0	26.9	26.6	25.8	25.5	24.4
Panama		51.0	34.0	37.3	38.8	40.2	37.4	36.5	34.6	32.5
Paraguay	124.0	48.3	61.4	124.1	121.3	120.7	117.5	112.9	107.5	105.1
Peru				550.2	558.9	572.9	501.8	534.6	529.2	518.4
Puerto Rico	120.3	118.6	127.6	112.5	110.5	108.3	107.8	109.5	111.6	112.1
St Kitts	1.5									
St Lucia										
St Vincent and the Grenadines										
Suriname		5.2	4.9							
Trinidad and Tobago	72.4	59.1	32.8	39.4	39.7	39.1	38.9	39.6	40.4	38.8
Uruguay	139.6	122.4								
Venezuela				969.0	960.0	957.0	952.0	948.5	1,040.9	1,030.0

Source: International Labour Organisation/Euromonitor
Notes: (a) Data refers to Gran Buenos Aires pre 1996 and 28 urban agglomerations post 1996, (b) Excl. rural population of Rondonia, Acre, Amazonas, Roraima, Para and Amapa, (c) 7 main cities, (d) Establishments with 10 or more persons employed., (e) Incl. mining and quarrying., (f) Prior to 1999: state-owned enterprises., (g) Public sector and establishments of non-agricultural private sector with 10 or more persons employed, (h) Employees and working proprietors, (i) Incl. working proprietors., (j) From 1996: establishments with 2 or more persons employed., (k) Excl. Transkei, Bophuthaswania, Venda, Ciskey; other geographical coverage of samples not specified.

Level of Paid Employment in Manufacturing 1977-2002

● '000

	1977	1985	1990	1996	1997	1998	1999	2000	2001	2002
Asia Pacific										
Afghanistan										
American Samoa										
Armenia										
Azerbaijan (e)		446.2	409.1	252.4	186.5	151.4	137.2	131.7	116.5	
Bangladesh	368.4	468.6								
Bhutan										
Brunei		2.9								
Cambodia										
China (f)		29,743.0	34,193.0	41,104.3	37,785.1	35,989.6	34,957.0	34,296.3	36,598.2	34,679.4
Fiji	10.9	16.7	19.2	24.6	27.0	29.2	30.3	31.5	32.2	34.3
French Polynesia	2.9	1.8								
Guam	1.0	1.1	1.9	2.2	2.2	1.9	1.7	1.6	1.5	1.4
Hong Kong, China	755.1	847.6	715.6	325.1	288.9	263.7	247.8	232.0	212.0	195.9
India (g, h)	5,391.0	6,183.0	6,118.0	6,600.0	7,137.0	7,251.0	7,273.0	7,383.8	7,573.1	7,616.1
Indonesia	4,171.0	1,684.7	3,049.0	9,373.0	9,624.0	9,917.0	9,973.0	10,070.1	10,616.8	10,714.6
Japan	13,400.0	12,350.0	13,060.0	13,074.0	13,067.0	12,581.0	13,445.0	13,208.0	12,840.0	12,600.9
Kazakhstan		1,083.0	1,237.0	575.0	577.0	508.0	574.3	574.8	616.1	625.4
Kiribati										
Kyrgyzstan			1,237.0	607.3	584.1	577.6	570.4	565.5	560.5	527.7
Laos										
Macau		59.6	63.0	39.8	38.2	37.6	37.0	36.5	36.0	34.9
Malaysia	349.2	473.3	841.8	1,298.2	1,313.7	1,324.2	1,332.2	1,338.3	1,346.2	1,361.0
Maldives										
Mongolia										
Myanmar	913.0	1,234.0								
Nauru										
Nepal										
New Caledonia		4.3	4.9	5.4	5.7	5.8	5.4	6.1	6.5	6.1
North Korea										
Pakistan	2,989.0	3,568.0								
Papua New Guinea	12.6									
Philippines	803.7	618.3	1,108.5	1,052.0	1,097.2	1,106.7	1,057.4	1,027.0	1,131.5	1,114.0
Singapore	219.1	254.0	351.8	352.9	345.2	337.2	332.5	328.3	325.8	309.5
Solomon Islands	1.0	1.8	2.3							
South Korea	1,702.0	2,997.0	4,260.0	4,677.0	4,474.0	3,898.0	4,006.0	4,198.0	4,357.8	4,293.6
Sri Lanka			236.8	362.7	288.3	309.5	264.1	399.7	405.6	421.3
Taiwan	1,767.0	2,488.0	2,653.0	2,427.0	2,570.0	2,645.0	2,691.0	2,714.7	2,760.2	2,792.4
Tajikistan										
Thailand				4,682.0	4,644.0	4,577.0	4,611.0	5,005.0	5,014.0	5,172.5
Tonga		1.0	1.2							
Turkmenistan										
Tuvalu										
Uzbekistan						1,114.0				
Vanuatu										
Vietnam				3,288.8	3,292.5	3,314.4	3,387.1	3,426.1	3,670.0	3,720.0
Western Samoa										
Australasia										
Australia (i)	1,175.8	1,018.5	1,007.3	957.9	949.3	922.7	893.9	883.7	870.6	870.6
New Zealand (i)	316.0	279.3	225.6	223.3	214.7	206.0	202.1	219.4	218.8	222.3

Source: *International Labour Organisation/Euromonitor*
Notes: *(a) Data refers to Gran Buenos Aires pre 1996 and 28 urban agglomerations post 1996, (b) Excl. rural population of Rondonia, Acre, Amazonas, Roraima, Para and Amapa, (c) 7 main cities, (d) Establishments with 10 or more persons employed., (e) Incl. mining and quarrying., (f) Prior to 1999: state-owned enterprises., (g) Public sector and establishments of non-agricultural private sector with 10 or more persons employed, (h) Employees and working proprietors, (i) Incl. working proprietors., (j) From 1996: establishments with 2 or more persons employed., (k) Excl. Transkei, Bophuthaswania,Venda, Ciskey; other geographical coverage of samples not specified.*

◘ Total Employment

Level of Paid Employment in Manufacturing 1977-2002

● '000

	1977	1985	1990	1996	1997	1998	1999	2000	2001	2002
Africa and Middle East										
Algeria										
Angola		62.0								
Bahrain	10.2	17.6								
Benin	1.6	8.3								
Botswana	4.2	9.9	24.3	24.3	23.8	23.5	25.9	25.6	26.0	26.1
Burkina Faso										
Burundi	2.8	5.6	7.0	5.4	5.4	5.3	5.2	5.2	5.8	5.6
Cameroon	49.9	114.1	63.9							
Cape Verde										
Central African Republic		7.8	4.0							
Chad			4.7							
Comoros										
Congo Dem Rep										
Congo-Brazzaville										
Côte d'Ivoire										
Djibouti										
Egypt	1,353.4	1,318.4	1,510.4	1,654.2	1,756.9	1,805.4	1,816.7	1,805.8	1,802.1	1,811.1
Equatorial Guinea										
Eritrea										
Ethiopia		88.1								
Gabon	17.1									
Gambia	3.9	1.4								
Ghana		51.7	28.7							
Guinea										
Guinea-Bissau										
Iran										
Iraq										
Israel	277.6	301.2	315.0	358.1	353.8	346.4	342.5	348.3	339.5	339.1
Jordan	26.6	36.1	56.6	68.2	69.7	70.4	70.1	70.5	74.9	
Kenya	118.0	158.8	187.7	210.5	214.5	217.9	218.0	220.4	224.8	225.3
Kuwait		45.5	55.8	53.8	54.2	54.0	53.5	53.3	59.3	56.3
Lebanon										
Lesotho										
Liberia	1.5									
Libya	41.7									
Madagascar			91.0							
Malawi	33.7	46.2	63.4	80.7	81.6	82.4	81.8	82.4	82.5	82.4
Mali										
Mauritania										
Mauritius	33.2	56.1	110.4	107.4	105.9	111.2	115.3	114.5	117.0	118.7
Morocco										
Mozambique										
Namibia										
Niger	1.5	2.4	2.0							
Nigeria										
Oman										
Qatar										
Réunion										
Rwanda										
Sao Tomé e Príncipe										
Saudi Arabia										
Senegal	30.5									
Seychelles	0.8	1.1	2.6	2.4	2.8	2.9	3.7	3.8	3.9	4.4
Sierra Leone	6.0	8.1								
Somalia										
South Africa [k]	1,323.8	1,429.0	1,525.2	1,438.1	1,383.8	1,351.6	1,314.5	1,306.8	1,269.1	1,250.0
Sudan										
Swaziland	8.4	10.6	14.2	16.0	15.5	15.2	15.2	15.5	15.6	15.5
Syria	256.3	284.3	100.3							
Tanzania	101.8									
Togo		5.2	4.7							
Tunisia	289.0									
Uganda										
United Arab Emirates										
Yemen										
Zambia	45.8	48.5								
Zimbabwe	145.1	169.6	197.1	183.3	197.8	207.6	200.7	198.2	195.5	

Source: International Labour Organisation/Euromonitor
Notes: (a) Data refers to Gran Buenos Aires pre 1996 and 28 urban agglomerations post 1996, (b) Excl. rural population of Rondonia, Acre, Amazonas, Roraima, Para and Amapa, (c) 7 main cities, (d) Establishments with 10 or more persons employed., (e) Incl. mining and quarrying., (f) Prior to 1999: state-owned enterprises., (g) Public sector and establishments of non-agricultural private sector with 10 or more persons employed, (h) Employees and working proprietors, (i) Incl. working proprietors., (j) From 1996: establishments with 2 or more persons employed., (k) Excl. Transkei, Bophuthaswania, Venda, Ciskey; other geographical coverage of samples not specified.

Total Unemployed 1977-2002

• '000

	1977	1985	1990	1996	1997	1998	1999	2000	2001	2002
North America										
Canada [a]	882.1	1,380.8	1,165.4	1,469.0	1,413.4	1,314.8	1,190.7	1,089.5	1,169.4	1,132.1
USA	6,991.0	8,312.0	7,044.0	7,236.0	6,422.0	6,208.0	5,878.0	5,655.0	6,742.0	7,282.0
Latin America										
Anguilla										
Antigua										
Argentina [b]	251.2	525.7	807.5	1,532.5	1,375.5	1,218.8	1,359.8	1,460.1	1,576.6	1,701.2
Aruba				3.2	3.3	3.4	3.5	3.5	3.6	3.8
Bahamas	19.4	11.7	15.3	16.9	14.7	12.1	11.5	11.6	11.7	11.8
Barbados	16.2	21.2	18.6	21.1	19.6	16.7	14.3	13.1	13.5	12.9
Belize										
Bermuda	0.1	0.0	0.1	0.2	0.2	0.2	0.2	0.2	0.2	0.2
Bolivia [c, d]			67.8	73.6	72.5	103.9	160.6	167.5	173.9	180.7
Brazil [e]	953.0	1,875.0	2,367.0	5,077.0	5,882.0	6,921.0	7,636.0	6,478.0	5,642.0	5,313.7
British Virgin Islands										
Cayman Islands										
Chile	378.4	515.4	268.1	302.2	303.6	419.2	529.1	489.4	469.4	494.8
Colombia [f, g]	261.0	499.9	491.9	735.4	782.4	998.0	1,415.5	1,526.1	1,625.9	1,704.0
Costa Rica	31.8	60.8	49.5	75.9	74.3	76.5	83.3	71.9	67.8	60.3
Cuba										
Dominica										
Dominican Republic				505.7	503.7	507.3	503.4	500.6	498.3	496.3
Ecuador	32.5	81.1	191.2	337.4	311.6	408.3	543.5	333.1	451.0	480.1
El Salvador	47.3	280.2	97.9	171.0	180.0	175.7	170.2	208.2	259.0	292.3
French Guiana	0.8	4.2	4.4	14.0	17.0	18.2	18.9	19.9	22.0	23.4
Grenada										
Guadeloupe	13.4	24.2	29.4	44.9	46.4	47.2	47.7	48.4	49.5	50.4
Guatemala		2.7	1.8	1.5	1.6	1.6	1.5	1.5	1.5	1.6
Guyana	2.4	13.3								
Haiti			339.7							
Honduras		49.3	61.7	89.4	69.4	87.7	89.3	98.6	103.9	109.2
Jamaica	215.1	260.8	166.6	183.0	186.9	175.0	170.8	163.3	168.8	164.2
Martinique		29.5	30.2	45.2	45.8	47.3	48.3	49.6	50.9	51.9
Mexico			707.1	1,355.0	984.8	889.4	682.0	650.9	678.5	682.2
Netherlands Antilles			9.8	9.3	10.1	10.5	9.2	8.5	8.2	7.5
Nicaragua		34.6	145.6	225.1	208.4	215.5	221.3	228.1	228.3	228.2
Panama		88.3	135.6	144.9	140.3	147.1	128.0	140.8	156.4	166.7
Paraguay		216.0	160.0	172.0	176.0	175.0	153.0	132.0	121.9	102.5
Peru [c]			476.5	461.6	565.0	582.5	624.9	566.5	651.5	676.9
Puerto Rico	174.0	216.0	160.0	172.0	176.0	175.0	153.7	131.9	126.6	108.1
St Kitts										
St Lucia										
St Vincent and the Grenadines										
Suriname	3.0	17.0	15.4	10.7	9.7	10.5	11.8	13.7	14.9	16.3
Trinidad and Tobago	57.5	72.8	93.6	86.1	81.2	79.4	74.0	70.5	66.9	62.2
Uruguay		135.4	105.7	141.8	134.2	123.8	137.7	167.7	188.0	210.5
Venezuela			767.1	996.2	924.2	916.2	879.5	842.7	883.5	929.6

Source: International Labour Organisation/Euromonitor
Notes: (a) Excluding indigenous populations living on reserves and full-time members of the armed forces, (b) Data refer to 28 urban agglomerations, (c) Urban areas, (d) Prior 1996: main towns, (e) Excl. rural population of Rondonia, Acre, Amazonas, Roraima, Para and Amapa., (f) 7 main cities, (g) Excluding armed forces and conscripts, (h) Civilian labour force

■ Total Unemployed Population

Total Unemployed 1977-2002

● '000

	1977	1985	1990	1996	1997	1998	1999	2000	2001	2002
Asia Pacific										
Afghanistan										
American Samoa	1.4	1.5	6.7	15.5	15.8	16.0	16.1	16.3	16.3	16.5
Armenia					423.7	354.8	335.4	313.0	283.0	260.0
Azerbaijan										
Bangladesh		336.0	997.0	1,417.0	1,439.0	1,443.0	1,450.0	1,455.8	1,463.5	1,469.0
Bhutan										
Brunei	1.9									
Cambodia										
China		1,969.0	3,127.0	5,528.0	5,768.0	5,710.0	5,750.0	5,950.0	6,393.8	6,511.0
Fiji		18.6	16.0	15.2	15.2	15.4	15.9	16.3	17.5	18.2
French Polynesia	0.1	0.9	0.6	1.8	2.7	3.4	3.7	4.3	4.5	5.1
Guam	2.0	2.7	1.3	4.0	4.8	3.7	3.4	3.6	3.6	3.8
Hong Kong, China	80.0	83.7	36.5	87.5	71.4	154.3	207.3	166.7	174.2	186.2
India	10,513.0	24,861.0	34,631.0	37,428.0	39,140.0	40,088.0	40,371.0	41,345.0	41,995.0	42,728.0
Indonesia	623.3	1,368.5	2,068.0	3,624.8	4,197.3	5,062.5	6,030.3	5,872.0	6,636.7	6,662.3
Japan	1,100.0	1,560.0	1,340.0	2,270.0	2,290.0	2,770.0	3,170.0	3,210.0	3,380.0	3,563.0
Kazakhstan										
Kiribati	2.0									
Kyrgyzstan				77.2	54.6	55.9	54.7	58.4	60.3	63.5
Laos										
Macau			5.3	8.7	6.5	9.6	11.8	12.5	11.8	11.9
Malaysia		414.5	315.3	217.0	214.9	284.0	313.8	294.4	290.9	264.7
Maldives										
Mongolia						48.3	48.5			
Myanmar	296.8	337.9	555.3	539.7	535.3	451.5	425.3	382.1	338.1	288.7
Nauru										
Nepal										
New Caledonia		64.8	12.8	10.4	10.7	10.7	12.1	18.0	20.0	24.1
North Korea										
Pakistan	986.0	2,337.0	2,055.0	1,845.0	2,254.0	2,279.0	2,334.0	3,127.0	3,411.0	3,816.0
Papua New Guinea										
Philippines	985.0	1,989.0	1,993.0	2,196.0	2,377.0	3,014.0	2,931.0	3,134.0	3,268.0	3,478.0
Singapore	36.9	53.2	25.9	54.0	45.5	62.6	90.2	97.1	72.9	67.1
Solomon Islands										
South Korea	511.0	621.0	454.0	427.0	559.0	1,459.0	1,354.0	890.0	821.0	686.0
Sri Lanka		840.3	1,005.1	710.3	704.6	701.0	612.7	497.0	534.6	460.6
Taiwan	89.0	213.0	140.0	242.0	256.0	267.0	273.2	320.7	286.9	366.6
Tajikistan				45.7	51.1	53.7	54.9	56.9	53.8	53.0
Thailand	168.5	1,336.3	709.2	353.2	292.6	1,137.1	984.8	811.6	687.6	610.9
Tonga										
Turkmenistan										
Tuvalu										
Uzbekistan				34.6	37.3	38.1	38.5	39.1	40.4	40.4
Vanuatu										
Vietnam										
Western Samoa										
Australasia										
Australia (h)	359.3	602.8	584.9	750.7	769.0	728.2	660.8	615.7	666.7	672.7
New Zealand	18.2	53.2	124.8	112.2	123.4	139.3	127.7	113.4	102.3	91.8

Source: International Labour Organisation/Euromonitor
Notes: *(a) Excluding indigenous populations living on reserves and full-time members of the armed forces, (b) Data refer to 28 urban agglomerations, (c) Urban areas, (d) Prior 1996: main towns, (e) Excl. rural population of Rondonia, Acre,Amazonas, Roraima, Para and Amapa., (f) 7 main cities, (g) Excluding armed forces and conscripts, (h) Civilian labour force*

▫ Total Unemployed Population

Total Unemployed 1977-2002

● '000

	1977	1985	1990	1996	1997	1998	1999	2000	2001	2002
Africa and Middle East										
Algeria			1,156.0	2,514.7	2,311.0	2,104.0	2,057.0	2,483.3	2,456.8	2,338.9
Angola		56.1	68.3	19.0	18.5	18.3	18.2	18.1	17.8	17.7
Bahrain		6.3	3.0	5.7	6.1	4.1	3.8	6.2	6.8	8.6
Benin										
Botswana										
Burkina Faso	5.0	32.5	42.0	13.5	9.2	9.4	7.5	6.6	5.4	4.8
Burundi		1.9	14.5							
Cameroon	38.4	14.3								
Cape Verde			0.3	0.7	0.7	0.7	0.6	0.6	0.6	0.6
Central African Republic	7.3	8.2	7.8	6.8	6.5	6.4	6.5	6.6	6.9	7.3
Chad										
Comoros										
Congo Dem Rep										
Congo-Brazzaville										
Côte d'Ivoire		86.4	140.3							
Djibouti										
Egypt	357.8	1,000.0	1,430.0	1,667.7	1,448.2	1,449.8	1,482.0	1,702.5	1,736.3	1,829.2
Equatorial Guinea										
Eritrea										
Ethiopia		56.4	44.2	28.3	34.6	29.5	25.7	23.2	20.7	18.0
Gabon										
Gambia										
Ghana	31.9	24.2	30.2	43.2	44.8	45.3	45.6	46.1	46.5	46.9
Guinea										
Guinea-Bissau										
Iran										
Iraq	9.6									
Israel	47.4	96.6	158.1	144.1	169.8	193.7	208.6	214.0	233.0	248.0
Jordan										
Kenya										
Kuwait				8.4	8.6	8.9	9.1	9.5	9.7	10.5
Lebanon					116.1					
Lesotho										
Liberia										
Libya										
Madagascar	46.5	28.8	16.8	3.2	3.1	3.2	3.1	3.1	3.2	3.3
Malawi										
Mali										
Mauritania										
Mauritius	17.1	64.8	12.8	10.4	10.7	10.7	10.4	10.3	11.5	11.9
Morocco			601.0	871.3	844.7	969.1	1,161.7	1,152.0	1,205.0	1,233.9
Mozambique										
Namibia										
Niger	9.5	29.0	20.9							
Nigeria	15.8	28.3	57.1	79.4	81.2	84.3	85.6	89.3	88.3	89.7
Oman										
Qatar										
Réunion	17.3	45.0	53.8	92.4	93.6	93.0	93.8	93.9	93.7	91.8
Rwanda										
Sao Tomé e Príncipe										
Saudi Arabia										
Senegal	4.6	10.8	10.4							
Seychelles		5.7								
Sierra Leone	9.2	0.3								
Somalia										
South Africa										
Sudan		45.0	53.8							
Swaziland										
Syria	100.3	128.3	198.6							
Tanzania										
Togo		4.1								
Tunisia			56.2	31.6	26.8	102.1	91.3	74.6	115.0	119.2
Uganda										
United Arab Emirates								41.0		
Yemen										
Zambia										
Zimbabwe										

Source: International Labour Organisation/Euromonitor
Notes: (a) Excluding indigenous populations living on reserves and full-time members of the armed forces, (b) Data refer to 28 urban agglomerations, (c) Urban areas, (d) Prior 1996: main towns, (e) Excl. rural population of Rondonia, Acre,Amazonas, Roraima, Para and Amapa., (f) 7 main cities, (g) Excluding armed forces and conscripts, (h) Civilian labour force

| ▫ Trends in Unemployment Rate | | | | | | | | | **Table 19.5** |

Unemployment Rate 1980-2002

- % of economically active population

	1980	1985	1990	1996	1997	1998	1999	2000	2001	2002
North America										
Canada [a]	7.9	11.0	8.5	9.7	9.2	8.4	7.6	6.8	7.2	6.9
USA	7.2	7.2	5.6	5.4	4.7	4.5	4.2	4.0	4.8	5.1
Latin America										
Anguilla										
Antigua										
Argentina [b]			10.2	17.2	14.9	12.8	14.1	15.0	16.6	19.0
Aruba										
Bahamas	12.4	11.2	11.9	11.5	9.8	7.7	7.3	7.1	6.9	6.7
Barbados	11.4	18.7	15.0	15.8	14.5	12.3	11.1	10.5	10.0	9.2
Belize										
Bermuda										
Bolivia [c, d]			6.9	3.8	3.7	5.0	7.4	7.4	7.5	7.6
Brazil [e]	3.4	3.4	3.7	7.0	7.8	9.0	9.6	8.0	6.8	6.2
British Virgin Islands										
Cayman Islands										
Chile	10.4	12.2	5.7	5.4	5.3	7.2	8.9	8.3	7.9	8.2
Colombia [f, g]	9.1	13.9	10.2	11.9	12.1	15.0	20.1	20.5	21.5	21.6
Costa Rica	5.9	6.8	4.6	6.2	5.7	5.6	6.0	5.2	4.8	4.2
Cuba										
Dominica										
Dominican Republic				16.6	15.9	15.7	15.4	15.2	15.0	14.7
Ecuador			7.5	10.5	9.2	11.5	14.8	8.8	10.9	11.0
El Salvador	12.9	16.9	10.0	7.7	8.0	7.3	7.0	8.3	10.0	11.0
French Guiana	7.1	13.5	13.9	18.3	19.7	19.7	20.1	20.2	20.5	20.6
Grenada										
Guadeloupe		22.0	17.0	25.8	26.4	26.6	26.8	27.0	27.4	27.6
Guatemala										
Guyana										
Haiti										
Honduras		10.4	4.8	4.3	3.2	3.9	3.7	4.0	4.1	4.2
Jamaica	27.3	25.0	15.7	16.0	16.3	15.2	14.8	16.0	16.4	16.3
Martinique										
Mexico			2.4	3.7	2.6	2.3	1.7	1.6	1.7	1.7
Netherlands Antilles			17.0	14.0	15.3	16.7	15.2	14.0	13.2	12.2
Nicaragua		3.2	11.1	14.9	13.3	13.3	10.9	9.8	9.0	9.2
Panama		12.3	16.3	14.3	13.4	13.6	11.8	13.0	14.5	15.3
Paraguay	4.1	5.1	6.6	8.2	10.3	10.5	8.3	7.1	6.8	6.2
Peru [c]			8.6	7.0	7.7	7.8	8.0	7.4	7.9	7.9
Puerto Rico	17.1	21.8	14.1	13.4	13.5	13.3	11.8	10.1	9.6	8.8
St Kitts										
St Lucia										
St Vincent and the Grenadines										
Suriname			15.8	11.0	10.5	10.6	14.0	16.0	17.2	17.9
Trinidad and Tobago	10.0	15.5	22.0	16.2	15.0	14.2	13.1	12.5	11.8	11.2
Uruguay		12.4	8.5	10.9	10.7	10.1	11.3	13.6	15.2	16.7
Venezuela			10.6	11.0	9.7	9.5	8.9	8.4	8.6	8.8

Source: International Labour Organisation/Euromonitor
Notes: (a) Excluding indigenous populations living on reserves and full-time members of the armed forces, (b) Data refer to 28 urban agglomerations, (c) Urban areas, (d) Prior 1996: main towns, (e) Excl. rural population of Rondonia, Acre,Amazonas, Roraima, Para and Amapa., (f) 7 main cities, (g) Excluding armed forces and conscripts, (h) Civilian labour force

◘ Trends in Unemployment Rate

Unemployment Rate 1980-2002

• % of economically active population

	1980	1985	1990	1996	1997	1998	1999	2000	2001	2002
Asia Pacific										
Afghanistan										
American Samoa										
Armenia					36.4	35.2	33.8	32.3	29.9	28.1
Azerbaijan										
Bangladesh		0.6	1.9	2.5	2.5	2.4	2.4	2.4	2.3	2.3
Bhutan										
Brunei										
Cambodia										
China			0.5	0.8	0.8	0.8	0.8	0.8	0.9	0.9
Fiji		8.1	6.4	5.9	6.4	6.9	7.6	8.4	8.9	9.4
French Polynesia										
Guam	9.9	7.8	2.8	8.3	9.6	7.7	7.2	7.5	7.6	7.8
Hong Kong, China	4.4	3.2	1.3	2.8	2.2	4.6	6.1	4.9	5.1	5.3
India	6.4	9.1	11.3	10.6	10.9	10.9	10.7	10.8	10.9	10.8
Indonesia			2.7	4.0	4.6	5.4	6.2	6.0	6.7	6.5
Japan	2.0	2.6	2.1	3.4	3.4	4.1	4.7	4.7	5.0	5.3
Kazakhstan										
Kiribati										
Kyrgyzstan										
Laos										
Macau			3.2	4.3	3.2	4.6	6.4	6.8	6.5	6.7
Malaysia		6.8	4.6	2.5	2.5	3.2	3.4	3.1	3.0	2.6
Maldives										
Mongolia						5.7				
Myanmar										
Nauru										
Nepal										
New Caledonia										
North Korea										
Pakistan	8.8	8.1	6.4	5.4	6.2	6.0	6.0	7.8	8.4	9.2
Papua New Guinea										
Philippines	6.9	8.9	8.1	7.4	7.8	9.6	9.2	10.1	9.8	10.2
Singapore	2.8	3.9	1.7	3.0	2.4	3.2	4.4	4.4	3.4	3.1
Solomon Islands										
South Korea	5.2	4.0	2.5	2.0	2.6	6.8	6.3	4.0	3.7	3.1
Sri Lanka		13.5	14.4	11.3	10.7	10.6	9.1	7.4	7.7	7.1
Taiwan	1.2	2.8	1.7	2.6	2.7	2.8	2.8	3.2	2.9	3.6
Tajikistan				2.6	2.7	2.8	2.8	2.9	3.0	3.1
Thailand	0.9	4.9	2.2	1.1	0.9	3.4	3.0	2.4	2.0	1.8
Tonga										
Turkmenistan										
Tuvalu										
Uzbekistan				0.4	0.5	0.5	0.5	0.5	0.5	0.5
Vanuatu										
Vietnam										
Western Samoa										
Australasia										
Australia [h]	5.9	8.3	6.9	8.2	8.3	7.8	7.0	6.4	6.8	6.7
New Zealand	2.3	3.4	7.9	6.2	6.6	7.5	6.8	6.0	5.3	4.7

Source: *International Labour Organisation/Euromonitor*
Notes: *(a) Excluding indigenous populations living on reserves and full-time members of the armed forces, (b) Data refer to 28 urban agglomerations, (c) Urban areas, (d) Prior 1996: main towns, (e) Excl. rural population of Rondonia, Acre,Amazonas, Roraima, Para and Amapa., (f) 7 main cities, (g) Excluding armed forces and conscripts, (h) Civilian labour force*

□ Trends in Unemployment Rate
Unemployment Rate 1980-2002

- % of economically active population

Africa and Middle East	1980	1985	1990	1996	1997	1998	1999	2000	2001	2002
Algeria			22.4	31.8	28.7	26.0	25.3	30.5	30.1	29.7
Angola										
Bahrain										
Benin										
Botswana										
Burkina Faso										
Burundi										
Cameroon										
Cape Verde										
Central African Republic										
Chad										
Comoros										
Congo Dem Rep										
Congo-Brazzaville										
Côte d'Ivoire										
Djibouti										
Egypt	6.3	7.7	8.7	9.3	8.0	7.9	7.8	8.9	9.0	9.3
Equatorial Guinea										
Eritrea										
Ethiopia										
Gabon										
Gambia										
Ghana										
Guinea										
Guinea-Bissau										
Iran										
Iraq										
Israel	4.8	6.7	9.6	6.7	7.7	8.6	8.9	8.8	9.3	9.6
Jordan										
Kenya										
Kuwait				1.1	1.1	1.0	1.0	1.0	1.0	1.0
Lebanon										
Lesotho										
Liberia										
Libya										
Madagascar										
Malawi										
Mali										
Mauritania										
Mauritius	7.9	16.1	2.7	5.5	5.9	5.9	6.7	8.0	8.6	9.2
Morocco			15.4	17.8	16.6	18.9	21.8	20.8	21.3	21.2
Mozambique										
Namibia										
Niger										
Nigeria										
Oman										
Qatar										
Réunion			23.0	39.6	40.0	39.8	40.1	39.9	39.7	39.4
Rwanda										
Sao Tomé e Príncipe										
Saudi Arabia										
Senegal										
Seychelles										
Sierra Leone										
Somalia										
South Africa										
Sudan										
Swaziland										
Syria	3.7	5.2	6.1							
Tanzania										
Togo										
Tunisia			2.2	1.1	0.9	3.4	3.0	2.4	3.5	3.5
Uganda										
United Arab Emirates										
Yemen										
Zambia										
Zimbabwe										

Source: International Labour Organisation/Euromonitor
Notes: (a) Excluding indigenous populations living on reserves and full-time members of the armed forces, (b) Data refer to 28 urban agglomerations, (c) Urban areas, (d) Prior 1996: main towns, (e) Excl. rural population of Rondonia, Acre,Amazonas, Roraima, Para and Amapa., (f) 7 main cities, (g) Excluding armed forces and conscripts, (h) Civilian labour force

Average Working Week in Non-Agricultural Activities 1977-2002

● Hours

	1977	1985	1990	1996	1997	1998	1999	2000	2001	2002
Algeria										
Argentina			41.8	42.4	42.6	42.7	42.6	42.0	42.1	42.0
Australia	35.0	33.0	33.3	35.0	34.8	34.8	34.9	34.8	34.7	34.8
Azerbaijan										
Bolivia			43.3	41.4	41.8	41.8	41.9	41.5	41.5	41.6
Brazil			43.1	41.7	41.4	41.6	40.9	40.8	40.5	40.3
Canada		32.0	31.3	30.7	31.3	31.2	31.4	31.6	31.6	31.8
Chile		43.0	44.9	44.6	43.9	43.9	43.3	43.9	43.4	43.3
China			38.6	37.5	36.9	36.5	36.2	36.0	35.8	35.6
Colombia			49.0	48.9	49.0	47.7	47.5	46.7	46.4	46.0
Ecuador			45.3	44.4	44.6	44.5	44.3	44.0	44.1	44.1
Egypt	56.0	56.0	55.0	56.0	53.0	52.0	53.1	52.2	52.0	52.0
Hong Kong, China		48.9	45.6	46.1	45.2	45.2	46.0	46.6	46.3	46.8
India			47.8	46.7	46.7	46.6	46.3	46.6	46.5	46.6
Indonesia			47.7	47.4	47.4	47.5	47.4	47.4	47.1	47.0
Israel	36.5	35.3	35.4	37.7	37.1	37.0	37.3	37.7	36.8	36.8
Japan	47.4	47.3	46.1	43.3	42.7	42.5	42.5	43.0	42.4	42.4
Jordan			54.3	56.4	56.5	56.1	55.3	55.4	55.8	55.9
Kazakhstan										
Kuwait										
Malaysia		45.2	45.2	44.3	44.1	44.0	43.8	43.7	43.4	43.4
Mexico				44.2	44.7	43.9	44.6	43.8	44.1	44.3
Morocco										
New Zealand	39.4	39.6	38.7	39.1	39.2	38.3	38.2	38.2	38.0	38.0
Nigeria										
Pakistan										
Peru	46.9	46.5	48.5	50.5	50.1	49.8	50.3	49.8	50.4	50.6
Philippines		47.8	47.6	46.2	45.9	45.5	46.3	45.8	46.1	46.3
Saudi Arabia										
Singapore		44.6	46.5	47.3	47.4	46.7	46.8	47.0	46.7	46.8
South Africa			45.4	45.4	45.5	40.5	40.7	41.2	41.5	41.9
South Korea	51.4	51.9	48.2	47.3	46.7	45.9	46.2	46.3	46.1	46.3
Taiwan			48.5	47.5	47.2	47.0	47.0	47.0	47.3	47.6
Thailand			49.1	50.1	49.2	51.3	50.0	50.5	50.8	50.8
Tunisia				44.0	44.1	44.2	44.2	44.3	44.4	44.5
Turkmenistan										
United Arab Emirates										
USA	36.0	34.9	34.5	34.4	34.6	34.6	34.5	34.5	34.2	33.6
Venezuela	42.9	40.7	41.8	41.6	41.6	41.5	41.3	41.4	41.7	41.8
Vietnam			44.6	44.2	44.1	43.9	43.7	43.6	43.9	44.0

Source: International Labour Organisation/Euromonitor
Notes: Hours actually worked by wage earners, unless otherwise stated

◫ Hours of Work

Table 19.7

Average Working Week in Manufacturing 1977-2002

● Hours

	1977	1985	1990	1996	1997	1998	1999	2000	2001	2002
Algeria										
Argentina			44.3	46.3	46.5	46.5	45.8	45.4	45.9	45.8
Australia	37.6	36.9	38.1	38.7	38.5	38.6	38.9	38.5	38.5	38.5
Azerbaijan										
Bolivia			47.5	44.7	44.2	44.0	43.5	43.7	43.8	43.8
Brazil			43.1	42.5	42.5	42.4	41.8	41.9	41.8	41.7
Canada	38.7	38.6	38.2	38.4	39.3	38.6	38.7	38.9	39.0	39.3
Chile		43.1	44.9	44.9	44.2	43.7	43.2	43.6	43.5	43.5
China	12.6	24.3	43.4	37.2	33.9	40.7	39.7	38.6	37.6	36.7
Colombia			47.5	47.5	47.5	47.1	46.8	46.0	45.9	45.5
Ecuador		44.0	45.3	45.4	45.6	45.8	45.9	45.8	45.8	45.9
Egypt	54.0	56.0	56.0	57.0	54.0	52.0	53.0	53.3	53.0	53.5
Hong Kong, China	51.8	44.8	44.2	45.0	43.8	44.0	44.9	45.2	45.0	45.3
India		45.9	46.4	46.7	46.5	47.0	47.0	47.0	47.0	47.1
Indonesia			48.5	46.5	46.5	46.4	46.3	46.2	46.1	46.1
Israel	38.8	38.6	38.8	41.8	42.1	42.0	41.7	42.6	41.5	41.4
Japan	46.0	46.2	45.7	43.3	42.7	42.5	42.7	43.7	42.9	42.9
Jordan			61.7	63.1	63.2	62.7	62.4	62.1	61.7	61.4
Kazakhstan			37.0	34.0	33.7	33.5	33.3	33.3	33.5	33.5
Kuwait										
Malaysia		45.8	45.3	45.6	45.6	45.7	45.6	45.4	45.2	45.2
Mexico	45.5	46.4	45.4	45.5	46.2	45.0	45.4	44.4	44.8	44.9
Morocco										
New Zealand	40.3	40.7	41.1	41.4	41.0	41.0	40.9	41.0	40.7	40.7
Nigeria										
Pakistan										
Peru	45.4	44.8	47.5	49.2	47.7	48.5	49.6	49.1	49.3	49.7
Philippines		44.8	44.9	44.0	44.3	43.9	44.5	43.9	44.3	44.5
Saudi Arabia										
Singapore		46.5	48.5	49.4	49.5	48.4	49.2	49.8	48.8	49.2
South Africa	46.5	45.9	45.4	45.4	45.5	45.3	45.1	44.7	44.4	44.2
South Korea	52.9	53.8	49.8	48.4	47.8	46.1	48.2	49.1	47.7	48.3
Taiwan		51.4	50.4	50.3	50.1	50.0	49.4	49.2	49.6	49.6
Thailand			48.3	49.4	49.1	50.5	50.1	50.2	50.4	50.5
Tunisia										
Turkmenistan										
United Arab Emirates										
USA	40.3	40.5	40.8	41.6	42.0	41.7	41.7	41.6	40.7	40.4
Venezuela	43.7	40.6	41.5	41.8	41.8	41.7	41.5	41.9	42.0	42.3
Vietnam			49.2	48.9	48.9	48.8	48.5	48.3	48.2	48.1

Source: International Labour Organisation/Euromonitor
Notes: Hours actually worked by wage earners, unless otherwise stated

☐ Economically Active Population

Table 19.8

Economically Active Population by Age Group 2002

● '000

	Under 15	15-19	20-24	25-29	30-34	35-39	40-44
Algeria		1,086.7	1,454.1	1,321.7	1,016.9	778.2	672.2
Argentina	13.2	437.9	1,239.5	1,212.9	1,061.3	1,012.7	1,024.2
Australia		822.3	1,132.9	1,189.0	1,191.1	1,181.5	1,243.6
Azerbaijan							
Bolivia	149.3	229.7	293.3	292.5	249.6	260.4	244.6
Brazil	2,791.1	9,133.6	11,942.3	10,707.4		20,833.2	
Canada		1,092.4	1,609.4	1,763.4	1,862.9	2,196.5	2,394.2
Chile		157.8	616.5	795.2	764.6	816.2	806.6
China		66,700.0	79,660.8	114,275.1	121,452.6	94,424.8	74,316.4
Colombia	37.1	641.6		2,329.2		2,246.1	
Ecuador	134.0	410.7	648.0	546.7	550.1	519.8	450.8
Egypt		2,118.1	2,859.5	2,185.6		4,496.2	
Hong Kong, China		69.7	332.3	476.3	490.2	554.3	560.3
India	11,691.8	34,113.5	51,514.7	55,117.2	50,577.9	46,005.4	
Indonesia	1,597.2	8,588.2	13,173.1	12,652.5	12,112.2	13,488.2	11,171.7
Israel		34.4	334.7		740.9		601.1
Japan		1,283.0	5,756.0	8,380.0	7,397.0	6,488.0	6,345.0
Jordan							
Kazakhstan	502.6	765.7	732.3	753.7	647.9	828.2	795.0
Kuwait							
Malaysia		645.2	1,636.3	1,762.7	1,459.9	1,265.7	1,124.4
Mexico	873.7	4,222.7	5,003.5	5,385.8	5,054.6	4,790.9	4,417.4
Morocco			1,287.8				3,460.8
New Zealand		147.9	186.0	195.4	216.9	243.9	258.3
Nigeria							
Pakistan	1,995.0	5,318.0	5,501.0	5,170.0	4,583.0	4,590.0	3,865.0
Peru	95.9	873.9	1,128.0	1,237.6	1,096.7	1,003.8	938.6
Philippines		3,299.0	4,749.0		7,327.0		7,636.0
Saudi Arabia							
Singapore		46.8	229.3	319.2	307.4	319.5	312.8
South Africa							
South Korea		412.0	1,615.0	2,589.0	2,679.0	3,157.0	3,506.0
Taiwan		337.6	861.9	1,428.6	1,571.2	1,687.9	1,510.2
Thailand	145.0	1,720.1	3,846.7	4,826.3	4,691.0	4,427.6	
Tunisia		387.1	479.8	502.8	461.5	438.8	432.3
Turkmenistan							
United Arab Emirates							
USA		8,150.0	14,832.0	14,419.0	16,248.0	18,114.0	19,749.0
Venezuela			2,592.8				5,373.9
Vietnam							

Source: *International Labour Organisation/Euromonitor*

Economically Active Population

Economically Active Population by Age Group 2002 (continued)

- '000

	45-49	50-54	55-59	60-64	Over 65	Total
Algeria	618.6	382.2	322.9	214.5		7,868.0
Argentina	956.2	791.6	563.8	339.8	283.7	8,936.8
Australia	1,131.1	1,008.7	649.9	293.7	150.6	9,994.4
Azerbaijan						
Bolivia	220.3	136.1	112.5	71.2	120.7	2,380.1
Brazil	16,119.4		9,151.7		5,292.4	85,971.1
Canada	2,024.2	1,794.0	1,059.7	484.0	221.3	16,502.0
Chile	655.2	580.1	401.8	240.6	195.9	6,030.5
China	75,957.9	42,999.8	28,799.8	18,916.0	18,043.9	735,547.1
Colombia	1,508.0		778.0		343.2	7,883.2
Ecuador	329.1	325.4	172.3	106.9	155.4	4,349.1
Egypt	4,442.2		2,681.1	536.0	378.0	19,696.7
Hong Kong, China	426.6	338.6	145.4	72.2	41.1	3,507.0
India	73,921.3		45,066.2	18,992.6	7,978.2	394,978.8
Indonesia	9,655.0	6,767.2	4,661.7	4,199.7	3,722.9	101,789.7
Israel		582.5	146.2	90.7	59.3	2,589.8
Japan	6,920.0	9,468.0	6,364.0	4,316.0	4,977.0	67,694.0
Jordan						
Kazakhstan	609.3	419.6	126.5	238.7	142.6	6,562.2
Kuwait						1,034.0
Malaysia	906.8	654.0	368.7	229.8		10,053.5
Mexico	3,326.3	2,572.0	1,761.9	1,228.8	1,791.2	40,428.7
Morocco			889.5		193.3	5,831.4
New Zealand	227.5	210.3	138.1	90.2	40.6	1,955.1
Nigeria						
Pakistan	3,394.0	2,477.0	1,747.0	1,406.0	1,641.0	41,687.0
Peru	692.8	591.2	344.0	272.5	307.0	8,582.0
Philippines		6,213.0		3,280.0	1,753.0	34,257.0
Saudi Arabia						
Singapore	264.1	216.3	83.0	55.3	34.3	2,188.0
South Africa						
South Korea	2,719.0	1,979.0	1,337.0	1,163.0	1,238.0	22,394.0
Taiwan	1,336.8	479.3	524.4	219.6	135.1	10,092.6
Thailand	7,627.5		4,421.5		2,045.1	33,750.8
Tunisia	242.2	159.1	95.3	74.4	114.2	3,387.5
Turkmenistan						
United Arab Emirates						
USA	17,634.0	15,077.0	9,700.0	5,437.0	4,414.0	143,774.0
Venezuela				2,277.1	293.6	10,537.4
Vietnam						

Source: International Labour Organisation/Euromonitor

Economically Active Population by Age Group 2002 (% Analysis)

• % of total EAP

	Under 15	15-19	20-24	25-29	30-34	35-39	40-44
Algeria		13.8	18.5	16.8	12.9	9.9	8.5
Argentina	0.1	4.9	13.9	13.6	11.9	11.3	11.5
Australia		8.2	11.3	11.9	11.9	11.8	12.4
Azerbaijan							
Bolivia	6.3	9.7	12.3	12.3	10.5	10.9	10.3
Brazil	3.2	10.6	13.9	12.5		24.2	
Canada		6.6	9.8	10.7	11.3	13.3	14.5
Chile		2.6	10.2	13.2	12.7	13.5	13.4
China		9.1	10.8	15.5	16.5	12.8	10.1
Colombia	0.5	8.1		29.5		28.5	
Ecuador	3.1	9.4	14.9	12.6	12.6	12.0	10.4
Egypt		10.8	14.5	11.1		22.8	
Hong Kong, China		2.0	9.5	13.6	14.0	15.8	16.0
India	3.0	8.6	13.0	14.0	12.8	11.6	
Indonesia	1.6	8.4	12.9	12.4	11.9	13.3	11.0
Israel		1.3	12.9		28.6		23.2
Japan		1.9	8.5	12.4	10.9	9.6	9.4
Jordan							
Kazakhstan	7.7	11.7	11.2	11.5	9.9	12.6	12.1
Kuwait							
Malaysia		6.4	16.3	17.5	14.5	12.6	11.2
Mexico	2.2	10.4	12.4	13.3	12.5	11.9	10.9
Morocco			22.1				59.3
New Zealand		7.6	9.5	10.0	11.1	12.5	13.2
Nigeria							
Pakistan	4.8	12.8	13.2	12.4	11.0	11.0	9.3
Peru	1.1	10.2	13.1	14.4	12.8	11.7	10.9
Philippines		9.6	13.9		21.4		22.3
Saudi Arabia							
Singapore		2.1	10.5	14.6	14.0	14.6	14.3
South Africa							
South Korea		1.8	7.2	11.6	12.0	14.1	15.7
Taiwan		3.3	8.5	14.2	15.6	16.7	15.0
Thailand	0.4	5.1	11.4	14.3	13.9	13.1	
Tunisia		11.4	14.2	14.8	13.6	13.0	12.8
Turkmenistan							
United Arab Emirates							
USA		5.7	10.3	10.0	11.3	12.6	13.7
Venezuela			24.6				51.0
Vietnam							

Source: *International Labour Organisation/Euromonitor*

◘ Economically Active Population

Economically Active Population by Age Group 2002 (% Analysis) (continued)

• % of total EAP

	45-49	50-54	55-59	60-64	Over 65	Total
Algeria	7.9	4.9	4.1	2.7		100.0
Argentina	10.7	8.9	6.3	3.8	3.2	100.0
Australia	11.3	10.1	6.5	2.9	1.5	100.0
Azerbaijan						
Bolivia	9.3	5.7	4.7	3.0	5.1	100.0
Brazil	18.7		10.6		6.2	100.0
Canada	12.3	10.9	6.4	2.9	1.3	100.0
Chile	10.9	9.6	6.7	4.0	3.2	100.0
China	10.3	5.8	3.9	2.6	2.5	100.0
Colombia	19.1		9.9		4.4	100.0
Ecuador	7.6	7.5	4.0	2.5	3.6	100.0
Egypt	22.6		13.6	2.7	1.9	100.0
Hong Kong, China	12.2	9.7	4.1	2.1	1.2	100.0
India	18.7		11.4	4.8	2.0	100.0
Indonesia	9.5	6.6	4.6	4.1	3.7	100.0
Israel		22.5	5.6	3.5	2.3	100.0
Japan	10.2	14.0	9.4	6.4	7.4	100.0
Jordan						
Kazakhstan	9.3	6.4	1.9	3.6	2.2	100.0
Kuwait						100.0
Malaysia	9.0	6.5	3.7	2.3		100.0
Mexico	8.2	6.4	4.4	3.0	4.4	100.0
Morocco			15.3		3.3	100.0
New Zealand	11.6	10.8	7.1	4.6	2.1	100.0
Nigeria						
Pakistan	8.1	5.9	4.2	3.4	3.9	100.0
Peru	8.1	6.9	4.0	3.2	3.6	100.0
Philippines		18.1		9.6	5.1	100.0
Saudi Arabia						
Singapore	12.1	9.9	3.8	2.5	1.6	100.0
South Africa						
South Korea	12.1	8.8	6.0	5.2	5.5	100.0
Taiwan	13.2	4.7	5.2	2.2	1.3	100.0
Thailand	22.6		13.1		6.1	100.0
Tunisia	7.1	4.7	2.8	2.2	3.4	100.0
Turkmenistan						
United Arab Emirates						
USA	12.3	10.5	6.7	3.8	3.1	100.0
Venezuela				21.6	2.8	100.0
Vietnam						

Source: *International Labour Organisation/Euromonitor*

Economically Active Population by Sex 2002

● As stated

	Total ('000)	EAP as % Total Population	Males ('000)	Males as % Total EAP	Females ('000)	Females as % Total EAP
Algeria	7,868	25.7	6,848	87.0	1,020	13.0
Argentina	8,937	23.7	5,303	59.3	3,634	40.7
Australia	9,994	51.4	5,562	55.7	4,432	44.3
Azerbaijan						
Bolivia	2,380	27.6	1,043	43.8	1,337	56.2
Brazil	85,971	49.8	49,588	57.7	36,383	42.3
Canada	16,502	53.2	8,873	53.8	7,630	46.2
Chile	6,030	38.9	4,010	66.5	2,021	33.5
China	735,547	56.8	429,958	58.5	305,589	41.5
Colombia	7,883	19.7	4,051	51.4	3,833	48.6
Ecuador	4,349	33.2	2,486	57.2	1,863	42.8
Egypt	19,697	30.6	15,618	79.3	4,079	20.7
Hong Kong, China	3,507	48.6	1,985	56.6	1,522	43.4
India	394,979	38.1	295,038	74.7	99,941	25.3
Indonesia	101,790	47.1	63,040	61.9	38,750	38.1
Israel	2,590	40.3	1,393	53.8	1,197	46.2
Japan	67,694	53.3	39,989	59.1	27,705	40.9
Jordan						
Kazakhstan	6,562	40.8	3,823	58.3	2,739	41.7
Kuwait	1,034	44.1	715	69.1	319	30.9
Malaysia	10,054	43.4	6,722	66.9	3,331	33.1
Mexico	40,429	39.7	26,550	65.7	13,879	34.3
Morocco	5,831	20.0	4,524	77.6	1,308	22.4
New Zealand	1,955	50.1	1,062	54.3	894	45.7
Nigeria						
Pakistan	41,687	25.6	34,884	83.7	6,803	16.3
Peru	8,582	32.4	4,716	55.0	3,866	45.0
Philippines	34,257	43.2	20,640	60.3	13,617	39.7
Saudi Arabia						
Singapore	2,188	65.5	1,216	55.6	972	44.4
South Africa						
South Korea	22,394	46.5	13,095	58.5	9,299	41.5
Taiwan	10,093	44.7	5,614	55.6	4,478	44.4
Thailand	33,751	54.2	18,532	54.9	15,219	45.1
Tunisia	3,387	35.0	2,524	74.5	863	25.5
Turkmenistan						
United Arab Emirates						
USA	143,774	51.5	76,561	53.3	67,213	46.7
Venezuela	10,537	42.0	6,705	63.6	3,833	36.4
Vietnam						

Source: *International Labour Organisation/Euromonitor*

Literacy and Education

Higher and University Education: Establishments, Staff and Students: 2002

● As stated

	Establish-ments	Teaching Staff ('000)	Students ('000)	Student to Staff Ratio	University Teachers ('000)	University Teachers (% of total)	University Students ('000)	University Students (% of total)	University Students to Staff Ratio
Algeria	383		547.4		22.6		384.7	70.3	17.1
Argentina	1,633	151.1			29.4	19.5	487.5		16.6
Australia		77.4	1,607.8	20.8	25.9	33.5			
Azerbaijan	48	17.1			12.7	74.5	84.4		6.6
Bolivia					9.1		183.3		20.2
Brazil		172.7	2,286.7	13.2					
Canada		188.9	1,470.2	7.8	31.8	16.8	839.3	57.1	26.4
Chile			710.6		30.1		348.7	49.1	11.6
China	1,031	493.5							
Colombia		72.5	778.1	10.7			643.9	82.8	
Ecuador									
Egypt							1,721.7		
Hong Kong, China		7.8	157.6	20.2	5.4	69.2	83.1	52.7	15.4
India									
Indonesia		214.7	3,458.5	16.1	197.8	92.1	3,388.3	98.0	17.1
Israel			289.6		13.4		118.3	40.8	8.8
Japan	673	385.2	6,935.3	18.0	288.1	74.8	2,817.7	40.6	9.8
Jordan	23	7.2	132.3	18.4	5.3	73.0	126.5	95.6	24.1
Kazakhstan	162				24.1		231.5		9.6
Kuwait		2.2			1.0	47.1	19.9		19.0
Malaysia	56	23.4			8.5	36.3	406.6		47.7
Mexico	4,921	195.2	1,908.9	9.8					
Morocco	51	12.5	400.6	32.0	14.1	112.6	279.9	69.9	19.8
New Zealand	42	10.8	216.4	20.1	5.1	47.0	108.1	49.9	21.3
Nigeria					19.0		282.1		14.9
Pakistan	1,286						129.2		
Peru	1,045	58.9			33.0	56.0	473.8		14.3
Philippines	1,793		2,725.8		76.0		2,142.8	78.6	28.2
Saudi Arabia		17.7	431.4	24.4	15.9	90.3	264.9	61.4	16.6
Singapore	21	7.7	128.3	16.7	3.2	41.7	51.0	39.7	15.9
South Africa		33.3	981.3	29.5	14.9	44.8	389.3	39.7	26.1
South Korea	431	89.5	3,266.0	36.5	63.4	70.8	1,724.4	52.8	27.2
Taiwan	148	50.0			33.9	67.9	427.3		12.6
Thailand			2,206.5						
Tunisia	124	8.5	183.1	21.5	7.0	82.7	157.3	85.9	22.4
Turkmenistan	19								
United Arab Emirates			18.3		0.8		13.1	71.9	15.5
USA	3,915	987.8	14,736.8	14.9					
Venezuela									
Vietnam	95	26.1							

Source: *Euromonitor from UNESCO*

Adult Literacy Rates and School Leaving Age: 2002

● As stated

	Adult Literacy Rate (%)	Compulsory Education Commencement Age	School Leaving Age
North America			
Canada	99.3	6	16
USA	99.9	6	16
Latin America			
Anguilla	95.7		
Antigua			
Argentina	97.0	6	14
Aruba			
Bahamas	94.7		
Barbados	99.7		
Belize	93.7		
Bermuda			
Bolivia	86.7	6	13
Brazil	86.0	7	14
British Virgin Islands			
Cayman Islands	98.2		
Chile	96.1	6	13
Colombia	92.2	6	12
Costa Rica	95.8		
Cuba	96.9		
Dominica			
Dominican Republic	84.3		
Ecuador	92.2	6	14
El Salvador	79.7		
French Guiana			
Grenada			
Guadeloupe			
Guatemala	70.0		
Guyana	98.7		
Haiti	51.9		
Honduras	75.7		
Jamaica	87.6		
Martinique	97.6		
Mexico	91.9	6	14
Netherlands Antilles	96.7		
Nicaragua	67.9		
Panama	92.3		
Paraguay	93.7		
Peru	90.6	6	16
Puerto Rico	94.1		
St Kitts			
St Lucia			
St Vincent and the Grenadines			
Suriname			
Trinidad and Tobago	98.5		
Uruguay	97.9		
Venezuela	93.2	5	15

Adult Literacy Rates and School Leaving Age: 2002

● As stated

	Adult Literacy Rate (%)	Compulsory Education Commencement Age	School Leaving Age
Asia Pacific			
Afghanistan			
American Samoa			
Armenia	98.6		
Azerbaijan	99.4	6	17
Bangladesh	35.0		
Bhutan			
Brunei	91.5		
Cambodia	69.2		
China	85.4	7	19
Fiji	93.5		
French Polynesia			
Guam	99.1		
Hong Kong, China	93.8	6	19
India	58.8	6	14
Indonesia	87.9	6	18
Japan	99.9	6	15
Kazakhstan	99.5	6	18
Kiribati			
Kyrgyzstan			
Laos	51.4		
Macau	94.3		
Malaysia	88.4	6	16
Maldives	97.0		
Mongolia	99.0		
Myanmar	85.3		
Nauru			
Nepal	44.1		
New Caledonia			
North Korea			
Pakistan	44.9	6	14
Papua New Guinea	65.3		
Philippines	95.7	7	13
Singapore	92.9	6	16
Solomon Islands			
South Korea	97.8	6	12
Sri Lanka	92.1		
Taiwan	96.4	6	18
Tajikistan	99.3		
Thailand	95.8	6	18
Tonga			
Turkmenistan	99.0	6	15
Tuvalu			
Uzbekistan	99.3		
Vanuatu			
Vietnam	93.8	6	18
Western Samoa	98.8		
Australasia			
Australia	99.9	6	16
New Zealand	99.9	5	16

Adult Literacy Rates and School Leaving Age: 2002

● As stated

	Adult Literacy Rate (%)	Compulsory Education Commencement Age	School Leaving Age
Africa and Middle East			
Algeria	68.9	6	15
Angola			
Bahrain	82.4		
Benin	39.8		
Botswana	78.9		
Burkina Faso	25.7		
Burundi	50.4		
Cameroon	77.9		
Cape Verde	75.8		
Central African Republic	49.6		
Chad	45.8		
Comoros	56.3		
Congo Dem Rep	64.1		
Congo-Brazzaville	82.8		
Côte d'Ivoire	49.6		
Djibouti	66.5		
Egypt	56.9	6	11
Equatorial Guinea	84.8		
Eritrea	57.6		
Ethiopia	41.5		
Gabon			
Gambia	38.9		
Ghana	73.7		
Guinea			
Guinea-Bissau	41.0		
Iran	78.4		
Iraq	40.0		
Israel	95.1	5	16
Jordan	90.8	6	15
Kenya	84.3		
Kuwait	83.0	6	14
Lebanon	86.9		
Lesotho	84.3		
Liberia	56.4		
Libya	81.7		
Madagascar	68.1		
Malawi	61.8		
Mali	44.8		
Mauritania	41.2		
Mauritius	85.3		
Morocco	50.8	7	13
Mozambique	46.5		
Namibia	83.3		
Niger	17.0		
Nigeria	66.7	6	12
Oman	74.4		
Qatar	82.1		
Réunion	88.5		
Rwanda	69.2		
Sao Tomé e Príncipe			
Saudi Arabia	78.0	6	12
Senegal	39.2		
Seychelles			
Sierra Leone			
Somalia			
South Africa	86.0	7	16
Sudan	60.0		
Swaziland	80.9		
Syria	76.1		
Tanzania	75.5		
Togo	59.6		
Tunisia	73.2	6	16
Uganda	68.9		
United Arab Emirates	77.4	6	12
Yemen	48.9		
Zambia	79.8		
Zimbabwe	90.0		

Pre-primary Education: Schools, Staff and Pupils: 2002

● As stated

	Pre-Primary Schools	Staff ('000)	Pupils ('000)	Pupil to Staff Ratio
Algeria		1.5	31.9	21.3
Argentina	15,180	82.0	1,380.8	16.8
Australia		11.0	197.5	18.0
Azerbaijan	1,978	16.0	99.6	6.2
Bolivia		8.2	304.7	37.0
Brazil	149,485	290.5	5,819.6	20.0
Canada		12.6	538.0	42.8
Chile	5,969	10.9	327.8	30.1
China	164,349	835.8	19,531.5	23.4
Colombia	20,523	59.5	2,232.9	37.5
Ecuador	4,620	17.0	225.6	13.3
Egypt	3,838	16.9	363.4	21.5
Hong Kong, China	757	10.1	172.2	17.0
India	51,506		4,433.9	
Indonesia	43,799	111.6	2,032.9	18.2
Israel			315.0	
Japan	14,765	108.8	1,763.9	16.2
Jordan	1,235	4.4	64.4	14.8
Kazakhstan	5,117	34.0	173.5	5.1
Kuwait	247	4.0	85.0	21.3
Malaysia	17,213	29.2	378.3	12.9
Mexico	73,869	161.5	3,603.5	22.3
Morocco	36,360	44.0	974.1	22.1
New Zealand	4,194	11.0	119.8	10.9
Nigeria				
Pakistan				
Peru	18,959	37.7	800.1	21.2
Philippines	7,815		331.1	
Saudi Arabia	1,053	8.1	78.7	9.7
Singapore				
South Africa	11,037	40.3	397.3	9.9
South Korea	8,180	30.5	589.7	19.3
Taiwan	2,948	16.8		
Thailand	31,647	89.9	1,945.4	21.6
Tunisia	1,353		54.1	
Turkmenistan	1,155	10.9		
United Arab Emirates	105	3.2	47.6	14.7
USA			8,329.9	
Venezuela		61.2	690.9	11.3
Vietnam	7,972	106.2	3,114.0	29.3

Source: Euromonitor from UNESCO

Primary Education: Schools, Staff and Pupils: 2002

• As stated

	Primary Schools	Staff ('000)	Pupils ('000)	Pupil to Staff Ratio
Algeria	16,603	197.2	4,983.9	25.3
Argentina	22,485	292.6	5,878.6	20.1
Australia	7,696	112.6	1,919.8	17.0
Azerbaijan	4,356	232.2	1,784.1	7.7
Bolivia	14,362	81.9	1,962.7	24.0
Brazil	196,796	1,479.7	36,029.7	24.3
Canada	13,034	143.3	2,515.0	17.6
Chile	11,312	74.7	2,495.5	33.4
China	503,899	5,921.9	124,198.5	21.0
Colombia	56,667	225.2	5,406.8	24.0
Ecuador	19,679	91.2	2,319.3	25.4
Egypt	15,588	409.8	6,853.6	16.7
Hong Kong, China	828	22.0	455.6	20.7
India	600,731	2,154.4	113,231.6	52.6
Indonesia	149,874	1,124.2	25,454.9	22.6
Israel	2,470	68.0	778.8	11.5
Japan	24,276	419.6	7,596.0	18.1
Jordan	2,813	43.8	1,175.1	26.8
Kazakhstan	3,413	73.1	1,380.4	18.9
Kuwait	280	10.1	138.9	13.8
Malaysia	7,355	158.3	2,939.4	18.6
Mexico	102,293	560.8	14,864.3	26.5
Morocco	5,991	135.4	3,992.7	29.5
New Zealand	2,297	24.3	509.7	20.9
Nigeria	50,357	481.7	15,659.9	32.5
Pakistan	171,073	386.1	21,569.9	55.9
Peru	34,767	179.1	3,658.4	20.4
Philippines	42,179	333.6	12,942.6	38.8
Saudi Arabia	13,343	188.9	2,311.9	12.2
Singapore	195	12.5	311.6	25.0
South Africa	21,751	247.9	8,937.6	36.0
South Korea	5,111	142.7	4,182.1	29.3
Taiwan	2,643	109.8	1,991.7	18.1
Thailand	39,254	314.1	6,200.0	19.7
Tunisia	4,527	60.7	1,291.2	21.3
Turkmenistan	1,942	18.4	421.0	22.9
United Arab Emirates		20.8	332.5	16.0
USA		2,033.0	49,126.2	24.2
Venezuela	17,287	171.8	4,845.3	28.2
Vietnam	23,542	376.6	10,249.3	27.2

Source: Euromonitor from UNESCO

■ Secondary Education

Table 20.5

Secondary Education: Staff and Pupils: 2002

● As stated

	Staff ('000)	Total Pupils ('000)	Pupils in Training Colleges ('000)	Pupils in Technical Colleges ('000)	Pupil to Staff Ratio
Algeria	163.7	2,898.0	149.1		17.7
Argentina	326.9	2,826.6			8.6
Australia	229.1	3,434.6	1,515.0	1,355.4	15.0
Azerbaijan		76.0	34.7	25.0	
Bolivia	27.5	388.5			14.1
Brazil	474.5	7,646.4			16.1
Canada	125.7	2,654.1			21.1
Chile	58.8	849.5	402.9		14.5
China	5,134.5	94,860.7	664.3	4,025.7	18.5
Colombia	230.0	3,750.4	1,027.0		16.3
Ecuador					
Egypt	614.5	3,722.0	1,672.3	2,049.7	6.1
Hong Kong, China	23.5	524.4		53.0	22.4
India	3,206.0	77,485.1	805.4		24.2
Indonesia	782.9	12,678.6		862.4	16.2
Israel	77.8	584.1	126.2	22.9	7.5
Japan	475.3	8,154.6	1,292.0	57.4	17.2
Jordan	18.0	180.6	23.2		10.0
Kazakhstan	261.9	1,945.7	92.8	201.8	7.4
Kuwait	22.5	247.2	3.4		11.0
Malaysia	121.8	2,030.9	0.7	43.9	16.7
Mexico	642.1	7,266.9			11.3
Morocco	86.3	1,610.6			18.7
New Zealand	15.6	242.9			15.5
Nigeria	170.4	4,280.2		150.4	25.1
Pakistan	271.3	6,229.6		80.0	23.0
Peru	127.6	2,661.6			20.9
Philippines	179.5	5,832.0			32.5
Saudi Arabia	71.3	971.1	86.0	16.6	13.6
Singapore	9.7	182.2	3.3	18.3	18.9
South Africa					
South Korea	204.5	4,242.1	980.2		20.7
Taiwan	101.8	1,661.7		405.7	16.3
Thailand	203.6	4,386.5	656.6	699.5	21.5
Tunisia	60.5	1,113.0	64.7		18.4
Turkmenistan	76.0		30.2	7.9	
United Arab Emirates	10.3	132.9	3.0		12.9
USA	1,453.6	31,835.2			21.9
Venezuela	58.6	443.4			7.6
Vietnam	72.1	2,429.9		139.5	33.7

Source: Euromonitor from UNESCO

Population

Total Population 1977-2003: National Estimates at Mid-Year

● '000

	1977	1980	1985	1990	1992	1993	1994	1995
North America								
Canada	23,496	24,264	25,595	27,366	28,031	28,379	28,703	29,036
USA	217,569	223,614	234,726	246,777	252,153	255,031	257,782	260,328
Latin America								
Anguilla	6	7	7	7	7	8	8	8
Antigua	60	61	62	64	65	65	65	66
Argentina	26,498	27,709	29,890	32,080	32,974	33,421	33,869	34,318
Aruba	61	60	63	64	69	73	77	82
Bahamas	197	210	232	255	265	270	275	280
Barbados	247	249	253	257	260	261	263	264
Belize	138	146	166	187	197	203	208	213
Bermuda	53	54	57	59	60	61	61	62
Bolivia	4,876	5,223	5,750	6,416	6,729	6,894	7,064	7,238
Brazil	108,783	116,664	129,658	141,774	146,408	148,684	150,933	153,143
British Virgin Islands	11	12	14	16	17	18	19	19
Cayman Islands	16	17	21	26	25	29	30	32
Chile	10,480	10,961	11,846	12,879	13,320	13,545	13,771	13,994
Colombia	25,008	26,788	29,812	32,918	34,211	34,856	35,496	36,128
Costa Rica	2,031	2,224	2,572	2,956	3,113	3,191	3,269	3,347
Cuba	9,442	9,650	10,053	10,547	10,708	10,780	10,845	10,906
Dominica	73	74	72	71	71	71	71	71
Dominican Republic	5,200	5,584	6,250	6,966	7,255	7,399	7,542	7,684
Ecuador	7,406	8,059	9,211	10,383	10,861	11,101	11,341	11,579
El Salvador	4,151	4,399	4,574	4,922	5,139	5,262	5,395	5,530
French Guiana	61	68	91	117	128	134	140	147
Grenada	90	89	90	91	91	91	91	92
Guadeloupe	327	327	355	391	405	411	418	424
Guatemala	6,159	6,635	7,528	8,520	8,978	9,215	9,462	9,715
Guyana	743	759	793	795	806	814	822	830
Haiti	4,706	5,017	5,636	6,353	6,619	6,754	6,893	7,035
Honduras	3,125	3,459	4,057	4,730	5,028	5,180	5,336	5,494
Jamaica	2,060	2,133	2,297	2,369	2,406	2,428	2,451	2,473
Martinique	327	326	341	360	370	380	380	379
Mexico	63,157	68,239	76,212	84,014	87,187	88,777	90,358	91,929
Netherlands Antilles	169	174	182	188	194	198	202	205
Nicaragua	2,405	2,641	3,077	3,469	3,667	3,776	3,891	4,008
Panama	1,779	1,912	2,125	2,351	2,444	2,491	2,538	2,585
Paraguay	2,750	3,028	3,509	4,098	4,340	4,460	4,580	4,703
Peru	16,180	17,506	19,697	21,768	22,547	22,935	23,331	23,739
Puerto Rico	3,044	3,197	3,378	3,529	3,601	3,640	3,679	3,715
St Kitts	45	44	44	42	41	41	40	40
St Lucia	111	115	125	134	138	140	142	144
St Vincent and the Grenadines	95	98	102	106	107	108	109	110
Suriname	358	355	384	402	405	407	408	409
Trinidad and Tobago	1,035	1,082	1,178	1,215	1,233	1,244	1,254	1,262
Uruguay	2,830	2,889	2,983	3,076	3,112	3,131	3,149	3,168
Venezuela	13,864	15,299	17,375	19,737	20,676	21,144	21,611	22,078

Source: *National statistical offices/UN/Euromonitor*

■ Total Population: National Estimates at Mid-Year

Total Population 1977-2003: National Estimates at Mid-Year (continued)

● '000

	1996	1997	1998	1999	2000	2001	2002	2003	% Growth 1977-2003
North America									
Canada	29,354	29,672	30,004	30,481	30,491	30,734	30,880	31,173	32.7
USA	262,803	265,230	267,786	270,249	272,820	275,306	277,803	280,306	28.8
Latin America									
Anguilla	8	8	8	8	8	8	8	8	33.3
Antigua	66	66	67	68	69	70	71	72	20.0
Argentina	34,768	35,220	35,672	36,125	36,578	37,032	37,487	37,944	43.2
Aruba	86	90	94	100	107	114	121	128	110.6
Bahamas	286	292	296	303	312	321	329	338	71.4
Barbados	265	267	268	269	271	273	275	277	12.2
Belize	220	226	230	237	245	252	259	266	92.9
Bermuda	63	63	64	65	66	67	68	69	30.2
Bolivia	7,414	7,592	7,773	7,957	8,143	8,329	8,516	8,705	78.5
Brazil	155,320	157,482	159,636	161,790	163,948	166,113	171,728	173,837	59.8
British Virgin Islands	19	20	20	21	21	22	23	24	118.6
Cayman Islands	33	34	36	37	39	40	42	44	172.2
Chile	14,210	14,419	14,622	14,822	15,018	15,211	15,402	15,589	48.8
Colombia	36,754	37,374	37,990	38,601	39,206	39,806	40,400	40,991	63.9
Costa Rica	3,424	3,500	3,575	3,649	3,724	3,798	3,872	3,945	94.2
Cuba	10,964	11,019	11,069	11,115	11,159	11,201	11,239	11,275	19.4
Dominica	71	71	71	71	71	71	71	71	-2.7
Dominican Republic	7,823	7,961	8,097	8,232	8,364	8,495	8,624	8,752	68.3
Ecuador	11,818	12,056	12,293	12,529	12,763	12,996	13,227	13,457	81.7
El Salvador	5,662	5,792	5,924	6,057	6,189	6,319	6,449	6,578	58.5
French Guiana	153	160	167	176	187	199	211	224	266.8
Grenada	92	93	93	94	94	95	96	97	7.8
Guadeloupe	432	438	443	451	464	479	491	505	54.4
Guatemala	9,976	10,244	10,519	10,802	11,091	11,385	11,687	11,995	94.7
Guyana	838	844	850	857	866	876	886	896	20.6
Haiti	7,180	7,329	7,482	7,637	7,797	7,959	8,125	8,294	76.2
Honduras	5,654	5,816	5,981	6,148	6,316	6,485	6,656	6,828	118.5
Jamaica	2,499	2,523	2,538	2,566	2,609	2,655	2,697	2,742	33.1
Martinique	383	387	389	393	399	404	409	414	26.6
Mexico	93,494	95,052	96,598	98,124	99,627	101,110	102,574	104,018	64.7
Netherlands Antilles	208	210	213	216	219	223	227	231	36.7
Nicaragua	4,124	4,236	4,349	4,463	4,578	4,694	4,813	4,932	105.1
Panama	2,631	2,677	2,722	2,767	2,812	2,856	2,899	2,942	65.4
Paraguay	4,828	4,958	5,089	5,223	5,359	5,496	5,636	5,778	110.1
Peru	24,159	24,586	25,017	25,447	25,876	26,305	26,736	27,165	67.9
Puerto Rico	3,752	3,786	3,810	3,847	3,904	3,967	4,025	4,086	34.2
St Kitts	40	39	39	38	38	38	38	38	-15.6
St Lucia	146	148	150	153	156	159	162	165	48.7
St Vincent and the Grenadines	111	112	112	113	115	117	119	121	27.4
Suriname	411	413	414	416	419	423	426	430	20.0
Trinidad and Tobago	1,270	1,277	1,283	1,291	1,301	1,313	1,324	1,336	29.0
Uruguay	3,186	3,204	3,221	3,239	3,257	3,274	3,293	3,311	17.0
Venezuela	22,544	23,010	23,475	23,938	24,401	24,863	25,323	25,783	86.0

Source: *National statistical offices/UN/Euromonitor*

Total Population 1977-2003: National Estimates at Mid-Year (continued)

● '000

	1977	1980	1985	1990	1992	1993	1994	1995
Asia Pacific								
Afghanistan	14,804	14,963	13,525	14,017	15,493	16,494	17,633	18,731
American Samoa	30	32	39	47	51	53	55	57
Armenia	3,157	3,327	3,588	3,783	3,795	3,793	3,784	3,776
Azerbaijan	5,769	6,047	6,548	7,066	7,336	7,495	7,597	7,685
Bangladesh	79,822	86,794	97,765	107,617	111,315	113,114	114,900	116,722
Bhutan	1,213	1,298	1,464	1,665	1,728	1,755	1,781	1,810
Brunei	169	187	216	250	264	272	279	287
Cambodia	6,621	6,302	7,136	8,383	8,922	9,192	9,460	9,724
China	956,753	997,121	1,068,294	1,150,780	1,178,440	1,191,835	1,204,855	1,217,550
Fiji	591	627	691	720	733	741	749	759
French Polynesia	135	148	170	192	200	204	207	211
Guam	97	104	116	131	137	141	144	148
Hong Kong, China	4,626	5,011	5,425	5,657	5,752	5,801	5,901	6,035
India	644,640	686,091	764,760	850,398	891,087	907,502	924,097	940,664
Indonesia	140,615	149,751	165,994	181,385	187,589	190,676	193,750	196,813
Japan	113,994	116,922	120,955	123,664	124,609	124,899	125,237	125,653
Kazakhstan	14,825	15,297	16,228	16,759	16,712	16,633	16,548	16,472
Kiribati	58	61	67	72	74	76	77	78
Kyrgyzstan	3,397	3,596	3,979	4,344	4,445	4,486	4,518	4,546
Laos	3,007	3,112	3,489	4,030	4,273	4,396	4,520	4,646
Macau	241	244	296	360	385	397	408	419
Malaysia	13,004	13,949	15,889	18,071	18,980	19,434	19,885	20,329
Maldives	135	145	174	209	222	229	235	242
Mongolia	1,498	1,627	1,868	2,163	2,269	2,318	2,364	2,408
Myanmar	31,408	33,437	37,118	40,025	41,015	41,480	41,932	42,392
Nauru	7	7	8	10	10	10	11	11
Nepal	13,098	14,122	16,075	18,288	19,255	19,748	20,250	20,758
New Caledonia	134	139	150	163	172	177	182	188
North Korea	16,624	17,369	18,624	20,122	20,799	21,148	21,506	21,871
Pakistan	79,916	86,794	102,976	120,866	127,566	130,935	134,445	138,150
Papua New Guinea	2,801	3,014	3,361	3,752	3,926	4,017	4,110	4,205
Philippines	45,509	48,776	55,188	61,396	64,402	65,984	67,565	69,148
Singapore	2,035	2,121	2,379	2,648	2,761	2,817	2,874	2,930
Solomon Islands	197	219	261	310	332	344	355	367
South Korea	36,610	38,276	40,969	43,078	43,972	44,419	44,870	45,321
Sri Lanka	13,929	14,668	15,882	16,865	17,226	17,401	17,574	17,746
Taiwan		18,084	19,567	20,504	20,899	21,087	21,268	21,441
Tajikistan	3,579	3,886	4,489	5,192	5,414	5,508	5,590	5,669
Thailand	44,005	47,167	51,637	55,949	57,219	57,782	58,334	58,891
Tonga	90	92	94	96	96	97	97	97
Turkmenistan	2,692	2,901	3,275	3,711	3,878	3,959	4,038	4,117
Tuvalu	7	8	8	9	9	9	10	10
Uzbekistan	14,476	15,643	17,796	20,091	20,939	21,343	21,730	22,108
Vanuatu	105	114	129	146	153	157	161	165
Vietnam	50,813	54,303	60,558	67,412	70,337	71,785	73,183	74,513
Western Samoa	152	154	156	159	161	162	164	166
Australasia								
Australia	14,291	14,657	15,735	16,924	17,284	17,489	17,656	17,838
New Zealand	3,215	3,219	3,358	3,477	3,557	3,605	3,660	3,716

Source: *National statistical offices/UN/Euromonitor*

Total Population: National Estimates at Mid-Year

Total Population 1977-2003: National Estimates at Mid-Year (continued)

• '000

	1996	1997	1998	1999	2000	2001	2002	2003	% Growth 1977-2003
Asia Pacific									
Afghanistan	19,663	20,368	20,893	21,354	21,923	22,421	22,879	23,795	60.7
American Samoa	59	61	63	66	70	74	78	82	174.1
Armenia	3,777	3,786	3,795	3,803	3,809	3,812	3,817	3,822	21.1
Azerbaijan	7,763	7,838	7,913	7,987	8,045	8,108	8,192	8,275	43.4
Bangladesh	118,616	120,594	122,650	124,774	126,947	129,087	130,337	132,837	66.4
Bhutan	1,847	1,893	1,945	2,004	2,064	2,123	2,160	2,235	84.3
Brunei	294	301	308	315	322	328	333	341	101.9
Cambodia	9,982	10,234	10,478	10,716	10,945	11,180	11,334	11,641	75.8
China	1,230,075	1,242,180	1,255,388	1,269,205	1,278,768	1,287,868	1,300,001	1,312,133	37.1
Fiji	768	777	786	796	806	816	822	833	40.8
French Polynesia	215	219	223	227	231	235	238	242	79.6
Guam	151	155	158	161	164	168	170	174	79.2
Hong Kong, China	6,156	6,311	6,502	6,687	6,843	7,018	7,118	7,318	58.2
India	957,122	973,500	989,779	1,002,874	1,012,611	1,026,878	1,045,899	1,064,921	65.2
Indonesia	199,867	202,907	205,932	208,939	211,388	214,237	218,035	221,833	57.8
Japan	126,017	126,327	126,585	126,819	126,968	127,014	127,074	127,134	11.5
Kazakhstan	16,405	16,346	16,294	16,237	16,187	16,132	16,057	15,983	7.8
Kiribati	79	80	81	82	84	85	86	87	50.0
Kyrgyzstan	4,571	4,596	4,619	4,643	4,669	4,694	4,704	4,724	39.1
Laos	4,773	4,902	5,032	5,163	5,297	5,429	5,517	5,695	89.4
Macau	430	440	450	459	467	476	481	491	103.7
Malaysia	20,766	21,196	21,620	22,068	22,450	22,881	23,455	24,029	84.8
Maldives	249	256	263	271	278	286	291	300	122.2
Mongolia	2,451	2,495	2,537	2,579	2,621	2,663	2,684	2,726	82.0
Myanmar	42,877	43,393	43,936	44,497	45,059	45,620	45,940	46,580	48.3
Nauru	11	11	11	12	13	14	15	16	129.6
Nepal	21,272	21,791	22,316	22,847	23,385	23,919	24,267	24,964	90.6
New Caledonia	193	198	202	206	210	214	217	223	66.7
North Korea	22,239	22,610	22,981	23,348	23,702	24,065	24,307	24,790	49.1
Pakistan	142,051	146,106	150,248	153,758	156,451	160,251	165,317	170,383	113.2
Papua New Guinea	4,301	4,399	4,499	4,600	4,702	4,804	4,872	5,008	78.8
Philippines	70,742	72,335	73,927	75,522	76,823	78,330	80,340	82,351	81.0
Singapore	2,987	3,044	3,104	3,164	3,218	3,274	3,308	3,374	65.8
Solomon Islands	379	392	404	417	430	443	452	470	138.4
South Korea	45,769	46,211	46,644	47,074	47,437	47,874	48,456	49,038	33.9
Sri Lanka	17,920	18,096	18,274	18,455	18,639	18,822	18,922	19,122	37.3
Taiwan	21,634	21,836	22,010	22,182	22,321	22,470	22,668	22,867	
Tajikistan	5,750	5,836	5,925	6,015	6,104	6,195	6,247	6,349	77.4
Thailand	59,454	60,018	60,578	61,163	61,601	61,992	62,514	63,035	43.2
Tonga	97	98	98	99	99	99	100	101	11.7
Turkmenistan	4,194	4,271	4,346	4,427	4,493	4,563	4,656	4,749	76.4
Tuvalu	11	11	11	12	12	12	12	12	71.4
Uzbekistan	22,480	22,848	23,212	23,574	23,942	24,306	24,521	24,951	72.4
Vanuatu	169	173	177	182	186	190	193	199	88.9
Vietnam	75,773	76,975	78,134	79,531	80,706	81,750	83,143	84,535	66.4
Western Samoa	168	170	172	174	177	180	181	184	21.4
Australasia									
Australia	18,072	18,311	18,524	18,730	18,967	19,183	19,312	19,572	36.9
New Zealand	3,762	3,793	3,816	3,837	3,858	3,884	3,920	3,956	23.0

Source: *National statistical offices/UN/Euromonitor*

■ Total Population: National Estimates at Mid-Year

Total Population 1977-2003: National Estimates at Mid-Year (continued)

● '000

	1977	1980	1985	1990	1992	1993	1994	1995
Africa and Middle East								
Algeria	17,048	18,738	21,885	24,954	26,261	26,915	27,568	28,222
Angola	6,450	7,019	8,005	9,230	9,880	10,237	10,603	10,972
Bahrain	300	340	410	500	520	540	560	580
Benin	3,198	3,459	4,019	4,660	4,924	5,058	5,195	5,336
Botswana	815	906	1,081	1,276	1,358	1,399	1,437	1,474
Burkina Faso	6,412	6,909	7,879	9,060	9,582	9,854	10,131	10,415
Burundi	3,826	4,130	4,741	5,456	5,751	5,896	6,032	6,156
Cameroon	7,953	8,655	9,970	11,472	12,131	12,473	12,823	13,182
Cape Verde	290	300	330	340	360	370	380	381
Central African Republic	2,154	2,313	2,607	2,942	3,082	3,151	3,220	3,288
Chad	4,192	4,477	5,116	5,746	6,105	6,306	6,509	6,707
Comoros	344	388	456	527	557	573	589	606
Congo Dem Rep	24,649	27,009	31,669	37,363	40,532	42,245	43,901	45,421
Congo-Brazzaville	1,532	1,669	1,922	2,220	2,351	2,419	2,489	2,590
Côte d'Ivoire	7,303	8,194	9,878	11,635	12,423	12,821	13,194	13,528
Djibouti	232	281	391	517	557	574	589	601
Egypt	37,110	39,958	45,438	51,037	52,585	54,081	54,872	56,344
Equatorial Guinea	209	217	312	352	369	379	389	399
Eritrea	2,201	2,382	2,701	2,889	3,000	3,028	3,097	3,187
Ethiopia	33,807	36,375	41,150	48,093	51,010	52,463	53,911	55,354
Gabon	633	692	803	935	991	1,019	1,048	1,077
Gambia	584	641	745	920	996	1,034	1,072	1,111
Ghana	10,190	10,833	12,933	15,128	16,112	16,624	17,138	17,649
Guinea	4,255	4,461	4,987	5,755	6,338	6,660	6,942	7,153
Guinea-Bissau	696	795	877	973	1,016	1,039	1,062	1,086
Iran	34,726	38,402	46,588	54,908	57,711	58,962	60,107	61,212
Iraq	11,777	13,007	15,317	18,078	18,897	19,260	19,649	20,095
Israel	3,294	3,515	3,836	4,372	4,946	5,123	5,261	5,400
Jordan	1,956	2,276	2,753	3,585	3,919	4,066	4,215	4,366
Kenya	14,834	16,632	19,871	23,552	25,070	25,817	26,536	27,216
Kuwait	1,012	1,213	1,518	1,756	1,515	1,630	1,763	1,848
Lebanon	2,754	2,669	2,668	2,555	2,699	2,807	2,915	3,009
Lesotho	1,247	1,346	1,526	1,722	1,802	1,843	1,884	1,926
Liberia	1,711	1,876	2,193	2,579	2,360	2,204	2,099	2,090
Libya	2,665	3,043	3,786	4,416	4,636	4,744	4,853	4,967
Madagascar	8,226	8,873	10,123	11,632	12,426	12,860	13,302	13,744
Malawi	5,606	6,183	7,243	9,335	9,575	9,576	9,589	9,670
Mali	6,425	6,863	7,915	8,842	9,258	9,479	9,709	9,944
Mauritania	1,439	1,551	1,776	2,026	2,142	2,203	2,265	2,329
Mauritius	922	966	1,016	1,057	1,079	1,091	1,103	1,114
Morocco	18,539	19,832	22,150	24,337	24,940	25,241	25,542	25,926
Mozambique	11,099	12,095	13,535	14,198	15,303	16,021	16,738	17,388
Namibia	949	1,029	1,178	1,350	1,426	1,465	1,504	1,543
Niger	5,069	5,586	6,608	7,731	8,268	8,555	8,850	9,150
Nigeria	60,838	66,237	78,754	87,824	93,746	96,694	99,469	102,070
Oman	971	1,130	1,425	1,785	1,932	2,006	2,081	2,155
Qatar	191	229	358	485	516	528	538	548
Réunion	490	506	555	604	625	635	645	655
Rwanda	4,681	5,163	6,054	6,987	6,251	5,740	5,365	5,259
Sao Tomé e Príncipe	86	94	106	119	124	127	130	133
Saudi Arabia	6,157	7,297	9,608	13,671	14,909	15,487	16,061	16,646
Senegal	5,088	5,538	6,375	7,327	7,718	7,916	8,120	8,330
Seychelles	61	63	65	70	70	70	70	73
Sierra Leone	3,049	3,236	3,583	3,994	4,061	4,083	4,121	4,188
Somalia	4,791	5,853	6,547	7,773	7,931	7,962	8,037	8,201
South Africa	27,263	29,095	32,410	35,896	37,397	38,216	39,054	39,785
Sudan	17,038	18,681	21,459	24,062	25,070	25,576	26,090	26,617
Swaziland	511	560	649	753	799	823	847	873
Syria	7,918	8,708	10,397	12,386	13,125	13,481	13,837	14,200
Tanzania	16,911	18,581	21,775	25,470	27,252	28,181	29,082	29,925
Togo	2,406	2,615	3,026	3,512	3,726	3,837	3,948	4,060
Tunisia	6,046	6,548	7,448	8,237	8,481	8,603	8,725	8,847
Uganda	11,926	13,120	14,736	16,457	17,373	17,882	18,406	18,935
United Arab Emirates	622	915	1,400	1,772	1,985	2,091	2,198	2,304
Yemen	7,426	8,219	9,698	11,590	12,864	13,593	14,324	15,022
Zambia	5,196	5,738	6,410	7,239	7,611	7,804	7,998	8,193
Zimbabwe	6,514	7,126	8,388	9,863	10,318	10,512	10,694	10,871

Source: National statistical offices/UN/Euromonitor

◘ Total Population: National Estimates at Mid-Year

Total Population 1977-2003: National Estimates at Mid-Year (continued)

● '000

	1996	1997	1998	1999	2000	2001	2002	2003	% Growth 1977-2003
Africa and Middle East									
Algeria	28,725	29,080	29,300	29,625	30,029	30,385	30,860	31,336	83.8
Angola	11,429	11,849	12,095	12,582	13,224	13,877	14,463	15,111	134.3
Bahrain	594	607	604	609	625	637	647	658	119.4
Benin	5,519	5,686	5,782	5,978	6,252	6,532	6,788	7,067	121.0
Botswana	1,510	1,542	1,570	1,603	1,645	1,691	1,731	1,775	117.8
Burkina Faso	10,780	11,115	11,307	11,699	12,288	12,898	13,403	13,985	118.1
Burundi	6,285	6,404	6,460	6,603	6,806	7,007	7,189	7,386	93.0
Cameroon	13,639	14,057	14,307	14,792	15,505	16,254	16,861	17,568	120.9
Cape Verde	392	403	408	421	437	453	467	483	66.4
Central African Republic	3,367	3,439	3,485	3,566	3,669	3,769	3,861	3,959	83.8
Chad	6,933	7,141	7,271	7,508	7,804	8,096	8,380	8,678	107.0
Comoros	627	647	658	681	714	750	779	813	136.3
Congo Dem Rep	46,917	48,288	49,150	50,696	52,876	55,111	57,191	59,435	141.1
Congo-Brazzaville	2,682	2,766	2,864	2,924	2,956	2,999	3,070	3,128	104.2
Côte d'Ivoire	13,830	14,106	14,294	14,598	15,060	15,551	15,994	16,475	125.6
Djibouti	610	618	623	632	647	663	676	691	197.8
Egypt	57,510	59,313	60,080	61,345	62,278	63,294	63,843	64,942	75.0
Equatorial Guinea	412	423	431	445	463	481	498	516	147.0
Eritrea	3,346	3,492	3,577	3,749	3,970	4,195	4,395	4,619	109.8
Ethiopia	57,085	58,671	59,653	61,469	63,813	66,105	68,281	70,592	108.8
Gabon	1,113	1,145	1,167	1,204	1,253	1,302	1,349	1,399	121.0
Gambia	1,158	1,201	1,229	1,277	1,338	1,400	1,455	1,516	159.6
Ghana	18,264	18,828	19,165	19,816	20,653	21,496	22,301	23,157	127.3
Guinea	7,220	7,281	7,340	7,389	7,504	7,620	7,735	7,852	84.5
Guinea-Bissau	1,116	1,144	1,161	1,194	1,237	1,282	1,321	1,364	96.0
Iran	62,324	63,469	64,628	65,758	66,796	67,896	68,566	69,906	101.3
Iraq	20,820	21,484	21,808	22,620	23,723	24,845	25,849	26,959	128.9
Israel	5,545	5,685	5,824	5,960	6,098	6,235	6,329	6,516	97.8
Jordan	4,520	4,678	4,828	4,987	5,143	5,284	5,427	5,571	184.8
Kenya	27,904	28,534	29,003	29,679	30,921	32,265	33,278	34,501	132.6
Kuwait	1,937	2,003	2,067	2,148	2,215	2,292	2,394	2,497	146.7
Lebanon	3,075	3,135	3,190	3,248	3,336	3,427	3,517	3,610	31.1
Lesotho	1,980	2,030	2,062	2,119	2,197	2,278	2,352	2,432	95.0
Liberia	2,345	2,579	2,666	2,976	3,369	3,802	4,201	4,666	172.7
Libya	5,120	5,260	5,483	5,505	5,718	5,851	6,011	6,161	131.2
Madagascar	14,271	14,755	15,058	15,610	16,373	17,156	17,830	18,590	126.0
Malawi	9,971	10,247	10,350	10,709	11,248	11,807	12,271	12,805	128.4
Mali	10,254	10,537	10,696	11,031	11,475	11,907	12,308	12,739	98.3
Mauritania	2,411	2,486	2,529	2,617	2,738	2,860	2,974	3,097	115.2
Mauritius	1,125	1,134	1,141	1,152	1,165	1,178	1,194	1,209	31.1
Morocco	26,386	26,848	27,310	27,775	28,238	28,703	28,956	29,461	58.9
Mozambique	17,938	18,443	18,872	19,382	20,146	20,975	21,681	22,477	102.5
Namibia	1,587	1,627	1,659	1,702	1,753	1,805	1,853	1,904	100.7
Niger	9,529	9,877	10,080	10,485	11,019	11,557	12,037	12,569	148.0
Nigeria	105,045	108,502	111,999	115,534	119,101	122,697	126,315	129,970	113.6
Oman	2,248	2,333	2,382	2,482	2,614	2,750	2,874	3,010	210.0
Qatar	560	571	579	592	609	627	643	660	245.8
Réunion	666	675	682	693	706	720	734	748	52.7
Rwanda	5,853	6,397	6,601	7,326	8,200	9,150	10,015	11,018	135.4
Sao Tomé e Príncipe	135	138	141	145	149	154	159	164	90.9
Saudi Arabia	17,405	18,345	19,362	20,378	21,364	22,354	23,358	24,376	295.9
Senegal	8,606	8,859	9,005	9,301	9,705	10,110	10,488	10,895	114.1
Seychelles	74	75	76	77	77	78	79	80	31.2
Sierra Leone	4,348	4,494	4,568	4,748	4,975	5,209	5,420	5,652	85.4
Somalia	8,656	9,073	9,242	9,776	10,494	11,226	11,845	12,563	162.2
South Africa	40,338	40,905	41,679	42,592	43,278	43,949	44,844	45,739	67.8
Sudan	27,306	27,938	28,296	29,039	30,226	31,490	32,536	33,735	98.0
Swaziland	905	935	952	987	1,034	1,081	1,122	1,168	128.5
Syria	14,662	15,085	15,335	15,827	16,477	17,141	17,733	18,385	132.2
Tanzania	30,787	31,577	32,104	32,982	34,142	35,279	36,312	37,431	121.3
Togo	4,197	4,322	4,398	4,542	4,737	4,931	5,114	5,310	120.7
Tunisia	8,969	9,089	9,215	9,333	9,437	9,550	9,619	9,758	61.4
Uganda	19,617	20,243	20,563	21,313	22,420	23,563	24,500	25,588	114.6
United Arab Emirates	2,411	2,517	2,624	2,759	2,938	3,088	3,178	3,359	439.8
Yemen	15,764	16,444	16,888	17,650	18,744	19,859	20,874	21,998	196.2
Zambia	8,427	8,642	8,634	8,975	9,418	9,859	10,211	10,624	104.5
Zimbabwe	11,062	11,238	11,251	11,521	11,840	12,159	12,440	12,748	95.7

Source: National statistical offices/UN/Euromonitor

Total Population 1978-2003: National Estimates at January 1st

● '000

	1978	1980	1985	1990	1992	1993	1994	1995
North America								
Canada	23,759	24,264	25,595	27,366	28,031	28,379	28,703	29,036
USA	219,539	223,614	234,726	246,777	252,153	255,031	257,782	260,328
Latin America								
Anguilla	6	7	7	7	7	8	8	8
Antigua	60	61	62	64	65	65	65	66
Argentina	26,895	27,709	29,890	32,080	32,974	33,421	33,869	34,318
Aruba	61	60	63	64	69	73	77	82
Bahamas	201	210	232	255	265	270	275	280
Barbados	248	249	253	257	260	261	263	264
Belize	140	146	166	187	197	203	208	213
Bermuda	53	54	57	59	60	61	61	62
Bolivia	4,995	5,223	5,750	6,416	6,729	6,894	7,064	7,238
Brazil	111,396	116,664	129,658	141,774	146,408	148,684	150,933	153,143
British Virgin Islands	11	12	14	16	17	18	19	19
Cayman Islands	16	17	21	26	25	29	30	32
Chile	10,637	10,961	11,846	12,879	13,320	13,545	13,771	13,994
Colombia	25,608	26,788	29,812	32,918	34,211	34,856	35,496	36,128
Costa Rica	2,093	2,224	2,572	2,956	3,113	3,191	3,269	3,347
Cuba	9,514	9,650	10,053	10,547	10,708	10,780	10,845	10,906
Dominica	73	74	72	71	71	71	71	71
Dominican Republic	5,327	5,584	6,250	6,966	7,255	7,399	7,542	7,684
Ecuador	7,620	8,059	9,211	10,383	10,861	11,101	11,341	11,579
El Salvador	4,247	4,399	4,574	4,922	5,139	5,262	5,395	5,530
French Guiana	63	68	91	117	128	134	140	147
Grenada	90	89	90	91	91	91	91	92
Guadeloupe	326	327	355	391	405	411	418	424
Guatemala	6,314	6,635	7,528	8,520	8,978	9,215	9,462	9,715
Guyana	748	759	793	795	806	814	822	830
Haiti	4,805	5,017	5,636	6,353	6,619	6,754	6,893	7,035
Honduras	3,234	3,459	4,057	4,730	5,028	5,180	5,336	5,494
Jamaica	2,082	2,133	2,297	2,369	2,406	2,428	2,451	2,473
Martinique	326	326	341	360	370	380	380	379
Mexico	64,874	68,239	76,212	84,014	87,187	88,777	90,358	91,929
Netherlands Antilles	171	174	182	188	194	198	202	205
Nicaragua	2,481	2,641	3,077	3,469	3,667	3,776	3,891	4,008
Panama	1,824	1,912	2,125	2,351	2,444	2,491	2,538	2,585
Paraguay	2,841	3,028	3,509	4,098	4,340	4,460	4,580	4,703
Peru	16,621	17,506	19,697	21,768	22,547	22,935	23,331	23,739
Puerto Rico	3,098	3,197	3,378	3,529	3,601	3,640	3,679	3,715
St Kitts	45	44	44	42	41	41	40	40
St Lucia	112	115	125	134	138	140	142	144
St Vincent and the Grenadines	96	98	102	106	107	108	109	110
Suriname	355	355	384	402	405	407	408	409
Trinidad and Tobago	1,049	1,082	1,178	1,215	1,233	1,244	1,254	1,262
Uruguay	2,849	2,889	2,983	3,076	3,112	3,131	3,149	3,168
Venezuela	14,357	15,299	17,375	19,737	20,676	21,144	21,611	22,078

Source: *National statistical offices/Eurostat/UN/Euromonitor*

□ Total Population: National Estimates at January 1st

Total Population 1978-2003: National Estimates at January 1st (continued)

- '000

	1996	1997	1998	1999	2000	2001	2002	2003	% Growth 1978-2003
North America									
Canada	29,354	29,672	30,004	30,481	30,491	30,734	30,880	31,173	31.2
USA	262,803	265,230	267,786	270,249	272,820	275,306	277,803	280,306	27.7
Latin America									
Anguilla	8	8	8	8	8	8	8	8	33.3
Antigua	66	66	67	68	69	70	71	72	20.0
Argentina	34,768	35,220	35,672	36,125	36,578	37,032	37,487	37,944	41.1
Aruba	86	90	94	100	107	114	121	128	110.6
Bahamas	286	292	296	303	312	321	329	338	68.0
Barbados	265	267	268	269	271	273	275	277	11.7
Belize	220	226	230	237	245	252	259	266	90.1
Bermuda	63	63	64	65	66	67	68	69	30.2
Bolivia	7,414	7,592	7,773	7,957	8,143	8,329	8,516	8,705	74.3
Brazil	155,320	157,482	159,636	161,790	163,948	166,113	171,728	173,837	56.1
British Virgin Islands	19	20	20	21	21	22	23	24	118.6
Cayman Islands	33	34	36	37	39	40	42	44	172.2
Chile	14,210	14,419	14,622	14,822	15,018	15,211	15,402	15,589	46.6
Colombia	36,754	37,374	37,990	38,601	39,206	39,806	40,400	40,991	60.1
Costa Rica	3,424	3,500	3,575	3,649	3,724	3,798	3,872	3,945	88.4
Cuba	10,964	11,019	11,069	11,115	11,159	11,201	11,239	11,275	18.5
Dominica	71	71	71	71	71	71	71	71	-2.7
Dominican Republic	7,823	7,961	8,097	8,232	8,364	8,495	8,624	8,752	64.3
Ecuador	11,818	12,056	12,293	12,529	12,763	12,996	13,227	13,457	76.6
El Salvador	5,662	5,792	5,924	6,057	6,189	6,319	6,449	6,578	54.9
French Guiana	153	160	167	176	187	199	211	224	255.2
Grenada	92	93	93	94	94	95	96	97	7.8
Guadeloupe	432	438	443	451	464	479	491	505	54.9
Guatemala	9,976	10,244	10,519	10,802	11,091	11,385	11,687	11,995	90.0
Guyana	838	844	850	857	866	876	886	896	19.8
Haiti	7,180	7,329	7,482	7,637	7,797	7,959	8,125	8,294	72.6
Honduras	5,654	5,816	5,981	6,148	6,316	6,485	6,656	6,828	111.1
Jamaica	2,499	2,523	2,538	2,566	2,609	2,655	2,697	2,742	31.7
Martinique	383	387	389	393	399	404	409	414	27.0
Mexico	93,494	95,052	96,598	98,124	99,627	101,110	102,574	104,018	60.3
Netherlands Antilles	208	210	213	216	219	223	227	231	35.1
Nicaragua	4,124	4,236	4,349	4,463	4,578	4,694	4,813	4,932	98.8
Panama	2,631	2,677	2,722	2,767	2,812	2,856	2,899	2,942	61.3
Paraguay	4,828	4,958	5,089	5,223	5,359	5,496	5,636	5,778	103.4
Peru	24,159	24,586	25,017	25,447	25,876	26,305	26,736	27,165	63.4
Puerto Rico	3,752	3,786	3,810	3,847	3,904	3,967	4,025	4,086	31.9
St Kitts	40	39	39	38	38	38	38	38	-15.6
St Lucia	146	148	150	153	156	159	162	165	47.4
St Vincent and the Grenadines	111	112	112	113	115	117	119	121	26.1
Suriname	411	413	414	416	419	423	426	430	21.0
Trinidad and Tobago	1,270	1,277	1,283	1,291	1,301	1,313	1,324	1,336	27.3
Uruguay	3,186	3,204	3,221	3,239	3,257	3,274	3,293	3,311	16.2
Venezuela	22,544	23,010	23,475	23,938	24,401	24,863	25,323	25,783	79.6

Source: *National statistical offices/Eurostat/UN/Euromonitor*

■ Total Population: National Estimates at January 1st

Total Population 1978-2003: National Estimates at January 1st (continued)

● '000

	1978	1980	1985	1990	1992	1993	1994	1995
Asia Pacific								
Afghanistan	14,964	14,963	13,525	14,017	15,493	16,494	17,633	18,731
American Samoa	31	32	39	47	51	53	55	57
Armenia	3,215	3,327	3,588	3,783	3,795	3,793	3,784	3,776
Azerbaijan	5,860	6,047	6,548	7,066	7,336	7,495	7,597	7,685
Bangladesh	82,150	86,794	97,765	107,617	111,315	113,114	114,900	116,722
Bhutan	1,240	1,298	1,464	1,665	1,728	1,755	1,781	1,810
Brunei	175	187	216	250	264	272	279	287
Cambodia	6,459	6,302	7,136	8,383	8,922	9,192	9,460	9,724
China	970,429	997,121	1,068,294	1,150,780	1,178,440	1,191,835	1,204,855	1,217,550
Fiji	602	627	691	720	733	741	749	759
French Polynesia	139	148	170	192	200	204	207	211
Guam	99	104	116	131	137	141	144	148
Hong Kong, China	4,761	5,011	5,425	5,657	5,752	5,801	5,901	6,035
India	658,012	686,091	764,760	850,398	891,087	907,502	924,097	940,664
Indonesia	143,606	149,751	165,994	181,385	187,589	190,676	193,750	196,813
Japan	115,022	116,922	120,955	123,664	124,609	124,899	125,237	125,653
Kazakhstan	14,979	15,297	16,228	16,759	16,712	16,633	16,548	16,472
Kiribati	59	61	67	72	74	76	77	78
Kyrgyzstan	3,460	3,596	3,979	4,344	4,445	4,486	4,518	4,546
Laos	3,035	3,112	3,489	4,030	4,273	4,396	4,520	4,646
Macau	240	244	296	360	385	397	408	419
Malaysia	13,303	13,949	15,889	18,071	18,980	19,434	19,885	20,329
Maldives	145	145	174	209	222	229	235	242
Mongolia	1,540	1,627	1,868	2,163	2,269	2,318	2,364	2,408
Myanmar	32,064	33,437	37,118	40,025	41,015	41,480	41,932	42,392
Nauru	7	7	8	10	10	10	11	11
Nepal	13,427	14,122	16,075	18,288	19,255	19,748	20,250	20,758
New Caledonia	136	139	150	163	172	177	182	188
North Korea	16,881	17,369	18,624	20,122	20,799	21,148	21,506	21,871
Pakistan	81,984	86,794	102,976	120,866	127,566	130,935	134,445	138,150
Papua New Guinea	2,872	3,014	3,361	3,752	3,926	4,017	4,110	4,205
Philippines	46,550	48,776	55,188	61,396	64,402	65,984	67,565	69,148
Singapore	2,058	2,121	2,379	2,648	2,761	2,817	2,874	2,930
Solomon Islands	204	219	261	310	332	344	355	367
South Korea	37,170	38,276	40,969	43,078	43,972	44,419	44,870	45,321
Sri Lanka	14,173	14,668	15,882	16,865	17,226	17,401	17,574	17,746
Taiwan		18,084	19,567	20,504	20,899	21,087	21,268	21,441
Tajikistan	3,678	3,886	4,489	5,192	5,414	5,508	5,590	5,669
Thailand	45,100	47,167	51,637	55,949	57,219	57,782	58,334	58,891
Tonga	91	92	94	96	96	97	97	97
Turkmenistan	2,761	2,901	3,275	3,711	3,878	3,959	4,038	4,117
Tuvalu	7	8	8	9	9	9	10	10
Uzbekistan	14,856	15,643	17,796	20,091	20,939	21,343	21,730	22,108
Vanuatu	108	114	129	146	153	157	161	165
Vietnam	51,956	54,303	60,558	67,412	70,337	71,785	73,183	74,513
Western Samoa	153	154	156	159	161	162	164	166
Australasia								
Australia	14,400	14,657	15,735	16,924	17,284	17,489	17,656	17,838
New Zealand	3,213	3,219	3,358	3,477	3,557	3,605	3,660	3,716

Source: National statistical offices/Eurostat/UN/Euromonitor

☒   Total Population: National Estimates at January 1st

Total Population 1978-2003: National Estimates at January 1st (continued)

● '000

	1996	1997	1998	1999	2000	2001	2002	2003	% Growth 1978-2003
Asia Pacific									
Afghanistan	19,663	20,368	20,893	21,354	21,923	22,421	22,879	23,795	59.0
American Samoa	59	61	63	66	70	74	78	82	165.2
Armenia	3,777	3,786	3,795	3,803	3,809	3,812	3,817	3,822	18.9
Azerbaijan	7,763	7,838	7,913	7,987	8,045	8,108	8,192	8,275	41.2
Bangladesh	118,616	120,594	122,650	124,774	126,947	129,087	130,337	132,837	61.7
Bhutan	1,847	1,893	1,945	2,004	2,064	2,123	2,160	2,235	80.2
Brunei	294	301	308	315	322	328	333	341	95.2
Cambodia	9,982	10,234	10,478	10,716	10,945	11,180	11,334	11,641	80.2
China	1,230,075	1,242,180	1,255,388	1,269,205	1,278,768	1,287,868	1,300,001	1,312,133	35.2
Fiji	768	777	786	796	806	816	822	833	38.3
French Polynesia	215	219	223	227	231	235	238	242	74.6
Guam	151	155	158	161	164	168	170	174	75.7
Hong Kong, China	6,156	6,311	6,502	6,687	6,843	7,018	7,118	7,318	53.7
India	957,122	973,500	989,779	1,002,874	1,012,611	1,026,878	1,045,899	1,064,921	61.8
Indonesia	199,867	202,907	205,932	208,939	211,388	214,237	218,035	221,833	54.5
Japan	126,017	126,327	126,585	126,819	126,968	127,014	127,074	127,134	10.5
Kazakhstan	16,405	16,346	16,294	16,237	16,187	16,132	16,057	15,983	6.7
Kiribati	79	80	81	82	84	85	86	87	47.5
Kyrgyzstan	4,571	4,596	4,619	4,643	4,669	4,694	4,704	4,724	36.5
Laos	4,773	4,902	5,032	5,163	5,297	5,429	5,517	5,695	87.6
Macau	430	440	450	459	467	476	481	491	104.6
Malaysia	20,766	21,196	21,620	22,068	22,450	22,881	23,455	24,029	80.6
Maldives	249	256	263	271	278	286	291	300	107.4
Mongolia	2,451	2,495	2,537	2,579	2,621	2,663	2,684	2,726	77.0
Myanmar	42,877	43,393	43,936	44,497	45,059	45,620	45,940	46,580	45.3
Nauru	11	11	11	12	13	14	15	16	129.6
Nepal	21,272	21,791	22,316	22,847	23,385	23,919	24,267	24,964	85.9
New Caledonia	193	198	202	206	210	214	217	223	64.3
North Korea	22,239	22,610	22,981	23,348	23,702	24,065	24,307	24,790	46.9
Pakistan	142,051	146,106	150,248	153,758	156,451	160,251	165,317	170,383	107.8
Papua New Guinea	4,301	4,399	4,499	4,600	4,702	4,804	4,872	5,008	74.3
Philippines	70,742	72,335	73,927	75,522	76,823	78,330	80,340	82,351	76.9
Singapore	2,987	3,044	3,104	3,164	3,218	3,274	3,308	3,374	63.9
Solomon Islands	379	392	404	417	430	443	452	470	130.5
South Korea	45,769	46,211	46,644	47,074	47,437	47,874	48,456	49,038	31.9
Sri Lanka	17,920	18,096	18,274	18,455	18,639	18,822	18,922	19,122	34.9
Taiwan	21,634	21,836	22,010	22,182	22,321	22,470	22,668	22,867	
Tajikistan	5,750	5,836	5,925	6,015	6,104	6,195	6,247	6,349	72.6
Thailand	59,454	60,018	60,578	61,163	61,601	61,992	62,514	63,035	39.8
Tonga	97	98	98	99	99	99	100	101	10.4
Turkmenistan	4,194	4,271	4,346	4,427	4,493	4,563	4,656	4,749	72.0
Tuvalu	11	11	11	12	12	12	12	12	71.4
Uzbekistan	22,480	22,848	23,212	23,574	23,942	24,306	24,521	24,951	68.0
Vanuatu	169	173	177	182	186	190	193	199	83.8
Vietnam	75,773	76,975	78,134	79,531	80,706	81,750	83,143	84,535	62.7
Western Samoa	168	170	172	174	177	180	181	184	20.6
Australasia									
Australia	18,072	18,311	18,524	18,730	18,967	19,183	19,312	19,572	35.9
New Zealand	3,762	3,793	3,816	3,837	3,858	3,884	3,920	3,956	23.1

Source: *National statistical offices/Eurostat/UN/Euromonitor*

■ Total Population: National Estimates at January 1st

Total Population 1978-2003: National Estimates at January 1st (continued)

● '000

	1978	1980	1985	1990	1992	1993	1994	1995
Africa and Middle East								
Algeria	17,590	18,738	21,885	24,954	26,261	26,915	27,568	28,222
Angola	6,636	7,019	8,005	9,230	9,880	10,237	10,603	10,972
Bahrain	320	340	410	500	520	540	560	580
Benin	3,279	3,459	4,019	4,660	4,924	5,058	5,195	5,336
Botswana	844	906	1,081	1,276	1,358	1,399	1,437	1,474
Burkina Faso	6,571	6,909	7,879	9,060	9,582	9,854	10,131	10,415
Burundi	3,920	4,130	4,741	5,456	5,751	5,896	6,032	6,156
Cameroon	8,180	8,655	9,970	11,472	12,131	12,473	12,823	13,182
Cape Verde	290	300	330	340	360	370	380	381
Central African Republic	2,206	2,313	2,607	2,942	3,082	3,151	3,220	3,288
Chad	4,278	4,477	5,116	5,746	6,105	6,306	6,509	6,707
Comoros	359	388	456	527	557	573	589	606
Congo Dem Rep	25,401	27,009	31,669	37,363	40,532	42,245	43,901	45,421
Congo-Brazzaville	1,576	1,669	1,922	2,220	2,351	2,419	2,489	2,590
Côte d'Ivoire	7,589	8,194	9,878	11,635	12,423	12,821	13,194	13,528
Djibouti	247	281	391	517	557	574	589	601
Egypt	38,015	39,958	45,438	51,037	52,585	54,081	54,872	56,344
Equatorial Guinea	207	217	312	352	369	379	389	399
Eritrea	2,259	2,382	2,701	2,889	3,000	3,028	3,097	3,187
Ethiopia	34,650	36,375	41,150	48,093	51,010	52,463	53,911	55,354
Gabon	652	692	803	935	991	1,019	1,048	1,077
Gambia	603	641	745	920	996	1,034	1,072	1,111
Ghana	10,359	10,833	12,933	15,128	16,112	16,624	17,138	17,649
Guinea	4,316	4,461	4,987	5,755	6,338	6,660	6,942	7,153
Guinea-Bissau	732	795	877	973	1,016	1,039	1,062	1,086
Iran	35,846	38,402	46,588	54,908	57,711	58,962	60,107	61,212
Iraq	12,175	13,007	15,317	18,078	18,897	19,260	19,649	20,095
Israel	3,371	3,515	3,836	4,372	4,946	5,123	5,261	5,400
Jordan	2,059	2,276	2,753	3,585	3,919	4,066	4,215	4,366
Kenya	15,418	16,632	19,871	23,552	25,070	25,817	26,536	27,216
Kuwait	1,080	1,213	1,518	1,756	1,515	1,630	1,763	1,848
Lebanon	2,722	2,669	2,668	2,555	2,699	2,807	2,915	3,009
Lesotho	1,279	1,346	1,526	1,722	1,802	1,843	1,884	1,926
Liberia	1,764	1,876	2,193	2,579	2,360	2,204	2,099	2,090
Libya	2,783	3,043	3,786	4,416	4,636	4,744	4,853	4,967
Madagascar	8,435	8,873	10,123	11,632	12,426	12,860	13,302	13,744
Malawi	5,800	6,183	7,243	9,335	9,575	9,576	9,589	9,670
Mali	6,554	6,863	7,915	8,842	9,258	9,479	9,709	9,944
Mauritania	1,475	1,551	1,776	2,026	2,142	2,203	2,265	2,329
Mauritius	938	966	1,016	1,057	1,079	1,091	1,103	1,114
Morocco	18,961	19,832	22,150	24,337	24,940	25,241	25,542	25,926
Mozambique	11,429	12,095	13,535	14,198	15,303	16,021	16,738	17,388
Namibia	975	1,029	1,178	1,350	1,426	1,465	1,504	1,543
Niger	5,232	5,586	6,608	7,731	8,268	8,555	8,850	9,150
Nigeria	62,564	66,237	78,754	87,824	93,746	96,694	99,469	102,070
Oman	1,022	1,130	1,425	1,785	1,932	2,006	2,081	2,155
Qatar	200	229	358	485	516	528	538	548
Réunion	494	506	555	604	625	635	645	655
Rwanda	4,836	5,163	6,054	6,987	6,251	5,740	5,365	5,259
Sao Tomé e Príncipe	88	94	106	119	124	127	130	133
Saudi Arabia	6,518	7,297	9,608	13,671	14,909	15,487	16,061	16,646
Senegal	5,234	5,538	6,375	7,327	7,718	7,916	8,120	8,330
Seychelles	62	63	65	70	70	70	70	73
Sierra Leone	3,110	3,236	3,583	3,994	4,061	4,083	4,121	4,188
Somalia	5,188	5,853	6,547	7,773	7,931	7,962	8,037	8,201
South Africa	27,860	29,095	32,410	35,896	37,397	38,216	39,054	39,785
Sudan	17,577	18,681	21,459	24,062	25,070	25,576	26,090	26,617
Swaziland	527	560	649	753	799	823	847	873
Syria	8,163	8,708	10,397	12,386	13,125	13,481	13,837	14,200
Tanzania	17,447	18,581	21,775	25,470	27,252	28,181	29,082	29,925
Togo	2,473	2,615	3,026	3,512	3,726	3,837	3,948	4,060
Tunisia	6,207	6,548	7,448	8,237	8,481	8,603	8,725	8,847
Uganda	12,336	13,120	14,736	16,457	17,373	17,882	18,406	18,935
United Arab Emirates	717	915	1,400	1,772	1,985	2,091	2,198	2,304
Yemen	7,680	8,219	9,698	11,590	12,864	13,593	14,324	15,022
Zambia	5,386	5,738	6,410	7,239	7,611	7,804	7,998	8,193
Zimbabwe	6,707	7,126	8,388	9,863	10,318	10,512	10,694	10,871

Source: *National statistical offices/Eurostat/UN/Euromonitor*

Total Population 1978-2003: National Estimates at January 1st (continued)

- '000

Africa and Middle East	1996	1997	1998	1999	2000	2001	2002	2003	% Growth 1978-2003
Algeria	28,725	29,080	29,300	29,625	30,029	30,385	30,860	31,336	78.1
Angola	11,429	11,849	12,095	12,582	13,224	13,877	14,463	15,111	127.7
Bahrain	594	607	604	609	625	637	647	658	105.7
Benin	5,519	5,686	5,782	5,978	6,252	6,532	6,788	7,067	115.5
Botswana	1,510	1,542	1,570	1,603	1,645	1,691	1,731	1,775	110.3
Burkina Faso	10,780	11,115	11,307	11,699	12,288	12,898	13,403	13,985	112.8
Burundi	6,285	6,404	6,460	6,603	6,806	7,007	7,189	7,386	88.4
Cameroon	13,639	14,057	14,307	14,792	15,505	16,254	16,861	17,568	114.8
Cape Verde	392	403	408	421	437	453	467	483	66.4
Central African Republic	3,367	3,439	3,485	3,566	3,669	3,769	3,861	3,959	79.5
Chad	6,933	7,141	7,271	7,508	7,804	8,096	8,380	8,678	102.9
Comoros	627	647	658	681	714	750	779	813	126.5
Congo Dem Rep	46,917	48,288	49,150	50,696	52,876	55,111	57,191	59,435	134.0
Congo-Brazzaville	2,682	2,766	2,864	2,924	2,956	2,999	3,070	3,128	98.5
Côte d'Ivoire	13,830	14,106	14,294	14,598	15,060	15,551	15,994	16,475	117.1
Djibouti	610	618	623	632	647	663	676	691	179.7
Egypt	57,510	59,313	60,080	61,345	62,278	63,294	63,843	64,942	70.8
Equatorial Guinea	412	423	431	445	463	481	498	516	149.3
Eritrea	3,346	3,492	3,577	3,749	3,970	4,195	4,395	4,619	104.5
Ethiopia	57,085	58,671	59,653	61,469	63,813	66,105	68,281	70,592	103.7
Gabon	1,113	1,145	1,167	1,204	1,253	1,302	1,349	1,399	114.5
Gambia	1,158	1,201	1,229	1,277	1,338	1,400	1,455	1,516	151.4
Ghana	18,264	18,828	19,165	19,816	20,653	21,496	22,301	23,157	123.5
Guinea	7,220	7,281	7,340	7,389	7,504	7,620	7,735	7,852	81.9
Guinea-Bissau	1,116	1,144	1,161	1,194	1,237	1,282	1,321	1,364	86.4
Iran	62,324	63,469	64,628	65,758	66,796	67,896	68,566	69,906	95.0
Iraq	20,820	21,484	21,808	22,620	23,723	24,845	25,849	26,959	121.4
Israel	5,545	5,685	5,824	5,960	6,098	6,235	6,329	6,516	93.3
Jordan	4,520	4,678	4,828	4,987	5,143	5,284	5,427	5,571	170.6
Kenya	27,904	28,534	29,003	29,679	30,921	32,265	33,278	34,501	123.8
Kuwait	1,937	2,003	2,067	2,148	2,215	2,292	2,394	2,497	131.2
Lebanon	3,075	3,135	3,190	3,248	3,336	3,427	3,517	3,610	32.6
Lesotho	1,980	2,030	2,062	2,119	2,197	2,278	2,352	2,432	90.2
Liberia	2,345	2,579	2,666	2,976	3,369	3,802	4,201	4,666	164.5
Libya	5,120	5,260	5,483	5,505	5,718	5,851	6,011	6,161	121.4
Madagascar	14,271	14,755	15,058	15,610	16,373	17,156	17,830	18,590	120.4
Malawi	9,971	10,247	10,350	10,709	11,248	11,807	12,271	12,805	120.8
Mali	10,254	10,537	10,696	11,031	11,475	11,907	12,308	12,739	94.4
Mauritania	2,411	2,486	2,529	2,617	2,738	2,860	2,974	3,097	110.0
Mauritius	1,125	1,134	1,141	1,152	1,165	1,178	1,194	1,209	28.9
Morocco	26,386	26,848	27,310	27,775	28,238	28,703	28,956	29,461	55.4
Mozambique	17,938	18,443	18,872	19,382	20,146	20,975	21,681	22,477	96.7
Namibia	1,587	1,627	1,659	1,702	1,753	1,805	1,853	1,904	95.3
Niger	9,529	9,877	10,080	10,485	11,019	11,557	12,037	12,569	140.2
Nigeria	105,045	108,502	111,999	115,534	119,101	122,697	126,315	129,970	107.7
Oman	2,248	2,333	2,382	2,482	2,614	2,750	2,874	3,010	194.6
Qatar	560	571	579	592	609	627	643	660	230.2
Réunion	666	675	682	693	706	720	734	748	51.5
Rwanda	5,853	6,397	6,601	7,326	8,200	9,150	10,015	11,018	127.8
Sao Tomé e Príncipe	135	138	141	145	149	154	159	164	86.6
Saudi Arabia	17,405	18,345	19,362	20,378	21,364	22,354	23,358	24,376	273.9
Senegal	8,606	8,859	9,005	9,301	9,705	10,110	10,488	10,895	108.2
Seychelles	74	75	76	77	77	78	79	80	29.1
Sierra Leone	4,348	4,494	4,568	4,748	4,975	5,209	5,420	5,652	81.7
Somalia	8,656	9,073	9,242	9,776	10,494	11,226	11,845	12,563	142.2
South Africa	40,338	40,905	41,679	42,592	43,278	43,949	44,844	45,739	64.2
Sudan	27,306	27,938	28,296	29,039	30,226	31,490	32,536	33,735	91.9
Swaziland	905	935	952	987	1,034	1,081	1,122	1,168	121.6
Syria	14,662	15,085	15,335	15,827	16,477	17,141	17,733	18,385	125.2
Tanzania	30,787	31,577	32,104	32,982	34,142	35,279	36,312	37,431	114.5
Togo	4,197	4,322	4,398	4,542	4,737	4,931	5,114	5,310	114.7
Tunisia	8,969	9,089	9,215	9,333	9,437	9,550	9,619	9,758	57.2
Uganda	19,617	20,243	20,563	21,313	22,420	23,563	24,500	25,588	107.4
United Arab Emirates	2,411	2,517	2,624	2,759	2,938	3,088	3,178	3,359	368.5
Yemen	15,764	16,444	16,888	17,650	18,744	19,859	20,874	21,998	186.4
Zambia	8,427	8,642	8,634	8,975	9,418	9,859	10,211	10,624	97.3
Zimbabwe	11,062	11,238	11,251	11,521	11,840	12,159	12,440	12,748	90.1

Source: National statistical offices/Eurostat/UN/Euromonitor

					Table 21.3

Total Population: National Estimates at January 1st

Population by Sex and Age at January 1st 2003

• '000

	Total	Male	Female	0-14	15-64	65+
North America						
Canada	31,320	15,530	15,790	5,754	21,588	3,978
USA	281,552	137,652	143,900	58,944	187,140	35,469
Latin America						
Anguilla	8	4	4	2	5	1
Antigua	71	34	37	21	45	5
Argentina	38,172	18,724	19,448	10,384	24,053	3,736
Aruba	124	62	63	37	79	8
Bahamas	335	164	171	96	199	41
Barbados	277	130	146	60	186	30
Belize	264	133	131	109	144	11
Bermuda	68	33	35	20	44	4
Bolivia	8,799	4,382	4,417	3,429	5,008	363
Brazil	174,893	86,307	88,586	47,250	117,983	9,660
British Virgin Islands	22	11	11	7	14	1
Cayman Islands	43	22	21	13	27	3
Chile	15,681	7,766	7,915	4,325	10,191	1,165
Colombia	40,696	20,189	20,507	12,688	26,039	1,970
Costa Rica	3,981	2,013	1,969	1,273	2,495	213
Cuba	11,291	5,653	5,639	2,265	7,880	1,146
Dominica	71	35	36	21	45	5
Dominican Republic	8,814	4,482	4,332	2,801	5,594	420
Ecuador	13,343	6,698	6,645	4,323	8,360	659
El Salvador	6,642	3,264	3,378	2,303	4,013	325
French Guiana	217	109	108	66	136	15
Grenada	95	47	48	29	60	6
Guadeloupe	499	255	245	154	311	34
Guatemala	12,152	6,124	6,028	5,205	6,512	436
Guyana	892	441	451	280	574	37
Haiti	8,380	4,121	4,259	3,314	4,747	320
Honduras	6,915	3,485	3,430	2,794	3,872	248
Jamaica	2,722	1,376	1,346	851	1,676	195
Martinique	413	200	213	92	277	44
Mexico	103,301	51,064	52,237	32,795	65,325	5,181
Netherlands Antilles	229	113	116	56	155	17
Nicaragua	4,992	2,494	2,498	1,980	2,848	164
Panama	2,963	1,494	1,470	893	1,899	171
Paraguay	5,850	2,951	2,899	2,251	3,391	208
Peru	26,951	13,362	13,588	8,578	16,994	1,380
Puerto Rico	4,060	1,936	2,124	982	2,667	412
St Kitts	37	19	19	11	25	2
St Lucia	164	81	83	50	106	8
St Vincent and the Grenadines	120	60	60	40	75	5
Suriname	428	208	220	141	265	22
Trinidad and Tobago	1,331	661	670	356	888	88
Uruguay	3,320	1,618	1,702	786	2,114	420
Venezuela	25,554	12,849	12,704	8,322	16,038	1,194

Source: *National statistical offices/Eurostat/UN/Euromonitor*

Population by Sex and Age at January 1st 2003

• '000

	Total	Male	Female	0-14	15-64	65+
Asia Pacific						
Afghanistan	24,254	12,444	11,809	11,006	12,527	721
American Samoa	80	42	38	27	42	10
Armenia	3,819	1,861	1,959	828	2,600	391
Azerbaijan	8,233	4,037	4,197	2,636	5,121	476
Bangladesh	134,087	68,693	65,394	44,399	85,154	4,534
Bhutan	2,273	1,149	1,124	955	1,224	94
Brunei	345	180	165	106	226	13
Cambodia	11,795	5,745	6,050	4,635	6,786	374
China	1,306,067	661,523	644,544	295,398	914,954	95,715
Fiji	838	426	412	252	544	43
French Polynesia	245	126	119	78	156	11
Guam	177	93	84	58	108	10
Hong Kong, China	7,417	3,738	3,679	1,121	5,469	828
India	1,055,410	549,802	505,608	343,047	661,248	51,116
Indonesia	219,940	109,704	110,230	64,712	144,372	10,850
Japan	127,104	62,150	64,954	18,114	85,679	23,312
Kazakhstan	16,020	7,798	8,222	4,154	10,559	1,308
Kiribati	88	45	43	31	46	11
Kyrgyzstan	4,734	2,321	2,413	1,580	2,855	299
Laos	5,783	2,915	2,868	2,483	3,102	198
Macau	497	244	253	103	360	34
Malaysia	23,742	12,029	11,713	7,881	14,786	1,075
Maldives	305	157	148	126	169	11
Mongolia	2,747	1,380	1,367	864	1,772	111
Myanmar	46,900	23,353	23,547	12,487	32,027	2,387
Nauru	15					
Nepal	25,313	12,844	12,469	10,055	14,337	920
New Caledonia	226	115	110	67	146	13
North Korea	25,032	12,567	12,466	6,916	16,702	1,414
Pakistan	167,850	86,468	81,382	67,923	94,358	5,568
Papua New Guinea	5,076	2,614	2,461	1,929	2,987	160
Philippines	81,346	40,930	40,415	28,134	49,723	3,488
Singapore	3,407	1,704	1,703	726	2,420	261
Solomon Islands	479	246	233	201	263	15
South Korea	48,747	24,607	24,140	10,551	34,245	3,951
Sri Lanka	19,222	9,488	9,734	4,817	13,057	1,348
Taiwan	22,768	11,598	11,169	4,541	16,137	2,089
Tajikistan	6,401	3,190	3,211	2,449	3,650	303
Thailand	62,775	31,273	31,502	14,485	44,233	4,056
Tonga	99	50	49	35	52	12
Turkmenistan	4,702	2,329	2,373	1,665	2,824	213
Tuvalu	13	6	6	4	7	2
Uzbekistan	25,166	12,511	12,654	8,939	15,005	1,222
Vanuatu	202	101	101	81	114	7
Vietnam	83,839	41,490	42,349	25,639	53,684	4,517
Western Samoa	186	96	89	69	108	9
Australasia						
Australia	19,701	9,815	9,886	3,931	13,313	2,458
New Zealand	3,938	1,940	1,998	878	2,588	472

Source: *National statistical offices/Eurostat/UN/Euromonitor*

□ Total Population: National Estimates at January 1st

Population by Sex and Age at January 1st 2003

• '000

	Total	Male	Female	0-14	15-64	65+
Africa and Middle East						
Algeria	31,098	16,065	15,033	9,850	19,632	1,616
Angola	14,869	7,356	7,513	6,967	7,474	428
Bahrain	653	376	277	204	430	19
Benin	6,948	3,451	3,497	3,214	3,234	501
Botswana	1,760	862	898	756	958	45
Burkina Faso	13,796	6,768	7,029	6,541	6,887	367
Burundi	7,304	3,598	3,705	3,379	3,729	195
Cameroon	17,369	8,662	8,707	7,565	9,188	616
Cape Verde	477	220	257	188	267	21
Central African Republic	3,916	1,858	2,059	1,677	2,089	150
Chad	8,536	4,191	4,346	3,876	4,378	283
Comoros	802	393	408	345	436	21
Congo Dem Rep	58,453	28,502	29,952	27,369	29,478	1,610
Congo-Brazzaville	3,072	1,485	1,587	1,425	1,544	103
Côte d'Ivoire	16,274	8,265	8,009	7,191	8,595	488
Djibouti	685	337	348	289	375	22
Egypt	65,491	33,469	32,022	22,650	40,525	2,316
Equatorial Guinea	509	248	261	224	265	20
Eritrea	4,539	2,342	2,197	2,005	2,400	135
Ethiopia	69,521	35,274	34,250	32,311	35,220	1,992
Gabon	1,376	674	702	558	736	83
Gambia	1,494	762	732	610	839	46
Ghana	22,776	11,561	11,217	9,946	12,115	715
Guinea	7,780	3,963	3,817	3,415	4,162	203
Guinea-Bissau	1,349	653	696	580	714	54
Iran	70,576	35,826	34,749	23,169	44,212	3,195
Iraq	26,533	13,594	12,939	10,951	14,755	829
Israel	6,609	3,275	3,334	1,877	4,063	670
Jordan	5,499	2,872	2,627	2,061	3,299	138
Kenya	34,173	17,615	16,562	15,560	17,586	1,030
Kuwait	2,445	1,452	993	549	1,852	44
Lebanon	3,558	1,741	1,816	1,208	2,143	207
Lesotho	2,398	1,165	1,233	971	1,325	101
Liberia	4,510	2,281	2,229	2,210	2,166	134
Libya	6,007	3,030	2,978	2,425	3,398	185
Madagascar	18,328	9,086	9,242	8,074	9,711	543
Malawi	12,633	6,265	6,367	5,924	6,368	341
Mali	12,546	6,270	6,276	5,708	6,402	445
Mauritania	3,044	1,520	1,524	1,367	1,578	100
Mauritius	1,198	592	606	307	818	74
Morocco	29,714	14,791	14,922	9,018	19,165	1,530
Mozambique	22,202	10,917	11,285	10,124	11,300	780
Namibia	1,885	945	940	797	1,015	73
Niger	12,370	6,038	6,332	6,055	6,010	306
Nigeria	128,129	64,318	63,811	54,798	69,563	3,768
Oman	2,956	1,557	1,399	1,289	1,594	74
Qatar	653	422	231	172	470	12
Réunion	741	362	378	205	488	48
Rwanda	10,695	5,258	5,437	4,981	5,467	247
Sao Tomé e Príncipe	161	84	77	56	84	21
Saudi Arabia	23,876	13,492	10,384	9,436	13,642	797
Senegal	10,713	5,493	5,221	4,943	5,503	267
Seychelles	79	41	38	27	42	11
Sierra Leone	5,566	2,729	2,837	2,462	2,942	163
Somalia	12,345	6,223	6,123	5,849	6,190	306
South Africa	45,291	22,025	23,266	15,155	27,799	2,337
Sudan	33,336	16,673	16,663	13,453	18,863	1,020
Swaziland	1,152	550	602	491	631	30
Syria	18,144	9,149	8,995	7,731	9,860	553
Tanzania	36,968	18,451	18,518	16,814	19,171	984
Togo	5,219	2,589	2,630	2,399	2,665	156
Tunisia	9,827	4,952	4,876	2,699	6,458	670
Uganda	25,266	12,652	12,615	12,327	12,400	541
United Arab Emirates	3,449	2,327	1,122	893	2,517	39
Yemen	21,528	11,039	10,491	10,383	10,698	448
Zambia	10,514	5,370	5,146	5,067	5,204	244
Zimbabwe	12,634	6,055	6,580	5,299	6,978	357

Source: *National statistical offices/Eurostat/UN/Euromonitor*

Population by Sex and Age (%) at January 1st 2003

- % of total

	Total	Male	Female	0-14	15-64	65+
North America						
Canada	100.00	49.58	50.42	18.37	68.93	12.70
USA	100.00	48.89	51.11	20.94	66.47	12.60
Latin America						
Anguilla	100.00	48.38	51.62	29.72	63.55	6.73
Antigua	100.00	48.07	51.94	29.60	63.50	6.90
Argentina	100.00	49.05	50.95	27.20	63.01	9.79
Aruba	100.00	49.56	50.44	29.52	63.67	6.81
Bahamas	100.00	49.03	50.97	28.53	59.30	12.17
Barbados	100.00	47.09	52.91	21.66	67.35	11.00
Belize	100.00	50.28	49.72	41.26	54.62	4.12
Bermuda	100.00	48.66	51.34	29.38	64.06	6.58
Bolivia	100.00	49.80	50.20	38.97	56.91	4.12
Brazil	100.00	49.35	50.65	27.02	67.46	5.52
British Virgin Islands	100.00	49.67	50.33	30.51	62.90	6.59
Cayman Islands	100.00	50.64	49.36	30.62	62.60	6.78
Chile	100.00	49.52	50.48	27.58	64.99	7.43
Colombia	100.00	49.61	50.39	31.18	63.98	4.84
Costa Rica	100.00	50.55	49.45	31.99	62.67	5.34
Cuba	100.00	50.06	49.94	20.06	69.79	10.15
Dominica	100.00	49.94	50.06	29.80	63.33	6.88
Dominican Republic	100.00	50.85	49.15	31.77	63.46	4.76
Ecuador	100.00	50.20	49.80	32.40	62.66	4.94
El Salvador	100.00	49.14	50.86	34.67	60.43	4.90
French Guiana	100.00	50.15	49.85	30.60	62.70	6.70
Grenada	100.00	49.47	50.53	30.18	63.06	6.76
Guadeloupe	100.00	50.98	49.03	30.87	62.35	6.79
Guatemala	100.00	50.39	49.61	42.83	53.58	3.59
Guyana	100.00	49.42	50.58	31.45	64.38	4.17
Haiti	100.00	49.18	50.82	39.54	56.64	3.82
Honduras	100.00	50.40	49.60	40.41	56.00	3.59
Jamaica	100.00	50.56	49.45	31.28	61.58	7.15
Martinique	100.00	48.33	51.67	22.21	67.11	10.69
Mexico	100.00	49.43	50.57	31.75	63.24	5.02
Netherlands Antilles	100.00	49.38	50.63	24.56	67.87	7.58
Nicaragua	100.00	49.96	50.04	39.67	57.06	3.28
Panama	100.00	50.40	49.60	30.13	64.10	5.77
Paraguay	100.00	50.44	49.56	38.47	57.97	3.56
Peru	100.00	49.58	50.42	31.83	63.05	5.12
Puerto Rico	100.00	47.69	52.32	24.17	65.69	10.14
St Kitts	100.00	49.83	50.12	29.45	66.51	4.05
St Lucia	100.00	49.56	50.49	30.31	64.63	5.06
St Vincent and the Grenadines	100.00	50.33	49.68	33.24	62.48	4.29
Suriname	100.00	48.69	51.32	32.92	61.92	5.16
Trinidad and Tobago	100.00	49.64	50.36	26.72	66.69	6.59
Uruguay	100.00	48.74	51.26	23.66	63.69	12.65
Venezuela	100.00	50.28	49.72	32.57	62.76	4.67

Source: National statistical offices/Eurostat/UN/Euromonitor

◻ Total Population: National Estimates at January 1st

Population by Sex and Age (%) at January 1st 2003

● % of total

	Total	Male	Female	0-14	15-64	65+
Asia Pacific						
Afghanistan	100.00	51.31	48.69	45.38	51.65	2.97
American Samoa	100.00	52.18	47.82	34.06	53.23	12.71
Armenia	100.00	48.72	51.28	21.69	68.07	10.23
Azerbaijan	100.00	49.03	50.97	32.01	62.20	5.78
Bangladesh	100.00	51.23	48.77	33.11	63.51	3.38
Bhutan	100.00	50.53	49.47	42.01	53.83	4.16
Brunei	100.00	52.16	47.84	30.77	65.58	3.64
Cambodia	100.00	48.71	51.29	39.30	57.53	3.17
China	100.00	50.65	49.35	22.62	70.05	7.33
Fiji	100.00	50.82	49.18	30.01	64.84	5.15
French Polynesia	100.00	51.28	48.72	31.75	63.60	4.65
Guam	100.00	52.55	47.45	32.92	61.30	5.78
Hong Kong, China	100.00	50.40	49.60	15.11	73.73	11.16
India	100.00	52.09	47.91	32.50	62.65	4.84
Indonesia	100.00	49.88	50.12	29.42	65.64	4.93
Japan	100.00	48.90	51.10	14.25	67.41	18.34
Kazakhstan	100.00	48.68	51.32	25.93	65.91	8.16
Kiribati	100.00	51.12	48.88	34.82	52.39	12.80
Kyrgyzstan	100.00	49.04	50.96	33.37	60.31	6.32
Laos	100.00	50.40	49.60	42.93	53.64	3.43
Macau	100.00	49.14	50.86	20.74	72.45	6.80
Malaysia	100.00	50.67	49.33	33.19	62.28	4.53
Maldives	100.00	51.45	48.55	41.24	55.21	3.55
Mongolia	100.00	50.22	49.78	31.46	64.50	4.04
Myanmar	100.00	49.79	50.21	26.62	68.29	5.09
Nauru	100.00					
Nepal	100.00	50.74	49.26	39.72	56.64	3.64
New Caledonia	100.00	51.10	48.90	29.81	64.58	5.62
North Korea	100.00	50.20	49.80	27.63	66.72	5.65
Pakistan	100.00	51.51	48.49	40.47	56.22	3.32
Papua New Guinea	100.00	51.51	48.49	38.01	58.84	3.15
Philippines	100.00	50.32	49.68	34.59	61.13	4.29
Singapore	100.00	50.01	49.99	21.32	71.02	7.66
Solomon Islands	100.00	51.38	48.62	41.98	54.87	3.16
South Korea	100.00	50.48	49.52	21.64	70.25	8.11
Sri Lanka	100.00	49.36	50.64	25.06	67.93	7.01
Taiwan	100.00	50.94	49.06	19.95	70.88	9.18
Tajikistan	100.00	49.83	50.17	38.26	57.02	4.73
Thailand	100.00	49.82	50.18	23.08	70.46	6.46
Tonga	100.00	50.93	49.07	35.17	52.24	12.60
Turkmenistan	100.00	49.53	50.47	35.40	60.06	4.54
Tuvalu	100.00	49.76	50.25	34.65	52.02	13.34
Uzbekistan	100.00	49.72	50.28	35.52	59.63	4.85
Vanuatu	100.00	50.05	49.95	40.01	56.65	3.34
Vietnam	100.00	49.49	50.51	30.58	64.03	5.39
Western Samoa	100.00	51.91	48.09	37.29	58.05	4.66
Australasia						
Australia	100.00	49.82	50.18	19.95	67.57	12.48
New Zealand	100.00	49.26	50.74	22.31	65.71	11.98

Source: National statistical offices/Eurostat/UN/Euromonitor

▣ Total Population: National Estimates at January 1st

Population by Sex and Age (%) at January 1st 2003

● % of total

	Total	Male	Female	0-14	15-64	65+
Africa and Middle East						
Algeria	100.00	51.66	48.34	31.67	63.13	5.20
Angola	100.00	49.48	50.53	46.86	50.27	2.88
Bahrain	100.00	57.57	42.43	31.33	65.83	2.84
Benin	100.00	49.67	50.33	46.26	46.55	7.20
Botswana	100.00	48.97	51.03	42.98	54.47	2.55
Burkina Faso	100.00	49.06	50.95	47.41	49.92	2.66
Burundi	100.00	49.27	50.73	46.27	51.06	2.67
Cameroon	100.00	49.87	50.13	43.55	52.90	3.55
Cape Verde	100.00	46.16	53.84	39.42	56.09	4.50
Central African Republic	100.00	47.44	52.56	42.82	53.35	3.83
Chad	100.00	49.09	50.91	45.40	51.28	3.31
Comoros	100.00	49.08	50.92	43.07	54.36	2.57
Congo Dem Rep	100.00	48.76	51.24	46.82	50.43	2.75
Congo-Brazzaville	100.00	48.34	51.66	46.39	50.27	3.34
Côte d'Ivoire	100.00	50.79	49.21	44.18	52.82	3.00
Djibouti	100.00	49.16	50.84	42.10	54.73	3.18
Egypt	100.00	51.10	48.90	34.58	61.88	3.54
Equatorial Guinea	100.00	48.79	51.21	43.95	52.11	3.94
Eritrea	100.00	51.60	48.40	44.16	52.86	2.98
Ethiopia	100.00	50.74	49.26	46.48	50.66	2.86
Gabon	100.00	48.99	51.01	40.51	53.47	6.02
Gambia	100.00	51.01	49.01	40.83	56.13	3.05
Ghana	100.00	50.76	49.25	43.67	53.19	3.14
Guinea	100.00	50.94	49.07	43.90	53.50	2.61
Guinea-Bissau	100.00	48.39	51.62	43.02	52.95	4.03
Iran	100.00	50.76	49.24	32.83	62.64	4.53
Iraq	100.00	51.24	48.77	41.27	55.61	3.12
Israel	100.00	49.56	50.44	28.39	61.47	10.13
Jordan	100.00	52.23	47.77	37.49	60.00	2.51
Kenya	100.00	51.55	48.47	45.53	51.46	3.01
Kuwait	100.00	59.39	40.61	22.46	75.75	1.79
Lebanon	100.00	48.95	51.06	33.96	60.24	5.81
Lesotho	100.00	48.60	51.41	40.51	55.26	4.23
Liberia	100.00	50.58	49.42	49.01	48.03	2.97
Libya	100.00	50.44	49.57	40.36	56.56	3.09
Madagascar	100.00	49.57	50.43	44.05	52.98	2.96
Malawi	100.00	49.60	50.40	46.89	50.41	2.70
Mali	100.00	49.98	50.02	45.49	51.03	3.54
Mauritania	100.00	49.93	50.07	44.90	51.83	3.29
Mauritius	100.00	49.41	50.60	25.59	68.27	6.15
Morocco	100.00	49.78	50.22	30.35	64.50	5.15
Mozambique	100.00	49.17	50.83	45.60	50.90	3.51
Namibia	100.00	50.11	49.89	42.29	53.83	3.88
Niger	100.00	48.81	51.19	48.95	48.58	2.47
Nigeria	100.00	50.20	49.80	42.77	54.29	2.94
Oman	100.00	52.67	47.34	43.61	53.91	2.50
Qatar	100.00	64.59	35.42	26.30	71.89	1.81
Réunion	100.00	48.92	51.08	27.65	65.92	6.43
Rwanda	100.00	49.16	50.84	46.57	51.11	2.31
Sao Tomé e Príncipe	100.00	52.15	47.85	34.62	52.11	13.27
Saudi Arabia	100.00	56.51	43.49	39.52	57.14	3.34
Senegal	100.00	51.28	48.73	46.14	51.37	2.50
Seychelles	100.00	51.52	48.48	33.85	52.80	13.35
Sierra Leone	100.00	49.03	50.97	44.23	52.85	2.92
Somalia	100.00	50.41	49.60	47.38	50.14	2.48
South Africa	100.00	48.63	51.37	33.46	61.38	5.16
Sudan	100.00	50.01	49.99	40.36	56.58	3.06
Swaziland	100.00	47.76	52.25	42.64	54.76	2.61
Syria	100.00	50.42	49.58	42.61	54.34	3.05
Tanzania	100.00	49.91	50.09	45.48	51.86	2.66
Togo	100.00	49.61	50.39	45.97	51.05	2.98
Tunisia	100.00	50.39	49.61	27.47	65.72	6.82
Uganda	100.00	50.08	49.93	48.79	49.08	2.14
United Arab Emirates	100.00	67.47	32.53	25.88	72.99	1.13
Yemen	100.00	51.28	48.73	48.23	49.69	2.08
Zambia	100.00	51.07	48.94	48.19	49.49	2.32
Zimbabwe	100.00	47.93	52.08	41.94	55.23	2.83

Source: *National statistical offices/Eurostat/UN/Euromonitor*

Number of Live Births 1977-2002

● '000

	1977	1980	1985	1990	1995	1997	1998	1999	2000	2001	2002
North America											
Canada	364.9	374.2	370.6	418.7	367.6	353.1	352.2	352.4	346.4	342.4	336.6
USA	3,285.3	3,546.5	3,689.9	4,121.2	3,889.3	3,845.8	3,822.9	3,790.0	3,749.6	3,699.0	3,639.2
Latin America											
Anguilla				0.1	0.1	0.1	0.1	0.1	0.1	0.1	0.1
Antigua			1.4	1.3	1.2	1.2	1.2	1.1	1.1	1.1	1.1
Argentina	651.1	684.4	641.4	686.5	695.2	700.5	704.7	707.8	710.1	711.6	712.3
Aruba	1.0	1.1	1.2	1.0	1.2	1.3	1.3	1.4	1.4	1.5	1.5
Bahamas	5.4	5.7	5.9	6.0	6.2	6.2	6.2	6.2	6.3	6.4	6.4
Barbados	4.4	4.4	4.2	3.8	3.6	3.5	3.4	3.4	3.4	3.4	3.4
Belize	5.6	5.7	6.0	6.4	6.5	6.4	6.4	6.5	6.5	6.6	6.5
Bermuda	0.9	0.9	0.9	0.9	0.8	0.8	0.8	0.8	0.8	0.8	0.7
Bolivia	200.0	206.2	214.6	231.6	248.7	252.3	254.7	256.9	258.5	259.4	259.5
Brazil	3,542.7	3,606.7	3,555.2	3,372.1	3,243.0	3,196.9	3,212.5	3,223.8	3,230.7	3,233.2	3,297.2
British Virgin Islands				0.3	0.3	0.3	0.3	0.3	0.3	0.3	0.4
Cayman Islands	0.4	0.5	0.6	0.5	0.5	0.5	0.5	0.5	0.5	0.5	0.5
Chile	251.8	256.9	274.1	289.7	290.6	286.7	286.7	286.1	284.8	282.7	280.0
Colombia	815.2	833.6	857.0	900.3	925.6	914.4	916.1	915.6	912.7	907.4	899.6
Costa Rica	64.4	68.6	75.9	81.0	81.1	81.7	82.6	83.4	84.1	84.5	84.9
Cuba	162.5	160.8	169.3	169.4	152.1	144.5	142.5	140.3	137.7	134.8	131.0
Dominica	1.6	1.9	1.5	1.4	1.3	1.3	1.3	1.2	1.2	1.2	1.2
Dominican Republic	181.3	191.6	200.5	199.6	197.3	195.6	197.3	198.7	199.8	200.5	200.9
Ecuador	282.8	292.9	301.3	306.2	310.8	309.1	310.0	310.5	310.2	309.0	307.4
El Salvador	167.1	161.3	146.6	148.1	158.0	160.6	162.0	162.9	163.5	163.5	163.1
French Guiana	1.6	1.9	2.7	3.7	4.6	4.9	5.1	5.3	5.5	5.7	6.0
Grenada	2.4				2.7	2.7	2.6	2.6	2.6	2.6	2.6
Guadeloupe	6.4	6.5	7.0	7.2	7.4	7.5	7.5	7.6	7.7	7.8	7.9
Guatemala	272.2	289.1	313.2	335.8	364.4	374.7	380.7	386.2	391.2	395.5	399.2
Guyana	23.4	23.1	21.7	19.8	20.0	20.0	19.9	19.8	19.7	19.5	19.3
Haiti	192.9	211.0	238.0	237.1	230.0	233.6	236.9	240.1	243.1	245.9	248.5
Honduras	140.3	150.5	165.3	180.6	193.3	195.0	197.3	199.0	200.1	200.6	200.4
Jamaica	59.3	59.2	57.9	56.8	56.3	54.4	54.2	54.2	54.4	54.0	54.6
Martinique	5.7	5.5	5.9	6.2	5.9	5.7	5.7	5.6	5.6	5.5	5.5
Mexico	2,344.3	2,341.7	2,324.9	2,358.2	2,364.4	2,339.1	2,339.5	2,333.5	2,320.8	2,301.2	2,274.7
Netherlands Antilles	3.6	3.6	3.6	3.6	3.6	3.4	3.4	3.4	3.4	3.5	3.5
Nicaragua	110.0	120.3	129.0	133.4	146.6	149.7	151.5	152.9	154.0	154.7	155.0
Panama	55.1	56.8	59.2	61.1	61.1	60.3	60.3	60.2	59.9	59.5	59.0
Paraguay	98.7	112.6	131.1	144.3	153.2	155.2	157.9	160.5	162.8	164.9	167.1
Peru	614.2	624.8	631.6	630.8	620.3	612.2	613.7	613.7	612.2	609.0	603.2
Puerto Rico	72.6	70.4	66.1	64.5	62.8	61.0	60.8	60.7	60.9	61.0	61.0
St Kitts	1.4	1.3	0.9	0.8	1.0	0.9	0.9	0.9	0.8	0.8	0.8
St Lucia	3.8	3.7	3.5	3.5	3.6	3.6	3.6	3.6	3.6	3.7	3.7
St Vincent and the Grenadines	3.0	3.0	2.7	2.5	2.5	2.2	2.2	2.2	2.2	2.2	2.2
Suriname	10.6	10.7	10.6	9.6	8.7	8.4	8.3	8.2	8.1	8.0	7.8
Trinidad and Tobago	30.4	31.1	30.3	24.7	19.8	17.9	17.9	17.9	17.8	17.9	17.8
Uruguay	57.2	55.5	54.6	56.1	56.7	56.5	56.4	56.3	56.1	55.8	55.5
Venezuela	474.7	502.1	503.9	566.8	571.8	572.3	576.2	578.8	580.1	579.9	578.3

Source: *National statistical offices/UN/Euromonitor*

□ Births

Number of Live Births 1977-2002

● '000

	1977	1980	1985	1990	1995	1997	1998	1999	2000	2001	2002
Asia Pacific											
Afghanistan	738.4	747.8	669.3	679.1	895.0	969.8	993.6	1,014.1	1,039.6	1,061.4	1,081.1
American Samoa	1.0	1.2	1.5	1.7	1.6	1.7	1.8	1.8	1.9	2.0	2.1
Armenia	71.2	76.9	82.8	75.6	53.6	42.5	41.5	40.3	38.9	37.4	35.7
Azerbaijan	145.0	154.8	172.1	175.4	149.6	126.3	123.1	119.4	114.7	109.5	103.9
Bangladesh	3,395.5	3,635.3	3,893.4	3,948.5	3,867.5	3,792.6	3,827.0	3,858.8	3,886.9	3,908.8	3,898.5
Bhutan	50.5	53.9	60.2	66.0	67.5	68.5	70.0	71.7	73.4	75.1	75.1
Brunei	5.2	5.7	6.2	6.7	7.0	6.7	6.7	6.7	6.6	6.5	6.3
Cambodia	221.4	289.2	365.0	367.2	385.3	389.7	393.7	396.5	398.0	398.7	395.5
China	20,522.4	20,833.1	22,851.3	23,125.8	20,894.4	20,123.3	19,955.6	19,837.7	19,598.4	19,395.3	18,617.3
Fiji	19.6	20.4	21.2	20.5	20.2	20.1	20.2	20.2	20.2	20.2	20.0
French Polynesia	4.3	4.6	5.1	5.3	4.9	4.7	4.8	4.8	4.8	4.9	4.8
Guam	2.8	2.9	3.1	3.7	4.3	4.4	4.4	4.5	4.5	4.5	4.5
Hong Kong, China	79.6	82.1	76.7	68.3	65.1	64.8	66.0	67.0	67.5	68.2	67.9
India	22,433.5	23,454.7	24,827.3	25,567.6	25,819.9	25,524.2	25,564.9	25,463.1	25,216.5	25,021.0	24,872.5
Indonesia	4,999.3	5,017.4	4,935.5	4,773.1	4,617.2	4,565.4	4,551.1	4,544.4	4,513.1	4,499.0	4,360.3
Japan	1,756.6	1,578.4	1,433.3	1,224.3	1,226.4	1,238.0	1,228.4	1,220.0	1,209.2	1,199.0	1,163.8
Kazakhstan	369.1	380.5	401.1	368.3	299.7	276.0	273.7	271.1	268.5	266.8	262.4
Kiribati					2.2	2.2	2.3	2.3	2.3	2.3	2.3
Kyrgyzstan	101.6	113.0	131.2	130.8	114.5	106.7	104.5	102.0	99.1	95.8	91.8
Laos	135.6	140.3	156.4	172.6	184.1	187.0	190.0	192.7	195.1	197.1	197.1
Macau	4.1	4.2	7.4	6.9	5.7	4.8	4.7	4.6	4.5	4.4	4.2
Malaysia	381.7	433.5	516.7	552.8	547.7	534.4	535.1	534.9	531.3	527.0	524.1
Maldives	5.7	6.1	7.3	8.3	9.0	9.5	9.7	9.9	10.1	10.4	10.5
Mongolia	58.7	62.3	67.9	69.4	64.1	60.5	60.5	60.3	59.9	59.3	58.1
Myanmar	1,191.4	1,202.7	1,214.7	1,224.6	1,189.0	1,147.7	1,139.5	1,128.3	1,113.6	1,095.2	1,067.4
Nauru					0.2	0.2	0.2	0.2	0.2	0.3	0.3
Nepal	520.4	556.2	623.8	699.0	768.7	790.2	801.3	811.2	819.9	826.8	825.9
New Caledonia	3.8	3.7	3.8	3.9	4.2	4.2	4.3	4.3	4.3	4.3	4.2
North Korea	341.1	359.7	386.0	416.3	429.0	421.5	421.3	419.9	417.1	413.2	406.0
Pakistan	3,441.2	3,716.9	4,324.1	4,909.5	5,362.0	5,534.4	5,653.9	5,743.1	5,795.1	5,881.1	6,005.5
Papua New Guinea	114.8	119.5	127.4	140.9	150.0	149.4	151.4	153.1	154.6	155.9	155.7
Philippines	1,708.3	1,780.1	1,908.1	2,000.3	2,068.2	2,057.3	2,073.3	2,084.3	2,082.0	2,080.1	2,085.6
Singapore	33.5	36.3	39.5	45.0	45.8	43.2	42.4	41.7	40.7	39.8	42.6
Solomon Islands	8.9	9.3	10.4	12.3	14.6	15.5	15.9	16.3	16.6	16.9	17.1
South Korea	862.9	850.9	771.3	700.9	662.6	631.8	631.1	629.3	625.7	622.0	619.1
Sri Lanka	380.3	395.6	386.9	354.1	328.3	314.2	317.1	320.1	323.2	326.1	327.7
Taiwan		419.5	350.4	321.9	332.3	329.1	332.8	331.8	334.1	334.3	339.8
Tajikistan	133.3	144.7	173.3	191.4	176.7	167.9	165.0	161.3	156.6	151.1	143.8
Thailand	1,332.3	1,315.1	1,231.8	1,170.5	1,160.5	1,174.6	1,168.3	1,159.9	1,146.3	1,129.3	1,112.1
Tonga		2.7	2.6	2.4	2.6	2.5	2.5	2.5	2.5	2.4	2.4
Turkmenistan	95.1	102.3	116.1	125.9	125.1	122.1	122.0	121.6	120.5	119.1	117.9
Tuvalu					0.2	0.3	0.3	0.3	0.3	0.3	0.3
Uzbekistan	504.5	553.1	639.3	668.2	605.8	558.1	552.3	544.0	533.5	520.4	501.6
Vanuatu	4.3	4.5	4.9	5.4	5.8	5.8	5.9	6.0	6.0	6.1	6.1
Vietnam	1,832.3	1,893.9	2,005.6	2,036.2	1,834.7	1,656.3	1,658.6	1,662.2	1,657.4	1,646.2	1,638.0
Western Samoa	5.3	5.5	5.8	5.4	5.0	4.9	5.0	5.0	5.0	5.1	5.1
Australasia											
Australia	227.9	224.8	246.4	260.6	248.3	245.4	246.1	246.5	247.0	246.8	245.3
New Zealand	55.2	53.2	55.4	59.2	59.2	56.7	56.3	55.7	55.1	54.4	53.7

Source: *National statistical offices/UN/Euromonitor*

Number of Live Births 1977-2002
● '000

Africa and Middle East

	1977	1980	1985	1990	1995	1997	1998	1999	2000	2001	2002
Algeria	767.2	798.2	807.8	779.5	768.9	747.8	743.2	739.8	736.8	730.9	726.2
Angola	324.3	355.3	410.0	472.7	559.3	604.1	617.2	642.7	676.3	710.6	741.6
Bahrain	10.3	11.4	13.1	14.0	12.7	11.5	11.2	10.9	10.8	10.5	10.2
Benin	164.3	177.9	201.5	219.8	235.1	243.1	245.7	252.2	261.7	271.0	278.9
Botswana	37.3	40.6	45.3	49.0	51.7	51.8	52.0	52.2	52.6	53.0	53.0
Burkina Faso	321.8	344.1	384.4	430.9	487.6	518.5	527.8	546.4	574.3	603.2	627.4
Burundi	170.9	188.8	222.7	253.1	272.4	275.8	278.6	285.3	294.6	304.0	312.6
Cameroon	359.1	390.7	439.1	479.4	513.8	527.9	534.4	549.2	571.8	594.9	612.1
Cape Verde	10.3	11.1	12.2	11.8	12.5	12.8	12.8	13.0	13.3	13.5	13.6
Central African Republic	94.9	100.1	110.3	122.2	132.4	136.0	136.7	138.6	141.1	143.3	144.9
Chad	202.1	215.5	246.4	278.3	325.0	345.3	351.7	363.3	377.8	392.1	406.0
Comoros	16.8	18.9	20.6	21.5	23.7	25.2	25.5	26.2	27.3	28.5	29.3
Congo Dem Rep	1,174.8	1,295.7	1,520.7	1,795.3	2,176.9	2,301.6	2,338.7	2,407.6	2,505.7	2,605.5	2,696.8
Congo-Brazzaville	70.2	74.8	84.8	98.7	115.5	123.2	127.4	129.9	131.1	132.8	135.7
Côte d'Ivoire	372.1	416.2	474.5	486.3	501.9	508.0	513.1	522.1	536.5	551.5	564.4
Djibouti	13.0	14.9	19.0	23.6	25.6	25.2	25.1	25.2	25.4	25.6	25.7
Egypt	1,442.1	1,550.5	1,662.8	1,612.4	1,545.6	1,552.8	1,545.0	1,545.5	1,532.9	1,517.5	1,486.3
Equatorial Guinea	8.9	9.3	13.6	15.4	17.3	18.3	18.6	19.2	20.0	20.8	21.5
Eritrea	99.2	107.5	121.5	127.1	133.8	142.7	144.8	150.2	157.2	163.9	169.2
Ethiopia	1,579.6	1,688.0	1,922.9	2,228.4	2,492.9	2,615.9	2,651.9	2,723.7	2,817.2	2,906.5	2,988.9
Gabon	20.8	22.8	27.8	34.0	40.2	43.2	44.0	45.4	47.2	49.0	50.7
Gambia	28.5	31.0	35.1	41.1	46.3	48.6	49.1	50.2	51.7	53.1	54.1
Ghana	477.4	498.7	556.7	591.2	627.0	639.3	646.6	663.9	686.4	708.1	727.5
Guinea	219.5	229.6	243.8	260.6	321.3	332.7	332.7	331.9	333.6	334.9	335.7
Guinea-Bissau	31.2	35.8	39.6	43.9	48.7	51.2	52.0	53.4	55.3	57.3	58.9
Iran	1,464.3	1,707.5	2,003.8	1,945.0	1,662.7	1,493.1	1,505.4	1,514.7	1,519.3	1,522.7	1,513.9
Iraq	493.5	538.7	622.1	709.8	750.8	784.0	786.9	805.9	833.1	858.6	877.5
Israel	85.8	87.4	89.1	97.1	115.8	121.8	123.2	124.4	125.3	126.9	125.3
Jordan	88.0	99.1	112.8	137.1	154.8	160.4	164.4	168.5	172.2	173.1	178.1
Kenya	768.1	846.3	953.4	984.8	997.0	1,009.2	1,020.0	1,037.2	1,073.0	1,092.6	1,135.9
Kuwait	40.6	45.0	47.2	42.4	33.5	32.0	34.1	36.7	39.2	41.2	46.0
Lebanon	83.0	79.2	76.1	68.1	68.4	63.6	64.1	64.5	65.4	66.2	66.8
Lesotho	52.2	55.2	60.0	64.5	68.8	71.0	71.3	72.3	73.9	75.4	76.5
Liberia	81.1	88.5	99.1	108.8	95.9	129.2	135.8	154.5	178.5	205.9	233.0
Libya	126.1	141.2	144.7	123.8	127.3	138.8	145.0	145.9	152.0	156.0	160.9
Madagascar	376.7	404.6	457.6	520.4	608.1	649.6	656.8	673.7	698.3	722.0	739.4
Malawi	320.7	341.3	381.4	476.2	470.0	483.8	484.8	497.1	516.8	536.4	550.6
Mali	326.1	346.2	397.0	443.2	497.4	526.0	533.5	549.6	571.0	591.8	610.8
Mauritania	64.3	67.3	77.0	89.2	101.7	108.2	110.2	114.1	119.4	124.8	129.9
Mauritius	24.6	23.3	21.1	21.3	20.7	19.3	19.2	19.1	19.0	18.9	18.8
Morocco	730.4	756.7	770.3	749.7	718.7	720.8	724.1	725.9	726.2	725.0	716.8
Mozambique	515.8	556.9	615.4	641.5	780.4	824.4	834.5	846.6	867.9	889.8	905.1
Namibia	40.6	43.5	49.6	56.3	60.5	61.1	61.5	62.1	62.9	63.5	63.8
Niger	288.3	316.7	370.8	429.1	506.4	547.2	558.1	580.2	609.3	638.5	664.3
Nigeria	2,906.6	3,155.3	3,673.1	3,938.4	4,360.5	4,521.5	4,628.2	4,728.9	4,823.0	4,909.8	4,988.6
Oman	44.8	51.4	63.3	73.7	79.7	82.4	84.4	88.2	93.3	98.5	103.3
Qatar	5.7	6.7	9.7	10.9	10.9	11.4	11.3	11.3	11.3	11.3	11.2
Réunion	12.4	12.3	12.9	13.4	13.5	13.4	13.3	13.3	13.2	13.1	13.0
Rwanda	247.1	265.8	284.3	304.1	224.7	271.5	279.9	310.2	346.6	386.1	421.8
Sao Tomé e Príncipe	3.8	3.7	3.8		5.6	5.9	6.0	6.1	6.2	6.4	6.5
Saudi Arabia	282.5	316.4	390.8	529.9	600.8	640.1	672.0	703.2	732.3	760.6	788.4
Senegal	250.7	266.6	294.9	317.2	336.2	349.6	352.7	361.1	373.2	384.6	394.2
Seychelles	1.6	1.9	1.6	1.6	1.5	1.5	1.5	1.5	1.5	1.5	1.5
Sierra Leone	148.7	158.1	175.7	196.9	207.3	222.6	225.9	234.4	245.1	256.1	265.9
Somalia	247.8	302.9	338.8	403.4	427.7	474.1	482.6	509.6	546.0	582.9	613.8
South Africa	958.3	1,000.0	1,032.4	1,024.1	1,067.9	1,091.1	1,098.0	1,106.3	1,106.2	1,103.5	1,103.7
Sudan	745.4	794.4	860.6	923.6	982.5	1,007.2	1,009.0	1,022.7	1,049.7	1,076.7	1,093.3
Swaziland	23.2	24.2	26.8	29.8	32.2	33.3	33.6	34.4	35.6	36.7	37.5
Syria	364.2	399.2	458.5	465.2	449.3	457.7	463.3	476.0	492.9	509.8	524.1
Tanzania	794.5	867.4	991.9	1,110.7	1,239.8	1,277.1	1,285.6	1,305.8	1,334.7	1,359.6	1,377.6
Togo	113.9	121.0	134.9	151.2	167.7	174.8	176.7	181.0	187.1	192.8	197.7
Tunisia	219.8	231.1	238.1	227.7	194.2	170.4	172.5	174.5	176.1	177.9	178.8
Uganda	600.3	660.8	743.7	831.1	955.0	1,020.4	1,037.2	1,075.8	1,132.7	1,191.5	1,240.1
United Arab Emirates	19.0	27.4	39.4	40.8	40.7	40.2	41.8	43.8	46.5	48.7	49.9
Yemen	398.8	422.7	479.0	591.8	780.2	845.2	861.0	891.6	937.1	981.5	1,018.4
Zambia	247.4	266.2	288.2	324.5	363.2	378.1	374.7	386.0	400.9	414.8	424.2
Zimbabwe	295.3	317.7	361.4	408.9	422.7	419.8	416.2	421.5	427.8	433.2	436.4

Source: *National statistical offices/UN/Euromonitor*

Deaths | Table 21.6

Number of Deaths 1977-2002

'000

	1977	1980	1985	1990	1995	1997	1998	1999	2000	2001	2002
North America											
Canada	169.2	173.0	183.0	246.3	209.6	216.6	220.9	226.7	229.2	233.7	237.8
USA	1,877.6	1,954.4	2,051.5	2,147.0	2,264.9	2,254.5	2,271.9	2,287.9	2,304.2	2,319.2	2,333.5
Latin America											
Anguilla			0.1		0.0	0.0	0.0	0.0	0.0	0.0	0.0
Antigua	0.4	0.3	0.3	0.4	0.4	0.4	0.4	0.4	0.4	0.4	0.4
Argentina	237.0	241.8	254.0	267.0	276.7	279.8	282.5	285.0	287.4	289.7	291.8
Aruba	0.3	0.3	0.4		0.5	0.6	0.6	0.6	0.7	0.7	0.7
Bahamas	1.1	1.2	1.4	1.6	1.9	2.0	2.0	2.1	2.2	2.3	2.3
Barbados	2.1	2.1	2.1	2.3	2.3	2.2	2.2	2.2	2.2	2.2	2.1
Belize	0.9	0.9	0.9	0.9	1.0	1.0	1.0	1.0	1.1	1.1	1.1
Bermuda	0.4	0.4	0.4	0.4	0.5	0.5	0.5	0.5	0.5	0.5	0.5
Bolivia	78.2	76.5	71.5	69.4	69.5	69.1	69.6	69.9	70.1	70.0	69.6
Brazil	987.6	1,013.1	1,031.5	1,049.1	1,091.2	1,110.7	1,125.6	1,140.5	1,155.3	1,170.2	1,209.3
British Virgin Islands	0.1	0.1	0.1		0.1	0.1	0.1	0.1	0.1	0.1	0.1
Cayman Islands	0.1	0.1	0.1	0.1	0.2	0.2	0.2	0.2	0.2	0.2	0.2
Chile	78.1	75.4	72.6	73.6	77.9	80.7	82.1	83.6	85.2	86.8	88.4
Colombia	193.5	192.0	195.5	212.3	220.3	216.8	224.1	231.9	240.4	249.4	259.1
Costa Rica	9.7	9.7	10.1	11.3	12.7	13.4	13.8	14.2	14.6	15.0	15.4
Cuba	57.1	60.3	66.1	71.6	76.0	77.8	78.5	79.2	79.9	80.6	81.3
Dominica	0.5			0.6	0.4	0.4	0.4	0.4	0.4	0.4	0.4
Dominican Republic	43.8	45.3	46.4	46.9	49.1	50.4	52.0	53.7	55.4	57.3	59.3
Ecuador	72.8	71.7	68.5	67.8	70.5	71.9	73.0	74.1	75.1	76.0	76.9
El Salvador	47.3	49.3	43.1	36.1	35.4	35.4	36.1	36.7	37.3	37.8	38.3
French Guiana	0.4	0.5	0.5	0.6	0.7	0.7	0.7	0.8	0.8	0.9	0.9
Grenada	0.7				0.5	0.5	0.5	0.5	0.5	0.5	0.5
Guadeloupe	2.2	2.2	2.3	2.4	2.6	2.6	2.7	2.7	2.8	2.9	3.0
Guatemala	75.1	76.3	77.7	75.7	75.0	75.6	76.6	77.5	78.2	78.7	79.1
Guyana	6.8	6.9	6.9	6.5	6.8	7.1	7.2	7.5	7.7	8.0	8.3
Haiti	77.6	81.2	86.9	90.7	95.0	97.8	99.0	100.0	100.9	101.7	102.4
Honduras	34.6	34.5	32.7	33.3	36.8	38.1	39.2	40.3	41.4	42.4	43.5
Jamaica	15.2	15.0	15.2	15.3	15.2	15.0	15.0	15.0	15.2	15.0	15.4
Martinique	2.2	2.1	2.1	2.2	2.4	2.4	2.5	2.5	2.6	2.7	2.7
Mexico	484.2	476.3	457.0	454.4	471.2	481.3	489.3	497.2	505.0	512.7	520.4
Netherlands Antilles	1.1	1.1	1.1	1.2	1.3	1.3	1.3	1.3	1.4	1.4	1.4
Nicaragua	27.1	28.2	28.2	25.2	24.0	23.9	24.2	24.5	24.7	24.9	25.0
Panama	11.1	11.3	11.8	12.6	13.4	13.7	13.9	14.1	14.4	14.6	14.8
Paraguay	21.5	22.9	24.5	25.9	26.8	26.9	27.3	27.7	28.1	28.3	28.6
Peru	176.1	173.3	164.7	158.7	157.8	158.5	160.1	161.5	162.8	163.9	164.7
Puerto Rico	19.7	20.8	23.2	26.5	28.7	29.0	29.3	29.7	30.3	30.9	31.6
St Kitts	0.6	0.5	0.4		0.3	0.3	0.3	0.3	0.3	0.3	0.3
St Lucia	0.8	0.8	0.8	0.8	0.9	0.8	0.9	0.9	0.9	0.9	0.9
St Vincent and the Grenadines	0.7	0.7	0.7		0.7	0.7	0.6	0.7	0.7	0.7	0.7
Suriname	2.6	2.5	2.6	2.5	2.5	2.5	2.5	2.5	2.5	2.5	2.5
Trinidad and Tobago	7.4	7.7	8.2	7.8	7.5	7.5	7.6	7.7	7.8	7.9	8.0
Uruguay	28.6	28.9	29.6	30.4	30.4	30.2	30.3	30.4	30.5	30.6	30.7
Venezuela	81.0	86.6	90.8	95.6	103.5	107.1	109.4	111.7	114.0	116.3	118.6

Source: *National statistical offices/UN/Euromonitor*

◻ Deaths

Number of Deaths 1977-2002

● '000

	1977	1980	1985	1990	1995	1997	1998	1999	2000	2001	2002
Asia Pacific											
Afghanistan	367.3	370.1	327.4	323.9	416.8	448.8	458.2	465.8	475.4	482.9	489.2
American Samoa		0.2	0.2		0.2	0.2	0.3	0.3	0.3	0.3	0.3
Armenia	17.4	18.5	22.3	25.7	26.8	27.8	27.9	28.0	28.1	28.3	28.4
Azerbaijan	39.2	41.0	43.6	47.0	49.6	48.6	49.0	49.4	49.7	50.1	50.5
Bangladesh	1,434.8	1,448.8	1,404.7	1,322.1	1,230.0	1,181.8	1,179.4	1,174.0	1,165.3	1,152.3	1,127.5
Bhutan	23.2	23.7	23.2	21.3	19.1	18.5	18.6	18.8	18.8	18.8	18.6
Brunei	0.9	0.9	0.8	0.8	0.9	0.9	0.9	1.0	1.0	1.0	1.1
Cambodia	264.9	172.2	106.5	105.3	109.1	110.5	112.8	114.9	116.9	118.9	120.0
China	6,393.0	6,644.5	7,132.0	8,007.9	8,590.2	8,633.2	8,728.3	8,828.1	8,898.9	8,966.9	9,056.5
Fiji	3.9	3.9	4.1	4.4	4.5	4.3	4.4	4.4	4.4	4.5	4.5
French Polynesia	1.0	1.0	1.0	1.0	1.0	1.1	1.1	1.1	1.1	1.1	1.1
Guam	0.4	0.4	0.5	0.6	0.7	0.7	0.8	0.8	0.8	0.8	0.8
Hong Kong, China	23.3	24.6	26.3	29.8	33.4	34.6	36.1	37.6	39.0	40.6	41.8
India	8,960.5	9,114.7	9,164.8	9,040.9	8,928.5	8,782.9	8,825.6	8,823.6	8,776.0	8,751.0	8,747.9
Indonesia	1,886.1	1,837.7	1,696.2	1,589.1	1,551.0	1,525.9	1,533.5	1,538.8	1,537.5	1,536.7	1,540.0
Japan	690.8	723.7	753.6	828.5	902.2	960.1	976.2	997.6	1,020.1	1,036.4	1,117.9
Kazakhstan	130.3	130.2	129.6	144.0	159.8	164.0	163.6	163.1	162.6	162.5	161.5
Kiribati		0.3	0.6	0.9	0.6	0.6	0.6	0.6	0.6	0.6	
Kyrgyzstan	32.5	32.8	32.5	32.9	34.3	34.9	34.7	34.5	34.2	33.9	33.4
Laos	62.3	61.0	64.3	68.1	69.1	69.1	69.7	70.1	70.3	70.2	69.4
Macau	1.6	1.6	1.8	1.8	1.8	1.9	2.0	2.0	2.1	2.2	2.2
Malaysia	100.1	96.1	93.4	96.6	100.6	101.7	103.5	105.4	106.9	108.6	111.0
Maldives	1.9	1.9	1.9	1.9	1.8	1.8	1.8	1.8	1.8	1.8	1.7
Mongolia	17.1	17.3	17.4	19.0	20.4	20.2	20.1	20.1	19.9	19.7	19.3
Myanmar	493.4	503.1	512.3	507.8	508.2	511.2	516.5	521.9	527.1	532.2	534.2
Nauru					0.1	0.1	0.1	0.1	0.1	0.1	0.1
Nepal	240.3	243.6	246.2	249.0	249.0	244.7	245.7	245.9	245.2	243.5	239.0
New Caledonia	0.9	0.9	0.9	0.9	1.0	1.0	1.0	1.0	1.0	1.1	1.1
North Korea	105.1	106.0	109.1	130.3	194.1	236.0	238.0	239.6	240.9	241.9	241.3
Pakistan	1,279.7	1,325.2	1,432.9	1,525.2	1,567.7	1,572.2	1,590.9	1,598.2	1,592.4	1,593.0	1,600.6
Papua New Guinea	44.8	45.1	46.1	47.4	47.2	46.7	47.0	47.2	47.3	47.2	46.6
Philippines	419.9	422.8	423.8	412.7	404.7	397.1	401.9	406.0	407.9	410.1	414.2
Singapore	10.4	11.2	12.8	13.6	14.4	15.0	15.5	16.0	16.5	17.1	17.5
Solomon Islands	1.5	1.4	1.8	2.2	2.1	2.1	2.1	2.1	2.1	2.1	2.1
South Korea	259.9	260.2	258.9	254.7	253.4	253.1	258.5	264.3	270.2	277.0	285.1
Sri Lanka	96.7	99.3	102.5	105.3	109.1	110.6	112.2	113.8	115.6	117.3	118.7
Taiwan			93.5	104.6	120.1	122.1	124.4	126.1	127.0	131.4	129.1
Tajikistan	31.7	32.7	34.2	37.2	39.0	39.2	39.3	39.4	39.4	39.4	39.0
Thailand	364.7	353.4	329.4	326.8	347.6	364.6	369.4	374.6	379.1	383.5	388.9
Tonga			0.3	0.5	0.6	0.6	0.6	0.6	0.6	0.6	0.6
Turkmenistan	25.8	26.5	27.7	29.1	30.3	31.0	31.0	31.0	30.8	30.6	30.4
Tuvalu			0.1	0.1	0.1	0.1	0.1	0.1	0.1	0.1	0.1
Uzbekistan	123.2	127.3	133.0	139.9	142.8	141.3	142.0	142.4	142.6	142.5	141.3
Vanuatu	1.1	1.1	1.1	1.1	1.1	1.1	1.1	1.1	1.1	1.1	1.0
Vietnam	656.1	650.6	614.6	580.7	556.3	535.5	537.0	539.0	538.4	535.9	534.4
Western Samoa	1.3	1.2	1.1	1.1	1.1	1.0	1.0	1.0	1.0	1.0	1.0
Australasia											
Australia	109.6	108.3	118.3	118.5	125.9	130.0	132.4	134.9	137.7	140.6	142.9
New Zealand	26.4	26.3	27.5	27.8	28.7	28.9	29.1	29.3	29.5	29.8	30.1

Source: *National statistical offices/UN/Euromonitor*

Deaths

Number of Deaths 1977-2002

• '000

	1977	1980	1985	1990	1995	1997	1998	1999	2000	2001	2002
Africa and Middle East											
Algeria	228.4	220.6	196.9	178.2	172.5	166.4	165.8	165.5	165.4	164.7	164.3
Angola	157.6	165.7	177.6	190.7	220.0	239.4	242.1	249.2	258.9	268.1	275.4
Bahrain	1.9	1.8	1.7	1.9	2.1	2.1	2.1	2.2	2.2	2.3	2.4
Benin	67.6	67.1	68.5	71.3	73.1	74.3	74.9	76.7	79.2	81.7	83.7
Botswana	9.2	9.3	9.2	10.5	19.3	26.2	28.5	31.3	34.6	38.3	42.3
Burkina Faso	133.0	134.4	142.1	161.7	186.7	199.4	199.0	201.6	206.6	210.9	212.5
Burundi	71.9	75.7	85.5	110.3	133.0	136.3	137.0	139.4	143.1	146.6	149.6
Cameroon	139.7	144.4	151.5	162.9	189.9	208.5	211.7	218.2	228.0	238.2	246.1
Cape Verde	2.9	3.1	3.2	2.8	2.7	2.6	2.5	2.6	2.6	2.6	2.6
Central African Republic	44.4	45.2	47.9	53.0	61.0	65.5	66.2	67.4	69.0	70.6	71.9
Chad	99.8	103.0	109.7	117.8	133.9	140.2	141.6	144.9	149.0	152.8	156.1
Comoros	5.3	5.6	5.8	5.8	6.0	6.2	6.2	6.3	6.4	6.6	6.7
Congo Dem Rep	431.8	456.1	498.3	561.0	679.0	725.8	727.2	736.8	753.0	767.1	776.0
Congo-Brazzaville	26.6	27.4	29.4	33.3	38.3	40.5	41.7	42.2	42.2	42.4	42.9
Côte d'Ivoire	127.4	135.4	150.1	170.5	203.2	217.0	219.8	224.4	231.4	238.8	245.5
Djibouti	5.1	5.9	7.4	9.1	10.6	11.1	11.5	12.0	12.6	13.4	14.1
Egypt	525.8	533.6	499.2	441.1	410.6	403.3	402.2	403.3	401.2	398.6	391.9
Equatorial Guinea	4.7	4.7	6.3	6.6	6.9	7.0	7.0	7.1	7.3	7.4	7.5
Eritrea	41.5	46.5	49.8	46.5	46.6	48.9	49.7	51.5	54.0	56.3	58.2
Ethiopia	711.0	760.8	824.5	906.4	1,037.4	1,116.6	1,139.0	1,178.1	1,228.0	1,277.8	1,326.4
Gabon	12.2	12.9	14.1	15.5	17.3	18.1	18.3	18.8	19.4	19.9	20.5
Gambia	14.5	15.4	16.6	19.0	21.3	22.2	22.4	23.0	23.7	24.3	24.7
Ghana	151.6	151.0	161.9	175.3	194.3	203.4	205.9	211.5	218.8	225.8	232.2
Guinea	107.6	109.5	112.3	115.5	133.0	132.9	132.2	131.2	131.0	130.6	129.9
Guinea-Bissau	18.3	20.3	20.9	21.7	22.8	23.4	23.5	23.9	24.5	25.1	25.5
Iran	417.9	437.6	438.3	395.8	354.2	335.1	337.9	340.1	341.2	342.1	340.2
Iraq	103.8	111.6	118.8	161.9	204.0	213.0	205.9	201.5	197.2	190.4	179.7
Israel	22.5	23.9	25.6	28.2	33.9	35.7	36.3	36.9	37.4	38.3	38.1
Jordan	18.8	20.9	21.8	22.9	22.6	21.7	22.1	22.5	22.9	22.9	23.2
Kenya	214.5	223.3	233.4	252.8	308.9	345.6	358.8	375.8	401.6	422.4	457.0
Kuwait	4.3	4.4	4.2	3.9	4.0	4.5	4.8	5.1	5.5	5.8	6.4
Lebanon	23.9	23.3	22.0	18.5	18.2	17.0	17.3	17.6	18.0	18.5	18.9
Lesotho	19.3	19.8	20.2	20.7	25.4	29.7	32.5	36.2	40.7	45.8	51.4
Liberia	31.0	31.8	32.9	49.3	41.2	42.8	42.4	45.0	48.0	50.5	51.4
Libya	33.8	35.6	29.7	21.7	23.0	24.7	25.8	26.0	27.1	27.8	28.6
Madagascar	148.8	156.9	174.5	191.8	209.6	216.4	217.3	221.1	227.1	232.4	235.2
Malawi	134.5	140.0	151.8	194.5	209.8	227.5	230.4	239.1	251.9	265.3	276.7
Mali	154.5	152.0	158.2	170.8	186.7	194.6	195.6	199.5	205.0	209.7	213.4
Mauritania	28.8	29.7	31.3	33.4	36.7	38.3	38.5	39.2	40.3	41.4	42.1
Mauritius	5.8	6.2	6.4	6.8	7.5	7.6	7.7	7.8	7.9	7.9	8.0
Morocco	241.0	240.2	222.7	199.5	183.0	177.9	178.2	178.0	177.4	176.2	173.3
Mozambique	233.4	253.0	279.7	290.5	373.4	413.0	427.0	443.7	467.1	493.1	517.4
Namibia	14.2	14.4	14.8	17.1	24.1	28.7	29.3	30.1	31.1	32.1	33.0
Niger	127.9	137.9	157.7	175.8	195.3	204.9	206.4	211.6	218.7	225.2	229.8
Nigeria	1,154.3	1,201.0	1,309.4	1,354.5	1,481.4	1,532.6	1,567.2	1,599.5	1,629.2	1,656.2	1,680.0
Oman	12.0	11.2	9.3	9.1	9.7	10.0	10.1	10.4	10.9	11.3	11.7
Qatar	1.8	1.6	1.5	1.7	2.0	2.2	2.3	2.3	2.4	2.5	2.6
Réunion	3.1	3.1	3.2	3.3	3.6	3.8	3.9	4.0	4.0	4.1	4.2
Rwanda	94.4	101.1	111.5	229.1	171.8	138.9	142.2	156.3	173.1	190.9	206.2
Sao Tomé e Príncipe	0.9		1.0		1.2	1.2	1.2	1.2	1.2	1.2	1.3
Saudi Arabia	65.9	67.4	66.7	74.8	77.6	80.5	84.1	87.5	90.5	93.3	95.9
Senegal	110.5	113.5	118.0	118.0	115.0	115.2	115.0	116.5	118.8	120.7	121.5
Seychelles	0.5	0.5	0.4	0.5	0.5	0.5	0.5	0.5	0.5	0.5	0.5
Sierra Leone	88.3	93.1	100.0	114.6	117.2	118.7	118.4	120.5	123.2	125.4	126.5
Somalia	109.7	131.2	137.9	177.7	176.4	167.7	168.6	175.7	185.4	194.6	201.0
South Africa	321.9	328.2	331.9	329.7	392.1	442.8	493.0	551.9	615.1	685.3	766.8
Sudan	305.4	314.7	325.9	334.6	338.2	339.6	339.0	342.2	349.6	356.6	359.9
Swaziland	8.2	8.3	8.4	8.8	11.1	13.1	14.7	16.9	19.5	22.6	25.8
Syria	70.2	76.4	81.0	75.1	67.3	64.9	65.2	66.4	68.1	69.7	70.8
Tanzania	276.7	284.4	298.6	330.2	390.8	418.5	424.5	434.9	448.8	462.3	474.1
Togo	42.4	43.3	45.3	50.0	56.9	60.2	60.7	62.1	64.1	65.9	67.5
Tunisia	60.7	59.6	57.7	55.6	57.6	60.9	61.3	61.5	61.6	61.7	61.4
Uganda	219.3	240.0	280.5	338.3	393.1	411.8	408.0	410.8	418.0	423.0	421.3
United Arab Emirates	4.6	5.1	5.5	6.7	8.3	9.0	9.5	10.2	11.2	12.0	12.7
Yemen	153.7	151.5	145.9	151.6	166.7	163.3	163.3	165.4	169.5	172.3	172.8
Zambia	85.4	88.9	93.6	118.2	158.7	178.7	176.0	179.9	185.3	190.0	192.3
Zimbabwe	71.9	75.0	87.2	126.2	178.6	202.2	202.1	206.5	211.8	217.0	221.5

Source: National statistical offices/UN/Euromonitor

Birth Rates 1977-2002

● Per '000 inhabitants

	1977	1980	1985	1990	1995	1997	1998	1999	2000	2001	2002
North America											
Canada	15.5	15.4	14.5	15.3	12.7	11.9	11.7	11.6	11.4	11.1	10.9
USA	15.1	15.9	15.7	16.7	14.9	14.5	14.3	14.0	13.7	13.4	13.1
Latin America											
Anguilla				19.8	17.8	17.1	16.9	16.6	16.2	15.9	15.5
Antigua			22.4	20.6	18.1	17.4	17.2	16.9	16.5	16.2	16.0
Argentina	24.6	24.7	21.5	21.4	20.3	19.9	19.8	19.6	19.4	19.2	19.0
Aruba	16.6	18.8	18.5	15.7	14.8	14.1	13.8	13.5	13.2	12.8	12.6
Bahamas	27.5	27.3	25.3	23.6	22.2	21.1	20.9	20.6	20.3	19.9	19.6
Barbados	17.7	17.5	16.5	14.9	13.6	12.9	12.8	12.7	12.5	12.4	12.2
Belize	40.9	39.0	36.4	34.2	30.6	28.5	27.9	27.4	26.7	26.0	25.2
Bermuda	16.2	16.1	15.2	14.6	13.2	12.5	12.2	11.9	11.6	11.2	11.0
Bolivia	41.0	39.5	37.3	36.1	34.4	33.2	32.8	32.3	31.7	31.1	30.5
Brazil	32.6	30.9	27.4	23.8	21.2	20.3	20.1	19.9	19.7	19.5	19.2
British Virgin Islands				18.5	17.6	17.0	16.7	16.4	16.1	15.7	15.5
Cayman Islands	24.4	28.9	30.6	18.5	15.2	14.5	14.2	13.9	13.6	13.2	13.0
Chile	24.0	23.4	23.1	22.5	20.8	19.9	19.6	19.3	19.0	18.6	18.2
Colombia	32.6	31.1	28.7	27.4	25.6	24.5	24.1	23.7	23.3	22.8	22.3
Costa Rica	31.7	30.9	29.5	27.4	24.2	23.3	23.1	22.9	22.6	22.3	21.9
Cuba	17.2	16.7	16.8	16.1	13.9	13.1	12.9	12.6	12.3	12.0	11.7
Dominica	21.8	26.0	21.4	19.5	18.8	18.1	17.8	17.5	17.2	16.8	16.6
Dominican Republic	34.9	34.3	32.1	28.7	25.7	24.6	24.4	24.1	23.9	23.6	23.3
Ecuador	38.2	36.3	32.7	29.5	26.8	25.6	25.2	24.8	24.3	23.8	23.2
El Salvador	40.2	36.7	32.1	30.1	28.6	27.7	27.3	26.9	26.4	25.9	25.3
French Guiana	25.8	27.3	29.5	31.3	31.4	30.6	30.3	29.8	29.4	28.9	28.3
Grenada	26.3				29.3	28.7	28.4	28.1	27.8	27.4	27.2
Guadeloupe	19.6	19.9	19.6	18.5	17.5	17.2	17.0	16.8	16.6	16.3	16.0
Guatemala	44.2	43.6	41.6	39.4	37.5	36.6	36.2	35.8	35.3	34.7	34.2
Guyana	31.5	30.5	27.3	24.9	24.1	23.7	23.4	23.1	22.7	22.3	21.8
Haiti	41.0	42.0	42.2	37.3	32.7	31.9	31.7	31.4	31.2	30.9	30.6
Honduras	44.9	43.5	40.8	38.2	35.2	33.5	33.0	32.4	31.7	30.9	30.1
Jamaica	28.8	27.8	25.2	24.0	22.7	21.6	21.3	21.1	20.8	20.5	20.2
Martinique	17.4	16.9	17.3	17.1	15.5	14.8	14.6	14.3	14.0	13.7	13.4
Mexico	37.1	34.3	30.5	28.1	25.7	24.6	24.2	23.8	23.3	22.8	22.2
Netherlands Antilles	21.5	20.8	19.7	19.2	17.5	16.1	16.0	15.8	15.7	15.5	15.3
Nicaragua	45.7	45.6	41.9	38.4	36.6	35.3	34.8	34.3	33.6	33.0	32.2
Panama	31.0	29.7	27.9	26.0	23.6	22.5	22.1	21.8	21.3	20.8	20.3
Paraguay	35.9	37.2	37.4	35.2	32.6	31.3	31.0	30.7	30.4	30.0	29.6
Peru	38.0	35.7	32.1	29.0	26.1	24.9	24.5	24.1	23.7	23.2	22.6
Puerto Rico	23.8	22.0	19.6	18.3	16.9	16.1	16.0	15.8	15.6	15.4	15.1
St Kitts	30.3	29.3	20.5	20.0	23.9	23.3	23.0	22.7	22.4	22.0	21.8
St Lucia	33.8	32.3	28.3	25.8	24.8	24.0	23.8	23.6	23.3	23.0	22.7
St Vincent and the Grenadines	31.5	30.8	26.4	23.4	22.4	19.8	19.5	19.2	18.9	18.5	18.3
Suriname	29.5	30.0	27.7	23.8	21.2	20.2	19.9	19.6	19.3	18.9	18.4
Trinidad and Tobago	29.3	28.8	25.7	20.3	15.7	14.0	13.9	13.8	13.7	13.6	13.5
Uruguay	20.2	19.2	18.3	18.2	17.9	17.6	17.5	17.4	17.2	17.1	16.9
Venezuela	34.2	32.8	29.0	28.7	25.9	24.9	24.5	24.2	23.8	23.3	22.8

Source: *National statistical offices/UN/Euromonitor*

□ Births

Birth Rates 1977-2002

● Per '000 inhabitants

	1977	1980	1985	1990	1995	1997	1998	1999	2000	2001	2002
Asia Pacific											
Afghanistan	49.9	50.0	49.5	48.4	47.8	47.6	47.6	47.5	47.4	47.3	47.3
American Samoa	34.3	36.5	38.1	36.2	28.7	28.1	27.8	27.5	27.2	27.0	26.9
Armenia	22.6	23.1	23.1	20.0	14.2	11.2	10.9	10.6	10.2	9.8	9.4
Azerbaijan	25.1	25.6	26.3	24.8	19.5	16.1	15.6	14.9	14.3	13.5	12.7
Bangladesh	42.5	41.9	39.8	36.7	33.1	31.4	31.2	30.9	30.6	30.3	29.9
Bhutan	41.6	41.5	41.1	39.6	37.3	36.2	36.0	35.8	35.6	35.4	34.8
Brunei	30.9	30.6	28.7	26.9	24.3	22.2	21.7	21.1	20.5	19.7	19.0
Cambodia	33.4	45.9	51.1	43.8	39.6	38.1	37.6	37.0	36.4	35.7	34.9
China	21.4	20.9	21.4	20.1	17.2	16.2	15.9	15.6	15.3	15.1	14.3
Fiji	33.2	32.5	30.7	28.4	26.6	25.9	25.7	25.4	25.1	24.7	24.4
French Polynesia	32.0	31.2	30.1	27.4	23.3	21.5	21.3	21.1	20.9	20.7	20.4
Guam	29.0	27.8	26.4	28.1	29.1	28.4	28.1	27.7	27.3	26.9	26.4
Hong Kong, China	17.2	16.4	14.1	12.1	10.8	10.3	10.1	10.0	9.9	9.7	9.5
India	34.8	34.2	32.5	30.1	27.4	26.2	25.8	25.4	24.9	24.4	23.8
Indonesia	35.6	33.5	29.7	26.3	23.5	22.5	22.1	21.8	21.4	21.0	20.0
Japan	15.4	13.5	11.9	9.9	9.8	9.8	9.7	9.6	9.5	9.4	9.2
Kazakhstan	24.9	24.9	24.7	22.0	18.2	16.9	16.8	16.7	16.6	16.5	16.3
Kiribati					28.7	28.1	27.8	27.5	27.2	26.9	26.7
Kyrgyzstan	29.9	31.4	33.0	30.1	25.2	23.2	22.6	22.0	21.2	20.4	19.5
Laos	45.1	45.1	44.8	42.8	39.6	38.2	37.8	37.3	36.8	36.3	35.7
Macau	17.1	17.1	24.8	19.2	13.5	10.8	10.5	10.1	9.7	9.2	8.8
Malaysia	29.4	31.1	32.5	30.6	26.9	25.2	24.8	24.2	23.7	23.0	22.3
Maldives	42.0	41.8	41.7	39.6	37.3	37.0	36.8	36.6	36.4	36.2	36.0
Mongolia	39.2	38.3	36.3	32.1	26.6	24.3	23.8	23.4	22.8	22.3	21.6
Myanmar	37.9	36.0	32.7	30.6	28.0	26.4	25.9	25.4	24.7	24.0	23.2
Nauru					20.2	19.5	19.3	19.0	18.7	18.4	18.2
Nepal	39.7	39.4	38.8	38.2	37.0	36.3	35.9	35.5	35.1	34.6	34.0
New Caledonia	28.5	26.9	25.1	24.2	22.5	21.4	21.1	20.8	20.4	20.0	19.5
North Korea	20.5	20.7	20.7	20.7	19.6	18.6	18.3	18.0	17.6	17.2	16.7
Pakistan	43.1	42.8	42.0	40.6	38.8	37.9	37.6	37.4	37.0	36.7	36.3
Papua New Guinea	41.0	39.6	37.9	37.5	35.7	34.0	33.6	33.3	32.9	32.4	32.0
Philippines	37.5	36.5	34.6	32.6	29.9	28.4	28.0	27.6	27.1	26.6	26.0
Singapore	16.5	17.1	16.6	17.0	15.6	14.2	13.7	13.2	12.6	12.2	12.9
Solomon Islands	45.0	42.5	39.9	39.6	39.7	39.6	39.3	39.0	38.6	38.2	37.7
South Korea	23.6	22.2	18.8	16.3	14.6	13.7	13.5	13.4	13.2	13.0	12.8
Sri Lanka	27.3	27.0	24.4	21.0	18.5	17.4	17.4	17.3	17.3	17.3	17.3
Taiwan		23.2	17.9	15.7	15.5	15.1	15.1	15.0	15.0	14.9	15.0
Tajikistan	37.2	37.2	38.6	36.9	31.2	28.8	27.8	26.8	25.7	24.4	23.0
Thailand	30.3	27.9	23.9	20.9	19.7	19.6	19.3	19.0	18.6	18.2	17.8
Tonga		29.6	28.1	24.8	26.4	25.7	25.5	25.2	24.9	24.6	24.4
Turkmenistan	35.3	35.3	35.4	33.9	30.4	28.6	28.1	27.5	26.8	26.1	25.3
Tuvalu					23.7	23.1	22.9	22.6	22.3	22.0	21.8
Uzbekistan	34.8	35.4	35.9	33.3	27.4	24.4	23.8	23.1	22.3	21.4	20.5
Vanuatu	41.0	39.8	37.9	36.7	35.0	33.7	33.3	32.9	32.5	31.9	31.4
Vietnam	36.1	34.9	33.1	30.2	24.6	21.5	21.2	20.9	20.5	20.1	19.7
Western Samoa	34.8	35.9	37.3	34.1	30.0	29.0	28.8	28.6	28.4	28.2	27.9
Australasia											
Australia	16.0	15.3	15.7	15.4	13.9	13.4	13.3	13.2	13.0	12.9	12.7
New Zealand	17.2	16.5	16.5	17.0	15.9	14.9	14.7	14.5	14.3	14.0	13.7

Source: *National statistical offices/UN/Euromonitor*

■ Births

Birth Rates 1977-2002

● Per '000 inhabitants

	1977	1980	1985	1990	1995	1997	1998	1999	2000	2001	2002
Africa and Middle East											
Algeria	45.0	42.6	36.9	31.2	27.2	25.7	25.4	25.0	24.5	24.1	23.5
Angola	50.3	50.6	51.2	51.2	51.0	51.0	51.0	51.1	51.1	51.2	51.3
Bahrain	34.4	33.5	31.9	28.1	22.0	19.0	18.5	17.9	17.2	16.5	15.7
Benin	51.4	51.4	50.1	47.2	44.1	42.8	42.5	42.2	41.9	41.5	41.1
Botswana	45.8	44.8	41.9	38.4	35.1	33.6	33.1	32.6	32.0	31.4	30.6
Burkina Faso	50.2	49.8	48.8	47.6	46.8	46.7	46.7	46.7	46.7	46.8	46.8
Burundi	44.7	45.7	47.0	46.4	44.2	43.1	43.1	43.2	43.3	43.4	43.5
Cameroon	45.2	45.1	44.0	41.8	39.0	37.6	37.4	37.1	36.9	36.6	36.3
Cape Verde	35.4	37.0	37.0	34.7	32.8	31.8	31.4	30.9	30.4	29.8	29.1
Central African Republic	44.1	43.3	42.3	41.5	40.3	39.6	39.2	38.9	38.5	38.0	37.5
Chad	48.2	48.1	48.2	48.4	48.5	48.4	48.4	48.4	48.4	48.4	48.5
Comoros	48.7	48.6	45.2	40.8	39.1	38.9	38.7	38.5	38.3	38.0	37.7
Congo Dem Rep	47.7	48.0	48.0	48.1	47.9	47.7	47.6	47.5	47.4	47.3	47.2
Congo-Brazzaville	45.8	44.8	44.1	44.5	44.6	44.5	44.5	44.4	44.4	44.3	44.2
Côte d'Ivoire	51.0	50.8	48.0	41.8	37.1	36.0	35.9	35.8	35.6	35.5	35.3
Djibouti	56.2	53.1	48.6	45.7	42.5	40.7	40.3	39.8	39.2	38.6	38.0
Egypt	38.9	38.8	36.6	31.6	27.4	26.2	25.7	25.2	24.6	24.0	23.3
Equatorial Guinea	42.7	43.0	43.6	43.6	43.3	43.2	43.2	43.2	43.2	43.2	43.2
Eritrea	45.1	45.1	45.0	44.0	42.0	40.9	40.5	40.1	39.6	39.1	38.5
Ethiopia	46.7	46.4	46.7	46.3	45.0	44.6	44.5	44.3	44.1	44.0	43.8
Gabon	32.8	32.9	34.6	36.4	37.3	37.8	37.7	37.7	37.7	37.6	37.6
Gambia	48.8	48.4	47.2	44.7	41.7	40.4	39.9	39.3	38.7	37.9	37.2
Ghana	46.8	46.0	43.0	39.1	35.5	34.0	33.7	33.5	33.2	32.9	32.6
Guinea	51.6	51.5	48.9	45.3	44.9	45.7	45.3	44.9	44.5	43.9	43.4
Guinea-Bissau	44.8	45.0	45.2	45.1	44.9	44.8	44.8	44.7	44.7	44.7	44.6
Iran	42.2	44.5	43.0	35.4	27.2	23.5	23.3	23.0	22.7	22.4	22.1
Iraq	41.9	41.4	40.6	39.3	37.4	36.5	36.1	35.6	35.1	34.6	33.9
Israel	26.0	24.9	23.2	22.2	21.4	21.4	21.2	20.9	20.5	20.2	19.8
Jordan	45.0	43.5	41.0	38.3	35.5	34.3	34.0	33.8	33.5	33.2	32.8
Kenya	51.8	50.9	48.0	41.8	36.6	35.4	35.2	34.9	34.7	34.4	34.1
Kuwait	40.1	37.1	31.1	24.1	18.1	15.9	16.5	17.1	17.7	18.4	19.2
Lebanon	30.1	29.7	28.5	26.7	22.7	20.3	20.1	19.9	19.6	19.3	19.0
Lesotho	41.8	41.0	39.3	37.4	35.7	35.0	34.6	34.1	33.6	33.1	32.5
Liberia	47.4	47.2	45.2	42.2	45.9	50.1	50.9	51.9	53.0	54.2	55.5
Libya	47.3	46.4	38.2	28.0	25.6	26.4	26.4	26.5	26.6	26.7	26.8
Madagascar	45.8	45.6	45.2	44.7	44.2	44.0	43.6	43.2	42.6	42.1	41.5
Malawi	57.2	55.2	52.7	51.0	48.6	47.2	46.8	46.4	45.9	45.4	44.9
Mali	50.8	50.4	50.2	50.1	50.0	49.9	49.9	49.8	49.8	49.7	49.6
Mauritania	44.7	43.4	43.4	44.1	43.7	43.5	43.6	43.6	43.6	43.6	43.7
Mauritius	26.7	24.1	20.8	20.1	18.6	17.1	16.8	16.6	16.3	16.1	15.7
Morocco	39.4	38.2	34.8	30.8	27.7	26.8	26.5	26.1	25.7	25.3	24.8
Mozambique	46.5	46.0	45.5	45.2	44.9	44.7	44.2	43.7	43.1	42.4	41.7
Namibia	42.8	42.3	42.1	41.7	39.2	37.6	37.1	36.5	35.9	35.2	34.5
Niger	56.9	56.7	56.1	55.5	55.3	55.4	55.4	55.3	55.3	55.2	55.2
Nigeria	47.8	47.6	46.6	44.8	42.7	41.7	41.3	40.9	40.5	40.0	39.5
Oman	46.1	45.5	44.4	41.3	37.0	35.3	35.4	35.5	35.7	35.8	36.0
Qatar	29.9	29.2	27.0	22.5	20.0	20.0	19.6	19.1	18.6	18.0	17.4
Réunion	25.3	24.4	23.3	22.2	20.6	19.9	19.5	19.2	18.7	18.2	17.7
Rwanda	52.8	51.5	47.0	43.5	42.7	42.4	42.4	42.3	42.3	42.2	42.1
Sao Tomé e Príncipe	44.4	39.2	35.7		42.0	42.7	42.4	42.1	41.8	41.5	41.1
Saudi Arabia	45.9	43.4	40.7	38.8	36.1	34.9	34.7	34.5	34.3	34.0	33.8
Senegal	49.3	48.1	46.3	43.3	40.4	39.5	39.2	38.8	38.5	38.0	37.6
Seychelles	26.7	30.5	24.7	23.1	20.9	20.2	20.0	19.7	19.4	19.0	18.7
Sierra Leone	48.8	48.8	49.0	49.3	49.5	49.5	49.5	49.4	49.3	49.2	49.1
Somalia	51.7	51.8	51.8	51.9	52.2	52.3	52.2	52.1	52.0	51.9	51.8
South Africa	35.1	34.4	31.9	28.5	26.8	26.7	26.3	26.0	25.6	25.1	24.6
Sudan	43.7	42.5	40.1	38.4	36.9	36.1	35.7	35.2	34.7	34.2	33.6
Swaziland	45.3	43.3	41.2	39.6	36.9	35.6	35.3	34.9	34.4	34.0	33.4
Syria	46.0	45.8	44.1	37.6	31.6	30.3	30.2	30.1	29.9	29.7	29.6
Tanzania	47.0	46.7	45.6	43.6	41.4	40.4	40.0	39.6	39.1	38.5	37.9
Togo	47.3	46.3	44.6	43.0	41.3	40.5	40.2	39.8	39.5	39.1	38.7
Tunisia	36.4	35.3	32.0	27.6	22.0	18.7	18.7	18.7	18.7	18.6	18.6
Uganda	50.3	50.4	50.5	50.5	50.4	50.4	50.4	50.5	50.5	50.6	50.6
United Arab Emirates	30.5	30.0	28.2	23.0	17.6	16.0	15.9	15.9	15.8	15.8	15.7
Yemen	53.7	51.4	49.4	51.1	51.9	51.4	51.0	50.5	50.0	49.4	48.8
Zambia	47.6	46.4	45.0	44.8	44.3	43.8	43.4	43.0	42.6	42.1	41.5
Zimbabwe	45.3	44.6	43.1	41.5	38.9	37.4	37.0	36.6	36.1	35.6	35.1

Source: National statistical offices/UN/Euromonitor

Table 21.8

Deaths

Death Rates 1977-2002

- Per '000 inhabitants

	1977	1980	1985	1990	1995	1997	1998	1999	2000	2001	2002
North America											
Canada	7.2	7.1	7.2	9.0	7.2	7.3	7.4	7.4	7.5	7.6	7.7
USA	8.6	8.7	8.7	8.7	8.7	8.5	8.5	8.5	8.4	8.4	8.4
Latin America											
Anguilla			10.4		6.0	5.9	5.5	5.9	5.9	5.8	5.8
Antigua	7.0	4.8	5.1	6.8	6.0	6.0	5.9	5.9	5.9	5.9	5.9
Argentina	8.9	8.7	8.5	8.3	8.1	7.9	7.9	7.9	7.9	7.8	7.8
Aruba	5.3	4.8	5.6		6.2	6.2	6.4	6.1	6.1	6.1	6.1
Bahamas	5.6	5.8	6.0	6.2	6.7	6.8	6.8	6.9	7.0	7.0	7.1
Barbados	8.7	8.3	8.4	8.9	8.7	8.3	8.2	8.1	8.0	7.9	7.8
Belize	6.5	6.1	5.4	5.0	4.7	4.5	4.5	4.4	4.4	4.3	4.3
Bermuda	7.5	7.9	7.0	7.3	7.3	7.2	7.2	7.2	7.2	7.2	7.1
Bolivia	16.0	14.6	12.4	10.8	9.6	9.1	9.0	8.8	8.6	8.4	8.2
Brazil	9.1	8.7	8.0	7.4	7.1	7.1	7.1	7.0	7.0	7.0	7.0
British Virgin Islands	5.8	6.3	5.0		5.2	5.2	4.8	5.1	5.1	5.1	5.1
Cayman Islands	5.2	6.2	5.9	4.1	5.0	5.0	5.0	4.9	4.9	4.9	4.9
Chile	7.5	6.9	6.1	5.7	5.6	5.6	5.6	5.6	5.7	5.7	5.7
Colombia	7.7	7.2	6.6	6.4	6.1	5.8	5.9	6.0	6.1	6.3	6.4
Costa Rica	4.8	4.4	3.9	3.8	3.8	3.8	3.9	3.9	3.9	3.9	4.0
Cuba	6.0	6.2	6.6	6.8	7.0	7.1	7.1	7.1	7.2	7.2	7.2
Dominica	6.7			8.6	6.1	6.1	6.3	6.0	6.0	6.0	6.0
Dominican Republic	8.4	8.1	7.4	6.7	6.4	6.3	6.4	6.5	6.6	6.7	6.9
Ecuador	9.8	8.9	7.4	6.5	6.1	6.0	5.9	5.9	5.9	5.9	5.8
El Salvador	11.4	11.2	9.4	7.3	6.4	6.1	6.1	6.1	6.0	6.0	5.9
French Guiana	7.2	6.6	5.6	5.0	4.6	4.4	4.4	4.4	4.3	4.3	4.2
Grenada	8.1				5.7	5.6	5.3	5.6	5.6	5.5	5.5
Guadeloupe	6.9	6.8	6.4	6.2	6.1	6.0	6.0	6.0	6.1	6.1	6.1
Guatemala	12.2	11.5	10.3	8.9	7.7	7.4	7.3	7.2	7.1	6.9	6.8
Guyana	9.2	9.1	8.7	8.2	8.1	8.4	8.5	8.7	8.9	9.1	9.4
Haiti	16.5	16.2	15.4	14.3	13.5	13.4	13.2	13.1	12.9	12.8	12.6
Honduras	11.1	10.0	8.1	7.0	6.7	6.6	6.6	6.6	6.5	6.5	6.5
Jamaica	7.4	7.0	6.6	6.5	6.2	5.9	5.9	5.9	5.8	5.7	5.7
Martinique	6.8	6.5	6.2	6.2	6.3	6.2	6.3	6.4	6.5	6.6	6.7
Mexico	7.7	7.0	6.0	5.4	5.1	5.1	5.1	5.1	5.1	5.1	5.1
Netherlands Antilles	6.6	6.4	6.2	6.3	6.3	6.2	6.2	6.2	6.2	6.2	6.2
Nicaragua	11.3	10.7	9.2	7.3	6.0	5.6	5.6	5.5	5.4	5.3	5.2
Panama	6.3	5.9	5.6	5.4	5.2	5.1	5.1	5.1	5.1	5.1	5.1
Paraguay	7.8	7.6	7.0	6.3	5.7	5.4	5.4	5.3	5.2	5.2	5.1
Peru	10.9	9.9	8.4	7.3	6.6	6.4	6.4	6.3	6.3	6.2	6.2
Puerto Rico	6.5	6.5	6.9	7.5	7.7	7.7	7.7	7.7	7.8	7.8	7.8
St Kitts	12.6	12.3	8.8		8.7	8.7	8.5	8.6	8.6	8.6	8.5
St Lucia	7.1	6.6	6.2	6.2	5.9	5.7	5.7	5.6	5.6	5.5	5.4
St Vincent and the Grenadines	7.3	7.3	6.5		5.9	5.9	5.3	5.9	5.8	5.8	5.8
Suriname	7.3	7.2	6.7	6.3	6.1	6.0	6.0	6.0	6.0	6.0	6.0
Trinidad and Tobago	7.1	7.1	6.9	6.4	6.0	5.9	5.9	5.9	6.0	6.0	6.0
Uruguay	10.1	10.0	9.9	9.9	9.6	9.4	9.4	9.4	9.4	9.3	9.3
Venezuela	5.8	5.7	5.2	4.8	4.7	4.7	4.7	4.7	4.7	4.7	4.7

Source: National statistical offices/UN/Euromonitor

■ Deaths

Death Rates 1977-2002

● Per '000 inhabitants

	1977	1980	1985	1990	1995	1997	1998	1999	2000	2001	2002
Asia Pacific											
Afghanistan	24.8	24.7	24.2	23.1	22.3	22.0	21.9	21.8	21.7	21.5	21.4
American Samoa		5.0	3.9		4.3	4.1	4.0	3.8	3.7	3.7	3.5
Armenia	5.5	5.5	6.2	6.8	7.1	7.3	7.3	7.4	7.4	7.4	7.4
Azerbaijan	6.8	6.8	6.7	6.7	6.4	6.2	6.2	6.2	6.2	6.2	6.2
Bangladesh	18.0	16.7	14.4	12.3	10.5	9.8	9.6	9.4	9.2	8.9	8.7
Bhutan	19.1	18.3	15.8	12.8	10.5	9.8	9.6	9.4	9.1	8.9	8.6
Brunei	5.4	4.7	3.8	3.4	3.1	3.0	3.1	3.1	3.1	3.1	3.2
Cambodia	40.0	27.3	14.9	12.6	11.2	10.8	10.8	10.7	10.7	10.6	10.6
China	6.7	6.7	6.7	7.0	7.1	7.0	7.0	7.0	7.0	7.0	7.0
Fiji	6.6	6.3	6.0	6.1	5.9	5.6	5.5	5.5	5.5	5.5	5.5
French Polynesia	7.8	6.9	5.8	5.3	4.9	4.9	4.8	4.8	4.8	4.8	4.8
Guam	4.1	4.0	3.9	4.4	4.7	4.7	4.8	4.8	4.8	4.8	4.9
Hong Kong, China	5.0	4.9	4.8	5.3	5.5	5.5	5.5	5.6	5.7	5.8	5.9
India	13.9	13.3	12.0	10.6	9.5	9.0	8.9	8.8	8.7	8.5	8.4
Indonesia	13.4	12.3	10.2	8.8	7.9	7.5	7.4	7.4	7.3	7.2	7.1
Japan	6.1	6.2	6.2	6.7	7.2	7.6	7.7	7.9	8.0	8.2	8.8
Kazakhstan	8.8	8.5	8.0	8.6	9.7	10.0	10.0	10.0	10.0	10.1	10.1
Kiribati		5.2	8.8	12.7	8.1	7.8	7.6	7.6	7.5	7.4	
Kyrgyzstan	9.6	9.1	8.2	7.6	7.5	7.6	7.5	7.4	7.3	7.2	7.1
Laos	20.7	19.6	18.4	16.9	14.9	14.1	13.9	13.6	13.3	12.9	12.6
Macau	6.6	6.5	5.9	4.9	4.4	4.3	4.4	4.4	4.5	4.6	4.6
Malaysia	7.7	6.9	5.9	5.3	4.9	4.8	4.8	4.8	4.8	4.7	4.7
Maldives	13.9	12.8	10.8	8.9	7.4	6.9	6.7	6.6	6.4	6.2	6.0
Mongolia	11.4	10.7	9.3	8.8	8.5	8.1	7.9	7.8	7.6	7.4	7.2
Myanmar	15.7	15.0	13.8	12.7	12.0	11.8	11.8	11.7	11.7	11.7	11.6
Nauru					5.3	5.1	5.1	4.9	4.8	4.7	4.5
Nepal	18.3	17.2	15.3	13.6	12.0	11.2	11.0	10.8	10.5	10.2	9.8
New Caledonia	7.1	6.6	5.9	5.6	5.2	4.9	4.9	4.9	4.9	4.9	4.9
North Korea	6.3	6.1	5.9	6.5	8.9	10.4	10.4	10.3	10.2	10.1	9.9
Pakistan	16.0	15.3	13.9	12.6	11.3	10.8	10.6	10.4	10.2	9.9	9.7
Papua New Guinea	16.0	15.0	13.7	12.6	11.2	10.6	10.4	10.3	10.0	9.8	9.6
Philippines	9.2	8.7	7.7	6.7	5.9	5.5	5.4	5.4	5.3	5.2	5.2
Singapore	5.1	5.3	5.4	5.1	4.9	4.9	5.0	5.1	5.1	5.2	5.3
Solomon Islands	7.4	6.6	6.9	7.0	5.8	5.3	5.2	5.1	4.9	4.8	4.6
South Korea	7.1	6.8	6.3	5.9	5.6	5.5	5.5	5.6	5.7	5.8	5.9
Sri Lanka	6.9	6.8	6.5	6.2	6.1	6.1	6.1	6.2	6.2	6.2	6.3
Taiwan			4.8	5.1	5.6	5.6	5.7	5.7	5.7	5.8	5.7
Tajikistan	8.8	8.4	7.6	7.2	6.9	6.7	6.6	6.6	6.5	6.4	6.2
Thailand	8.3	7.5	6.4	5.8	5.9	6.1	6.1	6.1	6.2	6.2	6.2
Tonga			3.4	5.1	6.6	6.3	6.1	6.1	6.0	5.9	5.8
Turkmenistan	9.6	9.1	8.5	7.8	7.4	7.2	7.1	7.0	6.9	6.7	6.5
Tuvalu				11.0	9.1	8.8	8.6	8.6	8.5	8.4	8.3
Uzbekistan	8.5	8.1	7.5	7.0	6.5	6.2	6.1	6.0	6.0	5.9	5.8
Vanuatu	10.4	9.8	8.4	7.3	6.6	6.1	6.0	5.9	5.7	5.6	5.4
Vietnam	12.9	12.0	10.1	8.6	7.5	7.0	6.9	6.8	6.7	6.6	6.4
Western Samoa	8.3	7.9	7.2	6.8	6.4	6.0	5.9	5.9	5.8	5.7	5.6
Australasia											
Australia	7.7	7.4	7.5	7.0	7.1	7.1	7.1	7.2	7.3	7.3	7.4
New Zealand	8.2	8.2	8.2	8.0	7.7	7.6	7.6	7.6	7.7	7.7	7.7

Source: *National statistical offices/UN/Euromonitor*

◘ Deaths
Death Rates 1977-2002

● Per '000 inhabitants

	1977	1980	1985	1990	1995	1997	1998	1999	2000	2001	2002
Africa and Middle East											
Algeria	13.4	11.8	9.0	7.1	6.1	5.7	5.7	5.6	5.5	5.4	5.3
Angola	24.4	23.6	22.2	20.7	20.1	20.2	20.0	19.8	19.6	19.3	19.0
Bahrain	6.3	5.3	4.2	3.8	3.6	3.5	3.5	3.6	3.6	3.6	3.7
Benin	21.1	19.4	17.0	15.3	13.7	13.1	13.0	12.8	12.7	12.5	12.3
Botswana	11.3	10.3	8.5	8.2	13.1	17.0	18.2	19.5	21.0	22.7	24.5
Burkina Faso	20.8	19.5	18.0	17.9	17.9	17.9	17.6	17.2	16.8	16.4	15.9
Burundi	18.8	18.3	18.0	20.2	21.6	21.3	21.2	21.1	21.0	20.9	20.8
Cameroon	17.6	16.7	15.2	14.2	14.4	14.8	14.8	14.8	14.7	14.7	14.6
Cape Verde	10.0	10.3	9.8	8.3	7.0	6.4	6.2	6.1	5.9	5.8	5.6
Central African Republic	20.6	19.5	18.4	18.0	18.5	19.1	19.0	18.9	18.8	18.7	18.6
Chad	23.8	23.0	21.4	20.5	20.0	19.6	19.5	19.3	19.1	18.9	18.6
Comoros	15.3	14.5	12.8	11.1	9.9	9.5	9.4	9.2	9.0	8.8	8.5
Congo Dem Rep	17.5	16.9	15.7	15.0	14.9	15.0	14.8	14.5	14.2	13.9	13.6
Congo-Brazzaville	17.4	16.4	15.3	15.0	14.8	14.7	14.5	14.4	14.3	14.1	14.0
Côte d'Ivoire	17.4	16.5	15.2	14.7	15.0	15.4	15.4	15.4	15.4	15.4	15.3
Djibouti	22.2	21.0	18.8	17.6	17.7	18.0	18.4	19.0	19.5	20.2	20.8
Egypt	14.2	13.4	11.0	8.6	7.3	6.8	6.7	6.6	6.4	6.3	6.1
Equatorial Guinea	22.7	21.8	20.3	18.7	17.2	16.5	16.3	16.0	15.7	15.4	15.1
Eritrea	18.9	19.5	18.4	16.1	14.6	14.0	13.9	13.7	13.6	13.4	13.3
Ethiopia	21.0	20.9	20.0	18.8	18.7	19.0	19.1	19.2	19.2	19.3	19.4
Gabon	19.2	18.6	17.5	16.6	16.0	15.8	15.7	15.6	15.5	15.3	15.2
Gambia	24.9	24.0	22.3	20.6	19.1	18.5	18.3	18.0	17.7	17.4	17.0
Ghana	14.9	13.9	12.5	11.6	11.0	10.8	10.7	10.7	10.6	10.5	10.4
Guinea	25.3	24.6	22.5	20.1	18.6	18.2	18.0	17.8	17.5	17.1	16.8
Guinea-Bissau	26.3	25.5	23.8	22.3	21.0	20.4	20.3	20.1	19.8	19.6	19.3
Iran	12.0	11.4	9.4	7.2	5.8	5.3	5.2	5.2	5.1	5.0	5.0
Iraq	8.8	8.6	7.8	9.0	10.2	9.9	9.4	8.9	8.3	7.7	7.0
Israel	6.8	6.8	6.7	6.4	6.3	6.3	6.2	6.2	6.1	6.1	6.0
Jordan	9.6	9.2	7.9	6.4	5.2	4.6	4.6	4.5	4.4	4.4	4.3
Kenya	14.5	13.4	11.7	10.7	11.4	12.1	12.4	12.7	13.0	13.3	13.7
Kuwait	4.2	3.6	2.7	2.2	2.2	2.2	2.3	2.4	2.5	2.6	2.7
Lebanon	8.7	8.7	8.2	7.2	6.0	5.4	5.4	5.4	5.4	5.4	5.4
Lesotho	15.5	14.7	13.3	12.0	13.2	14.6	15.8	17.1	18.5	20.1	21.9
Liberia	18.1	16.9	15.0	19.1	19.7	16.6	15.9	15.1	14.2	13.3	12.2
Libya	12.7	11.7	7.9	4.9	4.6	4.7	4.7	4.7	4.7	4.7	4.8
Madagascar	18.1	17.7	17.2	16.5	15.3	14.7	14.4	14.2	13.9	13.5	13.2
Malawi	24.0	22.6	21.0	20.8	21.7	22.2	22.3	22.3	22.4	22.5	22.6
Mali	24.1	22.1	20.0	19.3	18.8	18.5	18.3	18.1	17.9	17.6	17.3
Mauritania	20.0	19.2	17.6	16.5	15.8	15.4	15.2	15.0	14.7	14.5	14.2
Mauritius	6.3	6.4	6.3	6.4	6.7	6.7	6.7	6.7	6.7	6.7	6.7
Morocco	13.0	12.1	10.1	8.2	7.1	6.6	6.5	6.4	6.3	6.1	6.0
Mozambique	21.0	20.9	20.7	20.5	21.5	22.4	22.6	22.9	23.2	23.5	23.9
Namibia	14.9	14.0	12.5	12.6	15.6	17.6	17.7	17.7	17.7	17.8	17.8
Niger	25.2	24.7	23.9	22.7	21.3	20.7	20.5	20.2	19.8	19.5	19.1
Nigeria	19.0	18.1	16.6	15.4	14.5	14.1	14.0	13.8	13.7	13.5	13.3
Oman	12.4	9.9	6.5	5.1	4.5	4.3	4.2	4.2	4.2	4.1	4.1
Qatar	9.4	6.9	4.1	3.4	3.6	3.9	3.9	3.9	4.0	4.0	4.1
Réunion	6.3	6.1	5.7	5.4	5.6	5.7	5.7	5.7	5.7	5.7	5.8
Rwanda	20.2	19.6	18.4	32.8	32.7	21.7	21.5	21.3	21.1	20.9	20.6
Sao Tomé e Príncipe	10.7		9.7		8.8	8.5	8.3	8.3	8.2	8.1	7.9
Saudi Arabia	10.7	9.2	6.9	5.5	4.7	4.4	4.3	4.3	4.2	4.2	4.1
Senegal	21.7	20.5	18.5	16.1	13.8	13.0	12.8	12.5	12.2	11.9	11.6
Seychelles	8.0	7.4	6.7	7.8	7.0	6.7	6.6	6.5	6.4	6.3	6.1
Sierra Leone	29.0	28.8	27.9	28.7	28.0	26.4	25.9	25.4	24.8	24.1	23.3
Somalia	22.9	22.4	21.1	22.9	21.5	18.5	18.2	18.0	17.7	17.3	17.0
South Africa	11.8	11.3	10.2	9.2	9.9	10.8	11.8	13.0	14.2	15.6	17.1
Sudan	17.9	16.8	15.2	13.9	12.7	12.2	12.0	11.8	11.6	11.3	11.1
Swaziland	16.0	14.8	13.0	11.7	12.7	14.0	15.5	17.1	18.9	20.9	23.0
Syria	8.9	8.8	7.8	6.1	4.7	4.3	4.3	4.2	4.1	4.1	4.0
Tanzania	16.4	15.3	13.7	13.0	13.1	13.3	13.2	13.2	13.1	13.1	13.1
Togo	17.6	16.6	15.0	14.2	14.0	13.9	13.8	13.7	13.5	13.4	13.2
Tunisia	10.0	9.1	7.7	6.7	6.5	6.7	6.6	6.6	6.5	6.5	6.4
Uganda	18.4	18.3	19.0	20.6	20.8	20.3	19.8	19.3	18.6	18.0	17.2
United Arab Emirates	7.4	5.5	4.0	3.8	3.6	3.6	3.6	3.7	3.8	3.9	4.0
Yemen	20.7	18.4	15.0	13.1	11.1	9.9	9.7	9.4	9.0	8.7	8.3
Zambia	16.4	15.5	14.6	16.3	19.4	20.7	20.4	20.0	19.7	19.3	18.8
Zimbabwe	11.0	10.5	10.4	12.8	16.4	18.0	18.0	17.9	17.9	17.8	17.8

Source: National statistical offices/UN/Euromonitor

■ Deaths

Table 21.9

Infant Mortality Rates 1977-2002

● Deaths per '000 live births

	1977	1980	1985	1990	1995	1997	1998	1999	2000	2001	2002
North America											
Canada	12.4	10.4	7.9	6.8	5.8	5.5	5.5	5.5	5.4	5.4	5.4
USA	14.1	12.6	10.6	9.2	8.0	7.6	7.5	7.4	7.2	7.0	6.8
Latin America											
Anguilla					22.4	21.5	20.9	20.2	19.5	18.7	18.2
Antigua			24.4		22.4	21.9	21.3	20.6	19.9	19.0	18.5
Argentina	39.1	35.4	29.5	25.6	23.0	21.8	21.5	21.2	20.8	20.4	20.0
Aruba				24.4	8.7	8.2	7.6	6.9	6.2	5.3	5.1
Bahamas	35.4	32.9	26.4	21.7	19.7	18.7	18.5	18.2	17.9	17.6	17.2
Barbados	27.0	21.5	16.0	14.5	13.1	12.4	12.1	11.9	11.6	11.2	10.9
Belize			37.5	35.0	33.3	32.5	32.1	31.6	31.1	30.6	30.0
Bermuda				7.0	10.4	9.8	9.2	8.6	7.8	7.0	6.6
Bolivia	138.2	126.3	98.9	82.0	69.4	65.6	64.0	62.2	60.2	58.0	55.6
Brazil	78.8	71.5	59.9	50.7	44.3	42.1	41.5	40.8	40.1	39.2	38.3
British Virgin Islands	12.4	10.4			21.8	21.2	20.6	19.9	19.2	19.1	18.7
Cayman Islands				9.0	9.0	8.5	7.9	7.3	6.5	5.7	5.4
Chile	45.2	33.6	20.8	16.0	13.3	12.8	12.6	12.4	12.1	11.9	11.6
Colombia	56.7	52.2	44.6	38.0	32.4	30.0	29.3	28.5	27.6	26.6	25.6
Costa Rica	30.4	24.4	17.5	14.8	12.8	12.1	11.9	11.7	11.5	11.2	10.9
Cuba	22.5	19.5	14.8	11.4	8.7	7.5	7.5	7.4	7.4	7.3	7.3
Dominica				18.4	9.4	9.1	8.9	8.6	8.5	8.3	8.3
Dominican Republic	84.3	73.3	58.9	50.3	43.3	40.6	39.9	39.1	38.3	37.3	36.3
Ecuador	82.4	74.8	62.3	53.1	47.4	45.6	44.9	44.2	43.3	42.4	41.5
El Salvador	95.0	85.3	64.6	46.6	35.8	32.0	31.1	30.1	29.0	27.8	26.4
French Guiana	56.2	50.5	41.3	36.2	33.3	31.9	31.4	30.8	30.2	29.5	28.7
Grenada		25.0		15.0	12.9	12.4	11.8	11.5	11.4	11.1	10.9
Guadeloupe	31.9	28.0	23.2	15.1	8.7	8.3	7.8	7.7	7.5	7.2	7.4
Guatemala	90.9	84.4	71.4	57.5	48.3	46.0	45.2	44.4	43.4	42.3	41.2
Guyana	67.0	69.2	66.8	59.3	56.1	56.2	55.6	54.9	54.2	53.4	52.5
Haiti	139.2	130.9	114.2	88.6	70.8	68.3	67.2	65.9	64.5	63.0	61.3
Honduras	81.0	72.6	58.9	49.0	40.9	37.1	36.5	35.7	34.9	34.0	33.1
Jamaica	37.0	33.5	28.6	25.5	23.0	21.9	21.6	21.2	20.8	20.3	19.9
Martinique	21.9	17.6	11.9	8.8	7.3	7.0	7.0	6.9	6.9	6.9	6.8
Mexico	56.8	51.5	43.0	36.5	32.3	31.0	30.5	30.0	29.5	28.9	28.2
Netherlands Antilles	22.0	19.8	17.5	16.6	15.2	14.2	14.0	13.7	13.4	13.0	12.6
Nicaragua	90.1	84.6	71.8	55.8	43.4	39.5	38.9	38.2	37.5	36.6	35.7
Panama	35.4	32.7	29.3	26.6	23.1	21.4	21.0	20.5	19.9	19.3	18.6
Paraguay	51.0	49.9	47.7	44.9	41.1	39.2	38.8	38.4	38.0	37.5	37.0
Peru	99.1	89.7	74.3	61.2	49.8	45.0	43.8	42.4	40.9	39.2	37.4
Puerto Rico	19.7	18.4	15.4	12.6	11.3	11.0	10.9	10.8	10.6	10.5	10.3
St Kitts				24.0	19.2	18.6	18.4	18.1	17.9	17.6	17.3
St Lucia	29.3	25.7	21.3	17.9	15.1	14.3	14.1	13.9	13.6	13.4	13.1
St Vincent and the Grenadines		60.2			16.8	16.3	16.0	15.7	15.5	15.2	14.7
Suriname	44.0	42.0	38.1	34.6	31.1	29.1	28.6	28.0	27.3	26.5	25.7
Trinidad and Tobago	32.0	28.4	22.3	17.7	15.1	14.3	14.0	13.7	13.3	12.9	12.5
Uruguay	42.4	37.6	27.6	21.2	18.7	17.5	16.8	16.0	15.1	14.1	13.1
Venezuela	39.3	36.2	30.0	24.9	22.0	20.9	20.6	20.2	19.8	19.4	18.9

Source: Euromonitor from UN/national statistical offices/Eurostat
Notes: Rates refer to deaths of infants under one year

Deaths

Infant Mortality Rates 1977-2002

- Deaths per '000 live births

	1977	1980	1985	1990	1995	1997	1998	1999	2000	2001	2002
Asia Pacific											
Afghanistan	164.7	164.0	174.9	169.8	165.8	164.7	164.2	163.6	162.9	162.1	161.3
American Samoa					12.1	11.1	10.5	9.9	9.6	9.3	9.3
Armenia	21.7	21.9	24.2	21.3	17.0	16.9	16.6	16.3	16.0	15.7	15.4
Azerbaijan			36.7	34.6	33.4	32.5	32.0	31.4	30.8	30.1	29.3
Bangladesh	139.1	129.7	112.6	97.5	84.5	78.8	76.9	74.8	72.5	69.9	67.0
Bhutan	129.6	123.5	106.0	83.0	67.6	62.9	61.4	59.7	57.9	55.9	53.6
Brunei	23.0	18.1	11.8	10.4	10.1	9.6	9.4	9.2	9.1	8.9	8.6
Cambodia	263.2	190.8	113.7	95.5	87.1	83.4	81.7	79.7	77.5	75.1	72.5
China	52.6	52.3	50.9	48.2	43.8	41.4	40.7	39.8	38.8	37.7	36.5
Fiji	46.1	42.9	37.0	34.6	26.6	19.6	19.3	18.9	18.5	18.0	17.5
French Polynesia	56.0	42.0	23.4	14.3	10.4	9.7	9.5	9.3	9.2	8.9	8.7
Guam	34.2	31.1	26.0	17.6	11.6	11.0	10.8	10.7	10.5	10.2	9.8
Hong Kong, China	12.9	11.1	8.0	5.8	4.6	4.2	4.2	4.2	4.1	4.1	4.1
India	129.0	117.1	99.8	85.6	75.4	72.5	71.3	69.9	68.3	66.6	64.7
Indonesia	106.4	96.9	78.5	63.7	53.1	48.4	47.0	45.4	43.6	41.7	39.5
Japan	8.9	7.5	5.5	4.6	3.9	3.5	3.5	3.5	3.4	3.4	3.3
Kazakhstan	45.0	42.2	37.5	38.4	43.0	44.8	44.3	43.8	43.3	42.7	42.1
Kiribati				59.0	51.4	50.8	50.7	50.5	50.3		50.0
Kyrgyzstan	55.0	52.8	47.9	42.8	42.1	43.2	42.2	41.1	39.9	37.0	
Laos	135.0	135.0	121.5	109.7	100.2	96.6	95.2	93.7	91.9	90.0	88.0
Macau	31.0	22.9	13.8	10.8	9.3	8.9	8.8	8.7	8.5	8.4	8.2
Malaysia	33.8	30.7	22.1	16.0	13.2	11.6	11.4	11.2	10.9	10.6	10.3
Maldives	105.5	99.1	87.4	68.3	51.1	46.4	44.9	43.3	41.5	39.5	37.3
Mongolia	87.7	82.4	72.8	68.2	66.8	65.8	64.6	63.2	61.7	60.0	58.2
Myanmar	116.6	113.7	107.1	100.8	95.1	92.2	91.4	90.5	89.5	88.4	87.2
Nauru					42.5	41.9	41.8	41.7	41.5	41.2	40.1
Nepal	142.4	133.3	116.9	102.3	88.9	82.6	80.8	78.6	76.3	73.7	70.9
New Caledonia	32.0	26.1	17.8	12.8	8.9	7.2	7.1	7.0	6.9	6.7	6.6
North Korea	33.9	30.7	25.8	26.1	37.2	45.1	44.2	43.1	41.9	40.6	39.1
Pakistan	132.2	127.1	117.8	108.6	99.5	95.3	93.9	92.3	90.6	88.6	86.5
Papua New Guinea	101.2	95.8	88.8	81.1	72.3	69.0	67.9	66.7	65.3	63.7	62.1
Philippines	70.3	65.4	56.3	47.0	38.1	34.4	33.5	32.5	31.5	30.3	29.0
Singapore	12.5	10.3	7.8	6.6	5.4	4.9	4.8	4.8	4.7	4.6	4.6
Solomon Islands	47.0	42.1	35.2	30.4	25.9	24.0	23.5	22.9	22.2	21.5	20.7
South Korea	30.0	26.2	18.3	13.0	9.7	7.9	7.8	7.6	7.5	7.3	7.1
Sri Lanka	41.7	38.5	33.1	28.6	24.6	22.9	22.4	21.9	21.4	20.8	20.1
Taiwan					10.7	9.9	9.5	9.1	8.6	8.3	8.1
Tajikistan	69.0	66.8	61.2	57.3	56.6	56.6	56.1	55.5	54.8	54.1	53.3
Thailand	64.3	56.3	43.5	33.6	27.2	25.4	24.7	23.8	22.9	21.9	20.8
Tonga			5.0		41.2	40.3	40.0	39.5	39.1	38.7	38.5
Turkmenistan	73.0	66.0	59.0	56.3	54.8	54.8	53.8	52.7	51.5	50.1	48.6
Tuvalu					28.1	27.2	26.8	26.4	26.0	26.0	25.8
Uzbekistan	70.1	66.6	61.2	51.2	42.6	41.0	40.3	39.5	38.7	37.7	36.7
Vanuatu	84.0	76.4	63.0	46.8	35.1	32.5	31.9	31.1	30.4	29.5	28.5
Vietnam	82.5	76.0	62.6	51.3	43.5	40.1	39.1	37.9	36.6	35.1	33.6
Western Samoa	59.8	55.4	47.3	39.6	32.7	29.8	29.2	28.5	27.7	26.9	25.9
Australasia											
Australia	12.5	11.0	9.9	8.2	5.9	5.4	5.4	5.3	5.3	5.2	5.2
New Zealand	13.8	12.8	11.1	8.8	7.0	6.6	6.5	6.5	6.4	6.3	6.2

Source: Euromonitor from UN/national statistical offices/Eurostat
Notes: Rates refer to deaths of infants under one year

▫ Deaths

Infant Mortality Rates 1977-2002

● Deaths per '000 live births

	1977	1980	1985	1990	1995	1997	1998	1999	2000	2001	2002
Africa and Middle East											
Algeria	112.0	99.0	78.1	64.5	54.6	50.0	48.8	47.5	46.1	44.5	42.8
Angola	160.4	153.8	142.9	131.5	125.9	126.2	124.8	123.3	121.6	119.7	117.7
Bahrain	43.0	31.7	21.5	20.3	17.9	16.4	16.1	15.7	15.3	14.9	14.4
Benin	121.6	116.1	107.6	99.6	91.3	87.7	86.5	85.3	83.9	82.3	80.6
Botswana	76.3	72.0	62.2	59.3	68.1	73.9	72.9	71.6	70.3	68.8	67.2
Burkina Faso	134.2	125.9	116.3	110.4	102.8	99.1	97.1	94.9	92.3	89.6	86.6
Burundi	127.0	122.6	118.7	128.0	127.3	120.0	118.6	117.1	115.4	113.5	111.5
Cameroon	114.7	109.1	98.9	90.1	87.0	87.3	86.0	84.5	82.9	81.2	79.3
Cape Verde	86.0	85.0	78.8	68.9	59.7	55.6	54.6	53.5	52.3	51.0	49.6
Central African Republic	122.0	117.8	109.5	104.8	102.6	101.2	99.9	98.5	96.9	95.2	93.3
Chad	154.6	149.0	138.3	130.9	125.5	122.5	121.5	120.4	119.1	117.7	116.1
Comoros	116.3	110.5	100.0	89.0	79.7	76.3	74.8	73.1	71.3	69.2	67.0
Congo Dem Rep	117.1	112.5	103.6	96.7	92.4	90.6	88.5	86.1	83.4	80.4	77.2
Congo-Brazzaville	91.0	88.5	84.3	80.1	74.8	72.1	71.1	69.9	68.7	67.3	65.8
Côte d'Ivoire	117.0	112.4	105.2	97.9	91.3	89.0	87.7	86.2	84.5	82.7	80.8
Djibouti	143.2	136.6	126.1	121.6	118.8	116.6	116.7	116.8	116.9	117.0	117.1
Egypt	131.0	122.4	93.4	68.5	56.4	50.8	49.2	47.3	45.2	43.0	40.5
Equatorial Guinea	148.8	142.8	131.9	121.7	112.0	107.7	106.3	104.7	102.9	100.9	98.8
Eritrea	123.0	127.6	121.9	107.2	95.0	89.3	88.2	86.9	85.5	84.0	82.4
Ethiopia	143.8	141.6	135.4	126.0	117.8	114.8	113.4	111.8	110.1	108.2	106.1
Gabon	122.0	115.2	105.6	97.9	90.7	87.7	86.5	85.1	83.6	81.9	80.0
Gambia	166.5	159.5	148.6	139.0	129.4	125.3	123.6	121.8	119.7	117.4	115.0
Ghana	98.8	94.7	86.8	79.6	72.3	68.6	67.6	66.4	65.1	63.7	62.1
Guinea	167.5	161.9	150.9	139.7	128.4	124.2	122.7	120.9	118.9	116.8	114.4
Guinea-Bissau	176.2	170.2	157.5	145.5	135.5	130.8	129.3	127.5	125.6	123.5	121.2
Iran	106.8	98.9	80.3	62.0	49.1	44.0	42.7	41.2	39.6	37.8	35.9
Iraq	84.0	80.9	70.2	97.8	107.9	91.7	87.2	82.1	76.5	70.3	63.5
Israel	17.9	15.9	12.2	9.6	7.5	6.3	6.3	6.2	6.1	6.0	5.9
Jordan	65.0	59.1	54.1	38.1	29.6	26.6	26.0	25.3	24.4	23.6	22.6
Kenya	92.6	87.2	79.1	71.2	65.7	64.7	63.7	62.6	61.5		58.7
Kuwait	34.0	27.4	18.8	15.0	13.1	12.3	12.1	11.8	11.5	11.2	10.8
Lebanon	48.0	46.1	42.3	35.7	25.3	20.0	19.5	19.0	18.5	17.9	17.2
Lesotho	125.5	120.9	111.6	104.1	105.1	108.1	108.6	109.2	109.8	110.5	111.2
Liberia	166.7	140.5	112.4	138.9	136.4	111.4	106.3	100.5	94.1	87.0	79.3
Libya	63.0	54.4	41.5	33.1	28.8	27.8	27.4	26.9	26.4	25.8	25.2
Madagascar	121.8	119.2	116.4	111.9	104.0	100.2	98.8	97.2	95.5	93.6	91.5
Malawi	177.0	167.6	157.1	152.8	144.9	139.8	138.2	136.5	134.6	132.5	130.1
Mali	180.0	163.9	145.9	139.6	133.5	130.3	128.7	127.0	125.0	122.8	120.5
Mauritania	125.0	120.7	115.8	112.3	107.7	105.6	104.2	102.6	100.8	98.8	96.7
Mauritius	38.3	33.0	25.8	22.0	19.5	18.5	18.5	18.0	17.4	16.7	16.0
Morocco	110.0	102.4	85.2	69.0	57.1	52.2	50.6	48.8	46.7	44.5	42.1
Mozambique	140.4	140.4	138.8	135.8	135.7	136.7	135.3	133.7	131.9	129.9	127.7
Namibia	98.8	91.6	82.1	81.2	80.5	78.5	75.9	73.6	71.0	68.1	64.7
Niger	161.9	158.7	154.3	148.3	139.9	136.1	134.5	132.6	130.5	128.2	125.7
Nigeria	125.9	120.5	110.5	101.4	92.4	88.1	86.6	84.8	82.9	80.8	78.5
Oman	95.0	74.5	45.9	33.6	28.7	26.6	26.0	25.3	24.6	23.8	22.9
Qatar	46.0	39.5	28.1	21.4	16.2	13.6	13.2	12.8	12.3	11.8	11.2
Réunion	21.2	17.3	11.8	9.5	9.0	9.0	8.9	8.7	8.6	8.4	8.2
Rwanda	133.0	130.8	125.7	129.8	128.2	121.9	121.5	121.0	120.4	119.7	119.2
Sao Tomé e Príncipe	57.1		65.5	43.0	56.2	55.9	55.7	55.6	55.4	55.2	55.0
Saudi Arabia	75.0	66.0	49.3	36.0	27.8	25.0	24.3	23.5	22.6	21.6	20.6
Senegal	97.0	91.6	81.1	71.6	64.9	62.4	61.5	60.5	59.4	58.2	56.8
Seychelles				13.0	16.6	16.2	16.1	16.0	15.8	15.4	14.9
Sierra Leone	191.5	189.7	185.1	189.2	178.9	165.4	162.4	158.9	155.1	150.9	146.3
Somalia	148.8	145.8	137.4	149.8	141.7	122.3	120.8	119.0	117.1	115.0	112.7
South Africa	72.1	70.1	64.6	57.4	56.2	58.2	58.3	58.5	58.7	59.0	59.2
Sudan	123.6	117.1	107.1	98.6	89.9	85.9	84.6	83.1	81.5	79.6	77.7
Swaziland	108.0	100.4	90.1	82.7	83.4	86.9	87.7	88.6	89.5	90.6	91.7
Syria	67.0	62.8	53.7	42.1	31.3	26.9	26.1	25.3	24.4	23.4	22.3
Tanzania	113.0	106.2	96.0	89.4	83.9	81.3	79.9	78.4	76.6	74.7	72.7
Togo	117.1	110.5	100.7	93.6	86.5	83.1	81.8	80.3	78.6	76.8	74.8
Tunisia	88.0	78.8	59.1	41.4	32.5	30.3	29.5	28.7	27.7	26.7	25.5
Uganda	122.1	121.2	122.5	121.2	112.0	106.5	104.5	102.2	99.7	96.9	93.9
United Arab Emirates	38.0	34.5	26.1	18.3	13.7	12.0	11.8	11.6	11.4	11.2	10.9
Yemen	158.0	140.7	114.7	98.2	82.4	73.8	72.0	70.0	67.7	65.2	62.5
Zambia	111.0	105.2	99.0	99.2	96.7	93.6	91.3	88.8	86.0	83.0	79.6
Zimbabwe	73.1	70.0	67.4	69.2	67.6	65.0	63.4	61.6	59.6	57.4	55.0

Source: Euromonitor from UN/national statistical offices/Eurostat
Notes: Rates refer to deaths of infants under one year

Table 21.10

Marriage Rates

Marriage Rates 1977-2002

- Per '000 inhabitants

	1977	1980	1985	1990	1995	1997	1998	1999	2000	2001	2002
North America											
Canada	8.1	7.9	7.3	7.1	5.4	5.0	5.0	4.9	4.8	4.7	4.6
USA	9.9	10.5	10.2	9.8	8.9	8.9	8.5	8.6	8.5	8.4	8.4
Latin America											
Anguilla			13.8								
Antigua	2.5	2.7	3.5		21.0						
Argentina	6.9	5.9		5.7	4.6	3.9	3.9	3.8	3.8	3.7	3.7
Aruba			7.0		7.3						
Bahamas	6.6	6.6	8.5	8.6	9.0						
Barbados	2.8	4.2	4.7	7.4	13.5						
Belize			6.0	6.2	6.2						
Bermuda	8.6	10.2	12.4	15.0	16.8						
Bolivia	5.5	4.8									
Brazil	8.0	7.8	7.0	5.2	4.9	4.7	4.6	4.6	4.5	4.5	4.4
British Virgin Islands		10.0	13.0								
Cayman Islands		10.6	8.5	10.5							
Chile	7.0	7.7	7.5	7.5	6.1	5.8	5.5	5.3	5.1	4.9	4.7
Colombia	3.5	3.9	3.3								
Costa Rica	7.5	7.8	8.0	7.6	7.3						
Cuba	6.5	7.1	8.0	9.6	6.4	5.4					
Dominica				3.2							
Dominican Republic	4.3	5.3	3.3								
Ecuador	6.2	5.9	6.0	6.3	6.1	5.8	5.7	5.6	5.5	5.3	5.2
El Salvador	4.2	4.8	3.8	4.5							
French Guiana	3.3	2.8	3.8								
Grenada											
Guadeloupe	4.4	4.9	4.8								
Guatemala	4.4	4.5	4.8	5.1							
Guyana											
Haiti											
Honduras	4.2	4.0									
Jamaica	4.1	3.6	5.1	5.4	6.6						
Martinique	3.9	3.6	4.0	4.3							
Mexico	7.3	7.2	6.6	7.5	7.3	7.2	7.1	7.0	6.9	6.8	6.7
Netherlands Antilles				6.7	5.2						
Nicaragua	5.3	6.3									
Panama	5.0	5.2	5.7	5.2	3.4						
Paraguay	6.4	5.4	5.0								
Peru	2.3	2.8			4.0	4.0	4.0	4.1	4.1	4.1	4.1
Puerto Rico	11.3	10.3	9.2	9.4							
St Kitts	2.6										
St Lucia	3.5	3.6	3.1		3.4						
St Vincent and the Grenadines	3.2	3.4			4.8	4.6					
Suriname		6.7		4.7	5.5						
Trinidad and Tobago	7.3	8.2	6.7	5.4	5.3						
Uruguay	7.8	7.7	7.4	6.5	5.5						
Venezuela	7.1	6.2	5.4	5.5	3.9	3.8	3.7	3.8	3.8	3.9	4.0

Source: National statistical offices/Council of Europe/UN/Euromonitor
Notes: Rates refer to legal marriages (recognised marriages performed and registered)

Marriage Rates

Marriage Rates 1977-2002

● Per '000 inhabitants

	1977	1980	1985	1990	1995	1997	1998	1999	2000	2001	2002
Asia Pacific											
Afghanistan											
American Samoa		10.6	11.2								
Armenia				8.0	4.2	3.3	3.0	3.0			
Azerbaijan		9.8	10.5	10.2	5.6	6.0	5.2	4.8	4.7	4.6	4.5
Bangladesh		9.1	10.2		11.2	9.7					
Bhutan											
Brunei	6.6	5.3	8.6	6.8	6.1						
Cambodia											
China					7.5	7.1	6.9	6.7	6.6	6.5	6.4
Fiji	9.6	9.8	9.5		9.9						
French Polynesia			7.2	6.1							
Guam	17.2	15.3	13.1		10.1						
Hong Kong, China	9.0	10.1	8.3	8.3	6.3	5.7	4.7	4.4	4.2	4.1	4.0
India											
Indonesia	7.9	8.1	6.7								
Japan	7.2	6.6	6.1	5.8	6.3	6.2	6.3	6.2	6.1	6.0	5.9
Kazakhstan				9.9	7.2	6.4	6.3	6.2	6.0	5.8	5.5
Kiribati											
Kyrgyzstan				9.9	6.0						
Laos											
Macau	2.8	3.2	8.3	3.7	5.2						
Malaysia	1.8		3.1								
Maldives	24.4	34.2		10.6	19.7						
Mongolia		5.6	6.6								
Myanmar											
Nauru											
Nepal											
New Caledonia	5.4	5.6	5.0	5.2							
North Korea											
Pakistan											
Papua New Guinea											
Philippines	7.3	7.3	6.9	6.9	7.1	7.0	6.9	6.9	6.9	6.8	6.7
Singapore	9.0	9.8	9.2	9.0	8.4	6.9	6.7	6.6	6.5	6.5	6.4
Solomon Islands											
South Korea	8.1	9.7	9.0	9.2	7.1	7.0	7.0	6.8	6.7	6.6	6.5
Sri Lanka	7.6	8.2	8.1	8.9	9.3						
Taiwan			8.0	7.1	7.5	7.7	7.8	7.9	7.9	7.7	7.5
Tajikistan											
Thailand		6.6	6.6	8.2	7.5	7.2	7.0	7.0	6.9	6.8	6.7
Tonga			6.6	7.2							
Turkmenistan				10.2	7.4	6.2	6.0	5.9	5.8	5.7	5.6
Tuvalu											
Uzbekistan											
Vanuatu											
Vietnam											
Western Samoa	4.9	5.4									
Australasia											
Australia	7.4	7.4	7.3	6.8	6.1	5.8	5.9	6.9	6.9	6.8	6.8
New Zealand	7.2	7.4	7.6	7.0	5.6	5.3	5.3	5.1	5.0	4.9	4.8

Source: National statistical offices/Council of Europe/UN/Euromonitor
Notes: Rates refer to legal marriages (recognised marriages performed and registered)

Marriage Rates

Marriage Rates 1977-2002

- Per '000 inhabitants

	1977	1980	1985	1990	1995	1997	1998	1999	2000	2001	2002
Africa and Middle East											
Algeria		6.9	6.0	6.0	5.3	5.4	5.5	5.5	5.5	5.6	5.6
Angola											
Bahrain	5.0	6.8	6.3	5.8	5.7						
Benin											
Botswana											
Burkina Faso											
Burundi											
Cameroon											
Cape Verde				4.8							
Central African Republic											
Chad											
Comoros											
Congo Dem Rep											
Congo-Brazzaville											
Côte d'Ivoire											
Djibouti											
Egypt	9.5	9.1	8.5	7.6	7.9	9.7	10.2	9.9	10.1	10.3	10.6
Equatorial Guinea											
Eritrea											
Ethiopia											
Gabon											
Gambia											
Ghana											
Guinea											
Guinea-Bissau											
Iran	5.2	8.8		8.3							
Iraq	11.1										
Israel	8.1	7.6	6.9	7.0	6.1	5.6	6.1	4.7	4.6	4.6	4.5
Jordan	5.2	5.3	5.7	7.7	6.6	6.2	5.8	5.5	5.4	5.3	5.2
Kenya											
Kuwait	5.0	6.2	5.6	5.9	5.6	4.8	4.9	4.7	4.6	4.6	4.5
Lebanon											
Lesotho											
Liberia											
Libya	6.8	5.9	5.6	4.9							
Madagascar											
Malawi											
Mali											
Mauritania											
Mauritius	9.5	9.3	11.3	10.6	9.5	9.5	9.4	8.6			
Morocco											
Mozambique											
Namibia											
Niger											
Nigeria											
Oman											
Qatar	3.1	3.8	3.7	2.8							
Réunion	6.4	6.3	5.8	6.2							
Rwanda		2.7									
Sao Tomé e Príncipe											
Saudi Arabia					3.4	3.1	3.1	3.1	3.0	3.0	3.0
Senegal											
Seychelles	4.5	5.6	8.9	14.9	11.7						
Sierra Leone											
Somalia											
South Africa					3.6	3.8	3.9	4.0	4.1	4.1	4.2
Sudan											
Swaziland											
Syria	9.0	10.1	9.4	7.5							
Tanzania											
Togo											
Tunisia	8.1	7.5	6.9	6.9	6.0	5.6	5.6	5.5	5.4	5.3	5.2
Uganda											
United Arab Emirates				4.0	2.8	3.8	3.8	3.6	3.5	3.4	3.3
Yemen											
Zambia											
Zimbabwe											

Source: National statistical offices/Council of Europe/UN/Euromonitor
Notes: Rates refer to legal marriages (recognised marriages performed and registered)

Table 21.11

Divorce Rates

Divorce Rates 1977-2002

● Per '000 inhabitants

	1977	1980	1985	1990	1995	1997	1998	1999	2000	2001	2002
North America											
Canada	2.4	2.6	2.5	2.9	2.6	2.2	2.2	2.2	2.2	2.2	2.3
USA	4.7	4.6	4.6	4.7	4.4	4.5	4.6	4.7	4.6	4.7	4.7
Latin America											
Anguilla			0.9								
Antigua			0.5								
Argentina											
Aruba	1.6	2.0	2.8								
Bahamas	0.7	0.7	1.5	1.4							
Barbados	0.6		1.2		1.4						
Belize				0.6							
Bermuda	4.6	5.5	3.7								
Bolivia											
Brazil			0.3	0.5	0.7	0.7	0.7	0.8	0.8	0.7	0.7
British Virgin Islands											
Cayman Islands				4.2							
Chile	0.3	0.3	0.4	0.5	0.4	0.5	0.5	0.6	0.5	0.5	0.5
Colombia				0.1	0.1	0.1	0.2	0.2	0.2	0.2	0.2
Costa Rica	0.5	0.8		1.1							
Cuba	2.4	2.5	2.9	3.5							
Dominica											
Dominican Republic	1.7	2.1	1.2								
Ecuador	0.3	0.3	0.4	0.6	0.6	0.7	0.7	0.7	0.7	0.7	0.7
El Salvador	0.3	0.3	0.4								
French Guiana											
Grenada											
Guadeloupe	0.9	1.4	1.2	1.3							
Guatemala	0.1	0.1	0.2								
Guyana											
Haiti											
Honduras	0.2	0.2									
Jamaica	0.3	0.4	0.4	0.3							
Martinique	1.2	1.2	1.1	0.7							
Mexico	0.5	0.4	0.5	0.5	0.4	0.5	0.5	0.5	0.5	0.5	0.5
Netherlands Antilles	2.5	2.2		2.1	2.6						
Nicaragua	0.3	0.3		0.2							
Panama	0.6	0.6	0.7								
Paraguay											
Peru											
Puerto Rico	4.0	4.8	4.5	3.9							
St Kitts											
St Lucia											
St Vincent and the Grenadines											
Suriname		1.1		2.0							
Trinidad and Tobago	0.6	0.9	0.8	1.0							
Uruguay	1.8	1.6	1.4	2.2							
Venezuela	1.1	0.9	0.9	1.1	0.7	0.9	0.9	1.0	1.0	0.9	0.9

Source: National statistical offices/Council of Europe/UN/Euromonitor
Notes: Rates refer to final divorce decrees granted under civil law

■ Divorce Rates

Divorce Rates 1977-2002

● Per '000 inhabitants

	1977	1980	1985	1990	1995	1997	1998	1999	2000	2001	2002
Asia Pacific											
Afghanistan											
American Samoa											
Armenia				1.2	0.7	0.6	0.4	0.4	0.4		
Azerbaijan		1.2	1.2	2.0	0.8	0.8	0.8	0.7	0.7	0.7	0.7
Bangladesh											
Bhutan											
Brunei			0.7	0.8							
Cambodia											
China				0.7	0.8	0.8	0.8	0.9	0.9	0.9	0.8
Fiji											
French Polynesia											
Guam	3.1	4.6	7.7		4.3						
Hong Kong, China			0.8	1.0	1.5	1.6	1.7	1.7	1.7	1.8	1.8
India											
Indonesia	1.2	1.4	1.0								
Japan	1.3	1.5	1.7	1.3	1.6	1.7	1.7	1.8	1.8	1.8	1.9
Kazakhstan	2.6	2.7	2.4	2.6	2.4	2.3	2.4	2.2	2.2	2.2	2.2
Kiribati											
Kyrgyzstan				1.8							
Laos											
Macau											
Malaysia											
Maldives				7.9	10.8						
Mongolia		0.3	0.4								
Myanmar											
Nauru											
Nepal											
New Caledonia	0.8	0.9	1.1								
North Korea											
Pakistan											
Papua New Guinea											
Philippines											
Singapore	1.2	1.3	1.7	1.2	1.4	1.6	1.7	1.9	1.8	1.8	1.8
Solomon Islands											
South Korea	1.0	1.2	1.5	1.0	1.2	1.4	1.5	1.5	1.5	1.5	1.6
Sri Lanka		0.2	0.2								
Taiwan	1.3	1.5	1.8		1.6	1.8	1.8	1.8	1.8	1.8	1.9
Tajikistan				1.5							
Thailand	0.8	0.8	1.0		0.9	0.9	1.0	1.2	1.1	1.0	1.0
Tonga			0.6								
Turkmenistan	1.4	1.4	1.4	1.4	1.3	1.5	1.4	1.3	1.3	1.3	1.2
Tuvalu											
Uzbekistan				1.5							
Vanuatu											
Vietnam											
Western Samoa		0.3									
Australasia											
Australia	3.2	2.7	2.5	2.5	2.8	2.8	2.7	2.7	2.7	2.7	2.8
New Zealand	2.7	2.6	3.1	2.7	2.8	3.0	3.1	3.2	3.2	3.2	3.3

Source: National statistical offices/Council of Europe/UN/Euromonitor
Notes: Rates refer to final divorce decrees granted under civil law

■ Divorce Rates
Divorce Rates 1977-2002

● Per '000 inhabitants

	1977	1980	1985	1990	1995	1997	1998	1999	2000	2001	2002
Africa and Middle East											
Algeria											
Angola											
Bahrain		4.2	1.1	1.2							
Benin											
Botswana											
Burkina Faso											
Burundi											
Cameroon											
Cape Verde											
Central African Republic											
Chad											
Comoros											
Congo Dem Rep											
Congo-Brazzaville											
Côte d'Ivoire											
Djibouti											
Egypt	2.0	1.6	1.5	1.3	1.1	1.5	1.5	1.6	1.6	1.6	1.5
Equatorial Guinea											
Eritrea											
Ethiopia											
Gabon											
Gambia											
Ghana											
Guinea											
Guinea-Bissau											
Iran	0.5	0.6		0.7							
Iraq	0.8										
Israel	1.4	1.4	1.9	1.4	1.6	1.9	1.9	2.0	2.0	2.0	2.0
Jordan	1.2	1.2	1.3	1.2	1.2	1.3	1.3	1.3	1.3	1.3	1.3
Kenya											
Kuwait	1.3	1.8	1.6	1.3	1.8	1.6	1.6	1.5	1.5	1.5	1.5
Lebanon											
Lesotho											
Liberia											
Libya	1.8	1.3	1.0	0.6							
Madagascar											
Malawi											
Mali											
Mauritania											
Mauritius	0.2	0.4	0.5	0.7							
Morocco											
Mozambique											
Namibia											
Niger											
Nigeria											
Oman											
Qatar	1.6	1.7	1.0	0.7							
Réunion	0.7	0.8	1.2	1.3							
Rwanda											
Sao Tomé e Príncipe											
Saudi Arabia											
Senegal											
Seychelles											
Sierra Leone											
Somalia											
South Africa	0.7	0.7	0.8		0.8	0.8	0.8	0.9	0.9	0.9	0.9
Sudan											
Swaziland											
Syria	0.6	0.6	0.7	0.7							
Tanzania											
Togo											
Tunisia	1.4	0.9	1.0	1.4	0.9	1.0	1.0	1.1	1.1	1.1	1.1
Uganda											
United Arab Emirates	0.9	0.9	1.1		0.9	1.0	1.1	1.1	1.1	1.1	1.1
Yemen											
Zambia											
Zimbabwe											

Source: National statistical offices/Council of Europe/UN/Euromonitor
Notes: Rates refer to final divorce decrees granted under civil law

Population Density 1977-2003

● Persons per sq km

	1977	1985	1990	1995	1997	1998	1999	2000	2001	2002	2003
North America											
Canada	2.3	2.8	3.0	3.2	3.2	3.3	3.3	3.3	3.3	3.4	3.4
USA	23.5	25.8	27.1	28.6	29.1	29.4	29.6	29.9	30.2	30.5	30.7
Latin America											
Anguilla		76.9	87.9	87.9	87.9	87.9	87.9	87.9	87.9	87.9	
Antigua			136.4	154.5	150.0	151.1	152.3	154.5	157.3	159.3	161.8
Argentina	9.7	11.0	11.8	12.6	13.0	13.1	13.3	13.4	13.6	13.8	13.9
Aruba	310.9	315.8	368.4	442.1	463.2	484.2	505.3	542.1	580.1	615.2	654.1
Bahamas	14.4	23.0	25.5	27.5	28.8	29.3	29.8	30.7	31.7	32.5	33.4
Barbados	581.4	581.4	605.8	609.3	619.8	622.1	624.4	627.9	632.8	638.0	643.2
Belize	6.1	7.2	8.1	9.3	9.7	10.0	10.2	10.6	10.9	11.2	11.6
Bermuda	925.9	1,200.0	1,200.0	1,220.0	1,260.0	1,270.0	1,280.0	1,300.0	1,322.2	1,338.8	1,358.5
Bolivia	4.7	5.8	6.0	6.8	7.1	7.3	7.4	7.6	7.8	7.9	8.1
Brazil	12.9	15.8	16.9	18.2	18.7	19.0	19.3	19.5	20.0	20.4	20.7
British Virgin Islands				55.9	57.4	58.8	60.3	61.8	63.0	64.6	66.0
Cayman Islands				119.2	128.8	134.6	140.4	146.2	151.9	158.5	164.9
Chile	14.0	16.0	17.3	18.8	19.4	19.7	19.9	20.2	20.4	20.7	20.9
Colombia	21.5	27.8	31.4	34.5	35.7	36.3	36.9	37.5	38.0	38.6	39.2
Costa Rica	40.7	50.2	58.7	66.3	69.3	70.7	72.2	73.7	75.1	76.5	78.0
Cuba	83.4	91.9	96.4	99.6	100.6	101.0	101.4	101.8	102.2	102.5	102.8
Dominica		106.5	93.3	94.0	94.7	94.7	94.7	94.7	94.7	94.7	94.7
Dominican Republic	103.8	126.7	145.5	160.3	166.0	168.8	171.5	174.2	176.9	179.6	182.2
Ecuador	28.2	33.3	37.1	41.4	43.1	44.0	44.8	45.7	46.5	47.4	48.2
El Salvador	199.1	219.4	240.2	270.1	282.7	289.1	295.5	301.8	308.1	314.3	320.5
French Guiana	0.7	1.0	1.3	1.6	1.8	1.9	1.9	2.1	2.2	2.3	2.5
Grenada	289.9	279.4	264.7	267.6	272.1	273.5	273.5	276.5	277.4	278.9	280.0
Guadeloupe	185.4	201.2	227.8	249.7	256.8	260.4	264.2	269.8	279.8	286.8	295.5
Guatemala	58.4	72.4	79.6	90.8	95.7	98.3	101.0	103.6	106.4	109.2	112.1
Guyana	3.8	4.4	4.0	4.2	4.3	4.3	4.3	4.4	4.4	4.5	4.5
Haiti	171.2	210.5	232.9	257.9	268.7	274.3	280.0	285.8	291.8	297.9	304.1
Honduras	29.6	36.7	42.9	49.8	52.7	54.2	55.7	57.2	58.7	60.3	61.8
Jamaica	183.8	211.9	221.6	228.2	231.3	233.3	235.4	238.5	243.4	247.0	251.3
Martinique	305.8	320.8	339.6	358.0	362.3	365.6	368.4	372.6	379.4	383.8	389.5
Mexico	32.3	39.5	43.6	47.8	49.4	50.2	51.0	51.8	52.6	53.4	54.1
Netherlands Antilles	181.3	225.0	237.5	253.1	261.9	265.0	267.5	271.3	276.7	280.9	285.8
Nicaragua	15.7	24.6	29.0	33.5	35.4	36.3	37.2	38.2	39.2	40.1	41.1
Panama	22.8	28.9	31.9	35.0	36.3	36.9	37.5	38.1	38.7	39.2	39.8
Paraguay	7.1	9.1	10.5	12.0	12.6	13.0	13.3	13.7	14.0	14.4	14.7
Peru	12.5	15.2	16.9	18.4	19.0	19.4	19.7	20.0	20.4	20.7	21.1
Puerto Rico	343.8	369.2	396.3	417.4	424.4	427.8	431.2	436.2	444.0	450.5	457.8
St Kitts	153.3	138.9	111.1	111.1	109.7	108.3	108.3	105.5	105.6	104.6	104.2
St Lucia	194.8	221.3	229.5	232.8	241.0	244.3	247.5	252.7	257.8	263.0	268.2
St Vincent and the Grenadines	257.1	269.2	282.1	282.1	285.9	287.2	288.5	292.3	298.1	302.3	307.3
Suriname	2.2	2.4	2.6	2.6	2.6	2.6	2.7	2.7	2.7	2.7	2.7
Trinidad and Tobago	202.7	229.0	236.8	244.8	248.2	249.5	250.7	252.4	254.7	257.1	259.5
Uruguay	15.3	17.1	17.6	18.2	18.4	18.5	18.6	18.7	18.8	18.9	19.0
Venezuela	14.9	19.8	22.1	24.8	25.8	26.4	26.9	27.4	27.9	28.4	29.0

Source: *National statistical offices/UN/Euromonitor*

■ Population Density

Population Density 1977-2003

● Persons per sq km

	1977	1985	1990	1995	1997	1998	1999	2000	2001	2002	2003
Asia Pacific											
Afghanistan	19.5	23.9	22.1	29.4	31.6	32.4	33.2	34.0	34.7	35.8	37.2
American Samoa	152.3	175.0	250.0	267.5	300.0	310.0	322.5	340.0	360.1	378.0	398.0
Armenia			134.1	134.0	134.1	134.4	134.7	135.0	135.1	135.3	135.4
Azerbaijan			81.0	88.3	90.1	91.0	91.8	92.7	93.1	94.1	95.1
Bangladesh	574.4	762.3	833.8	904.0	934.3	950.4	966.9	983.5	996.5	1,010.9	1,030.1
Bhutan	26.0	32.4	35.8	38.9	40.8	42.0	43.3	44.5	45.6	46.8	48.4
Brunei	29.5	42.0	48.1	55.2	57.9	59.2	60.4	61.7	62.7	63.9	65.5
Cambodia	37.5	40.5	48.3	55.8	58.7	60.0	61.4	62.7	63.8	65.1	66.8
China	99.8	113.8	122.6	129.9	132.5	133.8	135.4	136.8	137.4	138.7	140.0
Fiji	32.7	37.8	39.6	41.8	42.8	43.3	43.9	44.4	44.8	45.3	45.9
French Polynesia	35.5	46.4	52.9	58.3	60.4	61.5	62.6	63.7	64.6	65.6	66.9
Guam	222.2	216.6	240.5	271.6	284.0	290.1	296.1	302.0	307.0	313.1	321.2
Hong Kong, China	4,246.7	5,459.3	5,738.1	6,157.3	6,471.3	6,661.3	6,833.4	7,000.7	7,139.6	7,290.8	7,492.4
India	197.6	250.5	280.5	313.6	324.7	330.2	335.6	339.0	342.2	348.6	355.0
Indonesia	71.2	89.7	99.3	107.8	111.2	112.8	114.5	116.2	117.2	119.3	121.4
Japan	308.1	319.4	327.4	344.0	346.1	347.0	347.6	348.3	348.4	348.5	348.7
Kazakhstan			6.3	6.1	6.1	6.0	6.0	6.0	6.0	6.0	5.9
Kiribati	87.7	89.0	95.9	108.2	108.9	110.3	111.6	113.7	116.0	117.9	120.1
Kyrgyzstan			22.8	23.8	24.0	24.1	24.3	24.4	24.5	24.6	24.7
Laos	14.9	15.2	17.7	20.4	21.5	22.1	22.7	23.2	23.7	24.3	25.1
Macau	17,500.0	15,528.2	18,295.5	21,215.5	22,246.3	22,722.5	23,149.6	23,566.7	23,916.4	24,310.1	24,834.9
Malaysia	37.8	47.7	54.3	61.2	63.9	65.2	66.4	67.9	68.8	70.5	72.3
Maldives	469.8	586.4	707.9	818.7	865.9	890.4	915.5	940.7	961.2	985.4	1,017.7
Mongolia	1.0	1.2	1.4	1.6	1.6	1.6	1.7	1.7	1.7	1.7	1.8
Myanmar	46.5	56.9	61.2	64.8	66.4	67.2	68.1	69.0	69.6	70.4	71.3
Nauru				550.0	550.0	550.0	550.0	605.4	660.8	693.5	740.8
Nepal	92.9	118.5	129.6	147.0	154.2	157.9	161.7	165.4	168.5	172.1	177.0
New Caledonia	7.3	8.0	9.0	10.4	10.9	11.2	11.4	11.6	11.8	12.0	12.4
North Korea	136.5	154.4	168.5	183.2	189.3	192.4	195.4	198.4	200.9	203.9	207.9
Pakistan	93.8	132.4	154.6	176.7	186.9	192.2	197.6	201.3	204.6	211.2	217.7
Papua New Guinea	6.1	7.5	8.4	9.4	9.8	10.0	10.3	10.5	10.7	10.9	11.2
Philippines	148.6	180.7	203.5	229.2	239.9	245.3	250.6	256.0	259.3	266.1	272.8
Singapore	3,782.5	4,101.8	4,387.9	4,849.8	5,039.2	5,136.9	5,230.3	5,321.3	5,395.2	5,476.8	5,585.5
Solomon Islands	7.0	9.5	11.3	13.3	14.2	14.7	15.1	15.6	16.0	16.5	17.1
South Korea	369.9	413.5	434.1	456.8	465.8	470.3	474.6	479.0	481.9	487.8	493.7
Sri Lanka	212.5	244.2	262.3	275.9	281.4	284.1	287.0	289.8	292.0	294.3	297.4
Taiwan	467.1	535.1	561.3	588.4	588.4	588.4	588.4	588.4	588.4	588.4	588.4
Tajikistan			37.3	40.6	41.8	42.5	43.1	43.7	44.2	44.8	45.5
Thailand	85.7	100.4	108.8	114.7	116.9	118.0	119.1	120.3	120.8	121.9	122.9
Tonga	128.8	138.9	138.9	136.8	135.4	136.1	136.1	137.5	137.5	137.5	137.5
Turkmenistan			7.8	8.7	9.0	9.2	9.3	9.5	9.6	9.8	10.0
Tuvalu				333.3	366.7	366.7	366.7	400.0	406.7	418.3	427.7
Uzbekistan			49.0	53.8	55.6	56.5	57.4	58.2	58.9	59.7	60.8
Vanuatu	6.8	11.0	12.1	13.7	14.4	14.7	15.1	15.4	15.7	16.1	16.5
Vietnam	153.2	185.0	204.9	226.9	234.7	238.3	241.8	246.9	249.0	253.3	257.6
Western Samoa	52.8	55.9	56.3	58.9	60.4	61.2	62.1	63.0	63.8	64.6	65.7
Australasia											
Australia	1.8	2.1	2.2	2.3	2.4	2.4	2.5	2.5	2.5	2.5	2.6
New Zealand	11.8	12.4	12.9	13.8	14.1	14.2	14.3	14.4	14.4	14.6	14.7

Source: *National statistical offices/UN/Euromonitor*

◻ Population Density

Population Density 1977-2003

● Persons per sq km

	1977	1985	1990	1995	1997	1998	1999	2000	2001	2002	2003
Africa and Middle East											
Algeria	7.2	9.2	10.3	11.7	12.1	12.3	12.3	12.6	12.7	12.9	13.1
Angola	5.6	6.3	7.9	8.6	9.2	9.5	9.9	10.3	10.9	11.4	11.9
Bahrain	453.9	594.2	717.4	802.8	859.2	855.6	845.8	869.0	891.2	902.2	919.1
Benin	29.2	36.1	42.3	47.8	50.2	51.6	53.0	55.1	57.9	60.2	62.8
Botswana	1.3	1.9	2.2	2.6	2.7	2.7	2.8	2.9	2.9	3.0	3.1
Burkina Faso	21.3	28.5	32.5	37.6	39.7	40.8	41.9	43.6	46.2	48.1	50.4
Burundi	140.1	181.3	209.5	234.2	245.9	249.6	253.5	260.7	269.3	276.4	284.4
Cameroon	17.0	21.5	24.8	27.9	29.5	30.3	31.2	32.4	34.2	35.6	37.3
Cape Verde	71.9	80.6	83.1	94.4	97.8	100.1	102.5	106.2	110.7	114.1	118.3
Central African Republic	3.5	4.2	4.8	5.0	5.4	5.5	5.6	5.8	6.0	6.1	6.3
Chad	3.3	3.9	4.5	5.1	5.6	5.7	5.8	6.1	6.3	6.5	6.8
Comoros	188.2	208.5	237.7	268.2	283.2	291.0	299.1	311.2	329.6	342.9	359.5
Congo Dem Rep	10.2	13.4	15.4	19.7	20.9	21.4	21.9	22.8	23.9	24.8	25.8
Congo-Brazzaville		5.6	6.4	7.5	8.0	8.3	8.5	8.6	8.7	8.9	9.0
Côte d'Ivoire	22.6	30.6	36.1	42.8	43.8	44.6	45.3	46.5	48.2	49.6	51.2
Djibouti	10.9	18.1	22.0	25.5	26.5	26.7	27.0	27.5	28.3	28.9	29.6
Egypt	38.9	45.7	51.7	57.2	60.0	61.0	62.1	63.1	63.9	64.7	65.8
Equatorial Guinea	11.8	10.7	12.3	14.1	14.8	15.2	15.6	16.1	16.9	17.5	18.2
Eritrea				32.0	33.3	34.7	36.1	38.1	40.5	42.6	44.9
Ethiopia	35.1	38.1	43.3	55.1	57.5	58.9	60.4	62.6	65.1	67.1	69.5
Gabon	3.7	3.8	4.4	4.1	4.4	4.5	4.6	4.8	5.0	5.1	5.3
Gambia	51.5	73.0	90.0	109.6	117.0	120.9	124.8	130.5	137.1	142.9	149.4
Ghana	43.9	55.2	65.0	75.8	80.9	83.1	85.3	88.8	92.7	96.2	100.1
Guinea	20.6	18.7	23.1	29.0	29.7	29.8	29.9	30.2	30.8	31.2	31.7
Guinea-Bissau	19.4	30.6	33.8	38.0	40.0	40.8	41.7	43.1	44.8	46.3	48.0
Iran	21.0	29.9	34.3	37.8	39.1	39.8	40.5	41.2	41.7	42.3	43.1
Iraq	27.4	35.1	40.7	45.4	47.8	49.1	50.6	52.8	55.6	58.0	60.7
Israel	173.8	194.2	219.0	265.4	279.1	285.7	292.4	299.1	304.6	311.4	320.5
Jordan	29.9	29.5	38.8	48.3	51.7	53.5	55.1	57.1	58.6	60.2	61.8
Kenya	24.6	35.0	43.0	49.6	49.5	50.5	51.4	52.9	55.8	57.6	60.0
Kuwait	47.0	116.1	120.2	101.1	111.1	113.8	118.2	122.9	125.7	131.5	137.2
Lebanon	265.4	261.0	248.8	289.3	304.3	309.6	314.1	320.8	331.4	338.6	347.8
Lesotho	40.9	48.9	57.5	64.3	65.7	67.2	68.7	70.9	73.8	76.2	79.0
Liberia	15.0	22.2	25.2	24.9	23.9	26.3	29.0	32.7	37.2	41.7	46.8
Libya	1.5	2.0	2.3	2.9	3.2	3.2	3.1	3.2	3.3	3.3	3.4
Madagascar	13.5	17.1	20.1	24.2	24.8	25.5	26.3	27.4	28.9	30.1	31.5
Malawi	58.9	73.9	86.7	101.7	105.8	108.5	111.5	116.1	123.0	128.0	134.3
Mali	5.2	6.6	6.6	8.4	8.5	8.7	8.9	9.2	9.6	9.9	10.3
Mauritania	1.5	1.7	1.9	2.2	2.4	2.4	2.5	2.6	2.7	2.8	3.0
Mauritius	471.9	485.2	517.2	540.4	555.9	560.1	564.3	570.4	577.5	583.6	590.2
Morocco	40.0	49.6	54.9	58.6	60.7	61.7	62.8	63.8	64.6	65.4	66.6
Mozambique	13.6	17.4	17.9	21.7	23.2	23.8	24.3	25.1	26.3	27.2	28.3
Namibia	1.1	1.4	1.6	1.8	1.9	2.0	2.0	2.1	2.2	2.2	2.3
Niger	4.1	5.1	6.0	7.1	7.6	7.8	8.1	8.5	8.9	9.3	9.8
Nigeria	78.6	103.8	104.0	110.7	117.2	121.0	124.9	128.8	132.7	136.7	140.7
Oman	3.1	7.5	8.0	6.9	7.3	7.6	7.8	8.2	8.7	9.1	9.6
Qatar	16.6	29.1	43.2	51.7	51.2	52.2	53.1	54.5	56.3	57.7	59.4
Réunion	195.2	218.0	238.0	259.0	267.4	271.0	274.6	279.6	285.5	290.7	296.4
Rwanda	165.6	243.2	283.3	214.0	231.8	254.7	280.5	313.5	351.3	390.5	433.5
Sao Tomé e Príncipe	83.0	99.0	125.0	131.8	142.2	145.3	148.4	153.1	158.0	162.8	167.7
Saudi Arabia	2.8	4.3	6.2	7.6	8.3	8.8	9.3	9.7	10.2	10.6	11.1
Senegal	26.7	33.6	38.4	42.7	45.0	46.2	47.4	49.2	51.6	53.5	55.6
Seychelles	148.5	144.4	155.6	158.9	165.6	167.8	170.0	171.1	171.7	173.6	174.9
Sierra Leone	43.4	49.7	55.2	60.0	60.8	62.7	64.8	67.8	71.2	74.3	77.7
Somalia	5.7	12.4	13.7	13.8	13.8	14.4	15.1	16.1	17.4	18.4	19.7
South Africa	22.5	26.3	29.1	32.3	33.2	33.8	34.5	35.3	35.6	36.4	37.1
Sudan	6.8	9.1	10.7	11.7	11.5	11.8	12.0	12.4	13.0	13.5	14.0
Swaziland	28.8	36.9	43.9	50.9	53.0	54.6	56.2	58.6	61.6	64.1	67.0
Syria	42.4	55.0	64.9	76.3	80.3	82.4	84.5	87.7	91.6	95.0	98.7
Tanzania	18.0	24.2	28.5	33.4	35.2	35.9	36.7	37.9	39.3	40.5	41.8
Togo	41.4	54.2	63.9	73.5	77.7	79.8	81.9	85.1	89.1	92.2	96.0
Tunisia	36.1	48.0	53.4	57.3	58.9	59.7	60.4	61.1	61.7	62.4	63.3
Uganda	52.2	74.4	88.3	96.4	100.1	102.9	105.8	110.5	117.0	122.1	128.2
United Arab Emirates	9.2	17.2	21.8	28.2	30.8	32.2	34.1	36.0	37.5	39.1	41.3
Yemen	13.9	17.4	21.1	28.3	30.3	31.4	32.6	34.3	36.7	38.5	40.8
Zambia	7.0	8.9	10.7	11.6	11.2	11.4	11.8	12.3	13.0	13.5	14.1
Zimbabwe	16.7	21.1	23.9	29.3	28.3	28.8	29.4	30.2	31.0	31.8	32.7

Source: National statistical offices/UN/Euromonitor

Urban Population 1980-2002

- % of total population

	1980	1985	1990	1995	1997	1998	1999	2000	2001	2002
North America										
Canada	75.7	76.4	76.6	76.7	76.9	76.9	77.0	77.1	77.2	77.3
USA	73.7	74.5	75.2	76.1	76.5	76.8	77.0	77.1	77.3	77.5
Latin America										
Anguilla				11.0	11.4	11.6	11.8	12.0	12.3	12.5
Antigua			35.4	35.8	36.2	36.4	36.6	36.8	37.1	37.3
Argentina	82.9	84.8	86.5	88.4	89.0	89.3	89.6	89.3	89.6	89.9
Aruba										
Bahamas	75.1	79.7	83.6	86.5	87.3	87.7	88.1	88.5	88.7	89.0
Barbados	40.2	42.5	44.8	47.3	48.4	48.9	49.5	50.0	50.4	51.0
Belize	49.4	48.4	47.5	50.4	51.9	52.7	53.4	54.1	54.7	55.4
Bermuda	100.0	100.0	100.0	100.0	100.0	100.0	100.0	100.0	100.0	100.0
Bolivia	45.5	50.5	55.6	59.5	60.7	61.3	61.9	62.6	62.8	63.0
Brazil	66.2	70.7	74.7	78.4	79.6	80.1	80.7	80.9	81.3	81.8
British Virgin Islands				56.0	58.0	59.1	60.1	61.1	61.8	62.5
Cayman Islands				100.0	100.0	100.0	100.0	100.0	100.0	100.0
Chile	81.2	82.6	83.3	84.4	84.9	85.2	85.4	84.6	85.0	85.3
Colombia	63.9	67.0	69.5	71.8	72.6	73.1	73.5	74.6	74.8	75.0
Costa Rica	43.1	44.7	45.8	46.8	47.2	47.4	47.6	47.8	48.0	48.3
Cuba	68.1	71.1	73.7	74.6	74.9	75.0	75.2	75.3	75.4	75.6
Dominica			67.7	69.3	70.0	70.3	70.7	71.0	71.3	71.6
Dominican Republic	50.5	54.6	58.3	61.8	63.1	63.7	64.4	65.0	65.5	66.0
Ecuador	47.0	51.2	55.1	60.3	62.3	63.3	64.3	65.3	66.0	66.8
El Salvador	41.6	42.7	43.9	45.0	45.6	46.0	46.3	46.6	46.9	47.3
French Guiana	70.8	72.7	74.6	76.4	77.1	77.4	77.8	78.1	78.4	78.6
Grenada	32.9	33.3	34.2	35.8	36.6	37.1	37.5	37.9	38.3	38.8
Guadeloupe	88.5	95.2	98.5	99.4	99.5	99.6	99.6	99.7	99.7	99.7
Guatemala	37.4	37.8	38.1	38.6	39.0	39.3	39.5	39.7	39.9	40.2
Guyana	30.5	31.6	33.2	35.4	36.5	37.1	37.6	38.2	38.2	38.3
Haiti	23.7	26.3	29.5	32.6	33.8	34.5	35.1	35.7	36.2	36.8
Honduras	34.9	37.7	41.8	47.5	49.6	50.6	51.7	52.6	53.3	54.2
Jamaica	46.8	49.2	51.5	53.7	54.7	55.1	55.6	56.1	56.5	56.9
Martinique	79.6	86.0	90.5	93.3	93.9	94.3	94.6	94.9	95.0	95.2
Mexico	66.3	69.6	72.5	73.4	73.8	74.0	74.2	74.4	74.6	74.8
Netherlands Antilles	67.9	67.9	68.4	69.2	69.7	69.9	70.2	70.4	70.7	70.9
Nicaragua	50.3	51.7	53.1	54.5	55.1	55.5	55.8	56.0	56.3	56.7
Panama	50.4	52.1	53.7	55.0	55.5	55.8	56.0	56.3	56.5	56.8
Paraguay	41.7	45.0	48.7	52.4	53.8	54.6	55.3	56.0	56.5	57.1
Peru	64.6	66.9	68.9	70.9	71.7	72.0	72.4	72.6	72.9	73.3
Puerto Rico	66.9	69.2	71.3	73.3	74.1	74.4	74.8	75.2	75.5	75.8
St Kitts	35.9	35.2	34.6	34.0	34.0	34.1	34.1	34.1	34.2	34.4
St Lucia	37.3	37.3	37.2	37.2	37.4	37.6	37.7	37.8	38.0	38.2
St Vincent and the Grenadines	27.2	33.6	40.6	48.1	50.8	52.1	53.5	54.8	55.7	56.7
Suriname	55.0	60.3	65.5	70.3	71.9	72.6	73.4	74.2	74.7	75.3
Trinidad and Tobago	63.1	66.2	69.1	71.7	72.7	73.1	73.6	73.9	74.2	74.6
Uruguay	85.2	87.2	88.7	90.0	90.5	90.8	91.0	91.4	91.5	91.6
Venezuela	79.4	81.9	84.0	85.5	86.1	86.3	86.6	87.3	87.4	87.6

Source: National statistical offices/UN/Euromonitor

◻ Urban Population

Urban Population 1980-2002

• % of total population

	1980	1985	1990	1995	1997	1998	1999	2000	2001	2002
Asia Pacific										
Afghanistan	15.6	16.9	18.2	19.9	20.7	21.1	21.5	21.9	22.3	22.7
American Samoa	44.2	46.1	48.1	50.3	51.3	51.7	52.2	52.7	53.1	53.6
Armenia			67.5	68.6	69.2	69.4	69.7	70.0	70.2	70.5
Azerbaijan			54.4	55.7	56.3	56.7	57.0	57.1	57.4	57.8
Bangladesh	14.4	17.0	19.3	21.8	22.9	23.4	24.0	24.5	24.9	25.5
Bhutan	3.9	4.4	5.2	6.0	6.4	6.7	6.9	7.1	7.3	7.5
Brunei	59.9	62.3	65.8	69.2	70.4	71.0	71.6	72.2	72.6	73.1
Cambodia	12.4	12.6	12.6	14.2	14.9	15.2	15.6	15.8	16.2	16.5
China	19.6	23.0	27.4	29.7	30.7	31.1	31.6	32.1	32.5	33.0
Fiji	37.8	38.5	41.6	45.5	47.1	47.8	48.6	49.2	49.8	50.6
French Polynesia	57.1	57.3	56.1	54.4	53.7	53.4	53.0	52.9	52.9	52.8
Guam	39.5	38.8	38.2	38.3	38.7	38.8	39.0	39.2	39.5	39.8
Hong Kong, China	91.5	92.9	99.9	100.0	100.0	100.0	100.0	100.0	100.0	100.0
India	23.1	24.3	25.5	26.8	27.4	27.8	28.1	28.4	28.7	29.1
Indonesia	22.2	26.1	30.6	35.6	37.7	38.8	39.8	40.2	41.1	42.2
Japan	76.2	76.7	77.4	78.1	78.4	78.5	78.7	78.9	79.0	79.2
Kazakhstan			57.0	56.4	56.5	56.5	56.6	56.6	56.7	56.8
Kiribati	31.7	33.5	34.6	36.8	37.8	38.2	38.7	39.1	39.5	40.0
Kyrgyzstan			37.4	34.9	34.3	33.9	33.6	33.3	33.3	33.3
Laos	13.4	15.6	18.1	20.7	21.8	22.4	22.9	23.5	24.0	24.6
Macau	98.1	98.5	98.7	98.8	98.8	98.8	98.8	98.8	98.8	98.8
Malaysia	42.0	45.9	49.8	53.7	55.2	55.9	56.7	56.8	57.4	58.2
Maldives	22.3	25.5	25.9	25.7	25.9	25.9	26.0	27.0	27.0	27.1
Mongolia	52.1	55.0	58.0	60.8	61.9	62.4	63.0	63.5	63.9	64.3
Myanmar	24.0	24.0	24.6	25.8	26.6	26.9	27.3	27.7	28.1	28.6
Nauru				100.0	100.0	100.0	100.0	100.0	100.0	100.0
Nepal	6.5	7.8	8.9	10.3	10.9	11.3	11.6	11.9	12.2	12.5
New Caledonia	56.3	58.8	61.6	69.8	72.6	74.1	75.5	76.8	77.6	78.6
North Korea	56.9	57.6	58.4	59.1	59.5	59.8	60.0	60.1	60.3	60.6
Pakistan	28.1	29.8	31.9	34.3	35.4	35.9	36.5	37.0	37.5	38.1
Papua New Guinea	13.0	14.0	15.0	16.0	16.6	16.8	17.1	17.4	17.7	18.0
Philippines	37.5	43.0	48.8	54.0	55.8	56.8	57.7	58.2	58.9	59.6
Singapore	100.0	100.0	100.0	100.0	100.0	100.0	100.0	100.0	100.0	100.0
Solomon Islands	10.5	12.4	14.6	17.0	18.1	18.6	19.2	19.7	20.1	20.7
South Korea	56.9	64.9	73.8	78.2	79.7	80.4	81.2	81.9	82.3	82.8
Sri Lanka	21.6	21.1	21.3	22.1	22.7	23.0	23.3	23.6	24.0	24.3
Taiwan			67.8	69.1	69.3	69.2	69.3	77.5	77.7	77.9
Tajikistan			31.7	27.5	27.3	27.4	27.7	27.5	27.6	27.6
Thailand	17.0	17.9	18.7	20.0	20.6	21.0	21.3	21.6	21.9	22.3
Tonga	27.0	29.9	32.6	35.2	36.3	36.9	37.4	38.2	38.7	39.1
Turkmenistan			45.1	44.5	44.6	44.7	44.7	44.8	45.0	45.1
Tuvalu				46.8	49.0	50.0	51.1	52.2	53.0	53.8
Uzbekistan			40.1	38.5	37.9	37.5	37.2	37.0	37.0	37.0
Vanuatu	17.9	18.0	18.2	18.9	19.3	19.6	19.8	20.0	20.3	20.6
Vietnam	19.2	19.6	19.7	19.4	19.5	19.6	19.6	19.7	19.8	20.0
Western Samoa	21.2	21.1	21.0	21.0	21.2	21.3	21.4	21.5	21.6	21.7
Australasia										
Australia	85.8	85.5	85.1	84.7	84.7	84.7	84.7	84.7	84.7	84.7
New Zealand	83.3	83.7	84.7	85.3	85.5	85.6	85.7	86.9	86.8	86.7

Source: *National statistical offices/UN/Euromonitor*

■ Urban Population

Urban Population 1980-2002

● % of total population

	1980	1985	1990	1995	1997	1998	1999	2000	2001	2002
Africa and Middle East										
Algeria	43.5	48.0	52.4	56.6	58.1	58.8	59.6	59.3	60.0	60.7
Angola	20.9	24.2	27.6	31.0	32.3	32.9	33.6	34.0	34.6	35.2
Bahrain	80.5	84.2	87.6	90.3	91.1	91.4	91.8	92.2	92.4	92.6
Benin	27.3	30.8	34.5	38.4	40.0	40.7	41.5	42.3	42.9	43.6
Botswana	15.1	25.2	41.5	47.7	48.7	49.3	49.8	50.2	50.6	51.1
Burkina Faso	8.5	11.4	13.6	15.9	16.9	17.5	18.0	18.5	18.9	19.5
Burundi	4.3	5.2	6.3	7.5	8.1	8.4	8.7	9.0	9.3	9.5
Cameroon	31.4	35.7	40.3	44.7	46.4	47.2	48.1	48.9	49.5	50.2
Cape Verde	23.5	33.0	44.2	54.2	57.4	59.0	60.6	62.2	63.1	64.1
Central African Republic	35.1	36.3	37.5	39.1	39.9	40.4	40.8	41.2	41.6	42.1
Chad	18.8	19.9	21.1	22.2	22.8	23.2	23.5	23.8	24.1	24.4
Comoros	23.2	25.5	27.9	30.4	31.5	32.1	32.6	33.2	33.7	34.2
Congo Dem Rep	28.7	27.9	27.9	28.7	29.3	29.7	30.0	30.3	30.7	31.1
Congo-Brazzaville	41.0	47.5	53.4	58.4	60.0	60.9	61.7	62.5	63.0	63.6
Côte d'Ivoire	34.7	37.5	40.3	43.3	44.5	45.2	45.8	46.3	46.8	47.4
Djibouti	73.6	77.5	80.2	82.1	82.6	82.8	83.1	83.3	83.5	83.7
Egypt	43.8	43.9	44.1	44.4	44.7	44.9	45.0	45.9	46.0	46.1
Equatorial Guinea	27.4	29.8	35.7	42.2	44.6	45.8	47.0	48.2	49.0	50.0
Eritrea				17.1	17.7	18.1	18.4	18.7	19.0	19.4
Ethiopia	10.5	11.7	13.4	15.4	16.3	16.7	17.2	17.6	18.0	18.4
Gabon	49.6	59.2	68.1	75.9	78.1	79.2	80.3	81.0	81.6	82.4
Gambia	19.6	22.5	25.7	29.0	30.4	31.1	31.8	32.5	33.0	33.7
Ghana	31.2	32.3	33.9	35.9	36.9	37.4	37.9	38.4	38.8	39.2
Guinea	19.1	22.3	25.7	29.2	30.6	31.4	32.1	32.8	33.4	34.0
Guinea-Bissau	16.9	18.4	20.0	21.7	22.5	22.9	23.3	23.7	24.1	24.5
Iran	49.6	53.4	56.3	59.0	60.0	60.6	61.1	61.6	62.0	62.4
Iraq	65.5	68.8	71.8	74.5	75.4	75.9	76.3	76.8	77.1	77.4
Israel	88.6	89.8	90.3	90.7	90.9	91.0	91.1	91.2	91.3	91.3
Jordan	59.9	64.1	68.0	71.4	72.5	73.1	73.6	73.8	74.2	74.7
Kenya	16.1	19.8	24.1	28.6	30.4	31.3	32.2	33.1	33.8	34.6
Kuwait	90.2	93.8	95.8	97.0	97.2	97.4	97.5	97.6	97.6	97.7
Lebanon	73.7	79.4	84.2	87.5	88.4	88.8	89.3	89.7	89.9	90.2
Lesotho	13.4	16.5	20.1	24.0	25.6	26.4	27.2	28.0	28.6	29.3
Liberia	35.0	39.3	42.0	42.0	43.2	43.7	44.3	45.0	45.4	46.0
Libya	69.3	76.7	81.8	85.3	86.2	86.7	87.1	87.6	87.8	88.1
Madagascar	18.3	20.8	23.5	26.5	27.7	28.4	29.0	29.6	30.1	30.7
Malawi	9.1	10.4	13.3	18.4	21.0	22.3	23.6	24.3	25.5	26.8
Mali	18.5	21.0	23.8	26.8	28.1	28.7	29.4	30.0	30.5	31.2
Mauritania	27.4	35.0	43.5	51.2	53.8	55.1	56.4	57.7	58.5	59.4
Mauritius	42.4	41.4	40.5	40.5	40.8	41.0	41.1	41.3	41.6	41.8
Morocco	41.1	44.6	48.2	52.1	53.7	54.5	55.3	55.1	55.8	56.7
Mozambique	13.1	19.4	26.6	33.8	36.4	37.6	38.9	40.2	41.0	41.9
Namibia	22.8	24.7	26.6	28.6	29.5	30.0	30.4	30.8	31.2	31.7
Niger	12.6	14.3	16.1	18.2	19.2	19.6	20.1	20.6	21.0	21.5
Nigeria	26.9	30.7	35.0	39.5	41.3	42.2	43.1	43.4	44.2	45.0
Oman	31.5	46.5	62.1	75.6	79.0	80.6	82.3	84.0	84.8	85.6
Qatar	85.6	87.9	89.9	91.4	91.8	92.1	92.3	92.5	92.6	92.8
Réunion	54.7	59.5	63.9	67.7	69.0	69.6	70.3	70.9	71.3	71.8
Rwanda	4.7	5.0	5.3	5.7	5.9	6.0	6.1	6.2	5.2	4.1
Sao Tomé e Príncipe	30.7	34.8	38.9	42.9	44.4	45.2	45.9	46.0	46.7	47.5
Saudi Arabia	65.9	72.6	78.5	82.8	84.0	84.5	85.1	85.3	85.7	86.1
Senegal	35.7	37.5	40.0	43.8	45.2	46.0	46.7	47.2	47.8	48.5
Seychelles	40.8	47.1	53.5	59.1	61.0	61.9	62.9	63.8	64.4	65.0
Sierra Leone	24.1	26.9	30.0	33.3	34.6	35.3	35.9	36.6	37.2	37.8
Somalia	22.2	23.2	24.2	25.6	26.4	26.7	27.1	27.5	27.9	28.3
South Africa	48.1	48.3	48.8	49.3	49.7	50.0	50.2	50.4	50.6	50.9
Sudan	20.0	22.4	26.6	31.3	33.2	34.2	35.1	36.1	36.8	37.7
Swaziland	17.8	21.8	23.8	25.0	25.6	25.8	26.1	26.4	26.6	27.0
Syria	46.7	48.4	50.2	52.2	53.1	53.6	54.0	54.5	54.9	55.3
Tanzania	14.8	17.6	20.8	26.9	29.3	30.5	31.7	32.1	33.1	34.1
Togo	22.9	26.5	28.5	30.7	31.7	32.3	32.8	33.3	33.7	34.3
Tunisia	51.5	53.8	57.9	61.9	63.3	64.1	64.8	65.5	66.0	66.6
Uganda	8.8	9.9	11.2	12.5	13.2	13.5	13.9	14.2	14.5	14.8
United Arab Emirates	71.5	76.9	80.9	83.8	84.6	85.1	85.5	85.6	85.9	86.2
Yemen	20.2	24.4	28.9	33.5	35.3	36.2	37.1	38.0	36.1	34.0
Zambia	39.8	40.9	42.0	43.0	43.6	43.9	44.2	44.5	43.9	43.2
Zimbabwe	22.3	25.2	28.5	31.8	33.2	33.9	34.6	35.3	35.9	36.5

Source: *National statistical offices/UN/Euromonitor*

Table 21.14

▣ Rural Population

Rural Population 1980-2002

● % of total population

	1980	1985	1990	1995	1997	1998	1999	2000	2001	2002
North America										
Canada	24.3	23.6	23.4	23.3	23.1	23.1	23.0	22.9	22.8	22.7
USA	26.3	25.5	24.8	23.9	23.5	23.2	23.0	22.9	22.7	22.5
Latin America										
Anguilla			100.0	89.0	88.6	88.4	88.2	88.0	87.7	87.5
Antigua			64.6	64.2	63.8	63.6	63.4	63.2	62.9	62.7
Argentina	17.1	15.2	13.5	11.6	11.0	10.7	10.4	10.7	10.4	10.1
Aruba										
Bahamas	24.9	20.3	16.4	13.5	12.7	12.3	11.9	11.5	11.3	11.0
Barbados	59.8	57.5	55.2	52.7	51.6	51.1	50.5	50.0	49.6	49.0
Belize	50.6	51.6	52.5	49.6	48.1	47.3	46.6	45.9	45.3	44.6
Bermuda										
Bolivia	54.5	49.5	44.4	40.5	39.3	38.7	38.1	37.4	37.2	37.0
Brazil	33.8	29.3	25.3	21.6	20.4	19.9	19.3	19.1	18.7	18.2
British Virgin Islands				44.0	42.0	40.9	39.9	38.9	38.2	37.5
Cayman Islands										
Chile	18.8	17.4	16.7	15.6	15.1	14.8	14.6	15.4	15.0	14.7
Colombia	36.1	33.0	30.5	28.2	27.4	26.9	26.5	25.4	25.2	25.0
Costa Rica	56.9	55.3	54.2	53.2	52.8	52.6	52.4	52.2	52.0	51.7
Cuba	31.9	28.9	26.3	25.4	25.1	25.0	24.8	24.7	24.6	24.4
Dominica			32.3	30.7	30.0	29.7	29.3	29.0	28.7	28.4
Dominican Republic	49.5	45.4	41.7	38.2	36.9	36.3	35.6	35.0	34.5	34.0
Ecuador	53.0	48.8	44.9	39.7	37.7	36.7	35.7	34.7	34.0	33.2
El Salvador	58.4	57.3	56.1	55.0	54.4	54.0	53.7	53.4	53.1	52.7
French Guiana	29.2	27.3	25.4	23.6	22.9	22.6	22.2	21.9	21.6	21.4
Grenada	67.1	66.7	65.8	64.2	63.4	62.9	62.5	62.1	61.7	61.2
Guadeloupe	11.5	4.8	1.5	0.6	0.5	0.4	0.4	0.3	0.3	0.3
Guatemala	62.6	62.2	61.9	61.4	61.0	60.7	60.5	60.3	60.1	59.8
Guyana	69.5	68.4	66.8	64.6	63.5	62.9	62.4	61.8	61.8	61.7
Haiti	76.3	73.7	70.5	67.4	66.2	65.5	64.9	64.3	63.8	63.2
Honduras	65.1	62.3	58.2	52.5	50.4	49.4	48.3	47.4	46.7	45.8
Jamaica	53.2	50.8	48.5	46.3	45.3	44.9	44.4	43.9	43.5	43.1
Martinique	20.4	14.0	9.5	6.7	6.1	5.7	5.4	5.1	5.0	4.8
Mexico	33.7	30.4	27.5	26.6	26.2	26.0	25.8	25.6	25.4	25.2
Netherlands Antilles	32.1	32.1	31.6	30.8	30.3	30.1	29.8	29.6	29.3	29.1
Nicaragua	49.7	48.3	46.9	45.5	44.9	44.5	44.2	44.0	43.7	43.3
Panama	49.6	47.9	46.3	45.0	44.5	44.2	44.0	43.7	43.5	43.2
Paraguay	58.3	55.0	51.3	47.6	46.2	45.4	44.7	44.0	43.5	42.9
Peru	35.4	33.1	31.1	29.1	28.3	28.0	27.6	27.4	27.1	26.7
Puerto Rico	33.1	30.8	28.7	26.7	25.9	25.6	25.2	24.8	24.5	24.2
St Kitts	64.1	64.8	65.4	66.0	66.0	65.9	65.9	65.9	65.8	65.6
St Lucia	62.7	62.7	62.8	62.8	62.6	62.4	62.3	62.2	62.0	61.8
St Vincent and the Grenadines	72.8	66.4	59.4	51.9	49.2	47.9	46.5	45.2	44.3	43.3
Suriname	45.0	39.7	34.5	29.7	28.1	27.4	26.6	25.8	25.3	24.7
Trinidad and Tobago	36.9	33.8	30.9	28.3	27.3	26.9	26.4	26.1	25.8	25.4
Uruguay	14.8	12.8	11.3	10.0	9.5	9.2	9.0	8.7	8.5	8.4
Venezuela	20.6	18.1	16.0	14.5	13.9	13.7	13.4	12.7	12.6	12.4

Source: *National statistical offices/UN/Euromonitor*

▣ Rural Population
Rural Population 1980-2002

● % of total population

	1980	1985	1990	1995	1997	1998	1999	2000	2001	2002
Asia Pacific										
Afghanistan	84.4	83.1	81.8	80.1	79.3	78.9	78.5	78.1	77.7	77.3
American Samoa	55.8	53.9	51.9	49.7	48.7	48.3	47.8	47.3	46.9	46.4
Armenia			32.5	31.4	30.8	30.6	30.3	30.0	29.8	29.5
Azerbaijan			45.6	44.3	43.7	43.3	43.0	42.9	42.6	42.2
Bangladesh	85.6	83.0	80.7	78.2	77.1	76.6	76.0	75.5	75.1	74.5
Bhutan	96.1	95.6	94.8	94.0	93.6	93.3	93.1	92.9	92.7	92.5
Brunei	40.1	37.7	34.2	30.8	29.6	29.0	28.4	27.8	27.4	26.9
Cambodia	87.6	87.4	87.4	85.8	85.1	84.8	84.4	84.2	83.9	83.5
China	80.4	77.0	72.6	70.3	69.3	68.9	68.4	67.9	67.5	67.0
Fiji	62.2	61.5	58.4	54.5	52.9	52.2	51.4	50.8	50.2	49.4
French Polynesia	42.9	42.7	43.9	45.6	46.3	46.6	47.0	47.1	47.1	47.2
Guam	60.5	61.2	61.8	61.7	61.3	61.2	61.0	60.8	60.5	60.2
Hong Kong, China	8.5	7.1	0.1	0.0	0.0	0.0	0.0	0.0	0.0	0.0
India	76.9	75.7	74.5	73.2	72.6	72.2	71.9	71.6	71.3	70.9
Indonesia	77.8	73.9	69.4	64.4	62.3	61.2	60.2	59.8	58.9	57.8
Japan	23.8	23.3	22.6	21.9	21.6	21.5	21.3	21.1	21.0	20.8
Kazakhstan			43.0	43.6	43.5	43.5	43.4	43.4	43.3	43.2
Kiribati	68.3	66.5	65.4	63.2	62.2	61.8	61.3	60.9	60.5	60.0
Kyrgyzstan			62.6	65.1	65.7	66.1	66.4	66.7	66.7	66.7
Laos	86.6	84.4	81.9	79.3	78.2	77.6	77.1	76.5	76.0	75.4
Macau	1.9	1.5	1.3	1.2	1.2	1.2	1.2	1.2	1.2	1.2
Malaysia	58.0	54.1	50.2	46.3	44.8	44.1	43.3	43.2	42.6	41.8
Maldives	77.7	74.5	74.1	74.3	74.1	74.1	74.0	73.0	73.0	72.9
Mongolia	47.9	45.0	42.0	39.2	38.1	37.6	37.0	36.5	36.1	35.6
Myanmar	76.0	76.0	75.4	74.2	73.4	73.1	72.7	72.3	71.9	71.5
Nauru										
Nepal	93.5	92.2	91.1	89.7	89.1	88.7	88.4	88.1	87.8	87.5
New Caledonia	43.7	41.2	38.4	30.2	27.4	25.9	24.5	23.2	22.4	21.4
North Korea	43.1	42.4	41.6	40.9	40.5	40.2	40.0	39.9	39.7	39.4
Pakistan	71.9	70.2	68.1	65.7	64.6	64.1	63.5	63.0	62.5	61.9
Papua New Guinea	87.0	86.0	85.0	84.0	83.4	83.2	82.9	82.6	82.3	82.0
Philippines	62.5	57.0	51.2	46.0	44.2	43.2	42.3	41.8	41.1	40.4
Singapore										
Solomon Islands	89.5	87.6	85.4	83.0	81.9	81.4	80.8	80.3	79.9	79.3
South Korea	43.1	35.1	26.2	21.8	20.3	19.6	18.8	18.1	17.7	17.2
Sri Lanka	78.4	78.9	78.7	77.9	77.3	77.0	76.7	76.4	76.0	75.7
Taiwan		100.0	32.2	30.9	30.7	30.8	30.7	22.5	22.3	22.1
Tajikistan			68.3	72.5	72.7	72.6	72.3	72.5	72.4	72.4
Thailand	83.0	82.1	81.3	80.0	79.4	79.0	78.7	78.4	78.1	77.7
Tonga	73.0	70.1	67.4	64.8	63.7	63.1	62.6	61.8	61.3	60.9
Turkmenistan			54.9	55.5	55.4	55.3	55.3	55.2	55.0	54.9
Tuvalu				53.2	51.0	50.0	48.9	47.8	47.0	46.2
Uzbekistan			59.9	61.5	62.1	62.5	62.8	63.0	63.0	63.0
Vanuatu	82.1	82.0	81.8	81.1	80.7	80.4	80.2	80.0	79.7	79.4
Vietnam	80.8	80.4	80.3	80.6	80.5	80.4	80.4	80.3	80.2	80.0
Western Samoa	78.8	78.9	79.0	79.0	78.8	78.7	78.6	78.5	78.4	78.3
Australasia										
Australia	14.2	14.5	14.9	15.3	15.3	15.3	15.3	15.3	15.3	15.3
New Zealand	16.7	16.3	15.3	14.7	14.5	14.4	14.3	13.1	13.2	13.3

Source: *National statistical offices/UN/Euromonitor*

Rural Population

Rural Population 1980-2002

• % of total population

	1980	1985	1990	1995	1997	1998	1999	2000	2001	2002
Africa and Middle East										
Algeria	56.5	52.0	47.6	43.4	41.9	41.2	40.4	40.7	40.0	39.3
Angola	79.1	75.8	72.4	69.0	67.7	67.1	66.4	66.0	65.4	64.8
Bahrain	19.5	15.8	12.4	9.7	8.9	8.6	8.2	7.8	7.6	7.4
Benin	72.7	69.2	65.5	61.6	60.0	59.3	58.5	57.7	57.1	56.4
Botswana	84.9	74.8	58.5	52.3	51.3	50.7	50.2	49.8	49.4	48.9
Burkina Faso	91.5	88.6	86.4	84.1	83.1	82.5	82.0	81.5	81.1	80.5
Burundi	95.7	94.8	93.7	92.5	91.9	91.6	91.3	91.0	90.7	90.5
Cameroon	68.6	64.3	59.7	55.3	53.6	52.8	51.9	51.1	50.5	49.8
Cape Verde	76.5	67.0	55.8	45.8	42.6	41.0	39.4	37.8	36.9	35.9
Central African Republic	64.9	63.7	62.5	60.9	60.1	59.6	59.2	58.8	58.4	58.0
Chad	81.2	80.1	78.9	77.8	77.2	76.8	76.5	76.2	75.9	75.6
Comoros	76.8	74.5	72.1	69.6	68.5	67.9	67.4	66.8	66.3	65.8
Congo Dem Rep	71.3	72.1	72.1	71.3	70.7	70.3	70.0	69.7	69.3	68.9
Congo-Brazzaville	59.0	52.5	46.6	41.6	40.0	39.1	38.3	37.5	37.0	36.4
Côte d'Ivoire	65.3	62.5	59.7	56.7	55.5	54.8	54.2	53.7	53.2	52.6
Djibouti	26.4	22.5	19.8	17.9	17.4	17.2	16.9	16.7	16.5	16.3
Egypt	56.2	56.1	55.9	55.6	55.3	55.1	55.0	54.1	54.0	53.9
Equatorial Guinea	72.6	70.2	64.3	57.8	55.4	54.2	53.0	51.8	51.0	50.0
Eritrea				82.9	82.3	81.9	81.6	81.3	81.0	80.6
Ethiopia	89.5	88.3	86.6	84.6	83.7	83.3	82.8	82.4	82.0	81.5
Gabon	50.4	40.8	31.9	24.1	21.9	20.8	19.7	19.0	18.4	17.6
Gambia	80.4	77.5	74.3	71.0	69.6	68.9	68.2	67.5	67.0	66.3
Ghana	68.8	67.7	66.1	64.1	63.1	62.6	62.1	61.6	61.2	60.8
Guinea	80.9	77.7	74.3	70.8	69.4	68.6	67.9	67.2	66.6	66.0
Guinea-Bissau	83.1	81.6	80.0	78.3	77.5	77.1	76.7	76.3	75.9	75.5
Iran	50.4	46.6	43.7	41.0	40.0	39.4	38.9	38.4	38.0	37.6
Iraq	34.5	31.2	28.2	25.5	24.6	24.1	23.7	23.2	22.9	22.6
Israel	11.4	10.2	9.7	9.3	9.1	9.0	8.9	8.8	8.7	8.7
Jordan	40.1	35.9	32.0	28.6	27.5	26.9	26.4	26.2	25.8	25.3
Kenya	83.9	80.2	75.9	71.4	69.6	68.7	67.8	66.9	66.2	65.4
Kuwait	9.8	6.2	4.2	3.0	2.8	2.6	2.5	2.4	2.4	2.3
Lebanon	26.3	20.6	15.8	12.5	11.6	11.2	10.7	10.3	10.1	9.8
Lesotho	86.6	83.5	79.9	76.0	74.4	73.6	72.8	72.0	71.4	70.7
Liberia	65.0	60.7	58.0	58.0	56.8	56.3	55.7	55.0	54.6	54.0
Libya	30.7	23.3	18.2	14.7	13.8	13.3	12.9	12.4	12.2	11.9
Madagascar	81.7	79.2	76.5	73.5	72.3	71.6	71.0	70.4	69.9	69.3
Malawi	90.9	89.6	86.7	81.6	79.0	77.7	76.4	75.7	74.5	73.1
Mali	81.5	79.0	76.2	73.2	71.9	71.3	70.6	70.0	69.5	68.8
Mauritania	72.6	65.0	56.5	48.8	46.2	44.9	43.6	42.3	41.5	40.6
Mauritius	57.6	58.6	59.5	59.5	59.2	59.0	58.9	58.7	58.4	58.2
Morocco	58.9	55.4	51.8	47.9	46.3	45.5	44.7	44.9	44.2	43.3
Mozambique	86.9	80.6	73.4	66.2	63.6	62.4	61.1	59.8	59.0	58.1
Namibia	77.2	75.3	73.4	71.4	70.5	70.0	69.6	69.2	68.8	68.3
Niger	87.4	85.7	83.9	81.8	80.8	80.4	79.9	79.4	79.0	78.5
Nigeria	73.1	69.3	65.0	60.5	58.7	57.8	56.9	56.6	55.8	55.0
Oman	68.5	53.5	37.9	24.4	21.0	19.4	17.7	16.0	15.2	14.4
Qatar	14.4	12.1	10.1	8.6	8.2	7.9	7.7	7.5	7.4	7.2
Réunion	45.3	40.5	36.1	32.3	31.0	30.4	29.7	29.1	28.7	28.2
Rwanda	95.3	95.0	94.7	94.3	94.1	94.0	93.9	93.8	94.8	95.9
Sao Tomé e Príncipe	69.3	65.2	61.1	57.1	55.6	54.8	54.1	54.0	53.3	52.5
Saudi Arabia	34.1	27.4	21.5	17.2	16.0	15.5	14.9	14.7	14.3	13.9
Senegal	64.3	62.5	60.0	56.2	54.8	54.0	53.3	52.8	52.2	51.5
Seychelles	59.2	52.9	46.5	40.9	39.0	38.1	37.1	36.2	35.6	35.0
Sierra Leone	75.9	73.1	70.0	66.7	65.4	64.7	64.1	63.4	62.8	62.2
Somalia	77.8	76.8	75.8	74.4	73.6	73.3	72.9	72.5	72.1	71.7
South Africa	51.9	51.7	51.2	50.7	50.3	50.0	49.8	49.6	49.4	49.1
Sudan	80.0	77.6	73.4	68.7	66.8	65.8	64.9	63.9	63.2	62.3
Swaziland	82.2	78.2	76.2	75.0	74.4	74.2	73.9	73.6	73.4	73.0
Syria	53.3	51.6	49.8	47.8	46.9	46.4	46.0	45.5	45.1	44.7
Tanzania	85.2	82.4	79.2	73.1	70.7	69.5	68.3	67.9	66.9	65.9
Togo	77.1	73.5	71.5	69.3	68.3	67.7	67.2	66.7	66.3	65.7
Tunisia	48.5	46.2	42.1	38.1	36.7	35.9	35.2	34.5	34.0	33.4
Uganda	91.2	90.1	88.8	87.5	86.8	86.5	86.1	85.8	85.5	85.2
United Arab Emirates	28.5	23.1	19.1	16.2	15.4	14.9	14.5	14.4	14.1	13.8
Yemen	79.8	75.6	71.1	66.5	64.7	63.8	62.9	62.0	63.9	66.0
Zambia	60.2	59.1	58.0	57.0	56.4	56.1	55.8	55.5	56.1	56.8
Zimbabwe	77.7	74.8	71.5	68.2	66.8	66.1	65.4	64.7	64.1	63.5

Source: National statistical offices/UN/Euromonitor

Total Population: National Estimates at January 1st				Table 21.15	

Males and Females by Age at January 1st 2003

● '000

	Males			Females		
	0-14	15-64	65+	0-14	15-64	65+
North America						
Canada	2,952	10,863	1,715	2,802	10,726	2,262
USA	30,148	92,665	14,839	28,796	94,474	20,630
Latin America						
Anguilla						
Antigua						
Argentina	5,276	11,923	1,526	5,108	12,130	2,210
Aruba						
Bahamas						
Barbados						
Belize						
Bermuda						
Bolivia	1,747	2,474	162	1,682	2,534	201
Brazil	24,027	58,102	4,178	23,224	59,881	5,482
British Virgin Islands						
Cayman Islands						
Chile	2,201	5,079	486	2,124	5,113	679
Colombia	6,468	12,837	884	6,220	13,202	1,085
Costa Rica	651	1,264	98	622	1,232	115
Cuba	1,161	3,951	541	1,104	3,929	606
Dominica						
Dominican Republic	1,426	2,852	204	1,374	2,741	216
Ecuador	2,200	4,195	303	2,124	4,165	357
El Salvador	1,174	1,943	147	1,129	2,070	179
French Guiana						
Grenada						
Guadeloupe						
Guatemala	2,657	3,259	208	2,548	3,253	228
Guyana						
Haiti	1,672	2,303	145	1,641	2,443	174
Honduras	1,423	1,947	115	1,371	1,925	134
Jamaica						
Martinique						
Mexico	16,736	31,996	2,332	16,058	33,329	2,850
Netherlands Antilles						
Nicaragua	1,008	1,412	74	973	1,437	89
Panama	456	955	82	436	944	89
Paraguay	1,146	1,717	88	1,105	1,674	120
Peru	4,360	8,372	630	4,218	8,621	749
Puerto Rico						
St Kitts						
St Lucia						
St Vincent and the Grenadines						
Suriname						
Trinidad and Tobago						
Uruguay	402	1,045	172	384	1,070	248
Venezuela	4,249	8,061	539	4,073	7,976	655

Source: National statistical offices/Eurostat/UN/Euromonitor

Males and Females by Age at January 1st 2003

• '000

	Males 0-14	Males 15-64	Males 65+	Females 0-14	Females 15-64	Females 65+
Asia Pacific						
Afghanistan	5,654	6,440	350	5,352	6,087	371
American Samoa						
Armenia	424	1,273	164	405	1,327	227
Azerbaijan	1,352	2,504	180	1,284	2,617	296
Bangladesh	22,826	43,592	2,275	21,573	41,561	2,260
Bhutan	487	617	44	468	606	50
Brunei	55	119	6	52	107	6
Cambodia	2,354	3,262	128	2,281	3,524	246
China	153,365	464,529	43,629	142,033	450,425	52,086
Fiji	129	277	20	123	267	23
French Polynesia	40	80	6	38	76	6
Guam	30	58	5	28	50	5
Hong Kong, China	582	2,765	392	539	2,704	436
India	176,501	347,410	25,890	166,545	313,837	25,225
Indonesia	32,886	71,860	4,957	31,826	72,512	5,893
Japan	9,275	42,998	9,877	8,839	42,681	13,434
Kazakhstan	2,122	5,204	472	2,032	5,354	836
Kiribati						
Kyrgyzstan	797	1,410	114	783	1,445	185
Laos	1,264	1,558	93	1,219	1,544	106
Macau	53	176	14	50	183	19
Malaysia	4,048	7,481	501	3,833	7,305	575
Maldives	65	86	6	61	82	5
Mongolia	443	888	49	422	884	62
Myanmar	6,328	15,930	1,095	6,159	16,097	1,291
Nauru						
Nepal	5,193	7,192	459	4,862	7,146	461
New Caledonia	35	75	6	33	71	7
North Korea	3,537	8,508	521	3,379	8,194	893
Pakistan	34,724	49,013	2,731	33,200	45,345	2,837
Papua New Guinea	995	1,546	73	934	1,441	87
Philippines	14,378	24,940	1,612	13,756	24,783	1,876
Singapore	375	1,211	117	351	1,208	144
Solomon Islands	103	135	7	98	127	8
South Korea	5,622	17,408	1,577	4,928	16,838	2,374
Sri Lanka	2,465	6,392	631	2,352	6,665	717
Taiwan	2,367	8,166	1,065	2,174	7,971	1,024
Tajikistan	1,241	1,819	129	1,207	1,830	173
Thailand	7,371	22,145	1,757	7,115	22,089	2,298
Tonga						
Turkmenistan	844	1,399	87	821	1,425	127
Tuvalu						
Uzbekistan	4,546	7,460	505	4,393	7,545	716
Vanuatu	41	56	3	39	58	3
Vietnam	13,160	26,536	1,793	12,479	27,147	2,723
Western Samoa	36	57	4	34	51	5
Australasia						
Australia	2,017	6,706	1,092	1,914	6,606	1,366
New Zealand	452	1,279	209	427	1,309	263

Source: National statistical offices/Eurostat/UN/Euromonitor

◙ Total Population: National Estimates at January 1st

Males and Females by Age at January 1st 2003

● '000

	Males			Females		
	0-14	15-64	65+	0-14	15-64	65+
Africa and Middle East						
Algeria	5,159	10,075	831	4,690	9,557	785
Angola						
Bahrain						
Benin						
Botswana						
Burkina Faso						
Burundi						
Cameroon						
Cape Verde						
Central African Republic						
Chad						
Comoros						
Congo Dem Rep						
Congo-Brazzaville						
Côte d'Ivoire						
Djibouti						
Egypt	11,694	20,547	1,228	10,956	19,979	1,087
Equatorial Guinea						
Eritrea						
Ethiopia						
Gabon						
Gambia						
Ghana						
Guinea						
Guinea-Bissau						
Iran	11,885	22,337	1,604	11,284	21,875	1,591
Iraq						
Israel	963	2,027	285	913	2,035	385
Jordan	1,055	1,749	68	1,006	1,550	70
Kenya						
Kuwait	262	1,165	25	287	687	19
Lebanon						
Lesotho						
Liberia						
Libya						
Madagascar						
Malawi						
Mali						
Mauritania						
Mauritius						
Morocco	4,605	9,450	736	4,413	9,715	794
Mozambique						
Namibia						
Niger						
Nigeria	27,826	34,440	2,052	26,972	35,123	1,717
Oman						
Qatar						
Réunion						
Rwanda						
Sao Tomé e Príncipe						
Saudi Arabia	4,904	8,088	500	4,532	5,554	298
Senegal						
Seychelles						
Sierra Leone						
Somalia						
South Africa	7,759	13,372	894	7,396	14,427	1,443
Sudan						
Swaziland						
Syria						
Tanzania						
Togo						
Tunisia	1,392	3,212	347	1,307	3,246	323
Uganda						
United Arab Emirates	471	1,836	20	422	681	19
Yemen						
Zambia						
Zimbabwe						

Source: National statistical offices/Eurostat/UN/Euromonitor

Population Projections by Age and Sex 2013: National and UN Estimates

● '000/% of total

	Total	Male	Female	% 0-14	% 15-64	% 65+
North America						
Canada	33,180	16,503	16,677	15.2	70.1	14.7
USA	306,007	149,691	156,316	19.8	66.3	13.9
Latin America						
Anguilla						
Antigua						
Argentina	42,505	20,866	21,639	25.1	64.5	10.4
Aruba						
Bahamas						
Barbados						
Belize						
Bermuda						
Bolivia	10,723	5,357	5,365	34.8	60.5	4.6
Brazil	195,903	96,295	99,608	24.5	68.6	6.9
British Virgin Islands						
Cayman Islands						
Chile	17,462	8,650	8,811	24.2	66.6	9.1
Colombia	46,458	23,030	23,428	27.1	66.8	6.1
Costa Rica						
Cuba						
Dominica						
Dominican Republic						
Ecuador	15,529	7,783	7,746	27.9	66.2	5.9
El Salvador						
French Guiana						
Grenada						
Guadeloupe						
Guatemala						
Guyana						
Haiti						
Honduras						
Jamaica						
Martinique						
Mexico	116,720	57,500	59,221	27.1	66.5	6.4
Netherlands Antilles						
Nicaragua						
Panama						
Paraguay						
Peru	31,092	15,409	15,683	27.4	66.4	6.2
Puerto Rico						
St Kitts						
St Lucia						
St Vincent and the Grenadines						
Suriname						
Trinidad and Tobago						
Uruguay						
Venezuela	30,026	15,066	14,961	28.3	65.6	6.1

Source: *National statistical offices/Eurostat/UN/Euromonitor*

■ Total Population: National Estimates at January 1st

Population Projections by Age and Sex 2013: National and UN Estimates

● '000/% of total

	Total	Male	Female	% 0-14	% 15-64	% 65+
Asia Pacific						
Afghanistan						
American Samoa						
Armenia						
Azerbaijan	8,833	4,329	4,504	28.9	65.4	5.6
Bangladesh						
Bhutan						
Brunei						
Cambodia						
China	1,371,737	689,072	682,664	16.8	73.9	9.3
Fiji						
French Polynesia						
Guam						
Hong Kong, China	8,869	4,498	4,371	10.5	77.0	12.5
India	1,206,652	632,039	574,613	29.1	65.0	6.0
Indonesia	249,144	124,406	124,738	26.4	67.6	6.0
Japan	125,541	61,468	64,073	13.6	63.3	23.1
Kazakhstan	15,243	7,437	7,806	24.7	67.5	7.8
Kiribati						
Kyrgyzstan						
Laos						
Macau						
Malaysia	28,502	14,433	14,069	29.4	64.5	6.1
Maldives						
Mongolia						
Myanmar						
Nauru						
Nepal						
New Caledonia						
North Korea						
Pakistan	211,336	108,548	102,789	36.4	59.8	3.8
Papua New Guinea						
Philippines	97,374	48,741	48,633	29.8	64.3	5.8
Singapore	3,892	1,937	1,954	17.5	73.0	9.4
Solomon Islands						
South Korea	53,424	27,142	26,282	21.6	67.4	11.0
Sri Lanka						
Taiwan	23,905	12,022	11,884	17.0	72.2	10.8
Tajikistan						
Thailand	65,513	32,515	32,998	17.6	73.7	8.7
Tonga						
Turkmenistan	5,391	2,676	2,714	29.2	66.5	4.3
Tuvalu						
Uzbekistan						
Vanuatu						
Vietnam	92,839	46,191	46,649	22.2	72.3	5.4
Western Samoa						
Australasia						
Australia	21,567	10,769	10,798	18.0	68.0	14.0
New Zealand	4,182	2,060	2,123	20.3	66.0	13.8

Source: National statistical offices/Eurostat/UN/Euromonitor

■ Total Population: National Estimates at January 1st

Population Projections by Age and Sex 2013: National and UN Estimates

● '000/% of total

	Total	Male	Female	% 0-14	% 15-64	% 65+
Africa and Middle East						
Algeria	34,735	18,263	16,472	25.0	68.5	6.5
Angola						
Bahrain						
Benin						
Botswana						
Burkina Faso						
Burundi						
Cameroon						
Cape Verde						
Central African Republic						
Chad						
Comoros						
Congo Dem Rep						
Congo-Brazzaville						
Côte d'Ivoire						
Djibouti						
Egypt	72,612	37,089	35,523	22.5	73.3	4.2
Equatorial Guinea						
Eritrea						
Ethiopia						
Gabon						
Gambia						
Ghana						
Guinea						
Guinea-Bissau						
Iran						
Iraq						
Israel	8,157	4,061	4,096	27.8	61.5	10.7
Jordan	7,008	3,651	3,358	34.6	63.1	2.3
Kenya						
Kuwait	3,306	1,979	1,327	19.3	77.2	3.4
Lebanon						
Lesotho						
Liberia						
Libya						
Madagascar						
Malawi						
Mali						
Mauritania						
Mauritius						
Morocco	33,253	16,588	16,665	23.4	70.7	5.8
Mozambique						
Namibia						
Niger						
Nigeria	165,010	82,995	82,014	41.6	54.8	3.7
Oman						
Qatar						
Réunion						
Rwanda						
Sao Tomé e Príncipe						
Saudi Arabia	33,604	20,633	12,971	36.0	59.1	4.9
Senegal						
Seychelles						
Sierra Leone						
Somalia						
South Africa	52,508	26,073	26,436	30.2	64.3	5.5
Sudan						
Swaziland						
Syria						
Tanzania						
Togo						
Tunisia	10,698	5,373	5,326	20.1	71.8	8.0
Uganda						
United Arab Emirates	4,998	3,381	1,616	24.3	74.1	1.7
Yemen						
Zambia						
Zimbabwe						

Source: *National statistical offices/Eurostat/UN/Euromonitor*

Possession of Household Durables

Possession of Household Durables 2002

● % of total households

	Air Cond-itioner	Bicycle	Black/White TV	Camera	CD Player	Colour TV	Dish-washer	Freezer
Algeria	49.7	19.1	31.3	6.5	8.3	71.7	3.3	2.5
Argentina	3.2	22.9	5.8	29.8	24.0	90.1	14.7	17.8
Australia	66.3	33.3	3.0	88.6	82.3	91.7	34.9	49.5
Azerbaijan	3.1	14.3	19.9	29.5	1.1	55.2	1.2	2.3
Bolivia	1.6	9.2	13.0	12.8	13.0	61.3	0.3	5.0
Brazil	1.8	11.8	8.9	15.9	15.2	86.6	6.1	7.4
Canada	36.0	57.2	8.2	91.7	76.1	98.7	53.0	58.9
Chile	3.1	13.6	33.1	17.8	11.2	60.9	2.2	16.4
China	0.3	89.8	39.7	17.2	2.0	45.5	1.3	0.5
Colombia	2.2	14.4	4.9	18.3	22.1	85.8	3.7	15.0
Ecuador	1.9	10.4	10.7	20.5	5.7	68.6	0.3	5.0
Egypt	1.9	9.2	61.8	3.6	3.9	48.4	0.3	2.9
Hong Kong, China	68.0	53.7	0.6	85.1	56.1	99.1	27.2	33.0
India	0.5	64.2	38.2	3.1	1.4	32.4	1.1	1.2
Indonesia	2.3	74.5	40.4	10.2	1.4	48.5	1.0	0.6
Israel	51.6	30.0	3.1	83.5	19.6	96.5	31.5	18.0
Japan	88.3	82.3	1.7	85.2	65.8	99.1	55.9	33.8
Jordan	56.6	15.2	5.2	10.8	11.5	92.2	6.5	17.3
Kazakhstan	2.6	43.8	22.7	22.1	1.3	58.5	1.2	2.9
Kuwait	81.5	40.8	1.6	18.2	19.5	89.4	10.3	21.5
Malaysia	45.4	84.9	5.6	85.3	16.7	90.2	2.0	3.6
Mexico	2.5	20.8	3.6	23.8	9.6	89.7	7.1	5.6
Morocco	7.8	16.7	29.7	16.6	8.6	45.3	0.2	1.3
New Zealand	78.3	44.3	7.5	91.0	86.4	97.4	39.4	55.1
Nigeria	14.5	28.1	17.4	3.5	4.3	50.0	2.8	3.0
Pakistan	11.4	23.1	18.0	3.0	4.7	36.0	2.9	3.2
Peru	1.6	10.4	6.9	23.0	31.7	47.6	0.5	5.1
Philippines	4.1	79.0	27.0	61.2	3.6	65.2	0.6	1.4
Saudi Arabia	84.9	20.8	1.3	30.4	31.5	99.1	21.1	25.8
Singapore	55.9	83.3	1.5	84.8	56.4	98.6	30.4	21.9
South Africa	17.4	14.8	4.7	10.7	6.8	64.4	16.6	21.8
South Korea	51.7	76.7	4.2	85.6	20.4	93.1	2.7	3.2
Taiwan	72.8	68.5	2.0	85.9	69.1	99.4	4.3	15.3
Thailand	24.5	81.9	25.1	73.2	5.1	82.3	1.0	2.1
Tunisia	21.0	25.5	3.3	9.6	7.8	89.9	7.9	3.2
Turkmenistan	0.7	31.4	29.7	11.2	1.4	69.6	0.2	0.4
United Arab Emirates	83.8	40.2	3.9	14.0	28.0	96.1	18.1	19.6
USA	75.9	42.1	0.9	95.9	56.8	99.5	56.4	35.7
Venezuela	3.2	15.2	6.2	20.1	9.5	92.8	3.0	20.5
Vietnam	0.2	83.9	40.9	3.3	1.2	38.6	0.7	0.1

Source: *National statistical offices/Euromonitor*

Possession of Household Durables 2002

% of total households	Hi-fi Stereo	Microwave Oven	Motor-cycle	Passenger Car	Personal Computer	Piano	Refrig-erator	Sewing Machine
Algeria	27.1	4.5	11.1	26.7	5.3	0.3	77.7	2.9
Argentina	52.2	13.7	14.7	57.4	24.6	1.2	83.3	33.3
Australia	66.4	77.0	15.1	81.3	41.5	7.2	81.5	45.2
Azerbaijan	10.1	2.4	5.1	20.6	2.7	2.1	55.8	51.7
Bolivia	25.5	1.6	6.2	13.7	2.4	0.3	54.8	15.2
Brazil	31.2	5.2	6.9	44.6	25.9	1.3	82.8	22.9
Canada	71.1	90.5	6.0	85.9	56.3	6.9	99.0	45.3
Chile	29.9	8.8	2.2	45.2	20.6	1.5	62.9	41.2
China	6.1	0.4	8.2	2.9	15.4	1.2	6.3	51.5
Colombia	37.9	8.5	4.6	33.8	12.3	0.8	67.0	32.1
Ecuador	21.0	0.7	1.8	13.2	17.6	0.6	59.4	25.7
Egypt	25.5	2.3	7.2	10.8	2.7	0.2	70.4	4.7
Hong Kong, China	56.3	79.1	31.3	74.1	26.9	12.5	96.2	51.2
India	12.4	0.4	4.3	0.6	0.9	0.7	13.3	10.7
Indonesia	20.8	0.7	8.2	3.9	0.8	1.0	25.7	37.7
Israel	54.4	79.6	6.3	84.3	38.0	11.3	99.7	41.0
Japan	57.2	90.7	17.3	81.5	42.2	21.8	97.4	62.9
Jordan	20.2	5.0	19.9	28.6	11.4	2.4	68.2	8.6
Kazakhstan	10.3	2.2	12.1	29.3	3.9	1.1	80.1	54.1
Kuwait	54.3	20.3	4.6	99.3	64.4	1.0	94.4	7.5
Malaysia	58.6	64.6	51.5	63.9	25.1	16.3	97.1	36.9
Mexico	43.4	21.5	1.6	22.5	8.0	3.0	67.8	37.4
Morocco	6.9	0.3	12.5	10.1	2.1	1.4	44.0	10.6
New Zealand	71.8	81.5	4.5	82.5	49.8	7.2	83.0	39.1
Nigeria	16.6	0.8	15.1	0.4	12.5	0.2	41.2	3.4
Pakistan	8.8	1.9	13.7	5.5	2.0	0.7	16.8	20.8
Peru	33.1	0.9	3.0	17.9	5.8	1.3	45.9	28.3
Philippines	31.3	0.5	31.4	7.7	2.6	1.2	41.0	45.5
Saudi Arabia	56.7	23.6	14.6	99.1	26.6	1.9	98.3	4.5
Singapore	56.6	52.8	7.5	41.2	59.8	9.5	99.2	49.8
South Africa	21.4	6.4	8.4	8.9	7.8	6.0	79.2	23.8
South Korea	58.1	46.1	47.3	43.9	29.4	18.8	97.3	39.8
Taiwan	61.5	44.4	82.2	51.3	36.0	12.0	99.5	17.1
Thailand	44.9	3.0	18.3	35.8	8.3	1.6	69.3	34.7
Tunisia	25.2	3.0	22.1	18.6	12.5	1.5	68.5	4.0
Turkmenistan	12.1	0.2	11.2	29.3	2.2	2.3	52.8	30.7
United Arab Emirates	57.1	19.8	10.6	96.3	45.5	1.9	95.2	2.1
USA	74.2	85.0	4.5	92.9	70.3	7.2	99.6	38.1
Venezuela	45.8	12.1	8.8	47.4	11.2	1.4	81.7	31.3
Vietnam	6.1	0.5	8.5	1.7	0.6	0.7	18.1	17.7

Source: *National statistical offices/Euromonitor*

□ Possession of Household Durables

Possession of Household Durables 2002

- % of total households

	Shower	Telephone	Tumble Drier	Vacuum Cleaner	Video Camera	Videotape Recorder	Washing Machine
Algeria	76.0	31.8	2.9	4.0	4.2	8.3	6.8
Argentina	92.3	66.3	7.1	53.0	6.5	35.9	49.1
Australia	99.1	80.5	55.2	98.7	20.3	80.9	91.4
Azerbaijan	64.6	40.5	0.6	26.0	0.2	7.1	2.5
Bolivia	53.1	12.4	3.2	13.6	2.7	11.7	17.4
Brazil	74.7	39.9	2.0	34.4	3.3	18.1	24.2
Canada	99.1	88.8	83.1	98.1	23.2	90.3	84.2
Chile	87.8	78.5	7.3	50.4	5.2	30.9	46.4
China	41.7	24.6	1.5	1.7	0.2	0.9	2.4
Colombia	96.7	50.3	3.8	48.0	4.8	25.7	38.4
Ecuador	56.3	18.5	3.1	12.0	4.2	26.8	23.3
Egypt	75.4	17.1	1.8	3.3	4.1	7.4	4.6
Hong Kong, China	97.7	96.4	27.0	75.2	30.4	72.8	96.3
India	41.3	15.1	1.1	0.1	0.1	2.2	4.7
Indonesia	45.6	11.7	1.5	1.3	0.2	2.2	5.1
Israel	96.8	89.7	35.5	68.9	9.3	71.1	93.9
Japan	99.9	86.8	35.5	99.4	38.1	77.5	99.0
Jordan	80.4	22.3	2.8	6.1	7.2	28.3	11.0
Kazakhstan	66.3	26.8	0.8	37.0	0.2	7.3	2.3
Kuwait	93.8	72.7	4.4	19.0	12.7	46.9	36.4
Malaysia	98.6	77.2	25.4	69.1	20.8	66.9	80.0
Mexico	67.0	30.7	4.9	10.6	1.7	37.5	40.3
Morocco	75.1	28.0	1.7	2.2	1.1	18.3	9.6
New Zealand	99.9	83.1	69.2	98.3	21.7	81.4	98.0
Nigeria	55.3	1.9	1.0	0.6	0.3	3.8	2.3
Pakistan	64.4	10.1	0.6	0.8	0.3	1.3	1.8
Peru	59.5	41.1	4.0	15.9	1.7	16.5	26.1
Philippines	82.8	10.8	1.6	1.4	0.1	24.0	8.0
Saudi Arabia	98.4	64.3	6.5	17.1	24.4	51.8	33.5
Singapore	99.6	96.6	26.8	77.9	11.9	80.9	93.8
South Africa	58.9	28.5	3.6	20.3	2.6	29.2	24.2
South Korea	95.2	98.2	33.8	60.0	22.7	68.1	68.0
Taiwan	98.2	98.2	23.2	50.3	7.1	58.0	94.2
Thailand	64.3	26.8	2.3	2.8	2.8	45.5	5.0
Tunisia	74.0	35.2	2.0	4.8	6.2	14.6	25.2
Turkmenistan	62.2	27.4	0.4	15.7	0.2	13.1	1.6
United Arab Emirates	99.1	99.1	7.2	9.7	12.3	51.6	35.0
USA	99.5	85.5	69.9	98.4	39.0	85.0	80.1
Venezuela	91.8	42.3	5.4	42.1	5.0	28.5	38.7
Vietnam	36.0	6.8	0.8	0.1	0.1	1.9	2.4

Source: *National statistical offices/Euromonitor*

Retailing

Table 23.1

◘ Retail Industry

Total Retail Sales 1997-2002

• US$ billion

	1997	1998	1999	2000	2001	2002
Argentina	57.0	59.3	58.0	57.5	55.0	17.9
Australia	87.3	78.3	84.9	80.9	75.6	85.6
Brazil	139.8	127.3	81.7	88.0	73.0	68.5
Canada	124.5	121.3	127.3	131.0	129.4	133.6
Chile	17.8	17.2	16.4	16.1	14.1	14.2
China	308.4	329.3	353.8	370.7	390.3	408.3
Colombia	24.4	22.2	18.7	17.5	16.2	16.2
Egypt	21.7	23.1	24.2	25.6	23.8	22.5
Hong Kong, China	29.3	24.0	22.8	23.2	24.6	24.6
India	191.8	191.0	206.1	221.8	238.0	268.2
Indonesia	66.9	21.8	31.5	33.5	31.2	43.0
Israel	21.5	21.6	21.5	23.2	23.8	23.6
Japan	986.6	905.1	1,032.8	1,084.5	951.0	912.6
Malaysia	17.6	10.0	11.0	11.9	12.4	13.2
Mexico	91.2	84.1	85.3	91.0	94.8	98.8
Morocco	14.0	15.0	15.8	15.9	15.4	16.9
New Zealand	13.6	11.5	12.1	11.0	10.8	12.9
Philippines	35.2	24.8	30.4	30.9	29.9	34.5
Saudi Arabia	30.9	32.0	33.3	35.0	35.8	36.4
Singapore	11.6	9.2	9.7	9.9	9.7	9.9
South Africa	28.5	25.1	24.4	23.2	19.2	17.7
South Korea	96.8	59.7	79.2	89.7	87.1	99.5
Taiwan	36.7	34.3	36.9	37.3	39.7	39.4
Thailand	30.7	16.1	23.0	26.7	27.0	30.2
USA	1,910.2	2,041.7	2,205.8	2,375.6	2,527.0	2,743.4
Venezuela	35.9	38.1	36.3	38.5	38.8	29.8
Vietnam	13.3	13.9	13.9	14.9	16.2	16.9

Source: Euromonitor from national sources

Table 23.2

◘ Retailers

Retail Sales by Type 2002

• US$ billion

	Food Retail Sales	Non-Food Retail Sales	Total Retail Sales
Argentina	9.7	8.2	17.9
Australia	38.0	47.6	85.6
Brazil	28.7	39.8	68.5
Canada	41.8	91.8	133.6
Chile	6.9	7.3	14.2
China	243.1	165.2	408.3
Colombia	10.2	6.0	16.2
Egypt	14.2	8.3	22.5
Hong Kong, China	6.5	18.1	24.6
India	168.0	100.2	268.2
Indonesia	26.3	16.7	43.0
Israel	8.4	15.3	23.6
Japan	416.0	496.7	912.6
Malaysia	3.4	9.8	13.2
Mexico	53.1	45.7	98.8
Morocco	10.4	6.5	16.9
New Zealand	5.2	7.7	12.9
Philippines	18.0	16.6	34.5
Saudi Arabia	6.3	30.1	36.4
Singapore	2.7	7.2	9.9
South Africa	9.7	8.1	17.7
South Korea	39.6	59.9	99.5
Taiwan	15.0	24.4	39.4
Thailand	10.9	19.4	30.2
USA	728.8	2,014.6	2,743.4
Venezuela	21.0	8.8	29.8
Vietnam	7.3	9.5	16.9

Source: Euromonitor from national sources

□ Retailers   **Table 23.3**

Number of Retailers by Type 2002

• No of Outlets	Food Retailers	Non-Food Retailers	Total Retailers
Argentina	197,869	98,119	295,988
Australia	36,864	56,321	93,185
Brazil	813,183	925,269	1,738,452
Canada	45,811	65,748	111,559
Chile	102,565	44,673	147,238
China	14,109,883	7,078,480	21,188,363
Colombia	238,341	100,089	338,431
Egypt	366,138	189,419	555,557
Hong Kong, China	18,345	40,415	58,760
India	3,891,621	7,966,423	11,858,044
Indonesia	161,687	77,308	238,995
Israel	19,866	33,348	53,214
Japan	470,201	731,703	1,201,904
Malaysia	130,306	24,374	154,679
Mexico	633,502	460,434	1,093,936
Morocco	234,006	34,824	268,830
New Zealand	5,934	21,993	27,927
Philippines	91,941	51,612	143,553
Saudi Arabia	48,173	55,435	103,608
Singapore	4,266	13,952	18,218
South Africa	55,241	38,025	93,266
South Korea	296,460	449,967	746,427
Taiwan	29,781	89,654	119,435
Thailand	293,232	77,955	371,188
USA	149,682	552,311	701,993
Venezuela	63,673	82,802	146,475
Vietnam	597,235	143,945	741,180

Source: Euromonitor from national sources

□ Retailers   **Table 23.4**

Retail Market Percentage Shares of Food Retailers by Type 2002

• % of total retail market	Super-markets	Hyper-markets	Co-ops	Dis-counters	Conven-ience stores	Inde-pendent grocers	Food specialists	Other food retailers
Argentina	25.2	11.5		1.5	4.7	19.1	12.7	25.3
Australia	66.3			0.2	4.0	9.8	19.7	
Brazil	58.1	21.0		7.8	1.6	7.5	2.8	1.2
Canada	81.9				8.2	3.8	6.1	
Chile	36.7	26.3			1.2	21.5	14.3	
China	36.5	2.2	6.9	3.0	3.9	17.3	17.5	12.7
Colombia	27.0	10.9			0.1	36.1	12.6	13.3
Egypt	6.2	1.1	2.2	4.3	0.3	38.9	47.1	
Hong Kong, China	49.8			0.5	13.3	2.9	30.2	3.4
India	0.2		0.1	0.1	0.1	71.2	12.0	16.4
Indonesia	5.7	0.7	27.1		0.2	0.5	0.1	65.8
Israel	19.4	15.3	27.7	3.4		24.3	9.9	
Japan	31.0	15.4	6.7	1.4	11.6	11.0	22.8	
Malaysia	30.7	15.4			2.7	31.8	3.6	15.9
Mexico	10.5	24.7		7.6	2.3	29.0	21.4	4.5
Morocco	8.1	2.1	2.7		5.3	24.5	47.1	10.2
New Zealand	79.2				5.3	5.9	9.6	
Philippines	16.6				1.9	4.9	4.8	71.7
Saudi Arabia	20.1	16.7	1.5	2.5	6.3	26.2	16.4	10.3
Singapore	47.6	4.9	4.9		16.3	14.9	8.9	2.4
South Africa	39.6	8.8		1.5	6.3	16.2	11.8	15.8
South Korea	18.5	34.8	7.4		3.6	13.0	19.0	3.7
Taiwan	14.7	31.2	1.7		24.2	3.7	3.6	20.9
Thailand	4.9	17.2	0.2		5.1	27.6	1.2	43.8
USA	50.7	18.9	11.2	12.7	4.3	1.0	1.2	
Venezuela	13.1	28.4	0.2		0.2	28.8	16.5	12.7
Vietnam	11.2		0.2	0.4		70.7	6.5	11.0

Source: Euromonitor from national sources

■ Retailers **Table 23.5**

Number of Food Retailers by Type 2002

● No of Outlets

	Super-markets	Hyper-markets	Co-ops	Dis-counters	Conven-ience stores	Inde-pendent grocers	Food specialists	Other food retailers
Argentina	1,014	59		518	5,389	105,168	72,970	12,751
Australia	2,265			30	2,355	4,295	27,918	
Brazil	69,812	7,377		32,518	5,040	243,808	327,775	126,853
Canada	4,854				7,159	11,505	22,294	
Chile	603	54			469	69,476	31,963	
China	838,762	206	10,697	678,797	670,843	7,717,715	4,082,050	110,813
Colombia	1,139	32			13	133,300	52,818	51,039
Egypt	494	5	239	66	373	305,390	59,571	
Hong Kong, China	1,241			229	714	2,004	13,945	212
India	425		1,533	264	2,961	2,608,478	771,207	506,755
Indonesia	1,298	10	136,035		1,035	8,720	4,092	10,497
Israel	736	80	321	108		7,178	11,444	
Japan	15,001	1,499	2,943	1,045	35,608	62,046	352,059	
Malaysia	795	42			767	127,132	635	935
Mexico	989	673		227	2,303	336,922	274,208	18,180
Morocco	100	7	202		6,890	162,686	33,993	30,129
New Zealand	926				789	1,769	2,450	
Philippines	4,380				966	2,114	29,806	54,675
Saudi Arabia	352	15	569	233	2,966	18,607	24,994	436
Singapore	193	4	293		377	2,328	969	102
South Africa	1,418	33		29	1,743	43,295	5,939	2,783
South Korea	2,437	230	24,119		3,655	102,003	144,644	19,372
Taiwan	982	125	165		7,466	12,227	7,274	1,543
Thailand	171	114	340		3,145	270,018	10,724	8,721
USA	43,735	3,146	10,999	27,150	32,571	9,653	22,430	
Venezuela	1,275	27	2		313	42,634	15,962	3,460
Vietnam	138		985	3		486,461	48,635	61,013

Source: Euromonitor from national sources

■ Retailers **Table 23.6**

Retail Market Percentage Shares of Food Specialists by Type 2002

● % of Food Specialists

	Bakers	Butchers	Fish-mongers	Green-grocers	Other Food Specialists
Argentina	9.0	36.9	1.2	14.3	38.6
Australia	9.2	13.0	4.5	14.6	58.7
Brazil	49.1	10.0	7.0	34.0	
Canada	23.2	22.3	7.8	14.7	31.9
Chile	23.8	18.5	3.8	17.0	37.0
China	5.6	57.8	20.5	12.3	3.8
Colombia	43.7	25.7	2.3	25.6	2.8
Egypt	31.4	46.7	8.5	10.0	3.3
Hong Kong, China	25.1	24.0	15.0	23.1	12.7
India	9.1	4.9	3.3	5.2	77.5
Indonesia	94.4			5.6	
Israel	20.5	26.4	2.2	26.9	24.0
Japan	18.7	6.0	8.2	8.3	58.8
Malaysia	54.8				45.2
Mexico	5.6	21.7	1.2	0.1	71.4
Morocco	29.6	24.0	6.3	37.0	3.0
New Zealand	16.1	17.9	4.6	17.9	43.4
Philippines	71.0				29.0
Saudi Arabia	25.4	28.8	17.5	22.1	6.2
Singapore					100.0
South Africa	19.0	67.7	9.3	4.0	
South Korea	2.0	36.1	19.8	19.8	22.3
Taiwan	90.5				9.5
Thailand	100.0				
USA	8.0	41.1	9.0	20.1	21.7
Venezuela	28.7	4.7	2.9	2.8	60.8
Vietnam	61.8	38.2			

Source: Euromonitor from national sources

Retail Market Number of Food Specialists by Type 2002

- No of Outlets

	Bakers	Butchers	Fish-mongers	Green-grocers	Other Food Specialists
Argentina	6,135	24,494	810	14,563	26,969
Australia	3,915	2,652	1,487	1,516	18,348
Brazil	161,591	36,414	25,615	104,155	
Canada	5,210	4,780	2,000	5,000	5,304
Chile	9,247	4,545	1,133	5,958	11,080
China	877,080	1,047,754	871,589	1,209,959	75,667
Colombia	24,297	11,707	1,497	13,733	1,584
Egypt	37,805	3,984	2,851	10,962	3,969
Hong Kong, China	1,124	3,041	1,994	3,995	3,790
India	93,137	34,358	17,340	54,766	571,607
Indonesia	3,506			586	
Israel	2,146	2,222	227	5,821	1,027
Japan	74,671	16,356	26,962	27,733	206,338
Malaysia	391				245
Mexico	32,950	71,292	5,081	5,212	159,674
Morocco	8,677	7,713	3,549	12,295	1,759
New Zealand	853	734	332	306	226
Philippines	28,756				1,050
Saudi Arabia	5,898	6,345	3,803	6,115	2,834
Singapore					969
South Africa	1,055	4,350	485	49	
South Korea	3,843	35,850	24,283	46,228	34,440
Taiwan	6,923				351
Thailand	10,724				
USA	2,808	8,029	1,581	3,311	6,700
Venezuela	5,694	671	524	758	8,316
Vietnam	21,944	26,690			

Source: Euromonitor from national sources

Retail Market Percentage Shares of Non-Food Retailers by Type 2002

- % of Total

	Book-sellers and Stationers	Chemists and Druggists	Clothing, Footwear, Leather-wear, Accessory Outlets	CTNs	Department Stores	DIY, Garden-ing and Hardware Outlets	Electrical, Electronic and Com-puter Outlets	Home Furniture and Funish-ing Outlets
Argentina	0.9	26.8	38.2		0.4	1.5	3.3	11.6
Australia	6.9	11.6	11.9	2.1	6.9	12.0	10.0	7.8
Brazil	4.0	5.3	13.4	0.4	17.2	10.7	29.8	4.9
Canada	1.7	9.9	12.0	0.9	12.5	9.2	3.8	10.0
Chile	3.8	15.4	13.4	3.3	31.1	14.6	6.7	5.8
China	3.5	12.2	8.7	1.4	24.9	12.5	15.2	3.3
Colombia	3.7	10.1	24.4	7.4	7.1	16.4	4.1	5.8
Egypt	19.0	13.1	21.5	0.5	6.0	2.5	5.2	6.0
Hong Kong, China	4.1	4.6	16.8		12.7	2.2	10.0	12.6
India	0.8	8.6	23.4	4.2	0.2	1.2	6.4	4.6
Indonesia	1.7	2.8	6.2		62.7	0.7	3.6	0.8
Israel	1.3	5.5	10.9		28.5	10.3	8.8	20.5
Japan	5.8	8.6	19.9	0.0	13.1	3.1	13.3	3.9
Malaysia	2.7	4.8	20.7	0.4	17.6	2.8	17.1	11.1
Mexico	8.2	9.4	19.2		18.4	8.8	5.1	3.1
Morocco	3.2	8.1	14.4	4.6	8.7	7.8	4.9	8.7
New Zealand	4.4	8.3	12.4	0.2	18.2	5.6	9.5	7.1
Philippines	4.4	9.8	12.4	2.1	17.3	5.8	20.8	11.3
Saudi Arabia	3.4	4.5	11.4	2.6	22.7	5.5	8.5	7.8
Singapore	4.6	2.1	13.1	0.0	13.2	2.2	8.8	21.3
South Africa	3.7	11.0	33.5		18.2	3.3	3.5	16.6
South Korea	4.7	4.9	18.6	5.9	21.7	4.9	20.4	11.0
Taiwan	1.6	4.5	36.7	0.0	17.9	3.0	6.3	8.2
Thailand	1.7	2.4	5.0	0.2	15.9	2.2	8.6	3.1
USA	1.0	9.2	8.5	1.1	12.0	6.2	10.0	5.8
Venezuela	3.5	10.8	23.5	0.9	7.8	5.9	8.6	1.0
Vietnam	8.6	0.9	18.6		0.2		21.7	12.6

Source: Euromonitor from national sources

■ Retailers

Retail Market Percentage Shares of Non-Food Retailers by Type 2002 (continued)

● % of Total

	Jewellers	Mail Order	Record/ Video Games Outlets	Sports Goods Outlets	Toy Shops	Variety Stores	Other Non-Food Specialists	Other Non-Food Retailers
Argentina	2.0		1.4	1.3	0.8		11.8	
Australia	2.1	3.2	1.9	2.1	0.8	12.9	7.7	
Brazil	2.1	0.0	2.5	5.1	0.5	2.0	1.4	0.6
Canada	1.5	1.4	1.3	1.4	2.2	7.3	5.5	19.5
Chile	0.1		2.0	1.3	1.2		1.4	
China	1.7	0.1	6.6	1.2	4.9		1.8	2.0
Colombia	2.0		1.9	0.3	0.4		6.9	9.4
Egypt	9.0	0.3	0.4	0.3	0.5	10.7	5.0	
Hong Kong, China	14.8		0.3	0.6	0.5		4.1	16.7
India	10.0		0.6	0.9	0.1		1.7	37.1
Indonesia	0.6		3.2	0.2	0.9	6.4		10.2
Israel	0.7		0.7	1.4	0.7	5.8	4.8	
Japan	1.7		1.3	2.6	2.7	1.3	22.6	
Malaysia	5.4	0.3	1.5	2.3	0.9		10.7	1.8
Mexico	1.6		0.8	0.8	0.5	1.7	2.7	19.6
Morocco	3.0		1.9	3.1	0.9	5.2	1.1	24.4
New Zealand	3.2	0.5	1.6	9.6	0.2		18.9	0.4
Philippines	4.0		0.9	1.1	1.0		5.6	3.5
Saudi Arabia	5.0		0.8	2.6	0.2	15.5	6.3	3.0
Singapore	10.8	0.0	1.6	2.0	0.6		12.4	7.1
South Africa	1.7		0.9	1.5	0.5		1.0	4.5
South Korea		0.0	0.6	2.0			3.2	2.1
Taiwan	3.9	0.6	1.2	0.2	0.5		12.9	2.3
Thailand	4.1	0.2	0.7	0.3	0.0		43.7	11.9
USA	1.5	9.9	1.7	1.6	2.7	22.2	6.0	0.7
Venezuela	5.9		3.6	0.8	0.3		27.5	
Vietnam	5.8		14.6	8.6	3.6	4.4	0.1	

Source: Euromonitor from national sources

■ Retailers   **Table 23.9**

Number of Non-Food Retailers by Type 2002

● No of Outlets

	Book-sellers and Stationers	Chemists and Druggists	Clothing, Footwear, Leather-wear, Accessory Outlets	CTNs	Department Stores	DIY, Garden-ing and Hardware Outlets	Electrical, Electronic and Com-puter Outlets	Home Furniture and Furnish-ing Outlets
Argentina	3,605	1,126	49,055		5	2,417	18,881	3,755
Australia	8,468	4,762	18,723	692	110	4,550	4,329	3,026
Brazil	47,759	30,996	202,316	194,328	44,667	45,899	51,522	42,339
Canada	1,069	6,047	10,026	4,533	395	2,303	17,261	1,539
Chile	3,035	1,321	17,293	7,612	200	1,789	1,645	1,835
China	880,418	938,130	1,550,896	68,158	10,990	916,718	525,458	115,194
Colombia	7,724	11,439	26,500	11,193	147	8,001	5,218	5,263
Egypt	8,876	22,033	89,632	15,770	434	6,451	4,366	5,216
Hong Kong, China	2,575	3,788	12,599		206	1,972	3,094	2,748
India	282,890	678,000	1,517,000	526,843	88	310,070	206,857	412,000
Indonesia	7,964	7,578	13,403		595	2,271	8,219	1,732
Israel	1,203	1,374	9,662		206	2,415	1,142	3,341
Japan	36,950	83,330	188,131	1,016	315	19,424	61,872	38,728
Malaysia	507	590	9,143	1,575	171	632	2,330	1,032
Mexico	38,911	8,745	119,373		620	28,406	10,425	14,220
Morocco	885	4,577	14,166	4,640	31	2,753	1,077	269
New Zealand	917	1,117	5,982	136	313	1,562	941	776
Philippines	1,193	5,652	5,006	5,967	2,311	2,932	1,764	2,722
Saudi Arabia	4,436	2,683	19,143	1,471	350	5,237	5,438	548
Singapore	926	177	3,101	50	41	497	851	1,792
South Africa	1,415	2,677	21,259		348	968	824	7,098
South Korea	49,984	39,813	135,634	39,119	160	35,842	43,181	47,998
Taiwan	304	2,311	21,587	110	65	81	1,681	3,307
Thailand	754	4,155	18,789	1,551	70	1,628	24,573	1,660
USA	12,680	47,445	116,339	37,964	13,472	28,894	30,320	28,201
Venezuela	2,582	3,807	12,903	7,034	455	4,005	3,597	483
Vietnam	3,264	15,410	21,258		4		10,415	10,764

Source: Euromonitor from national sources

Number of Non-Food Retailers by Type 2002 (continued)

- No of Outlets

	Jewellers	Mail Order	Record/ Video Games Outlets	Sports Goods Outlets	Toy Shops	Variety Stores	Other Non-food Specialists	Other Non-food Retailers
Argentina	1,835		705	6,587	3,960		6,187	
Australia	2,763	323	1,273	2,894	625	1,703	2,081	
Brazil	9,451		9,671	27,289	8,708	404	54,190	155,732
Canada	524	2,445	918	969	2,016	468	7,894	7,341
Chile	85		2,004	1,034	2,059		4,761	
China	22,044		868,470	143,432	346,921		113,144	578,506
Colombia	2,513		949	510	544		2,137	17,951
Egypt	5,876		693	482	869	3,497	25,222	
Hong Kong, China	2,203		240	563	678		3,252	6,496
India	632,462		58,399	77,912	35,280		733,714	2,494,907
Indonesia	2,313		3,830	386	2,468	26,499		50
Israel	2,343		2,621	3,734	2,020	335	2,951	
Japan	14,075		6,924	19,290	12,131	856	248,660	
Malaysia	508		588	322	242		6,725	9
Mexico	9,238		4,475	3,683	4,920	165	46,200	171,051
Morocco	1,356		562	522	172	73	3,133	608
New Zealand	993	92	698	917	189		6,873	488
Philippines	2,333		4,036	1,367	1,729		9,598	5,002
Saudi Arabia	717		1,062	569	331	1,277	11,735	437
Singapore	708	2	239	277	152		3,589	1,550
South Africa	1,243		400	903	290		103	498
South Korea		104	4,155	8,459			34,851	10,667
Taiwan	1,142		659	162	250		44,133	13,862
Thailand	1,518	92	6,970	468	224		8,465	7,039
USA	28,744	12,148	11,027	23,240	17,981	13,213	119,761	10,881
Venezuela	1,064		1,972	628	356		43,916	
Vietnam	11,036		20,979	5,261	21,444	3,078	21,032	

Source: Euromonitor from national sources

Travel and Tourism

▣ Length of Tourist Stay										Table 24.1

Average Tourist Stay in Accommodation Establishment 1991-2002

● Nights

	1991	1993	1995	1996	1997	1998	1999	2000	2001	2002
North America										
Canada	5.6	5.4	5.4	5.6	5.5	5.2	5.4	5.2	5.1	5.2
USA										
Latin America										
Anguilla										
Antigua										
Argentina	2.6	2.5	2.6	2.6	2.7	2.7	2.8	2.9	2.9	3.0
Aruba										
Bahamas	4.8	4.8	4.7					6.5	6.4	6.5
Barbados	7.0	7.3	6.9	7.2	6.6	6.6	7.6	7.3	7.4	7.4
Belize	6.0	6.0	5.0							
Bermuda	5.7	5.2			5.2	5.3	5.4	5.4	5.5	5.6
Bolivia	3.3	3.1	2.8	2.3	2.3	2.3	2.2	2.2	2.2	2.2
Brazil	2.6	2.1	2.1	2.1	2.2	2.2	2.2	2.2	2.2	2.2
British Virgin Islands			7.1	7.1	7.0	7.1	7.7	7.3	7.1	7.1
Cayman Islands			4.7	4.5	4.9	5.3	5.0	4.9	4.6	4.6
Chile	2.3	2.3	2.2	2.2	2.3	2.2	2.0	2.1	2.1	2.1
Colombia	3.6	2.5	2.6	2.6	2.6	2.7	2.7	2.7	2.7	2.7
Costa Rica	2.6									
Cuba	2.9	3.0	3.2	3.1	3.1	3.3	3.0	3.0	3.0	3.0
Dominica										
Dominican Republic										
Ecuador	2.0	2.0	2.1	2.2	2.2	2.3	2.3	2.3	2.4	2.4
El Salvador	2.9	2.5	2.2	2.3	2.5	3.0	4.0	4.0	4.0	4.0
French Guiana										
Grenada	6.5	7.2	7.4	7.5	7.4	7.4	7.3	7.2	7.1	7.0
Guadeloupe	5.5	6.3	6.1	6.0	5.7	6.1	5.8	5.2	5.3	5.3
Guatemala	4.0	3.9	4.0							
Guyana										
Haiti	9.4	7.4	9.6							
Honduras	3.2									
Jamaica	7.7	7.8	7.1	7.1	7.1	7.0	6.9	6.6	6.4	6.1
Martinique	8.1	9.3	10.0	8.0	9.4	8.8	8.5	8.4	8.2	7.9
Mexico	3.9	3.8	3.7	3.8	3.8	3.6	3.6	3.4	3.4	3.4
Netherlands Antilles										
Nicaragua	1.7	2.2	2.8	2.8	3.0	3.2	3.3	3.3	3.3	3.3
Panama	2.6	2.3	2.4	2.4	2.3	2.2	2.3	2.5	2.6	2.6
Paraguay		3.0	3.0	3.0	2.5	2.5	3.0	4.0	4.6	5.2
Peru	1.6	1.4	1.4	1.4	1.4	1.4	1.4	1.4	1.5	1.4
Puerto Rico	2.7	2.7	2.8	2.6	2.7	2.7	3.0	2.5	2.4	2.2
St Kitts										
St Lucia	10.8	10.6	9.0	8.7	8.8	8.7	8.7	9.6	9.7	9.7
St Vincent and the Grenadines	11.1									
Suriname										
Trinidad and Tobago										
Uruguay			8.2			7.1	7.6	4.4	3.9	4.0
Venezuela	2.3	3.1	4.0	4.2	10.0	10.0	7.0	7.0	7.0	7.0

Source: *Euromonitor from World Tourism Organisation*

Average Tourist Stay in Accommodation Establishment 1991-2002 (continued)

● Nights

	1991	1993	1995	1996	1997	1998	1999	2000	2001	2002
Asia Pacific										
Afghanistan										
American Samoa										
Armenia			6.0	6.5	6.5	6.5	6.8	6.7	6.3	6.7
Azerbaijan										
Bangladesh										
Bhutan								7.0	7.1	6.9
Brunei		2.5	3.0	2.6	2.1	1.8	2.9	1.9	1.8	1.8
Cambodia		2.4								
China	1.9	2.3	2.5	2.4	2.4	2.6	2.5	2.5	2.5	2.5
Fiji	8.6	8.6	8.6	8.3	8.2	8.5	8.4	8.5	8.4	8.5
French Polynesia	8.3	8.7	9.6	9.1	9.5	9.2	9.2	10.6	10.7	10.9
Guam	3.5	3.0	3.0							
Hong Kong, China										
India										
Indonesia	2.7	2.7	2.5	2.7	2.8	2.6	2.4	2.3	2.2	2.1
Japan										
Kazakhstan										
Kiribati		21.0	19.0	21.0	21.0	18.0	16.1	15.0	14.4	13.9
Kyrgyzstan										
Laos										
Macau	1.4	1.4	1.3	1.3	1.3	1.4	1.4	1.3	1.3	1.3
Malaysia	1.8	1.7	1.6	1.6	1.7	1.6	1.5	1.5	1.6	1.6
Maldives	8.8	8.7	8.4	9.0	8.9	8.8	8.7	8.4	8.2	8.1
Mongolia										
Myanmar	2.5	2.3	3.0	4.0	4.0	4.0	4.0	4.0	4.0	4.0
Nauru										
Nepal	2.6	2.3								
New Caledonia			5.3	4.6	4.7	4.5	4.4	4.4	4.4	4.4
North Korea										
Pakistan		1.3	1.2	1.1	1.0	1.2	1.2	1.2	1.2	1.1
Papua New Guinea	2.6									
Philippines		2.8	2.7	2.9	2.6	2.6	2.9	2.7	2.7	2.5
Singapore	3.0	2.8	3.1	2.8	2.8	2.9	2.7	2.7	2.7	2.7
Solomon Islands										
South Korea										
Sri Lanka										
Taiwan										
Tajikistan										
Thailand										
Tonga										
Turkmenistan										
Tuvalu										
Uzbekistan										
Vanuatu								6.9	6.8	6.7
Vietnam			2.6	2.4	2.2	2.2	2.4	2.4	2.4	2.5
Western Samoa										
Australasia										
Australia	7.9	7.5	7.2	2.1	2.0	2.2	2.2	2.3	2.2	2.3
New Zealand					1.7	1.8	1.8	1.8	1.8	1.8

Source: *Euromonitor from World Tourism Organisation*

◻ Length of Tourist Stay

Average Tourist Stay in Accommodation Establishment 1991-2002 (continued)

● Nights

	1991	1993	1995	1996	1997	1998	1999	2000	2001	2002
Africa and Middle East										
Algeria		3.3								
Angola		8.4								
Bahrain										
Benin		8.6								
Botswana						9.4	9.8	10.0	9.8	9.7
Burkina Faso										
Burundi	3.3	2.3	1.5	1.2	1.1	2.0	2.1	2.0	2.1	2.2
Cameroon										
Cape Verde							3.8	4.2	4.6	5.0
Central African Republic										
Chad	3.7	3.0	3.0	2.0	2.0	3.0	3.0	3.6	4.2	4.9
Comoros			7.0							
Congo Dem Rep			5.0				7.0	7.0	7.0	7.0
Congo-Brazzaville				3.0	3.7	2.7	4.1	3.7	3.3	3.0
Côte d'Ivoire	3.1		3.4		3.4	3.4	3.4	3.4	3.4	3.4
Djibouti										
Egypt							4.0	6.0	6.8	7.9
Equatorial Guinea										
Eritrea										
Ethiopia	4.4	3.1	4.4	5.3	2.4	4.5	3.8	2.1	2.0	1.8
Gabon										
Gambia										
Ghana										
Guinea										
Guinea-Bissau										
Iran			2.6	2.5	2.7	3.0	3.0	3.0	2.9	2.6
Iraq										
Israel		3.3	3.2	3.2	3.3	3.4	2.6	3.1	3.4	3.6
Jordan										
Kenya	13.7	13.9	12.5	14.2	11.8	9.8	9.4	8.7	8.4	7.6
Kuwait			3.3							
Lebanon										
Lesotho										
Liberia										
Libya										
Madagascar	4.0	4.0	5.1	4.0	4.0	4.0	4.0	4.0	4.0	4.0
Malawi										
Mali	2.1	2.1	2.4	2.0	2.0	2.0	3.0	2.0	1.8	1.8
Mauritania										
Mauritius										
Morocco		7.8	7.5	7.0	7.1	7.3	7.0	6.3	6.0	5.8
Mozambique										
Namibia					1.8	1.9	2.0	2.1	1.9	1.9
Niger	1.9	2.8	3.0	5.0	5.0	5.0	5.0	5.0	5.0	5.0
Nigeria										
Oman										
Qatar	1.8	2.1								
Réunion		5.8	6.4	6.3	6.7	7.2	7.1	6.7	6.5	6.4
Rwanda	4.3									
Sao Tomé e Príncipe										
Saudi Arabia										
Senegal	4.3	4.0	3.8	3.8	4.0	4.1	4.1	3.6	3.4	3.1
Seychelles										
Sierra Leone	8.0	7.0	7.0							
Somalia										
South Africa										
Sudan										
Swaziland	1.1	1.0	1.0	1.1	1.1	1.0	1.0	0.8	0.8	0.7
Syria		2.5	2.3	2.2	3.6	2.5	2.0	1.6	1.4	1.3
Tanzania		8.0	8.0	7.3	7.5	7.6	7.7	8.0	8.2	8.6
Togo	2.5	2.3	2.3	2.3	2.3	2.1	2.2	2.1	1.9	1.7
Tunisia		6.2	6.6	6.5	6.4	6.2	6.4	6.5	6.3	6.0
Uganda										
United Arab Emirates										
Yemen										
Zambia										
Zimbabwe										

Source: Euromonitor from World Tourism Organisation

Length of Tourist Stay

Table 24.2

Average Tourist Stay in the Country 1991-2002

● Nights

	1991	1993	1995	1996	1997	1998	1999	2000	2001	2002
North America										
Canada	5.6	5.4	5.4	5.6	5.5	5.2	5.4	5.2	5.1	5.2
USA										
Latin America										
Anguilla	10.3	9.7	9.5	9.4	9.5	9.2	8.5	8.6	8.7	9.2
Antigua										
Argentina	14.5	13.8	14.4	14.6	14.9	15.3	15.8	16.0	16.3	16.9
Aruba	7.5	7.2	7.2	7.4	7.5	8.5	9.3	8.6	8.5	8.5
Bahamas	5.9	5.8	5.7	5.8	6.0	5.4	5.4	6.2	6.4	6.7
Barbados	10.9	11.2	11.0	10.7	10.5	11.1	10.1	10.1	10.3	10.3
Belize	10.0	10.0	9.0	7.0	7.0	7.1	7.1	7.6	7.7	7.7
Bermuda	6.6	6.2	6.3	6.1	6.1	6.2	6.2	6.2	6.3	6.3
Bolivia	6.5	9.6	11.0	11.0	10.0	10.0	10.1	10.0	10.0	10.0
Brazil	16.1	13.1	13.1	13.2	12.9	13.0	14.0	12.1	11.8	11.2
British Virgin Islands	9.5	7.0	7.2	7.4	8.0	8.4	9.4	8.9	8.5	8.3
Cayman Islands	4.9	7.0	7.0	6.9	7.4	6.9	6.5	6.4	6.4	6.3
Chile	11.7	10.8	11.5	11.3	11.0	11.6	10.0	10.1	10.1	10.1
Colombia	14.0	3.0	3.0	3.0	2.6	2.7	3.0	3.1	3.0	3.0
Costa Rica	8.9	10.4	10.0	10.4	9.7	9.5	11.1	11.3	11.5	11.1
Cuba	8.9	9.6	8.7	11.7	11.3	11.3	10.0	10.5	10.4	10.4
Dominica	12.0	14.4	11.2							
Dominican Republic	10.5	10.2	10.6	10.6	10.4	10.0	11.1	11.1	11.0	11.0
Ecuador	10.5	10.3	11.2	11.5	11.5	11.7	11.8	11.8	12.0	12.0
El Salvador	4.3		2.2	2.3	2.5	3.0	4.0	4.0	4.0	4.0
French Guiana										
Grenada								7.2	7.1	7.0
Guadeloupe										
Guatemala	6.7	6.8	7.1	7.3	7.5	7.5	7.5	7.6	7.6	7.6
Guyana					19.0	19.0	19.0	19.0	19.0	19.0
Haiti										
Honduras		4.8		7.4	7.6	7.8	9.3	10.4	10.9	11.3
Jamaica	10.9	11.0	10.9	11.1	10.8	10.9	10.3	10.1	9.9	9.7
Martinique	13.5	14.1	14.6	13.0	12.9	14.4	13.0	13.2	13.1	12.8
Mexico	10.5	11.3	10.7	10.2	10.1	9.6	9.7	9.9	10.2	10.5
Netherlands Antilles										
Nicaragua										
Panama	9.7	9.7	9.8	8.2	9.4	10.6	10.0	9.7	9.9	10.2
Paraguay				3.3	3.3	4.0	3.5	6.0	6.4	6.9
Peru	13.4	15.9	16.6	9.5	9.5	10.2	10.4	10.5	10.8	10.6
Puerto Rico										
St Kitts	8.1	8.0	9.4	8.8	8.3	8.7	8.7	8.6	8.5	8.5
St Lucia										
St Vincent and the Grenadines		10.3	11.7	10.7	10.3	11.1	10.6	10.6	10.5	10.3
Suriname										
Trinidad and Tobago										
Uruguay										
Venezuela	11.0	15.0	19.0	18.0	18.0	18.0	13.0	14.0	14.1	13.9

Source: *Euromonitor from World Tourism Organisation*

◘ Length of Tourist Stay

Average Tourist Stay in the Country 1991-2002 (continued)

● Nights

	1991	1993	1995	1996	1997	1998	1999	2000	2001	2002
Asia Pacific										
Afghanistan										
American Samoa										
Armenia		5.6	6.0	6.5	6.5	6.5	6.8	6.7	6.4	6.7
Azerbaijan	3.0	4.0	5.0	5.0	5.0	5.0	5.0	4.9	4.8	4.8
Bangladesh	13.0	9.5	10.0	9.5	9.0	8.5	7.0	6.5	6.3	6.0
Bhutan								7.0	7.1	6.9
Brunei		2.5	3.6							
Cambodia			8.0	7.5	6.4	5.2	5.5	5.5	5.8	5.8
China	1.9	2.3	2.5	2.4	2.5	2.7	2.6	2.6	2.6	2.5
Fiji										
French Polynesia	10.3	10.6	12.0	11.6	12.0	11.7	11.8	12.1	12.2	12.4
Guam										
Hong Kong, China	3.4	3.8	3.9	3.7	3.6	3.4	3.4	3.0	2.9	2.8
India		27.9	29.5	29.8	30.8	31.2	31.9	32.1	32.5	32.8
Indonesia	11.8	10.7	10.2	10.5	10.6	9.2	10.5	12.3	12.6	13.1
Japan	12.3	10.2	9.4	8.4	8.6	8.8	8.0	8.0	8.2	8.7
Kazakhstan										
Kiribati	22.0									
Kyrgyzstan										
Laos		3.5	4.3	4.1	5.0	5.0	5.5	5.5	5.6	5.6
Macau										
Malaysia	4.6	4.7	4.8	5.4	5.3	5.5	6.0	5.8	5.6	5.4
Maldives	8.8	8.6	8.4	9.0						
Mongolia										
Myanmar	6.3	6.7	7.0	7.0	7.0	7.0	7.0	7.0	7.0	7.0
Nauru										
Nepal	9.3	11.9	11.3	13.5	10.5	10.8	12.3	11.9	11.2	10.7
New Caledonia			18.0	17.0	16.0	16.0	16.0	16.0	16.0	16.0
North Korea										
Pakistan		30.0	30.0	30.0	30.0	30.0	25.0	25.0	25.0	25.0
Papua New Guinea				11.0	10.0	9.4	8.0	10.2	10.1	9.8
Philippines	12.0	12.3	10.1	9.9	9.5	9.1	8.9	8.8	8.7	8.4
Singapore	3.3	3.0	3.7	3.3	3.3	3.4	3.2	3.2	3.1	3.1
Solomon Islands	13.0									
South Korea	5.2	5.3	5.3	5.7	5.5	4.9	4.7	4.9	5.0	5.3
Sri Lanka	11.4	10.6	10.0	9.8	10.1	10.4	10.3	10.1	10.0	9.9
Taiwan	7.3	8.0	7.4	7.4	7.4	7.7	7.7	7.4	7.4	7.3
Tajikistan										
Thailand	7.1	6.9	7.4	8.2	8.3	8.4	8.0	7.8	7.8	7.6
Tonga	16.0	20.2								
Turkmenistan										
Tuvalu	7.6									
Uzbekistan										
Vanuatu	9.2	9.1	9.1	9.1	8.8	8.2	7.2	7.6	7.3	7.1
Vietnam			4.7	4.5	4.5	5.6	5.6	6.0	6.0	6.0
Western Samoa					7.6	7.6	8.6	8.9	9.0	9.2
Australasia										
Australia	29.0	23.0	23.0	24.0	23.0	25.0	26.0	26.0	27.0	27.0
New Zealand	20.0	19.2	19.0	19.3	20.0	19.6	20.0	20.1	20.1	19.8

Source: *Euromonitor from World Tourism Organisation*

Length of Tourist Stay

Average Tourist Stay in the Country 1991-2002 (continued)

● Nights

	1991	1993	1995	1996	1997	1998	1999	2000	2001	2002
Africa and Middle East										
Algeria										
Angola		20.0								
Bahrain										
Benin	5.0	6.7								
Botswana	4.7	4.9								
Burkina Faso	2.4	2.3	2.3	2.3	2.3	3.6	3.8	3.8	3.6	3.4
Burundi										
Cameroon	2.2									
Cape Verde					7.0	7.0	7.0	7.0	7.0	7.0
Central African Republic										
Chad										
Comoros			7.0							
Congo Dem Rep	15.0									
Congo-Brazzaville										
Côte d'Ivoire			3.6		3.6	3.6	3.6	3.6	3.6	3.6
Djibouti										
Egypt		6.0	6.5	6.1	6.7	5.8	6.5	6.0	7.1	8.3
Equatorial Guinea										
Eritrea				14.0	19.0	22.0	24.0	17.0	15.5	16.2
Ethiopia										
Gabon										
Gambia	11.8	12.1	13.2	12.3	13.4	13.8	14.3	14.0	14.7	15.0
Ghana		10.2	10.2	10.4	10.4	10.4	10.9	11.0	10.8	10.6
Guinea								4.4	4.9	5.2
Guinea-Bissau										
Iran						5.0	5.0	5.0	5.0	5.0
Iraq	3.0									
Israel		17.6	16.1	15.6	15.4	16.2	15.0	15.0	14.9	14.8
Jordan		4.8	3.8	3.6	3.9	4.1	4.2	4.3	4.3	4.4
Kenya										
Kuwait										
Lebanon		3.2								
Lesotho	2.1	2.1								
Liberia										
Libya										
Madagascar	15.0	17.0	15.0	15.0	15.0	20.0	20.0	20.0	20.0	20.0
Malawi	9.2	7.0	8.0	8.0	9.0	8.0	8.0	7.0	7.0	6.0
Mali										
Mauritania								5.3	5.7	6.3
Mauritius	12.3	12.3	10.7	10.6	10.5	10.3	10.4	10.4	10.5	10.4
Morocco		11.6	12.1	12.0	10.7	10.4	10.0	9.4	8.9	8.2
Mozambique										
Namibia					19.6					
Niger	13.2	5.3	16.0	10.0	10.0	10.0	10.0	10.0	10.0	10.0
Nigeria										
Oman										
Qatar										
Réunion	19.3	18.2	16.4	17.0	15.8	16.4	15.7	15.7	15.3	15.0
Rwanda										
Sao Tomé e Príncipe										
Saudi Arabia										
Senegal					4.2	4.2	4.2	4.2	4.2	4.2
Seychelles	10.5	9.6	9.5	9.7	10.3	10.5	10.4	10.4	10.3	10.3
Sierra Leone										
Somalia										
South Africa										
Sudan										
Swaziland		1.0	1.0	1.1	1.1	1.0	1.0	0.8	0.8	0.7
Syria	2.8	2.0	2.0	1.9	1.8	3.5	4.4	4.5	4.6	4.8
Tanzania	7.0		8.0							
Togo										
Tunisia		6.1	5.7	6.2	6.5	6.1	6.9	6.6	6.5	6.1
Uganda	14.8	10.0	14.0	14.0						
United Arab Emirates										
Yemen	4.0	5.0	6.0	5.0	5.7	6.0	6.5	6.5	6.6	6.6
Zambia	11.0	11.0	8.0	10.0	9.0	8.0	8.0	8.0	8.0	8.0
Zimbabwe	5.8	5.3	4.6	4.5	5.2	3.4	3.6	3.0	3.1	2.8

Source: Euromonitor from World Tourism Organisation

□ Length of Tourist Stay										Table 24.3
Domestic Tourist Nights 1991-2002										
● '000 nights	**1991**	**1993**	**1995**	**1996**	**1997**	**1998**	**1999**	**2000**	**2001**	**2002**
North America										
Canada	50,368	48,793	37,256	39,002	37,597	44,653	43,980	43,484	43,746	44,760
USA										
Latin America										
Anguilla										
Antigua										
Argentina										
Aruba										
Bahamas										
Barbados										
Belize			65	55	58	53	59	61	64	66
Bermuda										
Bolivia	1,234	1,259	1,329	1,380	1,420	1,443	1,365	1,293	1,251	1,183
Brazil	53,645	73,440	89,532	95,752	124,844	200,432	210,211	215,528	218,677	220,813
British Virgin Islands										
Cayman Islands										
Chile	2,668	3,027	3,683	4,051	4,321	5,116	5,027	4,224	4,049	3,957
Colombia	12,027	10,263	9,476	10,441	9,825	10,197	10,337	10,403	10,393	10,334
Costa Rica										
Cuba	7,715	3,220	3,308	3,308	3,500	3,285	3,154	3,261	3,287	3,247
Dominica										
Dominican Republic										
Ecuador										
El Salvador		34	31	38	47	51	59	63	73	82
French Guiana										
Grenada										
Guadeloupe										
Guatemala		1,940	1,983							
Guyana										
Haiti										
Honduras		793								
Jamaica										
Martinique										
Mexico	32,654	35,250	41,244	42,604	45,581	48,763	63,082	69,377	70,370	75,531
Netherlands Antilles										
Nicaragua	56	26	45	66	56	63	89	96	102	106
Panama										
Paraguay										
Peru	10,434	9,246	10,166	10,130	10,326	10,964	11,516	11,917	12,153	12,263
Puerto Rico										
St Kitts										
St Lucia										
St Vincent and the Grenadines						12	11	10	10	10
Suriname										
Trinidad and Tobago										
Uruguay										
Venezuela										

Source: *Euromonitor from World Tourism Organisation*

◻ Length of Tourist Stay

Domestic Tourist Nights 1991-2002 (continued)

• '000 nights

	1991	1993	1995	1996	1997	1998	1999	2000	2001	2002
Asia Pacific										
Afghanistan										
American Samoa										
Armenia										
Azerbaijan										
Bangladesh										
Bhutan										
Brunei										
Cambodia										
China	101,399	149,687	176,679	160,975	185,250	207,078	313,904	354,031	339,623	392,720
Fiji		237	286	299	301	320	344	330	319	310
French Polynesia										
Guam										
Hong Kong, China										
India										
Indonesia										
Japan	378,000	369,000	328,000	329,000	349,000	345,000	333,000	313,000	321,800	326,752
Kazakhstan								844	813	795
Kiribati										
Kyrgyzstan			50							
Laos										
Macau		146	179	188	172	181	204	227	236	253
Malaysia			10,716	13,473	15,635	14,182	16,166	19,344	20,378	22,649
Maldives										
Mongolia										
Myanmar		599								
Nauru										
Nepal										
New Caledonia		200	194	167	159	140	166	181	193	199
North Korea										
Pakistan		4,545	4,449	3,457	2,710	2,470	3,036	3,574	3,586	3,543
Papua New Guinea										
Philippines										
Singapore										
Solomon Islands										
South Korea	11,278	11,728	15,083	11,748	11,017	11,367	11,500	11,806	12,831	14,395
Sri Lanka		463	611	678	769	857	874	952	982	1,036
Taiwan										
Tajikistan										
Thailand										
Tonga										
Turkmenistan										
Tuvalu										
Uzbekistan										
Vanuatu										
Vietnam			9,910	9,885	13,085	14,784	17,096	17,920	18,871	19,072
Western Samoa										
Australasia										
Australia	39,750	37,793	44,341	52,784	50,661	66,687	69,005	67,284	73,572	77,863
New Zealand							5,718	5,056	4,957	4,932

Source: *Euromonitor from World Tourism Organisation*

Length of Tourist Stay

Domestic Tourist Nights 1991-2002 (continued)

● '000 nights

	1991	1993	1995	1996	1997	1998	1999	2000	2001	2002
Africa and Middle East										
Algeria		3,338	3,573	3,487	3,404	2,775	3,275	3,111	3,058	3,221
Angola		32	9	9	37	7	24	11	12	15
Bahrain										
Benin		806								
Botswana										
Burkina Faso		59	114	120	126	138	144	152	156	162
Burundi										
Cameroon			346	350	468	475	524	634	744	854
Cape Verde										
Central African Republic						5	5	5	5	5
Chad		2	1	1	2	3	3	10	6	6
Comoros										
Congo Dem Rep			80							
Congo-Brazzaville				66	78	40	27	25	19	17
Côte d'Ivoire	413				413	413	413	413	413	413
Djibouti										
Egypt					3,592	3,425	3,768	3,955	4,083	4,336
Equatorial Guinea										
Eritrea										
Ethiopia										
Gabon										
Gambia										
Ghana										
Guinea										
Guinea-Bissau										
Iran		5,458	6,908	8,289	7,065	8,266	9,610	9,765	9,985	10,715
Iraq										
Israel	6,090	5,856	6,737	7,238	7,978	9,742	9,635	9,870	9,907	9,777
Jordan				519	529	498	577	541	528	527
Kenya		895	689	783	777	697	654	794	758	811
Kuwait										
Lebanon										
Lesotho				45	51	57	66	74	82	91
Liberia										
Libya				978	950	960	969	962	961	958
Madagascar		70	35							
Malawi										
Mali		9	15	38	46	51	5	6	7	8
Mauritania										
Mauritius										
Morocco		2,283	3,951	3,876	4,062	4,114	4,088	4,211	4,230	4,246
Mozambique										
Namibia			213	194	194	224	161	156	163	157
Niger		137	13	16	18	20	112	124	146	158
Nigeria										
Oman			182	215	218	263	247	253	257	265
Qatar										
Réunion										
Rwanda										
Sao Tomé e Príncipe										
Saudi Arabia								14,540	18,080	20,620
Senegal	68	57	85	79	100	77	91	106	100	102
Seychelles		9	7	6	7	9	11	12	13	14
Sierra Leone										
Somalia										
South Africa	9,188	8,597	11,390	12,100	13,415	14,006	14,098	14,407	14,148	14,254
Sudan										
Swaziland	28			22	26	22	23	24	25	25
Syria	2,982	2,600	1,338	1,247	1,124	1,158	1,133	1,081	1,065	1,095
Tanzania		906	120	150						
Togo		24	39	45	40	44	43	26	21	19
Tunisia	1,305	1,574	1,832	1,995	2,112	2,194	2,169	2,255	2,298	2,250
Uganda		52								
United Arab Emirates										
Yemen										
Zambia										
Zimbabwe										

Source: Euromonitor from World Tourism Organisation

Length of Tourist Stay

Table 24.4

International Tourist Nights 1991-2002

- '000 nights

	1991	1993	1995	1996	1997	1998	1999	2000	2001	2002
North America										
Canada	82,773	82,080	91,983	96,685	96,648	98,283	105,720	109,660	107,769	108,677
USA										
Latin America										
Anguilla			366	352	408	404	400	377	353	368
Antigua										
Argentina	21,961	26,003	31,227	33,561	36,209	39,334	32,423	36,622	36,772	36,519
Aruba	3,768	3,317	3,726	3,824	3,879	3,959	3,998	4,250	4,330	4,295
Bahamas	8,402	5,975	6,405							
Barbados	2,082	2,314	2,542	2,603	2,434	2,303	2,412	2,297	2,270	2,292
Belize			446	416	455	432	489	516	531	509
Bermuda	2,538	2,516	2,421	2,365	2,283	2,274	2,144	1,966	1,864	1,810
Bolivia	738	835	976	1,041	1,109	1,142	1,095	991	934	902
Brazil	17,511	20,038	22,300	29,816	31,211	50,108	52,553	46,676	46,736	47,886
British Virgin Islands										
Cayman Islands										
Chile	1,968	2,116	2,145	2,650	2,953	2,657	2,108	2,181	2,244	2,235
Colombia	1,777	3,575	5,947	3,414	5,214	5,350	4,888	4,969	4,645	4,618
Costa Rica										
Cuba	4,132	4,809	6,631	6,631	7,400	9,164	9,824	10,323	11,043	10,856
Dominica										
Dominican Republic			15,596	16,812	18,884	18,942	29,390	32,849	35,678	34,336
Ecuador	1,129	1,284	1,488	1,592	1,720	1,843	1,895	2,096	2,284	2,231
El Salvador		153	128	608	937	1,584	2,590	3,133	3,646	3,960
French Guiana										
Grenada								329	331	331
Guadeloupe		778	926	876	849	850	847	3,233	2,951	2,912
Guatemala	3,437	3,822	3,195	3,691	4,380	4,853	5,511	5,899	5,837	5,817
Guyana										
Haiti		44	105							
Honduras		554								
Jamaica	9,212	5,760	5,427	5,698	5,763	5,959	5,903	6,066	6,169	6,230
Martinique	4,251	1,723	2,288	2,102	2,497	2,625	2,573	2,441	2,362	2,359
Mexico	19,414	19,888	24,910	28,278	30,574	29,723	34,361	33,970	35,907	34,917
Netherlands Antilles										
Nicaragua	121	139	172	170	260	280	247	300	316	324
Panama		879	875	956	1,035	1,074	1,094	1,161	1,180	1,252
Paraguay				921	851	641	560	755	724	729
Peru	1,078	943	1,887	2,035	2,099	2,173	2,703	3,075	3,015	3,025
Puerto Rico				893	949	1,065	1,095	1,103	1,142	1,188
St Kitts										
St Lucia										
St Vincent and the Grenadines						33	35	36	37	38
Suriname										
Trinidad and Tobago										
Uruguay				2,291	2,888	2,509	2,566	2,577	2,575	2,576
Venezuela	1,355	2,163	2,579	9,956	9,440	7,949	5,571	5,338	5,021	4,836

Source: Euromonitor from World Tourism Organisation

Length of Tourist Stay

International Tourist Nights 1991-2002 (continued)

● '000 nights

	1991	1993	1995	1996	1997	1998	1999	2000	2001	2002
Asia Pacific										
Afghanistan										
American Samoa										
Armenia			78	89	116	161	204	222	236	257
Azerbaijan	3,944	1,555	862	158	67	143	34	82	124	124
Bangladesh										
Bhutan						46	53	61	61	60
Brunei										
Cambodia										
China	25,741	37,633	42,829	47,340	53,200	57,925	63,104	78,310	87,398	93,434
Fiji		1,520	1,682	1,716	1,806	1,991	2,143	1,519	1,482	1,470
French Polynesia	1,240	957	1,264	1,250	1,431	1,467	1,645	2,137	2,095	2,091
Guam	2,580	2,352	4,086							
Hong Kong, China										
India										
Indonesia	30,429	36,277	44,265	51,397	54,702	42,287	46,520	50,887	51,341	49,814
Japan										
Kazakhstan								281	274	264
Kiribati										
Kyrgyzstan			37							
Laos										
Macau		2,578	2,930	3,250	2,672	2,753	2,885	3,219	3,499	3,567
Malaysia			11,554	12,463	14,652	16,215	17,493	21,295	23,038	24,423
Maldives	1,725	2,351	3,039	3,039	3,271	3,467	3,718	3,937	4,024	4,186
Mongolia										
Myanmar		379	833	1,225	1,323	1,407	1,386	1,442	1,512	1,428
Nauru										
Nepal	550		799	1,017	1,030	1,043	1,056	1,069	1,081	1,091
New Caledonia		307	313	321	385	391	350	372	383	378
North Korea										
Pakistan	743	834	622	640	567	623	706	620	638	601
Papua New Guinea			109	115	117	117	117	114	114	113
Philippines						13,577	13,731	13,063	13,020	12,851
Singapore		6,252	6,902	7,074	6,923	6,944	7,054	7,110	7,054	7,055
Solomon Islands										
South Korea	9,483	8,162	8,693	7,813	7,132	7,067	7,192	7,219	7,721	8,443
Sri Lanka	3,633	3,380	3,308	2,399	3,123	3,455	4,048	3,735	3,278	2,979
Taiwan	12,782	13,182	14,834	15,145	15,199	15,058	15,966	16,487	16,882	16,544
Tajikistan										
Thailand	36,089	39,952	52,375	59,212	60,120	65,232	68,293	73,855	84,020	86,656
Tonga	352	515	488							
Turkmenistan										
Tuvalu										
Uzbekistan				843	1,294	1,445	1,696	1,947	1,952	1,873
Vanuatu		248				465	343	321	284	236
Vietnam			4,515	4,157	4,642	4,104	4,816	6,307	7,218	7,821
Western Samoa										
Australasia										
Australia	16,421	14,319	17,047	19,139	18,112	17,731	19,128	21,040	21,685	22,460
New Zealand	19,289	22,248	26,782	29,577	7,637	7,470	8,230	9,115	9,382	9,415

Source: *Euromonitor from World Tourism Organisation*

International Tourist Nights 1991-2002 (continued)

- '000 nights

	1991	1993	1995	1996	1997	1998	1999	2000	2001	2002
Africa and Middle East										
Algeria	669	364	364	354	85	132	159	190	221	252
Angola	74	78	33	33	89	95	48	77	77	91
Bahrain	834	1,119		1,123	1,563	1,287	1,263	1,764	1,828	1,993
Benin	161	302	314	362	445	525	486	566	600	613
Botswana										
Burkina Faso		300	288	304	320	613	579	670	626	688
Burundi		55	53	52	47	82	83	84	88	89
Cameroon		215	224	227	239	240	246	260	273	285
Cape Verde										
Central African Republic		28	37	31	29	30	25	23	21	19
Chad		27	26	42	46	116	121	107	122	128
Comoros	181	209	184	190						
Congo Dem Rep	40	40	119	98	56	37	32	27	22	17
Congo-Brazzaville				119	93	55	63	76	89	102
Côte d'Ivoire			1,009	1,314	1,479	1,511	1,829	2,132	2,435	2,737
Djibouti		98			38	27	26	36	39	43
Egypt	16,231	15,089	20,451	23,765	26,579	20,151	31,002	32,788	37,373	41,646
Equatorial Guinea										
Eritrea										
Ethiopia		72	90	103	143	73	74	210	243	255
Gabon						203	252	250	262	287
Gambia										
Ghana		2,616	2,906	3,172	3,393	3,601	3,919	4,226	4,500	4,778
Guinea	143						90	82	75	65
Guinea-Bissau							70	70	70	70
Iran				967	798	933	977	962	974	1,000
Iraq										
Israel	4,663	8,273	9,790	9,180	8,396	8,865	9,047	9,676	9,748	9,986
Jordan	1,544	2,294	3,505	2,836	2,720	2,682	3,154	3,291	3,135	3,320
Kenya		5,294	4,366	4,279	4,133	2,116	2,241	2,823	3,190	2,660
Kuwait	13	259	239	252	266	272	271	246	265	263
Lebanon										
Lesotho				150	169	141	165	169	175	178
Liberia										
Libya				699	397	253	320	286	278	262
Madagascar		989	1,249	1,240	1,511	2,424	2,627	3,041	3,619	4,182
Malawi	1,164	1,120	1,536	1,355	1,436	1,235	1,013	1,235	1,227	1,234
Mali		48	102	194	148	163	165	174	166	163
Mauritania							168	162	158	157
Mauritius		4,610	4,435	4,958	5,451	5,568	5,729	6,413	6,740	7,003
Morocco	13,392	9,310	8,502	8,719	9,560	10,676	11,891	12,313	12,991	13,175
Mozambique										
Namibia			403	393	393	497	399	383	422	424
Niger				180	195	198	208	224	235	228
Nigeria										
Oman		861	881	873	939	1,122	1,092	1,190	1,274	1,366
Qatar	255	340	427	386	502	403	487	490	492	500
Réunion		507	637	690	715	912	1,032	1,081	1,153	1,298
Rwanda										
Sao Tomé e Príncipe				9						
Saudi Arabia										
Senegal	1,016	673	1,139	1,127	1,329	1,449	1,469	1,401	1,583	1,611
Seychelles	946	830	835	933	948	910	904	933	986	1,037
Sierra Leone		364	309	374	448	390	390	383	405	405
Somalia										
South Africa	1,321	1,321	2,546	2,790	2,928	3,126	4,027	3,625	3,557	3,651
Sudan										
Swaziland										
Syria		1,759	1,823	1,851	1,837	1,804	1,845	1,837	1,829	1,821
Tanzania	1,543	1,841	2,308	2,550	2,829	3,657	4,868	3,766	3,234	2,802
Togo		60	127	145	154	153	162	132	136	134
Tunisia	12,443	22,119	23,514	24,130	27,684	28,788	33,151	33,168	35,303	36,913
Uganda		1,030	1,471	1,647						
United Arab Emirates				7,004	7,009	7,984	8,554	10,313	10,110	10,106
Yemen		349	307	373	483	526	379	473	446	428
Zambia							2,301	2,646	2,856	3,191	3,496
Zimbabwe		1,200	1,542	1,684	2,857	3,087	3,824	2,120	2,505	2,411

Source: *Euromonitor from World Tourism Organisation*

■ Tourism Expenditure **Table 24.5**

Tourist Expenditure 1985-2002

● US$ million

	1985	1990	1995	1996	1997	1998	1999	2000	2001	2002
North America										
Canada	4,130	10,401	10,220	11,090	11,268	10,765	11,345	12,412	10,237	10,209
USA	24,517	37,349	44,916	48,739	51,220	56,509	59,351	65,044	58,008	58,716
Latin America										
Anguilla			6							
Antigua	13	17	23	26						
Argentina	671	1,171	3,190	2,340	2,680	3,993	4,107	4,449	1,719	1,341
Aruba	17	40	73	120	130	111	122	144	161	183
Bahamas	123	196	213	235	250	256	309	303	310	332
Barbados	23	47		74	81	90	91	98	79	77
Belize	5	7	25	23	30	24	24	31	27	29
Bermuda	76	119	145							
Bolivia	30	130	152	162	172	172	165	130	171	171
Brazil	1,145	1,505	3,412	5,825	5,446	5,731	3,059	3,932	3,253	2,987
British Virgin Islands			40							
Cayman Islands										
Chile	269	426	774	806	946	906	806	865	684	628
Colombia	169	454	878	856	958	1,120	1,078	1,057	904	843
Costa Rica	53	148	321	335	358	408	428	449	489	563
Cuba		246								
Dominica	3	4	6	7	7	8	8	8	8	8
Dominican Republic	84	101	173	203	221	254	282	291	334	368
Ecuador	196	175	235	219	227	241	271	299	262	271
El Salvador	89	55	72	73	75	77	80	80	95	103
French Guiana										
Grenada	3	5	4	5	5	5	5	6	6	7
Guadeloupe										
Guatemala	61	100	141	135	119	157	183	187	225	254
Guyana			21							
Haiti	43	32	35	36	35	37	33	46	37	38
Honduras	27	38	57	60	62	61	60	99	85	87
Jamaica	32	54	148	157	181	198	227	198	156	146
Martinique										
Mexico	2,262	5,519	3,171	3,387	3,892	4,209	4,541	5,499	4,825	5,136
Netherlands Antilles										
Nicaragua	6	15	40	60	65	70	78	79	85	91
Panama	65	99	128	136	164	176	184	191	178	179
Paraguay	47	58	133	224	195	143	109	93	177	198
Peru	163	495	297	351	485	452	443	531	315	281
Puerto Rico	411	630	833	821	869	874	815	883	811	796
St Kitts	5	4	5	6	6	6	6	7	7	8
St Lucia		18	25	29	29	30	31	35	32	32
St Vincent and the Grenadines	7	7	6	7	8	8	9	9	8	8
Suriname	13	12	3	8	11	11				
Trinidad and Tobago	219	112	69	76	72	67				
Uruguay	162	111	236	192	264	265	280	281	250	246
Venezuela	597	1,023	1,865	2,251	2,381	2,451	1,646	2,040	2,213	2,217

Source: *Euromonitor from World Tourism Organisation*

Tourist Expenditure 1985-2002 (continued)

- US$ million

	1985	1990	1995	1996	1997	1998	1999	2000	2001	2002
Asia Pacific										
Afghanistan	2		1							
American Samoa										
Armenia			3	22	41	45	34	38	45	46
Azerbaijan			146	329	621	170	139	543	642	737
Bangladesh	45	78	229	200	170	198	212	292	221	231
Bhutan										
Brunei										
Cambodia			8	13	12	7	8	12	11	13
China	314	470	3,688	4,278	10,166	9,205	10,864	8,640	9,799	10,181
Fiji	18	41	64	58	53	52	66	46	50	51
French Polynesia										
Guam	226									
Hong Kong, China										
India	354	393	996	1,040	1,342	1,713	2,010	1,407	1,639	1,667
Indonesia	591	836	2,172	2,300	2,436	2,102	2,353	1,995	1,641	1,531
Japan	4,814	24,928	36,792	37,040	33,041	28,815	32,808	31,480	28,764	29,094
Kazakhstan			283	319	445	498	394	363	363	328
Kiribati		2	3	4	4	2	2			
Kyrgyzstan			7	6	4	3	3	4	5	5
Laos			30	22	21	23	12	17	27	32
Macau		39	137	137	153	146	131	161	169	180
Malaysia	1,158	1,450	2,314	4,101	2,478	1,785	1,973	2,725	2,826	3,325
Maldives	5	15	30	30	39	42	45	46	45	48
Mongolia			20	19	14	45	41	51	55	58
Myanmar		2	18	28	33	27	18	36	39	49
Nauru										
Nepal	29	45	136	125	103	78	71	136	134	171
New Caledonia										
North Korea										
Pakistan	202	440	449	900	364	352	180	267	426	508
Papua New Guinea	21		58	72	78	52	53	45	40	37
Philippines	37	111	422	450	1,936	1,950	1,308	954	1,001	819
Singapore	613	1,803	4,655	6,139	2,676	4,707	4,666	4,970	4,112	4,813
Solomon Islands	4	11	13	15	6	6	7	6	7	7
South Korea	606	3,166	5,903	6,963	6,262	2,640	3,975	6,377	4,712	5,817
Sri Lanka	46	74	186	176	180	202	219	225	188	184
Taiwan		4,984	7,149	6,493	5,981	5,050	5,635	6,185	5,473	5,656
Tajikistan										
Thailand	280	854	3,372	4,171	1,888	1,448	1,843	2,065	1,767	1,923
Tonga	3	1	3							
Turkmenistan				73	125					
Tuvalu										
Uzbekistan										
Vanuatu	2	1	5			8	9	9	9	9
Vietnam										
Western Samoa	1	2	3	4	5	4	4	4	4	4
Australasia										
Australia	1,918	4,535	4,979	5,322	6,129	5,418	6,048	6,024	6,653	7,011
New Zealand	389	958	1,289	1,480	1,451	1,438	1,493	1,346	1,258	1,210

Source: *Euromonitor from World Tourism Organisation*

■ Tourism Expenditure

Tourist Expenditure 1985-2002 (continued)

● US$ million

Africa and Middle East

	1985	1990	1995	1996	1997	1998	1999	2000	2001	2002
Algeria	606	149	42	40	40	170	139	152	92	78
Angola		38	75	73	70	59	31	60	53	59
Bahrain			122			142	159			
Benin	7	12	5	6	7	7	8	7	6	6
Botswana	17	39	145	140	157	126	143	163	137	143
Burkina Faso	20	35								
Burundi	9	17	25	12	10	11	8	11	9	9
Cameroon	130	280	105							
Cape Verde			16	18	17	24	19	21	22	21
Central African Republic	24		37							
Chad	20	36	23							
Comoros	7	6	7			3				
Congo Dem Rep	35	16	10							
Congo-Brazzaville	63	114	52	40	36	57	60	58	45	42
Côte d'Ivoire	106	221	190	248	282	237	306	238	227	230
Djibouti		25	4							
Egypt	106	129	1,278	1,317	1,347	1,148	1,078	1,000	1,238	1,320
Equatorial Guinea			7							
Eritrea										
Ethiopia	4	11	25	25	40	46	55	65	48	49
Gabon	83	137	173	176	178	180	183	175	154	147
Gambia	2	8	14	15	16	16	16	16	14	14
Ghana	10	13	21	22	24	27	31	36	17	15
Guinea		30	21	27	23	27	31	36	31	32
Guinea-Bissau										
Iran	508	340	241	529	677	788	918	1,350	1,999	2,745
Iraq										
Israel	549	1,442	2,120	3,304	3,570	2,376	2,566	2,700	3,128	3,128
Jordan	424	336	425	381	398	353	355	367	368	382
Kenya	15	38	145	167	194	147	115	95	94	81
Kuwait	1,988	1,837	2,248	2,492	2,558	2,517	2,510	3,140	2,975	3,180
Lebanon										
Lesotho	5	12	13	12	13	12	12	12	9	8
Liberia										
Libya	487	414	212	215	154	143	150	172	149	152
Madagascar	24	40	59	52	48	119	111	113	119	121
Malawi	8		16							
Mali	37	62	49	46	42	29	29	29	42	48
Mauritania	17		23	36	48	42	55	26	24	22
Mauritius	19	94	159	179	177	185	187	194	156	149
Morocco	88	184	302	316	316	424	440	434	344	324
Mozambique										
Namibia		63	82	89	99	88	86	80	67	61
Niger	9	44	21	23	24	25	25	28	21	20
Nigeria	200	576	906	1,304	1,816	1,567	620	730	921	873
Oman		47	47	47	47	47	47	64	57	62
Qatar										
Réunion										
Rwanda	11	23	10			17	18			
Sao Tomé e Príncipe	1	2	1							
Saudi Arabia										
Senegal	38	105	75							
Seychelles	9	20	39	30	30	26	21	20	36	43
Sierra Leone	1	4	2	2	2	4	4	6	3	2
Somalia										
South Africa	413	1,117	1,849	1,754	1,947	1,842	1,806	1,603	1,407	1,293
Sudan	43	51	43	28	34	29	35	37	32	34
Swaziland	11	14	43	42	37	42	45	38	32	29
Syria	302	249	498	513	545	580	630	700	535	525
Tanzania	16	19	360	412	407	493	550	569	544	564
Togo	22	43	18	12	5	3	3	2	5	6
Tunisia	126	179	251	174	160	235	239	250	212	206
Uganda		8	80	135	137	95	141	108	112	123
United Arab Emirates	409									
Yemen	67		76	78	81	83	75	90	108	119
Zambia	22	49	57							
Zimbabwe	58	66	106	118	120	131	110	103	95	90

Source: Euromonitor from World Tourism Organisation

Tourism Receipts 1985-2002

US$ million

	1985	1990	1995	1996	1997	1998	1999	2000	2001	2002
North America										
Canada	3,103	5,612	7,882	8,623	8,763	9,396	10,171	10,768	10,800	10,994
USA	17,937	43,007	63,395	69,751	73,268	71,286	74,881	85,153	72,295	67,451
Latin America										
Anguilla	12	35	49	48	57	58	56	56	52	47
Antigua	133	298	247	258	269	256	291	312	272	253
Argentina	523	1,976	2,144	4,572	5,069	2,888	2,812	2,903	2,534	4,361
Aruba	117	353	621	614	666	730	782	773	688	640
Bahamas	995	1,333	1,346	1,398	1,416	1,354	1,503	1,816	1,575	1,436
Barbados	309	494	612	685	717	703	677	863	719	706
Belize	12	91	77	89	87	108	112	104	99	101
Bermuda	357	490	488	472	478	487	480	431	448	458
Bolivia	30	84	146	159	170	174	179	160	171	177
Brazil	1,739	1,444	2,097	2,469	2,595	3,678	3,994	4,228	3,701	2,419
British Virgin Islands	68	132	205	268	210	232	300	324	251	244
Cayman Islands	86	236	394	368	493	450	439	607	407	369
Chile	123	540	900	905	1,021	1,062	894	827	794	649
Colombia	287	406	657	909	955	929	928	1,028	792	996
Costa Rica	118	275	660	689	719	884	1,002	1,102	896	925
Cuba	96	199	977	1,231	1,354	1,571	1,714	1,795	1,463	1,390
Dominica	10	20	34	37	40	38	49	46	35	34
Dominican Republic	368	890	1,576	1,783	2,099	2,142	2,524	2,918	2,689	2,622
Ecuador	133	188	255	281	290	291	343	402	294	300
El Salvador	43	145	41	44	75	125	211	239	199	257
French Guiana						51	50	53	57	58
Grenada	26	38	54	60	59	59	63	75	61	66
Guadeloupe	95	197	458	496	372	466	375	418	339	327
Guatemala	67	185	277	284	325	394	570	518	557	571
Guyana	18	27	78	38	60	54	59	53	47	47
Haiti	93	46	56	58	57	57	55	69	56	54
Honduras	25	29	107	115	146	168	195	240	188	199
Jamaica	407	740	1,069	1,092	1,131	1,197	1,279	1,333	1,106	1,321
Martinique	93	240	384	382	400	415	404	302	341	337
Mexico	2,900	5,467	6,179	6,934	7,593	7,493	7,223	8,295	8,401	8,342
Netherlands Antilles	233									
Nicaragua	7	12	50	54	74	90	107	116	72	70
Panama	200	172	367	343	369	494	538	576	690	710
Paraguay	105	112	137	140	128	111	81	66	183	186
Peru	231	259	428	632	805	845	890	1,001	683	705
Puerto Rico	758	1,366	1,828	1,898	2,046	2,233	2,138	2,547	2,728	2,744
St Kitts	31	63	65	67	72	76	70	84	73	71
St Lucia	56	154	268	269	282	293	311	332	234	237
St Vincent and the Grenadines	23	54	41	64	70	72	77	82	57	55
Suriname	5	11	31	17	43	61	53	58	60	62
Trinidad and Tobago	97	95	73	108	193	201	210	226	191	189
Uruguay	235	238	611	717	759	695	653	652	561	576
Venezuela	416	496	951	945	1,086	961	656	765	831	801

Source: *Euromonitor from World Tourism Organisation*

◻ Tourism Receipts

Tourism Receipts 1985-2002 (continued)

● US$ million

	1985	1990	1995	1996	1997	1998	1999	2000	2001	2002
Asia Pacific										
Afghanistan	1		7							
American Samoa	7	10	10			10				
Armenia			5	5	7	10	27	45	8	9
Azerbaijan			70	46	162	125	81	109	120	145
Bangladesh	23	11	23	32	59	51	50	59	49	53
Bhutan	1	2	5	6	6	8	9	8	9	9
Brunei	19		37			37				
Cambodia	2		100	118	143	166	190	228	162	169
China	1,250	2,218	8,733	10,200	12,602	14,098	16,231	14,433	17,792	19,749
Fiji	147	227	283	299	294	244	275	171	255	291
French Polynesia	98	171	326	322	345	354	394	357	266	263
Guam	231	936	1,275		2,361	1,908	1,908			
Hong Kong, China	1,788	5,032	9,604	11,994	9,979	7,496	7,210	7,886	8,200	9,897
India			2,583	2,963	3,152	2,935	3,009	3,296	3,042	2,841
Indonesia	548	2,153	5,228	6,087	5,437	4,331	4,710	5,749	5,411	5,287
Japan	1,137	3,578	3,226	4,078	4,326	3,742	3,428	3,374	2,736	3,301
Kazakhstan			122	199	289	407	363	370	412	261
Kiribati	1	2	1		2	2	2	2		2
Kyrgyzstan			5	4	7	8	4	4	5	5
Laos	4		25	44	73	80	97	114	126	129
Macau	150	1,473	3,090	3,127	2,947	2,638	2,466	3,083	1,769	1,989
Malaysia	622	1,667	3,909	4,142	2,490	2,456	3,540	4,563	2,515	2,616
Maldives	41	81	210	266	286	303	325	321	344	362
Mongolia			21	10	13	33	28	37	20	23
Myanmar		9	38	33	34	35	35	43	37	37
Nauru										
Nepal	39	109	117	117	116	153	168	167	137	143
New Caledonia			108	109	111	111				
North Korea	10									
Pakistan	186	156	114	146	117	98	76	86	92	61
Papua New Guinea	10	41	60	68	71	75	76	64	34	35
Philippines	994	1,306	2,454	2,700	2,831	2,413	2,534	2,514	1,649	1,774
Singapore	1,660	4,719	8,390	7,961	6,843	5,402	5,974	6,370	6,162	6,223
Solomon Islands	3	4	16	14	16	7	6	7	6	7
South Korea	784	3,559	5,587	5,430	5,116	6,865	6,802	6,609	6,294	6,539
Sri Lanka	82	132	225	173	212	231	275	253	211	246
Taiwan	963	1,740	3,286	3,636	3,402	3,372	3,571	3,605	3,013	3,140
Tajikistan										
Thailand	1,171	4,326	7,664	8,664	7,048	5,934	6,695	7,119	6,731	7,222
Tonga	5	9	11	13	16	8	9	9	8	9
Turkmenistan			192	66	74	192	71	119	117	120
Tuvalu										
Uzbekistan			21	15	19	13	15	18	10	10
Vanuatu	19	22	58	50	46	52	56	58	43	44
Vietnam		64	86	539	506	480	518	560	583	612
Western Samoa	7	20	33	40	39	38	42	49	34	35
Australasia										
Australia	1,062	4,088	7,857	9,113	9,057	7,335	8,017	8,442	7,600	6,477
New Zealand	413	1,019	2,318	2,432	2,093	1,726	2,083	2,068	1,592	1,705

Source: Euromonitor from World Tourism Organisation

Tourism Receipts 1985-2002 (continued)

● US$ million

	1985	1990	1995	1996	1997	1998	1999	2000	2001	2002
Africa and Middle East										
Algeria	137	84	24	24	20	23	21	20	28	28
Angola		13	10	9	9	8	13	18	8	9
Bahrain	175	135	247	263	311	366	408	396	364	379
Benin	9	28	27	29	31	33	34	31	35	37
Botswana	24	65	162	181	203	175	234	223	191	196
Burkina Faso	5	8	25	31	39	42	40	32	33	34
Burundi	1	3	1	1	1		1	1	1	1
Cameroon	45	21	36			40				
Cape Verde			10	11	15	20	23	16	16	17
Central African Republic	2		8							
Chad	7	12	10							
Comoros	2	2	21	23	26	16	19	20	15	15
Congo Dem Rep	8	7	5			2				
Congo-Brazzaville	6	8	14	8	3	9	12	11	8	8
Côte d'Ivoire	36	48	89	75	88	108	95	74	77	74
Djibouti	5	5	4			4				
Egypt	901	1,994	2,684	3,896	3,727	2,565	3,903	4,357	3,800	4,279
Equatorial Guinea			2			2				
Eritrea			58	69	90	34	28	36	44	44
Ethiopia	9	26	26	28	36	16	16	24	26	27
Gabon	9	3	7			8	11	7	9	10
Gambia	19	46	21	31	32	49	32	37	42	43
Ghana	20	81	233	249	266	284	304	202	178	181
Guinea			1	6	6	1	7	12	3	3
Guinea-Bissau		36	1							
Iran	27	62	190	244	327	477	662	850	1,122	1,149
Iraq	181		13							
Israel	1,101	1,382	2,938	2,942	2,741	2,657	2,974	3,100	1,653	1,712
Jordan	518	512	660	743	774	773	795	772	519	700
Kenya	249	466	486	426	377	290	304	433	321	308
Kuwait	103	132	121	184	188	207	243	213	178	193
Lebanon			710	715	1,000	1,221	673	742	837	956
Lesotho	7	17	27	32	22	18	19	22	25	29
Liberia	6									
Libya	3	6		6	6	18	28	35	17	16
Madagascar	5	40	58	65	73	91	100	116	97	100
Malawi	5	11	9	5	6	15	20	27	18	19
Mali	25	47	25	29	26	50	50	51	33	32
Mauritania	5		11	19	21	20	28	25	27	28
Mauritius	55	244	430	452	485	503	545	585	493	509
Morocco	606	1,259	1,304	1,712	1,449	1,712	1,880	2,040	2,460	2,443
Mozambique										
Namibia	15	61	278	297	336	288	295	261	203	210
Niger	6	17	15	17	18	18	24	17	18	19
Nigeria	33	25	54	85	118	142	133	118	156	117
Oman	52	69	92	99	108	113	105	138	95	98
Qatar	120									
Réunion			216	258	249	265	270			
Rwanda	7	10	2			19	17	18	20	21
Sao Tomé e Príncipe	1		2			2				
Saudi Arabia	2,378		1,210			673	742		3,420	3,464
Senegal	85	168	161	150	153	178	166	181	164	156
Seychelles	51	120	97	108	122	111	112	110	90	92
Sierra Leone	7	19	6	10	9	8	8	12	5	5
Somalia	8									
South Africa	425	992	1,595	2,125	2,439	2,738	2,526	2,012	1,779	1,973
Sudan	62	21	8	8	4	2	2	6	6	6
Swaziland	13	25	48	38	40	37	35	37	32	33
Syria	395	320	1,338	1,206	1,035	1,190	1,360	474	1,300	1,277
Tanzania	20	65	258	322	392	570	733	739	542	527
Togo	25	58	13			11	6	6	5	5
Tunisia	551	953	1,393	1,557	1,414	1,557	1,560	1,496	1,605	1,509
Uganda	2	10	79	117	135	144	149	152	105	101
United Arab Emirates	4									
Yemen	106	200	50	46	69	84	60	76	68	69
Zambia	8	41	47	60	75	75	85	91	53	51
Zimbabwe	26	64	154	219	230	177	202	156	125	118

Source: Euromonitor from World Tourism Organisation

Total Number of Rooms in Tourist Accommodation 1991-2002

● '000

	1991	1993	1995	1996	1997	1998	1999	2000	2001	2002
North America										
Canada			280.0	332.0	327.0	330.0	352.1	378.0	349.2	356.5
USA	3,080.0									
Latin America										
Anguilla	0.9	1.0	1.0	0.9	0.9	1.0	1.1	1.1	1.0	1.0
Antigua	3.3	3.0	3.0	3.2	3.2	3.2	3.2	3.2	3.2	3.2
Argentina	89.8	98.0	112.0	85.2	155.4	162.5	162.2	166.1	168.0	177.0
Aruba	5.2	6.0	6.0	6.8	7.2	7.2	7.8	7.8	7.7	8.1
Bahamas	13.2	14.0	13.0	13.3	13.3	14.2	14.2	14.7	14.3	14.8
Barbados	5.4	6.0	5.0	6.3	5.3	5.8	5.8	6.5	6.5	6.8
Belize	2.8	3.0	4.0	4.0	4.0	4.0	4.0	4.0	4.0	4.0
Bermuda	4.3	4.0	4.0	4.0	4.0	4.0	3.0	3.0	3.0	3.0
Bolivia	11.0	12.0	14.0	14.0	14.0	15.0	15.0	15.8	16.0	16.3
Brazil	138.0	139.0	140.0	139.0	213.0	234.0	245.0	278.0	282.0	295.0
British Virgin Islands	1.2	1.0	1.0	2.0	2.0	2.0	2.0	2.0	2.0	2.0
Cayman Islands	3.3	3.0	4.0	4.5	4.5	4.2	4.3	4.4	4.7	4.7
Chile	25.8	33.0	39.0	40.0	41.0	45.0	46.0	47.0	48.0	49.0
Colombia	40.2	44.0	49.0	52.0	53.0	53.0	53.2	54.0	54.0	54.0
Costa Rica	7.2	9.0	25.3	27.1	27.9	28.1	28.8	29.5	30.4	31.0
Cuba	22.2	26.0	28.0	30.0	32.0	36.0	37.0	38.1	40.0	41.0
Dominica	0.6	1.0	1.0	0.8	0.8	0.8	0.9	0.9	0.9	0.9
Dominican Republic	22.6	27.0	32.0	35.0	39.0	43.0	49.4	52.2	54.0	56.2
Ecuador	29.5	32.0	39.0	32.0	32.4	33.3	34.0	36.7	39.0	42.0
El Salvador	3.2	3.0	3.0	3.5	3.8	4.0	4.5	4.9	5.0	5.1
French Guiana						1.3	1.0	1.0	1.0	1.0
Grenada	1.1	1.0	2.0	2.0	2.0	2.0	2.0	1.8	2.0	2.0
Guadeloupe	7.0	8.0	8.0	8.0	9.0	8.0	8.3	8.1	8.1	8.1
Guatemala	9.0	10.0	12.0	13.0	14.0	15.0	16.3	17.0	18.0	19.0
Guyana	0.5	1.0	1.0	0.6	0.7	0.7	0.7	0.7	0.7	0.7
Haiti	1.2	1.0	2.0	1.8	1.8	1.8	1.8	1.8	1.8	1.8
Honduras	6.7	8.0	10.0	11.0	11.0	12.0	12.9	13.9	14.3	14.9
Jamaica	17.3	16.0	18.0	19.0	19.0	19.0	19.0	19.9	19.8	19.8
Martinique		5.0	5.0	5.0	6.0	6.0	6.8	6.8	6.9	6.9
Mexico	345.2	366.0	370.0	382.0	382.0	397.0	419.6	421.9	426.4	432.5
Netherlands Antilles										
Nicaragua	1.5	1.0	2.0	2.0	2.0	3.0	2.8	3.3	3.4	3.4
Panama	5.6	9.0	9.0	10.0	11.5	12.0	12.5	13.7	14.5	15.0
Paraguay	4.8	5.0	5.0	5.0	5.0	5.0	4.9	4.9	4.7	4.7
Peru	55.2	64.0				98.0	99.0	100.0	103.1	105.4
Puerto Rico	7.9	9.0	10.0	10.0	11.0	12.0	11.0	11.9	12.0	11.8
St Kitts	1.4	2.0	2.0	2.0	2.0	2.0	2.0	2.0	2.0	2.0
St Lucia	2.5	3.0	4.0	4.0	4.0	4.0	4.1	4.4	4.5	4.7
St Vincent and the Grenadines	1.1	1.0	1.0	1.0	1.0	2.0	1.5	1.7	1.9	1.9
Suriname	1.6		1.0	1.1	1.3	1.3	1.3	1.3	1.3	1.3
Trinidad and Tobago	2.1	3.0	3.0	4.0	4.0	4.0	4.2	4.5	4.7	4.8
Uruguay		11.0	13.0	14.0	15.0	16.0	14.0	13.7	13.5	13.1
Venezuela	68.5	59.0	65.0	67.2	71.7	73.8	75.4	76.0	76.9	78.2

Source: Euromonitor from World Tourism Organisation

Total Number of Rooms in Tourist Accommodation 1991-2002 (continued)

● '000

	1991	1993	1995	1996	1997	1998	1999	2000	2001	2002
Asia Pacific										
Afghanistan										
American Samoa	0.3									
Armenia					3.5	3.6	3.8	3.9	4.0	4.1
Azerbaijan	2.5	2.0	2.0	5.6	6.0	6.4	6.9	7.0	6.8	7.0
Bangladesh	3.1	3.0	4.0	4.2	4.2	4.5	4.5	4.5	5.0	6.0
Bhutan								1.2	1.2	1.1
Brunei		1.0	1.0	1.2	1.1	1.2	1.7	2.4	2.4	2.4
Cambodia		5.0	5.0	6.0	6.0	8.0	9.0	9.0	9.0	9.0
China	321.1	386.0	486.0	594.0	702.0	765.0	889.0	948.0	974.5	1,004.6
Fiji	4.5	5.0	5.0	5.0	5.0	6.0	5.8	5.3	5.2	4.9
French Polynesia	2.8	3.0	3.0	3.0	3.0	3.0	3.0	3.4	3.4	3.4
Guam	5.2	6.0	7.0	8.0	8.0	9.0	10.0	10.1	10.2	10.3
Hong Kong, China	31.2	34.0	33.0	34.0	33.0	34.0	35.0	36.4	37.4	38.0
India			57.0	62.0	65.0	67.0	72.1	75.0	77.8	76.0
Indonesia	150.2	175.0	193.0	197.0	185.0	232.0	248.0	253.0	262.7	269.4
Japan	217.0	242.0	1,540.0	1,559.0	1,565.0	1,570.0	1,580.2	1,617.0	1,704.0	1,832.0
Kazakhstan				2.3	2.3	1.7	3.0	9.1	9.7	10.9
Kiribati	0.1	0.1	0.4	0.4	0.4	0.4	0.5	0.5	0.5	0.5
Kyrgyzstan			3.0							
Laos		2.0	3.0	3.7	4.1	5.0	5.5	7.3	8.2	8.7
Macau	4.9	8.0	9.0	8.5	9.0	9.0	9.4	9.2	9.2	9.2
Malaysia	49.9	61.0	76.0	86.0	98.0	108.0	109.0	134.5	149.7	172.0
Maldives	4.0	5.0	6.0	5.9	6.1	7.1	7.8	8.3	8.7	9.0
Mongolia										
Myanmar	1.3	2.0	8.0	12.0	13.0	14.0	14.7	16.2	17.1	18.4
Nauru										
Nepal	5.6	6.0	11.0	13.0	14.0	15.0	16.7	18.2	19.2	20.1
New Caledonia	1.8	2.0	2.0	2.0	2.0	2.0	2.4	2.4	2.4	2.5
North Korea										
Pakistan			30.0	32.0	32.0	34.9	35.1	35.5	36.9	37.4
Papua New Guinea	2.6	3.0	3.0							
Philippines	13.3	13.0	31.0	21.0	30.0	38.0	36.5	29.8	29.4	28.6
Singapore	25.6		30.0	32.3	33.2	35.1	34.9	35.6	36.8	38.6
Solomon Islands	0.3	1.0			0.9	0.9	1.0	1.0	1.0	1.0
South Korea	42.5	56.0	59.0	45.1	46.6	47.0	47.5	51.2	52.7	55.6
Sri Lanka	10.9	12.0	14.0	14.0	15.0	15.0	16.0	15.9	15.9	16.7
Taiwan	19.8	20.0	20.0	20.0	19.0	19.0	20.3	19.9	19.8	19.7
Tajikistan										
Thailand	190.5	212.0	256.0	266.0	273.0	279.1	279.9	318.8	356.5	386.6
Tonga	0.6	1.0	1.0	0.6	0.6	0.6	1.0	1.0	1.0	1.0
Turkmenistan			2.0	2.7	2.6	2.2	2.0	1.9	1.9	1.7
Tuvalu				0.1	0.1	0.1	0.1	0.1	0.1	0.1
Uzbekistan										
Vanuatu	0.5	1.0	1.0	0.7	0.7	0.7	0.8	1.1	1.2	1.3
Vietnam		34.0	50.0	56.0	56.0	60.0	63.6	67.0	69.8	71.3
Western Samoa			1.0	1.0	1.0	1.0	1.0	1.0	1.0	1.0
Australasia										
Australia	161.9	167.0	170.0	173.9	172.3	182.1	190.1	194.9	198.0	202.0
New Zealand		26.0	27.0	30.0	23.0	23.9	24.9	25.9	26.3	27.1

Source: Euromonitor from World Tourism Organisation

◻ Tourist Accommodation

Total Number of Rooms in Tourist Accommodation 1991-2002 (continued)

● '000

	1991	1993	1995	1996	1997	1998	1999	2000	2001	2002
Africa and Middle East										
Algeria			32.0	32.3	32.8	34.1	35.1	35.0	34.6	34.9
Angola	3.2	1.0	5.0	4.9	6.2	6.2	6.2	6.2	5.8	6.0
Bahrain			5.0	4.9	5.1	6.1	6.2	6.8	7.3	7.9
Benin	1.5	2.0								
Botswana	1.4	2.0	2.0	2.0	2.0	2.0	2.0	2.0	2.0	2.0
Burkina Faso	2.8									
Burundi	0.7	1.0	1.0	0.6	0.6	0.6	1.0	1.0	1.0	1.0
Cameroon	7.4	11.0								
Cape Verde			1.0	1.0	1.5	1.8	1.8	2.4	3.0	3.0
Central African Republic	0.2	0.2	0.2	0.2	0.2	0.2	0.2	0.3	0.3	0.3
Chad	0.3	0.3	0.4	0.4	0.4	0.4	0.6	0.7	0.6	0.7
Comoros	0.4	0.4	0.4	0.4	0.4	0.4	0.4	0.4	0.4	0.4
Congo Dem Rep	3.4	22.0	22.0				6.0	6.0	6.0	6.0
Congo-Brazzaville	3.4			3.0	3.8	1.9	2.0	2.5	3.0	3.3
Côte d'Ivoire	6.0	5.0	5.0	8.0	8.0	10.1	12.2	12.0	12.4	12.6
Djibouti	0.3		0.3	0.3	0.3	0.4	0.4	0.4	0.3	0.3
Egypt	60.5	59.0	65.0	70.0	76.0	83.0	94.0	113.6	123.2	136.8
Equatorial Guinea										
Eritrea			3.0	3.0	4.0	4.0	4.0	4.5	5.0	5.0
Ethiopia	2.8	3.0	3.0	2.0	6.0	2.0	2.8	6.5	8.2	8.8
Gabon	2.8	3.0	2.0	2.0	2.0	2.0	2.0	2.5	2.7	2.9
Gambia										
Ghana	6.3	9.0	9.0	10.0	11.0	11.0	11.0	11.0	11.0	11.0
Guinea				2.0	2.0	3.1	3.6	4.1	4.5	
Guinea-Bissau										
Iran	16.8	19.0	21.0	24.0	25.0	27.0	22.0	22.0	22.6	23.0
Iraq	31.5		25.0	26.0	26.0	25.9	21.6	26.7	29.8	31.9
Israel		33.0	36.0	37.0	38.0	40.0	43.0	45.6	48.2	50.8
Jordan	7.6	9.0	10.0	11.0	12.0	14.0	16.2	17.5	18.5	19.1
Kenya		18.0	18.0							
Kuwait			3.0	2.4	2.8	2.2	2.3	2.0	1.9	1.8
Lebanon			10.0	10.0	9.7	11.0	14.3	14.5	14.8	14.8
Lesotho	0.8	1.0	1.0	2.0	1.0	1.4	1.5	2.0	2.5	3.0
Liberia										
Libya		8.0			7.8					
Madagascar	3.0	3.0	3.0	5.0	5.0	6.0	6.0	6.7	7.4	8.1
Malawi	1.0	1.0	2.0	2.0	2.0	2.0	3.6	4.2	4.7	5.2
Mali	1.3	1.0	2.0	2.0	2.0	2.0	2.0	2.7	3.3	3.6
Mauritania							2.0	2.0	2.0	2.0
Mauritius	5.1	5.0	6.0	7.0	7.0	7.0	8.3	8.7	8.9	9.3
Morocco		60.0	63.0	64.0	63.0	64.9	66.1	66.8	68.1	68.3
Mozambique										
Namibia	2.4	2.0	3.0	5.0	3.0	3.0	3.0	3.0	3.0	3.0
Niger	1.5	1.0	2.0	1.5	1.5	1.5	1.2	1.1	1.1	1.1
Nigeria		30.0								
Oman	2.2	2.0	3.0	3.1	3.5	4.7	5.1	5.3	5.5	5.7
Qatar	1.7	2.0	2.0	3.0	2.0	1.8	2.0	2.0	2.0	2.0
Réunion	1.6	2.0	2.0	2.0	2.0	2.0	2.5	2.7	3.1	3.2
Rwanda	1.0									
Sao Tomé e Príncipe	0.1	0.2	0.2	0.2	0.2	0.3	0.3	0.3	0.3	0.3
Saudi Arabia			25.0					55.9	61.8	67.7
Senegal	6.8	8.0	8.0	7.8	8.2	8.2	8.5	8.8	9.3	9.6
Seychelles	1.8	2.0	2.0	2.2	2.3	2.3	2.4	2.5	2.7	2.7
Sierra Leone	1.1	1.0	1.0	0.7	0.7	0.3	0.4	0.4	0.4	0.4
Somalia										
South Africa	45.2	43.0	46.0	47.2	50.0	52.0	53.3	51.9	51.5	52.7
Sudan		3.0	3.0	4.0	3.7	3.5	4.5	4.6	4.9	4.7
Swaziland	1.2	1.0	1.0	1.2	1.2	1.2	1.1	1.2	1.2	1.2
Syria	14.0	14.0	14.0	15.0	15.0	15.0	15.4	15.5	15.6	15.9
Tanzania		6.0	7.0	7.0	7.0	7.5	9.6	10.0	10.3	10.6
Togo	2.1	2.0	2.0	2.0	2.0	2.0	2.3	2.4	2.6	2.8
Tunisia			81.0	85.0	89.1	92.3	96.0	102.0	108.0	113.0
Uganda	2.7	3.0	4.0	3.9						
United Arab Emirates				21.6	23.2	26.5	28.3	30.2	31.1	33.0
Yemen	4.0	5.0	7.0	7.0	7.7	8.8	9.7	10.4	11.1	11.7
Zambia	3.7	4.0	4.0	4.1	4.2	4.3	4.0	4.0	4.1	4.4
Zimbabwe	4.1	4.0	4.0	4.4	4.5	4.9	5.1	5.2	5.3	5.4

Source: Euromonitor from World Tourism Organisation

Hotel Bed Occupancy Rates 1991-2002

- % of beds occupied

	1991	1993	1995	1996	1997	1998	1999	2000	2001	2002
North America										
Canada	55.9	56.7	61.1	62.4	63.7	64.0	63.4	63.0	62.9	62.8
USA										
Latin America										
Anguilla	33.3	37.4				80.3	80.3	80.3	80.3	80.3
Antigua			81.4	81.4	81.4	81.4	81.4	81.4	81.4	81.4
Argentina										
Aruba	68.9	79.5	72.2	71.5	73.5	78.5	78.6	74.0	72.3	73.4
Bahamas	56.3	56.8	66.5	66.4	68.0	68.7	68.6	67.2	67.0	66.4
Barbados	50.5	53.7	57.9	60.6	57.2	58.6	55.9	56.9	57.2	56.8
Belize	24.0	30.0	29.5	26.9	27.1	29.9	31.4	41.7	45.6	44.1
Bermuda	58.8	59.4	58.3	57.0	58.4	60.0	61.3	61.0	60.5	60.6
Bolivia	27.5	28.5	28.4	29.1	29.7	28.3	26.1	23.6	22.1	20.5
Brazil					62.4	61.7	59.3	60.8	61.0	61.5
British Virgin Islands	59.3	56.6	57.7	56.5	52.4	59.3	58.8	62.0	59.1	59.0
Cayman Islands	60.0	71.3	75.3	66.0	62.9	68.1	64.7	70.0	76.1	79.0
Chile	39.5	37.7	34.9	34.7	36.1	35.0	30.2	30.8	31.1	30.7
Colombia	55.3	53.2	53.4	48.3	49.0	40.0	39.1	41.8	42.1	42.5
Costa Rica	67.9	71.0	54.0	48.1	46.7	51.0	53.0	59.6	62.9	65.7
Cuba	69.8	57.9	62.9	64.9	75.4	76.1	71.7	74.2	75.3	73.9
Dominica										
Dominican Republic	68.3	74.7	76.8	72.8	76.3	69.7	66.9	70.2	71.3	70.8
Ecuador										
El Salvador	25.5	35.0	53.0	58.0	65.0	68.0	70.0	61.0	60.5	62.7
French Guiana						50.0	50.0	50.0	50.0	50.0
Grenada	65.0	68.8	65.9	59.3	62.1	62.3	64.8	71.0	73.6	75.8
Guadeloupe	62.5	60.7	67.3	68.9	69.8	65.3	66.3	56.9	52.3	50.4
Guatemala	83.5	78.4	71.4	61.2	63.4	57.5	56.8	56.3	55.4	55.0
Guyana										
Haiti										
Honduras							47.3	48.6	49.7	50.0
Jamaica	57.9	60.3	60.8	57.7	55.7	58.7	57.0	58.5	58.3	58.4
Martinique	56.3	59.3	51.4	54.2	55.8	58.0	58.1	52.0	53.0	51.3
Mexico	53.9	51.3	51.2	53.3	56.4	56.4	50.5	54.8	55.2	56.7
Netherlands Antilles										
Nicaragua	58.2	65.0	65.0	65.0	65.0	66.0	65.0	65.8	66.1	66.1
Panama	45.0	49.1	53.6	54.3	52.5	49.5	43.6	40.1	39.5	38.1
Paraguay	30.7	60.0	66.0	61.0	58.0	52.0	47.0	45.0	43.1	40.3
Peru	30.7	32.3	34.7	33.1	32.3	29.9	28.9	28.2	27.6	27.2
Puerto Rico	69.0	68.5	68.0	69.0	69.8	67.3	72.0	70.7	71.2	70.3
St Kitts										
St Lucia	72.2	67.9	73.2	66.6	71.4	75.3	72.5	67.0	65.1	62.4
St Vincent and the Grenadines										
Suriname										
Trinidad and Tobago	50.3	54.5	47.2	49.2	50.0	54.1	55.6	56.1	56.7	56.9
Uruguay										
Venezuela	69.6	68.6	64.2	62.1	60.3	58.2	56.4	54.0	53.2	51.4

Source: *Euromonitor from World Tourism Organisation*

◻ Tourist Accommodation

Hotel Bed Occupancy Rates 1991-2002 (continued)

● % of beds occupied

	1991	1993	1995	1996	1997	1998	1999	2000	2001	2002
Asia Pacific										
Afghanistan										
American Samoa										
Armenia					16.0	17.0	19.3	21.0	22.3	23.1
Azerbaijan	47.0	60.0	80.0	70.0	49.8	37.0	31.5	30.8	30.1	29.8
Bangladesh	48.6	50.0	59.0	39.5	45.0	42.0	42.0	49.1	47.7	50.3
Bhutan								50.3	49.6	47.4
Brunei		64.7	71.0	66.9	61.2	54.5	49.1	62.8	62.0	61.5
Cambodia		24.8	37.0	40.0	30.0	40.0	44.0	45.0	46.9	47.1
China	61.4	67.7	58.1	55.3	53.8	51.7	53.4	55.9	57.7	60.7
Fiji	51.9	48.4	53.8	53.5	54.4	50.8	51.1	51.6	50.2	49.6
French Polynesia	51.3	57.4	60.0	53.3	54.1	59.2	57.5	60.3	60.6	60.8
Guam	79.0	61.0	87.0	85.0	82.0	67.0	61.0	63.0	64.2	62.9
Hong Kong, China	75.0	87.0	85.0	88.0	76.0	76.0	79.0	83.0	84.8	86.3
India			73.7	71.1	62.9	59.4	50.4	49.1	47.3	45.2
Indonesia	54.2	51.1	52.3	52.9	48.4	38.1	42.2	43.2	44.2	44.7
Japan	75.9	67.1	67.8	68.4	70.3	68.6	68.2	69.2	72.4	75.2
Kazakhstan										
Kiribati	36.0									
Kyrgyzstan			25.4							
Laos					62.0	47.0	45.0	42.1	39.7	36.5
Macau	78.7	57.0	57.0	64.1	52.1	53.1	55.4	59.1	60.3	62.7
Malaysia	72.1	61.4	65.5	62.3	58.0	49.9	51.7	50.7	50.6	50.6
Maldives	63.2	64.8	70.5	72.8	77.4	76.2	69.7	68.2	66.8	65.1
Mongolia										
Myanmar	57.8	58.8	50.0	32.0	26.0	28.0	30.0	26.6	25.1	22.8
Nauru										
Nepal	34.9	30.2	49.0	50.0						
New Caledonia	50.7	59.6	48.9	50.5	57.0	56.6	54.0	51.6	50.3	48.7
North Korea										
Pakistan		62.0	53.6	52.0	47.1	46.4	41.1	39.0	37.9	36.2
Papua New Guinea			54.0	60.0	61.6	61.9	61.9	59.1	58.9	58.4
Philippines	64.8	59.9	62.1	70.0	69.1	56.9	59.2	58.8	58.5	57.7
Singapore	76.8	83.4	84.1	82.3	79.4	71.3	74.9	83.5	83.9	85.1
Solomon Islands										
South Korea	64.3	63.2	67.4	65.8	62.7	58.1	61.8	65.1	67.2	71.9
Sri Lanka	48.4	57.0	53.0	40.3	49.1	52.8	57.6	52.3	50.8	47.1
Taiwan	55.0	53.8	61.5	62.3	63.5	62.2	60.6	63.9	65.1	63.7
Tajikistan										
Thailand		50.3	53.6	51.4	46.6	47.5	49.5	50.8	51.6	52.1
Tonga										
Turkmenistan					24.0					
Tuvalu										
Uzbekistan				35.7	44.8	53.9	63.0	72.1	73.5	72.6
Vanuatu	55.5	55.7	51.9	50.7	55.3	59.1	51.9	52.0	52.6	54.8
Vietnam		48.3	51.0	43.1	43.0	42.7	45.2	50.1	51.2	52.1
Western Samoa			70.0							
Australasia										
Australia	50.1	53.3	58.5	58.4	57.4	57.7	58.7	58.1	58.4	59.5
New Zealand					50.0	48.0	50.8	52.0	51.8	51.9

Source: *Euromonitor from World Tourism Organisation*

Hotel Bed Occupancy Rates 1991-2002 (continued)

- % of beds occupied

	1991	1993	1995	1996	1997	1998	1999	2000	2001	2002
Africa and Middle East										
Algeria		41.0	33.3	33.6	40.2	37.0	38.0	41.9	39.1	39.3
Angola	66.0	51.0	33.0	44.0	45.0	92.0	68.0	46.0	38.0	45.6
Bahrain			6.0				48.0	55.4	62.8	70.3
Benin	58.0	31.6	32.4	34.0	36.0	33.0	34.4	36.0	36.6	40.3
Botswana	57.2	53.5	50.6	51.5	57.9	48.0	53.3	53.6	52.8	52.5
Burkina Faso	25.5	45.7	48.9	54.2	59.9	58.5	57.6	57.0	56.4	55.9
Burundi	49.1	49.8	36.1	32.1	15.4	18.2	19.9	17.0	16.1	16.7
Cameroon		16.7	16.9	16.1	16.3	16.1	16.5	15.8	15.6	
Cape Verde			60.0	70.0	70.0	80.0	41.0	52.0	53.1	54.8
Central African Republic	43.1	38.2	43.0	51.7	55.4	49.1	51.2	50.7	51.1	51.9
Chad	8.1	24.0	19.5	18.5	23.3	79.7	83.1	84.5	79.9	82.1
Comoros						45.0	30.0	27.0	26.5	26.3
Congo Dem Rep	30.7	50.0	39.9				40.0	40.0	40.0	40.0
Congo-Brazzaville	30.7	44.6	35.4	48.7	68.5	55.7	39.8	40.7	44.8	47.1
Côte d'Ivoire	39.0	40.3	40.3	52.0	70.0	75.0	89.5	88.0	90.6	91.9
Djibouti	22.9	49.3								
Egypt		43.0	57.0	63.0	62.0	46.0	67.0	73.0	76.0	81.5
Equatorial Guinea										
Eritrea			37.0	55.0	57.0	44.0	37.0	45.0	45.3	42.8
Ethiopia		36.9	51.8	60.5				40.0	42.4	49.3
Gabon			60.0	60.0	60.0	60.0	70.0	70.0	70.0	70.0
Gambia		54.6	43.6	37.6	59.3	44.7	42.7	53.0	58.3	62.7
Ghana	70.0	71.0		69.0	71.0	70.6	70.5	70.7	70.8	70.6
Guinea										
Guinea-Bissau										
Iran			53.0	54.0	53.0	53.5	53.3	53.3	53.3	53.4
Iraq	29.3									
Israel		60.2	60.3	58.2	54.3	58.8	61.8	60.0	61.4	60.1
Jordan		47.0	52.6	46.8	43.6	37.9	34.9	39.5	33.1	33.0
Kenya	59.1	52.0	43.7	44.6	51.6	35.3	33.9	39.3	44.7	48.1
Kuwait										
Lebanon			36.4	27.3	32.0	36.7	28.0	28.0	27.8	27.9
Lesotho	28.1	22.3	21.8	20.5	20.8	17.8	22.1	19.8	19.6	19.6
Liberia										
Libya				71.0	57.0	51.0	53.0	50.0	48.0	44.0
Madagascar	39.8	45.0	48.0	57.0	57.0	58.0	60.0	63.0	65.2	67.2
Malawi	42.7	34.5	39.0	38.0	37.0	38.0	40.0	39.0	40.0	40.5
Mali	36.3	21.9	40.0	50.9	43.9	35.7	42.6	50.2	55.7	58.7
Mauritania							47.0	49.5	51.0	54.5
Mauritius	66.1	68.5	66.0	68.0	72.0	72.0	71.0	70.0	71.7	71.0
Morocco		51.6	45.8	41.0	43.9	48.2	51.6	47.6	51.5	52.4
Mozambique										
Namibia		39.4	39.7	38.2	32.9	35.9	37.2	36.4	36.4	35.8
Niger	33.5	28.3	37.0	37.5	37.8	45.0	39.3	38.6	39.9	39.1
Nigeria										
Oman	45.2	51.0	52.0	49.0	51.0	47.0	41.0	42.0	41.2	40.8
Qatar	29.3	39.4	57.3	65.8	78.3	79.0	60.6	64.6	68.2	70.2
Réunion	53.8	48.0	56.5	59.3	61.5	64.0	63.9	64.8	67.5	67.4
Rwanda	16.0									
Sao Tomé e Príncipe										
Saudi Arabia								42.0	54.0	62.0
Senegal	34.5	27.2	35.0	34.4	38.0	40.0	42.8	35.4	40.6	40.9
Seychelles	56.0	58.0	53.0	57.0	56.0	53.0	53.0	52.0	52.5	51.2
Sierra Leone	22.0	18.0	14.1	17.0	20.0	20.2	19.6	19.6	19.7	19.6
Somalia										
South Africa	49.6	46.4	57.1	56.4	53.5	52.5	52.4	53.6	53.3	52.5
Sudan										
Swaziland	37.4	36.3	45.0	40.9	36.9	34.3	36.9	47.0	38.8	38.9
Syria	34.0	30.0	28.0	28.0	32.0	34.0	28.0	23.0	25.8	24.6
Tanzania		68.9	52.0	57.0	56.3	59.9	63.7	54.2	59.3	59.2
Togo	19.6	10.3	25.0	21.9	23.1	20.0	21.4	19.1	18.1	16.8
Tunisia		51.6	48.7	48.0	52.7	52.5	56.5	55.8	59.6	62.0
Uganda	32.0	49.0	56.0	63.0						
United Arab Emirates				64.0	61.0	58.0	58.0	62.0	63.8	66.2
Yemen	41.0	60.0	60.0	60.0	60.0	73.5	83.0	69.0	81.0	83.8
Zambia	54.0	46.0	47.0	48.5	49.4	40.3	46.0	49.0	48.4	49.5
Zimbabwe	50.1	41.1	49.1	50.3	52.0	49.0	42.0	29.0	37.5	32.4

Source: Euromonitor from World Tourism Organisation

◙ Tourist Accommodation   **Table 24.9**

Total Number of Bed Places in Tourist Accommodation 1991-2002

● '000

	1991	1993	1995	1996	1997	1998	1999	2000	2001	2002
North America										
Canada										
USA	5,544.0									
Latin America										
Anguilla										
Antigua	6.6									
Argentina	222.3	255.0	277.0	317.5	390.1	364.7	368.9	378.2	349.6	365.0
Aruba	10.4	12.0	13.0	13.6	14.5	14.5	15.6	15.6	16.7	16.7
Bahamas	26.3	27.0	27.0	26.6	26.6	28.5	28.3	29.4	28.2	29.0
Barbados	11.7	12.0	10.0	11.4	10.3	11.7	12.3	12.2	12.4	12.5
Belize	4.7	5.0	6.0	6.0	6.0	7.0	6.8	7.0	7.0	7.0
Bermuda	8.5	9.0								
Bolivia	19.6	21.0	24.0	24.0	23.6	25.0	26.2	26.9	27.0	27.3
Brazil	276.0	278.0	279.0	279.0	425.0	429.0	502.0	579.0	479.0	574.0
British Virgin Islands										
Cayman Islands	6.5	7.0	7.0	13.2	13.3	12.2	11.8	11.0	11.2	11.4
Chile	62.3	77.0	89.0	91.0	92.0	102.4	108.1	110.1	112.0	114.3
Colombia	72.4	78.0	93.0	98.0	100.0	101.0	103.0	104.1	105.0	106.0
Costa Rica										
Cuba	44.4	53.0	58.0	61.0	64.0	72.0	76.4	77.6	80.0	81.4
Dominica										
Dominican Republic	45.1	54.0	65.0	88.6	96.3	107.6	123.5	130.5	135.0	139.0
Ecuador	58.6	61.0	77.0	64.5	67.6	69.4	70.8	78.3	82.0	87.0
El Salvador	6.0	6.0	7.0	7.0	7.5	8.0	9.1	9.8	10.5	10.9
French Guiana										
Grenada	2.3	3.0	3.0	3.0	3.0	3.0	3.0	3.0	3.0	3.0
Guadeloupe										
Guatemala	23.0	27.0	30.0	33.0	36.0	38.0	41.0	44.0	44.9	45.3
Guyana										
Haiti										
Honduras	11.9	13.0	17.0	18.0	20.0	21.0	20.0	22.3	22.7	23.2
Jamaica	35.4	33.0	37.0	39.0	40.0	39.0	40.0	41.5	41.6	42.3
Martinique		10.0	11.0	11.0	12.0	13.0	14.6	14.6	16.3	16.3
Mexico	690.3	733.0	741.0	763.0	765.0	794.0	839.2	864.0	876.0	903.0
Netherlands Antilles										
Nicaragua	2.6	2.0	3.0	4.0	4.0	5.0	4.9	5.8	5.9	6.0
Panama	10.8	15.0	15.0	19.7	22.9	24.4	25.0	27.3	27.9	28.6
Paraguay				10.4	10.4	10.8	10.7	10.7	10.6	10.6
Peru	95.1	111.0				157.0	166.0	175.0	179.0	183.0
Puerto Rico	15.8	17.0	21.0	21.0	22.0	24.0	22.2	23.9	25.1	26.3
St Kitts	2.8	3.0								
St Lucia	5.1		7.0	7.0	6.0	6.8	7.4	8.2	8.6	8.9
St Vincent and the Grenadines	2.2	2.0	2.0	3.0	3.0	3.0	3.1	3.5	3.6	3.9
Suriname										
Trinidad and Tobago										
Uruguay				34.5	36.1	37.9	36.5	37.2	37.0	36.2
Venezuela	142.0	122.0	138.0	144.0	155.0	159.0	163.1	164.7	165.3	166.9

Source: *Euromonitor from World Tourism Organisation*

Total Number of Bed Places in Tourist Accommodation 1991-2002 (continued)

'000

	1991	1993	1995	1996	1997	1998	1999	2000	2001	2002
Asia Pacific										
Afghanistan										
American Samoa	0.5									
Armenia					10.3	10.8	12.1	13.0	13.9	14.7
Azerbaijan	4.9	4.0	4.0	26.0	26.0					
Bangladesh	6.3	6.0	8.0	8.4	8.6	9.4	9.5	9.8	11.0	11.0
Bhutan								2.2	2.0	1.9
Brunei										
Cambodia		8.0	8.0	10.0	11.0	13.0	15.0	16.3	16.8	17.2
China	679.5	812.0	987.0	1,200.0	1,412.0	1,524.0	1,769.8	1,856.0	1,923.8	1,951.0
Fiji	12.1	13.0	13.0	13.0	14.0	14.7	14.2	13.5	12.2	11.4
French Polynesia	5.5	6.0	6.0	6.0	6.0	6.0	7.0	6.7	6.7	6.5
Guam										
Hong Kong, China										
India	89.0	98.0	115.0	124.0	129.0	133.0	144.2	151.0	156.0	160.0
Indonesia	271.8	305.0	338.0	370.0	395.0	414.0	416.0	422.3	428.9	431.5
Japan										
Kazakhstan				5.1	5.1	3.9	6.1	6.4	6.9	7.5
Kiribati	0.2	0.2								
Kyrgyzstan			5.0							
Laos					7.1	8.7	9.6	12.9	13.2	14.0
Macau	10.1	16.0	18.0	18.0	20.0	19.0	19.9	19.1	18.9	18.6
Malaysia										
Maldives	8.0	10.0	12.0	11.8	12.2	14.2	15.5	16.7	17.6	18.4
Mongolia										
Myanmar	2.8	4.0	15.0	23.7	26.7	29.8	29.4	32.3	32.0	31.7
Nauru										
Nepal	11.2	13.0	22.0	26.0	28.0	29.0	32.2	35.0	36.7	39.1
New Caledonia										
North Korea										
Pakistan	39.5	44.0	45.0	47.0	48.0	52.3	52.7	53.3	53.8	53.4
Papua New Guinea	5.3	5.0	5.0							
Philippines	26.5	26.0	62.0	42.0	59.0	77.0	73.0	53.8	49.8	46.7
Singapore										
Solomon Islands	0.7	1.0								
South Korea	85.0	113.0	117.0	123.0	135.0	139.0	147.7	159.0	161.3	168.5
Sri Lanka	21.3	23.0	26.0	26.6	28.0	29.0	28.9	29.4	29.4	29.6
Taiwan										
Tajikistan										
Thailand										
Tonga	1.3	1.0	1.0	1.4	1.0	1.0	1.1	1.0	1.0	1.0
Turkmenistan			7.0	7.2	6.6	3.9	3.7	3.6	3.4	3.2
Tuvalu	0.1	0.1								
Uzbekistan										
Vanuatu	1.2	1.0	2.0					2.9	2.8	2.8
Vietnam		68.0	98.0	108.0	106.0	114.0	116.3	121.0	125.4	127.7
Western Samoa		1.0	2.0	2.0	2.0	2.0	2.0	2.0	2.0	2.0
Australasia										
Australia	464.6	478.0	489.0	504.1	507.8	536.8	559.7	567.5	572.0	588.0
New Zealand										

Source: Euromonitor from World Tourism Organisation

◻ Tourist Accommodation

Total Number of Bed Places in Tourist Accommodation 1991-2002 (continued)

● '000

	1991	1993	1995	1996	1997	1998	1999	2000	2001	2002
Africa and Middle East										
Algeria	55.0	57.0	64.0	64.7	65.7	71.0	72.4	72.7	70.1	71.8
Angola	6.8	6.2	7.0	6.8	9.0	9.0	9.0	9.0	9.0	9.0
Bahrain				6.6	6.5	8.1	8.4	9.0	9.9	10.7
Benin	3.2	5.0								
Botswana	2.6	3.0	3.0	3.0	4.0	3.0	4.0	3.0	4.0	3.0
Burkina Faso	4.2									
Burundi	1.4	1.0	1.0	0.9	0.9	0.9	1.0	1.0	1.0	1.0
Cameroon	10.6	13.0								
Cape Verde			3.0	3.0	3.0	3.0	3.2	4.5	4.4	4.5
Central African Republic	0.3	0.3	0.4	0.3	0.3	0.3	0.4	0.4	0.4	0.4
Chad	0.6	1.0	1.0	0.7	0.7	0.7	1.0	1.3	1.1	1.3
Comoros	0.8	1.0	1.0	0.8	0.7	0.8	0.8	0.8	0.8	0.8
Congo Dem Rep		27.0	27.0				9.0	9.0	9.0	9.0
Congo-Brazzaville										
Côte d'Ivoire	12.0	10.0	10.0	11.0	11.0	11.8	12.5	12.5	12.6	12.7
Djibouti	0.5	1.0	0.5	0.5	0.6	0.6	0.6	0.6	0.6	0.6
Egypt	105.8	117.0	129.0	141.0	151.0	167.0	187.0	227.2	246.3	273.2
Equatorial Guinea										
Eritrea			7.0	7.0	8.0	9.0	9.0	9.3	10.2	10.2
Ethiopia	4.9	5.0	5.0	4.0	8.0	4.0	6.4	9.4	8.4	6.8
Gabon										
Gambia		5.0	6.0	6.0	6.0	6.0	6.0	6.0	6.0	6.0
Ghana	9.2	12.0	9.0	13.8	14.2	14.3	11.0	7.7	4.4	1.1
Guinea										
Guinea-Bissau										
Iran	32.4	37.0	42.0	49.0	51.0	55.0	47.1	47.1	48.4	49.6
Iraq	74.0		53.0	55.0	54.0	51.0	42.2	58.1	56.0	68.5
Israel	60.0	66.0	75.0	81.0	86.0	90.0	116.0	106.8	121.2	157.5
Jordan	15.6	17.0	21.0	23.0	24.0	27.0	31.8	34.4	33.6	36.3
Kenya	26.5	34.0	34.0	31.0	26.0	22.0	20.6	22.0	23.4	24.8
Kuwait			3.0	3.5	3.3	3.3	3.2	2.9	3.1	3.3
Lebanon			16.0	15.0	18.0	25.0	25.4	25.6	25.7	25.7
Lesotho	1.7	2.0	2.0	4.0	2.0	2.8	3.0	4.0	5.0	5.9
Liberia										
Libya		15.0			15.3					
Madagascar	6.9	7.0	7.0	9.6	10.0	10.0	11.0	11.9	12.6	13.3
Malawi										
Mali	1.9	2.0	2.0	2.2	2.0	3.0	2.9	3.1	3.6	3.8
Mauritania							4.0	4.0	4.0	4.0
Mauritius	10.5	11.0	12.0	14.0	14.0	15.0	16.9	17.8	18.3	19.3
Morocco	116.2	116.0	123.0	124.0	123.0	125.1	127.5	128.4	130.1	130.5
Mozambique										
Namibia	4.7	4.0	6.0	11.0	6.0	6.0	6.0	6.0	6.0	6.0
Niger	3.0	3.0	3.0	3.0	3.0	3.0	2.3	2.8	2.7	2.6
Nigeria	55.0	75.0								
Oman	3.1	3.0	4.0	4.5	5.0	6.5	7.6	7.9	8.1	8.3
Qatar	2.4	2.0	3.0	2.6	2.7	2.7	2.5	2.6	2.7	2.7
Réunion	3.2	4.0	4.0	4.0	4.0	4.0	5.0	5.4	6.2	6.3
Rwanda	2.0									
Sao Tomé e Príncipe	0.1	0.3	0.4	0.3	0.4	0.5	0.4	0.5	0.5	0.6
Saudi Arabia										
Senegal	13.7	15.0	16.0	16.1	17.0	17.1	17.6	18.3	19.5	20.1
Seychelles	3.7	4.0	4.0	4.5	4.6	4.7	4.8	5.0	5.4	5.6
Sierra Leone	2.2	2.0	2.0	1.4	1.4	0.6	0.8	0.8	0.9	0.9
Somalia										
South Africa	88.7	87.0	95.0	96.0	103.0	107.0	110.4	108.0	106.3	109.2
Sudan		10.0	10.0	9.0	8.7	8.0	7.9	7.8	7.5	7.8
Swaziland	2.5	2.0	2.0	2.3	2.3	2.3	2.0	2.2	2.3	2.6
Syria	30.1	30.0	31.0	31.0	31.0	32.0	33.4	34.2	33.4	35.4
Tanzania	9.9	11.0	12.0	12.0	13.0	13.0	17.2	17.3	18.1	18.6
Togo	3.7	4.0	2.0	4.0	5.0	4.0	4.3	4.4	4.8	4.8
Tunisia	123.2	144.0	161.0	170.0	178.0	185.0	191.9	197.4	211.0	218.9
Uganda	4.6	6.0	6.0	6.6						
United Arab Emirates				36.6	39.1	44.4	45.8	49.3	50.5	53.2
Yemen	8.5	11.0	14.0	15.0	16.4	18.6	20.9	26.0	26.5	28.2
Zambia	6.9	8.0	6.3	6.7	7.3	7.4	7.1	7.0	7.0	7.4
Zimbabwe	6.9	8.0	9.0	8.7	9.2	9.5	8.6	9.4	9.2	9.3

Source: Euromonitor from World Tourism Organisation

Tourist Arrivals								Table 24.10	

International Tourist Arrivals 1990-2002

● '000

	1990	1995	1996	1997	1998	1999	2000	2001	2002
North America									
Canada	15,209	16,932	17,329	17,669	18,869	19,411	19,650	19,630	19,492
USA	33,663	36,355	39,293	42,211	40,491	42,219	44,687	43,968	44,986
Latin America									
Anguilla	91	106	86	114	114	107	112	106	120
Antigua	197	211	220	232	226	232	232	233	231
Argentina	1,661	2,496	2,609	2,764	3,012	2,898	2,949	2,687	2,624
Aruba	433	619	641	646	647	687	726	732	749
Bahamas	3,629	3,239	3,416	3,446	3,348	3,648	4,204	4,287	4,508
Barbados	794	442	447	472	512	515	545	548	570
Belize		329	350	304	299	340	373	383	401
Bermuda	548	557	570	562	558	547	538	528	524
Bolivia	217	283	313	355	387	342	306	280	253
Brazil	1,091	1,991	2,665	2,850	4,818	5,107	5,313	5,246	5,491
British Virgin Islands		357	412	378	392	421	436	442	447
Cayman Islands	615	1,044	1,173	1,248	1,275	1,430	1,385	1,404	1,442
Chile	943	1,540	1,449	1,643	1,757	1,622	1,742	1,692	1,704
Colombia	812	1,399	756	639	674	546	557	551	522
Costa Rica	435	785	781	812	942	1,031	1,088	1,109	1,162
Cuba	327	742	999	1,153	1,390	1,561	1,741	1,782	1,837
Dominica	45	68	69	68	67	75	70	68	67
Dominican Republic	1,533	1,806	2,037	2,482	2,702	2,932	3,154	3,186	3,373
Ecuador	362	439	494	529	511	517	615	644	746
El Salvador	73	238	288	387	541	658	795	840	960
French Guiana					68	70	72	73	76
Grenada	76	108	108	111	116	125	128	131	138
Guadeloupe	418	1,059	1,236	1,204	1,111	940	1,015	1,019	1,055
Guatemala	509	563	520	577	634	823	826	821	853
Guyana	64	95	92	75	68	75	105	111	143
Haiti	120	145	150	149	147	143	140	138	136
Honduras	290	270	263	306	321	371	471	502	563
Jamaica	841	1,147	1,162	1,192	1,225	1,248	1,323	1,345	1,392
Martinique	703	885	477	513	549	564	526	520	512
Mexico	17,176	20,241	21,405	19,351	19,392	19,043	20,641	19,814	20,785
Netherlands Antilles									
Nicaragua	106	281	302	358	406	468	486	483	502
Panama	278	345	362	402	410	436	456	468	502
Paraguay	280	438	425	395	350	269	323	337	384
Peru	316	477	584	650	724	857	896	881	965
Puerto Rico	3,426	4,086	4,110	4,350	4,671	4,221	4,566	4,544	4,690
St Kitts	110	203	172	195	250	224	214	213	217
St Lucia	248	549	422	563	629	636	727	756	836
St Vincent and the Grenadines	158	218	216	200	202	223	256	278	324
Suriname		69	74	78	69	75	79	81	85
Trinidad and Tobago	227	282	317	360	377	421	481	500	564
Uruguay			2,259	2,463	2,323	2,273	2,236	2,303	2,232
Venezuela	519	700	758	814	695	606	469	450	422

Source: Euromonitor from World Tourism Organisation

■ Tourist Arrivals

International Tourist Arrivals 1990-2002

● '000

	1990	1995	1996	1997	1998	1999	2000	2001	2002
Asia Pacific									
Afghanistan	6								
American Samoa	100	18	21						
Armenia		12	13	23	32	41	45	42	47
Azerbaijan		174	210	306	483	602	681	669	684
Bangladesh	115	156	166	182	172	173	199	197	203
Bhutan	2	5	5	5	6	7	8	8	8
Brunei	377	498	837	643	964	967	984	943	1,023
Cambodia	17	220	260	219	286	368	466	476	517
China	27,463	46,389	51,127	57,588	63,478	72,796	83,443	88,003	96,780
Fiji	307	336	357	372	384	429	377	359	338
French Polynesia	132	172	164	180	189	211	252	250	270
Guam	780	1,361	1,362	1,381	1,137	1,162	1,288	1,290	1,364
Hong Kong, China	5,933	10,200	12,974	11,274	10,160	11,327	13,059	13,725	15,179
India	1,707	2,124	2,288	2,374	2,359	2,482	2,641	2,663	2,601
Indonesia	2,177	4,324	5,034	5,185	4,607	4,728	5,064	5,126	5,444
Japan	3,505	3,732	4,245	4,670	4,557	4,903	5,272	5,362	5,906
Kazakhstan			203	284	257	394	1,683	1,606	1,699
Kiribati	3	3	4	5	2	1	1	1	1
Kyrgyzstan		12	42	87	59	69	74	77	81
Laos		346	403	463	500	614	737	788	876
Macau	5,942	7,753	8,151	7,000	6,948	7,444	9,162	9,279	9,612
Malaysia		7,122	6,775	5,859	5,203	7,456	9,583	10,440	11,816
Maldives	195	315	339	366	396	430	467	486	504
Mongolia	147	108	71	82	197	159	158	157	155
Myanmar	21	194	490	491	478	434	416	410	377
Nauru									
Nepal	255	363	393	422	464	491	464	451	432
New Caledonia	123	86	91	105	106	101	111	109	107
North Korea		128							
Pakistan	424	378	369	376	429	432	557	555	503
Papua New Guinea	41	42	67	66	67	67	58	57	56
Philippines	1,024	1,760	2,049	2,223	2,149	2,171	1,992	1,952	1,905
Singapore	5,322	7,137	7,292	7,198	6,241	6,958	7,692	7,858	8,410
Solomon Islands	9	12	11	16	13	21	26	29	37
South Korea	2,266	2,922	2,879	3,087	3,503	3,917	4,368	4,461	4,842
Sri Lanka	298	403	302	366	381	436	400	378	351
Taiwan	1,934	2,332	2,358	2,372	2,298	2,411	2,624	2,671	2,912
Tajikistan									
Thailand	5,299	6,951	7,244	7,294	7,843	8,651	9,579	9,923	10,923
Tonga	29	33	31	29	34	44	43	44	46
Turkmenistan		233	271	332	380	437	462	470	481
Tuvalu	1	1	1	1	1	1	1	1	1
Uzbekistan		92	174	253	272	299	349	348	366
Vanuatu	35	44	102	81	78	97	106	105	103
Vietnam		1,351	1,607	1,715	1,520	1,782	2,140	2,169	2,418
Western Samoa	48	68	73	68	78	85	88	87	91
Australasia									
Australia	2,215	3,726	4,164	4,318	4,167	4,459	4,946	5,122	5,268
New Zealand	976	1,409	1,529	1,497	1,485	1,607	1,787	1,812	1,887

Source: Euromonitor from World Tourism Organisation

◻ Tourist Arrivals

International Tourist Arrivals 1990-2002

● '000

	1990	1995	1996	1997	1998	1999	2000	2001	2002
Africa and Middle East									
Algeria	1,137	519	605	635	678	749	866	758	797
Angola		9	21	45	52	45	51	48	51
Bahrain	2,051	3,047	1,988	2,600	2,897	3,280	3,869	4,109	4,695
Benin	247	580							
Botswana	829	1,021	512	604	747	839	989	1,025	1,128
Burkina Faso	74	124	131	138	160	165	175	169	175
Burundi	109	33	27	9	15	26	27	26	25
Cameroon	100	100	101	133	135	148	178	181	212
Cape Verde		28	37	45	52	67	83	88	106
Central African Republic		26	21	17	7	10	12	11	13
Chad	9	7	8	41	41	46	54	53	55
Comoros	8	23	24	26	27	24	24	22	23
Congo Dem Rep		35	37	30	53	80	103	107	139
Congo-Brazzaville	33	28	39	27	20	14	19	17	16
Côte d'Ivoire	196	188	237	274	301	355	423	431	479
Djibouti	33	21	20	20	21	20	19	18	17
Egypt		3,134	3,896	3,961	3,454	4,797	5,506	6,015	7,024
Equatorial Guinea									
Eritrea		315	417	410	188	57	70	74	89
Ethiopia	79	103	109	115	91	92	136	148	170
Gabon	108	125	145	167	195	178	155	132	109
Gambia	101	45	77	85	91	96	105	107	113
Ghana	146	286	305	325	348	373	398	403	438
Guinea	100	99	12	17	23	27	33	34	41
Guinea-Bissau									
Iran	153	452	567	740	1,007	1,321	1,385	1,421	1,398
Iraq	748	61	51	15	45	30	78	83	69
Israel	1,063	2,215	2,100	2,010	1,942	2,313	2,417	2,312	2,227
Jordan		3,277	3,164	3,068	3,303	3,314	3,019	2,824	2,709
Kenya	768	931	1,003	1,001	894	969	1,037	1,028	1,079
Kuwait		2,299	1,565	1,637	1,763	1,884	1,944	1,908	1,904
Lebanon		450	424	557	603	673	742	769	752
Lesotho	242	209	312	313	289	333	382	385	400
Liberia									
Libya	789	1,832	1,276	913	850	965	963	934	879
Madagascar	82	85	83	101	121	138	160	169	188
Malawi	130	190	193	207	220	254	227	226	234
Mali	44	42	98	75	83	87	86	84	83
Mauritania						24	30	33	38
Mauritius	292	422	486	536	558	578	656	665	726
Morocco		2,602	2,693	3,072	3,242	3,817	4,113	4,187	4,461
Mozambique									
Namibia		453	494	551	666	703	749	753	819
Niger	21	17	38	44	42	43	50	53	60
Nigeria		467	822	611	739	776	813	821	887
Oman	149	279	349	376	424	503	571	597	707
Qatar	136	294	327	435	507	611	642	660	693
Réunion	200	304	350	374	400	394	430	440	479
Rwanda	16	1							
Sao Tomé e Príncipe		6	6	5	4	4	5	5	5
Saudi Arabia		4,400							
Senegal	246	280	288	320	365	378	400	409	446
Seychelles	112	121	131	130	128	124	130	133	142
Sierra Leone	98	38	38	23	22	22	21	21	20
Somalia									
South Africa	1,030	4,561	5,187	5,170	5,898	6,026	6,000	5,952	6,022
Sudan	33	63	57	29	27	31	40	43	41
Swaziland	287	347	1,337	1,635	985	1,252	1,151	1,069	968
Syria	1,442	2,252	2,435	2,332	2,463	2,681	3,014	3,009	2,909
Tanzania		295	326	360	482	627	501	433	399
Togo	103	53	58	92	69	70	60	53	42
Tunisia	3,204	4,119	3,884	4,264	4,718	4,832	5,057	5,153	5,187
Uganda	69	185	174	171	192	187	191	192	197
United Arab Emirates		1,601	2,572	2,476	2,991	3,393	3,907	3,922	3,920
Yemen	52	61	74	80	88	58	73	76	71
Zambia	141	163	264	341	362	456	511	526	579
Zimbabwe	605	1,582	1,597	1,336	2,087	2,250	1,967	1,794	1,611

Source: *Euromonitor from World Tourism Organisation*

Tourist Arrivals by Method 2002

● '000

	Air	Rail	Road	Sea	Total
North America					
Canada	7,290	117	11,554	531	19,492
USA	31,061		13,459	466	44,986
Latin America					
Anguilla	28			92	120
Antigua	204			27	231
Argentina	1,108		1,237	279	2,624
Aruba	742			6	749
Bahamas	1,287			3,221	4,508
Barbados	557			6	570
Belize	139		181	81	401
Bermuda	301			223	524
Bolivia	200	5	43	4	253
Brazil	2,915		2,397	179	5,491
British Virgin Islands	130			317	447
Cayman Islands	306			1,136	1,442
Chile	644	48	974	39	1,704
Colombia	431		41	50	522
Costa Rica	877		254	31	1,162
Cuba	1,837				1,837
Dominica	45			22	67
Dominican Republic	3,228			145	3,373
Ecuador	398		332	16	746
El Salvador	241		714	5	960
French Guiana					76
Grenada	127			11	138
Guadeloupe	634			421	1,055
Guatemala	466		304	83	853
Guyana	137			6	143
Haiti	136				136
Honduras	271		273	19	563
Jamaica	1,392				1,392
Martinique	463			49	512
Mexico	8,242		12,544		20,785
Netherlands Antilles					
Nicaragua	206		275	21	502
Panama	401		92	9	502
Paraguay	52		326	6	384
Peru	666		294	5	965
Puerto Rico	3,378			1,311	4,690
St Kitts	61			156	217
St Lucia	285			551	836
St Vincent and the Grenadines	93			231	324
Suriname	61			23	85
Trinidad and Tobago	458			106	564
Uruguay	341		804	1,087	2,232
Venezuela	404		4	13	422

Source: Euromonitor from World Tourism Organisation

☐ Tourist Arrivals

Tourist Arrivals by Method 2002

● '000

	Air	Rail	Road	Sea	Total
Asia Pacific					
Afghanistan					
American Samoa					
Armenia	42	1	4		47
Azerbaijan	653	3	21	1	684
Bangladesh	145		58		203
Bhutan	8				8
Brunei					1,023
Cambodia	390		127		517
China	8,281	1,313	83,179	4,007	96,780
Fiji	326			12	338
French Polynesia	270				270
Guam	1,353			11	1,364
Hong Kong, China	7,864		5,025	2,290	15,179
India	2,107	16	478		2,601
Indonesia	3,042		53	2,349	5,444
Japan	5,672			235	5,906
Kazakhstan					1,699
Kiribati	1				1
Kyrgyzstan	81				81
Laos	101		775		876
Macau	927		3,691	4,995	9,612
Malaysia	3,848	269	7,484	214	11,816
Maldives	504				504
Mongolia					155
Myanmar	203		173	1	377
Nauru					
Nepal	330		102		432
New Caledonia	106			1	107
North Korea					
Pakistan	419	42	38	4	503
Papua New Guinea	56				56
Philippines	1,881			25	1,905
Singapore	6,322		901	1,187	8,410
Solomon Islands	17			20	37
South Korea	4,488			354	4,842
Sri Lanka	351			0	351
Taiwan	2,900			12	2,912
Tajikistan					
Thailand	9,177		1,465	281	10,923
Tonga	39			7	46
Turkmenistan	113		369		481
Tuvalu					1
Uzbekistan	328	36	2		366
Vanuatu	51			52	103
Vietnam	1,118		968	332	2,418
Western Samoa	89			3	91
Australasia					
Australia	5,218			50	5,268
New Zealand	1,877			10	1,887

Source: *Euromonitor from World Tourism Organisation*

□ Tourist Arrivals

Tourist Arrivals by Method 2002

● '000

	Air	Rail	Road	Sea	Total
Africa and Middle East					
Algeria	311		213	273	797
Angola	49		2		51
Bahrain	796		3,891	8	4,695
Benin					
Botswana	51	10	1,067		1,128
Burkina Faso					175
Burundi	10		13	1	25
Cameroon					212
Cape Verde	106				106
Central African Republic	13				13
Chad	37		18		55
Comoros	23				23
Congo Dem Rep					139
Congo-Brazzaville					16
Côte d'Ivoire	465		14		479
Djibouti					17
Egypt	5,586		599	839	7,024
Equatorial Guinea					
Eritrea	42		43	4	89
Ethiopia	132	16	22		170
Gabon	109				109
Gambia	113				113
Ghana					438
Guinea	41				41
Guinea-Bissau					
Iran	168		1,223	7	1,398
Iraq					69
Israel	1,813		402	12	2,227
Jordan	574	1	2,030	104	2,709
Kenya					1,079
Kuwait	847		991	66	1,904
Lebanon	488		263	1	752
Lesotho	11		386		400
Liberia					
Libya					879
Madagascar	188				188
Malawi	128	9	97		234
Mali	83				83
Mauritania					38
Mauritius	719			7	726
Morocco	2,177		476	1,808	4,461
Mozambique					
Namibia	187		632		819
Niger	60				60
Nigeria	553	236	77	21	887
Oman					707
Qatar					693
Réunion	477			2	479
Rwanda					
Sao Tomé e Príncipe	5				5
Saudi Arabia					
Senegal	431			15	446
Seychelles	139			3	142
Sierra Leone	4		16		20
Somalia					
South Africa	1,785	16	4,201	20	6,022
Sudan	39			2	41
Swaziland	25		943		968
Syria	322		2,560	27	2,909
Tanzania	263	13	96	27	399
Togo					42
Tunisia	3,865		1,278	44	5,187
Uganda					197
United Arab Emirates					3,920
Yemen					71
Zambia	59	31	489		579
Zimbabwe	401	142	1,068		1,611

Source: *Euromonitor from World Tourism Organisation*

Tourist Arrivals by Region 2002

● '000

	Africa	Americas	East Asia/Pacifc	Europe	Middle East	South Asia
Algeria	64	3	9	120	10	
Argentina		2,309		315		
Australia	110	634	2,852	1,554	41	77
Azerbaijan		2		409		202
Bolivia	1	154	22	76		
Brazil	34	4,006	98	1,338		13
Canada	74	16,377	1,000	1,949	35	57
Chile	3	1,419	38	239	1	4
China	61	679	3,419	1,447	52	249
Colombia		459		63		
Ecuador	1	614	19	112		
Egypt	178	358	294	5,302	843	49
Hong Kong, China	91	1,290	12,295	1,175	30	256
India	160	390	383	906	91	670
Indonesia	46	154	4,237	825	128	54
Israel	33	612	111	1,345	102	22
Japan	17	947	3,859	832	3	80
Jordan	23	81	62	406	2,098	39
Kazakhstan						
Kuwait	20	43	103	57	1,166	500
Malaysia	89	177	10,810	473	46	221
Mexico		20,369		416		
Morocco	102	157	41	2,468	86	7
New Zealand	21	220	1,138	362	6	12
Nigeria	1,197	32	100	227	27	37
Pakistan	15	60	50	191	35	151
Peru	4	715	19	217		9
Philippines	1	286	1,349	229	15	26
Saudi Arabia						
Singapore	84	421	5,994	1,177	84	650
South Africa	4,674	151	176	968	8	45
South Korea	17	478	4,713	389	6	94
Taiwan	7	345	1,786	138	12	14
Thailand	110	725	6,866	2,693	177	353
Tunisia	541	21	7	3,905	713	
Turkmenistan		1	9	23		82
United Arab Emirates	152	76	280	948	1,692	645
USA	270	31,670	5,848	6,748	90	360
Venezuela	2	224	6	189	1	1
Vietnam	2	155	1,987	266		8

Source: Euromonitor from World Tourism Organisation

Index

General Index (A-Z)

D

E

F

G

H

I

J

W

Y

Z

□ Also available from Euromonitor

■ Country Data

Country data is essential background information when writing business proposals and reports. Using Euromonitor's research it is easy to build a detailed profile of a country. We have data back to 1977 so you can analyse historic as well as recent trends.

- **Asian Marketing Data and Statistics**
  www.euromonitor.com/amdas
- **European Marketing Data and Statistics**
  www.euromonitor.com/emdas
- **International Marketing Data and Statistics**
  www.euromonitor.com/imdas
- **Latin American Marketing Data and Statistics**
  www.euromonitor.com/lamdas
- **World Economic Factbook**
  www.euromonitor.com/factbook
- **World Economic Prospects**
  www.euromonitor.com/worldeconomicprospects
- **The Enlarged European Union: A Statistical Handbook**
  www.euromonitor.com/neweu
- **The Future Demographic: Global Population Trends and Forecasts**
  www.euromonitor.com/futuredemographic

■ Lifestyle Data

It is important when researching a new market to understand national habits and lifestyle choices. Euromonitor can help because we research a huge range of lifestyle statistics for 71 countries, including eating and drinking habits, home ownership patterns, income and earning trends, employment, and travel and tourism.

- **World Consumer Lifestyles Databook: Key Trends**
  www.euromonitor.com/lifestylesdata
- **World Consumer Income and Expenditure Patterns**
  www.euromonitor.com/incomeexpenditure

■ Market Size Data and Forecasts

Euromonitor's consumer market directories provide an excellent starting point to investigate international markets. They enable you to understand consumer trends in 52 countries by providing up-to-date market size statistics for more than 330 consumer products. It is easy to identify the largest markets, those forecast to grow, which are static and which are in decline.

- **Consumer Europe**
  www.euromonitor.com/consumereuroope
- **Consumer USA**
  www.euromonitor.com/consumerusa
- **Consumer Asia**
  www.euromonitor.com/consumerasia
- **Consumer Latin America**
  www.euromonitor.com/consumerlatinamerica
- **Consumer Middle East**
  www.euromonitor.com/consumermiddleeast
- **Consumer Eastern Europe**
  www.euromonitor.com/consumereasterneurope
- **Consumer International**
  www.euromonitor.com/consumerinternational
- **Consumer China**
  www.euromonitor.com/consumerchina
- **European Marketing Forecasts**
  www.euromonitor.com/europeanforecasts
- **International Marketing Forecasts**
  www.euromonitor.com/internationalforecasts

- **Retail Trade International**
  www.euromonitor.com/retailtradeinternational
- **World Retail Data and Statistics**
  www.euromonitor.com/retailstatistics

■ Company Directories

Euromonitor's company directories allow you to identify the top players in the food, drinks, household and personal care industries on a national, regional and international level, based on their market share ranking. Our profiles are much more detailed than traditional company directories, you can understand who owns the leading brands in a market, identify the ultimate parent company and learn about a company's key strategies for success

- **Global Market Share Planner**
  www.euromonitor.com/globalmarketshareplanner
- **Market Share Tracker**
  Www.euromonitor.com/marketsharetracker
- **Major Performance Rankings**
  www.euromonitor.com/performancerankings
- **World Leading Global Brand Owners**
  www.euromonitor.com/globalbrandowners
- **Major Market Share Companies: Americas**
  www.euromonitor.com/companiesamericas
- **Major Market Share Companies: Asia-Pacific**
  www.euromonitor.com/companiesasia
- **Major Market Share Companies: Western Europe**
  www.euromonitor.com/companieswe
- **Major Market Share Companies: Eastern Europe, Middle East & Africa**
  www.euromonitor.com/companiesee_me_af
- **World Cosmetics and Toiletries Marketing Directory**
  www.euromonitor.com/cosmeticsdirectory
- **World Drinks Marketing Directory**
  www.euromonitor.com/drinksdirectory
- **World Food Marketing Directory**
  www.euromonitor.com/fooddirectory
- **World Retail Directory and Sourcebook**
  www.euromonitor.com/retaildirectory

■ Information Source Directories

Euromonitor analysts carry out thousands of research projects every year and consequently have a huge database of business information sources, ranging from trade associations and government departments to online databases and industry journals. Buy one of our directories and you can have access to the same information sources that Euromonitor researchers use when starting new research projects. They are an invaluable reference for librarians who receive requests for information across a broad range of subjects

- **World Directory of Business Information Libraries**
  www.euromonitor.com/
- **World Directory of Business Information Websites**
  www.euromonitor.com/
- **World Directory of Non-official Statistical Sources**
  www.euromonitor.com/
- **World Directory of Trade and Business Associations**
  www.euromonitor.com/
- **World Directory of Trade and Business Journals**
  www.euromonitor.com/
- **World Directory of Marketing Information Sources**
  www.euromonitor.com/